CONTENTS

LIBRARY ASSOCIATION
LONDON AND HOME COUNTIES BRANCH
KENT SUB-BRANCH

THE KENT BIBLIOGRAPHY

A finding list of Kent material in the
Public Libraries of the County and of
the adjoining London Boroughs

Compiled by the late George Bennett

Hon. Editors: Wyn Bergess and Carleton Earl

Supplement compiled and edited by
Wyn Bergess

ERRATA

Pages 322 - 327 are incorrectly numbered. For the correct
alphabetical order of the Author/Title Index consult pages
in the following sequence: 321, 325, 324, 323, 322, 327.

LIBRARY ASSOCIATION
LONDON AND HOME COUNTIES BRANCH
1981

© LONDON AND HOME COUNTIES BRANCH
OF THE LIBRARY ASSOCIATION
7 RIDGMOUNT STREET
LONDON WC1E 7AE

To past and present members of the Kent
Sub-Branch on the occasion of the Centenary
of the Library Association, 1877-1977

ISBN 0 902119 30 3

Printed and bound in England by
STAPLES PRINTERS LIMITED
at The Stanhope Press, Rochester, Kent.

EDITOR'S NOTES

The Supplement to the Kent Bibliography includes items reported by contributing libraries from April 1973 to December 1980.

In general, three categories of material have been excluded from the Bibliography:

1) Newspapers and Periodicals - these are listed in "The Kent Union List of Periodicals", compiled by Brian Bishop and Carleton Earl. (London and Home Counties Branch of the Library Association).

2) Electoral Registers, Poll Books and Directories (until 1974) - these are included in "Kent Directories Located", compiled by W.F. Bergess and B.R.M. Riddell. (Kent County Library).

3) Maps and Plans relating to Kent which are held in the libraries of Kent - a Union List is being compiled by members of a Sub-committee of the Kent Sub-Branch of the Library Association.

The arrangement of the Supplement follows that of the original volume. Additional subject headings and individual sections for prominent historical personages have been included. Several complex subject groups have been sub-divided: eg. Kent Authors and Literature is now comprised of sections headed General, Collections, Fiction, Plays and Poetry. Added entries have been made for items with multiple content wherever feasible. If the subject matter relates to Kent in general, the item appears under the subject heading only; if a specific place is mentioned, then the entry appears under both subject and place headings.

      eg. A Flora of Kent   - Natural History
         A Flora of Maidstone - Natural History and Maidstone.

In some cases, an assessment of author, or date, has been made from sources available; this is indicated by brackets in the case of an author. eg. (Black, William Henry) and by brackets, "circa" or a question mark in reference to a date. eg. (1901), c.1900, 1901?. Brackets may also be used to indicate an assumption in part of a title, but those used in relation to a note, extract etc., are enclosing information. Abbreviations are few and may easily be discerned eg. n.d. = not dated; pseud. = pseudonym. Abbreviations of publishers are used only in the case of those easily known by initials - eg. Kent County Council (K.C.C), Kent County Library (K.C.L.), Kent Archaeological Society (K.A.S.).

The main index links authors, titles (where not indicative of content) publishers etc., with the main place and subject arrangement. A subject index and an index to biographees have been added in the Supplement.

Following the re-organisation of Kent County Library in 1974, Ashford and Tonbridge Libraries became Divisional Headquarters together with most of the former Borough Libraries. It is obviously unhelpful for these to be included in the blanket location 11. for Kent County Library, and so, with some large individual branch libraries with considerable local history collections, they have been given separate location numbers.

An asterisk * denotes either a revised entry from the original volume or an entry from the original volume with added locations.

The Editor would like to thank all the librarians involved for their co-operation and help in providing information, and Mrs. Jackie Lindley for her typing and patience with a difficult task.

Wyn Bergess.
Honorary Editor.

1. London Borough of BEXLEY: Local Studies
    Centre, Hall Place, Bourne Road, Bexley,
    Kent, DA5 IPQ.
    Telephone: Crayford (0322) 526574 Telex 896119

2. London Borough of BROMLEY: Local Studies
    Department, Central Library, High Street,
    Bromley, Kent, BR1 IEX.
    Telephone: 01-460-9955   Telex: 896712

    Note: It is advisable to contact the library
          before making a visit.

3. CANTERBURY Library,
    The Beaney Institute, High Street,
    Canterbury, Kent. CT1 2JP.
    Telephone: Canterbury 63608

4. CHATHAM Library,
    Riverside, Chatham, Kent. ME4 4HL.
    Telephone: Medway 43589

5. DARTFORD Library,
    Central Park, Dartford, Kent. DA1 IEU.
    Telephone: Dartford 21133.

6. DOVER Library,
    Maison Dieu House, Dover, Kent. CT16 IDW.
    Telephone Dover 204241

7. FOLKESTONE Library,
    Grace Hill, Folkestone, Kent. CT20 IHD
    Telephone: Folkestone 57583

8. GILLINGHAM Library,
    High Street, Gillingham, Kent. ME7 IBG.
    Telephone: Medway 51066

9. GRAVESEND Library,
    Windmill Street, Gravesend, Kent. DA12 IAQ.
    Telephone: Gravesend 52758

10. HYTHE Library,
    Stade Street, Hythe, Kent.
    Telephone: Hythe 67111

11. KENT COUNTY LIBRARY HEADQUARTERS,
    Springfield, Maidstone, Kent. ME14 2LH.
    Telephone: Maidstone 671411.   Telex:965212

    Note: This location represents the Local
          History collections of the libraries
          in the County system prior to the
          Local Government Reorganisation of
          April, 1974.

12. MAIDSTONE Library,
    St. Faith's Street, Maidstone, Kent. ME14 ILH
    Telephone: Maidstone 52344 and 677449

13. MARGATE Library,
    Cecil Square, Margate, Kent. CT9 IRE.
    Telephone: Thanet 23626 and 22895

14. RAMSGATE Library,
    Guildford Lawn, Ramsgate, Kent.
    Telephone: Thanet 53532

15. ROCHESTER Library,
    Northgate, Rochester, Kent. MEI ILS.
    Telephone: Medway 43837 and 42415

16. SEVENOAKS Library,
    The Drive, Sevenoaks, Kent. TN13 3AB.
    Telephone: Sevenoaks 453118.

17. London Borough of GREENWICH: Local Studies
    Centre, Woodlands, Mycenae Road, London, SE2.
    Telephone: 01-858-4631

18. London Borough of LEWISHAM:
    Manor House Library, Old Road, London, SE13 5SY
    Telephone: 01-852-5050

19. TUNBRIDGE WELLS Library,
    Mount Pleasant, Tunbridge Wells,
    Kent. TN1 INS
    Telephone: Tunbridge Wells 22352/3

20. SITTINGBOURNE Library,
    Central Avenue, Sittingbourne, Kent.
    ME10 4AH.
    Telephone: Sittingbourne 76545

21. WYE COLLEGE (UNIVERSITY OF LONDON),
    The Library, Wye College,
    6 Upper Street, Wye.
    Telephone: Wye 812699

22. ASHFORD Library,
    Church Road,   Ashford,   Kent.
    Telephone: Ashford 20649 and 35526

23. TONBRIDGE CENTRAL Library,
    4 High Street, Tonbridge, Kent.
    Telephone: Tonbridge 352754 and 350479

24. BROADSTAIRS Library,
    The Broadway, Broadstairs, Kent.
    Telephone: Thanet 62994

25. STROOD Library,
    32, Bryant Road, Strood, Rochester, Kent.
    Telephone: Medway 78161

26. FAVERSHAM Library,
    Newton Road, Faversham, Kent.
    Telephone: Faversham 2448

27. SHEERNESS Library,
    44 Trinity Road, Sheerness, Kent.
    Telephone: Sheerness 662618

28. DEAL Library,
    Broad Street, Deal, Kent.
    Telephone: Deal 2984 and 4726

29. SANDWICH Library,
    13 Market Street, Sandwich, Kent.
    Telephone: Sandwich 613819

30. HERNE BAY Library,
    High Street, Herne Bay, Kent.
    Telephone: Herne Bay 4896

31. WHITSTABLE Library,.
    31/33 Oxford Street,
    Whitstable,   Kent.
    Telephone: Whitstable 273309

32. CORPS Library,
    Royal School of Military Engineering,
    Brompton, Gillingham, Kent.
    Telephone: Medway 44555
                       Extension 309

*   It is advisable to contact a repository before a visit is made.

ADAMS, William, (1564 - 1620) PILOT OF GILLINGHAM & "THE FIRST ENGLISHMAN IN JAPAN".

ADAMS, William *
Captain Adam's junk sea adventure. Logbook
1615 and 1617 - 19. Microfilm of MS
original.
8
Letters, 1614 - 1617, Facsimile copies.
8.
Letters written by, and about, William Adams,
1614 - 1620. Facsimile copies.
8.
Logbook of William Adams, 1614 - 1619.
Transactions of the Asiatic Society of Japan,
Vol. XII, Part II, 1915. Microfilm.
8.

The original letters of the English pilot,
William Adams, written from Japan between
AD.1611 and 1617. Reprinted from the
Hakluyt Society Papers.
8.

ASIATIC SOCIETY OF JAPAN.
History of the English Factory of Hirado,
1613 - 1622. In the transactions.
Vol. XXVI. 1898.
Microfilm.
8.

BATE, J.
William Adams, the pilot-major of Gillingham,
the first Englishman who discovered Japan, by
J. Bate & others.
McKay. 1934
4,8,11,12

BLAKER, Richard. *
The needlewatcher. (A novel about William
Adams).
Heinemann. 1932.
8

BLUNDEN, Edmund. *
Poem of the commemoration for William
Adams at the site of the Memorial at Ito.
n.d.
8

BLYTHE, Norma E.
William Adams 1546 - 1620.
Unpublished thesis. (Sittingbourne College
of Education). 1970.
8

BRITISH PETROLEUM COMPANY.
B.P. Kent News, No 58, July 3rd, 1964.
Contains an article on William Adams.
8

GILLINGHAM BOROUGH COUNCIL *
Memorial to Will Adams: Gillingham's
tribute to its most famous son. 1930.
8

GILLINGHAM BOROUGH COUNCIL
The William Adams memorial: souvenir
programme. 1934.
8

GILLINGHAM PUBLIC LIBRARY *
William Adams, 1564 - 1620. An exhibition
& lecture to commemorate the 400th
anniversary of his birth.
K.C.C. 1964.
4, 8.

HARRIS, John *
A succinct account of......Mr William Adams.
Microfilm. n.d.
8

JAPANESE AIR LINES. GLOBAL COURIER. *
Japanese Air Line's Global Courier, Vol.2.,
No.9, September - October, 1964. Contains
article on William Adams.
8

LUND, Robert. *
Daishi-san. (William Adams of Gillingham):a novel.
Cassell. 1962.
4, 8.

MANNIN, Ethel. *
With William Adams through Japan.
F. Muller Ltd. 1962.
8,15.

MINAKAWA, Saburo.
Christian Activities, persecutions and revival
in Japan (1549 - 1873). Associations with
William Adams.
Tokyo, Kobunsha. 1966.
8

NICOLE, Christopher.
Lord of the golden fan. (a novel about William
Adams).
Cassell. 1973.
4

NORBURY, Paul.
Introducing Japan, edited by P. Norbury.
(Includes William Adams).
Paul Norbury. Caxton House,High St. Tenterden.1976.
8

PASKE-SMITH, M. *
A glimpse of the "English House" and English
life at Hirado, 1613 - 1623. (William Adams
interest).
Kobe, Japan. J.L. Thompson & Co Ltd. 1927.
8

ROGERS, Philip George. *
The First Englishman in Japan: the story of
William Adams.
Harvill Press, 1956.
4,5,8,11,12,15.

STONACH, George W. *
Lord of the wandering needle: an English
sailor in 17th Century Japan.
Chambers Journal. 1944.
8

SWANZY, Henry. *
The First Englishman in Japan.
B.B.C. 1964.
8

TAMES, Richard.
Will Adams 1564 - 1620: an illustrated
life of Will Adams.
Shire Pubns. 1973
11

THE WILL ADAMS MEMORIAL CEREMONY.
April 14th,1966. Yokosuka, Japan.
(Collection of photographs & Order of ceremony).
8.

THE WILL ADAMS MEMORIAL CEREMONY.
April 8th 1975, Yokosuka, Japan.
(Collection of photographs & order of ceremony).
8

YOKOSUKA CITY COUNCIL*
Paintings by Japanese schoolchildren of
Tsuaynana Park, site of Adams' Tomb. 1963.
Yokosuka City Council, Japan.
8

ADAMS, William. (1564 - 1620) PILOT OF
GILLINGHAM & "THE FIRST ENGLISHMAN IN JAPAN",
Cont'd.

YOKOSUKA CITY COUNCIL*
Programme of annual ceremony commemorating
William Adams. 1964.
Yokosuka City Council, Japan.
8

William Adams and Yokosuka. (Text in English
and Japanese). 1968.
Yokosuka City Council. Japan.
8

ADDINGTON

GENERAL REGISTER OFFICE
Census Returns 1841, 1851, 1861, 1871.
Addington. Microfilm.
23

ILLUSTRATED PARTICULARS, CONDITIONS, AND
PLAN OF...the residential sporting &
agricultural estate known as Addington Park
situate in the parishes of Addington,
Trottiscliffe, Offham, Ryarsh, Wrotham,
Leybourne and West Malling...about 2,404 acres.
Knight, Frank & Rutley. Auctioneers. 1923.
11

SWEETMAN, H.S,
A genealogical Memoir of the ancient,
honourable and extinct family of Leigh of
Addington.
P.P. 1887.
1

AGRICULTURE

AGRICULTURE & FISHERIES, Board of
Report on agricultural education in Kent.
H.M.S.O. (1915?).
11

AGRICULTURE & FISHERIES, Ministry of *
Hops: report of the second reorganisation
commission for England. (Economic series
no. 47).
H.M.S.O. 1947.
3,8

AGRICULTURE & FISHERIES & FOOD, Ministry of
Agricultural land classification of England
and Wales. Report to accompany Sheet 171
London S.E.
Min. of Agriculture, Fisheries & Food. 1975.
16

BAKER, Alan Reginald Harold.
Some Fields & Farms in medieval Kent.
Reprinted from Archaeologia Cantiana.
Vol. LXXX. 1965.
K.A.S. 1965.
11

BAKER, Dennis.
The marketing of corn in the first half
of the eighteenth century: North-east Kent.
An off-print from
The Agricultural History Review. Vol 18.
Part II, 1970. pp. 126 - 150.
British Agricultural History Society. 1970.
3,11

BEST, Robin Hewitson.*
The changing location of intensive crops:
an analysis of their spatial distribution
in Kent and the implications for land-use
planning.
Wye College. 1966.
2,4,5,7,11,12,19,21.

BIGNELL, Alan
Hopping down in Kent.
R. Hale. 1977.
2,3,4,5,6,7,11,12,16,19,22,25,28,30.

BODDINGTON, M.A. B.*
Pig production in Kent; 1967 - 1969:
results for a small sample of farms.
Wye College. 1970.
2,8,9,21.

BOYS, John *
A general view of the agriculture of the
County of Kent; with observations on the
means of improvement.
G. Nicol, London. 1796.
2

BRADE-BIRKS, Stanley Graham.
The soil as a natural object: pedology as
a branch of geology.
In The Journal of the Agricola Club &
Snarley Guild. Vol. VIII No.2. 1971-72.
pp. 42 - 50.
3

BULL, Christopher.
Farm based recreation in South East England:
the experiences of a random sample of farmers
in Kent, Surrey & Sussex, by Christopher Bull
and Gerald Wibberley (Studies & Rural Land
Use Report no.12)
Wye College. December 1976.
1,2,3,4,5,11,19,21

BUNYARD, George.
Fruit farming for profit (up to date):
a practical treatise, embracing chapters on
all the most profitable fruits with detailed
instructions for successful culture. 3rd &
4th eds
Frederick Bunyard, Maidstone 1890.
11
(Bunyard's was a well-known Maidstone nursery
until the early 1960's).

Chater, G.P.*
Report on hop-picking by machine, by
G.P. Chater & Miss C.L. Jary.
Wye College. 1955.
4.21.

CLINCH, George.*
English hops; a history of cultivation and
preparation for the market from the earliest
times. (mainly in relation to Kent).
McCorquedale and Co. 1919.
5, 25.

COLTHUP, William.*
A man of Kent at home and abroad.
(The author was a Kent Farmer, Chairman of the
Finance Committee of K.C.C. for seventeen years,
High Sheriff of Kent...page 12 has information
about the hop industry). Privately printed
for the author by Messrs. J.A. Jennings,
Canterbury. 1953.
11, 12.

DANKS, William.
The diary of William Danks of East Down,
Shoreham 1806 - 1810. MSS and another
typescript copy. (Agricultural diary).
16

DICKIE, A.J.
Centralised grain storage: a Kent feasibility
study.
Home Grown Cereals Authority. 1972.
4

DORLING, M.J.*
East Kent Horticulture by M.J. Dorling and
R.R.W. Folley. (results from 6 holdings
for 1953 - 1955).
Wye College. 1957.
3,8,11,12,19,21.

EAST MALLING RESEARCH STATION.
Annual Report
1st Oct.1970 - 30th Sept. 1971. 12.
1st Oct.1971 - 30th Sept. 1972.   4, 11, 12.
1st Oct.1973 - 30th Sept. 1974. 11.
1st Oct.1974 - 30th Sept. 1975. 11.
1st Oct.1975 - 30th Sept. 1976. 11.

FARLEY, James George Wilson.*
Pull no more poles: an account of a venture
among hop pickers.
Faith Press. 1962.
2, 19.

FOLLEY, Roger Roland Westwell.
Culinary apples in 1973: time to start again?
Studies in the economics of Fruit Farming.
Report no.12. (Wye College. Farm Business
Unit, School of Rural Economics & Related
Studies).
Wye College. 1975.
11,21,23.

Dessert apples & pears in 1972 - 73: Financial
results for a sample of growers. Agricultural
Enterprise Studies in England & Wales, Report
no. 27. (Wye College Farm Business Unit,
School of Rural Economics & Related Studies).
Wye College. 1974.
11,21.

FORDHAM, S.J.
Soils in Kent II. Sheet TR35 (Deal) by
S.J. Fordham & R.D. Green. Soil Survey
Record no. 15.
Harpenden Soil Survey of G.B. Rothamsted
Experimental Station. 1973.
2,4,6,7,11,13.

Soils in Kent III. Sheet TQ06 (Rainham)
by S.J. Fordham & R.D. Green. Soil Survey
Record no. 37
Harpenden Soil Survey of G.B. Rothamsted
Experimental Station. 1976.
3,8,11,20.

GARRAD, G.H.*
A survey of the agriculture of Kent.
(County Agricultural Surveys no.1.)
Royal Agricultural Society of England. 1954.
13,25,26

GREEN, R.D.
Soils in Kent I. Sheet TR04 (Ashford)
by R.D. Green & S.J. Fordham. Soil Survey
Record no.14.
Harpenden Soil Survey of G.B. Rothamsted
Experimental Station. 1973.
2,4,6,7,11,13,19.

                    *

The Soils of Romney Marsh by R.D. Green.
(Bulletin no.4.)
Harpenden Soil Survey of G.B. Rothamsted
Experimental Station. 1968.
11.

HAGGAR, R.J. *
Kent wild white clover: the growth and
management of wild clover with special
reference to seed production by R.J. Haggar
& W. Holmes.
Wye College. 1963.
3.

HALL, Sir Alfred Daniel. *
A report on the agriculture and soils of Kent,
Surrey & Sussex,by Sir A.D. Hall and Sir E.J.
Russell.
H.M.S.O. (Board of Agriculture & Fisheries)
1911.
9.

THE HOP GARDEN, or directions for planting
& managing hops. (Dedication signed J.A.)
Printed for J. Roberts. London, 1721.
11.

HYAMS, Edward.
Not in our stars. A novel set on a Kent Fruit
Farm. (The Author lives at Chilham).
Longmans Green. 1949.
11.

IRVING, R.W.
Green money & the common agricultural policy.
Wye College. 1975.
11,21.

JERMY, A.C.
Chalk grassland: studies in conservation &
management in South-East England, by A.C.Jermy
& P.A. Stott. (Kent properties pp.55-56.)
Kent Trust for Nature Conservation. 1973.
2,3,4,6,11,12,

KENT BEE-KEEPERS' ASSOCIATION YEAR BOOK, 1973.
K.B-K.A. 1973.
11,20.

KENT COUNTY AGRICULTURAL SOCIETY.
Catalogue of horses, cattle, sheep....at
the County Agricultural Show at Maidstone
(later held at Detling, Nr. Maidstone).
11. 1948 - 1972 (with gaps)
3. 4. 48th Show (at Detling) on July 14th,
        15th and 16th. 1977. entitled KENT
        COUNTY SHOW, Detling, Maidstone -
        official handbook
Printed by Geerings for the Society. 1977.

Preview of the Kent County Show, Detling
Maidstone on July 12th,13th,14th, 1979. In
Living in Kent. 1979.
4.

KENT COUNTY COUNCIL: COUNTY SECRETARY'S DEPT.
Research & Intelligence Unit.
Farm open day at Reed Court Farm, Chainhurst,
Marden, 17th August, 1975, results of a
survey of visitors' opinion on the day.
K.C.C. 1975.
11.

KENT COUNTY COUNCIL: DISEASES OF ANIMALS BRANCH.
Diseases of animals inspectors: (a list)
K.C.C. 1975.
12.

KENT COUNTY COUNCIL: PLANNING DEPT.
Kent County structure plan. (a) Report on
agriculture. (b) Report on forestry (adopted
by the Local Planning Authority (a) in May,1975
(b) in February 1975. Serial no. 8B.
K.C.C. 1975.
3,4,9,11,13,16.

KENT COUNTY FEDERATION OF YOUNG FARMERS' CLUBS
Year Book 1971.
Kent County Federation of Young Farmers' Clubs.
1971.
12.

LAIRD, A. Bonnet.*
My part of the Country.
Jenkins. 1925.
4

LEWIS, Mary. *
Old days in the Kent hop gardens,
edited by M. Lewis.
West Kent Federation of Womens'
Insts. Tonbridge. 1962.
1,2,3,4,5,6,7,8,9,11,12,15,19,24,30.

McRAE, Stuart Gordon.
The rural landscape of Kent, by S.G. McRae
and C.P. Burnham.
Wye College. 1973.
1,2,4,5,6,9,11,19,20,24,25,26,27,28,30.

MARKHAM, Gervase.*
The inrichment of the Weald of Kent: or,
a direction to the husbandman for the true
ordering, manuring & inriching of all the
grounds within the Wealds of Kent and Sussex
......revised, inlarged & corrected........
Printed by Eliz. Purflow for John Harison,
London, 1649.
11.

The inrichment of the Weald of Kent........
Printed   for George Sawbridge. 1675
2.

The inrichment of the Weald of Kent...
(Facsimile reprint of 1625 edition).
Theatrum Orbis Terrarum Ltd. Da Capo Press.
1973.
11. 19

MARSHALL, William.
Minutes, experiments, observations &
general remarks on agriculture in the
Southern Counties: a new edition....2 vols.
Printed for. G. Nicol, G.G. & J. Robinson &
J. Debrett. 1799.
11.

The review and abstract of the county reports
to the Board of Agriculture. 1817.
David & Charles Reprints. Newton Abbott. n.d.
12.

Review and abstracts of the County Reports to
the Board of Agriculture....vol.5 (includes
summary of Boys' Agriculture of Kent) 1818.
David & Charles Reprints. Newton Abbott. 1968.
2.

MARSTON, Louise.
Cripple Jess, the hop-picker's daughter.
(a novel).
John F. Shaw & Co. Ltd. London. (c.1900)
1,11.

MELLING, Elizabeth*
Aspects of agriculture and industry...
Kentish sources III, edited by E. Melling.
K.C.C. 1961.
1,13,30,31.

A NOTE OF SUCH AS HAVE BEEN EXPENDITED AND
HAVE PRESSED THEIR ACCOUNT... (List of
landowners responsible for marsh or grazing
land in Dartford & district 1626 - 85).
Typescript from the original in the
Dunkin Collection, Kent County Library.1973.
5.

OAKSEY, John
Pride of the Shires: The story of the
Whitbread Horses.
Hutchinson. 1979.
12.

PARKER, Hubert H. *
The hop industry.
P.S. King & Son, London, 1934.
11.

PRICE, Daniel
A system of sheep grazing and management
as practised in Romney Marsh.
R. Phillips. 1809.
1,21.

REID, Ian G.*
The Small Farm on heavy land: a study of
the problems of Farming in the Wealden
area of South East England. (Wye College:
Farm Business Unit: School of Rural Economics
& Related Subjects).
Wye College. 1958.
11,12,21.

RICHARDSON, T.L.
The agricultural labourers' standard of
living in Kent, 1790 - 1840.
In ODDY, Derek,
    The making of the modern British Diet,
    by Derek Oddy and Derek Miller. pp.103-116.
Croom Helm. 1976.
3.

SACKVILLE-WEST, Victoria (afterwards Lady
Country notes   Nicolson)*
(includes "The Kentish Landscape";"The Hop
Picking Season"; "The Garden & the Oast".
M. Joseph. 1939
11.12.23.

The Women's Land Army.
M. Joseph. 1944.
11,12.23

SARGENT, Miles.*
Saint Francis of the hop-fields.
Philip Allan. 1933.
2.

SCOT, Reginald
Perfite platforme of a hoppe garden.(Facsimile
reprint of the 1574 edition).
Da Capo Press. Theatrum Orbis Terrarum Ltd.
1973.
11,19.

SELBY, Prideaux George. *
The Faversham farmers Club & its members.
Gibbs, Canterbury. 1927.
26.

SMALL, Julia
East Kent Ploughing Match Association:
ploughing matches from 1840
Kent Ploughing Match Association. 1979.
6,16,23,28.

SMITH, A.
A geographical study of the agriculture on
the Kentish Manors of Canterbury Cathedral
Priory, 1272 - 1379.
(M.A. Dissertation, University of Liverpool)
Photocopy. n.d.
3.

STRATTON, John Young.*
Hops and hop-pickers.
S.P.C.K. 1883.
2.

SYKES, Joseph Donald. *
Profits and problems of farming in South-
East England, by J.D. Sykes & G.P. Wibberley.
(Wye College, Farm Management Survey.
Report 7).
Wye College. 1956.
4, 21.

AGRICULTURE   Cont'd.

THE TESTON SYSTEM OF FARMING...together with
the Courland Method of Making Clover......
(Sir Charles Middleton, afterwards Lord
Barham, answers questions concerning his farm.
W. Wildash, Rochester.   1816.
11,12.

THOMAS, Helen
A remembered harvest.   (Hop-picking in the
Weald).
Tragara Press.   1970.
11,19.

TOPLEY, William
On the agricultural geology of the Weald.
(From the Journal of the Royal Agricultural
Society of England. Vol.VIII, Pt.II).
William Clowes.   1872.
7.

WAUGH, Mary.*
Fruit and hop growing in Kent. (written for
children).
O.U.P.   1962.
20,26,27.

WHITEHEAD, Sir Charles.*
A sketch of the Agriculture of Kent, with
an introduction by the Chairman of the
Technical Education Committee of the County
Council of Kent. (G.M. Arnold, Esq.) (Sir
Charles Whitehead was an Alderman of
Faversham Council)
Reprinted from the Journal of the Royal
Agricultural Society of England, Third
Series, Vol.X. Part III, 1899.
Spottiswoode.   1899.
11. 26.

WHITEHEAD, R.A.
Steam in the village.
(Kentish author - passing references to
Kent throughout, including Horton Kirby
& Darenth).
David & Charles, Newton Abbott.   1977.
5.

WIGAN RICHARDSON INTERNATIONAL LTD.
Hop Report 1973.
Hop Report 1974.
8.

WORMALD, H. *
Diseases of Fruit and crops.
(The Author worked at East Malling
Research Station).
Crosby Lockwood.   1939.
11.

WRIGHT, Tom.
The gardens of Britain, Volume 4: Kent,
East and West Sussex and Surrey, by
Tom Wright in Association with the
Royal Horticultural Society .
B.T. Batsford.   1978.
1,2,5,11,12,13,16,19,23.

WYE COLLEGE
A catalogue of agricultural & horticultural
books, 1543 - 1918, in Wye College Library.
Wye College.   1977.
11, 21, 23.

The Journal of the South- eastern Agricultural
College, Wye, Kent. No17.   1908
Printed by Headley Bros. Ashford. 1908.
11. 21.

WYE COLLEGE: Prospectus 1972 - 76.
Wye College.   1972.
11.

WYE COLLEGE:CENTRE FOR EUROPEAN
AGRICULTURAL STUDIES.
Survey of the potato industry in the E.E.C.
Wye College. 1975.
11,12.

WYE COLLEGE: School of Rural Economics
and related studies.
The British Isles Tomato Survey.   3rd
report 1968 crop.
Wye College. 1971
8.21.

Farm business statistics for South-East
England.
Wye College
3.5.   1975; 1977.
11.   1973; 1977.
21.   1973; 1975; 1977

YOUNG, Arthur.
A six weeks tour through the Southern
Counties of England & Wales....2nd edition
corrected.... by W. Strahan. (North Kent
Farming mentioned in Letter 3).
W. Nicoll, London. 1769.
11.

YOUNGMAN, James.
Wye Farm management game, description
& administrators' manual.
Wye College (Farm Business Unit). 1975.
11.21.

AIRPORTS

CONNOLLY, P.A.
Gravesend Airport, 1932 - 1958.
Compiled by P.A. Connolly and C.R. Munday.
K.C.L. Gravesham Division. 1975.
4.9.20.

GREAT BRITAIN, Laws etc. (Eliz. II).
Maplin Development act. 1973. Ch.64.
H.M.S.O. 1973.
4.

KENT COUNTY COUNCIL: PLANNING DEPARTMENT.*
The search for a site for a third London
Airport. Part I. Background information
concerning Sheppey & Cliffe.
K.C.C. 1968.
4.9.11.20.25.

ROYAL AERONAUTICAL SOCIETY: MEDWAY BRANCH.
A brief history of Rochester Airport.
Rochester. Marconi Avionics. 1979.
4,9,15,23

SHEPPEY GROUP.
Synopsis of the evidence given at the
Foulness Enquiry.
The Sheppey Group. 1969.
4.

TRADE AND INDUSTRY. Dept of:
ACCIDENTS INVESTIGATION BRANCH.
Aero Commander 680 G-ASHI. Report of the
accident at approximately ¼ mile south
of Rochester City Airport, Kent, on 19th
February, 1975.
H.M.S.O. 1976.
11.

Avions Pierre Robin DR360, Robin Knight
G-AZOX. Report on the accident at Biggin
Hill Aerodrome, Kent on 21st July, 1973.
Civil Aircraft Accident Report 17/74.
H.M.S.O. 1974.
11.23.

ALDINGTON

ELLISTON-ERWOOD, Frank Charles.*
Notes on the Architecture of Aldington
Church, Kent, and the Chapel at Court-
at-Street, called "Bellirica".
Kent Archaeological Society. n.d.
1.11.17.

GREAT BRITAIN: Laws etc. (Geo.III)
An act for inclosing Aldington Freight,
otherwise Aldington Frith, in the parish
of Aldington in the County of Kent.
(59 Geo.3. C.31. Private Act.)   Printed by:
George Eyre & Andrew Strahan. 1819.
11.

LONG, G.S. *
A short life of Erasmus, Formerly Rector
of Aldington.   Printed by:
Fleetway Press. London. 1929.
11.12.

NEAME, Alan.*
The holy maid of Kent: the life of
Elizabeth Barton 1506 - 1534. (Born at
Aldington).
Hodder & Stoughton. 1971.
2.3.4.6.7.8.11.12.19.

ALLHALLOWS.

DUNCAN, Leland Lewis.*
A short guide to the church pf
All Hallows, Hoo.
n.d.
4.

HAMMOND, F.J. *
The story of an outpost Parish, Allhallows,
Hoo.
Society for Promoting Christian Knowledge.
1928.
2,25.

McLELLAN, Doreen.
Allhallows railway. Compiled by Doreen
McLellan. (Local History Pamphlet no.4)
K.C.L. Gravesham Division. 1975.
4.12.20.

ALLINGTON

CONWAY, Agnes C.
The owners of Allington Castle, Maidstone.
(1086 - 1279).Reprinted from Archaeologia
Cantiana. Vol.29. 1911.
(Bound with 4 other pamphlets: title,
Allington Castle).
4.

CONWAY, William Martin.   1st Baron Conway
                             of Allington
Allington Castle. photos, plans. Reprinted
from Archaeologia Cantiana. Vol.27 1909.
(Bound in with 4 other pamphlets; title,
Allington Castle).
4.

FRIENDS OF ALLINGTON CASTLE
Guide to Allington Castle.
Friends of Allington Castle. n.d.
30.

KIELY, M.B.
Allington Castle: the medieval phase.
Faversham Carmelite Press.
1974.
11.12.

McGREAL, Father Wilfrid.
An introduction to Allington Castle
Carmelite Press, Faversham. 1971?
11,12,25.

TILDEN, Philip
True remembrances.
(Allington Castle, Lympne Castle,
Saltwood Castle, Chartwell).
Country Life. 1954.
7,12.

TOWN & COUNTRY MAGAZINE.
Includes Information on:- Allington Castle.
Virtue, London. 1837 - 8.
4.

WYATT, Sir Stanley Charles*
Cheneys & Wyatts. (The Cheyneys of
Chilham Castle & the Wyatts of Allington
Castle).
Carey & Claridge. 1960.
11.

ANERLEY

JOBSON, A. *
South London sepia (memories of childhood
& youth in Anerley - Typescript).
1967.
2.

WAINWRIGHT, J.G.
The District School System (the North
Surrey District School, Anerley). (photocopy)
Printed by order of the Managers. 1896.
2.

WAITE, H.E.
The story of Methodism in Anerley.
The Trustees of the Methodist Church. 1928.
2.

APPLEDORE

CATALOGUE OF THE INTERESTING AND EXTENSIVE
LIBRARY OF....the late Dr. F.W. Cock, The
Well House, Appledore, Kent,comprising books
& manuscripts relating to Kent...which will
be sold on Monday, May 8th, 1944.
Sotheby & Co. 1944.
1,7,11

COCK, Frederick William
Additional notes on the Horne and Chute
Families of Appledore. (Reprinted from
Archaeologia Cantiana Vol.49. 1935.
K.A.S. 1935.
11.

Notes from the transcripts and registers
of Appledore, Kent. (Sold for the benefit
of the Village Hall Fund).
1927.
1,3,12.

ST. PETER & ST. PAUL, APPLEDORE: a short guide.
Printed by Thompson, Ashford. 1973.
11.

WINNIFRITH, Sir John.
Appledore, Kent: a short history.
The Author, Hall House Farm, Appledore. 1973.
1,7,11,22.

ARCHITECTURE -
See also Towns, Villages etc.

ARCHIBALD, John.*
Kentish architecture as influenced by
geology.
The Monastery Press. Ramsgate, 1934.
25.

ARMSTRONG, J.R.
Weald & Downland Open Air Museum, edited
by J.R. Armstrong, and J. Lowe.
Phillimore & Co. Chichester, Sussex.
3.   1975.
8.   1973.
11. 1974.

BARLEY, Maurice Willmore.
English Farmhouse & cottage.
Routledge & Kegan Paul. 1961.
11.

BATES, Harry.
The English Cottage, by H. Bates & C.Fry.
2nd edn. revised.
Batsford, 1944.
11.

BIDDLE, Gordon
Victorian Stations.
David & Charles, 1973.
11.

BLACKHEATH SOCIETY.
Some hints on the maintenance and repair
of 17th and 18th Century premises.
(Originally produced by the York Georgian
Society. Reprinted with local photographs
and list of buildings in Blackheath,
Lewisham & Greenwich).
Blackheath Society. 1949.
11.

BRAUN, Hugh.
The English castle. 3rd ed. rev.
Batsford. 1947/8
13.

CHALKLIN, Christopher William.
The provincial towns of Georgian England:
a study of the building process. 1740 -
1820.
D. Arnold. 1974.
11.

DEEBLE, E.B.
Plan for the introduction of the patent
metallic caisson, in forming piers,
harbours, breakwaters, basins, locks,
quays, docks, mill-dams, roads through
morasses and foundations to lighthouses
on sands or marshy soil, fortifications,
aquaducts, etc. (References to Kent and
Dover).
Ridgway, Piccadilly. n.d.
11.

DITCHFIELD, Peter Hampson.
The Manor houses of England.
Batsford. 1910.
11.

ELLISTON-ERWOOD, Frank Charles.
Plans of, and brief architectural notes on,
Kent Churches. Series 1. 4 parts.
Reprinted from Archaeologia Cantiana.
Vol. 59 - 62. 1949 - 1962.   Printed by:
Headley Bros. Ashford. 1946 - 49.
4.11.

ENVIRONMENT, Dept. of the
Lists of buildings of historical &
architectural interest. See
Individual Towns etc.

ENVIRONMENT, Dept. of the: ANCIENT
MONUMENTS AND HISTORIC BUILDINGS.
An illustrated guide to the ancient
monuments maintained by the Dept. of the
Environment. Southern England.
H.M.S.O, 1973.
12.

ERRAND, J.
Secret Passages and Hiding Places.
N. Kaye. 1974.
22.

ESAM, Frank.*
The manors and farmhouses of Kent: a series
of 44 pen and ink sketches illustrating the
development of domestic architecture in Kent
from the 13th century.
South Eastern Gazette. Maidstone. 1906?
1,2,3,5,6,8,11,12,16.

FRY, Plantagenet Somerset.
British mediaeval castles.
David & Charles. 1974.
11.

GLENCROSS, Alan.
The Buildings of Greenwich.
L.B. of Greenwich. 1974.
1,2,11,18.

GRAVETT, Kenneth.*
Timber and brickbuilding in Kent: a selection
from the J.Fremlyn Streatfeild collection.
Phillimore. 1971.
For Kent Archaeological Society Records Branch
2,5,6,7,8,12,20.   (Vol.20)

HAGUE, Douglas B.
Lighthouses: their architecture, history
and archaeology, by D.B. Hague & R. Christie.
Gower Press. 1975.
24.

HARRIS, Richard.
Discovering Timber Framed buildings.
Shire Pubns. 1978.
11.

HOPKINS, Robert Thurston.
Moated houses of England. (pp.71 - 106,Kent).
Country Life. 1935.
5,11,15,18.

HUSSEY, Christopher.
The old homes of Britain: the southern counties-
Kent, Sussex, Hampshire, Surrey and Middlesex,
edited by Christopher Hussey.
Country Life. 1928.
6,8,11.12.

JESSUP, Frank William.
The Eighteenth Century Country House
in Kent. (100 copies printed).
Privately Printed at Canterbury College of Art.
1966.
3.

JONES, Barbara.
Follies and grottoes. 2nd edition revised and
enlarged.
Constable. 1974.
11.

KENT COUNTY COUNCIL
Heritage Year 1975: Kent Bulletin. No 1. 1975.
K.C.C. 1975.
12.

KENT COUNTY COUNCIL, Planning Dept
Housing Design Guide.
K.C.C. 1976.
3,4,11,13,16,23.

"75 for 75" An exhibition of photographs
of some of the best buildings in Kent.
European Architectural Heritage Year. 1975.
K.C.C. 1975.
3,20.

KENWARD. James.*
The roof tree
O.U.P. 1941 (1938)
9

KERSHAW, S. Wayland.*
Famous Kentish houses: their history and
architecture.
B.T. Batsford. 1880.
3,11,15,16,26

LINDLEY, Kenneth Arthur
Seaside architecture.
Hugh Evelyn. 1973
7,14

MADDEN, Len
Kent: a building survey. Extracted from
Building 7th and 14th April, 1972, by
Len Madden and others.
4

MASON, Reginald Thomas.*
Framed buildings of the Weald.
The Author, Handcross, Sussex. 1964.
24, 25
2nd edition. Coach Publishing House,Ltd.Horsham.
1969.
2,12,16
3rd edition. Coach Publishing House,Ltd.Horsmam.
1973.
16

MELLING, Elizabeth.*
Some Kentish Houses Kentish Sources V,
edited by E. Melling.
K.C.C. 1965.
2,3,4,5,6,7,8,11,12,14,15,16,18,19,20,21,25,
27,30,31

MERCER, Eric
English vernacular houses: a study of trad-
itional farmhouses and cottages. (Kent 173 -
178 and passim).
H.M.S.O. 1975
11,17,19

NEWMAN, John.
North East and East Kent. (The buildings of
England series No. 39, edited by N.Pevsner).
Penguin. 1969*
2,3,4,5,7,8,9,11,12,19,21,24,25,28.
Penguin. 1976 2nd edition.
2,3,7,11,12,15,19,20,26,27,30

West Kent and the Weald. (The buildings of
England series No. 38, edited by N.Pevsner).
Penguin. 1969*
2,3,4,5,7,8,9,19,21,24,25,28
Penguin. 1976 2nd edition.
2,3,7,8,11,12,15,19,20,23,24,27,28,30

OSWALD, Arthur.*
Country houses of Kent
Country Life. 1933.
1,2,3,4,5,6,7,8,9,11,12,14,15,19,20,21,24,25

SACKVILLE-WEST, Victoria
          afterwards Lady Nicolson
English country houses, 2nd ed.
Collins, 1942.
23

SEABOURNE M.
The English School: its architecture and
organisation, 1370 - 1970. Vols. I and II
by M. Seabourne and M. Lowe(Includes Canterbury:
King's School and St. Mildred's C.of E. School;
Brabourn National: Hytne National;Ightham
National; Monks Horton National; Ramsgate R.C.
School; Sittingbourne National (and briefly)
Tonbridge School).
Routledge. 1977.
3.

SIMPSON, W. Douglas
Castles from the air
Country Life. London. 1949.
12

SOUTH-EASTERN SOCIETY OF ARCHITECTS.*
Architecture in Kent, Surrey & Sussex:the year
book of the South-Eastern Society of Architects
in alliance with the Royal Institute of
British Architects, 1952 - 53.
The Society. 1953.
11

SQUIERS, William
Secret hiding places: the origins,histories and
descriptions of English secret hiding places
used by priests,cavaliers, Jacobites, and
smugglers. (pp.261-275, Kent).
S. Paul. 1934.
11

STEPHENSON, D.
Balcony railings in Kent. Reprinted from
Archaeologia Cantiana Vol 86. 1971.
K.A.S. 1971
9

SYMES, Rodney
Railway architecture of the south-east,by
R. Symes and David Cole.
Osprey Pubns. 1972.
4,7,9,11,19

WEBB, William
Kent's Historic Buildings.
R. Hale. 1977
1,3,5,6,7,9,11,15,16,19,20,22,23,25,26,27.28.30

WIKELEY,Nigel.*
Railway Stations: Southern Region,by
N. Wikeley and J. Middleton.
Peco Pubns. 1971.
3,4,7,9,11,12,30

ASH BY WROTHAM

LAMBARDE, Fane F.*
Notes on the Parish Church of Ash-by-Wrotham,
Kent.
Typescript. 1909.
11

ASH-NEXT-SANDWICH

THE CHURCH OF ST. NICHOLAS at Ash-next-
Sandwich(First edition 1928 by Sir Reginald
Thomas Tower). Revised in 1951 and 1972.
Printed by A.J. Snowden. 1972.
3,11

DILNOT, Frank.*
The squire of Ash. A novel.
Brentano. 1929, 1930.
11,25

PLANCHÉ, J.R.*
A corner of Kent,or some account of Ash-next-
R. Hardwicke. 1864.   Sandwich.
2.

ASHFORD

ASHFORD 1974: guide to the Borough of Ashford
and Tenterden.
The Ashford Advertiser & Rider. 1974.
11

ASHFORD BOROUGH COUNCIL
Ashford Borough: official guide.
Service Publications Ltd for Ashford Borough
Council. 1975.
11

ASHFORD BOROUGH COUNCIL: PLANNING DEPARTMENT.
Ashford   Borough planning handbook.
Ashford Borough Council, Planning Dept. 1977.
4,6,11

ASHFORD LOCAL HISTORY GROUP
Ashford's past at present.
L.R.B. Hist. Pubns. Kennington. 1976.
1,2,3,6,7,8,11,12,16,19,22

ASHFORD URBAN DISTRICT COUNCIL.
Ashford official guide.
Home Publishing Co.(Southern) Croydon. 1972.
4,22

BOORMAN, Henry Roy Pratt.
Ashford's progress: the development of an
important town.
Kent Messenger, Maidstone. 1977.
3,4,11,12,15,19,22,23,25

CHUDLEY, John A.
Letraset, a lesson in growth.
(Letraset Factory at Ashford was built
in 1968).
Business Books Ltd. 1974.
11

"DAY BY DAY" DIRECTORY OF ASHFORD,
KENNINGTON and WILLESBOROUGH.
Redmans. Ashford.
5th edn. 1965.   12, 19
6th edn. 1970.   11

GLOUCESTER, J.H. Comber. (J.H.C. pseud).*
St. Mary's Church Ashford, Kent. compiled
by J.H.C.
British Publishing Co. Ltd,.
3.   1958
4.   1956 & 1961
7.   1956
8.   1956 & 1970
11.   1956, 1966 & 1970.
12.   1966.

GREAT BRITAIN, Laws etc. (Vic)
An act for making railways between
Maidstone and Ashford. 1880.
7

HEADLEY'S DIRECTORY OF ASHFORD & DISTRICT.
Headley Bros. Invicta Press. Ashford.
2nd edn. 1933.   11.
4th edn. 1938/9   11.

HEADLEY'S GUIDE TO ASHFORD & DISTRICT,*
illustrated; issued under the auspices
of the Ashford Chamber of Commerce.
Headley Bros. Invicta Press, Ashford.
1900, 1931. etc.
1.3.4.7.11.12.13.15.19

IGGLESDEN, Sir Charles.*
Ashford Church
Kentish Express, 1901.
2

Crimson Glow.(A novel set in the Ashford
Area during World War 1).
Kentish Express. 1925
11.22
4 6. (2nd edition 1940)

KENT COUNTY COUNCIL: COUNTY SECRETARY'S DEPT.
RESEARCH AND INTELLIGENCE UNIT.
Survey of attendance at Ashford North Youth
Wing; Final report. (A youth club).
K.C.C. 1975.
11

KENT COUNTY COUNCIL: PLANNING DEPT.
Administrative County of Kent Town and
Country Planning Act 1971. Kent Development
Plan (1967 Revision). Amendment No.30,
comprehensive development area No.14.
Singleton, Ashford (comprising part of the
Ashford Borough). Scale 1:2,500. Size 84 x
120 cm.
K.C.C. 1976.
11

Administrative County of Kent, Town and
Country Planning Act 1971. Kent development
Plan (1967 revision). Ashford Town Map
Amendment No.30. Comprehensive development
area No.14. Singleton, Ashford (comprising
part of the Ashford Borough). Town map
amendment map.....For use with written statement.
K.C.C. 1976.
11

Expansion at Ashford: an appraisal of its*
impact on East Kent.
K.C.C. 1967.
13,24

Kent Development Plan (1967 revision) Town
& Country Planning Act, 1971. Comprehensive
development area No.14 Amendment No.30.
Singleton, Ashford. (comprising part of the
Ashford Borough). Written statement.
K.C.C. 1976.
11

Singleton informal action area plan.
(A proposed development between Ashford
& Great Chart).
K.C.C. 1977.
11

Singleton informal action area plan: proposals
map. Scale 1:2500. Size 77 cm x 1.32 metres.
For use with written statement.
K.C.C. 1977.
11

"KENT COUNTY EXAMINER" DIRECTORY OF ASHFORD,
and popular calendar for 1896.
B.P. Boorman, Ashford. 1896.
11

"KENTISH EXPRESS"
Guide and directory to Ashford, Romney
Marsh, Tenterden & Elham districts.
Kentish Express, Ashford. c.1923
3

A MASTER OF HOUNDS*: being the life story of
Harry Buckland of Ashford by one who knows him.
Faber. 1931.
1,7,11,22

METROPOLITAN PUBLISHING.
Ashford, Kent: guide and street plan.
Metropolitan Publishing. 1974.
11

PEARMAN, Rev. Augustus John.*
Ashford: its Church, Vicars, College &
Grammar School.
Thompson, Ashford. 1886.
26

ASHFORD Cont'd

ROCHARD, J.*
Ashford illustrated and historical being a
concise and comprehensive account of this
picturesque and interesting neighbourhood.
J. Rochard. Gravesend. 1897?
22

SOROPTOMIST CLUB OF ASHFORD.
Ashford: a guide for the disabled.
Soroptomist Club of Ashford. 1973?
11

AUSTEN. JANE (1775-1817)

CONNECTIONS WITH ASHFORD, GODMERSHAM,
TONBRIDGE. ETC.

ANDREWS, S.M.*
Jane Austen.....her Tonbridge connections.
Tonbridge Free Press. 1949.
11,12,19

BARR, John.
Jane Austen, 1775 - 1817: catalogue of an
exhibition held in the King's library,
British Library Reference Division.
B.M. Publications. 1975.
3

CECIL, David.
A portrait of Jane Austen.
Constable. 1978.
3

KENT COUNTY LIBRARY
J.A. 1775-1975; marking the
bicentenary of the birth of Jane Austen on
16 December, 1775.
K.C.L. 1975.
3

LLEWELYN, Margaret
Jane Austen: a character study.
W. Kimber. 1977.
3

SOUTHAM, B.C.
Jane Austen.
Longman for British Council. 1975.
3

WILKS, Brian.
Jane Austen
Hamlyn. 1978.
3

AVIATION

BARNES, C.H.*
Shorts' aircraft since 1900. (Short
Brothers' Aircraft works were in
Rochester until 1948).
Putnam. 1967.
4,25

BOWYER, Chaz.
Sunderland at War.
(Sunderland Flying boats were built by
the Short Brothers at Rochester).
Ian Allan. 1976.
11

BRUCE, Gordon.
C.S. Rolls, pioneer aviator: an account of
the contribution made to British aviation
by Charles Stewart Rolls, 1877 -1910.
(Many of Rolls' Flights were made from Kent).
Monmouth District Museum Service. 1978.
2,11

CHAPMAN, T.
The Cornwall Aviation Company. (The Company
which gave aerial joy rides).
Glasney. 1979.
13

CIVIL AVIATION AUTHORITY.
A study of general aviation in the South
East of England: a report to the Civil
Aviation Authority and the Standing
Conference on London and South East Regional
Planning. (Kent Airfields mentioned).
Civil Aviation Authority. 1974.
11

JABLONSKI, Edward.
Seawings: an illustrated history of flying
boats. (Section on Short Bros. of Rochester).
R. Hale. 1974.
4

KENT AVIATION HISTORICAL AND RESEARCH SOCIETY.
Wings over Kent. No.1 (1st of a series on
Aviation history).
The Society. 1979.
2,6,16,28

POOLMAN, Kenneth.*
Flying Boat: the story of the "Sunderland".
(Short Brothers of Rochester).
Kimber. 1962.
15

PRESTON, James M.
A Short History: a history of Short Bros.
Aircraft activities in Kent, 1908 - 1964.
North Kent Books. 1978.
3,4,5,12.
2 Corrected reprint. 1979.

SHORT BROTHERS (ROCHESTER & BEDFORD LTD).*
Pamphlets describing the aircraft and history
of the firm. c.1920 - 1945.
4

TRADE & INDUSTRY, Dept. of: ACCIDENTS INVESTI-
GATION BRANCH.
Aero Commander 680 G-ASHI. Report of the
accident at approximately ¼ mile South of
Rochester City Airport, Kent, on 19th February,
1975.
H.M.S.O. 1976.
11

Avions Pierre Robin DR 360, Robin Knight
G-AZOX. Report on the accident at Biggin
Hill Aerodrome, Kent, on 21st July, 1973.
Civil Aircraft Accident Report 17/74.
H.M.S.O. 1974.
11,23

Beagle A61 Series 2. (Terrier) G-ARTZ.
Report on the accident at Home Farm,
Leigh near Tonbridge, Kent,on 15th August,
1973.
H.M.S.O. 1974.
11

Owl Racer 65 - 2G - AYNS. Report on the
accident at Greenwich Reach, River Thames..
on 31st May, 1971.
H.M.S.O. 1974.
11.

Piper PA 32R (Cherokee Lance) PH-PLY
Report on the accident at Holly Hill, near
Snodland, Kent,on the 29th April, 1978.
H.M.S.O. 1979.
11,23

AYLESFORD

AYLESFORD PARISH COUNCIL.
Aylesford, Kent: Official guide.
Issued by the authority of the Aylesford
Parish Council. Text by L.H. Smith, illust-
rated by Frank A. Oakley.
Forward Publicity Ltd. 1975.
4,6,11,12,25

BROWN, Anthony
Red for Remembrance: British Legion 1921-71.
Heinemann. 1971.
12

CARMELITE FRIARS
Aylesford priory: a guide.
Carmelite Press. Faversham. 197-?
12

The friars: Aylesford.
Carmelite Press. Faversham. 1977.
12

Return of the White Friars.
Carmelite Press. Faversham. 1974.
12

CLEEVES, Janet D. *
Guide to the Friars, Aylesford.
British Legion Press. Maidstone. 1954.
11

COPSEY, Alan Charles.
Aylesford Priory, Kent, some chronological
notes on the Carmelite Period: 1242-1538.
Duplicated text. 197-?
11

THE FRIARS GUIDE BOOK., Aylesford.
Kent, England.
Carmelite Press, Faversham. 195-?
11,25

GENERAL REGISTER OFFICE
Census Returns, 1841,1851,1861,1871,
Aylesford.
Microfilm.
23

INGLE, Joy *
Preston Hall; history and legend.
British Legion Press.
9,11   1962
4   1965
15   1957

KENT COUNTY COUNCIL: PLANNING DEPT.
Aylesford Conservation Study.
K.C.C. 1972.
1,2,3,4,7,8,12,16,20,25,30

LYNCH, E. Killiai.
The Order of Carmelites.
Carmelite Press, Aylesford. c.1950
11

NATIONAL BOOK LEAGUE.
An exhibition of the work of three private
presses; St. Dominics Press/Ditchling;
Edward Walters/Primrose Hill and Saint
Alberts' Press/Aylesford. Devised and
presented by Brocard Sewell under the
sponsorship of Linotype U.K. and the
National Book League. Catalogue by Joseph
Jerome.
St. Alberts' Press, Faversham. 1976.
11

REED PAPER GROUP. *
A tour of the Aylesford Paper Mills &
associated Factories.
Reed Paper & Board Group. n.d.
8,11

ROUND ABOUT KIT'S COTY HOUSE: * an essay in
popular topography.
Bell & Daldy, 1861.
8

ROYAL BRITISH LEGION.
The British Legion Village, Preston Hall,
Maidstone, Kent. 1925 to 1970.
British Legion Press 197-?
11,12

Into the future: the story of the Royal
British Legion.
British Legion Press. 1976.
11
Kent County Branch Handbook - see ORGANISATIONS

1921-1971. Fifty years. The British Legion,
Kent. British Legion Press, 1971.
30

The Royal British Legion Village 50th
anniversary open day: the record of 50
years of treating, training and rehabilitating
disabled ex-servicemen and women.
British Legion Press. 1975.
11

SHEPPARD, Lancelot Capel.
The English Carmelites. (Refers to the
Aylesford Carmelite Priory throughout)
Burns Oates. 1943.
11

VIGAR, J.E.
Forgotten facts of Aylesford and District.
The White House, Aylesford. 1976.
4,12,25.

AYLESHAM

AYLESHAM FESTIVAL COMMITTEE
A festival of Aylesham, to celebrate H.M.
The Queen's Silver Jubilee and Aylesham's
Golden anniversary. 4th,5th,6th,7th June,1977
Aylesham Festival Committee. 1977.
6.

BAPCHILD

AVENT, A.E.
The Church of St. Laurence, Bapchild: a
brief guide for visitors.
Bapchild Parochial Church Council. 1973.
20

**CHEMPSTEAD HOUSE, Bapchild. By order of the
executors of the late Lady Doubleday.....the
remaining contents of the residence for sale
by auction....Wednesday 24th March and
Thursday 25th March, 1976.**
Finn-Kelsey, Collier-Ashenden. 1976.
20

BARFRESTON

CLARKE, Charles.*
An attempt to ascertain the age of the church
of Barfreston, in Kent: with remarks on the
architecture of that building, in a letter
from Charles Clarke to John Britton.
Britton's Architectural Antiquities of
Great Britain. 1812.
11.

GOODSALL, Robert Harold .*
The church of St. Mary, Barfreston.
S.P.C.K. 19--?
6

WORSFOLD, Frederick Henry.*
A guide to Barfreystone Church and its
world famous carvings.
Kentish Gazette, Canterbury.
12   1949
30   3rd edn. 1958
11   8th edn. 1978 Printed by Kent County
                           Printers.

BARHAM

BARHAM WOMEN'S INSTITUTE.
History of Barham.
Printed by A. & J. Purchase. Canterbury.
6.7. New Edition. 1966.
3,7,28.   1977.

EDWARDS, Frank.
Dear old Barham. (7 duplicated sheets)
Reprinted for the Silver Jubilee Fete.   1977.
3

PARTICULARS & SPECIAL CONDITIONS OF SALE
relating to Elmstone Court, Barham. No.2. Out
Elmsted Lane, Barham & Building Plot. out
Elmsted Lane, Barham....28th July, 1972.
Collier & Gardener. Canterbury. 1972.
3

PRICE, F.H.
Nature notes (first appeared in
Barham Parish Magazine 1971 - 75).
1976.
3

BARMING

IMPERIAL GROUP REVIEW. Vol.5 No.1
Nov. 1973. Imperial Group Ltd.
Smedleys at Barming & Faversham are
owned by the Imperial Group Ltd.
11

BEARSTED

BEARSTED & THURNHAM HISTORY BOOK COMMITTEE
History of Bearsted & Thurnham.
Bearsted & Thurnham History Book Committee. 1978.
3,11,12,15,23

CHURCH OF THE HOLY CROSS, BEARSTED.
Church Magazine for August, 1972.
Bearsted Parochial Church Council. 1972.
11

HOLY CROSS CHURCH:* a short account.
Kent Messenger. Maidstone. 1955.
12

BECKENHAM

BECKENHAM, BOROUGH COUNCIL.*
Official guide to the Borough of Beckenham
Pyramid Press. 1960
4

BECKENHAM JOURNAL; Diamond Jubilee supplement..
1876 - 1936 (includes references to important
events within the period)
T.W. Thornton. 1936.
2

BECKENHAM LIBRARY.
A brief introduction to the history of
Beckenham. (duplicated transcript)
Bromley Public Library, 1977.
2,3

BECKENHAM PUBLIC LIBRARIES.
Beckenham classified trades directory.
Beckenham Public Library. 1956.
2

BORROWMAN, Robert.
Short description of the parish church
of Beckenham, Kent.
T.W. Thornton, Beckenham. 1906.
11

BRASSELL, K.W.
St. James's Church, Elmers End. 1879 - 1979.
centenary booklet,by K.W. Brassell and others.
(Elmers End, Beckenham)
The Parish. 1978.
2

COLLINS, J.P.
Distribution of retailing in Beckenham,Kent
1885 - 1915 (photocopy of transcript).
1976.
2

COPELAND, H. Robert.
100 years of change in Beckenham 1874 - 1974.
H.R. Copeland & Son. 1974.
2,18.

The village of old Beckenham.*
H.R. Copeland & Son. 1970.
30

DYER, Albert.
The ups and downs of my life: the memoirs of
Albert Dyer 1908 - 1970. (Duplicated typescript:
life and trade in Penge and Beckenham).
n.d.
2

FORSTER, John Lord Harraby
Master, the Lord Forster of Harraby:
an obituary by Geoffrey Tookey. (Lord
Forster was a resident of Beckenham).
In Granya, No.76, 1973, pp 75 - 79.
Honourable Society of Gray's Inn. London. 1973.
2.

KELLY'S DIRECTORIES LTD.
Kelly's Directory of Beckenham, Penge and
neighbourhood. 43rd edition.
Kelly's Directories Ltd. 1938.
11

LUCAS, Meriel.
James William Wells. 1847 - 1902.
Typescript. (J.W. Wells was a resident of
Beckenham, 1884 - 1900).
1976.
2

MACDONALD, Gilbert.
One hundred years: Wellcome, 1880 - 1980.
In pursuit of excellence.
Wellcome Foundation. 1980.
2,5.

2

PORTEOUS, Chris.
Seeing and serving Christ for 100 years.
(history of Christ Church,Beckenham).
The Author, Christ Church, Beckenham.1975.
2,11

TONKIN, Nancy and MANNING, Patricia.
Reminiscences of the Adrenian Association
(Cover title - Langley Park 1919 - 1979)
Note: Langley Park School for Girls, was
formerly Beckenham/Beckenham County
Grammar School for Girls.
Langley Park School for Girls. 1979.
2

TOOKEY, G.W.
The acquisition of the Langley Estate
(Beckenham) by the Style family.
Typescript n.d.
2
The History of Kelsey Park, Beckenham.
Typescript, 1975.
2
The History of Langley Park, Beckenham.
Typescript, 1975.
2
The story of Park Langley, Beckenham.
Typescript, 1952, with addendum 1964.
2

WELLCOME FOUNDATION LIMITED.

(Administrative Headquarters and Research
Labatory at Beckenham, also at Dartford).

Foundation News, 1970 - 71; 1972 - 73.
Burroughs Wellcome.
5.

Some achievements of the Wellcome Foundation.
Burroughs Wellcome. 1965.

2
The Wellcome Foundation: Company with a
difference. The Wellcome Foundation. 1980.
2

BECKET, SAINT THOMAS, ARCHBISHOP OF
CANTERBURY (1162 - 1170)

ABBOTT, Edwin A.*
St. Thomas of Canterbury, 2 vols.
Black 1898.
1.3.11.12.17.

ANOUILH, Jean
Becket: or the honour of God
Eyre Methuen. 1963.
3

BALL, Mia.
Worshipful Company of Brewers: a short
history.
(pp.19 - 70 Canterbury & St. Thomas á
Becket mentioned).
Hutchinson. 1977.
11

BARONIUS, Caesar. (B.A. pseud)
The life or the Ecclesiastical Historie
of St. Thomas, Archbishop of Canterbury.
1639.
17
1975. Reprinted by the Scholar Press.
3,17

BEAZELEY, M.*
"On certain human remains found in the crypt
of Canterbury Cathedral Church & supposed by
some to be those of Archbishop Becket" From
the Proceedings of the Society of Antiquaries,
25, XXII, 15, December 5th 1907.
3

BECKET, Thomas. Archbishop of Canterbury.*
The prophecie of Thomas Becket....concerning
the wars betwixt England, France and Holland.
G. Freeman. 1666
3

BELLOC, HILAIRE.*
Becket: St. Thomas of Canterbury.
Catholic Truth Society. London. 1933
3,11

BENEDICT, Abbot of Peterborough.*
The Life and miracles of St. Thomas of
Canterbury.
Caxton Society. 1850.
3

BENSON, Robert Hugh.*
The Holy Blissful Martyr, Saint Thomas of
Canterbury.
Macdonald & Evans. 1908.
1,3

BORENIUS, Tancred.
Addenda to the iconography of St. Thomas of
Canterbury. Read to the Society of Antiquaries
of London, 26th February, 1931.
The Society. 1931.
11
The Iconography of St. Thomas of Canterbury*
read to the Society of Antiquaries of London,
28th February, 1929.
The Society, 1929.
11,12
Some further aspects of the iconography of
St. Thomas of Canterbury read to the Society
of Antiquaries of London, 9th February, 1933.
The Society, 1933.
11
St. Thomas Becket in Art.
Methuen. 1932
3,6,12

BROMLEY, Francis E.*
Note on the corona of St. Thomas of Canterbury.
In Archaeologia Cantiana Vol.46. 1934.
17

BUSHELL, W.D.*
Saint Thomas of Canterbury. Extracts from
the biographies, translated into English
with explanatory notes.
Macmillan & Bowes. 1896.
11

CANTERBURY CATHEDRAL LIBRARY
Thomas Becket anniversary. Exhibition of
treasures in the Cathedral Library 26th June
to 18th July, 1970.
Canterbury Cathedral, 1970.
3

COMPTON, Piers.*
The Turbulent Priest: a life of St. Thomas
of Canterbury.
Staples Press. 1957.
4,11,12.

COOLE, Albert.*
The Life of Thomas Becket.
P.D. Eastes & Co. Ltd. Canterbury. 1927.
3,11

DARK, Sidney.*
St. Thomas of Canterbury.
Macmillan. 1927.
3,7,11,12

Seven Archbishops.* (Chapter entitled
"The Saint")
Eyre & Spottiswoode. 1944.
1,11

DE VERE, Aubrey Thomas*
St. Thomas of Canterbury. (poem)
King. 1876.
11,17

BECKET, SAINT THOMAS, ARCHBISHOP OF
CANTERBURY (1162 - 1170).

DUGGAN, Alfred.*
Thomas Becket of Canterbury.
Faber. 1952.etc.
1,3,5,11,12,21

DWYER, J.J.
Saint Thomas of Canterbury, 1118 - 1170.
Revised edition.
Catholic Truth Society, 1948.
3

ELIOT, Thomas Stearns.
Film of "Murder in the Cathedral", by
T.S. Eliot & George Hoellering.
Faber, London. 1952.
3
Murder in the Cathedral.
Faber, London. 1935
3,6
Murder in the Cathedral: a screen play
(programme)
Westminster Press, London. 1951.
3
Murder in the Cathedral (television
camera script) 1964.
3

FITZSTEPHEN, William.*
The life and death of Thomas Becket,
Chancellor of England & Archbishop of
Canterbury based on the account of
William Fitzstephen....translated and
edited by George Greenaway.
Folio Society. 1961.
3,4,11

FOREVILLE, Raymonde.*
La Jubile de Saint Thomas Becket du
XIIIe au XVe Siècle.
Paris Imprimeries Oberthur. 1959.
3

FOWLER, Montagu.*
Some notable Archbishops of Canterbury.
(Includes Thomas Becket).
S.P.C.K. 1895.
1,11

GALLAGHER, Michael Paul.
T.S. Eliot. Murder in the Cathedral.
(Study guide series).
Gill & Macmillan. Dublin. 1977.
3

GARNIER OF PONT-SAINTE-MAXENCE.
Garnier's Becket: translated from the 12th
Century "Vie Saint Thomas" ...by Janet Shirley.
Phillimore. 1975.
3,11

GILES, J.A. *
Life and letters of Thomas à Becket, 2 vols.
London, Whittaker & Co. 1846.
3,17

GITTINGS, Robert.
Conflict at Canterbury: an entertainment in
Sound and light, specially commissioned.....
For the Festival of Canterbury, 1970.
Heinemann Educational. 1970.
11

HALL, D.J.*
English Mediaeval pilgrimage.
(Chapter 6: St. Thomas Becket p.130-165)
C. Chivers
4. 1965.
3. 1973.

HOOK, Walter Farquhar.*
Lives of the Archbishops of Canterbury, 12 vols.
Vol.II includes Thomas Becket.
Richard Bentley. 1860 - 84.
1,3,4,6,7,11,12,17

HOPE, Anne.
The life of St. Thomas à Becket of Canterbury.
Burns & Oates. 1868.
11

HUMPHREY-SMITH, Cecil R.
Heraldry associated with the martyrdom of
Archbishop Thomas Becket.
(Photocopy of p.371 - 375 of Proceedings,the
10th International Congress of Genealogical
& Heraldic Sciences. Vienna 14 - 19 Sept. 1970)
Heralaisch-Genealogische Gesellschaft. 1970.
3

HUMPHREY-SMITH, Cecil R.
Heraldry associated with the martyrdom
of Archbishop Thomas Becket (photocopy of
p.18 - 28 of 'The Coat of Arms' Vol.XII
Heraldry Society. 1971.
3

HUTTON, William Holden.*
Saint Thomas of Canterbury....from contemporary
biographers and other chroniclers.
D. Nott. London. 1899.
3

Thomas Becket: Archbishop of Canterbury.*
C.U.P.
3   1910 and(1926   2nd edn)
3,6.1926 2nd edn.

JEEVES, Mary Angela.
St. Thomas Becket "Most Mighty in England";
a psychological study.
Arthur H. Stockwell, Ilfracombe.Devon. 1956
3

BECKET AND CANTERBURY, a book list.
K.C.L. Maidstone. 1970.
3

KNOWLES, Dom David.*
Archbishop Thomas Becket From The Proceedings
of the British Academy Vol.35.
O.U.P. London. 1949.
3
The episcopal colleagues of Archbishop Thomas
Becket.
Cambridge U.P. 1951.
3
Thomas Becket.
A.&.C. Black. 1970.
11,12

LAWLER, Ray.*
A breach in the wall: a play about the tomb of
Becket in a village church.
William Doran. 1971.
3

LEE, Laurie.
Peasants' Priest: a play. Acting edition
for the Festival of the Friends of Canterbury
Cathedral. 1947.
H.J. Goulden. Canterbury, 1952.
1,12

McKILLIAM, A.E. *
A Chronical of the Archbishops of Canterbury.
(Includes Thomas Becket).
J. Clarke. 1913.
1,2,3,4,8,11,12

BECKET, SAINT THOMAS, ARCHBISHOP OF CANTERBURY (1162 - 1170).

MILLS, Dorothy.*
Thomas Becket, 1118 - 1170, Archbishop of
Canterbury.
Friends of Canterbury Cathedral. Canterbury.
1960.
3,4,7,11,19

MILMAN, Henry Salisbury.
The vanished memorials of St. Thomas
of Canterbury. Read to the Society of
Antiquaries of London on February 26th and
March 12th 1891.
The Society. 1891.
11

MORRIS, John.
The relics of St. Thomas of Canterbury.
n.d.
1,3,11,15,17

MYDANS, Sheila.*
Thomas: a novel of the life of Becket.
Collins, London. 1965.
3

PAIN, Nesta.
The King and Becket.
Eyre & Spottiswoode. 1964.
4.

Thomas Becket: B.B.C. TV Camera script.*
1968.
3

PATCH, Rev. John D.H.*
Guide to the Parish Church of St. Thomas the
Martyr, Winchelsea. Revised edition.
Adam & Son. Rye.
15. 1913.
3. 1933.

POLLEN, John Hungerford.*
King Henry VIII and St.Thomas Becket, being
a history of the burning of the Saint's bones
and the reports thereon,by Thomas Derby,
William Thomas & P. Crisestone Henriquez.
Reprinted from The Month, February & April.1912.
3

REYNOLDS, Ernest Edwin.
St. Thomas Becket.
Catholic Truth Society, 1970.
3

ROBERTSON, James C.*
Becket, Archbishop of Canterbury.
Murray. 1859.
12,17
Materials for the history of Thomas Becket,
Archbishop of Canterbury.
Longman, London. 1875.
3,17

ROUTLEDGE, Charles Francis.*
Short summary of the controversy as to
"Becket's bones"
Crow. Canterbury. 1888.
1
Survey of the "Becket bones" controversy
by C. Routledge & others. 1888
17

RYE, Walter.
Some new facts as to the life of St. Thomas à
Becket, tending to show that he was probably
early educated in, and closely connected in
many ways with Norfolk.
W.H. Hunt, Norwich. 1924.
11

SCOTT, Patrick.
Thomas á Becket and other poems. 1853
17

SPEAIGHT, Robert.*
Thomas Becket.
Longmans.1949.
3   1938
4 12   1949

STEDDY, George S.
The greatest of the English Martyrs. A short
account of the relics of St. Thomas of
Canterbury and of the replica of his shrine,
in the Catholic Church dedicated to him at
Canterbury.(Photocopy)
David H.E. King. 1920.
3

TENNYSON, Alfred. 1st Baron Tennyson.*
Becket; a play.
Macmillan
3   1884, 1888 and 1933
11   1932
Souvenir of Becket*...First presented at the
Lyceum Theatre, 6th February, 1893,by Henry
Irving.
Black & White. London. 1893
3

THOMPSON, Robert Anchor.*
Thomas Becket: martyr patriot.
Kegan, Paul, Trench & Co. London. 1889.
3

THORNTON, W. Pugin.*
Becket's bones.
Cross & Jackman. Canterbury. 1901.
7,12,13,14.
Report on a human skeleton found in the
crypt of Canterbury Cathedral, supposed to
be Thomas a Becket s
Crow, Canterbury, 1888.
1.17.

TOUT, Thomas Frederick.*
The place of St. Thomas of Canterbury in
history.
(Reprinted from the Collected Papers of
T.F. Tout. Vol. III)
Manchester University Press. 1934.
3

URRY, William.
Some notes on the two resting places of
St. Thomas Becket at Canterbury. (Pages 195 -
209 of "Thomas Becket; actes du colloque
international de Sédières 19-24 Août 1973")
Beauchesne. Raymonde Foreville. 1973?
3

Two notes on Cuernes de Pont Sainte
Maxence:*Vie de Saint Tomas. Reprinted from
Archaeologia Cantiana. Vol.LXVI. 1953.
3,17

VITA ET PROCESSUS S. THOMAE.* 1495-6
17

WADDAMS, Herbert Montagu.
Saint Thomas Becket.
Pitkin. 1971.
11

WHEELER, Clifford.
The life of Thomas á Becket, Archbishop of
Canterbury, Saint and Martyr, presented in
a vivid poem.
Cross & Jackman, Canterbury. 1924.
11

WILLIAMSON, Hugh Ross.*
The arrow and the sword...being an enquiry
into the nature of the deaths of
William Rufus and Thomas Becket.
Faber. 1955.
3

BECKET, SAINT THOMAS, ARCHBISHOP OF CANTERBURY (1162 - 1170)

WINSTON, Richard.*
Thomas Becket.
Constable, 1967.
1,5,12

WOODGATE, Mildred Violet.*
Thomas Becket, 1118 - 1170.
St. Paul Publishers. 1971.
11

BEDGEBURY

MITCHELL, A.F.*
Bedgebury Pinetum & Forest Plots. 4th
edition, edited by A.F. Mitchell and A.W.
Westall for the Forestry Commission.
H.M.S.O. 1972.
11,19

Short guide to Bedgebury Pinetum and Forest
Plots, with illustrations and plans by
A.F. Mitchell. (Forestry Commission Guides).
H.M.S.O. 1969.
2,4,8,9,11

BEKESBOURNE

ASPINALL, John
The Best of Friends.
(Zoo parks at Howletts, Bekesbourne and at
Port Lympne).
McMillan. 1976.
3,7

FIFTY YEARS AGO: a description of the villages
of Bridge, Patrixbourne & Bekesbourne, taken
from "Saunters through Kent with pen and pencil"
by Charles Igglesden.
Bekesbourne Parochial Church Council. 1977.
3

A TRUE & PERFECT TERRIER. (This terrier
for the Parish of Bekesbourne was made out in
1695 for the Rev. Nicholas Batteley).
A.&.J. Purchese. Canterbury. 1977?
3

BELTRING

WHITBREAD AND CO. LTD.*
A souvenir of your visit to Whitbread's hop
garden at Beltring, Paddock Wood.
Whitbread & Co. 195-?
19

BELVEDERE

ALL SAINTS CHURCH, BELVEDERE.
(A collection of pamphlets produced by the Church).
1856.
1

PRITCHARD, John A.
Belvedere and Bostall, a brief history.
London Borough of Bexley, Library & Museum
Services. 1974.
1

BENENDEN

B.,K.
The Benenden Angel & other fables, by K.B.
Illustrations by Penelope Cox. 1954.
11

BENENDEN CHEST HOSPITAL, Staff Gazette.
No.20. Summer 1972.
Benenden Chest Hospital. 1972.
11

BIRD, K.
Ballad of Benenden: being the history of
the manor of Hemsted. (Benenden School)
Printed by Elvey & Gibbs. (1934). 1969
reprint with additions & alterations.
The ballad was first performed in 1934 for
the tenth anniversary of the founding of
Benenden School
11

CRAN, Marian
The story of my ruin. (The author's
account of how she discovered a cottage
& garden in a "village near Tenterden",
that is, Benenden).
Herbert Jenkins. 1924.
4,11

HASLEWOOD, Rev. Francis F.*
The parish of Benenden, Kent: its monuments,
vicars, and persons of note. Also a reprint
of "This winter's wonders". 1673.
P.P. 1889.
2,19

LEBON, Cicely.*
St. George's Church, Benenden: a guide and
brief architectural history, by C. Lebon and
M. Price.   Printed by The
Courier Coy. Tunbridge Wells. 1962.
11

BESSELS GREEN

GROSER, William.
Memoirs of Mr. John Stanger, late Pastor of
a Baptist Church at Bessels Green, Kent.
(Author lived at Maidstone)
Printed by Milne and Banfield. 1824.
11.

BEULT RIVER & VALLEY

KLOEDEN, Judith L.
An ecological assessment of allurial
grassland in the Beult River Valley, Kent.
(Discussion papers in Conservation no.11)
University College, London. 1975.
2

BEWL RIVER & VALLEY

CROSSLEY, David.
The Bewl Valley ironworks. c.1300 - 1730.
Royal Archaeological Institute. 1975.
2,3,6,8,11,12

BEXLEY

ARCHAEOLOGIA, OR MISCELLANEOUS TRACTS
RELATING TO ANTIQUITY.
Proceedings of the Society of Antiquaries,
Vol.XC. 1944.
1

BEXLEY CIVIC SOCIETY.
Borough Walk 2. Around old Bexley
Bexley Civic Society. 1977.
1

BEXLEY CRICKET CLUB.
150th Anniversary handbook.
Bexley Cricket Club. 1955.
1

BEXLEY, LONDON BOROUGH COUNCIL.
Bexley street atlas.
Ed. J. Burrow. 1976.
4

The Civic Centre.
London Borough of Bexley. 1973.
1

BOROUGH ENGINEERS' DEPARTMENT.
Old Bexley Conservation Area.
As Author. 1973.
1

PUBLIC RELATIONS DIVISION.
Bexley: Official Guide.
G.W. May Ltd. London.
11   1974 & 1977
4,25 1975

TOWN PLANNING DIVISION.
Green Belt.
Discussion paper and interim policy
(2 pamphlets).
London Borough of Bexley 1974?
2

Planning for the
people of Bexley: a guide to town planning
in the borough, 1971.
Pyramid Press. 1971.
11

BUTLER, L.
Growth and development of industry in the
Greater London Borough of Bexley. Thesis.
1972.
1

ELLISTON-ERWOOD, Frank Charles.
The Roman antiquities of N.W. Kent with
special reference to the site of Noviomagus,
....with an account of the excavations...at
Joyden's Wood, Bexley.....1926-27. From the
Journal of the British Archaeological
Association. Vol. XXXIV, 1928.
Bound with   The earthworks at Charlton,*
London S.E. From Journal of the British
Archaeological Association Vols XXII & XXIX,
1916 and 1923.
11.

ENVIRONMENT, Department of the.*
Railway Accident. Report on the collision
that occurred on 12th November 1970 at
Bexley Station, in the Southern Region:
British Railways.
H.M.S.O. 1972.
8

FOSTER, M.C.
The Flora of Bexley
London Borough of Bexley, Libraries and
Museums Dept. 1972.
1,5,11.

GODDARD, Rev. Charles (Vicar of Bexley).*
Bexley Tracts. No.1. January 1832.
Printed by F.H. Wall of Richmond. 1833.
1,11

GREAT BRITAIN, Laws etc. (Geo.III).
An act for paving, cleaning and lighting
the High Street, East Street and West Street.
...George III, 1773.
Fyre Books. 1974.
1

HUTCHERSON, Ruth.
The history of Danson, from Saxon settlement
to public park.
The Author. 1978.
5

THE KENT PAEDIATRIC SOCIETY.*
A study in the epidemiology of health:
being an investigation into the incidence
and causation of health among....schoolchildren
in the Borough of Bexley, Kent.
Bexleyheath, Health Department. 1952.
11

LEVY, L.A. *
Education in Bexley; a history in the
area of the London Borough to 1970,by L.A. &
L.M. Levy.
L.B. Bexley. Libraries & Museums Dept. 1971.
2,11

MORRIS, P.E.
Hall Place, Bexley.
London Borough of Bexley, Libraries &
Museums Dept. 1970.
7,12

NEWMAN, Leonard Hugh.*
Butterfly farmer.
Phoenix House. 1953.
2

ROOME, K.M. comp.
A history of the parish church of St. Mary
the Virgin,Bexley, Kent, compiled by
K.M. Roome.
St. Mary's P.C.C. 1974.
1,2

SAYNOR, Joy.
Bexley Mosaic, edited by Joy Saynor.
W.E.A. Bexley Branch. 1977.
1,2,5,23

TESTER, P.J.
Bexley Village - a short history.
London Borough of Bexley. Libraries and
Museums Department. 1975.
1,2,5,11,18.

THRELFALL, W.
Bexley in 1830 - 1832. Typescript.
1955.
1

BEXLEYHEATH

BEXLEY, LONDON BOROUGH COUNCIL:
DIRECTORATE OF DEVELOPMENT SERVICES.
Bexleyheath town centre: interim policies.
Bexley London. B.C. 1977
Bexleyheath town centre: report of survey.
Bexley London. B.C. 1977.
11

COURSE, Edwin A.*
The Bexleyheath Railway. 1883 - 1900.
(Proceedings of the Woolwich & District
Antiquarian Society Vol XXX 1954)
1,4,5,8,11,12.

BEXLEYHEATH   Cont'd

FOXLEY, Gladys L.
A history of Bexleyheath Golf Club,
1907 - 1977.
Bexleyheath Golf Club. 1977.
1

FRISWELL, Laura Hain. (Mrs. Ambrose Myall)
James Hain Friswell: a memoir.
(J.H. Friswell was a resident and a writer
in Bexleyheath).
George Redway. 1898.
1

LOCKHART, J.G.
Blenden Hall.
Philip Allan. 1930.
1

ST. PETER'S BEXLEYHEATH.   This is your Church.
1961.
1

BIBLIOGRAPHY

BARBER, Melanie.
Index to the letters & papers of Frederick
Temple, Archbishop of Canterbury, 1846 - 1902,
in Lambeth Palace Library, Compiled by
Melanie Barber.
Mansell. 1975.
3,11

BENNETT, George
The Kent Bibliography: a finding list of Kent
material in the public libraries of the
County, and of the adjoining London Boroughs.
Compiled by G. Bennett and edited by W.Bergess
and C. Earl. (For the Kent Sub-Branch of the
L.A.)
Library Association, London & Home Counties
Branch. 1977.
1,2,3,4,5,6,7,8,9,10,11,12,13,14,15,16,17,18,
19,20,22,23,24,25,26,27,28,30,

BERGESS, Winifred F.
Kent directories located; compiled, edited
and analysed by W.F. Bergess and Barbara
R.M. Riddell.
Kent C.C. Maidstone, 1973.
1,2,3,4,5,6,7,8,9,10,11,12,13,14,15,16,17,18
19,20,21,22,23,24,25,26,27,28,29,30

Kent Directories located - 2nd ed. Compiled,
edited and analysed by W.F. Bergess and
B.R.M. Riddell.
K.C.C. Maidstone, 1978.
1.2.3.4.5.6.7.8.9.10,11,12,13,14,15,16,17,18,
19,20,21,22,23,24,25,26,27,28,29.

BISHOP, Brian.
Kent union list of periodicals. 2nd ed.
Compiled by B. Bishop & C. Earl.
London & Home Counties Branch, Kent Sub Branch.
Library Association. 1973.
1.2.3.4.5.6.7.8.9.10.11.12.13.14.15.16.17.18,
19,20,21,22,23,24,25,26,27,28,29

BLACK, William Henry.
Catalogue of....(Colfes' Library) in the year
1652. (The library in the Free School,
Lewisham). 1831
17,18

BRITISH MUSEUM.
Dickens: an excerpt from the "General Catalogue
of Printed Books" in the British Museum.
British Museum. 1960.
12

BRITISH MUSEUM: NATURAL HISTORY*-
DEPARTMENT OF GEOLOGY.
Catalogue of the Mesozoic Plants in the
Department of Geology, The British Museum
(Natural History): The Wealden Flora by
A.C. Seward.
British Museum. 1894 - 5.
4,11

BROWN, Christopher. R.
Kentish Tales. (Annotated list of
books set in Kent).
Kent County Library - School Library Service.
1976.
3,4,5,8,

BROWN, M.D.
David Salomon's House: Catalogue of
momentos. (Southborough).
M.D. Brown. 1968.
12

CANTERBURY CITY MUSEUMS.
Buffs' Museum: Catalogue of books.
Duplicated typescript. 1976.
3

CATALOGUE OF A WHITSUNTIDE EXHIBITION OF
family and village treasures,
& bygones held at St. Nicholas-at-Wade.
pre 1970.
13

CATALOGUE OF HALE'S, LATE NUCKELL'S,
Royal Kent Marine Library, Broadstairs.   1847
24

CATALOGUE OF MAMMALIA AND BIRDS
in the Museum of the Army Medical
Department at Fort Pitt, Chatham.
Burrill. Chatham.
11.

CATALOGUE OF THE COLLECTION OF PICTURES
at Broomhill, Kent.
A.K. Baldwin, 1881.
19.

CATALOGUE OF THE FIRST PORTION of the
Important Library of Thomas Willement,
Esq, F.S.A.   Compiled by C.R. Smith.
(Sotheby, Williamson & Hodge). (Thomas
Willement lived at Davington).
Printed Davy and Sons, London. 1865.
11.26.

CATALOGUE OF THE INTERESTING AND
EXTENSIVE LIBRARY OF...the late Dr. F.W.
Cock, The Well House, Appledore, Kent,
comprising books and manuscripts
relating to Kent....which will be
sold on Monday 8th May, 1944.
Sotheby and Co. London. 1944.
1,7,11.

CATALOGUE OF THE LITURGICAL LIBRARIES OF
THE LATE. Rev. Robt. Charles Jenkins. Honorary Canon of Canterbury Cathedral, and of
a well-known collector, recently deceased,
.....which will be sold by auction...
1897.
3

A CATALOGUE OF THE SYDNEY COLLECTION at
Frognal, Chislehurst. Kent.
Knight, Frank and Rutley, Auctioneers.
Dryden Press. 1915.
1.4.12.17.

BIBLIOGRAPHY   Cont'd

CATALOGUE OF THE WORKING LIBRARY OF ELLEN
TERRY at Smallhythe Place, Tenterden, Kent.
National Trust. 1977.
11

CHATHAM BOROUGH COUNCIL: PUBLIC LIBRARIES.
Book List & Bulletin Nos. 1 - 4.
Chatham Borough Council. 1944 - 45.
4
Care, welfare & housing of old people: a
list of books in stock.
Chatham Borough Council. 1962.
4
Catalogue of the books in the reference &
lending departments. Mackay. 1904.
4
Catalogue of the books in the adult
lending department & reference department.
2nd edition.
Wood & Co. 1913.
4
Supplementary Catalogue of books in the
lending library, with key to the indicator
Class F.
Chatham Borough Council. 1926.
4

CHURCHILL, Irene Josephine.*
Calendar of Kent Feet of Fines to the
end of Henry III's reign, compiled by I.J.
Churchill & others. (Kent Records Vol.15).
K.A.S. Records Branch. 1956.
12

CURLL, Edmund.
A catalogue of books sold by Edmund Curll.
(Tunbridge Wells bookseller).
n.d.
19

DAVIES, Geoffrey Alun.
The Channel tunnel: a bibliography of the
fixed link.
Cadig Liaison Centre.   Coventry. 1973.
2,3,6

DAVIS, Godfrey Rupert Charles.
Mediaeval cartularies of Great Britain:
a short catalogue.
Longmans Green. 1958.
11

DUNKIN, Edwin Hadlow Wise.*
Index to the Act Books of the Archbishops
of Canterbury, 1663 - 1859 compiled by
E.H.W. Dunkin. 2 parts.
British Record Society. 1938.
Part I. (A-K) edited by C. Jenkins &
C.A. Fry.
3,11
Part II (L-Z) edited by C. Jenkins.
2,11

EMDEN, Alfred Brotherston.*
Donors of books to St. Augustines' Abbey,
Canterbury. (Oxford Bibliographical
Society Occasional Papers No.4).
Oxford Bibliographical Society. 1968.
3,4,11,24.

FOLKESTONE PUBLIC LIBRARY.
Some sources of information on places in Kent
Folkestone Public Library. 1931.
4

GANN, P.D.
Unpublished works on Kentish Natural
History in Kent Libraries.
(From the transactions of the Kent
Field Club, Vol.5, Part 2,1974).
Kent Field Club. 1974.
11

GIBSON, J.S.W.
Census Returns, 1841,1851,1861 & 1871, on
microfilm. A directory of local holdings.
2nd Edn, compiled by J.S.W. Gibson.
Gulliver Press. 1980.
13.

GIRAUD, Francis F.*
Catalogue of books preserved in the library
of the Free Grammar School of Elizabeth,
Queen of England, in Faversham. Compiled by
F.F. Giraud.
J. Higham. Faversham. 1895.
26

GOMME, George Laurence.
The literature of local institutions.
Elliot Stock. London. 1886.
11

GREAT BRITAIN: PARLIAMENT — HOUSE OF COMMONS.
General index to the reports from Committees
of the House of Commons, 1715 - 1801. Printed
but not inserted in the journals of the
House, 1803, with a new introduction by
John Brooke. (Reports are held on microfilm).
Chadwyck Healey. 1973.
11

GRIMSDELL, Mrs. N.L.
The Isle of Sheppey: a list of books
relating to Sheppey in the Kent County
Libraries. compiled by Mrs. N.L. Grimsdell.
KCL. Swale Division. 1978.
3,4,11,20,27

GRITTEN, A.J.*
Catalogue of books, pamphlets and excerpts
dealing with Margate, the Isle of Thanet
and the County of Kent, in the local
collection of the Borough of Margate Public
Library, compiled by A.J. Gritten.
Margate Library Committee. 1934.
1,3,4,7,11,13

HOUSTON, Jane.
Index of cases in the records of the
Court of Arches at Lambeth Palace Library,
1660 - 1913, edited by J. Houston.
Phillimore. 1972.
5,23

HULL, Dr. Felix.*
A calendar of the White and Black Books
of the Cinque Ports, 1432 - 1955,
edited by Dr. F. Hull.
H.M.S.O. 1966.
1,2,3,4,5,6,7,8,10,11,12,13,14,15

HYTHE BOROUGH COUNCIL.*
Catalogue of documents, compiled by
H.D. Dale & C. Chidell.
Hythe Borough Council. n.d.
11

INDEXES OF THE GREAT WHITE BOOK,*
and of the Black Book of the Cinque Ports.
Elliott Stock. 1905.
1,3,4,6,7,10,11,12,13,14,17

JESSUP, Frank William.*
The History of Kent: a select bibliography
compiled by F.W. Jessup.
Kent Education Committee. Maidstone. 1966.
1.2.3.4.5.7.8.10.11.12.13.15.16.18.19.21
2nd edition 1974. 20,27

KENT ARCHAEOLOGICAL SOCIETY: RECORDS BRANCH.
Publications of the Society 1912 - 1934.
Microfiche 73 slides.
Chadwyck Healey Ltd. 1979.
11

BIBLIOGRAPHY Cont'd

KENT COUNTY COUNCIL; ARCHIVES OFFICE
Calendar of early Quarter Sessions Rolls
1596 - 1605.
(K.A.O., Q/SRG; Q/SR 1 - 5)
K.C.C. 1975?
2,3,6,7,8,9,11,12,13,16,20,24,25,28,29,30,31

Calendar of Quarter Sessions Records
1574 - 1622, Parts 1 - 4
(K.A.O., QM/JC; QM/SB,SP,SRO).
K.C.C. 1976
2,3,6,7,8,9,11,12,13,15,20,24,28,29,30,31

Calendar of Quarter Sessions Records.
Sessions Papers 1639 - 1677.
(K.A.O., Q/SBI-12)
K.C.C. 1978
2,3,4,5,8,9,11,13,15,24,30,31

Catalogue of estate maps 1590 - 1840 in
the Kent County Archives Office,edited by
Felix Hull...County Archivist.
K.C.C. 1973.
4,5,6,7,9,11,12,13,16,20,25,30

Catalogue of medieval fragments, catalogued
by S. Freeth.
K.C.C. 1974.
3,4,8,9,11,12,13,15,16,20,24,25,30

Catalogue of the Amherst MSS. (KAO, U1350).
Deposited by the Rt. Hon. the Earl Amherst
per the India Office Library, February,1968.
Catalogued by F. Hull, April - Dec. 1968
K.C.C. 1977.
3,5,8,9,11,13,15,23,24,30,31

Catalogue of the archives of the Confederation
of the Cinque Ports and of the Lord Warden
of the Cinque Ports. Rev. edn. First
Published. 1963.
K.C.C. Maidstone. 1979.
4,12,13,23,24

Catalogue of the Cecil-Maxse MSS.
Deposited by Helen, Lady Hardinge of Penshurst
& the Hon. Julian Hardinge, 1st July, 1971.
Catalogued by Jacqueline A.V. Rose, 1973,
& Margaret Scally 1974 - 5.
2 parts. (K.A.O. U1599)
K.A.O. 1977.
3,4,6,8,9,11,15,20,23,24

Catalogue of the Cobb MSS Part I - IV:
records of the Cobbs of Margate family
and business concerns. (U1450).
K.C.C. Maidstone. 1979.
4,5,12,13,23,24.

Catalogue of the De L'Isle manuscripts.
3 parts. (KAO.1475).
K.C.C. 1974 - 75
3,11,12,13,24,25,30,31
Part 1. 1,8,9,16,20
Part 2. 1,2,8,16,20
Part 3. 3,4,15

KENT COUNTY COUNCIL, ARCHIVES OFFICE
Catalogue of the MANN (Cornwallis) MSS.
Manorial documents, deeds, estate papers
etc. of the Mann & (related) Cornwallis
Families. (KAO U24).
Catalogued by D.M.M. Shorrocks.
K.C.C. 1977.
3,4,9,15,20,23,24,30,31

Catalogue of the records of Dover Harbour
Board from 1682. Catalogued by M. Scally
1975 - 6. (KAO DHB)
K.C.C. 1977.
3,4,5,6,9,11,12,30,31

Catalogue of the Romney of the Mote MSS,
1461 - 1957. 2 parts. Catalogued by D.Gibson
(U1644 - U1515).
K.C.C. 1975.
3,7,8,9,12,13,15,20,24,25,26,27,30,31.

Catalogue of the Stern MSS. Deposited by
J. Stern, 8 Langton Way, Croydon. 3 March
1975. KAO U 1883 Catalogued by Felix Hull
April-May, 1975.
K.C.C. 1976.
3,4,8,9,11,12,15,24,30,31

Catalogue of the Twysden and Twisden MSS
(K.A.O., U48,48,47/47. 655.1655.1823/2).
K.C.C. 1977.
3,6,8,9,11,15,20,23,24,30.

Faversham Borough Records, 1282 - 1950,
deposited by the Corporation of Faversham
on the 3rd November, 1958. Catalogued by
C.W. Chalklin, January 1960 - June 1962.
Photocopy of the catalogue.
K.C.C. Archives Office. 1963?
26

Guide to the Kent County Archives Office,*
compiled by Felix Hull.
K.C.C. 1958.
20,24,25,29,30,31

Guide to the Kent County Archives Office.*
First Supplement 1957-1968,
compiled by Felix Hull.
K.C.C. 1971.
6,12,19,20,25,30,31

Handlist of Kent County Council Records,
1889 - 1945, prepared for County Council
by Felix Hull.
K.C.C. 1972.
2,4,5,6,7,8,11,19,20,25,30.

KENT COUNTY LIBRARY
Becket & Canterbury, a book list.
K.C.L. Maidstone. 1970.
3

Edward Hasted: the history & topographical
survey of the County of Kent, an index to
parishes, hundreds and lathes.
K.C.C. 1972.
2,4,11,12

The Isle of Sheppey.* Part I - Libraries
on the Isle of Sheppey. Part II - A
select list of books relating to the Isle
of Sheppey in Kent County Libraries.
K.C.L. 1956.
1,2,3,4,7,8,11,12,15,27.

KENT COUNTY LIBRARY.
Kent: a list of books added to the County
Library during 1966; 1973 and 1974 - 1976.
K.C.C. 1967; 1974 and 1978.
1966. 4,7,11,13,25
1973. 4,7,11,13,25
1974 - 76.   3,4,5,6,7,8,9,10,11,12,13,14,
             15,16,20,22,23,24,25,26,27,
             28,29,30,31

Kent: a select list of references in
periodical articles published during 1971
and 1972.
K.C.L. Maidstone. 1973.
3,11

List of books concerning Herne Bay, Herne
& Reculver.*
K.C.L. 1951.
3

Local History Catalogue. *
K.C.C. 1939.
3,11,12,13

KENT COUNTY LIBRARY - SWALE DIVISION.
Faversham: a list of publications
in the local collection of Faversham library.
K.C.C. c1978.
3,20,26

KENT COUNTY LIBRARY - THANET DIVISION.
Punch and Judy: a bibliography.
K.C.C. 1976.
4,13

KESTON FOREIGN BIRD FARM..
A descriptive catalogue.
Keston Foreign Bird Farm. c.1960.
2

KEYNES, Geoffrey.*
Bibliography of the writings of Dr.William
Harvey. 2nd edn.
Cambridge University Press. 1953.
7

LEGOUIX, Susan (Later Mrs. Sloman).
Maidstone Museum & Art Gallery: Foreign
paintings catalogue.
Maidstone Borough Council. 1976.
4,6,11

LIBRARY ASSOCIATION.
Subject index to periodicals:
regional lists: Kent. 1954.
Library Association. 1954 etc.
1,2,3,6,7,8,9,11,12
1957. 4.
1962. 15.
1964. 17.
1966. 17.

LIBRARY ASSOCIATION: COUNTY LIBRARIES GROUP.
Readers' guide to books on sources of
local history. 4th edition.
As Author. 1971.
11

LINDSEY, C.F.
Windmills: bibliographical guide .
The author. London. 1974.
11

MAIDSTONE MUSEUM & ART GALLERY.
Catalogue of the Guy Mannering Collection
of British Birds....in the Maidstone
Museum.
Maidstone Borough Council. 1960.
4,11

MAIDSTONE PUBLIC LIBRARY.
Victoria Library: list of books added to
the Library July 1903; January to March 1906;
1907 - 19.
Maidstone Public Library.
12

MULLINS, E.L.C.
A guide to the historical and archaeological
publications of societies in England and
Wales, 1901 - 1933. Compiled for the
Institute of Historical Research by E.L.C.Mullins.
Athlone Press. 1968.
11

NATIONAL MARITIME MUSEUM-GREENWICH.
Catalogue (of the collections) (under
revision).
As author. 1937.
11

NORTON, Jane E.
Guide to the national and provincial directories
of England and Wales, excluding London, and
Published before 1856. (pp. 111 - 117 Kent)
offices of the Royal Historical Society. 1950
7,11

OWEN. D.M.*
A catalogue of Lambeth manuscripts, 889
to 901 (Carte antique et miscellannee)
Lambeth Palace Library. 1968.
11

RAYER, Felicity.
Record repositories in Great Britain, 5th
edition, revised and re-edited by Felicity
Rayer. The Royal Commission on Historical
Manuscripts. (pp. 32 - 33 Kent)
H.M.S.O. 1973
11

ROCHESTER BRIDGE TRUST.
Guide to classification and indexing
of records at the Bridge Chamber, Rochester.
Printed by Mackays, Rochester, for the Trust.
1954.
4,11

ROYAL COLLEGE OF SURGEONS OF ENGLAND.*
Historical & descriptive Catalogue of
the Darwin Memorial at Down House, Downe,
Kent.
E.&.S. Livingstone. 1969.
8

SAWYER, P.H.
Anglo Saxon Charters, an annotated list
and bibliography.
Royal Historical Society. 1968.
11

SAYERS, Jane E.
Calendar of the papers of Charles Thomas
Longley, Archbishop of Canterbury, 1862-
1868, in Lambeth Palace Library, by J.E.
Sayers and E.G.W. Bill.
Mansell, 1976.
3,11

Estate documents at Lambeth Palace Library:
a short catalogue.*
Leicester Univ. Press. 1965.
1,5,7,11,13,30.

SCHEDULE OF KENTISH NEWSPAPERS stored in
the strong room of the Beaney Institute,
Canterbury. Includes "Man of Kent".
3

SLATER, Michael.
The catalogue of the Suzannet Charles Dickens
Collection: edited and with an introduction by
Michael Slater.
Sotheby, Parke Bernet Publications in association
with the Trustees of the Dickens House.
11.

BIBLIOGRAPHY Cont'd

SMITH, Charles Roach.
Catalogue of Anglo-Saxon and other antiquities
discovered at Faversham in Kent....in the South
Kensington Museum, compiled by C.R. Roach.
Chapman & Hall. 1871.
26

SMITH, Gerard Edwards.*
Catalogue of rare, or remarkable phaenogamous,
plants collected in South Kent with descriptive
notices.
Longman etc. 1829.
1,2,6,7,11,12,15,17,19

SMITH, John Russell*.
Bibliotheca Cantiana: a bibliographical
account of what has been published on the
history, topography, antiquities, customs,
and family history of the County of Kent.
John Russell Smith. 1837.
1,2,3,4,5,6,7,8,9,11,12,13,14,15,
16,17,18,19,20,24,26

SOTHEBY & CO. Auctioneers.
Catalogue of printed books comprising
extensive collections of English topographical
books, mainly relating to the County of Kent
To be sold on 4th and 5th Frebruary, 1974.
Sotheby and Co. London. 1974.
1

THORPE, John Senior*
Index to the monumental inscriptions in the
"Registrum Roffense", edited by F.A. Crisp.
Limited edition.
Privately published by F.A. Crisp. 1885.
2,11,12

TUNBRIDGE WELLS PUBLIC LIBRARY.
Local History Catalogue. 1966
Tunbridge Wells Public Library. 1966.
30

UNIVERSITY OF KENT.
Research completed...on Kentish history.
(a list of theses and essays).
Typescript. 1973.
4

WATKINS, Albert Henry.
Catalogue of the H.G.Wells collection in
the Bromley Public libraries, edited by
A.H. Watkins.
London Borough of Bromley.Public Libraries
1974.
11

WATT, John Y.
Catalogue of the books and papers in the
Fitzgerald Collection relating to Charles
Dickens in Eastgate House Museum, Rochester.
Photocopy of typescript. 1935.
25

WOODS, Frederick.*
Bibliography of the works of Winston Churchill.
Nicholas Vane 1963.
12
2nd revised edn. Kaye & Ward. 1969.
12

WRIGHT,Samuel.
A bibliography of the writings of Walter H.
Pater.
(Walter Pater was at School in Canterbury)
Dawson. Folkestone. 1975.
3

WYE COLLEGE.
A catalogue of agricultural and horticultural
books, 1543 - 1918, in Wye College Library.
Wye College. 1977.
11,21,23

BICKLEY

ATTENBOROUGH, John.
A living memory: Hodder & Stoughton,
Publishers 1868 - 1975.
(The Hodder-Williams Family were residents
of Bromley. The firm evacuated to Bickley
during the Second World War, and now operates
at Dunton Green).
Hodder & Stoughton. Dunton Green. 1975.
2,16

GORDON, Richard pseud (i.e. OSTLERE, Gordon).
Good neighbours: suburbia observed. (the
suburb observed is Bickley).
Heinemann. 1976.
2

BIDDENDEN

BIDDENDEN LOCAL HISTORY SOCIETY.*
The story of Biddenden.
The Society.
1953.   8   New edition 1957. 2
n.d.   22

DUNCAN, Leland Lewis.
Abstract of all the wills of Biddenden
Folk proved in the Prerogative Court of
Canterbury, extracted and edited by
Leland L. Duncan. Typewritten copy.
n.d.
11

JONES, H. Gordon.*
A short guide to the Church of All Saints,
Biddenden. 3rd edition revised by Betty
Gordon Jones.   Printed by:
Elvy & Gibbs. Canterbury. 1965.
11

KEMP, John.*
Memoir of John Kent, First pastor of
"Ebenezer" Strict Baptist Chapel, Bounds
Cross, Biddenden, Kent. Including autobiography,
extracts from letters, meditations, verses
and sermons.
Published by his widow and printed by
C.J. Farncombe. 1933.
11

KENT COUNTY COUNCIL: PLANNING DEPT.
Biddenden village study.
K.C.C. 1969.
4,7,8,12,13,16,19,20,25,30

BIGGIN HILL

CORBELL, P.M.
Royal Air Force Station, Biggin Hill,
compiled by P.M. Corbell. (photocopy).
Air-Britain. 1967.
2

ODLE, Mrs Rose
Salt of our youth
(autobiography of a Biggin Hill resident
Wonders of Cornwall. Penzance. 1972.
2

ROHAN, John J.
Hells Kitchen.
(Autobiography of a Biggin Hill doctor).
Photocopy of typescript.
c.1967
2

ROYAL AIR FORCE, Biggin Hill*
1917 - 1954.
R.A.F. Biggin Hill. 1954.
1.

WRIGHT, Nicholas.
The Bump; Battle of Britain 4th Anniversary
Reunion; Royal Air Force 21st September,1980.
R.A.F. Biggin Hill. 1980.
2,12

BILSINGTON

KENDON, Margery.
Bilsington people. 1800 - 1900
M. Kendon. Bilsington. 1974.
7,11

LIST OF INSCRIPTIONS ON MEMORIALS AT
BILSINGTON CHURCH. (1967?)
(Typed list signed Thomas P. Church 1967)

PARTICULARS AND CONDITIONS OF SALE OF...*
excellent and rich pasture land in the
parishes of Newchurch and Bilsington,
Romney Marsh...for sale by auction...
on Tuesday July 14th 1885...by
order of the Trustees...of the late
Thos. Kingsnorth, Esq.
Messrs Cobb. 1885
7

BIOGRAPHY

ADAMSON. J.H.
Sir Harry Vane, his life and times, 1613 -
1662, by J.H. Adamson and H.F. Folland.
(the family home was Fairlawne House,
Plaxtol).
Bodley Head. 1973.
23

ALLDERIDGE, Patricia.
The Late Richard Dadd, 1817 - 1886
(the artist, and family, lived in Chatham
prior to the murder of his father in
Cobham Woods, thereafter in Bethlem
Hospital, London).
Tate Gallery Academy Editions. 1974.
4,11,12,15,25

Midsummer nightmare (Richard Dadd).
In Sunday Times Magazine, September
24th 1972.
4

Richard Dadd: Midsummer Nightmare.
(From Sunday Times Magazine,
September 24th 1972. Original version).
typescript.
4

ALSOP, Susan Mary.
Lady Sackville: a biography.
(Lady Victoria Sackville West, 1862 -
1936, married Lord Lionel Sackville-West)
Weidenfeld & Nicolson. 1978.
11,12,16,23

ARDIZZONE, Edward.
Article from the "Daily Telegraph"
Magazine of 3/9/1976.
(Kent and Maidstone connections, died
November 1979 aged 80)
12

ARNOLD, Ralph.*
Orange Street and Brickhole Lane.(Autiobiography)
The author lived at Cobham).
Hart-Davis. 1963.
4,11,12

ARNOLD, Ralph.*
A very quiet war.
Rupert Hart Davis. 1962.
11, 12

A yeoman of Kent: an account of Richard
Hayes (1725 - 1790) and of the village of
Cobham.
Constable. 1949
1,2,3,4,5,6,7,9,11,12,15,17,18,19,25

ASHLEY, Evelyn.*
The life of John Henry Temple, Viscount
Palmerston. 2 vols.
(Lord Warden of the Cinque Ports. 1861 -
66).
R. Bentley. 1876.
6

ATKINS, Hedley.
Memoirs of a surgeon.
(the author lived at Down House from 1962)
Springwood Books. 1977.
2

BANKS, Adeline Mary.
Reverend Charles Waters Banks. (Charles
Banks was an Evangelical Preacher
who spent his early years at Ashford and
Cranbrook).
Robert Banks and Son. London. 1890.
11

BARRY, T.B.
George Payne F.S.A. 1848 - 1920:
an assessment of his archaeological career.
KBC. 1970
4

BARTLETT, C.J.
Castlereagh (Lord Castlereagh lived
at North Cray).
Macmillan. 1966.
1

BELL, Anthea.
E. Nesbit.
(Miss Nesbit lived at Eltham)
Contained in:Three Bodley Head Monographs.
Revised edition. Bodley Head. 1968.
1.

BELL, Neil.*
My writing life.
(Author lived at New Brompton).
Alvin Redman. 1955.
8, 11

BENTINE, Michael.
The Long banana skin.
(Michael Bentine spent his childhood in
Folkestone).
Wolfe. 1975.
7

(BLACK, William Henry).
Memorials of the family of Colfe and the
life and character of the late Abraham Colfe.
Leathersetter's Company. 1831.
1,3

BLAXLAND, Gregory.
J.H. Thomas: a life for Unity.
(James Henry Thomas b.3.10.1874. d.21.1.1949
J.P. for Kent,Governor of Dulwich College. M.P.)
The author lives in Canterbury.
F. Muller. 1964.
3

BOORMAN, Henry Roy Pratt.*
The spirit of Kent: the Right Hon. Lord
Cornwallis. K.C.V.O., K.B.E., M.C., D.C.L.
(Biography).
Kent Messenger. 1968.
4,5,6,9,11,28

BORTON, Lieut. Col. A.C.
My Warrior Sons the Borton family diary,
1914 - 1918; edited and with an introduction
by Guy Slater.
(The Diary of Lieut. Col. A.C. Borton who
lived at Cheveney House, Hunton.)
Davies. 1973.
11

BOSSOM, Alfred Charles, Lord Bossom of
Maidstone.
(Sir Alfred Bossom was M.P. for Maidstone).
Some reminiscences. Kent Messenger. 1959.
1931 - 1959.
11

BRADBURY, Janet
The Recollections of Janet Bradbury
nee Drummond. (The author lives in Sandgate)
Bradbury. 1976.
7

C., J. pseud.
The sunlit memories of childhood, or, passages
in the life of a pigmy.
(The Author lived at Fairlawn Park, Plaxtol
Nr. Tonbridge, for seven years).
Printed by G. Tolimin & Sons at the Guardian
Printing Works, Preston. (1909?).
11.

CARAMAN, Philip.
Henry Garnet, 1555 - 1606 and the gunpowder
plot.
(Garnet rented the Manor House at Erith)
Longmans. 1964.
1

CASSON, John.
Lewis and Sybil: a memoir.
(Lewis Casson & Sybil Thorndike) Sybil
Thorndike lived in Rochester and Aylesford
in her youth).
Collins. 1972.
4

CATHCART, Helen.
The Duchess of Kent.
W.H. Allen. 1971
12

CHURCH, Richard.*
The golden sovereign: a conclusion
to "Over the bridge" (autobiography)
Heinemann. 1957.
4,11,12

Kents' contribution*(People of England series)
Adams & Dart. 1972
2,4,6,7,8,

Over the bridge:*an essay in autobiography.
Heinemann Educational. 1966.
11
12 Heinemann 1955

The Voyage Home.*
Heinemann. 1964.
4.5.11.12.15.23

CLARK , Sir Kenneth.
Another part of the wood: a self portrait.
(Sir Kenneth Clark lived at Lympne during
the 1930s and at Saltwood From c.1950-
1970)
J. Murray. 1974.
7,
11 Coronet Books (Hodder) 1976.

The Other Half.
J. Murray. 1977
7

CLAYTON, F.S.*
John Wilson of Woolwich: a Baptist Pastorate
of fifty years.
Kingsgate Press. 1927
1,11

CLIFFORD, Lady Anne.* (1590 - 1676)
Diary of the Lady Anne Clifford, with an
introductory note by V. Sackville West.
(Lady Anne became wife to Richard, 3rd Earl
of Dorset).
Heinemann. 1923.
5.8.11.16

CLEARY, Frederick E.
"I'll do it yesterday" (an autobiography)
(F.E. Cleary resides at St. Margaret's Bay).
Carlos Press. 1979.
6

COLTHUP, William.*
A man of Kent at home and abroad.
(The author was a Kent Farmer, Kent
County Councillor and High Sheriff of Kent).
Privately printed for the author by
J.A. Jennings, Canterbury. 1953.
11, 12

CONNOLLY, Jane.
Old days and ways.
(Contains reminiscences of Woolwich and
Woolwich Dockyard).
Garsdale. 1912
1,11

CONWAY, William Martin.* 1st Baron Conway of
Allington.
Autobiography of a mountain climber.
Cape. 1933.
12

Episodes in a varied life.*
Country Life. 1932.
4,12

Mountain memories, a pilgrimage to romance.
Cassell, London. 1970.
4

The Pilgrim's quest for the divine.
Frederick Muller. 1936.
4

COOK, Raymond.
Life in Many parts.
(the author's life story as a Dover Travel
Agent, Rotarian and Methodist.)
National Childrens' Home. 1972.
6

CRAMP, Rev. Dr. John Mockett.
(Baptist Minister, St. Peters, Broadstairs).
Memoir of the Rev. Thomas Cramp, late of
St. Peters, Isle of Thanet. (Pastor of
the Baptist Church, St. Peters', Isle of
Thanet). 1852.
24

CRAN, Marian. (the author lived in Benenden)
The Gardens of Good Hope.
Herbert Jenkins. 1927.
11

Hagar's Garden.
Herbert Jenkins. 1941
11

Making the dovecot pay.
Herbert Jenkins. 1935
11

Squabbling garden.
Herbert Jenkins. 1924.
11

Story of my ruin
(The authors' account of how she discovered
a cottage and a garden in a village near
Tenterden)
Herbert Jenkins. 1924.
4, 11

CROFT-COOKE, Rupert.*
The Altar in the loft. (The author attended
Tonbridge School).
Putnam. 1960.
8,11,12,23

The days of peace.
W.H. Allen. 1973.
11

Gardens of Camelot (Childhood in West Kent,
mainly Chipstead.)
Putnam. 1958.
11,12

The last of spring. (Includes the authors'
experiences as a second-hand bookseller in
Rochester).
Putnam, 1964.
4

The life for me.
Macmillan. 1952.
11

The verdict of you all.
Secker & Warburg. 1955
11

CRONK, Anthony.
A Wealden Rector: the life and times of
William Marriott Smith-Marriott of Horsmonden.
(Vicar of Horsmonden from 1825)
Phillimore. 1975.
3,8,11,17,19

CURTIS, Anthony.
Somerset Maugham
(W. Somerset Maugham was a pupil at Kings
School,Canterbury).
Weidenfeld & Nicolson. 1978.
3

DALE, R.
Catland. (a biography of Louis Wain,
who lived at Westgate-on-Sea).
Duckworth. 1977.
13

DAUBENEY, Rev. Giles.*
Reminiscences of a country parson.
(Rev. Giles Daubeney was Vicar of Benenden
1895 - 1906 and Vicar of Herne, 1906 - 1945.
He died in 1960 age 99).
P.P.1950.
3,11.30.

DAY, J. Wentworth.*
H.R.H. Princess Marina, Duchess of Kent:
the first authentic life story.
R. Hale. 1962.
12

DENCE, Thomas.*
Reminiscences of a septuagenarian (The
author was a Bromley business man who gave
the money for the East Cliff Pavilion
at Herne Bay; he lived at Shortlands)
Sir Joseph Causton & Sons. London. 1911.
11,12

DERING, Rev. Cholmeley Edward. (Rector of
Pluckley).
By-gone hours.
Elliott & Son. 1842.
11

DERING, Sir Edward.
The diaries and papers of Sir Edward Dering,
Second Baronet 1644 - 1684,edited by
Maurice F. Bond.
(Sir E. Dering was mainly resident at
Surrenden Dering, Pluckley).
H.M.S.O. 1976.
11, 22, 23

DONALDSON, Christopher William.
Clara
(A tribute to Clara Elizabeth Tritton of
Canterbury, 26th July, 1883 -
11th November, 1975).
A.&.J. Purchese. 1976?
3

DUFF Mrs A.G*
Life-work of Lord Avebury 1834 - 1913,
edited by A.G. Duff. (M.P. for Maidstone).
Watts. 1924.
2,12

DUFF, David.
Edward of Kent: The life story of Queen
Victoria's Father.
Muller. 1973.
1

DUFFY, Maureen.
The passionate shepherdess Aphra Behn,
1640 - 89. (Authoress of plays, novels,
and poems born in, or near, Canterbury).
Jonathan Cape. London. 1977.
3,11,12

DYER, Albert.
The ups and downs of my life: the Memoirs
of Albert Dyer, 1908 - 1970.
(Life and Trade in Penge and Beckenham).
Duplicated typescript n.d.
2.

EHRMANN, Rev. Louis Emil Augustus.
The twist of the Collar, being memoirs
of one abandoning commerce for the ministry.
(The author was Vicar of Lynsted).
The Author. Lynsted,Sittingbourne. 1949.
11

ELWIG, Henry.*
A biographical dictionary of notable people
at Tunbridge Wells, 17th to the 20th Century,
also a list of local place names.
Stanford Printing Co. Tunbridge Wells. 1941
11,19

EWALD, Alexander Charles.
The life and times of the Hon. Algernon
Sydney, 1622 - 1683, by Alex Charles Ewald.
2 vols. (The second son of Robert, 2nd Earl
of Leicester. Penshurst connections).
Tinsley Bros. London. 1873.
11

FORSTER, John Lord Harraby
Master, the Lord Forster of Harraby:
an obituary by Geoffrey Tookey. (Lord
Forster was a resident of Beckenham).
In Granya, No.76, 1973, pp 75 - 79.
Honourable Society of Gray's Inn.
London. 1973.
2.

FREEMAN, Sarah.
Isabella and Sam: the story of Mrs.Beeton.
(Mrs. Beeton lived at Greenhithe for a time)
Gollancz. 1977
5

FRIEDMANN, Paul.
Anne Boleyn: a chapter of English history
1527 - 1536.
(Family home of the Boleyns was Hever Castle)
Macmillan. 1884.
12

FRISWELL, Laura Hain (Mrs. Ambrose Myall).
James Hain Friswell: a memoir. (J.H.Friswell
was a resident and a writer of Bexleyheath).
George Redway. 1898.
1

FULLER, Ronald.
Hell-fire Francis. (Connection with Bexley
village).
Chatto & Windus. 1939.
1

FULLER, Thomas.
The worthies of England: Kent to Leicestershire
section. (extracted from the main work).
Printed by J.Nichols,London. 1811
11

GANN, L.H.
Huggins of Rhodesia: the man and his
country, by L.H. Gann and M. Gelfand.
(Godfrey Huggins, 1st Viscount Malvern and
Bexley, politician and surgeon and a Prime
Minister of Rhodesia).
Allen and nwin. 1964.
1

GATTY, Richard.
Portrait of a Merchant Prince: James Morrison,
1789 - 1857.
(Morrison bought much property in the 1840's
including Hole Park, Rolvenden).
Pepper Arden, Northallerton, Yorks. 1976?
11

GILLEN, Mollie.
Royal Duke. (Prince Augustus Frederick,
Duke of Sussex, 1773 - 1843. His first wife,
Lady Augusta Murray and their children lived
in Ramsgate).
Sidgwick and Jackson. 1976.
14

GREYSMITH, David.
Richard Dadd; the rock and castle of
seclusion. (Richard Dadd spent his early
life in Chatham).
Studio Vista. 1973.
4,11

GUENTHER, John.*
Sidney Keyes. (Sidney Keyes lived at Dartford).
London Magazine. 1967.
5,12

GUNTHER, A.E.
John George Children, F.R.S. (1777 - 1852) of
the British Museum. Mineralogist and
reluctant keeper of Zoology).
(J.G. Children lived in Tonbridge and collaborated with Sir Humphry Davy in founding
the Ramhurst Gunpowder mills).
British Museum (Natural History) 1978.
23.

HACKETT, Benedict.
Blessed John Stone. (Saint John Stone was
martyred at the Dane John, Canterbury,
in 1539 and was canonised in 1970).
Office of the Vice-Postulation, n.d.
3,11,30

Saint John Stone: Austin Friar, Martyr.
Rome. Augustinian Postulation. 1970
3

HALFPENNY, HARRIETTE.
Wilderness records: or, a memorial of
H.H. of Chertsey, edited by J. White.
(Harriette Halfpenny was resident in the
Bexley area).
Hamilton, Adams and Co.
1843.
1

HANDLEY-TAYLOR, Geoffrey.
Kent Authors to-day: being a check-list
of authors born in Kent together with
brief particulars of authors born elsewhere
who are currently working or residing in Kent,
edited by G. Handley Taylor.
Eddison Press. 1973.
1,2,4,5,7,8,9,11,16,22,25,28,30

Sussex authors today: being a checklist of
authors born in Sussex together with brief
particulars of authors born elsewhere who are
currently working or residing in Sussex.
edited by G. Handley Taylor.
Eddison Press. 1973.
25

HARDIE, Martin.
John Pettie, R.A. F.R.S.A.
(John Pettie was the uncle of Martin Hardie;
Hardie being a Tonbridge resident in retirement)
A.&.C. Black. 1908
23

HAWKE, Martin Bladen, Baron Hawke.
Memorial biography of W.G. Grace, edited
by M.B. Hawke and others. (Grace was a
resident of Mottingham and Sydenham).
Constable. 1919.
2

HELPS, Sir Arthur.
Life and labours of Mr. Brassey.
(Preston Hall, Aylesford, was bought by Thomas
Brassey in 1855 and occupied by his son
Sir Henry Brassey).
First Publ. 1872.
Reprint, Evelyn, Adams & Mackay, 1969.
11

HICKEY, William.
Memoirs of William Hickey. edited by
Peter Quennell. (there is a short
connection with Erith).
Routledge and Kegan Paul. 1960.
1

HIGGS, Lionel F.
The life of J.E. Martin: an ordinary man
who did extraordinary things. (Bexley connections).
Kingsgate Press. 1942.
1

HILL, William Thomson.
Octavia Hill. Pioneer of the National
Trust and Housing Reformer. (Octavia Hill
lived at Crockham Hill).
Hutchinson. 1956.
25

HODGE, James.
Richard Trevithick (Pioneer of the great
mechanical developments of the XIX th century
and Father of the Steam locomotive). (Died in
Dartford in 1833).
Shire Publications. 1973.
5

HOLMES, Martin.
Proud Northern Lady: Lady Anne Clifford,
1590 - 1676. (Wife to Richard, 3rd Earl
of Dorset).
Phillimore. 1975.
16

IGGLESDEN, Sir Charles.*
A mere Englishman in America. (The author
lived in Ashford).
Kentish Express, Ashford. 1930.
6,7,11

JELF, Katherine Frances.*
George Edward Jelf: a memoir. (Canon Jelf
lived in Rochester for some years).
Skeffington. 1909.
11

JESSOPP, Augustus.
John Donne, sometime Dean of St. Paul's,
A.D. 1621 - 1631. (Donne was non-resident
Vicar of Sevenoaks).
Methuen. 1897
11

JESSUP, Ronald Frederick.
Man of many talents: an informal bio-
graphy of James Douglas, 1753 - 1819
(An early member of the Corps of Royal
Engineers at Chatham and lived in
Rochester during the 1780's.)
Phillimore. 1975.
11. 32.

KAMM, J.
The story of Sir Moses Montefiore.
(Sir Moses lived at East Cliff Lodge,
near Dumpton Stairs, and built the
Synagogue and College for Jewish studies)
Valentine Mitchell. 1960.
24

KEMP, Betty.
Sir Francis Dashwood: an eighteenth-century
independent. (Sir Francis, 1708 1781,
succeeded his brother-in-law, Sir Robert Austen
of Hall-Place, Bexley, as M.P. for New Romney,
a seat he held from 1747 - 1760).
Macmillan. 1967.
1

KENT COUNTY LIBRARY.
Who's Who in Kent County Library.
K.C.C. 1974
25

KENT: Historical, Biographical and Pictorial.*
Baxter. 1907.
4

KIDMAN, Brenda.
A handful of tears. (An account of many travels,
with the beginning of her life spent in
Tunbridge Wells).
B.B.C. 1975.
11

KINNAIRD, Emily.
Reminiscences. (E. Kinnaird was an Evangelist
and partly responsible for establishing the
Y.W.C.A. in India. Bromley pp. 7 - 8).
J. Murray. 1925.
11

KIRKBRIDE, Lt. Col. William.
Like it or not. (Reminiscences of life
as a Royal Engineer Officer in peace)
Arthur H. Stockwell. Ilfracombe. 1965.
4.32.

LONG, G.S.*
A short life of Erasmus, formerly
Rector of Aldington.
11,12

LOYD. Samuel J. Baron Overstone.
Correspondence. 3v. (includes biographical
note and many letters to and from George
Warde Norman of Bromley).
Cambridge U.P. 1971
2

LUCAS, Meriel.
James William Wells. 1847 - 1902.
(J.W. Wells was a Beckenham resident,
1884 - 1900). Typescript.
1976.
2

LUCY, Sir Henry William.
Nearing Jordan.
(Vol.3 of "Sixty years in the Wilderness"
1909 - 1916) The author lived at Hythe).
Smith Elder & Co. 1916
7

LYALL, Very Rev. William Rowe.*
Memoir of the late Dean of Canterbury, William
Rowe Lyall,...bound with other pamphlets
on William Rowe Lyall. 1857.
11,17

McCALL, Dorothy.
When that I was: autobiography. (Bexley
connections)
Faber. 1952
1

MARLOW, Louis.
Sackville of Drayton. (Known as Lord
George Sackville till 1770, Lord George
Germain, 1770 - 1782 and Viscount Sackville
from 1782)
Home and Van Thal. 1948.
11

MARLOWE, John.
Milner: apostle of Empire.
(Sir Alfred Milner was created 1st.Viscount
Milner in 1902. b.1854-d.1925.
He purchased Sturry Court, Sturry).
Hamilton. 1976.
3

MARPLES, Morris.
Wicked Uncles in love. (Includes Prince
Augustus Frederick, Duke of Sussex, whose
first wife, Lady Augusta Murray, and their
children lived in Ramsgate).
Michael Joseph. 1972.
14

MARSHALL, William M.
George Hooper, 1640 - 1727. Bishop
of Bath and Wells. (Dean of Canterbury
1691 - 1701).
Dorset Publishing Co. 1976.
3

MASON, John Neve.
The second book of reminiscences. (on the
Cinque Ports etc; the author lived in
Tenterden as a boy).
The Author. Cannon House, Rye. 1920?
11

MASSINGHAM, Betty.
Turn on the fountains: a life of Dean Hole.
(Dean of Rochester).
Gollancz. 1974.
11,15

MAURICE, C. Edmund.
The life of Octavia Hill as told in her letters
(Octavia Hill lived at Crockham Hill and
was a pioneer of The National Trust)
Macmillan. 1913.
25

MILLS, Anthony Reginald.*
The halls of Ravenswood: more pages from
the Journals of Emily and Ellen Hall.
(See next entry).
Muller. 1967.
2,8,11

Two Victorian ladies:* more pages from
the journals of Emily and Ellen Hall.
(Residents of Ravenswood House, West
Wickham) From 1842.
Muller. 1969.
2,8,11

MILNER, Violet Georgina Viscountess Milner
My portrait gallery. 1886 - 1901
(Lady Milner lived at Sturry Court, Sturry)
John Murray. 1951.
3

MOORE, Doris Langley.*
E. Nesbit, a biography.(E.Nesbit lived in Eltham).
Rich & Cowan. 1936.
2,12

MORGAN, Verne.
Yesterday's sunshine. (Includes childhood
memories of Bromley),
Bailey & Swinfen. 1974.
2

MORLEY, Sheridan.
Sybil Thorndike: a life in the Theatre.
(Sybil Thorndike spent early years in
Rochester and Aylesford).
Weidenfeld and Nicolson. 1977
15

NEAME, Alan.*
The Holy Maid of Kent: the life of Elizabeth
Barton 1506 - 1534.
(Born at Aldington; utterances and miracles
in the chapel at Court-at-Street; later a
nun at St. Sepulchre's, Canterbury).
Hodder & Stoughton. 1971
2,3,4,6,7,8,11,12,19

NICOLSON, Nigel.
Portrait of a marriage. (That between
V. Sackville-West and Sir Harold Nicolson)
Weidenfeld & Nicolson. 1973.
11,16

NORMAN, George Warde.
Autobiography...commenced 1857
(George Warde Norman
and family lived at The Rookery, Bromley
Common). (photocopy of typescript).
2

NORMAN, Geraldine.
The Fake's progress.   (Tom Keating,
b. Forest Hill).
Hutchinson. 1977.
7,18

ODLE, Mrs Rose.
Salt of our youth. Autobiography of a
Biggin Hill resident.
Wonders of Cornwall. Penzance. 1972.
2

PATTERSON, Rev. Robert. (Vicar of Littlebourne)
Richard Elwyn, Master of Charterhouse, 1885 -
1897: a brief record of his life.
(Richard Elwyn held the livings of East
Farleigh, 1880 - 1885 and Ramsgate, 1872 - 1880.
He was Rural Dean of Westbere in 1880 and of
North Malling 1883 - 1885).
Wells, Gardner, Darton & Co. London, 1900
3

PEARSON, Edward.
The history of Jimmy Lee, an
Ambassador of Christ.....(a biography in
verse. Jimmy Lee was a wandering preacher
in Ashford area. Edward Pearson was a
farm labourer from the same district).
Jabez Francis. Rochford.Essex. 1872.
22

PECK, Alan.
No time to lose, the fast moving world
of Bill Ivy (Motor cyclist from Maidstone)
Motor Racing Pubns. 1972.
4,12

PEMBERTON, Max.
Lord Northcliffe: a memoir. (Lord Northcliffe
lived at "Elmwood", Broadstairs, for several
years).
Hodder & Stoughton. 1922.
24

PETT, Phineas.
The autobiography of Phineas Pett, edited
by W.G. Perrin. (Master shipwright).
Printed for the Navy Records Soc. 1918.
11

POINTER, Thomas James.
Memories. (Handwritten manuscript;
gives a short biographical history from
1837 - 1912. A farmworker who lived in
Birchington, Margate and St. Peter's,
the latter from 1858).
1912.
24

POLE -STUART. Dr. E.
Who's Who in Folkestone. c1700 - 1840.
MSS. 1976.
7

PONSONBY, Sir Charles.
Ponsonby remembers. (The author was in
the West Kent (Queens Own) Yeomanry in
World War I and later M.P. for Sevenoaks)
Alden Press. Oxford. 1965.
16

POOLE, Keith B.
The two Beaux. (Nash and Brummell)
frequented Tunbridge Wells society.
EP Publishing Co. 1976.
19

POPE, Douglas.
Now I'm sixteen: an autobiography.
(The author moved to Cranbrook when he
was four years old)
Dent. 1937
11.

RAPHAEL, Fredric.
Somerset Maugham and his world.
(W.S. Maugham was a pupil at Kings School
Canterbury).
Thames & Hudson. 1976.
3

RAVEN, Margaret Maxwell.
I remember perfectly well. (member of
the Broadstairs Raven family).
Charles Clarke Ltd. Printers Haywards Heath.1941.
24

RAVEN, Dr. Martin Owen.
Reflections on retirement. (The author
lives at Broadstairs)
Privately published. 1968.
11.
See Also.
RAVEN. Mary.
Three Broadstairs Ravens
In BROADSTAIRS and FAMILY HISTORY Sections.

READ, Conyers.
Mr Secretary Walsingham...3Vols.
(Walsingham family owned Scadbury,Chislehurst
and Sir Francis was resident for a time at
Footscray).
Anchor. 1967.
2

REES, Jean A.
His name was Tom: the biography of Tom Rees.
(Tom Rees was an Evangelist who established
Conference centres at Hildenborough and
Otford).
Hodder and Stoughton. 1971
11

RICHARDS, Frank pseud Charles Hamilton.
Autobiography of Frank Richards (a
privately owned museum is situated in
Maidstone - The Charles Hamilton Museum).
Charles Skilton,Ltd. 1962.
12

RIOS, Dom Romanus.
A heroine of the Mission Field; Mother
Mary of the Heart of Jesus, foundress
of the Institute of Our Lady of the
Missions.
(The order had two Convents - the Convent
of Notre Dame des Missions at Deal and the
Convent of St. Anne, Sturry, where Mother
Mary is buried.)
George Gill & Sons Ltd. London. 1944
3

RODERICK, Colin.*
John Knatchbull: from quarter deck to
gallows.
Angus & Robertson. 1963.
3,7

ROHAN, John J.
Hell's Kitchen.
(An autobiography of a Biggin Hill Doctor).
Photocopy of typescript.
C. 1967.
2

ROSE, George.
Remembered mercies recorded: an account of
The Lord's leadings. (The Author was
pastor of the Cranbrook Strict Baptist
Chapel. pp. 140 - 252)
D.G. Woodham. Liverpool. 1952.
11

ROWE, Mrs Mercy Elizabeth.
John Tetley Rowe and his work: a brief
record of his life and work in London,
Chatham and Rochester, by his wife.
(Biography of an Archdeacon of Rochester).
Parrett & Neves. Chatham. 1915.
4.8.11.12.15

RUDGE, Charles.*
William Jeffery: the Puritan apostle
of Kent. (The Author was once Baptist
Minister of Sevenoaks.)
James Clarke Co. Kingsgate Press. London. 1904.
11,16

SACKVILLE-WEST, Victoria (afterwards Lady
Nicolson). Pepita.
Hogarth. 1937.
7.16

SANGER, "Lord" George. (1825-1911)
Seventy years a snowman.
(Owner of the largest English Circus of the
nineteenth century. His entertainment centre,
Marine Parade, Margate, flourished from 1874-1903)
First published 1910.
1926.   13
1966 Fitzroy edn-MacGibbon & Kee. 13.

SASSOON, Siegfried.
The old century and seven more years.
(The author's family lived in Matfield).
Faber. 1938.
11

Siegfried Sassoon: poets' pilgrimage;
assembled with an introduction by Felicitas
Corrigan. (includes some poetry and prose)
Gollancz. 1973.
11

Siegfried's journey, 1916 - 1920.
Faber, 1945.
4,12,23

The Weald of Youth.*
(Siegfried Sassoon's childhood was spent in
Matfield).
Faber, London. 1942.
4,23

SHEARS, Sarah.
Gather no moss.
(The second volume of an autobiography,
the author was born in Kent.)
Elek. 1972.
11

The seventh Commandment. (third volume
of an autobiography).
Elek. 1973
11

SHERRARD, Owen Aubrey.*
Two Victorian girls,with extracts from the
Hall diaries; edited by A.R. Mills.
(The Halls of Ravenswood House,West Wickham).
Muller. 1966.
2,8,11.

SIMMON, Jack.
English Country historians edited by Jack Simmon.
E.P. Publishing. Wakefield. 1978.
12.

SLIGHT, Rev. B.
Uncle Daniel, the pious farmer.
(Daniel Dickensen of Pembury).
Wm. Freeman. 1856.
19

SMETHAM, Henry.*
C.R.S. and his friends, being personal
recollections of Charles Roach Smith, F.S.A.
and his friends.
C.W. Daniel. London. 1929.
3.4.9.12.25

SMITH, Logan P.
The life and letters of Sir Henry Wotton.
(of Boughton Malherbe).
O.U.P. 1966.
12

SOUTH EAST ARTS ASSOCIATION.
Directory of writers in the South-East.
S.E.A.A. 1979.
4,5,

SPENCER, Herbert R.
William Perfect (1737 - 1809)
Reprinted from Herbert R. Spencer's
"History of British midwifery from 1650 -
1800". (Surgeon at West Malling).
John Bale, Sons. London. 19--
3

SPOONER, T.G.M.
Brother John: the life of the Rev. John
Hobbs.' (John Hobbs was born at St. Peters'
Broadstairs in 1800.
Wesley Historical Society. New Zealand,1955.
11

STEVENS, Michael.
V. Sackville-West: a critical biography.
(Victoria Sackville-West, authoress,
poetess etc. 1892 - 1962, married Sir
Harold Nicolson).
Michael Joseph. 1973.
11,12,16,19

SWAN, Mary Edwards.*
Sir Joseph Wilson Swan, F.R.S., inventor and
scientist. A memoir by M.E.Swan and K.R.Swan.
1883 - 1894. (Family resident in Bromley).
Benn. 1929.
2

Ditto.* reprinted with added appendix.
Oriel Press. 1968.
2

TAYLOR, Margaret.
E. Nesbit in Eltham.
The Eltham Society. 1974.
18.

TEICHMAN, Oska.*
Black horse News and other memories.(Including
childhood and youth at 'Sitka', Chislehurst,
and West Kent point-to-point).
P. Davies. 1957.
1,2,7

TENISON, E.M.
Alastair Gordon, R.N. A story of the present
day. (Alastair Gordon was a Sittingbourne man).
Printed by H. Watson & Viney. 1921.
20

THOMSON, Arthur Alexander.
Great men of Kent. (Men of the Counties
Series 1).
Bodley Head. 1955.
12

TICH, Mary (ie. POWELL, Mary Ralph).
Little Tich, giant of the Music Hall,
by M. Tich and Richard Findlater.
(Little Tich, Harry Ralph, was born at
the Blacksmith's Arms, Cudham).
Elm Tree Books. 1979.
2.

TIFFIN, Alfred.
Loving and serving: an account of the work
of J.W.C. Fegan, edited by G. Fielden Hughes.
(Blantyre House, Goudhurst, Detention Centre).
P.P. n.d.
17,19

TOMLINSON, Fred.
A Peter Warlock handbook. 2 vols., edited
by Fred Tomlinson.
Triad Press.
Vol 1. 1974. Vol II. 1977.
5

Warlock and Delius.
Thames Publishing. 1976.
5
(Peter Warlock (i.e. Philip Arnold
Heseltine) lived at Eynsford from 1925 to
1928).

TOMLINSON, Norman.
Louis Brennan. (Louis Brennan lived in
Gillingham and invented the Brennan Torpedo
and a monorail)
Hallewell Pubns. 1980
8,15,32.

TYRWHITT-DRAKE, Sir Hugh Garrard.*
My life with animals and other reminiscences.
(The author lived at Cobtree Manor, Maidstone,
and was Mayor of Maidstone).
Blackie. 1939.
11,12,15

UGLOW, Capt. Jim.
Sailorman: a barge master's story. (The
author was born at Gillingham and served on
seagoing barges from Rochester and Greenhithe).
Conway Maritime Press. 1975.
4,9,11,12,15,20,26,27.

VALENTINE, Alan.
Lord George Germain. (Known as Lord George
Sackville till 1770, Lord George Germain 1770 -
1782 and Viscount Sackville from 1782).
Clarendon Press. 1962.
11

WADE, Virginia.
Courting triumph. (Miss Wade's family own
Sharsted Court, Doddington).
Hodder & Stoughton. 1978.
11

WAINEMAN, Paul. (pseud of Mrs. Sylvia
Macdougall nee Börgstrom).
Let's light the candle: memoirs.
(The author lived at Provender, Nr Faversham)
Methuen. 1944.
11,26

WAKELEY, R.H.
Gathered fragments, a memorial of Thomas
S. Wakeley late pastor of Providence
Chapel, Rainham, Kent.
Oxford. 1902.
8

WARNICKE, Retha M.
William Lambarde, Elizabethan antiquary,
1536 - 1601.
Phillimore. 1973.
1,2,5,11,12,16,25

WATTS, Alan Wilson.
In my own way: an autobiography, 1915-1965.
(Includes childhood memories of Chislehurst)
Cape. 1973.
2.3

WAYLEN, Barbara.
The story of Frances Banks: the great seeker
(Frances Banks was tutor/organiser at
Maidstone Prison for some years from 1950)
Regency Press. 1972.
11

WELCH, Denton.
The Denton Welch journals; edited with an
introduction by Jocelyn Brooke new edition.
(Resided at Blackheath, Tonbridge, St.Mary
Platt, East Peckham & Crouch).
Hamilton. 1973.
11

WELCH, Denton.
Maiden voyage New edition. (Account of the early
years at College in Blackheath).
Hamilton. 1973.
11

WHEELER, J.M.
The family and friends of William Frederick
Wells, founder of the Society of Painters in
Water colours. (W.F. Wells, 1764 - 1836, was
born in Chislehurst and resided during summer
and autumn for many years at Knockholt).
Photocopy. The Author. 1970.
2

WHITE, John Baker.*
True blue: an autobiography 1902-1939. (The
author was MP for the Canterbury Division of
Kent, 1945 - 1953).
Muller. 1970.
3,6,11

WHO'S WHO IN KENT.
Ebenezer Baylis. Worcester. 1935.
13,19,25,28

WHO'S WHO IN KENT, SURREY & SUSSEX.
H. Cox. 1911
19

WHO'S WHO IN MAIDSTONE.*
Pullman Press.Ltd. 1960.
1,4,11,12,15

WILLIAMS, Marguerite.*
John Wilson of Woolwich, an apostle to the
people. (Sixty years Pastor of Woolwich
Tabernacle).
Marshall, Morgan & Scott. 1937.
1,11

WINGFIELD-STRATFORD, Esme.
This was a man: the biography of the Hon.
Edward Vesey Bligh, Diplomat-Parson-Squire.
Robt. Hale. 1949.
9,25

WINNIFRITH, Rev. Alfred.
The fair maids of Kent.
F.J. Parsons. Folkestone. 1921
2,25

Men of Kent & Kentish men;*biographical
notices of 680 worthies of Kent.
F.J. Parsons. Folkestone. 1913.
24,25.

WOOLF, Mrs Virginia (Stephen).
Orlands: a biography - (A fictional biography
connected with the Sackvilles).
L.&.V. Woolf at The Hogarth Press. 1928.
11

WYLLIE, M.A.
We were one: a life of W.L. Wyllie. (Wyllie
was a Kent Marine artist who lived at Hoo).
G. Bell. 1935.
11

YANDELL, Elizabeth.
Henry. (The account of a childhood spent
near Cranbrook).
Bodley Head. 1974.
7,11,19,22

BIRCHINGTON

Birchington-on-Sea. (1959 edn.)
Printed by Central Press.Margate. 1959.
11

Birchington-on-Sea. (1966 edn.)
Printed by Central Press.Margate. 1966.
11

BIRCHINGTON PUBLICITY COMMITTEE.
Sunny Birchington-on-Sea.
Printed by Central Press.Margate. 1967.
13

CLARK, M. Dudley.
Birchington, Kent. An appreciation of a quiet
Kentish health resort and a practical guide
to its most interesting features.
(Homeland Handy Guides No.11)
F.Warne. c.1900
11,13

COLES, Cyril A.G.*
Some notes concerning All Saints' Church,
Birchington.
Cooper Printers. Margate. 1945 (1950reprint)
2

MARGATE BOROUGH COUNCIL.
A new lease of life at Margate, Cliftonville,
Birchington, Westbrook & Westgate-on-Sea.
Margate Borough Council. n.d.
13

MAYHEW, Athol.
Birchington-on-Sea and its bungalows with an
historical sketch of Thanet, and notes on the
island, by S. Wayland Kershaw.
Batsford. 1881.
1,6,8,11,13,15,17.

NOTES ON QUEX HALL.
(Photocopied articles etc. From various sources)
11

POWELL-COTTON MUSEUM.
Guide to the big game and curios in the Quex
Museum, Birchington.
Lane, Gentry. 1920.
11

Illustrated guide to the Powell-Cotton Museum
of history and ethnography. Quex Park,
Birchington,Kent. Printed by:
Central Press,Margate, for Museum Trustees. 1969.
11,30

SPURGEON'S HOMES.
Within our gates: the Spurgeon's Homes quarterly
...Issues from Spring 1955 to Autumn 1973.
with some numbers missing.
Spurgeon's Homes. Birchington.
11

WALKER, Alfred T.
A guide to the Parish Church of All Saints,
Birchington.
Westwood. 1967.
4,13

WESTGATE ON SEA & BIRCHINGTON annual &
almanack for 1883.
Hinton. 1883
13

BIRLING

GENERAL REGISTER OFFICE.
Census Returns. 1841, 1851, 1861, 1871,
Birling, Microfilm.
23

BISHOPSBOURNE

CHARLTON PARK*, Bishopsbourne, near Canterbury
Kent: official guide.
English Life. 1971
30

BLACKFEN

ILOTT, SUSAN J.
Blackfen - From Country to Suburb.
London Borough of Bexley, Library and
Museums Department. 1977.
1,2,5,11,18.

BLACKHEATH.

BAKER, Gerard L.*
Blackheath: the story of the Royal Hundred.
Part 1. Blackheath & Greenwich.
Morden Society.   1925.
1,2,11,12,17,18

BATCHELOR, Richard.
Aspects of middle-class education, 1830-1864,
with special reference to Blackheath Proprietary School
Unpublished Thesis.   1977.
18

BINGHAM, Frederick.
The "Borough" pocket guide to Blackheath
(Kent), specially compiled by F.Bingham.
(Facsimile of 1909 Edward J. Burrow's Guide
to Blackheath).
Blackheath reprints.   1977?
11,17

BLACKHEATH PRESERVATION TRUST.
Martin House.
Blackheath Preservation Trust. 1975.
17,18

BLACKHEATH SOCIETY.
Some hints on the maintenance and repair of
17th & 18th Century premises. (Originally
produced by the York Georgian Society. Reprinted with local photographs and lists of
buildings in Blackheath,Lewisham & Greenwich)
Blackheath Society.   1949.
11

BONWITT. W.
The History of the Paragon, Paragon House,
and their residents. (Blackheath)
Blackheath Bookshop Ltd.   1976.
1,11,17,18

BUCHANAN, Colin and Partners.
Greenwich & Blackheath study.
Colin Buchanan & Partners. 1971.
2

CARNEGIE, Mori
Church plate in the Hundred of Blackheath
(reprinted from Transactions Greenwich and
Lewisham Antiquarian Society. V.4.
Blackheath Press. 1939.
2

GREAT BRITAIN: Laws etc.(Geo.III).
An Act for the more easy and speedy recovery
of small debts within the hundred of Blackheath
of Bromley....
1765
2,11.
An act to explain, amend and make more effectual,
an act...for the more easy and speedy recovery
of small debts within the hundred of Blackheath,
of Bromley.
Eyre & Strahan. 1770.
1,2,11,12

GREENWICH NATURAL HISTORY CLUB-ZOOLOGICAL
COMMITTEE. Fauna of Blackheath & its vicinity.
Part 1. Vertebrate animals.
Printed by Wm.Clowes. 1859.
2

MALIM Mary Charlotte.*
The book of the Blackheath High School,
edited by Mary Charlotte Malim and Henrietta
Caroline Escreet.
H.W.&.A.Mitchenall,Blackheath Press. 1927.
2,11.

MARTIN, A.R.
No 6, Eliot Place, Blackheath. The house and
its occupants, 1797 - 1972.
Greenwich & Lewisham Antiquarian Society. 1974.
17,18

RHIND, Neil.
Blackheath village and environs,1790 - 1970.
Vol.one The village & Blackheath Vale.
Blackheath Bookshop.Ltd. 1976.
1,2,11,17,18

Martin House.
Blackheath Preservation Society. 1975.
11,17

SAUNDERS, D.K.
The centenary history of the Blackheath Harriers
(1869-1969), by D.K.Saunders & A.J.Weeks-Pearson.
Blackheath Harriers Club. 1971.
2

STONE, John M.*
Underground passages, caverns etc. of
Greenwich & Blackheath.
Greenwich Antiquarian Society, 1914.
1,2,17

UNWIN, T. Fisher Publisher.*
Greenwich & Blackheath: a handy guide to
rambles in this district.
T.Fisher Unwin. 1883?
18

WEST, John.
The role of the justice of the peace for the
Hundred of Blackheath during the nineteenth
century.
Unpublished study. 1973.
18

WOLFFRAM, H.
Thirty years' work (1868-97) in preparing
candidates for the Army at Faraday House,
Blackheath, and the Manor House, Lee.
1898.
18

BLEAN

DAVID DANEL, Marie-Louise.
Iconographie des Saints medecins come et
Damien.
(Blean church of St. Cosmos,Damien mentioned)
Imp. Morel & Corduant:Lille. 1958.
3

NEWCOMBE, Martin J.
The natural history of the badger in Ellenden
Wood, Blean, offprint from Transactions
of the Kent Field Club. vol.6 Part 2.
pp.75 - 84.
(1977)
3

BONNINGTON

LIST OF INSCRIPTIONS ON MEMORIALS AT BONNINGTON
CHURCH. (1967?)
Typed list signed Thomas P. Church. 1967.
11

BORDEN

BORDEN PARISH COUNCIL.
An appraisal of the parish of Borden,
issued by the Borden Parish Council.
K.C.C. 1977
20

GLEDHILL, A.E.
Borden Cookery Book of tried recipes.
W.H. Parrett Ltd. Gazette Office. 1910.
11

HOVENDEN, Robert.*
Pedigree of the family of Hovenden in Borden,
Kent, England, shewing the descendants in
England and in the U.S.A. Compiled by
R. Hovenden.
P.P.1908
3,11

ST. PETER & ST.PAUL, Borden, Kent.
A Short History.
Church Publishers. (1974).

BOROUGH GREEN

ANNUAL HANDBOOK FOR WROTHAM AND BOROUGH GREEN,
Kent. 1923.
5.

BOROUGH GREEN, PARISH COUNCIL.
Borough Green Official Guide.
Forward Publicity. (1979).
4.

GENERAL REGISTER OFFICE.
Census Returns. 1841, 1851, 1861, 1871.
Borough Green. See Wrotham.
23

WROTHAM PARISH COUNCIL.
Official guide to Wrotham, Borough Green &
District, Kent.
Home Publishing Co. Croydon.
1952 etc. 1, 5.
1961. 4.
1965. 19.
Forward Publicity Ltd.
1974. 4, 11
1977. 7, 11

BORSTAL

CLOUT, Norman.
Borstal past and present: a history of
St. Matthew's church & the village of Borstal.
The Author. T.H. Printers, Rochester. 1978.
4,11,15,25

BOSTALL

PRICHARD. John A.
Belvedere and Bostall, a brief history.
London Borough of Bexley:
Library & Museum Services. 1974.
1,11

BOUGHTON MALHERBE

SMITH, Logan P.
The life and letters of Sir Henry Wotton.
(of Boughton Malherbe).
O.U.P. 1966
12

BOUGHTON MONCHELSEA

TYE, D.F.
Boughton Monchelsea School: (extracts from the
school log book, 1863 - 1963, selected and
edited by D.F.Tye).
(B.M. School Parent/Teacher Assoc. 1973).
11

BOXLEY

CAVE-BROWNE, Rev. John.*
History of Boxley Parish.
Dickinson. Maidstone 1892.
2

ELLISTON-ERWOOD, Frank Charles.
Plans of, and brief architectural notes on,
Kent Churches. 2nd series. Part III. The
Church of St. Mary, Boxley.
(Reprinted from Arch.Cant. Vol LXVl 1953).
Kent Archaeological Society. (1953).
11

HEATH, Sidney.
In the steps of the pilgrims. (pp.147-190,
Kent; pp. 185 - 190 The Boxley Rood of
Grace. Original edition entitled "Pilgrim
Life in the Middle Ages").
Rich and Cowan. (1950).
3,6,11

WYATT, George.
The papers of George Wyatt, Esquire, of
Boxley Abbey in the County of Kent.
Royal Historical Society. 1968.
1

BRABOURNE

SAMPSON, Aylwin.*
The church of St. Mary the Virgin, Brabourne,
Kent.
Cross & Jackman, Canterbury. 1954.
30

The Church of St. Mary the Virgin, Brabourne,
Kent. Revised edition.
Elvy Bros & Cross & Jackman,Canterbury. 1965
11

BRASTED

CAVE-BROWNE Rev. John Curate in Charge of
Brasted.*
The history of Brasted, its manor, parish and
church.
J.H. Jewell, Westerham. 1874.
16,25.

DURTNELL, Cyril Streeter.
From an acorn to an oak tree: a study in
continuity. (Extracts from the family history
of the Durtnell's who have lived at Brasted for
26 generations).
C.S.Durtnell. Printed by Hooker Bros.
Westerham. (1976?).
2,3,11,17,19.23.

PYM, Horace N.*
Odds and Ends at Foxwold: a guide for the
inquiring guest.
Ballantyre, Hanson & Co. 1887
1

SINGLETON, H.G.H.
Brasted Place and its owners. Printed by The
Courier & Co.Ltd. Tunbridge Wells. 1954
16

BRENCHLEY.

ALL SAINTS, BRENCHLEY, KENT. Printed
by Stonestreet & Sons. Tonbridge. 1934.
11

BRENCHLEY PARISH COUNCIL.
Brenchley & Matfield official guide. Issued by
authority of the Brenchley Parish Council.
Forward Publicity. 1972?
4

GENERAL REGISTER OFFICE.
Census Returns. 1861.
Brenchley (part of) photocopy.
23

HALE, Robert.
Plan of an estate called the Park Farm
and Cat's Place Farm situate in the parishes
of Brenchley & Yalding in the County of Kent.
Scale 21" = 1 mile. Size 65cm by 90cm.
1837.
11

KENT COUNTY COUNCIL: PLANNING DEPT.
Brenchley Village Study.
K.C.C. 1967.
19, 30

BRENZETT

EVERSON, Don.
The reluctant Messerschmitt (shot down in the
English Channel in October, 1940, found by
fishermen, retrieved and restored and now in
Brenzett Aeronautical Museum).
Portcullis Press. Redhill, Surrey. 1978.
7,12

BRIDGE

BOWTELL, Rev. John.
A sermon preached at Patrixbourne & Bridge.
Printed by J. Abree. Canterbury, 1749.
3

FIFTY YEARS AGO: a description of the villages
of Bridge, Patrixbourne & Bekesbourne, taken
from "Saunters through Kent with pen and pencil"
by Charles Igglesden.
Bekesbourne Parochial Church Council. 1977.
3

HILL, Michael.
The village that bent the A 2 In "The Sunday
Times Magazine" November 7 1978 pp. 78 - 87.
3.

UNIVERSITY OF KENT AT CANTERBURY.
Bridge as portrayed in historical sources
prior to 1939
(S214: Aspects of the economic and social
history of Kent, Group Research Project,1978).
University of Kent at Canterbury. 1978.
3,11

BRIDGES

ARNOLD, A.A.
Rochester Bridge in A.D. 1561.Reprinted from
Archaeologia Cantiana. Vol.17. 1887, pp.212-240.
25

BALSTON, John N,
Teston Bridge: an appreciation.
The author. 1978.
11,12

BECKER, M. Janet.*
Rochester Bridge, 1387 - 1856.
Constable 1930.
1,2,3,4,5,8,9,11,12,15,17,18,19,25

BROWN, Samuel.
King's Ferry Bridge. Design for a suspension
bridge over the Swale. Two views. (it is
believed that the Bridge was never built).
photocopies. 1833.
4

ENVIRONMENT. Department of the
Bridges of architectural or historic interest.
Dept. of Environment. (1977).
4

GREAT BRITAIN, Laws etc. (Eliz. II)
The Rochester Bridge Act, 1965.
H.M.S.O. 1965.
4,25

JERVOISE, E.*
The ancient bridges of the South of England.
Architectural Press. 1930.
13,15

KENT COUNTY LIBRARY.
Medway Bridges: eight historic prints published
on the occasion of the opening of the new bridge
at Maidstone, 1978, with text by Peter Richards,
Stella Hardy, Brenda Purle.
Kent County Library. 1978.
4,11,16,19,23

MELLING, Elizabeth.*
Some roads and bridges: a collection of examples.
Kentish Sources.1, edited by E.Melling.
K.C.C. Archives Office. 1959.
1,2,3,4,5,6,7,8,9,11,12,14,15,16,18,19,20,
30,31

REPORTS AND DOCUMENTS* relating to Rochester
Bridge, printed at the request of the
commonalty, assembled at a meeting at Rochester
on 27th February, 1832. The Wardens &
Associates of Rochester Bridge.
Printed by J & W.H. Sweet, Strood. 1832.
11,12,15

ROBINS, F.W.
The story of the bridge (contains references
to bridges in Rochester and Kent). n.d.
15

ROCHESTER BRIDGE See also ROCHESTER in both vols.

WHEATLEY, Rev. Sydney William, Hon. Canon
of Rochester Cathedral.
Heraldic decoration of the Drawbridge of the
Mediaeval Bridge of Rochester. Reprinted
from Archaeologia Cantiana. Vol.63. 1951.
pp.140 - 143.
Headley Bros. Ashford. 1951.
15,25

BROADOAK

MID KENT WATER COMPANY.
Report on Broadoak Resevoir May 1972 (by
Binnie and Partners, Chartered Engineers).
Binnie & Partners. 1972.
11.

SOUTHERN WATER AUTHORITY AND THE MID-KENT
WATER CO. Broad Oak Reservoir scheme.
The Authors.1975.
3

BROADSTAIRS   See also Isle of Thanet.

ARCHAEOLOGIA, OR MISCELLANEOUS TRACTS
RELATING TO ANTIQUITY.
Proceedings of the Society of Antiquaries,
Vol. LXI, 1809.
24.

BARBER, T.
Barber's picturesque illustrations of the
Isle of Wight comprising views of every object
of interest on the island.(The White & Culmer-
White family of Broadstairs were boatbuilders
& ancestors of Whites of Cowes,Shipbuilders).
Simpkin & Marshall. n.d.
24.

BARLOW. P.W. Junior.*
Broadstairs past and present.
Parsons, Broadstairs. 1882.
24.

BIRD, James Edward.
The story of Broadstairs & St. Peters.
Lanes (East Kent) Ltd. Broadstairs. 1974.
1,3,6,11,12,24.

BREEZY BROADSTAIRS.*
James Simson.Weekly News Office. Broadstairs.1897.
24

BRIGGS Enid Semple.*
Horses and donkeys in retirement: true
story of "the Ranch", Broadstairs.
Raleigh Press. Exmouth. 1955.
11,24

"The Ranch":*a paradise for horses.
Warne. 1946.
11,24

BROADSTAIRS & ST.PETER'S ARCHAEOLOGICAL
SOCIETY. Archaeological discoveries in
Broadstairs and St. Peter's up to 1972.
Broadstairs & St. Peter's Archaeological
7,11   Society.   1973.

BROADSTAIRS & ST. PETER'S CHAMBER OF COMMERCE.
The gateway to prosperity yearbook.
Broadstairs & St. Peter's Chamber of Commerce.1964.
24

BROADSTAIRS & ST. PETER'S DISTRICT Local Board.
The Public Health Act. 1875. Byelaws.
for the above district.
1881.
11

BROADSTAIRS & ST. PETER'S URBAN DISTRICT COUNCIL.
Annual report of the Medical Officer of Health.
1971.
13

Broadstairs & St. Peter's: Official Guide.
11   1948
24   1927,1928,1929,1939,1960,1961,1962,1963,
      1964,1966,1969.
25   1970

Committee Reports. 1888 - 1892.
24
Committee Reports. 1892 - 1898 (Finance excepted).
24
Committee Reports No 1. 1914-1921.
24
Committee Reports.Finance No.2 1917 - 1921.
24
Council Minutes. 1946 - 1973.
24
Letter Book 1880 - 1886
24
Letter Book 1900 - 1909
24
Pier and Harbour Sundry Debtors' Day book
No 1. 1915 - 1923.
24
Public Library Committee Minute Book. 1926-1950.
24

BROADSTAIRS & ST. PETER'S URBAN DISTRICT COUNCIL*
Souvenir Programme to commemorate the landing
of the Danish Viking Ship at Broadstairs Bay.
in the Isle of Thanet. Thursday 28th July,1949.
24

Sunny Broadstairs: official guide.
Broadstairs & St. Peter's U.D.C.
24.   1919; 1922;(1932);1933.

Year Book 1901.
Snow & Co. Printers
24

Year Books.
Vol I. 1899 - 1906.
Vol II 1907 - 1913.
24

BROADSTAIRS DURING THE TIME OF CHARLES DICKENS,*
1836 - 59.
Charles Ward & Sons. Broadstairs.1949
11,24

BROADSTAIRS PARISH CHURCH OF THE MOST
HOLY TRINITY. A brief History.
(Duplicated pamphlet). 1978.
13,24

BROADSTAIRS PIER.
Special Pier Committee Minute Book 1882.
24
Treasurer's Account Book 1831 - 1841.
24

BROADSTAIRS PIER AND HARBOUR.
Harbour Accounts Day Book, 1849 - 1857
24
Minute Books 1833 - 1847; 1853 - 1869;
1869 - 1883; 1883 - 1895; 1895 - 1911;
1911. 24.
Minute Book (Special Meetings) 1870-1880.
24.

Works Committee Minute Books 1880 - 1885;
1885 - 1890; 1890 - 1899; 1899 - 1911;
1911 - 1923.
24

BURROW, Edward J & Co. Publishers
The "Borough" Guide to Broadstairs.
E.J. Burrow & Co.Ltd. Cheltenham. c.1900.
11

CALLAM, Gertrude Marian Norwood.*
The Norwoods. 2 vols.
Vol 1. An introduction to their history.
Vol.II Heraldry and Brasses.
A.E. Callam. 1963 - 1965.
24,
27 (Vol II only)

A CATALOGUE OF HALE, late Nuckell's,Royal
Kent Marine Library. Broadstairs.
1847.
24

CHARLES DICKENS AND HIS BLEAK HOUSE.*
A story and guide.
Elvy & Gibbs. Printers. Canterbury. 1959 etc.
1. 1965 only
2. 1960
11. 1970.
4,6,8,12,15,19,24.   1959 etc.

COMMISSIONERS OF BROADSTAIRS PIER.
Resolutions Books: 1792 - 1814; 1814 - 1824;
1825; 1825 - 1843; 1843 - 1853.
24
Treasurer's Book. 1842 - 1852.
24

CRAMP, Rev. Dr. John Mockett. (Baptist
Minister, St. Peter's, Broadstairs).
Memoir of the Rev. Thomas Cramp, late of
St. Peter's, Isle of Thanet. (Pastor of
the Baptist Church, St. Peter's, Isle
of Thanet).
1852.
24

DALE, Rev. Thomas.
The believers' hiding place and shield.
A sermon preached in the Chapel of Ease,
Broadstairs, on Sunday, 29th July, 1832.
24

DAVIES, Rev. Charles Greenall.
A sermon preached in the Chapel of Ease,
Broadstairs, on Sunday, March 24th 1833.
24

DICKENS, Charles.
Our English watering place.
(Written in 1851 and first published in 1852).
Dickens House Museum, Broadstairs. 1973.
3

DICKENS HOUSE, Broadstairs.
1939.
24

EAST KENT (No.1) UNITED DISTRICTS FOR THE
APPOINTMENT OF MEDICAL OFFICERS OF HEALTH
Minute Book No. 1. 1920 - 1930.
24
Minute Book No. 2. 1931 - 1941.
24

EAST KENT TIMES AND BROADSTAIRS AND ST.
PETER'S MAIL.
Golden Jubilee Edition. Wednesday 25th
February, 1953.
East Kent Times. 1953.
24
Supplement. Trumans, Gwyn & Co.(Brewery).
Opening of the modern depot and offices at
Westwood, Broadstairs.
East Kent Times. 1964.
24

ENVIRONMENT, Department of the.
List of buildings of special architectural
or historic interest. District of Thanet, Kent.
(Broadstairs & St. Peters Area)
Department of the Environment 1974.
11.24.

GARDNER, Peter G.A. *
St. Peter's village community: a selection
of documents. c.1700 - c.1900., compiled
by P.G.A. Gardner and P.J. Hills. 1972.
24

GREAT BRITAIN. Laws etc. (Geo.III).*
An Act for repairing or rebuilding the pier
adjoining to the Harbour of Broadstairs.
1792.
13,24

AN ACT*for amending an Act...for the
repairing...of the pier adjoining to the
harbour of Broadstairs. 1805.
24

Broadstairs Harbour Act. 1792.
Broadstairs Harbour Act. 1805.
(Bound with Broadstairs & St. Peter's
Urban District Council Act., 1913).
24

GREAT BRITAIN. Laws etc. (Edw. VII).
Broadstairs and St. Peter's Water and
Improvement Act. 1901.
24.

GREAT BRITAIN, Laws etc. (Geo.V.)
Broadstairs & St. Peter's Urban
District Council Act, 1913.
(Bound with Broadstairs Harbour Acts
of 1792 and 1805).
24

HELLIAR, A.
A most strange and curious guide to
Broadstairs.
Broadstairs Printing & Publishing Co. n.d.
24.

HEYWOOD, John Publisher.*
Illustrated guide to Broadstairs.
J. Heywood. Manchester. n.d.
24

HILLS, Peter J.*
Dane Court, St. Peters-in-Thanet: a
Kentish manor and its families.
Printed by G.W. Belton. 1972.
7,8,24

The Parish Church of St. Peter in Thanet.
An introductory history and a guide.
Printed by G.W. Belton. 1970.
12,13,24

HURD, Howard.
On a late-Celtic village near Dumpton Gap,
Broadstairs. Read to the Society of
Anqiquaries of London. 27th May, 1909.
Extracted from Archaelogia Vol.LXI and bound.
Society of Antiquaries of London. 1909.
24

SOME NOTES*on recent archaeological discoveries
at Broadstairs. For Broadstairs and St. Peters
Archaeological Society.
Broadstairs Printing & Publishing Co. 1913
24

JOHNSON, H.C.*
Sunny Broadstairs, edited by H.C.Johnson.
Broadstairs & St. Peter's Advancement Assn.
c.1910.
4

JOINT THANET SPORTS CENTRE COMMITTEE.
Report and estimate of cost for the proposed
recreation centre at St. Peters' Court,
Broadstairs. 1970.
13

JOTTINGS OF KENT.
"A PARISHONER" Jottings of St. Peters including
Broadstairs.   (1).
24
History of Richborough Castle...   (2).
24
DOWKER, G. Ancient Church & Roman Castrum
at Reculver. (3).
24.
RUTTON, W.L. Sandgate Castle. (4).
24
"R.J.F." Annals of Sandgate Castle. (5).
24
ANDERSON, A.H. Sandwich, Kent. (6).
24
PAYNE, O.D.B. Soul of a Wooden Saint. (7).
24
CATHEDRAL & Metropolitan Church of
Christ, Canterbury.   (8).
24
THE QUEEN'S DIAMOND JUBILEE. 1897. (9).
24
A SHORT GUIDE TO Folkestone Parish Church.
24   4th edn (10).
DALE, Rev. H.D. Notes of the Parish church
of St. Leonard, Hythe. (11).
24
DALE, Rev H.D. Notes on the Crypt & Bones of
Hythe Church. (12).
(These twelve items are bound together and
can be found separately in their sections)

THE KING'S WORK: Parish Magazine of St.
Peter's-in-Thanet. For 1901,1904 and 1905.
1905.
24

LAPTHORNE, William H.*
A Broad place: an historical account of
Broadstairs from 1500 AD to the present:
illustrated with old views. 1st & 2nd
editions.
Thanet Antiquarian Book Club.
n.d. and 1971
24

Broadstairs Panorama.
Thanet Antiquarian Book Club. 1971
24

Historic Broadstairs.
Thanet Antiquarian Book Club. n.d.
24

Smugglers' Broadstairs:*an historical guide
to the smuggling annals of the ancient
town of Bradstow; illustrated with
old views.
Thanet Antiquarian Book Club
24   1970
11 & 24.   1971 2nd edn revised
24   1977

LISTER-HETHERINGTON. Rev. A.
Congregationalism in Broadstairs.
Printed by Lanes,Broadstairs. 1964.
24

MILVILLE, Hugh (pseud. for Hugh Raven)
There go the ships: a book of Broadstairs.
Typescript. n.d.
11,24.
See Also RAVEN, Mary
          Three Broadstairs Ravens.
          BROADSTAIRS: FAMILY HISTORY.

"A MINISTER OF THE GOSPEL" pseud.
An address to British Christians on the
importance and necessity of a revival of
religion. (The minister was almost certainly
the Rev. Dr. J.M. Cramp and the address was
given at Broadstairs).
1832.
24

MOCKETT, John.*
An address to the inhabitants and parishioners
of St. Peter's,Thanet,containing an account of
the proceedings of the Parish Officers.
1822.
24

A second address to the inhabitants and
parishioners of St. Peter's,Thanet.
1823.
24

NATIONAL PARKS & ACCESS TO THE COUNTRYSIDE
ACT. 1949. Pt.IV. Survey of Public Rights
of Way. Definitive Statement. County of Kent.
Broadstairs U.D.C.
H.M.S.O. 1952.
24

NEW MARGATE, RAMSGATE AND BROADSTAIRS GUIDE.
Printed by Thanet Press. 1801.
24

NEW RAMSGATE GUIDE WITH MAP, containing also
an account of Margate and Broadstairs, as well
as the life boat work on the coast of Kent.
S.R. Wilson. 1890.
24

NORCOTT, P.
Bigger and better earthquakes.
1970
24

"A PARISHIONER" pseud (R.R. Schartace).
Jottings of St. Peters', including Broadstairs.
Printed by Jennings & Son. 1876.
11
24 - Included in "Jottings of Kent"

PINKESS, F.E.
A short history of the Baptist Church,
St. Peter's-in-Thanet.
1963. (rev. 1970)
13

POINTER, Thomas James.
Memories. (Handwritten manuscript, gives
a short biographical history from 1837 - 1912!
Farmworker who lived in Birchington,Margate
and St. Peter's , the latter from 1858.
1912.
24

RAVEN, Mary.
Three Broadstairs Ravens: Dr Hugh Milville
Raven, 1877 - 1963; Miss Olive Margaret Raven
1881 - 1970; Dr. Martin Owen Raven, 1888-1976
compiled by Mary & David Raven.
Lanes (East Kent) Ltd. 1976.
3,24.

ROCHARD J.S. & Co. Publishers.
Illustrated and historical Broadstairs
(Title page "Broadstairs Illustrated")
Holiday guides published by J.S. Rochard & Co.,
Gravesend,of which there are three issues,
one dated 1900.
24

ST. PETER'S CHURCH HISTORY.
Margate.
Printed by Cooper. C.1930.
24

ST. PETER'S CHURCH HISTORY: Parish Church
of St. Peter's-in-Thanet.
Printed by Gibbs & Son. Canterbury (1950)
12

ST. PETER'S-IN-THANET.
(Notes on famous Churches and Abbeys series).
Soc. for promoting Christian Knowledge. c.1915
24

ST PETER THE APOSTLE IN THANET. Year book from
Easter, 1892. to Easter 1893. Alfred Whitehead,
Vicar.
Printed Kebles Gazette. 1893.
24

SANGSTER, Alfred.*
Historical notes on the Parish of St. Peter
the Apostle in Thanet.
Keble's Gazette. 1904.
13,24

SOCIETY OF ST. PETER AND ST PAUL LTD. Publishers.
The Parish church of Broadstairs.
Society of St. Peter & St. Paul. 1924.
24

SOUVENIR GUIDE TO THE HOUSE ON THE CLIFF
immortalised by Charles Dickens as the home
of Betsy Trotwood in the novel David Copperfield.
Dickens House Museum, Broadstairs. (1974).
3

STONE HOUSE, North Foreland Road, Broadstairs.
(A guide when Stone House was a School,now flats)
Published by Goodall, c.1960.
24

BROADSTAIRS   Cont'd

STORY OF THE VIKINGS and the VIKING SHIP
"HUGIN" (1949).
(Duplicated typescript account of the 1949
invasion by a replica of a Viking Ship &
crew from Denmark.   The landing was at
Broadstairs & the ship is preserved at Pegwell
Bay).
11

THE TAIT HOMES, "Old Girls" Annual Paper 1916.
Jubilee Number.
24
The Tait Homes Fellowship: Annual Paper 1936-
1937.
24

THANET DISTRICT COUNCIL, AMENITIES DEPARTMENT.
Broadstairs on the sunny Kent coast.
Thanet District Council. 1975.
13,24

WHITES OF COWES: SHIPBUILDERS.
(The White & Culmer-White family of Broadstairs
were boat builders & ancestors of Whites of
Cowes).
T. Samuel White & Co. n.d.
24

BROMLEY

ASHFORD, Anna.
Bromley Hospital 1869 - 1947.
(Essay for Open University course on History
of Architecture and design) Typescript.
1976.
2

ATTENBOROUGH, John.
A living memory: Hodder & Stoughton Publishers,
1868 - 1975.(The Hodder-Williams family were
residents of Bromley and the firm evacuated to
Bickley during the second world war. It is now
located at Dunton Green)
Hodder & Stoughton. Dunton Green. 1975.
2,16

BARTHOLOMEW, B.M.
A short history of St. Andrews, Bromley.
(4p. only but including account of the Burnt
Ash Lane area c.1910/20).
(1951)
2

BELSEY, Harry John.
Bromley memories: a working class childhood.
1917 - 21.
H.J. Belsey. 1977.
2

BERRY, C.F.
Five years in a pillbox, C6 Area.Memoirs of a
part-time Warden, 1939 - 1945. C6
Area was the Southborough District of Bromley,
Kent) Typescript. 1975?
2

BIBBY, Margaret.
Bromley Baptist Church, Park road...these
seventy five years. 1863 - 1938.
Bromley Printing Co. Printers. 1938.
2

BIRKBECK, Robert.
Notes on the history and genealogy of the
family of Lubbock.
Mitchell & Hughes Printers, 1891
2

BLAKE, Lewis pseud (i.e. G.L.Dennington).
Bromley in the front-line: The story of
the London Borough of Bromley under enemy
air attack in the second world war...
The Author. 1980.
2,5.

BROMLEY ASSOCIATION FOR THE HANDICAPPED
AND BROMLEY COUNCIL OF SOCIAL SERVICE.
Bromley for the disabled.
The Authors.1974.
2

BROMLEY CONGREGATIONAL CHURCH.
A short history of our War work...1914-
1918. (photocopy).
Bromley Congregational Church, 1919.
2

BROMLEY, LONDON BOROUGH COUNCIL.*
The London Borough of Bromley: introductory
handbook.
Bromley,London Borough Council. (1965).
11

The London Borough of Bromley: official guide
(1974). British Publishing Co., Ltd.,
Gloucester. (1974).
11

London Borough of Bromley:official street plan.
G.W. May. 1971 & 1973 edition.
4

BROMLEY, LONDON BOROUGH COUNCIL:EDUCATION COMMITTEE.
Ravensbourne College of Art & Design.
Prospectus. 1969 - 70.
As author. 1969.
11

BROMLEY PUBLIC LIBRARY.
Town Trail:around the High street, Bromley.
London Borough of Bromley Public Libraries. 1975.
18

Views of the London Borough of Bromley
in the 18th and 19th centuries. Historical
notes by A.H. Watkins.
London Borough of Bromley Public Libraries.1972
2.
Text only 11.

BROMLEY SOCIETY FOR MENTALLY HANDICAPPED CHILDREN.
A life apart. A survey of the problems and
needs of the mentally handicapped and their
families in the London Borough of Bromley.
The Society. 1975.
2

BURNHAM. T.G.
Branch to Bromley North. In. The Railway
Magazine Feb. 1975. pp. 56 - 59.
2

CAWSTON, Edward Percy.
Historical notes on Bromley Hill Court....
Duplicated Typescript .
Kent & Sussex Authors Conclave.(1972)
2

CHURCH MISSIONARY SOCIETY.
Celebration: Foxbury 1875-1975.
Foxbury was the home of the Tiarks
family then a Missionary Training College and
now a Retreat. Used by the Army and A.T.S. 1940-
45). Duplicated typescript
Church Missionary Society. 1975.
2

CONDIE, Stuart J.
Social segregation: a case study of the
Bromley area. 1870 - 1939. Unpublished thesis.
1978.
2

DANCE, G.W.
Bygone Bromley and District, compiled by
G.W. Dance.
John Hallewell. Rochester.   1980.
2

DUNKIN, John.*
Outlines of the history and antiquities of
Bromley. photocopy of the author's extra -
annotated copy. (original in Greenwich Local
History Collection).
J. Dunkin. 1815.
2

EAMES, Geoffrey L.
Bromley Hockey Club..notes on the years 1963 -
1978.
G.L. Eames. 1979.
2

ENVIRONMENT, Department of.
List of buildings of special architectural
or historic interest, London Borough of
Bromley (photocopy).
H.M.S.O. 1973.
2

FOX, Reg.
Bromley Common Methodist Church by, R.Fox and
Geoffrey Fletcher. 1877 - 1977.
The Church. 1976.
2

FREEMAN, Charles.*
History, antiquities, improvements etc...
of the parish of Bromley, Kent.
William Beckley. Bromley. 1832.
1,2,3,18

GAGE, W.L.
Churchill Theatre, Bromley. Case study,
Commissioned by the Arts Council to assist
in teaching arts administration by, W.L.
Gage and others. (Duplicated typescript).
Polytechnic of Central London. (1978).
2

GREAT BRITAIN: Laws etc. (Geo.III).
An Act for the more easy and speedy Recovery
of Small depts within the Hundreds of
Blackheath and of Bromley.... 1765.
2,11

An act to explain, amend and make more
effectual, an act...For the more easy and
speedy recovery of small debts within the
hundreds of Blackheath and of Bromley.
Charles Eyre and William Strahan. 1770.
1,2,11,12
GREAT BRITAIN:Laws etc.   (Vic.)
Act for the lease of...Mid-Kent Railway
(Bromley to St. Mary Cray) Coy., to the
London, Chatham & Dover Railway Company.
(25 - 26 Vic. Ch.224). 1862.
2

An act to amend the acts relating to The
Bromley Direct   Railway Co...1877
2

GREAT BRITAIN. Laws. (Eliz.II)
Bill to confirm a scheme of the Charity
Commissioners for the application or management
of Bromley College.
H.M.S.O. 1960.
2,8

HORSBURGH, Edward Lee Stuart.
Bromley, Kent, from the earliest times to the
present century...(1st edition published 1929)
1971 Facsimile Reprint. S.R. Robinson.*   11
1980 Reproduction of the original edition,
     slightly reduced in size and without
     blank pages, Lodgmark Press,Chislehurst.
     2.

HUGHES, Muriel.*
A short history of Bromley Parish Church.
British Publishing Co Ltd. Gloucester. 1971
8

JENKINS, Peggy.
A short history of St. John the Evangelist
Bromley, Kent. (Centenary history).
The Church, 1980.
2

KELLY, M.B.
A woodland walk at High Elms.
London Borough of Bromley. 1971?
2

KINNAIRD, Emily.
Reminiscences. (E. Kinnaird was an Evangelist
and partly responsible for establishing the
Y.W.C.A. in India. Bromley pp. 7-8)
J. Murray. 1925.
11

LOCAL HISTORY SOCIETY FOR THE LONDON BOROUGH
OF BROMLEY.
Bromley local history: aspects of the history
of the community in the London Borough of
Bromley   —expected to be annual
The Society. 1976.
2   No.1. 1976 in progress.
3   No.23 1978 Third series

MAGGS, K.R.A.
(Population statistics for the London Borough
of Bromley 1801 - 1965) in Croydon Field
Studies Bulletin 36 1972.
(Duplicated typescript).
2

MAY, Arthur.
A history of the Hervey Lodge no.1692 of the
...ancient free and accepted Masons of England
Centenary year 1977...(includes lists of
officers and members).
The Lodge. Province of Kent. 1977.
2

MISCELLANEA GENEALOGICA ET HERALDICA.
5th series v.4 parts 5 and 6 (containing
Charlton pedigree, some extracts from Kent
Wills, part of "Monumental Inscriptions in
Bromley Church"
(ed. Clarke & R. Holworthy)
Mitchell, Hughes & Clarke. 1921
2

MORGAN, Verne.
Yesterday's sunshine.(includes childhood
memories of Bromley)
Bailey Bros. & Swinfen. 1974.
2

MORLEY, Thomas William (1883-1931).
Exhibition of works by T.W. Morley at Bromley
Central Library...1979. (includes brief bio-
graphy of tne painter who lived at Hayes).
Bromley Central Library. 1979.
2

NORMAN, George Warde.
(George Warde Norman and family lived at the
Rookery, Bromley Common). Photocopy of typescript.
lived at The Rookery, Bromley Common).
2

NORTON, Ann.
Aspects of Bromley Union 1871 - 1910 with
special reference to unemployment and
emigration.(Unpublished thesis) 1978.
2

PARNELL, J.W.
Home for the weekend-back on Monday: a study
of a 5-day ward for the rehabilitation of
geriatric patients,by J.W.Parnell & R.Naylor.
(Experiment at the Leonard Hospital, Bromley)
Queens Institute of District Nursing. 1973.
2

POCKNELL, Edmund.
A short history of the Hervey Lodge no.1692 of
the...ancient free and accepted Masons of
England..Note(includes lists of officers and
members).   Province of Kent.   1937.
2

REEVES, M.
An index of Bromley, Kent, parish registers,
compiled by M. Reeves & others from the trans-
script in the library of the Society of
Genealogists. (Typescript).   1973.
2

SCOTT, F.
A double century 1772 - 1972: a history of
methodism in Widmore, Bromley,Kent.
Duplicated typescript.   1972.
2

SHAW,Herbert.
Tne story of Nalder and Collyer's Croydon
Brewery and its licensed houses in Bromley.
Typescript text of talk given..10th Nov.1977.
1977.
2

SMITH, Arthur William.
Wray (Optical Works) Ltd. 1850 - 1971.
(Wray moved to Bromley in 1915). Typescript
(1974).
2

SMITH, P.J.
Predicting school populations: a study for
the London Borough of Bromley,by P.J.Smith
and K.N. Groom.
Royal Institute of Public Admin. 1971
2

STOCKWELL College: the past one hundred years:
mainly photographs. The College moved to
Bromley Palace in 1935.
The College. 1975.
2

THURLEY, Elizabeth Fusae.
Research Project: understanding & perceptions of
London School children of Japanese Society.
(Based on research in 8 schools in the London
Borough of Bromley)
Japan Foundation. 1978.
2

TRANSPORTATION PLANNING ASSOCIATES.
Greater London Council heavy vehicle restraint
study: Scheme reports...London Borough of Bromley.
Transportation Planning Assoc. 1974.
2

TRANSPORTATION PLANNING ASSOCIATES.
Greater London Council heavy vehicle restraint
study. Borough report..London Borough of Bromley.
Transportation Planning Assoc. 1974.
2

WATKINS, Albert Henry.
The manor and town of Bromley. AD862 to 1934.
Duplicated typescript.
Bromley Public Library. 1972.
2

WERF, Philip van der.
A study of the development of commerce in Bromley
1800 - 1900...Photocopy of manuscript.
Teachers Training College Thesis. 1972.
2

WILSON, Jack F.
The Royal Observer Corps:a brief history...and
memories of the Bromley Group No.19 Operations
Room, who guarded the South Eastern approaches
to London.
Typescript. (1975).
2

WILTON, Eric.*
Centre Crew: a memory of the Royal Observer Corps.
Published privately for the members of "B" Crew
of the Royal Observer Corps Centre at Bromley,
Kent.
Printed by King & Jarrett. 1946.
2,11

BROMPTON

BRIDGE, Colin W.
An Urban trail in Victorian Gillingham around
New Brompton. (Let's explore Gillingham,2).
Rainham,Gillingham & Chatham Amenities Soc. 1978.
4

INSTITUTE OF THE ROYAL ENGINEERS.
South African Engineer Corps & Boer Leaders
Statues. Notes from the Corps library from
letters dated 17th April, 1964- 6th January,1970.
4

ROYAL SCHOOL OF MILITARY ENGINEERING, Brompton.
Open day, 1968.
4

A Manuscript history of the establishment.
n.d.
32

R.E. War Memorial. The unveiling by H.R.H.
the Duke of Connaught & Strathearn, 1922.
4

ST. LUKE'S CHURCH, New Brompton.
St. Luke's Book of Memories.
St. Luke's Church. 1906.
11

Service & ceremony to be used at the laying of
the foundation stone of St. Luke's Church, New
Brompton, by the Provincial Grand Master...9th
May, 1908.
Province of Kent (Freemasons) 1908.
11.

WARD, B.R.*
School of Military Engineering. 1812-1909.
R.E. Institute, Brompton. 1909.
15

BROOKLAND

ROPER, Anne.*
The Church of St. Augustine, Brookland.
Geerings, Ashford. 1953.
30

BROOMFIELD

CAVE-BROWN, Rev. John*
In and about Leeds & Broomfield parishes, Kent.
Read on 17th January 1894, to the British
Archaeological Association & extracted from the
Journal. (1894).
1,4,11,15

BROOMHILL   See   SOUTHBOROUGH

BUCKLAND-IN-DOVER

BUCKLAND CHURCH MAGAZINE, St. Andrew's Church,
Buckland, Dover. 1883-4, 1891-2, 1893-4,
1895-6, 1905-7. (Bound vols. each bound with
the Penny Post).
6.
ROOKWOOD, O.M.*
Buckland-in-Dover, 1852 - 1952.
Buckland Press, Dover. 1952
11

BURHAM

PATRICK, G.
Discovery of the remains of a Roman house at
Burham, Kent. 1897.
1

CANALS AND WATERWAYS

BELLARS, E.J.
The canal that failed: an account of the Croydon
Canal. Unpublished Thesis.   1975.
18

CALLAGHAN, W.H.
The Croydon Canal.
Unpublished Study. 1977.
18

DENNEY, Martyn.
London's waterways. (Covers Dartford and
Crayford Navigation).
Batsford. 1977.
5

GREAT BRITAIN, Laws Etc (William IV & Victoria)
An Act for transferring and vesting the Royal
Military Canal, Roads, Towing Paths...in the
Counties of Kent & Sussex, and also the Rates
and Tolls arising therefrom.
Printed by Eyre & Spottiswoode. 1837.
11

HADFIELD, Charles.
The canals of South and South East England.
David & Charles. 1969.
11

McLELLAN, Doreen E.
The Thames and Medway canal (Local history
pamphlet no 11.)
Kent County Library, Gravesham Division (1978).
3,4,6,9,11

MOULE, Thomas.
Inland navigation of England & Wales; maps by
Thomas Moule. 1836. Brian Stevens, Monmouth.
(1970?)
The maps give existing canals and proposed
canals from plans deposited for permission
for construction. Some of these canals were
not built.
11

SATURDAY MAGAZINE, 1834.
Includes items on Chatham Dockyard, Cinque Ports
Reculver, Ancient Church in Dover Castle, Thames
& Medway Canal.
S.P.C.K.   1834.
11

VINE, Paul Ashley Laurence.
London's lost route to the sea: an historical
account of the inland navigations which linked
the Thames to the English Channel. 3rd edition.
David & Charles. 1973.
1

The Royal Military Canal:* an historical account
of the waterway and military road from Shorncliffe
in Kent to Cliffe End in Sussex.
David & Charles. 1972.
2,3,4,6,7,11,12,19,32.

WATSON, K.
The Thames & Medway Canal: a study of recreational
potential. (Gravesham Borough Council: Planning
Dept.)
Gravesham Borough Council.
1st Edn. (1975) 4.9.11.15.
2nd Edn. (1976) 9.

WEST, R. George.
To Penge - by canal. Duplicated typescript. 1976.
2

CANTERBURY

AITKEN, George A.*
Defoe's "Apparition of Mrs. Veal". Photocopy of
an article appearing in The Nineteenth Century,
Vol. XXXVII, 1895.
3

ANGLICAN INTERNATIONAL CONFERENCE ON SPIRITUAL
RENEWAL. A new Canterbury tale; the reports of
the Anglican International Conference on
Spiritual Renewal held at Canterbury, July, 1978.
With an introduction by Michael Harper, Chair-
man of the Conference.
Grove Books, Bramcote, Notts. 1978.
3.
BAINE, Rodney M.*
The apparition of Mrs. Veal: a neglected account.
Photocopy of an article appearing in Proceedings
of the Modern Languages Association Vol. LXIX.
1954.
3
Defoe and Mrs. Bargrave's story. Photocopy
of an article in the Philological Quarterly.
Vol. XXXIII, IV. October 1954.
3

BALL, Mia.
Worshipful Company of Brewers: a short history.
(pp.19 - 70, Canterbury & St. Thomas a Becket
mentioned).
Hutchinson. 1977.
11

BARLEY, Maurice Willmore.
European towns, their archaeology and early
history. (contains 2 articles on Canterbury)
Academic Press. 1977.
3

BARTLETT, A.E.
Canterbury masters & their apprentices 1763 -
1777, with a few entries of 1758 - 1762, edited
by A.E. Bartlett.
Harrington Family Miscellany Record Pub. Canterbury.
1978.
3,23

BENNETT-GOLDNEY, Francis.*
The Royal and Ancient City of Canterbury.
Official Guide.
Canterbury & District Chamber of Trade.(1914).
11

The West Gate, Walls and Castle of
Canterbury.*
Gibbs. 1914
30

BERBIERS, John L.
Cole Craft Calendar. 1979. (Compiled from a
selection of original sketches of old Canterbury
by Mr. John Berbiers).
Cole Craft. (1978).
3

Planning in Canterbury In The Architect,
Jan, 1974. pp. 32 - 35.
3

BERRY, M.H.A.
Canterbury Chapters: a Kentish heritage for
tomorrow, edited by M.H.A. Berry and J.H.
Higginson.
Dejall & Meyorre, Liverpool for Christchurch
College, Canterbury. 1976.
1,2,3,4,6,7,11,15,16,20,22,23,24,28

BICKERSTETH, Samuel.
A note on the history of Meister Omers, The
Precincts, Canterbury.
(No publisher). 1936.
3

BOYLE, John.
Portrait of Canterbury.
Hale. 1974.
1,3,6,7,11,12,14,15,16,20,22,25,26,28,30

BRASIER, W. C. Publisher.*
The picturesque companion to the Isle of
Thanet, Dover, Canterbury & parts adjacent.
W.C. Brasier, Margate. c.1860.
24

BRENT, John.*
Canterbury in the olden time, 2nd. ed. enlarged...
Simpkin & Marshall & Co. 1879.
26,30.

BRETHERTON, Ralph Harold.*
The apparition of Mrs. Veal. Article in the
Gentleman's Magazine, December 1901.
3

BRITANNIA: a Journal of Romano-British and
kindred studies. Vol.I. 1970.
Includes articles on The Roman Theatre at
Canterbury and on Richborough.
Society for the Promotion of Roman Studies.1970.
11

BROOKS, Charles S.*
Roundabout to Canterbury.
Harcourt, Brace & Co. 1926.
11

BUNCE, Cyprian Rondeau.*
Ancient Canterbury: the records of Alderman
Bunce, re-published from the "Kentish Gazette"
of 1800 - 1801.
1924.
3

A translation of the several charters etc.*
granted by Edward IV, Henry VII, James I and
Charles II to the citizens of Canterbury, also
a list of the bailiffs and mayors. From the year
780, to the present period. With a description
of the boundaries of the city...by a citizen.
Translated by C.R. Bunce.
Printed by J. Greve. Canterbury. 1791.
II.

BUZZARD, T.C.
Canterbury 1851 census: Use in evaluating
population and social structure. Extended essay
Photocopy University of Kent at Canterbury. (197?)
3.

C., H.R.*
The Canterbury & Whitstable Railway. Article in
Southern Railway Magazine, Vol.VIII, No.90.
June 1930
3.30

CANTACUZINO, Sherban.*
Canterbury, by Sherban Cantacuzino & others.
Studio Vista. 1970.
3

CANTERBURY, (album of photographs).
Photographs date from the early 1900's
11

CANTERBURY.* Articles extracted
from the Penny Magazine, Monthly Supplement -
the issues of November 30th 1833 and
February 28th. 1832.
Society for the Diffusion of Useful Knowledge.
London. 1834.
4

CANTERBURY. (Epislide Beautiful Britain series).
Educational Productions Ltd. 1958.
24

CANTERBURY & DISTRICT FOOTBALL LEAGUE.
Handbook & directory of clubs. Season 1974-75.
The League. 1974.
3

CANTERBURY & THANET COMMUNITY HEALTH COUNCIL.
Annual Reports: for the year ending on March 31st..
3   1976
3,13   1977
3,13   1978

CANTERBURY & THANET HEALTH DISTRICT: Kent
Area Health Authority.
District Plan. 1980 - 81
1979.
13

CANTERBURY CATHEDRAL:ARCHIVES AND LIBRARY.
Aspects of Canterbury in the eighteenth century:
(catalogue of an exhibition). 22 June - 14 July,
1973.
4

CANTERBURY CHAMBER OF TRADE.
The ancient city of Canterbury: Mother-city of
the Anglo-Saxon race.
Canterbury Chamber of Trade. c.1903.
12, 30.

The Canterbury View Book: Seventy Views.
Canterbury Chamber of Trade. c.1910
11

The Canterbury View Book: Souvenir edition
of the visit by the Leeds Choral Union on
June 19th, 1914.
Canterbury Chamber of Trade.
11

The penny guide to the ancient City of Canterbury'
...(5th edition?)
Cross & Jackman. 1907.
8

The Pilgrims' guide to the Royal & Ancient
City of Canterbury: the official guide.
3 1922,1925,1927,1929,1933,1936,1938,1952,
   1953,1954,1957,1960,1961.
11 1926,1927,1961
24 1956.
30 1966.

CANTERBURY CITY COUNCIL.
Abstract of accounts & financial statistics
for the year 1974 - 75.
Canterbury City Council.   1975.
3

Canterbury Conservation study. 1979.
1979.
13

The Pilgrims' Guide*to the Royal & Ancient
City of Canterbury: the Official Guide.
Completely revised by John Boyle.
3   1967,1968,1975,1978
4   1968
13   1967,1968
20   1968,1975
24   1968
25   1968
28   1976

Presentation of the Honorary Freedom of the
City to His Grace the Lord Archbishop of
Canterbury the most Reverend and Right
Honourable Dr. Frederick Donald Coggan and
the Very Reverend Ian Hugh White-Thomson
on Friday 5th March, 1976. Canterbury Ltd. (1976)
Printed J.A. Jennings. Canterbury Ltd. (1976)
3

Presentation of the Honorary Freedom of the
City of Canterbury to His Royal Highness The
Prince of Wales (opening of Guildhall)
November 1978.
Canterbury City Council.   1978.
3

Presentation of the honorary Freedom of the
City to John George Bosworth Stone, Esquire,
Tuesday, 24th March, 1936.
11

Souvenir of the Royal Visit: City of
Canterbury, July 11th 1946.
11

Summary of accounts and financial statistics
for the year 1973 - 74.
Canterbury City Council.   1975.
3

CANTERBURY CITY COUNCIL: AMENITIES AND
RECREATION DEPARTMENT.
Canterbury, Herne Bay & Whitstable welcomes
you. Official Guide.
Canterbury City Council.
3   1975;1977; 1978.
11   1975.
12   1975.
31   1977.

CANTERBURY CITY COUNCIL: CITY ARCHITECT AND
PLANNING OFFICER.
Canterbury conservation study: consultation
draft.
Canterbury City Council.   1979.
2

Central area; report of the City Architect
and Planning Officer on the proposed traffic
network.
Canterbury City Council.   1972.
3

City of Canterbury: spaces around buildings.
Canterbury City Council.   1973.
3

The Marlowe development.
Canterbury City Council.   1977.
3

CANTERBURY CITY COUNCIL, CITY ARCHITECT
AND PLANNING OFFICER.
Planning for industry
Canterbury City Council.   1973.
3

Ring road:north east section. An appraisal
of the alternative routes.
Canterbury City Council.   1973.
3

Riverside area: footpaths & recreation
Canterbury City Council.   1973.
3

St. George's Street, Canterbury.
Canterbury City Council.   1973.
3

A sense of enclosure.
Canterbury City Council.   1973
3

Stour Street.
Canterbury City Council.   1972.
3

Tree planting: a feature of the urban
development.
Canterbury City Council.   1973.
3

CANTERBURY CITY COUNCIL: CITY ENGINEER.
Canterbury transportation study.Report on
surveys.
Canterbury City Council, Canterbury.
Kent County Council, Maidstone.(1976).
3

CANTERBURY CITY COUNCIL: DEPARTMENT OF ARCHITECTURE
AND PLANNING.
Canterbury central area interim office policy.
Canterbury City Council.   1975.
3

Canterbury: redevelopment of the Marlowe and
Watling Street Car Parks. A report of Canterbury
City Council prepared by Messrs.Healey &
Baker.
Healey & Baker.   1975.
3

City of Canterbury tourist study. 1975.
Canterbury City Council.   1975.
3

CANTERBURY CITY COUNCIL. MEDICAL OFFICER OF
HEALTH.
Annual report, 1971.
Canterbury City Council.   1973.
3

CANTERBURY CITY COUNCIL, PUBLICITY DEPARTMENT.
List of organisations.
Canterbury City Council.   1972.
4

CANTERBURY CITY COUNCIL. PUBLIC RELATIONS OFFICE.
City of Canterbury: guide to local services
and amenities.
Home Publishing.   1979.
4

Tower House & Westgate Gardens.
Canterbury City Council. (1978).
3

CANTERBURY CITY COUNCIL: SOCIAL SERVICES DEPT.
The Canterbury Survey of handicapped people.
Canterbury City Council.   1974.
3

CANTERBURY CITY MUSEUMS: Buffs Museum.
Buffs Museum: catalogue of books.
Duplicated typescript.
Canterbury City Museums. 1976.
3

Guide to the Museum of the Buffs.
Canterbury City Museums. 1975.
3

CANTERBURY CITY MUSEUMS & CANTERBURY
PUBLIC LIBRARY.
Good books: quarterly bulletin of the
Canterbury Royal Museum and Public
Library...with short articles of
archaeological and historical interest.
Kentish Gazette. Canterbury.
3   1947-1950
11 1947 summer.

A guide to the Canterbury museums (text
by Louise Millard, designed and illustrated
by Christopher Hills).
Jennings (printer) 1967.
30

T. Sidney Cooper, R.A. Exhibition of
paintings & drawings at the Royal Museum,
Canterbury, 20th August - 10th September,
1977. (Local artist).
3

CANTERBURY COMMISSION, 1880.
Report of the commissioners appointed....
to inquire into the existence of corrupt
practices in the City of Canterbury together
with the evidence taken before The
Commissioners; reprinted from the daily
reports published in "The Canterbury Press".
Cross & Jackman,"The Canterbury Press",
Canterbury. 1881.
11

CANTERBURY CRICKET WEEK:*   an authentic
narrative of the origin and career of the
institution, including the programmes of
the "Old Stagers" performances...Vol I.
Matches recorded 1839 - 1851.
William Davy. Canterbury. 1865.
1,3,4,11

CANTERBURY: Features of historical interest
& picturesque views by the City and neighbourhood.
No publisher. c.1900.
11

CANTERBURY: Map dated 1588 from the Sloane MSS
2596, British Museum in   Harrison, W.
Harrison's description in Shakespeare's youth,
having the second and third books of the
description of Britaine.
N. Trubner. 1877.
26

CANTERBURY NAVIGATION & SANDWICH HARBOUR
COMPANY. Report made by the directors of the
Canterbury Navigation & Sandwich Harbour
Company to the proprietors, at their second
general Assembly held at the Guildhall,
Canterbury on Tuesday, the 6th of December,1825.
Wood,Printer, Canterbury. 1825.
3

CANTERBURY. PHILOSOPHICAL AND LITERARY
INSTITUTION.*
Synopsis of the museum of the Philosophical
and Literary Institution, Canterbury.
Canterbury Philosophical & Literary Institution
printed by G. Wood. 1826.
3,11

CANTERBURY PROPERTIES: a manuscript book containing Abstracts of Title of various properties
during the 17th, 18th and 19th centuries.
n.d.
11

CANTERBURY SOCIETY FOR MENTALLY HANDICAPPED
CHILDREN.
Year Book 1977 - 78.
The Society. 1978.
3

CANTERBURY URBAN STUDIES CENTRE.
Canterbury City Trails no 1 & 2.
The Centre, Canterbury. 1977
3

CAVINESS, Madeline Harrison.
A lost cycle of Canterbury paintings of 1220.
In Antiquaries Journal. Vol.54. Part I. 1974.
Reprinted by O.U.P. 1974.
3,11

CHATTERTON, E. Keble.
T. Sidney Cooper. R.A., his life and art.
(local artist.)
Art Record Press. 1902.
3

CHURCH, Richard.
A portrait of Canterbury.
Hutchinson. 1968.
13,22

CITY OF CANTERBURY, 1970. FESTIVAL COMMITTEE.
Canterbury 1970: complete programme of events,
June to October.
Perfecta Publications for the Festival Committee
1970.
11

CITY OF CANTERBURY, SILVER JUBILEE COMMITTEE.
Programme of events(first edition) Produced
and printed by City Secretary's Dept. 1977.
3

CLUTTON & PARTNERS. Surveyors.
Cluttons. 1765 - 1965. (A London based
firm of surveyors who opened a Branch in
Canterbury after World War II. J.H.Clutton
was surveyor to the Medway Conservancy Board
in the late 19th century).
Clutton and Partners. (1965).
11

THE COBBLER OF CANTERBURY. Frederic Ouvry's
edition of 1862. reprinted.
D.S. Brewer. Cambridge. 1976.
3

COCK, F. William.*
The Kentish Post, or, The Canterbury Newsletter.
Alexander Moring. 1913.
3,12,23

COMMISSIONERS ON MUNICIPAL CORPORATIONS IN
ENGLAND AND WALES, Reports.
Report of the City of Canterbury (pages
683 - 712 of the reports).
(1834?)
3

COOPER, Thomas Sidney.*
Views in Canterbury and its environs, drawn from
nature and on stone...(portfolio of six engravings) (Canterbury artist)
Westmead Press. 1972.
1,3

COZENS, W.S. Builder & Decorator.
Discovering Canterbury: an interesting Tudor
building restored.
W.S. Cozens, Builder & Decorator,Canterbury.193-?
11

CANTERBURY Cont'd

CROSS, Francis W.*
Rambles round old Canterbury, by F.W.
Cross and J.R. Hall.
Simpkin Marshall & Co. 1884
2,8,26.

CROUCH, Marcus.*
Canterbury.
Longman. 1970.
3,23

DANKS, W.*
Canterbury. ("Beautiful England" Series).
Blackie. 1910.
3

DEFOE, Daniel.*
A true revelation of the apparition of
one Mrs. Veal....at Canterbury, the 8th
September, 1705.
10th edition n.d.
3

EAST KENT ROAD CAR COMPANY LTD.
Time table area No.5. Canterbury.
5th June 1977 until further notice.
East Kent Road Car Coy. Ltd. 1977
11

EIGHTEEN PHOTOGRAPHIC VIEWS OF
CANTERBURY.
Printed in Bavaria.
n.d. (190-?)
11

ENVIRONMENT, Dept. of the.
Canterbury Southern By-pass (A2):
alternative routes: a consultative document.
Department of the Environment. 1973.
11

List of buildings of special architectural
or historic interest. City of Canterbury.
H.M.S.O. 1973.
3,11

ERWOOD, Guy R.*
Panorama of Canterbury: the ancient and
modern city in eighty photographs.
Lambarde Press. Sidcup. 1963.
30

FELLOWS, Reginald B.*
History of the Canterbury and Whitstable
Railway.
J.A. Jennings. Canterbury. 1930.
31

GARDINER, Mrs. Dorothy.
Canterbury: photographs with a short text by
Dorothy Gardiner.
S.P.C.K. n.d.
11

The literary tradition of Canterbury:*
from Chaucer to Conrad.
Printed by Gibbs & Son. Canterbury, 1952.
30

The Mayor's insignia of the City of Canterbury:*
a lecture.
Gibbs & Son. Canterbury. n.d.
30

The story of Canterbury Castle with the
adjacent walls and the Dane John and its
manor.*
Jennings. Canterbury. 1951.
30

GARNETT, MEPHAM & FISHER LTD. Publishers
The Canterbury, Herne Bay & Whitstable Local
Directory.
Garnett, Mepham & Fisher Ltd. Brighton.
11 40th issue 1932 - 33
11 41st issue 1934.

GITTINGS, Robert.
Conflict at Canterbury: an entertainment in
sound and light. Specially commissioned....
for the Festival of Canterbury, 1970.
Heinemann Educational. 1970.
11

GLOVER, C. Gordon.
A Canterbury Tale.
In "In Britain", June 1975.
12

GOAD, Charles E. Ltd. Publisher.
Canterbury: Shopping centre plan. Scale 88feet=
1 inch. Size 46cm x 87cm.
C.E. Goad Ltd. Revised edition 1975. 3.
                Revised edition 1977. 3.

GOSTLING, William.*
A walk in and about the City of Canterbury,
with many observations not to be found in
any description hitherto published.....
3rd edition.
Simmons and Kirkby. 1779.
30

A walk in and about the City of Canterbury,*
with many observations not to be found in any
description hitherto published...A new edition
with considerable additions.
Wm. Blackley. Canterbury. 1825.
2,31

GOULDEN, H.J. Publisher.
Canterbury (photographs)
H.J. Goulden, Canterbury. c.1916.
11

Gems of Canterbury: a collection of permanent
photographs with descriptive sketch.
H.J. Goulden, Canterbury, n.d.
11

Gouldens' Canterbury Guide, containing an account
of whatever is...in and about that ancient city,
including....the Cathedral and St. Augustine's
Monastery.
H.J. Goulden. Stationer's Hall, Canterbury. 1897?
11

GREAT BRITAIN, Laws etc. (Geo.II).
An Act for repairing and widening the road from...
Chatham to St. Dunstan's Cross, Canterbury.
1729
3

An Act for repairing and widening the road
leading from St. Dunstan's Cross....to the
Waterside of Whitstable.
1736.
3

GREAT BRITAIN, Laws etc. (Geo IV).
An Act to authorise the company of proprietors
of the Canterbury & Whitstable Railway to
raise a further sum of money for completing
the undertaking....(9Geo4 CXXIX).
Wm. Gunnell, Agent. Curteis & Kingsford
Solicitors. 1828.
11

GREAT BRITAIN, Laws etc. (Wm.IV).
An Act for more effectually repairing...the
road from the Post Road near Faversham...
to Castle Street, Canterbury.
1831.
3

CANTERBURY, Cont'd

HACKETT, Benedict.*
Blessed John Stone. (Saint John Stone was
martyred at the Dane John, Canterbury in
1539 and was canonised in 1970)
Office of the Vice Postulation. n.d.
3,11,30

Saint John Stone: Austin Friar, Martyr.
Augustinian Postulation. Rome. 1970.
3

HALES PLACE, CITY OF CANTERBURY, KENT
Sale Catalogue (photocopy), 24th June
1925. Auctioneers: H, & R.L. Cobb. 1925.
3

Catalogue of the interior and exterior
fixtures and fittings in and about the
mansion which will be sold for demolition,
by auction on the site on February 1st,
2nd, 3rd, 6th, 7th, 8th & 9th 1928.
Auctioneers: Street & Lewis of London. 1928.
3

HARRINGTON, Duncan.
The memorial inscriptions of the Non-
Conformist Burial Ground in Wincheap,
Canterbury, transcribed by D. Harrington.
Kent Family History Society. 1976.
1,3,7,11

HEALTH AND SOCIAL SECURITY, Dept of.
A refuge for battered women: a study of the
role of a women's centre (at Canterbury).
H.M.S.O. 1978.
11

HIGENBOTTAM, Frank.*
The apparition of Mrs. Veal to Mrs Bargrave
at Canterbury, 8th September 1705. Reprinted
from Archaeologia Cantiana. Vol.73 1959.
3,11.17.

HILL, Jane M.
Leisure activities in Canterbury in selected
years of the 1840's (1840, '42, '46, '50)
according to the Kentish Gazette. (extended
essay).
University of Kent at Canterbury. 1972.
3

HOME, Gordon.*
Canterbury of our grandfathers and of to-day:
a pictorial presentation of the city as it was
and as it is. Revised edition.
Homeland Asscn. Canterbury. H.J.Goulden Printers.
11   1948.

INDEXES OF WILLS & ADMINISTRATIONS proved in
Canterbury Prerogative Court.
See GENEALOGICAL RECORDS.

KENT COUNTY COUNCIL. PLANNING DEPARTMENT
Kent County Structure plan. Summary.
Supplementary leaflet 7. Canterbury District.
K.C.C. (1977?).
3

KENT COUNTY LIBRARY.
Becket and Canterbury, a book list.
K.C.L. Maidstone. (1970).
3

KENT COUNTY WAR MEMORIAL.
(The War Memorial is in Canterbury City and
is in the custody of the Dean & Canons of
the Cathedral).
n.d.
11

KENT MESSENGER.
Canterbury, the first of June, 1942. (an
account of the air raid by the German Air Force)
Kent Messenger. 1942. (probably a very much
later reprint. c.1966)
30.

KENTISH GAZETTE.
Canterbury traffic study...Supplement to the
Kentish Gazette, Friday 16 January, 1970.
5

KENTISH GAZETTE & CANTERBURY PRESS.*
Mrs Veal's apparition. Reprinted from an
article in the Kentish Gazette & Canterbury
Press, May 19th, 1931.
3

LAWRENZ, Manfred.
Canterbury: funktions und strukturnandel
einer mittelaterlichen Stadt.
Keil University. 1974.
3

LOOMCRAFT.
Vol.I 1958 - vol 3. 1964.
3

LOXTON, Howard.
Pilgrimage to Canterbury.
David & Charles. 1978.
3,5,6,9,11,16

M'DIVITT, John.
Statistics of the Kent & Canterbury Hospital.
In British Medical Almanack 1839. pp.179-183.
3

MARCHANT, Bessie.
In perilous times: a tale of old Canterbury.
Gall & Inglis. (1901).
11

MARSHALL, Emma.*
In the service of Rachel, Lady Russell: a
story. (Partly set in Canterbury).
Seeley & Co.Ltd. London. 1893.
11

MARTIN, Norah Baldwin.*
Canterbury (Our Beautiful Homeland Series).
Blackie. 1951?
30

MAXTED, Ivan.*
The Canterbury & Whitstable Railway.
Oakwood Press. 1970.
3,11,12,15,31

MORRIS, John.*
Canterbury: a guide for Catholics.
Catholic Truth Society. , London.
11 1952.
3 1959 revised by Rev. L.E.Whatmore.

NEVE, Christopher.
William Townsend 1909-1973; retrospective
exhibition of paintings and drawings arr.by
C. Neve. Catalogue designed and printed by
Taylor Brothers. Bristol. (1978?)
(the artist lived at Rolvenden).
3

NEWMAN & CO. Publishers.
Thirty two views of Canterbury & Neighbourhood
(Engravings).
Newman & Co. London. (c.1880).
11

OLD PARK FARM, SAINT MARTIN, CANTERBURY.
Catalogue of the live and dead farming stock,
implements etc...sold by auction by Messrs.
Cooper ... Friday October 6th, 1865.
3

PACKE, Christopher.
Ankographia, sive convallium descriptio.
(Canterbury and East Kent).
J. Abnee. 1743.
30

PARKER, Michael St. John.*
Christian Canterbury, City of Pilgrims.
Pitkin. 1970
3

PILBROW, James.
Report to the local Board of Health, Canterbury,
on the sewerage and water supply of their
district .....
Canterbury Corporation. Canterbury. 1867.
3

PILGRIMS' MAP OF CANTERBURY.
(Scale 1 mile = 1.27cm. Size 30cm x 38cm)
Map shows places of religious significance.
The Catholic Shop. Canterbury. 1975.
11

PINNOCK, Kenneth.*
Canterbury.
Educational Publications. 1958.
3,8,11,12,13

THE POST OFFICE
Post codes, Canterbury, Kent and district.
The Post Office. 1973.
7

REYNOLDS, Charles & Co. Publishers.
Album of Canterbury Views.
Charles Reynolds & Co. c.1900
11

RICEMANS (CANTERBURY) LTD.
A new look at Ricemans': twelve years of
growth and achievement.
Ricemans(Canterbury) Ltd. 1975.
3

RIGDEN, George.
The sanatory condition of Canterbury (photocopy)
Henry Wood, Canterbury. 1847
3

THE ROYAL AND ANCIENT CITY OF CANTERBURY.
(Photographs & explanatory text.)
Walter Scott. Bradford. n.d.
3

ST. AUGUSTINE'S GAOL.*
Rules, orders and regulations for the management of the new gaol.
Printed by Cowtan & Colgate. Canterbury. 1812.
3

SANDYS, Charles.
The vindication "whereinne ye practices of a
countie-atturney bee notablie displaied and
sette forth to ye contentacyon and delite of
ye gentille reader". A romance of real life.
(Concerns the conduct of Kingsford and
Wightwick, Solicitors of Canterbury, in
connection with the inheritance of Miss Elizabeth
Fagge.)
John Russell. London. 1847.
3

SARTIN, Stephen.
Thomas Sidney Cooper, C.V.O., R.A., 1803 - 1902.
(Painter of Canterbury).
F. Lowis. 1976.
3

SCOUTEN, Arthur H *
An early printed report on the apparition of
Mrs. Veal. Photocopy of an article in the
Review of English Studies. July 1955.
3

At that moment in time: Defoe and the early
accounts of the apparition of Mistress Veal.
In Forum Vol.II, No.2., Winter 1961 - 62.
3.

SECORD, Arthur W.
A September day in Canterbury, the Veal-
Bargrave story.
Reprinted from the Journal of English and
German Philology Vol.LIV, No 4. October 1955.
3.

SMALL, E. Milton. Stationer.*
The Canterbury Pilgrim's guide, in, through and
around the ancient city. 2nd edition.
E. Milton Small.
Printed by Gibbs & Son, Canterbury. 1890.
11

SQUIBB, Fionna.
Information from local topography and guide
books on Canterbury 1800 - 1850. Photocopy of
extended essay.
University of Kent at Canterbury (197?).
3

STANLEY, Arthur Penrhyn.*
Historical memorials of Canterbury.
John Murray
13 1912.
20 1895
26 1895

SWANN, Edward.*
An artist in old Canterbury.
Charles Skilton. 1970.
3,4,6,7,8,11,12

THORNTON, W. Pugin.*
Descriptive and illustrated catalogue of two
old Dutch painted and stained windows in the
Royal Museum and Free Library at Canterbury.
Cross & Jackman. Canterbury. 1899.
11

THE TOPOGRAPHER FOR THE YEAR 1790, containing
a variety of original articles,...Vol.II, Nos.
X-XV, January-June, 1790.(Includes Canterbury
and Greenwich).
Printed for J. Robson...1790.
11

27 PALACE STREET, CANTERBURY, a Georgian house
with walled garden and garage. For sale freehold with vacant possession. (For sale by tender,
closing date Friday 1st September 1972).
MAXTON GRAHAM & CO. Auctioneers & Estate Agents.
3

UNIVERSITY OF KENT AT CANTERBURY.
Living in Victorian Canterbury as portrayed in
historical sources. 1857 - 1907. A Group
Research Project. 1979.
13

Tyler Hill: the changing scene since 1890.
(S214:Aspects of the
economic & social history of Kent, Group
Research Project 1976).
1977
3

URRY, William.*
Canterbury under the Angevin kings.
Athlone Press. 1967.
24,30

City of Canterbury. The chief citizens of
Canterbury. A list of Portreeves...Prepositi..
and of Mayors...compiled until the close of the
14th century by William Urry...and thereafter
by Cyprian Rondeau Bunce(and others) with a
list of sherriffs. Canterbury City Council. 1978
3

CANTERBURY   Cont'd

WARD, Henry Publisher.
The Canterbury guide containing a concise
account of whatever is curious and worthy of
observation in and about that ancient city and
its suburbs, also a description of the
Cathedral Priory of Christ Church and of St.
Augustines' Abbey.
Published & Printed by Henry Wood.
2   1827
11 1828; 5th edn. 1835.

WARNER, Harold William.
A history of Beverley Cricket Club, 1835 -
1959, with foreword by Leslie Ames. Autographed
copy. Plates, ports, facsim. tables.
Elvy Bros & Cross & Jackson Ltd. Canterbury. 1959.
3,4

The story of Canterbury Cricket Week, with
forewords by Colin Cowdrey, Desmond Eager and
Donald Carr. Illus, Ports, Tables.
J.A. Jennings. Ltd. Printers. Canterbury.
3,4

WATSON, William W.*
The visitors' guide to Herne Bay, Canterbury
and the most memorable spots in Kent. (photocopy).
John Dicks. 1855.
11,17,30

WATT, F.
Canterbury pilgrims and their ways.
Methuen. 1917
2

WEINER, J. Ltd. Publisher.
Canterbury & District Green Guide.
(Weiner's Neighbourhood guides).
J. Weiner Ltd. 1968.
30

WILLIAMSON, Catherine Ellis.
Though the streets burn (Canterbury). Paperback edition
The Merlin Press. 1966
3

WILSON, S. Gordon.
Canterbury and Charles Dickens.   Printed by:
J.H. Jennings for Canterbury Chamber of Trade.
1,3,6,11,15

The Pageant Book of Canterbury* through the
centuries, planned to assist the cause of
Charity by the Right Worshipful, the Mayor.
Kent Herald Press. Canterbury, 1930.
11

YOUNGMAN, E. & SON. Publishers.
The Black and White Concise Canterbury &
Cathedral Guide.
Youngman & Son. Canterbury. 192-?
11

Pen & ink drawings of Canterbury.
Youngman & Son. Canterbury. (19--).
3

CANTERBURY - ALMSHOUSES, HOSPITALS.

CHARITY COMMISSION.
Scheme including appointment of Trustees. In
the matter of the charity called the Vidgen-
Wilson Almshouses...regulated by a scheme...
of the 23rd November 1926, as varied by a
scheme...of the 18th May 1971...Sealed 25th
October 1978.
Charity Commission. 1978.
3

COTTON, Charles.*
The Canterbury charities and hospitals, in 1546
together with some others in the neighbourhood,
edited by C. Cotton.
K.A.S. 1934.
3,4,5,11,12,17,18

HILL, Rev. Derek Ingram.*
The ancient hospitals and almshouses of
Canterbury.
Archaeological Society. Canterbury. 1969.
2,3,4,6,11,12,24

Eastbridge Hospital and the ancient almshouses
of Canterbury.
A.J. Snowden, Canterbury. (1973).
3,11

HOBSON, John Morrison.*
Some early and late houses of pity.
Routledge. 1926.
3

WILSON, S. Gordon.
With the Pilgrims to Canterbury and the history
of the hospital of Saint Thomas.
S.P.C.K. 1934.
3,6,11,12,14

CANTERBURY,   ANTIQUITY & ARCHAEOLOGY.

CANTERBURY ARCHAEOLOGICAL SOCIETY.
Annual Report. 1973.
Canterbury Archaeological Society. 1974.
3

CANTERBURY ARCHAEOLOGICAL SOCIETY AND
CANTERBURY ARCHAEOLOGICAL TRUST.
Canterbury archaeology. 1975 - 76.
The Authors. 1976.
1,3,20,24

FRERE, Sheppard.*
Roman Canterbury; an account of the
excavations at the Rose Lane Sites, Summer 1946.
Reprinted from Archaeologia Cantiana.
Canterbury Excavation Committee. 1955.
2,3,4,6,30

Roman Canterbury:*the city of Durovernum:
an illustrated non-technical summary. 3rd edn.
Canterbury Excavation Committee. Printed-Jennings
1,2,3,4,6,7,8,11,12,23,30   1962.

The Roman theatre at Canterbury* (Reprinted from
Britannia Vol.1. 1970)
2,3,4,11,30

JENKINS, Frank.*
Roman Canterbury: an account of the excavations
at No.5. Watling Street. June-December 1947...
Canterbury Excavation Committee. 1953.
1,2,3,4,6,11,30

MILLARD, Louise.
The archaeological implications of development
in Canterbury.
Canterbury City Museums. 1974.
3

The archaeological implications of development
in Canterbury. Revised edition.
Canterbury City Museums. 1975.
3

PILBROW, James.*
Discoveries made during excavations at Canterbury
in 1868.
Society of Antiquaries of London. 1871
1,3

(ROYAL ARCHAEOLOGICAL INSTITUTE OF GREAT
BRITAIN AND IRELAND) Proceedings at
meetings of the Royal archaeological institute:
the Summer meeting at Canterbury, 15-24th July,
1929.
Royal Archaeological Institute. 1929.
3,7,11,30

Report of the summer meeting of the Royal
Arcnaeological Institute at Canterbury in 1969.
Royal Arch. Institute. 1970.
11,30

SOMNER, William.*
The Antiquities of Canterbury.
Richard Thrale - 1640.
6,7,8,11,14,15,19,31

The Antiquities of Canterbury in two
parts. 2nd edn. revised and enlarged by Nicolas
Batteley. Printed for R. Knaplock. 1703.
2

The Antiquities of Canterbury, with a new
introduction by William Urry. (Reprint of
the revised edition of 1703 published by
R. Knaplock).
E.P. Publishing. Ilkley. 1977.
3,11,23,30

(S.P.Q.R.).
Canterbury in Roman times.
K. Gazette. 192-?
4,30

TATTON-BROWN, Tim.
Canterbury included in"Current Archaeology"
Vol VI No 3. No 62 June 1978. pp.78 - 83
3

WILLIAMS, Audrey.*
An account of the excavations carried out
during September-October 1944. (Roman
Canterbury No.2 - Reprinted from Archaeologia
Cantiana Vol 59 1946)
Medici Society. 1947
1,2,3,6,17

An account of the excavations carried out
during 1945. (Roman Canterbury No.3 -
Reprinted from Archaeologia Cantiana Vol.
60 1947).
Medici Society. 1948.
1,2,3,6,17.

An account of the excavations in Butchery Lane,
Christma 1945 and Easter 1946. (Roman
Canterbury No.4 by A. Williams & S. Frere.
Reprinted from Archaeologia Cantiana. Vol 61.
1948).
Medici Society. 1949.
1,2,3,6,11,17,21

CANTERBURY   CATHEDRAL

ALTHEA pseud.
A visit to Canterbury Cathedral
Cathedral Gifts Ltd. 1974.
3

BABINGTON Margaret Agnes.*
Canterbury Cathedral, illustrated.
Dent, Toronto.
4 1948 (revised edn)
26 1933

BABINGTON, Margaret Agnes.*
(A Friend of Canterbury Cathedral)
The romance of Canterbury Cathedral.
Raphael Tuck. Canterbury. 1932.
13,23

BARNES, Philip.
Five Cathedral poems.
Author. 1974.
3

BLAKENEY, H.E.
Building dates of English medieval cathedrals.
Elvy & Gibbs. Canterbury. (1976).
3

BLANCHET, Wendy.
The tale of Canterbury Cathedral (in verse for
children).
Elvy & Gibb, Canterbury. 1975.
3,11

BORENIUS, Tancred.
Addenda to the Iconography of St. Thomas of
Canterbury. Read to the Society of Antiquaries
of London., 26th February, 1931.
The Society, 1931.
11

The Iconography of St. Thomas of Canterbury.*
read to the Society of Antiquaries of London,
28th February, 1929.
The Society. 1929.
11

Some further aspects of Iconography of St.
Thomas of Canterbury read to the Society of
Antiquaries of London, 9th February, 1933.
The Society. 1933
11.
BRITTON, John.*
The history and antiques of the Metropolitan
Church of Canterbury.
Nattali. 1836.
8

BUMPUS, T. Francis.
The cathedrals of England and Wales. Standard
edition. (Includes Canterbury pp.18-31:
Rochester pp. 92 - 102).
T. Werner Laurie. 1937.
3.

BURNBY, John.*
An historical description of the Cathedral and
Metropolitan Church of Christ, Canterbury.
T. Smith & Son. 1772
2

CANTERBURY: official guide to the Cathedral
Church & handbook to the City.
E. Crow, Canterbury. n.d.
11

CANTERBURY CATHEDRAL: DEAN & CHAPTER.
La Cathèdrale de Canterbury: guide pour les
visiteurs Français.
Canterbury Cathedral*Dean & Chapter. n.d.
11

The Cathedral and Metropolitical Church of
Christ, Canterbury.*
Canterbury Cathedral.Dean & Chapter. (1951)
30

THE CANTERBURY PILGRIM'S PROGRESS.
Printed by Arthurs' Press. Stroud, Glos. c.1947
3,8,11

THE CATHEDRAL & METROPOLITAN CHURCH OF CHRIST,
CANTERBURY. A handbook for Pilgrims. Printed
for the Dean & Chapter of Canterbury Cathedral
by:Gibbs & Sons Printers, Canterbury
3 1954; 1925 rep. 1938; 1931.
11 1925
24 1925. Included in "Jottings of Kent"

CAVINESS, Madeline Harrison.
The early stained glass of Canterbury Cathedral
circa 1175 - 1220.
Princeton University Press. New Jersey. U.S.A. 1971.
3,11.

CANTERBURY CATHEDRAL Cont'd

CAWLEY, David L.
Canterbury bells: the bells of Canterbury
Cathedral.
Cathedral Gifts Ltd. Canterbury. (1978?)
3

COTTON, Charles.*
The Saxon Cathedral at Canterbury and the
Saxon saints buried therein.
Manchester University Press. 1929.
25

DUNCOMBE, John.*
An historical description of the Metropolitical
Church of Christ, Canterbury 2nd edition.
Simmons & Kirkby. 1783
31

FAIRBAIRNS, W.H.
Canterbury. (Notes on Cathedrals series)
S.P.C.K.c1903 & c.1919
3

FRIENDS OF CANTERBURY CATHEDRAL.*
The ANNUAL REPORT and CHRONICLE were separate
publications up to and including 1973. From
1974 onwards, the Chronicle alone has been
published but a Report is included.
3 Annual Report and Chronicle 1928-1973.
   Chronicle 1974 in progress.
4 Annual Report 1973. Chronicle 1972
11 Annual Report 1973. Chronicle 1975
24 Annual Report 1931. Chronicle 1932.

The Canterbury Festival, Saturday 12th June
to Saturday 19th June 1937: souvenir programme.
Friends of Canterbury Cathedral. 1937.
11

GEM, R.D.H. *
The Anglo-Saxon Cathedral Church at Canterbury:
a further contribution. Reprinted from "The
Archaeological Journal", Vol. CXXVII pp.196-201.
Royal Archaeological Institute. 1971.
3,4

GERVASE Of Canterbury.*
Of the burning and repair of the Church of
Canterbury in the year 1174. From the Latin
of Gervase. Edited by Charles Cotton.
Canterbury Papers No 3. (Friends of
Canterbury Cathedral),
Cambridge University Press.
7   1930
1   1932 (2nd edn)
1,4,11   1937
3   1951

GILBERT, E.C.*
The date of the late Saxon Cathedral at
Canterbury. Reprinted from "The Archaeological
Journal", Vol. CXXVII pp. 202-210.
Royal Archaeological Institute. 1971.
3,4

GOSTLING, Frances M.
The lure of English Cathedrals (Southern)
Mills & Boon. 1925.
11

GRIERSON, Elizabeth.*
Canterbury (Tales of English Minsters)
For younger readers.
A.&.C. Black. 1910
11

HANDBOOK TO THE CATHEDRALS OF ENGLAND.*
Southern Division, Part 2.
(Canterbury, Rochester.etc).
John Murray, London.
4   1876
26 1861

HARRISON, Rev. Benjamin.*
Patient waiting: sermons preached in Canterbury
Cathedral. (The author was Archdeacon of
Maidstone).
Rivingtons. 1889.
3,11

HAYES, Dagmar.*
Ervin Bossanyi: the splendour of stained glass.
Friends of Canterbury Cathedral. 1965
3,4,11,21

HENDERSON, Arthur E.*
Canterbury Cathedral, then and now.
S.P.C.K. 1938
7,30

HEWS, Evelyn Mary.
A service of thanksgiving for the life of
Evelyn Mary Hews 18th January 1887 -9th May 1970.
on Tues. 26th May, 1970.
Canterbury Cathedral. 1970.
3

HILL, Rev. Derek Ingram.
Christ's glorious church: the story of Canterbury
Cathedral.
S.P.C.K. 1976
3,5,8,11,12,15,23,30

HISTORICAL MANUSCRIPTS COMMISSION.
Ninth report of the Royal Commission on Historical
Manuscripts...Part I. Report and Index. pp. 72 -
177 Canterbury Cathedral MSS. pp. 285 - 291
Rochester MSS.
H.M.S.O. 1883
11

JAMES, Montague Rhodes.
The verses formerly inscribed on twelve windows
in the choir of Canterbury Cathedral.
(Cambridge Antiquarian Society. Octavo
publications. No. XXXVIII),
Cambridge University Press for the Society.1901.
3

KEATES, Jonothan,
Canterbury Cathedral,
Summerfield. 1980.
6,28.

LANG-SIMS,Lois.
Canterbury Cathedral:Mother Church of Holy Trinity.
Cassell. 1979.
6,12,23.

LEE, Lawrence,
Stained Glass.
(Sections on Canterbury Cathedral stained glass).
M. Beazley, 1976.
3.

LES TAPISSERIES DE LA VIE DU CHRIST ET DE
LA VIERGE D'AIX-EN-PROVENCE.

16th Century Canterbury Cathedral
tapestries were sold in the 17th Century.
They were in Aix Cathedral and on
exhibition in Aix Tapestry Museum in 1977.
Some of them have since been stolen from
Aix Cathedral.
Aix Tapestry Museum. 1977.
3.

LORD, Mrs. Freisen.*
Tales from Canterbury Cathedral (told
to Children).
Sampson, Low, Marston. 1897.
26.

LYALL, Very Rev. William Rowe.*
Memoir of the Late Dean of Canterbury,
William Rowe Lyall...bound with other
pamphlets on William Rowe Lyall. 1857.
11,17.

MACLEISH , Kenneth.
Canterbury Cathedral in National
Geographic March 1976 p.364-379.
3.

MANN, Sir James.*
The funeral achievements of Edward, The Black
Prince. 3rd edition revised. Printed by
W.M. Clowes, London,   1951.
4,11

and the 1972 edition, reprinted 1975.
Canterbury: The Cathedral Gift shop. with
Mills, Dorothy. Edward the Black Prince;
a short history.
(The achievements hung over the Black
Prince's tomb in Canterbury Cathedral until 1949)
3,30.

MARSHALL, William M.
George Hooper 1640- 1727, Bishop of Bath and
Wells. (Dean of Canterbury 1691 - 1701)
Dorset Publishing Company. 1976.
3

MILMAN, Henry Salisbury.
The vanished memorials of St. Thomas of
Canterbury. Read to The Society of
Antiquaries of London, February 26th and
March 12th, 1891.
The Society. 1891.
11

MORRIS, John.*
The tombs of the Archbishops in Canterbury
Cathedral.
E. Crow, Canterbury. 1890.
1,3,6,11,15,17.

RACKHAM, Bernard.*
The stained glass windows of Canterbury
Cathedral: a guide for visitors and students.
S.P.C.K. 1957.
30

RAMSAY, Arthur Michael, Archbishop of
Canterbury.
Canterbury Pilgrim.
S.P.C.K. 1974.
3,15

ROBERTSON, Rev. William Archibald Scott.*
The crypt of Canterbury Cathedral, (and
two further essays).
Extracted from Archaeologia Cantiana and
bound together.
K.A.S. n.d.
11

Obituary notice of the Rev. W.A. Scott
Robertson, M.A., Honorary Canon of
Canterbury Cathedral, composed by George
Payne. Reprinted from Archaeologia
Cantiana.
Mitchell & Hughes. 1898.
3

ROUSHAM, Sally.
Canterbury: the story of the Cathedral.
Carlton Cleeve, for the Dean and Chapter of
Canterbury Cathedral. 1975.
1,3,7,11

S., G. *
Chronological history of Canterbury Cathedral.
H.S. Claris, Kent Herald. 1885.
2

SERMONS PREACHED IN THE CATHEDRAL,*
at the Commemoration of the Founders of the
King's School, Canterbury, on Speech Day from
1887 to 1896.
Longmans. 1897.
3

SHIRLEY, John.
Canterbury Cathedral in five languages.
Pitkin. 1972.
3

Pictorial history of Canterbury Cathedral.*
Pitkin, 1971.
3.30

Pictorial history of Canterbury Cathedral.
Pitkin. 1974.
3

SIBREE, James.
Our English Cathedrals; their architectural
beauties and characteristics and their
historical associations.   Vol 2. The Southern
Cathedrals.
Francis Griffiths.   London. 1911.
11

"T.F."
(Address) to the members of the"Greater
Chapter" of the Cathedral Church of Christ,
Canterbury,28th October, 1896.
3

TAYLOR, H.M.*
The Anglo-Saxon Cathedral Church at Canterbury.
Reprinted from "The Archaeological Journal"
Vol. CXXVI 1970. pp.101-130.
Royal Archaeological Institute. 1970.
3,4

TICEHURST, Norman F.
On some sixteenth century bird drawings from
"William Burch's Common Place Book" in
Canterbury Cathedral Library.
Reprinted from British Birds. Vol. XVII No.1
June 1st 1923.
3

THE TIMES OF EDWARD THE BLACK PRINCE: replicas
of his achievements. Knights of the Garter,
past and present(Canterbury papers no.8)
Friends of Canterbury Cathedral. 1954 Repr.1959
4

TRISTRAM. Ernest William.*
The paintings of Canterbury Cathedral.
(Canterbury Papers No.6).
Friends of Canterbury Cathedral. 1951.
24

URRY, William.*
A pictorial guide to Canterbury Cathedral.
Willett. 1950.
3,7,11

WADDAMS, Herbert Montagu
Canterbury Cathedral.
Pitkin Pictorials Ltd. 1975.
3
11 1968 & 1969

WARD, H. Snowden.*
The Canterbury Pilgrimages.
A.&.C. Black. 1904.
2,26

WARNER, S.A.*
Canterbury Cathedral.
S.P.C.K. 1923
2

WEBB, Brian.
Graffiti, recorded by Brian Webb from Dover
Castle & Canterbury Cathedral with an intro-
ductory note by Barry Kirk.
College of Art Press. Canterbury. 1967.
11

WHITE, Joseph William Gleeson.*
The Cathedral Church of Canterbury, edited
by J.W.G. White.
Bell. 1896.
1

WILLIS, Robert.
Architectural history of Canterbury Cathedral.
Longman, Pickering & Bell. 1895.
2

WITHERS, Hartley.*
Canterbury & Rochester with Minster-in-
Sheppey, by Hartley Withers and others.
G. Bell and Sons. 1929.
6,7,17

The Cathedral Church of Canterbury: a des-
scription of its fabric, and a brief history
of the Archiepiscopal See. 3rd edition Revised.
By Hartley Withers (Bells Cathedral Series).
George Bell and Sons. 1899 reprinted 1904.
4

WOODRUFF, Charles Eveleigh.*
Memorials of the Cathedral & Priory of Christ
in Canterbury, by C.E.Woodruff & W. Danks.
Chapman & Hall. 1912.
26

WOOLNOTH, William.*
A graphical illustration of the Metropolitan
Cathedral Church of Canterbury; accompanied
by a history and description......and historical
notes of the...Convent of Christchurch.
T. Cadell & W. Davies. 1816.
2

YOUNGMAN, E. and Son. Publishers.
The Black and White Concise Canterbury and
Cathedral Guide.
E. Youngman & Son. Canterbury. (192-?).
11

CANTERBURY CATHEDRAL - ARCHBISHOPS

AITKEN, William Francis.
Frederick Temple, Archbishop of Canterbury.
S.W. Partridge. London. 1901.
11

ARNOTT, Anne.
Wife to the Archbishop. (Jean Braithwaite
Coggan, wife of Dr. Donald Coggan, Archbishop
of Canterbury).
3.   Mowbray 1976
11   Mowbray 1976 & Hodder & Stoughton 1978.

BARBER Melanie.
Index to the letters and papers of Frederick
Temple, Archbishop of Canterbury, 1846 - 1902,
in Lambeth Palace Library. Compiled by
Melanie Barber.
Mansell. 1975.
3,11

BECKET, Saint Thomas Archbishop of Canterbury
See separate section.

BENEDICTA, Sister.
Anselm of Canterbury, a monastic scholar: an
expanded version of a paper given to the
Anselm Society, St. Augustine's College,
Canterbury in May, 1973.
S.L.G. Press, Oxford. 1977
3,6

BROMILEY, G.W.*
Thomas Cranmer, Archbishop and martyr.
Church Book Room Press. 1956.
4

Thomas Cranmer, theologian.*
Lutterworth Press. 1956.
4

CARPENTER, Edward.*
Cantuar:the Archbishops in their office.
Cassell. 1971.
11,12

A CHURCHMAN OF THE DIOCESE OF CANTERBURY pseud.
Laud and Tait:an ecclesiastical study & review.
James Parker & Co. London. 1883.
3

CUTTS, Edward L.*
Augustine of Canterbury.
Methuen. 1895.
4

DARK, Sidney.*
Archbishop Davidson and the English Church.
Philip Allan. 1929.
11
(Dr.Davidson was Archbishop of Canterbury
1903 - 1928).

Seven archbishops.*
Eyre & Spottiswoode. 1944.
1,11

DAVIDSON, Randall Thomas. Bishop of Rochester*
Life of Archibald Campbell Tait, Archbishop of
Canterbury. 2 vols by R.T.Davidson and W.
Benham. (Rev. Davidson became Archbishop of
Canterbury).
Macmillan. 1891
11,15

DUCKETT, Eleanor Shipley.*
Saint Dunstan of Canterbury: a study of monastic
reform in the tenth century.
Collins. 1955.
3,4,8,11,12

DUNKIN, Edwin Hadlow Wise.*
Index to the Act Books of the Archbishops
of Canterbury, 1663 - 1859, compiled by
E.H.W. Dunkin. 2 parts.
British Record Society. 1938.
Part I. (A-K) edited by C. Jenkins and C.A.Fry.
2.3.11
Part II (L-Z) edited by C. Jenkins
2,3,11

FISHER, Geoffrey Francis. Archbishop of
Canterbury.
The Archbishop speaks.
Evans Bros. (1958).
3

The order of service for the enthronement of the
Most Reverend Father in God Geoffrey Lord
Archbishop of Canterbury Primate of All England
...Thurs 19th April, 1945.
J.A. Jennings. Canterbury. 1945
3

FOWLER, Montagu.*
Some notable Archbishops of Canterbury.
S.P.C.K. 1895.
1,11

GIBSON, Margaret.
Lanfranc of Bec. (Archbishop of Canterbury
29.8.1070 - 28.5.1089: responsible for the
rebuilding of Canterbury Cathedral, reconsecrated
on 4.10.1077).
Clarendon Press. 1978.
3

HOOK, Walter Farquhar.*
Lives of the Archbishops of Canterbury, 12
Vols. Vol I. Anglo-Saxon period.
Richard Bentley. 1860 - 84.
26

HOPKINS, Jasper.
Anselm of Canterbury Vol.1. by J. Hopkins
and H. Richardson.
S.C.M. 1974.
3

IREMONGER, F.A.*
William Temple, Archbishop of Canterbury: his
life and letters. (William Temple was
Archbishop from 1942 - 1944).
O.U.P. 1948.
11

JACOB, Ernest Fraser.*
Archbishop Henry Chichele.
Nelson. 1967.
26

LAMB, John William*
The Archbishopric of Canterbury from
its foundation to the Norman
Conquest:with a foreword by the
Archbishop of Canterbury.
Faith Press. 1971.
3,4,8,11,12.

LOCKHART, J.G*
Cosmo Gordon Lang.
Hodder & Stoughton. 1949.
11.

McKILLIAM, A.E*
A Chronicle of the Archbishops of Canterbury.
J. Clarke. 1913.
1,2,3,4,8,11,12.

MORRIS, John.*
The tombs of the Archbishops in Canterbury
Cathedral.
E. Crow. Canterbury. 1890.
1.3.6.11.15.17

PECHAM JOHANNIS,or PECKHAM JOHANNIS/JOHN.
Archbishop of Canterbury, 1279 - 1292
Registrum.
See CANTERBURY DIOCESE & PROVINCE.

PERRY, Edith Weir.
Under four Tudors: being the story of Matthew
Parker sometime Archbishop of Canterbury.
2nd edition.
Allen & Unwin. 1964.
11

POPE, Fred.
The Canterbury Pewside Book, compiled by
Fred Pope. (Photographs of Archbishop
Ramsey with humorous captions)
Leslie Frewin. 1966.
11

POULTON, John.
Dear Archbishop.
A report on the letters to the Archbishop
of Canterbury after his "Call to the Nation."
Hodder & Stoughton. 1976.
11

THE REGISTER OF THE ARCHBISHOPS OF CANTERBURY.
(13th - 17th Centuries).
Twenty reels of microfilm.
World Microfilms. 197- ?
11

ROBERTSON, Rev. William Archibald Scott.*
Archbishop Hubert Walter and his tomb in
Canterbury Cathedral Church.(Reliquary
Vol.IV (New Series)
Printed by Bemrose & Sons. 1890.
3

ROBINSON, J. Armitage.
The times of Saint Dunstan.
Clarendon Press. 1922.
3

ST. JOHN THE BAPTIST COLLEGE, OXFORD.
The Canterbury Quadrangle, 1636 - 1936.
(William Laud was president of St. John's
and was responsible for the building of the
quadrangle, prior to becoming Archbishop of
Canterbury.
Oxford University Press. 1936.
11

SAYERS, Jane E.
Calendar of the papers of Charles Thomas
Longley, Archbishop of Canterbury, 1862 - 1868,
in Lambeth Palace Library, by J.E. Sayers &
E.G.W. Bill.
Mansell. 1976.
3,11

SIMPSON, James Beasley.*
The Hundredth Archbishop of Canterbury.
(Dr. Ramsey).
Harper & Row, New York, U.S.A. 1962.
11

TEMPLE, William Archbishop of Canterbury
(1942-1944).
The order of service for the enthronement
of the Most Reverend Father in God William
Lord Archbishop of Canterbury Primate of
All England...Thursday 23rd April, 1942.
J.A. Jennings. Canterbury. 1942.
3

TILLOTSON, John, Archbishop of Canterbury*
1630 - 1694.
The golden book of Tillotson; selections from
the writings of the Rev. John Tillotson D.D.
Archbishop of Canterbury, edited with a
sketch of his life by James Moffatt.
Hodder & Stoughton. 1926.
4

TREVOR-ROPER, Hugh Redwald.*
Archbishop Laud, 1573 - 1645. 2nd edition
Macmillan. 1962.
11,12

WARD, Bernard.*
St. Edmund, Archbishop of Canterbury: his life
as told by old English writers, edited by
Bernard Ward.
Sands & Co. London. 1903.
11

CANTERBURY - CHURCHES

BOUGHEN, Rev. Edward.
Two sermons: the first preached at Canterbury
at the visitation of the Lord Archbishop's
Peculiar in St. Margaret's Church, April 14th
1635.
Printed by R.B. 1835.
3

CARPENTER, R. Herbert.*
History of the church of St. Alphege,Canterbury.
Gibbs, Canterbury. 1888
3,11,15

CANTERBURY - CHURCHES Cont'd

COTTON, Charles.*
Churchwardens' accounts of the parish of St.
Andrew, Canterbury (1485 - 1625),
transcribed by Charles Cotton.
(5 parts bound together and reprinted from
Archaeologia Cantiana. Vols. 32 - 36 1917-23)
Mitchell Hughes & Clarke. (1923?)
11,14

COUSINS, David Stanley.
Catholic Canterbury: St. Thomas's Church,
Canterbury, 1875 - 1975; a short guide issued
to commemorate the centenary of the parish of
St. Thomas in that City, compiled by D.S.Cousins
and D.G. Steddy; edited by C.R. Humphery-Smith.
Church Publishers Ramsgate. (1975).
3,6,11

DONALDSON, Christopher William.*
A short history and guide of St. Martin's
Church, Canterbury.
Church Publishers. Ramsgate. 1967.
Revised Reprint. (1977?).
3,4,12,30

A short history and guide of St. Paul's church,
Canterbury.*
Church Publishers. 1964 etc.
1,3,4,8,11,12,30

THE PARISH OF ST. MARTIN AND ST. PAUL CANTERBURY.
Historical essays in memory of James Hobbs.
Friends of St. Martins. 1980.
28.

ST.GEORGE'S PLACE BAPTIST CHURCH, CANTERBURY.
History and manual, 1948. Souvenir brochure
commemorating the 125th anniversary of the
opening of the Church.
11.

THE TOPOGRAPHER FOR THE YEAR 1791, containing
a variety of original articles...Vol.IV, Nos.
XXII - XXVII, January - June 1791. pp. 165 -
174. The Church of St. Andrew in Canterbury.
Printed for J. Robson. 1791.
11

WARNER, Kenneth.
A walk in the garden of God with Saint Mildred,
Canterbury,
A devotional pamphlet produced on the occasion
of a flower festival at St. Mildred's Church,
Canterbury
Printed by Elvy and Gibbs. 1969.
11

CANTERBURY DIOCESE AND PROVINCE.

ARCHBISHOP OF CANTERBURY'S COMMISSION on the
organisation of the church by dioceses in
London and the South-East of England.
Diocesan boundaries: report of the
Commission 1965/67.
Church Information Office. 1967.
3

BUCKINGHAM, Christopher.
The movement of Clergy in the Diocese of
Canterbury, 1552 - 62.
Offprint from "Recusant History", Vol.14,
No 47. October. 1978.
3

CANTERBURY CATHEDRAL: Dean & Chapter.
Calendar of Institutions by the Chapter of
Canterbury sede vacante.
K.A.S. 1924.
5

CANTERBURY DIOCESAN DIRECTORY. Published by
The Diocesan Board of Finance.
1958 - 59   7
1960 - 61   4
1963 - 66*   4
1964 - 65*   7
1971 - 72*   6,7,8,13.
1972 - 73*   4
1973 - 74   13.
1975 - 76   6
1976 - 77   3,12.
1977 - 78   6,12,13.
See also CANTERBURY CATHEDRAL in original volume.

CANTERBURY DIOCESAN DIRECTORY SUPPLEMENT,
Published by the Diocesan Board of Finance.
1958 - 59*   4
1959 - 60*   4
1961 - 62   4
1962 - 63*   4
1964 - 65*   4
1965 - 66   4
1967 - 68   4
1968 - 69*   4,8.
1969 - 70*   4
1970 - 71*   4
1972 - 73   4
See also CANTERBURY CATHEDRAL in original volume.

CHURCHILL, Irene Josephine.*
Mediaeval records of the Archbishops of Canterbury:
a course of public lectures delivered in Lambeth
Palace Library in 1960 by I.J. Churchill and
others. (The Lambeth Lectures).
Faith Press. 1962.
1,4,11,12,15,19

DUNKIN, Edwin Hadlow Wise.*
Index to the Act books of the Archbishops of
Canterbury, 1663 - 1859, compiled by E.H.W.
Dunkin. 2 parts.
British Record Socy. (1938).
Part I (A - K) edited by C. Jenkins and C.A.Fry.
2.3.11
Part. II (L-Z) edited by C. Jenkins.
2,3,11

FIELD, Colin Walter.
The province of Canterbury and the Elizabethan
settlement of religion.
C.W. Field. Robertsbridge. 1973.
1,3,11,12,20,26,27

HOUSTON, Jane.
Index of cases in the records of the Court of
Arches at Lambeth Palace Library, 1660 - 1913,
edited by J. Houston. Phillimore. 1972.
5

HUSSEY, Arthur,
Archbishop Parker's visitation 1569.
in Home Counties Magazine. Vol.V. 1903.
17.

LAMB, John William*
The Archbishopric of Canterbury from its
foundation to the Norman Conquest: with a
foreword by the Archbishop of Canterbury.
Faith Press. 1971.
3,4,8,11,12.

LE NEVE, John.
Fasti Ecclesiae Anglicanae, 1541 to 1857,III.
the Canterbury, Rochester and Winchester
dioceses. Athlone Press. 1974.
11

OYLER, Thomas H.
Parish churches of the diocese of Canterbury.
Hunter & Longhurst. London. 1910.
2,24,30

PECHAM, Johannis, Archbishop of Canterbury.*
(Registrum Johannis Pecham) The register of
John Pecham, Archbishop of Canterbury, 1279-
1292. 2 vols.
Canterbury & York Society. 1908-10; 1968-9
11

PECKHAM, John Archbishop of Canterbury
1279 - 1292.
Registrum epistolarum Fratris Johannis
Peckham. 2 vols.
Longman. 1882.
3

PECKHAM Johannis.
Rerum Britannicarum medii aevi scriptores, or,
Chronicles and memorials of Great Britain
and Ireland during the Middle Ages: Vol.77:
Registrum epistolarum fratris Johannis
Peckham; edited...
Public Record Office. Kraus Reprint.1965.
11

RAIT, Robert Sangster.*
English Episcopal Palaces. Part I The
Province of Canterbury edited by R.S. Rait.
(pp.3 - 4 Canterbury: pp 51 - 89 Lambeth;
P.8 brief mentions of the Bishop of
Rochester's palaces at Halling & Trottiscliffe).
Constable. 1910.
3,4,12

THE REGISTER OF THE ARCHBISHOPS OF CANTERBURY
(13th - 17th centuries) Twenty reels of
microfilm.
World Microfilms. 197-?
11

THE REPORT OF THE LAMBETH CONFERENCE. 1978.
C.I.O. Publishing. 1978.
3

RICHTER, Michael.
Canterbury professions, edited by Michael Richter.
Canterbury & York Society. 1973.
11

WHATMORE, Rev. Leonard. E.*
Archdeacon Harpsfields' Visitation, 1557.
Vol.1,transcribed by L.E.Whatmore & W.Sharp. Vol II.
transcribed by L.E. Whatmore, with notes.
Catholic Record Society. 1950 and 1951.
3,6,8

WILLIS, A.J.
Church. life in Kent: being church court records
of the Canterbury Diocese 1559 - 1565,
compiled by A.J. Willis.
Phillimore. 1975.
1,3,5,6,7,8,11,13,19,20,22,26,27

CANTERBURY - EDUCATION

BOGGIS, Robert James Edmund.*
A history of St. Augustine's College, Canterbury.
Cross and Jackman. 1907.
1,3,6,11,15,17

CANTERBURY ADULT STUDIES CENTRE.
Prospectus. 1976 - 1977,   1977 - 1978.
K.C.C. 1976 & 1977.
3

CANTERBURY COLLEGE OF ART.
Canterbury College of Art Prospectus.
College of Art. Canterbury.
3 1974, 1978.
11 1968-69 and 1972 - 73

CANTERBURY COLLEGE OF ART:SCHOOL OF ARCHITECTURE.
Immaterial. April 1975 No.1,edited by Alex Brown
and Archie Duncan.
College of Art. Canterbury. 1975.
3

CANTERBURY COLLEGE OF TECHNOLOGY.
Prospectus.
3 1974-75, 1975-76, 1976-77, 1977-78,
   1978-79
11 1974 - 75

CANTERBURY TAILS 1975.
Canterbury students rag. Not less than 18 pence.
East Kent Students Assoc. 1975.
3

CANTERBURY URBAN STUDIES CENTRE.
Newsletter. Issue No.1 March 1978.
Canterbury Urban Studies Centre. Canterbury.1978.
3

EDWARDS, David Lawrence.*
A history of the Kings School, Canterbury.
Faber & Faber. London. 1957.
2,3,4,6,8,11,14,15,21.

GILBERT, R.G.*
St. Augustine's College, Canterbury:
a brief guide...by R.G. Gilbert and F.H.
Maycock.
Printed by A.J. Snowden,Canterbury.1971.
11, 30

KENT COLLEGE. 1885 - 1935.*
Kent County Newspapers Ltd. 1937.
2,4,7,11,19

KING'S SCHOOL: CANTERBURY.
The Cantuarian. Vol. XVIII. No.3. July 1939.
Kings School. 1939.
Magazine of Kings School, Canterbury.
11

King's School, Canterbury*(founded in the 7th
Century), the ancient school of the Archbishop
and the City, refounded by Henry VIII in 1541.
Printed by H.J. Goulden, Canterbury. (c.1920).
11.

New buildings for the King's School, in the
precincts of Canterbury Cathedral...June 1978.
A report. duplicated. 1978.
3.

Register. 1859 - 1931*
Old Kings' Scholars Association 1932.
2,3,11.

Register. 1931-1970* with alphabetical index.
1971
2,3.

Visit of H.R.H. the Duke of Kent, K.G., on
Thursday May 12th 1938. Programme and order
of proceedings for the opening of the new
dining hall...etc.
King's School. 1938.
11

THE LANGTONIAN, January 1947, Vol 21. No.6
(Magazine of the Simon Langton School)
J.A. Jennings. 1947.
3

OLD LANGTONIAN NEWSLETTER. No. 11,12,13.
(Simon Langton School)
Old Langtonian Association.Canterbury.1974,5,6.
3

PERCIVAL, Alicia Constance.
Very superior men: some early public school
headmasters and their achievements.
(Includes Canterbury and Tonbridge).
C. Knight. 1973.
3

SEABORNE. M.
The English School: its architecture and
organisation, 1370 - 1970. Vols I and II
by M. Seaborne and R. Lowe. (Includes The
King's School and St. Mildred's Church of
England School, Canterbury).
Routledge. 1977.
3

SERMONS PREACHED IN THE CATHEDRAL at the
Commemoration of Founders of the Kings'
School, Canterbury, on Speech Day from 1887
to 1896.
Longmans. 1897.
3

SIMON LANGTON HIGH SCHOOL FOR GIRLS.
Jubilee, 1881 - 1931
The School. 1931
11

UNIVERSITY OF KENT AT CANTERBURY.
Gazette. No.8. Sept. 1973
        No 9. Oct. 1973
4

Library handbook.
University of Kent at Canterbury. 1968.
13

Prospectus for admission in 1975, 1976,
1977 and 1978.
University of Kent at Canterbury.
3.

University of Kent at Canterbury - Students
Union Workshop Manual 78/79 (Student Union
handbook).
University of Kent at Canterbury Student's Union. 1978.
3.

CANTERBURY - MONASTIC HOUSES

BOGGIS, Robert James Edmund.
A history of St. Augustine's Monastery, Canterbury.
Cross & Jackson. 1901.
2

CHRISTCHURCH PRIORY: CANTERBURY.
Compotus Johannis Pritirwell de Festo Sancti
Michaelis AD 1364 per annum integrum.
Taylor and Co. 1870.
3

CLAPHAM, Sir. Alfred William.*
St. Augustine's Abbey, Canterbury, Kent.
HMSO. 1955.
1,3,4,8,12,20,26,27,30.
11 1955 and 1972 reprint

COTTON, Charles.
The Grey Friars of Canterbury, 1224 - 1538.
2nd edition.
Manchester University Press Longmans, 1926.
11

DOYLE, Eric.
Canterbury and the Franciscans 1224 - 1974,
a commemorative essay.
Franciscan Study Centre. Canterbury, 1974.
3,11

EMDEN, Alfred Brotherston.*
Donors of books to St. Augustine's Abbey,
Canterbury. (Oxford Bibliographical Society
Occasional Papers No.4).
Oxford Bibliographical Society. 1968.
3,4,11,24

FRANCE, Walter Frederick.
St. Augustine's Canterbury; a story of enduring
life.
S.P.C.K. 1952
11

FRENCH, Katherine.
The house of the Grey Friars, Canterbury. 2nd edition.
The Courier, Tunbridge Wells. 1937.
24

GOULDEN, H.J. Publisher.
Goulden's Canterbury Guide, containing an account
of whatever is...in and about that ancient City,
including...the Cathedral & St. Augustine's
Monastery
H.J. Goulden. Canterbury. 1892.
11

MACLEAR, George Frederick.*
St. Augustine's Canterbury, its rise,
ruin and restoration.
Wells, Gardner Darton & Co. 1888.
1,3,4,6,11,12,15,30

MARTIN, Alan R.
The Grey Friars, Canterbury. Reprinted by kind
permission of the Royal Archaeological Institute..
with additional notes.
Cambridge University Press. 1930.
3.

SEARLE, William George.*
Christ Church, Canterbury. I. The Chronicle of
John Stone, Monk of Christchurch 1415 - 1470.
II Lists of deans, priors and monks of Christ-
Church Monastery, edited by W.G. Searle.
Printed for Cambridge Antiquarian Society, Cambridge.
1902.
1,3,11,12

SMITH, A.
A geographical study of agriculture on the Kentish
manors of Canterbury Cathedral Priory 1272 - 1379.
(M.A. Dissertation. University of Liverpool)
Photocopy from University of Liverpool. n.d.
3

THORNE, William.*
Chronicle of St. Augustine's Abbey Canterbury.
Now rendered into English by A.H. Davis.
Blackwell   1934.
1.3.7.11.12.13.14.17.18.24.

TOPOGRAPHICAL MISCELLANIES.
Includes:- Blackfriars at Canterbury.
Robson. 1792.
3,12

TURNER, G.J..*
The register of St. Augustine's Abbey, Canterbury,
commonly called the Black Book. Pt.1 edited by
G.J. Turner and Rev. H.E. Salter.
Oxford University Press. 1915.
1,11,12,17

WARD, Gordon Reginald.
The Domesday Book of the Monks of Canterbury.
Friends of Canterbury Cathedral. 1931
23

WARD, Henry Publisher.
The Canterbury Guide containing a concise
account of whatever is curious and worthy of
observation in and about that ancient City and
its suburbs, also a description of the Cathedral
Priory of Christchurch and of St. Augustine's
Abbey.
Published and Printed by Henry Ward.
2   1827
11 1828: 5th edition. 1835.

WOODRUFF, Charles Eveleigh.*
Memorials of the Cathedral & Priory of Christ
in Canterbury, by C.E. Woodruff and W. Danks.
Chapman and Hall. 1912.
1,3,4,6,7,8,11,12,13,14,15,19,26.

WOOLNOTH, William.*
A graphical illustration of the Metropolitan
Cathedral Church of Canterbury; accompanied by
a history and description...and historical notes
of the...Convent of Christchurch.
T. Cadell and W. Davies. 1816.
1.2.3.6.7.8.11.12.15.16

CAPEL-LE-FERNE

THE CLIFFS ESTATE, overlooking the Warren,
Folkestone. Seventh Sale. 120 plots of....
freehold building land comprising the Seventh
portion of the estate. To be sold by auction
...on...August 29th 1901. (Vendor Mr. Joseph
Henry Retallack-Moloney. Auctioneers. Messrs
Protheroe and Morris).
Protheroe and Morris (Auctioneers). 1901
7

CASTLES & HOUSES
See also Architecture, Kent, Towns & Villages.

BRAUN, Hugh.
The English Castle. 3rd edition .
Batsford. 1947/8
13

CONRAD, Borys,
Coach tour of Joseph Conrad's homes in Kent.
Printed by Farnham Printing Company,Farnham,1974.
3,8,11,26

ESAM, Frank.*
The manors and farmhouses of Kent; a series of
44 pen and ink sketches illustrating the
development of domestic architecture in Kent
from the 13th century.
South Eastern Gazette. Maidstone. (1906?).
1,2,3,5,6,8,11,12,16

FLETCHER, Benton.*
Royal homes near London.
Bodley Head. 1930.
5,17,18

FRY, Plantagenet Somerset.
British mediaeval castles.
David and Charles. 1974.
11

GUY, John.
Kent Castles.
Meresborough Books 1980.
2,6,11,13,23,28

Kent, castles, gardens and ancient houses.
James Pike. St. Ives. 1977
3,6,11,28

HARRIS, John.
A Country house index. An index to over 2000
country houses illustrated in 107 books of
country views published between 1715 and 1872.
Pinhorns. 1971.
7,23.

HOPE, Lady Elizabeth Reid.*
English homes and villages - Kent and Sussex.
(Early colour photography).
Salmon. Sevenoaks. 1909.
1,2,3,4,5,6,7,8,11,12,15,16,17,18,19

HOPKINS, Robert Thurston.
Moated houses of England. (pp.71 - 106,Kent)
Country Life. 1935.
5,11,15,18

HUSSEY, Christopher.*
The old homes of Britain: the Southern Counties-
Kent, Sussex, Hampshire, Surrey & Middlesex,
edited by C. Hussey.
Country Life. 1928.
6.8.11.12.

IVIMEY, Alan.*
Who Slept here? ("A new guide to the romantic
south-eastern counties" - cover title).
Newnes. 1961.
4,11,19

JESSUP, Frank William.
The Eighteenth Century Country house in Kent.
(one hundred copies printed).
P.P.at Canterbury College of Art. 1966.
3

KENT COUNTY COUNCIL:ARCHIVES OFFICE
Notes on records: how to trace the history
of your house.
K.C.C. (1973).
4

KENT MESSENGER.
Castles in Kent - Calendar 1978.
Kent Messenger. 1978.
12

KERSHAW, S. Wayland.*
Famous Kentish houses: their history and
Architecture.
Batsford. 1880.
3,11,15,16,26

MELLING, Elizabeth.*
Some Kentish Houses. Kentish Sources V, edited
by Elizabeth Melling.
K.C.C. 1965.
2,3,4,5,6,7,8,11,12,14,15,16,18,19,20,21,25,
27,30,31

NEWMAN, John.
North East & East Kent. West Kent and The
Weald.
See ARCHITECTURE

OSWALD, Arthur.*
Country houses of Kent
Country Life. 1933.
1,2,3,4,5,6,7,8,9,11,12,14,15,19,20,21,24,25.

SACKVILLE-WEST Victoria,(Afterwards Lady
Nicolson).
English Country houses. 2nd edition.
Collins. 1942.
23

SIMPSON, W. Douglas.
Castles from the air.
Country Life. 1949.
12

SMITHERS, David Waldron.
Castles in Kent.
John Hallewell Publications. Rochester. 1980.
2,6,9,11,12,13,23,24,28,

STRONG, Roy.
The destruction of the Country house 1875 -
1975 (County lists of Houses demolished,
including 45 in Kent, with demolition dates
and photographs).
Thames and Hudson. 1974.
16

WEBB, William.
Kent's Historic Buildings.
Hale 1977.
1,3,5,6,7,9,11,15,16,19,20,22,23,25,26,27,28,30

CAVES AND TUNNELS

See also CHANNEL TUNNEL
DARTFORD TUNNEL

BROOK, Cyril A.*
Deneholes-Dartford District. Observations
taken August 3rd - 12th 1935, by C.A. Brook
and S. Priest.
Typescript.
5.

CHANDLER, Raymond H.*
The implements and caves of Crayford,
1915 - 16.
17

CHELSEA SPELEOLOGICAL SOCIETY.
Deneholes, part II. (Many deneholes
in Dartford area).
Chelsea Speleological Society. 1979.
5

LE GEAR, R.F.
Deneholes-Part 2. comp. by R.F. LeGear.
Chelsea Speleological Society Records V.10.
1979.
2

PEARMAN, Harry.
Caves and tunnels in Kent. Records of the
Chelsea Speleological Society Vol.6. 1973.
1,2,3,5,6,9,11,19,30.

Caves and Tunnels in South East England.
Part I. Chelsea Speleological Society.
Records Vol.7. 1976.
1,4,11,19
Part II. Chelsea Speleological Society
Records. Vol.8. 1978.
4

PEARMAN, Harry.*
Deneholes and kindred phenomenen.
Records of the Chelsea Speleological Society.
Vol4. 1966.
1,2,3,4,5,7,8,9,11,15,19,25,30.

REEVE, Terry.
Caves and tunnels in South-East England.
Part three. Records of the Chelsea
Speleological Society Vol.9
1979.
2,4

STONE, John M.*
Underground passages, caverns etc. of
Greenwich and Blackheath.
Greenwich Antiquarian Society, 1914.
1.2.17.

CAXTON, William (1422(?) - 1491).
Believed to have been born in Tenterden.

BLADES, William.
The biography and typography of William
Caxton, England's first printer.
Muller. 1971
12   1971 & 1st edition Published by Trubner.1882.

BLAKE, Norman Francis.
Caxton: England's first publisher.
Osprey. 1976.
8,11

BLAKE, Norman Francis.*
Caxton and his world.
Andre Deutsch. 1969.
12

BRITISH LIBRARY:REFERENCE DIVISION.
William Caxton: an exhibition to commemorate
the quincentenary of the introduction of
printing into England. British Library
Reference Division. 24 September, 1976-
31st January 1977.
British Museum Publications for British
Library. 1976.
11

CAXTON, William.
Tne prologues and epilogues of William Caxton.
Edited and with a biographical introduction
by W.J.R. Gotch.
Oxford University Press for Early English
Text Society. 1928. 1958 Reprint.
11.

CHILDS, Edmund.
William Caxton; a portrait in background.
Northwood Publications. 1976.
3

CUNNINGTON, Susan.*
Story of William Caxton.
Harrap. 1917
12

DEACON, Richard.
A Biography of William Caxton, the first
English editor, printer merchant and trans-
lator.
F. Muller. 1976.
8,11,22

DIBDEN, Thomas Frognal.*
Typographical antiquities Vol.I, by T.F. Dibden
and others (Includes Caxton).
Miller. 1809.
12

INKPEN, H.
Playn rude and curyous: a brief introduction
to the work of Caxton....
Barton Court School, Canterbury...1976.
11

LARKEN, H.W.*
At the sign of the Red Pole: a short account
of the life and work of William Caxton. Printed at
Maidstone College of Art for the Author. 1961.
8,11,12

PLOMER, Henry Robert.*
William Caxton. Parsons, 1924.
12,15

WHO WAS CAXTON?* William Caxton, merchant,
historian...a monograph.
Hardwicke & Bogue, 1877.
12

CENSUS

CENSUS-ENUMERATORS BOOKS (Census Returns)
See GENEALOGICAL RECORDS

THE DOMESDAY BOOK FOR THE COUNTY OF KENT.*
- portion of a return of Owners of Land, 1873.
Sussex Express. Lewes. 1877.
1,2,5,6,11,12,14,15,17,18,20.

GENERAL REGISTER OFFICE
Comparative statement of population and abstract
of answers and returns. Photo-copies of Kent
extracts for 1801, 1811, 1821, and 1831.
H.M.S.O. n.d.
23

GENERAL REGISTER OFFICE.*
Census 1961. England and Wales. Population
dwellings, households, Kent, Surrey/Occupation
Industry Socio-Economic Groups: Kent/Birthplace
and nationality tables/County Report Kent.
(4 vols).
H.M.S.O. 1963-65
13 25.

Sample census 1966 England and Wales.County
Reports, Kent.
H.M.S.O. 1967-68
25

Sample Census 1966 England and Wales. Economic
activity County leaflet:Kent.
H.M.S.O. 1968.
20

LOCAL GOVERNMENT BOARD.
Return of owners of land, 1873 2 vols. Vol I
Counties - includes Kent.
Eyre and Spottiswoode. for H.M.S.O. 1875.
2.3.8.11.

CENSUS   Cont'd

OFFICE OF POPULATION, Censuses and Surveys.*
Census 1971; England and Wales. Advance Analysis:
Kent.
H.M.S.O.   1972.
2,7,8,20,28

Census 1971, England and Wales: County report:
Kent   3 parts.
H.M.S.O.   1973.
1,2,4,7,8,9,11,12,16,20,25,28

Census 1971.   England and Wales. Economic
activity.   County leaflet: Kent.
H.M.S.O.   1975.
3,4,11,12,20,23,26,27

Census 1971: Great Britain: Economic activity
County leaflets: General Explanatory notes.
H.M.S.O.   1975.
23.

CENSUS 1971. England and Wales. Migration
Regional Report (10% sample) South East
Region. Parts I and II
H.M.S.O.   1976
4,11,

Census 1971. England and Wales Migration
regional report (10% sample) South East
Region Part III(B)
1978.
4. 23.

Census, 1971, England and Wales report for
the County of Kent as constituted on
1st April 1974.
H.M.S.O.   1976.
3.4.9.11.20,26,27

Census 1971. Small Area Statistics. Ward and
Civil Parish lists for the Medway area
(Includes Rochester, Chatham and Strood
Rural District).
H.M.S.O.   1971
15

The Registrar General's Annual estimates of
the population of England and Wales and of
Local Authority Areas.   1973.
H.M.S.O.   1974.
28.

Registrar General's Annual Estimates of the
population of England and Wales and of Local
Authority Areas 1973 and 1974.
H.M.S.O.   1975.
28.

The Registrar General's revised estimates
of the population of England and Wales Regions
and Local Authority Areas.   1961 and 1971.
H.M.S.O.   1975.
28.

The Registrar General's revised estimates of
the population of England and Wales regions
and ocal Authority Areas in 1971 and 1972.
H.M.S.O.   1973.

REGISTRAR GENERAL'S OFFICE
Census of England and Wales 1911.
Area, families or separate occupiers, and
population. Vol.1. Administration areas,
counties, urban and rural districts etc.
H.M.S.O.   1914.
3,11

REGISTER GENERAL'S OFFICE.
Population Tables 1.
Number of the inhabitants in the years 1801,
1811, 1821, 1831, 1841 and 1851. England and
Wales II, South Eastern Division comprising
Surrey,Kent, Sussex.....
H.M.S.O. (1852)
11

CHALLOCK

ST. COSMAS & ST. DAMIEN, Challock.*
Revised edition
Printed by Home Words, London N1.   1966.
11

CHALK

GRAVESHAM BOROUGH COUNCIL - PLANNING DEPARTMENT.
The Castle Lane, Chalk, development
brief. consultation draft.
1978.
9,11

CHANNEL TUNNEL

AFCO ASSOCIATES.
The Channel Tunnel project: an answer: a
report prepared by Afco Associates, transport
consultants for the Channel Tunnel Opposition
Association.
AFCO Associates.   1973.
2,3,4,6,7,11

The Channel Tunnel Project: Key issues: (a
dialogue of dissent, published in the
interest of the British taxpayer): a report
prepared for the Channel Tunnel Opposition
Association by AFCO Associates, Transport
Consultants, AFCO Associates.1973.
2,3,4,7,11

BRITISH CHANNEL TUNNEL COMPANY LTD.
The Channel Tunnel-economic and financial
studies: a report.
Coopers and Lybrand Associates Ltd.   1973.
4.7

Statement following completion of economic
technical financial studies..
British Channel Tunnel Company. 1973.
4,7

Channel Tunnel: summary report 1973.
R.T.Z. Development Enterprises. 1973.
7

BRITISH RAILWAYS BOARD.
Channel Tunnel: London-Tunnel new rail link.
A document for consultation.
British Railways Board.   Jan. 1974.
20

Express link with Europe: British Rail - the
Channel Tunnel.
British Railways Board.   1973.
4

CALVERT, Roger.
The Chunnel replanned.
Typescript.   1975.
2,3,6,7

CHALMERS, James.
The Channel Railway connecting England and France.
E.&.F.N. Spon. London.   1861.
11

CHANNEL TUNNEL ADVISORY GROUP.
The Channel tunnel and alternative cross-
channel services: a report presented to the
Secretary of State for the Environment by
the Channel Tunnel Advisory Group.
(Chairman: Sir Alec Cairncross)
H.M.S.O. 1975.
2,3,4,6,7,11

CHANNEL TUNNEL OPPOSITION ASSOCIATION.
The Channel Tunnel project: an independent
appraisal.
Folkestone Channel Tunnel Opposition Association.
1973.
2.3.4.7.11.16.

The Channel Tunnel - the reasons why it
should not be built.
Folkestone Channel Tunnel Opposition Association.
Folkestone. (1973?).
3.4.
Notes on the aims of the Society.
Duplicated sheets. 1971.
4

The White Paper on the Channel Tunnel,
(cmnd 5430): a reply by the Channel Tunnel
Opposition Association.
Channel Tunnel Opposition Association,Folkestone.
1974.
2,3,4,6,7,11,16.

CHANNEL TUNNEL STUDY GROUP .
Why Britain needs a Channel Tunnel.
Channel Tunnel Study Group. 1962.
7

COLLARD, William.*
Proposed London and Paris railway...
(Channel Tunnel).
P.S. King & Son and Clowes 1928.
1.2.4.6.7.8.11.12.

CONSERVATION SOCIETY (LTD.) KENT BRANCH
A rail only link through the Tunnel...Paper
No 2.
1973.
4

COOPERS AND LYBRAND ASSOCIATES LTD.
The Channel Tunnel: a United Kingdom transport
cost benefit study: report presented to the
Secretary of State for the Environment,
31st May, 1973.
H.M.S.O. 1973.
2,3,4,6,7,9,11

DAVIES, Geoffrey Alun.
The Channel Tunnel: a bibliography of the
fixed link.
Cadig Liaison Centre, Coventry. 1973
2,3,6

DESTOMBES, J.P.*
Geological results of the Channel Tunnel
site investigation 1964 - 65, by J.P.
Destombes and E.R. Shephard-Thorn.
H.M.S.O. 1971
4,6

ENVIRONMENT, Department of the
The Channel Tunnel: its economic and social
impact on Kent. Report by Economic
Consultants Ltd. in association with the
Shankland/Cox partnership.
H.M.S.O. 1973.
1.2.3.4.6.7.11.12.16,19,22,28

The Channel Tunnel project: extracts
from a report...on the economic and social
impact of the Tunnel on Kent. (i.e. on the
Ashford Area) by Economic Consultants Ltd
with the Shankland/Cox partnership. 1973.
2,4,6,7,9,19

The Channel Tunnel project; presented to
Parliament by the Secretary of State for the
Environment. March 1973. Cmnd.5256
H.M.S.O. 1973.
4,7,9,11,16,20.

The Channel Tunnel; presented to Parliament
by the Secretary of State for the Environment,
September, 1973. Cmnd. 5430.
H.M.S.O. 1973.
2.3.4.6.11.12.16.22.

EUROPEAN FERRIES LTD.
The Channel Tunnel project: an objective
appraisal.
European Ferries Limited. 1973.
2.4.6.7.

FOREIGN AND COMMONWEALTH OFFICE.
The Channel tunnel:agreement for the settlement
of disputes between the Government of the
United Kingdom of Great Britain and Northern
Ireland, the Government of the French Republic,
the British Channel Company Ltd., and the Societe
Francaise du Tunnel sous la Manche Paris 16 May,1974.
France No.2 (1974) (Comnd 5762).
H.M.S.O. 1974.
6.

GIBBONS Gavin.*
Trains under the Channel.
Advertiser Press.Huddersfield. (1970).
4,6,7,11

GREAT BRITAIN, Laws etc. (Eliz.II)
Channel Tunnel: a bill to provide for the
construction and operation of a railway tunnel
system under the English Channel...
H.M.S.O. 1973.
11

Channel Tunnel (initial finance): a bill....
brought from the Commons, 13th November, 1973.
H.M.S.O. 1973.
6,11

Channel Tunnel (Initial finance) Act, 1973.
H.M.S.O. 1973.
6.7.11

A Bill (as amended by the select committee
and by standing committee E)to provide for
the construction...railway tunnel system
under the English Channel.
H.M.S.O. 1974.
3

GREAT BRITAIN. Parliament House of Commons.
Parliamentary debates, official report
Standing Committee E. Channel Tunnel Bill.
2nd sitting Tues. 16th July, 1974.
H.M.S.O. 1974.
3

Parliamentary debates, official report. Standing
Committee E. Channel Tunnel Bill. Third
sitting. Thurs. 18th July, 1974.
H.M.S.O. 1974.
3

Parliamentary debates, official report.
Standing Committee E. Channel Tunnel Bill.
Fourth sitting. Tues. 23rd July, 1974.
H.M.S.O. 1974.
3

Special report from the Select Committee on
The Channel Tunnel Bill, together with minutes
of evidence and the proceedings of the Committee.
Session 1974.
H.M.S.O. 1974.
3.6.11

CHANNEL TUNNEL   Cont'd

GREAT BRITAIN. Treaties etc., France. 1971.
Exchange of notes between....the United Kingdom
and French Republic concerning the Channel
Tunnel project.
H.M.S.O. 1971.
7

GREAT BRITAIN. Treaties, etc., France, 17th
                    November, 1973
Treaty between the United Kingdom...and the
French Republic concerning the construction and
operation of a railway tunnel system under the
English Channel...17th November, 1973,
presented to Parliament.
H.M.S.O. 1973.
11

HAINING, Peter.
Eurotunnel: an illustrated history of the
Channel Tunnel scheme.
New English Library. 1973.
1.4.6.7.9,11,12

KENT COUNTY COUNCIL: PLANNING DEPARTMENT.*
The Channel Tunnel: a discussion of terminal
requirements on the British side and of a possible
location for terminal facilities in Kent.
K.C.C. 1968.
9,20

KENT FIELD CLUB.
Transactions Vol.6. Part 1. Channel Tunnel Survey.
1976.
4

KYD, Tony.
Who fancies the Chunnel? and What chance for
the Tunnel? (Extracts from Motor. 22nd and
29th December. 1973)
4

LEROI, David.*
The Channel Tunnel.
Clifton Books. 1969.
11

MOTSON, Anne.
Is this the gateway to Europe. (Daily
Telegraph.16.11.73)
4.

PEQUIGNOT, Clifford Alfred.*
Chunnel: everyman's guide to the
technicalities of building a Channel Tunnel.
C.R. Brooks. London. 1965.
11

ROYAL INSTITUTE OF BRITISH ARCHITECTS:
Channel Tunnel Study Group.
Channel Tunnel rail link: an appraisal of the
proposals of the British Railways Board.
Royal Industute of British Architects.1974.
3,11

ROYAL SOCIETY OF ARTS.
The Channel Tunnel: a public discussion held
at the Society's House in John Adam Street,
Adelphi, London on 5th June 1973:
Supplement to the Society's"Journal".
1973.
3.4.6.11

SLATER, Humphrey.*
The Channel Tunnel,(by) Humphrey Slater and
Correlli Barnett.
Alan Wingate. 1958.
11

THE SUBMARINE CONTINENTAL RAILWAY CO.
Channel Tunnel: report of a meeting of the
members...Friday the 20th January, 1882
(also of)....an extraordinary general meeting
on Thursday August 17th 1882.
The Company. 1882.
2

THOME DE GAMOND. N.A.
Etude pour l'avant-projet d'un tunnel sous-
marin entre L'Angleterre et La France
reliant sans rompre charge les chemins de Fer de
ces deux pays par la ligne de Grinez á
Eastware.
(A feasibility study of the Channel Tunnel
from France to England)
Victor Dabmont, Editeur Paris. 1857
11

TRANSPORT, Ministry of.*
Proposals for a fixed Channel link, presented
to Parliament by the Minister of Transport,
September 1963. (Cmnd.2137).
H.M.S.O. 1963 reprinted 1973.
16

WEALD OF KENT PRESERVATION SOCIETY.
Committee on the Channel Tunnel - 1973.
Report to the Council.
Duplicated sheet, 5 pages, 1973.
4

WHITESIDE, Thomas.*
The tunnel under the Channel.
Hart Davis. 1962.
2,3

CHARING

CHARING CHURCH AND PARISH. (197-?)
11

HASTED, Edward.
Charing, its families, manors, church and
archbishop's palace with the village charities,
as extracted from the 1798 edition of "History and
Topographical Survey of the County of Kent"...
Archive & Palaeographical Group of the
Charing & District Local History Society,1978.
3,11

CHARITIES

BELL, Leonard H.*
Where Travellers rest: the story of Richard
Watt's Charity in Rochester.
Rochester Printing Company. 1926.
1,3,4,8,11,12,13,15,25

BOARD OF EDUCATION.*
Administrative County of Kent: endowed charities
(elementary education): report made to the
Board of Education....on endowments.
Printed for H.M.S.O. 1907.
11

CARLISLE, Nicholas.
A concise description of the endowed grammar
schools; Vol.I. Essex, Kent, London,
Middlesex and Surrey. First published in 1818.
Richmond Publishing. 1973.
3.7.12

CHAMPION, George J.
In the matter of Mrs. Mary Wiseman's Charity,
being partially educational, in the parish of
Woolwich, in the County of Kent, extracted from
official records and compiled.by Geo.J.Champion.
W.J. Squires, Bookseller,Woolwich. 1886.
11

CHARITY COMMISSION.
Scheme for the application of the property of
the late Corporation of the Mayor,Jurats & Commonalty
of the town of Fordwich. Sealed 10th Sept. 1888
(photocopy) Eyre & Spottiswoode for HMSO 1888
3

Scheme including the appointment of Trustees in
the matter of the Charity called the Vidgen-
Wilson Almshouses...regulated by a scheme...of
23 November 1926,as varied by a scheme...of the
18th May 1971. Sealed 25 October.1978.
Charity Commission. 1978
3

COMMISSION (on) Charities and Education
Reports.(on)...Charities & education..Kent.
1815 to 1839
2

DICKENS, Charles.
The Seven Poor Travellers,in three chapters. Local
notes by Edwin Harris.(Short novel of the Richard
Watts Charity,Rochester;Published in 1854)
Edwin Harris & Son.Rochester. 1926.
11

GREAT BRITAIN, Laws,statutes,etc. (Vic.)
An act for confirming a scheme of the Charity
Commissioners for Sir Eliab Harvey's Charity,in
the town of Folkestone.(28thJune, 1858)
Eyre & Spottiswoode. 1858.
11

GREAT BRITAIN, Laws,statutes,etc. (Eliz.II)
Chatham Intra Charity of Richard Watts and other
charities. A bill to confirm a Scheme of the
Charity Commissioners for the application or
management of certain charities in the County
of Kent. (3 Eliz.2)
H.M.S.O. 1954
4

Chatham Intra Charity of Richard Watts and other
charities. A bill instituted an Act to confirm
a scheme of the Charity Commissioners. for the
application or management of certain charities
in the County of Kent.
H.M.S.O. 1955.
4

Bill to confirm a scheme of the Charity Commissioners for the application or management of
Bromley College.
H.M.S.O. 1960
2.8

HARRIS, Edwin.*
Richard Watts' Charity(Old Rochester Series No.20)
Edwin Harris & Sons. Rochester.
3 - 1912.
4 - 1906

HINKLEY, E.J.F.
A history of the Richard Watts Charity.
Richard Watts Almshouses.Rochester. 1979
4

LANSDELL, Henry.*
Princess Aelfrida's Charity,3 vols,(Lands in
Greenwich,Lewisham & Woolwich which became an
endowment of Morden College.
Burnside Ltd. Blackheath 1911-16
2,11,17,18

LAWSON, A.W.
Charities of the parish of West Malling,Kent.
Printed by Stedman. 1918?
11

RICHARD WATTS CHARITY.*
The scheme for the management of the charity
and for the application of the income thereof..
Richard Watts Charity. 1934.
8

The Scheme for Watt's Charity, Rochester.
Charles & Tiver. 1855.
25

RICHARD WATTS CHARITY.*
A terrier or rental of the estate of Watts'
Charity Rochester. 1859...
Richard Watts Charity. 1860
11

A terrier or rental of the estates of Watts'
Charity, Rochester, as let at Midsummer,1885.
Original record.
Richard Watts Charity. 1885.
4

THE SCHEME for the Management and regulation
of Several Charities in Faversham...as approved
by the Court of Chancery by an order dated
5th April, 1836.
C. Roworth, London. 1856.
26

TWO SCHEMES relating to Faversham Grammar School
and other charities approved by the Queen's
Most Excellent Majesty on the 24th day of March
1876.
James Higham. Faversham
26

WARREN, Charles.
Westbere, Kent; history of the Bread and Cheese
Field Trust from 1833 to 1914-(photocopy)
The Author. Westbere.(1915).
3

CHARLTON

CHARLTON SOCIETY.
St. Luke Charlton:Parish Register for 1653 -
1753 and for 1754 - 1798.
Charlton Soc. & Greenwich Arts Council.(1977).
11

ELLISTON-ERWOOD, Frank Charles.*
The earthworks at Charlton.London S.E. From
"The Journal of the British Archaeological Association
Vols XXII and XXIX 1916 & 1923.
Bound with
ELLISTON ERWOOD, Frank Charles.*
The Roman antiquities of NW Kent, with special
reference to the site of Noviomagus...with an
account of the excavations...at Joyden's Wood,
Bexley...1926-27. From "Journal of the British
Archaeological Association. Vol.XXXIV. 1928.
2,11

MAY, Leonard Morgan.*
Charlton:near Woolwich,Kent. Full & complete
copies of all inscriptions in the old Parish
Church and Churchyard..(limited edition).
Charles North. 1908.
1,2,11,15,17,18

ST.LUKE THE EVANGELIST'S CHURCH, Charlton.
Parish Registers. 4 vols.
J.G.Smith.1977- (1978).
2

SMITH, John Gilbert.
Charlton: a compilation of the parish and its
people.vol.1 (13 pamphlets & index in box)
The Charlton Society 1970.
3

CHARLTON-IN-DOVER See DOVER

CHARTHAM

CANTERBURY AND THANET HEALTH DISTRICT:KENT AREA
HEALTH AUTHORITY.
St. Augustine's Hospital, Chartham,Canterbury,Kent.
A guide to patients on their admission to Hospital.
Kent Area Health Authority.(1975).
3

SOUTH EAST THAMES REGIONAL HEALTH AUTHORITY.
Report of committee of enquiry on St.Augustine's
Hospital, Chartham, Canterbury.
As Author. 1976.
3,11

CHART SUTTON

FRANKLYN, Charles Aubrey Hamilton .
The Genealogy of Anne the Quene,(Anne Bullen)
and other English Families (including) Francklyn
of Chart Sutton.
Privately printed by Foto direct,Brighton. 1977.
11

MAYO, Owen.
St.Michael's Church Chart Sutton:the history of
St.Michael's Church,Chart Sutton,Kent.(The Church)
1976.
11

CHARTWELL See WESTERHAM

CHATHAM

BELL, John Amy Bird Defendant.*
Trial of John Amy Bird Bell, 1831. See MAIDSTONE

THE BOUNDS OF CHATHAM PARISH. 18th September.1811.
(Cutting). 1817.
4

BRASS TO STEPHEN BOROUGH, 1584. St. Mary's Chatham.
(M.S., bound. A description of his achievement and
a coloured drawing of his coat-of-arms)
4

THE BROOK PENTAGON. Two scrapbooks of articles
compiled from local papers etc. from 1965-1977.
4

BURROW, Edward J. Ltd. Publisher.
The directional pointer guide-map to Rochester
and Chatham.
Ed. J. Burrow Ltd. (C.1920).
4

CATALOGUE...of mammalia and birds in the Museum
of the Army Medical Deptartment at Fort Pitt.
Burrill, Chatham. 1838
11

CHATHAM BOROUGH COUNCIL.
Chatham Corporation Minutes, 1929
(copy belonged to Councillor
A. Vallence)
1929.
11.

Chatham: Official Guide.*
Mowbray
4   17th edn. 1969
25 1960, 1961

Chatham; the souvenir and programme of events and
festivities in this historic Borough for
Coronation Year. 1953.

4

Conferment of the Freedom of the Borough on
H.M.S. Pembroke at the Medway Barracks- Foolscap
Scrapbook containing photographs,cuttings and
the Official Programme.   1955.
4

First draft Town Centre Map with written explanation.
Chatham Borough Council. Nov. 1963.
4,11

Hardstown redevelopment area.New houses in Upbury
Way.
Chatham Borough Council. Nov. 1963.
4

Housing.....and you.
Chatham Borough Council. 1962.
8

The Municipal Borough of Chatham;Official Guide.
Edward J. Burrows and Co Ltd. 1970.
4

Municipal Offices, Riverside: Borough Treasurer's
Dept., Housing Dept. Public Health Dept. Official
opening 5th Oct.1960.Historical & Descriptive notes.
Chatham Borough Council. 1960.
4

Official souvenir programme of the celebration
of the Coronation of their majesties King George
VI & Queen Elizabeth 1937. (Presented from the
collection of the late Capt. P.F.Hogg by his son
1962).
Chatham Borough Council.
4

Souvenir of the completion of the scheme of
sewerage of the Borough. Official opening of the
Chatham pumping station by Ald. E.A. Billinghurst.
25.9.29
Mackays Ltd. 1929.
4

CHATHAM BOROUGH COUNCIL: BOROUGH ENGINEER
AND SURVEYOR.
Bills of Quantity for Junior Boys' School,
Luton Road, Chatham.   April 1930.
4
Bills of Quantity for Senior Boys' School,
at Ordnance Place, Chatham. Bound typescript,
1938.
4

Contractors record showing contractor's name,
address, job to be done, estimated price &
remarks.
MS. 1906-36
4

Specification for three-bedroom houses- type
1/45 at Wayfields Avenue, Chatham.
Typescript. August 1945.
4

CHATHAM BOROUGH COUNCIL -PUBLIC HEALTH DEPARTMENT.
List of houses (inspected for Fitness)MS.1917-35
4
Record of houses inspected under Housing and
Town Planning Act,1909.MS.1922-35.
4
Register of houses in clearance area.MS.1932-39
4
Record of houses inspected under Housing and
Planning Act. 1930.MS. 1935-1937.
4.

CHATHAM BOROUGH COUNCIL-PUBLIC LIBRARIES.
Annual report.   1953-4,'54-5,'55-6,'56-7,'57-8,
'58-9,'59-60,'61-63.
Chatham Borough Council.
4
8 1953-54

Book list and bulletin. Nos 1-4
Chatham Borough Council. 1944 - 45.
4

Care,welfare and housing of old people. A list
of books in stock.
Chatham Borough Council.1962.
4

Catalogue of the books in the lending &
reference departments.
Mackay. 1904.
4

Catalogue of the books in the adult lending
department and reference departents, 2nd edition.
Wood & Co. 1913
4

Chatham public libraries jubilee. 1904-1964.
compiled by H. James & I.G.R. Stacey. Illus.
tables.
Chatham Borough Council. 1964.
4.8

Official opening of the New Junior Library
2nd May, 1962.
Chatham Borough Council. 1962.
8

Press cuttings on the library, with some on
local lectures, exhibitions and concerts.
April 1949 - March, 1951. Cuttings pasted into
quarto exercise book.
4

Public library regulations.
Chatham Borough Council. 1962.
4

CHATHAM BOROUGH COUNCIL - PUBLIC LIBRARIES.
Supplementary catalogue of books in the
lending library, with key to the indicator
Class F(fiction).
Chatham Borough Council. 1926.
4

CHATHAM FESTIVAL CARNIVAL COMMITTEE. 1951.
Borough of Chatham Festival Carnival and
£150 firework display on Wednesday 23rd
May, 1951. Souvenir programme No.4923.
(Festival of Britain 1951).

4

CHATHAM GRAMMAR SCHOOL FOR GIRLS.
School Magazine. Diamond Jubilee number
1907 - 67.
Issue(s) for 1874.
4.

CHATHAM THEATRE PROGRAMMES, bills and other
small items, 1954 - 55.
4

COOPER, John.
Fort Pitt: some notes on the history of a
Napoleonic Fort, Military hospital and
technical school.
Kent County Library for the Author. 1976.
3,5,6,7,8,9,11,13,15,20,25,32

CRAWSHAW, J.D.
Rome house and some of its occupants. Based
on a talk given to Chatham Historical Society.
(1977).
4

CULL, Frederick.*
Chatham- the Hill House(1567 - 1805)
Reprinted from Archaeologia Cantiana.Vol.LXXVII
1962.
Headley Bros. Ashford. 1962.
4

DAVIES, Hamlyn L. Rees.
The Guild of St. Helena-Chatham Garrison
Branch.(Some notes on the origin and object of
the Guild and on its work in Chatham).
Typescript. 1963.
4

DUGDALE, Thomas.
England and Wales delineated:historical
entertaining and commercial, alphabetically
arranged Vol 3 CA-DE (includes Chatham).
J. Tallis. 1835
4

ENVIRONMENT; Department of.
List of buildings of special architectural
or historic interest:Borough of Chatham,
Kent.
H.M.S.O. 1971.
11

FORT PITT GIRLS' SCHOOL, Fort Pitt, Chatham.1974.
4

FRANCIS ILES GALLERIES, CHATHAM.
Sir William Russell Flint, an exhibition of
paintings, 7th March - 4th April 1970.
(Catalogue).
1971
4

GORMAN, J.T.
The Jubilee Book of King George V. 1935.
Photographic issue presented by Chatham Borough
Council as a souvenir with portraits of Mayor
and Mayoress, Councillor Peter Ansell and
Miss Maude Ansell.
1935.
4

GRAY, Adrian A.
The Chatham Central Branch:notes by A.A.Gray
(4 typed sheets). August 1975.
4

GREAT BRITAIN, Laws etc. (Geo.II)
An act for repairing...the road from...Chatham
to St. Dunstan's Cross...Canterbury. 1729.
3

GREAT BRITAIN, Laws etc. (Geo.III)
An Act for the purchase of certain lands,tenements
and hereditaments at Sheerness and Chatham,for
the use of the Navy (24 June 1816)
Printed by Eyre & Strahan. 1816.
11

An act for enlarging the present or providing
an additional workhouse for the parish of
Chatham 42 Geo III. 1802.
William Burrill. 1826.
4

An act for enlarging the present,or providing
an additional workhouse for the parish of
Chatham in the County of Kent;for raising money
for that purpose; for the better ascertaining
& collecting the poor rates etc. 42 Geo III 1802.
Ambrose Etherington. 1841.
4

GREAT BRITAIN: Laws etc. (Vic.)
An act for enabling the Commissioners of the
Admiralty to purchase certain lands in the Parish
of Chatham in the County of Kent, and to stop up,
divert, or alter certain ways in the said parish...
Printed by Eyre & Spottiswoode. 1857
11

GREAT BRITAIN: Laws etc (Edw.VII)
Pier and harbour orders confirmation (Ch.cci)
(No.3) Act, 1902.(Provisional order relating
to the Sun Pier). Photocopy.
H.M.S.O. (1903).
4

GREAT BRITAIN: Laws etc. (Geo V)
Chatham Corporation Act. 1923
4

G.B. PARLIAMENT :HOUSE OF COMMONS SELECT COMMITTEE
ON THE CHATHAM ELECTION PETITION. 1853.
Chatham Election. Minutes ot evidence taken
before the select committee; together with
the proceedings of the committee. (1853).
4

GRIFFITHS, Arthur.
Fifty years of Public Service. (Writer was Deputy
Governor of Chatham Convict Prison.1870-1872)
Cassell. 1905.
8

GULVIN, Keith.
Chatham's concrete Ring.
Medway Military Research Group. 1979.
4.12.32

Fort Amherst: illustrated booklet .
Medway Military Research Group. 1977
2,4,11,15,25,32

The Napoleonic Defences of Rochester & Chatham.
Medway Military Research Group. 1978
4,6,11,15

HARRIS, Edwin .
The history of St Mary's Church, Chatham.
(Eastgate Series No.18)
John Hallewell, Rochester. 1978reprint
4.11.25

JONES, G.W.
Chatham in the'40's by G.W. Jones & M.Shortland
Fort Research Group, Chatham, 1978.
4

Fort Horsted by G.W. Jones & M. Shortland
Fort Research Group, Chatham. 1979.
4,11,12,32

Fort Luton 1892 by G.W. Jones & M. Shortland
Fort Research Group. Chatham, 1979.
4,11,15,32

KENT COUNTY COUNCIL:PLANNING DEPT.
Proposed Chatham Town Centre Ring Road -
Western End. Alternative route. Railway Street
to Dock Road Diagram...of exhibition. Jan. 1973.
K.C.C. 1977.
4

KENT MUSICAL COMPETITIVE FESTIVAL.
Thirty-fourth annual Kent Music Competitive
Festival. Chatham. 1950 Programme.
4

LOFTS, John Publisher.
Pictorial guide to Chatham.
John Lofts. (c.1850).
15

MARRINER, Edmund Hayes.
The genealogy of the Marriner family, Chatham,
Kent, England. by E.H. & H.A. Marriner.
Privately Printed. 1975.
4

MARSHALL, Elizabeth.
Special licence for the marriage of Elizabeth
Marshall of Chatham and Robert Creasey.
28 September 1741. MS.
4

MEDWAY CONSERVANCY BOARD.
Petition of the Conservation of the River Medway
against the confirmation of the provisional
order relating to the Chatham Sun Pier i.e.
Pier and Harbour provisional order (no.3) Bill
to authorise the extension of the pier.
photocopy. H.M.S.O.   1902.
4

MINUTES OF THE COURT LEET OF CHATHAM from
October 1756. Extracted from old records by
Wm. Marsh 1811 and continued to 1866.
Photocopy of MS in Rochester Museum.
4

MINUTES OF THE COURT LEET...October 1866 to
1888 List of High Constables 1756 - 1889.
List of Lords and Ladies of the Manor.
Photocopy of MS in Rochester Museum
4

MUNRO. A.G.
Rochester and Chatham with pen and camera.
Homeland Association 1898 etc.
1,5,7,9,11,12,15,17

Rochester and Chatham with their surroundings
3rd edn. by A.G. Munro and B.P. Row.
(Homeland handbooks)
Homeland Association (1911).
2

ORDNANCE SURVEY: ARCHAEOLOGICAL SECTION.
Set of Archaeological records cards for
Chatham and Rochester.
Ordnance Survey. (1976?).
4

THE PARISH CHURCH OF ST. STEPHEN, CHATHAM.
The Collation of the Rev. Ian Alexander Hardaker
B.D, A.K.C., by the Lord Bishop Suffragen of
Tonbridge and the Induction by the Archdeacon
of Rochester. Wed. 4th Nov 1970.
1970
4.

(PINN,WILLIAM).
Scrapbook containing newspaper cuttings
handwritten bills. etc. many on local (i.e.
Chatham) affairs. 1812.
4

THE POLL OF THE ELECTORS for a Member of
Parliament to represent the Borough of
Chatham...Wed. 22 June 1853.
(photocopy of original)
G.H. Windeyer(Printers)   1853.
4

PRENTIS, Walter.*
Notes on the Birds of Rainham...Chatham and
Sittingbourne.
Gurney & Jackson. 1894.
1,2,3,4,5,6,8,11,12,15,17,20

PRESNAIL, James.
Chatham: the story of a Dockyard town and the
birth place of the British Navy.
25 1952 Chatham Borough Council.*
3,30 1976. Medway Council.

A PROPOSAL TO DEVELOP FORT AMHERST situated
between Chatham and Gillingham as a Military
Engineering Open Air Museum.
(1973).
4

REYNOLDS, Charles & Co. Publisher.
The album of Rochester & Chatham Views.
Charles Reynolds & Company, London. (1890).
4 Photocopy
8,11,12,15

ROW, B. Prescott.
Rochester & Chatham with their surroundings
a handbook for visitors & residents, by
B.P. Row and A.H. Anderson.
Homeland Association Handbooks. C1911.
25

SACRED MELODIES for the use of Sabbath schools
4th ed
A.T. Fordham.   Chatham. 1867.
4

ST. JOHN'S SCHOOL, New Road Avenue, Chatham.
Diary 1859 - 1937, copied into an exercise
book, handwritten.
1943.
4

ST. MARY'S CHURCH, Chatham. Town Centre:
the magazine of Chatham Parish Church.
Editor: The Rector of Chatham.
July 1950.
4

SALVATION ARMY.
Chatham Citadel (Salvation Army) 100th
anniversary celebrations 1972-3.Souvenir
programme. 1973.
4

SANDERS, Frederick.
Trade cards trail to the year 1781. in
Cartophilic notes & news.Vol.6. July/Aug,
1976. No.70 .
4

SCAMMELL, S.D.*
Chatham long ago and now. A lecture delivered
under the auspices of the Town Council of
Chatham...to commemorate the incorporation
of the Borough...showing the unique history
...of the Mayoral Chain. New and enlarged edition
London Publishing Office. 1903.
2,11

SMITH, Victor. T.C.
Chatham's defences in the 19th century.
Reprinted from Post Mediaeval Archaeology. 1976.
11

The later nineteenth-century land defences of
Chatham.
Kent Defence Research Group (1976).
9,23,25,32

SMITH, W.E.J.
The story of Ebenezer Craded Sunday School
Printed by W.& J. Mackay,Chatham. 1949.
4,11.

THOMPSON, Fred.
A brief history of Christchurch, Luton,
and Luton Methodist Church.   (c. 1970).
11

CHATHAM Cont'd

WHYMAN, John.
From Leith to Lordswood; being a short history
of W. and J. Mackay Ltd. to mark their
centenary 1875 - 1975.
W.&.J. Mackay Ltd. 1976.
11,15

YOUNG, Percy.
The Tide Mill Secret. (The mill was moved from
Buckinghamshire to Luton by barge via Canals
and Rivers 1848).
Stockwell. n.d.
8

CHATHAM DOCKYARD

ARUP ASSOCIATES.
The Gun Wharf,Chatham: 400 years of maritime
history.
ARUP Associates. 1975.
4,11,15,25

CHATHAM BOROUGH COUNCIL.
Conferment of the Freedom of the borough on
H.M.S. Pembroke at the Medway Barracks Foolscap
scrap-book containing photographs,cuttings and
the official programme. 1955.
4

CHATHAM DOCKYARD EXTENSION, 1866.
Photograph album showing the construction of
the Extension. 1866.
32

CRACE, Admiral Sir John Gregory.*
Some notes on the history of Chatham Dockyard.
Privately printed. 1946?
25

CULL, Frederick.*
Chatham Dockyard Reprinted from Archaeologia
Cantiania. Vol. LXXIII 1959.
4

GREAT BRITAIN, Laws. etc. (Geo.II).
An Act for making compensation to the proprietors of such lands and hereditaments as
have been purchased for the better securing
of His Majesty's Docks, Ships and Stores at
Chatham, Portsmouth and Plymouth...1758.
Printed by Thomas Backett. 1759.
11

GREAT BRITAIN, Laws etc. (Geo III)
An Act for making compensation to the proprietors of certain tenements, and hereditaments
in the County of Kent purchased in pursuance of
an act...to rest certain messuages, lands...in
trustees for the better Securing of His
Majesty's Docks,Ships & Stores at Portsmouth and
Chatham. (1783).
11.
An Act for the purchase of certain lands,tenements
and hereditaments at Sheerness & Chatham, for the
use of the Navy. 24th June. 1816.
Printed by Eyre & Strahan. 1816.
11.

LEFRANQ, Paul.
La carriere movementee de Louis Alexandre
de Marolles inginieu Francais.
Circle Arch et Historique. Valenciennes. 1963.
4.

LLOYDS, Corporation of.
The Gun Wharf, Chatham.
Corporation of Lloyds. 1976.
15,25
NAVY DAYS CHATHAM. May 28-29th 1977.
Souvenir booklet.
8.

NAVY DEPARTMENT.
Meet the Royal Navy. Pamphlets in a folder,
including five on the history of Chatham
Dockyard.
H.M.S.O. & Chatham Dockyard. 1975.
11

PETT, Phineas.
The autobiography of Phineas Pett; edited by
W.G. Perrin. (Master Shipwright).
Printed for the Navy Records Society 1918.
11

PLAN SHOWING EXTENSION OF CHATHAM DOCKYARD
at St. Mary's Island. Scale 1in = c.550ft.
1869.
4

THE ROYAL DOCKYARD CHURCH, CHATHAM.*
H.M. Naval Dockyard. Chatham. 1969.
25

ST GEORGE'S CHURCH,Royal Naval Barracks, Chatham.
The memorial of the Chatham Port Division dedicated
to those from this division who gave their lives
in the Second World War. 1939 - 45.
4

SATURDAY MAGAZINE, 1834.
Includes items on Chatham Dockyard, Cinque
Ports, Reculver, Ancient Church in Dover Castle,
Thames and Medway Canal.
S.P.C.K. 1834
11

THOMPSON, Philip.
Success to H.M.S. "Hawkins"(poems to commemorate
the launching at H.M. Dockyard, Chatham...1st
October, 1917).
Printed on Silk. 1917.
4

WITCOMBE, Oliver.
Chatham Dockyard - past and present; by
Oliver Witcombe.
n.d.
4

CHAUCER, GEOFFREY. (1340(?) - 1400)

CHAUCER, Geoffrey.
The Canterbury Pilgrims, being Chaucer's
Canterbury Tales retold for children by
M. Sturt and E.C. Oakden.
Dent. 1954.
11

The Canterbury Tales: an illustrated selection
rendered into modern English by Nevill Coghill.
Allen Lane. 1977.
3

Canterbury Tales;*rendered into modern English by
J.U. Nicolson, with illustrations by Rockwell Kent.
Garden City Pub Co. New York, U.S.A. 1934
(also Published by W.H. Allen, 1934)
11

Chaucer's Canterbury Tales retold by
Katherine Lee Bates.
Rand McNally, U.S.A. 1914?
11

The Ellesmere miniatures of the Canterbury
Pilgrims. Edited by Theo Stemmler. 2nd ed
English Department,University of Mannheim,
Mannheim, 1977.
3.
BREWER, Derek Stanley.
Chaucer.
Longmans. 1953.
3

Chaucer and his World.
Eyre & Methuen.
1978.
3

CHUTE, M.
Geoffrey Chaucer of England.
Souvenir Press. 1977.
3

CHAUCER, Geoffrey (1340(?) - 1400) Cont'd

DILLON, Bert.
A Chaucer dictionary: proper names and
allusions, excluding place names.
G.K. Hall, Boston, Mass. (1974).
3

DUDENEY, Henry Ernest.
The Canterbury puzzles and other curious
problems. (Book of indoor games.
The Canterbury puzzles are based on "The
Canterbury Tales")
Heinemann. 1907.
11

GARDNER, John.
The life and times of Chaucer.
J. Casper. 1977
3

HADOW, Grace E.
Chaucer and his times.
Williams and Norgate. 1914.
3

HOWARD, Donald R.
The idea of Canterbury Tales.
University of California, Berkeley. (1976).
3

HOWARD, Edwin J.
Geoffrey Chaucer.
Macmillan. 1976.
3

MANLY , John Matthew.
The text of the Canterbury Tales -
Studies on the basis of all known manuscripts.
by John M. Manly and E. Rickert. 8 vols.
Chicago University Press, 1940.
3

SCOTT, A.F.
Who's Who in Chaucer.
Elm Tree. 1974.
3

STANLEY-WRENCH, Margaret.*
Chaucer: teller of tales.
The World's Work. 1967
3

WARD, Adolphus William.*
Chaucer.
Macmillan   1881
3,12

CHELSFIELD

BROWN, Theodore.
Half-Lights on Chelsfield Court Lodge.
Privately Printed. 1933.
11

THE CHURCH OF ST MARTIN OF TOURS,
Chelsfield
The Church. (1974).
2

DEWDNEY, W.S.
A history of Cannock School. Volume 1.
1905-1978 by W.S. Dewdney and L.F. Baker.
(At Eltham until 1960 then Chelsfield)
The School. 1979.
2.

CHERITON

ROBERTSON, William Archibald Scott.
Cheriton Church. Reprinted from Archaeologia
Cantiana. Vol.18
Mitchell & Hughes. 1889.
11

CHESTFIELD

DEBENHAM, Betty.*
Chestfield(Whitstable) Golf Club.
Golf Clubs Association (G.W.May Ltd). (197-?).
11,30,31

KENT COUNTY COUNCIL: PLANNING DEPT.
Chestfield informal district plan.
K.C.C. 1975.
1

CHETNEY

HARRISON, Jeffery.*
The nesting birds of Chetney Marsh, Kent.
Kent Ornithological Society. 1971.
12,16,25

CHEVENING

BARHAM, Abraham.
An address to the Right Honourable Philip Henry,
Earl Stanhope on the subject of a survey of
Chevening Park made for his Lordship in 1817.
1831.
16

GREAT BRITAIN, Laws etc. (Eliz. II)*
Act to confirm and give effect to a vesting Deed
and Trust instrument relating to the Chevening
Estate.
H.M.S.O. 1959.
4

NEWMAN, Aubrey.*
The Stanhopes of Chevening:a family biography.
Macmillan. 1969.
2,4,11,12,16,19

PARISH CHURCH OF St. Botolph's; Chevening:
a short guide for visitors.
J. Collard & Sons. 1965.
16

CHIDDINGSTONE

CHIDDINGSTONE: short particulars of the village
and parish church of Chidingstone now called
Chiddingstone.
A.P. Blundell Taylor & Co. Printer, London. n.d.
16

GENERAL REGISTER OFFICE.
Census Returns. 1851. Chiddingstone. photocopy
23

NEWTON, Jill.
Chiddingstone, a closer look, illustrations
by David Newton.
1973
16.19

A SHORT GUIDE TO CHIDDINGSTONE CASTLE AND ITS
COLLECTIONS.*
Stanford Printing Company,Tunbridge Wells.(195-?).
4,8,11.

CHILHAM

CHILHAM CASTLE. English Life Publications.(1974?).
11,19

CHILHAM CASTLE, KENT; its history and guide
to the ancient castle and keep (1972 edition).
Printed by Thompsons, 1972.
11

CHILHAM PARISH COUNCIL.
Chilham parish appraisal.
(Chilham Parish Council) 1978.
3

HERON, J.
Antiquities of Chilham. Photocopy of five
handwritten sheets. 1791
3

ILLUSTRATED PARTICULARS, plans and conditions
of sale of....Chilham Castle(estate) including
...the famous Jacobean residence...the historic
Norman Keep...in all about1,405 acres. For
sale by auction by Amos & Dawton & John D.Wood
& Co. 1949.
11

ILOTT, C.H.
The village of Chilham.
P.K. Osmond. 1975.
3,30

JESSUP, Frank William.*
Court rolls of the manor of Chilham 1654 -56
edited by F.W. Jessup.
K.A. Society. 1960.
4

OSWALD, C.A.
Chilham Castle.
English Life Publications. (1975).
2,3

THE TOPOGRAPHER FOR THE YEAR 1791, containing
a variety of original articles...Vol IV, Nos
XXII-XXVII, January - June 1791.
(pp.80 - 112, Chilham)
Printed for J. Robson. 1791
11

WYATT, Sir Stanley Charles.*
Cheneys and Wyatts...
Carey & Claridge. 1960.
11

CHISLEHURST

BRITISH SCIENTIFIC INSTRUMENT RESEARCH ASSOCIATION
Sira institute (Chislehurst) (Brochure of
Services).
Sira Institute. c.1970
2

BUSHELL, Thomas A.
The Blackney forges at Chislehurst (4p.
typescript notes).
1973.
2

Imperial Chislehurst: The story of a Kentish
Village.
Barracuda Books. 1974.
1,11,18.

CATALOGUE OF THE SYDNEY COLLECTION AT FROGNAL,
CHISLEHURST, KENT.*
(Auctioneers: Knight, Frank & Rutley).
Dryden Press 1915.
1,4, 12,17

CHISLEHURST URBAN DISTRICT COUNCIL.*
Chislehurst & Sidcup, Kent: the official guide.
E.J. Burrows & Co. Cheltenham, 1954 etc.
1,2   1951 - 59
4.   1951
5,11 1954 etc.
CHRIST CHURCH, CHISLEHURST.
Calendar of forthcoming events for October,
November & December, 1951.
11

DUFF, David.
Eugenie and Napoleon IIl: (includes
account of exile in Chislehurst)
Collins. 1978
2

GEE, Laurence E.
A survey of the rich and poor of Chislehurst,
1845 - 1900. (photocopy of thesis)
(1973)
2

GRADIDGE, Roderick.
Daylight saving in the suburbs: a tour of
Chislehurst, compiled by R. Gradidge.
(Notes for an architectural tour (duplicated
typescript).
Victorian Society. 1979.
2

LAGDON, G.J.
(Camden Place) a dissertation. Unpublished thesis
1978.
2

PLATT, Clifford L.
In trust for Chislehurst: an account of the
Commons of Chislehurst and St. Pauls Cray and
the National trust lands adjoining. Printed by
Pentagon Print for the Author. 1975.
2,11

ROBERTSON, Rev William Archibald Scott.*
Kentish Archaeology, 7 vols.(mostly reprinted
from Archaeologia Cantiana) Vol.4 - Romney Marsh
Chislehurst, Orpington.
Mitchell and Hughes. 1880
1

TSCHUDI, Clara
Eugenie, Empress of the French (section at
end on residence in Chislehurst).
Swan Sonnenschein 1900
2

WATTS,Alan Wilson.
In my own way: an autobiography, 1915 - 1965.
(Includes childhood memories of Chislehurst)
Cape 1973.
2,3

WEBBER, C.J.
History of Frognal, the estate and mansion.
typescript. 1971
2

(WESTERN MOTOR WORKS (CHISLEHURST) LTD.
The horseless carriage. (history of
Western Motor Works, originally established
at Frognal, Chislehurst)
1955
2

CHISLET

COOPER, J.E.*
The Mollusca of Chislet Marshes. Reprinted
from the Journal of Conchology: Vol.19, No.10,
June 1933. pp. 317-321.
11

DAVIES, Griffith James.
The Chislet Colliery, Ltd; outline of history
1913 to 1946, by Griffith James Davies,
Photocopy of typescript. 1946?
3

HASLEWOOD, Rev. Francis. F.*
The Parish of Chislet.
Privately printed. 1887.
2

HOVENDEN, Robert.*
The register of all the christenings, marriages
and burials in the parish of St. Mary,Chislet...
From 1538 - 1707, edited by R. Hovenden.
Mitchell & Hughes. n.d.
3,4,11,12
17 MSS copy in Latin

McINTOSH, Kinn H.
Chislet and Westbere, villages of the Stour
Lathe.
K.H. McIntosh, Sturry. 1979.
23,28

CHURCH HISTORY

ANDREWS, William.
Antiquities & Curiosities of the Church,
edited by W. Andrews.
W. Andrews & Co. 1897.
11

ANIMADVERSIONS on Lord Bexley's letter to the
Freeholders of Kent*(The Catholic Question)
British Catholic Association. 1829.
4,14

BASKERVILLE, Geoffrey.*
English Monks and the suppression of the
monasteries.
Cape. 1937.
3,11

BUCKINGHAM, Christopher.
The movement of clergy in the Diocese of
Canterbury, 1552 - 62. (Offprint from
'Recusant History' Vol.14. No.47
October. 1978).
3

CRAMP, Rev. Dr. John Mockett.
Letters on church rates addressed to the
Rev.J.E.N. Molesworth, M.A. of Canterbury.
(Dr. Cramp was Baptist Minister, St. Peters
Broadstairs)
G. Wightman. 1837.
24

CRANAGE, David Herbert Somerset.
The home of the monk: an account of English
Monastic life and buildings in the Middle
Ages.
Cambridge
11

CULMER, Richard (Minister at Harbledown)
The Ministers' hue and cry, or, a true
discovery of the insufferable injuries,
robberies, cozenages and oppressions now
acted against Ministers and Impropriators
Printed by Abraham Miller. London. 1651.
11

DERING, Sir Edward.
A collection of speeches made by Sir
Edward Dering...in matter of religion,
some formerly printed and divers more
now added; all of them revived for the
vindication of his name from weake
and wilfull calumnie;...
E. Dering. London. 1642.
11

The fower Cardinall - Vertues of a
Carmelite-Fryar, fraud, folly, foul-language,
blasphemy. Discovered by Sir Edward Dering,
knight and baronet. And by him sent backe
againe to their author Simon Stocke...
Printed by I.R. for R. Whitaker, St. Pauls
Churchyard, London. 1641.
11

DU BOULAY Francis Robinson Houssemayne.
A handlist of mediaeval ecclesiastical terms.
National Council of Social Service. 1952.

ELLISTON-ERWOOD, Frank Charles.*
The present state of monastic archaeology
in Kent. Reprinted from "The South
Eastern Naturalist and Antiquary" Vol.LIX
1954.
1,11,12

FIELD, Colin Walter.
The Province of Canterbury and the Elizabethan
Settlement of Religion.
C.W. Field.Robertsbridge. 1973.
1,3,11,12,20,26,27

FINUCANE, Ronald C.
Miracles and pilgrims:popular beliefs in
medieval England.
Dent. 1977.
3

GALLYON, Margaret.
The early church in Eastern England.
T. Dalton. Lavenham,Suffolk. 1973.
6,7,11,23

HUTCHINSON, C.B.
The Fanes of Thanet - 13 articles on the
development of Thanet as reflected in
church history.
Thanet Advertiser. 1917.
24

"A KENT INCUMBENT" pseud.
(probably Rev. Joseph Hall)
An easy solution and amicable settlement of
the Church-Rate question, suggested by a
Kent Incumbent. (Bound with "A Letter to
His Grace" by Joseph Hall).
Shaw & Sons. London. 1861.
3.

KEPLER, J.S.
The exchange of Christendom: the international
entrepot at Dover 1622 - 1651.
Leicester 1976.
11

ORDNANCE SURVEY.
Monastic Britain. 3rd ed. Maps - Scale 1:625,000
(folded with text)
Ordnance Survey 1978
23

PEARMAN, Rev. Augustus John*
Diocesan histories: Rochester.
S.P.C.K. 1897
1,2,3,4,5,8,11,12,15,17,18

PUBLIC RECORD OFFICE.*
List of the lands of dissolved religious houses,
Kent-Middlesex.
H.M.S.O. 1964.
4,7,8

RICHTER, Michael.
Canterbury professions: edited by
Michael Richter...
Canterbury & York Society. 1973.
11

ROBERTSON, Rev. William Archibald Scott.
Queen Mary's responsibility for parish
church goods seized by the Commissioners of
King Edward VI Reprinted from Archaeologia
Cantiana Vol.XIV 1881.
Mitchell & Hughes. 1881.
4

WALCOTT, Mackenzie E.C.
Inventions and valuations of Religious
houses at the time of the Dissolution,
from the Public Record Office. With
prefatory remarks....Read to the Society of
Antiquaries of London on 3rd March, 1870.
The Society. 1870.
11

WHATMORE, Rev. Leonard E.
Recusancy in Kent; studies and documents.
Colin W. Field. Robertsbridge. 1973
3,4,8,19.20.26.27

WILLIS, A.J.
Church life in Kent being Church Court records
of the Canterbury Diocese 1559 - 1565.
Compiled by A.J. Willis.
Phillimore. 1975.
1.3.5.6.7.8.11.13.19.20.22.26.27

CHURCHES See also TOWNS, VILLAGES ETC.

ADDYMAN,Peter.
The archaeological study of churches, edited by
Peter Addyman and Richard Morris.
Council for British Archaeology. 1976.
23

BOORMAN, Henry Roy Pratt.
Kent Churches by H.R.P. Boorman and V.J. Torr.
Kent Messenger. 1954.
24

CLINCH, George.
Old English Churches: their architecture,
furniture, decoration, monuments, Vestments
and plate. 2nd and enlarged edition
L. Upcott Gill. London. 1903.
11

DITCHFIELD, Peter Hampson.
The Village Church. (First Published. 1914)
E.P. Publishing 1975.
11

ELLISTON-ERWOOD Frank Charles.
Plans of, and brief architectural notes on,
Kent Churches, series 1. 4 parts.
Reprinted from Archaeologia Cantiana,
Volumes 59 - 62.
Printed by Headley Bros. Ashford.1946-49.
4,11

ESDAILE, Mrs Katherine Ada.*
English church monuments 1510 - 1840.
Batsford. London & Malvern Wells. (1946).
11

GLYNNE, Sir Stephen R.*
Notes on the churches of Kent.
Murray. 1877
20,25,26

GRAYLING, Francis.*
County Churches: Kent. 2 vols.
George Allen. 1913.
20, 24,25,30

HOPPER, H.C.
Thirty Kent churches.
(Text by H.C. Hopper, illustrations by
L.T. Hopper) An edition of 750 copies
Great Stour Publications. Canterbury. 1978.
2,3,4,11,13,15,16,23,28
5 - Copy 315

HUSSEY, Arthur.*
Notes on the churches in the counties of Kent,
Sussex & Surrey....mentioned in the
Domesday Book.
John Russell Smith. London. 1852.
25

MAXWELL, Donald.*
Adventures among churches. Contents include:-
Tenterden, Fairfield, Brookland, Harbledown.
Cuxton, Little Chart, Stone, Rainham.
Faith Press. 1928.
4,11

More Adventures among churches.*
(pp.67 - 102, pp. 127 - 8 Kent)
Faith Press. 1929.
4,11

OYLER, Thomas H.*
The parish churches of the Diocese of
Canterbury, with descriptive
notes.
Hunter & Longhurst. London. 1910.
2,24,30

ROBERTSON, Rev. William Archibald Scott.*
Church plate in Kent Reprinted from
Archaeologia Cantiana Vol. XVII 1886.
Mitchell & Hughes. 1886.
4

SMETHAM, Henry.*
Rambles round churches 4 vols.
Parrett & Neves. 1925 - 29
25

VALLANCE, Aymer.
Old crosses and lychgates(Kentish Author)
Batsford 1920 (rev.1933)
3

WALCOTT, Mackenzie, E.C.*
Parish church goods in Kent, A.D. 1552 (Edward
VI): inventories Part 1, edited by the Rev.
Mackenzie E.C. Walcott and the Rev.W.A. Scott
Robertson.
Printed by Taylor & Co. London. 1872.
4

YATES, E.
Church chests.(references to Kent Churches) In
Vol.50. South Eastern Naturalist & Antiquary.
South East Union of Scientific Services. 1946.
11

CHURCHILL, SIR WINSTON L.S. (1874-1965)
COUNTRY HOME AT CHARTWELL, NEAR WESTERHAM.

AMERICAN HERITAGE MAGAZINE & UNITED PRESS
INTERNATIONAL.*
Churchill: the life triumphant, the historical
record of ninety years.
American Heritage Publishing Coy. 1965.
12

ARTHUR, Sir George.*
Concerning Winston Spencer Churchill.
Heinemann. 1940.
12

BROAD, Lewis.*
The adventures of Sir Winston.
Hutchinson. 1957.
12

Winston Churchill, 1874 - 1952.
Hutchinson. 1952.
12

BURRIDGE, William F.*
The Right Honourable Winston Leonard Spencer
Churchill.
John Crowther. 1943.
12

CARTER, Violet Bonham.*
Winston Churchill, as I knew him.
Eyre & Spottiswoode and Collins. 1965
12

CHURCHILL, Randolph Spencer.*
Churchill:his life in photographs, edited by
R.S. Churchill and H. Gernsheim.
Weidenfeld & Nicolson. 1955.
12

Winston S. Churchill,*
Heinemann. 1966.
Vol I. Youth 1874 - 1900.
        Companion Vol.1. Part 1. 1874-1896.
Part 2. 1896 - 1900
        Companion Vol.II. 3 parts.
        Young Statesman 1901 - 1914.
12

CHURCHILL, Sir Winston Leonard Spencer.
My early life.
Odhams Press. 1947
12

Sir Winston Churchill.
Daily Mail. 1954
12

A speech by the Prime Minister...in the House of
Commons, August 20th 1940.
n.p. 1940.
12

Step by step 1936 - 1939
Butterworth. 1939.
12

CHURCHILL, Sir Winston Leonard Spencer.
Victory: war speeches 1945.
Cassell. 1946
12

War speeches...compiled by Charles Eade.
Cassell. 1952
12

The wisdom of Winston Churchill.
Allen & Unwin. 1956
12

The wit of Winston Churchill.
Parrish. 1955.
12

COOTE, C.R.*
Churchill: a self portrait, edited by C.R.
Coote.
Eyre & Spottiswoode. 1954.
12

COWLES, Virginia.
Winston Churchill:the era and the man.
Hamilton. 1953.
12

DAVENPORT, John.*
The lives of Winston Churchill by J. Davenport
and C.J.V. Murphy.
Charles Scribner & Sons, 1945.
12

MACRAE, R. Stuart.
Winston Churchill's Toyshop (Secret "Workshop"
for new weapons)
Roundwood Press. 1971
12

NORRIS, A.G.S.
A very great soul: a biographical character
study of the Rt. Hon. Sir Winston S.Churchill.
International Publishing Company, 1957.
12

THOMPSON, W.H.
I was Churchill's Shadow.
Christopher Johnson. 1951.
12

WINSTON CHURCHILL: tributes broadcast by the
B.B.C., 24th to 30th January, 1965.
B.B.C. 1965.
12

WOODS, Frederick.*
Bibliography of the works of Winston Churchill.
Nicholas Vane. 1963.
12
2nd revised edition.
Kaye & Ward. 1969
12

CINQUE PORTS

BAGLEY, G.S.
Edwardian Rye from contemporary pictures.
Rye Museums Association. 1974.
7

BOORMAN, Henry Roy Pratt.*
Kent & the Cinque Ports.
Kent Messenger   1957.
1,3,4,5,6,7,8,9,10,11,12,14,15,17,18,20,24

BRADLEY, Arthur Granville.*
Englands' outpost:the country of the Kentish
Cinque Ports.
Robert Scott. 1921.
24.25
*
An old gate of England: Rye, Romney Marsh
and the Western Cinque Ports.
Robert Scott. 1918.
24

BRAYLEY, Edward Wedlake.*
Deliniations historical and topographical of
the Isle of Thanet and the Cinque Ports.
Vols.I and II illustrated by William Deeble.
Sherwood,Neely & Jones.   1817 & 1818
3,7,11,12,13,14,15,16,17,24
6,8,10 Vol I. only
1,4,   Vol II only

BRENTNALL, Margaret.*
The Cinque Ports and Romney Marsh.
John Gifford. 1972.
2,3,4,6,7,19,22,23,25,28,30

BURROWS, Montagu.
The antiquity of the Cinque Ports Charters.
Reprinted from Archaeological Review. n.d.
8

CLARK, Kenneth M.
Many a bloody affray: the story of smuggling
in the port of Rye and district.
Rye Museum. 1968.
11

CLARK, Kenneth M.
Smuggling in Rye and district.
Rye Museums Publications. 1977.
7

COLBRAN, John Publisher.
Osborne's Strangers' Guide to Hastings & St.
Leonards. bound with The Handbook & Visitors'
Guide for Tunbridge Wells and its neighbourhood.
J Colbran. Tunbridge Wells. 1855.
11

COLLARD, John A.
A Maritime history of Rye.
J.A. Collard. 1978.
6,7,28

COLLINS, Greenville.
Rye Harbour area: plate 8 taken from
"Great Britain's Coasting Pilot".
Richard Mount. 1693?
11

COMPARATIVE, Dr. Junior pseud.*
A sentimental journey through Margate and
Hastings.
Printed for Henry Colburn,London.1814.
11
Newman. 1819.
3,6,12,13,15,17.

DEACON, J.L.*
Ancient Rye: an illustrated historical handbook
Printing & Publishing House. Rye. 1927.
1,11

EAST KENT ROAD CAR COMPANY LTD.
Descriptive and pictorial guide to East Kent
and Rye, Winchelsea & Hastings, with map and
street plans of 1949. edited by Alfred Baynton.
East Kent Road Car Company and Cook's Publicity
Services. 1949.
2   1934
7,11 1949
3.   1952.
AN ENTIRE & COMPLETE HISTORY, political and
personal of the Boroughs of Great Britain together
with the Cinque Ports. 3 vols.
G. Riley. 1792.
11,26
4 Vol 3
10 Vol 2

FORD, Ford Madox.*
(Title page HUEFFER, FORD MADOX).
The Cinque Ports.
W. Blackwood. 1900.
3,7

GILBERT, W.G.L.*
Rye reformed: being some account of the political
scene in Rye after the year 1832.
Rye Museum. 1958
11

CLIFFE - AT - HOO   Cont'd

ROBERTSON, Rev William Archbald Scott.
The Rectors of Cliffe-at-Hoo.
n.d.
1

SMITH, J.J.*
The Story of Cliffe-at-Hoo, or Cloveshoo.
Lithographed by Brown's Typewriting
Service. (197-?)
9,11

CLIFTONVILLE - See   MARGATE

COAL

ARBER, Edward Alexander Newell.
On the fossil plants of the Waldershare and
Fredville series of the Kent coalfield.
Reprinted from the "Quarterly Journal of the
Geological Society" Vol. LXV 1909
11

ARNOT, R. Page.
The Miners: a history of the Miners' Federation
of Great Britain, 1889 - 1910.
Allen & Unwin. 1949.
13

The Miners: a history of the Miners' Federation
of Great Britain: the years of struggle from
1910 - 1930.
Allen & Unwin. 1953.
13

The Miners: a history of the Miners' Federation
of Great Britain: the Miners in crisis and war
from 1930 onwards.
Allen & Unwin. 1961.
13

BOLTON, Herbert.*
The Fauna and Stratigraphy of the Kent coalfield.
Reprinted from the Transactions of the Institute
of Mining Engineers. Vol.49. 1915.
2

DAVIES, Griffith James.
The Chislet Colliery Limited: outline of history
1913 - 1946, by Griffith James Davies.
Photocopy of typescript. 1946?
3

FORSTER BROWN, Edward Otto.
Underground waters in the Kent coalfield and
their incidence in mining development, with an
abstract of the discussion.....
Institute of Civil Engineers. 1923.
11

FRANKS, E.
Draft of a paper written for the Rev. S.D.
Scammell on the history of coal mining, with
particular reference to wages in the industry
with cuttings about the prospecting for coal
in the Dover area, 1890.
M.S. 1890.
4

FUEL AND POWER, Ministry of.*
Kent Coalfield. Regional Survey Report.
H.M.S.O. 1945.
3,15.
13 - photocopy

HARRISON, Norman.*
Once a miner.
Oxford University Press. 1954.
3

JOB, Robert R.
The Kent Coalfield.
(typescript) 1966.
3

JOHNSON, Walford.
The development of the Kent coalfield
1896 - 1939. Extended Essay.
Typescript (photocopy)
University of Kent at Canterbury.1967.
3,11

NAIL, Martin.
The coal duties of the City of London and their
boundary marks. (The boundary runs through
Downe and Orpington)
PP.   1972
9

PITT, Malcolm.
The world on our backs: the Kent miners and the
1972 miners' strike.
Lawrence and Wisehart. London. 1979.
5,6,12,22,28

RITCHIE, A.E.*
The Kent Coalfield: its evolution and development.
Iron and Coal Trades Review. 1919.
2
14 Photocopy.

COASTAL DEFENCES

BENNETT, D.H.
A handbook of Kent's defences from 1540 until
1945, listed by D.H. Bennett.
Kent Defence Research Group. 1977.
2,3,4,6,9,11,13,16,22,23

COTTRELL, Leonard.*
The Roman Forts of the Saxon Shore.
H.M.S.O. 1964.
25

GREAT BRITAIN, Laws etc (Geo.III).*
An Act for making compensation to the proprietors
of certain lands and Hereditaments purchased
pursuance of an Act, made in the thirty-fourth
year of the Reign of His present Majesty, for
better securing His Majesty's batteries and other
works in the Counties of Kent and Devon.
Printed by Eyre & Strahan. 1798.
11

GREAT BRITAIN, Laws etc (Vic.)
An Act for defraying the expenses of constructing
fortifications for the protection of the Royal
Arsenals and Dockyards and the Ports of Dover
and Portland and of creating a Central Arsenal.
Printed by Eyre & Spottiswoode. 1860.1860.
11

HOGG, Ian Vernon.
Coast defences of England and Wales, 1856 - 1956.
David and Charles, Newton Abbott. 1974.
4,6,15

Fortress.
(Includes Dover, Deal and Walmer)
Macdonald and Jane. 1975.
15

HUNTER, G.Y.
Refuge harbours and coast defences.
W.C. Brasier, 1853.
13

JOHNSON, Stephen.
The Roman Forts of the Saxon Shore. (Kent Forts
pp. 44 - 56 and throughout the text)
Elek. 1976.
3,6,8,12,13,28.

Roman Fortifications on the "Saxon Shore".
(Kent Forts pp. 19 - 25).
H.M.S.O. 1977.
3,6,7,11

KENYON, J.R.
A note on two original drawings by William
Stukeley, depicting "The Three Castles which
keep the Downs".
Reprinted from The Antiquaries Journal Vol.
LVIII, Part I, 1978. pp. 162 - 163.
Oxford University Press. 1978.
11

LANAWAY, Hugh.*
The nine fortresses on the Saxon shore erected
during the Roman era (Antiquarian pamphlets)
V.V. Swinfield. Eastbourne. 1920.
25

COASTAL DEFENCES   Cont'd

LEWIN, Thomas.
On the castra of the Littus Saxonicum and
particularly the castrum of Othona.
Read to the Society of Antiquaries of London
on June 20th 1867.
Society of Antiquaries of London, 1867.
11

MACDOUGALL, Philip.
The Isle of Grain defences.
Kent Defence Research Group.   1980.
6,22,28

MORLEY, B.M.
Henry VIII and the development of coastal
defence. (Dept. of the Environment).
H.M.S.O.   1976.
3,6,7,11,15,28

PHILP, Brian J.
The discovery of the "Classis Britannia"
and "Saxon shore" Forts at Dover and
"The Port of Dover", past and present.
Duplicated sheets. 1970.
11

SOMNER, William.*
A treatise of the Roman Ports and Forts in
Kent..... Published by the Rev. James Brome,
Rector of Cheriton and Chaplain of the
Cinque Ports.
Printed at the Theater, Oxford by
George West, John Crosley and Henry Clements.
1693.
 1,2,3,4,6,7,8,11,12,13,14,15,17,18,21

SUTCLIFFE, Sheila.
Martello towers.
David & Charles, Newton Abbott. 1972.
2,5,7,11,12,19

COASTAL WATERS

ADMIRALTY
ADMIRALTY:HYDROGRAPHIC DEPT.
Coastal & Estuary Charts   See
SEA AND RIVER CHARTS.

ALLENDALE, John
Sailorman between the wars; being the journal
of a Thames, Medway and coastal bargeman.
John Hallewell, Rochester. 1978.
3,4,5,11,12,15,22,23,25

BAYLEY, George Bethel.*
Seamen of the Downs: a retrospective sketch
of the historic roadstead and a sequel to
Treasurers' "Heroes of the Goodwin Sands"
by G.B. Bayley and William Adams.
Blackwood. 1929.
1,3,4,6,7,11,13,14

BENHAM, Hervey.*
Down tops'l   the story of the east coast
sailing barges....with additional material.
Harrap. 1951
3,4,11,15
and 2nd edition. 1971
11

BLANDFORD, Percy William.*
South Eastern England(Regional Sailing
Guides I)
Constable. 1971.
11

BOUQUET, Michael Rome.*
South Eastern sail from the Medway to the
Solent. 1840 - 1940.
David & Charles, Newton Abbott. 1972.
3,6,7,12,25,28

BRADFORD, Ernle.*
Wall of England:the Channel's 2000 years of
history.
Country Life. 1966.
11

BUCKNALL, Rixon.*
Boat Trains and Channel packets:the English
short sea routes.
Vincent Stuart. 1957.
11

CAPPER, Douglas Parode.*
Moat defensive: a history of the waters of
the Nore Command, 55 BC to 1961. (The Nore
Command covers the Kent coastline).
Barker. 1963.
4,8,11,12,15

CLARKE, Derrick Harry.
East coast passage:the voyage of a Thames
Sailing barge.
Longman. 1971.
11

COLES, R.A.
The Shell pilot to the south coast harbours.
Faber and Faber. 1977
15

CRITCHETT & WOODS.
A new guide to stage-coaches, wagons, carts,
vessels etc, for 1822. 20th edition by
Critchett & Woods.
Published by T. Maiden. 1822.
11

DINGWALL, R.G.
The structural and stratigraphical geology of
a portion of the Eastern English Channel.
H.M.S.O. 1971
8

DUCKWORTH, C.L.D.
Railways & other steamers, by C.L.D. Duckworth
and G.E. Langmuir. (Includes ferries operating
from Kent Ports).
Shipping Histories Ltd. 1948.
13

FINCH, Roger.
Coals from Newcastle:the story of the North
East Coal Trade in the days of sail.
Terence Dalton. Lavenham. 1973.
11

FINDLAY, Alexander George.*
A handbook for the navigation of the different
channels of the Thames & Medway and the coast
between Folkestone and Orfordness.
R.H. Laurie. 1887
1.8.11.12

GARRETT, Richard.*
Cross Channel -transport across the channel;by
sea, air and discusses Channel Tunnel.
Hutchinson. 1972.
7,11

GOOCH, R.
Tales of the sea
P.P. 1886.
13

GRASEMANN, C.
English packet boats by C. Grasemann and
G.W.P. Maclachlan.
(Chronological table of ships 1790 - 1939)
Syren and Shipping Ltd. London. 1939.
11

GREAT BRITAIN, Laws Etc. (Geo.III).*
An Act to continue several laws for the better
regulating of pilots for the conducting of
ships and vessels from Dover, Deal and Isle
of Thanet, up the rivers of Thames & Medway.1763.
Printed by Mark Baskett. 1764.
9

COASTAL WATERS   Cont'd

STANFORD, Edward Ltd., Publisher.
Coloured charts for coastal navigation,
edited by Captain O.M.Watts.
No.1. The English Channel.
Stanford Marine Ltd.
4   1950
4   1960 new edn.

Stanford's Chart of the English Channel
from Lands' End to Flushing (Eastern Section)
edited by Capt. O.M. Watts. Revised edition.
Scale 6 miles = 1": Size 26" x 37".
Stanford Marine Ltd. 1975
11

Stanford's Chart of the English Channel
from the Goodwins to Selsey Bill, edited
by Capt. O.M. Watts. New edition. Scale 2½
miles = 1" approx. Size 24" x 37"
Stanford Marine Ltd. 1973.
11

Stanford's Harbour Guide: North Foreland to
the Needles, edited by Capt. F.S. Campbell.
Stanford Marine Ltd. 1975.
11

STANTON, William.*
Journal of William Stanton,pilot,of Deal,
1811 - 1867.
Simpkin Marshall. 1929.
24

STOKER, Hugh.*
Sea fishing in Kent.
E. Mart. Publishing, Peterborough, 1965.
1,2,4,5,6,7,8,11,12,15,
30 1967 Benn Ltd.
22 1973 Benn Ltd.

STREATER, Ronald A.
Cross Channel ferries from Kent. 2nd edition.
edited by R.A. Streater.
Marinart Ltd. Sandwich. 1978.
3,5,6,11,13

SUMMERS, Dorothy.
The East coast floods.
David & Charles. Newton Abbott. 1978.
4,9,11,28

THANET SAILING WEEK. 1974. - Programme
13

TOPLEY, William.
Geology of the straits of Dover. Reprinted
from the Quarterly Journal of Science
April 1872
7.

TRADE & INDUSTRY. Department of.
Safety in the Channel: a report by the
Anglo-French Safety of Navigation Group.
H.M.S.O. 1978.
7

TRIPP, Sir Herbert Alker.* ("Leighhoe")
Shoalwater and fairway: the casual explorations
of a sailing man in the shoal seas and tidal
waters of Essex and Kent. (First printed in
1924).
Conway Maritime Press. 1972.
3,9
11 and 1924

VEALE, Ernest William Partington.*
Gateway to the continent: a history of cross-
channel travel.
Ian Allen. 1955
1,6,7,8,11,12

WILLIAMSON, James Alexander.*
The English Channel: a history.
Collins. 1959.
11,13,29

COASTAL WATERS - SAFETY AT SEA

ADAMS, W.H. Davenport.
The story of our lighthouses & lightships.
Nelson. 1891.
24

BIGGS, Howard.
The sound of maroons:the story of life-
saving services on the Kent & Sussex coasts.
Terence Dalton Ltd. Lavenham. 1977.
1,2,3,4,5,7,11,12,19,23,24,30

CARTER, George Goldsmith.
Looming lights: a true story of the lightships
(Includes lightships off the Kent Coast).
13 Constable 1945.
11 Readers Union & Constable 1947.

COOKE, Arthur O.
Life on a lightship.
Hodder & Stoughton. 1914.
14

HAGUE, Douglas B.
Lighthouses: their architecture, history
and archaeology by D.B. Hague and R.Christie.
Gomer Press. 1975.
24

JACKSON, Derrick.
Lighthouses of England and Wales, including
the Channel Islands and the Isle of Man.
Illustrated by the author.
David & Charles, Newton Abbott, 1975.
11

MALSTER, Robert.
Wreck and rescue on the Essex coast the
story of the Essex lifeboats. (Thames Estuary)
D. Bradford Barton, Truro. 1968.
27

NEW RAMSGATE GUIDE WITH MAP, containing
also an account of Margate and Broadstairs
as well as lifeboat work on the coast of Kent.
S.R. Wilson. 1890.
24

WEBB, W.
Coastguard 1: an official history of
H.M. Coastguard.
H.M.S.O. 1976.
28.

COASTLINE

ADAMSON, Simon H.
Seaside Piers (Kent piers mentioned throughout)
Batsford 1977.
3,11,30

ANDERSON, Janice.
The Victorian and Edwardian seaside,by
J. Anderson and E. Swinglehurst. (Includes
information on Herne-Bay, Margate, Ramsgate,
Broadstairs)
Country Life. 1978.
3,13

BAILEY, B.V.
Kent's Best Beaches.
James Pike, St. Ives. 1977.
11,22

BEATTIE, William.*
The ports, harbours, watering-places and coast
scenery of Great Britain Vols I and II.
Views taken on the spot by W.H. Bartlett.
G. Virtue. 1842.
13,24

BLANCHARD, Edward Litt. L.*
Adams's descriptive guide to the watering places
of England and companion to the coast (Dover,
Folkestone, Margate, Ramsgate, Gravesend, Herne
Bay).
W.J. Adams.
9,13 1848, 1849
13   1850
9,11,13,24 1851

COASTLINE   Cont'd

BOORMAN, L.A.
Ecology of Maplin Sands and the coastal zones
of Suffolk, Essex and North Kent,by L.A.Boorman
& D.S. Ranwell, Institute of Terrestrial Ecology.
Institute of Terrestrial Ecology, Natural
Environmental Research Council.   1977
3,4,11

BOOTH, Kenneth.
Comparative studies of landscape schemes 1 & 2.
and
Landscape scheme 1.
(Kenneth Booth FILA, Tunbridge Wells).
Whitstable Central Area Coast Protection. 1973.
31

BURNARD, F.C.*
The ZZG or Zig Zag Guide round & about the
bold and beautiful Kentish Coast.
A.&.C. Black Ltd 1897.
1,2,3,6,7,8,11,12,13,14,15,17,18,21,24

CHAMBERS, W. and R. Publishers*
Chambers' Handy Guide to the Kent & Sussex
Coast:- in six routes or districts.
W.&.R. Chambers, Edinburgh. 1863.
1,6,13,17,19.

COGHLAN, Francis.*
The steam-packet and coast companion, or
general guide to Gravesend, Herne Bay,
Canterbury, Margate, Broadstairs, Ramsgate,
Dover....
H. Hughes, London.   1832 etc.
6,9,11,12,13,14

CORDELL, Alan.
Old postcard views from the Walter Dowsett
Collection: compiled by Alan Cordell, Peter
Ferguson and Alan Pearsall. No 2.   The
Rivers and Coast of Kent.
Nautical Pictorial. 1978
11,12,23

DE SELINCOURT, Aubrey
The Channel Shore. (pp. 1 - 34 Kent Coast)
R. Hale. 1953.
11

DIXON-SCOTT, J. Photographer.*
Kent Coast & Countryside: camera pictures
of the county by J. Dixon-Scott, selected
by B. Prescott Row.
Homeland Association, 1929.
2,8,11,12

DOVER DISTRICT COUNCIL.
Further Report on coast protection at Deal
in Kent.
Dover District Council. 1979.
28
Preliminary Report on Coast protection
at Deal in Kent.
Dover District Council. 1979.
28

FINDEN, E.
Views of ports and harbours, watering places,
fishing villages and other picturesque objects
on the English coast.....
7   Tilt 1836
11 E.P. Publishing 1974.

FUSSELL, L.*
A journey round the coast of Kent....
Baldwin, Cradock & Joy.   1818
2,31

GRANVILLE, Augustus Bozzi.*
The Spas of England and principal Sea Bathing
places.   Southern Spas.
Henry Colburn, London 1841
11

GREY, H.
The Victorians by the seaside by H. Grey &
G. Stuart.
Academy. 1973.
13

GRIMSON, John.
Channel coasts of England.
Robert Hale. 1978
3,12,13,14

A GUIDE TO ALL THE WATERING & SEA BATHING PLACES,
by the Editor of "The Picture of London".
Longman. 1815.
13

HARPER, Charles George.*
The Kentish Coast.
Chapman & Hall.
22   1910
31   1914

HOWELL, S.
The Seaside.
Studio Vista. 1974.
13

HUNTER, G.Y.
Refuge harbours and coast defences.
W.C. Brasier. 1853
13

JOHN, Malcolm.
Bygone Thanet and Channel Coastlands.
Chambers Green Ltd. 1980.
28

THE KENT COAST GUIDE.
Constitutional Press. n.d.
24

KENT COUNTY COUNCIL: PLANNING DEPARTMENT
Kent County Structure Plan.   The Undeveloped
Coast. Report prepared in December 1976.
(Serial no. E.12)
K.C.C. 1976.
3,4,5,9,11,12,13,15

KENT RIGHTS OF WAY COUNCIL.
The Saxon Shore Way.
Kent Rights of Way Council, Teynham. 1980.
12

LACEY, Joseph Melville.*
Littoral drift along the North-east coast of
Kent, and the erosion of the Beltinge cliffs
near Herne Bay. Selected engineering papers No.72.
The Institute of Civil Engineers. 1929.
11,30

LEWIS, Arthur D.*
The Kent Coast.
T. Fisher Unwin. 1911
24,31

LINDLEY, Kenneth.
Seaside Architecture.
Hugh Evelyn. 1973.
7,14

MILLWARD, Ray.
S.E. England: The Channel Coastlands,by
R. Millward and A. Robinson
Macmillan. 1973.
14

NATIONAL PARKS COMMISSION: COASTAL PRESERVATION
AND DEVELOPMENT.
The coasts of Kent and Sussex. Report of the
Regional Coastal Conference held in London on
27th May 1966.
H.M.S.O. 1967
24,25

A NAVAL OFFICER. pseud (ROGIER,E.)*
A brief history of Dover & Ramsgate harbours,
with a description of the coasts between Dungeness
and the Isle of Thanet and remarks on the probable
construction of a harbour between the South
Foreland & Sandwich Haven, by a Naval Officer.
W.H. Brewer, Ramsgate 1837
1,11

COASTLINE Cont'd

PHILLIPS, Richard Publisher.
Guide to all the watering places and sea-
bathing places.
Richard Phillips. 1808.
19

REYNOLDS, Christopher.
Creatures of the bay.
Andre Deutsch. 1974.
3,24

RUSKIN, John.
The harbours of England, with thirteen
illustrations by J.M.W. Turner. Ruskins'
Commentaries on twelve Turner engravings
of English Harbours.
George Allen. 1895.
11

RUSSELL, W. Clark.*
Betwixt the Forelands.
Sampson Low. 1889
1,6,7,11,12,13,18

SEARLE, Muriel V.
Bathine machines and bloomers.
Midas. 1977
30

SEASIDE PIERS
A special issue of The Architects' Journal.
Vol. 162 No.39 24th September 1975.
(includes Herne Bay Pier)
3

SEYMOUR, John.
The companion guide to the coast of South-
East England.
Collins. 1975.
6,11,12,15,22,28

SMITH, Baker Peter.*
A journal of an excursion round the south-
eastern coast of England.
Printed by Gilbert & Rivington. 1834.
11

SMITH, W.H. & Sons. Publishers.*
Environs of Dover and the watering places of
Kent. (c.1865 - 70).
W.H. Smith & Son. n.d.
11

SO, C.L.
Some coastal changes between Whitstable and
Reculver, Kent.
In Proceedings of the Geologists' Association
Vol.77, pp. 475 - 490, 1966
30

STANFIELD, Clarkson.
Stanfield's coast scenery. A series of views
in the British Channel.
Smith Elder & Co. 1836.
24

STEERS, James Alfred.
The sea coast.
Collins. 1972.
28

THORNTON, Edward Charles Bexley.*
South Coast pleasure steamers.
Stephenson & Sons. Prescot.
12   1962
19   1969

THORPE, Teresa.*
The development of the coastline between Hampton
Pier and Reculver at Herne Bay. (Thesis).
Photocopy. 1970.
11,30

TITTLEY, Ian.
An Atlas of the Seaweeds of Kent by I. Tittley
and J.H. Price. Transactions of the Kent Field
Club. Vol.7 . 1977.
3,6,7,8,11,13,23.

TURNER, Keith.
Pier Railways.
(includes Herne Bay & Hythe pp. 9 - 17)
Oakwood Press. 1972.
11,30

A VISITOR'S GUIDE TO THE WATERING PLACES or
a summer excursion round the coast of England.
W. Strange. 1842.
24

WALCOTT, Mackenzie E.C.*
A guide to the coast of Kent: descriptive of
scenery, historical legendary and archaeological.
E. Stanford. 1859.
24

WARD LOCK & CO. LTD. Publishers.
The complete South-East Coast: the coast resorts
from Whitstable to Selsey and excursions inland,
edited by Reginald J.W. Hammond.
Ward Lock. 1974.
11,26,28,30

Herne Bay, Whitstable, Seasalter and the Kent
Coast.*
n.d.
Ward Lock.
30

The Kent Coast (Red Guides).*
Ward Lock & Co. 1961
30

THE WATERING PLACES OF GREAT BRITAIN.* and
fashionable directory.
Hinton, London.
11,17,18,24   1831
6,13   1833

WHITSTABLE CIVIC SOCIETY.*
Coastal preservation and development.
Whitstable Civic Society. 1964.
31

YOUNG, Kenneth.
Music's great days in the Spas and Watering places.
Macmillan 1968
13

COASTLINE-SEA DEFENCES

DU-PLAT-TAYLOR, M.*
A sea wall in Kent (A paper read to the British
Section of the Société des Ingenieurs Civils de
France, 14th April, 1932.
The Societé. 1932
7

ROYAL COMMISSION ON COAST EROSION.
First report of the Royal Commission appointed
to enquire into and to report on certain questions
affecting coast erosion and the reclamation of
tidal lands in the United Kingdom.Vol 1.
Parts I and II.
Part I First Report
Part II Minutes of evidence and appendices.
H.M.S.O. 1907.
11

Third (and final) report of the Royal Commission
appointed to inquire into and to report on
certain questions affecting coast erosion, the
reclamation of tidal lands, and afforestation in
the United Kingdom. Vol III. Parts I and II
Part I Report
Part II Minutes of evidence and appendices.
H.M.S.O. 1911
11

COASTLINE - SEA DEFENCES Cont'd

THORN, Roland Berkeley.*
The design of sea defence works.
Butterworth. 1960.
8,12

Sea defence works: design, construction and
emergency works. 2nd edited, by R.B. Thorn
and J.C.F. Simmons.
Butterworth. 1971
7,11

COBHAM

ARNOLD, Ralph.*
Cobham Hall - Kent; notes on the house, its
owners and the gardens and park and objects
of special interest.
Westwood Educational Trust. 1951?
11,25

A yeoman of Kent: an account of Richard Hayes
(1725 - 1790) and of the village of Cobham.
Constable. 1949.
1,2,3,4,5,6,7,9,11,12,15,17,18,19,25

BAKER, Alfred.
The parish church of St. Mary Magdelene, Cobham,
Kent, compiled by Mr & Mrs. Alfred Baker
Brewsters, Rochester. (1973?).
11

COBHAM HALL, KENT. formerly the seat of the
Dukes of Lennox and Richmond and their des-
cendents the Blighs, Earls of Darnley, and
now the property of the Westwood Educational
Trust.
English Life Publications. 1973.
2,7,9,11,19,25,30

COBHAM PAROCHIAL CHURCH COUNCIL.*
History of the Parish Church of Cobham,
(St. Mary Magdalene).
Cobham Parochial Church Council.
9 1970
9 1973 revised edition

KENT COUNTY COUNCIL:PLANNING DEPARTMENT.*
Cobham:Village study.
K.C.C. 1970.
8,12,13,16,19,20,25,30

THE SEALED KNOT AT COBHAM HALL, 2nd-3rd
September, 1978. Souvenir programme.
4

SMITH, Charles Roach.
On a hoard of Roman Coins discovered
in Cobham Park and preserved by the
Earl of Darnley - 1883.
Anglebooks. 1973.
1

TESTER, P.J.
Notes on the medieval chantry college of
Cobham.
Reprinted from Archaeologia Cantiana,
Vol. LXXIX 1964.
11.

UGARTE, F. Perez.
The Cads of Cobham: a history of the Cobham
Amateur Dramatic Society.
Cobham Amateur Dramatic Society. 1974.
9

WALLER, John G.
On the fate of Henry Brooke, tenth Lord
Cobham. Read to the Society of Antiquaries
of London on December 6th 1877.
The Society. 1877
11

YE OLDE LEATHER BOTTLE, Cobham, Kent,
immortalised by Charles Dickens.
printed by F.A. Clements, Chatham. (19--?).
(Leaflet issued by The Leather Bottle)
11

COINS & TOKENS

JENKINSON, Hilary.
Mediaeval tallies, public and private.
Read to the Society of Antiquaries of London,
31st January, 1924.
From the Proceedings. Vol.LXXIV. 1924.
11

ROLFE, H.W.*
Plates taken from "Kentish tokens of the
seventeenth century" communicated to the
Numismatic Society of London.
The Society. (1862)
11

SMITH, Charles Roach.
On a hoard of Roman Coins discovered in
Cobham Park and preserved by the Earl of
Darnley...in 1883.
Anglebooks. 1973.
1

THOMPSON, R.H.
John Boxer and the nineteenth century silver
tokens of Kent.
Oxford University Press. 1972.
7

TILLEY, Ernest W.
The seventeenth-century token issues of
Gravesend & Milton-next-Gravesend.
Reprinted from Archaeologia Cantiana. Vol.
LXXXV 1970.
Printed by Headley Bros. Ashford. 1971.
9

TRADESMEN'S TOKENS issued in the Isle of
Thanet...and the Cinque Ports. (From Bibliotheca
Topographica Britannica).
1,11

COMMUNICATIONS

WILSON, Geoffrey.
The old telegraphs.
(London to South Foreland telegraph p.86-91)
Phillimore. 1976.
3,11,28

CONRAD, JOSEPH. (1857 - 1924)
HAD VARIOUS RESIDENCES WITHIN KENT.

CONRAD, Borys.
Coach tour of Joseph Conrad's homes in Kent.
Written and published by Joseph Conrad's Son,
Borys Conrad.
Printed by Farnham Printing Company,Farnham. 1974.
3,8,11,26

DALESKI, H.M.
Joseph Conrad: the way of dispossesion
Faber & Faber. 1977
3

SHERRY, Norman.
Joseph Conrad: a commemoration, edited by N.Sherry
Macmillan. 1976.
3

STALLMAN, R.W.
The art of Joseph Conrad; a critical symposium
edited by R.W. Stallman.
Michigan State University Press. 1960.
3

CONSERVATION See also
NATURAL HISTORY, TOWNS VILLAGES ETC.

ANDERSON, Peggy.
A proposed plan and management scheme for the
North Downs Country Park near Trottiscliffe.
(Discussion papers in Conservation No.10)
University College, London. 1975.
2

CIVIC TRUST.
Index of conservation areas. (pp.22 - 26
Kent Section)
Civic Trust. 1974.
11

Supplement to the Index of Conservation areas.
(p.7 Kent Section).
Civic Trust. 1976.
11

CONSERVATION SOCIETY (LTD) KENT BRANCH.
Comments on the Kent County Council's con-
sultation documents in connection with the
County Structure Plan.
Conservation Society Ltd. April 1976.
4

DEFEND KENT: a conservation magazine published
in Kent, edited by Brian Hawkes and Brian
Mitchell. Annual publication.
"Defend Kent".
Orcombe, Peckham Bush.
24   1968, 1969, 1970, 1972, 1973
4,7,11,30   1973
13   1968

JERMY, A.C.
Chalk grassland: studies on its conservation and
management in South-East England, by A.C. Jermy
and P.A. Stott. (pp. 55 - 56 Kent Properties)
Kent Trust for Nature Conservation.
1973   2,3,4,6,11,12
1975   2nd edition. 2,4,6,

KENT COUNCIL OF SOCIAL SERVICE.- COMMITTEE FOR
THE PRESERVATION OF RURAL KENT.*
Kent today
Kent Council of Social Service. 1938.
1,2,4,6,8,11,12,16,26

KENT COUNTY COUNCIL: PLANNING DEPARTMENT.
Conservation Policy Statement.
K.C.C. 1973.
3,4,7,8,11,12,13,16,19,20,25

Kent County Structure Plan. Conservation and
character of the built environment. (Adopted
by Local Planning Authority in June, 1975).
(Serial No. 5B).
K.C.C. 1975
3,4,9,11,13,16

Kent County Structure Plan. Rural Conservation.
(a) Landscape, (b) Nature conservation.
(Serial no. 7B).
K.C.C. 1975.
3,4,9,11,13,16

KLOEDEN, Judith L.
An ecological assessment of alluvial grassland
in the Beult River Valley, Kent - (Discussion
Papers in Conservation No.11)
University College, London. 1975.
2

MEDWAY PRESERVATION SOCIETY.*
The effects of a M.I.D.A. (Medway Industrial ˙
Development Area) on the Medway Estuary: a report
prepared by the Medway Preservation Society.
(Includes lists of birds and flowers)
Medway Preservation Society. 1971.
4,8,11

The future of the North Kent Marshes: a survey.*
The Society. 1974.
4,11,20,27

WEALD OF KENT PRESERVATION SOCIETY.
The first ten years, 1960 - 1970, the record
of an Amenity Society.
Elvey & Gibbs Partnership, Ashford. 1970.
7

WHITSTABLE CIVIC SOCIETY.*
Coastal Preservation and development.
The Society. 1964.
11,31

CONYER

SATTIN, Donald L.
Just off the Swale: the story of the Barge
Building village of Conyer.
Meresborough Books. 1978.
3,12,22,23

COOLING

NICHOLS, W.N.
Cooling, Kent, and its castle.
W.N. Nichols. Redhill, 1980.
4,6,22,28

COURT-AT-STREET

ELLISTON-ERWOOD, Frank Charles.*
Notes on the Architecture of Aldington Church,
Kent, and the Chapel at Court-at-Street, called
"Bellirica".
Kent Archaeological Society. n.d.
1,11,17

MOULTON, W.R.
Guide to Lympne Church and Castle, Studfall,
Shepway, West Hythe and Court-at-Street.
F.J. Parsons. (c. 1926).
7,11.

COURTENAY, SIR WILLIAM. P.H.
PSEUD. JOHN NICHOLS THOM (OR TOM). 1796 - 1838.

"CANTERBURIENSIS" pseud.*
The life and extraordinary adventures of Sir
William Courtenay, Knight of Malta, alias
John Nichols Tom....
James Hunt, Canterbury. 1838.
3,6,7,11,12,13,14,26

CANTERBURY TALE OF FIFTY YEARS AGO*-
the extraordinary career of Sir William Courtenay.
Cross & Jackman, Canterbury. 1888
3,6,11,12,19
17   1882

A COMPLETE AND CORRECT BIOGRAPHICAL HISTORY
of Sir William Courtenay.*
S. Prentice. Canterbury. 1838.
3

THE ECCENTRIC AND SINGULAR PRODUCTIONS OF SIR*
William Courtenay, K.M. alias Mr. Tom.
Henry Ward, Canterbury. n.d.
3,11.14

AN ESSAY ON THE CHARACTER OF Sir W. Courtenay.*
Henry Ward. Canterbury 183- etc.
3,6,14,17.

LIFE OF SIR WILLIAM COURTENAY.*
An article in the Penny Satirist, No.60.
June 9th 1838.
3.

ROGERS, Philip George.*
Battle in Bossenden Wood: the strange story of
Sir William Courtenay.
Oxford University Press. 1961.
1,3,4,5,6,7,8,11,12,15,17,18,20.
Reader's Union Edition. O.U.P. 1962.
2,11,20,25,26,

COURTENAY, Sir William Cont'd

THE TRIAL AND SENTENCE OF THE KNIGHT OF MALTA,
for perjury, being the second part of the
Canterbury Tale of the year 1833.
(Tracts No.4)   (Sir William Courtenay).
Elizabeth Wood, Canterbury. (1833).
3

COWDEN

DUNCAN, Leland L.*
The rectory and rectors of Cowden, Kent.
Pamphlet reprinted from Archaelogia Cantiana
Vol.XXI.   1895
Mitchell & Hughes.   London.   1895.
11,17,18

CRANBROOK

CRANBROOK RURAL DISTRICT COUNCIL,
Cranbrook, Kent. Official Guide.
Directory Publishing Ltd. (c.1965)
11

CURTIS, Henry.
Pedigree of Joyce of Boxford, near Newbury,
Co. Berks, and of Cranbrook, Co. Kent; with
notes of the origin of the name Joyce and
pedigrees of the various other early
families named Joyce.
(Grangerised copy of original work)   1917
11

DAVISON, Ian.*
Chimes of Cranbrook.
Eagle Printing Works, Cranbrook, 1938.
3,19

KENT COUNTY COUNCIL: PLANNING DEPT.
Cranbrook:informal district plan,
including a conservation study. Draft.
K.C.C.   1974.
19
Cranbrook: informal district plan, including
a conservation study.
K.C.C.   1976.
2,11
Cranbrook: informal district plan. Proposals
Map A. Structure.   Scale 1 = 2500.
Size 70cm x 66cm.
KCC.   1975.
11
Cranbrook: informal district plan. Proposals
Map B. Environment.   Scale 1 - 2500
Size 80 cm x 67cm.
For use with written statement.
K.C.C. 1975.
11

NOYES, Robert.*
Nehemiah's advice to the Jews....a sermon...
preached at Cranbrook, 1755.
P.P. 1756.
11

The substance of a sermon, occasioned by the
death of Mr. William Roffey, who departed
this life at Cranbrook in Kent on the 12th of
December, 1771, aged 67 years and 7 days.
Preached on the evening of his interment.
Printed and Sold by T. Smith & Son. (1771?)
Canterbury.
3

PILE, Cecil Charles Relf.*
Cranbrook: a Wealden Town.
Cranbrook & Sissinghurst Local History Society 1955.
2
Cranbrook broadcloth and the clothiers. 2nd
edition.
Cranbrook & Sissinghurst Local History Society 1967.
7,11

ROBINSON, Duncan H.*
Cranbrook School. A Brief History.
(Cranbrook notes and records No.9)
Cranbrook & District Local History Society 1971.
2,8

ROSE, George.
Remembered mercies recorded: an account of the
Lord's leadings. (The author was pastor of the
Cranbrook Strict Baptist Chapel. pp.140-252)
D.G. Woodham, Liverpool.   1952.
11

SIMMONS, W.T. Publisher.
Cranbrook almanac for 1915.
W.T. Simmons, Cranbrook.   1915.
19

TARBUTT, William.*
The ancient cloth trade of Cranbrook. Reprinted
from Archaeologia Cantiana Vol. IX 1874.
4

VALLANCE, Aymer.
A curious case at Cranbrook in 1437. Reprinted
from Archaeologia Cantiana Vol. XLIII, 1931.
11.

WAILES, Rex.*
The English Windmill.
Routledge & Kegan Paul.   1954.
11 1954
23 1977

WATERS, H. Bookseller.
Book of views of the Cranbrook area.
H. Waters, Bookseller, Cranbrook.   190-?
11

WOLVERHAMPTON CENTRAL ART GALLERY.
The Cranbrook Colony(Exhibition catalogue
Jan 22nd - March 12th 1977)
Cranbrook Colony - F.D. Hardy, G. Hardy,
J.C. Horsley, A.E. Mulready, G.B.O'Neil,
T. Webster.
Central Art Gallery, Wolverhampton. 1977.
11,19,23

CRAY, RIVER

BERENS, Edward.*
The Seven churches on the River Cray.
Printed by Gilbert & Rivington.   1830
1,5,11,17
2 photocopy

ROLES, Stephen.
Manufacturing industry of the Cray Valley.
Unpublished thesis.   1978.
2

CRAYFORD

BARNETT, E.J.
Crayford.   1889 - 1949
Typescript.
1

BEXLEY CIVIC SOCIETY.
Borough Walk I. Around old Crayford.
As author. 1977.
1

CHANDLER, Raymond H.*
The implements and caves of Crayford. 1915-16
17

DENNEY, Martin.
London's Waterways. (covers the Dartford
and Crayford Navigation)
Batsford. 1977
5

EVANS, Harold.
Vickers: against the odds, 1956 - 1977
(Works at Crayford & Dartford).
Hodder & Stoughton.   1978.
5

TREBILCOCK, Clive.
The Vickers Brothers: armaments and enterprise
1854 - 1914.
Europa Publications. 1977.
5.

CRICKET

ARROWSMITH, Robert Langford.*
Kent (History of County Cricket - Series)
Arthur Barker. 1971
2,12

ASHLEY-COOPER, F.S.
John Wisden's cricket match histories, I.
- Kent v. Surrey. 1731 - 1921
Wisden. 1921
11

ASSOCIATION OF KENT CRICKET CLUBS.
Cricket in Kent. Nos 1 & 2 edited by
H.A.W. Daniels: No.3 edited by E.W.Duckett.
Published by the Association.
*No 1. 1954. 3,6,20
*No 2. 1955. 2,4,6,11,20
*No 3. 1956. 1,3,6,11,20
 No 5. 1958 (West Kent Zone edition) 20
 No 6. 1959 20
 No 24. 1977 9

BARTY-KING, Hugh.
Quilt winders and pod shavers. (the history
of cricket bat and ball manufacture, a
Tonbridge area industry)
Macdonald and Jane's 1979
23

BENNETT, Walter.
Sidcup Cricket Club, 1877-1977: a history
and reference book compiled by W. Bennett on
behalf of the Club. (250 copies printed)
Sidcup Cricket Club. 1977
1,11

BEXLEY CRICKET CLUB.
150th Anniversary handbook.
Bexley Cricket Club. 1955.
1

BLANCHE, Robin.
"M.C.C.": a survey of the Maxton Cricket Club
during the period 1964 - 74 (Dover.)
P.P. 1975
6

CANTERBURY CRICKET WEEK:* an authentic
narrative of the origin and career of the
institution, including the programmes of the
"Old Stagers" performances...Vol I.
Matches recorded: 1839 - 1851.
William Davy. Canterbury. 1865.
1,3,4,11

CARDUS, Neville.
The noblest game: a book of fine cricket
prints by N. Cardus and John Arlott.
Harrap. 1969
23

CHEESEMAN, Dick.
The Sennocke Cricket Club, 1942 - 1963,
a short history. Typescript. n.d.
16

COWDREY, Michael Colin (Captain of Kent
1967 - 72).
The incomparable game.
Hodder & Stoughton. 1970.
11
M.C.C. - the autobiography of a cricketer.
Hodder & Stoughton. 1976.
3.8.11.12.15
Tackle cricket.Revised edition.
S. Paul 1974
11
Time for reflection.*
Muller, 1962.
11

DARTFORD CRICKET FESTIVAL COMMITTEE.
History of cricket in Dartford,250 years.
Dartford Cricket Festival Committee. 1978.
5

DENNESS, Mike (Kent Cricketer 1962-1977).
I declare.
A. Barker. 1977
3,11

DIMONT, Charles.
Brian Luckhurst Benefit, 1973.
Contributors: L.E.G. Ames & others; edited by
C. Dimont.   Printed by:
J.A. Jennings for Kent County Cricket Club,
Canterbury. 1973.
11,30

EVANS, Godfrey (Kent & England Wicket-*
Keeper 1946 - 59).
Behind the stumps.
Hodder & Stoughton. 1951
11
The gloves are off.*
Hodder & Stoughton. 1960
11

EVANS, John.
Kent, the winning eleven.
Kent County Cricket Club. Canterbury. 1978
3

FOWLE, Dennis.
Kent - the glory years (Cricket 1967-73),
edited by D. Fowle.
Everest Books. 1973.
6,11,28

GOULSTONE, John.*
Cricket in Kent, compiled by J. Goulstone
(Limited edition of 50 copies)
International Research Publications.
9, 23, 1972
12   1974
Early Club and Village Cricket. (General book
on the history of the clubs with a Kent Section).
Typescript 100 copies.
3.4.5.6.7.8. 1972
Early Kent Cricketers, 2nd edition.
International Research Publications, 1972.
3,9

GUNYON, William P.
A history of Meopham Cricket Club.
Meopham Cricket Club. 1976.
4,8,9,11,15,25

HARRIS, George Robert Canning 4th Baron Harris
1851 - 1932.
A few short runs.*
J. Murray. 1921.
11
Hints to young cricketers, by Lord Harris; also
the laws of cricket and other useful matter
connected with the game.
John Wisden:London
J. Burgess-Brown, Maidstone (1895?)
3
The History of Kent County Cricket.* edited
by G.R.C. Harris.
Eyre & Spottiswoode. 1907.
25
The History of Kent County Cricket,*
Appendix F. 1910 - 1923.
Gibbs & Sons, Canterbury. 1924.
3
The History of Kent County Cricket,*
Appendix H. 1946 - 1963.
Kent County Cricket Club. Canterbury. 1964.
1,2,3,4,5,11,20,30
Kent Cricket Matches, 1719 - 1880.*
edited by G.R.C. Harris & F.S. Ashley-Cooper.
Gibbs & Sons, Canterbury. 1929.
2,3,23

HAWKE, Martin Bladen Baron Hawke.
Memorial Biography of W.G. Grace, edited by
M.B. Hawke and others. (W.G. Grace was a
resident of Mottingham & Sydenham).
Constable 1919.
2

CRICKET Cont'd

IGGLESDEN, Sir Charles.*
Sixty-six years' memories of Kent Cricket
Kentish Express, Ashford. 1947.
26

KENT COUNTY CRICKET CLUB.
Annual (Entitled "Yearbook" up to 1951)
J.A. Jennings. Canterbury.
* 3 1948 in progress
* 4 1953-54; 1957-1966; 1969 - 70; 1973.
* 6 1933 (first year of issue).
* 8 1971
* 9 1954;1957;1960-63; 1969-72; 1974 in
  11 1973   progress
  12 1974
* 13 1934-36; 1965; 1971
  15 1969; 1976
  23 1973
* 30 1933; 1950; 1952-53; 1955-62; 1964; 1966 -
     1978 in progress

Centenary Appeal 1870 - 1970.
Kent County Cricket Club. 1969
3

Gillette Cup Final, 1971. (Kent Cricketers'
Souvenir Programme.
Kent County Cricket Club. 1971
3

One Hundred years of Kent Cricket, 1870-1970.*
Kent County Cricket Club. 1970
4,30

Rules, lists of subscribers, matches played in 1935*.
J.A. Jennings, Canterbury. 1935
30

KNOTT, Alan.*
(Kent & England Wicket-Keeper).
Stumper's View.
S. Paul. 1972.
8

MARRIOTT, Charles Stowel
(Played for Kent, Leg-break bowler)
The Complete leg-break Bowler.
Eyre & Spottiswoode. 1968
12

NEW ARTICLES OF THE GAME OF CRICKET. as settled
and revised at the Stour and Garter, Pall Mall,
February 25th 1774, by a committee of
noblemen and gentlemen of Kent, etc....
J. Blake. Maidstone. 1774.
11

NORMAN GRAHAM Benefit Souvenir. 1977.
(Kent Bowler)
1977
3

PEEBLES, Ian.*
Woolley - the pride of Kent.
(Kent & England Cricketer)
Hutchinson. 1969.
3

TAYLOR, Alfred D.*
The story of a cricket picture (Sussex & Kent)
(First published by Emery in 1923)
SR Publishers. 1972.
6,11

THOMPSON, P.A.
History of the Hayes (Kent) Cricket Club.
1828 - 1978.
Hayes Cricket Club. 1978.
2

UNDERWOOD, Derek.
(Kent and England Cricketer)
Beating the Bat.
Hutchinson. 1975.
8

WARNER, Harold William.
A History of Beverley Cricket Club, 1835 -
1959.
J.A. Jennings, Canterbury. (1959).
3,4,8,12

Story of Canterbury Cricket Week.
J.A. Jennings, Canterbury.(1959).
3,4,7,8,11,12,15

WARNER, Oliver.*
Frank Woolley.
Phoenix House. 1952.
11

WOOLLEY, Frank.
Early memories, as told to Martha Wilson Woolley.
The Cricketer Ltd. 1976.
7,11,19

The King of Games.*
Stanley Paul. 1935.
11

CRIME

BOTTOMS, A.E.
Criminals coming of age: a study of institutional
adaptation in the treatment of adolescent
offenders by A.E. Bottoms and F.H. McClintock.
(A study based on Dover Borstal).
Heinemann. 1973.
11

CHATHAM STANDARD.
Crimes that shocked the Medway Towns: a series of
articles from the Chatham Standard.
Parrett & Neves. 1973.
3,4,8,11,20,25

CLARK, Tim.
Psychopath; the case of Patrick Mackay by
Tim Clark and John Penycate. (Gravesend
connection).
Routledge and Kegan Paul. 1976.
9

KENT COUNTY CONSTABULARY.
Analysis of crime in 1963
(Supplement 'A' Chief Constable's Report)
Kent County Constabulary. Maidstone. 1964.
4

LLOYD, John.
Anecdotes of John Lloyd, a pretended clergyman, who was committed to prison on Friday,
September 6th 1782, charged with several highway robberies...(and the) remarkable sermon
he preached at Gravesend....
Printed for A. Milne. 202 High Holborn,London 1782.
11

MELLING, Elizabeth.*
Crime and punishment: a collection of examples
from original sources in the Kent County Archives
Office from the 16th to the 19th century,
edited by Elizabeth Melling.
K.C.C. 1969.
3,20,25,27,31

REES-DAVIES, William Rupert.
The Conquest of crime.
(The author is M.P. for Thanet West).
Conservative Political Centre.
1970.
13

CROCKHAM HILL

WESTERHAM PARISH COUNCIL.
Westerham & Crockham Hill, Kent. Official
Guide. Published with the authority of the
Westerham Parish Council.
Forward Publicity Ltd. 1975.
4,11

CRYSTAL PALACE

BEAVER, Patrick.*
Crystal Palace, 1851 - 1936; a portrait of
Victorian Enterprise.
Hugh Evelyn. 1970.
11

BELL-KNIGHT, C.A.
The Crystal Palace: its rise, its decline,
its fall.
The Author. 1976.
18

CRYSTAL PALACE PENNY GUIDE.*
Robert K. Burt. Crystal Palace Printing
Office. (1867).
11

MEASOM, George.
The official illustrated guide to the Brighton
& South Coast Railway and its branches,
including a descriptive guide to the Crystal
Palace at Sydenham.
Waterlow, London. 1859.
11

CUSTOMS

FIELD, Bartlett.
The Hodden Horse of East Kent.
The Author. 1967.
7

HARRIS, Edwin.*
Curious Kentish customs.
E. Harris, Rochester. 1899.
4

HARROD, Henry.
On the mantle and the ring of widowhood. Read
to the Society of Antiquaries of London on
February 16th 1865.
11.

JEWELL, Brian.
Fairs and Revels.
Midas Books. 1976.
23

THE KENTISH HOODEN HORSE TODAY, in English
Dance and Song May/June 1957. Vol.XXI No.5
7

NEILSON, N.
Custom and the common law in Kent in
Harvard Law Review v.38 No.4
Feb. 1925.
2

SMALL, Julia.
The Hooden Horse: an East Kent Custom.
Maritime & Local History Museum, Deal. (1975).
3

TYRWHITT-DRAKE, Sir Hugh Garrard.
The English Circus & Fairground.
The Author lived at Cobtree Manor, Maidstone).
Methuen.
12 1946 1st edition
11 1947 2nd edition

WHITLOCK, Ralph.
A calendar of Country Customs.
B.T. Batsford. 1978.
11

CUXTON

CHURCH, Derek.
Cuxton: a Kentish village.
A.J. Cassell, Sheerness. 1976.
2,3,4,6,8,9,11,13,15,16,22,25,30

DARENT, RIVER & VALLEY

BRADLEY, Arthur Granville.
The rivers and streams of England, painted by
Sutton Palmer. (Includes River Darent).
A.&.C. Black. 1909.
4

DARTFORD BOROUGH COUNCIL.
Darent Valley in Dartford: its problems and
opportunities. (Report).
Dartford Borough Council. 1979.
5

PHILP, Brian.
Archaeological excavations in the Darent
Valley by Brian and Edna Philp.
Kent Archaeological Rescue Unit (CIB).
1974.   2.3.5.6.8.9.11.16
1975.   2,5,6,8,9,16
1977   11.

ROGERS, Philip George.*
A Vale in Kent: a historical guide to the
Darent Valley.
P.M.E. Erwood(Publications)Ltd. Welling. 1955.
13,16,26

WHITNEY, John.
The genteel recreation.....(Poetical description
of the Rivers Darent and Medway).
Johnson. 1820.
11

DARENTH

CAIGER, John E.L.
Two Brasses:
The Crepehege Brass at Darenth, by J.E.L.
Caiger.
Reprinted from Archaeologia Cantiana. Vol.67 1962.
Headley Bros. Ashford. 1962.
30

LITTLE CHURCH OVER THE HILL (St. Margaret's
Darenth).
Rev. Griffin, Dartford, Kent. 1980.
5

DARTFORD

ATKIN, Stanley.
50 years of service: Rotary Club of Dartford,
1929 - 79.
Rotary Club. Dartford. 1979.
5

BROOK, Cyril A.*
Deneholes - Dartford District: observations
taken Autust 3rd - 12th 1935, by C.A. Brook
and S. Priest.
Typescript.
5

DARTFORD BOROUGH COUNCIL.
Darent Valley in Dartford: its problems and
opportunities. (Report).
Dartford Borough Council. 1979.
5

Official guide.Commemorative edition.
Home Publishing Company Ltd(1974).
4

Official Guide, Dartford Borough.
Home Publishing Company.Ltd. 1980.
5

DARTFORD CONGREGATIONAL CHURCH.
Church accounts, 1885 - 1905.
5

Church Meeting Minutes, 1847 - 1877; 1905-1908
1908 - 1911, 1911 - 1926; 1926-1951.5 vols.
5

Deacons' Meeting Minutes, 1905 - 1918; 1918 -
1951. 2 vols.
5

DARTFORD CONSTITUENCY CONSERVATIVE ASSOCIATION.
Dartford: town and rural.
Conservative Association, Dartford. 1978.
5

DARTFORD CRICKET FESTIVAL COMMITTEE.
History of Cricket in Dartford, 250 years.
Dartford Cricket Festical Committee.1978.
5

DARTFORD DISTRICT ANTIQUARIAN SOCIETY.*
Report, balance sheet and list of members.
Dartford District Antiquarian Society. n.d.
5

DARTFORD FIRE BRIGADE.
Claims and reports, 4th December, 1897.
- 29th October, 1916.
Dartford Fire Brigade. 1897 - 1916.
5

DARTFORD FOOTBALL CLUB.
Official handbook, 1972 - 73.
Dartford Football Club. 1972.
5

DARTFORD OVERSEERS OF THE POOR.
An assessment...For and toward the necessary
relief of the poor of the parish of Dartford
...at one shilling in the pound full rents.
(Covers part of 1760 and part of 1761)
Photocopy of original material in Kent
County Library.
5

DARTFORD URBAN DISTRICT COUNCIL.
Official guide to Dartford, Kent.
Edward J. Burrow. (1930).
11

DAVIS, William J.*
An illustrated guide to Dartford.
J.&.W. Davis. 1902
5

DENNEY,Martin.
London's Waterways.
(Covers Dartford & Crayford Navigation).
Batsford. 1977.
5

ENVIRONMENT. Department of the
List of buildings of special architectural
or historic interest: District of
Dartford, Kent. Dartford area.
H.M.S.O. 1975.
11

EVANS, Harold.
Vickers: against the odds, 1956 - 1977.
(Works at Crayford & Dartford).
Hodder & Stoughton.
1978.
5

GOULSTONE, John.
Records of the Scudder and Skudder families
in the Dartford district. (Dartford wills
and connections with Cobham, Darenth &
Erith). Typescript. 1973.
5

GREAT BRITAIN, Laws etc. (Eliz.II).
STATUTORY INSTRUMENTS.
Highways, England & Wales. The London -
Canterbury - Dover Trunk Road. Dartford Diversion
Order 1963.
H.M.S.O. 1963.
8

The South Orbital Road (Princes Road to
Dartford Diversion)Order 1965.
H.M.S.O. 1965.
8

HALL-THERMOTANK LTD.
Hall-Thermotank Ltd, 100 years cold, 1877 -
1977. (Contribution to a centenary of
refrigeration).
Hall-Thermotank. Dartford. 1977.
5

Hall-Thermotank Products Ltd.
Hall-Thermotank, Dartford. 1977
5

HODGE, James.
Richard Trevithick. (Pioneer of the great
mechanical developments of tne XIXth Century
and "Father" of the Steam locomotive, died
at Dartford in 1833).
Shire Publications Ltd. 1973.
5

HOLY TRINITY, PARISH CHURCH OF DARTFORD.
Holy Trinity Review, January 1970 -
December 1971
5

KENT COUNTY COUNCIL: EDUCATION DEPARTMENT.
Dartford Adult Education Centre: Adult
Education in and around Dartford 1976 - 77
K.C.C.(1976).
11

KENT COUNTY LIBRARY: DARTFORD DIVISION.
Halls for hire in the Dartford district.
Dartford Divisional Library.
5   1st edition 1977 and 2nd Edition 1980

LOVEJOY,(Derek)& Partners.
Littlebrook Power Station (Dartford) landscape
plan.
The Authors. 1973.
5

MACDONALD, Gilbert.
One hundred years: Wellcome 1880 - 1980.
In pursuit of excellence.
(The Wellcome Research Laboratory is at
Beckenham, also at Dartford).
Wellcome Foundation. 1980.
2,5.

McFEE, William.
Sir Martin Frobisher.
(In 1557 Frobisher returned with a cargo of
ore from N. America, it was smelted at
Dartford. Found to be of no value and used
in rebuilding the precinct wall of the Priory
- part still remains at J.&.E. Hall's works).
John Lane. The Bodley Head. 1928.
5

A NOTE OF SUCH AS HAVE BEEN EXPENDITORS and
have passed their account...(list of landowners
responsible for marsh or grazing land in
Dartford and district, 1626 - 85) (Typewritten
transcript from original in Dunkin Collection,
Kent County Library, the Dunkin Collection. 1973.
5

PORTEUS, Geoff.
The book of Dartford.
Barracuda Books. Buckingham. 1979.
5,6,16,22,28

PORTEUS, Geoff.
Dartford Parish Church of the Holy Trinity,
900th anniversary appeal.
Anniversary Appeal Committee,Dartford. 1980
5

REDSHAW, Charles T.*
Dartford & neighbourhood.
Snowden Bros. Dartford, 1911?
1,5,11,15,17,25

ROBSON, George.*
A sermon preached at Dartford at the visitation
of the Right Reverend, the Lord Bishop of
Rochester...1800, by George Robson, Rector
of Snodland.
James Robson. 1800
5,15

DARTFORD Cont'd

THE TEMPLE HILL LINK.
New series 109 - 143. April 1968 - March 1971.
(St. Edmund's Parish Church, Dartford).
5

TREBILCOCK, Clive.
The Vickers Brothers: armaments and enterprise,
1854 - 1914.
(Factories at Dartford & Crayford).
Europa Pubns. 1977.
5

TREVITHICK SOCIETY.
The Journal of the Trevithick Society.
Vol.1: 1973.
Trevithick Society 1973.
5.

THE TRIAL.(at large) of Joseph Stacpoole,
William Capper & James Lagier for wilfully and
maliciously shooting at John Parker; tried...
1777... Taken in shorthand by Joseph Gurney.
Printed for G. Kearsly. 1777.
11

WELLCOME FOUNDATION LTD.

(Administrative Headquarters and Research
Laboratory at Beckenham, also at Dartford).

Foundation News, 1970 - 71; 1972 - 73.
Wellcome Foundation
5.

Some achievements of the Wellcome Foundation.
Wellcome Foundation. (1965).
2.

The Wellcome Foundation: Company with a
difference.
Wellcome Foundation. 1980.
2

WHARTON, Florence Ann.
The social conditions of Dartford.
Holograph copy, c.1910.
5

WHITING, Crispin.
Attitudes towards the poor in the first half
of the eighteenth century; the aims and
actualities of the Parish Workhouse at
Dartford in Kent. (photocopy of typescript -
thesis for the University of Kent). 1978.
5

WIGGINS TEAPE.*
Dartford paper mills:issued to commemorate their
opening.
Wiggins Teape. (1958).
1,4,5,7,8,11,12,17,

DARTFORD TUNNEL

COODE, FITZMAURICE, WILSON & MITCHELL.
(Consulting Engineers).
Letterbook containing copies of letters sent
between 5th February, 1924 - 13th September
1930 concerning the proposed Gravesend -
Tilbury and Dartford - Purfleet tunnels.
(The Gravesend Tilbury Tunnel was not built)
1930?
11

DARTFORD TUNNEL JOINT COMMITTEE.
General Manager's Reports.
Printed by K.C.C. Supplies Dep.
* 3,4,11   1972
* 5   1963 in progress
  8   1973; 1976
  12   1973; 1974
*13   1969;1971;1972;1973;1974;1976.

DARTFORD TUNNEL JOINT COMMITTEE.*
A new Thames tunnel.
Printed by K.C.C. Supplies Department. 1964.
3,13

DARTFORD TUNNEL JOINT CONSULTATIVE COMMITTEE.
The Second Dartford Tunnel.
Dartford Tunnel Joint Committee. 1980.
5

DARWIN, CHARLES ROBERT. (1809 - 1882)
LIVED AT DOWNE

ALLEN, Grant.*
Charles Darwin.
Longmans,Green. 1885.
12

BRITISH MUSEUM: NATURAL HISTORY
Memorials of Charles Darwin: a collection of
manuscripts,portraits,medals,books and natural
history specimens to commemorate the centenary
of his birth and the fiftieth anniversary of
the publication of the "Origin of the Species".
British Museum. 1909.
11

DARWIN,Charles.
Darwin's notebooks on the transmutation of
species Part 1. First notebook(July 1837 -
February 1838), edited by Sir Gavin de Beer.
1960.
4

DARWIN,Charles Robert.*
The life and letters of Charles Darwin,
including an autobiographical chapter, 2ndedition
John Murray. 1887.
2,4,

FLETCHER, F.D.
Darwin: an illustrated life of Charles Darwin,
1809 - 1882.
Shire Publications. 1975.
11

FREEMAN, R.B.
Charles Darwin: a companion (note: biographical
rather than critical).
Dawson. 1978.
2

HIMMELFARB, Gertrude.
Darwin and the Darwinian revolution.
Chatto & Windus. 1959.
2

MOOREHEAD, Alan.*
Darwin and the Beagle.
Hamish Hamilton. 1969.
2

ROYAL COLLEGE OF SURGEONS OF ENGLAND.
Charles Darwin and Down House, prepared by Jessie
Dobson, Curator of the Anatomy Museum, Royal
College of Surgeons. (Guide book to the house).
E.&.S. Livingstone. 1959.
* 2,11   1959
Charles Darwin and Down House...
Churchill & Livingstone. 1971
8

Historical & descriptive catalogue of the *
Darwin Memorial at Down House, Downe, Kent.
E.&.S. Livingstone. 1969.
8.

DAVINGTON

BY ORDER OF THE CANTERBURY DIOCESAN BOARD OF
FINANCE;   For sale by Auction...on Thursday
6th April, 1972...Davington Priory and Nos.
3,4,5,6,7,& 8. Davington Hill, Faversham.
Burrows & Co. Auctioneers. (1972).
3

DAVINGTON   Cont'd

CATALOGUE OF THE FIRST PORTION OF THE
IMPORTANT LIBRARY OF THOMAS WILLEMENT,Esq.,
F.S.A,* compiled by C.R. Smith. (Thomas
Willement lived at Davington).
Printed by Davy & Sons, London. 1865.
11,26

GIBBS, Christopher.
Davington Priory: Admission brochure,
Saturday June 1st, Sunday June 2nd. (1973)
Faversham Society. (1973).
11

Davington Priory: admission brochure,
June 7th & 8th 1974.
Faversham Society (1974).
11

TAYLOR, Michael Minter.*
The Davington Light Railway. Locomotive
Papers No.40.
Oakwood Press. 1968.
2,20,26.

WAINWRIGHT, Clive.
Davington Priory. Reprinted from Country
Life of 9th & 16th December, 1971.
(The home of the late Mr. George Roberts).
11,20

WILLEMENT, Thomas.*
Historical sketch of the parish of Davington
in the County of Kent and of the priory
there dedicated to St. Mary Magdalene.
Basil MontaguePickering. 1862.
25,26

DEAL

CAMPBELL, Sir Guy.
Golf at Prince's (Sandwich) and at Deal.
Newman Neame Ltd. 195-?
11

COLLINS, Barbara.*
Discovering Deal (historic guide). Deal
entertainments & Publicity Committee.
Deal Borough Council. 1969.
30

DEAL AND WALMER COMMUNITY ASSOCIATION.
Proposed centre for the Deal & Walmer
Community Association: Report to the Dover
District Council.
Deal & Walmer Community Association. 1979.
28

DEAL BI-MILLENARY PAGEANT, 55 BC - AD1949,
at Walmer Castle, August 4th - 6th, 1949.
Souvenir Programme.   Printed by:
T.F. Pain & Sons, Deal. 1949.
11

DEAL BOROUGH COUNCIL.
Deal & Walmer: the historic holiday resort.
Official Guide.
Deal Borough Council. (1939)
11

DEAL BOROUGH COUNCIL: ENTERTAINMENTS DEPT.
Deal: official guide.   Printed by:
Thanet Printing Works - Ramsgate. 1974.
11,12,28

DEAL BOROUGH COUNCIL: PUBLICITY DEPARTMENT.
Deal: the early story of Deal, its people and
Roman invaders.
Deal Borough Council. 1970.
12

DEAL,WALMER & DISTRICT HISTORY SOCIETY.
Deal and its place in the European
Architectural Heritage.
The Society. (197-).
6,28,29

DEAL, WALMER AND DISTRICT HISTORY SOCIETY.
Deal for the visitor, with street map.
The Society. 1976.
11

The Deal scene, 1887 - 1977.
(illustrations with commentaries. In memory
of HARRY FRANKS, Local Historian).
Deal,Walmer & District History Society
and Deal Maritime & Local History Museum. 1977.
3,6,11

DOVER & DEAL PARLIAMENTARY CONSTITUENCY.
Register of Electors. 1975. (In 2 vols)
6

DOVER DISTRICT COUNCIL.
Further report on Coast Protection at Deal
in Kent.
Dover District Council. 1979.
28

Preliminary Report on Coast Protection at
Deal in Kent.
Dover District Council. 1979.
28

Sandwich, Deal & Dover.
Dover District Council.Printed Buckland Press,
Dover.
28 1973; 1976; 1977.

ENVIRONMENT, Dept of.
List of buildings of special archaeological
interest in the Borough of Deal.
H.M.S.O. 1974.
7.11

FRANKLIN, W.H. Photographer*
The new view album of Deal & Walmer, photographed..
by W.H. Franklin.
W.H. Franklin. Deal c.1900.
11

GREAT BRITAIN, Laws etc. (Geo.I).
Act of Parliament for the pilots of Dover,
Deal and Thanet, 1714 - 20.
(1721)
13

HUNT, F.J.
Deal, Walmer and Kingsdown Amateur Rowing
Club. 1927 - 1977.
Kent County Printers. 1929.
28

KENT COUNTY COUNCIL: PLANNING DEPARTMENT.*
Deal: draft town plan.
K.C.C. 1971.
8

Deal: informal district plan.
K.C.C. 1974.
11

Deal:*Middle Street Conservation Area: an
architectural appraisal.
K.C.C. 1971.
2.4.8.12,13,16,19,20,25.

Deal: a plan for the town centre. New edition.
K.C.C. 1974.
11

LAKER, John.*
History of Deal.2nd edition.
T.F. Pain. 1921
13

A LETTER TO THE OVERSEERS OF THE POOR.of the
Parish of Deal, in Kent, respecting the great
increase of their poor rates. With remarks on
the general duty of overseers. 2nd ed. Printed by:
Simmons & Kirkby. Canterbury. 1778.
3

DEAL Cont'd

MINERVA RAILWAY GUIDE and visitor's handbook for Deal, Walmer, Sandwich and District.
Minerva. 1907.
12

O'NEIL, Bryan Hugh St.John.*
Deal Castle by B.H. John O'Neil and
G.C. Dunning.
H.M.S.O. 1966.
20, 26, 27

PHIPPEN, James,Publisher.
The new handbook to Deal, Walmer,
Sandwich and their environs.
J. Phippen. 1852.
8,11,17

ROCHE, T.W.E.
Ships of Dover, Folkestone, Deal and Thanet..
A. Coles Ltd. Southampton. (1959).
30

ROGET, John Lewis.*
Sketches of Deal, Walmer and Sandwich.
Longmans,Green & Company. 1911.
1,2,3,4,6,11,12,15,17,18,

SAUNDERS, A.D.*
Deal and Walmer Castles.
H.M.S.O. 1963.
3,12,25

STANTON, William.*
The journal of William Stanton, pilot, of Deal,
1811 - 1867.
Simpkin Marshall 1929.
24

TOMASZEWSKI, N.E.
Deal before the Conquest, through
archaeological evidence.
Deal & Walmer Local History & Research Group.1978.
3,6,11,28.

Eight hundred years of worship: St. Leonard's
Church, Deal.
St. Leonards Parochial Church Council. 1980.
28

TRENDELL, John.
Operation Music-Maker: the story of the
Royal Marines Band.
John Trendell. 1979.
28

DEPTFORD

DEPTFORD BOROUGH COUNCIL.*
The Metropolitan Borough of Deptford: the
official guide.
Edward J.Burrow & Co. Cheltenham. c.1960.
11

DEWS, Nathan.*
History of Deptford. 2nd edition, revised
and enlarged.(Thamesmead histories Series).
First Published in 1884.
Reprinted in 1971 by the Conway Maritime
Press.
2

DOBSON, Howard E.
A comparative study of the Royal Dockyard.
at Deptford within two periods, 1689 -
1697 and 1739 - 1748.
Unpublished Thesis. 1974.
18

GREAT BRITAIN: Laws Etc. (Geo.III).
An act for the better regulation and government
of pilots licensed by the Corporation of
Trinity of Deptford Strand in the County of
Kent, and to prevent mischiefs and annoyances
upon the river of Thames below London Bridge.
1786.
12

HARRIS, G.G.
The Trinity House of Deptford, 1514 - 1660.
Athlone Press. 1969.
11

JONES, Graham G.
The Geographical analysis of social class;
a study of Deptford, South London, 1871 - 1901.
Unpublished Thesis. 1974.
18

JONES, P.E.
Some Bridge House properties. In
Journal of British Architects' Association.
Vol. XVI. 1953.
18

LEWISHAM: LONDON BOROUGH COUNCIL.
Town trail - Butt Lane to Deptford High Street.
London Borough of Lewisham. 1978.
18

RIGDEN, Reg.
The floating prisons of Woolwich & Deptford.
London Borough of Greenwich. 1976.
2,4,11,12,25.

ST. NICHOLAS' CHURCH: the ancient Parish
Church of Deptford.
St. Nicholas Parochial Church Council. 1975.
18

WEST, John.
Borough byways 1: New Cross and Deptford.
(Town Trail).
Lewisham Local History Society. n.d.
18.

DETLING

CAVE-BROWNE, Rev. John.*
Detling in Days gone by.
Simpkin Marshall. 1880.
7

DIALECTS

BAKER, Dick,pseud.
Guide to Tunbridge Wells, wid summat bout
de Town Hall writ and prented in de old
Kentish Dialect.
J. Richards. 1932.
19

BLAKE, Norman Francis.
"Born in Kent". From Lore and Language,
Vol.2, No.5. July 1976.
The Centre for English Cultural Tradition
& Language. 1976.
11

BRITTEN, James.
Old Country and farming words; gleaned from
Agricultural books. Published for the
English Dialect Society by Trubner & Co. 1880.
11

CARR, Barbara M.H.
Neglected sources for the vocabulary of
Kentish and some neighbouring dialects in
the eighteenth and nineteenth centuries.
Reprinted from "Transactions of the Philological
Society", 1950.
11

(MASTERS, John White)*
Dick and Sal: or, Jack and Joanses Fair:
a doggerel poem. 3rd edition.
Printed by Z. Warren. Dover 1830.
3,11

Dick and Sal at Canterbury Fair: an early
nineteenth century poem in the Kentish
dialect of the period. Limited edition of
228. Introductory note by Christopher Buckingham.
Ben Sands. Shoestring Press. Whitstable. 1973.
1,3,6,26
11 and another copy of earlier date minus
      cover and title page.

DIALECTS. Cont'd

MICHEL, Dan.*
Ayenbite of Inwyt; or, Remorse of conscience.
In the Kentish dialect, 1340 A.D.; edited from
the autographed MS in the British Museum...
with an introduction on the peculiarities of
the Southern Dialect..and a glossary index, by
Richard Morris.
N. Trubner for the Early English Text Society
1866.
11

PARISH, William Douglas.*
A dictionary of the Kentish dialect and
provincialisms in use in the County of Kent,
by W.D. Parish and W.A. Shaw.
Farncombe & Company. Lewes. 1889.
11 Grangerised copy
25, 26

PEGGE, Samuel.*
An alphabet of Kenticisms...to which is added
a collection of proverbs and old sayings.
K.A.S. 1874.
9

SKEAT, Walter William.
Reprinted glossaries....XI.Words used in the
Isle of Thanet,by J. Lewis, 1736.
Edited by W.W. Skeat.
English Dialect Soc   1874.repr. 1881.
4

DICKENS. CHARLES JOHN HUFFAM (1812 - 1870).

ADDISON, William.*
In the steps of Charles Dickens.
Rich & Cowan. 1955.
25

ALLBUT, Robert.
London & Country rambles with Charles Dickens.
Revised ed.
Sheppard & St. John. London. 1894.
11

Rambles in Dickens-land.*
Chapman & Hall.London. 1899
Truslove,Hanson & Comba. New York. 1899
2,11

BRIGDEN, C.A.T. illustrator.
Characters of Charles Dickens as depicted
by "Kyd"; drawn by C.A.T. Brigden. (Original
work by "Kyd"; Characters of Charles Dickens
portrayed in a series of original water colour
sketches by "Kyd" i.e. Joseph Clayton Clarke.
R. Tuck 1899).
John Hallewell Publications.Rochester. 1978.
11,15

BRITISH MUSEUM.
Dickens; an excerpt from the 'General Catalogue
of Printed Books' in the British Museum.
British Museum. 1960.
12

CARDEW, Percy T.*
The Murder of Edwin Drood recounted by John
Jasper; being an attempted solution of the
mystery based on Dickens' manuscript and
memoranda.
Cecil Palmer. 1920.
8,11

CARLTON, William J.*
Charles Dickens, shorthand writer; the
'prentice days...
Cecil Palmer. 1926.
12

CHARLES DICKENS and his Bleak House.* A story
and guide.
Gibbs & Company,Canterbury. 1959 etc.
4,6,8,11,12,15,19,24
1 1963 only
2 1960

CITY OF ROCHESTER SOCIETY.
Charles Dickens & the Medway Towns.
City of Rochester Society. 1976.
8

CLARK, W.A.
Edwin Drood again. in The Dickensian; a
quarterly magazine for Dickens lovers.
Vol. XXXIII. No. 243. Summer number. 1937.
The Dickens Fellowship. London. 1937.
11

COLLINS, Philip Arthur W.
Dickens; the critical heritage,edited by
P.A.W. Collins.
Routledge & Kegan Paul. 1971.
12

DeVRIES, Duane
Dickens' apprentice years.
Harvestor Press. 1976.
8

DEXTER, Walter.
The love romance of Charles Dickens.
Argonaut Press, London. 1936.
25.

DICKENS, Charles.
The battle of life.
Collins Clear Type Press. n.d.
12

Household words. A weekly journal conducted
by Charles Dickens. (a broken run)
Bradbury & Evans, 1850-9
4

Mystery of Edwin Drood.*
Chapman & Hall. 1870.
11

The seven poor travellers, in three chapters.*
Local notes by Edwin Harris. (Short novel
of the Richard Watts Charity, Rochester.
Published in 1854).
Edwin Harris & Son. Rochester. 1926.
11

The Old Curiosity Shop.
Routledge & Sons Ltd. 1895.
24

DICKENS FESTIVAL PAGEANT,*1951,
Rochester Souvenir Programme.
25

DICKENS HOUSE, Broadstairs.
1939.
24

DOLBY, George.*
Charles Dickens as I knew him; the story of
the reading tours in Great Britain and
America (1866 - 1870).
Unwin. 1885.
25

FITZGERALD, Percy.*
Bozland, Dickens' places and people.
Downey & Company. 1895.
24

Memories of Charles Dickens.* With an account
of "Household Words" and "All the Year Round"...
J. Arrowsmith, Bristol. 1913.
25

FORSTER, John.
The life of Charles Dickens. 2 vols.
Memorial edition, especially prepared for
subscribers by the Waverley Book Co. Ltd. n.d.
25

FROST, Thomas.*
In Kent with Charles Dickens.
Tinsley Brothers. 1880.
26

GISSING, George.
Charles Dickens; a critical study.
Blackie and Son. Glasgow and Dublin. 1898.
25

GOMME, A.H.
Dickens: (Literature in Perspective).
Evans. 1971.
12

GREAVES, John.
Who's who in Dickens.
Elm Tree Books Ltd. 1972.
8

HAINES, Charles.
Charles Dickens.
Franklin Watts. 1969.
12

HARDWICK, Michael John.
As they saw him....Charles Dickens by
M.J. &. M. Hardwick.
Harrap. 1970.
12

Dickens' England by M.J. & M. Hardwick.
Dent
1 1976
11 1970

The Charles Dickens Encyclopedia; compiled
by M.J. & M. Hardwick.
Osprey Publications. 1973.
11

HARRIS, Edwin.*
Gads Hill: the home of Charles Dickens.
(Eastgate Series No.35)
Mackays Ltd. Chatham. c.1930.
12

John Jasper's gatehouse:*a sequel to the
unfinished novel "The Mystery of Edwin
Drood", by Charles Dickens.
Mackays Ltd. Chatham.1931.
25

HAYWARD, Arthur L.
The Dickens Encyclopaedia; an alphabetical
dictionary of references to every character
and place mentioned in the works of Fiction,
with explanatory notes...
Routledge.   1931.
8

HIBBERT, Christopher.*
The making of Charles Dickens.
Longmans. 1967.
12

HOBSBAUM, Philip.
A reader's guide to Charles Dickens.
Thames and Hudson. 1972.
4

HOLLIDAY, A.C.*
Where Dickens Walked,
Solus Arts Advertising Service, Chatham for
Dickens Fellowship,Rochester Branch. 1951.
7

JONES, Charles Sheridan.*
The Country of Charles Dickens. Illustrated
by Ernest Coffin.
McCorqurdale. 1923?
8,9.

KITTON, Frederick G.*
Charles Dickens; his life, writings and
personality. Vols 1 and 2.
Caxton Publishing Company.London.1902.
25

LANG, Andrew.*
The puzzle of Dicken's last plot.
Chapman & Hall. London. 1905.
25

LANGTON, Robert.*
Charles Dickens and Rochester. (An essay read
to the Manchester Literary Club, 1880).
Chapman & Hall.
1880. 1,4,8,9,11,15,18
1888. T. Olroyd. Rochester.   4th edition.
      3,6,7,11,12,13

LANGTON, Robert.*
The childhood & youth of Charles Dickens, with
retrospective notes and elucidations from his
books and letters.
Hutchinson & Company. 1912.
11,25

LEY, J.W.T.*
The Dickens circle: a narrative of the
novelist's friendships.
Chapman & Hall. 1918.
25

McLELLAN, Doreen.
Dickens in Gravesham.
Kent County Library, Gravesham Division. 1977.
20,26

MARZIALS, Frank T.*
Life of Charles Dickens.
Walter Scott, London. 1887.
25

MATZ, B.W.
Dickensian inns and taverns.
Palmer? London. 1922.
4,8

The inns and taverns of "Pickwick" with
some observations on their other associations.
Palmer. London. 1921.
1,3,4,5,8,9,12,15,25.

NICKLIN, J.A.*
Dickens-land. (Illus. E.W. Haslehurst)
Blackie, 1911.
1.2.3.4.5.7.8.9.11.12.15.18.25.

NICOLL, Sir W(illiam) Robertson.*
The problem of"Edwin Drood"; a study in the
methods of Dickens.
Hodder & Stoughton. London. 1912.
11

OLIVER, John.
Dickens' Rochester.
John Hallewell Publications. Rochester. 1978.
3.4.11.12.23.25.

PARKER, Michael St. John .
Charles Dickens.
Pitkin. 1973.
11

PATTEN, Robert L.
Charles Dickens and his publishers.
Oxford University Press. 1978.
12

PUGH, Edwin.*
The Charles Dickens originals.
T.N. Foulis. London & Edinburgh. 1913.
25

RIMMER, Alfred.
About England with Dickens.
Chatto & Windus. 1883.
26

STIWELL, Osbert.
Dickens.
Chatto & Windus. 1932.
12,24

SLATER, Michael.
The catalogue of the Suzannet Charles Dickens
Collection: edited, and with an introduction
by Michael Slater.
Sotheby Parke Bernet Publications in association
with the Trustees of the Dickens House.1975.
11

THE TIMES.
A Dickens Pilgrimage.
Murray.   1914.
11

VICTORIA & ALBERT MUSEUM.
Charles Dickens; (catalogue of) an exhibition
to commemorate the centenary of his death.
June - Sept. 1970.
Victoria & Albert Museum. 1970.
8

DICKENS, CHARLES JOHN HUFFAM (1812-1870)Cont'd

WATT, John Y.
Catalogue of the books and papers in the
Fitzgerald collection relating to Charles
Dickens in Eastgate House Museum,Rochester.
Photocopy of typescript. 1935.
25

WELLS, George.*
The tale of Charles Dickens. Printed by
"The Journal" Company. Rochester. 1906.
11

WILLIAMS, Emlyn.
Readings from Dickens.
Heinemann. 1954.
24

WILSON, Angus.
The World of Charles Dickens.
Penguin. 1972.
11

WILSON, S. Gordon.*
Canterbury & Charles Dickens.
Canterbury Chamber of Commerce. 1927.
1,3,6,11,15,

DITTON

GENERAL REGISTER OFFICE.
Census Returns 1841, 1851, 1861, 1871.
Ditton. Microfilm.
23

DODDINGTON

BALL. W.A.R.
Doddington Parish Church.
Doddington Parochial Church Council? 1951.
20

DODE

ARNOLD, George Matthews.*
Dode, in Kent, with some account of its
little Norman Church, and of its early
extinguishment.
Caddel & Son. 1905.
2

DOVER

ADMIRALTY.
Dover bay, surveyed by Staff Commander
T.H. Tizard... H.M.S. Triton, 1885. Engraved
by Davies & Company. Admiralty under the
Superintendence of Captain F.J. Evans, 1874.
Scale 1:4900 (1 mile = 12") Size -25"x 32".
Hydrographic Chart.
Town Details From Ordnance Survey.
11

ALBUM OF DOVER VIEWS.
Charles Reynolds & Company.London. c.1900.
11

AMOS, J. Publisher.*
Amos's Guide to Dover and its vicinity.
J. Amos. Biggin St. Dover. (1887).
11

ARMSTRONG, Thomas.*
Dover Harbour. A novel.
Collins, 1942.
11

Dover Harbour. Reprint of the 1949 edition.
Collins. 1975.
11

BACON, Sir Reginald Hugh Spencer.*
The Concise story of the Dover Patrol.
Hutchinson. 1932.
4,6,11,12,

The Dover Patrol 1915 - 1917. 2 vols.
Hutchinson (1919)   11
Doran. 1919.   4,6,7,12

BAKER, W.J.
Some notes on the Church of St. Mary the
Virgin, Dover.
Printed by Wright, Dover. c.1940.
11

BATCHELLER, W. Publisher.*
New Dover Guide.
W. Batcheller. Dover. 1845.
2

BENNETT, J.J. ("Jackstaff" pseud).*
The Dover Patrol: The Straights:Zeebrugge:
Ostend, including a narrative of the
operations in the Spring of 1918 by "Jackstaff"
(J.J. Bennett).
Grant Richards Ltd. 1919.
11,12

BLANCHE, Robin.
"M.C.C." a survey of the Maxton Cricket
Club during the period 1964 - 74. (Dover)
P.P. 1975.
6

BOTTOMS, A.E.
Criminals coming of age: a study of instit-
utional adaptation in the treatment of
adolescent offenders, by A.E. Bottoms and
F.H. McClintock. (A study focussed on
Dover Borstal)
Heinemann. 1973.
11

BRASIER, W.C. Publisher.*
The picturesque companion to the Isle of
Thanet, Dover, Canterbury and parts adjacent.
W.C. Brasier, Margate. c.1860.
24

BROME, Rev. James.
A sermon preached in St. Marie's Church in
Dover, June the First, 1694, before the
Right Honourable Henry, Earl of Romney,
being the day in which he entered upon the
Office of Constable of Dover Castle and
Lord Warden of the Cinque Ports. Printed
for Eben Tracey... and Rest Fenner, bookseller
in Canterbury. 1694.
James Brome was Rector of Cheriton and
Chaplain to the Lord Warden of the Cinque
Ports.
11.

BROWN, Reginald Allen.
Dover Castle, Kent. Official Guide.
H.M.S.O.
* 1966   30
2nd edition 1974 1.3,4,11,12,20,25,26,27,30

BUCKINGHAM, Christopher.*
Catholic Dover: a book to celebrate the
centennial anniversary of St. Paul's
Church.
Thomas Becket Books. 1968.
23,24,30

CLARK, R.G.A.
The development of the Dover Works of the
South Eastern Gas Board.
P.P. 1956.
6

COLLINS, P.R.
Political, social and economic developments of Dover (Course essay).
(197?).
3

CONNELL, Charles.
Crabble Mill.
Printed by Elvy & Gibbs, Canterbury. 1973.
11

COOK, A.M. and RIGOLD, S.E.
Excavations at Dover Castle, principally
in the Inner Bailey by A.M. Cook, and
D.C. Mynard
Photocopy from British Archaeological
Journal Vol.32 pp.54-104, 1969.
6

COOK, Raymond.
Life in many parts. (The author's life
story as a Dover Travel Agent, Rotarian
and Methodist).
National Children's Home. 1972.
6

COXON, Stanley W.*
Dover during the dark days, by a "Dug-
out"....with contributions by other
officers of the Dover Patrol.
John Lane. 1919.
7,8,11,12,28.

CRELLIN, T.D.
The History and Amenity Committee and the
York Street excavations, 1968 - 71.
New Dover Group. 1972.
6

DARELL, William.*
History of Dover Castle.
Printed for S. Hooper & Wigstead.London.
1786. 7.
1797. 2,11.

DARELL, William.*
The history of Dover Castle(bound with Dibdin's
History of Dover and three papers read
by Rev. Sam Denne). Hooper & Wigstead,
London. 1797.
Graingerised book consisting of several works
interleaved with plates, fold plans and map
Contents: Darell's History of Dover Castle.
Dibdin's History of Dover. Denne's
Additional remarks on the Helmdon mantle-tree
inscription. Memoir on Hokeday. Pett, P.
Life of Mr. Phineas Pette.
11

DEEBLE, E.B.
Plan for the introduction of the patent metallic
caisson, in forming piers, harbours, breakwaters,
basins, locks, quays, docks, mill-dams,
roads through morasses and foundations to lighthouses on sands or marshy soil, fortifications,
aquaducts etc.
(References to Kent and Dover).
Ridgway. London.
11

DOVER & DEAL PARLIAMENTARY CONSTITUENCY.
Register of Electors. 1975. (In 2 vols)
6

DOVER BOROUGH COUNCIL.
Annual reports of the Medical Officer of Health.
1920 - 1924. 1925 - 1930. 1931 - 1936.
3 bound vols.
Dover Corporation.
6

Borough of Dover, Financial statistics.1971/72
Dover Corporation. (1972).
6

Dover,the gateway of England;official guide.
Dover Borough Council.(Entertainments
Committee) 1939.
11

Dover, Official Guide.
Dover Borough Council 1955.
11

Dover, Official Guide.
Dover Borough Council. 1974.
11,13,25

DOVER BOROUGH COUNCIL: MUSEUM*
Illustrated official guide to the Dover
Corporation Museum (under re-organisation) by
Frederic Knocker.
G.W. Griff. St. George's Press. Dover. 1932.
1,7,11

DOVER COLLEGE JUNIOR SCHOOL.
Magazine: a scheme of work in art and
English with a mixed ability group of boys,
Form 5A, during the school year 1974 - 75.
Dover College. 1975?
7,11,

DOVER CORPORATION TRAMWAYS.
Reports. 1900 - 1901. 1902 - 1903.
1903 - 1904. 1904 - 1905.
1905 - 1906.
1906 - 1907(Supplement to Annual Report)
Dover Borough Council(1901 - 1908).
6

DOVER DISTRICT COUNCIL.
Dover, Deal & Sandwich.
Dover District Council. Printed:Buckland Press,
Dover. 1973; 1976; 1977.
28

Summons, Agenda & Minutes of Council and
Committee. April 1976.
Dover District Council.
28

DOVER HARBOUR BOARD.
Eastern Docks development, opened by the
Minister of Transport...1st May 1970.
Dover Harbour Board. 1970.
11

Proposed new Hoverport, Western Docks, Dover:
impact study.
Dover Harbour Board. 1975.
6

DOVER HOSPITAL AND DISPENSARY:MANAGING COMMITTEE.
Annual Reports (bound together) for the years
1876 - 1888.
Dover Hospital Managing Committee. 1876 - 1888
11

DOVER STANDARD.
The Dover Pageant; 32 views. Pageant pictures
(reproduced from The Dover Standard)
with complete list of performers.
Dover Standard. (1908).
11

DOVER - THE FRENCH CHURCH.*
Registers, 5th May 1646 - 15th November, 1726,
transcribed by F.A. Crisp.
P.P. 1888
2,7,11,12

THE DOVORIAN: (magazine of Dover College;
set of bound vols for 1899 - 1928). The
magazine is issued 4 times per year Bound in
three-yearly vols.
11

EAST KENT ROAD CAR COMPANY LTD.
Timetable area No.7. Dover.
8th January 1978 until further notice.
East Kent Road Car Company Ltd. 1978.
11

ELLIS, C.Hamilton.
British trains of yesteryear, edited by
C. Hamilton Ellis. (Contains early photographs
of trains at Dover).
Ian Allan. 1960 (Reprinted 1974)
6

ELVINS, S.W.G.
"Invicta" the story of a royal castle.
D. Weaver (printer) (197?).
30

EMDEN, Walter.*
Dover, Englands gate.
Carl Hentshel. 1909.
7.

DOVER.   Cont'd

ENVIRONMENT, Department of the
List of buildings of special architectural interest
Borough of Dover, Kent.
Dept. of Environment. 1973.
7,11

FIRTH, John B.*
Dover and the Great War.
Alfred Leney. Dover, 1919.
1,2,3,4,6,7,8,11,12,14,15,24.

FORD, Douglas Morey.
The raid of Dover: a romance of the reign of
woman: A.D. 1940.
King, Sell & Olding/Holbrook & Son. 1910.
11

FREELING, Arthur.*
Picturesque excursions: containing upwards
of 400 views at and near places of popular
resort,edited by A. Freeling. (Includes
Margate, Tunbridge Wells and Dover).
William S. Orr. 1840.
24

GOAD, Charles E. Ltd. Publisher.
Dover: shopping centre plan.
Scale 88 feet = 1 inch. Size 33cm x 102 cm.
C.E. Goad Ltd. Revised edition.   1977.
11.
GREAT BRITAIN,Laws etc (Geo. I).
ACT OF PARLIAMENT for the pilots of Dover,
Deal and Thanet. 1714 - 20
13

GREAT BRITAIN. Laws (Geo.II).
An Act for making more effectual an act...
(intituled: An act for completing the
repairs of the Harbour of Dover... and
for restoring the Harbour of Rye...)
so far as the same relates to the harbour of
Rye. Printed.. by John Baskett. 1723.
6.8.11.

An Act for enlarging the terms and powers
granted...by several Acts of Parliament,
for repairing the harbour of Dover...
(1758)
Printed by Thomas Baskett. 1758.
11

GREAT BRITAIN. Laws, etc. (Geo.III).*
An Act for the more easy and speedy
recovery of small debts within the town and
port of Dover, and the parishes of
Charlton, Buckland, River, Ewell, Lydden,
Coldred, East Langdon, Ringwould, St.
Margaret's-at-Cliffe, Whitfield, Guston,
Hougham, otherwise Huffam, Capel-le-Fern
and Alkham and also the Liberty of Dover
Castle.
Printed by Eyre and Strahan. 1784.
6,11

GREAT BRITAIN, Laws Etc. (Vic.)
An Act for defraying the expenses of
constructing fortifications for the
protection of the Royal Arsenals and
Dockyards and the Ports of Dover and
Portland and of creating a Central Arsenal.
Printed by Eyre & Spottiswoode. 1860.
11

GREAT BRITAIN, Laws etc. (Eliz.II)
STATUTORY INSTRUMENTS.
The London-Folkestone-Dover trunk road
(York Street to Snargate St, Dover) order 1959.
H.M.S.O. 1959.
12

The London-Canterbury-Dover trunk road
(Priory Road, Dover) order, 1959.
H.M.S.O. 1959.
12

GREEN, Ivan.
The book of Dover: Cinque port; port of the
passage; gateway to England.
Barracuda Books. Chesham. 1978.
3,4,6,11,12,13,15,23,28.

Yesterday's town: Dover: an illustrated
record recalling the town 1780 - 1914.
Barracuda Books. Chesham. 1978
4,6,11,16,28.

HAINES, Charles Reginald.*
Dover Priory.
Cambridge University Press. 1930.
2

HANNAVY, J.L.*
The libraries of Dover & Folkestone: thesis
submitted for the Fellowship of the Library
Association. 1968.
University Microfilms. 1968.
6,7.

HASENSON, Alec.
The history of Dover Harbour.
Aurum Press. 1980.
6,28

HAYDON, Walter.
What to find on Dover Beach: a concise and
handy guide written in popular language to
some of the Wonders of the Seashore at Dover.
Dover & County Chronicle. 1976.
11

HAYNES, Alfred Henry
This is Dover.
The Author. Marine Parade,Dover. 1967.
24

This is Dover. Revised ed.
Printed by Weavers, Dover. 1976.
6

HEYWOOD, John Publisher.
Illustrated guide to Dover with excursions.
John Heywood. (1896).
11

IRON, Captain John.*
Keeper of the gate: the reminiscences of
Captain John Iron, Harbourmaster of Dover.
Sampson,Low, Marston. (1936).
11

JARVIS, Margaret Ada.
Captain Webb, and 100 years of Channel
swimming.
David & Charles. 1975.
3,6,7,11.

JONES, John Bavington.*
Annals of Dover. 2nd edition.
Dover Express. Dover. 1938.
15.
The Key of Dover: a visitors' guide.
J.Bavington Jones. Dover. (189-?).
11,17.

Records of Dover.
Dover Express. Dover. 1920.
15.

KENT COUNTY COUNCIL:ARCHIVES OFFICE.
Catalogue of records of Dover Harbour Board from
1682. Catalogued by M. Scally. 1975-6. Deposited
by the Manager, Harbour House, Dover,in
December 1974. (K.A.O.., D.H.B.).
K.C.C. 1977.
3,4,5,6,9,11,12,15,30,31.

KENT COUNTY COUNCIL. COUNTY SECRETARY'S DEPARTMENT
RESEARCH AND INTELLIGENCE UNIT.
The need for meals-on-wheels and luncheon clubs
in the Dover district of Kent: final report.
K.C.C. 1975.
11

DOVER   Cont'd

KENT COUNTY COUNCIL.PLANNING DEPARTMENT AND
DOVER DISTRICT COUNCIL, PLANNING SERVICES.
Dover town centre: interim development brief.
K.C.C. 1975.
6,11.

Dover: interim development brief. The town
centre. Proposals map.   Scale 1: 1250
Size 42" x 21".
K.C.C. 1975.
6,11

KENT COUNTY LIBRARY, DOVER DIVISION.
Dover. 1939 - 45.
Kent County Library, Dover Division. 1980.
6,13.

KNOCKER, Edward.*
On the antiquities of Dover: a lecture delivered
before the members of the Dover Museum and
Philosophical Institution on November 24th 1857.
Printed by W. Batcheller, Dover. 1858.
11

LYON, John.*
History of the town and port of Dover...Dover
Castle & a Short account of the Cinque Ports.
2 vols.
Printed by Ledger & Shaw, 1813-14.
2

MARSHALL, M. A.N.
The armed ships of Dover.   In Mariners Mirror.
Vol. 42. No.1 Feb. 1956.
6

MILLER, Alastair.
Inside outside: the story of a prison governor.
(The author was a governor of both Dover Prison
and Dover Borstal).
Queensgate Press. 1976.
6

MILLER, Alice Duer.*
The White Cliffs. (A novel). 7th edition.
Methuen. 1941.
11

MOYSE-BARTLETT, Colonel H.
Dover at War. (Relates to the period 1797 -
1808 and the information is taken from the
diary of Thomas Pattenden, born in Dover in 1742)
The author lived in Folkestone.
Reprinted from The Journal of the Society
for Army Historical Research. Autumn. 1972.
6,7.

"A NAVAL OFFICER" (pseud of ROGIER, E.)*
A brief history of Dover and Ramsgate Harbours,
with a description of the coasts between
Dungeness and the Isle of Thanet and remarks
on the probable construction of a harbour
between the South Foreland and Sandwich
Haven, by A NAVAL OFFICER.
W.H. Brewer. Ramsgate. 1837.
1,11.

THE NEW ALBUM OF DOVER VIEWS.
Overseas publication (c.1900)
11

ONE HUNDRED AND ONE VIEWS, Folkestone, Dover,
Sandgate, Hythe and south-eastern Kent.
Percy Bessell, Folkestone. (190?).
11

OVEREND, G.H.
Strangers at Dover. in the Proceedings of
the Huguenot Society of London, Vol.3. No.2.1890.
2

PARKER, Louis N.
The Dover Pageant of 27th July to 1st August,
1908: Book of the Words.
G.W. Grigg. Dover. 1908.
6

PECK, W. Emerson.
Notes on the Keep, the Roman Pharos, and the
shafts at the Shot Yard Battery, Dover Castle.
Communicated through Her Majesty's Secretary
of State for War. Read to the Society of
Antiquaries of London on June 27th 1872.
The Society. 1872.
11

PERRY, John.*
An account of the stopping of Dagenham Breach:
with the accidents which have attended the same
from the first undertaking, containing also
proper rules for performing any the like work,
and proposals for rendering the ports of Dover
and Dublin (which the author has been employed
to survey) commodious for entertaining large
ships; to which is prefixed a plan of the levels
which were overflowed by the Breach.
Printed for Benjamin Tooke at the Middle Temple
Gate in Fleet Street and sold by J. Peele at
Lock's Head in Paternoster Row, 1721.
11

PHILIPOT, John.*
John Philipot's roll of the Constables of
Dover Castle and Lord Wardens of the Cinque
Ports, 1627.
G. Bell and Sons. 1956.
6,8,23,30

PHILP, Brian J,
Buried Dover: Britain's lost Pompeii -
the gateway to England - the richest ten
acres of buried history.
Kent Archaeological Rescue Unit. 1977.
3,6,11.

The discovery of the "Classis Britannia" and
"Saxon shore" Forts at Dover and"The Port of
Dover", past and present.
Duplicated sheets. (1970?).
11

Roman Dover: Britain's buried Pompeii.
Kent Archaeological Reserve Unit.CIB. 1973.
2,6,7,11,30.

The Roman Painted house at Dover.
Kent Archaeological Reserve Unit. CIB. 1977
3,6,11,28.

PIKE'S DOVER AND DISTRICT LOCAL DIRECTORY.
52nd Issue, 1939 - 40.
Garnett, Mepham & Fisher Ltd. Brighton. 1939.
11

PUCKLE, Rev. John.*
The church and the fortress of Dover Castle.
John Henry & James Parker. 1864.
2,25.

RADFORD, C.A. Ralegh.*
Dover Castle. Ministry of Works Guide.
H.M.S.O.
12   1954.
13   1950.

RAHTZ, Philip A.
Dover,Stembrook & St. Martin-le-Grand. In
Archaeologia Cantiana. Vol.72, 1958.
17

'RAMBLER' pseud (SMITH, Barry).
By the way: (a brief history of pubs and
hotels in Dover since 1970).
B. Smith. 1978.
6

RAMBLING RECOLLECTIONS of the neighbourhood
of Dover, consisting of light scribblings,
illustrated by slight sketches of various
scenes and many incidents connected with the
locality of this interesting port. Engraved
by William Burgess, and thought to have been
written by him in Dover.
Rigden. 1848.
6,11.

DOVER. Cont'd

RANDALL, J.
Captain Webb: the intrepid champion Channel
Swimmer.(Originally published by J.Randall,1875).
Salop County Library. 1975.
6

RIGOLD, S.E.*
The Roman haven of Dover. Reprinted from
"The Archaeological Journal", Vol. CXXVI 1970.
p.p. 78 - 98.
Royal Archaeological Institute. 1970.
3

ROCHE, T.W.E.
Ships of Dover, Folkestone, Deal and Thanet....
A. Coles Ltd. Southampton. (1959)
30

ROYAL VICTORIA HOSPITAL, DOVER. Report for 1932.
Royal Victoria Hospital. 1933.
6

ST. PETER & ST. PAUL, CHARLTON-IN-DOVER,*
1291 - 1894.
n.d.
11

SATURDAY MAGAZINE, 1834.
Includes items on Chatham Dockyard, Cinque
Ports, Reculver, Ancient Church in Dover
Castle, Thames & Medway Canal.
S.P.C.K. 1834.
11

SAVE OUR SEAFRONT ACTION COMMITTEE.
Proposed new hoverport, Western Docks, Dover:
report on Dover Harbour Boards impact study,
with counter proposals.
Save our Seafront Action Committee. 1976.
6

SAVILL. Mr.*
The trial of Mr. Savill, linen draper, of
Margate, who was falsely and maliciously
charged with assaulting Mary Bayley...and found
guilty...arter proving his innocence, at the
Quarter Sessions, Dover, on the 7th of June 1800.
Published by Savill. 1800.
6,11.

SCOTT, Rivers.*
The gateway of England: the story of Dover Harbour.
Dover Harbour Board.
1957. 1, 24.
1965 (2nd edition) 1,24

SMITH, W.H. & SONS. Publishers.*
Environs of Dover and the Watering Places of
Kent. (c.1865-70)
W.H. Smith & Son. n.d.
11

STATHAM, Samuel Percy Hammond.
A short account of the parish church of St.
Mary-in-the-Castle, Dover. 6th edition.
Dover Times Office. Dover. 1907.
11

STOCKS, Ronald.
(The author was Inspector of Weights and Measures,
Dover Corporation 1937 - 1974)
Control of pounds and pints: Dover's role
in the inspection of Weights and Measures.
Buckland Press, Dover. 1975.
6,13

SURVEYORS' INSTITUTION.
The Visit to Dover. Transactions of the
Surveyors' Institution, Vol.XL, Part XII.
1907 - 8.
Surveyors' Institution. 1908.
6

TANNER. Terence Edmund.*
St. Edmunds Chapel Dover, and its restoration.
T.E. Tanner. 1968.
30

TAYLOR, H.J.*
The Dover Pageant: the book of the music: the
words chiefly written by James Rhoades, the
music chiefly written by H.J. Taylor (under the
direction of Mr. Louis N. Parker).
Weekes & Co. 1908.
3,6,11

TURNER, R.
The graphic guide to Dover.
R. Turner.   Dover, (1913).
11

WALFORD, Edward.
Holidays in the Home Counties. New Edition.
(Chapters on Dover, Leeds and Rochester)
W.H. Allen. 1899.
11

WARNER, Philip.
The Zeebrugge Raid. (The Dover Patrol).
Kimber. 1978.
6

WEBB, Brian.
Graffiti, recorded by Brian Webb from
Dover Castle & Canterbury Cathedral with an
introductory note by Barry Kirk.
College of Art Press. Canterbury. 1967.
11

WELBY, Douglas.
The Church of St. Mary-in-the-Castle, Dover.
Crabwell Publications. 1979.
6,28.

Dover 1810 - 1910 in photographs, compiled by
D. Welby.
Crabwell Pubns. and Buckland Press, Dover. 1978.
3,6,11,12.

(The Tidy Ruin) the parish Church of St.
James the Apostle, Dover, Kent.
Dover Archaeological Association. 1976.
3,6,7,28.

WOODRUFF, Cumberland Henry.
An account of discoveries made in Celtic
tumuli near Dover, Kent.
Read to the Society of Antiquaries of London on
December 12th 1872.
The Society. 1872.
11

DOWNE

ATKINS, Sir Hedley.
Down, the House of the Darwins: the story of
a house and the people who lived there.
Royal College of Surgeons. London. 1974.
1,2,8,11,16

Revised impression 1976. Phillimore.
3,16,23.

BRIGHTMAN, F.H.
Survey of Cuckoo Wood, Downe, edited by
F.H. Brightman. (Flora of part of Cuckoo Wood).
Duplicated typescript. 1950.
2

LUBBOCK, Adelaide.(The Hon. Mrs. Maurice)
The Lubbocks - a short account of the family.
(photocopy of typescript). 1977.
(The family lived at Downe).
2

RIDLER, Anne.*
Olive Willis and Downe House: an adventure in
education.
Murray.   1967.
2,6,8,12.

ROYAL COLLEGE OF SURGEONS OF ENGLAND.*
Charles Darwin & Down House, prepared by
Jessie Dobson, Curator of the Anatomy Museum,
Royal College of Surgeons. (Guide book to the
House).
E.&.S. Livingstone. 1959.
2,11.
The Same. Churchill & Livingstone. 1971.
8

DOWNE, Cont'd

ROYAL COLLEGE OF SURGEONS OF ENGLAND.
Historical & descriptive catalogue of the
Darwin Memorial at Down House, Downe, Kent.
E.&.S. Livingstone. 1969.
8.

WOOD, J.C.
The changing form and functions of Downe,Kent.
Typescript. B.A. Hon
2.

DULWICH

ALLPORT, D.H.
Dulwich village...revised edition.
Cardcraft Pub. Co. 1950.
2

BLANCH, William H.
Dulwich College and Edward Alleyne.
E.W. Allen. 1877.
2

DULWICH COLLEGE.
Dulwich College War Record 1914 - 1919,
Compiled by Mc C. Christison.
Keliher and Company Printers. 1923.
2.

Dulwich College War Record, 1939 - 1945.
Keliher, Hudson & Kearns. 1949.
2

SOUTHWARK, LONDON BOROUGH COUNCIL LIBRARIES DEPT.
The story of Dulwich. Text by Mary Boast,
designed and illustrated by David Birch.
Council of the London Borough of Southwark.1975.
11

DUNGENESS

CENTRAL ELECTRICITY GENERATING BOARD.
An appraisal of the technical and economic
aspects of Dungeness B nuclear power station.
Central Electricity Generating Board. 1965.
11

Dungeness B (AGR) nuclear power station.
Central Electricity Generating Board. 1965.
11

Dungeness B - Nuclear Power Station(1973 edn)
Central Electricity Generating Board. 1973.
3,4,11,12,20

KENT COUNTY COUNCIL: PLANNING DEPT.
Dungeness draft country side plan: issues and
choices.
K.C.C. 1978.
11

Dungeness draft countryside plan: report of
survey. First draft.
K.C.C. 1978.
11

TICEHURST, Norman F.
Common gull breeding on Dungeness Beach.
Reprinted from British Birds. Vol.XIII No.12.
May 1st. 1920.
3

Some local heron history.
Hastings & East Sussex Naturalist. 1920.
12

DUNTON GREEN

ATTENBOROUGH, John.
A living memory: Hodder and Stoughton
Publishers, 1868 - 1975.
(The Hodder Williams family were residents of
Bromley and the firm evacuated to Bickley
during the Second World War).
Hodder and Stoughton. Dunton Green. 1975.
2,16

DYMCHURCH

KENT COUNTY COUNCIL - PLANNING DEPT.
Lydd, New Romney and Dymchurch: Local Plan.
K.C.C. 1968.
7

LANE, GENTRY & CO. Publishers.
The Holiday Handbook of Romney Marsh, including
New Romney, Dymchurch and district.
Lane Gentry & Company, Margate (1927?).
11

EAST FARLEIGH

FRITH HALL, East Farleigh, Kent. Particulars
of Sale, August 1979. Bernard Thorpe and Partners.
12

EAST MALLING

Clare Park Estate, (East Malling)...to be sold
by auction by Messrs. H.&.R.L. Cobb...at the
Royal Star Hotel, Maidstone, on 22nd October 1953.
A Photocopy.
1953.
11.

FULLER, M.J.
Watermills of the East Malling stream.
M.J. Fuller. 1973.
11,12,26,30.

GENERAL REGISTER OFFICE.
Census Returns 1841, 1851, 1861, 1871.
East Malling. Microfilm.
23

McNAY, Michael
Portrait of a Kentish village; East Malling,
827 - 1978.
Gollancz. 1980.
6,22.

MERCER, Richard C.H.*
The parish church of St. James, East Malling.
East Malling Parochial Church Council. 1966.
11

TONBRIDGE & MALLING DISTRICT COUNCIL:PLANNING DEPT.
East Malling conservation study.
Tonbridge & Malling District Council. 1980.
12,23.

EAST PECKHAM.

COOK, A.R.*
A   Manor through four centuries (East Peckham).
Oxford University Press. 1938.
2

EAST PECKHAM SILVER JUBILEE COMMITTEE.
H.M. Queen Elizabeth's Silver Jubilee,
1952 - 1977. East Peckham
celebration souvenir programme.
East Peckham Silver Jubilee Committee. 1977.
Printed voluntarily by G. Jenkins & B. Shead.
3,11

GENERAL REGISTER OFFICE.
Census Returns 1841, 1851, 1861, 1871.
East Peckham. Photocopy.
23

LAWRENCE, Margaret.
Peckham Pupils: the story of the development
of education in a Kentish Village.
Kent County Library. 1978.
11,23

Remember East Peckham.
Peter Morgan. 1979.
23.

Through this door: St. Michael's Church, East
Peckham, illustrated by the Parish registers,
1558 - 1972, and other source.   Printed by:
White Crescent Press. Luton. 1973.
1,2,4,11,12,19.

EAST PECKHAM Cont'd

SERGEANT, Rev. John Middlemore.
East Peckham: a short history.
John Hilton. Hadlow. 1976.
12

EAST SUTTON

OYLER, Thomas H.*
East Sutton Church.
Kentist Express Ltd.   Ashford. 1898.
2,7.

SKINNER-FARMER, J.W.
St. Peter and St. Paul, East Sutton,
Kent. Some notes on the history of
an ancient church, compiled by J.W. Skinner-
Farmer. 3rd edition.
Printed by Young & Cooper. 1978.
11,12

EAST WICKHAM
See also PLUMSTEAD

CALEY, Frank.
The churches of the Parish of St. Michael,
East Wickham, Welling, Kent. AD.1110-1967.
Church Publishing, Ramsgate. 1967.
1,11.

EASTRY

EASTRY PARISH COUNCIL.
Eastry village appraisal.
Eastry Parish Council. 1979.
28.

HUSSEY, Arthur.*
Eastry Wills (continued).
Reprinted from Archaeologia Cantiana,
Vol.39. 1927.
Headley Bros. Ashford. (1927).
4,10,11,17.

SANDWICH LOCAL HISTORY SOCIETY.
Eastry 979 - 1979. Lathe, hundred and
manor. A celebration of 1000 years of
Eastry History.
Sandwich Local History Society. 1979.
13.

EASTWELL

PHYSICK, John.
Five monuments from Eastwell.
Victoria & Albert Museum. 1973.
23.

EBBSFLEET

PARKER, J.R.
The Ebbsfleet Valley, with particular reference
to its archaeology, history,vegetation and
wild life,& to its value as a local amenity.
Gravesham Society. 1980.
9.

ECCLES

TONBRIDGE AND MALLING DISTRICT COUNCIL:
PLANNING DEPARTMENT.
Eccles Village: informal district plan.Draft.
Tonbridge & Malling District Council. 1977.
23.

ECOLOGY

BOORMAN, L.A.
Ecology of Maplin Sands and the coastal zones
of Suffolk, Essex and North Kent by
L.A. Boorman and D.S. Ranwell, Institute of
Terrestrial Ecology.
Institute of Terrestrial Ecology, Natural
Environmental Research Council. 1977.
3,4,11

KLOEDEN, Judith L.
An ecological assessment of alluvial grassland
in the Beult River Valley, Kent. (Discussion
papers in Conservation. No.11).
University College, London. 1975.
2

PHILLIPS, N.J.A.
Dykes of Romney Marsh. A Thesis for a degree
in landscape ecology. 1975.
11,22.

SIDE, Alice G.*
An atlas of the Bryophytes found in Kent: maps
compiled from the record cards with ecological
notes on the species.
Kent Field Club. 1970.
7,8,9,11,30.

EDENBRIDGE

CARLEY, James.
The Tunbridge Wells, Snodland and Edenbridge
suspension railway, an abortive scheme of
1825 - 6 with notes on two more.
Meopham Publications Committee. 1979.
2,4,13,23.

THE CHURCH AND PARISH OF EDENBRIDGE, KENT.*
The Church Publishers. Ramsgate. 1965.
16

COMPTON, Herbert.*
The undertakers' Field, or murder will out.
(Novel set near Edenbridge)
Bachelor & Benedict. 1906.
11,12

IRWIN, John.*
Place names of Edenbridge.
Edenbridge & District Historical Society.1964.
30

KENT COUNTY COUNCIL:PLANNING DEPARTMENT.*
Kent Development Plan (1967 Revision).
Edenbridge: a local plan for the control
of the future development of the town.
K.C.C. 1971.
7,12,16.

EDUCATION

ARNOLD, George Matthews.*
Some account of the work of education under
the Kent Technical Education Committee
set up on the 6th April, 1903.
Spottiswoode for Kent County Council. 1903.
9.

BANKS, Frances.
Teach them to live: a study of education in
English prisons. (Includes mention of work
in Maidstone and Eastchurch prisons).
Parrish. 1958.
11.

BARNETT, Rosa.
The work of the Erith School Board with
reference to Elementary Education, 1871 -1903
(Typescript - special exercise For the
Certificate of Education; University of
London, Institute of Education). 1977.
5.

EDUCATION cont'd

BATCHELOR, Richard.
Aspects of middle-class education, 1830 -
1864, with special reference to Blackheath
Proprietary School.
Unpublished Thesis. 1977.
18.

BOARD OF EDUCATION.*
Administrative county of Kent: endowed
charities (elementary education): report
made to the Board of Education...on endowments.
Printed for H.M.S.O. 1907.
11.

BRUXNER, Mervyn.
The story of the Kent Music School. 1948 - 1970.
K.C.C. 1970?
4.

CARLISLE, Nicholas.
A concise description of the endowed
grammar schools. Vol.I. Essex, Kent, London,
Middlesex, Surrey. First published in 1818.
Richmond Publishing. 1973.
3,7,12.

COMMISSION (on) CHARITIES AND EDUCATION.
Reports....(on) Charities and education....
in Kent.
1815 - 1839.
2.

CROOK, Diane K.
The development of technical education on
Thames-side from Erith to Gravesend and its
relationship to the needs of the local
community, 1890 - 1914.
College thesis, typescript.
1977.
5,9.

DOVER COLLEGE JUNIOR SCHOOL
Magazine: a scheme of work in art and English
with a mixed ability group of boys, Form 5A
during the school year 1974 - 75.
Dover College. (1975?).
7,11

EDUCATION AND SCIENCE, DEPARTMENT OF.
Report by H.M. Inspectors on a survey of
nursery education in Kent carried out
during the Autumn Term 1969 and the
Spring Term 1970.
H.M.S.O. (1971).
4

FOX, John.
Education in Gillingham before 1893. (Local
History Series No.8)
Gillingham Public Library 1974.
1,4,6,8,11,12.

Education in Gillingham 1893 - 1974.
(Local History Series No.9)
Gillingham Public Library 1974.
1,4,6,8,11,12.

KENT COUNTY COUNCIL: COUNCIO AND COMMITTEE MEETINGS.
Organisation of Secondary Education.
(Paragraph 9 of the Report of the Education
Committee). 20th November, 1974.
(Papers before the Committee during
consideration of this item on their Agenda)
K.C.C. 1974.
11

KENT COUNTY COUNCIL. COUNTY SECRETARY'S DEPARTMENT
RESEARCH AND INTELLIGENCE UNIT.
Reorganisation of secondary education in
Sevenoaks and Westerham: results of a public
opinion survey carried out in Summer 1975.
K.C.C. 1975.
5,11.

KENT COUNTY COUNCIL - EDUCATION DEPARTMENT
Administrative County of Kent.*
Development plan for primary and secondary
education as approved by the Minister of
Education: revised edition.
K.C.C. 1949.
13.

Aids & suggestions for the teaching of local
history with special reference to rural
schools in Kent, by H.W. Saunders.*
K.C.C. 1922.
24.

Education Act 1944; outline of educational policy.*
K.C.C. 1944.
26.

Education Act 1976-letter from the Department of
Education and Science (Paragraph 1 of the
Report of the Education Committee).
K.C.C. April 1977.
4,8,11.

Education Act 1976 - letter from the Department
of Education and Science. (Paragraph 2 of
the Report of the Education Committee).
K.C.C. July 1977.
4.

Education Act 1976. (Paragraph 1 of the Report
of the Education Committee).
K.C.C. Nov. 1977.
4

Education Act 1976. (Paragraph 2 of the
Report of the Education Committee)
K.C.C. May 1979.
4

Education in Kent.*
K.C.C.
1933 - 38.   9, 23.
1938 - 48.   9,12,20
1953 - 58.   9,20.
1963 - 68.   3,4,24.
1968 - 74.   1,4,6,7,8,16,20,24,25.

Educational broadcasting: report of a special
investigation in the County of Kent during the
Year 1927.
Carnegie U.K. Trustees. 1928.
4.

Education vouchers in Kent: a feasibility study
for the Education Department of the Kent County
Council. (Library Edition and Popular Edition)
K.C.C. 1978.
3,4,6,9,11,12,15,16.

Handbook for Managers of County Primary Schools.
K.C.C. 1977.
3,4,5,9,12.

Handbook for Governors of County Secondary Schools.
K.C.C. 1977.
3,4,5,9,12.

Handbook for Governors of County Special Schools.
K.C.C. 1977.
3,4,5,9.

Further Education scheme: amended 1954.*
K.C.C. 1954.
1,3,12.

Kent: Further Education Scheme & county
college plan.
K.C.C. 1948.
13.

Kent Training College for the youth employment
service.
K.C.C. (1970).
4

Official opening of Walderslade County Secondary
Schools, & Wayfield & Oaklands County Primary
Schools by E.W. Woodhead, on Wednesday 22nd June,
1960 at 2.30 p.m. Souvenir booklet.
K.C.C. 1960.
4

KENT COUNTY COUNCIL - EDUCATION DEPT.
Organisation of Secondary Education: Report
of the Education Committee, 27th November 1975.
K.C.C. 1976.
9

Paragraphs 1 and 3 with Minutes for the
July and November meetings.
11
Paragraph 2.   4,8.

Regulations for divisional executives, managers,
governors and teachers in County Divisions.
K.C.C. 1957.
11

Resources in Kent: a guide to resources for
Kent Schools. (Contains details of Teachers'
Centres and of the School Library Service).
K.C.C. (1977).
3

Second triennial report on higher education
in the County of Kent.*
K.C.C. London. 1910.
4,23.

Special report on higher education in the
County of Kent.*
K. .C. London. 1906.
4

KENT COUNTY COUNCIL - EDUCATION DEPARTMENT*
ADVISORY COMMITTEE OF TEACHERS.
Schools and the Community: a report of the
Advisory Committee of teachers prepared
for the K.E.C.
K.C.C. 1969.
30.

KENT COUNTY COUNCIL-EDUCATION DEPARTMENT
CAREERS SERVICE.
Annual Reports for the year ending on the
30th September...
3   1974; 1975; 1976; 1977;
4,12   1975

Survey of degree course offers: a survey of
the A-level examination results and the
offers made to Kent Students...
K.C.C. 1978.
11

KENT COUNTY COUNCIL-EDUCATION DEPARTMEMT
CAREERS SERVICE, CANTERBURY DIVISION.
Apprenticeship survey. 1977 - 78.
Duplicated typescript.
(1978?).
3

KENT COUNTY COUNCIL-EDUCATION DEPARTMENT
NORTH EAST KENT DIVISION.
Opportunities in Secondary Education
(February 1974)
(Secondary education in the Sittingbourne
area 1974).
K.C.C. 1974.
20.

KENT COUNTY COUNCIL-EDUCATION DEP
Thames-side Divisional Executive.
Thames-side Division. Reorganisation of
secondary education.
K.E.C.T.D.E. 1973.
9.

KENT COUNTY COUNCIL:EDUCATION DEPARTMENT.
YOUTH AND COMMUNITY SERVICE.
Divisional Conferences on the Youth and
Community service in Kent.
K.C.C. 1976.
4.

KENT COUNTY COUNCIL-EDUCATION DEPARTMENT*
YOUTH EMPLOYMENT SERVICE.
Annual Reports for the year ending on the
30th September...
13   1964; 1969; 1970; 1972.
7,11   1972
3,8   1973
25.   1973;1974.

KENT COUNTY COUNCIL: EDUCATION DEPARTMENT.
Youth Service.
Training programme. 1974 - 75.
K.C.C. (1974).
11

KENT COUNTY COUNCIL.TECHNICAL EDUCATION COMMITTEE
Reports of the Technical Education Committee,
from Feb. 19 to Nov. 19, 1902.
K.C.C. 1962.
11

KENT FEDERATION OF HEAD TEACHERS' ASSOCIATIONS.
Yearbooks.
11   1973; 1974.
20   1973.

KREMER, Tony.
Education in Yalding, edited from Local
Records by Tony Kremer. 1974.
11

LAWRENCE, Margaret.
Peckham pupils: the story of the development
of education in a Kentish Village.
K.C.L. 1978.
11,23.

LEVY, L.A.*
Education in Bexley: a history in the
area of the London Borough to 1970, by L.A. and
L.M. Levy.
London Borough of Bexley.Libraries & Museums Dept.
1971.
2,11.

LOCKE, M.
Traditions and controls in the making of
a polytechnic: Woolwich Polytechnic, 1890-1970.
Thames Polytechnic. 1978.
5

MERCHANT NAVY COLLEGE, GREENHITHE.
A century of nautical education at Greenhithe.
Merchant Navy College, Greenhithe. 1977.
5

MOUNSDON, David D.
Elementary education in Folkestone in the
Nineteenth Century. Thesis.
University College of Wales. 1971.
7

MUNDEN, Alan Frederick.*
Eight centuries of education in Faversham.
Faversham Papers No.9.
Faversham Society 1972.
2,3,4,6,7,8,11,12,19,20,30.

OXFORD UNIVERSITY:EXTERNAL STUDIES COMMITTEE.
Prospectus 1974 - 75: External studies in Kent.
(by) the University of Oxford, and the University
of Kent at Canterbury.
External Studies Committee. (1974).
11.

PERCIVAL, Alicia Constance.
Very superior men: some early Public School
headmasters and their achievements. (Includes
Canterbury & Tonbridge).
C. Knight. 1973.
3

PIKE, Elsie.
The story of Walthamstow Hall, a century of
girls' education. Material collected by
E. Pike and arranged by C.E. Curryer.
First Published, Carey Press. 1938.
Revised edition Longman Press Ltd. 1973.
16,19.

RAMSEY, Geoffrey. Archbishop of Canterbury.
Campaign for education. 1963. The case for advance,
by G. Ramsey, Archbishop of Canterbury and
others.
The Campaign. 1963.
12.

REED, W.F.
Spelling reform in our schools. (Simplified
Spelling Society Pamphlet No.10).
The author was formerly Headmaster of
Holy Trinity School, Broadstairs.
Simplified Spelling Society. 1959.
24

EDUCATION Cont'd

RIDLER, Anne.*
Olive Willis and Downe House; an adventure in Education,
Murray   1967.
2,6,8,12

SCHOOLS 1924.
Truman & Knightley. 1924.
7.

THE SCHOOLS OF KENT- a handbook.*
Directory Publications. 1964.
13.

SEABOURNE, M.
The English School: its architecture and organisation, 1370 - 1970. Vols I and II by M. Seabourne and R. Lowe. (Includes - Canterbury, The King's School and St. Mildreds' C of E. School; Brabourn National, Hythe National, Ightham National; Monks Horton National; Ramsgate R.C. School; Sittingbourne National and (briefly) Tonbridge School).
Routledge. 1977.
3

THURLEY, Elizabeth Fusae.
Research Project; understanding and perceptions of London School Children of Japanese Society. (based on research in 8 schools in London Borough of Bromley).
Japan Foundation. 1978.
2

WAINWRIGHT, J.G.
The District School System. (the North Surrey District School at Anerley).
Photocopy.
Printed by Order of the Managers. 1896.
2

WEDD, Mary R.
Born for joy: teacher and learner in a village school (Kentish school).
Macdonald. 1969.
12.

WHITE, Bob,
Experiments in education at Sevenoaks School by B. White and others - introduced by L.C. Taylor, contents by boys past and present.
Constable. 1965.
8,11,12,16.

EDWARD, THE BLACK PRINCE. 1330 - 1376.

ALLMAND, C.T.
The Black Prince contained in "History Today" Vol. XXVI. Feb. 1976. p.p.100-8.
3

CORYN, M.*
The Black Prince, 1330 - 1376.
Arthur Barker. 1934.
3

EMERSON, Barbara.
The Black Prince.
Weidenfeld & Nicholson   1976.
3

HARVEY, John.
The Black Prince and his age.
Batsford. 1976.
3.

MANN, Sir James.*
The funeral achievements of Edward, the Black Prince. 3rd edition Revised.
Printed by W.M. Clowes, London. 1951.
4,11.

and the 1972 edition, reprinted 1975.
Canterbury: Cathedral Gifts Ltd.Canterbury bound with Mills, Dorothy. Edward, the Black Prince: a short history.
3,30.

MILLS, Dorothy.
Edward, the Black Prince; a short history by Dorothy Mills and the funeral achievements of Edward the Black Prince by the late Sir James Mann.
Cathedral Gifts Ltd. Canterbury. 1972(repr.1975)
3,30.

THE TIMES OF EDWARD THE BLACK PRINCE.
Replicas of his achievements, Knights of the Garter, past and present.
(Canterbury Papers No.8)
Friends of Canterbury Cathedral.
1954 repr. 1959.
4

EGERTON

HOOKER, Charles E.
My seventy years with traction engines.
Charles Hooker Company of Egerton.
Oakwood Press. 1973.
4,11.

ELECTIONS

BOUNDARY COMMISSION FOR ENGLAND AND WALES.
General Review of Parliamentary Constituency Boundaries. House of Commons (Redistribution of Seats) Acts. 1949 and 1958.
Boundary Commission. 1979.
4.

Rochester: report upon the proposed municipal boundary and division into wards of the City of Rochester.
Boundary Commission. 1837.
15

DOVER AND DEAL PARLIAMENTARY CONSTITUENCY.
Register of electors. 1975. (In 2 vols)
6.

EVANS, Sir Francis H. vs. LORD CASTLEREAGH.*
Maidstone election petition: complete report of the enquiry by Justices Grantham and Lawrence. Reprinted...from...The Kent Messenger and Maidstone Telegraph...2nd edition.
Kent Messenger. 1906.
11
(used for Judicial reference during the enquiry).

GREAT BRITAIN, Laws, Etc. STATUTORY INSTRUMENTS.
(Eliz. II).
Local Government, England and Wales.
The Borough of Medway (Electoral Arrangements) Order 1976. (S.I. 1976 No. 1130)
H.M.S.O. 1976.
4
The District of Swale (Electoral Arrangements) Order 1976. (S.I. 1976 No. 1974)
H.M.S.O. 1976.
20, 26, 27.

GREAT BRITAIN - PARLIAMENT- HOUSE OF COMMONS.
Select Committee on the Chatham Election Petition. 1853.
Chatham Election. Minutes of evidence taken before the Select Committee; together with the proceedings of the Committee. 1853.
4

HISTORY OF PARLIAMENT:POLL BOOKS.*
Draft list covering Kent.
Typescript. 1954.
4.

KENT COUNTY COUNCIL.
Kent County Council Elections. 5th May, 1977.
K.C.C. 1977.
11

Review of Kent County Council Electoral divisions. (Proposals to be forwarded to the Boundary Commission for England, q.v.)
K.C.C. 1979.
4

ELECTIONS cont'd.

KENT COUNTY COUNCIL-COUNTY SECRETARY &
SOLICITORS' DEPARTMENT.
Kent County Council electoral divisions
(from) the Ordnance Survey, Kent.
prepared by the Member Information
Centre, County Secretary & Solicitors'
Department.
K.C.C. 1976.
11

MEDWAY BOROUGH COUNCIL.
Proposal for future electoral arrangements
for the Borough of Medway in the County of
Kent.
Medway Borough Council. 1978.
4

Proposed new polling districts (Local
Government Act 1972 - Schedule 6.
Alteration of Polling Districts) to be
effective February 1979.
Medway Borough Council. 1978.
4

THE POLL OF THE ELECTORS for a Member of
Parliament to represent the Borough of
Chatham...Wed. 22 June 1853.
(Photocopy of the original).
G.H. Windeyer (Printer). 1853.
4.

ROCHESTER CITY - Register of Electors
for 1949.
25.

SEVENOAKS CONSTITUENCY.
Register of Electors. For 1979.
23.

TELESCOPE, Thomas pseud.*
Sir Brook Bridges, Bart. M.P. and his
supporters, their principles and practice
together with the resuscitation of Sir E.C.
Dering, Bart. on Barham Downs, at the
General Election, 1852.
Published & Printed for R. Colegate,
Canterbury. 1852.
3,17.

THANET EAST AND WEST CONSTITUENCY.
Electoral Register For 1977.
13.

TONBRIDGE AND MALLING CONSTITUENCY.
Register of Electors. February 1979.
23.

WEST KENT POLL BOOK. 1852.
Smith and Son. Maidstone. 1852.
5.

ELHAM

ELHAM COTTAGE AND COUNTRY RECIPES.
Committee in aid of fabric fund of
St. Mary's Church, Elham. 1976.
7.

FORWOOD, Michael J.
The Elham Valley railway.
Phillimore. 1975.
1,3,5,6,7,8,11,12,13,15,22.

HOPKINS, Robert Thurston.
Moated houses of England.
(pp. 71 - 106, Kent)
Country Life. 1935.
5,11,15,18.

KENTISH EXPRESS.
Guide and Directory to Ashford, Romney Marsh,
Tenterden and Elham Districts.
Kentish Express. Ashford. (1923).
3

PARKIN, E.W.*
Elham: a village study. Committee for the
Preservation of Rural Kent.
Headley Bros. Printers, Ashford. 1968.
3,30.

STORY OF THE ABBOT'S FIRESIDE, with a short
history of the Manor of Elham.
(The Abbots' Fireside was built in the fifteenth
century and is now a Guest House).
The Proprietors of the Abbot's Fireside
Printed by Kentfield, Taylor & Co.Folkestone. n.d.
11.

WILLIAMS, R.H. Isaac.*
A short history of Elham and its Parish Church.
Printed by the Kent Messenger. Maidstone. 1959.
11.

ELTHAM

BROOK, Roy.*
The story of Eltham Palace.
Harrap. 1960.
23.

BROWNING, W.H.
Souvenir of Eltham, 1926. Eltham Chamber of
Commerce. 1926.
Published for Eltham's first Shopping Week,1926.
11.

DEWDNEY, W.S.
A history of Cannock School. Volume 1, 1905 -
1978,by W.S. Dewdney and L.F. Baker(At Eltham
until 1960 and then at Chelsfield)
The School. 1979.
2

DUNNAGE, H. Architect*
Plans, elevations, sections, details and views
of the Great Hall of the Royal Palace of Eltham, in
in Kent. Measured and delineated by H. Dunnage
and C. Laver, Architects, with an essay, historical
and descriptive.
Published for the authors by J. Taylor,
High Holborn, and Priestley and Weale, High St,
Bloomsbury. 1828.
1,2,8,11,12,17,18.

ELTHAM PALACE - information in Town and
Country Magazine.
Virtue. London. 1837 - 8.
4

THE ELTHAM SOCIETY.
Looking into Eltham.
The Society. 1980.
2

Some Eltham Local History Records.
The Society. 1977.
2.

ENVIRONMENT, Department of the.
Railway accident: report on the derailment
that occurred on 11th June, 1972. at
Eltham (Well Hall).
H.M.S.O. 1973.
1.

KENNETT, John.
Trams in Eltham. 1910 - 1922.
Eltham Society. 1972.
1.

TAYLOR, Margaret.
E. Nesbit in Eltham.
Eltham Society. 1974.
18.

ERITH

BALL, W.E.*
De Luci the Loyal (Chief Justiciar of England
and Founder of Lesnes Abbey): a paper read
before the Society, 11th November, 1891.
Lewisham Antiquarian Society 1891.
1,

ERITH.   Cont'd

BARNETT, Rosa.
The work of the Erith School Board with
reference to elementary education, 1871 -
1903. (Typescript - special exercise
for Certertificate of Education,University of
London, Institute of Education).
1977.
5.

BEXLEY CIVIC SOCIETY.
Borough Walks: 4.Around old Erith.
The Society. 1977.
1.

BURT, BOLTON AND HAYWOOD LTD.
A century of progress: 1848 - 1948.
Burt, Bolton and Haywood Ltd. 1949.
1.

ERITH THEATRE GUILD LTD.
Erith Playhouse. 1973.
The Erith Theatre Guild Ltd. (1973?)
1.

ERITH URBAN DISTRICT COUNCIL.
Electric Tramways.
Erith Urban District Council.
1905.
1.

A GUIDE TO ERITH PARISH CHURCH.(St. John's).
Church Publishers.Ramsgate/1967.
1.

McMILLAN, A. Stewart.
The Royal Alfred Story, edited by Joan A.
Lafferty.
Royal Alfred Merchant Seaman Society. 1965.
1.

MAJOR, John B.
Erith and Neighbourhood.
Lund Humphries and Company Ltd.
1901.
1.

MORELL, Miss.
A history of Erith.
Hope. 1855.
1.

PRICHARD, John. A.
A History of Erith.Parts I,II and III.
London Borough of Bexley, Library Service.
1976, 1977, 1978.
1,
2,   Parts I and II
11. Part I.

WOOLWICH & DISTRICT ANTIQUARIAN SOCIETY.*
Report on explorations at Lesnes Abbey,
1909 - 10. From Vol.15 of the
Proceedings of the Woolwich and District
Antiquarian Society. 1910.
2.

EYNSFORD

BASSETT, Herbert H.*
The village of Eynsford.
Simpkin Marshall. 1909.
2.

DUNKIN, Alfred John.*
Legendae Cantiana: William de Eynsford,
the excommunicate: a Kentish legend
illustrative of Eynsford Castle.
John Russell Smith. London. 1842.
11
3 Imperfect copy, lacks pp. 9 - 30.

HARVEY, C.
A guide to St. Martin's Church, Eynsford,
Kent. Reprinted with additional items
and illustrations by the Rev. D.H.Sweetmen.
Lund Humphries. 1973.
16.

KIDD, Evelyne Rose.*
Eynsford: a study of the Parish. A local
study submitted for the main History Course
at Hereford Training College.
Typescript.Photocopy.
E.R. Kidd. 1965.
5,16.

RIGOLD, S.E.*
Eynsford Castle.
(Department of the Environment. Ancient Monuments.
& Historic Buildings).
H.M.S.O. 1964.
3,12,16,20,25,26,27,30.

EYTHORNE

ABBOTT, William George.
Local Historian of Eythorne. Obituary.
In Eythorne and District Baptist News
Letter - "Our Link", June 1971.
3.

MILLER, Alfred.C. *
Eythorne: the story of a village Baptist
Church.
Baptist Union Publications Department. 1924.
4.

FAIRFIELD

CAWLEY, David Lewis.
The Parish Church of St.Thomas Becket,
Fairfield.
D.L. Cawley. 1972.
7.

FAMILY HISTORY

BERGESS, Winifred F.
Records of the Crow(e) Family of Wateringbury,
Kent; compiled by W.F. Bergess and Carolyn
Duffy. Manuscript Notes. 1973.
11.

BIRKBECK, Robert.
Notes on the history and genealogy of the
family of Lubbock.
Mitchell & Hughes, Printers. 1891.
2.

(BLACK, William Henry)
Memorials of the Family of Colfe & the life
and character of the late Abraham Colfe.
Leathersellers' Company. 1831.
1,3.

BLAXLAND, George Cuthbert.
Memorials of the Blaxland Family by
C.G. Blaxland and C. Winifrid.
Photocopy of Typescript. n.d.
3.

BROWN, L.
Staples family records, edited by L. Brown.
International Research Pubns.   1975?.
5,11.

BUCKINGHAM, Christopher.
The Hales family of Hackington
(Leaflet produced to assist the appeal for
funds to restore the little chapel at
Tenterden Drive, Hales Place, Canterbury).
The Author. 1976.
5.

BURCHALL, Michael J.
Southern Counties Family Register: family
interest of the Family History Societies of
Hampshire - Kent - Surrey and Sussex,
compiled and edited by Michael J. Burchall
and Judy Warren.
PP. Brighton. 1926.
2,5,7,11

FAMILY HISTORY Cont'd

CALLAM, G.M.N.*
The Norwoods 2 vols.
Vol 1. An introduction to their history.
Vol 2. Heraldry and Brasses.
A.E. Callam. Bushey Heath. Herts. 1963-65.
24
27 Vol 2 only.

CHILD, Kenneth.
Some account of the Child Family, 1550 - 1861.
Phillimore. 1973.
11

COCK, Frederick William.
Additional notes on the Horne and Chute families
of Appledore. Reprinted from Archaeologia
Cantiana. Vol. 49. 1935.
11.

COOK, J.
The Cook family history C.1694-1978. (Kent and
Sussex family. J.Cook now lives in Folkestone).
J. Cook. 1978.
7.

COPPEN, John Maurice.
The Coppyns of Kent, 1300 - 1800.
Privately printed at the Leadenhall Press. 1900.
11.

CURTIS, Henry.
Pedigree of Joyce, of Boxford near Newbury, Co.
Berks, and of Cranbrook Co. Kent; with notes of
the origin of the name Joyce and Pedigrees of
various other early families named Joyce. 1917.
11 Grangerised copy of original work.

DAUBENEY, Rev. Giles.
The history of the Daubenay family.
(The author was Vicar of Benenden and of Herne)
Author 1951
11,30.

DORRINTON, J.B.
Fielder Family records, edited by J. Dorrinton
and C. Fielder.
International Research Pubns. (1975).
11.

The Scudder Family records, edited by J.B.
Dorrinton. (North West and West Kent)
International Research Pubns. (1972).
11

DOUCHE, John.
The roaring Ransleys of Ruckinge.
The Author (1977).
6

DURTNELL, Lt. Col. Cyril Streeter.
From an acorn to an oak tree: a study in con-
tinuity.(Durtnell family of Brasted)
Privately Published.
Printed by Hooker Bros. Westerham. 1976.
2,3,11,17,19,23.

FILMER, John L.
Filmer:Seven centuries of a Kent Family.
Research Publishing Company. 1975.
1,2,3,6,8,9,11,16,19,20,26,27.

FILMER, Reginald Mead.
Deep-rooted in Kent:an account of the Filmer
Family.
Research Publishing Company. 1977.
2,3,11,12,19,22,23,30.

FRANKLYN, Charles Aubrey Hamilton.
The Genealogy of Anne the Quene (Ann Bullen) and
other English Families (including) Francklyn of
Chart Sutton.
Privately printed by Fotodirect,Brighton.1977.
11

GOULSTONE, John.
Records of the Scudder and Skudder Families in the
Dartford district. (Dartford Wills, and connections
with Cobham, Darenth and Erith).
Typescript. 1973.
5

GRUBB, Geoffrey Watkins.
The Grubbs of Tipperary. (Alexander Grubb, late
16th Century,resided at Stone Castle, Near
Greenhithe, 10pp. on Stone Castle).
Mercier Press. Cork. 1972.
5.

HAILES, W.L.*
Hales of Kent.
P.P. n.d.
3.

HALES, R. COX.*
Brief notes on the Hales Family, bound with
"The early history of Tenterden"by Robert Furley.
Kent Archaeological Society. (1884).
11

HARRINGTON, Duncan.
The Harrington Family Miscellany Vol.1. March 1975,
edited by Duncan Harrington
D. Harrington. 1975.
12.

HASELWOOD, Rev.Francis F.*
Genealogical Memoranda relating to the family
of Dering of Surrenden-Dering, Pluckley, edited
by F. Haslewood.
Mitchell & Hughes. 1876.
3,11,12.

HODSOLL FAMILY.
The ancient Kent family of Hodsoll.
(Typescript) 197-
2

Hodsoll of Loose, County of Kent.*
(pedigree) n.d.
12.

HOVENDEN, Robert.*
Pedigree of family of Hovenden in Borden, Kent,
England, shewing the descendants in England
and in the U.S.A.Compiled by R. Hovenden.
P.P. 1908.
3,11.

KEECH, Gertrude C.*
The history of the Pledge family with the Barrow
ancestry. Illustrated by Leslie W. Rowswell.
Research Publications Department. 1970.
7.

KENT FAMILY HISTORY SOCIETY JOURNAL.
Journal No 1...in progress.
8,11.

KING, William Louis.
A genealogical record of the families of King
and Henham in the County of Kent.
Mitchell & Hughes. 1899.
11.

KNATCHBULL-HUGESSEN, Sir Hughe.*
A Kentish family.
Methuen. 1960.
1,3,4,5,6,7,8,9,11,12,14,15,17,18,21,22.

LEACH, Peter E.
The Allen MSS.
P.E. Leach, Sevenoaks. 1974.
11

LEE-WARNER, Edward.*
The life of John Warner, Bishop of Rochester,
1637 - 1666, containing some account of his
successors, the Lee-Warner Family.
Mitchell & Hughes. 1901.
2,3,11.

LE MAY, Reginald.*
Records of the Le May family in England,(1630-1950).
Le May. 1958.
19.

LEWI, Angela.
The Thomas More family group.(Family tree included)
National Portrait Gallery.
H.M.S.O. 1974.
3,11.

LONGHURST, T.J.
Fenner family records, edited by T.J. Longhurst.
International Research Publication. 1975?
11.

LUBBOCK, Adelaide (The Hon.Mrs. Maurice).
The Lubbocks, a short account of the family.
The family lived at Downe.
(photocopy of a typescript). 1977.
2.

(M.,J.P.?).
Note: (The Manning family) incomplete
typescript. 1946.
2,

MARRINER, Edmund Hayes.
The Genealogy of the Marriner Family,
Chatham, Kent, England,by E.H. & H.A. Marriner.
P.P. 1975.
4.

MARSHALL, Elizabeth.
Special licence for the marriage of Elizabeth
Marshall of Chatham and Robert Creasey.
28th September, 1751.   MS.
4.

MARSHAM - TOWNSHEND, Robert.*
Chart and narrative pedigrees of the Marshams
of Kent down to the end of 1902.
Mitchell, Hughes & Clarke. 1908.
2.

MARTIN, Bina Elizabeth.
Edgcumbes of Edgcumbe: a supplement to
"Parsons and Prisons". (Family connections with
Brompton, Chatham, Gillingham, & Tunbridge Wells)
P.P. in South Africa. 1976.
8,19.

MAYLAM, Percy.*
Maylam family records.First series.Gravestone
Inscriptions.Compiled by Percy Maylam.
Printed by Cross & Jackman, Canterbury. 1932.
11.

NEWMAN, Aubrey.*
The Stanhopes of Chevening: a Family biography.
Macmillan. 1969.
2,4,11,12,16,19.

NORRINGTON, John.
A preliminary account of the Norrington family
in Kent from the 15th to 19th century.
Norrington. Epsom. 1969.
3,7.

PHILLIPS, Charles J.*
History of the Sackville family...with a
description of Knole. 2 vols.
Cassell 1929.
2,11,15,16.

POOLE, Keith B.
Historic heraldic families. (Section on
Badlesmere family).
David & Charles. 1975.
3.

QUEBEC HOUSE PERMANENT ADVISORY COMMITTEE.*
Wolfe: portaiture and genealogy.
Quebec House Permanent Advisory Committee. 1959.
11,12.

RAVEN, Mary.
Three Broadstairs Ravens, Dr.Hugh Milville
Raven 1877 - 1963; Miss Olive Margaret Raven
1881 - 1970; Dr.Martin Owen Raven 1888-1976.
compiled by Mary & David Raven.
Lanes (East Kent) Ltd. 1976.
3,24.

SACKVILLE-WEST, Victoria(afterwards Lady
Nicolson).*
Knole and the Sackvilles. 1922; 1923.
Heinemann.
1,2,3,7,11,12 (1922), 13,14,15,16,
17,(1922), 19,20.
Lindsay Drummond Ltd. 1947; 1948.
1947. 1,4,5,8,11.
1948. 15,16,18,21,25.
1958. Benn. 5,8,11,12.

SACKVILLE-WEST, Victoria (afterwards Lady
Nicholson).
Pepita (biography).
The Author at the Hogarth Press. 1937.
4,7,16.

SIDNEY, Philip.*
Memoirs of the Sidney Family(Penshurst)
T.F. Unwin. 1899.
12.

The Sidneys of Penshurst.*
Bonsfield. 1901.
1,2,4,7,11,12,15,16,17,18,19.

A"SMARDONIAN" pseud.*
The family names of the Weald of Kent,
particularly Smarden.
Ashford Express. 1901.
1,4,7,11,12.

STONE, Richard C.
Ulcombe, Ireland and the St. Legers.
Reprinted from Archaeologia Cantiana, Vol.XCI.
1975.
Printed by Headley Bros. Ashford. (1976).
11.

SWEETMAN, H.S.
A genealogical memoir of the ancient, honourable,
and extinct family of Leigh of Addington.
P.P. 1887.
1.

TWISDEN, Sir John Ramskill.*
The family of Twysden and Twisden: their
history and archives from an original by Sir
John Ramskill Twisden & completed by C.H.Dudley
Ward.
Murray, 1939.
23.

TWYMAN, Frank.*
An East Kent family.
The Author 1956.
1,3,4,6,7,8,11,14,15,17,23.

(WENBAN, A.A.).
Rude forefathers; Wenbourne Wenban, a family
and social history. (Associated with the Weald
of Kent, especially Sandhurst).
A.A. Wenban, Birmingham. (1978?)
3.

WEYBURN, S. Fletcher.
Weyburn-Wyborn genealogy; being a history and
pedigree of Thomas Wyborn of Boston...and Samuel
Weyburn of Pennsylvania with notes on the origin
of the family...in Kent County in particular.
(p.p. 105 - 184, English/Kent Section).
Frank Allaben Genealogical Company, New York.
U.S.A. 1911.
11.

WHEELER, J.M.
The family and friends of William Frederick Wells,
founder of the Society of Painters in Watercolours. (W.F. Wells, 1764 - 1836, - born in
Chislehurst and resided during Summer and Autumn
for many years at Knockholt.
(Photocopy only) The Author. 1970.
2.

WHITE & CULMER-WHITE FAMILY.
See BARBER, T. Broadstairs.
See also WHITES OF COWES, Broadstairs.

WYATT, Sir Stanley Charles.*
Cheneys & Wyatts.
Carey & Claridge. 1960.
11.

FARNBOROUGH

FARNBOROUGH BOARD SCHOOLS 1873-1973. A short
history.
The School. 1973.
2,11.

FARNBOROUGH. Cont'd

HACKWOOD, John F.
Reminiscences of Farnborough Hospital...
photocopy extracts from File nos 16-22 (the
Hospital Magazine) 1976 - 7
2.

SAUNDERS, Hope (Later Mrs Hardwick).
Individual study of Farnborough, Kent.
(photocopy of thesis).
1942.
2.

WATERS, S.C.
A talk on local administration (with
reference to Orpington, Farnborough etc.)
typescript. n.d.
2.

WELCH, Kate.
The Woodland Nature Journal: photocopy of an
MSS compiled by the author at the age of 15
when resident at the Parsonage, Farnborough.
1914.
2.

WHYLER, Fred.
The story of Farnborough Hospital.
(Typescript) (1978).
2.

FARNINGHAM

CAMPBELL, Donald.
A short guide to the church of St. Peter and
St. Paul, Farningnam.
Farningham Parish Church 1973.
2,12.

DREW, Bernard.*
Farningham against Hitler; the story of six
years of War in a Kentish Village amid
Barrage, Balloons and Bombs. Photocopy.
The Kentish District Times Co. Ltd. Bromley.1946.
5,11,16.

HESKETH. Major C.
(Farningham).Extracts from documents...quoted
by the late Major Hesketh in 1930. MSS
(photocopy).
5,16.

KENT COUNTY COUNCIL - PLANNING DEPT.
Farningham; village study.
K.C.C. 1967.
30.

PARISH OF FARNINGHAM IN THE COUNTY OF KENT,
(a series of display panels from an
exhibition held c.1946) (photocopies)
1972.
5.

NASH MAUSOLEUM, Farningham - List of Plaques
and Tablets connected with the Nash family,
1708 - 1857, transcribed by Mrs. Mary John.
4.

ROBSON, I.S.
The Story of the Little Boys.
Homes for Little Boys, Farningham & Swanley.
Kent. (1910).5th edition.
5.

FAVERSHAM.

ARDEN OF FEVERSHAM: A TRAGEDY.*
Reprinted from the edition of 1592 with an
introduction by A.H. Bullen.
J.W. Jarvis. 1887.
26.

ARDEN OF FEVERSHAM: edited with a preface,
notes and glossary by the Rev. Ronald Bayne.
Dent. 1926.
11

ARDEN OF FEVERSHAM: lamentable and true
tragedy of Mr. Arden of Feversham, 1592.
Facsimile of original text. 1588-1591.
Scolar Press. 1971.
11

BOROUGH DIRECTORIES LTD. Publisher.*
Business & residential directory of the Borough
of Faversham and the Urban District of Sittingbourne and Milton. 1963.
Borough Directories Ltd. 1963.
20.

BRADBURN, H.
A guide to Faversham Parish Church.
British Publishing Company. 19--?
26.

BRITISH PUBLISHING COMPANY LTD.
Official guide to Faversham, Kent.
British Publishing Company Ltd. (1976)
3,4.

BY ORDER OF THE CANTERBURY DIOCESAN BOARD OF
FINANCE: For sale by Auction..on Thursday 6th
April 1972...Davington Priory and Nos. 3,4,5,6,
7,8 Davington Hill, Faversham.
Burrows & Co. Auctioneers. (1972)
3.

BYWATER, Francis.*
The inns & taverns of Faversham.(About Faversham
No.3)
Faversham Society. 1967.
1,2,4,6,8,11,12,20,24,30.

CADMAN, John.
Faversham History Trails.
Faversham Society. 1975.
3,12,20,30.

Faversham History Trails by John Cadman &
Arthur Percival. 2nd edition.
Faversham Society. 1978.
11,30.

CHILD & SON (Faversham).
Jubilee Souvenir. 1864 - 1914. (Department store)
Printed by Austin. Faversham 1914.
11.

COOPER-KEY, A.
Explosion...2nd April, 1916 at Uplees Marshes,
Faversham. Report...17 April, 1916. PRO Ref.
Supps.332. XL00464. Accident No 110/1915.
No. CLXVII.
Photocopy from Public Record Office. 1916.
26.

COWELL, M.H.*
A floral guide for East Kent etc. (with Flora
of Faversham).
Ratcliffe, Faversham. 1839.
1,3,5,6,7,9,11,13,15,17,26.

DANE, Herbert.*
A hundred years of Faversham History 1854 -
1954, compiled by H. Dane.
Faversham Historical Society. 1954.
26,30.

Mayoralty of Faversham *(Faversham Papers No.1)
Faversham Society. 3rd edition, 1968.
2,20,30.

The story of a thousand years:* a chronology
of Faversham's history compiled by H. Dane.
Faversham Society. 1968.
4,30.

The story of a thousand years:*a chronology
of Faversham's history from the earliest times
to 1968, Compiled by H. Dane.
Faversham Society. Reprinted 1975.
1,3,15,26.

The war years 1939-1945 in Faversham and
district;*the Roll of Honour, compiled by H.Dane.
F. Austin and Sons. (195-?)& reprinted (1971).
4,6,11,26.
195-? 30.

DAVIDSON, Diane.
Feversham: a novel.
Crown Publishers. New York. 1969.
26.

DELIUS, Nicolaus.
Arden of Faversham ein Shakspere zugeschriebenes
drama.
Elberfelt Verlag von R.L. Friderichs. 1855.
26.

DONNE, C.E.*
An essay on the tragedy of "ARDEN of FAVERSHAM"
Russell Smith & Co. Higham, Faversham. 1873.
26.

ENVIRONMENT, Department of the
List of buildings of special architectural or
historic interest: Borough of Faversham.
Department of the Environment. 1973.
7,11.

EXTRACTS FROM WILLS AND OTHER DOCUMENTS.*
Containing benefactions to the town of
Faversham including a translation of the
foundation charter of the Free Grammar
School of Queen Elizabeth. (2 copies)
W. Ratcliffe. Faversham. 1844.
26.

FAVERSHAM & DISTRICT CHAMBER OF COMMERCE.*
The Official Guide to Faversham.
Faversham & District Chamber of Commerce. 1950.
26.

FAVERSHAM BOROUGH COUNCIL.
Abstract of accounts:-
1948 - 49; 49-50; 50-51; 51-52; 52-53;
53-54; 54-55.
Faversham Borough Council.
26.

Faversham, Kent. Official Guide.*
Home Publishing Company Croydon. (1969).
26.

Town & Port of Faversham 1252 - 1952.*
Souvenir of the Seven Hundredth Anniversary.
W.&.J. Mackay. Chatham. 1952.
4,20.

FAVERSHAM BOROUGH COUNCIL: HEALTH DEPT.
Annual Report of the Medical Officer of Health
for 1971.
Faversham Borough Council. 1971.
11.

FAVERSHAM CENTRAL NATIONAL SCHOOLS.
Annual reports of the Faversham Central
National Schools from 1855 - 1869.
(1856, 58, 61, 63 missing)   2 copies.
J. Harding. Faversham. 1855 - 69.
26.

THE FAVERSHAM DIRECTORY AND YEAR BOOK OF
USEFUL INFORMATION, with almanack for 1888.
J.T. Swinnock, Faversham. (1888).
11.

FAVERSHAM DISTRICT NATIONAL SCHOOLS.*
Annual Reports of the Faversham District
National Schools from 1867 - 1874.
(2 copies) (one volume)
H.J. Rook, printer, Faversham.
1867 - 1874.
26.

FAVERSHAM INSTITUTE.   Monthly Journal
1862 - 1920.
11.

FAVERSHAM NATIONAL & COMMERCIAL SCHOOLS.
Annual reports of the Faversham National
and commercial schools from 1857 - 1866
(2 copies).
James Higham, John Sherwood. Faversham.
1857 - 66.
26.

FAVERSHAM SOCIETY.
Annual Report. 10th: 1st October 1971 -
30th September 1972.
The Society.
4.

Faversham,*ancient town and port: evidence
submitted...at a public enquiry into the
Town Map.
The Society. 1967.
2,4,11.

FAVERSHAM SOCIETY.
Fleur de Lis: a museum for Faversham.
The Society. 1973?
4.

FAVERSHAM TOWN COUNCIL.
The Official Guide to Faversham, Kent, issued
with the Authority of Faversham Town Council.
(twinned with Hazebrouck, France).
British Publishing Company,Croydon. (1976)
6,7,11,20,25,26,27.

FILMER, Arthur N.
Souvenir of Faversham: a collection of permanent
photographs.
A.N. Filmer, 5 East Street, Faversham. (1900?)
11,26.

FORWARD PUBLICITY LTD.
Faversham: official street plan.
Forward Publicity Ltd. (1977).
4.

FRIED, Erich.*
(Arden must die): Arden muss sterben. An opera
on the death of the wealthy Arden of Faversham
in two acts (seven scenes): libretto by
Erich Fried, music by Alexander Goehr; English
translation by Geoffrey Skelton. Libretto only.
Schott. 1967.
11.

GIRAUD, Francis F. (A Town Clerk of Faversham).*
Catalogue of the books preserved in the library
of the Free Grammar School of Elizabeth, Queen
of England, in Faversham, compiled by F.F.
Giraud.
J. Higham, Faversham. (1895).
26.

Extracts from Faversham Town accounts in
the reigns of Edward I and Henry VIII.*
Reprinted from Archaeologia Cantiana. Vol. X.1876.
4.

Extracts from Wills & other documents relating to
the objects & endowment of the Faversham District
National Schools, compiled by F.F. Giraud.
J. Higham. Faversham. (1867).
26.

Faversham Regulations for the town porters, 1448.
Reprinted from Archaeologia Cantiana. Vol.XXII
4.   1893.

Faversham Town Charters. Reprinted from
Archaeologia Cantiana. Vol. IX 1874.
4.

Municipal archives of Faversham, A.D. 1304 -
1324. in Archaeologia Cantiana. Vol. XIV, 1882.
K.A.S. 4.

On goods, and ornaments at Faversham Church,
A.D. 1512. in Archaeologia Cantiana. Vol. XVIII.
1889.
K.A.S.4
26. Reprinted Mitchell & Hughes. 1889.

On the Insignia of the Corporation of the Town,
Port and Borough of Faversham.
F. Austin. Faversham. 1897.
26.

The Parish Church of St. Mary of Charity,
Faversham: a lecture delivered on August 21st, 1901.
Church Reading Society. 1901.
26.

A visitors' Guide to Faversham by F.F. Giraud
and C.E. Donne.
James Higham. Faversham. 1876.
26.

GREAT BRITAIN, Laws etc. (Geo.III).*
An Act for making compensation to the proprietors
of such Lands and hereditaments as have been
purchased for the more safe and convenient
carrying on of His Majesty's Gunpowder Works and
Mill at Faversham...George III 26 Cap XCIL.
C. Eyre & W. Strahan. 1786.
11,26.

GREAT BRITAIN, Laws etc(George III).*
An Act for the more easy and speedy recovery of
small debts within the town and port of
Faversham...Boughton...Ospringe, Seasalter, and
Whitstable...George III 25. Cap VII.
Printed by Eyre & Strahan. (1785).
1,11,26.

GREAT BRITAIN, Laws etc.   (Wm. IV)
An Act for more effectually repairing...the
road from the Post Road near Faversham...to
Castle Street, Canterbury.   1831.
3

GREENSTREET, James.
Subsidy Roll for the Hundred of Faversham,
A°14, Henry VIII...Transcribed by James
Greenstreet. In Archaeologia Cantiana
Vol. 13.   K.A.S. 1880.
4.

HASTED, Edward.*
The parish and town of Faversham. (Faversham
Papers No.6). Reprinted from "History...of the
County of Kent" Vol.6.
Faversham Society. 1969.
30.

HOLT, Anita.*
Arden of Feversham: a study of the play first
published in 1592.
Faversham Society. 1970.
12,20,30.

IMPERIAL GROUP REVIEW.   Vol.5. No.1.
November 1973.   Imperial Group. Ltd.
Smedley's. at Barming and Faversham are owned
by the Imperial Group.
11.

JACOB, Edward.*
The History of the town and port of Faversham.
Printed for the Author by J. March. 1774.
2.

History of (the town and port of) Faversham,
with an introduction by John Whyman and a
biographical note on Jacob by Arthur Percival.
2nd Facsimile edition. First published in 1774.
A.J. Cassell, Sheerness. For the Faversham
Society. 1974.
6,11,12,20,22,25,26.

Plantae Favershamienses: a catalogue of the
more perfect plants....
Printed by J. March. 1777.
26.

KENT COUNTY COUNCIL - ARCHIVES OFFICE.
Faversham Borough Records, 1282 - 1950,
deposited by the Corporation of Faversham on
3rd November, 1958. Catalogued by C.W.
Chalklin. January 1960 - June, 1962.
Photocopy of Catalogue.
K.C.C. (1963?).
26.

KENT COUNTY COUNCIL - PLANNING DEPT.
Faversham Conserved.
K.C.C. 1969.
20,25,26.

KENT COUNTY COUNCIL: PLANNING DEPT. &
FAVERSHAM BOROUGH COUNCIL.*
Faversham, its history, its present role and
the pattern for its future: a survey and
report with recommendations for the conservation
of the old town, by A. Swaine.
K.C.C. 1969.
3,4,8,12,13,16,20,30.

KENT COUNTY LIBRARY: SWALE DIVISION.
Faversham: a list of publications in the
Local Collection of Faversham Library.
K.C.L. c.1978.
3,20,28.

LAMBARDE, Fane F.*
The Easter Sepulchre in Faversham Church, with
a note by the editor, Aymer Vallance.
Reprinted from Archaeologia Cantiana. Vol. XLI
1929.
Headley Bros. Ashford. 1929.
11.

LEES COURT, Faversham, Kent: Particulars of
the properties. Joint Agents: Finn-Kelcey,
Collier & Ashenden, Ashford, and Cluttons,
Canterbury. 1974.
(A Prospectus describing the Flats into which
the Mansion was divided).
3.

LEWIS, John.*
History and antiquities of the Abbey Church
of Faversham...
1727.
26.

MUNDEN, Alan Frederick.*
Eight centuries of education in Faversham.
(Faversham papers, no.9).
Faversham Society. 1972.
2,3,4,6,7,8,11,12,19,20,30.

PERCIVAL, Arthur.*
The Faversham gunpowder industry and its
development. 2nd edition revised.
(Faversham Papers No.4).
Faversham Society. 1969.
20,30.

PERCIVAL, Dorothy.
Out of the frying-pan: a collection of recipes
from members and friends of The Faversham
Society, compiled by Dorothy Percival.
Faversham Society. (197-?).
8,11.

PERKS, Richard Hugh.*
A history of Faversham sailing barges.
Society for Spritsail Barge Research. 1967.
26.

THE SCHEME FOR THE MANAGEMENT and regulation
of the several charities in Faversham....
as approved by the Court of Chancery by an order
dated 5th April, 1856.
C. Roworth. London. 1856.
26.

SELBY, Prideaux George.*
The Faversham Farmers' Club and its members.
Gibbs, Canterbury. 1927.
26.

SMITH, C. Leslie W.
Stories of Faversham.
Privately Published. 1974.
6,11,19,20,22,26.

SMITH, Charles Roach.
Catalogue of Anglo-Saxon and other antiquities
discovered at Faversham in Kent....in South Kensington Museum,compiled by C.R. Smith.
Chapman and Hall. 1871.
26.

SOUTHOUSE, Thomas.*
Monasticon Favershamiense in agro Cantiano...
Printed for T. Passenger. 1671.
1,4,6,11,12,14,17,26.

TELFER, William.*
Faversham Abbey and its last Abbot, John
Caslock. (Faversham Papers No.2).
Faversham Society. 1965.
20,30.

TWIST, Sydney.
Faversham 1901 - 1910. Syd Twist remembers.
(About Faversham No.13).
Faversham Society. 1977.
1,3,6,11, 26.

TWO SCHEMES RELATING TO FAVERSHAM GRAMMAR SCHOOL
and other charities approved by the Queen's
Most Excellent Majesty on the 24th day of March,
1876.
James Higham, Faversham. 1876.
26.

FAVERSHAM Cont'd

WEEKS, W.R.
A hundred years and more: the history of
Faversham Baptist Church, edited by
A.F. Munden.
The Faversham Society. 1977.
3,11.

WILSON, Sydney.*
Faversham: the King's Port.
Carmelite Press, Faversham. 1963.
20.

A Guide to the Town & Port of Faversham.
Voile & Roberson, Faversham. 1936.
26.

FAWKHAM

PROUDFOOT, W. Frank.*
Fawkham: the story of a Kentish Village.
A. Barker. 1951.
2.

FLOODS

GREAT BRITAIN: Laws etc. (Eliz.II)
River Medway (Flood Relief) Act 1976.
(Chapter XXII).
HMSO. 1976.
11.

Thames Barrier and Flood prevention Act,
1972. (Ch. XLV).
HMSO. 1972 (1974 reprint).
9,11.

GREATER LONDON COUNCIL.*
Taming the Thames: Protecting London from
Flooding. Amended edition of the Report
of December. 1969.
Greater London Council. January. 1970.
4,9.

GREATER LONDON COUNCIL- DEPARTMENT OF PUBLIC
HEALTH ENGINEERING.
Thames Flood protection. Thames Barrier by
R.W. Horner.
Reproduced from "Journal of the Institution
of General Technician Engineers". Vol.85 No.2.
Feb. 1974.
4.

Thames Flood Defences.
Greater London Council (1977).
4.

KENT COUNTY COUNCIL - ROADS DEPARTMENT.*
Report of the County Surveyor on the problems
of Flooding.
K.C.C. 1969.
4,5,9,11.

KENT RIVER AUTHORITY.
River Stour Flood control: a summary of the
preliminary Flood Studies of 1974, contained
in the River Stour Flood Relief Study Report
(by) Sir M. Macdonald & Partners, consulting
engineers.
Kent River Authority. 1974.
11.

River Stour Flood relief studies (by) Sir
M. Macdonald & Partners, consulting engineers.
Kent River Authority. 1974.
11.

KENT RIVER BOARD.
Works inspection by the Board on Friday 23rd
July, 1954: itinerary and notes. Inspection
of the flood emergency works carried out after
the February 1953 Floods.
Copy of typewritten report and programme.
Kent River Board. 1954.
7.

LORD MAYOR OF LONDON'S NATIONAL FLOOD AND
TEMPEST DISTRESS FUND.
The sea came in: the history of the Lord Mayor
of London's National Flood and Tempest
Distress Fund.
Lord Mayor of London's National Flood & Tempest
Distress Fund. (1958?).
11.

POLLARD, Michael.
North Sea Surge; the story of the East Coast
Floods of 1953.
Terence Dalton Ltd. Lavenham. 1978.
3.

ROYAL SOCIETY.
A discussion on problems associated with the
subsidence of South Eastern England, 26th -
27th May 1971, Organised by K.C. Bunham & D.A.
Gray. Contents include: The Thames Barrier.
The Royal Society, London. 1972.
4.

SOUTHERN WATER AUTHORITY.
Thames tidal flood defences: do you know?
Southern Water Authority. (1965?).
3.

SUMMERS,Dorothy.
The East coast Floods.
David & Charles. 1978.
4,9,11,28.

VALENTINE & SONS. LTD. Publisher.
Photographic View Album of Whitstable containing
views of the Flood, November 29th 1897.
Photographed and printed by Valentine & Sons
Ltd. Dundee. (1897).
11,31.

WOODMAN, George.*
Taken at the Flood. A novel based on the Great
Flood at Whitstable, 1953. (Whitstable author).
Macmillan 1957.
3, 31.

FOLKESTONE

ADMIRALTY.
Folkestone harbour, surveyed by Staff Comdr.
J. Parsons...H.M.S. Porcupine, 1873. Drawn by
Naval Lieut. G.A. Browning. Engraved by Davis &
Company. Admiralty under the Superintendence
of Capt. F.J. Evans., 1874. Scale 1 sea mile=
15". Size 18" x 25"
Hydrographic Map.
Town details from Ordnance Survey.
11.

ALBUM OF VIEWS OF FOLKESTONE.
Publisher unknown. C.1930.
11.

ARTHUR BROUGH PLAYERS.
The Arthur Brough Players present "The School for
Scandal" by Richard Brinsley Sheridan for their
21st. birthday at the Lees Pavilion, Folkestone
1929 - 1950. (Programme).
Arthur Brough Players. 1950.
11.

BAKER, Thomas S.
Antiquities of Folkestone.
Manuscript account and commonplace book kept
between 1810 and 1830. The Author was Mayor
of Folkestone in 1817.
11.

BISHOP, C.H.
The Folkestone Fiery Serpent, and other Kentish
Poems: a selection compiled by C.H. Bishop.
Kent County Library. 1977.
3,4,5,7,11,12,23,25,30.

Folkestone: the story of a town.
Printed by Headley Bros. Ashford. 1973.
2,4,6,7,8,11,12,13,16,22,28,29,30.

Old Folkestone Pubs.
K.C.C. 1979.
6,28.

BRITISH SERVICES TATTOO - 20th & 21st JULY,1951.
Held on the Sports Ground, Cheriton Road,
Folkestone.   Producer - Lt. Col. G.E.F.
Oliver.   Held with the Folkestone Flower Show
for the Festival of Britain.
Printed by F.J. Parsons. Folkestone. 1951.
11.

CALLCUT & BEAVIS Publishers.
32 views of Folkestone and Neighbourhood.
Callcut and Beavis. London. (c.1900).
11.

CHRISTCHURCH, Folkestone. A scrapbook.
1939.
7.

CLUNN, Harold Philip.
Famous south coast pleasure resorts past and
present. (pp.303 - 343 Folkestone area).
T. Whittingham. 1929.
7,11,12,15.

THE "CONAMURITE": 1918 - 27; 1928 - 1937.
(Bound vols.of Conamur school Magazine)
Privately printed.
7.

COURT OF RECORD MINUTE BOOK. 1665 - 84.
7

DAVEY, Peter.*
Chronicles of the old country theatres of
Southern England.
(Photostat copy of the Folkestone section).
n.d.
7.

ENVIRONMENT, Department of the
List of buildings of special architectural
or historic interest: District of Shepway,
Kent, Folkestone Area.
HMSO. 1975.
11.

FLETCHER, Joseph Smith.
The passenger to Folkestone. (a novel).
Herbert Jenkins. n.d.
11.

FOLKESTONE ART SOCIETY.
Folkestone Art Society Exhibition, 26th
September to 8th October, 1955: Catalogue.
Folkestone Art Society. 1955.
11.

FOLKESTONE ASTORIA CINEMA OPENING,
Souvenir programme April 1935.
1935.
7.

THE FOLKESTONE BAPTISTS 1667 - 1974
Programme of The Centenary Celebrations....
together with a history of the Folkestone
Baptists.
Folkestone Baptist Church. 1974.
7.

FOLKESTONE BOROUGH COUNCIL.
Abstract of accounts 1972 - 3.
Folkestone Borough Council. 1973.
7.

Ceremony of admission of Alderman Leonard
Charles Aldridge, Alderman Thomas Leslie Elvy
Franks. J.P. and Noel Copeland Scragg, Esq,
Solicitor, as honary freemen of the Borough
of Folkestone...1974.
Folkestone Borough Council. 1974.
7.

Coronation of Her Majesty Queen Elizabeth II,
1953: official souvenir programme.
Folkestone Borough Council. 1953.
11.

Folkestone Official holiday guide book.
Folkestone Borough Council. 1973.
11.

Folkestone - past and present.
Printed by F.J. Parsons Ltd. Folkestone. (1954).
2,11.

FOLKESTONE BOROUGH COUNCIL.
Presentation of the Freedom of Folkestone to the
Queens Own Buffs, the Royal Kent Regiment,on
Saturday 6th May, 1961.
Printed by F.J. Parsons, Folkestone. 1961.
11.

FOLKESTONE BOROUGH COUNCIL - ENTERTAINMENTS
AND PUBLICITY COMMITTEE.
Folkestone Official Guide.
"An invitation to Folkestone in 1955".
Folkestone Borough Councio. 1955.
4.

FOLKESTONE BOROUGH COUNCIL and PORT HEALTH AUTHORITY.
Annual report of the Medical Officer of Health
for 1972.
Folkestone Borough Council. 1973.
7.

FOLKESTONE CHAMBER OF COMMERCE.*
Folkestone: the gem of the Kentish coast.
Official Handbook.
Folkestone Chamber of Commerce.
1929 edition -   38th edition 1938
33rd edition 1933?   39th edition 1939
11.

FOLKESTONE FLOWER SHOW & FLORAL ACADEMY.
West Cliff Gardens, Folkestone. Thursday, Friday
& Saturday, July 22nd, 23rd, & 24th, 1954.
Schedule & Year Book.
Folkestone Flower Show & Floral Academy. 1954.
11.

THE FOLKESTONE HERALD.
Souvenir album of views. Folkestone, Sandgate,
Hythe and neighbourhood.
The "Folkestone Herald". (1902?).
11.

FOLKESTONE, HYTHE & DISTRICT HOTEL & CATERING
ASSOCIATION.
Folkestone & Hythe, Kent. 10th edition.
The Association. 1951.
11.

FOLKESTONE ROTARY CLUB.
Folkestone Competitive Musical Festival 1939,
organised by the Rotary Club of Folkestone.
Programme of the 15th Festival to be held...
on Saturday March 18th, 1939.
The Rotary Club. 1939.
11.

FOLKESTONE SILVER JUBILEE COMMITTEE .
Folkestone Celebration 1977: the Queen's Silver
Jubilee.
Folkestone Silver Jubilee Committee. 1977.
7.

THE GRAND HOTEL, The Leas, Folkestone, Kent.
Auction sale of furniture and equipment to be
sold by Smith-Woolley and Perry, Chartered
Surveyors, on Tuesday and Wednesday 4th and 5th
June, 1974 and the following day if necessary.
1974.
7.

GREAT BRITAIN, Laws etc. (Vic.).
An Act for confirming a scheme of the Charity
Commissioners for Sir Eliab Harvey's Charity
in the town of Folkestone. (28th June 1858).
Eyre & Spottiswoode. 1858.
11.

GREAT BRITAIN,Laws Etc. (Eliz II). STATUTORY INSTRUMENTS.
The London - Folkestone - Dover Trunk Road
(Kellick's Corner Diversion, Folkestone).
Order 1959.
HMSO. 1959.
12.

GREAT BRITAIN: PARLIAMENT:HOUSE OF COMMONS
Folkestone Gas.
HMSO. 1916.
7.

HANNAVY, J.L.*
The libraries of Dover and Folkestone: thesis
submitted for Fellowship of the Library
Association, 1968.
University Microfilms. 1968.
6,7.

HARSH, Frances.
A romance of old Folkestone.
Arthur C. Fifield. London. 1906.
11.

JENKINS, Robert Charles.
Gossip from the Municipal Records of Folkestone
(Reprinted from Archaeologia Cantiana, Vol.10.
1876). (In Kent Archaeological Society 's
"Some Kentish Towns" etc.)
4.

KELLY'S DIRECTORIES LTD.
Kelly's Directory of Folkestone, Sandgate
and neighbourhood.
Kelly's Directories Ltd. 1936. & 1938.
11.

(KNOLLYS, E.E.)
A short guide to Folkestone Parish Church.
Skeffington.
7,10,24. n.d.
11.   8th edition 1920

LYON, John.*
An account of a subsidence of the ground near
Folkestone on the coast of Kent. In a letter
from the Rev. John Lyon, M.A. to Edward King.
From The Transactions of the Philosophical
Society. Vol. LXXVI, 1786.
(Read to the Society on February 16th 1786).
11.

MACKIE, S.J.*
A descriptive and historical account of
Folkestone and its neighbourhood.
Simpkin Marshall. Printed by J. English,
Folkestone. 1856.
25. 30.

MARSHALL, M.N.
The armed ships of Folkestone.
In Mariner's mirror Vol. 41. No.1. Feb. '55.
6.

MAUGHAM, H. Hamilton.
Seven Churches. (pp. 24 - 28 St. Peter's
Church, Folkestone).
The Coelian Press. Hove. 1947.
11.

MOUNSDON, David D.
Elementary education in Folkestone in the
19th century. Thesis.
University College of Wales. 1971.
7.

NATIONAL ASSOCIATION OF HEAD TEACHERS.
Annual Conference at Folkestone, 4th - 8th
June 1954. (souvenir guidebook). (Official
guide book to Folkestone for 1954 and list
of Conference Officials).
National Association of Head Teachers. 1954.
11.

NATIONAL UNION OF TEACHERS.*
Folkestone Conference Souvenir, 1932.
University of London Press. 1932.
8,11.

ONE HUNDRED AND ONE VIEWS, Folkestone,
Dover, Sandgate, Hythe and South-Eastern Kent.
Percy Bessell, Folkestone. (190?).
11.

THE PARISH CHURCH of St. Mary and St.
Eanswythe, Folkestone.*
Kentfield, Folkestone. 1956.
12.

POLE-STUART, Dr. E.
Who's Who in Folkestone c1700 - 1840.
MSS. 1976.
7.

RECOLLECTIONS OF FOLKESTONE.
A. Newman & Company. London. 1876.
11.

RICE, John.
Folkestone: a photographic record.
Aten Press. 1977.
6,7,8,11.

Folkestone: specious and gruesome.
Aten Press. 1976.
7.

Folkestone in the 1800's: a history in drawing
and poems, by J. Rice and C.O'Brien.
Aten Press. 1973.
1.

RIDSDALE, Charles Joseph VS. CLIFTON & others.
Folkestone ritual case: the substance of the
argument, delivered before the Judicial Committee
of the Privy Council by Benjamin Shaw.
Printed by W.J. Terry. 187-?
11,17.

ROCHE, T.W.E.
Ships of Dover, Folkestone, Deal and Thanet...
A. Coles Ltd. Southampton. (1959).
30.

ST. MARGARET'S (School) Magazine.
(average two issues per year)
1901 - 7; 1908 - 11; 1912 - 16;
1926 - 30. (New Series 1 - 4).
7.

A SHORT GUIDE TO FOLKESTONE PARISH CHURCH.*
(St. Mary & St. Eanswythe). 4th edition.
Printed by Skeffington & Son. Ltd.
24 Included in "Jottings of Kent".

THE SOUTH EASTERN, Folkestone and District
property register 1896 and February, 1902.
F. Wilson, Temple and Co.
7.

SOUTH EASTERN UNION OF SCIENTIFIC SOCIETIES.*
The South Eastern Naturalist, being the
Transactions of the South Eastern Union of
Scientific Societies...including the Proceedings
at the Seventeenth Annual Congress held at
Folkestone, 1912.
The Society 1912.
7,11.

The South Eastern Naturalist and Antiquary, being
the sixtieth volume of Transactions of the
South Eastern Union of Scientific Societies,
including the Proceedings of the sixtieth
Annual Congress held at Folkestone, 1955.
The Society. 1955.
11.

SOUVENIR ALBUM OF VIEWS.
Folkestone, Sandgate, Hythe and neighbourhood.
F.J. Parsons Ltd. (c.1900).
11.

STONE, B.
Old Corps musings. (The Salvation Army in
Folkestone).
MSS. 1976.
7.

STREATER, Ronald A.
Ships and Folkestone.
Marinart. 1973.
6,7.

TIFFEN William. Publisher.
Excursions from Folkestone, Sandgate, and Hythe...
W. Tiffen, Hythe & Folkestone.
3,6.

ULLYETT, Henry.
Rambles of a naturalist round Folkestone, with
occasional papers on the Fauna and Flora of the
District, to which are added lists of Plants,
Lepidoptera, Birds and Land and Freshwater Shells.
J. English, Printer. (Folkestone). 1880.
1,4,6,7,11,12,15,17,26.

VERKAIK, John.
Edwardian Folkestone, its growth, leisure &
pleasure.
(Unpublished thesis-Rank Xerox copy of Typescript)
April. 1975.
7.

FOLKESTONE   Cont'd

WALTON, George Chapman.
The Flora of Folkestone and its Vicinity.
Reprinted from the Transactions of the South
Eastern Union of Scientific Societies 1912).
3,8,11.

WALTON, G(eorge) C(hapman).
A list of flowering plants and ferns found in
the neighbourhood of Folkestone.
Folkestone Natural History Society.   1894.
7,17.

WALTON, John W.*
Folkestone and the country round ··· Survey of
the Natural History and Archaeology of the
District...edited by John W. Walton.
Printed by Parsons for Folkestone Natural
History and General Sciences Society. 1925.
1,2,4,6,7,8,11,12,17,21.

(Plants found in the immediate neighbourhood
of Folkestone)
Typescript MS.   n.d.
7

The wild flowers, ferns and mosses of the district
round Folkestone. Based on the work of the late
Mr. G.C. Walton as published in 1894. To which
is appended a catalogue of mosses of the area,
as recorded by E.C. Green.
Folkestone Natural History Society. . 1950.
1,3,4,6,7,8,11.

WHAT'S ON IN FOLKESTONE. Jan,-June, July -
December 1933. Jan.- June, July - December 1934.
Jan.- March, 1935.
F.J. Parsons. 1933 - 35.
7.

WHAT'S ON IN FOLKESTONE, Hythe & Sandgate.
April - June, July - December 1930;
Jan.- June, July - December   1931;
Jan.- June, July - December 1932.
F.J. Parsons. 1930 - 1933.
7.

WINBOLT, Samuel Edward.
Roman Folkestone.*
Methuen. 1925.
2,25.

Roman Site: East Cliff.
Borough Engineer's Office, Folkestone. 1924.
11.

WOODWARD, Matthew.*
The past and present of the parish church
of Folkestone.
Skeffington. 1892.
2.

FOOTPATHS & COMMONS

BRADDOCK, Joseph.*
Footpaths of the Kent-Sussex border.
Chatterson. 1947.
1,2,3,4,5,6,8,9,11,12,15,18,19,20.

COPUS, G.D.*
The Commons at Green Street Green and Pratts
Bottom, Chelsfield. (Typescript).
1955.
2.

HOSKINS, W.G.
The Common Lands of England and Wales.
(photocopied pages relating to Kent),
by W.G. Hoskins and L. Dudley Stamp.
12

LEWISHAM DISTRICT: BOARD OF WORKS.
(Poster giving notice) that on the 8th day of
April next, application will be made...at
the Quarter Sessions, at Maidstone,for an order
stopping up, or diverting the undermentioned
Footpaths...within the parish of Lewisham.
Lewisham District: Board of Works. 1875.
11.

NATIONAL PARKS AND ACCESS TO THE COUNTRYSIDE ACT
1949. Pt. IV. Survey of Public Rights of Way.
Definitive Statement. County of Kent.
Broadstairs Urban District Council. 1952.
24.

PLATT, Clifford L.
In trust for Chislehurst: an account of the
Commons of Chislehurst & St. Paul's Cray and
the National Trust lands adjoining.
Printed by Pentagon Print for The Author. 1975.
2,11.

FOOTPATHS - COUNTRY WALKS

ARIS, Ernest.
A walk over the Downs and what we find.
Fountain Press. 1948.
11.

ARROWSMITH, John.*
Hikes in Kent and Sussex.
Besant. 1932.
11,14.

BAGLEY, William Alfred.
London countryside walks for motorists: South-
Eastern area. Illustrated with sketch maps and
photographs by the author.
Gerrard Publications. Harrow. 1976.
2,11,16,22.

BAILEY, Margaret.
Walks in the Forest of Blean; Fourteen rambles
North and West of Canterbury, by M. Bailey and
A. Gray. 2nd edition.
Swale Footpaths Group. 1973.
4,12,19,20,30.

BASSETT, E.
On foot in Luddesdown.
Luddesdown Rights of Way Group. 1980.
15.

BOLTON, D.
Nature trails: Meopham and Culverstone, written
and illustrated by D. Bolton and D.P. Chubb.
(Meopham & District Footpaths Group)
Meopham Publications Committee. 1973.
9,11.

BRIDGE, Colin W.
Around and about Gillingham: twenty-five walks
in Gillingham from a suggestion in the
Gillingham Schools' Jubilee Competition,
compiled by Colin Bridge.(Gillingham Urban
Studies Centre).
Gillingham Borough Council. 1977.
4,12.

BRITISH TOURIST AUTHORITY.*
Nature Trails.
British Tourist Authority 1974.(Nature Trails
listed by County, pp.22 - 23 Kent).
11.

CAMPBELL, Ian.
South East England: a guide to family walks,
edited by Ian Campbell.
Croom Helm. 1975.
3,4,12,15,20,22,25,26,27,30.

CHAMPION, George H.J.
Stonebridge walks; thirteen rambles from
Faversham, by G.H.J. Champion.
Swale Footpaths Group. 1973.
3,4,11,12,20.

Ten walks around Faversham, by G.H.J. Champion
and C.R. Theobald.*
Faversham Papers no 8.
Faversham Society & Swale Footpaths Group. 1971.
2,3,6,8,11,12,30.

CHEESEMAN, Clive.
On Foot around Maidstone, compiled by Clive
Cheeseman, John Hill and David Thornewell.
Burham Hilt Services for the Ramblers'
Association. 1974.
11,12,15,25.

3rd edition. Larkfield Hilt Services for the
Ramblers Association. 1978.
12.

CHESTERTON, Keith.
A Guide to London's Country Way. (pp.193-242 Kent)
Constable.   1978.
2,3,11,22.

COUNTRYSIDE COMMISSION.
North Downs Way.
Countryside Commission.   1978.
2.

North Downs Way maps: the relevant 1:50,000
Ordnance Survey Maps are 178, 179, 186, 187,
188, 189.
Countryside Commission.   1978.
4,23.

COX, John Charles.*
Rambles in Kent.
Methuen.   1913.
1,2,4,5,6,7,8,9,11,12,13,14,15,16,17,18,19,23.

CROUCH, Marcus.
Discovering walks in West Kent.
Shire Publications. 1978.
2,3,5,7,11,16,23.

DANIELL, Philip A.
Country walks around Bromley, Downe, Biggin Hill.
Circle Publications. Ilford. 1976.
2,11.

DAVIS, Cyril.
Ten Walks from Bredhurst.
Swale Footpaths Group.   1972.
8.

Walks on the North Downs: Hollingbourne to the
Medway, by C. Davis and A. Gray.
Swale Footpaths Group.   1974.
8,11,25.

DOGGETT, Tom.
The North Downs Way, by Tom Doggett and John
Trevelyan.
The Ramblers' Association.   (1978?)
2,3,5,6,28,30.

DOUGALL, Donald.
Donald Dougall's T.V. Walkabout.
Midas Books.   1974.
1,3,5,6,11,19,20,22,25,26,27,30.

FEARON, Henry Bridges ("Fieldfare"   pseud).*
Twenty walks in Kent.
Associated Newspapers. London. (1955).
2,3,4,11,13.

FIFTEEN WALKS AROUND FOLKESTONE.
McNerlin Hughes Associates.   1973.
11.
FOURTEEN WALKS IN AND AROUND TONBRIDGE.
Tonbridge Civic Society. (197-?).
11.

"GEOGRAPHIA" RAMBLERS' MAP to London's
Countryside.   S.E. Section, Kent.
Scale 1" to 1 mile.
"Geographia" Ltd. (1921?).
5,11.

GOULDEN and CURRY. Publishers.
The "WALKS GUIDE" to Tunbridge Wells and the
surrounding country, being based upon the
well-known "Walks and Drives Guide" but
newly revised and amplified.
Goulden & Curry. Tunbridge Wells.   1937.
11.

HARDMAN, G.W.
East Kent Walks.
T.F. Pain. Sandwich & Deal. 1934.
11.

JENNETT, Sean.
South Downs Way.
H.M.S.O. 1977.
6.

KELLY, M.B.
A woodland walk at High Elms.
London Borough of Bromley. (1971).
2.

KEMSING PARISH COUNCIL.
A guide to the Footpaths of Kemsing.
Kemsing Parish Council. 1974.
2.

KENT RIGHTS OF WAY COUNCIL.
Keys to the Kent countryside: a map and booklist
for walkers and riders.
Kent Rights of Way Council. Teynham.
4,11. 1977.
11.   1978.

The Saxon Shore Way.
Kent Rights of Way Council. Teynham. 1980.
12.

KING, Geoffrey.
A Country walk: a section of the proposed
"Weald Way" long distance footpath, illustrated
and compiled by G. King. (Fully illustrated
route cards which describe the route from
Tonbridge to Uckfield).
Independent Design Executive, Tonbridge, on
behalf of the Tunbridge Wells CHA and HF
Rambling Club.
8,11,23.

THE KNOCKHOLT SOCIETY.
Footpaths of Knockholt.
The Knockholt Society. 1977.
2.

LONDON TRANSPORT BOARD.
Country Walks. Second Series. 4th edition.
Completely revised. (pp.54 - 73, Kent).
London Transport. 1954.
11.

Country Walks. Second Series. New edition.
(pp. 61 - 79, Kent).
London Transport, 1959.
11.

Country Walks. New Second series.
London Transport. 1963.
11.

Country Walks.
London Transport. 1978.
5.

LONDON'S UNDERGROUND Publisher.*
London's country. Guide No.2. By road, steam
and field path South of the Thames. 5th edition.
(pp. 91 - 103, Kent).
Londons Underground. (192-?).
2,11.

LONGLEY-COOK, Hilary.
Walks on Ashdown Forest and around Tunbridge
Wells.
Waterdown Press Frant. 1973.
11,19.

MAIS, Stuart Petrie Brodie.*
Hills of the South.
Southern Railway Station. 1939.
11,18.

Southern rambles for Londoners.*
Southern Railway Company. 1932.
1,2,5.

Southern rambles - Kent.*
British Railways Southern Region. 1950.
1,3,4,5,7,8,11,15.

MEAD, J. Publisher.*
Rambles in Kent.
J. Mead. (c.1845).
1,3,4,7,8,11,12,14,15,17,19.

MEOPHAM & DISTRICT FOOTPATHS GROUP.
Six Walks from Cobham, 1971.
9.

Six Walks from Harvel, 1971.
9,11.

Six Walks from Hodsoll Street. (197-?).
11.

Six walks from Meopham Church & Camer. 1974.
11.

MEOPHAM & DISTRICT FOOTPATHS GROUP.
Six Walks from Meopham Green.   1970.
11.

Six walks from Nurstead & Istead Rise. (197-?).
11.

Six walks From Shipbourne.   1978.
9.

Six walks from Shorne.   1974.
11.

Six walks from Trosley Country Park.   1978.
9,11.
Published by Meopham Publications Committee.

Twenty miles round Meopham. (A footpath walk).
Meopham Publications Committee.   1975.
9.

The "Wealdway": a walker's route from the
Thames to the English Channel: Section I
Gravesend to Tonbridge.   1973.
Meopham Publications Committee.   1973.
9,11.

MILES, Walker pseud of TAYLOR, Edmund S.*
Field-park rambles in West Kent...
a practical handbook for pedestrians.
(Seven parts complete in one volume).
R.E. Taylor & Son.   1893.
2,9.

MORECROFT, Victor Wesley.
Fifty weekend walks in Berkshire, Surrey,
Sussex & Kent.* (pp.88 - 111, Kent Footpaths).
Hodder & Stoughton.   1952.
2,11,12.

Rambling through Kent: thirty rambles, as
published in the "Kentish Times".
Kentish Times.   1973.
1,2,9,11,16.

A new selection of Kentish Times rambles..
Kentish Times.   1978.
2.

MOUL, Duncan.
Weekends in Dickens land: a handbook for
the Rambler.
Homeland Association. London n.d.
11.
(192-?) Goldwin,Rochester. 4,6,7,8,9,18.

MURR, David.
A Riverside walk in Gillingham's Country
Park. (Let's explore Gillingham 1.)
Rainham, Gillingham and Chatham Amenity
Society.   1978.
4.

OAKELEY, R.H.
Country walks around Sevenoaks.
(Eleven walks on separate sheets).   1974.
The Sevenoaks Society.
2,3,11,16.

More Country walks around Sevenoaks.
(Walks Nos.12-22. Loose leaf in a Folder).
The Sevenoaks Society.   (1976).
2,16.

PAGE, Hugh E.*
Ramblers' guide to London's countryside.
Pt. 5: Kent.   3rd edition.
"Geographia" Ltd.   c.1930.
2,3,5,9,11.

PAYNE, George.*
Walks by the Marshes: a lecture.
Edwin Harris. Rochester.   1901.
1,11,15,25.

PEGWELL BAY COMMITTEE.
Cliff top Footpath, Pegwell, Cliffsend.
Walker's Guide. (Duplicated pamphlet).
Pegwell Bay Committee.   n.d.
24.

PYATT, Edward C.
Chalkways of south and south-east England.
(pp.36 - 58 North Downs Way in Kent).
David & Charles.   1974.
3,8,11,22,28.

Climbing and Walking in South-East England.
David & Charles.   1970.
2,22.

RAMBLERS ASSOCIATION. S.E. LONDON & KENT GROUP.
Walking around Hawkhurst, Cranbrook and Goudhurst.
Ramblers Association.   1972.
11,12.

SMITH, Alan.
North Downs Walks: Doddington and Lenham.
14 Downland walks between Harrietsham and
Charing, edited by Alan Smith with illustrations
by May Gardiner.
Swale Footpaths Group.   1973.
3,4,6,11,12,30.

SOUTH-EASTERN RAILWAY COMPANY LTD.
The illustrated ramble book of the London and
Dover Railway.
Anglebooks.   n.d.
1.

Rambles in Kent.
J. Mead.(c.1847).
2.

SPAYNE, Janet.
Walks in the hills of Kent by Janet Spayne
and Audrey Krynski.
Spurbooks.   1976.
1,2,3,5,6,8,9,11,12,15,23,28,30.

STANSTED AND FAIRSEAT SOCIETY.
Stansted and Fairseat: a guide to the footpaths
in the Parish of Stansted.
The Society. (197-?).
11.

STOW VALLEY SOCIETY.
Stow Valley Walks.   Folder No.1.
Stow Valley Society.   1974.
3.

SWALE FOOTPATHS GROUP.
Five walks.....: a selection of country walks
on individual cards.
Swale Footpaths Group and K.C.C.

Between Chatham & Maidstone.   1977.
11.

East of Faversham.   1977.
3,11.

East of Sittingbourne.   1977.
3,11.

Near Boughton.   1977.
3,11.

Near Newington.   1977.
3,11.

Near Rainham.   1976.
3,11.

Near Selling.   1977.
3,11.

Near Teynham.   1977.
3,11.

On Sheppey.   1976.
11.

South of Faversham.   1977.
3,11.

South of Sittingbourne.   1977.
3, 11.

West of Faversham.   1976.
3,11.

West of Sittingbourne.   1977.
3,11.

FOOTPATHS & COUNTRY WALKS   Cont'd

UNWIN. T. Fisher. Publishers.*
Greenwich & Blackheath: a handy guide to rambles
in the district.
T. Fisher Unwin. (1883?)
18.

Round Bromley & Keston:* a handy guide to
rambles in the district.
T. Fisher Unwin. n.d.
2,11,17.

WALKING IN KENT - sixteen walks.
A supplementary edition of Kent Life.
South Eastern Magazines Ltd. Larkfield. 1976.
2,4,8,24.

WALKING IN KENT - (Country Living Handbook).
South Eastern Magazines Ltd. Larkfield. 1977.
2,13.

WALKING IN KENT: a Supplementary edition
of Kent Life, June 1978.
South Eastern Magazines Ltd. Larkfield.1978.
9.

WALKING IN KENT: a Supplementary edition of
Kent Life. 1979.
South Eastern Magazines Ltd. Larkfield, 1979.
12,23,24.

WEALD OF KENT PRESERVATION SOCIETY.
Walks in the Weald: Four miles from Tenterden.
The Society and K.C.C. 1977.
11.

Walks in the Weald; near Bewl Reservoir.
The Society and K.C.C. 1977.
11.

Walks in the Weald: No.1. - a ten mile walk
From Cranbrook.
The Society & K.C.C. 1977.
11.

Walks in the Weald: No.4. - From Goudhurst
through the Teise Valley.
The Society & K.C.C. 1977.
11.

WHITE, Charles.
Country Walks. First series. 4th revised edition.
London Transport Board. 1939.
11.

Country Walks. Third series. 3rd rev
London Transport Board. 1939.
11.

WRIGHT, Christopher John.
A guide to the Pilgrims' Way and North Downs
Way.*
Constable. 1971.
3,11,12,25.

A guide to the Pilgrim's Way and North Downs
Way. New Revised Edition.
Constable. 1977.
2,3,16.

YALDING & NETTLESTEAD PROTECTION SOCIETY.
Local Walks. Set 1 and Set 2.
(Cards each describing a local Country Walk.-
Linton, Yalding, Wateringbury, Hunton,
Nettlestead etc).
The Society. Yalding. 1977.
11,12.

FOOTPATHS - HORSE RIDING.

CARLEY, John M.
Byways and bridleways in Meopham and nearby
parishes: a map for riders.
Meopham Publications Committee . 1972.
9.

KENT RIGHTS OF WAY COUNCIL.
Keys to the Kent Countryside: a map and booklist
for walkers and riders.
K.C.C.
4 1977
11 1977 and 1978.

FOOTSCRAY

BEXLEY CIVIC SOCIETY.
Borough Walks 3. Around Old Footscray.
Bexley Civic Society. 1977
1.

PARSONS, J.A.
Footscray.
Thesis. n.d.
1.

FORD

WHITING, William.
Further Roman Finds in Kent.
2. Discoveries at Ford, near Reculver.
Reprinted from the Antiquarian Journal Vol.IV,
No.1. January 1924.
Society of Antiquaries of London. 1924.
11.

FORDWICH

BLAXLAND, Pamela.
The gentlemen Settlers: a romance of Colonial
Australia. (A novel featuring the Blaxland
Family of Fordwich) (The author lives in Dover).
Angus & Robertson. 1975.
6,11.

CHARITY COMMISSION.
Scheme for the application of the property of
the late Corporation of the Mayor and Jurats
& Commonalty of the Town of Fordwich. Sealed
10th Sept. 1888. (photocopy).
Eyre & Spottiswoode for H.M.S.O. 1888.
3.

DERHAM, Walter.*
The Fordwich Stone and its legend.
Harrison. 1918.
1.

McINTOSH, Kinn Hamilton.
Fordwich: the lost port. A collection of essays
by various authors. Edited by K.H. McIntosh.
K. McIntosh. Sturry. 1975.
1,2,3,6,8,11,13,15,19,24,28,30,31.

W.,D.*
FORDWICH CHURCH: guide with illustrations:
(compiled by D.W. from notes collected by
Charles Phillips, former rector of Fordwich).
Jennings. 1960.
1,4,8,11,12,30.

W., J.A. (Willmore, J.A.).
Fordwich; the ancient port of Canterbury.
"This guide, originally written by the late
Mr. J.A. Willmore, was revised and brought up-
to-date by the late Revd. Canon R.U. Potts in 1946.
Further slight amendments were made in 1956
when the guide was reprinted.
(1956?)
3.

Fordwich: the ancient port of Canterbury.
Printed by J.A. Jennings Ltd. Canterbury.
1963 (reprint).
11.

WOODRUFF, Charles Everleigh.*
A History of the town and Port of Fordwich....
Cross & Jackman. Canterbury. 1895.
26,30.

FOREST HILL

FLOWER, Margaret.
The Development of Forest Hill between 1801
and 1910. Unpublished Thesis.
1977.
18.

FORESTRY

KENT COUNTY COUNCIL: PLANNING DEPT.
Kent County Structure Plan a) Report on Agriculture
b) Report on Forestry. (Adopted by the Local
Planning Authority. a) in May 1975 and b)
in February 1975. Serial No.8B.
K.C.C. 1975.
3,4,9,11,13,16.

MITCHELL, A.F.*
Bedgebury Pinetum and Forest Plots.
4th edition, edited by A.F. Mitchell and
A.W. Westall.
H.M.S.O. 1972.
11,19.

Short Guide to Bedgebury Pinetum and Forest
Plots,*with illustrations and plans by A.F. Mitchell.
(Forestry Commission Guides).
H.M.S.O. 1969.
2,4,8,9,11.

FRINDSBURY

FRINDSBURY. All Saints Parish Magazine. 1904-5.
25.

ROCHESTER CITY COUNCIL.
Ground collapse into a shaft at Frindsbury on
21st November, 1967. Report on investigation.
W.S. Atkins & Partners. Epsom. 1970.
4.

THORNDYCRAFT, Colin.
Frindsbury: a historical review, being a
publication to celebrate the 900th anniversary of
All Saints' Church, one of the four churches in
the Parish of Strood.
1975.
3,11,25.

FROGNAL See
CHISLEHURST & SIDCUP.

GARDENS

ASTOR, Gavin. 2nd Baron Astor of Hever
Hever Castle and gardens: history and guide.
Jarrold & Sons Ltd.
1971   16
1973   11
1974   8

BATES, H.E.
A fountain of flowers.
M. Joseph. 1974.
3.

CRAN, Marion. (The author lived in Benenden).
The Garden of ignorance.
Herbert Jenkins. 192-
22.

The Gardens of Good Hope.
Herbert Jenkins. 1927.
11.

Hagar's Garden.
Herbert Jenkins. 1941.
11.

Making the dovecot pay.
Herbert Jenkins. 1935.
11.

Squabbling Garden.
Herbert Jenkins. (1924).
11.

GUY, J.
Kent Castles, gardens & ancient houses.
James Pike. St. Ives. 1977.
3,6,11,28.

THE ILLUSTRATED HANDBOOK to the Rosherville
Botanical & Zoological Gardens, County Kent.
(Rosherville Gardens Company) n.d.
11.

INTERNATIONAL COMMITTEE ON MONUMENTS AND SITES.
National Committee for the United Kingdom.
UK ICOMOS Historic Gardens Committee.
A preliminary and interim list of gardens and
parks of outstanding historic interest.
UK ICOMOS Historic Gardens Committee.(1980).
23.

ISAAC, A SON OF ABRAHAM pseud.*
A visit to the Rosherville Gardens.
Hart Street School. 1844.
9.

McLELLAN, Doreen.
Rosherville Gardens, compiled by Mrs. D.
McLellan. (Local History pamphlet No.6)
K.C.L. Gravesham Division. 1976.
4,9,20.

MELVILLE, Henry.*
Illustrated guide to the botanical gardens,
at Rosherville, near Gravesend.
Tyler and Reed.(1843).
2,9,17.

NATIONAL GARDENS SCHEME.*
Beautiful Kent Gardens. 1948.
17.

Gardens of Kent...open to the public.*
1951, 1952, 1954, 1955 to date.
Stanford Printing Company, Tunbridge Wells.
3.

SACKVILLE-WEST, Victoria (afterwards Lady
                              Nicolson)
Victoria Sackville-West's garden book: a coll-
ection from "In your garden" by Phillipa Nicolson.
M. Joseph. 1968.
Sixth impression. 1976.
11,23.

SCOTT-JAMES, Anne.
Sissinghurst: the making of a garden. (The
garden at Long Barn, near Knole is also
described).
M. Joseph. 1974.
3,6,8,11,12,15,16,22.

WHITE, John T.
Parklands of Kent.
A.J. Cassell. Sheerness. 1975.
2,3,4,5,6,7,8,9,11,15,16,22,28,30.

WOOLWICH BOROUGH COUNCIL.
Opening of the gardens at Well Hall by the
Worshipful, the Mayor of Woolwich on Thursday,
25th May, 1933.
11.

WRIGHT, Tom.
The gardens of Britain. Volume 4: Kent,
East & West Sussex and Surrey, by Tom Wright
in Association with the Royal Horticultural
Society.
Batsford. 1978.
1,2,3,5,11,12,13,16,19,23.

GAVELKIND

ROBINSON, Thomas.*
Common law of Kent: or, the customs of
Gavelkind with an appendix concerning Borough-
English.
Printed by R.&.B. Nutt & F. Gosling for
F. Cogan. London. 1741.
2,11,25.

SANDYS, Charles.*
Consuetudines Kanciae: a history of gavelkind
and other remarkable customs in the County of Kent.
John Russell Smith. London. 1851.
3,9,26.

SOMNER, William.*
Treatise of gavelkind, both name and thing.
2nd edition.
F. Gyles etc. 1776.
2.

TAYLOR, Silas.*
History of gavel-kind - with the etymology thereof.
John Starkey. 1663.
2.

GAVELKIND Cont'd

TAYLOR, Silas.
The history of gavel-kind with the etymology
there of. Facsimile reprint of 1663 edition.
Sherwin & Frentel. Los Angeles, 1970.
2.

GENEALOGICAL RECORDS

BLOMFIELD, Kathleen.*
National Index of parish register copies;
compiled for the Society of Genealogists, by
K. Blomfield & H.K. Percy-Smith.
Society of Genealogists. London. 1939.
3,11.

BRETT, Sir Henry.
White Wings. Vol.II. Founding of the
(New Zealand) Provinces and old-time passenger
lists, 1840 - 1885.
(Includes list of passenger ships to 1886).
Capper Press. New Zealand. 1976.
11.

BRIGG, William.*
Genealogical abstracts of wills proved in
the Prerogative Court of Canterbury.
Register "Wootton" 1658. 2vols.
The Authors. 1894- 1914.
2,12.

BURCHALL, Michael J.
Index of East-Sussex parish records, 1275 - 1870.
Manuscripts of Sussex for the Sussex Family
History Group. 1975.
11.

BURN, John Southerden.
The history of Parish Registers in England,
also of the register of Scotland, Ireland,
the East and West Indies, the Dissenters and
the episcopal chapels in and about London.
1st edition.1879.
2nd edition.1862. Published by J.R. Smith.
Reprinted by E.P. Publishing. 1976.
11,23.

CHARLTON SOCIETY.
St. Luke, Charlton: Parish Register 1653 - 1753.
Charlton Society /Greenwich Arts Council. (1977).
11.
St. Luke,Charlton: Parish Register 1754 - 1798.
Charlton Society /Greenwich Arts Council. (1977).
11.

CHESTER, J.L.*
Allegations for marriage licences issued from the
Faculty Office of the Archbishop of Canterbury...
1543 - 1869. Compiled by J.L. Chester and
edited by G.J. Armytage.
Harleian Society. 1886.
2.

COCK, Frederick William.*
Notes from the transcripts and registers of
Appledore, Kent.
(Sold for the benefit of the Village Hall Fund)
1927.
1,3,12.

THE COUNTY OF KENT and many of its family records.*
Truman Press. 1896.
2.

COWPER, Joseph Meadows.*
Canterbury Marriage Licences,compiled by
J.M.Cowper. Six series, 1568 - 1750.
Cross & Jackman. Canterbury. 1892 - 1906.
2.

Canterbury Marriage Licences.*
Third Series. 1661 - 1676, compiled by
J.M. Cowper.
Cross & Jackman. Canterbury. 1896.

Canterbury Marriage Licences. Fourth Series.
1677 - 1700, compiled by J.M. Cowper.
Cross & Jackman. Canterbury. 1898.
7.

COX, John Charles.
Parish Registers of England.
E.P. Publishing Ltd. 1974.
28.

DOVER - THE FRENCH CHURCH.*
Registers, 5th May 1646 - 15th November,
1726, transcribed by F.A. Crisp.
P.P. 1888.
2,7,11,12

DUNCAN, Leland Lewis.
Abstract of all the wills of Biddenden
folk proved in the Prerogative Court of
Canterbury, extracted and edited by Leland
L. Duncan. n.d.
(Typewritten copy).
11.

The register of all the marriages, christenings
and burials in the church of St. Margaret,
Lee,..., from 1579 - 1754,
edited by L.L. Duncan and A.O. Barron.
Antiquarian Society. Lewisham. 1888.
2.

ELECTORAL REGISTERS AND POLL BOOKS
See
Kent Directories Located until 1974.
After 1974.see ELECTIONS in this volume.

GENERAL REGISTER OFFICE.
Census Returns:
Brenchley (part of) 1861   23
Chiddingstone.   1851   23
Paddock Wood.   1871.   23.
Yalding.   1851   23.

Census Returns, 1841, 1851, 1861, 1871. Kent.
Microfilm.
11.

Census Returns, 1841, 1851, 1861, 1871.
Addington, Aylesford, Birling, Borough Green,
Ditton, East Malling, East Peckham, Hadlow,
Hildenborough, Ightham, Leybourne, Mereworth,
Offham, Paddlesworth, Platt, Plaxtol, Ryarsh,
Shipbourne, Snodland, Southborough, Stansted,
Tonbridge, Trottiscliffe, Wateringbury,
West Malling, West Peckham, Wouldham, Wrotham.
23.

GIBSON, J.S.W.
Census Returns, 1841, 1851, 1861, & 1871.
on microfilm. A directory of local holdings,
compiled by J.S.W. Gibson.
Gulliver Press & Federation of Family
History Societies.
1979.   23
1980.   13, 23.

GRAHAM, Norman H.
The genealogists' consolidated guide to Parish
Registers in the London area, 1538 to 1837.
Compiled and arranged by N.H. Graham.
The Author. Petts Wood. 1977.
11.

HOVENDEN, Robert.*
The register of all the christenings, marriages,
and burials in the parish of St. Mary, Chislet..
from...1538 to 1707, edited by R. Hovenden.
Mitchell & Hughes. 1887.
3,4,11,12,
17. (MSS copy in Latin).

HUSSEY, Arthur.*
Eastry Wills (continued). Reprinted from
Archaeologia Cantiana. Vol.XXXIX, 1927.
Headley Bros. Ashford. (1927).
11.

Hythe Wills, Third and final part.
Reprinted from Archaeologia Cantiana.
Vol. LI. 1940.
11.

HUSSEY, Arthur.*
Reculver and Hoath wills; transcribed by
A.H. Reprinted from Archaeologia Cantiana.
Vol. XXXII, 1917.
Mitchell, Hughes & Clarke. 1917.
4,8,10,11,30.

Sittingbourne Wills.* (concluded).
Reprinted from Archaeologia Cantiana. Vol. XLIII
1931.
Headley Bros. Ashford. 1931.
4,10,11,17.

INDEX OF ADMINISTRATIONS IN THE PREROGATIVE COURT
OF CANTERBURY.*
(5volumes in 7 lacking Volume 2. Part 1).
British Record Society. 1944 - 68.
2.

INDEX OF WILLS AND ADMINISTRATIONS*now preserved
in the probate registry at Canterbury, Vol 2,
edited by C.H. Ridge.
British Record Society. 1940.
1.

INDEX OF WILLS.* proved in the Prerogative Court
of Canterbury (12 volumes. Lacking Volumes 1,7,8).
British Record Society. 1895 - 1960 (some
reprinted).
2.

INDEX TO THE WILLS proved in the Prerogative
Court of Canterbury, 1750 - 1800.Volume 1.A-BH.
Vol.II BI-CE, compiled by Anthony J. Camp.
Society of Genealogists 1976 and 1977.
Vol 1. 2.3.5.11..
Vol II. 3,11.

JENKINS, Robert Charles.*
The Saxon dynasty. Pedigree of the Kentish Kings.
J. English, Folkestone. 1867.
2,4.

KENT COUNTY COUNCIL: ARCHIVES OFFICE.
Notes on records: sources of genealogical information.
K.C.C.   n.d.
4.

Parish records and transcripts in the Kent County
Archives Office.
K.C.C. 1977.
2,3,5,8,11,13,23.

MAIDSTONE CENSUS 1821.
Enumerator's Returns for two districts
of Maidstone taken on 28th May, 1821.
Photocopy of MSS.
12.

MATTHEWS, John.*
Year Books of the probates from 1607...Abstracts of
Probate Acts in the Prerogative Court of
Canterbury. 2vols edited by J & G.F. Matthews.
1903 - 7.
2.

MISCELLANEA GENEALOGICA ET HERALDICA.
Fifth Series Vol.4, parts 5 and 6, containing the
Charlton pedigree and some extracts from Kent Wills;
part of "Monumental Inscriptions in Bromley Church",
edited by Clarke & R. Holworthy.
Mitchell, Hughes and Clarke. 1921.
2.

MORRISON, John Harold.*
Prerogative Court of Canterbury:
Letters of Administration 1620 - 1630 inclusive,
edited by J.H. Morrison.
P.P. 1935.
2,3,11.

Register "Scroope" (1630) edited by J.H.Morrison,
Abstracts & index.
P.P. 1934.
2,3,11,12.

Wills, sentences and Probate Acts, 1661 - 1670
inclusive, edited by J.H. Morrison.
P.P. 1935.
3,5,12.

NORTH, Jon.
Quaker Records. Talk given by Jon North to the
Kent Family History Society in Canterbury
15th Nov. 1974.
Typescript. 1974.
3.

ORIGINAL PARISH REGISTERS IN RECORD OFFICES AND
LIBRARIES. Local Population Studies in
Association with the Cambridge Group For the
History of Population and Social Structure.
1974.
11.
First Supplement 1976. 23.
Second Supplement 1978. 23.

PARISH REGISTERS OF SHIPBOURNE, Co. Kent. 12th
June 1560 - 19th July, 1658. (Printed).
23.

PLUMER, Henry R.
Inhabitants of West Kent, 1487 - 8. (That is,
those paying tithes to Sir John Leigh).
Extracted from The British Archivist Vol.I.
No.5, July 1913.
11.

POLLBOOKS AND ELECTORAL REGISTERS NOT INCLUDED
IN KENT DIRECTORIES LOCATED. See
ELECTIONS.

PREROGATIVE COURT OF CANTERBURY.
Inventories-Series 2. Part I. 1702, 1718 - 1733;
Part II 1734 - 1782 with index.
List and Index Society. 1973.
12.

PUTNAM, Eben.*
Two early passenger lists, 1635 - 1637.
(Reprinted from the New England Historical and
Genealogical Society Register, July, 1921).
1921.
12.

REEVES, M.
An index of Bromley, Kent, parish registers,
compiled by M. Reeves and others from the
transcript in the Library of the Society of
Genealogists. (typescript). 1973.
2.

ROCHESTER CATHEDRAL.*
Registers of the Cathedral Church of Rochester,
1657 - 1837, edited by Thomas Schindler.
Cross & Jackman. Canterbury. 1892.
2,3,8,9,11,12,15.

ROCHESTER DIOCESAN CONFERENCE - ECCLESIASTICAL
RECORDS COMMITTEE.*
The Parish Registers and Records in the Diocese
of Rochester: a summary of information collected
by the Ecclesiastical Records Committee of the
Rochester Diocesan Conference, with an introduction
by Rev. W.E. Buckland M.A.
Kent Archaeological Society.
Printed by Mitchell, Hughes and Clarke. 1912.
25.

ST. BOTOLPH'S CHURCH, Northfleet.
Parish Registers - Baptisms 1539 - 1653 and
1680 - 1748. Transcript made by Thomas Colyer-
Ferguson from Northfleet Parish Church Records.
E. Green and C. Ford. 1972.
9.

ST. LUKE THE EVANGELIST'S CHURCH, CHARLTON.
Parish Registers. 4 vols.
J.G. Smith. 1977 - 1978.
2.

SIMS, Richard.
A manual for the genealogist, topographer,
antiquary and legal professor, consisting of
descriptions of public records: parochial and
other registers, wills, county and family
histories.....
Edward Avery, London. 1888.
11.

GENEALOGICAL RECORDS Cont'd

SOCIETY OF GENEALOGISTS.
A list of parishes in Boyd's marriage index.
(pp. 18 - 19 Kent).
Phillimore 1974, reprinted 1976.
23.
11. 1974.

SQUIBB, G.D.
Visitation pedigrees and the genealogist.
Pinhorns. 2nd edition. 1978.
23.

TELFORD, Christopher.
Some Seventeenth Century marriages of some
important Kent families. In Topographical
Quarterly, Vol. IV. No.2. (Spring). 1936.
11.

THE VISITATION OF ENGLAND AND WALES, Vol.4,
edited by J.J. Howard and A.J. Crisp.
P.P. 1896.
3.

THE VISITATION OF KENT TAKEN IN THE YEARS
1530 - 31*by Thomas Benolte, Clarenceux, and
in 1574. Part 1. A - H. by Robert Cooke,
Clarenceux, and edited by W.B.Bannerman.
Harleian Society. 1923.
2.

THE VISITATION OF KENT TAKEN IN THE YEARS
1574* Part 2, I - Z and in 1592, by Robert
Cooke, Clarenceux, and edited by W.B. Bannerman.
Harleian Society. 1924.
2.

THE VISITATION OF KENT TAKEN IN THE YEARS 1619-
1621.*.by John Philipott, edited by R. Hovenden.
The Harleian Society. 1898.
2,24.

WILLIS, Arthur J.*
Canterbury Marriage Licences (General)
1568 - 1646, compiled by A.J. Willis.
Phillimore. 1972.
2,6,7,12,24,28.

Canterbury Marriage Licences 1751 - 1780,
compiled by A.J. Willis.
A.J. Willis, Folkestone. 1967.
24,30.

Canterbury Marriage Licences 1781 - 1809,
compiled by A.J. Willis.
A.J. Willis, Folkestone. 1969.
6,7,11,12,24,30.

Canterbury marriage licences. 1810 - 1837,
compiled by A.J. Willis.
Phillimore. 1971.
2,6,7,12,24,28,30.

GEOGRAPHY

BOLTON, Thomas.
Geography through Fieldwork. Book 3.
Studies in Wales, Scotland and England.
pp. 54 - 87 - The Wealden District of
South East England.
Blandford Press. 1970.
11.

BOSWORTH, George F.*
Kent (Cambridge County Geographies).
Cambridge University Press.
1909. 1.3.4.5.6.7.8.9.13.14.17.18,21,25.
1922. Pocket edition. 8.

Kent: its geography and history. (For Schools)
G. Philip and Son. 1900.
11.

Kent past and present.*
(See also Kent Bibliography, for other editions).
George Philip 1901.
6,7,8,12,13,26.

COLEMAN, Alice Mary.*
East Kent: a description of the Ordnance Survey.
Seventh edition One-inch sheet 173, by
A.M. Coleman and C.T. Lukehurst.
(British Landscape through maps).
Geographical Association. 1967.
2,3,4,6,20,23,24,30.

Field excursions in South-East England.
(Field studies for schools:11), by Alice Mary
Coleman and Clare T. Lukehurst.
Rivingtons. 1974.
3,6,11,16.

DELANY, Mary Cecilia.*
The historical geography of the Wealden Iron
Industry.
Benn. 1921.
1,2,3,5,11,15,19,26.

DOBSON, F.R.*
The South-east: a Regional Study.
English University Press. 1968.
12,13.

McRAE, Stuart Gordon.
The rural landscape of Kent, by S.G. McRae and
C.P. Burnham.
Wye College. 1973.
1,2,4,5,6,9,11,19,20,24,25,26,27,28,30.

MARCHINGTON, Trevor.
Studies in South-East England, by Trevor
Marchington and Brian P. Price. (pp.55 - 65,
North-East Kent). School Text Book.
Oxford University Press.1973.
6,11,19.

MARTIN, J.E.
Greater London: an industrial geography.
G. Bell. 1966.
1.

MASON, Oliver.
South-East England.
John Bartholomew and Sons, Ltd. 1979.
12.

MILLWARD Roy.
East Kent, by R. Millward and A. Robinson.
Macmillan. 1973.
11.

The Hoo Peninsula and the Scarplands of Mid-
West Kent, by R. Millward and A. Robinson.
Macmillan. 1971.
4,6,8,11.

Lower Thameside, by R. Millward and A. Robinson.*
Macmillan. 1971.
4,5,8,11.

South-East England - the Channel Coastlands,
by Roy Millward and Adrian Robinson.
Macmillan. 1973.
11.

South-East England: Thameside and the Weald,
by R. Millward and A. Robinson. (Landscapes
of Britain).
Macmillan. 1971.
2,11,16.

South East England
The Low Weald and Downs, by Roy Millward and
Adrian Robinson. (Landscapes of Britain).
Macmillan. 1973.

Thameside and the Weald, by Roy Millward and
Adrian Robinson.
Macmillan. 1971.
2,3,4,5,9,11,12,16,19,21.

ROWSELL, E.H.
Rainfall over the areas of the Kent and East
and West Sussex River Boards. 1916 - 1950.
Meteoroligical Office. 1963. (1973 reprint).
2.

GEOGRAPHY Cont'd

SAVORY, Henry Jarvis.*
South East England.
(Geography of the British Isles Series).
Cambridge University Press.1972.
4,6,7,11.

SMITH, A.
A geographical study of the agriculture on
the Kentish Manors of Canterbury Cathedral
Priory, 1272 - 1379. (M.A. Dissertation,
University of Liverpool).
Photocopy. n.d.
3.

THORNHILL, J.F.P.*
Downs and Weald: a social geography of
South-East England.
Christophers. n.d.
1935. 2,11.
1937. 4,11.

GEOLOGY

ALLEN, P.*
Geology of the Central Weald: the Hastings
beds. Geologists' Association Guides. No.24.
Benham and Co. Ltd. 1958.
4,12,15,17,30.

BRADE-BIRKS, Stanley Graham.
The soil as a natural object: pedology on
a branch of geology.
In The Journal of the Agricola Club and Snarley
Guild. Vol.VIII No.2. 1971-72. pp.42-50?
3.

BRISTOW, Clement Roger.*
Geology of the country around Royal Tunbridge
Wells, by C.R. Bristow and R.A.Bazley. etc.
(Explanation of one-inch Geological Sheet 303-
new series).
H.M.S.O. 1972.
2,3,6,7,11,12,13,16.25.

BRITISH MUSEUM: NATURAL HISTORY - Dept. of GEOLOGY.
British Caenozoic Fossils. (Tertiary and
quaternary) 4th edn. (Herne Bay is an important
location for Fossils).
British Museum. 1971.
30.

Catalogue of the Mesozoic plants in the Department
of Geology, The British Museum (Natural History):*
The Wealden Flora by A.C. Seward.
British Museum. 1894 - 5.
4,11.

BROWN, E.E.S.
Report of field meetings at Herne Bay and
Reculver. In Proceedings of the Geologists'
Association. Vol.47. Part 4, 1936.
pp. 349 - 350.
30.

BUTTERWELL, W.*
Bulletin of the Geological Research of Great
Britain.
H.M.S.O. 1954.
6.

COOLING, Christine M.
Record of Wells in the area of Chatham (Explanation
of the one-inch geological sheet 272 -
New Series).
H.M.S.O. 1964.
20.

Record of Wells in the area of the new series one-
inch (geological) Faversham (273) and Ramsgate
(274) Sheets. Geological Survey and Museum,
Water Supply Papers: Well Catalogue.
H.M.S.O. 1964.
11,20.

COOLING, Christine M.
Record of Wells in the area of New Series one-
inch (Geological) Reigate (286) and Sevenoaks
(287) sheets, by Christine M. Cooling and others.
Institute of Geological Sciences, Water Supply
Papers, Well Catalogue Series.
Natural Environment Research Council: H.M.S.O.1968.
23.

COOPER, John.
The Palaeontology of the London Clay (Lower
Eocene) of the Herne Bay coastal sections, Kent,
England. In Proceedings of the Geological
Association Vol. 88(3) pp. 163 - 178. 1977.
30.

DAVIS, Arthur G.
The London clay of Sheppey and the location of
its Fossils. In Proceedings of the
Geologists' Association. Vol.47. Pt.4. 1936.
pp. 328 - 345.
30.

DESTOMBES, J.P.*
Geological results of the Channel Tunnel site
investigation 1964 - 65. by J.P. Destombes and
E.R. Shephard-Thorn.
H.M.S.O. 1971.
4,6.

DEWEY, Henry.*
Geology of the country around Dartford.
(Explanation of the one-inch Geological Sheet
271), by H. Dewey, C.E.N. Bromehead, C.P.
Chatwin and H.G. Dines.
H.M.S.O. 1924.
1,4,5,8,9,11,12,15,17,18,19.

DIBLEY, George Edward.
Additional notes on the chalk of the Medway
Valley, Gravesend, West Kent, North East Surrey
and Grays (Essex). Reprinted from Proceedings
of the Geologists' Association. Vol.XXIX 1918.
pp68 - 105. 1918.
9.

DINES, H.G.*
Geology of the country around Chatham, by
H.G. Dines and others. (Explanation of the
one-inch Geological Sheet 272. New series).
H.M.S.O. 1954.
1,2,4,5,6,8,9,11,12,15,16,19,20,25,26,27.

The same - 1954 edition reprinted with amendments
by H.G. Dines.
H.M.S.O. 1971.
1,2,4,5,6,7,9,11,12,13,19,20,26,27.

Geology of the country around Sevenoaks and
Tonbridge, by H.G. Dines and others. (Explanation
of the one-inch Geological Sheet 287. New Series).
H.M.S.O. 1969.
2,3,4,6,9,12,13,16.

DINGWALL, R.G.
The structural and stratigraphical geology of
a portion of the Eastern English Channel.
H.M.S.O. 1971.
8.

DREW, Frederic.*
Geology of the country between Folkestone and
Rye, including the whole of Romney Marsh.
Longman,Green, Longman, Roberts & Green. 1864.
11.

EDMUNDS, F.H.*
Geology of the Wealden District. (British Regional
Geology Series).
H.M.S.O.
1stedition1935. 1.2.4.7.8.11.17.
2ndedition1948. 1.3.4.5.6.7.9.11.13.15.19.20.25.
3rdedition1954. 17.

GEOLOGY.   Cont'd

GALLOIS, R.W.*
Geology of the Wealden district. 4th edition.
(British Regional Geology), by R.W. Gallois
based on the previous editions by the late
F.H. Edmunds.
H.M.S.O. 1965.
2,3,4,5,6,7,8,9,10,11,12,15,16,19,20,24,25,30.

GEOLOGICAL SURVEY OF ENGLAND AND WALES.
Geology of the Country around Dorking.
H.M.S.O./University Microfilms. (1924 Fac.reprint)
2.

GEOLOGICAL SURVEY OF GREAT BRITAIN.
Summary of the progress of the Geological
Survey of Great Britain, Part 2.*
H.M.S.O. 1932.
6.

GURR, Philip R.
A new Fish Fauna from the Woolwich bottom
bed (Sparnacian) of Herne Bay, Kent,
in Proceedings of the Geologists'
Association Vol. 73, 1962, pp.419 - 447.
30.

HARVEY, Betty, Ida.
Records of wells in the area around Dartford:
inventory for one-inch geological sheet 271,
new series, by Betty I Harvey and others.
(Institute of Geological Sciences, Well
Inventory Series: Metric Units).
H.M.S.O. 1975.
1,2,9,11,23.

HEPWORTH, J*.
Rochester and district. A sketch-guide to
its geology, flora and fauna, compiled by
J. Hepworth.
Parrett & Neves. 1913.
2.

KIRKALDY, John Francis.*
Geology of the Weald. (Geologists'
Association Guides No.29)
Benham & Son. Colchester.
1958.   1,3,4,5,7,8,9,11,12,15,17.
1960.   25.
1967.   2,6,30.
1976.3rd edition revised by F.A. Middlemiss and
       others.   3,6,12.

LAMPLUGH, G.W.*
Concealed mesozoic rocks in Kent,by G.W.
Lamplugh, F.L. Kitchin and J. Pringle.
(Geological Survey -memoirs).
H.M.S.O. 1923.
3,4,11,6,9,19.

LAPWORTH, Herbert.*
Hydro-geological survey: East Kent Water
Supply.   Report July 1st. 1930.
Austens. 1930.
3,7,11.

MAIZELS, Judith K.
Geology in Kent and East Sussex; an
illustrated Guide.
The Author, Printed by Colecraft.
Canterbury. 1975.
3,11,13,30.

MILBOURNE, Raymond A.*
The Gault at Greatness Lane, Sevenoaks, Kent.
(Proceedings of the Geologists' Association
Vol.66, Part 3, 1956. pp. 235 - 242). Photocopy.
Benham & Son. Colchester.
11,16.

Notes on the Gault near Sevenoaks, Kent.
(Proceedings of the Geologists' Association
Vol.72, Part 4, 1961 pp. 437 - 443).
Photocopy.
Benham & Son. Colchester.
16.

MURCHISON, Sir Frederick.
On the distribution of the flint drift of
the South-East of England to the South and
North of the Weald, and over the surface of
the South Downs.   From the Quarterly Journal
of the Geological Society of London. Vol.VII.1851.
11.

PITCHER, Wallace Spencer.*
The London Region (South of the Thames).
(Geologists' Association Guides No.30)
Benham & Son. Colchester. 1958.
4,12,17.

The London Region (South of the Thames).
(Geologists' Association Guides No.30B).
Revised edn. by W.S. Pitcher and others.
Benham and Son. Colchester. 1967.
2,3,4,9,11,20.

ROYAL SOCIETY.
A discussion on problems associated with the
subsidence of Southeastern England. Contents
include: The Thames Barrier (Phil. Trans.A.
Vol. 272. No. 1221).
Royal Society. 1972.
4.

SHEPHARD-THORN, E.R.*
Geology of the country around Tenterden by
E.R. Shephard-Thorn and others. (Explanation
of the one-inch Geological Sheet. No.304 New series).
H.M.S.O. 1966.
1,3,4,5,7,8,11,12,15,16,17,19.

S.E. England and the Thames: a field guide,
by E.R. Shephard-Thorn and J.J. Eymer.
Geo.Abstracts Ltd. Norwich. 1977.
5.

SHERLOCK, R.L.*
London and the Thames Valley. 2nd edition.
(British Regional Geology).
H.M.S.O. 1947.
4,9,19.

The Same.   3rd edn.
H.M.S.O. 1962.
2,5,8,16.

SMART, J.G.O.*
Geology of the country around Canterbury and
Folkestone,by J.G.O. Smart and others.
(Combined memoir in explanation of the one-
inch Geological Sheets 289, 305, and 306 -
New Series).
H.M.S.O. 1966.
1,2,3,4,5,6,7,8,9,10,11,14,15,16,19,24,30.

The same - H.M.S.O. 1975.
13.

SO, C.L.
Coastal platforms of the Isle of Thanet, Kent.
(photocopy of Ms).
1964.
24.

SPURRELL, F.C.J.*
A sketch of the history of the rivers and
denudation of West Kent. etc.
West Kent Natural History Society.
Printed by E.G. Berryman and Sons, Greenwich.1886.
11,17.

TOPLEY, William.
Geology of the Hythe District. (Kent Miscellanea
Vol.3). 1883.
11.

Geology of the Straits of Dover. Reprinted
from the Quarterly Journal of Science,
April. 1872.
7.

Geology of the Weald.
Longmans. 1875.
1.7,11,12.15,17,19.

On the Agricultural Geology of the Weald.
From The Journal of the Royal Agricultural
Society of England. Vol. VIII, Pt. II.
William Clowes. 1872.
7.

Proceedings of the Geologists' Association
Vol.86, Pt.4., commemorating the centenary
of the publication of "The Geology of the
Weald" by William Topley.
Geologists' Association. 1976.
2.

GEOLOGY Cont'd

WARD, D.J.
The Lower London Tertiary (palaeocene),
succession of Herne Bay, Kent.
(Inst. of Geological Sciences Report. 78/10)
H.M.S.O. 1978.
2.

WEALD RESEARCH COMMITTEE.
Report of the Weald Research Committee,
November 1928.
Reprinted from the Proceedings of the
Genealogical Association Vol XXXIX Pt.3.
1928.
3.

WEIR, A.H.
Post Facial Soil Formation in the Loess of
Pegwell Bay, by A.H. Weir and others.
From Geoderma Vol.5. 1971.
Elsevier. 1971.
24.

WHITAKER, William.*
Report of an excursion to Reculver. in
Proceedings of the Geologists' Association
Vol.23. Pt.4. 1912. pp. 247 - 249.
30.

The Water supply of Kent, with records of
Sinkings and borings, by W. Whitaker and
others. (Memoirs of the Geological Survey
of England and Wales).
H.M.S.O. 1908.
1,2,4,5,7,9,11,12,25.

WHITE, H.J. Osborne.*
Geology of the country near Hastings and
Dungeness (Explanation of the one-inch
Geological Sheets 320 and 321).
H.M.S.O. 1928.
7,11.

Geology of the country near Ramsgate and
Dover. (Explanation of the one-inch Geological
Sheets 274 and 290).
H.M.S.O. 1928.
1,6,7,11,13,14,17.

WORSSAM, Bernard Charles.*
Geology of the country around Maidstone.
(Explanation of the one-inch Geological
Sheet 288 - New Series).
H.M.S.O. 1963.
1,3,4,5,6,7,8,11,12,15,16,17,19,25.

Stratigraphy of the Weald Clay - Report 78/11.
Institute of Geological Sciences.
H.M.S.O. 1978.
2,11,23.

A new look at river capture and at the
denudation history of the Weald.
H.M.S.O. 1973.
5,7,11.

GHOSTS.

AITKEN, George A.*
Defoe's "Apparition of Mrs. Veal"
Photocopy of an article appearing in
The Nineteenth Century Vol. XXXVII, 1895.
3.

BAINE, Rodney.M.*
The apparition of Mrs. Veal: a neglected
account. Photocopy of an article appearing
in Proceedings of the Modern Language
Association, Vol.LXIX. 1954.
3.

Defoe and Mrs. Bargraves' Story.
Photocopy of an article in The Philological
Quarterly. Vol. XXXIII, IV, October, 1954.
3.

BRETHERTON, Ralph Harold.*
The apparition of Mrs. Veal. An article
appearing in the Gentleman's Magazine,
December 1901.
3.

COCK, Frederick William.
An old Kentish ghost story. Extracted from the
oldest Kentish newspaper, 'The Kentish Gazette'.
For March 17 - 20. 1779.
From the 'Kentish Express'
August 7th, 1915.
3.

DEFOE, Daniel.*
A true revelation of the apparition of one
Mrs Veal...at Canterbury, the 8th September,
1705. 10th edition. n.d.
3.

FORMAN, Joan.
The Haunted South.
Hale. 1978.
4,12.

GREEN, Andrew.
Ghosts of the South East.
David and Charles. 1976.
3,6,11,12,22,28.

Ghosts of Tunbridge Wells.
John Hilton. Hadlow. 1978.
11,12,19,23.

Phantom Ladies.
(Includes ghosts at Bridge, Broadstairs,
Chilham, Cranbrook, Fawkham Green, Folkestone,
Margate , New Romney, Oxney Bottom, Plaxtol
and Pluckley).
Bailey Bros. 1977.
3.

HIGENBOTTAM, Frank.*
The apparition of Mrs. Veal to Mrs. Bargrave
at Canterbury, 8th September, 1705.
Reprinted from Archaeologia Cantiana. Vol.73.
1959.
3,11,17.

KENTISH GAZETTE AND CANTERBURY PRESS.*
Mrs. Veal's apparition.
Reprinted from an article in the Kentish
Gazette and Canterbury Press. May 19th 1931.
3.

METCALFE, Leon.
Discovering ghosts.
Shire Publications. 1972.
11.

SCOUTEN, Arthur H.*
An early printed report on the apparition of
Mrs. Veal.
Photocopy of an article in the Review of
English Studies, July 1955.
3.

At that moment of time: Defoe and
the early accounts of the apparition of
Mistress Veal. in Forum, Vol.II. No.2.
Winter 1961 - 62.
3.

SECORD, Arthur W.*
A September day in Canterbury: the Veal-
Bargrave story.
Reprinted from the Journal of English and
Germanic Philology Vol. LIV, No.4. October 1955.
3.

WEAVER, G.
Kent Ghosts (Viewing Kent Series).
James Pike. St. Ives. 1977.
2,3,6,11,19,28.

GILLINGHAM. See also
MEDWAY TOWNS.

BALDWIN, Ronald Arthur.*
The Jezreelites, the rise and fall of a
remarkable prophetic movement.
Lambarde Press. Orpington. 1962.
1,4,7,8,11,12,15,17.

GILLINGHAM BOROUGH COUNCIL.
Souvenir of the completion of the Gillingham
Sewerage Scheme.
Gillingham Borough Council. 1935.
8.

Souvenir programme of official opening of
the new Municipal Building. 1937.
Gillingham Borough Council. 1937.
8.

The William Adams Memorial: Souvenir Programme.
Gillingham Borough Council. 1934.
8.

GILLINGHAM BOROUGH COUNCIL - FINANCE DEPARTMENT.
The Borough of Gillingham rent allowance
scheme 1972.
Gillingham Borough Council. 1972.
8.

The Borough of Gillingham rent rebate scheme
1972.
Gillingham Borough Council. 1972.
8.

GILLINGHAM BOROUGH COUNCIL:LIBRARY AND ARTS
COMMITTEE.
Development of the library service 1957-1971.
Gillingham Borough Council. 1971.
8.

GILLINGHAM BOROUGH COUNCIL: PARKS AND
CEMETERIES DEPARTMENT.
Brief details of the Parks and Cemeteries
Department. (Duplicated pamphlet).
Gillingham Borough Council. 1973.
11.

GILLINGHAM BOROUGH COUNCIL: ROAD SAFETY/
HOME SAFETY COMMITTEE.
Accident Prevention Handbook.
Gillingham Borough Council. 1969.
8.

"THE GILLINGHAM CITIZEN". No.15 July 1911.
(Coronation of King George V).
8.

GILLINGHAM DISTRICT SCOUT COUNCIL.
Official handbook. 1970-71.
Gillingham District Scout Council.   (1970)
8.

GILLINGHAM: King George V. Memorial
Houses for the aged.
1937.
8.

GILLINGHAM. PARISH OF SOUTH GILLINGHAM.
Welcome to our community of South
Gillingham: a directory.
South Gillingham Parish Office. Wigmore. 1973.
4.

GILLINGHAM PARISH MAGAZINE 1886 - 1903.
8.

GILLINGHAM PUBLIC LIBRARY.*
Archives Collection. 2nd.edition (Local
History Series 1).
Gillingham Public Library. 1972.
4,6,7,8,25.

The Bookman's Door: the quarterly magazine
of Gillingham Public Libraries.
No 1. November 1950.
No 4. November 1951.
4.

Directory of local societies and organisations
9th edition.
Gillingham Public Library. 1972.
4.

1971 entry to the John Cotton Dora Library
public relations award contest (2 vols).
Gillingham Library. 1971.
8.

GILLINGHAM PUBLIC LIBRARY
1972 entry to the John Cotton Dora library
public relations award contest (2 vols).
Gillingham Library. 1972.
8.

Will Adams 1564 - 1620:* an exhibition and
lecture to commemorate the 400th anniversary
of his birth.
K.C.C. 1964.
4,8.

GILLINGHAM TOWN CARNIVAL 1938.
(Official programme).
8.

GILLINGHAM WORKING MENS' CLUB & INSTITUTE
SOCIETY.
Rules, 1903.
8.

GRAY, Geoffrey T.
The Story of Gillingham Church.
?The Author. 1968?
8.

GREAT BRITAIN. Laws, etc. (Geo.V).*
Gillingham Corporation Act 1931. An Act to
confer further powers upon the Mayor, Aldermen
and Burgesses of the Borough of Gillingham with
regard to their electricity undertaking...
H.M.S.O. 1931.
8,11.

GREAT BRITAIN, Laws, etc. (Eliz.II)
STATUTORY INSTRUMENTS.
The Gillingham Link Trunk Road Order. 1962.
H.M.S.O. 1962.
8.

HARKNESS, Ariel Law.*
Gillingham parish church dedicated to St.
Mary Magdalene.
British Publishing Company. 1959.
11.

HARRIS, Edwin.*
The history of Gillingham.
(Eastgate series - No.30).
E. Harris. Rochester. 1922.
8.

The History of Gillingham Church.*
(Eastgate Series - No.31).
E. Harris. Rochester. 1922.
8.

Reminiscences of Gillingham.*
(Eastgate series - No.32).
E. Harris. Rochester. 1922.
8.

JONES, G.W.
Fort Darland, past and present.
Fort Research Group, Chatham (1978?).
11,32.

"KEARSNEY CHRONICLE" JUBILEE ISSUE, 1921-1971.
(Includes notes on Gillingham House(?) School).
Kearsney College. Natal S.A. 1971.
8.

KNIGHT, Charles.*
Gillingham Fort.
1935.
8,32.

The history of Gillingham Pier.
Reprinted from "Chatham,Rochester &
Gillingham News" 1935 .
8.

Shipbuilding at Gillingham.* Reprinted from
"Chatham,Rochester & Gillingham News". 1938.
4,8.

LANGDON, John A.*
The Fireman's Wedding Tragedy, 11th July, 1929.
(Local History Series No.3).
Gillingham Public Library. 1972.
4,6,7,12,25.

GILLINGHAM Cont'd

LEEDS, C.S.*
Chats about Gillingham: an outline of its
past and present history.
Parrett & Neves. Gillingham. 1906.
25.

McCUDDEN, James Thomas Byford.*
Documents relating to the presentation
of the Freedom of the Borough of Gillingham
to Major J.T.B. McCudden.
n.d.
8.

MURR, David.
A riverside walk in Gillingham's country
park. (Let's explore Gillingham 1).
Rainham,Gillingham & Chatham Amenity Society.
1978.
4.

NEWTON, A.P.*
Forge Lane School, 1872.
(Local History Series, No.4).
Gillingham Public Library. 1972.
4,6,7,11,12,25.

ROGERS, Philip George.*
A history of Gillingham (Kent).
Gillingham Borough Council. 1948.
2,25.

The sixth trumpeter:*the story of Jezreel
and his tower.
Oxford University Press. 1963.
1,2,3,4,6,7,8,9,11,12,15,25.
5 1970.

TOMLINSON, Norman.
The book of Gillingham.
Barracuda Books. Buckingham. 1979.
4,5,6,8,11,16,23.

Louis Brennan.
Hallewell Publications. 1980.
15.

TRIGGS, Roger.
Gillingham Football Club.
(Local History Series No.7).
Gillingham Public Library. 1973.
4,6,11,25.

UPBURY MANOR SCHOOL. A Summer Fair...
Souvenir programme in aid of the J.D.R. Mc.Vie
Commemoration Fund.
1970.
4.

WIGNALL, George Wilding.
Gillingham Grammar School. 1923 - 1973,
compiled by G.W. Wignall.
Kent Art Printers For Gillingham Grammar
School. (1974).
1,4,8,11,15.

WILKES, R.E.
Louis Brennan C.B. - Dirigible Torpedo.
Gillingham Public Library. 1973.
4,6,7,8,9,11,12,25.

Louis Brennan C.B. - Gyroscopic Monorail.
Gillingham Public Library. 1973.
4,6,7,8,9,11,12,25.

GODINTON PARK See GREAT CHART.

GODMERSHAM

HUSSEY, Christopher.
Godmersham Park, Kent: the home of Mr &
Mrs. Robert Tritton. (photocopy from
Country Life, Feb. 16 & 23, & 2 March 1945).
Country Life. 1945.
12.

GOODNESTONE

THE TOPOGRAPHER. No.XVIII, Sept. 1790,
being No. III of Vol. III.
Includes information of Goodnestone and
Nonington Church. (pp. 171 - 178 and pp. 150 -
155).
Robson. 1790.
11,12.

GOODWIN SANDS

CARTER, George Goldsmith.*
The Goodwin Sands.
Constable. 1953.
2,24,30.

GATTIE, George Byng.*
Memorials of the Goodwin Sands and their
surroundings, legendary and historical.
J.J. Keliher
1885. 2.
1904. 24.

ISLE OF THANET ARCHAEOLOGICAL UNIT.
Wreck of a British Man-of-War discovered on
the Goodwin Sands. (Interim Report). 1979.
Isle of Thanet Archaeological Unit. 1980.
13,24.

LARN, Richard.
Goodwin Sands Shipwrecks (Ships lost are
listed on pp. 165 - 174).
David & Charles. 1977.
3,5,6,7,11,13,14,15,19,22,23,28,29,30.

PAPERS RELATIVE TO AN ASYLUM for the ships
and mariners of all nations at the Goodwin Sands.
H. Baynes. 1853.
24.

TREANOR, Rev. Thomas Stanley.*
The cry from the sea and the answer from the shore.
Religious Tract Society. 1898.
6,22,24.

Heroes of the Goodwin Sands.*
Religious Tract Society.
24   1892.
22,13. 1898.
3.   1900.

GORDON, GENERAL CHARLES GEORGE R.E. 1833 - 1885.
(AT GRAVESEND 1865 - 1871).

ALLEN, Bernard H.
Gordon.
Duckworth. 1935.
32.

Gordon and the Sudan.
Macmillan. 1931.
32.

Gordon in China.*
Macmillan. 1933.
12,32.

ALLEN, Charles H.*
The Life of "Chinese" Gordon, R.E.C.B.,
Abraham Kingdon & Co. 1884.
9.

BEATTY, Charles.*
His country was the world: a study of Gordon
of Khartoum.
Chatto & Windus. 1954.
12.

BOULGER, D.C.*
The Life of Gordon. 2 vols.
Fisher Unwin. 1896.
12.

BUTLER, Sir William Francis.*
Charles George Gordon.
Macmillan. 1889.
9,12.

GORDON, GENERAL CHARLES GEORGE R.E. 1833-1885.
(AT GRAVESEND 1865-1871) Cont'd.

COMPTON, Piers.
The last days of General Gordon.
Hale.   1974.
9.

FRENCH, Lt. Col. the Hon. E. Gerald.*
Gordon Pasha of the Sudan: the life story of
an ill-requited Soldier.
Maclellan. Glasgow. 1958.
9,32.

GARRETT, Richard.
General Gordon.
Arthur Barker.   1974.
11.

GORDON, General Charles George.
Gordon's Campaigns in China.
Chapman and Hall. 1900.
32.

HANSON, Lawrence.
Gordon: the story of a hero, by Lawrence and
Elizabeth Hanson.
Peter Davies. 1953.
32.

HUTCHINSON, Lt. Col. G.S.
The Gordon Boys' School, Woking.
(A pamphlet). 1944.
32.

LIFE OF GENERAL GORDON.
Walter Scott, London. 1885.
11.

LILLEY, W.E.*
The Life and Work of General Gordon at
Gravesend.
Kingdom. (1885).
4,9,11.

McLELLAN, Doreen E.
General Gordon.
(Local History Pamphlet No.3).
K.C.L. Gravesham Division. (1976).
3,4,8,9,12,20.

MARLOWE, John.
Mission to Khartum: the apotheosis of
General Gordon.
Gollancz. 1969.
9.

NUTTING, Anthony.*
Gordon, martyr and misfit.
Constable. 1966.
12,32.

SMITH, George Barnett.
General Gordon: the Christian Soldier and hero.
S.M. Partridge & Co. Ltd. (1896).
11.

SPARROW, Gerald.
Gordon, Mandarin and Pasha.
Jarrolds. 1962.
32.

TAMES, Richard.
General Gordon: an illustrated life of Charles
George Gordon, 1833 - 1885.
Shire Publications. 1972.
9.

TRENCH, Charles Chenevix.
Charley Gordon: an eminent Victorian reassessed.
Allan Lane. 1978.
9,11.

TURNBULL, Patrick.
Gordon of Khartoum.
Bailey Bros. & Swinfen, Folkestone. 1975.
9.

WORTHAM, H.E.*
Gordon: an intimate portrait.
Harrap. 1933.
12,32.

GOUDHURST

GOUDHURST LADIES COLLEGE:Prospectus & particulars.
Selkirk Press for the College. 189?.
11.

GOUDHURST

KENT COUNTY COUNCIL: PLANNING DEPARTMENT*
Goudhurst: Village study.
K.C.C. 1967.
30.

THE LEGAT SCHOOL DEVELOPMENT FUND.
The Legat School,Finchcocks,Goudhurst,Kent.
(School for Ballet).
The Legat School Development Fund. 1966.
11.

(LIST OF INSCRIPTIONS ON MEMORIALS INSIDE
GOUDHURST CHURCH) (1967?).
Typewritten list signed Thomas Church July 1967.
11.

THE OLD BETHANIAN: Samuel Kendon, 20th December
1864 - 30th May 1945. (Headmaster of Bethany
School, Goudhurst, for Fifty one years, 1894 -
1945).
Knole Park Press. Sevenoaks. (1945?).
11.

THE OLD BETHANIAN: W.A. Benians 19th July 1851 -
11th May 1939. (Headmaster of Bethany School,
Goudhurst, 1878 - 1916).
Knole Park Press. Sevenoaks. (1939).
11.

TIFFIN, Alfred.
Loving and Serving: an account of the work of
J.W.C. Fegan, edited by G. Fielden Hughes.
(Blantyre House, Goudhurst, Detention Centre).
P.P. n.d.
17,19.

TIFFIN, A.W.*
Goudhurst Coronation Book; a record of celebrations
in Goudhurst & Kilndown on May 12th 1937...(Part
I. Coronation celebrations. Part II Reminiscences and Local Lore).Compiled by A.W.Tiffen.
Tunbridge Wells Courier.   1937.
1,2,3,4,5,8,11,12,15,19.

The Goudhurst jubilee book,* a record of
celebrations in Goudhurst & Kilndown on May 6th
1935...Compiled by A.W. Tiffin.
Tunbridge Wells Courier.   1935.
1,2,5,6,11,12,19.

GRAVENEY BOAT

EVANS, Angela C.
The Graveney Boat, by A.C. Evans & V.H. Fenwick.
The Graveney Boat was discovered in the Graveney
Marshes. It is now in the National Maritime
Museum, Greenwich.
In Antiquity Vol. XLV. June 1971.
11.

FENWICK, Valerie H.
The Graveney Boat: a Tenth-Century find from Kent.
Excavation and recording...edited by Valerie
Fenwick. (Archaeological Series, No.3. BAR
British Series 53).
National Maritime Museum & B.A.R. 1978.
2,4,

GREENHILL, Basil.
The Graveney Boat.
In Antiquity Vol. XLV. 1971. pp. 41 - 42.
11,17.

Three Major boat finds in Britain: papers read
at a symposium held at the National Maritime
Museum...16th October 1971. (Includes three
papers on the Graveney Boat). Maritime
Monographs and Reports No.6.
Maritime Museum, Greenwich. H.M.S.O. 1972.
11,20.

GRAVESEND

"AN OLD ST. JOHN'S BOY" pseud
St. John the Evangelist: the rise and progress
of Catholicity in the Borough of Gravesend,
1842 - 1884, by An Old St. John's Boy.
Thomas Hall. Gravesend. n.d.
11.

ARNOLD, George Matthews.*
A few remarks about Gravesend in olden days.
Robert Kerr. London. 1876.
11.

Fulborough Farmhouse, East Chalk, Gravesend,
with notes by Ralph Nevill. (Reprinted from
Archaeologia Cantiana. Vol. XXI. 1895).
Mitchell & Hughes. 189 .
11.

Gravesend Public Library. Opened by the
Worshipful the Mayor, George M. Arnold, Esq.,
28th September 1905.
G.M. Arnold. Printed by Caddel & Son. 1905.
11.

BENSON, James.
A history of Gravesend; or, A historical
perambulation of Gravesend & Northfleet. 1954.
Revised and edited by Robert Heath Hiscock. 1976.
Phillimore. 1976.
2,3,6,8,9,11,16,23,25.

BLANCHARD, Edward Litt. L.*
Adams' descriptive guide to the watering places
of England and companion to the coast.
(includes Gravesend). W.J. Adams.
9 1848, 1849, 1851.
11 1851
13 1848, 1849, 1850, 1851.
24 1851.

BURCHMORE, L.J.
Royal Air Force Station Gravesend goings on,
by Chiefy B.
The Author, Farnham. 1974.
9.

CARLEY, James.
The Gravesend to Wrotham Turnpike road.
Meopham Publications Committee. 1973.
2,9,11,23,25.

CENTRAL ELECTRICITY GENERATING BOARD.
SOUTH EASTERN REGION.
Scientific Services Centre, Gravesend.
Scientific Services Centre. C.E.G.B.
Central Electricity Generating Board. 197-?
11.

CLARK, Tim.
Psychopath: The case of Patrick Mackay by
Tim Clark and John Penyeate
Routledge & K. Paul. 1976.
9.

CLIFFORD, J.R.S.*
Gravesend and its neighbourhood.
Smither Bros. Gravesend. 1886.
5.

COGHLAN, Francis.*
The steam-packet and coast companion, or
general guide to Gravesend-Herne Bay-
Canterbury-Margate-Broadstairs-Ramsgate-
Dover....
H. Hughes. London. 1932 etc.
6,9,11,12,13,14.

CONNOLLY, P.A.
Gravesend airport, 1932 - 1958,
compiled by P.A. Connolly and C.R. Munday.
K.C.C. Gravesham Division. 1975.
4,9,20.

COODE, FITZMAURICE, WILSON and MITCHELL,
(Consulting engineers)
Letterbook containing copies of letters
sent between 5th Feb. 1924 - 13th Sept. 1930
concerning the proposed Gravesend-Tilbury and
Dartford-Purfleet tunnels. (1930).
The Gravesend-Tilbury tunnel was not built.
Several of the letters were short feasability
reports. Firm changed to Coode, Wilson,
Mitchell and Vaughan-Lee in Dec. 1925.
11.

CROCKER, R.J. & PARTNERS.
Royal Terrace Pier, Gravesend, Kent: report
on the existing structural condition and
restoration works necessary.
R.J. Crocker & Partners. 1972.
9.

CRUDEN, Robert Peirce.*
History of the town of Gravesend.
Wm. Pickering. 1843.
2.

DAUNTON-FEAR, RICHARD.
Pocahontas and St. Georges, Gravesend.
Photocopy. (19--?)
9.

DIBLEY, George Edward.
Additional notes on the chalk of the Medway
Valley, Gravesend, West Kent, North East Surrey
and Grays, Essex.
Reprinted from the Proceedings of the Geologists'
Association. Vol. XXIX. 1918. pp. 68 - 105.
9.

DONALDSON, Norman.
In search of Dr. Thorndyke.
University Press. Bowling Green, U.S.A. 1971.
9.

DOUGLASS, Rev. Douglas Alexander.
From Princes Street to Milton Mount: the story
of Congregationalism in Gravesend from its
beginnings in Princes Street Chapel, including
the development of Milton Congregational Church
and their reunion in 1953, and the formation of
the United Reformed Church in Old Road East
under the name Milton Mount.
Milton Mount United Reformed Church. 1975.
9.

ENVIRONMENT. Deptartment of the
List of buildings of special architectural or
historic interest: Borough of Gravesham, Kent:
Gravesend area.
H.M.S.O. 1975.
11.

GRAVESEND & DISTRICT COMMUNITY RELATIONS COMMITTEE.
Annual reports, 1975-76. 1976-77. 1977-78.
9.

GRAVESEND & DISTRICT COMMUNITY COUNCIL-
EDUCATION SUB-COMMITTEE.
Immigrants at School, March 1977.
Gravesend & District Community Council. 1977.
4,9.
Immigrants at School, March 1977, reprinted
January 1978.
Gravesend & District Community Council. 1978.
4,9,25.

GRAVESEND & NORTHFLEET FOOTBALL CLUB LTD.
Official handbook 1973 - 74.
Football Supporters Pub. 1973.
9.

GRAVESEND BOROUGH COUNCIL.
The Borough of Gravesend. Gravesend Borough Council
12.   1972.

Official guide to Gravesend, 1914*: an
appreciation of the Borough & surroundings.
(by W. Syms).
Gravesend Borough Council. 1914.
11.

Official Handbook, 1967-8.
Edward J. Burrow & Co. Cheltenham. (1967).
25.

Official Handbook, 1972/3.
Edward J. Burrow & Co. Cheltenham. (1972).
19.

GRAVESEND BOROUGH COUNCIL - TREASURER'S DEPT.
Abstract of accounts for the year ended
31st March, 1972.
Gravesend Borough Council. 1973.
9.

GRAVESEND CONGREGATIONAL MAGAZINE,
January-December 1919. New Series. Nos.37-48.
9.

GRAVESEND COUNTY SCHOOL FOR GIRLS.
School Magazine; twenty-third anniversary
number No.22. 1937.
Printed by Reporter Ltd. Gravesend. 1937.
11.

GRAVESEND HISTORICAL SOCIETY.
Transactions.
4   1955-56, 1956-57, 1957-58.
5   1954-55, 1955-56, 1956-57,
     1957-58, 1958-59, 1966-67.
9   1954-55 in progress
11   1955-56.

GRAVESHAM BOROUGH COUNCIL-PLANNING DEPT.
Central Gravesend Draft District Plan.
Project Report.   December,1977.
Gravesham Borough Council
9.

Industry and warehousing in Gravesend.
Gravesham Borough Council.1977.
9,11.

Perry Street Draft district plan. Report
of Survey.
Gravesham Borough Council.
9.

Windmill Hill, Gravesend, conservation area.
Gravesham Borough Council. 1975.
9,11.

GRAY, Adrian.
The unusual birth of the Gravesend and
Rochester Railway.
In Journal of the Railway & Canal Historical
Society. Vol. XXIV. No.2, 1978.
4.

GREAT BRITAIN, Laws, etc. (Vic.)
Gravesend Railway Act, 1882.
H.M.S.O. 1882.
9.

GREAT BRITAIN, Laws etc. (Edw. VII)
An act to confirm certain provisional orders
made by the Board of Trade under the Electric
Lighting Acts...relating to..Gravesend
(extension to Northfleet)...
H.M.S.O. 1905.
9.

GREEN, E.R.*
Field names of Gravesend.
Gravesham Historical Society. 1966.
11.

THE GRAVESEND CHRONOLOGY, 3 vols.,*
compiled by E.C. Gunkel.
(Vol.I - to 1700; Vol.II 1701 - 1900;
Vol.III 1900 to date).
Gravesend Public Library. 1971.
8,9,11,12,26.
2nd.edition. 1973. 23.
3rd.edition. 1974. (Part I).9,11,12.

GUNKEL, Emuel Charles.
St. Andrew's waterside Mission and Church
compiled by E.C. Gunkel. (Local History
Pamphlet No.2).
Gravesend P.L. 1973.
4,8,25.

H., W.T.
A new historical, topographical and
descriptive companion to the visitor of
Gravesend, Milton and their environs; interspersed with curious anecdotes, in a
series of letters from the author to a friend.
W. Holbert. Gravesend. (1843).
11.

IERADI, Eric J.
Gravesend: the home of Coney Island.
Vantage Press New York, U.S.A.1975.
9.

JONES, D. Glyn.
The story of Milton Road School, Gravesend,
1884 - 1976.
Printed by Lewis & Sons, Gravesend. 1976.
9,11.

JONES, Rosemary.
Steam packet trips from London and their effect
on Gravesend between 1810 and 1860.
MS. Thesis. University of Southampton. 1978.
9.

KEAN, J.S.*
Artists of Gravesend up to the end of the
nineteenth century.
Gravesend Historical Society. 1964.
4,9,11.

KENT COUNTY COUNCIL-PLANNING DEPT.*
Gravesend town centre map: with revised
explanatory notes.
K.C.C. 1970.
11.

KING'S FARM JUNIOR SCHOOL Our words: children's
writing from King's Farm Junior School.Spring 1978.
King's Farm Junior School. 1978.
9.

LILLEY, W.E.*
The life and work of General Gordon at Gravesend.
Kingdom. (1885).
4,9,11.

LITTLE, Jan.
The growth of civic responsibility in Gravesend,
with special reference to housing. (1825-1900)
Thesis,Dartford College of Education.1976(Typescript)
9.

LLOYD, John.
Anecdotes of John Lloyd, a pretended clergyman,
who was committed to prison on Friday, September
6th 1782, charged with several highway robberies..
(and the) remarkable sermon he preached at
Gravesend...
Printed for A. Milne, 202 High Holborn,London.1782.
11.

LYNE, R.M.*
The Gravesend Branch Railway.
E.M. Humphries. Longfield. 1972.
9,11.

McLELLAN, Doreen E.
The Clock Tower, Gravesend.
(Local History pamphlet No.9).
K.C.L. Gravesham Division. 1977.
3,4,9.

Gravesend Borough Market:a history
(Local History Pamphlet No.12).
Kent County Library,Gravesham Division. (1979).
4.

Gravesend Central Library, compiled by D.E.
McLellan). (Local History Pamphlet No.13).
Kent County Library,Gravesham Division. 1980.
4,9.

MUNICIPAL CORPORATIONS' COMMISSION FOR ENGLAND
AND WALES, 1834.
Report on the Corporation of Gravesend.
H.M.S.O. 1835.
9.

PHILIP, Alexander John.*
Gravesend, the watergate of London.2nd edition
1907-08.
Homeland Association. 1907.
11.

A history of Gravesend and its surroundings
from prehistoric times to the opening of the
Twentieth Century.*(Originally planned in 4
volumes).
1914 Vol. I. only.Stanley Paul.
1,5,9,11,15,25.
1954. Completed as a one volume work.
The Author. Wraysbury. 1954.
1.2.3.4.5.7.8.9.11.12.15.17.18.

ST. GEORGE'S CHURCH, GRAVESEND. A history of
the parish and notes for visitors.
St. George's Church. c.1971.
9.

ST. JAMES PARISH CHURCH, GRAVESEND:
Year Book, 1956 - 57.
9

ST. JOHN'S COMPREHENSIVE SCHOOL; information
for parents, September 1975.
9.

SHEEHAN, Faurie.
The ferry-boat children. A Story for
children concerning the Seventeenth Century
Long Ferry.
Bailey Bros. 1976.
9.

SMITH, Victor T.C.
The Gravesend Forts. (Local History Pamphlet
No 10).
KCL: Gravesham Division. 1978.
3,4,6,9,32.

New Tavern Fort.
Gravesend Historical Society. Printed by
Laverock Reprographics Ltd. Maidstone. 1975.
4,9,11,25,32.

TALLIS, John. Publisher.*
A Comprehensive Gazetteer of Gravesend with
its environs being a complete guide...for
visitors...to which is added a general
directory of Gravesend and illustrations
on steel.
Jonn Tallis 15 St. John's Lane.Smithfield,
London. 1839.
9,11.

THAMESIDE ARCHAEOLOGICAL GROUP.
The excavation of the Gravesend Blockhouse,
1975-76, written by Donald Thompson.
(Clarendon Hotel Site). Part typescript
in a binder.
The Group. 1977.
9,11,32.

The Tudor Blockhouse, Gravesend: the historical
background to the archaeological excavation
carried out at the Clarendon Royal Hotel.
The Group (1975)
9, 32.

TILLEY, Ernest W.
The seventeenth-century token issues of
Gravesend and Milton-next-Gravesend.
Reprinted from Archaeologia Cantiana
Vol. LXXXV. 1970.
Headley Bros. Ashford. 1971.
9.

THE TOWN CRIER, Gravesend & District Vol 1.
Nos 1 - 4. 5th Sept - 22nd Sept. 1934.
K. Everill, Queen St. Gravesend.
9.

THE WATERING-PLACES OF ENGLAND, Part II.
Gravesend, Sheerness, Southend and Herne
Bay.
(The Travellers' Magazine. 180-?)
9.

THE WHIGS DEFENDED: or, the High-Church Saint
detected and exposed. Being an account of
the infamous life and character of Mr.A.S., the
discarded curate and school-master of Gravesend..
Printed for A. Baldwin. 1713.
11.

WILLIS, Peter J.
Gravesend round and about.
Edition compiled by Peter J. Willis.
Gravesend Public Library. 1973.
11.

WORKERS' EDUCATION ASSOCIATION:S.E. DISTRICT.
Gravesend 1851 W.E.A. Class Study of the 1851:
Census Returns, 1970 - 71: some historical
notes on Gravesend and District.
Workers' Education Association:S.E. District.1972.
2,5,8,9.

GRAVESHAM

GRAVESHAM ADVENTURE PLAYGROUND.
Annual report, Sept. 1974-Sept. 1975.
(Subsequent reports incorporated in Gravesend
and District Community Relations Committee
annual report).
Gravesend & District Community Relations Comm. 1975.
9.

GRAVESHAM BOROUGH COUNCIL.
An A-Z of Gravesham advice from the Information
Services of the Borough Council & Divisional
Libraries.
Gravesham Borough Council. 1977 and 1979.
11.

Official Handbook. Produced with the co-operation
of the Divisional Librarian's Dept. and by the
Authority of Gravesham Borough Council.
Home Publishing (Southern) Ltd.
1974   4,11.16.
1977   11,20.
1978   25.
1980   13.

Members' tour of inspection of Gravesham
Borough, Saturday June 5th, 1976.
Gravesham. 1976.
9.

GRAVESHAM BOROUGH COUNCIL-PLANNING DEPT.
Conservation in Gravesham.
Gravesham Borough Council.
1976   9,11.
1977   9.
1977   2nd edition.   9.

Derelict and despoiled land in Gravesham,
by K. Watson.
Gravesham Borough Council. 1976.
4,9,11.

Employment in Gravesham: current trends and
policies.
Gravesham Borough Council.
1975   9
1977   2nd edition.   9,11.

Industry and warehousing in Gravesham.
Gravesham Borough Council. May 1977.
4.

Offices in Gravesham.
Gravesham Borough Council. 1976.
9,11.

GRAVESHAM BOROUGH COUNCIL- TREASURER.
Abstract of accounts for the two years ended
31st March 1975 and 31st March 1976.
Gravesham Borough Council. 1977
9.

GRAVESHAM TEACHERS' CENTRE - Primary English
Group.
Here and There No 1. 1978.
9.

GRAVESHAM VOLUNTARY AIDE SCHEME.
Handbook. (1977).
9.

GUNKEL, Emuel Charles.
Gravesham: a brief history,compiled by E.C.Gunkel.
Gravesend Public Library.1973.
4,8,11.

HARKER, Sydney R.
The book of Gravesham.
Barracuda Books, Buckingham. 1979.
2,4,5,6,9,11,16,23.

McLELLAN, Doreen E.
Cafès & Restaurants in Gravesham,compiled by
D.E. McLellan.
KCL, Gravesham Division. 1976.
20.

GRAVESHAM Cont'd

McLELLAN, Doreen E.
Dickens in Gravesham.
Kent County Library,Gravesham Division. 1977.
20,26.

WILLIS, Peter J.
Gravesham round & about, compiled by
P.J. Willis.
Kent County Library, Gravesham Division.
11 1976 and 1977
13 1976.

WOODS, Walter T.W.
Kent County Services in Gravesham.
KCL Gravesham Division. 1977.
3,11,12.

GREAT CHART

GODINTON PARK, Ashford Kent.*
English Life Publications. 1970.
8,11,30.

HUSSEY, Christopher.
Godington Park: the Home of Mr Alan
Wyndham-Green.(photocopy of series of
articles from Country Life, December 1962).
Country Life. 1962.
12.

KNOCKER, Herbert W.
The account book of a Kentish Estate,
1616-1704. A review by Capt. Herbert W.
Knocker. Reprinted from Archaeologia
Cantiana, Vol.39. 1927.
The account book of Nicholas Toke was
edited by Eleanor Lodge in 1927.
K.A.S. (1927).
11.

GREEN STREET GREEN (ORPINGTON)

COPUS, G.D.*
The Commons at Green Street Green and Pratts
Bottom, Chelsfield. (Typescript).
1955.
2.

GREENHITHE

CHRIST CHURCH, Greenhithe: Parish Magazine
1902 - 1904.
Society for Promotion of Christian Knowledge.
1902 - 1904.
5.

GREENHITHE Parish magazine and Penny
Post. 1871 - 1874.
5.

TOVEY, W.
A Short history of Greenhithe,edited by W.Tovey.
Copy of a typescript. 1962.
5.

MERCHANT NAVY COLLEGE, GREENHITHE.
A Century of nautical education at Greenhithe.
Merchant Navy College, Greenhithe. 1977.
5.

GREENWICH.

ADMIRALTY.
Regulations established by the Lords Commissioners
of the Admiralty for the government of
Greenwich Hospital.
Printed by H.S. Richardson.Greenwich 1853.
11.

BAKER, Gerard L.*
Blackheath: the story of the Royal Hundred.
Part I. Blackheath and Greenwich.
Morden Society. 1925.
1,2,11,12,17,18.

BENNETT, Alfred Rosling.*
The first railway in London, being the story of
the London & Greenwich Railway from 1832 to 1878.
(First published by the Locomotive Publishing
Company 1926). Reprinted edition.
Conway Maritime Press. Greenwich. 1971.
2,11.

BLACKHEATH SOCIETY.
Some hints on the maintenance and repair of
15th & 18th Century premises. Originally
produced by the York Georgian Society.
Reprinted with local photographs and lists
of buildings in Blackheath, Lewisham & Greenwich.
Blackheath Society. 1949.
11.

BUCHANAN, Colin & Partners.
Greenwich & Blackheath Study.
Colin Buchanan & Partners. 1971.
2.

BUDD, G.L. Culver.*
In and about old Greenwich.
South Eastern Press. Greenwich. 1910.
2,11.

CARR, Frank George Griffith.
The "Cutty Sark".
The "Cutty Sark" is in dry dock at Greenwich.
Pitkin Pictorials Ltd.
1970 5.
1976 11.

Gypsy Moth Mark IV: round the world with
Sir Francis Chichester.
Gypsy Moth is in dry dock at Greenwich.
Pitkin Pictorials Ltd.
1969.

Maritime Greenwich.
Pitkin Pictorials Ltd. 1974.
11.

CHARLTON, John.
The Queen's House, Greenwich.
H.M.S.O. 1976.
11,23.

CHETTLE, George H.*
The Queen's House, Greenwich.
National Maritime Museum. 1937.
2,18.

COLVIN, Howard Montague.
The History of the Kings Works.
(pp. 140 - 152 Greenwich Palace).
H.M.S.O. 1976.
11.

DAWSON, C.M.
The Story of Greenwich-Palace, Hospital,College.
Printed by Heathvale Press, Blackheath,
for The Author. July 1977.
2,11,18.

DE MONTMORENCY, James Edward Geoffrey.*
A brief history of the church of St. Alfege
(the parish church of Greenwich)....
Greenwich Antiquarian Society. 1923.
12.

DIXON, Philip.
Excavations at Greenwich Palace 1970-71.
An interim report.
Greenwich & Lewisham Antiquarian Society. 1972.
2.

ELLISTON-ERWOOD, Frank Charles.*
The Turnpike roads between Greenwich & Woolwich,
an account of the development of road communications between the Capital and the town of
Woolwich. Reprinted from the Proceedings
of the Woolwich & District Antiquarian Society
Vol. XXX .
Independent Printing Works. 1954.
1,8,11,15,18.

FORBES, Eric G.
The Royal Observatory at Greenwich & Herstmonceux.
Vol 1; Origins and Early History(1675-1835).
Taylor & Francis. 1975.
18.

GLENCROSS, Alan.
The Buildings of Greenwich.
London Borough of Greenwich. 1974.
1,2,11,18.

GREAT BRITAIN, Laws etc. (Geo II)
An Act for taking down & removing the
Magazine for Gunpowder, and all Buildings
thereto belonging, situate near Greenwich
in the County of Kent, and erecting, instead
thereof, a new Magazine for Gunpowder at Purfleet,
near the River of Thames. 1759.
Printed by Thomas Baskett. 1760.
11.

GREAT BRITAIN: Laws etc. (Vic.)
An Act to enable the Commissioners of
Greenwich Hospital to widen and improve Fisher
Lane in Greenwich; and for other purposes
connected with the estates of the said
Commissioners.
Printed by Eyre & Spottiswoode. 1845.
11.

An act to enable the Commissioners of
Greenwich Hospital to regulate and manage
the Markets held at Greenwich in the County
of Kent.
Printed by Eyre & Spottiswoode. 1849.
11.

An Act to enable the Commissioners of Greenwich
Hospital to improve the said Hospital and also
to enlarge and improve the said Hospital and
also to enlarge & improve the Billingsgate Dock
and widen Billingsgate Dock & widen Billingsgate
Street in Greenwich...
Printed by Eyre & Spottiswoode. 1850.
11.

GREENHILL, Basil.
A Victorian Maritime Album: 100 photographs
from the Francis Frith Collection at the National
Maritime Museum.
Stephens. 1974.
1.

GREENWICH & LEWISHAM ANTIQUARIAN SOCIETY.
Old Greenwich-a town in transition.
The Society. 1975.
1,11,17,18.

Transactions.
1   Incomplete File From 1907.
5   1905 - 1913
11   1929.
17,18. 5 vols. 1905.-current issue.

GREENWICH FESTIVAL COMMITTEE.
Greenwich Festival June 16th - 30th 1973.
Greenwich Festival Committee. 1973
1.

GREENWICH HOSPITAL & TRAVERS FOUNDATION.
Accounts 1972 - 1973. Accounts of the
receipt & expenditure of the capital and of
the income derived from the lands and other
property held for the benefit of Greenwich
Hospital, and the Foundation of Samuel
Travers, Esquire, for the year ending 31st
March, 1973.
H.M.S.O. 1974.
11.

GREENWICH, LONDON BOROUGH COUNCIL.
The London Borough of Greenwich:
Information handbook.
1   1973
11   1978.

The Metropolitan Borough of Greenwich -
the official guide.
Edward J. Burrow & Co. Cheltenham (1961).
11.

GREENWICH:LONDON BOROUGH COUNCIL LIBRARIES
LOCAL HISTORY DEPARTMENT.
Greenwich Riverside Walk; by Alan Glencross
and Julian Watson.   London Borough
of Greenwich Libraries,Local History Department.
1975.
1,11.

HACKNEY, Noel C.L.
Cutty Sark: classic ships No 3: their history
and how to model them.
Patrick Stevens, Airfix Products. 1974.
11.

HAMILTON, Nigel.
America began at Greenwich.
Poseidon Press. 1976.
11.

Greenwich in colour: a guide for the visitor
covering the National Maritime Museum, the Old
Royal Observatory, Royal Naval College, Cutty
Sark & Gypsy Moth IV.
Greenwich Bookshop. 1970.
8,11.

Guide to Greenwich: a personal guide to the
buildings and walks of one of England's most
beautiful and historic areas.
Greenwich Bookshop. 1972.
11.

HOWSE, Derek.
Francis Place and the early history of the
Greenwich Observatory.
Science History Publications. 1975.
2.

The Royal Observatory at Greenwich and Herstmonceux, 1675 - 1975. Volume 3. The Buildings
and Instruments.
Taylor & Francis. 1975.
11,18.

KIRBY, John William.*
History of the Roan School (The Greycoat School)
and its Founder.
Blackheath Press. 1929.
5,11,17,18.

LANSDELL, Henry.*
Princess Aelfrida's Charity.3 vols. (Lands in
Greenwich, Lewisham & Woolwich which became
the endowment of Morden College).
Burnside Ltd. Blackheath 1911-16.
2,11,17,18.

L'ESTRANGE, Alfred Guy K.*
Palace and hospital; or, chronicles of Greenwich.
Hurst & Blackett. 1886.
2.

LIPMAN, V.D.
Greenwich Palace, Park & Town.
In Ancient Monuments Society. Transactions.
New Series. Vol.20. 1975. pp. 25 - 47.

LLOYD, Christopher C.
Greenwich: Palace, Hospital, College.
Officers' Mess,Royal Naval College. 1961.
11.

LONGRIDGE, Charles Nepean.
The "Cutty Sark"; the ship and the model.
The "Cutty Sark" is now preserved at Greenwich.
Originally published P. Marshall, 1933 in 2 vols.
Model and Allied Publications. 1975.
11.

McCREA, William Hunter.
Royal Greenwich Observatory: an historical review
issued on the occasion of its Tercentenary.
H.M.S.O. 1975.
11.

MAUNDER, E. Walter.*
The Royal Observatory Greenwich: a glance at its
history and work.
Religious Tract Society. 1900.
2,11.

MEADOWS, A.J.
The Royal Observatory, at Greenwich and Herstmonceux, Volume 2, Recent History, 1836 - 1975.
Taylor & Francis. 1975.
18.

MEASOM, George.*
The Official illustrated guide to the South
Eastern railway and its branches, including
the North Kent and Greenwich lines.
(Facsimile of the 1858 ed
E & W. Books. 1970.
3,4,5,6,7,8,12,14,15,17,18,30.

GREENWICH Cont'd

NATIONAL MARITIME MUSEUM.
Catalogue (of the collection). Under revision.
1937.
11.

A Concise guide to the National Maritime
Museum, Greenwich. 2nd edition.
H.M.S.O. 1966.
30.

THE PARISH CHURCH OF GREENWICH, St. Alphege.
n.d.
11.

PLATTS, Beryl.
A history of Greenwich.
David & Charles. 1973.
2,7,11,12,18,23.

RIGDEN, Reg.
The Romans in the Greenwich District.
London Borough of Greenwich. 1974.
2,18.

RITCHIE, Carson.
Greenwich - A closer look.
Conway, Maritime Press. 1974.
11,18.

RONAN, Colin Alistair.
Greenwich Observatory: 300 years of astronomy,
edited by C.A. Ronan.
Times Books. Greenwich. 1976.
2.

THE ROYAL OBSERVATORY AT GREENWICH AND
HURSTMONCEUX. 3 VOLS.
See
FORBES, Eric.   Vol.I.
MEADOWS, A.J.   Vol.II.
HOWSE, Derek.   VOl.III.

SHOBERL, William.*
A summer's day of Greenwich, being a guide
to the Hospital and Park, with a history of
the ancient palace...and a catalogue of the
pictures in the Painted Hall.
Henry Colburn, London.   1840.
11.

STONE, John M.*
Underground passages, caverns etc. of
Greenwich and Blackheath.
Greenwich Antiquarian Society. 1914.
1,2,17.

TEMPEST, Paul.
Down stream to Greenwich: the heritage and
future of London river. A guide to the
river from Westminster to Greenwich and a
guide to Greenwich itself by Paul Tempest.
Conway Maritime Press. 1975.
11.

THOMAS, Ronald, H.G.*
London's first railway - the London & Greenwich.
Batsford. 1972.
11,12.

THE TOPOGRAPHER FOR THE YEAR 1790, containing
a variety of original articles.... Vol.II.
Nos X - XV. January - June 1790.
(Includes Canterbury & Greenwich).
Printed for J. Robson. 1790.
11.

UNWIN, T. Fisher. Publisher.*
Greenwich & Blackheath: a handy guide to
rambles in the District.
T. Fisher Unwin. (1883?).
18.

VILLIERS, Alan John.
The Cutty Sark, last of a glorious era.
Hodder & Stoughton. 1953.
11.

WATSON, Basil.
The Royal Naval College, Greenwich: a short
guide to the chapel of St. Peter & St. Paul.
E.G. Berryman & Sons, printers. Greenwich.
1969 (1972 reprint).
2,11.

WOODLANDS ART GALLERY.
Watercolours from 1840 to 1914 of places in
the Borough of Greenwich: a catalogue of
pictures in the collection.
London Borough of Greenwich.   1975.
11.

GROOMBRIDGE.

FURLONG, Monica.
Burrswood: home of healing. (Founded by
Dorothy Kerin, Faith Healer).
Hodder & Stoughton.   1978.
19,23.

LEE, Barbara.
Discovering Groombridge, edited by B. Lee.
Groombridge Women's Institute.   1978.
19.

Groombridge, old and new: memories of village
life in the first half of the 20th Century,
edited by B. Lee.
Groombridge Old People's Welfare Council. 1978.
19,23.

WHITE, Dorothy V.
The Groombridge diary.
Humphrey Milford and Oxford University Press.1924.
23.

GUSTON

BODIAM, M.E.
A short history of Guston.
M.E.Bodiam. 1975.
6.

GYPSIES

DODDS, Norman Noel.*
Gypsies, didikois, and other travellers.
Johnson Publications. 1966.
(The author was M.P. for Dartford and the
Erith and Crayford Constituencies).
1,5,11.

KENT COUNTY COUNCIL - PLANNING DEPT.*
Gypsies and other travellers in Kent. Report
on the survey carried out in 1951/52 by
J.W.R. Adams.
K.C.C. 1952.
24.

HACKINGTON

BUCKINGHAM, Christopher.
The Hales Family of Hackington. (Leaflet
produced to assist the appeal for funds to
restore the little Chapel at Tenterden Drive,
Hales Place, Canterbury).
P.P. 1976.
3.

HAYES, John.
The Church of St. Stephen, proto-martyr,
Hackington, Kent.
1978.
3.

TOWN & COUNTRY MAGAZINE.
Includes information on: St. Stephens' Church,
Hackington.
Virtue, London. 1837-8.
4.

HADLOW

BARNDEN, Clive.
Hadlow. a thousand years of village life.
(Hadlow Millenium souvenir brochure).
1975.
12,19.

HADLOW   Cont'd

D, W.V. (DUMBRECK, William V.)*
A village folly, being the history of Hadlow
Castle, Hadlow, Kent.
John Hilton for Hadlow Local History Society.
1964. 2nd edition.   1971.
11,12.

GENERAL REGISTER OFFICE.
Census Returns - 1841, 1851, 1861, 1871.
Hadlow.
Photocopy.
23.

HADLOW PARISH COUNCIL.
Hadlow: the official guide.
Forward Publicity Ltd.   (1974).
4.

TOWN & COUNTRY MAGAZINE.
Includes information on ..Hadlow Castle.
Virtue.London.   1837 - 8.
4.

HALLING

GOWERS, Edward.
Across the low meadow: Halling a village on
the Meadway,   by E. Gowers & Derek Church.
Christine Swift. Maidstone.   1979.
4,11,12,13,23.

KENT COUNTY COUNCIL - PLANNING DEPT.
Halling Village. Informal District Plan.
K.C.C.   1974.
2,4,8,25.

Halling Village - Informal District Plan.
Proposals map. Scale 1:25000.
Size. 84 cm x 93cm.
K.C.C. 1974.
11.

HALSTEAD.

KITCHENER, Geoffrey D.
Halstead in Kent: an historical guide.
G. Kitchener, Otford Lane, Halstead.1978.
2,16.

ROYAL ARMAMENT RESEARCH & DEVELOPMENT
ESTABLISHMENT.
RARDE News: the Royal Visit on November
10th 1972. (Fort Halstead, Nr. Sevenoaks).
Royal Armament Research & Development
Establishment. 1972.
11.

HAM STREET

NATURE CONSERVANCY COUNCIL:SOUTH EAST REGION.
Ham Street Woods National Nature Reserve.
Nature Conservancy Council, Banbury.   1976.
3,12.

HAMPTON

MOUNT, Frank.*
My recollections of Hampton.
Printed by Northover & Sons. (1942).
30.

HARBLEDOWN

GARDINER, Mrs Dorothy.*
Hospital of St. Nicholas, Harbledown.
Jennings, Canterbury.   1950.
3

HARRIETSHAM

GOODSALL, Robert Harold.*
Stede Hill: the annals of a Kentish home.
Headley Bros.   Ashford.   1949.
12,20.

HARRIETSHAM ARTS FESTIVAL. Programme, 1976.
12.

OLD KENT SNAPS (photograph album).
Small photographs with captions, mainly of
Chegworth (Harrietsham), and including Chilham,
Maidstone & Sturry etc., 1910 - 1930.
The Album belonged to Joyce Amos, Victoria House,
Victoria Rd. Margate .
11.

WEBB, A.E.
Wild flowers, trees and shrubs growing in
Lenham & Harrietsham...
Headley Bros. Ashford.   1939.
7,11.

HARTLEY

BANCKS, Gerard W.*
Hartley through the ages: the story of a Kentish
Village.   Photocopy.
The Author, Hartley Rectory, Longfield. 1927.
2,16.

ELLERBY, Charles M.
Hartley Village - 1912 - 1974; sketches by
the Author.
Author, Nineveh Press, Northfleet. (1975).
3,8,9,11,12,16.

HARVEY, DR. WILLIAM (1578 - 1657).
SURGEON OF FOLKESTONE.

ARDLEY, Susan P.*
William Harvey: a symposium.
In Guy's Hospital Gazette Vol.71.No. 1799. 1957.
7.

CHAUVOIS, Louis.*
William Harvey.
Hutchinson, 1957.
3,7.

DOBY, T.*
Discoverers of blood circulation. (Includes
William Harvey of Folkestone).
Abelard-Schuman.   1963.
12.

FRANKLIN, Kenneth J.*
King Charles I and William Harvey.
Reprinted from the Proceedings of the Royal
Society of Medicine, February 1961 .
7.

William Harvey, Englishman, 1578 - 1657.
MacGibbon, 1961.
3,7.

HARRISON, William C.*
Dr. William Harvey & the discovery of circulation.
Collier-Macmillan.   1967.
7.

HARVEY TERCENTENARY, 1878, MEMORIAL *
report of the proceedings at the Public Meeting...
on September 6th 1871.....
1878.
7.

HOLLOWAY, Mark.*
William Harvey, 1578 - 1657.
Tower Publications. 1957.
7.

HARVEY, DR. WILLIAM (1578 - 1657). Cont'd

KEELE, Kenneth D.*
William Harvey. (British Men of Science Series).
Nelson. 1965.
7,8.

KEYNES, Geoffrey.*
Bibliography of the writings of Dr. William
Harvey. 2nd edition.
Cambridge University Press. 1953.
7.

Harvey through John Aubrey's eyes.*.the 254th
Harveian Oration at the Royal College of
Physicians.
The Lancet. 1958.
7.

The life of William Harvey.*
Clarendon Press. Oxford University Press. 1966.
3.

The personality of William Harvey.*
Cambridge University Press. 1949.
7.

The portraiture of William Harvey.*
Royal College of Surgeons. 1949.
7.

NEIL, E.
William Harvey and the circulation of the blood.
Priory Press. 1975.
7.

HASTINGLEIGH.

HOUGH, Brenda.
Some historical notes on Coombe Manor,
Hastingleigh, Kent.
A.T. Stainton. Coombe Manor. 1973.
3.

HAWKHURST

JEFFREYS, H.A.*
The Church of St. Laurence, Hawkhurst;
its history and architecture.
First published in 1874.
Kent Archaeological Society. 1973.
1.

HAYES AND KESTON

ALLEN, Diane.
The Parish of Hayes, Kent. 1870 - 1914:
Social and economic structure.
Unpublished Thesis. 1978.
2.

COOPER, W.H. Hewlett.*
Old Keston.
E. Strong & Sons, Bromley. 1879.
11.

COWARD, Alice.
Hayes, village on the Heath.
Compiled by A. Coward.
Hayes (Kent) Village Assn. 1973(i.e. 1972).
2.

KESTON FOREIGN BIRD FARM.
A discriptive catalogue.
Keston Foreign Bird Farm. c.1960.
2.

KESTON PARISH CHURCH HISTORY.
Church Publishers Ramsgate. (1972).
2.

MAHIR, Tom.
Police dogs at work (including account of the
Metropolitan Police dog training establishment
at Keston).
Dent. 1970.
2.

MITCHELL, Frank.
800th Anniversary 1175 - 1975. (The Church of
St. Mary the Virgin, Hayes).
Duplicated typescript. 1975.
2.

THOMPSON, Henry Percy.*
History of Hayes...(reprinted with added forword,
notes etc). First published in 1935.
Jackdaw Publications,Beckenham. 1978.
2.

THOMPSON, P.A.
History of the Hayes (Kent) Cricket Club,
1828 - 1978.
Hayes Cricket Club. 1978.
2.

WELLS, Mrs. Hester
A Study of the village of Old Hayes from 1777 -
1827, when the Rev. John Till was Rector...
Thesis. Typescript. 1976.
2.

WEST KENT BORDER ARCHAEOLOGICAL GROUP.
A walk through Keston. 2nd revised edition.
West Kent Border Archaeological Group. 1976.
11.

HEADCORN

CHURCH OF ST. PETER & ST. PAUL, HEADCORN.
Church Publishers,Ramsgate. (1977?).
11.

GREAT TONG FARM, Headcorn: open day 25th
August, 1980.
K.C.C. Maidstone. 1980.
12.

HEALTH & WELFARE

ADAMS, Matthew Algernon.
Report to the Local Board on the outbreaks
of Smallpox in Maidstone, 1881.
Vivish. Maidstone. 1881.
12.

BRITISH ASSOCIATION OF SOCIAL WORKERS:KENT BRANCH.
Homelessness in Kent: a Survey.
Shelter. 1974.
1.

BROADSTAIRS & ST. PETERS' DISTRICT LOCAL BOARD.
The Public Health Act 1875. Byelaws for the
above district.
Broadstairs & St. Peters'District Local Board.1881.
11.

CANTERBURY & THANET COMMUNITY HEALTH COUNCIL.
Annual Reports: for the year ending on March 31st..
1976   3
1977   3,13.
1978   3.13.

CANTERBURY & THANET HEALTH DISTRICT: KENT
AREA HEALTH AUTHORITY.
District Plan. 1980-81.
Canterbury & Thanet Health District:
Kent Area Health Authority. 1979.
13.

CANTERBURY CITY COUNCIL - MEDICAL OFFICER OF HEALTH.
Annual Report, 1971.
Canterbury City Council. 1973.
3.

COMMUNITY HEALTH COUNCIL - MEDWAY HEALTH DISTRICT.
Annual report.....for the period April 1974
to March 1975.
Community Health Council-Medway Health District.1975.
4,8,25.

CRESWICK, Paul.
Kent's care of the wounded, by Paul Creswick,
G. Stanley Pond and T.H. Ashton.
Hodder & Stoughton. 1915.
11,19.

EAST ASHFORD RURAL DISTRICT COUNCIL.
Annual Report of the Public Health Inspector
for the year 1972.
East Ashford Rural District Council. 1972.
11.

EAST KENT JOINT COMMITTEE.
Annual reports of the Medical Officer 1916-1919.
(Bound vol.)
East Kent Joint Committee.
6.

HEALTH & WELFARE   Cont'd.

FAVERSHAM BOROUGH COUNCIL: HEALTH DEPT.
Annual Report of the Medical Officer of Health
for 1971.
Faversham Borough Council. 1971.
11.

FOLKESTONE BOROUGH COUNCIL & PORT HEALTH
AUTHORITY.
Annual report of the Medical Officer of Health
for 1972.
Folkestone Borough Council. 1973.
7.

HEALTH & SOCIAL SECURITY, DEPARTMENT OF
A refuge for battered women; a study of the
role of a women's centre. (at Canterbury).
H.M.S.O. 1978.
11.

HERITAGE OF KENT: (special issue of
"Photography", prepared on behalf of the forces
under the care of the Kent County Welfare
Organisation).
Worlds Press News Publishing Co. London. 1943.
4.

JEFFERYS, Hazel D.
Public health in the Medway Towns during the
nineteenth century and the implementation of
the Public Health Acts, 1848 and 1875. (An
extended essay).
Typescript. (1973?).
4.

KENT AREA HEALTH AUTHORITY.
Health Services in Kent; Guide and Directory.
Kent Area Health Authority. 1975.
8,9,12,13.

KENT COUNTY COUNCIL: COUNTY SECRETARY'S DEPARTMENT.
RESEARCH & INTELLIGENCE UNIT.
The need for meals-on-wheels and luncheon
clubs in the Dover dictrict of Kent:final report.
K.C.C. 1975.
11.

KENT COUNTY COUNCIL: EDUCATION DEPARTMENT.*
Report on the health of the school child for
the year 1964. A. Elliott, Principal School
Medical Officer.
K.C.C.
13.

KENT COUNTY COUNCIL: HEALTH DEPARTMENT.
Annual report of the Medical Officer of Health
& Principal School Medical Officer.
1970.   13.
1972.   7,8,9,11,12,25.
1973.   8,11,12,25.

KENT COUNTY COUNCIL: SOCIAL SERVICES DEPARTMENT.
Directory.
K.C.C. (Aug. 1979).
4.

First Report of the Special Family Placement
Project. Progress report for 1975 by Nancy
Hazel & Rosemary Cox.
K.C.C. Feb. 1976.
5,8,11,16,19,20,23,25.

Kent family placement project. Handbook.
K.C.C. n.d.
23.

Second Report of the Special Family Placement
Project. Progress report for 1976 by Nancy Hazel
& Rosemary Cox.
K.C.C. 1977.
23.

Kent family placement project. Third annual
report, 1976-77.
K.C.C. 1977.
23.
Report on the Survey of the Handicapped in Kent,
by Elizabeth J. Humphries.
K.C.C. 1972.
4,9,13.

KENT PAEDIATRIC SOCIETY.*
A Study in the epidemiology of health;
being an investigation into the incidence and
causation of health among...schoolchildren in
the Borough of Bexley, Kent.
Bexley   Health Dept. 1954.
11.

MAIDSTONE BOROUGH COUNCIL.
The health of Maidstone.
Maidstone Borough Council. 1972.
12.

MALLING RURAL DISTRICT COUNCIL:PUBLIC HEALTH DEPT.
Annual Report on the health of the Malling
district for the year 1972.
Malling Rural District Council.1972.
11.

MARGATE BOROUGH COUNCIL: HEALTH DEPT.
Annual report for 1970 on The Health of Margate
by The Medical Officer of Health. Report of the
Chief Public Health Inspector & Meteorological
Report.
Margate Borough Council. 1971.
13.

NATIONAL HEALTH SERVICE - KENT AND CANTERBURY
EXECUTIVE COUNCIL.
Health and allied services in the County of
Kent and the City of Rochester.
Malcolm Page Ltd. (1959).
4.
Health Services Handbook,1959.
As Author.
30.
NATIONAL HEALTH SERVICE - KENT FAMILY
PRACTITIONER COMMITTEE.
Medical List, July 1974 & Amendment List. No.1/74
to December 1974.
3,4.

Medical List,1977.
22.

Pharmaceutical List, September 1974.
3.

PARNELL, J.W.
Home for the weekend - back on Monday: a study
of a 5-day ward for the rehabilitation of
geriatric patients by J.W. Parnell and R.Naylor.
(Experiment at the Lennard Hospital, Bromley).
Queen's Institute of District Nursing. 1973.
2

ROYAL TUNBRIDGE WELLS BOROUGH COUNCIL.
Annual report of the Medical Officer of Health
1916 - 1920, and 1931 - 35.
Royal Tunbridge Wells Borough Council.
19.

SOUTH-EAST THAMES REGIONAL HEALTH AUTHORITY.
Directory.
S.E. Thames Regional Health Authority, Croydon.
1974. 1.
1976. 3,12.

Strategies and guidelines for the care of the
elderly.
S.E. Thames Regional Health Authority. Croydon.1978.
1,3,5,9,11,12.

Strategies & guidelines For the development
of obstetric services.
S.E. Thames Regional Health Authority.Croydon.1978.
1,5,9,11,12.

SWALE RURAL DISTRICT COUNCIL.
Annual Report of the Medical Officer of Health
for 1972.
Swale Rural District Council. 1972.
11.

TRADE AND INDUSTRY,Department of - WARREN SPRINGS
LABORATORY.
National Survey of Air Polution 1961 - 71.
v.1...South East Region.
H.M.S.O. 1972.
2.

TUNBRIDGE WELLS AND DISTRICT COUNCIL OF
SOCIAL SERVICE.
Directory of statutory and voluntary social
services in Royal Tunbridge Wells and District.
October. 1975.
19.

TUNBRIDGE WELLS HEALTH DISTRICT: COMMUNITY
HEALTH COUNCIL.
Annual Report 1974/75.
Tunbridge Wells Health District, Community
Health Council. 1975.
11,19.

TUNBRIDGE WELLS LOCAL BOARD.
Medical Officer of Health's Reports, 1885-1904.
19.

YELLOLY, Margaret.
Kent special family placement project.
Independent evaluation of twenty-five
placements.
Goldsmiths' College, University of London. 1978.
23.

HEATH, EDWARD RICHARD GEORGE (1916 -)
Born in Broadstairs and M.P. for Bexley.

EVANS, Marian.
Ted Heath: a family portrait.
Kimber. 1970.
1.

HEATH, Edward.
Music, a joy for life.
Sidgwick & Jackson. 1976.
24.

Sailing. A course of my life.
Sidgwick & Jackson. 1975.
24.

HUTCHINSON, George.
Edward Heath: A Personal and Political
Biography.
Longman. 1970.
1,11.

ROTH, Andrew.
Heath and the Heathmen.
Routledge & Kegan Paul. 1972.
1.

SPROAT, Iain.
The Picture life of Edward Heath.
Watts. 1971.
1.

HEMPSTEAD

MORGAN, W.L.
A brief history of the Hempstead Congregational
Church, 1900 - 1958.
Duplicated pamphlet. (1958).
11.

HERALDRY

CALLAM, G.M.N.*
The Norwoods 2 vols.
Vol.1. An introduction to their history.
Vol.2. Heraldry & Brasses.
A.E. Callam. Bushey Heath, Herts. 1963-65.
24
27 vol 2 only.

ELLISTON-ERWOOD, Frank Charles*
Two coats of arms from Kent in London.
In Archaeologia Cantiana. Vol.LVIII. 1944.
1.

HUMPHREY-SMITH, Cecil R.
Heraldry associated with the martyrdom of
Archbishop Thomas Becket. (Photocopy of pp.371-
375 of the Proceedings, 10th International
Congress of Genealogical & Heraldic Sciences,
Vienna. 14th - 19th Sept. 1970).
Heraldisch Genealogische Gesellshaft. 1970.
3.

Heraldry associated with the Martyrdom of
Archbishop Thomas Becket. (Photocopy of pp.18 -
28 of The Coat of Arms, Vol XII 1971.
Heraldry Society. 1971.
3.

JEWITT, Llewellyn.
The Corporation plate and insignia of Office
of the Cities and towns of England and Wales;
edited and completed with large additions by
W.M. St. John Hope. Vol.I. Anglesey to Kent.
(pp. 313 - 367, Kent).
Benrose, London 1895.
11.

KENT COUNTY COUNCIL: ARCHIVES DEPT.
Heraldry and heraldic documents: a display
of items from the Kent Archives Office c.1100 -
1927 at....Tunbridge Wells, 1st - 20th July 1963.
K.C.C. 1963.
11.

OAKLEY, Kenneth P.
Decorative and symbolic uses of vertebrate fossils.
Oxford University Press. 1975.
12.

POOLE, Keith B.
Historic heraldic families.
(Section on Badlesmere family).
David & Charles. 1975.
3.

WHEATLEY, Rev. Sydney William.
(Hon. Canon of Rochester Cathedral).
Heraldic decoration of the drawbridge of the
Mediaeval Bridge of Rochester. Reprinted from
Archaeologia Cantiana Vol.LXIII.1951.pp.140-143.
Headley Bros. Ashford. 1951.
15,25.

WILLIAMS, Geoffrey.*
The heraldry of the Cinque Ports.
David & Charles. 1971.
2,3,4,6,7,8,11,12,21,24,30.

HERNHILL

THE CHURCH AND PARISH OF HERNHILL.
Printed by The Riverside Press Ltd, London &
Whitstable, (197-?).
11.

CURLING, P.W.
The Dawes Institute Club Hernhill, Faversham...
1904 - 1954; compiled and edited by P.W. Curling
and K.C. Judges.
Printed by Peter Ness. Gravesend. 1954.
11.

JANES, Hurford.*
Centenary commemoration of the opening of
Hernhill School, 1872 - 1972. Historical
sketch (H. Janes) - personal memories (K.C.Judges)
Printed by South Litho Printing.Folkestone. 1972.
11,20,30.

The church and parish of Hernhill.
Printed by the Riverside Press. London & Whitstable.
1970?.
20.

A SHORT ACCOUNT OF THE PARISH AND CHURCH OF HERNHILL,
in Kent printed for distribution at the re-
opening, after restoration, of the parish church.
R. Lancefield. Faversham. 1878.
26.

HERNHILL   Cont'd

THORPE, Rev. J.F. (Vicar of Hernhill).
A Short account of the Parish & Church
of Hernhill in Kent.
Lancefield, Faversham - Printer. 1878.
26.

HERNE

BUCHANAN, James Robert.*
Memorials of Herne, Kent. 2nd edition 1887.
Elliot Stock. 1887.
30.

GOUGH, Harold Eric.
The ancient parish church of St. Martin-in-
Herne. Some information about the Kneelers,
compiled by H.E. Gough.
Herne Parochial Council. 1974.
30.

The Story of the Parish Church of Herne.
(1967?) British Publishing Co.Gloucester. 30
1972   "   "   "   "   2,7,8
1975 Kent County Printers. 2nd revised edition.30.

Two Brasses. No.1. A newly found brass
from Herne Church by H.E. Gough.
Reprinted From Archaeologia Cantiana. Vol.67,1962.
Headley Bros. Ashford. 1962.
30.

HERNE MILL KENT   (photocopy).
"An effort to raise funds to enable an 18th century
smock mill once more to work by wind."
1935.
30.

KENT COUNTY LIBRARY.*
List of Books concerning Herne Bay, Herne &
Reculver.
K.C.C. 1951.
3.

PHILP, Brian.
Early church discovered at Herne, by Brian Philp
and Harold Gough: in Kent Archaeological Review,
No 44. Summer, 1976. photocopy.
30.

STRODE PARK in Herne, the factory in a stately
home.
In Veteran and Vintage Magazine, Vol.14,
No.2. October 1969, pp.36 - 40.
(The Strode Engineering Works produced "Westcar"
cars - and a tram for Herne Bay Pier).
Pioneer Pub
30.

HERNE BAY

THE ALBUM OF HERNE BAY VIEWS   Entered at
Stationers Hall.
Charter, Reynolds & Co. 26 & 27 Milk St.
London. (189-?).
11,30.

ALL ABOUT MARGATE & HERNE BAY,* including
Draper's, St. Peter's, Salmestone,
Chapel Bottom, Hengrove, Twenties and Nash
Court, Kingsgate and its modern antiquities,
Garlinge, Dandelion.
W. Kent & Co. London. 1866.
11.

BEECHAM's PHOTO-FOLIO. 24 choice photographic
views.
Margate & Herne Bay.
13.

BOND, A. Winstan.
Herne Bay Pier - three tramways and a mystery.
In Modern Tramway & Light Railway Review. Vol.31,
April 1968, No. 364. pp. 127 - 136.
30.

BRITISH MUSEUM-NATURAL HISTORY. Dept. of:GEOLOGY.
British Caenozoic fossils. (Tertiary and
quaternary) 4th edition.
(Herne Bay is an important location for fossils).
British Museum - Natural History. 1971.
30.

BROWN, E.E.S.
Report of field meetings at Herne Bay & Reculver.
In Proceedings of the Geologists' Association,
Vol.47, Part 4. 1936. pp.349 - 350.
30.

BROWNING, Robert H.K.
The Herne Bay Golf Club.
Golf Clubs Association. n.d.
30.

CAMPBELL, Agnes.
Thoughts by the wayside.
(Poems on Herne Bay).
The Badenoch Record Office. 1914.
30.

CANTERBURY CITY COUNCIL-AMENITIES AND RECREATION
COMMITTEE.
Canterbury, Herne Bay and Whitstable welcome you!
Official Guide.
Canterbury City Council-Amenities & Recreation
Committee.
1975   11, 12.
1977   3, 31.

City of Canterbury, Herne Bay, and Whitstable -
(Holiday Guide).
Canterbury City Council-Amenities & Recreation
Committee. (1978).
3.

CLAGUE, John C.
Herne Bay Sports Pavilion: a brief explanatory
article by the Architect, In Portico Sept. 1976.
p.5 - 7 illus.
Faculty of Architects & Surveyors. 1976.
3.

COOPER, John.
The Palaeontology of the London Clay (Lower
Eocene) of the Herne Bay coastal section, Kent,
England. In Proceeds.Geological Association.88(3)
163 - 178.
Geological Association 1977
30.

ENVIRONMENT, Department of the
List of buildings of special architectural
or historic interest: District of Canterbury,
Kent (Herne Bay area).
H.M.S.O. 1976.
3,11.

GARNETT, MEPHAM & FISHER LTD. Publishers.
Canterbury, Herne Bay & Whitstable Local
Directory.* 40th issue. 1932 - 33.
Garnett, Mepham & Fisher Ltd. Brighton. 1932.
11.
Canterbury & District, Herne Bay & Whitstable
Local Directory. 41st issue.
Garnett, Mepham & Fisher Ltd. Brighton. 1934.
11.

GURR, Philip R.
A new Fish Fauna From the Woolwich bottom bed
(Sparnacian) of Herne Bay, Kent, by P.R. Gurr.
In Proceedings of the Geologists' Association
Vol.73, 1962. pp. 419 - 447.
Geologists' Association. 1962.
30.

HASLUCK, Eugene Lewis.*
Beyond the Forest of Blean: Chapters in the
history of Herne Bay...edited by H.E. Gough.
Herne Bay Press. 1966.
1,2,3,7,8,11,12,13,15,30.

HERNE BAY PRESS.
The Great East Coast Storm, 1953.* damage
at Herne Bay & Whitstable, Kent.
Herne Bay Press. 1953.
30,31.

Special Storm Edition.
Monday, January 16th 1978.
3,30.

HERNE BAY   Cont'd.

HERNE BAY URBAN DISTRICT COUNCIL.
Herne Bay & Whitstable.
Herne Bay Urban District Council.(190-?).
11.

Herne Bay: Official guide.
Herne Bay Urban District Council & Herne
Bay Advertising Association.
1933   30
1934   11

HEYWOOD, John. Publisher.*
John Heywood's illustrated guide to Herne
Bay & neighbourhood.
J. Heywood. 1891; 1903.
30
n.d. 11,17.

JEFFERIS, Roger.
The wreck hunters.
(Information on the Roman pottery find
at Pudding-Pan Rock, Herne Bay).
Harrap. 1966.
30.

KENT COUNTY LIBRARY.*
List of books concerning Herne Bay, Herne
and Reculver.
Kent County Library. 1951.
3.

KING, Richard S.*
Herne Bay humourously expressed and
illustrated. (Verse).
R.S. King. (c.1890?).
11,17,30.

MESSENGER and ADAMS, Architects,Surveyors &
Land Agents.
The Landbook, November 1897 - Dec. 1898.
An Ms Ledger relating to property in the
town of Herne Bay.
30.

(POUT, Roger).
History of the Herne United Roller Hockey Club.
(By Roger Pout).
The Club. 1976.
3,30.

SCOTT, Will.
The Herne Bay pageant in celebration of the
Coronation of Their Majesties King George VI
and Queen Elizabeth, at the Grand Pier
Pavilion, May 13th & 14th. 1937.
Herne Bay Borough Council. 1937.
11.

SHEPPARD, Alfred Tresidder.
Running Horse Inn. (A novel set in Herne Bay,
where the author also resided).
Macmillan. 1906.
3,11.

TURNER, Keith.
Pier Railways.
(pp.9 - 17. Herne Bay & Hythe).
Oakwood Press. 1972.
11,30.

VIEWS OF HERNE BAY.*
(?) c.1860.
30.

WARD, D.J.
The Lower London Tertiary (palaeocene)
succession of Herne Bay, Kent.
(Inst. of Geological Sciences Report 78/10).
H.M.S.O. 1978.
2.

THE WATERING-PLACES OF ENGLAND. (Part 2):
Gravesend, Sheerness, Southend and Herne Bay.
(The Travellers' Magazine (18--?).
9.

WATKINSON, J.*
Herne Bay Congregational Church: history of
the Church, with biographical notes of its
Ministers.
P.P. 1910.
11.

WATSON, William W.
Visitors' Guide to Herne Bay & Canterbury &
the most memorable spots in Kent.
1850 Dean & Sons. London.   11
1855* John Dicks. 11,17   30-photocopy.

WHITEHEAD, C.J.*
Herne Bay 1830 - 1870. A study of the development
of an English seaside resort in the mid 19th.
Century.
Photocopy of a Thesis. 1971.
30.

WHITSTABLE & HERNE BAY ALMANACK.
Eastes. Canterbury. 1887.
11.

HERNE HILL

OSBORNE, Brian M.
St. Jude, Herne Hill, S.E.24: a Souvenir of the
diamond jubilee, a record of sixty years, 1868-
1928.
Parochial Church Council. 1928.
11.

HERSDEN

COUSINS, Herbert Stanley.
Little school-big war; Hersden County Primary
School during the Second World War.
Photocopy of typescript. 1977.
3.

PARISH MAGAZINE FOR WESTBERE & HERSDEN
For 1931, 1932, 1933 (except March), 1934 -
1939. (Bound in one volume).
3.

HEVER

ASTOR, Gavin. 2nd Baron Astor of Hever.
Hever Castle and Gardens: history and guide.
Jarrold & Sons, Ltd.
1971* 8,16.
1973   11.
1974   8.

CORKE, C. Essenhigh
Hever, from original water colour paintings by
C. Essenhigh Corke.
J. Salmon. Sevenoaks. n.d.
11.

EASTMAN, John.*
Historic Hever: The Church, by the Parish Clerk.
John Eastman. Hever. 1905.
1,16.

FRANKLYN, Charles Aubrey Hamilton.
The Genealogy of Anne the Quene (Anne Bullen)
and other English Families (including)
Francklyn of Chart Sutton.
P.P. by Fotodirect, Brighton. 1977.
11.

HEXTABLE

BALLS, Horace J.*
Hextable: from a house in 1860 to a village in
1960. Typescript. Photocopy.
H.J. Balls. 1960.
5,16.

HIGH HALDEN

MARTIN, W.W.*
The Chequers Inn, memoirs of a nonagenarian
(High Halden).
Mitre Press. 1929.
2,3,6,11,12,13.

HIGHAM

JESSUP, Ronald Frank.
Notes on a Saxon charter of Higham.
Photocopied from Archaeologia Cantiana.
Vol.LV. 1942.
25.

NASH, E.K.
The Parish Church of St. Mary the Virgin,
Higham.
(c.1950).
11.

ROOTES, Andrew.
A mosaic history of Higham, by Andrew
Rootes and edited by Ian Craig.
D.A. Printers Ltd. 1974.
3,4,9,25.

HILDENBOROUGH

GENERAL REGISTER OFFICE.
Census Returns. 1841, 1851, 1861, 1871.
Hildenborough. Photocopy.
23.

KENT COUNTY COUNCIL: HIGHWAYS & TRANSPORTATION
DEPARTMENT.
Tonbridge & Hildenborough District Plan:
transport Issues & alternatives.
K.C.C. Jan. 1979.
23.

TONBRIDGE & MALLING DISTRICT COUNCIL:PLANNING DEPT.
Tonbridge & Hildenborough draft district plan:
project report.
Tonbridge & Malling District Council. 1977.
23.

HISTORY-ARCHAEOLOGY.
See also ARCHAEOLOGIA CANTIANA(History-General)
TOWNS, VILLAGES, etc.

BARRY, T.B.
George Payne F.S.A. (1848-1920): an assessment
of his archaeological career.
K.B.C? July 1970.
4.

BENNETT, F.J.
Kentish megaliths and alignments. (originally
published in the "South Eastern Naturalist,1904).
Fenris-Wolf, Cambridge. 1978.
3,4,12,19.
15 - 1904.

BRITISH ARCHAEOLOGICAL ASSOCIATION - Journal
Vol.40. 1884.
Contains articles on several Kentish towns.
(Dover, Canterbury, Sandwich, Sandown,
Sandgate, Richborough, St.Margaret-at-Cliffe).
3,6,12.

COGHLAN, H.H.
Some aspects of prehistoric metallurgy in
the South of England.
In Transactions of the South Eastern
Naturalist and Antiquary. Vol.56. 1951.
11.

COPLEY, Gordon J.*
An archaeology of South-East England: a study
in continuity.
Phoenix House. 1958.
2,5,10,12,13,14.

COUNCIL FOR BRITISH ARCHAEOLOGY.
The plans and topography of medieval towns
in England & Wales.
Council for British Archaeology. 1976.
3.

DUNNING, G.C.
Neolithic occupation sites in East Kent.
In The Antiquaries Journal. Vol.46,Part I.
1966.
Oxford University Press. 1966.
4,11.

DYER, James.
Southern England: an archaeological guide.
Faber. 1973.
3.

FAUSSETT, Rev. Bryan (Rector of Monks Horton).
Inventorium sepulchrale: an account of some
antiquities dug up at Gilton, Kingston,
Sibertswold, Barfriston, Beakesbourne, Chartham,
& Crundale, AD1757 - AD1773.
P.P. for Subscribers. 1856.
1,3,4,5,6,7,8,11,12,13,15,17,25.

HAWKES, Sonia Chadwick.
The Jutish Style A. A study of Germanic animal
art in Southern England in the fifth Century A.D.
Published with the aid of a grant from
The Council For British Archaeology. 1958.
11.

HOGARTH, A.C.
Structural features in Anglo-Saxon graves.
The Royal Archaeological Institute. 1973.
24.

JESSUP, Ronald Frank.
Anglo-Saxon jewellery. New edition.
Shire Publications. 1974.
3.

Archaeology of Kent.*
Methuen. 1930.
1,2,3,4,5,6,7,8,9,11,12,13,14,15,16,17,18,19,20,
24,25,26.

Curiosities of British Archaeology, compiled by
R.F. Jessup. 2nd edition.
Phillimore. 1974.
15.

KENT ARCHAEOLOGICAL RESEARCH GROUPS COUNCIL.*
Kent Archaeological Review
Kent Archaeological Research Groups Council.
1965 - 1978.
3. Nos 1 and 2. 1965.
5. Nos 1 - 30. 1965 - 1972/3
7. Vols. 41 - 50. -? - 1978.

ORDNANCE SURVEY: ARCHAEOLOGICAL SECTION.
Set of Archaeological records cards
for Chatham & Rochester.
Ordnance Survey. c.1976?
4.

PAYNE, George.*
An Archaeological survey of the County of Kent.
Read to the Society of Antiquaries of London
on 25th June 1888. (From Archaeologia Vol.Ll.
1888).
Nichols & Sons For Society of Antiquarians of
London. 1889.
1,2,9,11,13,15,16,17.

PHILP, Brian J.
Rescue excavations in Kent 1972 - 74,
by Brian & Edna Philp.   (Kent Archaeological
Rescue Unit).CIB.
Kent Archaeological Rescue Unit. c.1976.
1,2,6,8,9,11,16,17,19.

SAMMES, Edward.
Discovering Regional Archaeology: South-
Eastern England: guides to the Archaeological
sites of Greater London, Hants, Kent, Surrey
and Sussex.
Shire Publications. 1973.
6,7,11,26.

SMITH, Charles Roach.*
Collectanea Antiqua: etchings and engravings
of ancient remains.
J.R. Smith.
7 vols. 1848 - 1880. 3,12.
Vols.1-6only   15,20.
6 vols in 3 vols.1848-1868. 11.

WAINWRIGHT, Richard.
A guide to the prehistoric remains in Britain.
Vol.1; South and East.
Constable. 1978.
23.

See also ARCHAEOLOGIA CANTIANA (History-General)
TOWNS, VILLAGES, etc.

WOOD, Eric Stuart.
Collins' field Guide to Archaeology; with an
introduction by Sir Mortimer Wheeler. 4th edn.
Collins 1975.
11.

HISTORY - GENERAL.
(INCLUDING PRE 20 CENTURY TOPOGRAPHICAL AUTHORS).

ABELL, Henry Francis.*
History of Kent.
Kentish Express: Ashford. 1898.
1,2,3,4,5,6,7,8,10,11,12,13,15,16,17,18,19,20,25.

A Short History of Kent for the young.
Kentish Express: Ashford. 1895.
1,2,3,5,6,8,10,11,14,15,18,26.

ALLEN, Thomas.*
Picturesque beauties of Great Britain....Kent.
George Virtue. 1833.
1,2,17.

ARCHAEOLOGIA CANTIANA.* In progress.
Kent Archaeological Society.   Vol I. 1858.
1,2,3,4,5,6,7,8,9,10,11,12,13,14,15,16,17,18,19,
20,21,28.
25.   Vols 1-16; 19; 22-24; 26; 29-32; 34; 38-51;
           53-55; 57-89.
30.   Vol.19(1892); Vols 45-60; 62-93 in progress.

BAGSHAW, Samuel.*
History, Gazetteer and directory of the County of
Kent. 2 vols.
Ridge. Sheffield. 1847.
1,2,3,4,5,6,7,8,11,12,13,14,15,17,18,19,21,25,26.

BANNER, Hubert   Stewart.*
Kentish Fire.
Hurst & Blackett. 1944.
1,2,4,5,9,11,15,19,23.

BEVAN, G. Phillips.*
Handbook to the County of Kent.
E. Stanford.
3. 1882.
5. 6th edition 1887.

BIBLIOTHECA TOPOGRAPHICA BRITANNICA.* Vol.1. No.1.
containing
1. Queries for the better illustrating the
antiquities and natural history of Great Britain
and Ireland.
2. The history and antiquities of Tunstall in Kent,
by the late Mr. Edward Rowe Mores.
J. Nichols. 1780.
1,4,5,6,8,11,12,15,17,20.

BLACK, Adam & Charles Ltd. Publishers.*
Black's Guide to Kent.
A.&.C. Black Ltd.
1870. 24
1886. 10th edition. 1,15,31.
1890. 11th ed   11.
1915. 25

BRAYLEY, Edward Wedlake.*
The Beauties of England and Wales...or original
delinations...of each County.
Vernon, Hood & Sharpe. Printed by Thomas Maiden.
3. Vol.VIII. 1808.
30. Part of Vol.VII and the whole of Vol.VIII,
    Kent, 1806 and 1808.

BUSHELL, Thomas A.
Kent. (The Barracuda guide to County History
Series, Vol.1).
Barracuda Books Ltd. Chesham, Bucks. 1976.
1,2,3,4,5,6,7,9,11,12,13,15,16,20,25,26,27,28,28,30.
                   *
Kent: our County.*
Association of Men of Kent & Kentish Men.   1971.
3,4,5,6,7,8,9,11,12,30,31.

BYGONE KENT.
A Monthly Journal on all aspects of local history.
Vol.1. No.1. Jan. 1980.— in progress.
Meresborough Books. Rainham. 1980.
4.

CAMDEN, William.
Camden's Britannia: Kent, from the edition of
1789 by Richard Gough. Annotated and edited by
G.J. Copley.
Hutchinson.   1977.
1,3,5,6,8,9,11,19,20,22,23,25,26,27,28,

Cantium:*being an excerpt from Camden's Britannia.
Extract from the first edition in English.
London. 1610.
2,6,13,14.

Cantium:* being an excerpt from Camden's Brittania.
Holland's edition 1610 - 1637.
London 1637.
13.

Cantium:* being an excerpt from Camden's Brittania.
Gibson's edition, 1610 - 95.
A.S. Walle & A.&.J. Churchill. London. 1695.
2,13.
Gibson's edition 1610 - 1722. London. 1722.
13,14.

Cantium:* being an excerpt from Camden's Britannia.
Gough's edition, 1610 - 1789.
T. Payne & Son, G.&.J. Robinson, London. 1789.
8,11,13.

Remains Concerning Britain.
(Facsimile reprint of 1870 edition).
E.P. Publishing.   1974.
1.

CANTIUM - a magazine of Kent Local History,
1969 - 1974.
Phillimore.
4.   1970. Vol.2. - 1974. Vol.6.
7.   1969. Vol.1; 1970 Vol.2; 1971 Vol.3.
11. 1969 Vol.1 - 1974 Vol.6.
19. 1973 Vol.5; 1974 Vol.6.
24. 1969 Vol.1. - 1974 Vol.6.

CLAIR, Colin.*
A Kentish garner.
Bruce & Gawthorne. Watford   (195-?)
1,3,4,5,7,8,11,12,14,15,18,19,20,26,28,30.
2.   1962.
9.   1960.
17. 1961.

COBBETT, William.*
Rural rides in the Counties of Surrey, Kent,
& Sussex. (pp.159 - 217, Kent).
1853 etc. Cobbett, afterwards Dent,   6,13,15,16.
1958 (1975 impression). Macdonald   2.

COLLISS, William.
Sketches, drawings, scumblings, blottings and
blunderings, some taken hastily as memoranda
and records only made during visits into
Kent commencing in 1869. Vol.I.
(Original Water colours & sketches mounted in
a leather bound book, the artist painted mainly
in the Hundred of Hoo).
11.

COOKE, George Alexander.*
Topographical and statistical description of
the County of Kent..
Sherwood, Neely & Jones   1816.
2.

COX, Thomas.*
Magna Britannia et Hibernia, Antiqua et Nova,
by T. Cox & A. Hall. Section dealing with Kent
pp. 1,071 - 1,270.
London: in the Savoy. Sold by M. Nutt. 1727.
2,3,4,6,7,8,9,11,12,13,17,18,21.

CROMWELL, Thomas Kitson.*
Excursions through the Counties of Kent,
Surrey and Sussex....
Longman, Hurst, Rees, Orme & Brown.
1820. 13.
1822. 2,3.

CROUCH, Marcus.
A book of Kent:a series of vignettes on the life
and times of yesteryear, edited by M. Crouch and
made by the printers of Kent, commemorating 500
years of printing in England, 1476-1976.
Paul Norbury, Tenterden, 1976.
2,5,6,7,8,11,15,20,23,28.

DARTON, Frederick Joseph Harvey.
English Fabric: the story of village life.
Newnes. (1935).
11.

(DENNE, Rev. Samuel & SHRUBSOLE, W.).*
The History & Antiquities of Rochester and its
Environs; to which is added a description of the
towns, villages etc. situated on, or near, to the
road from London to Margate, Deal & Dover, by
S. Denne & W. Shrubsole.
Printed & sold by T. Fisher. Rochester.
Sold by S. Crowden. London. 1772.
11,25.

The History & antiquities of Rochester and its
environs;* to which is added a description of
the towns, villages etc. Situated on, or near,
to the road from London to Margate, Deal & Dover
by S. Denne & W. Shrubsole.
2nd edition edited by W. Wildash, with considerable
additions & improvements.
Printed & sold by W. Wildash. Rochester.
Sold by Longman, Rees, Orme & Brown. London. 1817.
1,4,5,15,25,26.

A DESCRIPTION OF ENGLAND WALES,* containing a
particular account of each County....Vol.V.
(includes Kent).
Printed for Newbery & Carnan, London.
No.65, the North Side of St. Paul's Churchyard,1769.
3,17.

DITCHFIELD, Peter Hampson.*
Memorials of Old Kent, by P.H. Ditchfield & G.Clinch.
Bemrose. 1907.
1,2,3,4,5,6,7,8,9,10,11,12,13,14,15,16,17,18,19,22,25,

DUGDALE, Thomas.
England & Wales delineated, historical, entertaining
and commercial, alphabetically arranged. Vols. 1 - 3.
J. Tallis. 1835.
13.

ENGLAND DISPLAYED.....revised by P. Russell. Section
from Vol.2. covering Kent.
Adlard & Browne. 1769.
2.

ENGLAND PICTORIAL AND DESCRIPTIVE.(p.9-64 on Kent).
J.B. Knapp. (c.1895?).
2.

AN ENTIRE & COMPLETE HISTORY,* political and
personal, of the BOROUGHS OF GREAT BRITAIN,
together with the Cinque Ports. 3 vols.
G. Riley. 1792.
11,26.
4.   Vol.3
10.   Vol.2

EVERITT, Alan Milner.
Ways & Means in local history. (Contains
information about Kent).
National Council of Social Service. 1971.
20,26,27.

FIENNES, Celia.*
Journeys of Celia Fiennes, edited by C. Morris.
(includes Tour of Kent 1697...).
Cresset Press.   1947.
2,15,19.

FINCH, William Coles.
Life in rural England: occupations and pastimes
in field and village, farm and home, watermill
& windmill. (with special reference to Kent.).
C.W. Daniel. 1928.
4,8,11,12,25.

GARDINER, Mrs. Dorothy.*
Some sources of Kent Local History.
K.C.C. 1938.
3,8,11,13,30.

GOMME, George Laurence.*
Court minutes of the Surrey and Kent Sewer
Commission. Vol.1, edited by G.L. Gomme.
1909.
12.

GOODSALL, Robert Harold.*
A Kentish Patchwork.
Constable. 1966.
2,3,4,6,7,8,10,11,12,14,15,16,18,19,25,31.

A Second Kentish Patchwork.*
Stede Hill Pubns. Harrietsham. 1968.
2,3,4,5,6,9,11,12,16,26,31.

A Third Kentish Patchwork.*
Stede Hill Pubns. Harrietsham. 1970.
2,3,4,5,6,7,9,11,12,16,31.

A Fourth Kentish Patchwork.*
Stede Hill Pubns. Harrietsham. 1974.
1,3,4,6,7,8,9,11,12,15,16,19,22,24,25,27,31.

GREENWOOD, C.*
An epitome of County History.
Published for the Proprieter. 1838.
1,2,3,4,5,6,7,8,11,12,14,15,16,17,18,19,25.

HARRIS, John.*
History of Kent in 5 parts...Book I - an
exact topography. Book II-The Civil History
of Kent. (Bound in one volume).
D. Midwinter. 1719.
1,2,3,4,5,6,7,8,9,11,12,13,14,15,16,17,19.

HASTED, Edward.*
The history and topographical survey of the
County of Kent. 4 vols. (1st Folio edition).
Simmons and Kirkby. 1778 - 9.
1,2,3,4,5,6,7,8,10,12,13,15,16,17,19.21.
11.   Grangerised 1st edn. 1778-1799. 4 vols in
       14 vols.

The history and topographical survey of the
County of Kent.* 12 Vols. 2nd edition.
W. Bristow. Canterbury. 1797 - 1801.
1,2,3,4,5,6,7,8,9,11,12,13,14,15,16,17,
19,20,21,26,32.
18 - Vol.1.

The history & topographical survey of the
County of Kent. 12 vols.
Facsimile reprint of the 2nd edition.
Biographical note by A.M. Everitt.
E.P. Publishing Ltd. with K.C.C. 1972.
3,4,9,11,12,20,22,25.
2.   Vol. I.
8.   Vol. 6.
16.   Vol. 3.

HEATH, Richard.
English peasant.
E.P. Publishing Ltd. 1978.
28.

THE HISTORY OF KENT, edited by Graham Cook.
Twenty Four parts, of which only six were
published.
2,11,19,24,28. Parts 1 - 6.
13.   Parts 1 - 5.

HOME COUNTIES MAGAZINE - devoted to the topography
of London, Middlesex, Essex, Herts, Bucks,
Berks, Surrey, Kent and Sussex. 14 vols.
Various Publishers. 1899 - 1912.
1,3,7,9,11,12,16,17.18.
4.   Vols. 12, 13 & 14.
13.   Vol.4.

HOSKINS, William George.
Local history in England. 2nd edition Paperback.
pp. 244 - 255. Bibliographical References.
Longman. 1974.
11.

The Making of the English landscape.
Penguin. 1970.
11.

HUGHES, William R.*
A week's tramp in Dickens-Land.
Chapman & Hall.
1891. 24, 25.
1893. 2nd edition 24.
1898. 2.

HISTORY - GENERAL Cont'd
(INCLUDING PRE 20th CENTURY TOPOGRAPHICAL AUTHORS).

HULL, Felix.
A Kentish Miscellany (Kent Archaeological Society.
Records Branch. Vol. XXI).
Phillimore & Co.Ltd. 1979.
9,12,16,23.

HUNTER, Henry.
(Kent) extract from the History of London and
its environs.....Likewise an account of all the
towns, villages, and country within twenty-five
miles of London. By...H. Hunter & other gentlemen.
With maps, plans and views. 2 vols.
John Stockdale. London. 1811.
2.

IRELAND, William Henry.*
England's topographer, or a new and complete
history of Kent. Vols I - 4.
G. Virtue. 1828 - 30.
1,2,3,4,5,6,7,8,9,10,11,12,14,15,17,19,20,21,25.
13.   Vol 3. 1829.
16.   3 vols.   18.   Vol.2.
                            22.   Vol.1. 1828.

JESSUP, Frank William.*
The History of Kent: a select bibliography,
compiled by F.W. Jessup.
Kent County Council. 1966.
1,2,3,4,5,7,8,10,11,12,13,15,16,18,19,21.
2nd. edition 1974   20,27.

A History of Kent with maps & pictures.*
Darwen Finlayson. 1958.
1,2,3,4,5,6,7,8,9,11,12,14,15,17,18,19,20,21,24,
25,26.

1974 New Revised edition. Phillimore.
2,6,7,9,11,12,16,19,25,26,28,29.

Kent History Illustrated.*
Kent Education Committee. 1966
1,2,3,4,5,6,7,8,9,10,11,12,14,15,16,17,18,19,
20,24,25,30,31.
2nd edn. 1973. 2,7,9,12,15,16,19,20,27.

KEATE, George.*
Sketches from nature taken and coloured in a
journey to Margate.
2 vols. Printed For J. Dodsley.
1779.   2nd edn. Vol.I. 24.   2 vols.   13.
1782.   3rd edn. 2 vols.   11.12.13.15.17.
1790.   4th edn. 2 vols. 13.
1802.   5th edn. 2 vols. 6.8.13.
1806.   6th edn. 2 vols. 24.

KENT COUNTY COUNCIL: ARCHIVES OFFICE.
A display of Royal autographs and portraits,
great seals,etc. found on documents in the
Kent Archives Office.
Presented by F. Hull.
K.C.C.1953.
4.

English history through Kentish eyes:*an introduction to an exhibition of documents...
from the collection housed in the Kent
Archives Office.
K.C.C. 1955.
1,2,4,8,11,15,17,20,31.

Guide to the Kent County Archives Office,*
compiled by Dr. F. Hull.
K.C.C. 1958.
2,3,6,11,12,16,17,18,20,24,25,29,30,31.

First supplement 1957 - 1968,compiled by
Dr. F. Hull.
K.C.C. 1972.
4,5,6,7,8,9,11,12,19,20,25,30,31.

Kent Archives Office.*
K.C.C. 1966.
2,4,

Notes on records:how to trace the history
of your house.
K.C.C. (1973).
4.

KENT COUNTY LIBRARY.
Edward Hasted: the history and topographical
survey of the County of Kent: an index to
parishes, hundreds and lathes.
K.C.C. 1972.
2,4,11,12.

Local History Catalogue.
K.C.C. 1939.
3,11,12,13.

KENT VOLUNTARY SERVICE COUNCIL.
Journal of Kent Local History.   Autumn 1975→
Kent Voluntary Service. 1975→
28.

THE KENTISH TOURIST,*or excursions in the
County of Kent.
J. Dowding. (1822).
1,4,8,11,12,17,24.

THE KENTISH TRAVELLER'S COMPANION,* in a
descriptive view of the towns, villages,
remarkable buildings and antiquities, situated
in or near the road from London to Margate,
Dover & Canterbury.
1776.   1st edn. Simmons & Kirkby; Canterbury;
T. Fisher, Rochester.
2,3,6,8,9,13,14,15,18,20.
1794.   4th edn. Simmons & Kirkby; Canterbury
T.&.A. Etherington. Rochester & Chatham.
2,6,13,19.

KERSHAW, S. Wayland.*
Foreign refugee Settlements in East Kent.
Cross & Jackman, Canterbury. 1883.
11,26.

KILBURNE, Richard.*
A topographie or survey of the County of Kent.
Printed by Thomas Mabb for Henry Atkinson. 1659.
1,2,3,4,5,6,7,8,11,12,13,14,15,16,17,18,19,20,21.

KNOCKER, Herbert Wheatley.*
Kentish manorial incidents.
Manorial Society. 1912.
3,11,16,23.

LAMBARDE, William.*
A perambulation of Kent...Written in the yeere
1570....
First published in 1576.
1826. Baldwin, Cradock & Joy. 20,24,26.
1970. Reprint of the 1826 edn. with an introduction
      by Richard Church.
      Adams & Dart.
      6,8,17,19,20,22,24,26,27,29,30.

LEWIS, W. Publisher.*
Lewis's new Traveller's guide or a pocket
edition of the English Counties.
W. Lewis. London. 1819.
6,13.

LYSONS, Daniel.*
The Environs of London....Volume the Fourth,
Counties of Herts, Essex and Kent.
Printed for T. Cadell & W. Davies.
1796. 1,2,17,18.
1811. 12.

MACLAREN, R.
Kent long ago.(Viewing Kent Series).
James Pike. 1977.
2,3,6,11,28.

MALCOLM, James Peller.*
Excursions in the counties of Kent...Gloucester,
Hereford,Monmouth and Somerset in the years
1802, 1803 and 1805 - illustrated by descriptive
sketches of the most interesting places & buildings,
particularly the Cathedrals of Canterbury,
Gloucester, Hereford & Bristol with deliniations
of character in different walks of life.
Nichols, Son & Bentley. 1814.
1,2,
6,7,8.12.also 1805.
17.   also 1822.

MALCOLM, James Peller.*
First impressions or sketches from art and
nature, animate and inanimate. (pp.6 - 51 Kent).
Printed by John Nichols & Son. 1807.
6,11,15.

MILLER, William*
Jottings of Kent. 2nd ed
Whittaker & Company, London.
Thomas Hall. Gravesend.
1864.
1,2,3,4,5,6,7,8,9,11,12,13,14,15,16,17,25.

MOCKETT, John.
Mocketts' journal: a collection of interesting
matters relating to remarkable personages,
ancient buildings, manners & customs etc.
beginning with the year 50 by John Mockett of
St. Peter's in the Isle of Thanet.
Kentish Observer, Canterbury. 1836.
1,6,11,13,14,17,24.

MORGAN, E. Victor.
The study of prices and the value of money.
Historical Association. 1950.
23.

MURRAY, John Publisher.*
Handbook for Travellers in Kent.
John Murray, 1858. etc.
1,2,3,4,5, (1877 4th edition).
7,8,9,11, (1858).
12,14,15,16,17,18,19, (1858).

"OBSERVANT PEDESTRIAN" pseud.
Further excursions of the Observant Pedestrian
exemplified in a tour to Margate. Vols.1.2.& 3 only.
Dutton. 1801.
13.

PAGE, William.*
Victoria History of the County of Kent, 3 vols,
edited by W. Page.
St. Catherine Press, London. 1908 - 1932.
1,2,3,4,5,6,7,8,9,11,12,13,14,15,16, (Vols1& 2 only),
17,18,19,20,21,24,25,30.

PAYNE, George.*
Merry makings in the olden times. Read before
the Maidstone & Mid-Kent Natural History and
Philosophical Society on the 15th January 1891).
Frederick Bunyard, The Library, Maidstone.1891.
11,12.

PENNANT, Thomas.*
Journey from London to the Isle of Wight.
Vol.1. from London to Dover.
Vol.II from Dover to the Isle of Wight.
E. Harding. Oriental Press. 1801.
1,6,7,12.
2,4,8,13, Vol I. only.

PHILIPOTT, Thomas.*
Villare Cantianum.
1659. William Godbid.
1.2.4.6.7.13.14.15.17.21.
1776. 2nd edn. Whittingham.
1,2,3,5,6,8,12,16,17,19,21.

PIMLOTT, John Alfred Ralph.
The Englishman's holiday: a social history.
(Vacations to 1945).
First published by Faber in 1947.
Reprinted by Harvester Press Ltd. 1976.
3.

PROSSER, Arthur.
Illustrated history of Kent.
(Many of the cartoon Strips appeared in
The Kent Evening Post).
South Eastern Newspapers Ltd. Larkfield. 1978.
3,4,5,8,11,12,15,25.

PUMPHREY, George Henry.*
Conquering the English Channel.
(The author lives in Dover).
Abelard Schuman. 1965.
3,6,11.

ROAKE, Margaret.
Essays in Kentish history; edited,and with
an introduction, by Margaret Roake and John Whyman.
Frank Cass. 1973.
1,2,3,5,6,7,8,11,14,22,24,25,30,31.

RUSSELL, W. Clark.*
Betwixt the Forelands.
Sampson Low. 1889.
1,6,7,11,12,13,18.

SAUNDERS, Herbert Washington.*
History of Kent from the earliest times to 1714.
John Murray. 1936.
1,3,4,5,11,12,14.

SEYMOUR, Charles.*
A new topographical, historical and commercial
survey of the cities, towns and villages of the
County of Kent.
Sold by T. Smith: Canterbury.
1776   25.
1782.   26 (lacks title page).

SHEPHERD, George.*
Picturesque beauties of Great Britain: illustrated
by topographical, historical and critical notices;
combining every interesting object, ancient and
modern from an elaborate survey, and original
designs taken upon the spot by G. Shepherd,
H. Gastineau and others.
George Virtue. London.
1828.   3, 6,13,18.
1829.   12,
1831 & 1840.   4.
1832.   1,8,9,11,15,17,19.

A Treasury of Kent prints: a series of views
from original drawings by G. Shepherd,
H. Gastineau (& others) contained in W.G. Ireland
- "A new and complete history of the County
of Kent (1828-1831). New edition.
A. Cassell. Sheerness. 1972.
3,4,5,8,11,12,24.

SIMPSON, Samuel.*
The Agreeable Historian, or, the Compleat
English Traveller, giving a geographical
description of every County in...England...
with a map of every County, after the designs
of H. Moll and others. 3 vols.
KENT SECTION. C. Walker. London. 1746.
2.

SOUTHERN HISTORY: a review of the history of
Southern England.
Vol.1. 1979, edition. J.R. Lowerson.
Dawson. 1979.
23.

SPENCER, Nathaniel.*
The County & ancient Kingdom of Kent.
From The Complete English Traveller: a
Survey and Description of England and Wales.
1772.
4,6,7.

SPURRELL, F.C.J.
Collection of pamphlets in one volume (27).
Subjects include archaeology, place-names,
geology, dene holes etc., mainly in Kent.
1880 - 1896.
2.

SQUIERS, William.
Secret hiding places: the origins, histories
and descriptions of English secret hiding
places used by priests, Cavaliers, Jacobites
and Smugglers. (pp. 261 - 275, Kent).
S. Paul. 1934.
11.

STEAD, Richard.*
Bygone Kent, edited by R. Stead
1892. H.J. Goulden. Canterbury.
1,2,3,4,5,7,8,9,11,12,13,14,15,17,18,19,30.
1972. Facsimile Reprint E.P. Publications Ltd.
11,12.

TIMBS, John.*
Abbeys, castles and ancient halls of
England and Wales: their legendary lore and
popular history, by John Timbs and
Alexander Gunn. 3 vols.
F. Warne & Co. c.1872.
5,6,24.
Vol.1. (The South) only (1925).   4,11.

TOPOGRAPHICAL ACCOUNT OF THE HUNDRED OF
DEWSBOROUGH in Old English Record Hand.
An Ms Book of c.1860. The contents are
concerned with parishes within the Hundred of
Bewsborough, near to Dover.
17.

TOWN & COUNTRY MAGAZINE.
An Account of Kent.
December 1713.
17.

UNIVERSITY OF KENT AT CANTERBURY
Research Completed...on Kentish history;
(a list of theses & essays).
Typescript (1973).
4.

VAUGHAN, John.
The English Guide Book, c.1780 - 1870;
an illustrated history.
David & Charles. 1974.
11.

WATSON, William W.*
The visitors' guide to Herne Bay, Canterbury
and the most memorable spots in Kent.
J. Dicks. 1855.
11,17.

WRIGHT, Christopher John.
Kent through the years.
Batsford. 1975.
1,2,3,4,5,6,7,8,9,11,12,13,15,16,19,20,22,24,
25,26,27,28,30.

WYMER, Norman.
English town crafts; a survey of their
development from early times to the present
day.(Some of the crafts are carried out in rural
Kent).
Batsford 1949.
11.
E.P. Publishing. 1975.
11.

HISTORY - TO 900 AD.

AIRY, George Biddell.
Essays on the invasion of Britain by Julius
Caesar...Plautius and...Claudius Caesar etc.
Nichols & Sons. printers. 1865.
2.

THE ANGLO-SAXON CHRONICLE.
(Extracts made in Ms...appertaining to Kent).
4.

BUSHELL, Thomas A.
Ancient history & legends of the county of Kent.
Association of Men of Kent & Kentish Men (197?).
12,25.

CHURCH, Alfred J.
The Count of the Saxon Shore; or the Villa in
Vectis: a tale of the departure of the
Romans from Britain: a novel.
Seeley. 1887.
11.

DUNKIN, Alfred John.*
History of the County of Kent. Vol.2.
Caesar's campaigns.
John Russell Smith. 1858.
4,11,17.

ELLIS, Peter Berresford.
Caesar's invasion of Britain.
Orbis Publishing. 1978.
3.

GROSE, Francis.
The Antiquities of England & Wales, Vol.3. Kent.
(1784) Wright.   2.
(1797) New edition, printed for S. Hooper. 3.

JENKINS, Frank.*
Men of Kent before the Romans, Cantium in the
Early Iron Age.
Canterbury Archaeological Society. 1962.
1,2,3,4,5,7,8,9,10,11,12,14,15,19,24.

Men of Kent in the Dark Ages, AD.449-597.
Canterbury Archaeological Society. 1964.
1,2,3,4,5,7,8,10,12,15,19,25.

Roman Kent, Cantium in Roman Times, AD43-449.
Canterbury Archaeological Society. 1966.
1,2,3,4,5,6,7,8,9,10,11,12,15,17,18,19,24.

JOLLIFFE, J.E.A.*
Pre-feudal England: the Jutes.
Cass 1933 reprinted. 1962.
3,4,5,11,12,15,23.

MOTHERSOLE, Jessie.*
The Saxon Shore.
John Lane, Bodley Head. 1924.
1,2,3,6,7,8,11,12,13,14,15,17,19,20,30.

ORDNANCE SURVEY.
Roman Britain. 4th edition. Maps & Scale1:625,000
(Folded with text).
Ordnance Survey. 1978.
23.

THE PARKER CHRONICLE (AD832-900),
edited by A.H. Smith.
(The oldest extant version of the Old English
Chronicles).
Methuen. 1935.
11.

SOCIETY OF ANTIQUARIES OF LONDON.
Correspondence between the Society of Antiquaries
and the Admiralty respecting the tides in the
Dover Channel, with reference to the landing of
Caesar in Britain BC 55....
Read to the Society of Antiquaries of London
on Feb. 12th 1863.
(Extracted From Archaeology Vol.XXXIX).
The Society. 1863.
11.

SOMNER, William.*
A treatise of the Roman ports and forts in Kent...
West, Crosley & Clements. 1693.
1,2,3,4,6,7,8,11,12,13,14,15,17,18,21.

STANHOPE, Phillip Henry 5th Earl Stanhope.
On the day of Caesars' landing in Britain.
Read to the Society of Antiquaries of London
on November 15th 1866.
Extracted From Archaeologia Vol. XLI.
The Society. 1866.
11.

SWEET, Henry.
(Kentish extracts removed from the "Anglo-
Saxon Reader in prose and Verse").
pp. 53 - 60 and 190 - 226.
11.

VINE, Francis Thomas.*
Caesar in Kent, an account of the landing of
Julius Caesar and his battles with the Ancient
Britons.
1886. Turnbull & Spears, printers:Edinburgh
1,2,4,5,7,8,11,12,13,15,30.
1887 Elliott Stock. 2nd edition.
1,2,3,4,5,6,11,12,13,14,15,16,17,21,24,25.

WARD, Gordon Reginald
Anglo-Saxon records of Kent. Unpublished notes.
11.

The Belgic Britons:* Men of Kent in BC55.
Caxton & Holmesdale Press. Sevenoaks, 1961.
1,2,4,5,6,7,8,11,12,13,14,15,16,17,19,21.

A Charter of Wintred,* King of Kent, AD.699.
K.C.C. 1948.
1,2,3,8,11,26.

WARD, Gordon Reginald.
Hengest.*....Reprinted From Archaeologia
Cantiana, Vol.61. 1948.
1,8,11,16.
1949, Printed by Headley Bros. Ashford.
2,24.
1949. Anglo-Danish Publishing Coy.Ltd.
11,16.

King Oswin - a Forgotten ruler of Kent.(c.673AD).
Reprinted From Archaeologia Cantiana,
Vol.50   1938.
11.

WITNEY,K.P.
The Jutish forest: a study of the Weald of
Kent from 450 to 1380 AD.
University of London:Athlone Press. 1976.
1,2,3,5,7,11,12,15,16,20,22,23,26,27,30.

HISTORY - 901AD - 1500 AD

ALDERMAN, Clifford Lindsey.
Flame of Freedom: the Peasants' Revolt of
1381 (A novel).
Bailey & Swinfen.   1974.
5,11.

BALLARD, Adolphus.
Domesday inquest.   2nd edition.
Methuen.   1923.
11.

BASKERVILLE, Geoffrey.*
English Monks and the suppression of the
monasteries.
Cape. 1937.
3,11.

BERESFORD, Maurice Warwick.
Deserted mediaeval villages: studies: edited
by M.W. Beresford & John G. Hurst.
(County Gazeteer of Known villages in 1968
pp.183-212; pp.191-2 Kent).
Lutterworth Press.   1971.

CHURCHILL, Irene Josephine.*
Calendar of Kent Feet of Fines to the end of
Henry III's reign, compiled by I.J. Churchill
and others.(Kent Records, Vol.15).
Kent Archaeological Society: Records Branch.1956.
1,2,3,4,7,8,11,12,17,18.

COWIE, Leonard W.
The Black Death and the Peasants' Revolt.
Wayland.   1972.
5.

DU BOULAY, Francis Robin Houssemayne.*
Documents illustrative of Mediaeval Kentish
Society, edited by F.R.H. DuBoulay. (Kent
Records Vol.18)
Kent Archaeological Society:Records Branch.1946.
2,3,4,5,7,8,9,10,11,12,15,17,18,24.30.

EADMER The Monk.*
(Historia novorum in Anglia). History of recent
events in England. Translated by Geoffrey
Bosanquet from the Latin.   (Eadmer was a
Canterbury Monk).
The Cresset Press.   1964.
3,12.

FILMER, Reginald Mead.*
A Chronicle of Kent, 1250 - 1760.
Clear Copies Ltd.   London.   1967.
1,2,3,4,5,6,7,8,9,10,11,12,17,18,19,20,25,26,30.

FINN, Rex Welldon.
Domesday Book: a guide.
Phillimore.Roman & Littlefield.   1973.
11.

GALBRAITH, Vivian Hunter.
Domesday Book: its' place in administrative
history.
Oxford University Press.   1974.
11.

GASQUET, Cardinal Francis Aidan.
Parish life in mediaeval England.
Methuen. 1906.
11.

HENSHALL, Samuel.*
Specimens and parts, containing a history of
the County of Kent...Edward the Confessour (sic)
to Edward the first...
Rivington.   1798.
1,2,4,5,6,7,8,11,12,13,15,16,17.

JUSSERAND, Jean Adriene Antoine Jules.
English wayfaring life in the Middle ages
(XIVth Century): translated from the French
by Lucy Toulmin Smith.   New, revised and enlarged,
3rd edition.
T. Fisher Unwin.   1925.
11.

LARKING, Lambert Blackwell.*
A description of the heart shrine in Leybourne
Church, with some account of Sir Roger de Leybourn
and his connection with the Wars of the Barons
in the thirteenth Century.(A letter to Thomas
Godfrey Fausset, Esq.). Reprinted with additional
notes from Archaeologia Cantiana. Vol. V, 1863,
pp.28 . 76.
Printed by John Edward Taylor. 1864.
11,25.

LINDSAY, Philip.*
The Peasant's Revolt, 1381, by Philip Lindsay
and Roy Groves.
Hutchinson.   1950.
5,11,12.

RICHARDS, Peter.
The mediaeval leper and his northern heirs.
(Kent Leper Hospitals mentioned at Dover,
Romney, Canterbury & Harbledown).
D.S. Brewer.Rowman & Littlefield.   1977.
11.

ROGERS, James Edwin Thorold.
Six centuries of work and wages; the history
of English labour. 5th edition Wat Tylers'
Rebellion pp.253-262).
Swan Sonnenshein & Co. Ltd.   London.   1921.
11.

STAPLETON, Thomas.
Observations upon the succession to the Barony of
William of Arques, in the County of Kent, during
the period between the conquest of England and
the reign of King John. Read to the Society of
Antiquaries of London on the 9th & 16th of
January 1845. (Extracted from Archaeologia
Vol. XXXl).   (William held land in East Kent).
The Society. 1845.
11.

WEBBER, Ronald.
The Peasants' revolt.
Terence Dalton. 1980.
23,28.

WITNEY, K.P.
The Jutish Forest: a study of the Weald of Kent
from 450 to 1380 AD.
University of London. Athlone Press. 1976.
1,2,3,5,7,11,12,15,16,20,22,23,26,27,30.

WOODS, William.
Thunder on Saturday.
(Fiction. Wat Tyler's rebellion).
Melrose. 1952.
4.

HISTORY - 1501AD ONWARDS

ABELL, Henry Francis.*
Kent and the Great Civil War.
Kentish Express. Ashford. 1901.
1,3,4,5,7,10,11,12,15,17,19.

ALMACK, Richard.*
Papers relating to proceedings in the County of
Kent, A.D. 1642 - A.D. 1646...edited by R.Almack.
(In Camden Miscellany, Volume 3, 1854).
Camden Society. 1855.
1,3,4,11,15,17.

AYLMER, G.E.
The Civil War and Interregnum:sources for
local historians by G.E. Aylmer and J.S. Morrill.
Standing Conference for Local History. 1979.
23.

BOXER, C.R.
The Anglo Dutch Wars of the 17th century.
1652-1674.
H.M.S.O. 1974.
27.

BRUCE, John.
Observations on a MS relation of the proceedings
in the last session of Parliament holden in the
fourth year of King Charles, A.D.1628, belonging
to the Earl of Verulam. Read on 31st March 1859
to the Society of Antiquaries of London, 1859.
(Sir John Finch, Speaker of the House of Commons,
lived at Fordwich).
Society of Antiquaries of London. 1859.
11.

BRUCE, John.
Particulars respecting Thomas Sackville, Lord
Buckhurst, with a fragment of the "Itinerarium
ad Windsor" written by Mr. Serjeant Fleetwood,
Recorder of London. Read on March 26th 1857
to the Society of Antiquaries of London.
The Society ... 1857.
11.

C., M. (CARTER, Matthew).*
A most true and exact relation of that honourable though unfortunate Expedition of
Kent, Essex and Colchester in 1648, by a
loyal actor in that engagement.
1650.
2,4,6,8,12,17.

CASSE, G.R. (of Rochester).
A prisoner of France (1809 - 1814).
(Originally published in 1841).
Howard Baker. 1976 reprint.
15.

THE CATHOLIC QUESTION (Catholic Emancipation
Bill).
The Great Brunswick Meeting on Penenden Heath,*
October 24th. 1828.
Smith. 1829.
11,17.

The Kent County Meeting:* a report of the
speeches delivered at the Kent County Meeting
holden on Penenden Heath, October 24th 1828,
with prefaratory remarks.
Ridgeway. London.
Burrill. Chatham. 1828.
1,3,4,11,12.

The Kent Meeting, Penenden Heath, Friday,
October 24th 1828. The Catholic Question.
Bradley & Dent for the British Catholic
Association. 1828.
4.

CHALKLIN, Christopher William.
The Provincial towns of England: a study of
the building process, 1740 - 1820.
E. Arnold. 1974.
11.

Rural Change and Urban growth 1500 - 1800:
essays in English Regional History,by C.W.
Chalklin and M.A. Havinden.
Longman. 1974.
3.

Seventeenth-century Kent:* a social and
economic history.
Longmans, 1965.
1,2,3,4,5,6,7,8,10,11,12,15,17,18,19,20,21,30.

The Same. John Hallewell, Rochester. 1978.
          (1965 edition reprinted).
3,11,16,25.

CLARK, Peter.
English provincial Society from the Reformation
to the Revolution: religion, politics and society
in Kent 1500 - 1640.
Harvester Press. 1977.
1,2,3,4,5,8,9,11,12,15,16,23.

English towns in transition, 1500 - 1700,
by Peter Clark and Paul Slack.
Oxford University Press. 1976.
11.

COLOMB, Colonel George Hatton.*
The Royalist Rising in Kent, A.D. 1648.
Reprinted from Archaeologia Cantiana.
Vol.IX 1874.
4,17.

CROSSICK, Geoffrey.
An artisan elite in Victorian Society:
Kentish London 1840 - 1880.
Croom Helm. 1978.
2,11.

CROUCH, Marcus.
Victorian and Edwardian Kent from old photographs;
introduction and commentaries by Marcus Crouch
and Wyn Bergess.
Batsford. 1974.
1,2,3,4,6,8,9,11,12,15,16,18,19,20,22,24,
25,26,27,28.

DAVIS, Ralph.
English Merchant Shipping and Anglo-Dutch
rivalry in the Seventeenth Century.
H.M.S.O. 1976.
15.

DELAWARE STATE BOARD OF EDUCATION.
Project BICEN; (arranged by) State Board of
Education, Delaware, U.S.A., Kent County Council
Education Department, Kent County, England. 2 vols.
Delaware Department of Public Instruction 1978.
(Papers by Kent and Delaware Students to
commemorate the American War of Independence 1776).
11.

DERING, Sir Edward.
The Parliamentary Diary of Sir Edward Dering
1670 - 1673, edited by Basil Duke Henning.
Yale University Press. Oxford University Press.
1940.
11.

The speeches of Sir Edward Dering in the
Commons House of Parliament,* 1641.
Printed for F.C. and D.B. 1641.
11.

DUNCAN, Leland Lewis.
Kentish Administration grants. Part II.
(1604-1649). Edited by L.L. Duncan.
Reprinted from Archaeologia Cantiana.
Vol 20. 1893.
11.

EVERITT, Alan Milner.*
The Community of Kent and the Great Rebellion.
1640 - 1660.
Leicester University Press. 1966.
1,2,3,4,5,6,7,8,9,11,12,15,17,18,19,20,28.

The local community and the Great Rebellion.
Pamphlet: General Series No.70.
Historical Association. 1969.
23.

EXTRACTS FROM KENTISH NEWSPAPERS.
1838 - 39.   1840 - 45.
5.

FARNOL, Jeffery.*
The Broad Highway: a romance of Kent.
Sampson,Low,Marston.
1910.   23,30.
1912.   11,12,30.

FILMER, Reginald Mead.*
A Chronicle of Kent, 1250 - 1760.
Clear Copies Ltd. London. 1967.
1,2,3,4,5,6,7,8,9,10,11,12,17,18,19,20,25,26,30.

GOMME, George Laurence.*
The Gentleman's Magazine Library, being a
classified collection of the chief contents
from 1731 - 1868.
English Topography Part VI, Kent;Lancashire,
edited by F.A. Milne.
Elliot Stock. 1895.
1,2,3,4,5,6,7,8,9,11,12,13,14,15,16,17,18,19,20,
25.26.

GREAT BRITAIN: PARLIAMENT*
A declaration of the several proceedings of both
Houses of Parliament, with those in the county
of Kent now in arms against the authority of
Parliament...
Printed by the Printer to the Honourable
House of Commons. 1648. E. Husband.
11,12.

A second remonstrance, or declaration, of the
Lords and Commons,...concerning the Commission
of Array,occasioned by a...booke lately published,
intituled: His Majesty's answer to the declaration
of both Houses of Parliament concerning the said
Commission.
This copy belonged to Sir Roger Twysden and
bears his signature and a note on the title-page;
also some annotation throughout.
Published for Parliament by John Wright and
Richard Best, 18th January, 1642.
11.

GREAT BRITAIN: PARLIAMENT, HOUSE OF COMMONS.
General Index to the reports from Committee of
the House of Commons, 1715 - 1801. Printed but
not inserted in the journals of the House, 1803,
with a new introduction by John Brooke.
(Reports are held on Microfilm).
Chadwyck Healey. 1973.
11.

HANNEN, Henry.*
An account of a map of Kent dated 1596.
Reprinted from Archaeologia Cantiana. Vol.30.1913.
Mitchell Hughes & Clarke. 1913.
11,17,18.

HART, W.H.*
A register of the lands held by Catholics and
Non-jurors in the County of Kent in the reign
of King George I, edited by W.H. Hart.
J.R. Smith. 1870.
1,4,11,17.

HOBSBAWN, Eric John.*
Captain Swing by E.J. Hobsbawm and G. Rude.
(includes a number of references to incidents
in Kent).
Lawrence & Wishart. 1969.
2,3,4,11.

HOLDERNESS, B.A.
Pre-industrial England, economy and Society,
1500 - 1750. (Kent items included).
Dent;Rowman & Littlefield. U.S.A. 1976.
11.

JAMES, Harold A.*
The Dutch in the Medway 1667.
Chatham Borough Council. 1967.
3,4,11,19,23,24,25,31.

JORDAN, Wilbur Kitchener.*
Social institutions in Kent, 1480 - 1660.
Kent Archaeological Society. 1961.
1.2.3.4.5.7.11.12.15.17.18.19.25.

KENT ILLUSTRATED: EXHIBITION 1952.*
Catalogue...drawings & prints of...Kent, 1760 -
1860. For Sale by F.T. Sabin.
Sabin Galleries. 1952.
2,13.

THE KENTISH COMPANION FOR THE YEAR OF OUR LORD 1818.
Addressed to the inhabitants of the County of
Kent and the public in general.
Rouse, Kirkby & Lawrence: Canterbury. 1818.
5,11.

KNATCHBULL, Sir Edward.
The parliamentary diary of Sir Edward Knatchbull
1722 - 1730, edited for The Royal Historical
Society by A.W. Norman. Camden Series.
3rd Series. Vol. 94.
Royal Historical Society. 1963.
11.

LAMBARDE, William.
William Lambarde's notes on the procedures and
privileges of the House of Commons. (1584);
edited with notes, introduction and appendices
by Paul L. Ward. (House of Commons Library
Document No.10). (The Editor discusses the
doubts of authorship with the possibility of
William Lambert, M.P. being the author).
H.M.S.O. 1977.
3,11.

MELLING, Elizabeth.*
Kent and the Civil War, edited by E. Melling.
Kentish Sources II.
K.C.C. 1960.
1,2,3,4,5,6,7,8,9,11,12,15,16,18,19,20,24.31.

The Poor: a collection of examples from original
sources in the Kent Archives Office from the
16th to the 19th centuries, edited by E. Melling.
Kentish Sources IV.
K.C.C. 1964.
1,2,3,4,5,6,7,8,9,11,12,15,16,17,18,19,20,25,31.

MOORE, Francis.
Vox Stellarum: or a loyal almanack: for the
year 1849, with Coulter's Appendix for Sittingbourne.
Printed for the Company of Stationers. 1849.
20.

MOWLL, John H.
The Coronation of George VI and Queen Elizabeth,
12th May 1937: a personal record.
(The author was a Dovorian and a Baron of the
Cinque Ports who saw the Coronation in London).
P.P. (1937).
6.

NATIONAL MARITIME MUSEUM.*
The Second Dutch War: De Tweede Engelse Oorlog,
1665 - 1667.
H.M.S.O. 1967.
4,8,12,15,25.

PHILLIPS, Margaret R.*
Some Kent Children. 1594 - 1875.
K.C.C. 1972.
2,3,4,6,7,8,9,11,19,25.

PLOMER, Henry Robert.*
The Kentish feast...being notes on the annual
meetings of the Honourable Society of Natives
of the County of Kent, 1657 - 1701,edited by
H.R. Plomer.
Cross & Jackman. Canterbury. 1916.
1,2,3,4,7,9,11,12,13,14,17,30.

PREROGATIVE COURT OF CANTERBURY.
Inventories,Series 2. Part I. 1702, 1718 -
1733; Part II 1734 - 1782 with index.
List and Index Society. 1973.
12.

THE QUEEN'S DIAMOND JUBILEE 1897.
Theobald & Co. 1897.
24.

RICHARDSON, T.L.
The agricultural labourer's standard of living
in Kent, 1790 - 1840.
In ODDY, Derek.
    The making of the modern British Diet,
    by Derek Oddy and Derek Miller.pp.103-116.
    Croom Helm. 1976.
    3.

HISTORY - 1501 AD ONWARDS   Cont'd

ROGERS, Philip George.*
The Dutch in the Medway.
Oxford University Press.   1970.
2,5,7,8,9,12,19.

ROWLES, Walter.*
The Kentish Chronology and Index to the
principal pieces and objects worthy of
observation in the County of Kent.
Comprising a list of the Nobility etc.
Vidion. Maidstone.   1807.
1.2.3.4.12.17.
Bound with Rowles, Walter. A general history
of Maidstone....1809.
11.

RUSHWORTH, John.
A letter sent to the Honourable William
Lenthal Esq., Speaker of the Honourable
House of Commons, on the fight between His
Excellency's the Lord Fairfax Forces at
Maidstone and the Kentish Forces on June 1st
1648.
Reprinted by Maidstone College of Art. 1959.
11.

SABINE, William Henry Waldo.
Murder 1776, and Washington's policy of
silence. (Has an important bearing on the
life of Oliver de Lancey, M.P. for Maidstone).
Theo. Gaus & Sons Inc. New York.   1973.
12.

SWING, Francis.*
The life and history of Swing, the Kent rick-
burner; Written by himself.
R. Carlile. London.   1830.
8,11,17.

SYCKLEMOORE, J.P.
Kentish village life in the nineteenth century.
Manuscript.   1903.
3.

(38 EIGHTEENTH CENTURY VIEWS OF KENTISH CASTLES,
MONASTERIES, ETC.).
(Title page missing). Includes short account
of each item mentioned.
(177?).
11.

TWYSDEN, Sir Roger.*
Certaine considerations upon the Government
of England... (Camden Society 45).
Camden Society.   1849.
4,12.

UNIVERSITY OF KENT - FACULTY OF SOCIAL SCIENCES.
Life in Kent during the First World War;
S214, Aspects of the economic and social history
of Kent. Group Research Project 1975.
Duplicated Typescript.
University of Kent. Canterbury.   1975.
11.

WHYMAN, John.*
A sketch of economic development in Kent. 1600-1900.
University of Kent. Canterbury.   1969.
3,24.

WICKWIRE, Franklin.
Cornwallis and the War of Independence,by
F. and M. Wickwire.
Faber.   1971.
12.

WINSTANLEY, Michael J.
Life in Kent at the turn of the century.
Dawson. Folkestone.   1978.
1,2,3,4,5,6,7,9,11,12,14,15,16,19,22,23,24,28,

WOOD, T.P.S.
Prelude to Civil War 1642: Mr. Justice Malet
and the Kentish Petitions.
Michael Russell Ltd. Salisbury.   1980.
12.

HITHER GREEN

MACARTNEY, Sylvia.
Borough Byways 2 - Hither Green: Point to Point
Walk. (Town Trail).
Lewisham Local History Society.   1975.
11.18.

PALLANT , N.
Hither Green Motive Power Depot
(Locomotion papers, 119).
Oakwood Press.   1979.
16.

HOATH

HUSSEY, Arthur.*
Reculver and Hoath Wills; transcribed by A.H.
Reprinted from Archaeologia Cantiana. Vol.XXXII
1917.
Mitchell, Hughes & Clarke.   1917.
4,8,10,11,30.

PAYNE, J. Lewin.
Reculver Parish Church of St. Mary the Virgin
together with the Chapelry of the Holy Cross,
Hoath, by J.L. Payne and W.T. Hill.
Printed by Ridout & Sons.   Herne Bay.   1931.
11.

HOLLINGBOURNE

HOLLINGBOURNE RURAL DISTRICT COUNCIL.*
The Official guide.
4.   1959 & 1961. Home Publishing Coy. Croydon.
4.   1964,1967,1970. British Publishing Coy.
                           Gloucester.

THOMAS, Louise.*
Hollingbourne 1851 (and) Lines to Kentish
Children. (Poetry with notes on Hollingbourne).
Printed by Vivish & Co. Maidstone.   1906.
11,15.

HOO PENINSULA

ARNOLD, Ralph.*
The Hundred of Hoo.
Constable.   1947.
1,2,3,4,5,6,7,8,9,11,12,14,15,17,18,20,25.

COLLISS, William.
Sketches, drawings, scumblings, blottings,
& blunderings, Some taken hastily as memoranda
& records only made during visits into Kent
commencing in 1869.   Vol.I.
(Original water colours & sketches mounted
in a leather bound book, the Artist painted
mainly in the Hundred of Hoo).
11.

GREAT BRITAIN, Laws etc. (Vic).
Hundred of Hoo Railway Act.(42 & 43 Victoria
Chapter CXXVI).
1879.
8.

MacDOUGALL, Philip.
The story of the Hoo Peninsula.
John Hallewell.   1980.
23.

MILLWARD, Roy.*
The Hoo Peninsula and the scarplands of
Mid-West Kent by R. Millward & A. Robinson.
Macmillan.   1971.
4,6.

ROWSELL, Mary C.
Thorndyke Manor: a tale of Jacobite times.
(Situated in the Hundred of Hoo).
Blackie & Son Ltd.   n.d.
11.

TRANSPORT 2000, Kent Group.
Passenger transport on the Hoo Peninsula:
a feasability study. 2 vols.
Transport 2,000, 1978
4,25.

The restoration of passenger Train Services
on the Hundred of Hoo Peninsula: a feasibility
study. A summary of the final report to the
Medway Borough Council.
Transport 2,000, 1978.
9.

HOO ST. WERBURGH.

HOO ST. WERBURGH. Women's Institute.
A village scrapbook: Hoo Saint Werburgh.
Photocopy of original scrapbook.
(1978).
4.

MOSELEY, Mary.
Church history of St. Werburgh, Hoo, compiled
by Mary Moseley.
Printed by the Brewster Printing Coy., Rochester.
1970.
11.

HOOK GREEN

GRAVESHAM BOROUGH COUNCIL: PLANNING DEPARTMENT.
Hook Green (Meopham) conservation area.
Gravesham Borough Council. 1975.
9,11.
and 2nd edition, 1975.
9.

HORSMONDEN

CRONK, Anthony.*
St. Margaret's Church, Horsmonden; an historical
and descriptive account.
A. Cronk. 1967.
3.

A Wealden Rector: the life and times of William
Marriott Smith-Marriott of Horsmonden.
(Vicar of Horsmonden from 1825).
Phillimore. 1975.
3,8,11,17,19.

HORSMONDEN VILLAGE FETE and Jubilee Celebrations;
Calendar of events and Souvenir programme.
1972.
11.

HORTON KIRBY

CRESY, Edward.*
Horton Kirby. Memorandum relating to my tour round
the Parish.
Typescript. Photocopy
1857.
16.

KENT COUNTY COUNCIL: EDUCATION DEPARTMENT.
Horton Kirby Field Centre.
K.C.C. 1973.
11.

LATHAM, Charles photographer.*
"Franks", a country seat of the sixteenth century,
illustrated in the nineteenth century, by C. Latham.
Hudson and Kearne. London. 1894.
11.

HOSPITALS

ASHFORD, Anna.
Bromley Hospital 1869 - 1947. Typescript.
(Essay for Open University Course on History
of Architecture & Design).
1976.
2.

BEECHER, W.J.
Kent County Ophthalmic & Aural Hospital,
Maidstone: a short history. Centenary 1846-1946.
The Hospital Board of Management.
Printed by Vivish & Baker. Maidstone. 1946.
11.

CANTERBURY & THANET HEALTH DISTRICT: KENT AREA
HEALTH AUTHORITY.
St. Augustine's Hospital, Chartham, Canterbury.
Kent. A guide to patients on their admission
to hospital.
Kent Area Health Authority. (1975).
3.

DOVER HOSPITAL & DISPENSARY: MANAGING COMMITTEE.
Annual Reports (bound together) for the years
1876 - 1888.
Dover Hospital Managing Committee. 1876-1888.
11.

HACKWOOD, John F.
Reminiscences of Farnborough Hospital...Photo-
copied extracts from FILE nos 16-22. 1976-77.
(Farnborough Hospital Magazine).
2.

McDivitt, John.
Statistics of the Kent and Canterbury Hospital
in British Medical Almanack. 1839. pp.179-183.
3.

ROYAL VICTORIA HOSPITAL, DOVER.
Report for 1932.
Royal Victoria Hospital. 1933.
6.

SAINT BARTHOLOMEW'S HOSPITAL, ROCHESTER.
Trustees Account Book. 1889 - 1899.
15.

SOUTH EAST METROPOLITAN REGIONAL HOSPITAL BOARD.*
Directory.
3 1971, 1972, 1973.
9 1973.
25 1973.

SOUTH EAST THAMES REGIONAL HEALTH AUTHORITY.
Report of Committee of Enquiry into St.
Augustines' Hospital, Chartham, Canterbury.
South East Thames Regional Health Authority.1976.
3,11.

WHYLER, Fred.
The story of Farnborough Hospital.
(Typescript) (1978)
2.

HOTELS, RESTAURANTS & CLUBS

BOOTH, John.
Booth's Guide to Good Eating in Kent and Sussex.
Midas Books. 1975.
2,6,8,11,12,16,19.

BURROW, Edward J. & Co. Ltd. Publishers.
South East England: Sussex,Kent & Surrey with
numerous Street plans,maps of touring districts &
full information as to hotels. (pp.69-116
Kent Section).
E.J. Burrow & Co. Ltd. Cheltenham. (193-?)
11.

A GUIDE TO THE ISLE OF THANET and the Cliftonville
Hotel, Margate. 1890-1.
1890.
13.

McLELLAN, Doreen E.
Cafes and restaurants in Gravesham,compiled by
D.E. McLellan.
Kent County Library,Gravesham Division.(1976).
20.

MARGATE BOROUGH COUNCIL.
Register of Hotels & Guest Houses.
Margate Borough Council. 1959.
13.

"RAMBLER" pseud (Barry Smith).
By the Way. (A brief history of pubs and hotels
in Dover since 1970).
B. Smith. 1978.
6.

HOTELS, RESTAURANTS & CLUBS.   Cont'd

ST. MILDRED'S HOTEL, Westgate-on-Sea.
Prospectus.   n.d.
13.

TAYLOR, Jonn.
The Carriers' Cosmographie.   Inns, hostelries
and other lodgings in and neere London.
Theatrum Orbis Terrarum Ltd.   1974.
11.

TOMLINSON, A.W.
Tales from a road house.
(The author owned tne Old Barn Tea House at
Hildenborough & Tudor House, Bearsted).
Printed by Stonestreet & Sons. Tonbridge. n.d.
11.

WHITBREAD & CO LTD.
Your Club.
Whitbread.   1950.
23.

HOTHFIELD

MORGAN, G.H.
A symposium on Hothfield local nature reserve,
edited by G.H. Morgan & A. Spain.
The Transactions of the Kent Field Club. Vol.5
Part 3.   1975.
3,4,11.

HOUSING

ABBEY PUBLICITY SERVICES LTD.   Publishers.*
Residential and holiday areas of South-West Kent,
including the Kentish Weald.   4th edition.
Abbey Publicity Service Ltd.   (1939?)
2,11.

ARCHER, R.W.
Regional planning, county planning and the
supply of land for new housing in the South-
East of England, 1960 - 1970.
University College, London.   School of
Environmental Studies.   c.1969.
6.

BRITISH ASSOCIATION OF SOCIAL WORKERS:KENT BRANCH.
Homelessness in Kent: A Survey.
Shelter.   1974.
1.

BUTLER, Susan later Mrs. Goddard.
A description and explanation of variations in
"residential desirability...in part of the South
East London suburbs".   (Photocopy of typescript).
Dissertation for B.Sc. Special Hons. Degree,
Sheffield University. Area Covered is Bromley,
Chislehurst, Sidcup, Bexley, Blackfen.
Unpublished Dissertation.   1968.
2.

THE ECONOMIST INTELLIGENCE UNIT LTD.
Housing land availability in the South East:
final report, June 1974, of the Consultants'
study for the Department of The Environment and
the Housing Research Ltd, in Association with
Halpern & Partners.
H.M.S.O.   1975.
3,12.

LEES COURT, Faversham. Kent: Particulars of
the properties. (A prospectus describing the
flats into which tne Mansion was divided).
Joint Agents: Finn-Kelsey, Collier & Ashenden,
Ashford, and Cluttons, Canterbury.   1974.
3.

MAIDSTONE BOROUGH COUNCIL - PLANNING DEPARTMENT.
Maidstone Town Centre - Housing & Population.
Maidstone Borough Council.   1980.
12.

MARGATE BOROUGH COUNCIL - PUBLICITY DEPARTMENT.
Residential guide - Borough of Margate,
including Cliftonville, Westbrook,
Westgate-on-Sea & Birchington.
Margate Borough Council.   (1958?).
13.

THE SOUTH EASTERN, FOLKESTONE & DISTRICT
PROPERTY REGISTER.
F. Wilson Temple & Co.   1896 & February 1902.
7.

WHEELER, Barnaby.
Dry Hill Park, Tonbridge.   (Part II of a
thesis on the Mid-Victorian Suburban House).
1976.
23.

HOVERPORTS

DOVER HARBOUR BOARD.
Proposed new Hoverport, Western Docks, Dover:
impact Study.
Dover Harbour Board.   1975.
6.

KENT COUNTY COUNCIL: PLANNING DEPARTMENT AND
THANET DISTRICT COUNCIL PLANNING DEPARTMENT.
Consultation Draft Development Study, Ramsgate
International Hoverport, Pegwell Bay.
1979.
13.

SAVE OUR SEAFRONT ACTION COMMITTEE.
Proposed new hoverport, Western Docks, Dover;
report on Dover Harbour Board's impact study,
with counter proposals.
Save our Seafront Action Committee.   1976.
6.

HUNTON

BORTON, Lieut. Col. A.C.
My Warrior Sons: the Borton family diary,
1914 - 1918; edited and with an introduction by
Guy Slater.
(The Diary of Lieut. Col. A.C. Borton who lived
at Cheveney House, Hunton).
Davics.   1973.
11.

HYTHE

ABSTRACT OF THE ACCOUNTS OF ST. LEONARD'S PARISH,
Hythe, from 1st April 1813 to 1st April, 1814.
Geo. Scott, acting overseer. (Accounts for
Workhouse and Poor relief).
Printed by W. Tiffen, Hythe, 1814.
11.

ALBUM OF PHOTOGRAPHS: HYTHE.
W.S. Paine. Hythe.   c.1900.
11.

BURROW, Edward J. & Co. Publisher,
"Borough" Pocket Guide to Hythe (Official Guide).
E.J. Burrow & Co.   1908 - 9.
11.

BUSK, Hans.*
Handbook for Hythe: comprising a Familiar
explanation of the laws of Projectiles.
(Hythe School of Musketry).
Routledge.   1860.
10.
Reprint of the 1860 edition by Richmond
Publications, 1971.
11,12.

DALE, Rev. Herbert Dixon.
Ancient town of Hythe & St. Leonard's Church,
Kent.
Kipps Bookshop, Hythe.   1958.
11.

Crypt of St. Leonard's Church, Hythe and its
contents.
Printed by J. Lovick, Hythe.   (192-?).
11.

Notes on the Crypt and bones of Hythe Church.*
5th edition.
Printed by W.S. Paine & Co. Hythe.   1917.
3.

DALE, Rev. Herbert Dixon.
Notes on Hythe Parish Church by Rev. H.D. Dale
and on the Bones of the Crypt by F.G. Parsons.
(Cover Title).   Contains:-

Notes on the Parish Church of St. Leonard,
Hythe. 3rd edition.
Printed & Published by J. Lovick. Hythe. 1905.
and
DALE, Rev. H.D.
Notes on the Crypt and Bones of Hythe Church,
by Rev. H.D. Dale and F.G. Parsons.
Printed by Adlard & Son. 1904.
24.   Also included in "Jottings of Kent".

St.Leonard's Church Hythe.* From its
foundation with some account of the life and
customs of the town of Hythe from Ancient
Sources.
Murray. 1931.
1.

ENVIRONMENT,DEPARTMENT OF THE.
List of Buildings of Special Architectural interest.
Borough of Hythe, Kent.
Department of Environment. 1973.
7,11.

FOLKESTONE HERALD.
Souvenir album of views. Folkestone, Sandgate,
Hythe and neighbourhood.
The Folkestone Herald (1902?).
11.

FOLKESTONE, HYTHE & DISTRICT HOTEL & CATERING
ASSOCIATION.
Folkestone & Hythe, Kent. 10th edition.
The Association. 1951.
11.

FULTON, Hamish.
Ten views of Brockman's Mount a naturally
formed hill near Hythe, Kent, England.
(19--?).
7.

HUSSEY, Arthur.*
Hythe Wills, third and final part.
Reprinted from Archaeologia Cantiania.
Vol.Ll. 1940.
11.

HYTHE BOROUGH COUNCIL.*
Catalogue of documents, compiled by
H.D. Dale & C. Chidell.
Hythe Borough Council. n.d.
11.

Hythe, Kent. Official Guide.*
Hythe Borough Council & Chamber of Commerce.1924.
11.

Hythe, Kent. Official Guide, 1929.*
Health Resorts Association. London. 1929.
11.

Official Guide to Hythe, Kent. (1974 edition).
Compiled and edited by J.F. Billington.
Hythe Borough Council & Chamber of Commerce.
11.

Official Guide to Hythe, Kent. (1975 edition).
Hythe Borough Council & Chamber of Commerce.1975.
4,10.

MAIDSTONE AND DISTRICT AND EAST KENT BUS CLUB.
Fleet History and Route Map of Newman's of
Hythe. (1934 - 1963).
Publications No.F.11.
4.

MOULTON, W.R.
Guide to Lympne Church and Castle, Studfall,
Shepway, West Hythe and Court-at-Street.
F.J. Parsons. (c.1926).
11.

O'GORMAN, Richard A.*
Haymo of Hythe, Bishop of Rochester, with some
account of the former state and works of
Catholicity in Hythe and its Second Spring in
that ancient Cinque Port. (Haymo was Bishop
of Rochester 1319 - 53).
Washbourne. 1895.
1,2,8,11,12,17.

ONE HUNDRED AND ONE VIEWS, Folkestone, Dover,
Sandgate, Hythe and South-eastern Kent.
Percy Bessell,Folkestone. (190?)
11.

SOUVENIR ALBUM OF VIEWS.
Folkestone, Sandgate, Hythe and neighbourhood.
F.J. Parsons Ltd. (c.1900).
11.

SPICER R.F.
A Speck of Spice.
(A history of Spicer's the Grocers
of Hythe),
Spicers Stores, Hythe. 1975.
7

2nd Edition, Illustrated. 1976.
7.

TIFFEN, William. Publisher.
Excursions from Folkestone, Sandgate, and Hythe
W. Tiffen. Hythe & Folkestone. n.d.
3,6.

TOPLEY, William.
Geology of the Hythe District.
(Kent Miscellanea Vol.3). 1883.
11.

TURNER, Keith.
Pier Railways. (pp.9-17. Herne Bay and Hythe).
Oakwood Press. 1972.
11,30.

WHAT'S ON IN FOLKESTONE, HYTHE AND SANDGATE.
April-June, July-December 1930; Jan-June,
July-December 1931; Jan-June, July-December 1932.
F.J. Parsons. 1930-1933.
7.

WHITNEY, C.E.
St. Leonards Church, Hythe, Historical Guide.
C.E. Whitney. 1976.
7.

WILKS, George.*
The Early History of Hythe. Part 1.
Printed by McCorquodale and Co. 1889.
1.

ICKHAM

COOMBS, Leonard C.
Ickham; the friendly village.
Barry Clayton Press. Nonington. (1978).
3.

IGHTHAM

BOWRA, Edward V.
Ightham; notes on local history.
Ightham & District Historical Society. 1978.
2,5,11,12,16,23.

GENERAL REGISTER OFFICE.
Census Returns. 1841,1851,1861,1871, Ightham.
Microfilm.
23.

HARRIS, Edwin.*
History of Ightham Mote. (Eastgate Series No.8).
E. Harris. Rochester. 1910.
11.

HARRISON, Sir Edward R.*
History & Records of Ightham Church.
Church Army Press, Printers. 1932.
2.

IGHTHAM Cont'd

HARRISON, Sir Edward R.*
The Story of Oldbury Hill.
W.H. Smith; Printed by the Caxton & Holmesdale
Press, Sevenoaks. 1953.
24.

TONBRIDGE & MALLING DISTRICT COUNCIL:PLANNING DEPT.
Ightham Conservation study, Ivy Hatch and
Ightham Mote.
Tonbridge & Malling District Council. 1980.
23.

INDUSTRIAL ARCHAEOLOGY

BAINES, Derek.
TIP Handbook 1977/78. Transport & Industrial
Preservation: a guide to What, Where and When.
Edited, produced and published by Derek Baines.
2nd edition.
Derek Baines, Crawley, 1977.
11.

BUCHANAN, Robert Angus.
Industrial archaeology in Britain. (includes Kent).
Allen Lane. 1974.
11.

HASELFOOT, A.J.
South-East England:Kent, Surrey, East Sussex,
West Sussex. (Batsford guide to industrial
archaeology Series).
Batsford. 1978.
2,3,4,5,11,12,13,19,22,23,30.

INDUSTRY & TRADE

ARMSTRONG, Lyn.
Wood Colliers and charcoal burning.
Coach Publishing House & The Weald & Downland
Open Air Museum. 1978.
23.

BAILEY, Jocelyn.
Country wheelwrights.
(Author's husband comes from a family of
Wheelwrights at Kingsnorth).
Batsford. 1978.
11.

BALL, Mia.
The Worshipful Company of Brewers: a short
history. (pp.19-70 Canterbury and St. Thomas
a Becket mentioned).
Hutchinson. 1977.
11.

BANBURY, Philip.
Shipbuilders of the Thames and Medway.
David & Charles. 1971.
2,12.20.

BARTLETT, A.E.
Canterbury masters and their apprentices
1763-1777, with a few entries of 1758-1762,
edited by A.E. Bartlett.
Harrington Family Miscellany Record Publication.
Canterbury, 1978.
3,23,

BARTY-KING, Hugh.
Quilt winders and pod shavers. (The history
of Cricket bat and ball manufacture, a
Tonbridge Area industry),
Macdonald & Janes. 1979.
23.

BEADLE, D.
Portland cement in the making. (APCM-
N.W. Kent connections).
Cement and Concrete Association, Slough. 1977.
5.

BENHAM, Hervey.
The Stowboaters.
The Sprat-fishing industry in the Thames Estuary.
Essex Co.

BERGESS, Winifred F.
The cement industry of the Medway Valley...from
Borstal to Eccles, Kent. Maps,
Manuscript notes. (1974).
11.

BOROUGH DIRECTORIES LTD.*
Business & residential directory of the Borough
of Faversham & the Urban District of Sittingbourne
& Milton.
Borough Directories Ltd. 1963.
4,7,8,20.

A BRIEF ACCOUNT OF THE CLOTH TRADE IN THE
MAIDSTONE AREA (pamphlet).
n.d.
12.

BUTLER, L.
Growth & development of Industry in the Greater
London Borough of Bexley.
Thesis. 1972.
1.

CANTERBURY CITY COUNCIL:CITY ARCHITECT & PLANNING
OFFICER.
Planning for industry.
Canterbury City Council. 1973.
3.

CARVER, Jean.
Brickmaking & the Gillingham Brickfield.
Gillingham Urban Studies Centre. 1976.
8,23.

CHARTRES, J.A.
Internal trade in England 1500-1700.
Macmillan. n.d.
11.

CITY OF ROCHESTER SOCIETY.
Rochester High Street Trading. Introducing some
of the shops, hotels and specialist trades in
the High Street in the Jubilee Years of 1897 and
1977. Compiled by Colin Whyman.
Kent Art Printers for the Society. 1977.
4,8,11,15.

CLEERE, H.
The Roman iron industry of the Weald and its
connections with the Classis Britannica.
Reprinted from The Archaeological Journal,
Vol.131. For 1974.
Royal Archaeological Institute. (1974?).
3.

COLLARD, Allan Ovenden.*
The oyster & dredgers of Whitstable.
Joseph Collard. 1902.
1,2,3,4,6,7,8,11,12,15,31.

COLLINS, J.P.
Distribution of retailing in Beckenham, Kent.
1885 - 1915 (photocopy of typescript).
1976.
2.

COOK, David.
The value and limitations of trade directories
between c.1840 and 1870 as a source on the
nature and distribution of industrial activity
in East Kent. Photocopy.Extended essay.
University of Kent,Canterbury. (197?).
3.

COOPER-KEY, A.
Explosion....2nd April 1916 at Uplees Marshes,
Faversham. Report....of the 17th April, 1916.
(PRO Reference Supp 5. 332 XLO0464). Accident No.
110/1916 No.CLXVII (Gunpowder Industry).
Photocopy from the Public Record Office. 1916.
26.

CORRAN, H.S.
A history of brewing.(Kent mentioned p56-58 &
241 - 243, 245-6).
David & Charles. 1975.
11.

COX, Alan.
Brickmaking: a history and gazetteer.
(Survey of Bedfordshire publication).
Bedfordshire County Council/Royal Commission
on Historical Monuments. 1979.
23

CROSSLEY, D.W.
The Bewl Valley Ironworks, Kent. c.1300-1730.
Royal Archaeological Institute. 1975.
2,3,6,8,11,12,

Sidney ironworks accounts 1541 - 1573,
edited by D.W. Crossley. Camden Fourth Series,
Vol.15. (Ironworks belonging to the Sidneys of
Penshurst).
Royal Historical Society. 1975.
23.

DAVEY, Norman.
Building stones of England and Wales.
(Lists the quarries still being worked).
Bedford Square Press for the Standing Conference
for Local History. 1976.
11.

DELANY, Mary Cecilia.
The historical geography of the Wealden iron
industry.
Benn. 1921.
1,2,3,5,11,15,19,26.

DYER, Albert.
The Ups and Downs of my life: the Memoirs of
Albert Dyer, 1908 - 1970. Life and trade in
Penge and Beckenham.
Duplicated Typescript. n.d.
2.

ECONOMIST INTELLIGENCE UNIT LTD.
The future for heavy industry in the Lower
Medway. Economist Intelligence Unit report
prepared for Kent County Council,July 1973.
Vol.I.   Part I.   The regional Setting
         Part II   The Lower Medway
Vol.II   Part III Industrial Site requirements.
         Part IV   Examination of patterns of
                   investment.
4,11.

ELLISTON-ERWOOD, Frank Charles.
Fifty years of Commerce in Woolwich.
Woolwich Chamber of Commerce. 1949.
11.

John Barker's Plan of Woolwich, 1949.
A description and a commentary.
Kent Archaeological Society. n.d.
1.

EMPLOYMENT SERVICE AGENCY (Medway District).
Labour Market intelligence bulletin June 1977.
Employment Services 1977.
8.

ESSEX. UNIVERSITY OF COLCHESTER,SALT CONFERENCE.
Salt: the study of an ancient industry.
Report on the salt weekend, held at the
University of Essex, 20,21,22 September 1974.
Edited by K.W. de Brisay, K.A. Evans.(Kent p.26-31)
Colchester Archaeological Group. 1975.
11.

FERGUSON, Rosemary.
Guide to the antique shops of Kent, 1978, compiled
by R. Ferguson.
Antique Collectors Club Ltd. 1978.
4,11,22.

FINCH, Roger.
Coals from Newcastle: the story of the North
East Coal Trade in the days of sail.
Terence Dalton, Lavenham, 1973.
11.

FITZRANDOLPH, Helen E.
The rural industries of England & Wales: a survey
made on behalf of the Agricultural Economics
Research Institute, Oxford, by Helen E.
Fitzrandolph and M. Doriel Hay. 2 vols.
E.P.Publishing. 1977.
11.

FRANCIS, A.J.
The cement Industry, 1796 - 1914: a History.
(Medway Industry. Chapter 11).
David and Charles. 1978.
1,3,11,15,19,25.

FULLMER, J.Z.
Humphry Davy and the gunpower manufactory.
In Annals of Science: a quarterly review...
Vol.20. No.3. September 1964. pp.165-194.
23

GIFFORD, Colin Telfer.
Steam railways in industry. (includes "Kentish
Paper - Sittingbourne", pp. 80 - 86).
B.T. Batsford. 1976.
11,20,27.

GIUSEPPI, M.S.
Some Fourteenth-century accounts of ironworks
at Tudeley, Kent. Read (to the Society of
Antiquaries) 5th December 1912. Extracted from
Archaeologia Vol. LXIV and bound. (Transcripts
of accounts 1330 - 1354).
Society of Antiquaries. 1912.
11.

GRAVESHAM BOROUGH COUNCIL:PLANNING DEPARTMENT
Employment in Gravesham:current trends & policies.
Gravesham Borough Council. 1975.
9.
1977 2nd edition. 9,11.

Industry & Warehousing in Gravesham.
Gravesend Borough Council, 1977.
4.

Offices in Gravesham.
Gravesham Borough Council. 1976.
9,11.

GREAT BRITAIN, Laws etc.(Geo.III).*
An Act for making compensation to the proprietors
of such lands and hereditaments as have been pur-
chased for the more safe & convenient carrying on of
His Majesty's Gunpowder Works & Mill at Faversham...
(Geo.III, 26, Chap.XCIV).
Printed by C. Eyre & W. Strahan. 1786.
11,26.

An Act to continue & amend so much of an Act made
in the thirty third year of the reign of His
Present Majesty as permits Sir William Bishop,
George Bishop & Argles Bishop to carry on the
Manufacture of Maidstone Gineva.
Printed by Eyre & Strahan. 1799.
11.

HAZELL, Martin.
The Sailing barges and the brick and other
industries of Milton Creek, Kent. c.1850-c.1970; a
social and economic history.
Thesis for Department of Teaching Studies,
North London Polytechnic.
Photocopy of Ms Rough Draft. Completed May. 1972.
20.

HOOLE, G.P.
Sir Humphry Davy: Tonbridge Associations.
P.P. by Bridge Chemicals Ltd. Tonbridge. 1978.
2,11,19,23.

INBUCON/AIC MANAGEMENT CONSULTANTS.
Strategy for Tourism.Conclusions & recommendations.
A report commissioned by the English Tourist Board
for the S.E. England Tourist Board.
Inbucon/AIC Management Consultants. 1974.
4,13.

INDUSTRIAL GREAT BRITAIN, Part II.
A Commercial review of leading firms selected
from important towns of many Counties.
(The Selection includes Chatham,Rochester & Strood).
1891.
4.

INDUSTRY, Deptartment of BUSINESS STATISTICS OFFICE
Business Monitor...Report on the Census of
distribution and other services 1971. Part 8. Area
tables London and South East Region.
H.M.S.O. 1975.
3.

INSURANCE COMPANIES IN KENT.
A brief history (pamphlet).
n.d.
12.

ISLE OF THANET PROMOTIONS BOARD.
Focus on Thanet.
Isle of Thanet Promotions Board. 1979.
13.

Thanet Industrial Directory.
Isle of Thanet Promotions Board. 1979.
13.

JOINT COMMITTEE OF LOCAL AUTHORITIES IN
SOUTH-EAST KENT.
Industries opportunities in South East Kent.
Joint Committee of Local Authorities in
South-East Kent. (1971).
11.

KENT AND EAST SUSSEX SAND AND GRAVEL
WORKING PARTY.
Sand and gravel extraction:first(interim)
report of the...Working Party, and report of
the Northern London Gravel Working Party.
Standing Conference on London and S.E.
Regional Planning. 1973.
2,6,9,11.

KENT AND ESSEX SEA FISHERIES COMMITTEE.
Report for...1972 and 1973.
K.C.C. 1973 & 1974.
4 1972
7 1973.

KENT AREA TRADES DIRECTORY.
Artrad.
1974-1975. 11.
1977-1978. 11,19,20,26,27.

KENT COUNTY COUNCIL:EDUCATION DEPT.-CAREERS
SERVICE:CANTERBURY DIVISION.
Apprenticeship Survey. 1977/78.
Duplicated typescript.
(1978?).
3.

KENT COUNTY COUNCIL:EMPLOYMENT OPPORTUNITIES
OFFICER.
Directory of Overseas Transportation Services
by Sea, Air and Road, operating to and from
places in the County of Kent.
K.C.C.
1973. 2,4,6,11,12,25.
1975. 2nd edition. 11,13,20.

Office development in Kent.
K.C.C. 1975.
4.

Industry in Kent.
K.C.C. 1977.
3,11.

Kent-Facts for business.
K.C.C. 1978.
1,2,11.

KENT COUNTY COUNCIL:INDUSTRIAL & COMMERCIAL
LIAISON OFFICER.
Basic Facts for businessmen.
K.C.C. 1975.
3,11,12,13.

Kent - an Invitation to Industry.
K.C.C. 1973.
1,2,3,4,7,8,11.

Kent carries it - International, road,
rail, sea, air.
K.C.C.
1977. 3,5,9,11,12.
1979. 4.

Kent for Industry.
K.C.C.
1977. 11.
1978. 3,4,5,9,13,

Kent for Offices.
K.C.C. 1979.
4.

KENT COUNTY COUNCIL:PLANNING DEPARTMENT.*
Influence of car ownership on shopping habits.
K.C.C. 1964.
1,11,13.

Kent County Structure plan: aspect report on
employment.(Adopted by Local Planning Authority
in July, 1975). Serial No.2B.
K.C.C. 1975.
3,4,9,11,13,16.

Kent County Structure Plan.
a) Formal Recreation. b) Informal Recreation
c) Water recreation. d) Tourism.
Serial No. 10B.
K.C.C. 1975.
3,4,9,11,13,16.

Kent County Structure plan: Mineral extraction
in Kent (Adopted by Local Planning Authority...
in 1975). Serial No. 9B.
K.C.C. 1975.
3,4,9,11,13,16.

Kent County Structure plan: Shopping. (Adopted
by Local Planning Authority in April, 1975).
Serial No. 3B.
K.C.C. 1975.
3,4,9,11,13,16.

The potential of the Medway Estuary as a
maritime industrial development area:*
a discussion of the economic factors and an
appraisal of its impact on Mid and North Kent,
by R.G. Clarke, County Planning Officer.
K.C.C. 1970.
2.3.4.8.11.20.24.25.

KENYON, G.H.*
The Glass Industry of the Weald.
Leicester University Press. 1967.
25.

KNIGHT, Charles.*
Shipbuilding at Gillingham. Reprinted
from'Chatham, Rochester & Gillingham News'.
1938.
4,8.

KOHLER, David F.
The Employment of Black People in a London
Borough (i.e. Lewisham).
Community Relations Commission. July. 1974.
2,18.

LABOUR, Ministry of:JOINT STANDING COMMITTEE
FOR PAPER MILLS.
Safety in Paper Mills:First Report.
H.M.S.O. 1964.
11.

THE LINK.
Maidstone & District Chamber of Commerce.
Official Journal. 1957 - 1959.
12.

LOVELAND, Isaac.
Some names of tradesmen who resided in Sevenoaks
about 1848 and later on.
Mss. and another copy.— Typescript. 1927
16.

MACARTNEY, Sylvia.
A history of Lewisham silk mills, by S.
Macartney and John West.
Lewisham Local History Society. 1979.
2.

MAIDSTONE BOROUGH COUNCIL:PLANNING DEPARTMENT.
Maidstone Town Centre:industry and commerce.
Maidstone Borough Council. 1980.
12.

Maidstone Town Centre - Offices.
Maidstone Borough Council. 1980.
12.

Maidstone Town Centre-Shopping.
Maidstone Borough Council. 1980.
12.

MARGARY, Ivan Donald.
Roman communications between Kent and East
Sussex Ironworks.
Reprinted from the Sussex Archaeological
Collections. n.d.
11.

MARTIN, J.E.
Greater London: an industrial geography.
G. Bell. 1966.
1.

MATHIAS, Peter.
The brewing industry in England 1700-1830.
Cambridge University Press. 1959.
11.

MAXWELL, Donald.
Excursions in Colour. (Includes a chapter
on the Medway Valley and a chapter on
the Iron industry).
Cassell. 1927.
11.

MEDWAY AND GILLINGHAM CHAMBER OF COMMERCE.
Brochure.
Medway & Gillingham Chamber of Commerce. 1979.
4.

MEDWAY AND MAIDSTONE COLLEGE OF TECHNOLOGY.
The Business Advisory Centre. Annual Report.
(Period covered 1st August 1974 to 31st
July 1975). Manager Dr. C.M. Fletcher. (1976).
4,11.

MEDWAY INDUSTRIES.
An Exhibition May 21st - 28th 1949.
Souvenir Guide.
25.

MEDWAY PORTS AUTHORITY.
Tonnage of Imports. 1970 - 1973.
(3 typescript sheets).
(1974).
4,8.

MEDWAY PRESERVATION SOCIETY.*
The effects of a Maritime Industrial Development
Area on the River Medway: a report prepared by
the Medway Preservation Society.
Medway Preservation Society. 1971.
4.

MELLING, Elizabeth.*
Aspects of agriculture & industry, edited by
E. Melling.   Kentish Sources III .
K.C.C. 1961.
1,13,30,31.

MONEY, James H.
Medieval iron-workings in Minepit Wood,
Rotherfield, Sussex.
Reprinted from 'Medieval Archaeology',
Vol.XV. 1971.
23.

MOON, John H.
A short history of Lamberhurst Iron Industry.
Lamberhurst Local History Society. 1977.
19.

MORRICE, Alexander.
A treatise on brewing:wherein is exhibited
the whole process of the art and mystery
of brewing the various sorts of malt liquor..
3rd edition.
Printed for the Author by Knight & Compton,
Middle Street Cloth Fair, London. 1802.
11.

NATIONAL MASTER FARRIERS BLACKSMITH AND
AGRICULTURAL ENGINEERS ASSOCIATIONS.
Blacksmiths of Kent and Sussex.
(1975).
4.

NORTH EAST KENT ECONOMIC DEVELOPMENT COMMITTEE.
Why East Kent? a guide for potential developers
of new factories, offices, warehouses.
North East Kent Economic Development Committee.
1971.
11.

OPPORTUNITIES FOR INDUSTRY AT SITTINGBOURNE.
Freeguard Press. Sittingbourne. (1971).
11.

PADDOCK WOOD & DISTRICT YEAR BOOK and trades
and services guide.   Summer. 1975.
Gordon Bringes. Paddock Wood. 1975.
11.

PERCIVAL, Arthur.*
The Faversham gunpowder industry and its development. 2nd edition-revised.(Faversham Papers No.4).
Faversham Society. 1969.
11.

PILE, Cecil Charles Relf.*
Cranbrook Broadcloth and the clothiers.
2nd edition.
Cranbrook & District Local History Society. 1967.
7.11.

PRESTON, James M.
Industrial Medway: an historical survey.
J.M. Preston. Borstal Rd. Rochester.
Printed by W.&.J. Mackay Ltd. Chatham. 1977.
1,2,3,4,5,7,8,9,11,12,15,16,19,20,22,23,25,26,
27,28.

RAND, Duncan.
An Industrial Review and Guide to the Medway,
edited by Duncan Rand.
Pyramid Press Ltd. 1971.
4,24,25,30.
12 1974.

READ ABOUT BLACKSMITH SHOPS.
(Mentions Edenbridge Smithy).
Colourmaster International. (1975).
11.

REGENCY PUBLICITY SERVICE LTD. Publisher
The Sevenoaks & District Directory of Commerce
& Trade. 2nd edition. 1966 - 67.
Regency Publicity Service Ltd.Folkestone. 1966.
16.

The Sevenoaks Book: the Sevenoaks, Kent, and
District Directory of Commerce & Trade. 3rd edn.
1968/69.
Regency Publicity Service Ltd.Folkestone.1968.
16.

ROLES, Stephen.
Manufacturing industry of the Cray Valley.
Unpublished thesis. 1978.
2.

SATTIN, Donald L.
Just off the Swale:the story of the barge
building village of Conyer.
Meresborough Books. 1978.
3,12,22,23.

SHORTER, Alfred Henry.
Paper Making in the British Isles:an historical
and geographical study.
David and Charles. 1971.
11,23.

Water paper mills in England.
Society for the Protection of Ancient
Buildings. 1966.
23.

SMITH, Reginald Anthony.*
A palaeolithic industry at Northfleet, Kent.
Read to the Society of Antiquaries of London
on the 4th May 1911. (Extracted from Archaeologia
Vol. LXXII).
The Society. 1911.
11.

SOUTH-EAST ENGLAND DEVELOPMENT BOARD.*
Industrial South-East England, the Official
handbook.
Edward J.Burrow & Co. Cheltenham.
1   n.d.
3   1972
4   1969
11 1969;1972.
20 1962;1971.

INDUSTRY & TRADE Cont'd

STANDING CONFERENCE ON LONDON & SOUTH EAST
REGIONAL PLANNING. KENT & EAST SUSSEX SAND
& GRAVEL WORKING PARTY.
Sand and Gravel Extraction. Final Report. 1977.
Standing Conference on London & South East
Regional Planning. 1977.
9.

STARKIE, David Nicholas Martin.
Traffic & Industry.
London School of Economics & Political
Science (Geography Department). 1967.
25.

STEVENS, J.E.
Whitstable natives: a short study of Whitstable
and Oysters.
K.C. Hall. 1977.
1,3,6,11,23,28,30,31.

STOYEL, B. Derek.
Cement railways of Kent, by B.D. Stoyel
and R.W. Kidner. (Locomotion papers No.70).
Oakwood Press. 1973.
1,2,4,5,7,11,12,20,25,30.

STUBBS DIRECTORIES LTD.
Stubbs Kent Trade Guide.
Stubbs Directories Ltd.
13. 1968-9; 1969-70.
20. 1969-70.

THAMESIDE DEVELOPMENT BOARD.
Thameside: Britain's largest workshop.
Thameside Development Board. 1976.
1.

TOWN & COUNTY DIRECTORIES.
Kent Trades' Directory, 1972: Margate,
Ramsgate and including Maidstone and Tunbridge
Wells.
Town & County Directories. 1972.
11.

Margate, Ramsgate and North Kent District
Trades Directory, 1927-28.
Town & County Directories. (1927).
24.

TRADE & INDUSTRY, DEPARTMENT OF*WARREN SPRINGS.
Laboratory.
National Survey of Air Pollution 1961-71.
Vol I....South East Region.
H.M.S.O. 1972.
2.

TUNBRIDGE WARE See Souvenirs; Tunbridge Wells.

WEALDEN IRON RESEARCH GROUP.
Bulletins Nos 1-7 1969-1974.
19

Wealden Iron: Spring 1976. Bulletin of the
Wealden Iron Research Group.
19.

WELLS, Arthur G.
Bowaters' Sittingbourne Railway. 2nd edition.
(First published in 1962).
Locomotive Club of Great Britain. 1971.
11,25.

WERF, Philip Van der.
A study of the development of Commerce in
Bromley 1800 - 1900. (Photocopy of Ms:
Teacher's Training College Thesis). 1972.
2.

WOOD, David.
Powder barge W ↑ D.
(The Barges belonged to the Waltham Abbey
Royal Gunpowder Factory and transported
Gunpowder between factories - including
Faversham, Gravesend & Woolwich).
Wareham & West country Barge Group of
SSBR, Twickenham. 1977.
11.

WOODFORDE, John.
Bricks to build a house. (History of brickmaking
with references to The London Brick Co., District
Sales Office, in Sevenoaks, and the Redland
Group of Companies, whose brickworks are in
the Sevenoaks area).
Routledge & Kegan Paul for The London Brick Co.
1976.
11,16.

INDUSTRY & TRADE - FIRMS

ARROWCROFT INVESTMENT LTD.
The Ramsgate Industrial Estate: an Arrowcroft
development in partnership with the Ramsgate
Corporation.
Arrowcroft Investment Ltd. n.d.
11.

ATTENBOROUGH, John.
A living memory: Hodder & Stoughton, Publishers,
1868-1975.
(The Hodder Williams Family were residents of
Bromley: the firm evacuated to Bickley during
World War II, it is now located at Dunton
Green, Kent).
Hodder & Stoughton. 1975.
2,16.

BARNES, C.H.*
Shorts' aircraft since 1900.
(Short Brothers' Aircraft Works at Rochester).
Putnam. 1967.
4,25.

BENNETT OPIE LTD.
Case for celebration: a short history of
Bennett Opie Limited.
Published for Bennett Opie Ltd by Harley
Publishing Company.(1955?).
20.

BLATCHER, Margaret.
The first four hundred, 1570 - 1970:
a history of the firm of Thomson, Snell and
Passmore, Solicitors, of Tonbridge, Kent.
P.P. 1970.
23.

BLAW KNOX LTD.*
General Catalogue. Blaw Knox Construction
Equipment (Loose-leaf).
Blaw Knox Ltd. Rochester. (196-?).
4.

BLUE CIRCLE GROUP: ASSOCIATED PORTLAND CEMENT
MANUFACTURERS LTD.
Barges:one hundred years of river trading.
(Published to mark the Blue Circle Group's
Jubilee Celebrations in 1977).
Blue Circle Group. 1977.
4,9,11,23.

BOWATER PAPER CORPORATION LTD.*
Bowaters in North America, written by
Robert Sinclair.
Bowater Paper Corporation. 1960.
11,12.

BRITISH PETROLEUM COMPANY LTD.*
B.P. Kent Refinery.
B.P. Company Ltd. 1959.
4,8,11.

A Technical Description of the B.P. Kent Oil
Refinery.
B.P. Company Ltd. 1955.
3.4.8.

A Visit to the Kent Oil Refinery.
B.P. Company Ltd. 1958 and 1965.
2,4,8,11.

BRITISH PETROLEUM OIL KENT REFINERY LTD.
The Kent Refinery: a guide for visitors to the
B.P. Oil Refinery on the Isle of Grain, Kent.
British Petroleum Oil Kent Refinery Ltd. 1975.
4.

BROWN, W. Henry.
A Century of Co-operation at Sheerness, being
a chronicle of the oldest Co-operative
Society in the United Kingdom.
Co-operative Wholesale Societies Printing Works
Redditch. (1919?).
11.
The Co-operatove Story of Kent.
Co-operative Union. n.d.
13.

BURT, BOULTON AND MAYWOOD LTD.
A Century of Progress: 1848-1948.
(The firm is located at Erith).
1949.
1.

CHAPMAN, T.
The Cornwall Aviation Company.
(The Company which gave aerial joy rides).
Glasney. 1979.
13.

CHILD AND SON (Faversham).
Jubilee Souvenir 1864 - 1914.(Department Store).
Printed by Austin. Faversham. 1914.
11.

CHUDLEY, John A.
Letraset: a lesson in growth.   (The Letraset
Factory at Ashford was built in 1960).
Business Books Ltd. 1974.
11.

CLUTTON & PARTNERS Surveyors.
Cluttons 1765 - 1965.
(A London based Firm of Surveyors who opened a
Branch in Canterbury after World War II.
J.H. Clutton was Surveyor to the Medway
Conservancy Board in the late 19th century.
Clutton & Partners. (1965).
11.

COLLINGWOOD, Frances.
Inheritor of the Whatman tradition: William
Balston, 1759 - 1849. (Paper Mill at Springfield,
Maidstone, opened in 1806).
Extract from "Sales and Wants Advertiser".1958.
4.

CORINA, Maurice.
Fine silks and oak counters; Debenhams. 1778-
1978. (There are Debenham Stores at Folkestone,
Gillingham & Canterbury).
Hutchinson.Benham. 1978.
3.

DURTNELL, Cyril Streeter.
From an acorn to an Oak Tree. new edition.
A History of the family and the firm(builders),
Brasted.
Printed by Hooker Bros.for Durtnell & Son Ltd.(1976).
2,3,11,17,19,23,

EAST KENT TIMES AND BROADSTAIRS & ST. PETER'S MAIL.
Supplement. Trumans, Gwyn and Company (Brewery).
Opening of the modern depot and offices at
Westwood, Broadstairs.
East Kent Times. 1964.
24.

EVANS, Harold.
Vickers: against the odds,1956-1977.(Local firm-
works at Dartford & Crayford).
Hodder & Stoughton. 1978.
5.

FUNNELL, K.J.
Snodland paper mill - C. Townsend Hook and Company
from 1854.
C. Townsend Hook & Company, Snodland. 1980.
4,12,23.

HALL-THERMOTANK LTD.
Hall-Thermotank Ltd., 100 years cold, 1877-1977.
(Contribution to a centenary of refrigeration).
Hall-Thermotank. Dartford. 1977.
5.
Hall-Thermotank Products Ltd.
Hall-Thermotank. Dartford. 1977.
5.

HALLAM, W.B.
Blowfire: a history of the Alexandra Towing Com.
Ltd.
Journal of Commerce. 1976.
9.

HILTON, John Anthony.
A history of the Medway Navigation Company.
Compiled from various sources.
John Hilton. Hadlow. 1977.
2,3,4,8,15,16,19,22,23,25.

Joseph Hatch: the Ulcombe bellfounder.
J. Hannon & Co. 1978.
1,12.

HONNORS LTD.
Your catalogue from the Store for the garden.
Honnors Ltd. Maidstone. 1974 and 1979.
11.

HOOKER, Charles E.
My seventy years with traction engines.
(Charles Hooker & Company of Egerton).
Oakwood Press. 1973.
4,11.

IMPERIAL GROUP REVIEW. Vol.5. No.1.
Smedleys at Barming & Faversham are owned
by Imperial Group.
Imperial Group Ltd. 1973.
11.

JABLONSKI, Edward.
Seawings: an illustrated history of flying boats.
(Section on Short Bros. of Rochester). 1974.
4.

KENT FIRE INSURANCE COMPANY.
Constitution and regulations of the Kent
Fire Insurance Company.
The Company. Printed by J.V. Hall, Kings'
Arms Office, Maidstone. 1816.
11.

Instructions for the agents of the Kent Fire
Insurance and the United Kent Life and
Annuity Institutions.
The Company. Printed by A. Austen.Maidstone(1833?).
11.

KLINGER OF MARGATE LTD.
Klinger; leader in the production of children's
socks.
Klinger of Margate Ltd. (1972).
13.

KNIGHT, M.T.
A History of J.P. Knight, Ltd.
(Typescript). 1977.
15.

LLOYD'S LIST.
Medway & Thanet Industrial Supplement,
February 13th 1975.
(Corporation of Lloyds now located in Chatham).
12.

MACDONALD, Gilbert.
Wellcome. One hundred years, 1880-1980.
In pursuit of excellence .
(The Wellcome Research Laboratory is at Beckenham,
also at Dartford).
Wellcome Foundation. 1980.
2.5.

MARGATE & THANET PERMANENT BENEFIT BUILDING SOCIETY.
Rules.
T. Keble. 1864.
13.

MARLEY TILE COMPANY LTD.
Technical Flooring Manual.
Marley, Sevenoaks. 1977.
4.

Technical Roofing manual.
Marley, Sevenoaks. 1975 rep. 1978.
4.

MEDWAY PAPER SACKS LTD.
Medway Multi-walls (Advertisement pamphlet).
Medway Paper Sacks Ltd. n.d.
11.

MORAN, James.*
Henry George: printer, bookseller, stationer
and binder, Westerham. 1830 - c.1846.
Westerham Press. 1972.
2,11,16,19.

OAKSEY, John.
Pride of the Shires: the story of the
Whitbread horses.
Hutchinson. 1979.
12.

PACKHOUSE: THE STORY OF EKP. (East Kent Packers).
East Kent Packers. 1970.
11.

PRESTON, J.M.
A short history: a history of Short Bros.
Aircraft Activities in Kent, 1908-1964.
North Kent Books. 1978.
2,3,4,5,12.

REED PAPER GROUP.
Paper material of a thousand uses: information
for school children.
Reed Paper & Board Ltd. n.d.
11.

A tour of the Aylesford Paper Mills & associated
factories.
Reed Paper & Board Ltd. n.d.
8,11.

REEVE & CO (MARGATE) LTD.
Past & present history.
(Mineral water manufacturer).
Reeve & Company, Margate Ltd. 1904.
13.

RICEMANS (CANTERBURY) LTD.
A new look at Ricemans: twelve years of growth
& achievement.
Ricemans. 1975.
3.

ROVEX LIMITED.
The Hornby book of trains 1954 - 1979,
Prototypes and models.
(Rovex Ltd. manufacture toys, model railways,
etc. in Margate & Ramsgate).
Rovex Ltd. Margate & Ramsgate. 1979.
13.

SHAW, Herbert.
The Story of Nalder & Collyers' Croydon Brewery
and its licensed houses in Bromley. (Typescript
of a talk given...10th November. 1977).
2.

SHORT BROTHERS (ROCHESTER & BEDFORD LTD.).
Pamphlets describing the aircraft and history
of the firm, c.1920 - 1945.
4.

SHORT BROTHERS (ROCHESTER & BEDFORD LTD.):
Joint Shop Stewards & Staff Committee.
Plan Medway with Shorts in the Plan.
1946.
4.

Why Close Shorts?.
1946.
4.

SITTINGBOURNE & KEMSLEY LIGHT RAILWAY COMPANY.
An introduction to the Sittingbourne & Kemsley
Light Railway (Formerly Bowaters' Sittingbourne
Railway).
Duplicated Sheet. 1973.
11.

S.K.L.R. Stockbook and guide.
Sittingbourne & Kemsley Light Railway Company. 1975.
11.

SIX GENERATIONS OF HAND PAPER-MAKERS.
The Green family celebrate 150 years continuous
direction of Hayle Mill.
(J. Barcham Green, Hayle Mill, Tovil. Started
by John Green, born in 1669).
From Worlds' Paper Trade Review. 1960.
4.

SMITH, Arthur William.
Wray (Optical Works) Ltd., 1850 - 1971.
(The Firm moved to Bromley in 1915).
Typescript. (1974).
2.

SOUTH-EAST ENGLAND TOURIST BOARD.
Discover the South-East: Kent, Surrey &
Sussex.
South-East England Tourist Board. Tunbridge Wells.
1973.
4,7.

Strategy for Tourism.
South-East England Tourist Board. Tunbridge Wells.
(1974).
7.

Study of Tourism in the Medway Borough Council
District.
South-East England Tourist Board. Tunbridge Wells.
Oct. 1974.
4,25.

SPICER, R.F.
A Speck of Spice.
(A history of Spicer's the Grocers of Hythe).
Spicers Stores, Hythe, 1975.
7.

2nd Edition, Illustrated. 1976.
7.

STOWELL, Gordon.
The Medway Story.
(The Story of Medway Paper Sacks Ltd., Reed
Paper Group).
Medway Paper Sacks Ltd. n.d.
11.

STRODE PARK IN HERNE, THE FACTORY IN A STATELY HOME.
In Veteran & Vintage Magazine Vol.14, No.2,
October 1969. pp.36 - 40.
(The Strode Engineering Works produced "Westcar"
Cars - and a tram for Herne Bay Pier).
Pioneer Publications. 1969.
30.

TREBILCOCK, Clive.
The Vickers brothers: armaments and enterprise,
1854 - 1914.
(Factories at Dartford & Crayford).
Europa Publications. 1977.
5.

WELLCOME FOUNDATION LTD.
(Administrative HQ & Research Laboratory at
Beckenham, also at Dartford).
Foundation News, 1970-71; 1972 - 73.
Burroughs Wellcome.
5.

Some achievements of the Wellcome Foundation.
Burroughs Wellcome. (1965).
2.

The Wellcome Foundation: Company with a
difference.
The Wellcome Foundation. 1980.
2.

WESTERN MOTOR WORKS (CHISLEHURST LTD).
The Horseless Carriage.
(History of Western Motor Works, originally
established at Frognal, Chislehurst).
1955.
2.

WHITBREAD & CO. LTD.
The Brewers' Art.
Whitbread & Company. Ltd.London. 1948.
3,4,11,23.

Whitbreads' Brewery, incorporating The Brewers'
Art.
Whitbread & Company Ltd. London.
1947. 15.
1951. 11,19,23.

WHITES OF COWES:SHIPBUILDERS.
(The White & Culmer-White family of Broadstairs
were boatbuilders & ancestors of Whites' of Cowes)
J. Samuel White & Company. n.d.
24.

WHYMAN, John,
From Leith to Lordswood:being a short history of
W.&.J. Mackay to mark their centenary 1875-1975.
W.&.J. Mackay Ltd. Chatham. 1976.
11,15.

WIGGINS TEAPE.*
Dartford Paper Mills: issued to commemorate their
opening.
Wiggins Teape. (1958).
1,4,5,7,8,11,12,17.

WILLMOTT, Frank G.
Bricks & "Brickies".
(Mainly concerns Eastwoods Ltd. of Lower Halstow
and Rainham).
F.G. Willmott. Rainham. 1972.
4,7,8,11,12,20,24,25,26,27,30.

Cement, mud and 'muddies' a history of APCM Barges.
Photography by Alan Cordell. (River Industries of
the River Medway).
Meresborough Books. Rainham. 1977.
1,3,4,5,7,8,9,11,15,20,23,25,26,27,30.

INLAND DEFENCES

BENNETT, D.H.
A handbook of Kent's defences from 1540 until 1945,
listed by D.H. Bennett.
Kent Defence Research Group. 1977.
2,3,4,6,9,11,13,16,22,23,32.

COOPER, John.
Fort Pitt. Some notes on the history of a
Napoleonic fort, Military hospital and Technical
school. (Chatham).
K.C.C. for J. Cooper. 1976.
3,5,6,7,8,9,11,13,15,20,25,32.

GREAT BRITAIN: Laws etc. (Vic.)
An Act for defraying the expenses of constructing
fortifications for the protection of the Royal
Arsenals and Dockyards and the Ports of Dover
and Portland and of creating a Central Arsenal.
Printed by Eyre & Spottiswoode. 1860.
11.

GULVIN, Keith R.
Chatham's Concrete Ring.
Medway Military Research Group. Chatham. (1979).
4,12,32.

Fort Amherst:illustrated booklet.
Medway Military Research Group. 1977.
2,4,6,11,15,25,32.

The Medway Forts: a short guide.
K.R. Gulvin. 1975.
4,9,20,25,32.

The Napoleonic Defences of Rochester and Chatham.
Medway Military Research Group. 1978.
4,11,15,32.

JONES, G.W.
Fort Bridge woods, by G.W. Jones and M.Shortland.
Fort Research Group. Chatham. 1979.
4,32.

Fort Darland, past and present.
Fort Research Group. Chatham. (1978).
4,11,12,32.

Fort Horsted, by G.W. Jones and M. Shortland.
Fort Research Group. Chatham. (1978).
4,11,12,32.

Fort Luton by G.W. Jones and M. Shortland.
Fort Research Group, Chatham. (1978).
4,11,15,32.

KNIGHT, Charles.*
Gillingham Fort.
1935.
8,32,

SMITH, Victor T.C.
Chatham's defences in the 19th Century.
Reprinted from Post Mediaeval Archaeology. 1976.
11,32.

The Gravesend Forts. (Local History Pamphlet
No 10).
Kent County Library, Gravesham Division. (1978).
3,4,6,9,32.

The Late nineteenth-century land defences
of Chatham.
Kent Defence Research Group (1976)
9,23,25,32.

New Tavern Fort.   Gravesend Historical Society.
Printed by Laverock Reprographics Ltd.Maidstone.
1975.
4,9,11,25,32.

Shornemead Fort.
Kent Defence Research Group. 1977.
9,32.

SOMNER, William.
A treatise of the Roman ports and forts in Kent.
George West, John Crosley & Henry Clements. 1693.
1,2,3,4,6,7,8,11,12,13,14,15,17,18,21.

THAMESIDE ARCHAEOLOGICAL GROUP.
The excavation of the Gravesend Blockhouse,
1975-76 (Clarendon Hotel Site), written by
Donald Thompson. (Typescript).
Thameside Archaeological Group. 1977.
9,32.

The Tudor Blockhouse, Gravesend: the historical
background to the archaeological excavation
carried out at the Clarendon Royal Hotel.
Thameside Archaeological Group. (1975).
9,32.

VINE, Paul Ashley Lawrence.*
The Royal Military Canal; an historial
account of the Waterway and Military Road from
Shornecliffe in Kent to Cliffe End in Sussex.
David & Charles. 1972.
2,3,4,6,7,11,12,19,32.

INNS

BARTHOLOMEW, John & Son Ltd. Publisher
The inns of Kent map, compiled by K.C. Jordan.
John Bartholomew & Son Ltd. 1973.
4,6.
7. 1976.

BISHOP, C.H.
Old Folkestone Pubs.
Kent County Council. 1979.
6,28.

BOOTH, John.
The drinking man's guide to Kent & Sussex Pubs.
Midas Books. 1974.
3,5,6,16,19.

BYWATER, Francis.*
The Inns and Taverns of Faversham.
(Faversham Papers No.3).
Faversham Historical Society.
1967. 1.2.4.6.8.11.12.24.30.
1968. 2nd edn. 20.

CAMPAIGN FOR REAL ALE.
A guide to real draught beer in Kent.
C.A.M.R.A. 1977
1,9.
4,5,11. 1978.

CARLEY, James.
Pubs of Meopham.
Meopham Publications Committee. 1975.
3,8,9,11.

DAY, J. Wentworth.*
Inns of Sport.
Naldrett Press for Whitbread & Co
1949. 3.4.15.
1949. 2nd edition. 15,23.

FAMOUS OLD INNS OF EAST KENT.
Hamilton-Fisher. Torquay. n.d.
24.

INNS

FINN, Timothy.
Pub games of England.
Queen Anne Press. 1975.
11.

GOOD BEER GUIDE 1977.
(pp.90-95 Kent Public Houses).
Campaign for Real Ale Ltd.
11.

GOOD BEER GUIDE 1978.
(pp. 88 - 93 Kent Public Houses).
Campaign for Real Ale Ltd.
11.

HARRIS, Edwin.*
Rochester Inns & Signs.
(Old Rochester Series no.19).
E. Harris & Sons. Rochester. 1905.
15.
Reprint of 1905 edition.
John Hallewell. Rochester. 1976.
3,11,25,30.

HILL, Brian.*
Inn-signia.
(Many of the signs are for Kent Whitbread Pubs).
Naldrett Press for Whitbread & Company. Ltd.
1945. 3,4,12.
1949. 2nd edition.

HISSEY, James John.
The road and the inn.
Macmillan. 1917.
11.

HOGG, Garry.
The English Country Inn.
(pp. 63 - 80 Kent Inns).
Batsford. n.d.
3.

HOPKINS, Robert Thurston.
Old English mills and inns,
West Kent mentioned throughout text.
Cecil Palmer. 1927.
4,5.11.

LAMB, Cadbury.
Inn Signs.
Shire Publications. 1976.
11.

MARTIN, W.W.*
The Chequers Inn, memoirs of a nonagenarian.
(High Halden).
Mitre Press. 1929.
2,3,6,11,12,13.

MATZ, B.W.
The Inns and taverns of 'Pickwick' with some
observations on their other associations.
Cecil Palmer. London. 1921.
1,3,4,5,8,9,11,12,15,25.

Dickensian Inns & Taverns.
Cecil Palmer. 1922.
4,8.

MAYNARD, D.C.*
The Old Inns of Kent.
Philip Allen. 1925.
22,24,25.

MOAD, Michael.
Yesterday's Medway: old inns, written by
by M. Moad for the Directorate of Leisure
Services.
Medway Borough Council. (1978).
11,15,25.

MOON, John H.
The George and Dragon, Lamberhurst. (Pamphlet).
J.H. Moon. Printed by the Crown Chemical Co
Ltd. 1978.
19.

RAINBIRD, G.M.*
Inns of Kent.
Naldrett Press for Whitbread & Co. Ltd. 1948.
2,20,23.
2nd edition. 1949.2,20,25.

"RAMBLER" pseud. (Barry Smith).
By the way: (a brief history of pubs and
hotels in Dover since 1900).
B. Smith. 1978.
6.

SHAW, Herbert.
The Story of Nalder and Collyer's Croydon
Brewery and its licensed houses in Bromley.
(Typescript of a talk given...10th Nov. 1977).
2.

SHEPHERD NEAME LTD.
Abbey Ale Houses in the Garden of England.
New edition.
Edward J. Burrow & Co. Cheltenham. 1973.
9,15,19.

SMITH, Rhona Madge.
Alka-Seltzer guide to the pubs of Kent, edited
by R.M. Smith.
Bayard Books Ltd. 1975.
2,3,5,7,8,11,12,16,20,25,26,27,28.

TAYLOR, John.
The Carriers' Cosmographie. Inns, hostelries
and other lodgings in and neare London.
De Capo Theatrum Orbis Ltd. 1974.
11.

WEAVER, G.
Kent pubs and Inns. (Viewing Kent Series).
James Pike. St. Ives. 1977.
2,3,6,11,28.

WHITBREAD & CO.LTD.*
Inn crafts and furnishings.
Whitbread & Co. Ltd. London. 1950.
23.

Outings in Kent.*
(Lists Whitbread Inns).
Whitbread & Co. Ltd. (c.1935?).
11,15.

YE OLDE LEATHER BOTTLE, Cobham, Kent.,
immortalised by Charles Dickens. (Leaflet
issued by The Leather Bottle, Cobham).
Printed by F.A. Clements, Chatham. (19--?).
11.

ISLE OF GRAIN

BRITISH PETROLEUM COMPANY LTD.
The B.P. Kent Refinery.
B.P. Company Ltd. 1959.
4,8,11.

A Technical description of the B.P. Kent Oil
Refinery.
B.P. Company Ltd. 1955.
3,4,8.

A Visit to the Kent Oil Refinery.
B.P. Company Ltd. 1955 & 1965.
2,4,8,11.

BRITISH PETROLEUM OIL KENT REFINERY LTD.
The Kent Refinery: a guide for visitors to
the B.P. Oil Refinery on the Isle of Grain, Kent.
British Petroleum Oil Kent Refinery Ltd. 1975.
4.

BURNETT, Charles Buxton.
A history of the Isle of Grain, an old time
village in Kent.
Rigg, Allen & Co. 1906.
25.

GRAY, Adrian.
Isle of Grain Railways. (Locomotion papers no.77).
Oakwood Press. 1974.
1,2,3,4,9,11,12,15,27.

MACDOUGALL, Philip.
The Isle of Grain defences.
Kent Defence Research Group. 1980.
6,22,28.

REX VERSUS JAMES MONTAGUE, W.L. NEWMAN, JOHN
NELSON AND FOUR OTHERS.* Report of the Trial.
(The defendants cut through the embankment
at Grain Bridge, Yautlet Creek, Isle of Grain).
Corporation of the City of London. 1824.
11.

ISLE OF OXNEY

KAYE-SMITH, Sheila.
The challenge to Sirius.   (A novel, partly
set in the Isle of Oxney).
Cassell. 1923.
11.

PERCY, Edward.*
Cowferry Isle: a novel of Kentish Life.
(Set in the Isle of Oxney).
Nicholson & Watson. 1934.
1,6,11.

ISLE OF SHEPPEY

BROWN, Samuel.
King's Ferry Bridge. Design for a suspension
bridge over the Swale. 2 views. (It is
believed that the Bridge was never built).
Photocopies. 1833.
4.

DALY, Augustus A.*
The History of the Isle of Sheppey from the
Roman occupation to the reign of His Most
Gracious Majesty, King Edward VII.
1904. Simpkin Marshall,Hamilton,Kent & Co. 1904.
26.
1975 Reprint of the 1904 edn. A.J. Cassell.
        Sheerness.
11,12,20,22,25.

DAVIS, Arthur G.
The London Clay of Sheppey and the location
of its fossils. In Proceeds of the Geologist's
Association. Vol.47. Pt.4. 1936. pp.328-345.
30.

DAWN OF THE DAY. Sheppey Church Magazine.
Vol.VII. Jan 1890 - Dec. 1890.
SPCK. 1890.
27.

GRIMSDELL, Mrs. N.L.
The Isle of Sheppey: a list of books relating to
Sheppey in the Kent County Libraries, compiled
by Mrs. N.L. Grinsdell.
Kent County Library, Swale Division. 1978.
3,4,11,20,27.

HOGARTH's FROLIC: the five days peregrination
around the Isle of Sheppey of William Hogarth
and his fellow pilgrims, Scott, Tothall, Thornhill
and Forrest. Written by E. Forrest & illustrated
by William Hogarth.
J. Holten, London. 1872.
26.

ISLE OF SHEPPEY CHAMBER OF COMMERCE.
Isle of Sheppey & Sheerness-on-Sea Official Guide.
1952.Home Publishing Coy. Croydon.   8.
1959.New Century Pubns. 1959.   8.

KENT COUNTY COUNCIL: PLANNING DEPT,
Kent County Structure Plan.
Future development possibilities in Kent,
the Medway Towns, Sittingbourne & Sheppey.
(Serial No. E4B).
K.C.C. Dec, 1975.
4.

The search for a site for a third London Airport.*
Pt. 1. Background information concerning Sheppey &
Cliffe.
K.C.C. 1968.
4,20,25.

KENT COUNTY LIBRARY.*
The Isle of Sheppey.
Part 1. Libraries on the Isle of Sheppey.
Part 11.A Select list of books relating to the
        Isle of Sheppey in Kent County Libraries.
Kent County Library. 1956.
1,2,3,4,7,8,11,12,15,27.

QUEENBOROUGH-IN-SHEPPEY BOROUGH COUNCIL-
PUBLICITY COMMITTEE.
The Isle of Sheppey. (Cover title: Sheppey
Official Guide).
Queenborough-in-Sheppey Borough Council. n.d.
20.

SHEPPEY GROUP.
Synopsis of the evidence given at the Foulness
Inquiry.
The Sheppey Group. 1969.
4.

SHEPPEY URBAN DISTRICT COUNCIL.
Sheerness-on-Sea and the Isle of Sheppey,
compiled by George Beynon.
Sheppey Urban District Council. 1927.
6.

SWALE FOOTPATHS GROUP.
Five walks on Sheppey: a selection of country
walks on individual cards.
Swale Footpaths Group/K.C.C. 1976.
11.

TOWN & COUNTRY MAGAZINE.
Includes:- A legend of Sheppey.
Virtue. London. 1837 - 38.
4.

WOODTHORPE, T.J.*
A history of the Isle of Sheppey, Kent.
Smith, Printers, Sheerness, for the Sheerness
and District Co-operative Society. 1951.
1,2,3,4,8,11,12,25,26.30.

ISLE OF THANET

ALL ABOUT MARGATE & HERNE BAY;*
including Drapers', St. Peters', Salmerstone,
Chapel Bottom, Hengrove, Twenties and Nash Court,
Kingsgate and its modern antiquities,Garlinge,
Dandelion.
W. Kent & Company. London. 1866.
11.

ARCHAEOLOGICAL NOTES ON THANET a collection from
Archaeologia Cantiana.
Kent Archaeological Society.
13.

BENEDICTINES OF THANET, 1856 - 1931.
Monastery Press. Ramsgate. 1931.
11.

BONSFIELD, Publisher.*
Picture of Margate, being a complete guide to
all persons visiting Margate, Ramsgate &
Broadstairs - with "The Margate Hoy", a poem.
Bonsfield. 1809.
1,12,13.

BRADEN, J.T. Publisher.
J.T. Braden's photographic views of Margate
and neighbourhood.
Braden. c.1890.
13.

BRASIER, W.C. Publisher.*
The picturesque companion to the Isle of Thanet,
Dover, Canterbury and parts adjacent.
W.C. Brasier. Margate. c.1860.
24.

BRAYLEY, Edward Wedlake.*
Deliniations historical and topographical of
the Isle of Thanet and the Cinque Ports.
Vols I and II, illustrated by William Deeble.
Sherwood, Neely and Jones.
Vol 1. 1817   6.8.10.
Vol 11. 1818   1.4.
Vols I and II 1817 and 1818. 3,7,11,12,13,14,
                            15,16,17,24.

CALLCUTT & BEAVIS, Publishers.*
(32) Views of Margate & District.
Callcut & Beavis, London. (1895?).
11,13.

CANTERBURY & THANET COMMUNITY HEALTH COUNCIL.
Annual Reports: for the year ending on March 31st...
1976. 3.
1977. 3,13.
1978. 3.13.

CLARKE, W.J. and KNAPP. Publishers
Lane's guide to Margate and the Isle of Thanet.
W.J. Clarke & Knapp. 1906.
13.

ISLE OF THANET

CORONATION VISIT OF...ARCHBISHOP OF CANTERBURY
TO THE ISLE OF THANET, 25th June, 1953.
Illustrated souvenir programme.
13.

(COZENS, Zachariah).*
A Tour through the Isle of Thanet and some other
parts of East Kent including a particular description of the churches...
J. Nichols.
1793. 3,4,12.
1795. 3,11,13,17.

THE EAST KENT CRITIC.
"Candide" Publishing Agency.
13. 1973;1975;1976;1977.
24. 1964 in progress.

EAST KENT ROAD CAR COMPANY LTD.
Timetable area No.6. Thanet.
2nd October, 1977 until further notice.
East Kent Road Car Coy. Ltd. 1977.
11.

EAST KENT TIMES & BROADSTAIRS & ST.PETER'S MAIL.
Thanet storm damage, Wednesday 11th January 1978;
a pictorial record.
Reprinted from The East Kent Times; taken by
camera men John Wilson & Brian Greene.
East Kent Times. 1978.
11.

GREAT BRITAIN, Laws etc. (Geo.I).
Act of Parliament for the pilots of Dover,
Deal and Thanet, 1714 - 20.
(1721).
13.

GRITTEN, A.J.
Catalogue of books, pamphlets and excerpts dealing
with Margate, the Isle of Thanet and the
County of Kent, in the Local Collection of
the Borough of Margate Public Library,
compiled by A.J. Critten.
Margate Library Committee. 1934.
1,3,4,7,11,13.

A GUIDE TO THE ISLE OF THANET & THE CLIFTONVILLE
HOTEL, Margate. 1890-1.
1890.
13.

HILLS, William.*
Jottings of history relating to the Isle of
Thanet.
H.E. Boulter:Kent Argus. Ramsgate. 1886.
24.

HOUGHTON, George E. Publisher.*
Photographic souvenir of Margate & neighbourhood,
photographed & published by G.E.Houghton.
1895. 13.
1898. 11,12,13.

HUDDLESTONE, John.*
"Discovering Thanet" in pictures.
J.H. Pictorial Features.
Herbert Marshall. Thanet Printing Works. (1954?).
13,24.

HUTCHINGS AND CROWSLEY. Publishers.*
Thanet: historical and descriptive guide to
the Isle of Thanet.
Hutchings & Crowsley. (1883?).
24.

HUTCHINSON, C.B.
The Fanes of Thanet - 13 articles on the
development of Thanet as reflected in Church
History.
Thanet Advertiser. 1917.
24.

THE ISLE OF THANET. A report on tidal invest-
igations. The Boroughs of Margate and Ramsgate
and the Urban District Council of Broadstairs
and St. Peters. 1972.
24.

ISLE OF THANET FIELD CLUB.
Fourth Annual Report, January 1950 -
April 1951.
Isle of Thanet Field Club. 1951.
11.

THE ISLE OF THANET GAZETTE: a short history.
Isle of Thanet Gazette. n.d.
13.

ISLE OF THANET GAZETTE & THANET TIMES.
Historic Thanet: 42 page supplement.
21st April, 1978.
W.J. Parrett. Ltd.
24.

ISLE OF THANET GEOGRAPHICAL ASSOCIATION.*
Panorama: a magazine of geographical interest.
Annual issue.
Nos.1 - 11, 1956 - 1966. 4.13.
Nos. 2,3,5,9,10. 24.
Nos. 3 - 10. 6.
No. 10. 11.
No. 11. 4,8,11,12.
No 12. 1967. Thanet Panorama, a modern guide to
the Island. 1,4,9,13.
No. 15.1977. 3,24.

ISLE OF THANET LIGHT RAILWAYS.
Board of Trade Order dated 13th August. 1898.
(Light Railways Act. 1896).
24.

ISLE OF THANET PROMOTION BOARD.
Focus on Thanet.
Isle of Thanet Promotion Board. 1979.
13,24.

Thanet Industrial Directory.
Isle of Thanet Promotion Board. 1979.
13.

THE ISLE OF THANET VISITOR'S GUIDE.*
1892.
24.

JOHN, Malcolm.
Bygone Thanet and Channel Coastlands.
Chambers Green Ltd. 1980.
28.

KEBLE, T.H. Publisher.*
Kebles illustrated penny guide to the Isle of
Thanet, Margate, Westgate, Broadstairs,
Birchington & St. Peters.
T.H. Keble. (1891).
13.

KELLY'S DIRECTORIES LTD.
Kelly's Directory of the Isle of Thanet, 1973.
Kelly's Directories Ltd. 1973.
13.

KENT COUNTY COUNCIL:EDUCATION DEPARTMENT.
Hilderstone. 1971-2.
K.C.C. 1971.
13.

Hilderstone adult studies. 1979/80.
K.C.C. 1979.
13.

Hilderstone - 3 centres for Thanet.
(Adult education).
K.C.C. 1973.
13.

Thanet at School:* a picture of education in Thanet.
K.C.C. 1950.
11,13.

Thanet Technical College: Prospectus,1974-75.
K.C.C. (1974).
11.

KIDD, William Publisher.*
The picturesque pocket companion to Margate,
Ramsgate, Broadstairs and the parts adjacent,
illustrated by G.W. Bonner.
William Kidd. 1831.
24.

LANE, GENTRY & CO. Publishers.*
Lane & Gentry's Standard Guide to Margate and
historical Thanet.
Lane,Gentry & Company (1906?).
24.

LETTERS CONCERNING THE THANET VOLUNTEER YEOMANRY.
Kentish Gazette. 1810.
24.

LEWIS, John.*
The history and antiquities, as well ecclesiastical
as civil, of the Isle of Tenet, in Kent. 2nd ed
For J. Ames etc. London. 1736.
24.

LLOYDS LIST.
Medway & Thanet industrial Supplement.
February 13th 1975.
12.

MARGATE & THANET PERMANENT BENEFIT BUILDING SOCIETY.
Rules.
T. Keble. 1864.
13.

MAYHEW, Athol.
Birchington-on-Sea and its bungalows, with
an historical sketch of Thanet, and notes on
the island by S. Wayland Kershaw.
Batsford. 1881.
1,6,8,11,13,15,17.

MOCKETT, John.*
A letter to Capt. Thamas Garrett commanding the
Thanet Troop of Volunteer Yeomanry
Printed for the author in Canterbury. 1810.
3,11,13.

ONE HUNDRED AND ONE VIEWS (of) the Isle of
Thanet and District.
Rock Bros. London (c.1900).
11.

OULTON, W.G.*
Picture of Margate and its vicinity, illustrated
with a map and twenty views engraved by J.J.
Shury from drawings by Captain G. Varle.
(Interleaved with some 200 engravings, some
of Kent interest).
Baldwin, Cradock & Joy. London. 1820.
11.
1821. 2nd edition. 24.

PARKER, John R.A.
In and around lovely Thanet. (Etchings).
John Parker. London. n.d.
11.

PHILPOTT, R.W. Stationer.
Photographic Album of Ramsgate, Margate,
Broadstairs & District containing 31
charming views.
R.W. Philpott, Stationer. Ramsgate. c.1900.
11.

PITTOCK, George. M.*
Flora of Thanet: a catalogue of the plants
indigenous to the island with a few rare
aliens, by G.M. Pittock & friends.
Printed by R. Robinson, Margate. 1903.
24.

ROCHE, T.W.E.*
Ships of Dover, Folkestone, Deal and Thanet...
A. Coles Ltd. Southampton. (1959).
30.

SEDGWICK, W.F.Ltd.
Pictures of Ramsgate and neighbourhood. (Most
of the photographs taken by H. Borton).
Lewis Hepworth & Co. Tunbridge Wells. c.1900
11.

SIMSON, James.*
Historic Thanet.
Elliot Stock. 1891.
24,30.

SKEAT, Walter William
Reprinted glossaries...XI. Words used in the
Isle of Thanet by...J. Lewis. 1736, edited
by W.W. Skeat.
English Dialect Society. 1874 rep. 1881.
4.

SO, C.L.
Coastal platforms of the Isle of Thanet, Kent.
(photocopy of M.S.).
1964.
24.

"A SOCIETY OF GENTLEMEN".*
The Thanet Magazine. June - Dec. 1817.
Denne. Margate.
24.

THANET ADVERTISER.*
Thanet's Raid History - raids,bombs, shells.
A record of the home line of trenches, compiled
from Official and private documents. 3rd.edition.
maps.
Thanet Advertiser. 1919.
11,13,24.

THANET CATHOLIC ANNUAL.
Church Publishers for St. Augustines' Abbey.
1972;1974;1976. 13.
1978.   3.
1979.   13.

THANET DISTRICT COUNCIL.
Abstract of Accounts. 1978-1979.
Abstract of Accounts. 1979-1980.
Thanet District Council. 1979 -80
13.

Minutes. 1973/4.
Thanet District Council.
13.

Year Book. 1974/75; 1975/76; 1977/78.
Thanet District Council. 1974-1977.
13.

THANET DISTRICT COUNCIL:AMENITIES DEPT. -PUB.DEPT.
Margate,Broadstairs,Ramsgate.-Enjoy Thanet.
1976.   11,13,24.
1977. Isle of Thanet:Official Guide. 13,24.
1978. Isle of Thanet:Tourist Guide. 12,24.
1979. Isle of Thanet:Official Guide. 11,13,24.

THANET EAST AND THANET WEST.
Constituencies.
Electoral Register. 1977.
13.

THE THANET FIGARO. From June 2nd 1877 to
September 29th 1877.
(Nos. 1,2,3,5,& 7 missing).
13.

THE THANET FREE PRESS AND GENERAL ADVERTISER.
No. 249. December 22nd. 1882.
1882.
13.

THE THANET GLOWWORM.
August 4th 1880 - July 28th 1881.
1880/1.
13.

THE THANET ITINERARY OR STEAM YACHT COMPANION,*
containing a sketch of the island....3rd edition.
Bettison, Garner & Denne. Margate. 1823.
24.

THANET SAILING WEEK, 1974.
Programme.
13.

THANET TIMES.
A Sea of ice off Margate, 4 pages of photographs
showing frozen seas around the Thanet Coast on
January 26th 1963.
A Supplement, Tuesday 12th February, 1963.
24.

THANET WATER BOARD.*
Annual Reports.
11. 1971/2; 1972/3.
13. 1957/8; 1959/60; 1961/2; 1962/3;
     1963/4; 1965/6; 1971/2.

TRADESMEN'S TOKENS issued in the Isle of Thanet..
and the Cinque Ports.
(Bibliotheca Topographica Britannica).
1,11.

WHITE, J.T.
Thanet delineated. (Commonplace book).
MSS.   c.1946.
13.

IVYHATCH

TONBRIDGE & MALLING DISTRICT COUNCIL:
PLANNING DEPARTMENT.
Ightham conservation study, Ivy Hatch and
Ightham Mote.
Tonbridge & Malling District Council. 1980.
23.

KEMSING

BOWDEN, V.E.
St. Mary the Virgin, Kemsing: a guide.
S.L. Hunt printers 1973.
2.

The Church of St. Mary, Kemsing.(believed to
be written by V.E. Bowden). c.1960?
12.

THE HISTORY OF ST.EDITH OF KEMSING* and
guide to the Church of St. Mary, Kemsing.
Caxton & Holmesdale Press. 1951.
11,16.

KEMSING PARISH COUNCIL.
A guide to Kemsing Down Nature reserve.
Kemsing Parish Council. 1980.
16.

A guide to the footpaths of Kemsing.
Kemsing Parish Council. 1974.
2.

A guide to the historic buildings of
Kemsing,edited by Victor E. Bowden.
Kemsing Parish Council. 1975.
1,2,8,11,12,17.

KEMSLEY

KENT COUNTY COUNCIL:PLANNING DEPARTMENT.
Milton and Kemsley:informal action area
plan Draft.
K.C.C. 1973.
11,20.

SITTINGBOURNE & KEMSLEY LIGHT RAILWAY.
An introduction to the Sittingbourne & Kemsley
Light Railway (formerly Bowaters' Sittingbourne
Railway).
Duplicated sheet. 1973.
4.

Stockbook and guide. 1975.
Sittingbourne & Kemsley Light Railway. 1975.
11.

WELLS, Arthur G.
Bowaters' Sittingbourne Railway. 2nd edition.
(First published in 1962).
Locomotive Club of Great Britain. 1971.
11,25.

KENNINGTON

"DAY BY DAY" DIRECTORY OF ASHFORD, KENNINGTON
AND WILLESBOROUGH.
Redman . Ashford.
1965. 5th edition.12,19.
1970. 6th edition.11.

ASSOCIATION OF THE MEN OF KENT & KENTISH MEN.
Kent: the journal of the Association of Men
of Kent and Kentish Men.
Printed Brewster. 1970. →
28.

BAINES, A.
The way about Kent, edited by A. Baines.
Iliffe. n.d.
24.

BANKS, F.R.*
Kent (The Penguin Guides).
Penguin. 1955.
24.

BARNETT, Michael.
Kent & Sussex ABC atlas & county gazeteer,
edited and compiled by M. Barnett.
G.I. Barnett. 196-?.
11.

BARTHOLOMEW, John & Son Ltd. Publishers,
Post Office Post Code Map: Kent. Great
Britain & N. Ireland. Sheet 10. Scale 1 mile =
½ inch).
J. Bartholomew & Son. Ltd. Publishers. 1970/75.
11.

BELL, Nancy R.E.(Mrs. Arthur G. Bell).
The Skirts of the Great City. (pp.87-130 Kent).
2nd edition.Methuen. 1908.
11.

BIGNELL, Alan.
Kent Villages.
R. Hale. 1975.
1,3,5,6,7,8,9,11,12,15,22,24,25,26.

BOORMAN, Henry Roy Pratt.*
Kent and the Cinque Ports.
Kent Messenger. Maidstone. 1957.
1,3,4,5,6,7,8,9,10,11,12,14,15,17,18,20,24.

"Kent Messenger" Centenary.*
Kent Messenger, Maidstone. 1959.
1,2,3,4,5,6,7,8,9,11,12,14,15,17,18,25.

Kent our County.
Kent Messenger, Larkfield. 1979.
5,6,11,12,13,16,23,28.

Kent, our glorious heritage*
Kent Messenger. Maidstone. 1951.
2,24.

Kent Unconquered.*
Kent Messenger. Maidstone. 1951.
2,26.

Kentish Pride.*
Kent Messenger. Maidstone. 1952.
29.

BOOTH, Stuart.
The Aerofilms book of England from the Air,
edited by S. Booth.
Blandford Press. 1979.
23.

BOYLE, John.
Rural Kent by John Boyle and with drawings by
John L. Berbiers.
Robert Hale. 1976.
1,2,3,4,5,6,8,9,11,12,13,14,15,20,22,26,27,28.

BRENTNALL, Margaret.*
Kent, Surrey & Sussex.
Charles Letts & Co. 1971.
26.

BRIERCLIFFE, Harold.
Southern England.
Temple Press. 1950.
11.

BURKE, John.
Discovering Britain:South East England.
Faber. 1975.
6,11,22.

BURNHAM, C. Paul.
Kent:the garden of England by C.P. Burnham
and Stuart Macrae.
Paul Norbury Pubns. Tenterden. 1978.
2,3,4,5,9,11,13,14,15,16,22,23,24,28.

BURROW, Edward J. & Co.Ltd. Publishers.*
Kent: an illustrated review of the holiday,
residential, sporting & industrial aspects
of the County. The County Handbook.
Edward J. Burrow & Company,Cheltenham
1936. 25.
1938. 16.

Kent: a guide to the County and an
industrial review. The County Handbook.
E.J. Burrow & Co. Ltd. Cheltenham.
Seven issues with no dates specified. 24.

Kent:*a guide to the County and an
Industrial review. The County Handbook.
Edward J. Burrow & Company,Cheltenham.
1955. 16.
(1958?) edited by John Adham. 16.30.
1960. 20.
1962. 4th edn. 30.
1967. 6th edn. 30.
1971. 4,12,30.
(1978). 2,4,11,12,15,16,19,23.

South East England:Sussex, Kent and Surrey.
With numerous street plans, maps of touring
districts and full information as to hotels.
(pp.69 - 116 Kent Section).
Edward J. Burrow and Co. Cheltenham. (193?).
11.

CARR, F.G.P.
Photograph album of Kentish Views, 1957-1959.
11.

CARTER, Judith.
Over the sea to Kent. (a photographic record
of a two day car trip through Kent) taken
from IN BRITAIN. March 1975.
12.

CATLING, Gordon.*
The beauty of Kent.
Jarrold. 1953.
2.

CHURCH, Richard.*
Kent.
Hale. 1948.
1948 (1966 impression). 25.
1948 (1973 impression). 12.
1974 (Reprint of the 1948 edn). 12,16.

CLARK, F.C.*
Kentish fire.
Adams & Son. Rye. 1947.
1,2,3,4,5,6,7,8,9,11,12,14,15,16,17,19,20,24.

CLINCH, George.*
Kent. Illustrated by F.D. Bedford and from
photographs. (Little Guides Series).
Methuen. 1903.
2,4,25.

CLUNN, Harold Philip.*
The face of the Home Counties portrayed in
a series of eighteen weekend drives from
London. (pp.208-315, Kent Section).
New & Revised edition. Spring Books. 1958.
2,5,11,12.

COME TO KENT ASSOCIATION.
Come to Kent. Official County guide.
Organ of the "Come to Kent" Association.
County Association Ltd. 1949?.
4,8.

CONSTAPLE, C.&.D. Ltd. Publishers.*
Visitors' guide to Kent.
C.&.D. Constaple. (1971?).
2,6,9,12,

COOPER, Gordon.*
A fortnight in Kent.
Percival Marshall. 1950.
28.

COURT, Alexander Norman.*
Kent in colour.
Jarrold & Sons. 1954. 25.
1970 New edition. 11.

South-East England: Surrey, Sussex and Kent.
Jarrold & Sons. 1972.
12.

COX, John Charles.*
Kent: with illustrations by F.D. Bedford
and from photographs with four maps and plans.
3rd edition. Methuen. 1920. 25.
4th edition. Methuen. 1923. 4,24.

Rambles in Kent.
Methuen. 1913.
1,2,4,5,6,7,8,9,11,12,13,14,15,16,17,18,19,23,24.

CROUCH, Marcus.
The cream of Kent.
A.J. Cassell. Sheerness. 1973.
1,2,4,5,8,9,11,20,22,26,28,29,30.

Detective in the landscape in South-east
England.*
Longman Young Books. 1972.
6,7.

Discovering Kent.
Shire Pubns. 1975.
2,3,5,7,8,9,11,12,13,16,22,30.

The Home Counties (Includes Kent).
Hale. 1975.
2,3,11,12,15,22,23,28.

Kent.*
Batsford.
1966. 22.
1967. Reprint. 24.

DEXTER, Walter.*
Days in Dickensland.
Methuen. 1933.
3,11.

The Kent of Dickens.
Cecil Palmer. 1924.
2,25.

DIXON-SCOTT, J. Photographer.*
Kent Coast and Countryside: camera pictures of
the County by J. Dixon-Scott, selected by B.
Prescott Row.
Homeland Association. 1929.
2,8,11,12.

ELLIOTT, R.L.
Where to go, what to do in the South East: 300
places to visit in the wet or dry. 3rd ed
Heritage Pubns. Tavistock. 1975.
6,19.

ELLISTON-ERWOOD, Frank Charles.
Scraps on the County of Kent, compiled by
F.C. Elliston-Erwood.
(General Scrapbook with some Kent items).
11.

ELVIRA. pseud.*
Kentish yesterdays.
Kentish District Times. (1947).
1,2,3,5,8,11,15,17.

ENVIRONMENT, Dept. of the. ANCIENT MONUMENTS
& HISTORIC BUILDINGS.
An illustrated guide to the ancient monuments
maintained by the Dept. of the Environment:
Southern England. 5th edn.
H.M.S.O. 1973.
3,12.

EVANS, A.A.
By Weald and Down.
Methuen. 1939.
12.

FITTER, Richard Sidney Richmond.*
Home Counties, with a portrait by R.S.R.
Fitter, and edited by G. Grigson.
About Britain Guide No.3.
Collins, for the Festival of Britain Office.1951.
4,7,8,12,23.

FROST, Thomas.*
In Kent with Charles Dickens.
(Short mention of Davington, Boughton (Bossenden
Wood) and other localities connected with
Dickens' Stories.
Tinsley Brothers, London. 1880.
1,2,3,4,6,8,11,12,15,17,18,26.

GARDINER, Mrs. Dorothy.*
Companion into Kent.
1934. Methuen. 25.
1949. 3rd edn. Methuen. 30.
1973. 2nd edn. reissued. Spurbooks.
1,9,11,19,22,26,28.

GARDNER, William Biscombe.
Dicken's Country: water colours by
W. Biscombe Gardner & others.
A.&.C. Black. 1920.
11.

Kent.* 2nd edn. by W.B. Gardner and W.T. Shore.
A.&.C. Black. 1924.
3.

Kent Watercolours.*
A.&.C. Black. 1914.
19.24.

GEOGRAPHIA GUIDE TO S.E. ENGLAND.
Geographia Publications (1974?).
20,26,27.

GLOVER, Judith.
The Batsford colour book of Kent; introduction
& commentaries by Judith Glover.
Batsford. 1976.
3,6,11,12,15,22,23,28,29.30.

GREEN, J.R.
Story studies, second series. (A Travelogue:
articles originally written for the Saturday
Review. pp.44-62. Rochester and Knole).
Macmillan. 1903.
15.

HARPER, Charles George.*
The Downs and the Sea, by C.G. Harper and
J.C. Kershaw.
(pp.45 - 94 Kent Section).
Cecil Palmer. 1923.
1,2,3,8,11,14.

HIGHAM, Roger.
Kent. (Batsford Britain Series).
Batsford.   . 1974.
1,2,3,6,7,9,11,12,14,15,16,22,25,27,28.

HOME PUBLISHING COMPANY Publisher.*
Kent: an illustrated guide to the County,
with a foreword by S.P.B. Mais. 2nd edition.
(Spine Title - Kent County Guide).
Home Publishing Company. Croydon. n.d.
30.
1954. 16.

HOPE, Lady Elizabeth Reid.*
English homes and villages - Kent and Sussex.
(Early colour photography).
Salmon, Sevenoaks. 1909.
1,2,3,4,5,6,7,8,11,12,15,16,17,18,19.

HUGHES, James Pennethorne.*
Kent: a Shell Guide.
Faber . 1969.
3,22,30.

HUTTON, Edward.*
England of my heart: spring. With many
illustrations by Gordon Home.
Vol.I of a 4 volume work. Kent. Chapters I-IX.
Dent. 1914.
4,11.

IGGLESDEN, Sir Charles.*
A saunter through Kent with pen & pencil. 34 vols.
Kentish Express. Ashford. 1900-47.
2. Vols. 22 and 24. 1928-30.
20. Vols. 6,12,24,31. 1909-(1937).
23. Vol.32.
24. Vol.18? 1926.
25. Vols. 1,3,5,-20, 24,26. 1900-1932.

THE INVICTA MAGAZINE.* for the homes and
people of Kent,edited by C.J. Redshaw.
Vols. 1,2,and 3.
Snowden Bros. Dartford.
Simpkin Marshall. London. 1908-1912.
11,12,25.

JESSUP, Ronald Frank.*
Kent (Little Guides Series based on the
original guide by J. Charles Cox).
Methuen. 1950.
24,25,26,30,31.

South East England.
Thames & Hudson. 1970.
3,25.

JOHN, Malcolm.
Around historic Kent...Drawings by C.A.T.Brigden.
Midas Books. Tunbridge Wells. 1978.
1,3,4,6,7,9,11,12,13,14,15,16,22,23,24,28,30.

KELLY'S DIRECTORIES.
Kelly's Directory of Kent with coloured map.
12th edition.
Kelly's Directories. 1915.
11.

Kelly's Directory of Kent & Sussex, edited by
A. Lindsay Kelly.
Kelly's Directories. 1927.
23.

Kelly's Directory of Kent, Surrey & Sussex.
with coloured maps.
Kelly's Directories. 1930.
11.

Kelly's directory of Kent, 1938.
Kelly's Directories. 1938.
12.

KENT COUNTY COUNCIL.
The film:the making of Kent.
K.C.C. (1975).
12.

KENT COUNTY COUNCIL:PLANNING DEPARTMENT.
Environmental handbook: produced by the
Kent County Council during European Architectural
Heritage Year. (A general handbook to Kent).
K.C.C. 1975.
3,4,7,8,9,11,12,13,16,20.

KENT COUNTY JOURNAL.
The quarterly magazine of Kent.
Pilgrim Press Ltd. Folkestone.
Vol.3. Nos 1 & 2: Spring & Summer. 1936.
Vol.4. 1936-1939.
Vol.5. Nos 1 - 3: Summer,Autumn,Winter. 1939.
4.

KENT COUNTY LIBRARY.
Kent: a list of books added to the County
Library during - 1966; 1973; 1974-76.
K.C.C. 1967, 1974, & 1978.
1966.   4.7.11.13,25.
1973.   4.7.11.13,25.
1974-76.3,4,5,6,7,8,9,10,11,12,13,14,15, 16,20.
      22,23,24,25,26,27,28,29,30,31.

Kent: a select list of references in periodical
articles published during 1971 and 1972.
Kent County Library. 1973.
3,11.

KENT COUNTY LIBRARY:SCHOOL MUSEUM SERVICE.
Places to visit.
Kent County Council.
1976. 2nd edn. 3.11.
1977-78.   8.
1978-79.   3.

KENT COUNTY YEAR BOOK.*
Kent Messenger. Maidstone.
1934-35 edited by S.C. Kendall. 30.
1948 edited by Dorothy Pitcher. 30
1950 edited by Dorothy Pitcher. 30.

KENT FEDERATION OF AMENITY SOCIETIES.
Kent Matters - a periodical.
No 13. 1974.   8.
No 15. 1976.   24.
No 16. 1977   24.

KENT LEISURE GUIDE.
Published with the approval of the County Council.
Pyramid Press. 1976.
11,13,20,26,27.

KITTON, Frederick G.*
The Dickens Country.
A.&.C. Black.
1911. 2nd edition. 11,25.
1925.   11.

LINES, Clifford John.
South East England.
Ginn. 1972.
7.

LOFTUS, Harry.
Letts Tour Southern England: Kent,Surrey and
Sussex, completely revised by H. Loftus.
Charles Letts & Co. 1975.
3,11,12.

McCOLL, P.J.
Kent Car Tours (Viewing Kent Series).
James Pike, St. Ives. 1977.
2,3,6,11,22,29.

MASON, John.
Kent in Photographs: Text by John & Anne Mason.
Photographs by Anthony Kersting.
Batsford. 1976.
3,4,5,6,7,8,9,11,12,13,15,16,22,23,28.

MASON, Oliver.
South-East England. (Mainly a Gazeteer).
John Bartholomew & Son Ltd. 1979.
11,12.

MAXWELL, Donald.*
A detective in Kent:landscape clues to the
discovery of lost seas.
Jonn Lane/Bodley Head 1929.
2,24,25,30.

Unknown Kent...being a series of unmethodical
explorations of the County.
John Lane/Bodley Head. 1921.
20.24.25.

MEE, Arthur.*
Kent (King's England Series).
Hodder & Stoughton.
1936.   26, 29.
1969. New edn, revised & reset. 11,20,22,28,29,
                                          30,31.
1974.   28.

NICKLIN, J.A.*
Dickens land. Illustrated by E.W. Haslehurst.
Blackie. 1911.
1,2,3,4,5,7,8,9,11,12,15,18,25.

NORMAN, S.N.
A descriptive and pictorial guide to those
areas of Kent and East Sussex served by the
Maidstone & District Motor Services Ltd.
John Langton. London. (196-?).
11.

NORWOOD, John C.*
The Glory of Kent.
Reprinted from the South Eastern Gazette.
1930.
5.

OLD KENT SNAPS (photograph album).
Small photographs with captions, mainly of
Chegworth (Harrietsham) and including Chilham,
Maidstone & Sturry etc., 1910 - 1930.
The Album belonged to Joyce Amos, Victoria
House, Victoria Road, Margate.
11.

PAGE, Andre.*
Kent and East Sussex by Wanderbus.
Midas Books. 1973.
1,2,3,6,7,9,11,12,26,30.

What do you know about Kent?
P.A.Publications,Speldhurst.1973.
1,2,3,4,6,7,8,9,11,19,22,25,26,27,30.

PEPIN, David.
Pilgrims' guide to the South East.
(pp.4 - 23, Kent).
Mowbrays. 1977.
3,5,11.

PUBLIC BUILDING AND WORKS, Ministry of.*
Ancient monuments in the care of the Ministry
of Public Buildings & Works. Illustrated
Regional Guide No.2. Southern England. 4th edn.
H.M.S.O. 1970.
30.

QUINTON, Alfred Robert C. (1853-1934).
The England of A.R. Quinton:rural scenes as
recorded by a Country artist. Biographical
details researched by Alan Roger Quinton.
(A.R.C. Quinton completed the bulk of his work
in association with J. Salmon, publishers, of
Sevenoaks, from 1911 - 1934. - 2,300 paintings
for postcards. He visited Salmon in Sevenoaks
frequently. The book includes paintings of
Penshurst, Loose, and Groombridge).
J. Salmon Ltd. Sevenoaks. 1978.
16,23.

ROYAL AUTOMOBILE CLUB.
Kent.   (No.4 of the RAC County Road Maps & Guides).
Edward J. Burrow & Company. (192-?).
11.

SCOTT-JOB, Derrick.*
County guide to Kent,edited by D. Scott-Job.
Graham Scott (Publishers) Ltd.   1958.
1,3,5,6,7,9,11,12,14,15,20,24.

SHORE, W. Teignmouth.*
Kent.
A.&.C. Black. 1907.
6,24.

SOUTH EAST ENGLAND TOURIST BOARD.
Discover the South East; Kent, Surrey, Sussex.
S.E. England Tourist Board.
3. 1975.
27. 1974.

SOUTHERN ENGLAND WITH COLOURMASTER.
Colourmaster. 1972.
29.

SOUTHERN RAILWAY COMPANY.
Lovely Kent:section of "Hints for holidays",
1926:official guide.
Southern Railway. 1926.
11.

SPENCE, Keith.
A Companion guide to Kent and Sussex.
Collins. 1973.
1,2,3,5,6,7,8,9,11,12,16,19,22,28,30.

TAYLOR, Leonard.*
London's coast & countryside. (Where shall
we go? No.1).
Nicholson & Watson. 1950.
8,11.

THOMAS, Richard.
Kent.(A County Guide).
Johnston & Bacon. 1976.
1,2,3,6,8,11,28,30.

THOMPSON, Gibson.*
Picturesque Kent, by G. Thompson & sketches
by D. Moul.
F.E. Robinson & Company. 1901.
1,2,3,4,5,6,7,8,9,11,12,15,17,18,19,20,24,26.

THORNE, John.*
Kent: Chambers' Illustrated Guide & Souvenir.
W.&.R. Chambers Ltd. Edinburgh. (1949).
2,3,4,11,25.

THE TIMES.
A Dickens Pilgrimage.
J. Murray. 1914.
11.

TOURISTE.
(English-French-German edition of guide to Kent).
Gem Holdings Ltd. Chislehurst. (1978?).
3.

TURNOR, Reginald.*
Kent. (Vision of England Series).
Paul Elek. 1950.
1,2,3,4,5,6,7,8,9 11,12,13,14,15,16,17,18.21.

Kent. First published by Paul Elek in 1950.
John Hallewell, Rochester. 1978.
2,5,9,11,16,28.

South-East England.* Kent & Sussex,by R. Turner
& P.F. Gaye.
Elek Books. 1956.
1,3,4,5,8,9,11,12,14,15,25.

VULLIAMY, Laurence.
William Cobbett's rural rides revisited: a
photographic exploration.
Pierrot Publishers Ltd. London. 1977.
12,14.

WEBB, M.*
Viewing South-East England,
Napier Publications. 1978.
15.

WHAT'S ON AND WHERE IN KENT.
Rakell Ltd. Brighton. 1977.
11.

WHITBREAD & CO. LTD.*
Outings in Kent. (Lists Whitbread Inns).
Whitbread & Company Limited. n.d.
11,15.

WHITE, John Talbot.
A Country diary: Kent.
A.J. Cassell. Sheerness. 1974.
1,2,3,6,8,9,11,12,15,20,22.

The Countryman's Guide to the South-East.
Routledge and Kegan Paul. 1978.
2,3,5,7,11,12,30.

The Parklands of Kent.
A.J. Cassell,Sheerness. 1974.
1,2,3,4,5,6,7,8,9,11,15,16,22,28,30.

The South East Down and Weald: Kent, Surrey and
Sussex.
Eyre,Methuen. 1977
2,3,5,6,7,9,11,15,16,19.20,22,23,26,27,30

WIGHTMAN, Ralph.
Rural Rides.
(The Author covered Cobbetts' "Rides"
for a BBC Programme. pp.113-128,Kent).
Cassell. 1957.
11.

WINBOLT, Samuel Edward.*
Kent, Sussex & Surrey.
Penguin Books.
1939. 1,2,3,6,8,9,11,15.
1947. 4,7,11.

WYNDHAM, Richard.*
South-East England (Face of Britain Series).
Revised by Ronald Jessup.
Batsford. 1951.
3,8,11,12,18,24.

WYNDHAM, Richard.
South-Eastern Survey: a last look round
Sussex, Kent and Surrey.
Batsford. 1940.
1,2,4,6,8,9,11,13,15.

KENT-EAST

ABERCROMBIE, Sir Patrick.*
East Kent Regional planning scheme preliminary
survey, prepared for the Joint Town Planning
Committee of local authorities, by Sir P.
Abercrombie and J. Archibald.
Liverpool University Press & Hodder & Stoughton.
1925.
24,25,30.

East Kent Regional Planning Scheme, Final Report,
by Sir P. Abercrombie and J. Archibald.
Austens. 1928.
24.

BAILEY, Margaret.
Walks in the Forest of Blean. Fourteen walks
North & West of Canterbury, by M. Bailey and
A. Gray. 2nd edition.
Swale Footpaths Group. 1973.
4,12,19,20,30.

BLACK, Adam & Charles Publishers.*
Black's guide to Canterbury and the Watering
places of East Kent, edited by E.D. Jordan.
A.&.C. Black.
1901. 14th edition. 3,24.
1915. 11.
1921. 11.

BRIDGE-BLEAN RURAL DISTRICT COUNCIL.*
Official Guide of Bridge-Blean Rural District.
Home Publishing Company, Croydon.
1962. 4.
1968. 3.
1969. 30.
1972. 3,4,6.

CANTERBURY & THANET HEALTH DISTRICT:
KENT AREA HEALTH AUTHORITY.
District Plan, 1980 - 81.
Canterbury & Thanet Health District. 1979.
13.

CANTERBURY CITY COUNCIL.
Local Government re-organisation in England:
proposed County of East Kent.
Printed by A.&.J. Purchese. Bridge. n.d.
11.

CANTERBURY, WHITSTABLE & HERNE BAY SCOUT COUNCIL.
Directory, July 1974.
Canterbury, Whitstable & Herne Bay Scout Council.
1974.
3.

CATT, Andrew Robert.*
The East Kent Railway.
Oakwood Press. 1970.
2,4,7,12,26.

CHAMPION, George H.J.
Stonebridge walks:thirteen rambles from Faversham,
by G.H.J. Champion.
Swale Footpaths Group. 1973.
3,4,11,12,20.

Ten walks around Faversham,by G.H.J. Champion
and C.R. Theobald.*
Faversham Papers No.8.
Faversham Society & Swale Footpaths Group. 1971
2,3,6,8,11,12,30.

COLEMAN, Alice Mary.*
East Kent: a description of the Ordnance Survey
Seventh Edition One-inch Sheet 173. (British
landscape through maps), by Alice Mary Coleman
and Clare T. Lukehurst.
Geographical Association 1967.
2,3,4,6,20,23,24,30.

COLLYER, David G.
Battle of Britain Diary: East Kent July-
September 1940.
Kent Defence Research Group:Kent Aviation
Research Society. 1980.
13,28.

COOK, David.
The value & limitations of trade directories
between c.1840 and 1870. Source on the
nature & distribution of industrial activity
in East Kent. Photocopy of extended essay.197-?
University of Kent, Canterbury.
3.

CCOLING, Christine M.
Record of wells in the area of new series one-
inch (geological) Faversham (273) and Ramsgate
(274) sheets.
Geological Survey & Museum, Water Supply Papers:
Well Catalogue.
H.M.S.O. 1964.
11,20.

COOPER, Thomas Sidney.*
Views in Canterbury and its environs, drawn
from Nature and on stone. (Portfolio of
six engravings).
Westmead Press. 1972.
1,3.

COWELL, M.H.*
A Floral guide for East Kent etc. (with those
of Faversham).
Ratcliffe. Faversham. 1839.
1,3,5,6,7,9,11,13,15,17,26.

COX, W.J. Publisher.*
W.J. Cox's Guide to Whitstable and its surroundings.
W.J. Cox. Whitstable. 1876.
8,11,31.

W.J. Cox's illustrated popular guide to Whitstable-
on-Sea and the surrounding neighbourhood.
W.J. Cox. Whitstable. (1884?).
31.

(COZENS, Zechariah).*
A tour through the Isle of Thanet and some other
parts of East Kent, including a particular
description of the Churches....
Nichols.
1793. 3.4.12.
1795. 3.11.13.17.

DILNOT, Frank.*
The Lady Jean.
(Novel set in East Kent).
Brentano's. 1930.
6,11,12.

DORLING, M.J.*
East Kent Horticulture, by M.J. Dorling and
R.R.W. Folley.
(results from 6 holdings for 1953-1955).
Wye College. 1957.
3,8,11,12,19,21.

DUNNING, G.C.*
Neolithic occupation sites in East Kent.
In The Antiquaries Journal, Vol.46, Part I.
1966.
Oxford University Press. 1966.
4,11.

DWELLY, Edward.
Dwelly's Parish Records, Vol.3. Kent M.I.,
being the monumental inscriptions in the
parishes of Reculver-with-Hoath, Herne,
and Herne Bay with tricks of all the Armorial
Bearings and rubbings of the old brasses.
Published by E. Dwelly, Herne Bay. 1914.
3,11,15.

THE EAST KENT CRITIC.
1964 to date.   24.
1973;1975;1976;1977.   13.

EAST KENT JOINT COMMITTEE.
Annual report of the Medical Officer 1916-1919.
(Bound volume).
East Kent Joint Committee.
6.

EAST KENT ROAD CAR COMPANY, LTD.
Descriptive & pictorial guide to East Kent and
Rye, Winchelsea, and Hastings, with map & street
plans, edited by Alfred Baynton.
Produced for the East Kent Car Co Ltd. by
Cooks' Publicity Service.
1934.   2.
(1949)   7,11.
1952.   3.

Descriptive & Pictorial guide to the areas of
East Kent and part of Sussex served by the East
Kent Road Car Company Ltd.
John Langdon Ltd. Kensington. 1962.
11.

EASTRY RURAL DISTRICT COUNCIL.
Official guide of the Eastry Rural District.
Home Publishing Company. Croydon.
1971. Revised edn. 6.
1973. Commemorative edn. 4.6.

ENVIRONMENT, Deptartment of the
List of buildings of special architectural, or
historic interest; Eastry Rural District,
Dover Rural District. (Photocopy of the list
kept by Dover District Council:Planning Dept.).
6.

FAMOUS OLD INNS OF EAST KENT.
Hamilton-Fisher.
24.

FAUSSETT, Rev. Bryan (Rector of Monks Horton)*
Inventorium sepulchrale: an account of some
antiquities dug up at Gilton, Kingston,
Sibertswold, Barfriston, Beakesbourne, Chartham
& Crundale. AD1757 - AD1773.
Privately Printed for Subscribers. 1856.
1,3,4,5,6,7,8,11,12,13,15,17,25.

FIELD, Bartlett.
The Hooden Horse of East Kent.
B. Field. 1967.
7.

GREAT BRITAIN, Laws etc. (Geo.III).*
An Act for the more easy & speedy recovery of
small debts within the Town and Port of
Faversham...Boughton...Ospringe, Seasalter
and Whitstable. (Geo.III.25. Chap. VII).
Printed by C. Eyre & W. Strahan. (1785).
1,11,26.

HARDMAN, G.W.
East Kent Walks.
T.F. Pain, Sandwich & Deal. 1934.
11.

HAYES, Frederick W.
A Kent Squire: being a record of certain
adventures of Ambrose Gwynett, Esquire, of
Thornhaugh. (An Eighteenth Century novel set
in East Kent).
Hutchinson. 1900.
11.

HERNE BAY, CANTERBURY AND WHITSTABLE ELECTRICITY
GAZETTE. No.11. December 1963.
3.

HEYWOOD, John Publisher.*
John Heywood's illustrated guide to Herne Bay
and neighbourhood.
J. Heywood.
11, 17. n.d.
30. 1891;1903.

IGGLESDEN, Sir Charles.*
History of the East Kent Volunteers.
Kentish Express. Ashford. 1899.
1,2,3,4,6,7,8,11,12,14,15,17,24.

A saunter through Kent with pen and pencil.*
Vol.X (Nettlestead, Whitstable, Seasalter,
Swalecliffe, Graveney, Monks Horton, Harrietsham.
Kentish Express. (1914).
31.

INGOLDSBY, Thomas pseud. (Richard Harris
BARHAM, 1788-1845).
The Ingoldsby Legends.
Victorian Edn. R. Bentley & Son. 1882.   3.
      Warne. (190-)   2,4,
      Cassell 1908   4.

"INVICTA"
The Tramways of Kent. Vol.2. East Kent, edited
by G.E. Baddeley.
Light Railway Transport League. 1975.
1,2,3,5,6,7,8,12,13,15,20,22,25,26,27,28.

JACOB, J.*
Wild flowers, grasses & ferns of East Kent.
Dover Express & East Kent News. 1936.
24,26.

KENT, Joan pseud.
Wood smoke and pigeon pie.
(Country life in the Canterbury area).
Bailey Bros & Swinfen Ltd. Folkestone. 1977.
1,3,5,11,12,28,30.

KENT COUNTY COUNCIL.
Local Government Act 1958.   Review of Local
Government in East Kent.   2nd report of
Officers.
K.C.C. 1965.
13.

KENT COUNTY COUNCIL:PLANNING DEPARTMENT.
Kent Development Plan.
Sample Survey of households.
East Kent. 1968.
K.C.C. 1968.
Rural Areas.   7,11,13,20.
Urban Areas.   7,13,20,24.

KERSHAW, S. Wayland.
Foreign refugee settlements in East Kent.
Cross & Jackman. Canterbury. 1883.
11,26.

LAPWORTH, Herbert.*
Hydrogeological Survey:East Kent Water Supply.
Report, July 1st. 1930.
Austens, 1930.
3,7,11.

LONDON, CHATHAM AND NORTH KENT RAILWAY.
Canterbury, Ramsgate and Margate branch.
(Coloured plan of proposed line). London,
Chatham & North Kent Railway (1845), (Part
12 of the London to Dover Railway Plan).
11.

MILLWARD, Roy.
East Kent, by Roy Millward and Adrian Robinson.
Macmillan. 1973.
11.

NEWMAN & COMPANY Publishers
Thirty-two views of Canterbury & neighbourhood.
(Engravings).
Newman & Company. London. (c.1880).
11.

NEWMAN, John.
North-East and East Kent.
(The Buildings of England Series. No.39, edited
by N. Pevsner).
Penguin.
1969*. 2,3,4,5,7,8,9,11,12,19,21,24,25.28.
1976 2nd edn. 2.3.7.11.12.15.16.19.20.23.26.27.30

THE POST OFFICE.
Post Codes, Canterbury, Kent,& District.
The Post Office. 1973.
7.

SMALL, Julia.
The Hooden Horse: an East Kent Custom.
Deal Maritime & Local History Museum. (1975).
3.

SMART, J.G.O.
Geology of the country around Canterbury and
Folkestone, by J.G.O. Smart and others. (Combined
memoir in explanation of the one-inch Geological
Sheets 289,305,306-new series).
H.M.S.O.
1966. 1.2.3.4.5.6.7.8.9.10.11.14.15.16.19.24.30.
1975. 13.

SO, C.L.
Some coastal changes between Whitstable and
Reculver, Kent. In Proceedings of the Geologists'
Association. Vol. 77. pp.475-490. 1966.
30.

SOUTH EASTERN ELECTRICITY BOARD:CANTERBURY DISTRICT.
Annual Report for the years: 1973/74;1975/76;
1976/77.
South Eastern Electricity Board. Canterbury.
3.

SOUTH EASTERN ELECTRICITY BOARD:EAST KENT DISTRICT.
Annual Report for the year. 1977/78.
South Eastern Electricity Board. East Kent
District. 1978.
3.

STOUR VALLEY SOCIETY.
Stour Valley Walks. Folder No.1.
Stour Valley Society. 1974.
3.

SUMMERS, Dorothy.
East Kent Floods.
David & Charles. 1979.
4,9,11.28.

SWALE FOOTPATHS GROUP.
Five walks near Selling: a selection of County
Walks on individual cards.
Swale Footpaths Group/K.C.C. 1977.
3,11.

THORPE, Teresa.*
The development of the coastline between
Hampton Pier and Reculver at Herne Bay.
Photocopy of Thesis. 1970.
11,30.

TWYMAN, Frank.*
An East Kent Family.
F. Twyman. 1956.
1,3,4,6,7,8,11,14,15,17,23.

UNIVERSITY OF KENT:CENTRE FOR RESEARCH IN THE
SOCIAL SCIENCES.
Basic data on East Kent, by Eileen Mitchelhill.
University of Kent. Canterbury. 1977.
3.

WARD LOCK & CO. LTD. Publishers.*
A Pictorial & Descriptive Guide to Broadstairs,
Margate, Ramsgate, Herne Bay, Canterbury &
North East Kent. (Various permutations of
title from 1899 - 1965).
Ward Lock & Co. Ltd.
1915. 2.
1922. 7th revised edition.30.
1926. 8th edition 30.
c.1929.   13.
1932. 9th edition 2.
1946. 10th edition 2.3.
(1950). 11th edition 2.24.

WEINER, J. Ltd. Publisher
Canterbury & District Green Guide. (Weiner's
Neighbourhood Guides).
J. Weiner Ltd. 1968.
30.

WHITE, H.J.O.*
Geology of the Country near Ramsgate and Dover.
H.M.S.O. 1928.
1,6,7,11,13,14,17.

KENT - MID.

ABBEY PUBLICITY SERVICES LTD.
Mid-Kent twixt Wrotham and Headcorn.
Abbey Publicity. Croydon. (1939).
12.

BRITON, D.A.
Summer wanderings in the neighbourhood of
Maidstone, Kent. Containing accounts of Allington,
Aylesford, Boughton Monchensie, Boxley, Cosington,
Kits-Coty House, Leeds, Maidstone, Otham,
Paddlesworth, Snodland etc.
Printed by J. Jacques, High St. Newington. 1829.
11.

CHEESEMAN, Clive.
On foot around Maidstone, compiled by C.Cheeseman,
John Hill & David Thornewell.
Burham Hilt Services for the Ramblers'Association.
1974.
11,12,15,25.

3rd edn. Larkfield Hilt Services for the
Ramblers' Association, 1978.
12.

DAVIS, Cyril.
Walks on the North Downs:Hollingbourne to the
Medway, by C. Davis and A. Gray.
Swale Footpaths Group. 1974.
8.

DEXTER, Walter.*
Mr. Pickwick's Pilgrimages.
Chapman & Hall. 1926.
6,8,11,17,19.

ENVIRONMENT, Department of
List of buildings of special architectural
or historic interest:District of Maidstone.
H.M.S.O. 1974.
11,12.

ENVIRONMENT, Department of the
Mid Kent Town Maps - Medway Gap Town Map;
Medway Towns Town Map; Maidstone & Vicinity
Town Map. The Secretary of State for the
Environment statementof reasons for
departing from Inspectors' recommendations.
Department of the Environment. (1978?).
4.

ESTATE PUBLICATIONS.
Maidstone Area (Maps).
Estate Publications.   1979.
4.

GREEN & CO. Publishers.
Green's Mid Kent Court Guide,gazeteer and
County Blue Book: a fashionable register
and general survey of the county,
with delineations, topographical,
historical and descriptive.
Green & Co. 1874.
11.

HALES, Irene.
Villages around old Maidstone: a selection of
postcards from the early years of this century.
Meresborough Books. Rainham. 1980.
12.

HOUSING & LOCAL GOVERNMENT, Ministry of.
Provisional List of buildings of Architectural
or historic interest.
Maidstone Borough & Maidstone Rural District.
H.M.S.O. 1949 and 1960.
12.

ILLUSTRATED PARTICULARS, CONDITIONS AND PLAN OF
....the residential sporting and agricultural
estate known as Addington Park situate in the
parishes of Addington, Trottiscliffe, Offham,
Ryarsh, Wrotham, Leybourne and West Malling.
....about 2,404 acres.
Knight, Frank & Rutley, Auctioneers. 1923.
11.

KELLY'S DIRECTORIES LTD.
Kelly's Directory of Maidstone and neighbourhood,
1973 - 74. 17th edition.
Kelly's Directories. 1974.
11,12.

KENT COUNTY COUNCIL - PLANNING DEP
Kent County Structure Plan.
Strategic Issues: Planning Area 2. Mid & North
West Kent. (Serial No. 11B).
K.C.C. 1975.
3,4,9,13,16.

KENT COUNTY COUNCIL - PLANNING DEPARTMENT
Kent Development Plan. (1967 Revision).
Maidstone & Vicinity and Medway Gap Town Maps.
Report on the survey and analysis.
K.C.C. 1970.
11,12.

Kent Development Plan. (1967 Revision).
Maidstone & Vicinity Town Map. Amendment to
Written Statement, approved by the Planning
Committee on 12th November, 1970.
K.C.C. 1970.
11,12.

Kent Development Plan (1967 Revision).
Medway Gap Town Map.
Amendment to Written statement.
K.C.C. 1970.
8,11,12.

Kent Development Plan (1967 Revision). Medway
Towns, Maidstone & Vicinity & Medway Gap Town
Maps. Report on population and employment studies
in Mid-Kent. Analysis of Shopping Centres
in Mid-Kent.
K.C.C. 1970.
8,11,12,25.

Kent Development Plan: Sample survey of households, Mid-Kent, 1971. Vol.1.
(Maidstone & Medway Gap).
K.C.C. 1975.
11,12.

Kent Development Plan: Town & Country Planning
Acts 1962-1971. Public local inquiry into
objections and representations concerning
the Kent County Development Plan.Maidstone and
Vicinity Town Map - Medway Gap Town maps...
held at County Hall, Maidstone & Town Hall,
Chatham. 12th October 1971 to 30th March,1972.
K.C.C. (1978).
4.

"KENT MESSENGER" DIRECTORY OF MAIDSTONE and
the Surrounding Villages.
1927-8. 24th edn. Kent Messenger. (1927). 11.
1930-31.   Kent Messenger. (1930). 11.
1937 - 38.   Kent Messenger. 1937. 11.

MAIDSTONE RURAL DISTRICT COUNCIL.
The Official Guide of Maidstone Rural District.
Home Publishing Company. Croydon.
1972.   12.
1973.   19.

MALLING RURAL DISTRICT COUNCIL.*
Official Guide of the Malling Rural District.
Home Publishing Company. Croydon.
1957;1960;1961.   4.
1973;1974.   7.

MALLING RURAL DISTRICT COUNCIL -PUBLIC HEALTH
DEPARTMENT.
Annual Report on the health of the Malling
District for the year 1972.
Malling Rural District Council. 1972.
11.

MUGGERIDGE, Sidney John.*
The Postal history of Maidstone and the
surrounding villages with notes on their
postal markings.
Postal History Society. 1972.
3,4,6,7,8,9,11.

ROW, B. Prescott.
Kent's Capital: a handbook to Maidstone on the
Medway and a guide to the district, by B.
Prescott Row and W.S. Martin. 2nd edition.
(Homeland Association's Handbooks No.6.)
Ruck, Maidstone.   London. 1899.
12.

SMITH, Alan.
North Downs Walks:Doddington and Lenham.
14 Downland Walks between Harrietsham and Charing.
Edited by Alan Smith, with illustrations by
May Gardiner.
Swale Footpaths Group. 1973.
3,4,6,11,12.

KENT-MID. Cont'd

SMITH, J.*
Topography of Maidstone and its environs...
J. Smith. 1839.
1,8,17.

SOUTH EASTERN ELECTRICITY BOARD:MAIDSTONE
DISTRICT.
Annual Report. 1974/75.
12.

SWALE FOOTPATHS GROUP.
Five Walks between Chatham and Maidstone:
A selection of country walks on individual
cards.
Swale Footpaths Group/K.C.C. 1977.
11.

Five Walks near Boughton: a selection of
country walks on individual cards.
Swale Footpaths Group/K.C.C. 1977.
3,11.

TONBRIDGE AND MALLING DISTRICT COUNCIL.
Medway Gap district Centre Study.
Tonbridge and Malling District Council.
August. 1979.
4,23.

The Official Guide of Tonbridge and Malling
District.
Home Publishing Company,Croydon/Wallington..
1976. 7,20.
1977. 3,11.
1978. 3.
1979. 4.12.

WORSSAM, Bernard Charles.*
Geology of the country around Maidstone.
(Explanation of the One-inch Geological Sheet
288 - new series).
H.M.S.O. 1963.
1,3,4,5,6,7,8,11,12,15,16,17,19,25.

YALDING & NETTLESTEAD PRESERVATION SOCIETY.
Local Walks, Set I and Set II.
(Cards, each describing a local Country Walk-
Linton, Yalding, Wateringbury, Hunton,
Nettlestead etc.).
Yalding & Nettlestead Preservation Society. 1977.
11,12.

KENT - NORTH

ARNOLD, Ralph.*
The Coronation Book...written for Strood Rural
District Council.
Constable. 1953.
9,11.

BOORMAN, L.A.
Ecology of Maplin Sands and the coastal zones of
Suffolk, Essex and North Kent, by L.A. Boorman
and D.S. Ranwell, Institute of Terrestrial
Ecology.
Institute of Terrestrial Ecology,Natural
Environmental Research Council. 1977.
3,4,11.

CHAMPION, Mrs. I.K.
Natural history in the Rochester area, edited
by Mrs. I.K. Champion and Miss E.E. Floodgate.
Published to mark the Centenary of the Society
by Meresborough Books, Rainham. 1977.
1,2,3,4,8,11,12,15,25.

KIDNER, Roger Wakely.
The North Kent Line. Locomotion Papers 104.
Oakwood Press/ 1977.
1,2,4,5,6,8,11,12,15,16,18,23,25,28.

MEASOM, George.*
The Official illustrated guide to the South-
Eastern railway and its branches including
the North Kent and Greenwich lines.
(Facsimile of 1858 edition).
E.&.W. Books. 1970.
3,4,5,6,7,8,12,14,15,17,18,30

NEWELL, G.E.
Animal zones of the North Kent Coast.
In South Eastern Naturalist and Antiquary
Vol.59. 1954.
South Eastern Union of Scientific Society.1954.
11.

OFFICE OF POPULATION, CENSUSES AND SURVEYS.
Census 1971. Small area statistics,
Ward and Civil Parish Lists for the Medway Area.
(Includes, Rochester, Chatham and Strood Rural
District).
H.M.S.O. 1971.
15.

TOWN & COUNTY DIRECTORIES.
Margate, Ramsgate and N. Kent District trades
directory.
Town & County Directories. 1927 - 28.
24.

YOUNG, Arthur.
A six weeks tour through the Southern Counties
of England & Wales....2nd edition corrected...
by W. Strahan. (North Kent Farming mentioned
in Letter 3.).
W. Nicoll. London. 1769.
11.

KENT, NORTH-EAST.

BAKER, Dennis.*
The marketing of corn in the first half of the
eighteenth century:North-east Kent.
An offprint from The Agricultural History
Review Vol.18. Part II. 1970. pp.126-150.
British Agricultural History Society. 1970.
3,11.

COOLING, Christine M.
Record of wells in the area of Chatham.
(Explanation of the one-inch geological sheet
272 - New Series).
H.M.S.O. 1964.
20.

DAVIS, Cyril.
Ten walks from Bredhurst.by C. Davis.
Swale Footpaths Group. 1972.
4,8,11,12.

DINES, H.G.*
Geology of the Country around Chatham, by
H.G. Dines and others.
(Explanation of one-inch Geological Sheet
272, New Series).
H.M.S.O. 1954.
1,2,4,5,6,8,9,11,12,15,16,19,20,25,26,27.

Geology of the Country around Chatham.*
(Explanation of the one-inch Geological Sheet
272 - New Series). 1954 edition reprinted with
amendments by H.G. Dines and others.
H.M.S.O. 1971.
1,2,4,5,6,7,9,11,12,13,19,20,26,27.

FORDHAM, S.J.
Soils in Kent III. Sheet TQ86 (Rainham), by
S.J. Fordham and R.D. Green.
Soil Survey Record No.37.
Soil Survey of Great Britain Rothamsted
Experimental Station. Harpenden. 1976.
8,11,20.

HOLLINGBOURNE RURAL DISTRICT COUNCIL.*
Official Guide of Hollingbourne Rural District.
1959 & 1961. Home Publishing Coy.Croydon.   4.
1964;1967;1970. British Publishing Coy.Ltd.
                    Gloucester.   4.

KENT, Joan pseud.
Binder Twine and rabbit stew. (A country
childhood in the 1930s spent in the Sittingbourne
area).
Bailey & Swinfen Ltd. Folkestone. 1976.
1,3,5,8,11,20,28,30.

KENT COUNTY COUNCIL:EDUCATION DEPARTMENT.
NORTH EAST KENT DIVISION.
Opportunities in Secondary Education.
February 1974.
Kent County Council, 1974.
20.

Secondary Education in the Sittingbourne Area.
Kent County Council, 1974.
20.

KENT COUNTY COUNCIL:PLANNING DEPARTMENT.
Kent County Structure Plan.
Future development possibilities in Kent,
the Medway Towns, Sittingbourne and Sheppey.
(Serial No. E4B).
K.C.C. December. 1975.
4.

Kent County structure plan. Strategic issues.
Planning area 19:North-East Kent. (Serial No.13B).
K.C.C. 1975.
3,4,9,11,13,16.

Kent Development Plan. Sample Survey of households. Mid Kent 1971. Vol.2. Medway and Swale.
K.C.C. (1971?).
4,11,15,20.

The Swale:Coastal and Countryside plan:draft.
K.C.C. 1974.
20.

The Swale:coastal and countryside plan.
A report upon the natural resources of The Swale
and the activities within the area, which could
form the basis for an Informal Local Plan.
Approved by the K.C.C. as Local Planning
Authority on the 14th February 1974 for the
purpose of public consultations.
K.C.C. 1974.
11.

MAIDSTONE & DISTRICT MOTOR SERVICES LTD.
Timetable, Area No.4. Swale, 12th June, 1977
until further notice.
Maidstone & District Motor Services Ltd. 1977.
11.

MARCHINGTON, Trevor.
Studies in South-East England, by Trevor
Marchington and Brian P. Price.
(pp.55-65 North East Kent). School Textbook.
Oxford University Press. 1973.
6,11,19.

MASON, L.*
Wanderings in North East Kent.
Herne Bay Press Ltd. 1961.
30.

NEWMAN, John.
North East and East Kent.
(The Buildings of England Series No.39, edited
by N. Pevsner).
Penguin.
1969.* 2,3,4,5,7,8,9,11,12,19,21,24,25,28.
1976. 2nd edn. 2.3.7.11.12.15.16.19.20.23.26.
27,30.

NORTH EAST KENT ECONOMIC DEVELOPMENT COMMITTEE.
Why East Kent? a guide for potential developers
of new factories, offices, warehouses.
North East Kent Economic Development Committee.1971.
11.

NORTH-EAST KENT JOINT TOWN PLANNING COMMITTEE.*
North-East Kent regional planning scheme.
Report prepared for the North-East Kent Joint
Town Planning Committee by Adams, Thompson
& Fry. Chatham. 1930.
2,4,8,11,12,13,14,15,25.

PAYNE. George.*
Collectanea Cantiana; or archaeological researches
in the neighbourhood of Sittingbourne.
Mitchell & Hughes. 1893.
1,2,3,4,5,6,8,11,12,14,15,17,18,20,25.

PEARMAN, Harry.*
Deneholes and kindred phenomena. Records
of the Chelsea Spelaeological Society. Vol.4. 1966.
The Chelsea Spelaeological Society. 1966.
1,2,3,4,5,7,8,9,11,15,24,25,30.

PUGH, Christine.*
Stockbury:a regional study in North-East Kent,
by C. Pugh and G.E. Hutchings.
The Hill Farm, Stockbury. 1928.
2,3,4,5,7,8,11,12,15,20,21.

SITTINGBOURNE & SWALE ARCHAEOLOGICAL RESEARCH GROUP.
SARG: journal of the Sittingbourne and Swale
Archaeological Research Group. No.1.
(Duplicated pamphlet).
Sittingbourne & Swale Archaeological Research
Group. 1974.
11.

SPURRELL, F.C.J.
Early sites and embankments on the Margins of
the Thames Estuary. Reprinted from the
Archaeological Journal Vol.XL11. c.1886.
9.

The Same. Anglebooks. 1973.
1.

SWALE DISTRICT COUNCIL.
Handbook 1974 - 76.
Swale District Council. 1974.
20.

Swale District Council Review.
Kent Evening Post. Chatham. 1977.
3.

Swale Guide: the official guide to the area
of North Kent administered by Swale District
Council.
Swale District Council. January, 1977.
11,20,26,27.

Your Council and your Councillors.
(Information Service).
Swale District Council. 1975.
11.20.

SWALE FOOTPATHS GROUP.
Five walks East of Faversham: a selection
of country walks on individual cards.
Swale Footpaths Group/K.C.C. 1977.
3,11.

Five walks east of Sittingbourne: a selection
of country walks on individual cards.
Swale Footpaths Group/K.C.C. 1977.
3,11.

Five walks near Newington: a selection of
country walks on individual cards.
Swale Footpaths Group/K.C.C. 1977.
3,11.

Five walks near Rainham: a selection of
country walks on individual cards.
Swale Footpaths Group/K.C.C. 1976.
3,11.

Five walks near Teynham: a selection of
country walks on individual cards.
Swale Footpaths Group/K.C.C. 1977.
3,11.

Five walks South of Faversham: a selection
of country walks on individual cards.
Swale Footpaths Group/K.C.C. 1977.
3,11.

Five walks South of Sittingbourne:a selection of
country walks on individual cards.
Swale Footpaths Group/K.C.C. 1977.
3,11.

SWALE FOOTPATHS GROUP.
Five walks West of Faversham: a selection
of country walks on individual cards.
Swale Footpaths Group/K.C.C. 1976.
3,11.

Five walks West of Sittingbourne: a selection
of country walks on individual cards.
Swale Footpaths Group/K.C.C. 1977.
3.

SWALE RURAL DISTRICT COUNCIL
Annual report of the Medical Officer of
Health for 1972.
Swale Rural District Council. 1972.
11.

Official Guide of Swale Rural District.
Home Publishing Company. Croydon.
1960. 20.
(1969?).20.
1973. 74th edition. 4.7,11.

WARD LOCK & CO. LTD. Publishers.*
A Pictorial & Descriptive Guide to
Broadstairs, Ramsgate, Margate, Herne Bay,
Canterbury & North East Kent.
(Various permutations of title from
1899 - 1965).
Ward Lock & Co. Ltd.
1915   2.
1922. 7th rev. edn.   30.
1926. 8th edn.   30.
c 1929.   13.

KENT, NORTH-WEST

BEADLE, D.
Portland Cement in the making.
(Associated Portland Cement Manufacturers
connections in North-West Kent).
Cement and Concrete Association. Slouth. 1977.
5.

BOLTON, D.
Nature Trails:Meopham and Culverstone.
Written and illustrated by D. Bolton & D.P. Chubb.
(Meopham & District Footpaths Group).
Meopham Publications Committee. 1973.
9,11.

BUTLER, Susan, later Mrs. Goddard.
A description & explanation of variations in
"residential desirability"...in part of the
South-East London Suburbs. (Photocopy
of typescript. Dissertation for B.Sc. Special
Honours Degree, Sheffield University, 1968).
Area Covered:Bromley, Chislehurst, Sidcup,
Bexley, Blackfen.
2

CARLEY, James.*
The lost roads of Meopham and nearby parishes.
Meopham Publications Committee. 1971.
25.

CARLEY, John M.
Byways and bridleways in Meopham and nearby
parishes: a map for riders.
Meopham Publications Committee. 1972.
9.

CHETWYND, Richard Walter.
The environs of London: a guide for team and
cycle, by R.W. Chetwynd and others.
Kegan Paul, Trench, Trubner and Co. 1897.
1.

CONNOR, James Edward.
Forgotten stations of Greater London, by J.E.
Connor & B.L. Halford.   New edn.
Forge Books. 1978.
11.

CROOK, Diane K.
The development of technical education on Thames-
side from Erith to Gravesend, and its relationship to the needs of the local community,
1890-1914. Typescript.
History Special Exercise (Dartford College
of Education). 1977.
5,9.

CROSSICK, Geoffrey.
An artisan elite in Victorian Society:
Kentish London 1840 - 1880.
Croom Helm.   1978.
2,11.

DANIEL, C. St. J.H.
Sundials:the common vertical in North-West Kent.
Institute of Craft Education.   1973.
5.

DANIELL, Philip A.
Country walks around Bromley, Downe & Biggin
Hill.
Circle Publications. Ilford.   1976.
2,11.

DARTFORD CONSITUENCY CONSERVATIVE ASSOCIATION.
Dartford:town and rural.
Conservative Association. Dartford. 1978.
5.

DEWEY, Henry.*
Geology of the Country around Dartford.
(Explanation of the one-inch Geological
Sheet 271), by H. Dewey, C.E.N. Bromehead,
C.P. Chatwin and H.G. Dines.
H.M.S.O. 1924.
1,4,5,8,9,11,12,15,17,18,19.

DEXTER, Walter.*
Mr. Pickwick's pilgrimages.
Chapman & Hall. 1926.
6,8,11,19.

ELLIS. Harry.
London tramway memories. New Cross and Holloway
Depots, 1946 - 1952. The Author worked on the
trams, 1946 - 1952. The routes extended to North
West Kent.
Light Railway Transport League.
32 Church Road West, Farnborough. 1975.
11.

ELLISTON-ERWOOD, Frank Charles.*
Roman antiquities of North West Kent with
special reference to the site of Noviomagus...
with an account of the excavations at Joyden's
Wood, Bexley...1926-27. From "Journal of the
British Archaeological Association. Vol. XXXIV. 1928.
(Bound with The Earthworks at Charlton).
2,11.

FARRIES, Kenneth G.
The Windmills of Surrey and Inner London, by
K.G. Farries and M.T. Mason.
Skilton. 1966.
1.

FLETCHER, Benton.*
Royal homes near London.
Bodley Head. 1930.
5,17,18.

GEOLOGICAL SURVEY OF ENGLAND AND WALES.
Geology of the country around Dorking.
Fascimile Reprint.
HMSO/University Microfilms. (1924).
2.

GREEN, Frank.
London Suburbs: old and new.
Souvenir. 1933.
1.

HALL, Hammond.*
Mr. Pickwick's Kent: a photographic record of
the tour of the corresponding Society of the
Pickwick Club in Rochester, Chatham, Muggleton,
Dingley Dell, Cobham and Gravesend.
MacKay & Company. 1899.
25.

HARPER, Charles George.*
Motor runs round London. (South of the Thames).
Edward J. Burrow. 1930.
8.

HARVEY, Betty Ida.
Records of wells in the area around Dartford:
inventory for one-inch geological sheet 271,
by B.I. Harvey and others. (Institute of
Geological Sciences, Well Inventory Series:Metric
Units).
H.M.S.O. 1975.
1,2,9,11,23.

KENT, NORTH WEST.   Cont'd

HARVIE, K.G.
The Tramways of South London and Croydon-
1899-1949. 5th edition.
London Borough of Lewisham. 1975.
1,11,18.

JACKSON, Alan A.
Semi-detached London. Suburban development,
life and transport, 1900 - 1939.
Allen & Unwin. 1973.
18.

KELLY'S DIRECTORIES LTD. Publisher.
Kelly's Directory of Beckenham, Penge and
Neighbourhood. 43rd edition.
Kelly's Directories Ltd. 1938.
11.

KENT COUNTY COUNCIL:EDUCATION DEP
North West Kent College of Technology.
Prospectus. 1974-75.
The College is situated at Dartford &
Gravesend.
K.C.C. 1974.
11.

KENT COUNTY COUNCIL - EDUCATION DEPARTMENT.
THAMESIDE DIVISIONAL EXECUTIVE.
Thameside Division re-organisation of
Secondary education.
K.C.C. 1973.
9.

KENT COUNTY COUNCIL-HIGHWAYS & TRANSPORTATION DEPT.
North-West Kent Transportation Study.
Report on Surveys.
K.C.C. 1977.
5,9.

KENT COUNTY COUNCIL:PLANNING DEP
Kent County structure plan. Strategic issues.
Planning Area 2: Mid and North-West Kent.
(Serial no. 116).
K.C.C. 1975.
3,4,9,13,16.

Kent Development Plan:sample Survey of Households: North West Kent. 1968.
K.C.C. 1968.
4,8,11,16.25.

Kent Development Plan.* (1967 Revision).
North West Kent draft Town Map:draft explanatory
report and written statement.
K.C.C. 1971.
11.

Kent Development Plan (1967 Revision).
North West Kent Town Map. Amendment to
written statement.
K.C.C. 1972.
16.

Kent Development Plan (1967 Revision). North
West Kent Town Map. Report of Survey and
Analysis.
K.C.C. 1972.
11,16.

KNIGHT-SWEENEY, Brian.
A tour from Meopham.
Meopham Publications Committee. 1973.
9,11.

LONDON COUNTRY BUS SERVICES.
The vital link in danger, London Country
Green Line: a special report on the problems
facing London Country Bus Services.
London Country Bus Services. Reigate. (1975).
11.

LONDON NATURAL HISTORY SOCIETY.
The London naturalist. Nos. 48 - 50: 1968 -
70.
The London Bird Report Nos. 32-36, 1967-71.
London Natural History Society.
1965 - 1972.
5.

MARTIN, J.E.
Greater London: an industrial geography.
G. Bell. 1966.
1.

MATTHEWS, Brian.*
A History of Strood Rural District.
Strood Rural District Council. 1971.
2,3,4,12,25.
1. 1971 and 1976.

MATZ, B.W.
Dickensian Inns and Taverns.
1922.
4,8.

Inns & taverns of "Pickwick", with some
observations on their other associations.
Palmer. London. 1921.
1,3,4,5,8,9,12,15,25.

MAXWELL, Gordon S.
The Fringe of London...illustrated by
Donald Maxwell.
Palmer. 1925.
4.

Just beyond London:home travellers' tales...
illustrated by Donald Maxwell.
(Donald Maxwell lived in Rochester & East
Farleigh).
Methuen. 1927.
4.

MEOPHAM & DISTRICT FOOTPATHS GROUP.
Six walks from Cobham. 1971.
Meopham Publications Committee.
9.

Six walks from Harvel. 1971.
Meopham Publications Committee.
9,11.

Six walks from Hodsoll Street. (197-?).
Meopham Publications Committee.
11.

Six walks from Meopham Church & Camer. 1974.
Meopham Publications Committee.
11.

Six walks from Meopham Green. 1970.
Meopham Publications Committee.
11.

Six walks from Nurstead & Istead Rise. (197-?).
Meopham Publications Committee.
11.

Six walks from Shipbourne. 1978.
Meopham Publications Committee.
9.

Six walks from Shorne. 1974.
Meopham Publications Committee.
11.

Six walks from Trosley Country Park. 1978.
Meopham Publications Committee.
9,11.

Twenty miles round Meopham. (A footpath walk).
1975.
Meopham Publications Committee.
9.

The "Wealdway": a walkers' route from the Thames
to the English Channel. Section 1. Gravesend
to Tonbridge.
Meopham Publications Committee. 1973.
9.11.

MILLWARD, Roy.*
South-East England: Thameside and the Weald,
by R. Millward and A. Robinson. (Landscapes
of Britain).
Macmillan. 1971.
2,11,16.

The Hoo Peninsula and the Scarplands of Mid-
West Kent, by R. Millward and A. Robinson.
Macmillan. 1971.
4,6,8,11.

KENT, NORTH-WEST Cont'd

MILLWARD, Roy.*
Lower Thameside, by R. Millward & A.Robinson.
Macmillan, 1971.
4,5,8,11.

MONTIER, David J.
Atlas of breeding birds of the London area,
edited by D.J. Montier.
Batsford. 1977.
5.

NAIL, Martin.
The coal duties of the City of London and
their boundary marks.
Note:the boundary was through Downe and
Orpington.
M. Nail. 1972.
2,9.

PEARMAN, Harry. *
Deneholes and kindred phenomena. Records of
the Chelsea Speleaological Society. Vol.4.
1966.
Chelsea Speleaological Society. 1966.
1,2,3,4,5,7,8,9,11,15,19,24,25,30.

PHIPPEN, James.
The Road guide from London to Tunbridge Wells,
through Lewisham, Bromley, Farnborough,
Sevenoaks, Tunbridge...
Joseph Thomas. 1836.
11,19.

PITCHER, Wallace Spencer.*
The London Region (South of the Thames).
(Geologists' Association Guides No.30).
Benham & Co. Colchester. 1958.
4,12,17.

The London Region (South of the Thames),
(Geologists' Association Guides No.30B)
by W.S. Pitcher and others. Revised edition.
Benham & Co. Colchester. 1967.
2,3,4,9,11,20.

PRYCE, H. and Son. Publishers.*
Views of Woolwich and Neighbourhood.
H.Pryce & Son. Woolwich. (c.1900).
1,11.

REDSHAW, Charles T.*
Dartford and neighbourhood.
Snowden Bros. Dartford. 1911?.
1,5,11,15,17,25.

SHAW, K.D.
Short history of Gramophone Society activities
in South East London and North-West Kent...
(typescript). 1974.
2.

SHERLOCK, R.L.*
London and the Thames Valley.
(British Regional Geology).
H.M.S.O.
1947. 2nd edn. 4,9,19.
1962. 3rd edn. 2,5,8,16.

"A SON OF THE MARSHES", pseud.
Within an hour of London town,among wild birds
and their haunts; edited by J.A. Owen.
Blackwood. 1892.
11,20.

SOUTHWARK CATHOLIC DIRECTORY.
Pyramid Press for Southwark Catholic Children's
Society.
Forty-Seventh Annual Publication 1975.   11.
Forth-eighth Annual Publication 1976.   11.
Fiftieth   Annual Publication 1978.   3.
Fifty First Annual Publication 1979.   3.

STROOD RURAL DISTRICT COUNCIL.
Review of Council Services.
Strood Rural District Council. 1969.
11.

UNWIN, T. Fisher. Publisher.*
Round Bromley & Keston:a handy guide to rambles
in the district.
T.Fisher Unwin. n.d.
2,11,17.

WILLIAMS, Guy R.
London in the Country:the Growth of Suburbia.
Hamish Hamilton. 1975.
18.

WILLIAMS, Harry.
South London.
Hale. 1949.
11.

WILLIS, Peter J.
Gravesend round and about, 6th edition,
compiled by Peter J. Willis.
Gravesend Public Library. 1973.
11.

Gravesend round and about.
Kent County Library, Gravesham Division.
11.   1976 and 1977.
13.   1976.

WILLOUGHBY, D.W.
Trams in South-East London,by D.W. Willoughby
and E.R. Oakley.
D.W. Willoughby & E.R. Oakley. 1977.
5.

WITTON, A.M.
Buses of South-East England. (Fleetbook No.11),
edited by A.M. Witton and R.L. Telfer.
A.M. Witton. Manchester. 1977.
3,6,11,25.

KENT, SOUTH

MILLWARD, Roy.*
South-East England - the Channel Coastlands, by
R. Millward and A. Robinson.
Macmillan. 1973.
11.

SMITH, Gerard Edwards.*
Catalogue of rare, or remarkable phaenogamous
plants collected in South Kent...with descriptive
notices.
Longman. 1829.
1,2,6,7,11,12,15,17,19.

KENT, SOUTH-EAST

AMOS, J. Publisher.
Amos's Guide to Dover and its vicinity.
J. Amos. Biggin Street, Dover. (1887).
11.

COOK, Raymond A.*
Shell-fire corner carries on: a graphic
description of the war's events at England's
gateway.
R.A. Cook. Printed by Headley Bros. Ashford. 1942.
3,6,7,11.

CROSS CHANNEL GUNS.
In "After the Battle" No.29 1980. (Articles on
the heavy guns stationed on the cliffs near
Dover during World War II).
Battle of Britain Prints International Ltd.
6,28.

DOVER DISTRICT COUNCIL.
Environmental Health Department. Annual
Report 1975-6.
Dover District Council.(1977)
6.

Official Guide of Dover District, produced by
the Leisure and Recreational Department of the
Dover District Council. 1975.
6.

DOVER RURAL DISTRICT COUNCIL.
Official Guide of Dover Rural District.
British Publishing Company, Gloucester.
1972.   6.   1973.   4,6,7.

DREW, Frederick.*
Geology of the country between Folkestone and
Rye, including the whole of Romney Marsh.
Longman,Green,Longman,Roberts and Green. 1864.
11.

EAST ASHFORD RURAL DISTRICT COUNCIL.
Annual report of the Public Health Inspector
for the year 1972.
East Ashford Rural District Council. 1972.
11.

175

EAST ASHFORD RURAL DISTRICT COUNCIL
Official Guide of East Ashford Rural District.
Century Press Ltd.
(194-?). 11.
(1952)   7.

ELHAM RURAL DISTRICT COUNCIL.
Official Guide of the Elham Rural District.
1960; 1962; 1973. 4.
1974. Commemorative ed

EMBRY, Bernard.*
The Butterflies and Moths found in the Dover
and Deal district of Kent, by B. Embry and
G.H. Youden.
Buckland Association Press. 1949.
2.

ENVIRONMENT, Department of the
The Channel Tunnel project - extracts from a
Report on the economic and social impact of
the Tunnel on Kent (i.e. on the Ashford area).
By Economic Consultants Ltd. with the
Shankland/Cox Partnership. 1973.
2,4,6,7,9,19.

List of buildings of special architectural or
historic interest: District of Shepway, Kent.
Folkestone Area.
H.M.S.O.
11.

List of buildings of special architectural or
historic interest: Eastry Rural District,
Dover Rural District.
(Photocopy of list kept by Dover District
Council Planning Department).
6.

FIFTEEN WALKS AROUND FOLKESTONE.
McNerlin Hughes Associates. 1973.
11.

FORDHAM, S.J.
Soils in Kent II. Sheet TR35 (Deal)
by S.J. Fordham and R.D. Green.
Soil Survey Record No.15.
Harpenden Soil Survey of G.B. Rothamsted
Experimental Station. 1973.
2,4,6,7,11,24.

FORWOOD, Michael J.
Elham Valley Railway.
Phillimore. 1975.
1,3,5,6,7,8,11,12,13,15,22.

FRANKS, E.
Draft of a paper written for the Rev. S.D.
Scammell on the history of coal mining,
with particular reference to wages...with...
cuttings about the prospecting for coal
in the Dover area. 1890.
MS. 1882-3.
4.

GREAT BRITAIN. Laws etc. (Geo.III).*
An Act for the more easy and speedy recovery
of small debts within the town and port of
Dover, and the parishes of Charlton,
Buckland, River, Ewell, Lydden, Coldred,
East Langdon, Ringwould, St.Margaret's-at-Cliffe,
Whitfield, Guston, Hougham, otherwise Huffam,
Capel-le-Ferne and Alkham and also the
Liberty of Dover Castle.
Printed by Eyre & Strahan. 1784.
6,11.

GREEN, R.D.
Soils in Kent I. Sheet TR04. (Ashford) by
R.D. Green and S.J. Fordham. Soil Survey Record
No.14.
Harpenden Soil Survey of Great Britain.
Rothamsted Experimental Station. 1973.
2,4,6,7,11,19,24.

HEADLEY BROS. Publishers
Headleys' Directory of Ashford & District.
2nd edition.
Headley Bros. Invicta Press. Ashford. 1933.
11.
11. As above but 1938/9.

HEADLEY BROS. Publishers.*
Headley's Guide to Ashford & District illustrated:
issued under the auspices of the Ashford Chamber
of Commerce.
Headley Bros. Invicta Press. Ashford. 1900,1931 etc.
1,3,4,7,11,12,13,15,19.

IGGLESDEN, Sir Charles.*
Clouds. A novel set in the Folkestone-Hythe area.
John Long. 1912.
6,11.

IRELAND, William Henry.
Kent:the Hundreds of Loningborough   Heane and
Hythe.
Anglebooks. 1973.
1.

KELLY'S DIRECTORIES LTD.
Kelly's Directory of Folkestone, Sandgate
and neighbourhood.
Kelly's Directories Ltd. 1936. and 1938.
11.

KENT COUNTY COUNCIL:PLANNING DEPARTMENT.
Kent County Structure plan. Strategic issues.
Planning area 20: South-East Kent. (Serial No.14B)
K.C.C. 1975.
3,4,9,11,13,16.

LONDON, CHATHAM & NORTH KENT RAILWAY:Plan (of
proposed) main line from London to Dover.
Scale 6 chains = 1". Coloured plan, part I.
From Boughton to Dover folded to 35 sheets.
11¼" x 7¾". Names of landowners en route given.
London,Chatham & North Kent Railway. (1845?).
11.

MILLWARD, Roy.
Landscapes of Britain:South-East England -
the Channel coastlands;by Roy Millward and
Adrian Robinson.
Macmillan. 1973.
2,6,7,11,16,22,26,29.

MOULTON, W.R.
Guide to Lympne Church and Castle, Studfall,
Shepway, West Hythe and Court-at-Street.
F.J. Parsons. (c.1926).
7,11.

RAMBLING RECOLLECTIONS OF THE NEIGHBOURHOOD OF
DOVER, consisting of light scribblings illustrated
by slight sketches of various scenes and many
incidents connected with the locality of this
interesting port.
Engraved by William Burgess and thought to have
been written by him in Dover.
Rigden. April 17th 1848.
6.11.

RURAL DIRECTORY OF SOUTH-EAST KENT.
Redmans, Ashford. 1966.
6.

SCOTT, Dr. Ernest.*
Annotated list of Lepidoptera (Macro and Micro)
occurring in the neighbourhood of Ashford,
Kent. Revised by Dr. E. Scott. 1964.
Transactions of the Kent Field Club. Vol.2.
3,4,7,11,22.

SMART, J.G.O.*
Geology of the country around Canterbury and
Folkestone,by J.G. Smart and others. (Combined
Memoir in explanation of the one-inch Geological
Sheets 289, 305 and 306 - new series).
H.M.S.O.
1966. 1.2.3.4.5.6.7.8.9.10.11.14.15.16.19.24.30.
1975. 13.

SOUTH EAST ECONOMIC PLANNING COUNCIL.*
South East Kent study: recommendations of the
South East Economic Planning Council.
H.M.S.O. 1969.
2,3,4,6,7,9,11.

THE SOUTH-EASTERN, FOLKESTONE AND DISTRICT
PROPERTY REGISTER, 1896 and February 1902.
F. Wilson Temple & Company.
7.

STOTT, P.L.B.
The Character of Shepway, edited by P.L.B. Stott.
Folkestone Adult Education Centre. (typescript).
1973.
7.

TOPOGRAPHICAL ACCOUNT OF THE HUNDRED OF DEWSBOROUGH
in Old English Record Hand.
An Ms. Book of c.1860. The contents are concerned
with parishes within the HUNDRED OF BEWSBOROUGH,
near to Dover.
17.

WALTON, John W.
Folkestone and the country around: a popular and
scientific survey of the natural history and
archaeology of the district...edited by
J.W. Walton.
Printed by J. Parsons for the Folkestone Natural
History & General Sciences Society. Folkestone.
1925.
1,2,4,6,7,8,11,12,17,21.

Plants found in the immediate neighbourhood of
Folkestone.
Typescript M.S. n.d.
7.

The Wild Flowers, Ferns and Mosses of the district
round Folkestone. Based on the work of the late
Mr. G.C.Walton as published in 1894, to which
is appended a catalogue of mosses of the area,
as recorded by Mr. E.C. Green.
Folkestone Natural History Society. 1950.
1,3,4,6,7,8,11.

WARD LOCK & CO. LTD. Publishers.
Complete South East Coast: the coast resorts
from Whitstable to Selsey, and excursions
inland, edited by R.J.W. Hammond.
Ward Lock & Co. Ltd. 1974.
11,15,26,27,28,30.

Guide to South-East Kent, Deal, Dover Etc.*
(Various Permutations of title 1904-1953).
Ward Lock & Co. Ltd. (1912).
2.

Pictorial & Descriptive Guide to Folkestone,
Sandgate, Hythe...2nd ed.
Ward Lock & Co. Ltd. 1904.
7.

WHITE, H.J.O.*
Geology of the Country near Ramsgate and Dover.
H.M.S.O. 1928.
1,6,7,11,13,14,17.

KENT, SOUTH-WEST.

ABBEY PUBLICITY SERVICE LTD. Publishers.*
Residential and holiday areas of South-West
Kent including the Kentish Weald. 4th Edition.
Abbey Publicity Services Ltd. (1939?).
2,11.

KENT COUNTY COUNCIL:PLANNING DEPARTMENT.
Kent County structure plan:Strategic issues.
Planning area 3:South-West Kent. (Serial
No.12B).
K.C.C. 1975.
3,4,9,11,13,16.

Kent development plan:sample survey of households. South-West Kent 1968. + maps.
K.C.C. 1968.
11,16,19.

MAIDSTONE & DISTRICT MOTOR SERVICES LTD.
Timetable, area No.10. Hastings and Rother,
5th June 1977 until further notice.
Maidstone & District Motor Services Ltd. 1977.
11.

SHEPHARD-THORN, E.R.*
Geology of the country around Tenterden by
E.R.Shephard-Thorn and others.
H.M.S.O. 1966.
1,3,4,5,7,8,11,12,15,16,17,19.

WHITE, H.J. Osborne.*
Geology of the Country near Hastings and Dungeness.
(Explanation of the one-inch Geological Sheets
320 and 321).
H.M.S.O. 1928.
7,11.

KENT, WEST

AGRICULTURE, FISHERIES AND FOOD, Ministry of.
Agricultural land Classification of England
and Wales. Report to accompany Sheet 171
London, S.E.
Ministry of Agriculture,Fisheries and Food.1975.
16.

ANCKORN, Gordon.
A Sevenoaks Camera:Sevenoaks, Westerham and
surrounding villages in old photographs.
Ashgrove Press. Sevenoaks. 1979.
16,23.

"BELL STREET" pseud.
East Surrey.
(The story of the East Surrey Traction Company
which extended to the Westerham area).
H.J. Publications. St. Albans. 1974.
11.

BLACK, ADAM AND CHARLES Publishers*
Black's Guide to West Kent, edited by J.E.Morris.
A.&.C. Black. 1876.
1.
Black's Guide to West Kent, edited by A.R.
Moncrieff. 2nd edition.
A.&.C. Black. 1906.
1906. 2nd edition. 19.
1909. 3rd edition. 11.
1915. 4th edition. 11.

BRADDOCK, Joseph.*
Footpaths by the Kent-Sussex Border.
Chatterson. 1947.
1,2,3,4,5,6,8,9,11,12,15,18,19,20.

BRISTOW, Clement Roger.*
Geology of the country around Royal Tunbridge Wells,
by C.R. Bristow and R.A. Bazley etc. (Explanation
of the one-inch Geological Sheet 303 -new
series).
H.M.S.O. 1972.
2,3,6,7,11,12,13,16,25.

CHESTERTON, Keith.
A guide to London's countryway.
Note:Sections in Kent, pp.193 - 242.
Constable. 1978.
2,3,11,22.

CLUCAS, Philip.
The history of Sevenoaks and district.
Design Practitioners Ltd. St. Julians.Sevenoaks.
1975.
16.

COLBRAN, John, Publisher*
Colbran's new guide for Tunbridge Wells, being
a full and accurate description of the Wells
and its neighbourhood within a circuit of
nearly twenty miles, edited by J. Phippen.
J. Colbran, Tunbridge Wells.
1839. 19. 1844 2nd edition. 11.

The Handbook & Visitors' Guide for Tunbridge
Wells and its neighbourhood.
J. Colbran. Tunbridge Wells.
1855. 5th edition. 19
1855. 5th edition. 11 bound with Osborne's Strangers'
        guide to Hastings & St.Leonards. J.Colbran.
        1855.
1857. 6th edition. 2.
1863. 8th edition. 19.

COOLING, Christine M.
Records of wells in the area of New Series One-
inch (Geological) Reigate (286) and Sevenoaks
(287) sheets, by Christine M. Cooling and others.
Institute of Geological Sciences, Water Supply
Papers, Well Catalogue Series.
Natural Environment Research Council. 1968.
23.

CROFT-COOKE, Rupert.*
Gardens of Camelot. (Childhood in West Kent,
mainly Chipstead).
Putnam. 1958.
11,12.

CROUCH , Marcus.
Discovering walks in West Kent.
Shire Publications Ltd. 1978
2,3,5,7,11,16,23.

DEAKIN, Richard.*
The Flowering plants of Tunbridge Wells
and neighbourhood.
Stidolph & Bellanmy, Tunbridge Wells. 1871.
2.

DIBLEY, George Edward.
Additional notes on the Chalk of the Medway
Valley, Gravesend, West Kent, North East
Surrey, and Grays (Essex). Reprinted from
Proceedings of the Geologists Association
Vol. XXXIX, 1918. pp68-1O5
9.

DINES, H.G.*
Geology of the country around Sevenoaks and
Tonbridge, by H.G. Dines and others. (Explanation
of the one-inch Geological Sheet 287-New Series)
H.M.S.O. 1969.
2,3,4,6,9,12,13,16.

ENVIRONMENT, Deptartment of the
List of buildings of special architectural
or historic interest:District of Sevenoaks,
Kent. (Sevenoaks rural area).
H.M.S.O. 1975.
11.

List of buildings of special architectural
or historic interest in the District
of Tunbridge Wells.
H.M.S.O. 1974.
11,19.

FOURTEEN WALKS IN AND AROUND TONBRIDGE.
Tonbridge Civic Society. (197?).
11.

GIRL GUIDES ASSOCIATION.
Kent West:County Directory 1975-76.
Girl Guides Association. 1975.
8.

GOULD, David.
Westerham Valley Railway.
(Locomotion Papers No.72)
Oakwood Press. 1974.
1,2,3,4,6,11,15,16.

GOULDEN & CURRY Publishers.
The "Walks Guide" to Tunbridge Wells and
the surrounding country, being based upon
the well-known "Walks and Drives Guide" but
newly revised and amplified.
Goulden & Curry, Tunbridge Wells. 1937.
11.

GREAT BRITAIN, Laws etc. (Vic.)
An Act to enable the South-eastern Railway
Company to make, or complete, a Branch
Railway from the South-eastern Railway at
Tunbridge to Tunbridge Wells. (31st July,
1845). Cap. CLXVII. 1845.
23.

GREAT BRITAIN, Laws etc. (Edw. VII)
West Kent Electric Power Act. 1909.
1.

HILTON, John Anthony.
Tonbridge tales: a series of occasional
papers on the history of Tonbridge and the
surrounding district.
John Hilton. Hadlow. (1977).
12,19.

HOOKER BROS. Publishers.
Hookers' Directory 1935.(Westerham & District).
Hooker Bros. Westerham. 1835.
16.

"INVICTA" pseud.
The tramways of Kent, edited by G.E. Baddeley.
Vol.I. West Kent.
Light Railway Transport League. 1971.
1,2,3,5,6,7,8,9,25.

JONES, Edgar Yoxall.*
A prospect of Tunbridge Wells and the adjacent
countryside.
Lambarde Press.1964.
1,2,4,5,8,1O,11,12,15,19.

KAYE-SMITH, Sheila.
Three against the World.
Novel set on the Kent/Sussex border.
Cassell. 1924.
11.

KELLY'S DIRECTORIES LTD.
Kelly's Directory of Tunbridge Wells, Tonbridge
and neighbourhood.
Kelly's Directories Ltd. 1936.
11.

KENT COUNTY LIBRARY, SEVENOAKS DIVISION.
(Societies): list of organisations in Sevenoaks,
Swanley, Hartley, Edenbridge and the surrounding
district,March 1978.
Kent County Library, Sevenoaks Division.
1978.
11.

KIDNER, Roger Wakeley.
The Oxted Line(Locomotion papers 58).
(Briefly touches Kent and Edenbridge/Groombridge).
Oakwood Press. 1972.
4,7,11.

The Reading to Tonbridge Line.
Oakwood Press. 1974.
2,7,11,15,19.

LONGLEY-COOK, Hilary.
Walks in Ashdown Forest and around Tunbridge Wells.
Waterdown Press. Frant. 1973.
11,19.

MARGARY, Ivan Donald.
Roman roads in West Kent. Reprinted from
Archaeologia Cantiana Vol. LIX. 1946.
11.

MEOPHAM & DISTRICT FOOTPATHS GROUP. The Weald Way,
a walkers' route from the Thames to the English
Channel: Section I: Gravesend to Tonbridge.
Meopham Publications Committee. 1973.
9,11.

MILES, Walker (pseud. of TAYLOR, Edmund S.).*
Field & path rambles in West Kent: a practical
handbook for pedestrians......
R.E. Taylor & Son. 1893.
2,9.

MOORE, Frank L.
History of the West Kent Golf Club 1916 - 1976.
by F.L. Moore and and Alan Newing. (8p.pamphlet).
West Kent Golf Club. (1976).
2.

MOUL, Duncan.
Weekends in hopland:No.1. (Sevenoaks and District)
Homeland Association. n.d.
16.

THE NEW TONBRIDGE VIEW BOOK, containing the
beautiful views of the town and places of
interest in the vicinity.
J.G. North,35 High St, Tonbridge. (196?).
11.

NEWMAN, John.
West Kent and the Weald.
(The buildings of England series. No.38,
edited by N. Pevsner).
Penguin.
1969.* 2,3,4,5,7,8,9,11,19.21,24,25,28.
1976 2nd edn. 2,3,7,8,11,12,15,16,19,2O,23,
24,27,28,30.

OAKELEY, R.H.
Country walks around Sevenoaks.
(11 walks on separate sheets).
The Sevenoaks Society 1974.
2,3,11,16.

More country walks around Sevenoaks.
(Walks Nos.12-22. Loose leaf in a Folder)
The Sevenoaks Society. 1976.
2,16.

PHILP, Brian J.
Excavations in West Kent, 1960 - 1970:the
discovery and excavation of prehistoric,
Roman, Saxon and medieval sites, mainly
in the Bromley area and in the Darent
valley (Second Research Report in the
Kent Series).
Kent Archaeological Rescue Unit. Dover. 1973.
2,4,5,6,7,9,11,12,16,25,30.

PHIPPEN, James.*
The road guide from London to Tunbridge Wells;
through Lewisham,Bromley,Farnborough,
Sevenoaks,Tunbridge...
Joseph Thomas. 1836.
11,19.

PLUMER, Henry R.
Inhabitants of West Kent, 1487-8. (That is,
those paying tithes to Sir John Leigh).
Extracted from The British Archivist, Vol.I
No.5. July 1913.
11.

PROVINCE OF WEST KENT:FREEMASONS.
Freemasons manual and Directory.
Provincial Grand Lodge of West Kent. 1978-79.
2.

ROYAL TUNBRIDGE WELLS BOROUGH COUNCIL.
Tunbridge Wells & District:Official guide.
G.M. Publications.Bournemouth, for Royal
Tunbridge Wells Borough Council.
1976. 11,16,20.
1977. 4,13,25.
1978. 11.

SEVENOAKS & DISTRICT CONSUMERS' GROUP.
Sevenoaks Consumer: the newsheet of the
Sevenoaks & District Consumers' Group. July
1971. pp.1-21 assesses the Sevenoaks
Library Service.
Sevenoaks & District Consumers' Group. 1971.
11.

SEVENOAKS DISTRICT COUNCIL.
Official Guide of Sevenoaks District.
British Publishing Company. Gloucester.
1975. 11.
1978. 12.

SEVENOAKS URBAN DISTRICT COUNCIL.*
Guide and handbook to Sevenoaks and district,
edited by George Bennett.
Caxton & Holmesdale Press. Sevenoaks. 1948.
1,2,5,11,16,23.

SPURRELL, F.C.J.*
A sketch of the history of the rivers and
denudation of West Kent etc.
West Kent Natural History Society. Printed
by E.G. Berryman & Sons. Greenwich. 1886.
11.17.

TONBRIDGE & MALLING DISTRICT COUNCIL.
Official Guide of Tonbridge & Malling District.
Home Publishing Company Ltd. Croydon/Wallington.
1976. 7.20.
1977. 3,11.
1978. 3.
1979. 4,12.

TONBRIDGE URBAN DISTRICT COUNCIL.*
The Official Guide to Tonbridge and District.
Pyramid Press. 1963.
30.

TUNBRIDGE WELLS & DISTRICT COUNCIL OF SOCIAL
SERVICE.
Directory of Statutory and Voluntary Social
Services in Royal Tunbridge Wells and District.
Tunbridge Wells & District Council of
Social Service. October. 1975.
19.

TUNBRIDGE WELLS HEALTH DISTRICT - COMMUNITY
HEALTH COUNCIL.
Annual report 1974/5
11,19.

WALTER AND GRIST <u>Publishers</u>.*
Pictorial History of Tunbridge Wells and District.
Walter and Grist. 1892.
4,19.

WEST KENT FEDERATION OF WOMENS INSTITUTES.*
Countryside in the 70's:West Kent Survey in 1968.
West Kent Federation of Womens Institutes.
Tonbridge. (1970).
12.

WEST KENT POLL BOOK, 1852.
Smith and Son. Maidstone. 1852.
5.

<u>KENT ARTISTS</u>

ALLDERIDGE, Patricia.
The Late Richard Dadd, 1817-1886.
(The artist and his family lived in Chatham)
Tate Gallery, Academy Editions. 1974.
4,11,12,15,25.

Richard Dadd: midsummer nightmare.
(From Sunday Times Magazine 24th September 1972.
Original Version). Typescript.
4.

ARDIZZONE, Edward.
Article from the "Daily Telegraph" Magazine
of September 3rd. 1976.
(The artist had Kent and Maidstone Connections).
12.

BRIGDEN, C.A.T. <u>Illustrator</u>.
Characters from <u>Charles Dickens</u> as depicted by
Kyd;drawn by C.A.T. Brigden. (Chatham artist).
John Hallewell, Rochester. 1978.
11,15.
<u>See also</u> JOHN, Malcolm. (Kent).

The Countryside sketchbook:a book of poems and
sketches.
John Hallewell Publications. Rochester. 1978.
3,5,11,15.

CANTERBURY CITY MUSEUMS AND CANTERBURY PUBLIC
LIBRARY.
T. Sidney Cooper, R.A. Exhibition of paintings
and drawings, Royal Museum Canterbury...20th
August - 10 September.
Royal Museum. Canterbury. (1977).
3.

CHATTERTON, E. Keble.
T. Sidney Cooper, R.A., his life and art.
(Canterbury Artist).
Art Record Press. 1902.
3.

COOPER, Thomas Sidney.*
Views in Canterbury and its environs. Drawn
from Nature and on Stone. (Portfolio of six
engravings).
Westmead Press. 1972.
1,3.

CORKE, C. Essenhigh.
Hever, from original water colour paintings,
by C. Essenhigh Corke. (The artist lived
at Sevenoaks).
J. Salmon. Sevenoaks. n.d.
11.

CORNFORTH, John.
Some early Victorians at home. (an appraisal
of Charlotte Bosanquet's Watercolours of
Vinters Park)
Taken from Country Life, December 4th. 1975.
12.

COUSENS, Ruth Margaret.
Paintings by R.M. Cousens. F.S.A.I...of
Ramsgate and a biographical note of the artist.
1976.
11,13.

DODD, Charles Tattersall.
Charles Tattersall Dodd:artist of Tunbridge Wells.
Centenary exhibition, Municipal Art Gallery,
Tunbridge Wells. 24th November - 15th December
1978. (Catalogue).
19.

DUNDEE ART GALLERY.
(Catalogue of) An exhibition of Watercolours,
drawings and etchings: Amelia Long, Lady Farnborough
(1772-1837). Note: (Lady Farnborough lived at
Bromley Hill).
Dundee Art Gallery. (1979).
2.

FALK, B.
Turner the painter:his hidden life.
(Connections with Margate,Whitstable and
Knockholt).
Hutchinson. 1938.
13.

FOLKESTONE ART SOCIETY.
Folkestone Art Society Exhibition, 26th September
to 8th October. 1955. Catalogue.
Folkestone Art Society. 1955.
11.

GARDNER, William Biscombe. See KENT-GENERAL WORKS.

GREYSMITH, David.
Richard Dadd, the rock and castle of seclusion.
Studio Vista. 1973.
4,11.

HERBERT, Agnes.
The Isle of Man...with...32 colour plates by
Donald Maxwell.
(Artist lived in Rochester & East Farleigh).
Lane. 1909.
4.

KEAN, J.S.*
Artists of Gravesend up to the end of the nineteenth century.
Gravesend Historical Society. 1964.
4,9,11.

KIMBALL, Katherine.
Rochester:a sketch book.
A.&.C. Black   1912.
25.

LEWIS, John.
Rowland Hilder;painter and illustrator.
(Roland Hilder lives at Blackheath).
Barrie and Jenkins. 1978.
3.

MAXWELL, Donald.
(The Artist lived in Rochester & East Farleigh)
See also KENT AUTHORS & LITERATURE -GENERAL. ETC.

Adventures with a sketch book...with over
200 notes in line and colour.
Lane. 1914.
4,12.

Colour sketching in Chalk.
Pitmans. 1934.
4.

Excursions in colour.
Cassell 1927.
4,11,15,

MAXWELL, Donald.
(Scrapbook consisting of drawings of Churches
and other religious subjects, mainly by
Donald Maxwell,
4.

Wembley in colour...the British Empire Exhibition
of 1924...With over one hundred sketches
in colour and monochrome.
Longmans Green. 1924.
4.

MORLEY, Thomas William (1883 - 1931).
Exhibition of Works by T.W. Morley at Bromley
Central Library....1979. (Includes brief
biography of the painter who lived at Hayes).
Bromley Central Library. 1979.
2.

MORTLOCK, C.B.
Famous London Churches...depicted by Donald
Maxwell.
Skeffington. (1934?).
4.

NEVE, Christopher.
William Townsend 1909 - 1973; retrospective
exhibition of paintings and drawings arranged
by C. Neve. Catalogue designed and printed
by Taylor Brothers, Bristol (1978?).
(The artist lived at Rolvenden).
3.

NOAKES, Aubrey.
Charles Spencelayh and his paintings.
(Rochester-artist).
Jupiter. 1978.
3,15.

PEACOCK, David.
David Peacock's Tunbridge Wells sketchbook,
described by Frank Chapman.
Perspective Press. 1978.
3,4,5,6,11,13,15,16,19,23,28.

RUSKIN, John.*
The harbours of England, with thirteen illustrations
by J.M.W. Turner.
Ruskin's commentaries on twelve Turner
engravings of English Harbours.
George Allen. 1895.
11.13.14.

SARTIN, Stephen.
Thomas Sidney Cooper. C.V.O., R.A., 1803-1902.
F.Lewis. 1976.
3.

TONBRIDGE OAST THEATRE AND ARTS CLUB.
Centenary exhibition of watercolours and
etchings by Martin Hardie (1875-1952)
at Tonbridge Castle (Catalogue)
(The artist lived at Tonbridge in retirement)
Tonbridge Oast Theatre and Arts Club. 1975.
11.

VICTORIA AND ALBERT MUSEUM.
The rediscovery of an artist:the drawings of
James Jefferys (1751-84).
(The artist was born in Maidstone).
Victoria and Albert Museum. 1976.
12.

WHEELER, J.M.
The family and friends of William Frederick
Wells, founder of the Society of Painters in
Water-colours.
(W.F. Wells, 1764 - 1836, was born in Chislehurst
and resided during Summer and Autumn for many
years at Knockholt). Photocopy.
J.M. Wheeler. 1970.
2.

WHITE, Gabriel.
Edward Ardizzone artist and illustrator.
(Maidstone and Kent Connections).
Bodley Head. 1979?
28.

WOLVERHAMPTON CENTRAL ART GALLERY.
The Cranbrook Colony (Exhibition Catalogue
January 22nd - March 12th 1977).
Cranbrook Colony - F.D. Hardy, G. Hardy,
J.C. Horsley, A.E. Mulready, G.B. O'Neil,
T. Webster.
Wolverhampton Central Art Gallery. 1977.
11.19.23.

WYLLIE, M.A.
We were one:a life of W.L. Wyllie.
Wyllie was a Kent Marine artist who lived at Hoo.
G. Bell. 1935.
11.

KENT AUTHORS & LITERATURE - GENERAL

ADAMS, James Whirter Renwick.
Modern town and country planning...
(Kent County Planning Officer)
Churchill. 1952.
12.

ALLISON, R.D.R.
Notes on personal religion:a memorial volume for
private circulation only.
(The author lived at Dover in retirement).
Printed by A.R. Adams. Dover. 1935.
11.

ANDREWS, Pamela M.
ARC Publications. (Ealing Miscellany No.2).
(ARC Publications are published in Gillingham).
Ealing Technical College School of Librarianship.
1973.
8.

ARC PUBLICATIONS (GILLINGHAM POETRY GROUP)
Published by A. Ward. Gillingham.
BROWN, Paul. Reclaimed land. 1973.
CHALONER, D. Year of the Meteors 1972.
LYKIARD, Alexix. Life Lines. 1973.
RILEY, Peter. The Canterbury Experimental Weekend.
1971.
THOMAS, D.M. The Shaft. 1973.
8.

ARYA, S.P.Y. Surendranath Voegeli.
My Jesus:a book of meditations.
(Calamus leaves. 2).
Order of the Great Companions. Chatham. 1934.
4.

BEHRENS, Lilian Boys.*
Battle Abbey under thirty-nine Kings:
legends and records.
Saint Catherine Press. 1937.
3,12.

BEVAN, J.O.
The invasion of England by a hostile fleet.
(The Author lived in Canterbury).
H.J. Goulden. Canterbury. 1910.
3.

BINYON, Lawrence.*
Akbar, a biography.
Nelson. 1939.
11,12.

BROWN, Christopher.
Kentish Tales.
(Annotated list of books set in Kent).
Kent County Library,School Library Service.1976.
3,4,5,8.

BRYDGES, Sir Samuel Egerton.*
The Sylvan Wanderer:consisting of a series of
moral, sentimental & critical essays. (2 vols)
Printed at the Private Press of Lee Priory 1813-1817.
3,11.

CHURCH, Richard.*
Green Tide.
Country Life. 1945.
3,11.

A Window on a Hill (Essays inspired by/at Goudhurst).
Hale. (1951).
4,5,11,12.

COGGAN, Dr. Frederick Donald. Archbishop of
Canterbury
The Prayers of the New Testament.
Hodder & Stoughton. 1974.
3.

These were his Gifts.
University of Exeter. 1974.
3.

Word and World. (Written when Archbishop of York)
Hodder & Stoughton. 1971.
3.

COOPER-MARSDIN, Rev A. (Vicar of Borstal)
Church, or Sect.
Journal Company. n.d.
11.

COTTON, Charles (of Canterbury).
The Bardon papers;a collection of contemporary
documents relating to the trial of Mary Queen of
Scots, 1586. (MS.Eg.2124).
Printed & Published by J.T.Savage.Ramsgate.1907.
3.

CRAMP, Rev.Dr. John Mockett.
An essay on the obligation of Christians to observe
the Lord's supper every Lord's day.
(Rev. Cramp was the Baptist Minister, St.Peters'
Broadstairs).
S. Burton. 1824.
24.

CRAN, Marian.
The Joy of the Ground. (Gardening).
Herbert Jenkins. 1928 & 1929.
11.

CREATON, David.
Beasts and babies. (The author lives at Marden)
Hodder & Stoughton. 1978.
3,11.

Beasts of my fields
Hodder & Stoughton. 1977.
11.

CROUCH, Marcus.
Treasure seekers and Borrowers.
Library Association. 1962.
15.

CUNNINGHAM, Dr. John S.
Kingdom in the Sky.
(Dr. Cunningham practises medicine in Tonbridge).
Souvenir Press. 1975.
23.

DOLDING, C.
Blueprint for happiness here and in the hereafter.
(The author was born in Kent and retired to Wye)
C. Dolding. Wye. 1977.
11,23.

DONALDSON, Christopher William.
A Small manual of prayer to help in the
stewardship of Time.
A&J.Purchese. 1975.
3.

DOUGLAS, Rev. Robert
God and Greater Britain:the British race from the
twentieth century BC to the twentieth century A.D.
(Vicar of Bredgar, Sittingbourne).
James Nisbet. 19--
20.

ELLIOTT, Douglas J.
Buckingham:the loyal and ancient Borough.
(The author resides in Tonbridge).
Phillimore. 1975.
23.

EVANS, Dr. (R.C.T.) of Herne Bay.
The Guidance Bible, contain the Authorized
Version...arranged as in the Paragraph Bible...
(Compiled by Dr. Evans of Herne Bay).
Parrett & Neves of Chatham. 1937.
4.

FINCH, William Coles.*
Water, its origin and use.
Alston Rivers Ltd. London. 1908.
4,8,12,25.

FLETCHER, J.
Spring now beyond the weather.
(Folkestone authoress).
Fletcher. 1976.
7.

FREE THOUGHTS ON THE EXTENT OF THE DEATH of
Cnrist,tne Doctrine of Reprobation,etc.
Jasper Sprange. Tunbridge Wells. 1787.
19.

FRY, Colin Richard.
New voice No.1. Autumn 1962,Edited by Colin
R. Fry. (The editor was born in Ashford).
Free School Lane. Rochester. 1962.
4.

GILLHAM, Philip.
Alternative energy:Methane,solar,wind.
Kent County Library,Technical Service. K.C.C.
(1978?).
8.

Computers.
Kent County Library Technical Service. K.C.C.
(1978?).
8.

GOFFIN, Magdalen.
Maria Pasqua.
(Mrs.Goffin is a Tonbridge authoress).
O.U.P. 1979.
23.

GOODSALL, Robert Harold.*
Palestine memories 1717-1918-1925.
(The author lived at Harrietsham).
Cross & Jackman. Canterbury. 1925.
3,11.

Photography in Winter.
R.H. Goodsall. 1931.
11.

GRANT, Charles.
The Ancient War Game. (The Author lives at Dover)
A.&.C. Black. 1974.
6.

Napoleonic Wargaming.
Model and Allied Publications. 1974.
6.

The War Game.
A.&.C. Black. 1971.
6.

HALL, Rev. Joseph.
A proposal and statement by the Rev. Joseph Hall,
incumbent of Knockholt, Kent. 1860.
(Bound with "A letter to his Grace the
Archbishop...)
1860.
3.

HANDLEY-TAYLOR, Geoffrey.
Kent Authors to-day;being a checklist of Authors
born in Kent together with brief particulars of
authors born elsewhere who are currently working
or residing in Kent, edited by G.Handley-Taylor.
Eddison Press. 1973.
1,2,4,5,7,8,9,11,16,22,25,28,30.

HATCH, P. Henry.
Poetic genius:an essay on poetical character...
a lecture delivered at the Assembly Room, Royal
Victoria and Sussex Hotel, Tunbridge Wells,
February 27th 1839.
J. Colbran. Tunbridge Wells. 1839.
19.

HAZLITT, William.
Character of John Bull. (Essays and miscellany.
The Author was born in Maidstone).
Florin Press. Staplehurst. 1978.
11.

HEWITT, Mrs. E.C.
Mind and its culture.
(The author lived at East Farleigh).
Ward & Co. 1855.
11.

HIGENBOTTAM, Frank.
Running a family history bulletin on a shoestring.
Federation of Family History Societies. 1975.
3.

HILTON, John.
Aspects of local history, compiled by John Hilton.
J. Hilton. Hadlow. (1977).
23.

HOBSON, Victor.G.
The Unified quantum field Theory.
(The author was born in Folkestone).
Austaprint. Australia. 1972.
7.

HOLE, Rev. Samuel Reynolds. Dean of Rochester.
A book about Roses.
Blackwood and Sons. 1885.
15.

A book about the garden and the gardener.
Nelson. 1892.
15.

HORN, Alfred Aloysius   pseud.(SMITH, Alfred
Aloysius).(The Author lived at Whitstable in later
years).
The Ivory Coast in the Earlies.
Cape 1927.
31.

Trader Horn:the Ivory Coast in the Earlies.
Edited by Etheldreda Lewis.(Florin Books).
Cape. 1932.
3.

Trader Horn:the Ivory Coast in the Earlies.
Edited by Etheldreda Lewis.
Remploy (Howard Baker). 1969.
31.

The Waters of Africa.
Cape. 1929.
31.

HOWE, P.P.
The best of Hazlitt.
(William Hazlitt was born in Maidstone)
Methuen. 1924 reprint 1965.
25.

JOSEPH, Jack.
Notes on music. (Gillingham author).
Lindley Press. 1975.
8.

LEWIS, Rev. John (Vicar of Margate).
The Church Catechism explained.
S.P.C.K. 1794.
13.

A Complete history of the several translations
of the Holy Bible and New Testament into English.
Pole. 1739.
13.

A Defence of the Communion Office and Catechism
of the Church of England.
Downing. 1742.
13.

A History of the life and sufferings of the
Reverend and Learned John Wycliffe.
Knaplock and Wilkin. 1720.
13.

The Life of Reynold Pecock.
John Moore. 1744.
13.

MACKLEY, George E.
Wood engraving. (A Tonbridge author).
National Magazine Co., London. 1948.
23.

MARLEY TILE COMPANY LTD.
Technical Flooring Manual.
Marley Group. Sevenoaks. 1977.
4.

Technical Roofing Manual.
Marley Group, Sevenoaks. 1975. Reprinted 1978.
4.

MAXWELL, Donald.
(The author lived in Rochester & East Farleigh).
Across India with the Prince...
(Limited edition of 150 copies).
D. Maxwell, Rochester. 1922.
4.

The book of the Clyde, being a connected
series of drawings.
Lane. 1927.
4.

A Cruise across Europe...with 100 illustrations
by the Author and Cottington Taylor.
Lane.   1925.
4,11.

A detective in Sussex...
Written and illustrated by Donald Maxwell.
Lane. 1932.
4.

A dweller in Mesopotamia...with sketches in
colour, monochrome and line.
Lane. 1921.
4.

The Landscape of Thomas Hardy.
Cassell. 1928.
4.

The last crusade...with 100 sketches in colour,
monochrome and line made by the Author in....
1918 when sent to Palestine...
Lane. 1920.
4.

The new lights O'London.
Jenkins. 1926.
4.

A painter in Palestine:being an impromptu
pilgrimage...with Bible and Sketch book.....
Lane. 1921.
4.

Unknown Dorset...in line and colour.
Lane. 1927.
4.

Unknown Norfolk...Illustrated in line and
colour.
Lane. 1925.
4.

Unknown Somerset....being a series of unmethodical explorations..in line and colour.
Lane. 1927.
4.

Unknown Suffolk...being a series of unmethodical explorations..in line and colour.
Lane. 1926.
4.

Unknown Surrey...illustrated in line and
colour by the author.
Lane. 1924.
4.

Unknown Sussex...illustrated in line and
colour by the author.
Lane. 1923.
4.

MEDWAY WRITERS CIRCLE.
Azimuth (quarterly magazine) Vol.1. No.1:
1967 -(in progress).
4,8,15.

A MINUTE JOURNAL OF A SHORT TOUR IN FLANDERS
AND FRANCE accurately kept for the
entertainment of a young family. MS. 1828.
(Diary of a Continental Holiday).

11.

MORECROFT, John H.
White tie and tails. A collection of after
dinner tales by a Dovorian and retired
journalist.
Bailey Bros & Swinfen. Folkestone. 1974.
6.

NARRATIVE OF THE INGRATITUDE AND ILL-TREATMENT
Mrs. K-TH-N P-Y-N hath received from Mr.
S-M-L ED-M-TT, with copies of the Letters
and other Transactions, that hath passed on
Account of that Affair. And of the misconduct
of the Rev. Mr. Josiah L-W-S and the Church
under his Care, at SM-RD-N, Kent, in their
dealings with him and me, by K-TH-N P-Y-N.
(Mrs. K-TH-N P-Y-N was aunt to Sarah, the
late wife of Samuel Edmett of Biddenden and
who died on July 12th 1761, leaving one son,
Thomas, whose financial security is the issue.
Josiah Lewis was Pastor of Tilden Chapel,
Smarden, 1766 - 1778)
Printed and Sold by Simmons and Kirkby.
Canterbury. 1770.
3.

NORTH, Dudley.   3rd Lord North.
A forest promiscuous of several seasons production.
(Lord North discovered the Chalybeate springs
at Tunbridge Wells, in 1606.)
Daniel Pakeman. 1659.
19.

ONCE A MONTH:a magazine of general literature.
No 1. June 1866, edited by H.A. Neame.
C.D. Dixon.
13.

OXENDEN, Rev. Ashton. (Rector of Pluckley).
The Christian Life.
Hatchards. London. 1870.
11.

The Home Beyond,* or, a happy old age.
William MacIntosh, London. 1863.
11.

The Pathway of Safety, or, Counsel to the
awakened.
Westheim, MacIntosh & Hunt. London. 1862.
11.

The Story of Ruth.
Hatchards. London. 1873.
11.

RAGGETT, G.F.*
Saint George the Martyr, the Patron Saint of
England. (The author lived at Sandwich).
PP. c.1918.
6,11.

ROUTLEY, Erik.
The Puritan pleasures of the detective story.
(The author lives at Dartford).
Gollancz. 1972.
5.

SACKVILLE-WEST, Victoria (Afterwards Lady Nicolson).*
Country notes. (Contents include "The Kentish
Landscape"; "The Hop Picking Season"; "The
garden and the oast").
M. Joseph. 1939.
11,12,23.

"SARA" pseud.
Tom's progress in dreams:fiction and truth for
the young. (Broadstairs Author).
Printed by the Thanet Printing Works. Ramsgate.
n.d.
24.

SCHWARTZ, John.
The nearness of God, a pledge of immortality.
(A souvenir of Lent, 1907 - articles published
in the Sevenoaks Chronicle).
The Author lived at Sevenoaks and was a Lay
Reader in the Diocese of Rochester.
Joseph Salmon, Sevenoaks. 1907.
11.

SIX, James. F.R.S.
Account of an improved thermometer...communicated
to the Royal Society by the Rev. Mr. Wollaston...
read on February 28th 1782.
(James Six lived in Canterbury and died
there in 1793. There was a memorial to him
in Holy Cross Church, now used as the Guildhall).
3.

Experiments to investigate the variation of
Local Heat...Read at the Royal Society on
June 10th 1784.
3.

SMITH, Clare Sydney.
The Golden Reign: story of friendship with
'Lawrence of Arabia' 3rd edition.
(The author lives in Deal).
Cassell. 1978.
28.

"A SON OF THE MARSHES" pseud.
On Surrey Hills.   2nd edition.
Blackwood. 1892.
20.

SOUTH EAST ARTS ASSOCIATION.
Directory of Writers in the South East of
England.
South East Arts Association. 1974.
4,5.

Review: a magazine of literature and the arts.
Spring 1977.
South East Arts Association. 1977.
4,19.

STEELE, Gordon.
To me God is real. (The author lives in Folkestone).
Stockwell, Ilfracombe. 1973.
7.

STOCK, John. (Minister of the Zion Chapel,
Chatham).
An essay on the mode and subjects of Christian
Baptism.
A.T. Fordham, Chatham. 1844.
4.

TOWNSEND, Rev. George.
The Replication;or, a familiar address to Mr.
William Frend, of Jesus College, Cambridge,
presenting him with the proofs required in
his public challenge...(The author was a
minister in Ramsgate.)
Printed by Simmons and Kirkby. 1789.
11.

A testimony for truth:in a brief vindication
of the divinity of Christ and a trinity in
Unity denied in Rev. Frends' address to the
Citizens of Canterbury.
Simmons & Kirkby. 1788.
3.

TREASURES OF THOUGHT:a collection of favourite
quotations with an introduction by Thomas
Harrison (Vicar of Margate).
J.C.Lane. Margate. 1917.
11.

TYRWHITT-DRAKE, Sir Hugh Garrard.*
(The Author lived at Cobtree Manor, Maidstone,
and was Mayor of Maidstone).
Beasts and circuses.
Arrowsmith. 1936.
12.

The English Circus and Fairground.
Methuen.
12. 1st edition. 1946.
11. 2nd edition. 1947.

WARREN, Clarence Henry.
The Happy Countryman.
(A biography of Mark Thurston, "Larkfield"
being in East Anglia).
(The author lived in Mereworth)
Bles. 1939.
11.

WEDMORE, Sir Frederick.
Certain comments, with introductory essays,
by Sir George Douglas and George C.Williamson.
(The author resided at White Mill End, South
Park, Sevenoaks).
Selwyn & Blount. London. 1925.
11.

On books and Art.
Hodder & Stoughton. 1899.
11.

WHITE, Th(omas) Henry.*
The Marigold Window, or, pictures of thought.
(Essays which include those on walks in the
Weald,Sevenoaks,Sandwich,Minster-in-Thanet).
(The author lived at Sevenoaks).
Longman,Brown,Green & Longman. London.
W. Batcheller. Dover. 1849.
6.11.

WILLETT, William.
The waste of daylight, with an account of the
progress of daylight saving, 19th edition.
(The author was a resident of Chislehurst).
W. Willett. 1914.
2.

WILLIAMSON, Catherine.
Death and its aftermath. (Canterbury authoress).
Headley Bros. Ashford. (1975).
3.

WINDUS, William Edward.
Literary scrapbook.
(The author lived in Deal circa 1900)
11.

WOOD, Dorothy.
Leo VI's concept of divine monarchy.
(The author lives in Canterbury).
The Monarchist Press. (1964).
3.

KENT AUTHORS AND LITERATURE -COLLECTIONS.

A.,R .G. (AYERST, R.G.J).
Bagatelles, by R.G.A.
(Collection of poems and pamphlets)
n.d.
3.

ADAMS, Henry Gardiner ("NEMO" pseud.)*
The Kentish Coronal; consisting of original
contributions, in prose and poetry, by persons
connected with the County of Kent.
Simpkin and Marshall. 1841.
1,2,4,6,7,8,11,12,15,17.

DOBELL, Leonora Olive.*
Prose and Verse. Privately published.
(The reprint of this work was commissioned
by the Author's daughter, who lives at
Sittingbourne).
Printed by Voile & Robertson. Faversham.
Reprint (1940).
1.11.

SMETHAM, Henry.*
Sketches:prose and rhyme. (The author lived at
Strood).
Whiting & Co. 1889.
8,11,12.

TUNBRIDGE MISCELLANY - consisting of poems etc.
2 parts.
E. Curll. 1713.
19.

WILMOT, John. 2nd Earl of Rochester.
The Works of the Earls of Rochester, Roscommon,
and Dorset:the Dukes of Devonshire, Buckinghamshire etc. with memoirs of their lives. In two
volumes bound as one with additions and
adorned with cuts.
(Poems by Charles Sackville, 6th Earl of Dorset,
pp. 27 - 53).
P.P. 1777.
11.

WOTTON, Sir Henry.
Reliquiae Wottoniae:or, a collection of lives,
letters, and poems;with characters of sundry
personages and other incomparable pieces
of language and art.   Includes biography by
Izak Walton. 4th edition.
Printed for T. Tooke...and T. Sawbridge. 1685.
11.

KENT AUTHORS AND LITERATURE - FICTION.

ALFORD, Elizabeth M.
Netherton-on-Sea; a story of Ars and Mentana.
(Edited by H. Alford).
Tinsley. 2nd edition. 1870.
17.

ARMIGER, Will.
A drama of death:a novel by Will Armiger.
The novel was published in serial form in
the "Bexhill-on-Sea Chronicle" and collected
into a scrapbook by W.E. Windus of Deal.
(1888).
11.

ARNOLD, Ralph.
Hands across the Water. (A novel).
(The author lived in Cobham).
Constable. 1946.
11.

BALDWIN. Michael.
A World of Men.
(The author was born in Gravesend).
Gollancz. 1962.
9.

BOSCAWEN, Gertrude.
Judith, the "Stranger"; a Kentish Story.
James Nisbet. 1887.
11.

COOKE, Canon Daniel. (Vicar of Brompton).
Soldier Tim, or, Something wanting.(A Novel).
Marshall Bros. London.
4. 1900.
11. 1897.

DOBELL, Leonora Olive.
Two women of Kent. A novel set in Mid and
North East Kent.
H.J. Drane. Old St. Bride's Press. 1905.
11.

DORLING, Henry Taprell.
Dover - Ostend.(A novel).
Hodder & Stoughton. 1933.
11.

FARNOL, Jeffery.
The honourable Mr. Tawnish:a romance
2nd edition.
Sampson Low. 1913.
30.

HOARE, E.N.
Between the locks;or, the adventures of a
water-party. A novel.
(Includes the River Medway, Hops & Hopping).
Society for Promoting Christian Knowledge.
(188 ?).
11.

HORN, Alfred Aloysius. pseud. (SMITH,
Alfred Aloysius).
Harold the webbed or The Young Vikings.   A
novel with autobiographical Facts).
(The author lived at Whitstable, in later years).
Cape. 1928.
31.

INGOLDSBY, Thomas pseud. (Richard Harris
BARHAM, 1788 - 1845).*
The Ingoldsby Legends.
Victoria Edn. R. Bentley & Son. 1882.   3.
                                    1894.   6,9.
            Warne. (190-).   2,4.
            Cassell. 1908.   4.

KAYE-SMITH, Sheila.
(Five novels set in Kent, Sussex and the Weald).
The end of the House of Alard.
Cassell. (1923).
11.

The Isle of Thorns.
Cassell. 1924.
11.

Starbrace.
Cassell 1923 & 1924 (reprints).
11.

Three Against the World. Sussex edn.
Cassell 1924 (reprint).
11.

The Tramping Methodist.
Cassell, 1922.
11.

KENT COUNTY LIBRARY
Pick of the year:selected fiction of 1979
reviewed by the staff of Kent County Library.
Kent County Library (1980).
23.

KNATCHBULL-HUGESSEN, Edward Hugessen
Baron Brabourne.
Moonshine:Fairy Stories, illustrated by
William Brunton. 3rd edition.
Macmillan. 1872.
11.

LOVE, Kathleen.
A strange experience. (New Canterbury Tales Vol.I).
A Story.
Published by the Canterbury Department of Adult
Studies for the Kent Literacy Scheme. (1978?).
3.

MARSH, Ronald J.
The Quarry.
Macdonald. 1962.
4.

NETHERSOLE, Susan Colyer.
Pounce,the Miller. A Novel set in Kent.
Mills and Boon. 1930.
11.

RICE, John. (Folkestone author).
Butterfly Ball.
Aten Press. 1975.
7.

SACKVILLE-WEST, Victoria (afterwards Lady Nicolson)
All passion spent.
V. Sackville-West at the Hogarth Press. 1932,
reprinted 1938.
4.

The death of noble Godavary:and Gottfried Kunster.
New Ninepenny Novels No.14.
Benn. 1882.
11.

WHEELER, Terence.
The wreck of the rat trap.
(The author lives at Whitstable and is a lecturer
at Christchurch College, Canterbury).
Macmillan. 1973.
31.

WINDUS, William Edward.
(Four short stories).
In manuscript. The author lived at Deal at one time.
11.

WOODMAN. George.*
The Heretic. A novel. (Whitstable author).
"Designed, illustrated and hand-printed by Ben
Sands, 97 Island Wall, Whitstable, Kent".
The Shipyard Press. 1963.
3,11,15,31.

No elastic under her chin. A Novel.
Stanley Paul. 1951.
31.

WOOLF, Mrs. Virginia (Stephen).
Orlando:a biography.
(A Fictional biography connected with the
Sackvilles).
L.&.V. Woolf at the Hogarth Press. 1928.
11.

KENT AUTHORS & LITERATURE - PLAYS.

BAKER, Thomas.*
Tunbridge Walks:or, the Yeoman of Kent, a
comedy by the Author of the "Humour o'the Ape".
Bernard and/or Henry Lintott 1703,1714,
1727,1736 and 1764.
1,11,17,19.

BARKAWAY, Charles.
He found adventure:a play in three acts.
(Tonbridge author).
Play Rights and Publications. 1937.
23.

BARKAWAY, Charles.
Peter lends a hand:a play in three acts.
French. 1938.
23.

BARWIS, Michael.
Mutiny at the Nore.
A project drama, first performed at Sevenoaks
School.
Heinemann Educational Books. 1969.
11,23,27.

CUMBERLAND, Richard.
The posthumous dramatick works of the late
Richard Cumberland Esq. 2 vols.
(Poet and dramatist who settled in Tunbridge
Wells).
G.&. W. Nicol. 1813.
19.

WINDUS, William Edward.
Illiam Dhône: a drama; bound with Fenella:
a drama. (The author lived at Deal at one time).
P.P. 1886 and 1890.
11.

KENT AUTHORS AND LITERATURE - POETRY.

A., R.G. (AYERST, R.G.J.).
Bagatelles, by R.G.A.
(Collection of poems and pamphlets).
n.d.
3.

ADAMS, Henry Gardiner (Nemo" pseud.)
The Kentish Coronal,* consisting of original
contributions in prose and poetry, by persons
connected with the County of Kent.
Simpkin and Marshall 1841.
1,2,4,6,7,8,11,12,15,17.

The Ocean Queen and other poems.
Etherington. Chatham. 1836.
11.

AESOP AT TONBRIDGE,*or, a few select Fables
in Verse.
E. Whitlock. 1698.
11,19.

BARBER, Mary.
Poems on several occasions.
(A Seasonal visitor to Tunbridge Wells -
some poems written in and about the town).
C. Rivington. 1735.
19.

BARNES, Philip.
Five Cathedral Poems.
P. Barnes. (1974).
3.

BINYON, Laurence.
The burning of Leaves and other poems.
Macmillan. 1944.
11.

BISHOP, C.H.
The Folkestone Fiery Serpent and other Kentish
poems: a selection compiled by C.H.Bishop.
Kent County Library. 1977.
3,4,5,7,11,12,23,25,30.

BLANFORD, John.
Poems (Kentish author:some poems about
Kent).
Mitre Press. 195-?.
11.

BLUNDEN, Edmund.
Shells by a stream:new poems.
Macmillan. 1945.
23.

BONE, David.
The Bees of Swanland:a poem with drawings by
Arthur Coombes and the author.
The Bee and Blackthorn Press, Beckenham. 1957.
11.

BONE, David.
A Lenten Pie.
The Bee & Blackthorn Press. Beckenham. 1960.
11.

Narrow days:poems. (Poems on the Coldrum Stones
and Dode Church).
Bee and Blackthorn Press. 1966.
11.

BRIGDEN, C.A.T. illustrator.
The Countryside sketchbook:a book of poems
and sketches.
John Hallewell Pubns. Rochester.   1978.
3,5,11,15.

BROWNING, Stella.
Pilgrimage, and other poems.
The author was educated at Southlands Grammar
School, New Romney.
London Literary Editions. 1972.
11.

BRYDGES, Sir Samuel Egerton.*
Sonnets and other poems.
New edition with additions. First published in 1785.
G.&.T. Wilkie. London. 1789.
3,6.

BUSH, A.E.
A selection of poems.
(The author lived at Folkestone).
Elwy Bros. Folkestone. 194-?.
11.

CAMPBELL, Agnes.
Thoughts by the wayside.
(Poems on Herne Bay).
The Badenoch Record Office. 1914.
30.

CARRICK, Charles.
Poems; serious,humourous and satirical.
A. Ginden. Canterbury. 1870.
3.

CINQUE PORTS POETRY SOCIETY.
The Cinque Ports Horizon No.1.
Cinque Ports Poetry Society. 1974.
7.

A CONTESTED ELECTION: or the rival Knights.
A Heroic poem by Lieut. Col. Sir Rhymester
Rhymeway Bard of Rhymeacre Hall.
H. Ward:Canterbury. 1852.
3.

COPE, Michael.
Sound-tweezered nights. (poems and pensées).
(Dartford poet).
Regency Press. 1972.
5.

CUMBERLAND, Richard.
A poetical version of certain Psalms of David,
by Richard Cumberland, Esq.
(Poet and dramatist who settled in Tunbridge
Wells).
J. Sprange. 1801.
19.

DEACON, M.
Poems.
(The poet has been connected with Harrietsham
and Lenham).
Stockwell. 1973.
11.

DOBELL, Leonora Olive.*
Prose and Verse. Privately published.
Printed by Voile & Roberson, Faversham
Reprint(1940).
1,11.

Songs of the sunshine and night. Privately published.
Printed by Voile and Roberson. Faversham.
(Reprinted 1940).
1,11.
(The reprint of these poems was commissioned
by the Author's daughter, who lives at Sittingbourne)

DODSWORTH, Mrs.
Fugitive pieces. (Author was formerly
Miss Barrell.   Two of the poems relate to
Margate).
Simmons & Kirkby, Canterbury. 1802.
11.

DONAGHEY, Betty.
Autumn green, and other poems.
(The poet was born at Wilmington).
Outposts Publications. Walton-on-Thames. 1977.
3,5.

DONALDSON, Christopher William.
Save the Stour and other poems.
SCOPS Press. 1974.
3,11,23.

EDWARDS, Thomas.
Nature-poems (and others).
Printed by Lewis,Hepworth & Morriss. Tunbridge
Wells. 1893.
11.

THE EIGHTEENTH OF NOVEMBER, 1852.
Printed for private circulation, 1853.
(Poem about the funeral of the Duke of
Wellington, Lord Warden of the Cinque Ports
and who died at Walmer).
11.

ELLIOTT, Christina.
Poems.
Arthur H. Stockwell Ltd. Ilfracombe. (196-?).
2. 23.

FAULKNER, Roger.
Winged Shadows (Poems)
(The Poet lives in Sittingbourne).
Outposts Publications. 1973.
20.

FENN-MARSHALL, Vera.
Poetic reflections:a collection of verse.
(A Dover Poetess. See pp.232-240).
Poetry Press. Ltd. (1974).
6.

FOURNIER, Freda.   (A Kentish poet).
At home and abroad in Verse.
Arthur H. Stockwell Ltd. Ilfracombe. 1973.
4,11.

Here and there in Verse.
Arthur H. Stockwell Ltd. Ilfracombe. 1975.
4,8,11,15,25.

GLADWELL, Miriam E.
In War-time: poems.   (The poetess lived
at Ramsgate).
Shandel and Flowerdew.
Thanet Advertiser Offices, Ramsgate. 1916.
11.

GREEN, Henry J.
First of the few. (Kentish poet).
Outposts Publications. 1977.
3.

Moments of pause:poems.
Duplicated typescript. (1977).
3.

Pebbles from the beach (Poems about Kent).
P.P. (1978).
3.

Varied impulses:poems.
Duplicated typescript. 1978.
3.

Where I make my home:poems.
Thanet Printing Works. Ramsgate. (1977).
3.

HENDERSON. D. Stella.
The Morals and wonders of life.
(The poet resides in Dartford).
A.H. Stockwell Ltd. Ilfracombe. 1978.
5.

HETHERINGTON, Tom.
Sing Jubilee! a Christ Church college anthology
of 25 poems to commemorate the Silver Jubilee
of H.M. Queen Elizabeth II.
(Christchurch College, Canterbury).
1977.
3.

HUNTER, Rex.
Through the Pain and other verses.
Rex Hunter. PP.   1978.
22.

IANDOLO, H.R.
Prelude to Heaven:a collection of Poems.
A Kentish poet - two poems on Kent are included.
Carmelite Press. Whitefriars, Faversham. 1977.
8,11.

IGNES-FATUI:or False Lights, a poem in
Hudibrastic verse, with notes. (The preface
indicates that the poet lived in East Kent,
near to Richborough).
Rouse,Kirkby & Lawrence. Canterbury. 1810.
3.

KENDON, Frank.
Arguments and emblems.
J. Lane. 1925.
11.

KENT AND SUSSEX POETRY SOCIETY.
Poetry Folio. Vol.XXVII. 1973. 9.
Poetry Folio. Vol.XXVIII. 1974. 11.

KING, William Louis.
Verses by the wayside.
(The poet lived at Paddock Wood).
The collection includes poems on the King and
Henham families.
PP. and printed by Francis & Co. London. 1915.
11.

LAKE, Phyllis.
A hornet in my hair. Poems.
(The poetess lives in Margate).
Mitre Press. 1976.
13.

THE MARGATE HOY - a poem.
In BONSFIELD, Publisher.
Picture of Margate, being a complete guide to all
persons visiting Margate,Ramsgate and Broadstairs.
Bonsfield, 1809,
1,12,13.

(MASTERS, John White).*
Dick and Sal;or, Jack and Joanses Fair: a
doggerel poem. 3rd edn.
Printed by Z. Warren. Dovor. 1830.
3,11.

Dick and Sal at Canterbury Fair:an early nineteenth century poem in the Kentish dialect of
the period.   Limited edition of 228.
Introductory note by Christopher Buckingham
Ben Sands. Shoestring Press. Whitstable. 1973.
1,3,6,26.
11 -and another copy of earlier date minus
     cover and title page.

MOORHOUSE, Rev. M.B.
Stories in Verse by land and sea from legendary
and other sources.
(The poet was vicar of St. Mary Bredin's,
Canterbury).
J.A. Jennings. Canterbury. 1898.
3.

MUSGRAVE, Rev. George (Vicar of Borden).
Costumes and Boots:a hudibrastic poem for the
days we live in.
Paternoster & Hales Printers. 1879.
20.

OSBOURN, H.J.L.
Selected poems.
(The poet lives in the Weald).
Welmont Publications, Beckenham. 1977.
11.

PAGDEN, S.
Songs from the Hillside.
(Poems by a poet who lived at Harbledown,
near Canterbury - some local poems included).
Walter Scott Publishing Co Ltd.   (1910).
3.

PEARSON, Edward.
The history of Jimmy Lee, an Ambassador of
Christ...(A biography in Verse. Jimmy Lee was a
wandering preacher in the Ashford area.
Edward Pearson was a farm labourer from the
same district).
Jabez Francis, Rochford. Essex. 1872.
22.

PINK PEACE No.9. Final edition.
(A poetry Magazine published in Folkestone).
Aten Press. 1974.
7.

POST, Thomas.*
Selection of verses written by Thomas Post of
Wye aged 84 and for many years a Shepherd.
Kentish Express. Ashford. (1902).
3,11,17,21.

PRICE, H.I.
Poems.
H.I. Price. (Printed in Sittingbourne).
October. 1975.
20.

RICHARD OF MAIDSTONE.
Alliterative poem on the deposition of King
Richard II, edited by Thomas Wright.
(Richard became a Carmelite Monk and
died at Aylesford).
Camden Society. 1838.
11.

ROBB, Brian.
And time stood still
(Includes poems about Kent).
Printed for the author by Sprint Print,
Chislet. 1977.
11.

ROGERS, B.
Diving and flying (poems and pictures)
Villiers. 1978.
13.

ROSE, Charles.   (Gillingham Poet).
From our garden:poems.
Hawthorn. n.d.
8.

Poems Dad did.
Hawthorn. n.d.
8.

SACKVILLE-WEST, Victoria.*(afterwards Lady
Nicolson).
The Land
Heinemann. 1926.
5,11,12,16,17,19,23.

Sissinghurst: a poem.
Hogarth Press. 1931. Reprinted by The
National Trust. 1972.
23.

SAYER, Bernadette.
I'm deaf - not daft.   (Tonbridge poet).
B. Sayer. (1978).
23.

SCOTT, Constance M.M.
Woven on a Kentish loom (poems)
(The poetess lived at Chatham).
Parrett & Neves. Chatham. 1942.
11.

SHAW, George Bernard.
Lady, Wilt thou Love Me?
(Love poems for Ellen Terry).
David and Charles. 1980.
22.

SLADDEN, Dilmot.*
The Northmen: a poem in Four cantos.
(The Sladden Family were connected with Canterbury)
Henry Wood,   Canterbury. 1834.
11.

SLUGS: illustrated by Bill Lewis.
(Poems by the Members of Outcrowd).
Outcrowd. Maidstone. 1975 and 1977.
11.

SMETHAM, Henry.*
Sketches:prose and rhyme.
(The author lived at Strood).
Whiting and Co. 1889.
8,11,12.

SOUTH EAST ARTS ASSOCIATION.
An Anthology of New Poetry.
Poetry South East 1. Selected and arranged by
Howard Sergeant. 1976.
3,4,5,6,7,11,19.

Poetry South East 2. Selected and arranged by
Laurence Lerner. 1978.
7,11,25,30.

Poetry South East 3. Selected and arranged by
John Rice. 1978.
7.

SPRANGE, J. Publisher.
On the High Rocks, near Tunbridge Wells:
a descriptive poem.
J. Sprange. Tunbridge Wells. 1777.
19.

STAP, Louise.
Poems by Louise Stap and Jane Emelie Stap.
(The Stap Family lived at Deal).
Barnicott & Pearce. The Wessex Press. 1920.
11.

THOMAS. Louise.*
Hollingbourne 1851 (and)Lines to Kentish Children.
(Poetry with notes on Hollingbourne).
Printed by Vivish and Co. Maidstone. 1906.
11.15.

TOPLEY,   Peter.
Poems from West Wickham.
(Photocopy of typescript - "Edition" limited
to 50 copies).
P. Topley. 1978.
2.

TUNBRIDGE EPISTLES, from Lady Margaret to the
Countess of B.. (Poems).
Johnson & Davenport. 1767.
19.

WAUGH, Marlene.
Verba ipsis loquitor. (The words speak for them-
selves).
(The poetess lives at Hartley)
Regency Press. 1973.
11.

WEDMORE, Sir Frederick
Poems of the love and pride of England, edited
by F. and M. Wedmore.
(The author resided at White Mill End, South Park
Sevenoaks. Millicent Wedmore was his wife).
Ward Lock. 1897.
11.

WEDMORE, Millicent (of Sevenoaks)
Chiefly of heroes:Poems.
Smith-Elder & Company. London. 1913.
11.

Collected poems.
Ingpen and Grant, London. 1930.
11.

In Many Keys:poems.
Elkin Matthews, London. 1921.
11.

A Minstrel in the South:Poems.
Smith-Elder & Company. London. 1909.
11.

WHITTAKER, Joseph.
The almond tree and other poems
(The poet was connected with Bexleyheath).
Kentish Indepependent. Woolwich. 1931.
11.

WILMOT, John. 2nd Earl of Rochester
The Works of the Earls of Rochester, Roscommon,
and Dorset:the Dukes of Devonshire,
Buckinghamshire etc., with memoirs of
their lives.   In two volumes bound as one
with additions and adorned with cuts.
(Poems by Charles Sackville. 6th Earl of
Dorset, pp. 27 - 53.
Privately published. 1777.
11.

WOODS, Nancy.
Kentish Poems.
PP. (197-?).
11.

WYATT, Sir Thomas.
Poetical Works.
(The Aldine edition of British Poets).
Bell and Daldy. n.d.
25.

KENT SONGS

DAVIDSON, John.
Ballads & Songs.
Contents include: In Romney Marsh, A
Cinque Port. etc.
Bodley Head. 1894.
11.

GOUGH, Benjamin.
Kentish lyrics:sacred, rural and miscellaneous.
Houlston and Wright. 1867.
3,25,26.

KENT GIRL GUIDE ASSOCIATION.
Kent County Hymn Book.
Published for the Kent Girl Guide Association
by Novello.
1939 2nd edition. 5
1950 (reprint) 11.

Kent County Song Book.
Songs chosen by the Association.
Novello. 1935.
11.

KIDBROOKE

DUNKIN, Edwin Hadlow Wise.*
Historical memoranda relating to the Liberty
or Parish of Kidbrooke in the County of Kent.
Bembrose & Sons. 1874.
5.

KILNDOWN

BATCHELOR, Gordon.
Kilndown 1977:an account of the village
Celebrations and other events during Silver
Jubilee Year.
Kilndown Jubilee Committee. (1978).
11.

KINGSDOWN

ELLISTON-ERWOOD, Frank Charles.*
Architectural notes on Kingsdown Church
near Sevenoaks (St. Edmund); reprinted from
Archaeologia Cantiana . v.35. 1921.
Mitchell Hughes & Clarke. London. 1921.
2.

HUNT, F.J.
Deal, Walmer & Kingsdown Amateur Rowing Club,
1927 - 1977.
Kent County Printers. 1979.
28.

REDMAN, Douglas S.R.
The Parish Church of St. Edmund, King and
Martyr, West Kingsdown in the County of Kent.
D.S.R. Redman. Printed by the Druid Press. 1974.
11.

KINGSNORTH MARSHES

HINES, J.
Barge remains in Kingsnorth Marshes. In Topsail;
the journal of the Society for Spritsail Barge
Research. Issue No.15, Autumn 1976. pp.48-50
11.

KIPPINGTON

STANDEN, Hugh Wyatt.*
Kippington in Kent:its History and its churches
with illustrations.
H.W. Standen. Sevenoaks. 1958.
2.

KITCHENER, Field Marshall Horatio Herbert, R.E. 1ST EARL KITCHENER OF KHARTOUM. (1850-1916). (RESIDENCE AT BROOME PARK, DENTON).

BALLARD, Brigadier General C.R.
Kitchener.
Faber and Faber. 1930.   32.
Newnes. n.d.   32.

CASSAR, George H.
Kitchener:architect of victory.
Wm. Kimber. 1977.
3,32.

GERMAINS, V.W.
Kitchener's Armies
Peter Davies. 1930.
32.

MAGNUS, Philip.
Kitchener:portrait of an imperialist.
Murray. 1958.
32.

KNOCKHOLT

BARROWS, V.
Changes in Knockholt Village,
from 1850 - 1880.
(Typescript photocopy of unpublished thesis)
1978
2.

THE KNOCKHOLT SOCIETY.
Footpaths of Knockholt
The Society. 1977.
2.

WARLOW, G.H.*
History of Knockholt.Collected from divers
sources by G.H. Warlow.
No Publisher. (1910?).
11.

KNOLE

ALSOP, Susan Mary.
Lady Sackville:a biography.
(Lady Victoria Sackville-West lived at Knole
from 1889).
Weidenfeld & Nicolson. 1978.
11,12,16,23.

BRADY, John G.*
Visitor's guide to Knole.
Payne. Sevenoaks. 1839.
16.

CLIFFORD, Lady Anne. (1590-1676).*
Diary of the Lady Anne Clifford, with an
introductory note by V. Sackville West.
(Lady Anne became wife to Richard, 3rd Earl
of Dorset).
Heinemann. 1923.
5,8,11,16.

KNOLE Cont'd

FAULKNER, P.A.
Some medieval archiepiscopal palaces.
Reprinted from The Archaeological Journal ,
Vol.CXXVII. pp.130-146 (Knole). 1971.
Royal Archaeological Institute. 1971.
3.

GUIDE TO KNOLE HOUSE, its state rooms.
pictures and antiquities, with an
account of "The Possessors and Park
of Knole". New authorised edition.
Printed by William Wicking. Sevenoaks. 1892.
11.

HOLMES, Martin.
Proud Northern Lady:Lady Anne Clifford,
1590 - 1676.
Phillimore. 1975.
16.

MACKIE, S.J.*
Knole House.
Harrison, Sevenoaks. 1858.
16.

PHILLIPS, Charles J.*
History of the Sackville Family...with
description of Knole...2 vols.
Cassell. 1929.
2,11,15,16.

SACKVILLE WEST, Victoria (afterwards
Lady Nicolson).*
Knole and the Sackvilles.
1922;1923. Heinemann.
1,2,3,7,11,12(1922)13,14,15,16,17(1922)19,20.
1947;1948. Lindsay Drummond Ltd.1.4.5.8.11.15.
                        16,18,21,25(1948).
1958 Benn. 4th edition.   5.8.11.12.16.

Knole, Kent.*
National Trust
1950.   12.
1956.   12.
1974. Reprinted with minor alterations to the
       description of contents. 11.16.
1976.   3,23.

LAMBERHURST

GREAT BRITAIN, Laws etc. (Geo.III).
Lamberhurst Road Act, 2d. Geo.III. Cap.67.
(1761).
23.

HUSSEY, Christopher.*
A short history of Scotney Castle.
Stanford Printing Company.Tunbridge Wells.1953.
8.11.

MOON, John H.
The Downhill path:the early history of Lamberhurst.
J.H. Moon. Printed by the Crown Chemical Coy. Ltd.
1974.
11,19.

The George & Dragon. Pamphlet.
J.H. Moon. Printed by the Crown Chemical
Coy. Ltd. 1978.
19.

A Short history of Lamberhurst.
Lamberhurst Local History Society. 1977.
19.

A Short history of the Lamberhurst Iron Industry.
Lamberhurst Local History Society. 1977.
19.

MORLAND, William
Lamberhurst school:the story of the voluntary
school in Lamberhurst, from...1833 to...1949.
Phillimore. 1972.
1,3,7,8,11,15,19.

A Tour of Saint Mary's Church, Lamberhurst.
W. Morland. n.d.
19.

LAMBETH PALACE

BARBER, Melanie.
Index to the letters and papers of Frederick
Temple, Archbishop of Canterbury, 1846-1902.
in Lambeth Palace Library, compiled by
Melanie Barber.
Mansell. 1975.
3,11.

CAVE-BROWNE, Rev. John.*
Lambeth Palace and its associations.
Blackwood. 1882.
12,17.

CHURCHILL, Irene Josephine.*
Mediaeval records of the Archbishops of
Canterbury:a course of public lectures delivered
in Lambeth Palace Library in 1960 by I.J.
Churchill and others.(The Lambeth Lectures).
Faith Press. 1962.
1,4,11,12,15,19.

HOUSTON, Jane.
Index of cases in the records of the Court of
Arches at Lambeth Palace Library, 1660-1913,
edited by Jane Houston.
Phillimore for British Record Society. 1972.
5,23.

KERSHAW, S. Wayland.
Lambeth Palace Library and its Kentish Memoranda.*
Reprinted from Archaeologia Cantiana.
Vol.IX. 1874.
4,17.

Lambeth Palace in olden times.
Reprinted from the Architect.1881.
26.

OWEN, D.M.
A Catalogue of Lambeth Manuscripts, AD889-901.
(Carte antique et miscellannee).
Lambeth Palace Library. 1968.
11.

SAYERS, Jane E.
Calendar of the papers of Charles Thomas Longley,
Archbishop of Canterbury,1862 - 1868, in
Lambeth Palace Library, by J.E. Sayers and
E.G.W. Bill.
Mansell. 1976.
3,11.

Estate documents at Lambeth Palace Library:*
a short catalogue.
Leicester University Press. 1965.
1,5,7,11,13,30.

LAND TENURE.

BARTHOLOMEW, Leonard.
A rental of the real estate of Leonard Bartholomew.
1752- 1757. (Manuscript Ledger, listing tenants
and actual rents for properties in various
parts of Kent and notes of payment from 1752-1757).
11.

CULPEPPER, Sir Thomas (The Elder, of Hollingbourne)
A tract against usurie.
Facsimile reprint of the 1621 edition.
Walter Johnson. Theatre Orbis Terrarum.1974.
11.

DAVIS, Godfrey Rupert Charles.
Mediaeval cartularies of Great Britain:a short
Catalogue.
Longmans Green. 1958.
11.

DEFENCE. Ministry of.
Report of the Defence Lands Committee. 1971-3.
(Chairman-Lord Nugent of Guildford).
H.M.S.O. 1973.
7.

THE DOMESDAY BOOK FOR THE COUNTY OF KENT.*
portion of a Return of Owners of Land, 1873.
Sussex Express. Lewes. 1877.
1,2,5,6,11,12,14,15,17,18,20.

ELTON, Charles I.*
The tenures of Kent.
J. Parker & Co. 1867.
1,2,3,4,8,11,15,17.

LAND TENURE Cont'd

GREY, Edmund   Earl of Kent.
The Grey of Ruthin Valor:the valor of the
English lands of Edmund Grey, Earl of Kent,
drawn up from the Minister's accounts of
1467-8, edited with an introduction by
R.I. Jack.
(Only the Earldom and not the lands refer to Kent).
Sydney University Press. 1965.
11.

LOCAL GOVERNMENT BOARD.*
Return of Owners of Land, 1873, 2 vols.
Vol I. Counties - includes Kent.
Eyre & Spottiswoode for H.M.S.O. 1875.
2,3,8,11.

TOPOGRAPHICAL QUARTERLY.
Palaeography, genealogy and topography: Kent.
(A list of Kent Deeds).
Research Publishing Company. 1938.
11.

LAND UTILISATION

BULL, Christopher.
Farm based recreation in South East England:
the experiences of a random sample of Farmers
in Kent, Surrey and Sussex, by Christopher Bull
and Gerald Wibberley. (Studies in Rural
Land Use No.12). (Wye College, Farm Business
Unit, School of Rural Economics and Related
Studies).
Wye College. December. 1976.
1,3,4,11,19,21.

HALL, Peter.
The future of the Green Belt.
College of Estate Management. 1974.
2.

KENT COUNTY COUNCIL:PLANNING DEPARTMENT.
Kent County Structure Plan: the Green Belt:
Report prepared in November 1976.Serial No.E.11.
Kent County Council. 1976.
3.4.5.9.11.12.13.15.

KENT COUNTY COUNCIL:PLANNING DEPARTMENT.
KENT COUNTY STRUCTURE PLAN.   See PLANNING.
See   KENT COUNTY COUNCIL:PLANNING DEPARTMENT
INDEX CARD.

WILLIAMS, Guy R.
London in the Country:the growth of suburbia.
Hamish Hamilton. 1975.
18.

LARKFIELD

KENT COUNTY COUNCIL:PLANNING DEPARTMENT.
North Larkfield:informal action area plan.
Kent County Council. 1973.
11.

LAW

GLEASON, J.H.
The Justices of the Peace in England 1558-1640.
A later Eiranarcha. (Appendix "A" is devoted
to Kent).
Oxford University Press. 1969.
25.

JUSTICES HANDBOOK, 1974. County of Kent.
Derry and Sons. Nottingham. 1974.
11.

LAMBARDE, William
Eirenarcha, or of the offices of the Justices
of the Peace, in Foure bookes. Revised,
corrected and enlarged....Printed for the
Company of Stationers. London. 1607.
11.

THE LAW SOCIETY.
The Legal Aid Solicitors' List. 1976 and 1978.
Law Society. 1976 and 1978.
3,9.

NEILSON, N.
Custom and the Common Law in Kent.
In Harvard Law Review.
Vol.38 No. 4. February 1925.
2.

LEE

BIRCHENOUGH, Edwyn.*
The Manor House, Lee and its associations,
by Edwyn and Josephine Birchenough. 2nd edition
revised and enlarged.
London Borough of Lewisham. 1971.
4.

Notes on Lee History, by Edwyn and Josephine
Birchenough.
Unpublished typescript. 1973.
18.

BIRCHENOUGH, Josephine.
Borough Byways - 3. A field path in Lee. ·
(Town trail).
Lewisham Local History Society. 1975.
18.

Borough Byways - 4. Hocus-pocus. (Town Trail
in Lewisham and Lee).
Lewisham Local History Society. 1975.
11,18.

Four hundred years in Lee.
Unpublished typescript. 1973.
18.

DUNCAN, Leland Lewis.
The Register of all the marriages, christenings
and burials in the Church of Saint Margaret,
Lee...from 1579 - 1754, edited by L.L.Duncan
and A.O. Barron.
Lewisham Antiquarian Society. 1888.
2.

ELLISTON-ERWOOD, Frank Charles.*
The making of the new road at Lee.1824-1828.
Blackheath Press For Kent Archaeological Society
1952.
2,11,18.

TATE, Rosemary.
A study of the growth and development of Lee,
with particular reference to population
changes in the nineteenth century.
Unpublished Thesis. August. 1973.
18.

WOLFFRAM, H.
Thirty years' work (1868-97) in preparing
candidates for the Army at Faraday House,
Blackheath, and The Manor House, Lee.
1898.
18.

LEEDS

CAVE-BROWNE, Rev. John.*
In and about Leeds and Broomfield parishes,
Kent. (Read on 17th January 1894 to the British
Archaeological Association and extracted from
the Journal).
1,4,11,15.

Leeds Priory, Kent.
British Archaeological Association. 1893.
1.4.6.11.12.15.

GEOFFREY-LLOYD, Lord Geoffrey William.
Leeds Castle:a brief history of the castle of
the Queens of Mediaeval England and a brief
guide to the rooms by Lord Geoffrey-Lloyd and
Peter Wilson.
Leeds Castle Foundation.
1976.   12,19.
1978 Revised edition. 11,23,28.
1980.   28.

GROVE, L.R. Allen.
The Church of St. Nicholas, Leeds, Kent.
P.P. 1980.
12.

HARRIS, Edwin.*
The Siege of Leeds Castle.
E. Harris. Rochester. 1906.
6.7.

LEEDS Cont'd

MARTIN, Charles Wykeham.*
History and description of Leeds Castle.
Nichols & Sons. 1869.
2.

ROYAL COLLEGE OF NURSING OF THE UNITED KINGDOM.
New horizons in clinical nursing: the report
of a seminar held at Leeds Castle, Kent,
from 14th - 17th October, 1975.
(pp.51-53, Information on the Leeds Castle
Charitable Trust).
Royal College of Nursing of the United Kingdom.
1976.
11.

WALFORD, Edward.
Holidays in the Home Counties. New Edition.
(Chapters on Dover, Leeds and Rochester).
W.H. Allen. 1899.
11.

LEGAL CUSTOMS

WILLIAM OF BYHOLTE.*
The Chronicle of William of Byholte (1310-
1320). An account of the legal system known
as Frankpledge,edited by Dom.D.Prangnell
Monastery Press. Ramsgate. 1967.
1,3,11,24,30.

LEGENDS & FOLKLORE

DYER, Thomas Firminger Thiselton.
English folk-lore.
Kent superstitions mentioned. (See index).
David Bogne, Trafalgar Square. 1883.
11.

IGGLESDEN, Sir Charles.*
Those superstitions;foreword by Marjorie
Bowen. (Includes some Kent Superstitions).
Jarrolds. 1932.
11.

SETFORD, L.
Kent legends and Folklore.
(Viewing Kent Series.)
James Pike. St. Ives. 1977.
3.4.6.11.19.28.

SWAINSON, Charles.
The Folklore and provincial names of
British Birds.
Elliott Stock for the Folklore Society.
London. 1886.
11.

TOWN AND COUNTRY MAGAZINE.
Includes:- A legend of Sheppey.
Virtue, London. 1837-38.
4.

LEIGH

TRADE AND INDUSTRY. Dept. of: ACCIDENTS
INVESTIGATION BRANCH.
Beagle A61 Series 2(Terrier) G-ArZT.
Report on the Accident at Home Farm,
Leigh, near Tonbridge, Kent. on 15th
August, 1973.
H.M.S.O. 1974.
11.

LENHAM

GOODSALL, Robert, H.
The Saxon Warriors of Lenham.
Taken from "Kent Life", May & June. 1963.
12.

KENT COUNTY COUNCIL:PLANNING DEPARTMENT.
Lenham Village:informal District Plan.
Kent County Council. 1974.
11,12.

WEBB, A.E.
Wild Flowers, trees and shrubs growing in
Lenham and Harrietsham.
Headley, Ashford. 1939.
7,11.

LESNES ABBEY - See ERITH.

LETTERS

ADAMS, William.*
Letters, 1614 - 1617,
Facsimile copies.
8.

Letters written by, and about William Adams,
1614 - 1620.
Facsimile Copies.
8.

The Original letters of the English Pilot,
William Adams, written from Japan between
A.D. 1611 and 1617. Reprinted from the
Hakluyt Society Papers.
8.

ANIMADVERSIONS ON LORD BEXLEY'S LETTER TO THE
FREEHOLDERS OF KENT.*
(The Catholic Question).
British Catholic Association. 1829.
4,14.

BARBER, Melanie.
Index to the letters and papers of Frederick
Temple, Archbishop of Canterbury, 1846 -
1902, in Lambeth Palace Library. Compiled
by Melanie Barber.
Mansell. 1975.
3,11.

BARTLETT, Rev. Thomas.
(Rector of Kingstone, near Canterbury).
A letter to Sir Edward Knatchbull, Bart,M.P.
for the County of Kent, in reply to the charges
brought by the Rev. G.R. Gleig, M.A. Rector of
Ivy Church...against the Church Missionary Society.
Printed by R. Watts. London. 1823.
3.

(Rector of Kingstone and of St. Mildred and
All Saints, Canterbury).
The protestant rule of faith vindicated:with a
glance at Popery:in reply to the letter of the
Rev. James Quin, upon the rule of faith and
Bible reading. (Note:Rev.Quin was the Roman
Catholic priest in Canterbury).
Henry Ward:Canterbury. 1832.
3.

Strictures upon the Rev. James Quin's "defence" of
his letter on the rule of faith and Bible reading.
Henry Ward. Canterbury. 1832.
3.

BLIGH, Edward. 5th Earl of Darnley.
Edward, Fifth Earl of Darnley and Emma Parnell,
his wife:the story of a short and happy married
life told in their own letters...edited..by
their daughter, Lady Elizabeth Cust and their
grand-daughter Evelyn Georgina Pelham.
(The Bligh Family lived at Cobham Hall).
Richard Jackson. Leeds. 1913.
11.

BRYDGES, Sir Samuel Egerton.
Letters written from the Continent.
John Warwick. Lee Priory Press. 1821.
3,11.

CARTER, Mrs. Elizabeth.*
Letters from Mrs. Elizabeth Carter to Mrs
Vesey, 1763-1787.
1809.
11.17.

CARTER, Mrs. Elizabeth.
Letters to Mrs. Montague. 1755 - 1800.
3 vols. 1817.
17.

Series of letters between Mrs. Elizabeth Carter
and Miss Catherine Talbot, 1741-1770.
1809.
11,17.

CRAMP, Rev. Dr. John Mockett.
Letters on Church rates addressed to the
Rev. J.E.N. Molesworth, M.A. of Canterbury.
(Rev. Cramp was Baptist Minister of St.
Peters, Broadstairs).
G. Wightman. 1837.
24.

DARWIN, Charles Robert.*
Life and letters of Charles Darwin
including an autobiographical chapter.
2nd edition.
John Murray. 1887.
2,4,

DERRICK, Samuel.
Letters written from Leverpoole, Chester,
Corke...Tunbridge Wells and Bath. 2 vols.
G. Faulkner, Dublin. 1762.
19.

DISRAELI, Benjamin Earl of Beaconsfield.
Lord Beaconsfield's letters, 1830 - 1852.
New edition of "Home Letters" and
"Correspondence with his sister", with
additional letters and notes - with a
portrait. Edited by his brother.
(Mentions Maidstone in 1837 and 1838;
Disraeli was M.P. for Maidstone).
Murray. 1887.
11.

GILES, J.A.*
Life and letters of Thomas a Becket. 2 vols.
Whittaker and Co. London. 1846.
3,17.

H.,W.T.
A new historical, topographical and descriptive
companion to the visitor of Gravesend,
Milton and their environs, interspersed
with curious anecdotes, in a series of
letters from the author to a friend.
W. Holbert. Gravesend. (1843).
11.

HALL, Rev. Joseph, (Incumbent of Knockholt,Kent)
A letter to His Grace the Archbishop of
Canterbury, Right Hon. Lord Campbell, Lord High
Chancellor, and Right Hon. Lord Palmerston,
K.G., M.P.,First Lord of the Treasury.
(For private circulation only).
1860.
3.

HAMPSON, John. (1760-1817).
A blow at the root of pretended Calvinism,
or real Antinomianism, in several letters to
a friend.
Jasper Sprange, Tunbridge Wells. 1788.
19.

HOLE, Samuel Reynolds. Dean of Rochester.*
The Letters of Samuel Reynolds Hole.
George Allen. 1907.
4,8,11,15.

IREMONGER, F.A.*
William Temple, Archbishop of Canterbury:
his life and letters. (William Temple was
Archbishop from 1942 - 1944).
Oxford University Press. 1948.
4,8,11,12.

KIRBY, Rev. F.
A Pastor's reverie, in a series of four
letters to his senior Deacons. 2nd edition.
(The author lived at Frittenden and was
Pastor at the Baptist Chapel at Staplehurst)
Sovereign Grace Union. London. 1931.
11.

A LETTER FROM A CITIZEN OF BATH TO HIS
EXCELLENCY, DR. R....at Tunbridge, 1705.
19.

A LETTER TO THE OVERSEERS OF THE POOR OF THE
PARISH OF DEAL, in Kent, respecting the great
increase of their poor rates. With remarks
on the general duty of overseers. 2nd edition.
Printed by Simmons & Kirkby, Canterbury, 1778.
3.

LETTERS CONCERNING THE THANET VOLUNTEER YEOMANRY.
Kentish Gazette. 1810.
24.

LEWIN, Thomas Herbert.
The Lewin Letters:a selection from the correspondence and diaries of an English family,
1756 - 1884. Vols I and II (Sidcup connections).
Constable. 1909.
1.

LLOYD, Samuel J. Baron Overstone.
Correspondence. 3 vols.
(Includes biographical note and many letters to
and from George Warde Norman of Bromley.)
Cambridge University Press. 1971.
2.

MAURICE, C. Edmund.
The life of Octavia Hill as told in her letters.
(Octavia Hill lived at Crockham Hill and was
a pioneer of the National Trust).
Macmillan. 1913.
25.

MOCKETT, John.*
A letter to Captain Thomas Garrett, commanding
the Thanet troop of Volunteer Yeomanry.
Printed for J. Mockett, Canterbury. 1810.
3,13.

MONTAGU, Mrs. Elizabeth.
The letters of Mrs. Elizabeth Montagu, with some of
the letters of her correspondents. 4 vols.
T. Cadell. 1809.
19.

MORE, Sir. Thomas.
St. Thomas More:selected letters edited by
Elizabeth Frances Rogers.
Yale University Press. New York. (1961).
3.

OXINDEN, Henry.*
The Oxinden Letters, 1607-1642, being the
correspondence of Henry Oxinden of Barham and
his circle, edited by Mrs. D. Gardiner.
Constable. 1933.
8,11,13,21,30.

RICHARDSON, Samuel.
The correspondence of Samuel Richardson, Vol.3.
(Connections with and visits to Tunbridge Wells).
Richard Phillips. 1804.
19.

RUSHWORTH, John.
A letter sent to the Honourable William Lenthal,
Esq., Speaker of the Honourable House of Commons,
on the Fight between His Excellency's the
Lord Fairfax Forces at Maidstone and the Kentish
Forces on June 1st. 1648.
Reprinted by Maidstone College of Art. 1959.
11.

SASSOON, Siegfried.
Letters to a critic. No.323 of an edition of 420.
Kent Editions. 1976.
11.

SMITH, Charles Roach.
On some Anglo-Saxon remains, discovered at Stowting,
in the County of Kent;in a letter from Charles
Roach Smith to Sir Henry Ellis, Secretary.
Read to the Society of Antiquaries of London on
29th February, 1844.
The Society. 1844.
11.

SMITH, Logan P.
The life and letters of Sir Henry Wotton.
(Of Boughton Malherbe).
Oxford University Press. 1966.
12.

LETTERS Cont'd

TOKE, Nicholas (Of Goddington or Godinton).
Five letters on the state of the poor in the
County of Kent, as first printed in the year
1770; to which is added - A short introduction
on the same subject...1808.
Printed by Rouse, Kirkby & Lawrence. Canterbury.
1808.
11.

LEWISHAM

BIRCHENOUGH, Edwyn.
Field Archaeology in Lewisham, by Edwyn and
Josephine Birchenough.
Unpublished Typescript. 1973.
18.

BIRCHENOUGH, Josephine.
Borough Byways-4. Hocus-Pocus.
(Town Trail in Lewisham and Lee).
Lewisham Local History Society. 1975.
11,18.

Borough Byways - 5. Romans and Railways
(A Lewisham Town Trail).
Lewisham Local History Society. 1975.
11,18.

(BLACK, William Henry).
Memorials of the family of Colfe, and of the
life and character of the Reverend Abraham Colfe.
Half-title:-Bibliothecae Colfanae Catalogus.
Leathersellers Company. 1831.
1,3,

Catalogue of...(Colfe's Library) in the year
1652. (The Library in the Free School,
Lewisham).
1831.
17,18.

BLACKHEATH SOCIETY.
Some hints on the maintenance and repair of
17th and 18th century premises. (Originally
produced by the York Georgian Society.
Reprinted with local photographs and lists
of buildings in Blackheath, Lewisham and
Greenwich.
Blackheath Society. 1949.
11.

BYRNE, Stephen P.
The Changing Face of Lewisham.
London Borough of Lewisham. 1965.
18.

DYMOND, Dorothy.
The Forge:the history of Goldsmith's College,
1905-1955, edited by Dorothy Dymond.
Methuen. 1955.
11.

GREENWICH & LEWISHAM ANTIQUARIAN SOCIETY.
Transactions.
Blackheath Press.
Incomplete File.   1.
5 vols. 1905 - current issue. 17,18.
1929.   11.

GUY, L.H.
Memoirs of a Light Reserve Leader - ordeal
of Lewisham 1939 - 1945.
Unpublished typescript. 1976.
18.

HEADLAND, Janice.
The Picture Palaces of Lewisham: notes to
accompany an exhibition held at the Manor
House, Lee, June to December 1976, by
J. Headland and K. George.
London Borough of Lewisham. 1976.
18.

HONOR OAK ESTATE NEIGHBOURHOOD ASSOCIATION.
A street door of our own:a short history of
life on an London County Council Estate.
Honor Oak Estate Neighbourhood Association.1977.
18.

JONES, P.E.
Some Bridge House properties.
In: Journal of British Archaeological Association
Vol.XVI. 1953.
18.

KIRBY, Herbert Charles.*
Monumental Inscriptions in the Church and
Churchyard of St. Mary, Lewisham, edited by
H.C. Kirby and L.L. Duncan.
Printed by C. North, Antiquarian Society,
Lewisham. 1889.
2,11,17,18.

KIRBY, John William.*
Lewisham, a historical record...
Lewisham Borough Council. 1950.
1,2,18.

KOHLER, David F.
Employment of black people in a London Borough
(i.e. Lewisham).
Community Relations Committee. 1974.
2,18.

LANSDELL, Henry.*
Princess Aelfrida's Charity. 3 vols.
(Lands in Greenwich, Lewisham and Woolwich
which became the endowment of Morden College).
Burnside Ltd. Blackheath. 1911-1916.
2,11,17,18.

LEWISHAM DISTRICT:Board of Works.
(Poster giving notice) that on the 8th day of
April next, application will be made...at
Quarter Sessions, at Maidstone for an order
stopping up, or diverting the undermentioned
footpaths....within the parish of Lewisham.
Lewisham District - Board of Works. 1875.
11.

LEWISHAM, LONDON BOROUGH COUNCIL.
Beckenham Place (Lewisham).
London Borough of Lewisham. 1973.
18.

Lewisham:a guide to the Borough. 1974-75.
G.W. May. 1974.
11.

Lewisham:the official guide.
Ed. J. Burrow and Co. Cheltenham (1977?).
11.

The Town Hall, Lewisham, 1875-1968.
London Borough of Lewisham. 1971.
2.

MACARTNEY, Sylvia.
A history of Lewisham silk mills,by S.Macartney
and John West.
Lewisham Local History Society. 1979.
2.

Sion House, Lewisham. Its site, owners, occupiers,
and Associations.
Unpublished study. 1973.
18.

PEDDY, D.P.R.
The Poor Law in Lewisham. 1814 - 1846.
Unpublished Thesis. 1976.
18.

PEET, J. Michael.
Of Lords and Landowners, of Battles and
Benefactors. A study of the origins of the
street names in the Parish of St. George's,
Perry Hill.
J.M. Peet. December. 1977.
18.

READ, Joan.
The Manor of Hatcham-aspects of its development
1600-1900.
Unpublished Thesis 1973.
18.

Read about Lewisham. (For young readers)
J. Read. 1976.
2,11.18.

WARD, Gordon Reginald.*
The Manor of Lewisham and its Wealden 'dens".
Reprinted from the 'Transactions of the Greenwich
and Lewisham Antiquarian Society Vol.IV. 1937.
2,11.

LEYBOURNE

GENERAL REGISTER OFFICE.
Census Returns. 1841,1851,1861,1871.
Leybourne. Microfilm.
23.

KENT COUNTY COUNCIL:PLANNING DEPARTMENT.*
Leybourne Lakes proposed country park:
a report on the Leybourne Lakes and adjoining
areas at Snodland and New Hythe...
Kent County Council. 1972.
4,8,12,13,16,19,20,25.

LARKING, Lambert Blackwell.*
A description of the heart-shrine in Leybourne
Church, with some account of Sir Roger de
Leybourn, Knt., and his connection with the
Wars of the Barons in the thirteenth century.
(A letter to Thomas Godfrey Faussett, Esq.).
Reprinted with additional notes from
Archaeologia Cantiana. Vol.5 1863, pp.28 -76.
Printed by John Edward Taylor. 1864.
11,25.

LIBRARIES

BEXLEY PUBLIC LIBRARIES.*
Kent library statistics 1960-61 and 1961-62.
4.

GASKIN, Valerie.
A comparison of the library services in
Sittingbourne and Milton Urban District
provided by the local council and the
library services in Tonbridge Urban District
provided by the County Council.
Typescript Thesis. n.d.
20.

GATE, John.
Maidstone public library 1855-1958.
(Typescript). 1969.
12.

GILLINGHAM BOROUGH COUNCIL-LIBRARY AND
ARTS COMMITTEE.
Development of the Library Service.1957-1971.
Gillingham Borough Council. 1971.
8.

GOSNEY, R.
Central Library for the Medway Towns:(a thesis
presented to the North-West Polytechnic).
Photocopied sheets. c.1970.
4.

HANNAVY, J.L.*
The Libraries of Dover and Folkestone:
thesis submitted for Fellowship of the
Library Association, 1968.
University Microfilms. 1968.
6,7.

HODGE, Gwenyth.
Library services in Tonbridge, 1826 - 1975.
(Duplicated typescript).
Kent County Library, Tonbridge and Malling
Division.   (1975).
3,23.

KENT COUNTY COUNCIL.
County Library Headquarters:opening and
dedication.
Kent County Council. 1965.
12.

KENT COUNTY LIBRARY.
Central lending library guide.
(Springfield, Maidstone).
Kent County Library. (1980).
4.

County Library directory. Revised 1978.
Kent County Library. 1978.
3.

The Isle of Sheppey. Part I - Libraries on
the Isle of Sheppey. Part II- A select
list of books relating to the Isle of Sheppey
in Kent County Libraries.
Kent County Library. 1956.
1,2,3,4,7,8,11,12,15,27.

KENT COUNTY LIBRARY
Rules and regulations for branch libraries
in force from 1937.
Kent County Library. 1937.
11.

Who's Who in Kent County Library.
Kent County Library. 1974.
25.

KENT COUNTY LIBRARY:TONBRIDGE/MALLING DIVISION.
Building an extension to Tonbridge Central
Library:some questions and answers.
Kent County Library:Tonbridge and Malling Division.
March 1980.
4.

MACKEAN, William Herbert,Canon of Rochester
Cathedral.*
Rochester Cathedral library:its fortunes and
adventures through nine centuries.
Printed by Staples. Rochester. 1953.
1,3,4,8,9,11,15,23.

McLELLAN, Doreen E.
Gravesend Central Library, compiled by
Doreen E. McLellan. (Local History Pamphlet
No 13).
Kent County Library. Gravesham Division. 1980.
4,9.

MARGATE PUBLIC LIBRARY.
Scrapbook 1951 - 60.
(Cuttings from local papers regarding library).
13.

MARSH, Ronald J.
Rochester Public Libraries.
3 typescript pp. 1974.
4.

STEWART, Bertram.
The library and the picture collection of the
Port of London Authority.
Richards Press. 1955.
9.

SWAN, Peter.
A short history of library services in
Sevenoaks. 1905-1980.
Kent County Library. 1980.
16,23.

LIGHTHOUSES, LIGHTSHIPS, LIFE SAVING SERVICES
See   COASTAL WATERS:SAFETY AT SEA.

LITTLESTONE

HODGSON, R.D.*
An eye off the ball at Littlestone:the rambling
discourse of a phytopsychologist.
Limited edition -350 copies.
Privately printed for the benefit of the
Littlestone Golf Club. 1939.
7,11.

LOCAL GOVERNMENT

ANATOMY OF A COUNCIL: MAIDSTONE
A Kent Messenger Supplement, November, 1975.
12.

BOUNDARY COMMISSION FOR ENGLAND AND WALES.
Report on the County of Kent.
Eyre and Spottiswoode. 1885.
9.

CANTERBURY CITY COUNCIL.
Local Government Re-organisation in England:
proposed County of East Kent.
Printed by A.&.J. Purchese. Bridge. n.d.
11.

FINANCIAL TIMES.
Medway Towns (Financial Times Report).
Monday, July 31st. 1972.
On Local Government organisation.
4.

KENT BOROUGH AND URBAN DISTRICTS ASSOCIATION.
Kent Statistics. 1972.
Kent Borough and Urban District Association.1972.
8.

LOCAL GOVERNMENT Cont'd

KENT COUNTY COUNCIL.
Annual report and financial statement for the
year ending 31 March, 1980.
K.C.C. 1980.
12.

Chief Executive's Corporate Review.
K.C.C. 1979.
4.

Committees' statements of objectives,
18th November. 1970.
K.C.C. 1970.
8,13.

Countrywise:a radio series devised by Kent
County Council and broadcast on B.B.C.
Radio Medway.
Printed by K.C.C. Supplies
Department, Maidstone. (1973).
3,11.

Handbook, 1950-51.
K.C.C. 1950.
3.

Kent County Council Election, 5th May, 1977.
K.C.C. 1977.
11.

Kent:The county administration in War.*
1939 - 45.
K.C.C. 1946
4,24,30.

Local Government Act 1958. Review of Local
Government in East Kent. 2nd Report of Officers.
K.C.C. 1965.
13.

Policy Review Statements.
1974.   4,11,13.   1975.   4.
K.C.C.

Report as to the work of the Council, 1946-1949.*
K.C.C. 1949.
9.

A review of events, trends and problems during
1965, compiled by G.T. Heckels.
K.C.C. 1966.
4,5,11,12,13,30.

Service rendered:a summary of the activities
of the Kent County Council.*
K.C.C. 1970.
13,24.25.

KENT COUNTY COUNCIL:AMENITIES AND COUNTRYSIDE
COMMISSION.
Grants towards capital expenditure on village
halls and community centres.
K.C.C. 1974.
12.

KENT COUNTY COUNCIL:ARCHIVES OFFICE.*
Handlist of Kent County Council Records, 1889-
1945,prepared by Dr. Felix Hull for the
County Council.
K.C.C. 1972.
2,4,5,6,7,8,11,19,20,25,30.

Report of the County Archivist in respect of
the three years ending 31st December, 1969.
K.C.C. 1970.
4.

Report of the County Archivist in respect of
the two years ending 31st December, 1971.
K.C.C. 1972.
13.
Report of the County Archivist in respect
of the year ending 31st December,
1972.   3,4.11.
1973.   3,11.
1974.   3,8.

Report of the County Archivist in respect of
the period 1st January, 1975 to 31st March, 1976.
K.C.C. 1976.
3,8,12.

KENT COUNTY COUNCIL - ARCHIVES OFFICE.
Report of the County Archivist in respect of the
period 1st April,1976 to 31st March,1977.
K.C.C. 1977.
3,8,13.

Report of the County Archivist in respect of
the period 1st April,1977 to 31st March,1978.
K.C.C. 1978.
8,13.

Report of the County Archivist, 1st April,1978
to 31st March, 1979.
K.C.C. 1979.
13.
Report of the County Archivist in respect of
the period 1st April,1979 to 31st March,1980.
K.C.C. 1980.
11,12.

Twenty-five years:a report on the work of the
Kent County Archives Office. 1933-1958.
K.C.C. April 1958.
4,30.

KENT COUNTY COUNCIL-CHILDRENS' COMMITTEE.*
Report on the work of the Childrens' Committee.
1953-58.   9.
1958-63.   13.
1963-70.   25.

KENT COUNTY COUNCIL-CONSUMER PROTECTION DEPARTMENT.
Consumer Advice Directory.
K.C.C.
1974.   3.12.
1976.   11,13.

KENT COUNTY COUNCIL-COUNCIL & COMMITTEE MEETINGS.
Key issues for 1977/78. Paragraph 1. of the
Report of the Policy and Resources Committee,
28th April, 1977.
K.C.C. 1977.
4,8,11.

Key issues for 1979/1980.(Paragraph 1. of the
Report of the Policy and Resources Committee).
K.C.C.   May. 1979.
4.

Meeting on the 19th February 1975.Part II
quarterly reports.
K.C.C. 1975.
11.

Minutes and Agenda.
4 1948 in progress   11   1948   in progress
5 1972 in progress   13   1973   in progress
8 1932 in progress   16   1948-1949; 1954 in progress
9 5 year file.   22   1964   in progress

Standing orders (for the regulation of
proceedings and business of the council).
Item No.26 (Paragraph 2 of report of Policy
and Resources Committee) on agenda of County
Council meeting on 19 February,1975.
K.C.C. 1975.
4,11.
KENT COUNTY COUNCIL:COUNTY SECRETARY AND
SOLICITORS' DEPARTMENT.
Kent County Council electoral divisions.
(From)the Ordnance Survey, Kent, prepared by
the Member Information Centre, County
Secretary and Solicitor's Department.
K.C.C. 1976
11.
KENT COUNTY COUNCIL:ESTABLISHMENT DIVISION.
Report of the County Establishment Officer
for the year ended 31st March, 1973.
K.C.C. 1973.
4,9,11,13.

KENT COUNTY COUNCIL:HEALTH DEPARTMENT.
Annual Report of the Medical Officer of Health
and Principal School Medical Officer for the year..
K.C.C. 1970.   13.
1972   7,8,9,11,12,25.
1973   3,8,11,12,25.

KENT COUNTY COUNCIL:HIGHWAYS AND TRANSPORTATION
DEPARTMENT.
Annual Report. 1974-1975.
K.C.C. 1975.
11,12.

KENT COUNTY COUNCIL:LIBRARIES,MUSEUMS AND
ARCHIVES SUB-COMMITTEE.
The County Archives service and the County
Library - policy statement.
K.C.C. 6th December, 1973.
4.

KENT COUNTY COUNCIL-PERSONNEL DEPARTMENT.
Manpower Budget 1975/76 and Forecasts 1977/80.
K.C.C. 1975.
11.

Manpower Budget 1976/77 and Forecasts 1978/81.
K.C.C. 1976.
13.

Manpower Budget 1977/78 and Forecasts 1979/82.
K.C.C. 1977.
3,5,13.

Manpower Budget 1978/79 and Forecasts 1980/83.
K.C.C. 1978.
3,8.

KENT COUNTY COUNCIL:POLICY AND RESOURCES COMMITTEE.
County of Kent Bill. Summary of latest
developments regarding the promotion of the
County of Kent Bill. Recommendation to
K.C.C. in the form required by law.
K.C.C. 28th February, 1980.
4.

KENT COUNTY COUNCIL:SOCIAL SERVICES DEPARTMENT.
Directory.
K.C.C. August 1979.
4.

Ten year plan for the development of the
personal Social Services.
K.C.C. 1973.
4.

KENT COUNTY COUNCIL:SUPPLIES DEPARTMENT.
Purchasing and supply in the County Administration,
1964 - 1969, by G. Carney.
K.C.C. 1970.
4.

KENT COUNTY COUNCIL:SURVEYORS DEPARTMENT.
Annual Report of the County Surveyor.
3.   1966/67; 1967/68;1968/69; 1970/71.
3,11.   1971/72
7,11,12. 1972/73
3.   1973/74
3,8.   1974/75
3,13.   1975/76
3,8,13.   1976/77
3,13.   1977/78
13.   1978/79
13.   1979/80

KENT COUNTY COUNCIL;TREASURER'S DEPARTMENT.
Abstract of accounts for the financial year
ended 31st March.
K.C.C.
1952 —1961.   4.

Abstract of accounts for the financial year
ended 31st March, 1961 with comparative
figures for the year ended 31st March,1960.
K.C.C. (1961).
11.

Budget for 1966-67 and forecasts 1967-71.
K.C.C.
12.

Budget for 1970/71 and accounts and statistics
for 1969.
K.C.C. 1970.
13.

Budget for 1971/72 and forecasts 1972/6
K.C.C. 1971.
13.

Budget for 1972/73 and forecasts 1973-7
K.C.C. 1972.
5,13,25.

KENT COUNTY COUNCIL:TREASURER'S DEPARTMENT.
Budget for 1973/74 and forecasts 1974-8,
K.C.C. 1973.
11,12,13,25.

Budget for 1975/76.
K.C.C. 1975.
11,25.

Budget for 1976/77.
K.C.C. 1976.
11,25.

Budget 1977/78.
K.C.C. 1977.
3,5,13.

Budget for 1978/79.and forecasts for 1980/83.
K.C.C. 1978.
3,5,8,13.

Capital Budget 1974/75.
K.C.C. 1974.
4.

Five Year Capital Plan. 1970/75.
K.C.C. 1970.
4,13.

Kent County Services (Facts & Figures)
(Variations in exact title).
1960-61.   9.
1972/73; 1973/74; 1974/75.   3.
1975/76.   3.12.
1976/77; 1977/78; 1978/79.   3.

KENT COUNTY COUNCIL;WEIGHTS AND MEASURES DEPARTMENT.
Report of the Chief Inspector for the year
ended 31st March.
1949-1967.   3.
1968/1969.   13.
1969/1970; 1970/1971:1971/1972. 3.
1972/1973.   7,11,12,13.

KENT COUNTY JOINT COMMITTEE.
The new Kent County Council;its management,
administration,function,relationships.
K.C.C. 1973.
4.

KENT FINANCIAL OFFICERS' ASSOCIATION.
The District Councils of Kent:Statistics
based on information supplied by the members
of the Kent Financial Officers' Association.
K.C.C.
1974/75.   4.11.12.13.
1975/76.   3,11,12.
1976/77.   3.

KENT FIRE BRIGADE.*
Annual Report for the year ending 31st March.
K.C.C.
1964/65. - 1972/73.   4.
1972/73.   11.

Fire prevention and safety handbook.*
Printed by Malcolm Page.
K.C.C.
1st edition 1959.   3.
2nd edition 1964.   30.
3rd edition 1971.   3.

An outline of the organisation of the
Kent Fire Brigade.
K.C.C. 1972.
4.

KENT MESSENGER.
Deadline for change:the new Kent.Local
Government reorganisation 1974.
A Kent Messenger Group supplement. 1974.
Kent Messenger, Larkfield.
4.

The New Kent-a Kent Messenger Special 1973.
Kent Messenger. Larkfield.
2.

What does it all mean? Local Government reorganisation '73 - '74.
A Kent Messenger Group Supplement. 1973.
Kent Messenger. Larkfield.
2.

LOCAL GOVERNMENT Cont'd

MELLING, Elizabeth.
History of the Kent County Council,
1889 - 1974, prepared for the County Council
by Elizabeth Melling, B.A., Assistant
County Archivist.
K.C.C. 1975.
1,2,3,4,6,7,8,9,11,12,13,14,15,16,17,18,19,20,
24,25,26,28,29,30.

MOYLAN, Prudence Ann.
The form and reform of County Government:
Kent 1889 - 1914.
Leicester University Press. 1978.
1,2,3,5,7,11,12,13,18,19,22,23.

ROCHESTER CITY COUNCIL.
Local Government Reorganisation:
Representations of Rochester City Council.
Rochester City Council. 1971
25.

SHAW'S LOCAL GOVERNMENT MANUAL and directory
for unions, urban, rural and port sanitary
authorities and school boards for 1876.
Shaw and Sons, Fetter Lane. 1876.
11.

STEPHENS, Sir Edgar.
The Clerks of the Counties, 1360 - 1960;
(photocopy of short sections).
Lists Clerks of the Peace for Kent,
1395-1960. Society of the Clerks
of the Peace of Counties and of the Clerks
of County Councils. 1961.
11.

STOCKS, Ronald.
Control of pounds and pints. Dover's role in the
inspection of Weights and Measures.
(The Author was Inspector of Weights and
Measures, Dover Corporation 1937-1974).
Buckland Press. Dover. 1975.
6,13.

STROOD RURAL DISTRICT COUNCIL.
Review of Council Services.
Strood Rural District Council. 1969.
11.

SWALE DISTRICT COUNCIL.
Handbook 1974 - 76.
Swale District Council. 1974.
20.

Your Council and your Councillors.
(Information Service).
Swale District Council. 1975.
11,20.

WATERS, S.C.
A talk on local administration.
(With reference to Orpington, Farnborough
etc).
Typescript. n.d.
2.

WOODS, Walter T.W.
Kent County Services in Gravesham.
Kent County Library, Gravesham Division. 1975.
3,11,12.

LOOSE

HODSOLL FAMILY.*
Hodsoll of Loose, County of Kent. (Pedigree).
n.d.
12.

KENT COUNTY COUNCIL: PLANNING DEPARTMENT.
Loose Valley study.
K.C.C. 1974.
11.

LOOSE AMENITIES ASSOCIATION
Programme for Loose Medieval Street Fayre, 1975.
Loose Amenities Association. 1975.
12.

THORNBURGH, Roger.*
Exploring Loose village: a walk through the
old village, and a glimpse of its buildings
and past.
Loose Amenities Association and Kent County
Library. 1978.
1,2,3,4,5,6,8,11,12,19,22.

LOWER HALSTOW

ROBBINS, Rev. Peter Tyndall.*
Lower Halstow: a brief history of the parish
and guide to the church.
Gibbs & Sons. Canterbury.
1962.   11,12.
1966 reprint.   4.
1973 reprint.   20.

SWALE DISTRICT COUNCIL.
Lower Halstow planning study.
Swale District Council. 1975.
20.

WILLMOTT, Frank G.
Bricks and 'brickies'
Mainly concerns Eastwoods Ltd. of Lower Halstow
and Rainham.
F.G. Willmott. Rainham. 1972.
4,7,8,11,12,20,24,25,26,27,30.

LUDDESDOWN

BASSETT, E.
On foot in Luddesdown.
Luddesdown Rights of Way Group. 1980.
15.

LULLINGSTONE

EVISON, Vera Ivy.*
A bronze mount from the Roman Villa at
Lullingstone.
In The Antiquaries Journal Vol.46, Part I.
1966.
11.

THE LEGEND OF THE HART DYKES: a curious delve
to link together philology, fact and fancy.
Typewritten text, inserted pamphlet of
Lullingstone Roman Villa.
Scrapbook. Was the property of Harold Miles.
(196-?).
11.

MEATES, Lieut. Col. Geoffrey Wells.*
Lullingstone Roman Villa, Kent.
Heinemann. 1955.
2,15.

Lullingstone Roman Villa, Kent.
(Ministry of Works Guide Books).
H.M.S.O. 1963.
12,20,25,26,27,30.

The Roman Villa at Lullingstone, Kent.
Typescript, 2 vols. - text and plans. 1973.
5.

The Roman Villa at Lullingstone, Kent.
Volume I. The Site. (Monograph series of the
Kent Archaeological Society No.1.)
Whitefriars Press for Kent Archaeological
Society. London/Tonbridge. 1979.
2,4,6,12,13,16,23.

LUTON See CHATHAM

LYDD

CARPENTER, Edward.
Lydd volunteer fire brigade. 1890-1940.
Margaret F. Bird. Lydd. (1978).
3,22.

CLARKE, G.S.
The Lydd experiments of 1886.
In Professional Papers of the Corps of
Royal Engineers. Vol. XII. 1886.
Mackay. 1887.
6.

198

LYDD   Cont'd

ENVIRONMENT, Dept. of
List of buildings of special architectural
or historic interest:Borough of Lydd.
Department of Environment. 1973.
7,11.

FINN, Arthur.*
Records of Lydd. Translated and transcribed
by Arthur Hussey and M.M. Hardy and
edited by A. Finn.
Kent Express
2.

KENT COUNTY COUNCIL:PLANNING DEPARTMENT
Lydd, New Romney and Dymchurch Local Plan.
K.C.C. 1968.
7.

LYDD CHURCH RESTORATION FUND-* an urgent
appeal.
(The Church was severely damaged in World
War II).
Lydd Church Restoration Fund Appeal
Committee, 1950.
11.

OYLER, Thomas H.*
Lydd and its church.
Kentish Express. Ashford. 1894.
2,22.

LYDDEN

BUCKINGHAM, Christopher.*
Lydden:a parish history.
Thomas Becket Books. 1967.
2,20.

LYMINGE

JENKINS, Robert Charles.*
Acta in Liminae:the history of the basilical
and conventual church of St. Mary and
St. Eadburg in Lyminge.
J. English. Folkestone. c.1880.
11.

Observations on the remains of the basilica of
Lyminge.
Reprinted from Archaeologia Cantiana.
Vol.IX. 1874.
Mitchell and Hughes. 1888?
11.

PRICE, Leonard Charles.
The Lyminge Scrapbooks;compiled by L.C. Price.
5 vols.
1870-1940.
11.

LYMPNE

ASPINALL, John.
The best of Friends.
(Zoo Parks at Howletts,Bekesbourne,and
Port Lympne).
McMillan. 1976.
3,7.

THE HISTORY OF LYMPNE AND ITS CASTLE.*
Headley Bros. Ashford. (1970).
30.

LYMPNE CASTLE ESTATE:Particulars, plan,
views and conditions of sale of...residential
and agricultural property...in all...333 acres
including the...castle and grounds...offered
for sale by auction on...February 12th 1919.
Tresidder & Co. (auctioneers) 1919.
7.

MOULTON, W.R.
Guide to Lympne Church and Castle, Studfall,
Shepway, West Hythe and Court-at-Street.
F.J. Parsons. Folkestone. (c.1926).
7,11.

SMITH, Charles Roach.*
The antiquities of Richborough, Reculver
and Lympne in Kent.
John Russell Smith. 1850.
2,24.

Report on the excavations made on the site
of the Roman Castrum at Lympne in Kent
in 1850.
First Published in 1852. Facsimile Edition,
H. Margary, Lympne. 1976.
3,7,8,19,23.

TILDEN, Philip.
True remembrances.
(Allington Castle, Lympne Castle, Saltwood
Castle, Chartwell).
Country Life. 1954.
7,12.

McCUDDEN, James Thomas Byford. V.C.
OF GILLINGHAM (WORLD WAR I)

CHADWICK, Ronald T.*
McCudden V.C. (Local History Series No.7).
Gillingham Public Library. 1972.
4,6,7,8,11,24.

COLE, Christopher.
McCudden V.C. with a forward by Air Vice
Marshal 'Johnnie' Johnson.
Kimber. 1967.
4.

JONES, William Earl Byford.*
Fighting planes and aces (includes a chapter
about J.T.B. McCudden).
J. Hamilton. 1932.
8.

McCUDDEN, James Thomas Byford.*
Documents relating to the presentation of
the freedom of the Borough of Gillingham
to Major J.T.B. McCudden.
n.d.
8.

Five years in the Royal Flying Corps.*
Edited by C.G. Grey.
Chivers' Reprint of the original edition,
edited by "Aeroplane and General Publishing
Company", 1918.
Reprinted 1965. Chivers of Bath.
4,8,15.

Flying Fury.* (Originally published as "Five
years in the Royal Flying Corps" in 1918).
Aviation Book Club. London. 1930.reprinted 1939.
4,8.

Flying Fury:five years in the Royal Flying Corps.
New edition edited by Stanley M. Ulanoff.
Prefatory notes by Hugh M. Trenchard and John
M. Salmond.
Bailey and Swinfen. Folkestone. 1973.
8,11,25.

WHITEHOUSE, Archibald.*
The years of the sky kings.
Macdonald. 1957.
8.

MAIDSTONE

ADAMS, Matthew Algernon.
Report to the Local Board on the outbreaks of
smallpox in Maidstone, 1881.
Vivish, Maidstone. 1881.
12.

ALL SAINTS, MAIDSTONE:our gift to the future?
All Saints Development Committee. 197-?.
11.

ANATOMY OF A COUNCIL:MAIDSTONE.
(Kent Messenger Supplement November,1975).
12.

APOTHECARIES COMPANY Vs. T.RYAN.
A correct report of the trial of the Apothecaries'
Company versus Ryan, March 17th,1831
at Kent Assizes.
(Mr. T. Ryan was the defendant and also
wrote up the article. The main characters
are connected with Eynsford and Farningham).
Royal Exchange, Effingham Wilson. 1831.
17.

BALDOCK, Kay.
Old Maidstone:a selection of postcards from
the early years of this century,compiled by
K. Baldock and Irene Hales.
Meresborough Books. 1980.
12,23.

BALSTON, Thomas.*
The Housekeeping Book of Susanna Whatman,
1776-1800,edited by Thomas Balston.
(The Whatman Family lived at Vinter's Park,
Maidstone).
Geoffrey Bles. 1956.
4.

BEECHER, W.H.
Kent County Ophthalmic and Aural Hospital,
Maidstone:a short history.
Centenary. 1846 - 1946.
The Hospital Board of Management.
Printed by Vivish & Baker. Maidstone (1946)
11.

BELL, John Any Bird Defendant.*
Narrative of the facts relative to the murder
of Richard Faulkner Taylor in the woods
between Rochester and Maidstone...March,1831
...together with the trial of John Any Bird
Bell for the murder...
Printed by S. Caddel, Rochester. (1831).
11,12.

BOREMAN, Robert.*
A mirrour of mercy and judgement, or, an
exact, true narrative of the life and death
of Freeman Sonds, Esquier, sonne to Sir
George Sonds of Lees Court in Sheldwich
in Kent. Who, for murthering his·elder
brother was arraigned and condemned at
Maidstone, executed there 1655.
Thomas Dring, Fleet Street. London. 1655.
11,26.

BOTTOMLEY, Horatio.*
Convict '13':A ballad of Maidstone Gaol.
Stanley Paul. (1927).
1,11,12.

BRIDGE, John W.*
All saints', Maidstone:a short guide to
the Church.
Printed by the "Kent Messenger". 1969.
2,11,12.

A BRIEF ACCOUNT OF THE CLOTH TRADE IN THE
MAIDSTONE AREA (pamphlet).
n.d.
12.

BUNYARD, George.
Fruit farming for profit (up to date):
a practical treatise, embracing chapters
on all the most profitable fruits with
detailed instructions for successful culture.
3rd and 4th editions.
(Maidstone Nursery until early 1960s)
Frederick Bunyard. Maidstone. 1890.
11.

THE CATHOLIC QUESTION *(Catholic Emancipation·
Bill).
The Great Brunswick Meeting on Penenden
Heath, October 24th,1828.
Smith. 1829.
11,17.

THE CATHOLIC QUESTION (Catholic Emancipation Bill)
The Kent County Meeting: a report of
the speeches delivered at the Kent County
Meeting holden on Penenden Heath, October 24th,1828,
with prefaratory remarks.
Ridgway - London.   1828.
Burrill - Chatham.
1,3,4,11,12.

The Kent Meeting, Penenden Heath, Friday,
October 24th,1828. The Catholic Question.
Bradley and Dent for the British Catholic
Association. 1828.
4.

COLLEGE OF ALL SAINTS, MAIDSTONE:
particulars, views, plans and conditions of
sale. Auctioneers:-Hampton and Sons Ltd.
Hampton and Sons Ltd. London. 1900.
12.

COLLINGWOOD, Frances.
Inheritor of the Whatman tradition.
William Balston, 1759 - 1849. (Papermaking)
(Balston Mill, Springfield, Maidstone).
Extract from Sales and Wants Advertiser 1958.
4.

COLLINS, Kenneth J.
The Queen's Own Royal West Kent Regimental
Museum. (at Maidstone Museum).
English Life Publications. 1973.
2,4,6,11,12,19,25.

CORNFORTH, John.
Some early Victorians at home (an appraisal of
Charlotte Bosanquet's watercolours of Vinters Park)
taken from Country Life. December 4th,1975.
December 4th,1975.
12.

DANIELS, Jack.
Bower and Fant, Maidstone:a prize winning
town walk in the competition sponsored by
the County Council. Devised and designed by
Jack Daniels.
Kent County Library. 1976.
4,8,11,17.19.

ELLISTON-ERWOOD, Frank Charles.*
Around Maidstone.
St. Catherine Press. London. 1947.
11.

ENVIRONMENT, Department of the
List of buildings of special architectural
or historic interest:District of Maidstone.
H.M.S.O.   1974.
11,12.

ESTATE PUBLICATIONS.
Maidstone area. (Maps).
Estate Publications. 1979.
4.

EVANS, Sir Francis H. Vs. LORD CASTLEREAGH.
Maidstone election petition:complete report of the
enquiry by Justices Grantham and Lawrence.
Reprinted...from...The Kent Messenger and
Maidstone Telegraph...2nd edition.
Kent Messenger. 1906.
11.

FULLJAMES, J.A.
Focus on All Saints C. of E. Primary School,
Maidstone. (Pamphlet 1975).
12.

GATE, John.
Maidstone Public Library, 1855 - 1958.
Typescript. 1969.
12.

GOAD, Charles E. Ltd.
Insurance plans of Maidstone, revised to 1929.
C.E. Goad. (1929).
12.

GREAT BRITAIN, Laws etc. (Geo.III).
An Act for widening, improving, regulating,
paving, cleansing and lighting the streets,
lanes, and other publick passages and places
within the King's Town of Maidstone...1791.
1791.
12.

An Act to continue and amend so much of an
Act made in the thirty third year of the
reign of His Present Majesty as permits Sir
William Bishop, George Bishop and Argles Bishop
to carry on the manufacture of Maidstone Geneva.
Printed by Eyre & Strahan. 1799.
11.

GREAT BRITAIN, Laws etc. (Geo.IV)
Acts of Parliament for the government and
regulation of the poor in the town and parish
of Maidstone 1828.
1828.
12.

GREAT BRITAIN, Laws etc. (Vic)
An Act for making railways between Maidstone
and Ashford...
1880.
7.

GROOM, J.B.*
A Maidstone naturalist's rambles during the
'Year of Rain' from March 1903 to March 1904.
South Eastern Gazette (Maidstone).   1904.
6,8,11,12,17.

GROVE, L.R. Allen.
Maidstone in 1650. From a 1650 written description
by Nicholas Wall. (Map). Research and mapping
by L.A.R. Grove and Robert Spain, 1974 - 75.
Supplemented and confirmed by information
from later maps.
Maidstone Museum. 1975.
11,12.

The story of Maidstone.
Maidstone Information Centre.   1975.
12.

HILTON, John (Anthony).
Maidstone:an outline history.
John Hilton. Hadlow. 1979.
11,12,23.

HONNORS LTD.
Your catalogue from the store for the garden.
(Honnors is a Maidstone garden supplies shop
established 1890. Picture of early premises)
Honnors Ltd. 19 Earl St. Maidstone.   1974.
11. 1979.

HOUSING AND LOCAL GOVERNMENT, Ministry of.
Provisional list of buildings of architectural
or historic interest. Maidstone Borough and
Maidstone Rural District.
H.M.S.O.   1949 and 1960.
12.

HUGHES, Reginald.
A history of the organs of the parish church
of All Saints, Maidstone, Kent.
Beacon Press. Lewes.   1980.
12.

KAIN, Daniel.
The trolleybuses of Maidstone; a survey of the
history of the Maidstone Corporation Trolleybus
system with fleet details and record of sold
vehicles,by D. Kain and M. Coates.
British Trolleybus Society. 1972.
2,4,7,9,12.

KELLY'S DIRECTORIES LTD.
Kelly's Directory of Maidstone and neighbourhood 1973 - 74. 17th edition.
Kelly's Directories Ltd.   1974.
11,12.

KENT AND SUSSEX BAPTIST ASSOCIATION.MAIDSTONE
AND DISTRICT MISSIONARY AUXILIARY.
Missionary reports presented to the spring and
autumn meetings of the Maidstone District of
the Kent and Sussex Baptist Association.
1951 - 1955.
(Copies of typewritten reports and one letter)
11.

KENT COUNTY COUNCIL.
County Library Headquarters: opening and dedication.
K.C.C. 1965.
12.

KENT COUNTY COUNCIL:HIGHWAYS & TRANSPORTATION
DEPARTMENT.
Maidstone transportation study:reports on surveys.
K.C.C. 1974.
11,12.

KENT COUNTY COUNCIL:PLANNING DEPARTMENT.
Kent Development Plan (1967 Revision) Maidstone
and Vicinity Town Map. Amendment to written
statement. Approved by the Planning Committee
on 12th November, 1970.
K.C.C. 1970.
11,12.

Kent Development plan (1967 Revision).
Maidstone and Vicinity Town Map. Medway Gap Town
Map. Report of Survey and analysis.
K.C.C. 1970.
11,12.

Kent Development Plan (1967 Revision).
Medway Towns, Maidstone and Vicinity and Medway
Gap Town Maps. Report on population and
employment studies in Mid-Kent.   Analysis
of shopping centres in Mid-Kent.
K.C.C. 1970.
8,11,12,25.

Kent Development Plan:sample survey of Households, Mid-Kent, 1971. Vol.1. (Maidstone and
Medway Gap).
K.C.C. 1975.
11,12,

(Kent Development Plan). Town and Country planning
Acts 1962 - 71. Public local inquiry into
objections and representations concerning the
Kent County development plan. Maidstone and
Vicinity town map, Medway Gap town map...held
at County Hall, Maidstone and Town Hall, Chatham,
12th October,1971 to 30 March,1972.
K.C.C. (1978).
4.

KENT COUNTY LIBRARY.
Central Lending Library Guide. (Springfield,
Maidstone).
K.C.C. (1980).
4.

THE KENT COUNTY MEETING.*
A report of the speeches delivered at the
Kent County Meeting, holden on Penenden Heath,
October 14th,1828.
Ridgeway, London.   Burrill, Chatham. 1828.
1,3,4,11,12.

THE KENT MEETING, Penenden Heath, Friday,
24th October,1828. The Catholic Question.
Bradley and Dent for The British Catholic
Association. 1828.
4.

"KENT MESSENGER" DIRECTORY OF MAIDSTONE and
the surrounding villages.
1927-8 24th edn. Kent Messenger. (1927).
1930-31   Kent Messenger. (1930).
1937-38   Kent Messenger. 1937.

KENT MUSICAL COMPETITIVE FESTIVAL.
Programme of the thirty-third Kent Musical
Competitive Festival to be held in Maidstone
on 14th, 21st, 25th and 28th May,1949.
Printed by W. Mackay, Chatham. 1949.
11.

L(AMPREY), S.C.*
Brief historical and descriptive account of
Maidstone...
J. Brown. Maidstone.1834.
4.

LEGOUIX, Susan (later Mrs. Sloman).
Maidstone Museum and Art Gallery:Foreign
paintings catalogue.
Maidstone Borough Council. 1976.
4,6,11.

"Maidstone our heritage"; an exhibition
illustrating some aspects of the appearance
and character of Maidstone, past and present.
Maidstone Area Arts Council (1975).
11,12.

MAIDSTONE:a short guide.
(Pamphlet).
1949.
12.

MAIDSTONE AND DISTRICT AND EAST KENT BUS CLUB.
The illustrated fleet history of Maidstone
Corporation 1904 - 1974, edited by
Nicholas King.
Maidstone & District & East Kent Bus Club.
Aylesford. 1975.
11,12.

Seventy-five years of municipal transport in
Maidstone, 1904 - 1979.
Maidstone and District and East Kent
Bus Club. Aylesford. 1979.
12,23.

MAIDSTONE AND DISTRICT CHAMBER OF COMMERCE.
Maidstone (Kent): the official guide.
Ed. J. Burrow & Co. (c.1930).
11.

THE MAIDSTONE BOOK: 4th edition.
Regency Publicity Services Ltd. 1971.
4.

MAIDSTONE BOROUGH COUNCIL.
Borough of Maidstone:Official Guide,*
by L.R.A. Grove and Alfred Joyce.
Published for Maidstone Borough Council by
the Suburban and Provincial Association.
1961 1st edn.   4.11.
(1964) 2nd edn. 11.
1970 5th edn.   4.
1974 G.W. May Ltd.   19.
1975 G.W. May Ltd.   12.

Corporation year book 1899 - 1900.
Young and Cooper. Maidstone. 1899.
12.

General improvement area two:Perryfield Street.
Maidstone Borough Council. 1974.
12.

The Health of Maidstone.
Maidstone Borough Council. 1972.
12.

Leisure facilities in Maidstone.
Maidstone Borough Council. 1975.
12.

Maidstone:features of historical interest
and picturesque views of the Borough and
neighbourhood.*
Maidstone Borough Council. (1903?).
11,12.

Maidstone:the souvenir and programme of
events and festivities in this historic
borough for Coronation year 1953.
Maidstone Borough Council. 1953.
11.

Mote swimming baths:official opening by the
Rt. Hon. the Lord Cornwallis, Saturday
6th October, 1973.
1973.
12.

Programme (for) Son et Lumière,
Maidstone 1968...Riverside, Lockmeadow,
31st August - 28th September.
(Production was written and directed by
Albert Seth).
Maidstone Borough Council. 1968.
11.

Museum, public library and Bentlif Art
Gallery:report...1907.
Maidstone Borough Council. 1908.
12.

Park and Ride scheme:an introductory leaflet.
Maidstone Borough Council. 1975.
12.

Peel Street area survey.
Maidstone Borough Council. 1973.
12.

Perryfield Street;housing survey.
Maidstone Borough Council. 1973.
12.

A walk around Maidstone.
Maidstone Borough Council. (1978).
12.

Warrants for collection of watch and library
rates, with bonds for collectors. 1843 - 63.
12.

Written statement and map showing the graves
and tombstones at the burial ground of the
Friends' Meeting House, Wheeler Street,Maidstone.
1975
12.

MAIDSTONE BOROUGH COUNCIL:BOROUGH ENGINEER'S
DEPARTMENT.
Albion Place Local plan.
Maidstone Borough Council. 1973.
12.

Height of buildings policy.
Maidstone Borough Council.1973.
12.

Maidstone-House improvement grants.
Information handbook.
Pyramid Press. c.1970.
12.

MAIDSTONE BOROUGH COUNCIL:INFORMATION OFFICE.
Maidstone:official guide.
British Publishing Co. Ltd., for Maidstone
Borough Council. Gloucester. 1978.
11,12.

MAIDSTONE BOROUGH COUNCIL:PLANNING DEPARTMENT.
Maidstone town centre:conservation and
townscape.
Maidstone Borough Council. 1980.
12.

Maidstone town centre:housing and population.
Maidstone Borough Council. 1980.
12.

Maidstone town centre:industry and commerce.
Maidstone Borough Council. 1980.
12.

Maidstone town centre:leisure and tourism.
Maidstone Borough Council. 1980.
12.

Maidstone town centre:main issues and choices
facing the future.
Maidstone Borough Council. 1980.
12.

Maidstone town centre:offices.
Maidstone Borough Council. 1980.
12.

Maidstone town centre report on public
consultation.
Maidstone Borough Council. 1980.
12.

MAIDSTONE BOROUGH COUNCIL:PLANNING DEPARTMENT.
Maidstone town centre;shopping.
Maidstone Borough Council. 1980.
12.

Maidstone town centre;transportation.
Maidstone Borough Council. 1980.
12.

Popular Grove; development brief.
Maidstone Borough Council. 1980.
12.

MAIDSTONE:CENSUS FOR 1821. The Enumerators'
returns for two districts of Maidstone,
taken on May 28th,1821.
(not for 1801 as in the Kent Bibliography).
12.

MAIDSTONE DISTRICT SCOUT COUNCIL.
Yearbook 1975 - 76.
Maidstone District Scout Movement. (1976).
11.

MAIDSTONE FESTIVAL, July 4th - 25th. 1976.
Souvenir programme and notes.
(The Festival was jointly sponsored by
Maidstone Borough Council, Festival Committee
and the Maidstone Area Arts Council).
11,12.

MAIDSTONE GRAMMAR SCHOOLS.
Journal (kept by Reginald Henry Freed).
The Grammar School. 1927 - 1930 3 vols.
This is a homework diary for three years.
1927 - 28; 1928 - 29; 1929 - 30.
11.

Maidstone Grammar School:album of photographic
Prints. Tonbridge Road/Westree Road Site.
1870 - 1929.
Commercial and General Photographic Co.
London. (c.1922).
12.

The Maidstonian:Magazine of the Grammar School.
1925 - 1932.
11.

Opening of the new buildings by the Right
Hon. Lord Cornwallis on 28th July, 1930.
(Includes a list of Headmasters of the
School from 1549 - 1925).
The Grammar School. 1930.
11.

School Magazine:Maidstone Grammar School
for Girls.
1957 in progress.   12.
1972 - 73.   11.

The Wasp:magazine of the Maidstone Grammar
School Natural History Society. 1962 and 1963.
11.

MAIDSTONE MUSEUM AND ART GALLERY.
A brief guide to Maidstone Museum and Art
Gallery, compiled by the Staff in 1970.
Maidstone Borough Council. 1970.
4.11.

Catalogue of the Guy Mannering collection of
British birds..in the Maidstone Museum.
Maidstone Borough Council. 1960.
4,11.

Notes on the Kentish Collections in the
County Room of Maidstone Museum.*
Reprinted from the General Guide.
Maidstone Borough Council. Printed by W.P.
Dickinson. 1909.
4.5,11,17.19.

A short guide to the Maidstone Museum and
Art Gallery, with plan .
Maidstone Borough Council. 1936 and 1952.
12.

MAIDSTONE MUSEUM AND ART GALLERY.*
The Tyrwhitt-Drake Museum of Carriages at the
Archbishop's Stables, Mill Street, Maidstone.
The Official Guide. (The Tyrwhitt-Drake
Collection) 8th edition.
Maidstone Borough Council, 1971.
4,11.

MAIDSTONE PUBLIC LIBRARY.
Victoria Library:list of books added to the
Library, July 1903; January - March 1906;
1907 - 19.
Maidstone Public Library.
12.

MAIDSTONE UNION.
Statement of accounts for the half year ended
Michaelmas 1878, with a list of persons
receiving indoor and outdoor relief.
T.B. Brown. Maidstone. 1878.
23.

MAIDSTONE WATERWORKS COMPANY.*
Scale of quarterly charges for the supply of
water for domestic consumption....with the
rules and regulations required to be observed.
Dickinson. 1884.
12.

MASON, Hilda Claire.
Maidstone Amateur Dramatic Society. 1920's
and 1930's. A scrapbook of newspaper
cuttings, programmes etc.
11.

MUGGERIDGE, Sidney John.*
The postal history of Maidstone and the surrounding
villages with notes on their postal markings.
Postal History Society. 1972.
3,4,6,7,8,9,11.

OSTEOPATHIC EDUCATION AND RESEARCH LTD.
École Européene d'Ostéopathie; (course information)
1975.(College in Tonbridge Road, Maidstone).
Osteopathic Education and Research Ltd. 1975.
12.

ROW, B. Prescott.*
Kent's capital:a handbook to Maidstone on the
Medway and guide to the district. 2nd edition.
by B.P. Row and W.S. Martin. (Homeland
Association's handbooks no.6).
Ruck - Maidstone. Beechings - London. 1899.
12.

ROWLES, Walter.*
A general history of Maidstone, the shire town of
the County of Kent;containing its ancient and
present state, civil and ecclesiastical.
(Bound with Rowles, Walter - The Kentish
Chronology and Index...1807).
W. Rowles. London 1809.
11.

THE ROYAL ENGINEERS:Maidstone Station families'
guide.
Method Publishing Co. 1975.
11.

RUSHWORTH, John.
A letter sent to the Honourable William
Lenthal, Esq., Speaker of the Honourable House
of Commons, on the Fight between His
Excellency's the Lord Fairfax Forces at
Maidstone and the Kentish Forces on June 1st,1648.
Reprinted by Maidstone College of Art. 1959.
11.

RUSSELL, J.M.*
The History of Maidstone.
W.S. Vivish and F. Bunyard. Maidstone. 1881.
2.

The History of Maidstone.
Limited edition reprinted from the 1881 edition.
John Hallewell. Rochester. 1978.
3,11,22.23.

SABINE. William Henry Waldo.
Murder, 1776, and Washington's policy
of silence.
(Has an important bearing on the life of
Oliver de Lancey M.P. for Maidstone).
Theo. Gaus' Sons Incorporated. New York.   1973.
12.

SCOTNEY, David James Stratton.
The Maidstone trolleybus, 1928-1967.
National Trolleybus Association. 1972.
6,7,11,12.

SMITH, J.*
Topography of Maidstone and its environs...
J. Smith.Maidstone. 1839.
1,8,17.

STREATFIELD, Frank.*
An account of the Grammar School in the
King's town and parish of Maidstone in
Kent.
Rogers and Brown. Oxford. 1915.
2.

THOMAS, Bernard G.
Fire-fighting in Maidstone.
Phillimore. 1976.
1,3,6,8,11,12,22,25.

TOWN AND COUNTY DIRECTORIES.
Kent Trades Directory, 1972; Margate,
Ramsgate and including Maidstone and
Tunbridge Wells.
Town and County Directories. 1972.
11.

TRIAL AT MAIDSTONE SPRING ASSIZES, 1837.
For the possession of a picture, the
supposed portrait of Charles I by Vandyke.
Newspaper cuttings referring to the trial.1837.
11.

TYRWHITT-DRAKE, Sir Hugh Garrard.*
Sir Hugh Garrard Tyrwhitt-Drake's Zoo Park:
official illustrated guide (1938).
(At Cobtree Manor, Maidstone)
12.

The Tyrwhitt-Drake Scrapbook:concerning the
private collection of animals kept near
Maidstone.
n.d.
12.

TYSON, R.G. and Co. Publisher .
Picturesque Maidstone:a collection of
permanent photographs with descriptive sketch.
(2nd series).
R.G. Tyson and Co. 14 Mill Street. Maidstone. n.d.
(? early 1900's.)
12.

VIDLER, John.*
If freedom fail, by John Vidler with Michael Wolff.
(John Vidler was governor of Maidstone Prison
for ten years).
Macmillan. 1964.
4,11.12.

WHO'S WHO IN MAIDSTONE.*
Pullman Press Ltd. 1960.
1,4,11,12,15.

MANSTON

FRASER, Flt. Lt. William*
The story of the Royal Air Force, Manston.
Royal Air Force. Manston.
1970. 1st edn.   7.9.
1972. 2nd edn.   3,11,30.
1976. 3rd edn.   13.

MAPS

BARNETT, Michael.
Kent and Sussex ABC Atlas and County Gazeteer,
edited and compiled by M. Barnett.
G.I. Barnett. (196-?).
11.

BARTHOLOMEW, John and Son. Publisher
The Inns of Kent Map, compiled by K.C. Jordan.
J. Bartholomew and Son Ltd.
6. 1973.
7. 1976.

Post Office:Post Office Code Map:Kent.
Great Britain & Northern Ireland Sheet 10.
Scale 1 mile = ½"
J. Bartholomew and Son Ltd. 1970/75.
11.

CARLEY, John M.
Byways and bridleways in Meopham and nearby
parishes:a map for riders.
Meopham Publications Committee. 1972.
9.

COLEMAN, Alice M.*
East Kent:a description of the Ordnance
Survey seventh edition one inch sheet, 173.
(British Landscape through Maps) by
A.M. Coleman and C.T. Lukehurst.
Geographical Association. 1967.
2,3,4,6,20,23,24,30.

COUNTRYSIDE COMMISSION.
North Downs Way maps:the relevant 1:50,000
Ordnance Survey maps are 178, 179, 186, 187, 188,
189.
Countryside Commission. 1978.
4,23.

"GEOGRAPHIA" Ramblers' Map to London's
Countryside. S.E. Section. Kent.
Scale 1" to 1 mile.
Geographia Ltd. (1921?).
5,11.

HANNEN, Henry.*
An account of a Map of Kent dated 1596.
Reprinted from Archaeologia Cantiana. Vol.30.1913.
Mitchell, Hughes and Clarke. 1913.
11,17,18.

HARLEY, John Brian.
Maps for the local historian:a guide to the
British Sources.
Reprinted from "The Local Historian".
National Council of Social Service for the
Standing Conference for Local History. 1972.
11.

Ordnance Survey maps: a descriptive manual
Ordnance Survey. 1975.
11.

KENT COUNTY COUNCIL:ARCHIVES OFFICE.
Catalogue of estate maps 1590 - 1840.
in the Kent County Archives Office,edited
by Felix Hull.
K.C.C.1973.
4,5,6,7,9,11,12,13,16,20,25,30.

Kentish estate maps, 1596 - 1861:an introduction
to the work of some local map-makers
as illustrated by a display held at County Hall,
Maidstone, 28th April - 4th June, 1954.
K.C.C. 1954.
3,4,9,11

Kentish Maps and Mapmakers,1590-1840,
prepared by F. Hull.
K.C.C. 1973.
1,2,3,5,8,11,15,16,20,30.

KENT RIGHTS OF WAY COUNCIL.
Keys to the Kent Countryside:a map book for
walkers and riders.
Kent Rights of Way Council. 1978.
13.

MONTIER, David J.
Atlas of breading birds of the London area,
edited by D.J. Montier.
Batsford. 1977.
5.

ORDNANCE SURVEY.
Monastic Britain. 3rd edition. Maps - Scale 1:
625,000. (Folded with text).
Ordnance Survey. 1978.
23.

MAPS. Cont'd

ORDNANCE SURVEY.
The old series Ordnance Survey maps of England
and Wales. A reproduction of the 110 sheets
of the survey in early state in 10 volumes.
Introduction by J.B. Harley and Yolande
O'Donoghue. Vol.I. Kent,Essex, East Sussex
and South Suffolk. Scale 1" = 1 mile.
Harry Margary. Lympne Castle. 1975.
5,8,9,11,16,19.

Roman Britain 4th edition. Maps - Scale
1:625,000 (Folded with text).
Ordnance Survey 1978.
23.

ROYAL AUTOMOBILE CLUB.
Kent. (No.4 of the R.A.C. County Road Maps
and Guides).
Ed. J. Burrow & Co. (192-?)
11.

SIDE, Alice G.*
An atlas of Bryophytes found in Kent:maps
compiled from the record cards with ecological
notes on the species.
Kent Field Club. 1970.
7,8,9,11,30.

TITTLEY, Ian.
An Atlas of the Seaweeds of Kent, by I. Tittley
and J.H. Price.
Transactions of the Kent Field Club,
Vol.7. 1977.
3,6,7,8,11,13,23.

TOMBLESON, W.
Panoramic Map of the Thames and Medway.
J. Reynolds. (183-?).
11.

MARDEN

KENT COUNTY COUNCIL:COUNTY SECRETARY'S DEPARTMENT:
RESEARCH AND INTELLIGENCE UNIT.
Farm Open Day at Reed Court Farm, Chainhurst,
Marden, 17th August,1975; results of a Survey
of visitors' opinion on the day.
K.C.C. 1975.
11.

KENT COUNTY COUNCIL:PLANNING DEPARTMENT.
Marden Village:Informal District Plan.
K.C.C. 1973.
11,12.

MARGATE
See also ISLE OF THANET

ALBUM OF VIEWS OF MARGATE.
Brown & Rawcliffe. c.1900.
11.

ALL ABOUT MARGATE AND HERNE BAY,*
including Drapers', St. Peters —
Salmerstone, Chapel Bottom, Hengrove, Twenties
and Nash Court, Kingsgate and its modern
antiquities, Garlinge, Dandelion.
W. Kent and Co. London. 1866.
11.

ATKINSON, G.
A sermon occasioned by the death of George III
and ....Edward, Duke of Kent,preached at
Ebenezer Chapel, Margate.
1820.
13.

BEECHAM'S PHOTO-FOLIO. 24 choice photographic
views. Margate and Herne Bay.
13.

BENHAM, W.
A sermon preached at St. John's church Margate...
following the funeral of Mr. T.F. Cobb.
Kebles' Gazette. 1882.
13.

BONSFIELD, Publisher.*
Picture of Margate, being a complete guide to
all persons visiting Margate, Ramsgate &
Broadstairs with the Margate Hoy, a poem.
Bonsfield. 1809.
1,12,13.

BRADEN, J.T. Publisher.
J.T. Braden's photographic views of Margate
and neighbourhood.
J.T. Braden c.1890.
13.

BRASIER, W.C. Publisher.*
Brasier's Companion to the Almanacks and
General Advertiser for the year....
W.C. Brasier.
1878   24.
1881/2 13.

BRIDGEWATER, Howard.*
The Grotto.
1948. Rydal Press. Keighley. 11,13,14.
(1952?) Cooper the Printer Ltd.Margate. 11.24.

CALLCUTT & BEAVIS, Publishers.*
Thirty-two views of Margate and District.
Callcutt and Beavis. c.1895.
11,13.

CHAPMAN, T.
Cornwall Aviation Company. (The company which
gave aerial joy rides).
Glasney. 1979.
13.

CHAPMAN, W. (Curate of Margate).
Two sermons preached at Margate; the first
on reading the occasional prayer for the
Victory of the Nile; the second on the day
appointed for a public thanksgiving.
Hatchard. 1799.
13.

CLARKE, George Ernest.*
Historic Margate.
(Reprinted article published in the Thanet
Gazette).
Margate Public Libraries.
1957   30.
1972.   24.
1975 reprint11.

CLARKE, W.J. and KNAPP, Publishers.
Clarke's Margate Almanack, 1904.
Clarke, W.J. & Knapp.
13.
Clarke's Margate domestic & weather Almanack,
Clarke W.J. & Knapp. 1901
13.

Lane's Guide to Margate and the Isle of Thanet.
Clarke W.J. & Knapp. n.d.
13.

CLOUD, Yvonne.*
Beside the seaside, six variations.
(pp.227 - 264. Margate).
Stanley Nott. London. 1934.
11,13,14.

COMPARATIVE, Dr. Junior pseud.*
A sentimental journey through Margate and
Hastings.
Printed for Henry Colburn, Hanover Square,
London.1814.
11.
Newman 1819.   3,6,12,13,15,17.

CORKILL, W.H.*
Avebury, Coldrum and Margate.
Harper Cory. c.1953.
3,13,24.

CORY, Harper.*
The goddess at Margate. Published under the
authority of the Borough of Margate.
Mayflower Publishing Coy. n.d.
11,12,13.

The Grotto.
Mayflower Publishing Coy. n.d.
24.

CROOK, Herbert Evelyn.*
Margate as a health resort.
Printed by Harman Keble. Margate.
1893. 13,14.
1895. 4th edition. 11.13.

DAY, T.J.
A mid-Victorian seaside resort: Margate 1846-
1863.
Manchester B.A. thesis Mod. Hist.and Economics 1978.
13.

MARGATE
See also   ISLE OF THANET.

DAY, T.J.
A mid-Victorian seaside resort.Margate
1846-1863.
University of Manchester. B.A. thesis.1978.
13.

DRAPER'S MILLS TRUST.
Draper's Mills.
Draper's Mills Trust. 1976.
11.13.

EAST KENT TIMES AND BROADSTAIRS & ST.PETERS MAIL.
Margate Centenary Souvenir Supplement.1857-1957.
East Kent Times,Broadstairs and Margate. 1957.
24.

EMANUEL, W.
The magic of Margate,from "Lady's Realm"
September 1908.
13.

ENVIRONMENT, Department of the
List of buildings of special architectural
or historic interest:Borough of Margate.
Department of the Environment.
7,11. 1973.
13.   1975.

FREELING, Arthur.*
Picturesque excursions:containing upwards
of 400 views at and near places of popular
resort, edited by A. Freeling. (Includes
Margate, Tunbridge Wells and Dover).
William S. Orr. 1840.
24.

GALTON, Capt. Douglas.*
Report on the scheme of drainage submitted
by Albert Latham.
Keble. 1881.
13.

GORE, T.R.
Mid-Victorian Margate, with reference to the
Margate census of 1851. 2 vols. Thesis.
Typescript. 1979.
13.

GREAT BRITAIN, Laws etc. (Geo.I).*
An Act to enable the pier-wardens of the town
of Margate...more effectually to recover the
ancient and accustomary droits for the support
and maintenance of the said pier.
1724.
13.

GREAT BRITAIN, Laws etc. (Vic)
Pier and harbour orders confirmation Act 1878.
H.M.S.O. 1875.
13.

Local Government Act 1888. Borough of Margate.
13.

GRITTEN, A.J.
Catalogue of books, pamphlets and excerpts
dealing with Margate, the Isle of Thanet
and the County of Kent, in the Local History
Collection of the Borough of Margate Public
Library, compiled by A.J. Gritten.
Margate Library Committee. 1934.
1,3,4,7,11,13.

A GUIDE TO THE ISLE OF THANET and the
Cliftonville Hotel, Margate, 1890-1.
1890.
13.

HAMBRIDGE, H.W. (Bill).
Westgate on sea. 1909 - 1969. typescript.
c.1977.
13.

HASLAM, Ruby M.
The Shell Temple (Margate).
Regency Press. 1974.
2,6,11,15.

HOUGHTON, George E. Publisher.*
Photographic souvenir of Margate and neighbourhood, photographed by G.E. Houghton.
G.E. Houghton. Margate.
1895.   13.
1898.   11.12.13.

HOUGHTON, George E. Publisher.
Photographic Souvenir of the Great Storm,
Margate,November 29th,1897.
G.E. Houghton. Margate.
1897. 3,13.
1898. 13.

ISLE OF THANET CONSERVATIVE ASSOCIATION.
Fete and pageant in the grounds of Northdown,
Margate...7th, 8th and 9th of July, 1932...
edited by Gordon W. Clark.
The Association. 3 Thanet Road, Margate. 1932.
11.

KAY, A.M.*
St. John the Baptist in Thanet. (Margate Parish
Church).
Parochial Church Council. Printed by Cooper
the Printer, Margate. 1951.
11.

KEATE, George.*
Sketches from nature taken, and coloured, in
a journey to Margate. 2 vols. Printed for
J. Dodsley.
1779. 2nd edn. Vol.I. 24.   2 vols. 13.
1782. 3rd edn. 2 vols. 11,12,13,15,17.
1790. 4th edn. 2 vols. 13.
1802. 5th edn. 2 vols. 6,8,13.
1806. 6th edn. 2 vols. 24.

KELLY'S DIRECTORIES LTD.
Kelly's Directory of the Isle of Thanet, 1973.
Kelly's Directories Ltd. 1973.
13.

KENT COUNTY COUNCIL:ARCHIVES OFFICE.
Catalogue of the Cobb MSS. Parts I - IV:
records of the Cobb of Margate,Family and
business concerns.
K.C.C. 1979.
4,5,12,13,23,24.

KLINGER OF MARGATE LTD.
Klinger:Leader in the Production of Childrens Socks.
Klinger of Margate Ltd. c.1972.
13.

KOPS, B.
On Margate sands;a novel.
Secker & Warburg. 1978.
13.

LANE, Gentry and Co. Publishers.
Lane & Gentry's Standard guide to Margate
and historical Thanet.
Lane, Gentry & Co. Hastings & Margate. (1906?).
24.

LIGHTHOUSE - School Magazine of the Dame
Janet Junior School.
Duplicated Typescript. 1978.
13.

LUDLOW, R. Nelson.
1808-1958. Margate Methodist Circuit Triple-
Jubilee souvenir brochure and plan. 1958.
13.

MARGATE AMBULANCE CORPS.
Celebrating 100 years voluntary service,1880-1980.
Margate Ambulance Corps. 1980.
13.

MARGATE BOROUGH COUNCIL.
Abstract of accounts 1882 - 5.
13.

Borough of Margate water undertaking 1879 - 1956.
Margate Borough Council. 1956.
13.

Building byelaws made under the Public Health
Act, 1936.
Shaw and Sons.
13.

Byelaws made by the ...council..for the good rule
and government of the Borough.
Margate Borough Council.1928 and 1932.
13.

Bye-laws made with respect to Hackney carriages.
Margate Borough Council. 1913.
13.

MARGATE OPERATIC SOCIETY.
Finian's Rainbow. Programme.   1976.
13.

MARGATE PUBLIC LIBRARY.
The Margate Bookshelf: Summer & Autumn issues
1948; Winter Issue 1949.
13.

Scrapbook 1951 - 60. (Cuttings from
local papers concerning the library).
13.

MARGATE SCHOOL BOARD.
Penny Dinners 1886 - 1917.
Ms notebook.
13.

MAYHEW, Athol.*
The Chronicles of Westgate-on-Sea.
"Kent County News" Office. Canterbury. 1880.
8,11.13.17.

MORLEY, Malcolm.*
Margate and its theatres, 1730 - 1965.
Museum Press.   1966.
1,3,4,6,7,11,13,15,19,23.

NATIONAL CO-OPERATIVE EDUCATION ASSOCIATION.
Official report of the proceedings.   Co-
operative education convention Margate,
Easter, 1958.
Co-operative Union.   1958.
13

THE NEW ALBUM OF MARGATE VIEWS.   (c.1900).
11.

NEW MARGATE, RAMSGATE AND BROADSTAIRS   GUIDE.
Printed by Thanet Press.   1801.
24.

NEW RAMSGATE GUIDE WITH MAP, containing also
an account of Margate and Broadstairs as
well as life-boat work on the coast of Kent.
S.R. Wilson. 1890.
24.

"OBSERVANT PEDESTRIAN"
Further excursions of the Observant Pedestrian
exemplified in a tour to Margate. Vols.1.2.3.only.
Dutton. 1801.
13.

OULTON W.G.*
Picture of Margate and its vicinity, illustrated
with a map and twenty views engraved by
J.J. Shury from drawings by Captain G. Varle.
Baldwin, Cradock and Joy. London. 1820.
1,6,7,11,12,13,14,15,17,
11.   a second copy with some 200 engravings inter-
      leaved, some of Kent interest.
1821. 2nd edition. 24.

PAVING AND LIGHTING RATE 1839 and 1840.
(MSS).
13.

PERRY, W. Publisher.
Twelve views (of) Margate, (drawn by W. Perry).
W. Perry, Publisher, Margate. c.1860.
11.

PILKINGTON, Mrs. Mary.*
Margate!!!
J. Harris . 1813.
24.

RECOLLECTIONS OF MARGATE.
(Album of photographs).
n.d.
13.

REEVE AND CO.(MARGATE) LTD.
Past and present history.
(Mineral water manufacturer).
Reeve and Co (Margate) Ltd. 1904.
13.

REYNOLDS, CHARLES AND CO.   Publisher.*
Album of Margate Views.
Charles Reynolds and Co. London.
c.1878. 13,14.
(1900). 11.

ROCK AND CO. Publishers.*
The Royal Cabinet Album of Margate.
Rock and Co.   London. c.1900.
11.

ROGERS, James R.*
The loss of nine gallant lives. Written on
the capsizing of the surf boat "Friend of
all Nations" off Margate on Thursday, December
2nd,1897.
R. Robinson and Co. Margate. (1898).
3.

ROTARY INTERNATIONAL 37th ANNUAL CONFERENCE,
Margate. 1966.
13.

ROYAL SCHOOL FOR DEAF AND DUMB CHILDREN.
Annual Report 1937 - 8.
13.

"The Royal School" Magazine.   175 years
commemorative issue, 1792 - 1967.
Royal School for Deaf & Dumb Children. 1967.
13.

ST. JAMES'S BUDGET. No. 911. Vol. XXXV.
Friday December 10, 1897.
13.

ST.JOHN THE BAPTIST-IN-THANET:the opening of
the new St. John's Community Centre, 1971.
13.

ST. MILDRED'S HOTEL, Westgate-on-Sea,
(prospectus).
n.d.
13.

ST. PAUL'S CHURCH, CLIFTONVILLE, centenary
brochure, 1873 - 1973.
Thanet Printing Works, Ramsgate. 1973.
13.

SALMERSTONE SCHOOL TREASURY, 1977.
(Poems, stories, drawings by pupils)
typescript. 1978.
13.

SANDERS, J & Co. Engravers & Publishers.*
Views of Margate:thirty engravings originally
published by J.S. and Company (J. Sanders) and
Kershaw and Sons. c.1870.
11.13.

SANGER, "Lord" George (1825 - 1911).
Seventy years a showman. (Owner of the
largest English Circus of the nineteenth century.
His entertainment centre, Marine Parade, Margate,
flourished from 1874 - 1903).
First published 1910.
1926.   13.
1966 Fitzroy edn. Macgibbon and Kee. 13.

SAVILL, Mr.*
The trial of Mr Savill, linen draper, of Margate,
who was falsely and maliciously charged with
assaulting Mary Bayly...and found guilty...
after proving his innocence, at the Quarter
Sessions, Dover, on the 7th June,1800.
Published by Savill. Printed by A. Young. 1800.
6,11.

THE SHELL TEMPLE OF MARGATE* known as The
Grotto. Guide Book.
Printed by Cooper, Margate. n.d.
11,13.

STAFFORD, F.
Margate 1876. Extracts from Keble's Gazette,
compiled by F. Stafford, for Margate Civic
Society.
Margate Civic Society. 1976.
13.

Margate 1879. Extracts from Keble's Margate and
Ramsgate Gazette, January - December 1879,
compiled by F. Stafford for Margate Civic Society.
Margate Civic Scoiety. 1979.
13.

T.,B.
Merry Margate:a reminiscence of a sunny
morning's ramble.
Royal Deaf School. 1890.
13.

MARGATE.   Cont'd

THANET DISTRICT COUNCIL.
Margate. A study of the old town area,
together with recommendations for its conservation
by A. Swaine.
Thanet District Council. 1975.
13.

THANET DISTRICT COUNCIL: AMENITIES DEPARTMENT.
Margate: official holiday guide.
Thanet District Council 1975.
11.

THANET DISTRICT COUNCIL: PLANNING DEPARTMENT.
Margate old town action area plan:
report of a survey December, 1976.
Thanet District Council. 1976.
13.

TOWN AND COUNTY DIRECTORIES.
Kent Trades Directory, 1972. Margate,
Ramsgate and including Maidstone and Tunbridge
Wells.
Town and County Directories 1972.
11.

Margate, Ramsgate and North Kent district
Trades' Directory.
Town and County Directories. 1927 - 28.
24.

WALTON, Hugh Mersey.*
A short history of Holy Trinity Church,
Margate, 1825 - 1932.
Printed by Simpson & Turner for H.M. Walton.
Margate. 1932.
3,11,12,13.

WALTERS, John.
Dreamland cinema and entertainments Complex,
Margate.
Open University project essay. MSS 1976.
13.

WATERHOUSE, F. Aelred, (W., F.A.).*
A short history of Salmestone Grange.
Printed by Cooper. Margate.
1939. 14.
1948. 2,13.

WESTGATE-on-SEA AND BIRCHINGTON
annual almanack for 1883.
Hinton.
13.

WESTGATE-ON-SEA: souvenir letter card.
Polden. Westgate-on-Sea. (c.1930).
11.

WILDE, Laurie A.
A short history of Margate College,
1873 - 1940.
Old Margatonian Association. 1970.
11.

MARLOWE, Christopher. (1564 - 1593)

HENDERSON, Philip.
Christopher Marlowe.
Harvester Press. Brighton. 1974.
3.

HILTON, Zella.
Who was Kit Marlowe?
Weidenfeld and Nicolson. 1977.
3.

HOTSON, John Leslie.*
The death of Christopher Marlowe.
Nonesuch Press. 1925.
11,18.

LOM. Herbert.
Enter a spy; the double life of Christopher
Marlowe.
Merlin Press. 1978.
3.

THE MAN WHO SLEW KIT MARLOWE...
In The Weekly Despatch, 17th May, 1925.
3.

MARLOWE, Christopher.
The amorous poem entitled Hero and Leander.
(Printed at the Chiswick Press, Copy No.64
of 206 copies).
Golden Hours Press. London. 1933.
3.

The Famous Tragedy of the Rich Jew of Malta.
(Printed at the Chiswick Press, copy no 64
of 250 copies printed).
Golden Hours Press. London. 1933.
3.

The Tragicall History of Doctor Faustus.
(Printed at the Chiswick Press, No. 64 of
250 copies printed).
Golden Hours Press. London. 1932.
3.

MATFIELD

BRENCHLEY PARISH COUNCIL.
Brenchley and Matfield official guide.
Issued by authority of the Brenchley Parish
Council.
Forward Publicity. 1972?
4.

TOMPSETT, B.P.
The making of a new garden: Crittenden House,
Matfield, Kent; reprinted from Journal of the Royal
Horticultural Society. LXXXV. Part 2. February 1960.
19.

MEDWAY GAP - See KENT-MID

MEDWAY, RIVER AND VALLEY

ADMIRALTY.
River Medway, Sheet I. Sheerness Bar to
Bishops Ness, surveyed by Staff Commander. J.W.
Dixon, 1886 - 7, the soundings east of Grain by
Staff Comdr. Tizard. Engraved by Davies and Co.
Admiralty under the Superintendance of Capt. W.J.L.
Wharton. 1889. Scale 1:12,230 (Sea-mile = 6")
Hydrographic Chart.
Topography taken from Ordnance Survey.
11.

ALLENDALE, John.
Sailorman between the wars: being the journal
of a Thames, Medway and Coastal bargeman.
John Hallewell, Rochester. 1978.
3,4,5,11,12,15,22,23,25.

BENNETT, A.S.
Us bargemen.
Meresborough books. Rainham. 1980.
11,12.

BRADLEY, Arthur Granville.
The rivers and streams of England.
Painted by Sutton Palmer. (Includes River Medway).
A.&.C. Black and Co. 1909.
4.

BRANCH-JOHNSON, William.*
The English prison hulks.
C. Johnson. London.
1957   8,11,15,25.
1970 Revised edition. Phillimore. 11.12.

COOMBE, Derek.
The Barleymen: fishermen and dredgermen of
the River Medway, with chapters by Leslie H. Hill
and Leonard J. Wadhams.
Pennant Books, Rainham. 1979.
2,4,5,23,28.

DANCE, Charles.
New Medway Steam Packets, 140 years.
In SEA BREEZES, the magazine of ships and
the sea. Vol.52, No. 393, September,
1978, pp. 569 - 579.
11.

DIBLEY, George Edward.
Additional notes on the chalk of the Medway
Valley, Gravesend, West Kent, North East
Surrey and Grays, Essex.
Reprinted from the Proceedings of the Geologists'
Association Vol. XXIX 1918, pp.68 - 105.
Geologists' Association. 1918.
9.

DUMPLETON, Bernard.
Story of the Paddle Steamer (includes
Medway and Thames paddlesteamers).
Colin Venton, Melksham, 1978.
11,27.
Excerpts from "The Story of the Paddlesteamer".
4.

ECONOMIST INTELLIGENCE UNIT LTD.
The future for heavy industry in the Lower
Medway. Economist Intelligence Unit report
prepared for Kent County Council, July 1973.
Vol.I. Part I. The regional setting.
       Part II The Lower Medway.
Vol.II Part III. Industrial Site requirements.
       Part IV Examination of patterns of
               investment.
4,11.

FEARNSIDE, William Gray.*
The Thames and Medway:a series of 80 splendid
engravings from drawings by Tombleson, with
interesting historical descriptions by
W.G. Fearnside.
Thomas Holmes (183-?)
1,4,7,11,12,15.

FINCH, William Coles.*
The Medway river and valley.
G.W. Daniel Co. 1929.
2,24,25.30.

FINDLAY, Alexander George.*
A hand-book for the navigation of the different
channels of the Thames & Medway and the coast
between Folkestone and Orfordness.
R. Holmes Laurie. 1877.
1, 8, 11, 12.

GILLHAM, Eric Howard.*
Census of the breeding birds of the Medway
Islands, June 3rd - 5th 1955, edited by
E.H. Gillham and others.
Members of the Medway Census in
conjunction with the Kent Ornithological
Society, Chatham. 1955.
1,2,4,8,11,25,26.

GOODSALL, Robert Harold.*
The Medway and its tributaries.
1955 Constable. 20, 25.
1970 Reprinted by S.R. Publishers Ltd. 3,6,11,
22,30.

GREAT BRITAIN, Laws etc. (Geo.III).*
An act for improving the navigation of the
River Medway, from the town of Maidstone,
through the several parishes of Maidstone,
Boxley, Allington and Aylesford, in the
County of Kent....1792.
1792.
8,12.

An Act for the better Security of His
Majesty's Naval Arsenals in the River Medway
and Portsmouth and Hamoaze Harbours and of
His Majesty's ships and vessels lying at
and resorting to the same.
Printed by George Eyre & Andrew Strahan, London.
1811.
11.

GREAT BRITAIN: Laws etc. (Eliz II).
River Medway (Flood Relief) Act 1976.
(Chap.XXII).
H.M.S.O. 1976.
11.

GREAT BRITAIN PARLIAMENT. BILLS.
(Medway Ports Authority Bill). A Bill to amend
the Medway Ports Reorganisation Scheme,1968...
Photocopy. 1972.
4.

HARRIS, Edwin.
The River side:an itinerary of the Medway,
within the City of Rochester and memories it
recalls. Reprint of the 1930 edition,
published by Edwin Harris
North Kent Books. 1979.
4,11.

HARRIS, Edwin.*
A trip down the Medway.
(Old Rochester Series No.5).
E. Harris. Rochester. 1897.
25.

A trip up the Medway.
(Old Rochester Series No.6).
E. Harris, Rochester. 1897.
25.

HARRISON, Jeffery.*
Breeding birds of the Medway estuary, by Jeffery
G. Harrison, J.N. Humphreys and Geoffrey Graves.
Illustrated by Pamela Harrison.
WAGBI. 1972.
15,16,25,27,30.

HILTON, John Anthony.
A history of the Medway Navigation Company,
compiled from various sources by
J.A. Hilton.
John Hilton, Hadlow. 1977.
2,3,4,8,15,16,19,22,23,25.

IRELAND, Samuel.*
Picturesque views, on the River Medway, from the
Nore to the vicinity of its source in Sussex.
T & J. Egerton. 1793.
2.

JAMES, Harold A.
The Dutch in the Medway 1667.
Chatham Borough Council. 1967.
3.4,11,19,23,24,25,30.

KENT COUNTY COUNCIL - PLANNING DEPARTMENT.*
The potential of the Medway Estuary as a
maritime industrial development area: a
discussion of the economic factors and an
appraisal of its impact on Mid and North Kent,
by R.G. Clarke, County Planning Officer.
K.C.C. 1970.
2,3,4,8,11,20,24,25.

Report and recommendations of the lower
Medway Working Party.
K.C.C. 1974.
4,11.

Report of the results of the consultations on
the recommendations of the Lower Medway Working
Party;interim decisions now to be taken on
the conclusions.
K.C.C. 1974.
4,11.

Structure plan. Potential development of the
Lower Medway (Report of the Lower Medway Working
Party as amended following consultations).
Serial No.4. Final Draft (Nov.74).
K.C.C. 1974.
11.

KENT COUNTY LIBRARY.
Medway Bridges;eight historic prints published
on the occasion of the opening of the new
Bridge at Maidstone 1978...with text by
Peter Richards,Stella Hardy and Brenda Purle.
Kent County Library. 1978.
4,11,16,19,23.

KENT COUNTY LIBRARY - MEDWAY DIVISION.
Sights along the Medway.
1973 (Chatham Public Libraries).   4.
1974 Kent County Library.   3,4,11.
1975 "   "   "   4,11,12.
1976 "   "   "   3,4,11.
1977 "   "   "   3,4,11.
1978 "   "   "   4,11,12.

LIST OF MERCANTILE VESSELS BUILT ALONG THE MEDWAY,
1823 - 1930, and in East Anglia, Kent and Sussex
from 1803.
From a photocopy in Rochester Museum.
4.

McCULLOCH, Rev. Joseph.*
Medway adventure.
(The author was Rector of Chatham from 1943).
M. Joseph. 1946.
7,11.

MARCH, Edgar James.*
Spritsail barges of Thames and Medway.
P. Marshall. 1948.
20,25.

THE MARITIME TRUST.
The story of the Cambria.
(Medway Barge anchored by Rochester Esplanade)
Ship's Monthly with the Maritime Trust.
4,11.25.

MARSH, Ronald.*
The conservancy of the river Medway 1889 -
1969;a history of the Medway Conservancy
Board.
Medway Conservancy Board. 1971.
2,12,20.

MAXWELL, Donald.
Excursions in colour.
(Includes a chapter on the Medway Valley).
Cassell. 1927.
11,15.

MEDWAY PORTS AUTHORITY.
Boating on the River:Medway and Swale.
Medway Ports Authority.
1969   8.   1970.   8.   1975.   8.

Medway Ports Authority;illustrated descriptive
booklet (1973).
8.

Medway Ports Authority:river Byelaws. 1973.
8.

Notice to Mariners:water ski-ing and aqua-planing.
(Notice 19 of 1973).
Medway Ports Authority 1973.
4,8.

Official Handbook.
E.J. Burrows and Co. Cheltenham. 1978.
3,4,15,25.

MEDWAY PRESERVATION SOCIETY.*
The effects of a M.I.D.A. (Medway Industrial
Development Area) on the Medway Estuary, a
report prepared by the Medway Preservation
Society. (Includes lists of birds and flowers)
Medway Preservation Society. 1971
4,8,11.

MEDWAY RIVER USERS ASSOCIATION. Rules.
(1974).
12.

MEDWAY '75: the River Medway, its
people, its places. Souvenir supplement
published by the Kent Evening Post to coincide
with the Medway Regatta. 1975.
9,11.

MEDWAY '76: the story of the River Medway
from dinosaurs to Cod War Frigates.
Souvenir supplement of the Kent Evening Post,1976.
9.

MEDWAY YACHTING ASSOCIATION.
Water based recreation in the tidal Medway
and the Swale. A study of the likely
requirements for yachting facilities over
the 1970's and of what can be done to provide
them.
Medway Yachting Association. 1970.
4.

MILLAR, J.B.
The story of Medway Queen, a paddle steamer that
went to war;(edited by J.B. Millar).
Paddle Steamer Preservation Society.1975.
3,4,8,11,20,25,26,27.

PERKS, Richard Hugh.
Sprits'I:a portrait of sailing barges and
sailormen, written in collaboration with
Patricia O'Driscoll and Alan Cordell.
(The author lives near Faversham. North Kent
barge building centres are given).
Conway Maritime Press. 1975.
3.4.9.11.12.15.20.22.25.

PRESTON, John M.
Industrial Medway:an historical survey.
Printed W.&.J. Mackay Ltd. for J.M. Preston,
Borstal Road, Rochester. 1977.
1.2.3.4.5.7.8.9,11,12,15,16,19,20,22,23,25,26,27,28.

SAGE, Stephen.
Sailing barges of the Medway.
Typescript Ms. 1973.
11.

SMITH, Peter C.
Heritage of the sea.
(Includes 7 ships with Medway connections).
Balfour Pubns. 1974.
4.

STANFORD, Edward Ltd. Publishers.
Coloured charts for coastal navigation. (Edited by
Capt. O.M. Watts) No.8. The River Medway and the
Swale.New edition correctd to November 1974.
Stanford Maritime Ltd. 1974.
4.

Stanford's Harbour Guide: River Medway and the
Swale. Edited by Capt. F.S. Campbell.
Stanford Maritime Ltd. 1975.
1,8,9,11,12,15,20,25,26,27.

TOMBLESON, W.
Panoramic Map of the Thames and Medway.
J. Reynolds. (183-?).
11.

TRANSPORT, Ministry of.
The reorganisation of the ports. Cmnd.3903.
(Includes Medway Ports).
H.M.S.O. 1969.
11.

UGLOW, Capt. Jim
Sailorman:a bargemaster's story. (The author was
born in Gillingham and served on seagoing barges
from Rochester to Greenhithe).
Conway Maritime Press. 1975.
4,9,11,12,15,20,26,27.

WHITNEY, John.
The genteel recreation. Poetical description
of the Darent and Medway Rivers.
Johnson. 1820.
11.

WILLIAMSON, W.S.
The upper reaches of the River Medway. 4th edition.
Scale:4" to 1 mile. Section A. Tonbridge to Yalding.
Section B. Yalding to Allington lock. Transit map,
Allington to Rochester Bridge.
Imray, Laurie, Norie and Wilson. 1975.
4.

WILLMOTT, Frank G.
Cement, mud and muddies;a history of APCM barges.
Photography by Alan Cordell.
(River industries of the River Medway).
Meresborough Books. Rainham. 1977.
1,3,4,5,7,8,9,11,15,20,23,25,26,27,30.

WILSON, Charles.Publisher.*
Sailing directions for the rivers Thames and Medway.
Charles Wilson. 1881.
2,15.

WOODTHORPE, T.J.*
The Tudor Navy and the Medway:Queenborough as a
Naval Port.
Typewritten script. n.d.
11,20,26,27.

MEDWAY TOWNS.
See also CHATHAM, GILLINGHAM, ROCHESTER, STROOD.

AZIMUTH: journal of the Medway writers' circle.
Vol.1. Nos. 1 - 5. 1967 - 72.
4.

BYEGONE MEDWAY: a calendar selected from "an
album of old views of Chatham, Gillingham,
Rochester and Strood area" for 1979.
John Hallewell. Rochester. 1978.
11.

MEDWAY TOWNS Cont'd
See also CHATHAM,GILLINGHAM,ROCHESTER,STROOD.

BYEGONE MEDWAY:an album of old views of the
Chatham,Gillingham,Rochester and Strood area.
Compiled from the collections of Malcolm John,
Jenifer Roberts and John Sifleet.
John Hallewell. Rochester.
Vol.I. 1978. Vol II. 1979.
4,11.

CHATHAM & DISTRICT LETTER CARD.
(Letter written by "Doris" from Gillingham,
probably in the 1930's). n.d.
11.

CHATHAM NEWS:Almanac and Yearbook. 1907.*
25.

CHATHAM,ROCHESTER,STROOD AND BROMPTON
MECHANICS INSTITUTION.
Prospectus for the erection of a building for
a Mechanics Institute, public hall and
lecture room for Chatham, Rochester, Strood
and Brompton.
R. Taylor, printer. Chatham. (1830?).
4.

CHATHAM STANDARD.
Crimes that shocked the Medway Towns:series
of articles from the Chatham Standard.
Parrett and Neves. Sittingbourne. 1973.
3,4,8,11,20,25.

CITY OF ROCHESTER SOCIETY.
Charles Dickens and the Medway Towns.
City of Rochester Society. 1976.
8.

COMMUNITY HEALTH COUNCIL:MEDWAY HEALTH DISTRICT.
Annual report...for period April 1974 to March 1975.
1975.
4.

EMPLOYMENT SERVICE AGENCY (Medway District).
Labour Market Intelligence Bulletin, June 1977.
Employment Services. 1977.
8.

FINANCIAL TIMES.
Medway Towns
Financial Times Report, Monday,
June 31st 1972).
(On Local Government Organisation)
4.

GOODHEW, R.C.
Continuity and change in the Medway Ports
since the 2nd World War: a short project
undertaken in partial fulfillment of the
requirements of the degree of B.Sc. at
Hull University.
Typescript (photocopy) 1965.
4,8.

GOSNEY, R.
Central Library for the Medway Towns (a thesis
presented to the North West Polytechnic).
Photocopied sheets. 1970.
4.

GREAT BRITAIN, Laws etc. (Eliz.II).
Medway Ports Authority Act. 1973. ch.xxi.
H.M.S.O. 1973.
1,4,11,12.

GULVIN, Keith R.
'The Medway forts':a short guide.
P.P. 1976.
4,9,20,25,32.

HEADWAY: the newsheet of the Medway Arts Council.
1965.in progress.
4 incomplete.
8.

INDUSTRIAL GREAT BRITAIN PART II:a commercial
review of leading firms selected from important
towns of many counties. (Selection including
Chatham, Rochester, Strood).
1891.
4.

JEFFERYS, Hazel D.
Public health in the Medway Towns during the
nineteenth century and the implementation of the
Public Health Acts 1848 and 1875. (An extended
essay). Typescript.
(1973?).
4.

KELLY'S DIRECTORIES LTD.
Kelly's Directory of Rochester, Strood, Chatham
and Gillingham.
Kelly's Directories Ltd. (1922).
11

Kelly's Directory of the Medway Towns.
Kelly's Directories Ltd. 1973.
7.

KENT COUNTY COUNCIL.
Application of the Medway Towns for amalgamation
and extension as a County Borough.
K.C.C. 1946.
1.

KENT COUNTY COUNCIL:EDUCATION DEPARTMENT.*
The Arts in the Medway Towns, 1951 - 1952.
K.C.C. (1953?).
25.

Medway and Maidstone College of Technology.
Part Time Courses 1975-76. K.C.C. 1975. 11.
Full Time Courses 1975-76. K.C.C. 1975. 11.
KENT COUNTY COUNCIL:HIGHWAYS AND TRANSPORTATION
DEPARTMENT.
Future of Transport in the Medway Towns.
K.C.C. 1974.
4,25.

Medway Towns Transportation Study:Technical
report.
K.C.C. 1974.
4,11,15.

KENT COUNTY COUNCIL:PLANNING DEPARTMENT.
Kent County Structure Plan.
Future development possibilities in Kent;
the Medway Towns, Sittingbourne and Sheppey.
(Serial No. E4B).
K.C.C. December 1975.
4.

Kent Development Plan (1967 Revision).
Medway Towns, Maidstone and vicinity and Medway Gap
Town Maps. Report on population and employment
studies in Mid Kent. Analysis of shopping centres
in Mid-Kent.
K.C.C. 1970.
8,11,12,25.

Kent Development Plan.*(1967 Revision) Medway
Towns Town Map (1970 Revision) Written statement,
(as approved by the Planning Committee at its
meeting on the 10th December 1970).
8,11.

Amendment to the written statement as approved
by the Planning Committee on the 12th December,
1970).
8 ,11,12,25.

Kent Development Plan*(1967 Revision).
Medway Towns Town Map (1970 Revision)
Report on the Survey and analysis.
K.C.C. 1970.
8,11,12,25.

Kent Development Plan. Sample survey of households. Mid Kent 1971. (Volume II, Medway and
Swale).
K.C.C. 1975.
4 ,11,15,20.

MEDWAY TOWNS Cont'd
See also CHATHAM, GILLINGHAM, ROCHESTER, STROOD.

RAND, Duncan.*
Industrial Review and Guide to the Medway,
edited by D. Rand.
Pyramid Press. (1971).
4,24,25,30.
1974.   12.

Theatre in Rochester and the Medway area.
(Photocopy of typescript, 1971).
4.

RAPLEY, Hazel E.
Enforcement of law and order in the
Medway Towns during the Nineteenth Century.
Typescript. Unpublished Thesis.
Sittingbourne College of Education. 1976.
4,8.25.

ROCK AND CO. Publishers.*
Rock's Royal Album (of) Rochester,
Chatham and neighbourhood.
Rock and Company. c.1890.
11.

ROWE, Mrs. Mercy Elizabeth.*
John Tetley Rowe and his work:a brief
record of his life and work in London,
Chatham and Rochester, by his wife.
(Biography of an Archdeacon of Rochester).
Parrett & Neves. Chatham. 1915.
4,8,11,12,15,25.

SOUTH EAST ENGLAND TOURIST BOARD.
Study of tourism in the Medway Borough
Council District.
South East England Tourist Board. 1974.
4,25.

WEINER, J. Ltd. Publisher.
Medway Towns' Green Guide.
(Weiner's Neighbourhood Guides).
J. Weiner Ltd. 1969.
8.

WHITTA, Terry.*
Art and entertainment in the Medway Towns:
a report produced from the findings of
Breakaway Arts, September,1964.
4,8.

Report on a Market Research project
(Medway Towns), 21st February,1970.
Concerned with entertainment.
Duplicated Typescript. (1972).
4.

WINSPUR, Catherine.
Look Medway (South) 76.
P.P. (1976).
4,8.

WRIGHT, I.G. Publisher.*
Wright's topography of Rochester, Chatham,
Strood, Brompton etc..
(Damaged copy).
I.G. Wright. 1838.
25.

MEOPHAM

BEAUMONT, Stephen.*
The Meopham Book, edited by Stephen
Beaumont and others.
Meopham Parish Council.
(c.1963)   5.9.
1970.   9,11.

CARLEY, James.
The lost roads of Meopham and nearby parishes.*
Meopham Publications Committee.   1971.
25.

Meopham Parish Council:the first 80 years.
Meopham Parish Council. 1980.
22.

Meopham Pictorial.
Meopham Publications Committee. 1978.
3,8,9,11.

CARLEY, James.
Pubs of Meopham.
Meopham Publications Committee, 1975.
3,8,9,11.

CARLEY, John M.
Byways and Bridleways in Meopham and
nearby parishes:a map for riders.
Meopham Publications Committee. 1972.

The story of Meopham Mill.*
Meopham Publications Committee. 1972.
2,4,9,11.

DAVIES, Michael W.
Meopham:a village and its church.
Meopham Parochial Church Council? 1975.
9,11.

GOLDING-BIRD, Cuthbert Hilton.*
The History of Meopham:a Kentish village from
Saxon times.
Williams and Norgate. 1934.
30.

The story of old Meopham.
Ash and Co. Ltd. 1918.
25.

GRAVESHAM BOROUGH COUNCIL:PLANNING DEPARTMENT.
Culverstone chalet area, Meopham, Kent.
Gravesham Borough Council. 1975.
11.

GUNYON, William P.
History of Meopham Cricket Club.
W.P. Gunyon, 3, Fox Cottages,Meopham.   1976.
4,8,9,11,15,25.

HAYES, Will.
Gray Ridge (and)the Book of Francis Howgill,
written and compiled by Will Hayes. Order of
the Great Companions, Hertha's Chapel, Meopham
Green. 1942.
(Francis Howgill was a Westmoreland Quaker).
11.

KNIGHT-SWEENEY, Brian.
Meopham Miscellany, 1895 - 1899, by B.
Knight-Sweeney and J. Carley.
Meopham Publications Committee. n.d.
2,9.11.

A tour from Meopham.
Meopham Publications Committee. 1973.
9,11.

MEOPHAM & DISTRICT FOOTPATHS GROUP.
Six walks from Meopham Church and Camer.
Meopham Publications Committee, 1974.
11.

Six walks from Meopham Green.
Meopham Publications Committee, 1970.
11.

Twenty walks round Meopham.
Meopham Publications Committee, 1975.
9,11.

See also. FOOTPATHS- COUNTRYWALKS.

MEOPHAM PUBLICATIONS COMMITTEE.
Meopham History trail.
Meopham Publications Committee. 1978.
9,11.

MEREWORTH

GENERAL REGISTER OFFICE.
Census Returns, 1841,1851,1861,1871.
Mereworth. Microfilm.
23.

LOWE, Jeremy B.
A short guide to the church of St.Lawrence,
Mereworth. (197?).
11.

MEREWORTH CASTLE near Maidstone, Kent:*
the residence of Mr. Michael and Lady Anne Tree.
1954. Reprinted brom the Antique Collector,
October, 1954.
11.

MEREWORTH Cont'd

TOOTELL, J.
A plan of an estate in the parish of Yalding
and in the hamlet of Old Hay in the Parish
of Mereworth in the County of Kent. The
property of Lord Strafford. Revised from The
Tithe Maps....1860.
Scale 1 mile = 26" (.744m.) Size 92cm x 110cm.
11.

WARREN, Clarence Henry.
A boy in Kent.
Geoffrey Bles. 1937.
6,11,25,26.

MERSHAM HATCH

KNATCHBULL-HUGESSEN, Sir Hughe.*
A Kentish Family.
Methuen. 1960.
1,3,4,5,6,7,8,9,11,12,14,15,17,18,21,22.

RODERICK, Colin.*
John Knatchbull:from quarterdeck to gallows.
Angus & Robertson. 1963.
3,7.

MILITARY & NAVAL HISTORY

ARUP ASSOCIATES.
The Gun Wharf, Chatham:400 years of
maritime history.
Arup Associates. 1975.
4,11.

ATKINSON, Christopher Thomas.*
The Queen's Own Royal West Kent Regiment 1914-19.
Simpkin,Marshall etc. 1924.
13.

BACON, Sir Reginald Hugh Spencer.*
The Concise Story of the Dover Patrol.
Hutchinson. 1932.
4,6,11,12.

The Dover Patrol, 1915 - 1917. 2 vols.
Hutchinson (1919) 11.
Doran 1919. 4,6,7,12.

See also DOVER & WORLD WAR I for other titles.

BARWIS, Michael.
Mutiny at the Nore, (project drama).
First performed at Sevenoaks School.
Heinemann Educational Books. 1969.
11,23,27.

BELL, Ernest W.
Soldiers killed on the first day of the Somme.
(Casualties listed by Regiment).
E.W. Bell, Bolton. 1977.
11.

BLAXLAND, Gregory.
The Buffs. (Men at Arms Series).
Osprey Publications. 1972.
6,7,14,28.

The Buffs:*Royal East Kent Regiment:
The Third Regiment of Foot.
Leo Cooper. 1972.
6,7,11,12,30.

The farewell years:* the final historical
records of the Buffs, Royal East Kent
Regiment (3rd. Foot), 1948 - 1967.
Queen's Own Buffs Office. Canterbury. 1967.
30.

A guide to the Queen's Regiment;* with maps
and sketches by the late D.G. Woodcock.
P.P. for The Queen's Regiment, Canterbury,1970.
11.

The Home Counties Brigade,*its members and
their integration.
Gibbs, Canterbury (1960?).
13,24.

BLAXLAND, Gregory.
The Queen's Own Buffs, the Royal Kent Regiment.
(3rd,50th and 97th of Foot).
Queen's Own Buffs Regimental Association,
Canterbury. 1974.
1,3,5,9,11,15,28.

The Story of the Queen's Own Buffs, the
Royal West Kent Regiment.
Gibbs, Canterbury. 1963.
30.

BOTZOW, Herman S.D.*
Monorails.(Louis Brennan).
M. Paterson. 1960.
8.

BOYD, Derek.
Royal Engineers (Famous Regiments Series).
Leo Cooper Ltd. 1975.
8,11,12,15,32.

THE BUFFS:History of 'A' Squadron, 141st
Regiment R.A.C. (The Buffs).
The Regiment 1946.
11.

THE BUFFS: Royal East Kent Regiment.
Malcolm Page Ltd. n.d.
13.

BURCHMORE, L.J.
Royal Air Force Station, Gravesend, goings on,
by"Chiefy B"
L.J. Burchmore. Farnham. 1974.
9.

BUSK, Hans.*
Handbook for Hythe:comprising a familiar
explanation of the laws of projectiles.
(Hythe School of Musketry).
Routledge. 1860.
10.

Reprint of the 1860 edition,by Richmond
Publications. 1971.
11.12.

CANTERBURY CITY MUSEUMS.
The Buff's Museum: Catalogue of Books.
Duplicated typescript.
Canterbury City Museums 1976.
3.

Guide to the Museum of the Buffs.
Canterbury City Museum. 1975.
3

CAPPER, Douglas Parode.*
Moat defensive:a history of the waters of
the Nore Command, 55BC to 1961.
 Barker 1963.
4,8,11,12,15.

CHAPLIN, Lt. Col. Howard Douglas.
The battle honours of the dirty half-hundred,
1756-1881.
Museum Committee,Queen's Own Royal West
Kent Regiment. Canterbury. 1976.
12.

The 97th, or Earl of Ulster's Regiment 1824 -
1881.*
The Queen's Own Royal West Kent Regimental
Museum Committee, Maidstone. 1973.
3,7,11,16,20,26,27.

The Queen's Own Royal West Kent Regiment,
1881 - 1914.*
Regimental History Committee. Maidstone. 1959.
6.

The Queen's Own Royal West Kent Regiment,
1920 - 1950.*
M. Joseph. 1954.
24.

The Queen's Own Royal West Kent Regiment,
1951 - 1961.*
Regimental Museum Committee, Maidstone. 1964.
12.

CHATHAM DOCKYARD EXTENSION, 1866.
Photograph Album showing the construction
of the extension. 1866.
32.

COLLINS, Kenneth J.
Queen's Own Royal West Kent Regimental
Museum (Maidstone Museum).
English Life Publications. Derby. 1973.
2,4,6,11,12,19,25.

COMMONWEALTH WAR GRAVES COMMISSION.
The war dead of the Commonwealth. The
register of the names of those who fell in the
1939-45 War and are buried in cemeteries
and churchyards in the County of Kent.
Parts I, II and III.
Commonwealth War Graves Commission. 1960 & 1961.
2,3,7.

CONNOLLY , T.W.J. (R.E.)
History of the Corps of Royal Sappers and Miners.
2 vols.
Longmans, Brown and Green.
1855 1st edition.   32.
1857. 2nd edition.   8,32.

Romance of the Ranks and Social Incidents
of Military Life. 2 vols.
Longmans, Brown and Green. 1859.
32.

THE CONNOLLY PAPERS (M/S) (CONNOLLY, T.W.J).
a) Notitia Historica,Royal Engineers.
b) SkeletonMemoirs of Royal Engineer Officers.
32.

CORBELL, P.M.
Royal Air Force Station, Biggin Hill,
compiled by P.M. Corbell. (Photocopy)
Air-Britain. 1967.
2.

DAVIES, Hamlyn L. Rees.
The Guild of St. Helena:Chatham Garrison Branch.
(Some notes on the origin and object of the
Guild and on its work in Chatham). Typescript.
1963.
4.

DEFENCE, Ministry of
Report of the Defence Lands Committee, 1971 - 73.
H.M.S.O. 1973.
7.

DIGGES, Thomas.
England's defence:a treatise concerning invasion,
or, a brief discourse of what orders were best for
repulsing of foreign forces, if at any time they
should invade us by sea in Kent...exhibited in
writing...a little before the Spanish invasion
in...1588, by Thomas Digges, Esq., Muster-Master-
General of all Her Majesty's Forces in the Low
Countries. To which is now added, an account
of such stories of War...collected by Thomas
Adamson...1763.
Printed for F. Haley. 1680.
11.

THE DRAGON: a paper for men of the Buffs and men
of Kent. The issues for 1921, bound together.
The Buffs (East Kent Regiment). 1921.
11.

DUGAN, James.*
The Great Mutiny.
Putnam. 1965.
11,15.

(DUNCAN, William Edmonstone).
The Royal Artillery commemoration book, 1939-1945,
(edited by W.E. Duncan, H.F. Ellis, R.L. Banks,
M. Scarfe).
Published on behalf of the Royal Artillery
Benevolent Fund by Bell. 1950.
11.

THE EAST KENT YEOMAN:official organ of the Royal
East Kent Mounted Rifles. Vol.VI. No.8, 1911.
The Regiment. 1911.
11.

EVERSON, Don.
The Reluctant Messerschmitt.
(Shot down in the English Channel in October, 1940,
found by fishermen,retrieved and restored and now
in Brenzett Aeronautical Museum)
Portcullis Press. Redhill,Surrey. 1978.
7.12.

FAZAN. E.A.C.*
Cinque Ports Battalion: the story of the 5th
(Cinque Ports) Battalion, the Royal Sussex
Regiment (T.A.),formerly the 1st. Cinque Ports
Rifle Volunteer Corps:its antecedents, traditions
and uniforms.
Royal Sussex Regimental Association. 1971.
6.

FIELD, C.
Louis Brennan:the man from Castlebar and Gillingham.
Printed by Reader & Phillips.Gillingham.1973.
11.

FOLKESTONE BOROUGH COUNCIL.
Presentation of the Freedom of Folkestone to the
Queen's Own Buffs, the Royal Kent Regiment
on Saturday 6th May, 1961.
Printed by F.J. Parsons. Folkestone. 1961.
11.

FRASER, Flt. Lt. William*
The Story of the Royal Air Force, Manston.
Royal Air Force, Manston.
1970. 1st ed   7.9.
1972 2nd ed   3,11,30.
1976 3rd ed   13.

FREESTON, Ewart Cecil.
Prisoner-of-war ship models, 1775 - 1825.
Nautical Publishing Co. 1973.
4.

GENERAL MOORE AT SHORNECLIFFE.
Sandgate Society, Sandgate. n.d.
11.

GILL, Conrad.*
The Naval Mutinies of 1797.
Manchester University Press.   1913.
4,11.

GLOVER, Richard.
Britain at bay;defence against Bonaparte 1803-1814.
Allen and Unwin. 1973.
3,4,11.

GREAT BRITAIN, Laws etc. (Geo.II)
An Act for taking down and removing the
Magazine for Gunpowder, and all Buildings thereto
belonging, situate near Greenwich in the County
of Kent, and erecting, instead thereof, a new
Magazine for Gunpowder at Purfleet, near the
River of Thames, 1759.
Printed by Thomas Baskett. 1760.
11.

GREAT BRITAIN, Laws etc. (Geo III).
An Act for the purchase of certain lands,
tenements and hereditaments at Sheerness
and Chatham for the use of the Navy. (24th
June,1816).
Printed by Eyre and Strahan. 1816.
11.

GULVIN, Keith R.
Kent Home Guard:a history.
North Kent Books in association with
Meresborough Books. 1980.
2,6,12,13,16,22,23,28.

H.M.S. KENT:a short history, 1653-1928.*
Sampson,Low,Marston. 1928.
4,6,11,16.

HALL, Eric Foster.*
A short history of the Buffs:Royal East Kent
Regiment (3rd Foot)... 2nd edition. 1950.
Medici Soc. 1950.
1,2,3,7,8,11,14,30.

HANGER, George.*
Reflections on the menaced invasion
and the means of protecting the capital by
preventing the enemy from landing in any part
contiguous to it...a correct military
description of Essex and Kent.
(facsimile reprint;original John Stockdale,
1804).
Paul B.Minet. 1972.
2.

HEAD, General Sir. Francis Bond.
The Royal Engineer.
Murray. 1869.
32.

HISTORICAL RECORDS OF THE BUFFS.*
(Royal East Kent Regiment) 5 vols.
Vol.5. KNIGHT, Charles Henry Bruere.1919-48.
Medici Society. 1951.
2.

HISTORY OF THE CORPS OF ROYAL ENGINEERS.*
9 vols. 1889 - 1958.
Vol.I. PORTER, Whitworth.
Longmans, Green & Co. 1889.
8,15,25,32.
Vol II. PORTER, Whitworth.
Longmans, Green & Co. 1889.
8,15,25,32.
Vol. III WATSON, Sir Charles M.
Institute of Royal Engineers,Chatham.1915.
8,15,25,32.
Vol. IV. BROWN, W. and BAKER,?
Institute of Royal Engineers, Chatham, 1952.
(Reprinted 1954).
8,32.
Vol. V. THE HOME FRONT, France,Flanders
and Italy in the First World War.
Institute of Royal Engineers. Chatham, 1952.
8,32.
Vol.VI GALLIPOLI, Macedonia, Egypt and
Palestine, 1914 - 1918.
Institute of Royal Engineers. Chatham. 1952.
8,32.
Vol VII CAMPAIGNS IN MESOPOTAMIA AND EAST AFRICA.
and the Inter-War Period, 1919 - 1938.
Institute of Royal Engineers. Chatham. 1952.
8,32.
VOL.VIII. PAKENHAM-WALSH, R.P. 1938-1948.
Campaigns in France & Belgium. 1939 - 40,
Norway, the Middle East, etc.
Institute of Royal Engineers. Chatham. n.d.
8,32.
Vol.IX. PAKENHAM-WALSH, R.P. 1938- 1948.
Campaigns in Sicily and Italy, the War
against Japan, North West Europe, 1944-45 etc.
Post-War. 1945 - 1948.
Institute of Royal Engineers. Chatham. n.d.
8,32.

HOLLOWAY, Roger.
The Queen's Own Royal West Kent Regiment:
the dirty half-hundred; (the 50th/97th Regiment
of foot).
Leo Cooper. 1973.
1,3,5,6,7,8,9,11,12,25.

HOWE, Capt. G.R.
Drums and drummers.
(A history of the drums and drummers of the
Buffs. (The author was a Captain in the Regiment).
Medici Society. 1932.
11.

IGGLESDEN, Sir Charles.*
History of the East Kent Volunteers.
Kentish Express. Ashford. 1899.
1,2,3,4,6,7,8,11,12,14,15,17,24.

JESSUP, Ronald Frederick.
Man of many talents: an informal biography of
James Douglas, 1753 - 1819. (An early member of
the Corps of Royal Engineers, Chatham, he lived
in Rochester during the 1780's).
Phillimore. 1975.
11.

JOURNAL OF THE UNITED SERVICES.
1829 - In progress.
32.

KENNEDY, Paul M.
The rise and fall of British naval mastery.
Allen Lane. 1976.
4.

KENT COUNTY WAR MEMORIAL.
(The War Memorial is in Canterbury City and is in
the custody of the Dean & Canons of the Cathedral).
n.d.
11

KIRKBRIDE, Lt. Col. William.
Like it or not. (Reminiscences of life as a
Royal Engineer Officer in Peace).
Arthur H. Stockwell, Ilfracombe. (1965).
4,32.

KNIGHT, Capt. Henry Raleigh.*
Brief digest of the services of the Buffs.
(East Kent Regiment) for the occasion of the
Presentation of the Colours to the 1st.
Battalion, by the Lord Mayor of London on the
16th May,1906. Compiled by Capt. H.R. Knight.
Gale & Polden. Aldershot. 1906.
11.

LETTERS CONCERNING THE THANET VOLUNTEER YEOMANRY.
Kentish Gazette. 1810.
24.

LEWIN, Thomas.
On the castra of the Littus Saxonicum and particularly the castrum of Othona. Read to the
Society of Antiquaries of London on June 20th,
1867.
Society of Antiquaries of London. 1867.
11.

LLOYDS, Corporation of.
The Gun Wharf Chatham.
Corporation of Lloyds. Chatham. 1976.
15,25

LUSHINGTON, Lt.Col. Franklin.*
Yeoman service. A short history of the Kent
Yeomanry 1939 - 1945.
Medici Society. 1947.
6,13.

MAURICE-JONES, K. W.*
The history of coast artillery in the British
Army.
Royal Artillery Institution. 1959.
11.

MEDWAY MILITARY RESEARCH GROUP.
Newsletter. No.1. In progress,
Medway Military Research Group. 1977.
4.

MOCKETT, John.*
The letter to Capt. Thomas Garrett commanding
the Thanet Troop of Volunteer Yeomanry.
Printed for J. Mockett in Canterbury. 1810.
3,11.

MOLLO, Boris.
The Sharpshooters: 3rd County of London Yeomanry
1900 - 61; Kent and County of London Yeomanry
1961 - 70.
Historical Research Unit. 1970.
2.

MOLONY, C.V.*
"Invicta" with the First Battalion the Queen's
Own Royal West Kent Regiment in the Great War.
Nisbet and Co. London. 1923.
1,2,4,5,6,7,8,9,11,12,17.

THE MUSEUM OF THE CORPS OF ROYAL ENGINEERS;
brochure designed by John Allwood.
Printed by Flo-Print for Brompton Barracks.(1974?).
4,32.

PARSONS, Capt. Edward.
Bible-Back: (the Royal Marines in New Zealand)
Printed DaiNippon Printing Co. Hong Kong. n.d.
28.

PENFOLD, Michael J.
The unfinished journey.
(Typescript. Loss of H.M.S. Hythe 1915).
19.

PERCIVAL, Charles Spencer.
On a list of the Royal Navy in 1660.
Read to the Society of Antiquaries of London,
February 16th,1882.
Societies of Antiquaries of London. 1882.
11.
PROFESSIONAL PAPERS OF THE CORPS OF ROYAL
ENGINEERS.
1837 - In progress.
32.

A PROPOSAL TO DEVELOP FORT AMHERST,
situated between Chatham and Gillingham,as a
Military Engineering Open Air Museum. (1973).
4.

QUEEN'S DIVISION OF INFANTRY.
A commission in one of the famous regiments of
the Queen's Division of Infantry.
Queen's Division. Bassingbourn. (1971?).
3.

ROYAL AIR FORCE:BIGGIN HILL, 1917 - 1954.*
Royal Air Force, Biggin Hill. 1954.
1.

ROYAL ENGINEER JOURNAL.
Vol. 1. 1870 - In progress.
32.
ROYAL ENGINEERS:Maidstone Station Families' Guide.
Method Publishing Co. 1975.
11.

ROYAL MARINES - Chatham division.
Notes, a cutting and a photocopied section of
Records of the Royal Marines..and about the Barracks.
4.

ROYAL MILITARY ACADEMY, WOOLWICH.
Records of the Royal Military Academy, 1741-1892.
F.J. Cattermole. Woolwich. 1892.
11.

ROYAL SCHOOL OF MILITARY ENGINEERING.
A History of the Establishment.
(M/S.) n.d.
32.

Open day Programmes
 4. 1968.   32. 1937*1962-1964;1969 in progress
4.

R.E. War Memorial:the Unveiling by H.R.H. The
Duke of Connaught and Strathearn in 1922.
4.

South African Engineer Corps and Boer Leaders'
Statues. Notes from the Corps Library from
Letters dated 17th April, 1946 - 6th January,1970.
4,32.

RUSSELL, R.O.*
The history of the 11th (Lewisham) Battalion,
the Queen's Own Royal West Kent Regiment.
Lewisham Newspaper Company.1934.
2.

THE SAPPER: Regimental Journal of the Corps of
Royal Engineers.
1895 - In progress.
32.

SMITH, Peter. C.
Per mare per terram:a history of the
Royal Marines.
Balfour Publication. 1974.
28.

TAYLOR, Arthur.
Discovering English County regiments.
Shire Publications. 1970.
11.

THOMPSON, Philip.
Success to H.M.S. 'Hawkins' (poems to commemorate
the launching at H.M. Dockyard, Chatham, 1st
October,1917. Printed on silk). 1917.
4.

TOMLINSON, Norman.
Louis Brennan.
Hallewell Publications. 1980.
5,11,15,32.

TRENDELL, John.
Operation music-maker:the story of the Royal
Marines Bands. (The Royal Marines Band
School is at Deal).
John Trendell. 1979.
28.

VINE, Paul Ashley Laurence.*
The Royal Military Canal:an historical account of
the waterway and military road from Shorncliffe
in Kent, to Cliff End in Sussex.
David & Charles. 1972.
2,3,4,6,7,11,12,19,32.

WARD, B.R.*
School of Military Engineering, 1812 - 1909.
(Brompton).
Royal Engineers' Institute. Brompton. 1909.
15.32.

WENYON, H.J.*
The history of the Eighth battalion, the Queens
Own Royal West Kent Regiment 1914 - 19,
by H.J. Wenyon and H.S. Brown.
Hazell, Watson & Viney,Printers. 1921.
2.

WEST KENT (QUEEN'S OWN) YEOMANRY.
Roll of honour.
Barnard & Crannis, Printers. (c.1919).
2.

WHITEHEAD, J.G.O.
Henry Yeveley,Military Engineer.
Reprint from 'The Royal Engineers Journal'
pp102-110.
(1974?).
3,32.

WILKES, R.E.
Louis Brennan, C.B. - Dirigible Torpedo.
Gillingham Public Library. 1973.
4,6,7,8,9,11,12,25.
Louis Brennan C.B.-Gyroscopic Monorail.
Gillingham Public Library. 1973.
4,6,7,8,9,11,12,25,
WILSON, Jack F.
The Royal Observer Corps:a brief history...
and memories of the Bromley Group No.19
Operations room who guarded the S.E. approaches
to London.
(typescript). (1975).
2.

WILTON, Eric.*
Centre Crew: a memory of the Royal Observer Corps.
Published privately for the members of "B"
Crew of the Royal Observer Corps Centre at
Bromley, Kent.
Printed by King and Jarrett. (1946).
2,11.

WOLFFRAM, H.
Thirty years' work (1867 - 97) in preparing
candidates for the Army at Faraday House,
Blackheath, and the Manor House, Lee.
1898.
18.

WOODTHORPE, T.J.*
The Tudor Navy and the Medway: Queenborough
as a Naval Port. Typewritten Script.
n.d.
11,20,26,27.

WRIGHT, Nicholas.
The Bump:Battle of Britain 40th anniversary
reunion, Royal Air Force,21st September, 1980.
Royal Air Force. Biggin Hill. 1980.
2,12.

MILTON-NEXT-GRAVESEND

DOUGLASS, Rev. Douglas Alexander.
From Princes Street to Milton Mount;the story
of Congregationalism in Gravesend from its beginnings in Princes Street Chapel, including the
developments of Milton Congregational Church and
their reunion in 1953, and the formation of the
United Reformed Church in Old Road East under
the name Milton Mount.
Milton Mount United Reformed Church. 1975.
9.

MILTON-NEXT-GRAVESEND Cont'd

H., W.T.
A new historical, topographical and descriptive
companion to the visitor of Gravesend, Milton and
their environs interspersed with curious anecdotes
in a series of letters from the author to a
friend.
W. Holbert. Gravesend. (184-?).
9,11.

SMITH, Paul R.
Milton Parish Church history.
Milton Church, Gravesend. 1975.
9.

TILLEY, Ernest W.
The Seventeenth-century token issuers of Gravesend
and Milton-next-Gravesend. Reprinted from
Archaeologia Cantiana Vol. LXXXV 1970.
Headley Bros. Ashford. 1971.
9.

MILTON REGIS

AN ACCOUNT OF SOME ANTIQUITIES discovered in
the winter of 1824 near the creek at Milton.
A photocopy taken from The Gentleman's Magazine,
December,1825. pp. 485-7.
20.

BAILEY, P.M.
Pollution! a survey of pollution in the area
of Milton Creek.
1974.
4,20.

BETHUNE, Ian.
The Church of the Holy Trinity, Milton Regis.
Freeguard Press, Sittingbourne. 1973.
1,11,20.

A Short history of the Court Hall, Milton
Regis, Kent.
Sittingbourne & Swale Archaeological Research
Group. 1974.
11,20.

BOROUGH DIRECTORIES LTD.*
Business and residential directory of the Borough
of Faversham and the Urban District of
Sittingbourne & Milton.
Borough Directories Ltd. 1963.
4,7,8,20.

ENVIRONMENT, Department of the.
List of Buildings of special architectural
or historic interest. District of Swale, Kent;
Sittingbourne and Milton Area.
H.M.S.O. 1974.
11,20.

GASKIN, Valerie.
A comparison of the library services in Sittingbourne and Milton Urban District provided
by the local council and the library services
in Tonbridge Urban District, provided by
the County Council.
Thesis - Typescript. n.d.
20.

GRAYLING, Francis.
The Churches of Sittingbourne and Milton.
Anglebooks. 1973.
1,11.

HAZELL, Martin.
The Sailing barges and the brick and other
industries of Milton Creek, Kent c.1850 - c.1970;
a social and economic history. Thesis for
Department of Teaching Studies. North London
Polytechnic.
Photocopy of MS Rough Draft. Completed May,1972.
20.

KENT COUNTY COUNCIL:PLANNING DEPARTMENT.
Milton and Kemsley;informal action area plan.Draft.
K.C.C. 1973.
11.20.

Sittingbourne and Milton Regis:Conservation
Study. Draft.
K.C.C. 1973.
11,20.

SITTINGBOURNE AND MILTON URBAN DISTRICT COUNCIL.
Sittingbourne and Milton, Kent,Official Guide.
Sittingbourne and Milton Urban District Council.
1963.
20.

"A SON OF THE MARSHES" pseud.*
Drift from Longshore, edited by J.A. Owen.
Hutchinson. 1898.
20.

Forest Tithes and other studies from nature,*
edited by J.A. Owen.
Smith Elder and Co. 1893.
11,20.

From Spring to Fall; or When life Stirs,*
edited by J.A. Owen.
Blackwood. 1894.
20.

In the green leaf and the Sere.*
K.Paul. 1896.
20.

MINSTER-IN-SHEPPEY

BRAMSTON, William.*
History of Abbey Church of Minster, Isle
of Sheppey, Kent.
Hazell, Watson & Viney. 1896.
2,27.

JONES, P.T.*
The Story of the Abbey and Gate House, Minster,
Isle of Sheppey.
Gibbs & Sons. Canterbury. n.d.
12.

The Story of the Abbey Church and Gate House,
Minster, Isle of Sheppey. 3rd edition.
British Publishing Company. Gloucester. 1950.
11,12.

WITHERS, Hartley.*
Canterbury & Rochester with Minster-in-Sheppey,
by H. Withers and others.
G. Bell & Sons. 1929.
6,7,17.

MINSTER-IN-THANET

BISH, Dom Gregory.*
Minster Abbey, Minster-in-Thanet, near Ramsgate,
Kent, 670 - 1947. A short historical and
architectural guide.
Minster Abbey, Ramsgate.
1947. 11,24.
1951. 13.
1965. 11.

FAGG, Brian R.
Minster Abbey, Thanet. In Ancient Monuments
Society Transactions,New Series Vol. 17, 1970.
pp. 39 - 50.
11.

GELL, Francis.*
The Minster of Minster-in-Thanet.
Jesse Pullen. Ramsgate. (1879).
24.

MINSTER ABBEY, Isle of Thanet, Kent.
Lane & Gentry, Printers. n.d.
30.
Standard Press, Printers. Margate. (1928).
11.

MINSTER PARISH COUNCIL.
Minster-in-Thanet, Kent; the official guide.
13th edition.
Norman Martell Ltd. Ramsgate. (1978?).
11.

MINSTER PARISH COUNCIL-VILLAGE STUDY COMMITTEE.
The Parish of Minster-in-Thanet; an appraisal
of current trends and future needs.
Minster Parish Council. 1978.
3,11,13.

ST. MARY'S CHURCH; Minster-in-Thanet.
W.H. Bligh. Ramsgate. 192-?
12,13.

ST. MILDRED 660 - 725, Abbess of Minster-in-
Thanet; St. Mildred and her kinsfolk.
1950.
12.

SALMESTONE: The story of a monastic grange
from the Middle Ages to the present day.
Printed by Thanet Printing Works. (197-?).
11.

TOWN AND COUNTRY MAGAZINE.
Includes information on:- Minster-in-Thanet.
Virtue, London. 1837 - 8.
4.

WHITING, William.
Further Roman finds in Kent...
1) Discoveries at Minster, Thanet.
Reprinted from the Antiquarian Journal.
Vol. IV, No.1. January, 1924.
Society of Antiquaries of London. 1924.
11.

MONUMENTAL INSCRIPTIONS

ASHMOLEAN MUSEUM.
Notes on brass rubbing, with...a summary of
the remaining figure brasses in the British
Isles. 6th edition. pp. 70 - 73 Kent.
Ashmolean Museum. Oxford. 1969.
11.

BLOXAM, Matthew Holbeche.
On the sepulchral monuments in Rochester
Cathedral.
PP. 1863.
8.

CAIGER, John E.L.
Two brasses.
2. The Crepehege brass at Darenth, by
John E.L. Caiger; reprinted from Archaeologia
Cantiana, Vol. 67, 1962.
Headley Bros. Ashford. 1962.
30.

COMPLETE BRASS-RUBBING GUIDE TO THE FIGURE
BRASSES IN THE COUNTY OF KENT.
Studio 69 (Phillips & Page). Norwich. 1974.
1,2,3,6,11,30.

D'ELBOUX, R.H.
Some Kentish Indents.
Reprinted from Archaeologia Cantiana. Vol.59.
1947.
11.

DUNCAN, Leland Lewis.*
Kentish Monumental Inscriptions at Tenterden,
edited by L.L. Duncan.
Kent Archaeological Society. 1919.
1,3,8,11,12,14,15,17,22.

DWELLY, Edward.
Dwelly's parish records. Vol.3. Kent M.I.
being the monumental inscriptions in the
parishes of Reculver-cum-Hoath, Herne & Herne
Bay, with tricks of all the Armorial
Bearings and rubbings of the old Brasses.
Published by E. Dwelly. Herne Bay. 1914.
3,11,15.

GOUGH, Harold Eric.
Two Brasses.
1. A newly-found brass from Herne Church, by
H.E. Gough; reprinted from Archaeologia
Cantiana. Vol.67.
Printed Headley Bros. Ashford. 1962.
30.

GRIFFIN, Ralph.*
List of Monumental brasses in the County
of Kent in 1922 (cover title Monumental brasses
in Kent), by R. Griffin and M. Stephenson.
Headley Bros. Ashford. 1922.
7.

HARRINGTON, Duncan.
The memorial inscriptions of the Nonconformist
Burial Ground in Wincheap, Canterbury, trans-
cribed by D. Harrington.
Kent Family History Society. 1976.
1,3,7,11.

HARRIS, Edwin.*
Quaint Kentish Epitaphs and Signs.
E. Harris, Rochester. 1899.
4.

KIRBY, Herbert Charles.*
Monumental Inscriptions in the Church and Church-
yard of St. Mary, Lewisham, edited by
H.C. Kirby and L.L. Duncan.
Lewisham Antiquarian Society. 1889.
2.

LIST OF INSCRIPTIONS ON MEMORIALS AT BILSINGTON
CHURCH.
Typewritten list signed Thomas Church. 1967
1967?.
11.

LIST OF INSCRIPTIONS ON MEMORIALS AT BONNINGTON
CHURCH.
Typewritten list signed Thomas Church. 1967.
1967?
11.

LIST OF INSCRIPTIONS ON MEMORIALS INSIDE
GOUDHURST CHURCH.
Typewritten list signed Thomas Church. 1967.
1967?
11.

MACKLIN, Herbert Walter.
Monumental brasses together with a selected
bibliography and county lists of brasses
remaining in the churches of the United Kingdom.
6th edition.
Allen & Unwin. 1913.
11.

MAIDSTONE BOROUGH COUNCIL.
Written Statement and map showing the graves
and tombstones at the burial ground of the
Friends' Meeting House, Wheeler Street, Maidstone.
Maidstone Borough Council. 1975.
12.

MAY, Leonard Morgan.*
Charlton; near Woolwich, Kent. Full and complete
copies of all inscriptions in the old Parish
Church and Churchyard. (Limited edition).
Charles North. 1908.
1,2,11,15,17,18.

MONUMENTAL INSCRIPTIONS. MISCELLANEA GENEALOGICA
ET HERALDICA.
Fifth series, Vol.4, parts 5 and 6. (Containing
Charlton pedigree, some extracts from Kent Wills,
part of "Monumental Inscriptions in Bromley
Church", edited by Clarke & R.Holworthy.
Mitchell, Hughes & Clarke. 1921.
2.

NASH MAUSOLEUM, FARNINGHAM. - LIST OF PLAQUES
AND TABLETS CONNECTED WITH THE NASH FAMILY.
1708 - 1857, transcribed by Mrs. Mary John.
4.

OYLER, Thomas H.*
Epitaphs and inscriptions from the churches
of Kent, edited by T.H. Oyler.
Kentish Express, Ashford. 1912.
2,25,30.

PULLEN, Doris E.
Inscriptions copied from the tombstones of
St. Bartholomew's Church, Sydenham.
Unpublished Typescript. 1976.
18.

SADLER, A.G.
The indents of lost monumental brasses in Kent.
Part 1 and Part 2.
A.G. Sadler. Ferring-on-Sea, Sussex. 1975 & 1976.
1,2,3,5,6,7,8,9,12,13,15,16,17,19,20,29.

SADLER, A.G.*
The indents of lost monumental brasses in Kent.
Appendix.
A.G. Sadler. Ferring-on-Sea.Sussex. (1979).
2,4,5,6,13,22,28.

THORPE, John Senior.*
Index to the Monumental Inscriptions in the
"Registrum Roffense", edited by F.A. Crisp.
Limited edition.
P.P. by F.A. Crisp. 1885.
2,11,12.

MORE, SIR THOMAS (1478 - 1535).

BOARDMAN, Brigid M.
The life of Thomas More, (for children).
Catholic Truth Society. (1978).
3.

ELLISTON-ERWOOD, Frank Charles.*
The end of the House of Roper.
Woolwich Antiquarian Society. 1935.
11.

JENKINS, Claude.*
Sir Thomas More; a commemoration lecture.
(Canterbury Papers No.5).
Jennings, Canterbury. 1935.
1,3,4,11,12.

LEWI, Angela.
The Thomas More family group.
(Family tree included).
National Portrait Gallery. H.M.S.O. 1974.
11.

McCONICA, James.
Thomas More; a short biography.
H.M.S.O. 1977.
3.

MANNING, Anne.*
The household of Sir Thomas More, with Roper's
life of More.
Dent, 1906.
3,12.

MORE, Margaret (1505 - 1544).*
The household of Sir Thomas More, or a diary of
his family circle, written by his daughter
Margaret. 3rd edition.
Hall, Virtue and Co. London. n.d.
3.

MORE, Sir Thomas.
St. Thomas More; selected letters, edited by
Elizabeth Frances Rogers.
Yale University Press. New York. (1961).
3.

MORISON, Stanley.
The likeness of Thomas More;an iconographical
survey of three centuries.
Burns & Oates. 1963.
3.

PAUL, Leslie.*
Sir Thomas More.
Faber. 1953.
12.

REYNOLDS, Ernest Edwin.
The life and death of St. Thomas More;
the field is won.
(Previously published as "The Field is Won").
Burns and Oates. 1968. (reproduced 1978).
3.

*

Margaret Roper, eldest daughter of Sir
Thomas More.
Burns & Oates. London. 1960 and 1963.
3

Sir Thomas More.
(Writers and their work:no 178).
Longmans for British Council. 1965
(reprinted with amendments 1970).
3.

RUPP, Gordon.
Thomas More;the King's good servant.
Collins. 1978.
3.

THOMAS MORE THROUGH MANY EYES. (Sermons preached
in Chelsea Old Church 1954 - 1977).
Leighton Thomson. 1978.
3.

TRAPP, J.B.
'The King's Good Servant'; Sir Thomas More
1477/8 - 1535.
National Portrait Gallery. (1977).
3.

MORRIS, WILLIAM (1834 - 1896)
LIVED AT BEXLEYHEATH.

BRADLEY, IAN.
William Morris and his World.
Thames & Hudson. 1978.
1.

DE CARLO, Giancarlo.
William Morris.
Il Balcone. 1947.
1.

FAULKNER, Peter.
William Morris;the critical heritage,
edited by Peter Faulkner.
Routledge and Kegan Paul.
1973.
1.

GODWIN, Edward.
Warrior Bard;the life of William Morris,
by E. & S. Godwin.
Harrap. 1947.
1.

HENDERSON, Philip.
William Morris; his life, work and friends.
Thames & Hudson. 1967.
1.

MACKAIL, J.W.
The life of William Morris, 2 vols.
Longmans. 1920.
1.

MARILLIER, H.C.
History of the Merton Abbey Tapestry Works.
Constable. 1927.
1.

MEIER, Paul.
William Morris;the Marxist Dreamer. Vols I and II.
Harvester Press. 1978.
1.

MORRIS, William.
The letters of William Morris to his family and
friends, edited by P. Henderson.
Longmans. 1950.
1.

MORRIS, William.
Political writings of William Morris, edited by
A.L. Morton.
Lawrence & Wishart. 1973.
1.

MORRIS, William.
William Morris;selected writings and designs,
edited by Asa Briggs.
Penguin. 1962.
1.

SHAW, Bernard.
Morris as I knew him.
William Morris Society. 1966.
1.

SPARLING, H. Halliday.
The Kelmscott Press and William Morris, Master-
Craftsman.
Macmillan. 1924.
1.

MORRIS, WILLIAM (1834 - 1896)   Cont'd
LIVED AT BEXLEYHEATH

TAMES, Richard.
William Morris: an illustrated life of
William Morris, 1834 - 1896.
Shire Publications. 1972.
1
11   1978.

THOMPSON, Paul.
The work of William Morris.
Heinemann. 1967.
1.

VALLANCE, Aymer.
William Morris: his art, his writings and
his public life.
George Bell and Sons. 1909.
1.

WILES, H.V.
William Morris of Walthamstow.
Walthamstow Press. 1951.
1.

WILLIAM MORRIS SOCIETY.
The Typographical adventure of William
Morris: an exhibition arranged by the
William Morris Society. 1957.
1.

MOTTINGHAM

HORSMAN, Elizabeth.
Centenary:the story of...St. Andrew,
Mottingham.
St. Andrew's Church Mottingham. (1980).
2.

PARKINSON, W.H.
Mottingham - from hamlet to urban village.
London Borough of Bromley Public Libraries. 1977.
18.

MURSTON

LUMAN, Rev. Arthur.
Murston Parish Church,by the Rev. Arthur and
Mrs Luman. (1947?).
20.

MURSTON PARISH COUNCIL.
The Parish Council of Murston, 1894 - 1930: a
concise report of the passing of the Council,
March 28th,1930.
Murston Parish Council. 1930.
20.

MUSEUMS

ARMSTRONG, J.R.
Weald and Downland Open Air Museum, by J.R.
Armstrong and J. Lowe.
Phillimore. Chichester.
1971. 11.
1973.   8.
1974. 11.
1975.   3.

CANTERBURY CITY MUSEUMS AND CANTERBURY
PUBLIC LIBRARY.
Buff's Museum: Catalogue of Books.
Duplicated typescript. 1976.
3.

Guide to the Museum of the Buffs.
1975.
3.

A guide to the Canterbury Museums.
(text by Louise Millard, designed and
illustrated by Christopher Hills).
Printed by Jennings. Canterbury. 1967.
30.

CANTERBURY PHILOSOPHICAL AND LITERARY INSTITUTION*
Synopsis of the museum of the Philosophical and
Literary Institution, Canterbury.
Canterbury Philosophical & Literary Institution.
Printed by G. Wood. 1826.
3.11.

COLLINS, Kenneth J.
The Queen's Own Royal West Kent Regimental
Museum (Maidstone Museum).
English Life Publications. 1973.
2,6,11,12,19.25.

DOVER BOROUGH COUNCIL, MUSEUM.
Illustrated official guide to The Dover Corporation
Museum (under reorganisation), by Frederick
Knocker.
G.W. Griff, St. George's Press. Dover. 1932.
1,7,11.

FAVERSHAM SOCIETY.
Fleur de Lis: a museum for Faversham.
1973?
4.

GREENHILL, Basil.
National Maritime Museum.
Pitkin. 1974.
11.

LEGOUIX, Susan (later Mrs. Sloman).
Maidstone Museum and Art Gallery: Foreign
paintings catalogue.
Maidstone Borough Council. 1976.
4.6.11.

MAIDSTONE MUSEUM AND ART GALLERY.
The Tyrwhitt-Drake Museum of Carriages at the
Archbishop's Stables, Mill Street, Maidstone.
Official Guide. (The Tyrwhitt-Drake
Collection) 8th edition.
Maidstone Borough Council. 1971.
4.11.

MOAD, Michael.
Eastgate House Museum: a brief guide to the
house and the museum collections, written by
M. Moad for the Directorate of Leisure
Services, Medway Borough Council. (1978).
11,15,25.

THE MUSEUM OF THE CORPS OF ROYAL ENGINEERS,
designed by John Allwood.
Printed by Flo-Print for Brompton Barracks.
(1974?).
4.

NATIONAL MARITIME MUSEUM
Catalogue (of the collections).
Under Revision.
National Maritime Museum, Greenwich. 1937.
11.

A concise guide to the National Maritime Museum,*
Greenwich. 2nd edition.
H.M.S.O. 1966.
30.

POWELL-COTTON MUSEUM.
Guide to the big game and curios in the Quex
Museum, Birchington.
Lane, Gentry, Margate. 1920.
11.

Illustrated guide to the Powell-Cotton Museum of
history and ethnography. Quex Park, Birchington.
Printed by the Central Press, Margate, for
the Museum Trustees. 1969.
11,30.

A PROPOSAL TO DEVELOP FORT AMHERST. Situated
between Chatham and Gillingham, as a Military
Engineering Open Air Museum. (1973).
4.

MUSIC

BLACK, Vera L.
A History of Rochester Choral Society, 1873 - 1973.
P.P. 1973.
4,11.

MUSIC Cont'd

BRUXNER, Mervyn.
The Story of the Kent Music School,1948-1970.
K.C.C. 1970?
4.

COPLEY, I.A.
The music of Peter Warlock;a critical survey.
(Peter Warlock lived in Eynsford).
Dennis Dobson. 1979.
5.

FOLKESTONE ROTARY CLUB.
Folkestone Competitive Musical Festival 1939,
organised by the Rotary Club of Folkestone.
Programme of the 15th Festival to be held...
on Saturday, March 18th,1939.
The Rotary Club. 1939.
11.

FOR THE WIDOW'S SUNDAY SCHOOL AND FOR YOUTH.
(Hymn Book).
Printed by J. Joffery at the Herald Office,
Christchurch Yard, Canterbury. 1807.
3.

FRIED, Erich.
(Arden must die) Arden muss sterben,
an opera on the death of the wealthy Arden
of Faversham in two acts. (Seven scenes);
libretto by Erich Fried, music by Alexander
Goehr, English translation by Geoffrey
Skelton.
Schott. 1967.
Libretto only. 11.

GILLINGHAM & MEDWAY MUSIC FESTIVAL.
Programme No.1. 1975. 4.
No.2. 1977. 4.
No.3. 1978. 4.

HEATH, Edward.
Music, a joy for life.
Sidgwick and Jackson. 1976.
24.

HUGHES, Reginald.
A history of the organs of the Parish
Church of All Saints, Maidstone, Kent.
Beacon Press. Lewes. 1980.
12.

JOSEPH, Jack.
Notes on music.(Gillingham author.)
Lindley Press. 1975.
8.

KENT COUNTY COUNCIL.
Kent County Youth Orchestra at National
Festival.(Press Notice 161/75.)
Gives a list of the players of the
Orchestra with addresses and instruments.
1st July, 1975.
4.

KENT MUSICAL COMPETITIVE FESTIVAL.
34th Annual Musical Competition Festival,
Chatham. 1950. Programme.
4.

Programme of the thirty-third Kent Musical
Competitive Festival to be held in Maidstone
on 14th, 21st, 24th and 25th May,1949.
Printed by W. Mackay.Chatham. 1949.
11.

KENT MUSIC SCHOOL.
Annual Report 1974 - 75.
Kent Music School. 1975.
3.

LONG, K.R.
The music of the English Church.
Hodder and Stoughton. 1972.
3.

MEDWAY TOWNS BAND.
Newsletter.
No 12. April 1980. in progress.
4.

SACRED MELODIES FOR THE USE OF SABBATH
SCHOOLS. 4th edition.
A.T. Fordham. Chatham. 1867.
4.

SHAW, K.D.
Short History of gramophone Society activities
in South-East London and North-West Kent...
(typescript).
1974.
2.

TAYLOR, H.J.*
The Dover Pageant:the book of the music;
the words chiefly written by James Rhoades;
the music chiefly written by H.J. Taylor (under
the direction of Mr. Louis N. Parker).
Weeks & Co. 1908.
3,6,11.

TRENDELL, John.
Operation Music-maker; the story of the
Royal Marines Band.
John Trendell. 1979.
28.

WROTHAM. ST. GEORGE'S CHURCH.
Wrotham Festival of Music, 22nd - 29th
September,1974 in aid of St. George's Church
Organ Restoration Fund.
4.

YOUNG, Kenneth.
Music's great days in the Spas and Watering places.
Macmillan. 1968.
13.

NACKINGTON

LOWER HARDRES AND NACKINGTON PAROCHIAL CHURCH COUNCIL.
The church of St. Mary The Virgin, Nackington.
A brief guide for pilgrims and visitors.
Published by Lower Hardres and Nackington
Parochial Church Council.
April, 1978.
3.

NATURAL HISTORY

ALEXANDER, Horace Gundry.
Seventy years of birdwatching; with drawings by
Robert Gilmor.
T. &. A.D. Poyser. 1974.
7,11,19.

BLACKSTONE, J.
Specimen Botanicum quo plantarum plurium
rariorum Angliae indigenarum loci natales,
illustrantur (includes Kent).
S. Birt (1745).
26.

BOTANICAL POCKET-BOOK with observations on some
of the rarer plants growing in the neighbourhood
of Tunbridge Wells.
J. Clifford. 1840.
19.

BOYD, Hugh.
Duck wings; a study of duck production, by
Hugh Boyd, Jeffery Harrison and Allan Allison:
Illustrated by Pamela Harrison.
WAGBI in co-operation with Marley Ltd.
and the Harrison Zoological Museum, Sevenoaks.
1975 reprinted 1977.
16.

BRIGHTMAN, F.H.
Survey of Cuckoo Wood, Downe, edited by
F.H. Brightman. (Flora of part of Cuckoo Wood)
Duplicated typescript. 1950.
2.

CATALOGUE...OF MAMMALIA AND BIRDS IN THE MUSEUM
of the Army Medical Department at Fort Pitt,
Chatham
Burrill. Chatham.1838.
11.

CHALMERS-HUNT, J.M.*
The butterflies and moths of Kent. Vol.I.
Rhopalocera. Vol.II. Heterocera.
Buncle & Co. Ltd. Arbroath. 1960 - 68.
6,7,11,15,30.

CHAMPION, Mrs. I.K.
Natural History in the Rochester area, edited by
Mrs. I.K. Champion and Miss E.E. Floodgate.
Published to mark the Centenary of the Society,
by Meresborough Books, Rainham. 1977.
1,2,3,4,8,11,12,15,25.

CHANDLER, Marjorie Elizabeth Jane.
The lower tertiary floras of Southern England.
I. Palaeocene floras: London Clay Flora
(Supplement).
British Museum (Natural History). 1961.
3.

COOPER, J.E.*
The mollusca of Chislet marshes.
Reprinted from the Journal of Conchology,
Vol.19, No.10. June,1933. pp. 317 - 321.
11.

COWELL, M.H.*
A floral guide for East Kent, etc... (with
those of Faversham).
W. Ratcliffe. Faversham. 1839.
1,3,5,6,7,9,11,13,15,17,26.

DEAKIN, Richard.*
The flowering plants of Tunbridge Wells and
neighbourhood.
Stidolph and Bellamy. Tunbridge Wells. 1871.
2,6,11,15,17,19.

EDWARDES, Edward Tickner.
Sidelights of nature in quill and crayon;
2nd edition.
Kegan Paul, Trench, Trubner. 1912.
11.

EMBRY, Bernard.*
The butterflies and moths found in the Dover
and Deal District of Kent, by B. Embry and
G.H. Youden.
Buckland Associated Press. 1949.
2,6,7,11.

FINCH, William Coles.*
The lure of the country side, a nature lover's
pot-pourrie.
C.W. Daniel. London. 1927.
4,8,11,12.

FOSTER, M.C.
The Flora of Bexley.
London Borough of Bexley. Libraries and
Museums Department. 1972.
1,5,11.

GANN, P.D.
Unpublished works on Kentish Natural History
in Kent Libraries. (From the Transactions of
The Kent Field Club, Vol.5, Part 2, 1974).
Kent Field Club. 1974.
11.

GILLHAM, Eric Howard.*
The birds of the North Kent Marshes, by
E.H. Gillham and R.C. Holmes.
Collins, 1950.
1,2,3,4,5,7,8,9,11,12,14,15,17,18,20,25,26.

Census of the breeding birds of the Medway
Islands,* June 3rd - 5th 1955;
edited by E.H. Gillham and others.
Members of the Medway Census in Conjunction
with the Kent Ornithological Society, Chatham 1955.
1,2,4,8,11,25,26.

GREENWICH NATURAL HISTORY CLUB, ZOOLIGICAL
COMMITTEE *
Fauna of Blackheath and its vicinity:-
part 1. Vertebrate animals.
William Clowes, printers. 1859
2,11.

GROOM, J.B.*
A Maidstone Naturalist's rambles during the
"Year of Rain" from March,1903 to March,1904.
South Eastern Gazette,(Maidstone). 1904.
6,8,11,12,17.

HAES, I.
Natural history of Sussex (viz Kent, West).
Harvester Press Ltd. 1977.
22.

HARRISON, James Maurice.*
The birds of Kent. 2 vols.
H.F. and G. Witherby. 1953.
1,2,3,4,5,6,7,8,9,11,14,15,16,19,20,22,26,30.

HARRISON, Jeffery Graham.*
Breeding birds of the Medway estuary, by
Jeffery G. Harrison, J.N. Humphreys and
Geoffrey Graves; illustrated by Pamela Harrison.
Kent Ornithological Society and W.A.G.B.I.
1972.
11,15,16,25,27.30.

The nesting birds of Chetney Marsh.*
Kent Ornithological Society. 1970.
2,7,12,16,25.

The Sevenoaks Gravel Pit Reserve: a joint
WAGBI- Wildfowl Trust experimental reserve.
WAGBI with Redland Ltd and the Harrison
Zoological Museum Trust. 1974.
1,8,11,16,17.

The Thames transformed: London's river and
its waterfowl, by J.G. Harrison and P. Grant.
André Deutsch. 1976.
1,2,4,9,15.

Wild fowl of the North Kent marshes;* illustrated
by Pamela Harrison and foreword by George
Atkinson-Willes.
W.A.G.B.I. 1972.
11,30.

HAYDON, Walter.
What to find on Dover Beach: a concise and
handy guide written in popular language to
some of the wonders of the seashore at Dover.
Dover and County Chronicle. 1976.
11.

HEPWORTH, J.*
Rochester and District. A sketch-guide to
its geology, flora and fauna,
compiled by J. Hepworth.
Parrett and Neves. Rochester. 1913.
2,4,5,8,11,12,15.

ISLE OF THANET FIELD CLUB.
Fourth Annual Report, January,1950 - April,1951.
Isle of Thanet Field Club. 1951.
11.

JACOB, Edward.*
Plantae Faversham ienses ..:a catalogue of
the more perfect plants.
J. March. 1777.
1,6,11,14,15,17,26.

JACOB, J.*
Wild flowers grasses and ferns of East Kent.
Dover Express, East Kent News. 1936.
3,6,7,11,13,14,24,26.

JERMY, A.C.
Chalk grassland: studies on its conservation
and management in South-east England, by
A.C. Jermy and P.A. Stott. (pp.55 - 56 Kent
Properties).
Kent Trust for Nature Conservation.
1973. 2.3.4.6.11.12.
1975. 2nd edition. 2.4.6.

JOHNSON, Thomas.*
Botanical journeys in Kent and Hampstead.
A facsimile reprint with introduction and
translation of his "Iter Plantarum" 1629, and
"Descriptio Iterneris Plantarum" 1632.
Edited by J.S. Gilmour.
Hunt Botanical Library, Pittsburgh,
Pennsylvania. U.S.A. 1972.
1,2,4,5,11.

KEMSING PARISH COUNCIL.
A guide to Kemsing Down Nature Reserve.
Kemsing Parish Council. 1980.
16.

NATURAL HISTORY Cont'd

KENT FIELD CLUB.
Bulletin of the Kent Field Club.
1973 No.18.   11.
1974 No.19, edited by A.G. Side.   11.

Transactions of the Kent Field Club,*edited
by L.R.A. Grove.
1957-63.   Vol.I. Parts 1-4.   2,3,4,8,11,31.
1964.   Vol.II   3,4,7,11,22.
1965-71   Vol III.   3,4.
1972.   Vol.IV   3,4.
1973-75   Vol.V. Parts 1-3   3,4.
                  Parts 2-3   11.
1976-77   Vol.VI Parts 1-2   4.
                  Part 2   3.
1977   Vol VII   3,4,6,7,8,11,13.

KENT ORNITHOLOGICAL SOCIETY.*
Kent Bird Report. No. 1. 1952.
1.   1952 in progress
2.   1952 in progress
3.   1952-1964; 1966-1970; 1973-1975.
4.   1954 in progress
6.   1952 in progress
7.   1952 in progress
8.   1952 in progress
9.   1967-1970
11.   1952 in progress
12.   1953 - 1965
14.   1952 in progress
15.   1952 in progress
20.   1956;1964;1966-1975.
24.   1953;1954.
25.   1974;1975.
30.   1968;1972.

KENT TRUST FOR NATURE CONSERVATION.*
(Formerly Kent Naturalists' Trust).
Annual Report.
1971   11
1974   19
1976   8
1977   4.
Bulletin No.1. 1978. 3.

The first 10 years, 1958 - 1968.*
Kent Trust for Nature Conservation. (1968).
2.

Ruxley Gravel Pit.
(Checklist of birds, animals, plants and
insects).
Kent Trust for Nature Conservation. (1979).
2.

KESTON FOREIGN BIRD FARM.
A descriptive catalogue.
Keston Foreign Bird Farm. c.1960.
2.

KNIGHT, Robert.
Will the people of Sandwich celebrate the
bicentennial of Walker and Boys (1784)?
Notes of the Foraminifera, especially those
of Pegwell Bay.
1980.
13.

LONDON NATURAL HISTORY SOCIETY.
The London Bird Report.
Nos. 32 - 36; 1967 - 71.
London Natural History Society. 1968 - 1972.
5.

The London Naturalist. Nos. 48-50, 1968-70.
London Natural History Society. 1969-71.
5.

MANNING, Stanley Arthur.
The Naturalist in South East England: Kent
Surrey and Sussex.
David and Charles. 1974.
2,3,6,7,9,11,25,28.30.

MONTIER, David J.
Atlas of breeding birds of the London Area,
edited by D.J. Montier.
Batsford. 1977.
5.

MORGAN, G.H.
A symposium on Hothfield Local Nature Reserve,
edited by G.H. Morgan and A. Spain.
Transactions of the Kent Field Club, Vol.5,
Part 3. 1975.
3,4,11.

NATURE CONSERVANCY COUNCIL - SOUTH EAST REGION.
Ham Street Woods - national nature reserve.
Nature Conservancy Council. 1976.
3,12.

Wye and Crundale Down - Nature Trail.
Nature Conservancy Council. 1977
3,7.

Stodmarsh Nature Reserve.
Nature Conservancy Council. (1976).
3.

Wildlife Conservation in the North Kent Marshes:*
report of a working Party, edited by B.H. Green.
Nature Conservancy Council. 1971.
2,3,4,5,9,11,12,15,27.

NEWCOMBE, Martin J.
The natural history of the badger in Ellenden
Wood, Blean.
Offprint from "Transactions of the Kent Field
Club" Vol.6. Part 2. pp.75-84.   (1977).
3.

NEWELL, G.E.
Animal Zones of the North Kent Coast.
In. South Eastern Naturalist and Antiquary,
Vol. 59.1954.
South Eastern Union of Scientific Societies.1954.
11.

The Marine Fauna of Whitstable.
In. The Annals and Magazine of Natural History,
May,1954, No. 77. (photocopy).
31.

PITTOCK, George M.*
Flora of Thanet. A catalogue of the plants
indigenous to the island, with a few rare
aliens,by G.M. Pittock and friends.
Printed by R. Robinson & Co. Margate. 1903.
11,12,13,14,17,24.

PRENTIS, Walter.*
Notes on the birds of Rainham...Chatham and
Sittingbourne.
Gurney and Jackson. 1894.
1,2,3,4,5,6,8,11,12,15,17,20.

PRICE, F.H.
Nature Notes. (First appeared in Barham
Parish Magazine 1971 - 75).
(1976).
3.

REYNOLDS, Christopher.
Creatures of the Bay.
André Deutsch. 1974.
3,24.

ROCHESTER NATURALISTS' CLUB.
The Rochester Naturalist: a quarterly record
of the Rochester Naturalists' Club. 1883-1948.
Vol.I.   4,7,15,17.
Vol.II.   4.
Vol.III. -
Vol.IV.   11,12.
Vol.V.   11.
Vol.VI.   11,17.

SANDWICH BAY BIRD OBSERVATORY.
Report for 1975.
Sandwich Bay Bird Observatory. 1976?
6.

SCOTT, Dr. Ernest.*
Annotated list of Lepidoptera (Macro and Micro)
occuring in the neighbourhood of Ashford, Kent.
Revised by Dr. E. Scott.
Transactions of the Kent Field Club. Vol.2.1964.
3,4,7,11,22.

SIDE, Alice, G.*
An atlas of the Bryophytes found in Kent: maps
compiled from the record cards with ecological
notes on the species.
Kent Field Club. 1970.
7,8,9,11,30.

SMITH, Gerard Edwards.*
Catalogue of rare, or remarkable,phaenogamus
plants collected in South Kent, with descriptive
notes.
Longman. 1829.
1,2,6,7,11,12,15,17,19.

"A SON OF THE MARSHES" pseud.
The wild-fowl and sea-fowl of Great Britain,
edited by J.A. Owen.
Chapman and Hall. 1895.
8,20.

Within an hour of London town among wild
birds and their haunts,edited by J.A. Owen.
Blackwood. 1892.
11,20.

Woodland, moor and stream;being the notes of
a naturalist.*
Smith Elder and Co.
20. 1889.
11. 2nd edition 1890.

SOUTH EASTERN UNION OF SCIENTIFIC SOCIETIES.*
South Eastern Bird Report, being an account of
bird-life in Hampshire, Kent, Surrey and Sussex.
3. 1938 - 1939.
4. 1936 - 1939; 1946 - 1947.
7. 1943.
11. 1939; 1942-1943; 1945; 1947.
15. 1938.

The South Eastern Naturalist and Antiquary:*
being the transactions of the South Eastern
Union of Scientific Societies.
4. 1906 - 1944; 1947 - 1949; 1956; 1958;
   1960 - 1966.
5. 1896 - 1958. (14 vols.).
7. 1912.
9. 1907; 1925 - 1934; 1939-1943.
11. 1912; 1955.
12. 1898 - 1943.
17. 1893; 1896-1931;1934 in progress.
19. 1946

STUBB, Michael.
The birds of Sussex;their present status.
Phillimore & Co. 1979.
4.

SWAIN, F.A.
Crofton Heath Surveys...review of the
scientific interest,by F.A. Swain and others.
(Typescript—natural history). 1973.
2.

SWIFT, John.
Ducks, ponds and people. A guide to the
management of small lakes and ponds for
wildfowl. (Includes information on
the Sevenoaks Gravel Pit Reserve).
WAGBI. 1976.
16.

THOMPSON, Edward Pett.
(Mayor of Dover, 1836 and 1838).
The notebook of a naturalist.
Smith Elder. 1845.
6.

TICEHURST, Norman F.
On some Sixteenth century bird drawings from
"William Burch's Commonplace Book"
in Canterbury Cathedral Library.
Reprinted from British Birds. Vol.XVII No.1.
June 1st,1923.
3.

Common gull breeding on Dungeness Beach.
Reprinted from British Birds, Vol. XIII,No.12,
May 1st, 1920.
3.

Some Local Heron history. (Dungeness).
East Sussex Naturalist. Hastings. 1920.
12.

TITTLEY, Ian.
An atlas of the seaweeds of Kent, by I.Tittley
and J.H. Price.
Transactions of the Kent Field Club. Vol.7.
1977.
3,6,7,8,11,13,23.

ULLYETT, Henry.
Rambles of a Naturalist round Folkestone, with
occasional papers on the fauna and flora of
the district, to which are added lists of
plants, lepidoptera, birds and land and
Freshwater shells.
J. English, Printer. Folkestone. 1880.
1,4,6,7,11,12,15,17,26.

WALTON, George Chapman.
The Flora of Folkestone and its Vicinity.
Reprinted from The Transactions of the
South Eastern Union of Scientific Societies,1912.
3.8.11.

A list of Flowering Plants and Ferns found in
the neighbourhood of Folkestone.
Folkestone Natural History Society.
1894.
7,17.

WALTON, John W.
Folkestone and the country around; a popular
and scientific survey of the natural history
and archaeology of the district.. edited by
J.W. Walton.
Printed by J. Parsons, Folkestone for Folkestone
Natural History and General Sciences Society.1925.
1,2,4,6,7,8,11,12,17,21.

Plants found in the immediate neighbourhood
of Folkestone.
Typescript MS. n.d.
7.

The wild flowers, ferns and mosses of the
district round Folkestone. Based on the work
of the late Mr. G.C. Walton as published in 1894,
to which is appended a catalogue of mosses of
the area, as recorded by E.C. Green.
Folkestone Natural History Society. 1950.
1,3,4,6,7,8,11.

WEBB, A.E.
Wild flowers, trees and shrubs growing in Lenham
and Harrietsham.
Headley Bros. Ashford. 1939.
7.11.

WELCH, Kate.
The Woodland Nature Journal;
(photocopy of MSS, compiled by the author at the
age of 15 when resident at The Parsonage,
Farnborough.
1914.
2.

WHEELER, Alwyne.
The Tidal Thames:the history of a river and
its fishes.
Routledge. 1979.
4.

WILDLIFE CONSERVATION AND A LIST OF NATURE
RESERVES IN KENT.
Photocopied articles.
25.

WYE ORNITHOLOGISTS' CLUB.
The Wye and District Bird Report;(edited by
Gwyn Williams) The Club, Wye College.
No.1. October,1975 - September,1976.   3.
No.2. October,1976 - September,1977.   3.

NATURE CONSERVATION See NATURAL HISTORY

NATURE WALKS

BOLTON, D.
Nature Trails: Meopham and Culverstone, written
and illustrated by D. Bolton and D.P. Chubb.
(Meopham and District Footpaths Group).
Meopham Publications Committee. 1973.
9.11.

NATURE WALKS Cont'd

BRITISH TOURIST AUTHORITY.
Nature trails. (Nature trails listed by
County. p.22 - 23 Kent).
British Tourist Authority. 1974.
11.

EDWARDES, Edward Tickner.
Sidelights of nature in quill and crayon.
2nd edition.
Kegan Paul, Trench, Trubner. 1912.
11.

NATURE CONSERVANCY COUNCIL-SOUTH EAST REGION.
Wye and Crundale Down - Nature Trail.
Nature Conservancy Council. 1977.
3.

TONBRIDGE AND MALLING DISTRICT COUNCIL.
Tonbridge Castle Nature Trail.
Tonbridge and Malling District Council. 1977.
4.

NETTLESTEAD

HILTON, John Anthony.*
Nettlestead, a village history.
John Hilton. Hadlow. 1964.
12.

NEW ASH GREEN

CLOUSTON, Brian & Partners.
New Ash Green:landscape master plan.
B. Clouston & Partners. Kingston. 1973.
11.

THOMAS, Denis.*
A village in Kent. The historic and cultural
heritage of New Ash Green edited by D.Thomas.
Quadrangle Books. 1967.
24,30.

NEWCHURCH

Particulars and conditions of sale of...*
excellent and rich pasture land in the parishes
of Newchurch and Bilsington, Romney Marsh...
For sale by auction....on Tuesday,July 14th,
1885...by order of the Trustees...of the
Late Thomas Kingsnorth,Esq.
Thomas Cobb. 1885. 7.
7.

NEW CROSS

WEST, John.
Borough Byways 1: New Cross and Deptford.
(Town trail).
Lewisham Local History Society.
18.

NEWNHAM

BERRY, W.T.
Newnham in Kent:a village of no importance.
Faversham Society. 1976.
3,6,11,20,26.

NEW ROMNEY

ENVIRONMENT, Department of the.
List of buildings of special architectural
or historic interest: Borough of New Romney,Kent.
H.M.S.O. 1973.
11.
FORSETT, John.*
The Custumal of New Romney, edited by F.W.
Jessup. New edition. Originally published 1564.
Phillimore. (1972?).
2.8.

KENT COUNTY COUNCIL:PLANNING DEPARTMENT.
Lydd, New Romney and Dymchurch:Local Plan.
K.C.C. 1968.
7.

LANE, GENTRY AND COMPANY Publishers
The Holiday Handbook of Romney Marsh, including
New Romney, Dymchurch and district.
Lane,Gentry & Co. Margate. (1927?).
11.

LIVETT, Greville Mauis.*
The Church of St. Nicholas, New Romney, with
additional notes by Rev. A.W. McMichael,
Vicar of New Romney.
W.R. Geering. Ashford. 1930.
2.

MARTON, Mrs. M.E.*
The church of St. Nicholas, New Romney.
W.R. Geering, Ashford. 1927.
1,11,12.

MURRAY, K.M. Elizabeth.*
The Register of Daniel Rough, Common Clerk of
Romney, 1353 - 1380, edited by K.M.E. Murray.
Kent Archaeological Society (Records Branch)1945.
5.

ST. NICHOLAS (Church) NEW ROMNEY, KENT.
Adams (of Rye). n.d.
30.

TEICHMAN-DERVILLE, Max.*
Annals of the town and port of New Romney.
Headley Bros. Ashford. 1929.
2.

NEWSPAPERS

BOORMAN, Henry Roy Pratt.*
"Kent Messenger" Centenary.
Kent Messenger. 1959.
1,2,3,4,5,6,7,8,9,11,12,14,15,17,18,25.

"No Mean Association": Diamond Jubilee 1916 -
1976. Kent Newspaper Proprietors' Association,
now the Kent and Downs Newspaper Association.
Kent Messenger. 1976.
5,6,7,11,23.

Your family newspaper, compiled by H.R.P.
Boorman.
Kent Messenger. 1968.
12.

COCK, F. William.*
'The Kentish Post or the Canterbury News-letter'.
Alexander Moring. 1913.
3,12,23.

DILNOT, George.
The romance of the Amalgamated Press, compiled
by George Dilnot.
Amalgamated Press. 1925.
11.

EAST KENT TIMES AND BROADSTAIRS AND ST. PETERS'
MAIL.
Centenary Supplement: 1866 - 1966.
East Kent Times. 1966.
24.

GREAT BRITAIN-MONOPOLIES COMMISSION.
Westminster Press Ltd., and Kentish Times Ltd.,
Gravesend and Dartford Reporter Ltd., and
F.J. Parsons Ltd.: subsiduaries of Morgan-
Grampian Ltd:a report.(HC1973. 460).
H.M.S.O. 1973.
2,4,7,9.

GREAT BRITAIN. PARLIAMENT. HOUSE OF COMMONS:Papers.
Courier Printing and Publishing Company Limited and
Associated Newspapers Group Limited:a report on
the transfer of five newspapers (H.C. 108).
H.M.S.O. 1974.
16.

ISLE OF THANET GAZETTE - a short history.
The Isle of Thanet Gazette. n.d.
13.

NEWSPAPERS Cont'd

KENT AND ESSEX MERCURY.
The issue of Tuesday, 17th December, 1822.
No.X of a Weekly newspaper.
17.

KENT AND SUSSEX COURIER AND SOUTHERN COUNTIES
HERALD.
Courier Centenary edition 1972, with page 1 of the
1st edition of Friday, October 4th, 1872.
4.

RALPH, Vic.
The first Kentish newspaper.
K.C.C. ? 1975.
12.

SCHEDULE OF KENTISH NEWSPAPERS STORED IN
THE STRONG ROOM OF THE BEANEY INSTITUTE CANTERBURY:
includes "Man of Kent".
3.

NONINGTON

SUTTON, Aubrey.
Nonington.
A. Sutton. 1975.
3,6,7,

THE TOPOGRAPHER, No.XVIII September,1790,
being No III of Vol III: includes Nonington
Church (pp.171 - 178) and Goodnestone Church
(pp.150 - 155).
Robson. 1790.
11,12.

TOPOGRAPHICAL MISCELLANIES.
Includes:- St. Alban's Court at Nonington.
Robson. 1792.
3,12.

NORTH DOWNS WAY

COUNTRYSIDE COMMISSION.
North Downs Way.
Countryside Commission. 1978.
2.

North Downs Way Maps.
Countryside Commission. (1978).
4,23.

DAVIS, Cyril.
Walks on the North Downs:Hollingbourne to
the Medway,by C. Davis and A. Gray.
Swale Footpaths Group. 1974.
8.

DOGGETT, Tom.
The North Downs Way,by T. Doggett and John
Trevelyan.
Ramblers Association. 1978.
2,3,5,6,28,30.

SMITH, Alan.
North Downs Walks:Doddington and Lenham.
14 Downland walks between Harrietsham and
Charing, edited by Alan Smith, with
illustrations by May Gardiner.
Swale Footpaths Group. 1973.
3,4,6,11,12.

WRIGHT, Christopher John.
A guide to the Pilgrim's Way and North
Downs Way.*
Constable, 1971.
3,11,12,25.

A guide to the Pilgrims' Way and North
Downs Way. New Revised edition.
Constable, 1977.
2,3,16.

NORTHFLEET

ARNOLD, George Matthew.*
On the Old Rectory at Northfleet.
Reprinted from Archaeologia Cantiana, Vol.20,
1893.
Mitchell & Hughes. (1893).
9,11,17.

BENSON, James.
A History of Gravesend, or a historical
perambulation of Gravesend and Northfleet,
revised and edited by Robert Heath Hiscock,
1954.
Phillimore. 1976.
3,6,8,9,11,16,23,25.

GREAT BRITAIN, Laws etc. (Edw. VII).
An Act to confirm certain provisional orders
made by the Board of Trade under the Electric
Lighting Acts....relating to....Gravesend
(extension to Northfleet). 1905.
9.

JOHNSON, Miss.
John Huggens and the college he founded, by Miss
Johnson and Rev. H. McCalman.
Huggens College (Northfleet). 1954.
5.

NORTHFLEET CONGREGATIONAL CHURCH.
Centenary Booklet, 1850 - 1950.
Northfleet Congregational Church. 1950.
9.

NORTHFLEET URBAN DISTRICT COUNCIL.
Building Byelaws made under the Public Health
Act, 1936.
Shaw and Son. (1953?).
9.

The Story behind the Council's emblem.
Northfleet Urban District Council. 1974.
9.

The Tenants' Handbook.* 3rd edition.
British Publishing Company for Northfleet
Urban District Council. 1960.
9.

ROSHERVILLE GARDENS
See GARDENS:ZOO PARKS ETC.
and GRAVESEND & NORTHFLEET IN KENT BIBLIOGRAPHY.

ST. BOTOLPH'S CHURCH - Northfleet.
Parish Registers - Baptisms 1539 - 1653
and 1680 - 1748. Transcript made by Thomas
Colyer - Ferguson from Northfleet Parish Church
Records.
E. Green and C. Ford. 1972.
9.

ST. BOTOLPH'S CHURCH, Northfleet - a short guide
and history.
British Publishing Company. 1960.
9.

SMITH, Reginald Anthony.*
A palaeolithic industry at Northfleet, Kent.
Read to the Society of Antiquaries of London on
the 4th May, 1911.
(Extracted from Archaeologia Vol. LXXll)
The Society of Antiquaries. 1911.
11.

NORTH KENT MARSHES

GILLHAM, Eric Howard.*
The Birds of the North Kent Marshes,by E.H.
Gillham and R.C. Holmes.
Collins. 1950.
1,2,3,4,5,7,8,9,11,12,14,15,17,18,20,25,26.

HARRISON, Jeffery Graham.*
Wildfowl of the North Kent Marshes; illustrated
by Pamela Harrison and foreword by George
Atkinson-Willes.
WAGBI. (1972).
11,30.

MEDWAY PRESERVATION SOCIETY.
The future of the North Kent Marshes.
Medway Preservation Society.   December, 1974.
4,11,20,27.

NATURE CONSERVANCY COUNCIL - SOUTH EAST REGION.*
Wildlife conservation in the North Kent
Marshes: a report of a working party. Edited
by B.H. Green.
Nature Conservancy Council.   1971.
2,3,4,5,9,11,12,27.

NICHOLS, W.N.
A history of the North Kent Marshes in the
area of Cliffe from Roman times including the
Roman Invasion AD43 and possible site
of the ancient Church councils
called Cloveshoh with a diversion of the
River Thames.
W.N. Nicholls. Redhill.   1979.
2,4,5,11,12.

PAYNE, George.*
Walks by the marshes: a lecture.....
Edwin Harris.   Rochester.   1901.
1,11,15,25.

NURSTEAD

PRYOR, C.A.
Nurstead Court.
Meopham Publications Committee (1975).
8,9,11,12,19.

OBITUARIES

ABBOTT, William George.
Local Historian of Eythorne. Obituary.
In. Eythorne and District Baptist News
Letter - "Our Link", June, 1971.
3.

BENIANS, W.A.
In memoriam: W.A. Benians, 19th July, 1851 -
11th May, 1939. (Headmaster of Bethany
School, Goudhurst, 1878 - 1916)
In. The Old Bethanian.
Knole Park Press. Sevenoaks.   (194-?).
11.

FORSTER, John, Lord Harraby.
Master the Lord Forster of Harraby, an
obituary composed by Geoffrey Tookey.
In. Graya, No.76, 1973. (pp75 - 79).
Lord Forster was a resident of Beckenham).
Hon. Society of Grays Inn.   1973.
2.

FRY, James Hockett.
Brief obituary of Mr. James Hockett Fry
(of Pembury).
J. Clifford. 1840.
19.

KENDON, Samuel.
In Memoriam; Samuel Kendon, 20th December, 1864-
30th May, 1945.
(Headmaster of Bethany School, Goudhurst for
fifty-one years, 1894 - 1945).
In. The Old Bethanian.
Knole Park Press, Sevenoaks. (1945?).
11.

MARRIOTT, Charles Stowel (1895 - 1966).
Obituary from the "Old Alleynian",
Winter, 1967.
C.S. Marriott, a leg-break bowler played for
Kent & Lancashire and taught English Literature
at Dulwich College.   Died. 13th October, 1966.
12.

MAXWELL, Donald.
Obituary notice from the Kent Messenger, 1st
August, 1936.   M/S.
12.

ROBERTSON, Rev. William Archibald Scott.
Obituary notice of the Rev. W.A. Scott
Robertson, M.A., Honorary Canon of Canterbury,
composed by George Payne. (Reprinted from
"Archaeologia Cantiana" Vol.23. 1898).
Mitchell & Hughes. London. 1898.
3.

SIX, James. F.R.S. (1730/1 - 1793).
Inventor of the variable thermometer and
carried out "experiments in Natural Philosophy."
Died in Canterbury on August 25th, 1793.
Obituary In: The Kentish Gazette of August 27th,
1793.
3.

OFFHAM

GENERAL REGISTER OFFICE.
Census Returns, 1841, 1851, 1861, 1871.
Offham.   Microfilm.
23.

OFFHAM PAROCHIAL CHURCH COUNCIL.
The Parish Church of St. Michael and All Angels,
Offham, Kent.
Offham Parochial Church Council. 1971
(1978 reprint).
11.

OLDBURY HILL

PAYNE, George.*
Oldbury and its surroundings, paper read before
the Maidstone and Mid-Kent Natural History and
Philosophical Society.
F. Bunyard, Printer.   1888.
2,11,14.

PERKINS, J.B. Ward.
Excavations on the Iron Age Hill Fort at
Oldbury, near Ightham, Kent.
In. Archaeologia, Vol.90, 1944.
Society of Antiquaries of London. 1944.
5.

ORGANISATIONS

ASSOCIATION OF MEN OF KENT AND KENTISH MEN.*
Annual Reports, Lists of Members, papers....
Association of Men of Kent and Kentish Men. 1900-
1902.
2.

Roll of Members, rules etc.
Association of Men of Kent and Kentish Men. 1950.
4.

ATKIN, Stanley.
50 years of service: Rotary Club of Dartford.
1929 - 1979.
Dartford Rotary Club.   1979.
5.

BRITISH RED CROSS SOCIETY - KENT BRANCH.*
Yearbook for 1973, including reports for 1972.
British Red Cross Society.   1973.
4,7.

Yearbook for 1975, including reports for 1974.
British Red Cross Society. 1975.
3.

BRITISH SCIENTIFIC INSTRUMENT RESEARCH ASSOCIATION.
Sira Institute (Chislehurst) (Brochure of
Services).
Scientific Instrument Research Association c.1970.
2.

BROWN, Anthony.
Red for Remembrance: British Legion 1921 - 71.
Heinemann. 1971.
12.

CAMPBELL, Marjorie A.*
The Story of Guiding in Kent, 1910 - 1960,
compiled by M.A. Campbell.
(The Author is a Kent Guide Commissioner).
Girl Guide Association. Printed by Perry
Son and Lack Ltd. Dartford. (1960).
4,5,8,11.

CAMPBELL, Robin.
The 1st - 70 years: a history of the 1st.
Sevenoaks (Hicks Own) Scout Group, 1909 -
1979.
1st Sevenoaks Scout Group. 1979.
16.

CANTERBURY CITY COUNCIL: PUBLICITY DEPARTMENT.
List of Organisations.
Canterbury City Council. 1972.
4.

CANTERBURY SOCIETY FOR MENTALLY HANDICAPPED
CHILDREN.
Year Book 1977/78.
Canterbury Society for Mentally Handicapped
Children. 1978.
3.

CANTERBURY, WHITSTABLE AND HERNE BAY SCOUT
COUNCIL.
Directory, July,1974.
Canterbury, Whitstable and Herne Bay
Scout Council. 1974.
3.

CITY OF ROCHESTER SOCIETY.
Best foot forward: a review of the
Society's achievements during the first
ten years.
Executive Committee of the City of
Rochester Society. (1977).
11.

GILLINGHAM DISTRICT SCOUT COUNCIL.
Official Handbook. 1970 - 71.
Gillingham District Scout Council. 1970?
8.

GILLINGHAM PUBLIC LIBRARY.
Directory of local societies and
organisations. 9th edition.
Gillingham Public Library. 1972.
4.

GILLINGHAM WORKING MEN'S CLUB AND INSTITUTE
SOCIETY.
Rules. 1903.
8.

GIRL GUIDES ASSOCIATION.
Kent West County Directory: 1975/76.
Girl Guides Association. 1975.
8.

HARRIS, Christopher W.J.
Fifty years of progress: the London and
Home Counties Branch of the Library
Association.
Library Association. 1976.
2.

HARTCUP, Adeline.
Kent Council of Social Service: the first
fifty years.
Kent Council of Social Services. 1973.
1,4,7,9,11,30.

INSURANCE INSTITUTE OF MID-KENT.
(List of officers 1974).
12.

JEFFRIES, E.S.
Short History of West Wickham Allotments
Society...and West Wickham Allotments
Association...
Duplicated Typescript. 1975.
2.

KENT AND ESSEX SEA FISHERIES COMMITTEE.*
Annual Reports. 1962 - 1973.
4.

KENT ARCHAEOLOGICAL SOCIETY.
Annual Report....1957.
Kent Archaeological Society.
4.

Members list: 1st January, 1977.
Kent Archaeological Society. 1977.
4.

KENT ASSOCIATION FOR THE BLIND.*
Annual Report.
Kent Association for the Blind.
1971 - 1972   4.
1973 - 1974. 12.

KENT ASSOCIATION FOR THE DISABLED.
Yearbook.
Magus Publications.
1975 - 76.   20.
1976 - 77.   11.
1977 - 78.   4,25.

KENT ASSOCIATION OF YOUTH CLUBS.*
Official Handbook. Printed by the Pyramid
Press for K.S.C. of National Voluntary
Youth Organisations.
1972.   30.
1974.   8,9,11,20.
1975.   20,26.

KENT COUNCIL OF SOCIAL SERVICE.*
Annual Reports.
1972.   4.
1973.   3,4,7,11. (50th Annual Report).
1974.   8.

An environmental directory for Kent:
statutory and voluntary organizations in Kent of
interest to those concerned with amenity and
the environment.
Kent Council of Social Service. 1975.
2,11,12,13,19,25,29.

KENT COUNTY AMATEUR SWIMMING ASSOCIATION.
Handbook. 1979.
Kent County Amateur Swimming Association. (1979).
4.

KENT COUNTY ASSOCIATION OF CHANGE RINGERS.
Outline of the Association.
Kent County Association of Change Ringers. 1974.
12.

KENT COUNTY LIBRARY - MEDWAY DIVISION
Medway Towns Societies.
Kent County Library, Medway Division.
1969 Chatham Public Library   4.
1975 Kent County Library   4.11.
1977 Kent County Library   4.

KENT COUNTY LIBRARY - SEVENOAKS DIVISION.
(Societies):a list of organisations in
Sevenoaks, Swanley, Hartley, Edenbridge and
the surrounding district, March 1978.
Kent County Library, Sevenoaks Division. 1978.
11,16.

KENT COUNTY SCOUT ASSOCIATION.
Kent County Scout Handbook, 1973.
Kent County Scout Association (1973).
11.

KENT STANDING CONFERENCE OF NATIONAL VOLUNTARY
YOUTH ORGANISATIONS.*
Handbook of Kent Youth Organisations, 1967.
Kent Standing Conference of National Voluntary
Youth Organisations.
13.

KENT VOLUNTARY SERVICE COUNCIL.
Annual Reports.
53rd 1976. 11.
54th 1977   3,11,13.
55th 1978   13.

LEWIS, J.D.*
W.V.S. in Kent, 1939 - 1945.
Kent Messenger, Maidstone. (1946).
23.

LIBRARY ASSOCIATION, Kent Sub-Branch.
Kent newsletter. Vol.8 nos. 4 - 6.
Vol.9. nos.2,4,6.Vol.10. nos.1-4, 6.
Vol.11 nos.1,2,6.Vol 12. nos.1.2.5.
Library Association. 1957 - 61.
4.

MAIDSTONE DISTRICT SCOUT COUNCIL.
Yearbook 1975 - 76.
Maidstone District Scout Movement. (1976).
11.

MARGATE AMBULANCE CORPS.
Celebrating 100 years voluntary service, 1880 -
1980.
Margate Ambulance Corps. 1980.
13.

MAY, Arthur.
A History of the Hervey Lodge No. 1692 of
the ....ancient, free and accepted Masons of
England: Centenary Year 1977.
(Includes lists of Officers and members).
The Lodge.   1977.
2.

MEDWAY AND GILLINGHAM COMMUNITY RELATIONS
COUNCIL,
Campaign for harmony:the annual edition of "Link";
prepared by S. Ikran Ali and M.A. Zaheer
Afridi. Presented to the Annual General
Meeting, Monday 16th July, 1979.
4.

MEDWAY AND NORTH KENT MARRIAGE GUIDANCE COUNCIL.
Annual report and accounts 1975 and minutes
of Annual General Meeting held on 10th July, 1975.
(1975).
4.

MEDWAY SOCIETY FOR MENTALLY HANDICAPPED CHILDREN.
Year Book.
1972.   8.
1974.   ("Their world our concern")   4.
1974 - 75.   8,25.
1977 - 78.   4.

MEDWAY YOUTH COMMITTEE.
Medway Youth Organisations.
Pyramid Press Ltd. n.d.
4.

NATIONAL UNION OF TOWNSWOMEN'S GUILDS.*
Kent County Yearbook 1966 and annual
report 1965.
13.

NORTH KENT YACHTING ASSOCIATION.
Gazetteer of Member clubs; 2nd edition.
North Kent Yachting Association.   1978.
9.

NORTH WEST KENT SPASTICS GROUP.
Yearbook. 1973, 1976, 1977.
North West Kent Spastics Group.
9.

POCKNELL, Edmund.
A short history of the Hervey Lodge No. 1692,
of the...ancient, free and accepted
Masons of England.
(Includes lists of Officers and Members).
The Lodge, Province of Kent. 1937.
2.

PROVINCE OF WEST KENT:FREEMASONS.
Freemasons' Manual and Directory.
Provincial Grand Lodge of West Kent.
1978 - 1979.
2.

ROYAL AGRICULTURAL BENEVOLENT INSTITUTION.
List of subscriptions and donations, etc.
(pp. 143 - 161, Kent).
Royal Agricultural Benevolent Institution.1889.
11.

ROYAL BRITISH LEGION - KENT BRANCH.
Kent County Branch Handbook.*
British Legion Press.
1971.   30.
1972.   7,30.
1973.   30.
1975.   12.
1977.   9.

Into the Future:the story of the Royal British
Legion.
British Legion Press. (1976).
11.

1921 - 1971. Fifty years: the British Legion,
Kent. *
British Legion Press. 1971.
30.

ROYAL BRITISH LEGION,WHITSTABLE BRANCH.
Loyalty and Service:year books and souvenir
1969 - 70.
British Legion Press. (1969).
31.

ROYAL LIFE SAVING SOCIETY - KENT BRANCH.
Annual Report, 1972.
Royal Life Saving Society.
4.

Kent Life Saving Handbook.
Royal Life Saving Society.
1972. 11.
1973.   4.8.

ROYAL MASONIC INSTITUTE FOR GIRLS.
Yearbook 1960: being some account of the history
of the objects and work of the Institution.
(pp. 14 - 35 Kent).
Royal Masonic Institute for Girls. 1960.
11.

ST. JOHN AMBULANCE ASSOCIATION AND BRIGADE -
KENT BRANCH.
Centenary Book, 1877 - 1977.
St. John Ambulance Association & Brigade. 1977.
5.

Yearbook and Directory.*
St. John Ambulance Association and Brigade.
1953;1963;1965;1967;1972;1973;1974.   4.
1973.   12.
1976.   20.26.
1978.   6.
1979.   6.

SHAW, K.D.
Short history of Gramophone Society
activities in South East London and North West
Kent (typescript).
1974.
2.

SITTINGBOURNE LITERARY AND SCIENTIFIC ASSOCIATION.
Proceedings.
Parrett. 1879.
20.

STANDING CONFERENCE FOR LOCAL HISTORY.
Local history societies in England and Wales:
a list.
Standing Conference for Local History. 1978.
11,28.

TONBRIDGE AND TUNBRIDGE WELLS SOCIETY FOR
MENTALLY HANDICAPPED CHILDREN.
Year Book,1976.
Tunbridge and Tunbridge Wells Society for
Mentally Handicapped Children.   (1976).
19.

TUNBRIDGE WELLS AND DISTRICT COUNCIL OF
SOCIAL SERVICE .
Directory of Statutory and voluntary Social
Services in Royal Tunbridge Wells and District.
Tunbridge Wells and District Council of
Social Service .   October, 1975.
19.

WEALD OF KENT PRESERVATION SOCIETY.
The first ten years, 1960 - 1970: the record
of an Amenity Society.
Elvey and Gibbs Partnership. Ashford. 1970.
7.

WEST-KENT FEDERATION OF WOMEN'S INSTITUTES.
Speaker's list and year book.
West Kent Federation of Women's Institutes.1978.
4.

WOMEN'S ROYAL VOLUNTARY SERVICE.
Annual report 1973.(South Eastern Region).
4.8.

ORPINGTON

ALL SAINTS CHURCH, ORPINGTON:
illustrated guide to the parish church....with
additional notes and corrections. Revised edition.
All Saints Church. 1980.
2.

ORPINGTON   Cont'd

BROMLEY PUBLIC LIBRARIES.
Introduction to the history of Orpington
(duplicated typescript). Revised edition.
London Borough of Bromley:Public Libraries. 1975.
1.2.3.12.16.18.

HANSON, Jack.
Residential care observed:an evaluation.
(Note:Manor Fields, Old People's Home,
Orpington)
National Institute for Social Work Training
and Age Concern. 1972.
2.

LAW, Maurice.
These forty years:a short history of Christ
Church, Orpington. (includes lists of
personalia).
(The Church). 1980.
2.

NEWBY, Donald.
The Orpington Story.
(Liberal Party in Orpington, 1954 to the
1962 Bye-Election win).
Prism Publications. 1962.
2.

PARKER, M.R.J.
Orpington:development and change 1930 - 1978
and the need for conservation   Unpublished
dissertation, B.A. (Hons) Geography,
University of Hull. (1979).
2.

PIPE, H.M.
Newstead Wood:the first twenty five years.
(Started as Orpington Grammar School for Girls)
The School. 1979.
2.

ROBERTSON, Rev. William Archibald Scott.*
Kentish Archaeology, 7 vols. (mostly
reprinted from Archaeologia Cantiana)
Vol.4 - Romney Marsh, Chislehurst, Orpington.
Mitchell & Hughes. 1880.
1.

TIMMIS, L.B.
Historical notes on the parish of Orpington,
and the so-called Priory (1977).
London Borough of Bromley Public Libraries. 1979.
2.

WATERS, S.C.
A talk on local administration: (with
reference to Orpington, Farnborough, etc).
Typescript. n.d.
2.

OSPRINGE

CLINCH, Phyllis E.
Painter's Forstal with Ospringe: an anthology
of legend and history, collected and illustrated
by P.E. Clinch. (Faversham papers No.15).
Faversham Society. 1978.
3,11.

DRAKE, Charles H.*
The hospital of St. Mary of Ospringe
commonly called Maison Dieu. Reprinted from
Archaeologia Cantiana Vol. XXX 1913.
Mitchell Hughes and Clarke.(1914).
26.

RIGOLD, S.E.*
Maison Dieu, Ospringe, Kent, by S.E.
Rigold and G.C. Dunning.
 Ministry of Works Ancient Monument Series
H.M.S.O.
1958 3,4,7,8,11,12,25,30.
1962. 5.
1969.20,26,27.
1972. 7.

WHITING, William.*
Report on the excavation of the Roman Cemetery
at Ospringe, by W. Whiting and others.
J. Johnson for Society of Antiquaries of London.
1931.
2.

OTFORD

CLARKE, Dennis.
Otford in Kent:a history, by D. Clarke and
Anthony Stoyel.
Otford and District Historical Society. 1975.
1,2,3,6,8,9,11,12,13,15,16,19,24,25.

ELDER, D.G.*
Otford past and present.
(1950).
2,16.

OTHAM

CAVE-BROWN, Rev. John.*
Otham Church and Parish. A paper read on
6th March, 1895. (Extract from the Journal
of the Kentish Archaeological Association,
June 1895).
3,11.

PADDLESWORTH

GENERAL REGISTER OFFICE.
Census Returns 1841, 1851, 1861, 1871.
Snodland and Paddlesworth. Microfilm.
23.

PADDOCK WOOD

GENERAL REGISTER OFFICE.
Census Returns. 1871.
Paddock Wood. Photocopy.
23.

PADDOCK WOOD AND DISTRICT YEAR BOOK, AND
TRADES AND SERVICES GUIDE.
Summer 1975.
Gordon Bringes, Paddock Wood. 1975.
11.

WALKER, Jack.
The history of Saint Andrews Church,Paddock
Wood, and guide of the present church.
1976.
17,19.

PALMER, SAMUEL. 1805 - 1881.
(LIVED FOR A TIME AT SHOREHAM)

LISTER, Raymond.
Samuel Palmer.
Faber. 1974.
5.

Samuel Palmer and his etchings.*
Faber, 1969.
12.

Samuel Palmer in Palmer Country.
Hugh Tempest Radford. East Bergholt. 1980.
16,23.

PEACOCK, Carlos.*
Samuel Palmer, Shoreham and after.
John Baker. 1968.
12,16.

PATRIXBOURNE

BOWTELL, Rev. John.
A sermon preached at Patrixbourne and Bridge.
Printed by J. Abree, Canterbury. 1749.
3.

PATRIXBOURNE Cont'd

FIFTY YEARS AGO: a description of the
villages of Bridge, Patrixbourne and
Bekesbourne taken from "Saunters through
Kent with pen and pencil"...by Charles
Igglesden.
Bekesbourne Parochial Church Council. 1977.
3.

ST. MARY'S, PATRIXBOURNE.
(Guide to the church).
Kent County Printers, Canterbury. 1965.
3.

PEGWELL BAY

KENT COUNTY COUNCIL: PLANNING DEPARTMENT and
THANET DISTRICT COUNCIL: PLANNING DEPARTMENT.
Consultation draft. Development Study.
Ramsgate International Hoverport, Pegwell Bay.
1979.
13.

KNIGHT, Robert.
Will the people of Sandwich celebrate the
bicentennial of Walker and Boys (1784)?
Notes on the Foraminifera, especially
those of Pegwell Bay.
1980.
13.

PEGWELL BAY COMMITTEE.
Clifftop footpath, Pegwell, Cliffsend:
walker's Guide.
(Duplicated pamphlet).
Pegwell Bay Committee. n.d.
24.

STORY OF THE VIKINGS AND THE VIKING SHIP
"HUGIN". (1949).
(Duplicated typescript account of the 1949
invasion by a replica of a Viking Ship and
crew from Denmark. The landing was at
Broadstairs and the ship is preserved at
Pegwell Bay).
11.

WEIR, A.H.
Post glacial soil formation in the
Loess of Pegwell Bay, by A.H. Weir and
others, from Geoderma Vol 5. 1971.
Elsesvier. 1971.
24.

PEMBURY

FRY, James Hockett.
A brief obituary of Mr. James Hockett Fry
(of Pembury).
J. Clifford. 1840.
19.

JENNINGS, Letitia.*
Margery Polley: the Pembury martyr.
(Photo-copy).
Protestant Reform Society. 1910.
23.

PEMBURY PARISH COUNCIL.
Pembury 2000: an analysis of the present
village and recommendations for the future,
plus map.
Pembury Parish Council. 1976.
19.

SLIGHT, Rev. B.
Uncle Daniel, the pious farmer.
(Daniel Dickensen of Pembury).
William Freeman. 1856.
19.

STANDEN, E.J.*
Just one village, 1910 - 60. (Pembury)
E.J. Standen. Privately Printed. (1972)
11,19.

PENGE

DOUGLAS-JONES, Ian E.
The first hundred years: the story of Penge
parish church, centenary souvenir booklet.
(St. John the Evangelist's Church)
Xerox copy only.
1950.
2.

DUDLEY, M.R.
The Parliamentary enclosure movement:
Penge Hamlet c.1780 - c.1860.
(Unpublished dissertation. B.A. Honours Course).
1980.
2.

DYER, Albert.
The ups and downs of my life: the memoirs of
Albert Dyer 1908 - 1970.
Duplicated typescript: life and trade in Penge
and Beckenham .
n.d.
2.

KELLY'S DIRECTORIES LTD.
Kelly's Directory of Beckenham, Penge and
neighbourhood. 43rd edition.
Kelly's Directories Ltd. 1938.
11.

REEVES, Graham.
A school for Penge: the story of St. John's
Schools, founded 1837.
The School Managers. 1978.
2.

SAMPSON, Mrs. P.M.
Social provision in the nineteenth century for
the members of the Company of Watermen and
Lightermen with special reference to the
Almshouses at Penge.
Thesis: photocopy of typescript. 1974.
2.

WEST, R. George.
To Penge - by canal.
(Duplicated typescript).
1976.
2.

PENSHURST

BINNEY, Marcus.
Penshurst Place, Kent, I - IV, the seat of Viscount
de L'Isle: home of the Sidneys. (Country Life -
March 9th and 16th; April 27th; May 4th, 1972).
Reprinted from Country Life. 1972.
11,19.

CHURCH OF ST JOHN THE BAPTIST, Penshurst.
(list of rectors).
1937.
12.

CROGGAN. Lucy E.*
Onward and Upward. (Includes a chapter on
Penshurst).
J. Read, Sittingbourne. 1853.
11.

KENT COUNTY COUNCIL: PLANNING DEPARTMENT.*
Penshurst: village study.
K.C.C. 1968 and 1974.
2,4,7,11,12,13,16,20,25,30.

MARSHALL, Emma.*
Penshurst Castle in the times of Sir Philip
Sidney. (historical novel).
Seeley. 1908.
2.

PENSHURST CHURCH AND VILLAGE.*
(Printed by Ashmead Press Limited, London.
S.E.10.). 1970.
4,7,11,12,16.

PENSHURST PLACE.
Printed by Arthurs Press. (1968?).
11.30.

PENSHURST Cont'd

PENSHURST PLACE, TONBRIDGE, KENT, the
home of Lord de L'Isle.
Printed at the Curwen Press. (1973?).
11.

PETLEY, Rev. J.L. Ward.*
Penshurst:the home of the Sidneys.
Goulden and Nye. 1890.
1,17,19.

SIDNEY, Hon. Mary.*
Historical guide to Penshurst Place.
Goulden and Co. Tunbridge Wells. 1903.
2,16.

SIDNEY, Philip.*
Memoirs of the Sidney Family.
T. Fisher Unwin. 1899.
12.

The Sidneys of Penshurst.
Bonsfield. 1901.
1,2,4,7,11,12,15,16,17,18,19.

STAGG, Frank Noel.
Penshurst historical notes.
Typescript. 1939.
16.

Some historical notes concerning Penshurst
Parish before the Sidneys.*
Typescript. 1946.
16.

WHAT YOU CAN SEE AT PENSHURST PLACE.
Guide Books. n.d.
11.

PETHAM

PETHAM PAROCHIAL CHURCH COUNCIL.
All Saints' Church, Petham:a short history
of the Church and Parish.
Petham Parochial Church Council. 1977.
3.

A SOUVENIR FROM STONE STREET FARM,
being a description of the old yeoman's
house together with side lights on smuggling
and the legend of Slippery Sam. 4th edition.
The Proprietors of Slippery Sam's.
1934.
11.

PETTS WOOD

EDWARDS, J.P.
History of the Petts Wood Sports Association.
Limited edition of 400 copies.
P.P., Printed by Ches F. Thorn & Son Ltd.
Erith. (1976?).
2,11.

WAYMARK, Peter.
A history of Petts Wood.
Petts Wood Residents' Association. 1979.
2.

PIERS See COASTLINE

PILGRIMS' WAY

ADAIR, John.
The Pilgrims' Way:shrines and saints in
Britain and Ireland.
Thames & Hudson. London. 1978.
3,12.

BELLOC, Hilaire.*
The Old Road from Canterbury to Winchester.
Constable.
1910. 2.8.26.
1952, reprint of 1910 edition. 2.8.

CAPPER, Douglas Parode.*
On the Pilgrims' Way.
Methuen and Co. 1928.
25.

CARTWRIGHT, Julia. (Mrs Henry Ady).*
The Pilgrims' Way from Winchester to Canterbury.
J. Murray, 1911.
9,25.

CLIFT, J.G.N.
The Pilgrims' Way between Farnham and Albury.
Reprinted from the South Eastern Naturalist,1910.
11.

COWLES, Frederick I.
Pilgrim Ways, with illustrations by Doris M. Cowles.
Burns, Oates and Washbourne. 1934.
4.

FEARON, Henry Bridges.(FIELDFARE pseud).*
The pilgrimage to Canterbury.
Associated Newspapers. (1956).
2,3.

FINCH, William Coles.*
In Kentish Pilgrim land:its ancient roads and
shrines.
C.W. Daniel. 1925. etc.
1,2,4,5,6,7,8,9,10,11,12,13,14,15,16,17,18,19,20,25.

GOODSALL, Robert Harold.*
The ancient road to Canterbury - a progress
through Kent.
1959. Subscription edition.Headley Bros. Ashford. 26.
1960. Constable. 2.

HAMILTON, Ronald.
Summer pilgrimage:a ruminative journey from
Winchester to Canterbury.
P.&.G. Wells Ltd. Canterbury. 1975.
3,9,11.

HEATH, Sidney.*
In the steps of the pilgrims.
(pp. 147 - 190 Kent; pp. 185 - 190 The Boxley
Rood of Grace. Original edition entitled
"Pilgrim life in the Middle Ages").
Rich and Cowan. 1950.
3,6,11.

JENNETT, Sean.*
The Pilgrims' Way from Winchester to Canterbury.
Cassell.
1971. 2.3.4.7.8.11.12.19.21.25.26.
1973. 11.22.

KIRKHAM, Nellie.*
The Pilgrims' Way - a series of Camera Studies,
with descriptive text by N. Kirkham and photographs
by W.E. Lake.
Muller. 1948.
1,3,4,8,9,11,12,15,18.

MAXWELL, Donald.*
The Pilgrims' Way in Kent.
Kent Messenger, Maidstone.
1932 1st edition. 6,11.
1933 3rd edition 2.
1959 9th edition 23,25.
1966 11th edition 25.
1969(12th edition?) 25.
1977(14th edition) 4.5.

PARR, Henry.*
New wheels in old ruts:a pilgrimage to Canterbury
via the ancient Pilgrims'Way.
T. Fisher Unwin. 1896.
3,4,8,11,12,15,17,18.

PENNELL, Joseph.*
A Canterbury Pilgrimage,by J. and E.R. Pennell.
Seeley and Company. 1885.
3,25.

WHITE, Charles.
The Pilgrims' Way.
Guide for walkers between Dorking and
Westerham Hill.
London General Omnibus Company. 1918.
11.

WILSON, S. Gordon.*
With the Pilgrims to Canterbury, and the
history of the hospital of Saint Thomas.
S.P.C.K. 1934.
3,6,11,12,14,

WRIGHT, Christopher John.*
A Guide to the Pilgrims' Way and the
North Downs Way.
Constable.
1971. 2.3.4.5.7.8.9.11.12.21.25.
1977. New Revised edition 2.3.16.

PITT, William.
(THE ELDER. 1708 - 1778)
(THE YOUNGER 1759-1806).

AYLING, Stanley.
The Elder Pitt; Earl of Chatham.
Collins. 1976.
2.

EHRMAN, J.
The younger Pitt:the years of acclaim.
(References to Hayes and Holwood).
Constable. 1969.
2.

JARRETT, Derek.
Pitt the younger.
(lived at Holwood, Keston).
Weidenfeld & Nicolson. 1974.
2.

PLACE NAMES AND SURNAMES

COUCHMAN, Conrad.*
Couchman:some notes and observations on the
antiquity and origin of the above name.
C.Couchman. Coulsden, Surrey. 1968.
4,9,11,22.

ELWIG, Henry.*
A biographical dictionary of notable people
at Tunbridge Wells, 17th to the 20th
Century, also a list of local place names.
Stanford Printing Company. Tunbridge Wells.
(1941).
11,19.

GLOVER, Judith.
The place names of Kent.
Batsford. 1976.
1,3,6,7,8,9,11,12,15,16,20,22,25,26,27,28,30.

GREEN, E.R.*
Field names of Gravesend.
Gravesend Historical Society. 1966.
11.

HARDMAN, Frederick William.*
The Danes in Kent:a survey of Kentish place-
names of Scandinavian origin. (A lecture
given at Walmer, on 7th February,1927).
2,26.

History in local place-names.*
T.F. Pain. 1926.
7.

The pronunciation of Kent place names.
Southwold. Walmer. 1933.
26.

HARRISON, Lewis.
What's in a name? a Kentish dictionary.
Part 1. only. Place-names and place-name
elements.
Parry & Herring. 1927.
2,25.

HORSLEY, John William.*
Place names in Kent.
South Eastern Gazette (Maidstone). 1921.
3,9,25.

IRWIN, John.*
Place names of Edenbridge.
Edenbridge & District Historical Society. 1964.
30.

PEET, J. Michael.
Of Lords and Landowners, of Battles and
Benefactors. A study of the origins of the
Street Names in the Parish of St. George's,
Perry Hill. (Lewisham).
J.M. Peet. December,1977.
18.

"SMARDONIAN", A. pseud.*
The family names of the Weald of Kent,
particularly Smarden.
Ashford Express . 1901.
1,4,7,11,12.

WALLENBERG, J.K.*
Kentish Place Names.
Appelbergs. Uppsala. 1931.
6,25,30.

The Place Names of Kent.
Appelbergs. Uppsala. 1934.
25,26,30.

PLAISTOW

MACFARLANE, William Angus.*
St. Mary's first hundred years, 1863 - 1963,
a history of Plaistow Parish Church.
Limited edition of 700.
Bookprint Ltd. Kingswood, Surrey. 1963.
2,11,12.

ST. MARY'S CHURCH, PLAISTOW, BROMLEY....
1863 - 1943.
Strong & Sons. printers. 1943.
2.

PLANNING - GENERAL
See also: SUBJECTS, TOWNS AND VILLAGES

ABERCROMBIE, Sir Patrick.*
East Kent Regional Planning Scheme Preliminary
Survey, prepared for the Joint Town Planning
Committee of local authorities by Sir P.
Abercrombie and J. Archibald.
Liverpool University Press & Hodder and
Stoughton. 1925.
24,25,30.

East Kent Regional Planning Scheme, Final
Report, by Sir P. Abercrombie and J. Archibald.
Austens. 1928.
24.

ARCHER, R.W.
Regional planning, county planning and the
supply of land for new housing in South
East England, 1960 to 1970.
University College, London.
School of Environmental Studies. c.1969.
6.

ENVIRONMENT, Department of the.
Strategic plan for the South East. Population
pressure and population change: a monitoring
report...
H.M.S.O. 1975.
2.

Strategic plan for the South East: Review:
Government statement 1978.
H.M.S.O. 1978.
2,3,11,23.

HOUSING AND LOCAL GOVERNMENT, Ministry of.*
The South East Study: 1961 - 1981.
H.M.S.O. 1964.
1,2,3,5,6,7,8,9,11,19,25.

KENT COUNTY COUNCIL:PLANNING DEPARTMENT.
Administration of the County of Kent.
Preliminary outline, county plan explanatory
statement.
K.C.C. 1949.
3,12,13.

POLICE Cont'd

RAPLEY, Hazel E.
Enforcement of Law & Order in the Medway Towns
during the Nineteenth Century. Unpublished thesis,
Sittingbourne College of Education. 1976
4,8.

POLLUTION

BAILEY,P.M.
Pollution! a survey of pollution in the area
of Milton Creek.
1974.
4, 20.

HOUSING AND LOCAL GOVERNMENT, Ministry of.
Pollution of the Tidal Thames:a report of the
Departmental Committee on the effects of
heated, and other, effluents and discharges
on the condition of the tidal reaches of the
River Thames.
H.M.S.O. 1961.
4.

THAMES SURVEY COMMITTEE.*
Effect of Polluting discharges on the Thames
Estuary: the reports of the Thames Survey
Committee and the Water Pollution Laboratory.
(Water Pollution Paper No.12).
H.M.S.O. 1964.
4,5,9.

TRADE & INDUSTRY,Department of WARREN SPRINGS
LABORATORY.
National Survey of Air Pollution, 1961 - 71.
Vol.1......South East Region.
H.M.S.O. 1972.
2.

POOR LAW

ABSTRACT OF THE ACCOUNTS of St. Leonard's
Parish, Hythe, from 1st April,1813, to 1st
April,1814. George Scott, acting overseer.
(Accounts for workhouse and poor relief).
Printed by W. Tiffen, Hythe. 1814.
11.

DARTFORD OVERSEERS OF THE POOR.
An Assessment...for and toward the necessary
relief of the poor of the parish of Dartford..
at one shilling in the pound full rents.
(Covers part 1760 and part 1761).
Photocopy from original in Kent County Library.
Photocopy. 1973.
5.

FRASER, Derek.
The new poor law in the nineteenth century.
edited by D. Fraser.
Macmillan. 1976.
11.

GREAT BRITAIN, Laws etc. (Geo.III)
An Act for enlarging the present, or providing
an additional, workhouse for the Parish of
Chatham. 42 Geo III 1802.
Wm. Burrill. 1826.
4.

An Act for enlarging the present, or providing
an additional, workhouse for the Parish of
Chatham in the County of Kent: for raising
money for that purpose: for the better
ascertaining and collecting the poor rates etc.
42 Geo. III 1802.
Ambrose Etherington. 1841.
4.

GREAT BRITAIN, Laws etc. (Geo. IV)
Acts of Parliament for the government and
regulation of the poor in the town and parish
of Maidstone. 1828.
12.

JENKIN, Austin Fleeming.
A manual for overseers, being a practical
treatise on the appointment, powers and
duties of overseers, assistant overseers, and
collectors of poor rates.
Knight & Co. 1896.
11.

A LETTER TO THE OVERSEERS OF THE POOR of the
parish of Deal, in Kent, respecting the great
increase of their poor rates. With remarks
on the general duties of overseers. 2nd edition.
Printed by Simmons & Kirkby, Canterbury. 1778.
3.

MAIDSTONE UNION.
Statement of accounts for the half year ended
Michaelmas 1878,with a list of persons
receiving in-door and outdoor relief.
T.B. Brown. Maidstone. 1878.
12.

MELLING, Elizabeth.*
The poor...from original sources in the Kent
Archives Office, edited by Elizabeth Melling.
K.C.C. 1964.   .
1,2,3,4,5,6,7,8,9,11,12,14,15,16,17,18,19,
20,25,31.

NORTON, Ann.
Aspects of Bromley Union 1871 - 1910 with
special reference to unemployment and emigration.
An unpublished thesis.
1978.
2.

OXLEY, Geoffrey W.
Poor relief in England and Wales.
David and Charles. 1974.
23.

PEDDY, D.P.R.
Poor Law in Lewisham 1814 - 1846.
Unpublished Thesis.
1976.
18.

TOKE, Nicholas (of Goddington
                    or Godinton).
Five letters on the state of the poor in the
County of Kent, as first printed in the year
1770: to which is added a short introduction
on the same subject...1808.
Printed by Rouse, Kirkby & Lawrence,
Canterbury. 1808.
11.

WHITING, Crispin.
Attitudes towards the poor in the first half
of the eighteenth century:the aims and
actualities of the Parish Workhouse at
Dartford in Kent.
(photocopy of typescript thesis for University
of Kent).
1978.
5.

POPULATION
See also CENSUS

ENVIRONMENT, Department of the.
Strategic plan for the South East.
Population pressure and population change.
A monitoring report....
Department of the Environment. 1975.
2.

HOLLIS, J.
Demographic projections for the counties
of S.E. England, 1975.
Greater London Council. 1976.
5.

KENT COUNTY COUNCIL:PLANNING DEPARTMENT.
Kent County Structure plan. Population(a)
Population basis and strategic demand for
dwellings. (b) Population change in Kent.
(Adopted by the Local Planning Authority (a) in
November,1974 and (b) in May,1975.
Serial No. 1B.
K.C.C. 1975.
3,4,9,11,13,16.

Kent Development Plan.(1967 Revision).
Medway Towns, Maidstone and vicinity and
Medway Gap Town Maps. Report on population
and employment studies in Mid-Kent
Analysis of Shopping Centres in Mid-Kent.
K.C.C. 1970.
8,11,12,25.

NOTTINGHAM UNIVERSITY:DEPARTMENT OF ADULT
EDUCATION.
Local population studies No.8.
Spring 1972.
Nottingham University, Department of
Adult Education. 1971.
13.

ORIGINAL PARISH REGISTERS in record offices and
libraries. Local Population Studies in
association with the Cambridge Group for
the History of Population and Social Structure.
1974.
11.
First Supplement 1976. 23.
Second Supplement 1978. 23.

POSTAL HISTORY

AUSTEN, Brian.
English provincial posts, 1633 - 1840: a
study based on Kent examples.
Phillimore. 1978.
2,3,4,5,11,12,16,19,22,23.

KENT POSTAL HISTORY GROUP.
The Kent Post. In Progress.
1973 Vol.I.   8,11,13.
1974 Vol II.   8,11,13.
1975 Vol.III.   8,11,13.
1976 Vol.IV   8,11,13.
1977 Vol.V   8,11,13.

MUGGERIDGE, Sidney John.*
The postal history of Maidstone and the
surrounding villages with notes on their
postal markings.
Postal History Society. 1972.
3,4,6,7,8,9,11.

POSTLING

POSTLING PAROCHIAL CHURCH COUNCIL.
The church of St. Mary and St. Radigund,
Postling, Kent; prepared and duplicated
by Postling Parochial Church Council.
Postling Parochial Church Council. (197-)
3.

PRATTS BOTTOM

COPUS, G.D.*
The Commons at Green Street Green and
Pratts Bottom, Chelsfield (Typescript).
1955.
2.

HOOK, Judith Ann.*
Pratts Bottom, an English Village.
Norman-Stahli Publishing Co., Pratts
Bottom. 1972.
2,11.

PRINTING AND PUBLISHING

BACON, Francis.
Of gardens, with illustrations by
Elizabeth Hammond
P.P. at the Maidstone School of
Arts and Crafts. 1946.
11.

BEVAN, Anthony.
Tillot blocks:18th and 19th century
applied woodcuts, written and designed by
Anthony Bevan and Julia Sambrook.
Tallot blocks were woodcuts used on the
outside of bales of cloth.
College of Art.Canterbury. 1966.
11.

BOORDE, Andrew.
Thoughts before building,with an introduction
and notes by H. Edmund Poole (illustrated
by students from the college).
College of Art Press, Canterbury. 1961.
11.

BRITISH LIBRARY, REFERENCE DIVISION.
William Caxton:an exhibition to commemorate
the quincentenary of the introduction of
printing into England.
British Library Reference Division, 24th
September, 1976 - 31st January,1977.
British Museum Publications for British
Library. 1976.
11.

BUNYAN, John.
The work of Jesus Christ, as an advocate,
clearly explained, and largely improved,
for the benefit of all believers. 2nd edition.
(Published and printed in Faversham).
Z. Warren, Faversham. 1816.
11.

BURA, Paul.
Behind the Joker.
(Published in Folkestone).
Aten Press. 1973.
7.

CANTERBURY COLLEGE OF ART, DEPARTMENT OF
HISTORY OF ART/DESIGN AND COMPLEMENTARY STUDIES.
Piranesi. Utopia, the furor of archaeology
and architecture against itself. A celebration
of the bicentenary 1778 - 1978.
Duplicated. 1978.
3.

CAUDWELL, Hugo.
Whitsun holiday, illustrated by Judy White.
College of Art, Canterbury. (1967).
11.

CROUCH, Marcus.
A Book of Kent:a series of vignettes on the
life and times of yesteryear, edited by
M. Crouch and made by the printers of Kent,
commemorating 500 years of printing in
England, 1476 - 1976.
Paul Norbury, Tenterden. 1976.
2,5,6,7,8,11,15,20,23,28.

DIBDEN, Thomas Frognal.*
Typographical antiquities Vol.I by
T.F. Dibden and others. (Includes Caxton).
Miller. (1809).
12.

HULBERT, D.P.M.
Reciprocity for 1851: or an "exhibition of
humanity and fraternity and divinity".
(Canterbury Printer).
Printed by Henry Chivers. Canterbury. (1851).
3.

LIPSCOMBE, Margaret.
Ten herbs and their uses,designed by
Jane E. Lines, illustrated by Charlotte Cox.
College of Art Press. Canterbury. 1969.
11.

MACKAYS, W.&.J. of Chatham.
Type for books.
Bodley Head 1976.
8.

MILES, Herbert W.
Corolla Cantiana: a garland of wild flowers;
(illustrated by Students from Canterbury
College of Art).
College of Art Press, Canterbury. 1963.
11.

NATIONAL BOOK LEAGUE.
An exhibition of the work of three private
presses: St. Dominics Press/Ditchling,
Edward Walters/Primrose Hill and Saint
Albert's Press/Aylesford. Devised and
presented by Brocard Sewell, under the spon-
sorship of Linotype U.K., and the National
Book League. Catalogue by Joseph Jerome.
St. Alberts' Press. Faversham. 1976.
11,26.

PICKERING, C.L.
An outline of the printing crafts.
Medway School of Art and Crafts.
Rochester. 1936.
4.

A POETIC LANDSCAPE: an anthology of
verse with six wood engravings,by Alan Burton.
College of Art Press. Canterbury, 1963.
11.

RALPH, Henry Victor.
Bookman and printer extraordinary: Brydges
and the Lee Priory Press.
In Country Life March 23rd,1978. pp. 778 - 79.
Country Life. 1978.
3.

RUSHWORTH, John.
A letter sent to the Honourable William Lenthal
Esq., Speaker of the Honourable House of
Commons, on the fight between His Excellency's
the Lord Fairfax Forces at Maidstone and the
Kentish Forces at Maidstone on June 1st, 1648.
Reprinted by Maidstone College of Art. 1959.
11.

"SARETAH" pseud.
Questioning.
(Published in Folkestone).
Deva. 12 Church Street, Folkestone. 1976.
7.

STIRLING, Dr. Leader.
Bush Doctor - being letters from Dr. Leader
Stirling of Tanganika Territory.
Printed and published by Parrett and
Neves,   Chatham,for the Universities'
Mission to Central Africa. 1947.
4.

WOODMAN, George.*
The heretic.
(Whitstable author, publisher and printer)
 Designed, illustrated and hand-printed by
Ben Sands, 97 Island Wall, Whitstable, Kent .
The Shipyard Press. 1963.
3,11,15,30.

PRISONS

BANKS, Frances.
Teach them to live: a study of education in
English prisons.
(Includes mention of work in Maidstone and
Eastchurch prisons).
Parrish. 1958.
11.

BOTTOMLEY, Horatio.*
Convict '13'; a ballad of Maidstone Goal.
Stanley Paul. (1927).
1,11,12.

BOTTOMS, A.E.
Criminals coming of age: a study of institutional
adaptation in the treatment of adolescent offenders,
by A.E. Bottoms and F.H. McClintock.
(A study focussed on Dover Borstal).
Heinemann. 1973.
11.

BRANCH-JOHNSON, William.*
English prison hulks.
1957 C. Johnson. 8,11,15,25.
1970. Revised edition. Phillimore. 11.12.

GRIFFITHS, Arthur.
Fifty years of Public Service.
(the author was Deputy Governor of Chatham
Convict Prison 1870 - 1872).
Cassell. 1905.
8.

MILLER, Alistair.
Inside outside:the story of a prison governor.
(The author was a governor of both Dover
Prison and Dover Borstal).
Queensgate Press. 1976.
6.

RIGDEN, Reg.
The floating prisons of Woolwich and Deptford.
London Borough of Greenwich. 1976.
2,11,12,25.

ST. AUGUSTINE'S GAOL.
Rules and Regulations for the County Prisons,
at St. Augustine's, Canterbury. Approved by
the Judges of Assize, 2nd August, 1819.
Printed   by Cowtan and Colegate, Canterbury. 1819.
11.

SUSSEX, John.
Community service by offenders:
Year One in Kent.
Barry Rose. 1974.
2,5,11,12.

TIFFIN, Alfred.
Loving and Serving:an account of the work of
J.W.C. Fegan; edited by G. Fielden Hughes.
(Blantyre House, Goudhurst, Detention Centre).
P.P.   n.d.
17,19.

VIDLER, John.*
If freedom fail by J. Vidler and M. Wolff.
(John Vidler was governor of Maidstone Prison
for ten years).
Macmillan. 1964.
4,11,12.

WAYLEN, Barbara.
The Story of Frances Banks:the great seeker.
(Frances Banks was Tutor/organiser at Maidstone
Prison for some years from 1950).
Regency Press. 1972.
11.

PUBLIC UTILITIES

CENTRAL ELECTRICITY GENERATING BOARD.
An appraisal of the technical   and economic
aspects of Dungeness B Nuclear Power Station.
Central Electricity Generating Board. 1965.
11.

Dungeness "B" (AGR) Nuclear Power Station.
Central Electricity Generating Board. 1965.
11.

Dungeness "B" Nuclear Power Station.
Central Electricity Generating Board. 1973.
3,4,11,12,20.

CENTRAL ELECTRICITY GENERATING BOARD, SOUTH
EASTERN REGION.
Scientific Services Centre, Gravesend.
Central Electricity Generating Board,
South East Region. (197-?)
11.

CLARK, R.G.A.
The development of the Dover Works
of the South Eastern Gas Board.
P.P. 1956.
11.

THE EAST KENT TIMES,BROADSTAIRS AND ST.
PETERS MAIL.
Supplement. Richborough Power Station,
Sandwich, Kent. 1963.
24.

GALTON, Captain Douglas.*
Report on the scheme of drainage submitted
by Albert Latham. (For Margate).
Keble. 1881.
13.

GILLINGHAM BOROUGH COUNCIL.
Souvenir of the completion of the Gillingham
Sewerage Scheme.
Gillingham Borough Council. 1935.
8.

GREAT BRITAIN, Laws etc. (Vic.)
Kent Watermarks Act, 1877.
40 and 41 Vict. 1877.
H.M.S.O. 1877.
1.

GREAT BRITAIN, Laws etc. (Vic.)
Kent Water Works Act 1888.
51, Vic. 1888.
H.M.S.O. 1888.
1.

GREAT BRITAIN, Laws etc. (Edw. VII)
An Act to confirm certain provisional
orders made by the Board of Trade under
the Electric Lighting Acts...relating to...
Gravesend (extension to Northfleet).
1905.
9.

Broadstairs and St. Peters' Water and
Improvement Act, 1901.
24.

Kent Electric Power Act, 1902.*
2 Edw. 7.
H.M.S.O. 1902.
1.

West Kent Electric Power Act, 1909.
H.M.S.O. 1909.
1.

GREAT BRITAIN, Laws etc. (Geo.V).*
Gillingham Corporation Act, 1931. An Act
to confer further powers upon the Mayor,
Aldermen and Burgesses of the Borough of
Gillingham with regard to their electricity
undertaking...
H.M.S.O. 1931.
8,11.

GREAT BRITAIN: PARLIAMENT. HOUSE OF COMMONS.
Folkestone Gas.
H.M.S.O. 1916.
7.

HERNE BAY, CANTERBURY & WHITSTABLE
ELECTRICITY GAZETTE No.11. December,1963.
3.

HOUSING AND LOCAL GOVERNMENT, Ministry of.
Provisional order confirmation (West Kent
main sewerage District) Act. 1968.
H.M.S.O. 1968.
4.

KENT COUNTY COUNCIL:PLANNING DEPARTMENT.
Kent Structure Plan: Waste disposal.
Adopted by the Local Authority, July,1976.
Serial No. 15B.
K.C.C. 1976.
3,4,9,11,13,15.

LOVEJOY (Derek) AND PARTNERS.
Littlebrook Power Station (Dartford).
Landscape plan.
D. Lovejoy and Partners. 1973.
5.

MAIDSTONE WATERWORKS COMPANY.
Scale of quarterly charges for the supply
of water for domestic consumption...
with the rules and regulations required
to be observed.
1884.
12.

MARGATE BOROUGH COUNCIL.
Borough of Margate Water Undertaking 1879 - 1956.
Margate Borough Council. 1856.
13.

MARGATE DRAINAGE CONTROVERSY.
from "Iron" 17th February - 16th March, 1888.
(See also Galton, Capt. Douglas; and
LATHAM, Albert).
13

MID-KENT WATER COMPANY.
Report on Broadoak Reservoir, May 1972.
by Binnie and Partners,Chartered Engineers.
Binnie and Partners. 1972.
11.

NORTON, TRIST, WATNEY AND COMPANY.
Plan showing estates of George Field, Esq.,
Rev. J.J. Saint and John Heugh, Esq., and the
land required for the Sewage Works. November, 1869.
6 chains = 1 inch.
(Tunbridge Wells).
19.

PILBROW, James.
Report to the Local Board of Health,
Canterbury, on the Sewerage and Water Supply
of that district....
Canterbury Corporation, Canterbury. 1867.
3.

RAMMELL, T.W.
Report to the General Board of Health on a
preliminary enquiry into the Sewerage...of
the inhabitants of Sandgate, by T.W. Rammell.
H.M.S.O. 1849.
7.

REES, Judith Anne.
Industrial demand for water:a study of
South East England.
Weidenfeld & Nicolson. 1969.
12.

ROBINSON, Sydney.
Seeboard, the first twenty-five years.
South Eastern Electricity Board. 1974.
5,6,8,11,12,15.

SOUTH EASTERN ELECTRICITY BOARD.*
Annual Report and Accounts.
1967 - 68; 1968 - 69; 1969 - 70; 1971 - 72. 3.
1972 - 73.   12.
1973 - 74.   3.8.
1974 - 75; 1975 - 76; 1976 - 77; 1977 - 78.   3.

SOUTH EASTERN ELECTRICITY BOARD: CANTERBURY DISTRICT.
Annual report for the year 1973/74
Annual report for the year 1975/76
Annual report for the year 1976/77
South Eastern Electricity Board, Canterbury.
3.

SOUTH EASTERN ELECTRICITY BOARD:EAST KENT DISTRICT.
Annual report for the year 1977/78.
South Eastern Electricity Board, East Kent District.
1978.
3.

SOUTH EASTERN ELECTRICITY BOARD:MAIDSTONE DISTRICT.
Annual Report for the Year 1974 - 75.
12.

SOUTH EASTERN GAS CONSULTATIVE COUNCIL.*
Annual Report.
1963 - 64; 1965 - 1966. 3.
1972. Terminal report. (Nine months ended
     31st December, 1972). 3.12.

SOUTH EASTERN GAS:CONSUMERS' COUNCIL.
Annual Report.
1973-74. First report:15 months to the
     31st March, 1974.   6.8.
1974 - 75. 3.6.12.
1975 - 76. 3.11.
1976 - 77; 1977 - 78. 3.

SOUTHERN WATER AUTHORITY.
Annual Report and accounts. Southern
Water Authority, Worthing.
1974 - 75 (First Annual Report of the
          Authority). 4.8.11.12.
1975 - 76. 5.
1976 - 77; 1977 - 78.   3.

The Southern Way with water:an explanatory
booklet on the work and responsibilities of
the Southern Water Authority, with an appendix
on careers.
Southern Water Authority. 1975.
3,4,8,11.

SOUTHERN WATER AUTHORITY & THE MID-KENT WATER COMPANY.
Broadoak Reservoir Scheme.
Southern Water Authority. 1975.
3.

STANDING CONFERENCE ON LONDON AND SOUTH EAST
REGIONAL PLANNING.
Waste Disposal in South East England.
Standing Conference on London and South
East Regional Planning. 1978.
23.

PUBLIC UTILITIES Cont'd

STROOD WATERWORKS COMPANY.
The Strood Waterworks Souvenir.
The Journal Co. Printers. 1903.
25.

THANET WATER BOARD.*
Annual Reports.
11. 1971/2; 1972/3.
13. 1957/8; 1959/60; 1961/62; 1962/63;
    1963/64; 1965/66; 1971/72.

WHITAKER, William.*
The water supply of Kent, with records of
Sinkings and borings, by W. Whitaker and
others. (Memoirs of the Geological
Survey of England and Wales).
H.M.S.O. 1908.
1,2,4,5,7,9,11,12,25.

QUEENBOROUGH

CASTLE, Joseph.*
Queenborough and its church.
Rigg. Sheerness. 1907.
26.

COPY OF THE CHARTER OF THE BOROUGH OF
QUEENBOROUGH.*
(Bound with newspaper cuttings, illustrations,
maps and MSS notes).
Printed by Ellerton and Henderson. (185-?).
11.

FAVRESFIELD, Charles.
The Constables of Queenborough Castle.
In The Invicta Magazine Vol. 3. 1913.
pp. 153 - 164.
4.

QUEENBOROUGH PARISH CHURCH.
H.I. Ford, Print Associates (1975?).
20.

QUEENBOROUGH:REPORT ON THE BOROUGH OF
QUEENBOROWE, OR QUEENBOROUGH.
Municipal Corporations in England and Wales.
(18--)
15.

WOODTHORPE, T.J.*
The Tudor Navy and the Medway:Queenborough
as a naval port.
Typewritten script. n.d.
11,20,26,27.

RAILWAYS

ABC OF SOUTHERN ELECTRIC TRAINS.*
Ian Allan. (1950?).
4.11.

ABC OF SOUTHERN LOCOMOTIVES.
Ian Allan.
1946.   7.
1947. 11th edition. 1.

ADAMS, John.
Southern Steam in Camera.
Ian Allan. 1977.
15.

ALLEN, Cecil J.
Salute to the Southern.
Ian Allan. 1974.
7.

BENNETT, Alfred Rosling.*
The first railway in London, being the
story of the London and Greenwich
Railway from 1832 to 1878.
(First published by Locomotive Publishing
Company, 1926).
Reprinted edition.
Conway Maritime Press. Greenwich. 1971.
2,11.

BIDDLE, Gordon.
Victorian Stations.
David and Charles. 1973.
11.

BLACK, G.T.*
Westerham Valley. (Railway). 2nd edition.
(Branch Line handbook No.8).
Branch-Line Handbooks Teddington, Middlesex.
April, 1962.
1,2,4,6,8,11,12,15,16,17.

BODDY, H.
Kent railway development between August
and December,1845. The Railway Times,
Vol.9. Part II as a source of information
concerning it.
(197-).
3.

BOND, A. Winstan.
Herne Bay Pier - three tramways and a mystery.
In. Modern Tramway and Light Railway Review.
Vol.31, April,1968, No. 364. pp. 127 - 136.
30.

BRADLEY, Donald Lawrence.*
The locomotives of the London, Chatham and
Dover Railway.
Railway Correspondence and Travel Society.
2. 1979.
25. 1960.

BRITISH RAILWAYS BOARD.
Channel Tunnel: London - Tunnel new rail link:
a document for consultation.
British Railways Board, January, 1974.
20.

Express Link with Europe:British Rail - The
Channel Tunnel.
British Railways Board. 1973.
4.

BRITISH RAILWAYS BOARD:SOUTHERN REGION.
Sectional appendix to the Working Timetable
and Books of Rules and Regulations: South
Eastern Division. BR 30020 ——1960.
Issued by the General Manager of Waterloo
Station - This is a Staff manual labelled
"Private and not for Publication".
11.

BRITISH RAILWAYS:SOUTHERN REGION.
Extension of electrification from Gillingham
to Sheerness-on-Sea, Ramsgate and Dover.*
British Rail (Southern). 1972.
9.

Higham and Strood tunnels.
British Rail (Southern). 1972.
4.

Kent Coast electric train services: London,
Sheerness, Margate, Ramsgate, Canterbury and
Dover. Timetables: November 2nd,1959 -
June 12th, 1960. June 15th - September 13th,
1959.
British Rail (Southern) 1959.
9.

The railway system in Southern England from 1803.
British Rail (Southern). (197-?).
3.

BUCKNALL, Rixon.*
Boat trains and Channel packets:the English
short sea routes.
Vincent Stuart. 1957.
11.

BULLEID, Henry Anthony Vaughan.
Bulleid of the Southern.
Ian Allan. 1977.
11.

BURNHAM, T.G.
Branch to Bromley North.
In. Railway Magazine February,1975. pp. 56 - 59.
2.

RAILWAYS Cont'd

C ., H.R.*
The Canterbury and Whitstable Railway.
 Article in Southern Railway Magazine
Vol. VIII, No.90, June 1930 .
3,30.

CARLEY, James.
The Tunbridge Wells, Snodland and Edenbridge
Suspension Railway:an abortive scheme of
1825-26 with notes on two more.
Meopham Publications Committee. 1979.
2,4,6,13,15,23.

CASSERLEY, Henry Cecil.
Locomotives at the grouping: Southern Railway,
by H.C. Casserley and S.W. Johnston.
(First published in 1965).
Ian Allan. 1974.
3.

Recollections of the Southern between the Wars.
D. Bradford Barton Ltd. 1976.
11.

CATT, Andrew Robert.*
The East Kent Railway.
Oakwood Press. 1970.
2,4,7,12,26.

CHALMERS, James.*
The Channel Railway connecting England and
France.
E. & F.N. Spon, 16 Bucklersbury, London. 1861.
11.

CHURTON, Edward.
The Rail Road Book of England Vol.1: All
routes from London.
Sidgwick & Jackson. 1973.
1.

CLARK, Ronald Harry.*
A Southern region record:
(Railway chronology and record 1803 - 1965).
Oakwood Press. 1964.
2,5,
11 plus extra pamphlet covering 1964 - 1974.

COLLARD, William.*
Proposed London and Paris railway....
P.S. King & Son & Clowes. 1928.
1,2,4,6,7,8,11,12.

CONNOR, James Edward.
Forgotton stations of Greater London, by
J.E. Connor and B.L. Halford.
New edition.
Forge Books. 1978.
11.

COURSE, Edwin A.
The Bexley Heath Railway, 1883 - 1900.*
 Proceedings of the Woolwich and District
Antiquarian Society, Vol. XXX 1954 .
1,4,5,8,11,12.

The Railways of Southern England: independent
and light railways.
Batsford. 1976.
1,2,3,5,6,7,8,11,15,20,26,27,29.

The Railways of Southern England: the main lines.
Batsford. 1973.
2,6,8,11,19,30.

The Railways of Southern England:secondary and
branch lines.
Batsford. 1974.
2,3,4,6,11,12,15,27.

CREER, Stanley.
Southern Steam - south and east.
(Photographs with captions).
D. Bradford Barton Ltd. 1973.
4,7.

More Southern Steam - south and east.
D. Bradford Barton Ltd.
1974. 6,11,12.
1976. 7.

CROSS, Derek.
Southern Steam from lineside.
D. Bradford Barton Ltd. 1974.
11,15,22.

DARWIN, Bernard.*
War on the line:the story of the Southern
Railway in War-time.
Southern Railway Company. 1946.
3,11.

DAVIES, William James Keith.
The Romney, Hythe and Dymchurch Railway.
David and Charles. 1975.
3,6,8,11,12,15,19,22.

DEVEREUX, Charles M.
Railways to Sevenoaks. (Locomotion Papers no.102).
Oakwood Press. 1977.
1,2,3,11,15,16,18.23

DIXON, Alan G.
Stockbook:the locomotives and stock of the Kent
and East Sussex Railway.
Tenterden Railway Company. 1978.
11,15.

DYER, B.R.
Kent railways.
James Pike. St. Ives. 1977.
3,6,11,28.

EARLEY, Maurice William.
The Southern scene:an album of photographs.
(Locomotives).
Oxford Publishing Company. 1973.
3.

ELLIS, C. Hamilton.
British Trains of yesteryear, edited by
C. Hamilton Ellis.
(Contains early photographs of trains at Dover).
Ian Allan. 1960 reprinted 1974.
6.

The London, Brighton and South Coast railway.
Ian Allan. 1971.
23.

ENVIRONMENT, Department of the.*
Railway Accident: report on the collision that
occurred on 12th November,1970 at Bexley Station,
in the Southern Region,British Railways.
H.M.S.O. 1972.
8,9.

Railway accident:report on the derailment that
occurred on 11th June, 1972, at Eltham (Well
Hall) Station, in the Southern Region, British
Railways.
H.M.S.O. 1973.
1,11.

FAIRCLOUGH, Tony.
Southern Branch Line Steam, III; edited by
T. Fairclough and Alan Wills.
D. Bradford Barton Ltd. 1976.
11.

Southern Branch Line Steam, IV; edited by
T. Fairclough and Alan Wills.
D. Bradford Barton Ltd. 1977.
11.

FELLOWS, Reginald B.*
History of the Canterbury and Whitstable
Railway.
J.A. Jennings, Canterbury. 1930.
1,2,3,4,6,7,8,11,12,15,17,19,31.

FORWOOD, Michael J.
Elham Valley Railway.
Phillimore. 1975.
1,3,5,6,7,8,11,12,13,15,22.

GAMMELL, Christopher John.
Southern branch lines 1955 - 1965.
Oxford Publishing Company, 1976.
3,11,15.

GARRETT, S.R.*
Kent and East Sussex Railway.
Oakwood Press. 1972.
6,7,30.

GIBBONS, Gavin.*
Trains under the Channel.
Advertiser Press Ltd. Huddersfield. (1970).
4,6,7,11.

GIFFORD, C.T.
Steam railways in industry.
(Includes "Kentish paper - Sittingbourne",
pp. 80 - 86).
Batsford.   1976.
11,20,27.

GOULD, David.
Carriage Stock of the South Eastern & Chatham
Oakwood Press. 1976.   Railway.
1,3,4,5,6,7,9,11,20,23,26,27.

Maunsell's Southern Railway Steam passenger
stock. 1923 - 39.
David Gould. 1978.
5.

Westerham Valley Railway.
(Locomotion Papers. No.72)
Oakwood Press, 1974.
1,2,3,4,6,11,15,16.

GRAY, Adrian A.
Isle of Grain Railways. (Locomotion Papers No.77).
Oakwood Press, 1974.
1,2,3,4,9,11,12,15,27.

Chatham Central Branch.
Notes on four typed sheets.
August 1975.
4.

London to Brighton Line, 1841 - 1977.
Oakwood Press. 1977.
18.

Unusual birth of the Gravesend and Rochester
Railway.
In Journal of the Railway and Canal Historical
Society. Vol. XXIV, No.2. July, 1978.
4.

GREAT BRITAIN, Laws etc. (Geo IV)
An Act to authorise the Company of proprietors
of the Canterbury and Whitstable railway, to
raise a further sum of money, for completing
the undertaking....(9 Geo.4. CXXIX).
Wm. Gunnell Agent. Curteis and Kingsford
Solicitors. 1828.
11.

GREAT BRITAIN, Laws etc. (Vic).
An Act to enable the South-eastern Railway
Company to make, or complete, a Branch Railway
from the South-eastern Railway at Tunbridge,
to Tunbridge Wells. (31st July,1845).
Cap. CLXVII.
1845.
23.

Act for lease of...Mid-Kent Railway
(Bromley to St. Mary's Cray) Company to the
London, Chatham and Dover Railway Company...
1862.
2.

The London, Chatham and Dover Railway Act 1873.
(36 Victoria Chapter XIV).
1873.
8.

Act to amend the Acts relating to "The
Bromley Direct Railway Company...."
1877.
2.

Hundred of Hoo Railway Act.
(42 and 43 Victoria, Chapter CXXVI).
1879.
8.

An Act for making railways between Maidstone
and Ashford.
1880.
7.

GREAT BRITAIN, Laws etc. (Vic.)
Gravesend Railway Act, 1882,
9,

South Eastern Railway Act, 1896.*(Ch. CXXVI).
9.

South Eastern Railway Act, 1897.*(Ch. CCXXVII).
9.

An Act to provide for the working union of
the South Eastern and the London, Chatham
and Dover Railway Companies...(1st August 1899).
H.M.S.O. 1899.
7.

GREEN, Simon B.
Kent and East Sussex railway guide.
Tenterden Railway Company Ltd. 1974.
11,23.

HARESNAPE, Brian.
Maunsell locomotives.
Ian Allan 1977.
3.

HASENSON, Alexander.*
The Golden Arrow:a history and contemporary
illustrated account.
Howard Baker. 1970.
11.

HILTON, John Anthony.
A History of the South Eastern and Chatham
Railway; compiled from various sources by
J.A. Hilton. Vol I. 1812 - 1845;
Vol.II 1845 - 1855.
J. Hilton. Hadlow. 1977 and (1979).
Vol.I. 1.2.3.4.6.7.9.11.15.16.23.30.
Vol.II. 4,15,23.

ISLE OF THANET LIGHT RAILWAYS. Board of
Trade Order dated 13th August, 1898. (Light
Railways Act 1896).
24.

JOHN, Malcolm.
Bygone South Eastern Steam, Vol 1,
edited by Malcolm John.
John Hallewell, Chatham. 1980.
12.

KALLA-BISHOP, P.M.
Locomotives at War.
Bradford Barton Ltd. 1980.
28.

THE KENT AND EAST SUSSEX RAILWAY.
Union Publications. London. 1963.
15,19.

KENT RAILWAYS - Twenty one articles taken from
"The Railway Magazine", including a list of the
Railways concerned.
4.

KIDNER, Roger Wakeley.
The North Kent Line. (Locomotion papers No. 103).
Oakwood Press. 1977.
1,2,4,5,6,11,12,15,16,18,23,25,28.

Notes on Southern Railway Rolling Stock.
Oakwood Press. 1974.
15.

The Oxted line.(Locomotion papers 58).
(Briefly touches Kent c. Edenbridge/Groombridge).
Oakwood Press. 1972.
4,7,11.

The Reading to Tonbridge line.
Oakwood Press. 1974.
2,7,11,15,19.

The Romney, Hythe and Dymchurch Railway.
(2nd revised edition). (Locomotion papers,
no. 35).
Oakwood Press. 1978.
2,3,11,16,25.

The South Eastern and Chatham Railway.
Oakwood Press. 1963.
1,25,26,
3.Reprinted with Corrections. 1977.
The South Eastern Railway and the
South Eastern & Chatham Railway.
Oakwood Press. 1953.
9.

RAILWAYS Cont'd

KIDNER, Roger Wakely.
Southern Railway Branch Lines in the 'thirties.
Oakwood Press. 1976.
1,3,5,7,11,15,30.

Southern Railway rolling stock.
Oakwood Press. 1974.
3,6,19.

LEIGH-BENNETT. E.P.
"Southern" ways and means,illustrated by Fougasse.
Southern Railway. (193?).
11.

LONDON, CHATHAM AND DOVER RAILWAY: Illustrated
Guide.
Newton(?) (1896).
2.

LONDON, CHATHAM AND NORTH KENT RAILWAY:
Plan (of proposed) main line from London to
Dover.   Scale 6 chains = 12". Comprises four
folding plans in a box. Size 11¼" x 7¾" ——
folded sheets.
1. Boughton-Dover. 35 sheets in 1 folded plan.
2. Boughton-Rochester. 38+4 in 1 folded plan
3. Rochester-Dartford. 23 sheets in 1 folded plan.
4. Dartford-London. 32 sheets in 2 folded plans.
1845.
11.

Plan (of proposed) main line from London to
Dover. Scale 6 chains = 1 inch. Coloured
Plan, Part I. From Boughton to Dover.
Folded to 35 sheets, 11¼" x 7¾".
1845.
11.

Canterbury, Ramsgate and Margate branch.
(Coloured plan of proposed line). Part XII
of the London to Dover railway plan.
1845.
11.

LONDON COMMUTER TERMINALS WORKING PARTY.
Report on rail commuting to London from Kent.
1971.
4.

LYNE, R.M.*
The Gravesend Branch Railway.
P.P. E.M. Humphries, Longfield. 1972.
9,11.

McLELLAN, Doreen.
The Allhallows Railway. (Local History
Pamphlet No.4).
Kent County Library, Gravesham Division.
1975.
4,12,20.

MAGGS, Colin.
The Weston Clevedon and Portishead railway.
(A Col. Stephens Railway; Col. Stephens
operated from Tonbridge).
Oakwood Press. First Published. 1964...
1976 reprint with addenda and corrigenda.
23.

MARSHALL, C.F. Dendy.*
A history of Southern Railway.
Southern Railway Company. 1936.
25.

MAXTED, Ivan.*
Canterbury and Whitstable Railway.
Oakwood Press. 1970.
3,11,12,15,31.

MEASOM, George.
The official illustrated guide to the Brighton
and South Coast Railway and its branches,
including a descriptive guide to the Crystal
Palace at Sydenham....
Waterlow, London. 1859.
11.

The official illustrated guide to the South
Eastern railway and its branches:*including
the North Kent and Greenwich lines.
(Facsimile of the 1858 edition).
E.&.W. Books. 1970.
3,4,5,6,7,8,12,14,15,17,18,30.

MINERVA RAILWAY GUIDE AND VISITORS' HANDBOOK
for Deal, Walmer, Sandwich and District.
Minerva. 1907.
12.

MITTON, Geraldine Edith.*
The Southern Railway. 2nd edition.
A.&.C. Black. 1925.
9.

MOODY, George Thomas.
Southern Electric:the history of the world's
largest suburban electrified system. (1909-1979)
Ian Allan. London.
1957* 11,25.
1968* 4th edition. 11.
1979. 5th revised edition. 2.5.6.

MORGAN, John Scott.
The Colonel Stephens' Railways:a pictorial
history. (Colonel Stephens operated from
Tonbridge: Chapter 6).
David and Charles. 1978.
3,7,11,23.

MORRIS, Owen James.*
The World's smallest public railway. (The
birth, progress and majority of the Romney,
Hythe and Dymchurch Railway).
Ian Allan.
1946. 4,7.
1949. 11.12.

NASH, Sidney Charles.
Southern Region Steam Album. 1948 - 1967.
Ian Allan. 1974.
3,6,12,15.

NEWTON, S.C.
Rails across the Weald.
(East Sussex Record Office - Handbook No.4).
East Sussex County Council. 1972.
7.

NOCK, Oswald Stevens.*
The South-Eastern and Chatham Railway.
Ian Allan.
1961   25.
1971. Revised edition. 2.7.20.26.27.

Southern Steam.
David and Charles. 1966.
11.

NOKES, George Augustus (BBKON, G. pseud).*
History of the South-Eastern Railway.
Railway Press Company. 1895.
2,7,8.

PALLANT, N.
Hither Green Motive Power Depot.
(Locomotion Papers, 119).
Oakwood Press. 1979.
16.

PRIDEAUX, J.D.C.A.
The English narrow gauge Railway.
David and Charles. 1978.
7.

PRYER, G.A.
A Pictorial record of Southern Signals.
Oxford Publishing Company. 1977.
5,7.

RANSOME-WALLIS, Patrick.
Roaming the Southern rails. (pp. 11 - 74, Kent).
(The author lives at Herne Bay).
Ian Allan. 1979.
11.

Southern album.*
Ian Allan. 1968.
3.

RAYNER, Bryan.
Southern electrics:a pictorial Survey;
edited by B. Rayner.
D. Bradford Barton, Ltd. 1975.
11.

ROMNEY, HYTHE AND DYMCHURCH RAILWAY.
The official Golden Jubilee edition guidebook,
1927 - 1977.
Photo Precision Ltd. 1977.

Timetable and guide. 1976.
3.

RAILWAYS, Cont'd

ROVEX LIMITED.
The Hornby book of trains 1954 - 1979,
Prototypes and models.
(Rovex Limited manufacture toys, model
railways etc., in Margate and Ramsgate).
Rovex Limited. Margate & Ramsgate. 1979.
13.

ROYAL INSTITUTE OF BRITISH ARCHITECTS:
CHANNEL TUNNEL STUDY GROUP.
The Channel Tunnel rail link:an appraisal
of the proposals of the British Railways
Board.
Royal Institute of British Architects. 1974.
3,11.

SAVILL, Raymond Arthur.*
The Southern Railway, 1923 - 1947: a chronicle
and record.
Oakwood Press. 1950.
11.

SITTINGBOURNE AND KEMSLEY LIGHT RAILWAY COMPANY.
An introduction to the Sittingbourne and
Kemsley Light Railway, (formerly Bowaters'
Sittingbourne Railway). Duplicated sheet.
1973.
4.

Sittingbourne and Kemsley Light Railway
Stockbook and guide. 1975.
Sittingbourne and Kemsley Light Railway. 1975.
11.

SMITH, John L.*
Rails to Tenterden.
Lens of Sutton, Surrey. 1967.
1.2.3.4.6.7.8.9.11.12.15.19.

SOUTH EASTERN AND CHATHAM RAILWAY COMPANY.
Passenger train working time table.
June 14th, 1920, and until further notice.
1920.
4.

Time tables. October 2nd, 1922, and until
further notice.
South Eastern and Chatham Railway Company. 1922.
23.

SOUTHERN RAILWAY COMPANY.
Modern Locomotives and electric traction of
the Southern Railway (1940).
Locomotive Publishing Company. 1940.
1.

SOUTHERN RAILWAY: SOUTH EASTERN AND CHATHAM SECTION.
Time tables.   July 9th, 1923, and until further
notice.
Southern Railway. 1923.
23.

SPENCE, Jeoffry
Victorian and Edwardian railways from old
photographs, introduction and commentaries
by Jeoffry Spence.
Batsford. 1975.
11.

STEEL, Ernest A.
The Miniature World of Henry Greenly,
by E.A. and E.H. Steel.
(pp. 169 - 193, Romney, Hythe and Dymchurch
Railway).
Model and Allied Publications. 1973.
7,11,12.

STOYEL, B. Derek.
Cement railways of Kent, by B.D. Stoyel and
R.W. Kidner.   (Locomotion Papers No.70).
Oakwood Press. 1973.
1,2,4,5,7,11,12,20,25,30.

THE SUBMARINE CONTINENTAL RAILWAY COMPANY.
Channel Tunnel:report of a meeting of the
members...Friday the 20th January,1882.
(Also of) an extraordinary general meeting
on Thursday August 17th,1882.
The Submarine Continental Railway Company. 1882.
2.

SYMES, Rodney.*
Railway architecture of the South East,
by R. Symes and D. Cole.
Osprey. 1972.
4,7,9,11,19.

TAYLOR, Michael Minter.*
The Davington Light Railway:(locomotion papers
No.40)
Oakwood Press. 1968.
2,20,26.

THOMAS, Ronald, H.G.*
London's First railway — the London and Greenwich.
Batsford. 1972.
11,12.

TOWNROE, S.C.
The Arthurs, Nelsons and Schools of the Southern.
Ian Allan. 1973.
3,11.

TRANSPORT 2000, KENT GROUP.
Passenger trains on the Hoo Peninsula: a
feasibility study.   2 volumes.
Transport 2000, Maidstone. 1978.
4,25.

The restoration of passenger train services
on the hundred of Hoo peninsula: a feasibility
study.   Tables of statistics to be presented
with the final report to Medway Borough Council.
Transport 2000. 1978.
9.

TURNER, J.T. Howard.
The London, Brighton, and South Coast Railway.
Vol. I.   Origins and Formation.
Vol. II.   Establishment and Growth
Vol. III. Completion and Maturity.
Batsford.   1978 - 79.
18, 19.   Vol. 1.
18, 19.   Vol. II.
4.   Vol. III.

TURNER, Keith.
Pier Railways.   (pp. 9 - 17, Herne Bay and Hythe).
Oakwood Press. 1972.
11,30.

WAKEMAN, Norman.*
The South Eastern and Chatham Railway Locomotive
List 1842 - 1952,compiled by N. Wakeman.
Oakwood Press. 1953.
25.

WELLS, Arthur G.
Bowater's Sittingbourne Railway. 2nd edition.
(First published in 1962).
Locomotive Club of Great Britain. 1971.
11,25.

WHITE, Henry Patrick.
Forgotten Railways: South-East England.
(Forgotton Railways series).
David and Charles. 1976.
3,4,6,8,11,12,15,19,28.

Southern England. (A Regional History of
the Railways of Great Britain, Vol.2).
3rd edition.
David and Charles. 1969.
3,12.

WIKELEY, Nigel.*
Railway stations:Southern region, by N. Wikeley
and J. Middleton.
Peco Publications, Seaton, Devon. 1971.
3,4,7,9,11,12,23,30.

WILLIAMS, Alan.
Southern Electric album.
Ian Allan. 1977.
11.

WOLFE, C.S.
Historical guide to the Romney, Hythe and
Dymchurch Light Railway.
Romney, Hythe and Dymchurch Railway Association,
New Romney. 1976.
1,4,6,7,9,11,15,28.

RAINHAM.

GILLINGHAM BOROUGH COUNCIL:BOROUGH ARCHITECTS'
AND PLANNING OFFICE.
Rainham district centre plan:proposals map,
second draft, land use framework...(and)
traffic network.
Gillingham Borough Council and K.C.C. (1972).
11.
GILLINGHAM BOROUGH COUNCIL:GENERAL PURPOSES
COMMITTEE.
Rainham District Centre Plan, 1972.
(To be used with proposals map indexed
under Gillingham Borough Council: Borough
Architect's and Planning Office)
Gillingham Borough Council and K.C.C. 1972.
11.
GREAT BRITAIN, Laws etc. (Eliz II)STATUTORY INSTRUMENTS.
The Rainham Creek (Closure) Order 1976.
(S.I. 1976 No. 2043).
H.M.S.O. 1976.
4.

HASLEWOOD, Rev. Francis F.
An address delivered at the opening of the new
school house at Rainham, Kent, on Monday,
November 8th,1846, by the Rev. F.F. Hazelwood,
to which is added the form of prayer used on
the occasion. (Photostat of the original
pamphlet).
J.E. Coulter. Sittingbourne. 1846.
8.

PEARMAN, Rev. Augustus John.*
Rainham Church.
Reprinted from Archaeologia Cantiana
Vol. 17. 1886.
Mitchell and Hughes. 1886.
20

PRENTIS, Walter.*
Notes on the birds of Rainham...Chatham and
Sittingbourne.
Gurney and Jackson. 1894.
1,2,3,4,5,6,8,11,12,15,17,20.

SMITH, Richard Allington.*
A new Guide to Rainham Parish Church.
R.A. Smith. 1969.
8.

STATION ROAD METHODIST CHURCH, RAINHAM.*
Jubilee Souvenir Handbook, 1900 - 1950.
Station Road Methodist Church. 1950.
4.

WAKELEY, R.H.
Gathered Fragments: a memorial of Thomas
S. Wakeley, late pastor of Providence
Chapel, Rainham, Kent.
Oxford (University Press). 1902.
8.

WILLMOTT, Frank G.
Bricks and "Brickies".
(Mainly concerns Eastwood's Ltd., of
Lower Halstow and Rainham).
F.G. Willmott. Rainham. 1972.
4,7,8,11,12,20,24,25,26,27,30.

RAMSGATE
See Also   ISLE OF THANET

ARROWCROFT INVESTMENT LTD.
Ramsgate Industrial Estate:an Arrowcroft
development in partnership with the
Ramsgate Corporation.
Arrowcroft Investment Ltd. n.d.
11.

BARLEY, H. Publisher
Views of Ramsgate. Engravings by
J.S. & Co., and Kershaw & Sons.
H. Barley. c.1870.
11.

BARNARD, Howard Clive.*
Records (1909 - 1922) of the Ramsgate
County school for boys, (now known as
Chatham House School). 2nd edition,
compiled by H.C. Barnard and F.N. Taylor.
Chatham House, Ramsgate. 1923.
24.

BEAR, J.*
The new Ramsgate guide containing all matters of
moment and places of interest in the town of
Ramsgate,combined with the most attractive
walks and drives...
J. Bear, Ramsgate. 1867.
11,13,14.

CARDOZO, D.A.*
Think and thank. The Montefiore synagogue
and college, Ramsgate, 1833 - 1933, by
D.A. Cardozo and P. Goodman.
Oxford University Press. 1933.
24.

COUSENS, Ruth Margaret.
Paintings by R.M. Cousens F.S.A.I.P. of
Ramsgate and a biographical note of the artist.
P.P. 1976.
11,13.

CUBITT, Sir William.
Report of Sir William Cubitt on Ramsgate Harbour.
Ordered by the House of Commons to be printed.
1853.
11.

FINN, Ralph.*
Romansgate in Thanet.
W.E. White. Ramsgate.
1969.   24. 30.
1972   Second edition. 2.7.8.

HUDDLESTONE, John.
The Ramsgate Story and Ramsgate.
(Duplicated sheets).
(197-?).
11.

HURD, A.G.
These 300 years. The story of Ramsgate
Congregational Church. 1662 - 1962.
1962.
13.

ISLE OF THANET ARCHAEOLOGICAL UNIT.
Publication no.1. Excavation of a Neolithic/
Bronze Age site at the Lord of the Manor,
Haine Road, Ramsgate.
Isle of Thanet Archaeological Unit. (1977).
13,14,24.

KAMM, J.
The Story of Sir Moses Montefiore.
(Sir Moses lived at East Cliff Lodge near
Dumpton Stairs and built the Synagogue and
College for Jewish studies).
Valentine Mitchell. 1960.
24.

KELLY'S DIRECTORIES LTD.
Kelly's directory of the Isle of Thanet 1973.
Kelly's Directories Ltd. 1973.
13.

MARTIN, Kennett Beecham.
Brief history of the origin and progress of
the Royal Harbour of Ramsgate.
Transcribed from the original by
Robert Matkin.
London. 1831.
14.

MATKIN, Robert B.
The Construction of Ramsgate Harbour.
In Transactions of the Newcomen Society,
Vol. 48, 1976 - 77.
13,24.

Smeaton at Ramsgate.
In Quest: the journal of the City University,
London. No. 28, Autumn 1974. pp. 14 - 19.
11.

"A NAVAL OFFICER" (pseud of ROGIER, E.).*
A brief history of Dover and Ramsgate Harbours,
with a description of the coasts between
Dungeness and the Isle of Thanet, and remarks
on the probable construction of a Harbour
between the South Foreland and Sandwich Haven,
by A Naval Officer.
W.H. Brewer, Ramsgate. 1837.
1,11.

RECIPES

DARTFORD AND DISTRICT CONSUMERS' GROUP.
The Consumers' cook-book.
Dartford and District Consumers' Group. 1971.
5.

DUFF, Gail.
Fresh all the year.
(The Author lives in North Kent).
Macmillan 1976.
11

Gail Duff's Vegetarian Cook Book.
Macmillan. 1978.
11.

ELHAM COTTAGE AND COUNTRY RECIPES.
Committee in Aid of the Fabric Fund of St.
Mary's Church, Elham 1976.
7.

FOAT, William.
Recipe book. (Small hand-written book of
recipes. William Foat was a "Family Butcher"
at St. Peters, Broadstairs).
Date on Front cover, 1936.
24.

GLEDHILL, A.E.
Borden Cookery Book of tried recipes.
W.J. Parrett Ltd. Gazette Office. 1910.
11.

HASTINGS, Macdonald.
Wheelers' fish cookery book;by Macdonald
Hastings and Carole Walsh. (Whitstable Oysters).
M. Joseph. 1974.
3.

A LITTLE BOOK OF RECIPES:for the benefit of the
Rye, Winchelsea and District Memorial Hospital
assembled from divers sources and embellished
by a learned disquisition by Miss Jane Findlater,
a diverting discourse on cooking by Edward
Percy, together with sundry discursive
decorations by R.H. Sauter.
Printed by Deacon's Printing Works, Rye. 1936.
11.

PALMER, Cecile.
Rochester Recipes:Food for hungry pilgrims,
compiled by C. Palmer.
Rochester Cathedral Book Stall. 1977.
11,15,25.

PERCIVAL, Dorothy.
Out of the frying-pan: a collection of
recipes from members and friends of the
Faversham Society;compiled by Dorothy Percival.
Faversham Society. (197-?).
8,11.

PIKE, Mary Ann.
Town and country Fare and Fables. (Section on Kent).
David and Charles. 1978.
11.

REVELL, Alison.
A Kentish cookery collection:a collection of
recipes taken from original sources in the Kent
Archives Office, from the seventeenth to the
nineteenth century, and edited by A. Revell.
K.C.C. 1978.
3,4,5,11,12,13,14,16,23,24,28,30.

SAMUELSON, M.K.
Sussex recipe book, with a few excursions into
Kent.
Country Life. 1937.
11.

SMITH, Joanna.
Village cooking: recipes from the Weald.
Sidgwick and Jackson. 1974.
3,5,11,19.

THOMPSON, E.
The Amateur jam-makers handbook.
(Folkestone author).

E. Thompson. Folkestone. 18--/1900s.
7.

WEST KENT FEDERATION OF WOMEN'S INSTITUTES.
The Country Housewife's handbook. 5th edition.
West Kent Federation of Women's Institutes.
Tonbridge. 1968.
11.

RECREATION AND ENTERTAINMENT.

ABERCROMBIE, Nigel.
The arts in the South East (Kent, Surrey and
East Sussex): a preliminary report.
(Art, Theatre and Music).
South East Arts Association. Canterbury.March,1974.
4,11,12,16,24,25.

BULL, Christopher.
Farm based recreation in South East England:
the experiences of a random sample of Farmers in
Kent, Surrey and Sussex,by Christopher Bull and
Gerald Wibberley. (Studies in Rural Land use
Report No. 12). (Wye College, Farm Business
Unit, School of Rural Economics and Related
Studies).
Wye College. December 1976.
1,3,4,5,11,19,21.

DUDENEY, Henry Ernest.
The Canterbury puzzles and other curious problems.
(Book of indoor games. The Canterbury puzzles
are based on "The Canterbury Tales).
Heinemann. 1907.
11.

FINN, Timothy.
Pub games of England.
Queen Anne Press. 1975.
11.

GREATER LONDON AND SOUTH EAST COUNCIL FOR SPORT
AND RECREATION.
Regional recreation strategy:issues report.
Greater London and South East Council
for Sport and Recreation. 1979.
2,11.

JOINT THANET SPORTS CENTRE COMMITTEE.
Report and estimate of cost for the proposed
recreation centre at St. Peter's Court,
Broadstairs.
Joint Thanet Sports Centre Committee. 1970.
13.

KENT COUNTY COUNCIL:PLANNING DEPARTMENT.
Kent County Structure Plan.
a) Formal recreation.   b) Informal recreation
c) Water recreation.   d) Tourism.
Serial No. 10B.
K.C.C. 1975.
3,4,9.11,13,16.

MAIDSTONE BOROUGH COUNCIL.
Leisure facilities in Maidstone.
Maidstone Borough Council. 1975.
12.

MAIDSTONE BOROUGH COUNCIL: PLANNING DEPARTMENT.
Maidstone Town Centre - Leisure and tourism.
Maidstone Borough Council. 1980.
12.

MOAD, Michael.
Yesterday's Medway: public entertainments,
written by M. Moad for the Directorate of
Leisure Services, Medway Borough Council. (1978).
11,15,25.

PIMLOTT,John Alfred Ralph.
The Englishman's holiday: a social history.
(Vacations to 1945). First published by
Faber in 1947. Reprinted by Harvester Press in
1976.
3.

SOUTH EAST ARTS ASSOCIATION.
The Gallery guide.
South East Arts Association. 1977?
19.

UNIVERSITY OF KENT:FACULTY OF SOCIAL SCIENCES.
Leisure pursuits in Kent, 1850 - 1914.
Group Research project 1973. Completed as part
of the course on aspects of the economic social
history of Kent in the Faculty of Social
Sciences.   Includes Horseracing and Cricket.
Duplicated Typescript. University of Kent. 1973.
4,11.

WHITTA, Terry.*
Art and entertainment in the Medway Towns:a report
produced from the findings of Breakaway Arts.
September 1964.
4,8.

Report on a Market Research project (Medway
Towns) 21st February,1970.   Concerned
with entertainment.
Duplicated Typescript.   (1972).
4.

RECULVER

BROWN, E.E.S.
Report of field meetings at Herne Bay and
Reculver. In Proceedings of the Geologists'
Association. Vol.47. Part 4. 1936. pp.349 & 350.
30.

CARTER, George Goldsmith.*
Forgotten ports of England. (Including Sandwich,
Reculver and Romney Marsh).
Evans Brothers. London. 1951.
1,3,4,6,7,8,11,12,13,14,15,25.

DOWKER, George.*
The ancient church and Roman Castrum at
Reculver. Reprinted by permission from the
Executrix of the late George Dowker, Esq.,
F.G.S.,to F.G. Holman.   Reprinted from
Archaeologia Cantiana, Vol. XII, 1878 .
J. Townsend. 1906.
11,17,19,24 Included in "Jottings of Kent".

GRAHAM, Rose.
Sidelights on the rectors and parishioners
of Reculver from the register of Archbishop
Winchelsey.
Reprinted from Archaeologia Cantiana,
Vol. LV11. 1944.
30.

HERNE BAY CENTRAL TOWNSWOMEN'S GUILD.
Reculver: A story of thoughtless
destruction.   A Study by Herne Bay Central
Townswomen's Guild.   1977.
Herne Bay Townswomen's Guild. October. 1977.
30.

HUSSEY, Arthur.*
Reculver and Hoath Wills: transcribed by A.H.
(Arthur Hussey).
Reprinted from Archaeologia Cantiana,
Vol. XXXII. 1917.
Mitchell, Hughes and Clarke. 1917.
4,8,10,11,30.

JESSUP, Ronald Frank.*
Reculver.
From Antiquity Vol. X. No. 38, June,1936.
pp. 179 - 194.
3,30.

KENT COUNTY LIBRARY.*
List of Books concerning Herne Bay,
Herne and Reculver.
K.C.C. 1951.
3.

MILLGATE'S HANDBOOK TO RECULVER.* 6th edition.
A.H. Sheppard. 1956.
30.

PAYNE, J. Lewin.*
Reculver Parish Church of St. Mary the
Virgin together with the Chapelry of the
Holy Cross, Hoath, by J.L. Payne and W.T. Hill.
Printed by Ridout. Herne Bay. 1931.
11.

PHILP, Brian J.
Recent discoveries at Reculver.
Reprinted from Archaeologia Cantiana, Vol. 71.
11.

The Roman Fort at Reculver.*
Reculver Excavation Group.
1962. 3rd edition. 3.5.8.30.
1969. 5th edition. 3,5,30.
1974. 6th edition (covers work until 1970). 1.11.

RECULVER PAROCHIAL CHURCH COUNCIL.*
St. Mary The Virgin, Revulver.
Published by Reculver Parochial Church Council
to commemorate the Foundation of the original
Church at Reculver, June,1969.
11,30.

SATURDAY MAGAZINE, 1834.
Includes items on Chatham Dockyard, Cinque
Ports, Reculver, Ancient Church in Dover
Castle, Thames and Medway Canal.
S.P.C.K. 1834.
11.

SMITH, Charles R.*
The antiquities of Richborough, Reculver and
Lymne in Kent.
J.R. Smith. 1850.
2,24.

TAYLOR, H.M.*
Reculver reconsidered. Reprinted from
"The Archaeological Journal", Vol. CXXV 1969,
pp. 291 - 6.
Royal Archaeological Institute. 1969.
3,4,11,30.

WHITAKER, W*
Report of an excursion to Reculver. (Proceedings
of the Geologists' Association Vol. 23, Part 4,
1912, pp. 247 - 249.
30.

WICKHAM, W.*
The Two sisters: a Tale of Reculver.
Reprinted from "The Ladies' Pocket Magazine". 1834.
24.
Printed by Ridout, Herne Bay. n.d.   3.

WORKS, Ministry of:ANCIENT MONUMENTS AND HISTORIC
BUILDINGS.
Reculver, Kent. (4 page leaflet).
H.M.S.O.
1947. 2.4.8.11.12.
1951. 4.

RELIGIOUS DENOMINATIONS.
See also TOWNS AND VILLAGES

ANIMADVERSIONS. ON LORD BEXLEY'S LETTER TO
THE FREEHOLDERS OF KENT.*
(The Catholic Question).
British Catholic Association. 1829.
4,14.

BALDWIN, Ronald Arthur.*
The Jezreelites, the rise and fall of a
remarkable prophetic movement.
(For additional material see Gillingham in both
volumes. Jezreel's Tower was in Gillingham)
Lambarde Press. Orpington. 1962.
1,4,7,8,11,12,15,17.

THE BENEDICTINES OF THANET, 1856 - 1931.
Monastery Press. Ramsgate. 1931.
11.

CANTERBURY DIOCESAN DIRECTORY AND SUPPLEMENT.
See Canterbury - Diocese and Province.

THE CATHOLIC QUESTION (Catholic Emancipation Bill).
The Great Brunswich Meeting on Penenden Heath,
October 24th, 1828*
Smith, 1829.
11,17.

THE CATHOLIC QUESTION (Catholic Emancipation Bill).
The Kent County Meeting: a report of the
Speeches delivered at the Kent County Meeting
holden on Penenden Heath, October 24th,1828,
with prefatory remarks.
Ridgeway-London. Burrill-Chatham. 1828.
1,3,4,11,12.

The Kent Meeting, Penenden Heath,Friday Oct.24th,
1828. The Catholic Question.
Bradley and Dent for the British Catholic
Association. 1828.
4.

CHAMBERS, Ralph Frederick.*
The Strict Baptist Chapels of England: Volume 3,
The Chapels of Kent.
Ralph Frederick Chambers. Thornton Heath,
Surrey. 1955.
2,11.

DOYLE, Eric.
Canterbury and the Franciscans, 1224 - 1974: a
commemorative essay.
Franciscan Study Centre. Canterbury. 1974.
3,11.

FIELD, Colin Walter.
The Province of Canterbury and the
Elizabethan settlement of religion.
C.W. Field. Robertsbridge. 1973.
1,3,11,12,20,26,27.

HAYES, Will.
Gray Ridge (and) The Book of Francis Howgill,
written and compiled by Will Hayes.
Order of the Great Companions, Hertha's Chapel,
Meopham Green. 1942.
(Francis Howgill was a Westmoreland Quaker).
11.

KENT AND SUSSEX BAPTIST ASSOCIATION.
Year book, 1972.
Kent and Sussex Baptist Association. 1972.
9.

KENT COUNTY COUNCIL: EDUCATION DEPARTMENT.*
Story of Christianity in Kent: for use by
teachers in schools in the County as a
supplement to the agreed syllabus for
Religious Teaching.
Kent Education Committee. 1961.
4,6,9,13,15,16,19,20,24,25,26,27,30.

KEPLER, J.S.
The exchange of Christendom:the international
entrepot at Dover, 1622 - 1651.
Leicester University Press. 1976.
11.

LE NEVE, John.
Fasti Ecclesiae Anglicanae, 1541 to 1857,
III: the Canterbury, Rochester and Winchester
dioceses.
Athlone Press. 1974.
11.

LIDBETTER, H.
The Friends Meeting House. 2nd edition.
Ebor Press. 1979.
15.

LYNCH, E. Killian.
The Order of Carmelites.
Printed at the Carmelite Press, Aylesford. c.1950.
11.

MACKESON, Charles.*
Illustrated Church Congress handbook for 1892.
3.

MODERN CANTERBURY PILGRIMS: the story of twenty-
three converts and why they chose the Anglican
Communion.
Mowbray. 1956.
11.

PAWLEY, Bernard.
Rome and Canterbury: through four centuries.
A study of the relations between the Church of
Rome and the Anglican churches; 1530 - 1973.
Mowbrays. 1974.
11.

ROCHESTER DIOCESAN DIRECTORY.
See Rochester Diocese

ROGERS, Philip George.*
The Sixth Trumpeter:the story of Jezreel and
his Tower.
Oxford University Press. 1963.
1,2,3,4,5 1970, 6,7,8,9,11,12,15,25.

ROTH, Cecil.
The rise of Provincial Jewry: the early history
of the Jewish communities in the English country-
side, 1740 - 1840.
(Includes Canterbury, Chatham, Dover, Ramsgate,
Sheerness).
The Jewish Monthly. 1950.
3.

SHEPPARD, Lancelot Capel.
The English Carmelites. (Refers to the Aylesford
Carmelite Priory throughout).
Burns Oates. 1943.
11.

SHOWLER, Karl.*
A review of the history of the Society of
Friends in Kent 1655 - 1966.
Canterbury Preparative Meeting of the
Society of Friends. 1970.
6,7,12.

SOUTHWARK CATHOLIC DIRECTORY.
Forty-seventh Annual Publication 1975. 11.
Forty-eigth   Annual Publication 1976. 11.
Fiftieth   Annual Publication 1978.   3.
Fifty-first   Annual Publication 1979.   3.
Pyramid Press for Southward Catholic Children's
Society.

THANET CATHOLIC ANNUAL.
Church Publishers for St. Augustine's Abbey.
1962. 13.
1974. 13.
1976. 13.
1978.   3.
1979. 13.

TIMPSON, Thomas.*
Church history of Kent: from the earliest period
to the year MDCCCLVIII (1858).
(Non-conformist).
Ward and Company. 1859.
2.

WHATMORE, Leonard E.
Recusancy in Kent:studies and documents.
Colin W. Field, 26 High Street, Robertsbridge,
Sussex. 1973.
4,8,19,20,26,27.

RICHBOROUGH

BRITANNIA:a Journal of Romano - British and
Kindred Studies. Vol.I. 1970.
(Includes articles on the Roman Theatre
at Canterbury and on Richborough).
Society for the Promotion of Roman Studies. 1970.
11.

BUSHE-FOX, J.P.*
Richborough Castle (Ministry of Works Guides).
H.M.S.O.
1922. 1.3.5.6.7.8.10.11.13.14.15.
1924. 3.11.17.30.
1930. 3.17.
1936. 8.
1955. 2.4.8.12.21.

EAST KENT TIMES, BROADSTAIRS AND ST. PETER'S MAIL.
Supplement: Richborough Power Station, Sandwich,
Kent. 1963.
24.

THE HISTORY OF RICHBOROUGH CASTLE, near Sandwich,
with historical notices of the ancient town of
Stonar.
Printed and published by Henry Jones. 1843.
24. Included in "Jottings of Kent".

LEWIS, Rev. John.*
A short dissertation on the antiquities of the two
ancient ports of Richborough and Sandwich, by the
Isle of Thanet in Kent. Communicated by the
Rev. Mr. John Lewis.
Read before the Society of Antiquaries of London
on October 11th, 1744.
11.

REPORTS ON THE EXCAVATION OF THE ROMAN
FORT AT RICHBOROUGH, KENT.*
Nos. 1.2.3 and 4 by J.P. Bushe-Fox.
No. 5 by B.W. Cunliffe.
Society of Antiquaries.
Nos. 1,2,& 3; 1926, 1928 and 1932. 24,29.
No. 4, 1949.   4,24,29.
No. 5, 1968.   12,24,29.

SMITH, Charles Roach.*
The antiquities of Richborough, Reculver
and Lymne in Kent.
J.R. Smith. 1850.
2,24.

RIPPLE

RIPPLE VILLAGE APPRAISAL COMMITTEE.
Ripple- Past and Present.
Ripple Village Appraisal Committee. 1980
28.

RIVER

WELBY, Douglas.
The Kentish village of River.
Crabwell Publications. 1977.
3,6,7,11,13,15,22,23,30.

RIVERS

COOTE, Jack Howard.
East Coast Rivers.
Yachting Monthly.
1956. 11.
1971. 7th edition. 11.
1974. 27.

CORDELL, Alan.
Old postcard views: from the Walter Dowsett
Collection; compiled by Alan Cordell, Peter
Ferguson and Alan Pearsall. Part II.
The rivers and Coast of Kent.
Nautical Pictorial. 1978.
11,12,23.

KENT RIVER AUTHORITY.
Kent River Handbook.
Ed. J. Burrow & Company Ltd. Cheltenham.
1972. 8.
1973. 1,8,11.
1974. 1,4,9.

KENT RIVER BOARD.
Report for the years ended 31st March, 1953
and 31st March, 1954.
23.

Works inspection by the Board on Friday
23rd July, 1954: itinerary and notes.
Inspection of the Flood emergency works
carried out after the February,1953 floods.
Copy of typewritten report and programme.
Kent River Board. 1954.
11.

MARTIN, Nancy.
Sea and river pilots.
Terence Dalton. Lavenham. 1977.
11.

MITCHELL, John.*
Kentish Waters.(Fishing Famous Rivers Series).
Rivers in Kent which come under the control
of the Kent River Board.
E.M. Art and Publishing, Peterborough for
Angling Times. 1965.
1,2,3,4,5,6,7,8,11,19,20,30.

SPURRELL, F.C.J.*
A sketch of the history of the rivers and
denudation of West Kent, etc.
West Kent Natural History Society.
Printed by E.G. Berryman and Sons. Greenwich.1886.
11,17.

WORSSAM, Bernard Charles.
A new look at river capture and at the
denudation history of the Weald.
H.M.S.O. 1973.
5,7,11.

ROAD TRANSPORT.

BARKER, Theodore Cardwell.
A History of London Transport, passenger travel
and the development of the Metropolis.
Vol.I. The Nineteenth Century. (1963).
Vol.II The Twentieth Century to 1970. (1974).
(includes Bus Companies operating in North
West Kent).
Allen and Unwin. 1963 and 1974.
1,11.

"BELL STREET" pseud.
East Surrey.
(The Story of the East Surrey Traction Company
which extended to the Westerham area).
H.J. Publications. St. Albans. 1974.
11.

BLACKER, Ken.
Trolleybus.
Capital Transport. 1975.
1.

CARLEY, James.*
Public transport timetables, 1838.
Part one. Kent and East Sussex, compiled
by James Carley. 1971.
4.8.30.

CHATHAM AND DISTRICT TRACTION COMPANY.
Official time-table. 1955.
(Last issued).
4.

COOPER, Terence.
The wheels used to talk to us, edited by
T. Cooper. Includes transcripts of taped
conservations with Stanley Guildford Collins.
(London trams. 1913 - 1951).
Tallis Publishing Company. 1977.
1.

COOPERS AND LYBRAND ASSOCIATES LIMITED.
Forecasts of cross-Channel road traffic
through Kent Ports. (Survey for the
Department of the Environment).
Coopers and Lybrand. (1975).
6,7.

CRITCHETT AND WOODS.
A new guide to Stage-coaches, wagons, carts,
vessels etc. for 1822.
20th edition by Critchett and Woods.
Printed by T. Maiden. 1822.
11.

DOVER CORPORATION TRAMWAYS.
Reports. 1900 - 1901; 1902 - 1903;
          1903 - 1904; 1904 - 1905
          1905 - 1906; 1906 - 1907
          1906 - 1907(Supplement to Annual Report)
Dover Corporation. (1901 - 1907).
6.

EAST KENT ROAD CAR COMPANY LIMITED.
East Kent 'bus and coach fares, from 21st
February,1971. Decimal edition.
6.

Timetable Area 5. Canterbury. 5th June,1977
until further notice.
11.

Timetable Area 6. Thanet. 2nd October,1977
until further notice.
11

Timetable Area 7. Dover 8th January 1978.
until further notice.
11.

ROAD TRANSPORT Cont'd

ELLIS, Harry.
London tramway memories. New Cross and Holloway
depots, 1946 - 1952.
(The author worked on the trams 1946 - 1952.
The routes extended to North West Kent.)
Light Railways Transport League, 32 Church Road
West, Farnborough. 1975.
11.

ERITH URBAN DISTRICT COUNCIL.
Electric tramways.
Erith Urban District Council. 1905.
1.

GRAY, J.A.
London's Country buses.
Ian Allan Ltd. Shepperton, Surrey. 1980.
5.

HARVIE, K.G.
The tramways of South London and Croydon.
1899 - 1949. 5th edition .
London Borough of Lewisham. 1975.
1,11,18.

"INVICTA" pseud.
The Tramways of Kent; edited by G.E. Baddeley.
Light Railway Transport League.
Vol.I.* West Kent. 1971.   1,2,3,4,5,6,7,8,9,11,
                           25,30.
Vol.II. East Kent. 1975.   1,2,3,5,6,7,8,11,12,
                           13,15,20,22,25,26,27,
                           28.
JENKINSON, Keith A.
Preserved buses.
Ian Allan. London. 1976.
12.

JOHN, Malcolm.
Bygone Buses. Volume 1.
Chambers Green Ltd. 1980.
28.

Bygone buses of Kent and Sussex.
John Hallewell Publications. 1980.
6.

KAIN, David.
The trolley buses of Maidstone: a survey
of the history of the Maidstone Corporation
trolleybus system...by D. Kain and M. Coates.
British Trolley bus Society. 1972.
2,4,7,12.

KENNETT, John.
Trams in Eltham,1910-1952,compiled by J.Kennett
Eltham Society. 1972.
1.

KING, John Thornton.
Buses and bathchairs...but not a tram in
sight:a review of public passenger road
transport in Tunbridge Wells from the late
Victorian era to the end of 1914.
Omnibus Society. 1976.
1,8,19,23.

KING, Nicholas.
Fleet History P.K.9. - the East Kent Road
Car Company Ltd, Compiled by N. King.
P.S.V. Circle. 1973.
7.

LONDON COUNTRY BUS SERVICES.
The vital link in danger, London Country Green
Line: a special report on the problems
facing London Country Bus Service.
London Country Bus Services, Reigate. (1975).
11.

McCALL, A.
Green Line:the history of London's Country
bus services.
New Cavendish Books. 1980.
5.

MAIDSTONE AND DISTRICT AND EAST KENT BUS CLUB.
Annual Report - 1963.
Maidstone and District and East Kent Bus
Club. Aylesford.
4.

MAIDSTONE AND DISTRICT AND EAST KENT BUS CLUB.
A current fleet list of East Kent, Maidstone
and District,and Maidstone Corporation Transport.
Maidstone and District and East Kent Bus Club.Aylesford.1973.
3,4,6,8,9,11,30.

A current fleet list of East Kent, Maidstone
and District,and Maidstone Borough Council.
Maidstone and District and East Kent Bus Club.
Aylesford. 2nd edition. 1975.
3,4,6,8,9,11.

A current fleet list of East Kent and Maidstone
and District,and Maidstone Borough Council.4th
edition.
Maidstone and District and East Kent Bus Club.
Aylesford. 1977.
6.11.

A current fleet list of East Kent, Maidstone
and District, and Maidstone Borough Council.
Maidstone and District and East Kent Bus Club.
Aylesford. 5th edition. 1978.
23.

A current fleet list of East Kent, Maidstone
and District, and Maidstone Borough Council.
Maidstone and District and East Kent Bus Club.
Aylesford. 6th edition. 1979.
23.

Fleet history and Route Map of Newman's of
Hythe. (1934 - 1963). Publication No.F.11.
Maidstone and District and East Kent Bus Club,
Aylesford.
4.

The Illustrated Fleet history of Maidstone
Corporation 1904 - 1974, edited by Nicholas King.
Maidstone and District and East Kent Bus Club.
Aylesford. 1975.
11,12.

The Maidstone and District Motor Services Ltd.
and subsidiaries:an illustrated fleet history
1911 - 1977.
Maidstone and District and East Kent Bus Club.
1977.
23.

Maidstone and District - unladen weights.
October 1969. Publication No. P.10. Single
duplicated sheet.
Maidstone and District and East Kent Bus Club.
Aylesford. 1969.
4.

Monthly news-sheet. No. 107 June,1961 -
(In progress).
Maidstone and District and East Kent Bus Club.
Aylesford.
4.

Route workings of the Maidstone and District
Motor Services Ltd., 4th edition.
Maidstone and District and East Kent Bus Club.
1974.
4.

75 years of municipal transport in Maidstone,
1904 - 1979.
Maidstone and District and East Kent Bus
Club. Aylesford. 1979.
12.23.

MAIDSTONE AND DISTRICT MOTOR SERVICES LIMITED.
Complete time-table. 15th June,1955.
Complete time-table. 17th June,1956.
Comprehensive time-table. 29th June,1958.
Comprehensive time-table. 3rd January,1960.
4.

Fare table. 26th February, 1956 with
revisions up to 17th June, 1956.
4.

Timetable Area 10. Hastings and Rother.
5th June,1977 until further notice.
11.

Timetable Area 4. Swale.
12th June,1977 until further notice.
11.

MAIDSTONE MUSEUM AND ART GALLERY.
The Tyrwhitt-Drake Museum of Carriages at
the Archbishop's Stables, Mill Street,
Maidstone - Official Guide.
(The Tyrwhitt-Drake Collection) 8th edition.
Maidstone Borough Council. 1971.
4.11.

MORRIS, C.
Regional history of British bus services.
Volume 1. South-east England.
Transport Publishing Company. 1980.
13.

PAGE, Andre.
Kent and East Sussex by wanderbus.
Midas Books, Speldhurst. 1973.
1,2,3,6,7,9,11,12,26,30.

SCOTNEY, David James Stratton.*
The Maidstone Trolleybus, 1928 - 67.
National Trolleybus Association. 1972.
6,7,11,12.

"SOUTHEASTERN". pseud (i.e. F.M. Atkins,
G.E. Baddeley, R.J. Durrant, R. Elliott and
A.A. Jackson).*
The tramways of Woolwich and South East London.
Light Railway Transport League. 1963.
2,4,5,8,12.

TAYLOR, John.
The Carriers' Cosmographie: Inns, hostelries
and other lodgings in and neare London.
De Capo Theatrum Orbis Terrarum Ltd. 1974.
11.

TRANSPORTATION PLANNING ASSOCIATES.
Greater London Council heavy vehicle restraint
study...Borough report...London Borough of Bromley.
Transportation Planning Associates. 1974.
2.

Greater London Council heavy vehicle restraint
study: Scheme reports....London Borough of Bromley.
Transporation Planning Associates. 1974.
2.

WILLOUGHBY, David William.
London Transport tramways handbook, by
D.W. Willoughby and E.R. Oakley.
Published by D.W. Willoughby and E.R. Oakley,
Hartley. 1972.
11.

Trams in South East London, by D.W. Willoughby
and E.R. Oakley.
D.W. Willoughby and E.R. Oakley. 1977.
5.

WITTON. A.M.
Buses of South-East England, (Fleetbook No.11),
Edited by A.M. Witton and R.L. Telfer.
A.M. Wilton. Manchester.
1977. 3.6.11.25.
1980. 2nd edition. 6,12,13.

ROADS

BRITISH ROAD FEDERATION.
County Road needs in East Sussex, Kent and
West Sussex.
British Road Federation. 1978.
1.

CANTERBURY CITY COUNCIL:CITY ARCHITECT AND
PLANNING OFFICER.
Central Area: report of the City Architect
and Planning Officer on the proposed traffic
network.
Canterbury City Council. 1972.
3.

Ring Road: North-East section. An appraisal
of the alternative routes.
Canterbury City Council. 1973.
3.

CARLEY, James.
The Gravesend to Wrotham turnpike road.
Meopham Publications Committee. 1973.
2,9,11,23,25.

The lost roads of Meopham and nearby parishes.*
Meopham Publications Committee. 1971.
25.

CARY, John.
Cary's new itinerary:or an accurate delineation
of the great roads, both direct and cross throughout England and Wales:with many of the principal
roads in Scotland, from an actual admeasurement
by John Cary, made by command of His Majesty's
Postmaster General for official purposes, under
the direction and inspection of Thomas Hasker.
11th edition.
G.&.J. Cary. 1828.
4.

DUNLOP RUBBER COMPANY LIMITED.
"On the road": the Dunlop pictorial road plans.
Vol.I. (South-eastern England). 2nd edition.
Ed. J. Burrow & Company. Cheltenham. 193-?
11.

ELLIS-MACE, J.
Old Tenterden Road, by J. Ellis-Mace, Esq.,
at the Ashford Road Mutual Improvement Society.
(Reproduced from Thomson's Almanac and Local
Directory for 1891).
W. Thomson. 1891.
11.

ELLISTON-ERWOOD, Frank Charles.*
The Biddenden and Boundgate Turnpike Road,
1766 - 1883.
Reprinted from Archaeologia Cantiana, Vol.LXXI.
1957.
Printed by Headley Brothers. Ashford. 1957.
1.11.

The making of the New Road at Lee,*1824-1828.
Blackheath Press for Kent Archaeological Society.
1952.
2,11,18.

Miscellaneous notes on some Kent Roads and
allied matters...*
Reprinted from Archaeologia Cantiana, Vol.LXX.
1956.
Printed by Headley Brothers. Ashford.
1,4,11.

More notes on Kentish Roads.*
Reprinted from Archaeologia Cantiana,
Vol. 73, 1959.
Printed by Headley Brothers. Ashford. 1959.
11.

Road works at Shooter's Hill, Kent, 1816.
Reprinted from Woolwich and District
Antiquarian Society Reports, 1947.
1,2,8,11,12,18.

The Turnpike roads between Greenwich and
Woolwich,*an account of the development of
road communications between the Capital
and the Town of Woolwich.
 Reprinted from the Proceedings of the Woolwich
and District Antiquarian Society. Vol. XXX.
1954
Independent Printing Works. 1954.
1.8.11.15.18.

ENVIRONMENT, Department of the.
A20 Sidcup by-pass proposals: Swanley by-pass
to Kemnal Corner.
Department of the Environment. 1974.
2.

Canterbury Southern by-pass (A2): alternative
routes: a consultative document.
Department of the Environment. 1973.
11.

GREAT BRITAIN: Laws etc. (Geo. II).*
An Act for repairing...the road leading from
the...Sign of the Bells...in Rochester...to
Maidstone. 1728.

ROADS Cont'd

GREAT BRITAIN:Laws, etc. (GEO.II).*
An Act for repairing..the road from...
Chatham...to St. Dunstan's Cross...Canterbury.
1729.
3.

An Act for repairing and widening the road
leading from Saint Dunstan's Cross...to the
water-side at Whitstable.*
H.M.S.O. 1736.
3.

An Act for explaining and amending...several
acts of Parliament made in the...reign of
His late Majesty, George the First...for
repairing the several roads therein mentioned
in the Counties of Surrey, Kent and Sussex.
Printed by John Baskett. 1737.
11.

GREAT BRITAIN, Laws etc. (GEO.III).
Lamberhurst Road Act. 2d. Geo. III. Cap. 67.
(1761).
23.

GREAT BRITAIN:Laws etc. (WILL. IV).
An Act for more effectually repairing...
the road from the Post Road near Faversham...
to Castle Street...Canterbury.
1831.
3.

The General Highway Act, (5 and 6 Wm. IV. Ch.50).
With notes and an index...by J. Bateman.
Maxwell, Sweet and Stevens. London. 1835.
11.

GREAT BRITAIN: Laws etc. (7 Will.IV and Vic).
An Act for transferring and vesting the
Royal Military Canal, Roads, Towing Paths,.....
in the Counties of Kent and Sussex, and also
the Rates and Tolls arising therefrom...
Printed by George Eyre and Andrew Spottiswoode.
1837.
11.

GREAT BRITAIN: Laws etc. (Eliz.II).
STATUTORY INSTRUMENTS.
The Gillingham Link Trunk Road, Order 1962.
H.M.S.O. 1962.
8.
The London - Canterbury - Dover Trunk Road.
(Priory Road, Dover) Order 1959.
H.M.S.O. 1959.
12.

(Highways, England and Wales).
The London - Canterbury - Dover Trunk Road.
Dartford Diversion Order 1963.
H.M.S.O. 1963.
8.

The London-Folkestone-Dover Trunk Road.
(Kellicks Corner Diversion, Folkestone)
Order 1959.
H.M.S.O. 1959.
12.

The London-Folkestone-Dover Trunk Road.
(York Street to Snargate Street, Dover).
Order 1959.
H.M.S.O. 1959.
12.

Sl No. 1605.
Tne Mid-Kent Motorway M20. (Swanley-Farningham
Section) Scheme 1973.
H.M.S.O. 1973.
8.

SI No. 1606.
The Mid-Kent Motorway M20 (Swanley-Farningham
Section) connecting roads (No.1).Scheme 1973.
H.M.S.O. 1973.
8.

The South Orbital Road,(Princes Road to
Dartford Diversion) Order 1965.
H.M.S.O. (1965).
8.

HARPER, Charles George.*
The Dover Road:annals of an ancient Turnpike.
Chapman and Hall.
2. 1895 and 1907.
25. 1895.

The Hastings road and "The Happy Springs of
Tunbridge".*
Chapman and Hall. 1906.
2,3,4.

HILL, Michael.
The Village that bent the A2. (Bridge).
In The Sunday Times Magazine, November 7th,1976.
pp. 78 - 87.
3.

HISSEY, James John.
On Southern English roads. (pp. 86 - 89
Tunbridge Wells).
Richard Bentley, London. 1896.
11.

The road and the inn.
(Chapters 21 and 22, Kent).
Macmillan. 1917.
11.

HUGHES, George Martin.*
Roman roads in South-East Britain: romance and
tragedy.
Allen and Unwin. 1936.
5.

JERROLD, Walter.*
Highways and Byways in Kent, with illustrations
by Hugh Thomson.
Macmillan.
1908 24.
1920 25.
1924 (1907 edition reprinted)   4.

KENT COUNTY CONSTABULARY.*
Analysis of road traffic accidents in the
Kent Police Area.
K.C.C.
1953 - 57; 1958 - 68; 1969 - 71.
4.

KENT COUNTY CONSTABULARY:TRAFFIC DIVISION.*
Accidents in the Kent Police Area.
K.C.C.
1968 - 70.   12.
1971.   5.12.25.
1972.   4.12.
1973.   4,8.
1974.   8,11,12.
1976.   8,13,28.
1977.   5,13.
1978.   5,13.
1979.   5.13.

KENT COUNTY COUNCIL.
Proposed Chatham Town Centre Ring Road - Western
End. Alternative routes, Railway Street to
Dock Road. Diagram...of exhibition January,1977.
K.C.C. 1977.

KENT COUNTY COUNCIL:PLANNING DEPARTMENT.*
Planning basis for Kent incorporating reports
upon the County Planning Survey and the County
Road Plan.
K.C.C. 1948.
1,2,3,4,5,6,7,8,9,11,13,15,17,19,21.

KENT COUNTY COUNCIL - ROADS DEPARTMENT*
Report of the County Surveyor on the
problems of Flooding.
K.C.C. 1969.
4,5,9,11.

KENT COUNTY COUNCIL:SURVEYOR'S DEPARTMENT*
County Road Plan Report,adapted by the Roads
Committee. 1945.
5,11,13,15.

Note for use of members on matters relating
to work of Roads Committee.*
K.C.C. 1970.

KENTISH GAZETTE.
Canterbury traffic study...Supplement to the
Kentish Gazette 16th January, 1970.
5.

ROADS Cont'd

MARGARY, Ivan Donald.
Roman communications between Kent and the East
Sussex Ironworks.
Reprinted from the Sussex Archaeological
Collections.
n.d.
11.

Roman roads in West Kent.
Reprinted from Archaeologia Cantiana. Vol.LIX.
1946.
11.

MAXWELL, Donald *
The enchanted road...
(Country between London and Weald of Kent).
Methuen. 1927.
2,25.

MEDWAY TOWNS - M2,M20 & M25 Two scrapbooks
compiled from local papers, 1956 - 1977.
4.

MELLING, Elizabeth.*
Some roads and bridges. Kentish Sources 1.
A collection of examples in the Kent County
Archives.edited by E. Melling.
K.C.C. Archives Office. 1959.
1,2,3,4,5,6,7,8,9,11,12,14,15,16,18,19,20,30,31.

PEEL, John Hugh Bignal.
Along the Roman roads of Britain.
(pp. 15 - 38, Watling Street, Dover - London).
Pan Books. 1976.
11.

PHIPPEN, James.*
The road guide from London to Tunbridge Wells,
through Lewisham, Bromley, Farnborough,
Sevenoaks, Tunbridge...
Joseph Thomas. 1836.
11,19.

STARKIE, David Nicholas Martin.
Traffic and industry.
London School of Economics and Political
Science. (Geography Department). 1967.
25.

VINE, Paul Ashley Larence. *
The Royal Military Canal: an historical account
of the waterway and military road from
Shorncliff in Kent to Cliff End in Sussex.
David and Charles. 1972.
2,3,4,6,7,11,12,19.

ROCHESTER
See also MEDWAY TOWNS.

ARNOLD, A.A.
Rochester Bridge in AD 1561, photocopied
article from Archaeologia Cantiana, Vol. 17.
1887. pp. 212 - 240.
25.

ARNOLD, Ralph.*
The Whiston matter: the Reverend Robert Whiston
VS. The Dean and Chapter of Rochester.
(Headmaster of the King's School, Rochester).
Rupert Hart-Davis. 1961.
25.

AN AUTHENTIC COPY OF THE CHARTER AND BYLAWS
OF THE CITY OF ROCHESTER.*
John Hughes. 1749.
25.

BARNES, C.H.*
Short's aircraft since 1900.
(Short Brothers' Aircraft Works were in
Rochester until 1948).
Putnam. 1967.
4,25.

BECKER, M. Janet.*
Rochester Bridge. 1387 - 1856.
Constable. 1930.
1,2,3,4,5,8,9,11,12,15,17,18,19,25.

BELL, Leonard.H.*
Where travellers rest:the story of Richard
Watts' Charity in Rochester.
Rochester Printing Company. 1926.
1,3,4,8,11,12,13,15,25.

BLACK, Vera L.
A history of Rochester Choral Society. 1873-1973.
P.P. 1973.
4,11.

BLAW KNOX LTD.*
General Catalogue. Blaw Knox Construction
Equipment (Loose leaf).
Blaw Knox Ltd., Rochester. (196-?).
4.

BOUNDARY COMMISSION FOR ENGLAND AND WALES.
Rochester:report upon the proposed municipal
boundary and division into wards of the
City of Rochester.
Boundary Commission for England and Wales. 1837.
15.

BOWYER, Chaz.
Sunderland at War.
(Sunderland Flying Boats were built by the
Short Brothers at Rochester).
Ian Allan. 1976.
11.

BROWN, Reginald Allen.*
Rochester Castle, Kent.
H.M.S.O. 1969.
3,12,20,25,26,27,30.

BURROW, Ed. J. Ltd. Publisher.
The directional pointer guide-map to Rochester
and Chatham.
Ed. J. Burrow Ltd. (c.1920).
4.

CAMPBELL, Alistair.
Charters of Rochester; edited by A. Campbell.
(Anglo Saxon Charters:I).
Oxford University Press for the British Academy.
1973.
1,2,3,4,5,8,11,12,25.

CATALOGUE OF THE COLLECTION OF ANTIQUE FURNITURE
AND EFFECTS, including a fascinating collection
of Dickensia.....15 Maidstone Road, Rochester on
Wednesday and Thursday,19th and 20th November,
1975. (W.G. Mason Collection).
Walter and Randall, Auctioneers.
4.

CHAMPION, Mrs. I.K.
Natural history in the Rochester area; edited
by Mrs. I.K. Champion and Miss E.E. Floodgate.
Published to mark the Centenary of the Society.
Meresborough Books, Rainham, for the
Rochester and District Natural History Society.
1977.
1,2,3,4,8,11,12,15,25.

CITY OF ROCHESTER SOCIETY.
Best foot forward: a review of The Society's
achievements during its first ten years....
Executive Committee of the City of Rochester
Society. (1977).
11.

Heritage cards.
1) The Guildhall. 2) The Bridge. 3) St.
Bartholomew's Hospital and Chapel.
City of Rochester Society. 1978.
4.

Rochester*a walk round the City.
Medway Borough Council. 1968.
11.
Rochester High Street trading: introducing some
of the shops, hotels and specialist trades in
the High Street in the Jubilee years of 1897 & 1977.
Compiled by Colin Whyman.
Kent Art Printers for City of Rochester Society. 1977
4,8,11,15.

CROFT-COOKE, Rupert.*
The Last of Spring.
(Includes the Author's experiences as a second-
hand bookseller in Rochester).
Putnam. 1964.
4.

ROCHESTER Cont'd

See also MEDWAY TOWNS

(DENNE, Samuel and SHRUBSOLE, W.)*
The History and Antiquities of Rochester and
its Environs: to which is added a description
of the towns, villages etc., situated on, or
near, to the road from London to Margate,
Deal and Dover, by S. Denne and W. Shrubsole.
Printed and sold by T.Fisher. Rochester.
Sold by S. Crowder. London. 1772
11,25.

The History and Antiquities of Rochester and
its Environs:*to which is added a description
of the towns, villages etc., situated on, or
near, to the road from London to Margate,
Deal and Dover, by S. Denne and W. Shrubsole.
2nd edition edited by W. Wildash with
considerable additions and improvements.
Printed and Sold by W. Wildash. Rochester.
Sold by Longman,Rees,Orme and Brown. London. 1817.
1,4,5,15,25,26.

DICKENS, Charles.
The Seven Poor Travellers, in three chapters.
Local notes by Edwin Harris.
(Short novel of the Richard Watts' Charity,
Rochester. Published in 1854).
Edwin Harris and Son. Rochester. 1926.
11.

DICKENS FESTIVAL PAGEANT.*
Rochester, 1951 Souvenir Programme.
25.

ENVIRONMENT, Department of the.
List of buildings of architectural or
historic interest in Rochester and Strood.
H.M.S.O. July 1969.
25.

FIELDING, Cecil Henry.*
Records of Rochester.
Snowden Brothers, Dartford. 1910.
7,25.

FRENCH PROTESTANT HOSPITAL.
The Charter and by-laws of the Corporation
of the Governor and Directors of the Hospital,
for poor French Protestants and their
descendants residing in Great Britain, 1718;
with lists of the Officers.(The French
Hospital moved to Rochester in 1960 and is now
a group of flats (La Providence) for the
elderly descendants of the French Huguenots).
La Providence, Rochester.
Printed for the French Hospital. 1972.
4,11.

GAUSDEN, John.
Rochester:an appreciation in words and pictures.
Cooks Publicity Service for the Corporation
of Rochester.
11. 1952 4th edition.
20. 1949.

GRAY, Adrian A.
The Unusual birth of the Gravesend and Rochester
Railway.
In Journal of the Railway and Canal
Historical Society, Vol. XXIV, No.2.
July 1978.
4.

GREAT BRITAIN. Laws etc. (Eliz. II).
Chatham Intra Charity of Richard Watts and
other Charities. A bill to confirm a scheme
of the Charity Commissioners for the
application or management of certain charities
in the County of Kent. (3 Eliz.2).
H.M.S.O. 1954.
4.

Chatham Intra Charity of Richard Watts and other
Charities. A bill intituled An Act to confirm
a scheme of the Charity Commissioners for
the application or management of certain
charities in the County of Kent.
H.M.S.O. 1955.
4.

257

GREAT BRITAIN, Laws etc. (Eliz.II).*
The Rochester Bridge Act, 1965.
H.M.S.O. 1965.
4,25.

GREENWOOD, E.J.*
The hospital of St. Bartholomew, Rochester.
E.J. Greenwood. 1962.
8,25.

GULVIN, Keith R.
The Napoleonic defences of Rochester and
Chatham.
Medway Military Research Group. 1977.
4,11,15,32.

HALLEWELL, John. Publisher
The complete tourists guide and handbook to
the ancient City of Rochester.
John Hallewell Publications. Rochester. 1979.
4.

HARRIS, Edwin.*
Gundulf the Good: or, Saxon Rochester.
E. Harris and Sons, Rochester. 1910.
7,11.

Historic houses of Old Rochester.*
(Old Rochester Series No.7).
E. Harris.& Sons. Rochester. n.d.
25.

The History and will of Sir Joseph Williamson.*
(Eastgate series - No.9).
E. Harris and Sons. Rochester. 1910.
8,15.

History of Rochester Castle.*
(Old Rochester Series No.2).
E. Harris.& Sons. Rochester. 1997.
25.

Odo: or the siege of Rochester Castle.
E. Harris and Sons. Rochester. 1900.
25.

Old Rochester. Numbers. 1 - 29.*
Edwin Harris and Sons. Rochester
Collected volume of the 29 parts. Various
editions from 1897 - 1930.
2.
Parts 1 - 8. 1896.
25.
Collected Volume of the 29 parts. Reprinted by
J. Hallewell, Rochester. 1974.
1.

Reminiscences of Old Rochester.*
(Old Rochester Series No.1).
E. Harris.& Sons. Rochester. n.d.
25.

Restoration House:or Rochester in the time
of the Commonwealth.*
E. Harris and Sons. Rochester. 1904.
7,25.

Richard Watts' Charity.*(Old Rochester Series
No.20).
Edwin Harris and Sons. Rochester.
3. 1912.
4. 1906.

Richard Watts:or Rochester in the time of the
Tudors.*
E. Harris and Sons. Rochester. 1903.
7,25.

The Riverside:*an itinerary of The Medway within
the City of Rochester and memories it recalls.
North Kent Books. 1930 reprinted 1979.
4.

Rochester Inns and Signs.* (Old Rochester
Series No.19).
E. Harris and Sons. Rochester.
1905   15.
1976.   Reprint of the 1905 edition by John
         Hallewell, Rochester.
3,11,25,30.

Simon De Montfort or the third Siege of
Rochester Castle.*
E. Harris and Sons. Rochester. 1902.
7,25.

HARRIS EDWIN.
Sir Robert Knowles:the founder of Rochester
Bridge.
Edwin Harris and Sons. Rochester. 1911.
25.

William D'Albini, or the second siege of
Rochester Castle.*
E. Harris and Sons. Rochester. 1901.
7,25.

HEARNDEN, Isaac.*
The lady of Rochester Castle;a romance in
rhyme. (photocopy).
J. Munday, Gravesend. 1891.
4.

HEPWORTH, J.
Rochester and district. A sketch-guide to
its geology, flora and fauna, compiled by
J. Hepworth.
Parrett and Neves, Rochester. 1913.
2,4,5,8,11,12,15.

HINKLEY, E.J.F.
A history of the Richard Watts Charity.
Richard Watts Almshouses, Rochester. 1979.
4.

JABLONSKI, Edward.
Seawings:an illustrated history of flying
boats.
(Section on Short Brothers, Rochester).
1974.
4.

JOHN, Malcolm.
Rochester:a sketch in pen and verse.
Prints based on sketches by Katherine
Kimball.
John Hallewell Publications. 1977.
4,8,11,15,25.

JONES, G.W.
Fort Bridgewoods, by G.W. Jones and M.Shortland.
Fort Research Group. Chatham 1979.
4,32.

KIMBALL, Katherine.*
Rochester:a sketch book.
A.&.C. Black.   1912.
25.

THE KING'S SCHOOL, ROCHESTER. (Founded in
the 7th Century, reconstituted in 1542 by
Henry VIII).
Printed by the Printing Company, Rochester,
for the Kings' School. c.1920.
11.

KNIGHT, M.T.
A history of J.P. Knight Ltd. (Typescript).
1977.
15.

LANGTON, Robert.*
Charles Dickens and Rochester.
(An essay read to the Manchester Literary
Club, 1880).
1880. Chapman and Hall. 1.4.8.9.11.15.18.
1888 T. Oldroyd. 4th edition. Rochester.
                    3,6,7,11,12,13.

LONDON AND MIDDLESEX ARCHAEOLOGICAL SOCIETY.*
Visit of the London and Middlesex Archaeological
Society to Rochester and Strood on Thursday,
26 June,1884, under the presidency of
C. Roach Smith, F.S.A.
Nichols and Sons. For the London and
Middlesex Archaeological Society. 1884.

11.

MARSH, Ronald,
The Conservancy of the River Medway,1881-1969.
(The Medway Conservancy Board sat in Rochester).
Medway Conservancy Board. 1971.
2,4,5,6,7,8,9,11,12,19,20.

Rochester:the evolution of the City & its government.
Rochester City Council. 1974.
1,2,4,5,6,7,9,11,13,15,16,20,25,26,27,

MARSH, Ronald.
Rochester Public Libraries.
Typescript, 3 pages. 1974.
4.

MOAD, Michael.
Eastgate House Museum, a brief guide to the
house and the museum collections, written by
Michael Moad for the Directorate of Leisure
Services.
Medway Borough Council. 1978.
11,15,25.

Yesterday's Medway: historic buildings.
(Corn Exchange and Guildhall, Rochester).
Medway Borough Council. (1978).
11

Yesterday's Medway: historic buildings.
(Rochester Bridge, the Bridge Chapel,
Watt's Charity).
Medway Borough Council. (1978).
11.

MUNRO, A.G.
Rochester and Chatham with pen and camera...
Homeland Association 1898 etc.
1,5,7,9,11,12,15,17.

Rochester and Chatham with their surroundings,
by A.G. Munro and B.P. Row. 3rd edition.
(Homeland Handbooks).
Homeland Association 1911?
2.

MURRAY, John Oliver.*
The martial, medical and social history of
the port of Rochester. (Photocopy of a
typescript).Rochester City Council. 1952.
11.

NOAKES, Aubrey.
Charles Spencerlagh and his paintings.
(Rochester Artist).
Jupiter. 1978.
3,15.

THE OLD HALL, BOLEY HILL, ROCHESTER.
The tour of the house. Notes.
n.d.
25.

OLIVER, John.
Dicken's Rochester.
John Hallewell Publications Rochester. 1978.
3,4,11,12,23,25.

ORDNANCE SURVEY;ARCHAEOLOGICAL SECTION.
Set of Archaeological records cards for
Chatham and Rochester.
Ordnance Survey. (c.1976?).
4.

PALMER, Cecilie.
Rochester recipes; food for hungry pilgrims,
compiled by C. Palmer.
Rochester Cathedral Book Stall. 1977.
11,15,25.

PARTICULARS, PLANS AND CONDITIONS OF SALE OF
FIFTEEN....villa residences....situate....
in the Borstal Road, St. Margaret's. By
order of the executors of the late Sir H.G.
Regnart. (Joint auctioneers). Maple and Co.,
in conjunction with Messrs Kidwell and Co.
(1914).
11.

POOLMAN, Kenneth.*
Flying boat:the story of the "Sunderland"
(Short Brothers of Rochester). Kimber. 1962.
15.

PRESTON, James M.
A Short History: a history of Short Brothers.
Aircraft activities in Kent, 1908 - 1964.
North Kent Books. (1978).
2,3,4,5,12.

RAND, Duncan.
Theatre in Rochester and the Medway area.
(Photocopy of a typescript, 1971).
4.

ROCHESTER Cont'd
See also MEDWAY TOWNS

REPORTS AND DOCUMENTS relating to Rochester
Bridge,*printed at the request of the
Commonalty, assembled at a meeting at
Rochester on the 27th February, 1832.
The Wardens and Assistants of Rochester Bridge.
Printed by J. & W.H. Sweet, Strood. 1832.
11,12,15.

REYNOLDS, Charles and Company. Publisher*
The Album of Rochester and Chatham views.
Charles Reynolds and Co. London. (1890).
4. Photocopy.
8,11,12.15.

RICHARD WATTS CHARITY.
The scheme for the management of the Charity
and for the application of the income thereof.
Richard Watts' Charity. 1934.
8.

The Scheme for Watts' Charity, Rochester.
Charles and Tiver. 1855.
25.

A terrier, or rental, of the Estates of
Watts' Charity, Rochester, 1859.....
Richard Watts' Charity. 1860.
11.

A terrier, or rental, of the Estates
of Watts' Charity, Rochester, as let
at Midsummer, 1885.
Original Record, Richard Watts' Charity.
1885.
4.

ROBINS, F.W.
The Story of the Bridge. (Contains
references to bridges in Rochester and
Kent).
n.d.
15.

ROCHESTER - an album of photographs.
E. Marshall. The Library. (1917?).
11.

ROCHESTER AND GILLINGHAM HOCKEY CLUB.
Brief history and guide.
c.1948.
25.

ROCHESTER BRIDGE TRUST.
Guide to classification and indexing of
records at the Bridge Chamber, Rochester.
Printed by Mackays, Rochester, for the Trust.
1954.
4,11.

ROCHESTER CITY: REGISTER OF ELECTORS.
Register of Electors 1949.
25.

ROCHESTER CITY COUNCIL.
A bill to extend the boundaries of the
City of Rochester to make further provision
with respect to the improvement, health, local
government and finances of the City.
Rochester City Council. 1951
15.
City of Rochester: souvenir of the visit
of the members of the Library Association.
Rochester City Council. 12th June 1936.
25.

A guide to house purchase.
Rochester City Council. 1962.
25.

Local Government reorganisation:
representations of the Rochester City Council.
Rochester City Council. 1971.
25.

Notes on Guildhall and the Guildhall portraits.
Typescript. Single leaf, folded.
(1973?).
4.

ROCHESTER CITY COUNCIL;PUBLIC LIBRARIES.
Annual Report: City of Rochester Public Libraries.
Rochester City Council, Public Libraries. 1961-2
8.

ROCHESTER CIVIC WEEK.
The Yeoman of the guard:the Peter Hudson Players.
Programme.
(1931?).
25.

ROCHESTER HISTORICAL PAGEANT COMMITTEE.
Rochester Historical Pageant, presented
during Civic Week in the Castle Gardens,
June 22nd - 27th,1931. Historical, industrial
and trades exhibition. 1931.
R.H.P. Committee.
15,25.

ROCHESTER NATURALISTS' CLUB.
The Rochester Naturalist; a quarterly record
of the Rochester Naturalists' Club. 1883- 1948.
Vol. I.   4,7,15,17.
Vol.II.   4.
Vol.III   -
Vol.IV.   11.12.
Vol.V.   11.
Vol. VI.   11.17.

ROCHESTER: Photograph Album of Scenes in
Rochester.
32.

ROCHESTER:REPORT ON THE BOROUGH OF ROCHESTER.
Municipal Corporations of England and Wales.
(18--).
15.

ROW, B. Prescott.
Rochester and Chatham, with their surroundings:
a handbook for visitors and residents,by
C.P. Row and A.H. Anderson.
(Homeland Handbooks).
Homeland Association. c. 1911.
25.

ROYAL AERONAUTICAL SOCIETY:MEDWAY BRANCH.
A brief history of Rochester Airport.
Marconi Avionics. Rochester. 1979.
4,9,15,23.

ST. BARTHOLOMEW'S HOSPITAL, ROCHESTER.
Trustees Account Book. 1889 - 1899.
15.

SHORT BROTHERS (ROCHESTER AND BEDFORD LIMITED).*
Pamphlets describing the aircraft and history
of the firm, c.1920 - 1945.
4.

SHORT BROTHERS (ROCHESTER AND BEDFORD LIMITED):
JOINT SHOP STEWARDS AND STAFF COMMITTEE.
Plan Medway with Shorts in the plan.
1946.
4.

Why close Shorts?
1946.
4.

SIR JOSEPH WILLIAMSON'S MATHEMATICAL SCHOOL.
A Service in praise and thanksgiving in
commemoration of the founder and benefactors
of the Mathematical School.
1973.
4.

SMITH, Frederick Francis.*
A History of Rochester.
1928. C.W. Daniel. 15.25.
1976 (reprint of the 1928 edition by J. Hallewell,
      Rochester). 3,8,11,22,25.

Rochester in Parliament 1295 - 1933.*
Simpkin Marshall Ltd. 1933.
25.

Rochester:with references to old records and
the Government of the City.*
W.&.J. Mackay, Chatham. 1923.
25.

ROCHESTER Cont'd
See also. MEDWAY TOWNS

TAYLOR, J.C.*
Guide to Rochester Castle and Keep,
compiled by J.C. Taylor, Curator for
the City of Rochester Council.
City of Rochester Council? 1951.
11.

THORNDIKE, Russell.*
The Slype. A novel set in Rochester and
in the Cathedral.
1927.Robert Holden.   4.8.11.
1927.Cape.   11.
1933.Robert Holden. 11.

WALFORD, Edward.
Holidays in the Home Counties.
(Chapters on Dover, Leeds, and Rochester).
New Edition.
W.H. Allen. 1899.
11.

WHEATLEY, Rev. Sydney William.
(Hon. Canon of Rochester Cathedral).
Heraldic Decoration of the Drawbridge of the
Medieval Bridge of Rochester.
(Reprinted from Archaeologia Cantiana,
Vol. 63. pp. 140 - 143). 1951.
Headley Brothers. Ashford.1951.
15,25.

WILDISH, W.T.
The History and Antiquities of Rochester:
its Cathedral, Castle etc.
Wildish, 1890.
20.

A short History of Rochester Castle from
the earliest period to the present century.
Wildish (c.1885).
20.

ROCHESTER CATHEDRAL

BEST-SHAW, J.K.
The Bells of Rochester Cathedral.
Kent Art Printers, for the Friends of
Rochester Cathedral. n.d.
4,11.

BLAKENEY, H.E.
Building dates of English Mediaeval Cathedrals.
Printed by Elvy and Gibbs. Canterbury. (1976).
3.

BLOXAM, Matthew Holbeche.
On the sepulchral monuments in Rochester
Cathedral.
P.P. 1863.
8.

BUMPUS, T. Francis.
The Cathedrals of England and Wales.
Standard Edition.
(pp. 18 - 31 Canterbury Cathedral; pp. 92 - 102
Rochester Cathedral).
T. Werner Laurie. 1937.
3.

D'ELBOUX, R.H.
Rochester Cathedral indents.
 Reprinted from Transactions of the
Monumental Brass Society, Vol. VIII. Part IV.
The Monumental Brass Society. 1946.
11.

FAIRWEATHER, F.H.*
Gundulf's Cathedral and Priory Church of
St. Andrew, Rochester..,by F.H. Fairweather.
(Reprinted from the Archaeological Journal,
Vol. 86; 2nd series. Vol. 36).
Royal Archaeological Institute. 1930.
1.

FRIENDS OF ROCHESTER CATHEDRAL.*
Annales Amicorum Cathedralis Roffensis,
being the Annual Reports of the Friends.
1947 - 1952; 1954 - 1972.   4.
1973.   4,11.
1974.   4.
1975, 1976.   8.

GARDINER, Rena.
The Story of Rochester Cathedral.
Rena Gardiner. 1978.
15.

GHOSTLING, Frances. M.
The Lure of English Cathedrals (Southern).
Mills and Boon. 1925.
11.

HANDBOOK TO THE CATHEDRALS OF ENGLAND,*
Southern Division, Part 2. Canterbury,
Rochester, etc.
John Murray. London.
1876. 4.
1861. 26.

HARRIS, Edwin.*
The Guide to Rochester Cathedral.
(Old Rochester Series No. 17).
E. Harris and Sons. Rochester. 1931.
25.

Rochester Cathedral.*
(Old Rochester Series No.3).
E. Harris,& Sons. Rochester. 1902.
25.

HISTORICAL MANUSCRIPTS COMMISSION.
Ninth report of the Royal Commission on
Historical Manuscripts. Part I.
Report and Index. pp. 72 - 177 Canterbury
Cathedral MSS. pp. 285 - 291 Rochester MSS.
H.M.S.O. 1883.
11.

HOPE, Sir William Henry St. John.*
The architectural history of the cathedral
church and monastery of St. Andrew at
Rochester.
Mitchell and Hughes. 1900.
25.

JOHNSTONE, Rupert.*
Rochester Cathedral Choir School:a short history.
R. Johnstone. Rochester. 1959.
4.

MACKEAN, Rev. William Herbert, Canon of Rochester
Cathedral.*
Rochester Cathedral Library: its fortunes and
adventures through nine centuries.
Printed by Staples. Rochester. 1953.
1,3,4,8,9,11,15,23.

THE MEN WHO TOOK THE MONEY:a tale of
Rochester Cathedral.
Cockshaw. 1851.
15.

PALMER, George Hendy.*
The Cathedral Church of Rochester: a description
of its fabric and a brief history of the Episcopal.
1st and 2nd editions.
George Bell and Sons. 1897 and 1899.
25.

RAWLINSON, Richard.*
The History and antiquities of the Cathedral
Church of Rochester...
1717. E. Curll. 4.
1723. W. Mears and J. Hooke. 2.

ROCHESTER CATHEDRAL FLOWER FESTIVAL. 1973.
Souvenir Guide.
4.

ROCHESTER CATHEDRAL.* Registers of the
Cathedral Church of Rochester. (1657 - 1837)..;
edited by Thomas Schindler.
Cross and Jackman. Canterbury. 1892.
2.

ROCHESTER CATHEDRAL VISITORS' GUIDE.
Pitkin Pictorials Ltd. 1975.
25.

SIBREE, James.
Our English cathedrals: their architectural
beauties and characteristics and their
historical associations. Vol. 2.
The Southern Cathedrals.
Francis Griffiths. London. 1911.
11.

ROCHESTER CATHEDRAL. Cont'd

UNDERHILL. Rev Francis.
Rochester Cathedral. Revised edition.
(Previous editions entitled "The Story of
Rochester Cathedral").
British Publishing Company. Gloucester. 1977.
11.

The Story of Rochester Cathedral.
British Publishing Company. Gloucester.
n.d. 7th edition. 11.
1964. 15th edition with additions and
      revisions by Guy Pentreath. 3,11.

WELSBY, Canon. Paul A.
Canon of Rochester Cathedral
Rochester Cathedral in the time of
Charles Dickens.
Printed by the Brewster Printing Company,
Rochester. 1976.
4,8,11,15.

WHEATLEY, Rev. Sydney William.*
Rochester Cathedral and its Priory: a brief
historical sketch of their buildings.
Parrett and Neves. Chatham. n.d.
25.

Rochester Cathedral:our monumental brasses,
a sad story.*
Parrett and Neves. Rochester. n.d.
25.

Rochester Cathedral: some notes on some
of its monuments.
Parrett and Neves. Rochester.
25.

Rochester Cathedral:notes on some of its
wall paintings and other coloured decorations.*
Parrett and Neves. Chatham. 1972.
25.

WHYMAN, John.
How the Victorians looked after Rochester
Cathedral. Typescript.
John Whyman. 1976.
15.

WITHERS, Hartley.*
Canterbury and Rochester with Minster-
in-Sheppey, by Hartley Withers and others.
G. Bell and Sons. 1929.
6,7,17.

ROCHESTER CATHEDRAL - BISHOPS, DEANS ETC.

ATTERBURY, Francis. Bishop of Rochester.*
Sermons and discourses on several subjects
and occasions.
Bowyer. 1723.
15.

BEECHING, Rev. H.C. Dean of Norwich.
Francis Atterbury. (Dean of Westminster
and Bishop of Rochester, 1713 - 1722).
The last 23 pages of a Pitman Catalogue.
Pitman. 1909.
11.

BRINTON, Thomas, Bishop of Rochester. 1373 - 1389.*
The sermons; edited by Sister Mary Aquinas
Devlin. 2 volumes.
Camden Series. 3rd Series. Vols. 85 and 86.
Royal Historical Society. 1954.
4,11,12,15.

HARRIS, Edwin.*
The Bishops of Rochester, AD 601 - 1897.
(Old Rochester Series. No.4).
E. Harris. Rochester. 1897.
25.

HOLE, Samuel Reynolds, Dean of Rochester.*
The Letters of Samuel Reynolds Hole.
George Allen. 1907.
4,8,11,15.

LEE-WARNER, Edward. Bishop of Rochester,
1637 - 1666.*
The Life of John Warner, Bishop of Rochester,
1637 - 1666, containing some account of his
successors, the Lee Warner Family.
Mitchell and Hughes, London. 1901.
2,3,11.

MASSINGHAM, Betty.
Turn on the Fountains: a life of Dean Hole
(Dean of Rochester).
Gollancz. 1974.
11,15

O'GORMAN, Richard A.*
Haymo of Hythe, Bishop of Rochester: with some
account of the former state and works of
Catholicity in Hythe, and its second spring
in that antient Cinque Port.
Washbourne. 1895.
1,2,8,11,12,17.

UNDERHILL, Francis.
John Fisher, Bishop of Rochester and Cardinal.
Published by Francis Underhill as a duplicated
pamphlet. n.d.
11.
1961. Church Literature Association. 4.
1977. Rochester Cathedral (1977).   3.

ROCHESTER DIOCESE

CUSTUMALE ROFFENSE....transcribed by John
Thorpe Junior.
John Nichols 1788.
5,11,12,15.

HAMO, OF HYTHE. Bishop of Rochester. (1319-53)*
Diocesis Roffensis: Registrum Hamonis Hethe.
Pts. 5 - 10 only.
Oxford University Press. 1934 - 48.
4.

Registrum Hamonis Hethe. Diocesis Roffensis.
AD 1319 - 1352; edited by Charles Johnson.
(Kent Records Vol. IV. Part I).
Kent Archaeological Society: Records Branch.
1915 - 1948.
12.

KENT ARCHAEOLOGICAL SOCIETY:RECORDS BRANCH.
The Parish Registers and Records in the
Diocese of Rochester...(Kent Records Vol.I)
Introduced by W.E. Buckland.
Kent Archaeological Society. 1912.
25.

LE NEVE, John.
Fasti Ecclesiae Anglicanae, 1541 to 1857, III;
the Canterbury, Rochester and Winchester
dioceses.
Athlone Press. 1974.
11.

PEARMAN, Rev. Augustus John.*
Diocesan Histories: Rochester.
S.P.C.K. 1897.
1,2,3,4,5,8,11,12,15,17,18.

RAIT, Robert Sangster.*
English Episcopal palaces. Part I. The
Province of Canterbury; edited by R.S. Rait.
(pp. 3 - 4 Canterbury; pp. 51 - 89 Lambeth;
p.8. brief mentions of the Bishop of Rochester's
palaces at Halling and Trottiscliffe).Constable.1910
3,4,12.

REGISTRUM ROFFENSE......transcribed from the
originals by John Thorpe Senior.
Richardson for John Thorpe Junior. 1769.
1,5,8,11,12,15,16,17,25.

ROCHESTER DIOCESE - Jubilee Festival: Exhibition
of photographs: a catalogue.
Jubilee Executive Committee. Rochester. 1954.
25.

ROCHESTER DIOCESE.*
Your Diocese, Rochester. 27th Jubilee Souvenir and
programme of events.
Jubilee Executive Committee. Rochester. 1954.
1,9.25.

A sketch of the history of the diocese of
Rochester,* with a short account of the
cathedral and precinct: a souvenir of the
Thanksgiving Anniversary. Office of the
Diocesan Chronicle. Chatham. 1926.
11,12,19,23,25,

ROCHESTER DIOCESAN DIRECTORY.
Various publishers.

1900.		11.
1903.		15.
1906.		4.
1932 - 33.		8.
1935 - 36; 1937		11.
1944 - 45.		4.
1947 - 48.		1.
1948 - 49.		11.
1951 - 52.		4.
1953 - 54.		4,11.
1955 - 56.		11.
1956 - 57; 1957 - 58.		4,11.
1958 - 59.		4.
1959 - 60; 1963 - 64.		4,11.
1965 - 66; 1968 - 69.		11.
1969 - 70.		11,25.
1971 - 72.		4,11.
1972 - 73.		4,11,12.
1973 - 74.		2,11,25.
1973 - 74 in progress		2.
1974 - 75 in progress		11.
1975 - 76.		8,15.
1976 - 77; 1977 - 78		12.
1978 - 79.		23.
1979 - 80.		23
1980 - 81.		15.

ROCHESTER DIOCESAN DIRECTORY-SUPPLEMENT.
1964; 1965 - 1973.   4.

THE SEE OF ROCHESTER, PAST AND PRESENT,*
with a plea for the restoration of
her ancient inheritance.
Parrett and Neves. Rochester. 1905.
7.

TEXTUS ROFFENSIS; edited by Thomas Hearne.*
E. Theatro Sheldoniano. Oxford. 1720.
2,8,15.

TEXTUS ROFFENSIS; edited by P. Sawyer.
Parts I and II. In. Early English
Manuscripts Vols. VII and XI, edited by
B. Colgrave.
Rosenkilde and Bagger. Copenhagen. 1957 - 1962.
11,15,
2. Part 1 only.

ROLVENDEN

BOWAN, Harold Townshend.*
Rolvenden, a parish and hundred of the Weald
of Kent.
Printed: Headley Brothers, Ashford for
Rolvenden Community Council. 1939.
2.

FAVIELL, John.
Great Maytham Hall.
Mutual Household Association Limited. 1978.
12.

GATTY, Richard.
Portrait of a Merchant Prince: James Morrison,
1789 - 1857. (Morrison bought much property
in the 1840's, including Hole Park, Rolvenden).
Limited edition of 250 copies.
Pepper Arden, Northallerton, Yorks. (1976?).
11.

ROMNEY MARSH

ABOUT THE ROMNEY MARSH: a miscellany.
Margaret F. Bird. Lydd. 1978.
3.

BRENTNALL, Margaret.
The Cinque Ports and Romney Marsh.
John Gifford.
1972. 2,3,4,6,7,11,19,22,25,30.
1980. 2nd edition. 6,23,28.

CARTER, George Goldsmith.*
Forgotten ports of England. (Including
Sandwich, Reculver and Romney Marsh).
Evans, 1951.
1,3,4,6,7,8,11,12,13,14,15,25.

DAVIES, William James Keith.
The Romney, Hythe and Dymchurch Railway.
David and Charles. 1975.
3,6,8,11,12,15,19,22.

DEANE, Spencer.
Sailor Smart: a novel.
(Part of the story is set in Romney Marsh).
C.S.S.M. London. 1934.
11.

DREW, Frederic.*
Geology of the Country between Folkestone and
Rye, including the whole of Romney Marsh.
Longman, Green, Longman, Roberts & Green. 1864.
11.

FERGUSON, John.
Murder on the Marsh. (Novel set in Romney Marsh).
John Lane. 1930.
11.

GREEN, R.D.*
Soils of Romney Marsh, by R.D. Green.
Bulletin No.4.
Soil Survey of Great Britain,
Rothamsted Experimental Station. 1968.
11.

JACOBS, Elsie M.
Across the Marshes. 2nd edition.
Published by Elsie M. Jacobs. 1959.
12.

KENTISH EXPRESS.
Guide and Directory to Ashford, Romney
Marsh, Tenterden and Elham Districts.
Kentish Express, Ashford. (1923).
3.

KIDNER, Roger Wakely.
The Romney, Hythe and Dymchurch Railway.
(2nd revised edition). (Locomotion Papers
No. 35).
Oakwood Press. 1978.
2,3,11,16,25.

LANE, GENTRY AND COMPANY. Publishers.
The Holiday Handbook of Romney Marsh, including
New Romney, Dymchurch and district.
Lane, Gentry and Co. Margate. (1927?).
11.

MORRIS, Owen James.*
The World's Smallest public railway.
(Birth, progress and majority of the Romney,
Hythe and Dymchurch Railway).
Ian Allan.
1946. 4,7.
1949. 11,12.

MURRAY, Walter John Campbell.
Romney Marsh.
Robert Hale.
1953 *   13, 30.
1972 * 2nd edition.   2, 3, 7, 8, 12, 22.
1975 3rd edition (?) 28.

ROMNEY MARSH Cont'd

PHILLIPS, N.J.A.
Dykes of Romney Marsh.
A Thesis for a degree in landscape ecology.
1975.
11,22.

PIPER, John.*
Romney Marsh.
Penguin Books. 1950.
6,13.

PRICE, Daniel.
A system of sheep grazing and management as
practised in Romney Marsh.
R. Phillips. 1809.
1,21.

ROBERTSON, Rev. William Archibald Scott.*
Kentish Archaeology, 7 volumes. (Mostly
reprinted from Archaeologia Cantiana).
Vol. 4. - Romney Marsh, Chislehurst,
Orpington.
Mitchell and Hughes. 1880.
1.

ROMNEY, HYTHE AND DYMCHURCH RAILWAY.
Official Golden Jubilee edition guidebook,
1927 - 1977.
Photoprecision Limited. 1977.
11.
Timetable and guide, 1976.
3,

SAVILLE, Malcolm.
The elusive grasshopper: a "Lone Pine" story.
(A children's story set on Romney Marsh).
Newnes. 1951.
11.

STEEL, Ernest Alfred.
The Miniature world of Henry Greenly, by
E.A. and E.H. Steel. (pp. 169 - 193
Romney, Hythe and Dymchurch Railway).
Model and Allied Publications. 1973.
7,11,12.

THORNDIKE, Russell.
Novels set on Romney Marsh.
Amazing quest of Doctor Syn.
Rich and Cowan. 1939.
4.

Courageous exploits of Doctor Syn.
Richard Cowan. 1942.
4.

Doctor Syn.
Richard Cowan. 1943.
4.

Doctor Syn on the high seas.
Richard Cowan. 1945.
4.

Doctor Syn returns.
Richard Cowan. 1948.
4.

Shadow of Doctor Syn.
Richard Cowan. 1948.
4.

WOLFE, C.S.
Historical Guide to the Romney, Hythe
and Dymchurch Light Railway.
Romney, Hythe and Dymchurch Railway
Association. 1976.
1,4,6,7,9,11,15,28.

ROTHER, RIVER

GOODSALL, Robert Harold.*
The Eastern Rother.
Constable. 1961.
26.

RUCKINGE

DOUCH, John.
The Roaring Ransleys of Ruckinge.
John Douch. P.P. (1977).
6.

RUSTHALL

ST. PAULS C. OF E. JUNIOR SCHOOL, RUSTHALL.
Environmental study of Rusthall village.
St. Pauls C. of E. Junior School. 1973.
19.

RUXLEY

KENT TRUST FOR NATURE CONSERVATION
Ruxley Gravel Pit.
(Checklists of birds, animals, plants and
insects....)
Kent Trust for Nature Conservation. (1979).
2.

RYARSH

GENERAL REGISTER OFFICE.
Census Returns. 1841, 1851, 1861, 1871.
Ryarsh.
Microfilm.
23.

ST. LAURENCE-IN-THANET

COTTON, Charles.*
History and antiquities of the church and
parish of St. Laurence, Thanet.
Simpkin Marshall. 1895.
2.

ST. MARGARET'S-AT-CLIFFE

COLLINS, Arthur H.
St. Margaret's-at-Cliffe.
S.P.C.K. n.d.
11.

JONES, John Bavington.*
St. Margarets-at-Cliffe Visitors' guide.
Dennis Weaver. 1972. (Reprint of 1907).
6,11.

KENT COUNTY COUNCIL:PLANNING DEPARTMENT.
St. Margaret's-at-Cliffe: informal district
plan.
K.C.C. 1973.
11.

MACFIE, A.L.
Historical sketches of St. Margarets-at-Cliffe,
1086 - 1911, edited by A.L. MacFie.
Printed at the Mana Press. Deal. 1977.
3,6,11,28.

ST. MARGARET'S BAY

CONNELL, Charles.
The house in the bay. The story of
South Sands House, formerly The Hermitage.
Lund Humphries. (1974).
3,6,11,24,28.

ST. MARY CRAY

BROMLEY PUBLIC LIBRARIES.
Town Trail. St. Mary Cray.
London Borough of Bromley. 1978.
18.

GREAT BRITAIN, Laws etc. (Vic.)
Act for the lease of...Mid-Kent Railway
(Bromley to St. Mary's Cray) Company,
to the London, Chatham and Dover Railway
Company. (25 - 26 Vic. Ch. 224).
1862.
2.

GREATER LONDON COUNCIL:HISTORIC BUILDINGS DIVISION.
St. Mary Cray: an appraisal of the Old
Village Centre.
(Limited number of copies issued;not formally
published.
Greater London Council. 1972.
2.

ST. MARY CRAY Cont'd

THE NEW ST. MARY OF THE CRAYS CHURCH,
CRAYFORD: Souvenir.
1973.
1.

ST. NICHOLAS-AT-WADE

CATALOGUE OF A WHITSUNTIDE EXHIBITION OF
FAMILY AND VILLAGE TREASURES AND BYGONES,
held at St. Nicholas at Wade.
n.d. (pre 1970).
13.

HELYER, Patrick J.
St. Nicholas-at-Wade. Thanet: an
interim guide to the Parish Church.
(pamphlet).
P.P. (1948?).
12.

JONES, A.
The Changing face of St. Nicholas at Wade,
edited by A. Jones. (In aid of restoration
fund).
1978.
13.

PARKER, Richard.*
The Schools of St. Nicholas-at-Wade, 1640 - 1957.
Gibbs and Sons. Canterbury. 1957.
30.

ST. PAUL'S CRAY

PLATT, Clifford L.
In trust for Chislehurst: an account of the
Commons of Chislehurst and St. Paul's Cray
and the National Trust lands adjoining.
Clifford L. Platt. 1975.
2.

SALTWOOD

DOTTRIDGE, H. Roland.
Slaybrook.
Published by Roland H. Dottridge. n.d.
11.

SALTWOOD CASTLE.
English Life Publications. 1975.
2,3,6,11.

TILDEN, Philip.
True remembrances.
(Allington Castle, Lympne Castle,
Saltwood Castle, Chartwell).
Country Life. 1954.
7,12.

VILLIERS, Olive G.*
Saltwood Parish Church:one thousand
years of history, edited by O.G. Villiers.
Kent Messenger. 1966.
7,11.

SANDGATE

CHAPLIN, Winifred Maud.*
Sandgate.
Sandgate Society. 1970.
11,30.

FOLKESTONE HERALD.
Souvenir album of views. Folkestone,
Sandgate, Hythe and neighbourhood.
The Folkestone Herald. (1902?)
11.

F(YNMORE) R.J.*
Annals of Sandgate Castle, 1539 - 1950,
compiled by R.J.F.
Printed and published by A.H. Couchman. (1951?)
7, 24 Included in "Jottings of Kent".

GERALD MOORE AT SHORNCLIFFE.
Sandgate Society. Sandgate n.d.
11.

IMPERIAL ALBUM OF SHORNCLIFFE CAMP AND
NEIGHBOURHOOD.
Reed, Stationer of Shorncliffe. c.1890.
11.

KELLY'S DIRECTORIES LIMITED.
Kelly's Directory of Folkestone, Sandgate
and neighbourhood.
Kelly's Directories Ltd. 1936 and 1938.
11.

ONE HUNDRED AND ONE VIEWS, Folkestone, Dover,
Sandgate, Hythe and South — Eastern Kent.
Percy Bessell, Folkestone. (190?).
11.

RAMMELL, T.W.
Report to the General Board of Health on a
preliminary enquiry into the Sewerage....
of the inhabitants of Sandgate,by T.W. Rammell.
H.M.S.O. 1849.
7.

RUTTON, W.L.*
Sandgate Castle, Kent. 1539 - 1894.
A.H. Couchman.
1894. 1.3.6.7.11.13.17.
13th revised edition n.d. 24.
        Included in "Jottings of Kent".

SOUVENIR ALBUM OF VIEWS.
Folkestone, Sandgate, Hythe and neighbourhood.
F.J. Parsons Ltd. (c.1900)
11.

TIFFEN, William Publisher.
Excursions from Folkestone, Sandgate and Hythe.
W. Tiffen. Hythe and Folkestone. n.d.
3.6.

TODD, A.
Encombe. 1821 - 1924.
(A house and estate in Sandgate).
P.P. 1968.
7.

WHATS ON IN FOLKESTONE, HYTHE AND SANDGATE.
April - June. July - December 1930; January -
June, July - December 1931; January - June,
July - December 1932.
F.J.Parsons. 1930 - 1933.
7.

SANDHURST

(WENBAN, A.A.)
Rude Forefathers: Wenbourne, Wenban, a family
and social history.
(Associated with the Weald of Kent, especially
Sandhurst).
A.A. Wenban. Birmingham. (1978?)
3.

SANDWICH

ANDERSON, Arthur Henry.
Sandwich, Kent. (Homeland Handy Guides)
Homeland Association. n.d.
24. Included in "Jottings of Kent"

BENTWICH, Helen C.*
History of Sandwich in Kent.
T.F. Pain. Deal.
1971. 1.6.
1972. 2nd edition. 2.7.11.29.30.

CAMPBELL, Sir Guy.
Golf at Prince's and Deal.
(6 - Fold Plate describes and illustrates
Prince's Course at Sandwich).
Newman Neame Limited. 195-?
11.

CARTER, George Goldsmith.*
Forgotten ports of England, (including
Sandwich, Reculver and Romney Marsh).
Evans. 1951.
1,3,4,6,7,8,11,12,13,14,15,25.

ADMIRALTY.
Folkestone harbour, surveyed by Staff Commander
J. Parsons...H.M.S. Porcupine, 1873.
Drawn by Naval Lieutenant G.A. Browning. Engraved
by Davies and Company. Admiralty under the
Superintendence of Captain F.J. Evans. 1874.
Scale 1 sea mile = 15". Size 18" x 25".
Hydrographic map. Town details from the
Ordnance Survey.
11.

River Medway, Sheet I, Sheerness Bar to
Bishops Ness, surveyed by Staff Commander
J.W. Dixon, 1886 - 7, the soundings east of
Grain by Staff Commander Tizard. Engraved
by Davies and Company. Admiralty under the
Superintendence of Captain W.J.L. Wharton.
1889. Scale 1: 12,230 (1 sea mile= 6")
Hydrographic Chart. Topography taken from the
Ordnance Survey.
11.

River Thames entrance, North Foreland to
The Nore. Surveyed by Staff Captain Tizard
and Officers of H.M.S. Triton, 1884 - 9., Margate
Sands and Queens Channel by Staff Captain
Parsons, 1875 - 6. Engraved by Davies and
Company, Admiralty under the Superintendence
of Captain W.J.L. Wharton. 1886.
Scale 7 sea miles = 9". Size 25" x 41".
Hydrographic chart. Topography taken from the
Ordnance Survey.
11.

ADMIRALTY; HYDROGRAPHIC DEPARTMENT.
Channel pilot. Part 1. South coast of England.
Originally compiled by Staff-Commander John
W. King. 10th edition.
H.M.S.O. 1908. (and 7th edition 1886).
11.

(Channel Pilot Part I). Supplement No.5 - 1937
relating to the Channel Pilot, Part I. 12th
edition 1931 corrected to 10th November, 1937.
H.M.S.O. 1937.
11.

(Channel Pilot Vol.I). Supplement No. 4 - 1965,
relating to the Channel Pilot Vol.I.
14th edition 1957, corrected to 9th November
1965.
H.M.S.O. 1965.
11.

COLES, K.A.
The Shell Pilot to the South Coast Harbours
Faber. 1977.
15.

COLLINS, Greenville.
Rye Harbour area:plate 8 taken from
"Great Britain's Coasting Pilot".
Richard Mount. 1693?
11.

FINDLAY, Alexander George.*
A handbook for the navigation of the different
channels of the Thames and Medway and the
coast between Folkestone and Orfordness.
R.H. Laurie. 1887.
1,8,11,12.

GROSVENOR, James.
A chart of the sands and channels, from The Nore
to Margate Road....by James Grosvenor, pilot.
Size 4½" = 4 miles.
Laurie and Whittle. 1794.
11.

HAY, John.
Pilotage of the British Channel from Scilly to
the Downs....in a series of Sectional Charts...
2nd edition.
C. Wilson. (1851).
11.

JEFFERYS, T(homas)
Second Chart of the coast of France from Ostend
to Ambleteuse (1761?). Scale 1" = 10 miles.
Size 7½" x 10" (Includes Kent Coast from
Margate Sands to Folkestone).
(1761?).
11.

NICHOLSON, R. Publisher.
Nicholson's guide to the Thames from source to
sea. 2nd edition.
Nicholson Publications. 1974.
15,27.

PENNEY, Stephen.*
Concise navigating directions for the River Thames,
including all the pools, reaches and channels
from London Bridge to the South Foreland and
Orfordness and the English Channel to Beachey Head.
J.D. Potter. 1896.
1,9.

REYNOLDS, James and Sons. Publishers.
Reynold's new chart of the Thames Estuary,
engraved by Ralph Welland and compiled from the
new Ordnance and Admiralty Surveys. Scale 1" =
2 nautical miles: Size 24" x 24". Also includes
map of the River Thames from Gravesend to
London. Scale 1" = 1 nautical mile: Size 4"
x 20".
James Reynolds and Sons. London. 1887.
11.

STANFORD, Edward Ltd. Publisher.
Coloured charts for coastal navigation; edited
by Captain O.M. Watts. No.1. The English Channel.
Stanford Maritime Ltd.
1950. 4.
1960. New edition. 4.

Coloured charts for coastal navigation, edited
by Captain O.M. Watts. No.8 - The River Medway
and The Swale. New edition corrected to
November,1974.
Stanford Maritime Ltd. 1974.
4,11.

Stanford's Chart of the English Channel from
Land's End to Flushing. (Eastern Section),
edited by Captain O.M. Watts. Revised edition.
Scale 6 miles = 1". Size. 26" x 37"
Stanford Maritime Ltd. 1975.
11.

Stanford's Chart of the English Channel,
from the Goodwins to Selsey Bill,edited by
Captain O.M. Watts. New edition. Scale 2½ miles
= 1" approx. Size 24" x 37".
Stanford Maritime Ltd. 1973.
11.

Stanford's Chart of the Lower Thames - Richmond to
the Nore. New edition. Scale 1 sea mile = 2¼".
Size 37" x 27".
Stanford Maritime Ltd.1973.
11.

Stanford's Chart of the Thames Estuary; initially
prepared under the supervision of Captain O.M.
Watts. Scale: 2 sea miles = 1". Size 27" x 28".
Stanford Maritime Ltd. 1975.
11.

Stanford's Harbour Guide: North Foreland to
the Needles, edited by Captain Forbes Sutherland
Campbell.
Stanford Maritime Ltd/ 1975.
11.

Stanford's Harbour Guide: River Medway and the
Swale, edited and prepared by Captain Forbes
Sutherland Campbell.
Stanford Maritime Ltd. 1975.
1,8,9,11,12,15,20,25,26,27.

WILLIAMSON, W.S.
The upper reaches of the River Medway. 4th edition.
Scale 4" to 1 mile. Section A - Tonbridge to
Yalding. Section B - Yalding to Allington Lock.
Transit map. Allington to Rochester Bridge.
Imray, Laurie, Norie and Wilson. 1975.
4.

WILSON, Charles Publisher.*
Sailing directions for the rivers Thames and
Medway...
Charles Wilson. 1881.
2,15.

WILSON, W. Eric.
The Pilots' Guide to the Thames Estuary and
the Norfolk Broads, compiled by W.E. Wilson
and Douglas Branson.
Imray, Laurie, Norie and Wilson. 1949.
25.

SEAL

BROWNLOW, Margaret Eileen.*
The delights of herb-growing. (Seal Herb Farm).
Seal Herb Farm Limited. 1965.
16.
Herbs and the fragrant garden.
Darton, Longman and Todd.
3rd edition Revised. 1978.
16.

STAGG, Frank Noel.*
Parish of St. Lawrence, Seal: historical notes.
(Typescript).
1946.
16.

SEASALTER

GOODSALL, Robert Harold.*
Whitstable, Seasalter and Swalecliffe.
Cross and Jackman. Canterbury. 1938.
17,19,30,31.

LUGARD, Cecil E.*
Communicants at Seasalter, 1615 - 1710,
edited by C.E. Lugard. (photocopy).
C.E. Lugard, Ashover, Derbyshire. 1929.
11,31.

Seasalter Borough, Manor and Parish,
edited by C.E. Lugard.
Elvy Brothers. Whitstable. n.d.
31.

The Sess of Seasalter 1653 - 1678 with index,
1704 - 1745 with index, and 1821,
Compiled by C.E. Lugard. (Photocopy).
C.E. Lugard, Ashover, Derbyshire. 1930.
31.

SERMONS

ASH, St. George Lord Bishop of Clogher.
Two sermons preached at Tunbridge Wells.
Dan Midwinter. 1714.
19.

ATKINSON, Rev. G.
A Sermon occasioned by the death of George
III and...Edward Duke of Kent, preached
at Ebenezer Chapel, Margate.
1820.
13.

ATTERBURY, Francis, Bishop of Rochester.*
Sermons and discourses on several subjects
and occasions.
Bowyer. 1773.
15.

BARNARD, Rev. S.
The fruits and effects of God's love....a
sermon preached at the Countess of Huntingdon's
Chapel, Tunbridge Wells. October 21st, 1787.
A. Lee, Lewes. 1787.
19.

BARTLETT, Rev Thomas.
The Church of England pastor: an address
delivered at the meeting of a clerical
association, in East Kent, on 17th of
November, 1840.
(Rector of Kingstone, and one of the six
preachers in Canterbury Cathedral).
John W. Parker. London. 1840.
3.

BENHAM, Rev. W.
A Sermon preached at St. John's Church, Margate...
following the funeral of Mr. T.F. Cobb.
Keble's Gazette. 1882.
13.

BENSON, Rev. Martin.
Tunbridge Wells Sermons, 1796 - 1828.
19.

BOUGHEN, Rev. Edward.
(Parson of Wood-church in Kent")-title page.
A sermon preached at Canterbury, at the
visitation of the Lord Archbishop's Peculiars:
in St. Margaret's church, April 14th,1635.
With a preface by Thomas Brett, L.C.D.,
Rector of Betteshanger in Kent.
Samuel Keble. London. 1714.
3.

Two sermons: the first preached at Canterbury,
at the visitation of the Lord Archbishops
Peculiars in St. Margaret's Church, April 14th,
1635....
Printed by R.B. 1635.
3.

BOWTELL, Rev. John.
A sermon preached at Patrixbourne and Bridge.
Printed by J. Abree. Canterbury. 1749.
3.

BRINTON, Thomas, Bishop of Rochester. 1373-1389.*
The Sermons; edited by Sister Mary Aquinas
Devlin. 2 vols.
Camden Series. 3rd Series. Vols. 85 and 86.
Royal Historical Society. 1954.
4,11,12,15.

BROME, Rev. James.
A sermon preached in St. Marie's church in Dover,
June the first, 1694, before the Right Honourable
Henry, Earl of Romney, being the day in which he
entered upon the office of Constable and Lord Warden of the
Dover-Castle and Lord Warden of the Cinque Ports.
Printed for Eben Tracey...and Rest Fenner, book-
seller in Canterbury. 1694.
James Brome was Rector of Cheriton and Chaplain
to The Lord Warden of the Cinque Ports.
11.

CHAPMAN, Rev. W. (Curate of Margate).
Two Sermons preached at Margate, the first on
reading the occasional prayer for the Victory
of the Nile; the second on the day appointed
for a Public Thanksgiving.
Hatchard. 1799.
13.

COOKE, Rev. Shadrach, (Vicar of Faversham).*
Legal Obedience, the Duty of a Subject: considered
in a sermon at the Archdeacon's visitation at
Sittingbourne.
Printed for Robert Knaplock. London. 1718.
3,11,26.

CRAMP, Rev. Dr. John Mockett.
(Baptist Minister, St. Peter's, Broadstairs).
Bartholomew-Day commemorated: a sermon delivered
at the Meeting House in Dean Street, Southwark.
August 24th, 1818.
1818.
24.

The inspiration of the Scriptures maintained and
defended. A sermon delivered at the Meeting
House in Dean Street, Southwark. November 10th,
1819.
1820.
24.

On the signs of the times: an address to Christians.
Wightman. 1829.
24.

A sermon delivered at the Meeting House in
Dean Street, Southwark, on Wednesday 16th February,
1820, being the day of the interment of his
late Majesty George III.
1820.
24.

A sermon occasioned by the death of his late
Majesty George IV, preached at St. Peters,
Thanet on Lord's Day, July 18th,1830.
Burgess and Hunt. 1830.
24.

Two sermons preached in the Meeting House, Dean
House, Dean Street, Southwark, on Lord's Day,
July 28th 1822.
1822.
24.

SERMONS Cont'd

DALE, Rev. Thomas.
The believer's hiding place and shield: a
sermon preached in the Chapel of Ease,
Broadstairs, on Sunday, 29th July, 1832.
24.

DAVIES, Rev. Charles Greenall
A sermon preached in the Chapel of Ease,
Broadstairs on Sunday March 24th 1833.
24.

DENNE, John.
The nature, design and benefits of confirmation:
a sermon preached in the parish church of
Westerham in Kent...1726, at a confirmation
held there by....Samuel, Lord Bishop of
Rochester.
R. Knaplock. London. 1726.
11.

HALL, Rev. Samuel Romilly.
A Weslyan Minister's address to the members
of Society in Tunbridge Wells; being a
reply to "A Clergyman's address to the
Weslyan Methodists in his parish".
John Mason. 1842.
19.

HARRISON, Rev. Benjamin.*
Patient waiting: sermons preached in
Canterbury Cathedral.
(The author was Archdeacon of Maidstone).
Rivingtons. 1889.
3,11.

LENG, Rev. John.
The duty of moderation to all men...
a sermon preached at Tunbridge Wells in
Kent on August 21st, 1715.
R. Knaplock, 1715.
19.

Knowledge of the nature and providence of
God...a sermon preach'd at Tunbridge Wells
in Kent, September 4th, 1715.
R. Knaplock. 1715.
19.

LLOYD, John.
Anecdotes of John Lloyd, a pretended clergyman, who was committed to prison on Friday,
September 6th, 1782, charged with
several highway robberies...(and the) remarkable
sermon he preached at Gravesend...
Printed for A. Milne, 202 High Holborn,
London. 1782.
11.

"A MINISTER OF THE GOSPEL".
An address to British Christians on the
importance and necessity of a revival of
religion. (The Minister was almost certainly
Rev. Dr. J.A. Cramp, and the address was
given at Broadstairs).
1832.
24.

NOYES, Rev Robert.*
Nehemiah's advice to the Jews...a sermon...
preached at Cranbrook. 1755.
1756.
11.

The substance of a sermon, occasioned by the
death of Mr. William Roffey, who departed this
life at Cranbrook in Kent, the 12th of
December, 1771, aged 67 years and 7 days.
Preached on the evening of his interment.
Printed and sold by T. Smith and Son. Canterbury.
(1771?).
3.

PEARSON, Rev. C. Ridley.
Two sermons preached at the commencement of
his Ministry in St. James' Church, 18th May, 1862.
H.S. Colbran. Tunbridge Wells. 1862.
19.

ROBSON, Rev George.*
A sermon preached at Dartford at the invitation
of the Right Reverend, the Lord Bishop of
Rochester....1800, by George Robson, Rector
of Snodland.
James Robson. 1800.
5,15.

ROSE, Rev. A.W.H.
Satisfaction in God's likeness. A Sermon
preached at Christchurch, Tunbridge Wells,
September 3rd, 1843.
W.E. Painter 1843.
19.

A SERMON PREACHED AT THE FUNERAL OF THE MOST
Reverend Father in God, John, by Divine Providence,
Lord Archbishop of Canterbury...who died at
Lambeth the 22nd Day of November, in the 65th
year of his age.
Printed for Chilwell, London. 1694.
3.

SERMONS PREACHED IN THE CATHEDRAL AT THE
commemoration of founders of the Kings School,
Canterbury on speech day from 1887 to 1896.
Longmans. 1897.
3.

SLIGHT, Rev. B.
The prevalence of Popery considered: a
sermon preached in Mount Sion Chapel, October
4th, 1835. (Tunbridge Wells).
W.E. Painter. 1835.
19.

SYDALL, Rev. Elias.
The true Protestant and Church of England Clergy..
a sermon preach'd at Tunbridge-Wells in Kent,
on Sunday, August 14th, 1715.
Printed for John Wyat. 1715.
11,20.

THOMAS MORE THROUGH MANY EYES.
(Sermons preached in Chelsea Old Church.
1954 - 1977).
Leighton Thomson. 1978.
3.

THORNTON, Rev. F.V.
Church Missions: a sermon preached in the Church
of the Holy Trinity, Tunbridge Wells,
August 26th, 1847.
Rivington. 1847.
19.

TOWERS, Rev. Johnson.
A sermon preached in St. Antholin's Church,
before the Worshipful Company of Skinners, on
...13th June, 1754.
(Tunbridge School was founded in 1573 by Sir
Andrew Judde and vested in the Skinner's
Company of London).
Hitch and Hawes. 1754.
11.

TRIMMELL, Charles. Bishop of Norwich.
A sermon preach'd in the Chappel at Tunbridge
Wells upon 19th August, 1711.
D. Midwinter. 1711.
19.

TUCKER, John.
A sermon preached at the consecration of Southborough
Chapel by...George, Lord Bishop of Rochester...
August 25th 1830.
J. Hatchard. 1830.
11.

WALLINGER, Rev. W.
A sermon preached in Holy Trinity Church,
Tunbridge Wells, June 28th, 1840, on the occasion
of the appointed thanks-giving for the preservation
of the Queen.
J. Colbran. Tunbridge Wells. 1840.
19.

WILLIAMS, Rev. W.
(Master of the Boarding School, Yalding)
A Sermon written on the death of Miss Mary Jeffery
of Tonbridge.
Waters and Son. Cranbrook. 1818.
19.

SEVENOAKS

ABBOTT, W.J. Lewis.*
Three papers: The Hastings Kitchen Middens -
notes on a remarkable barrow at Sevenoaks;notes
on some specialized and diminutive forms of flint
implements from Hastings Kitchen Midden and
Sevenoaks. (Journal of the Anthropological
Institute of Great Britain and Ireland. Vol.XXV,
November,1895. pp. 122 - 145).
Anthropological Institute of Great Britain
and Ireland. 1895.
16.

ALLNUT, Mrs.
Diary for 1831 and 1832. typescript copy.
16.

ANCKORN, Gordon.
A Sevenoaks camera: Sevenoaks, Westerham
and surrounding villages in old photographs.
Ashgrove Press. Sevenoaks. 1979.
16.23.

CAMPBELL, Robin.
The 1st - 70 years: a history of the 1st
Sevenoaks (Hicks Own) Scout Group, 1909 - 1979.
1st Sevenoaks Scout Group. 1979.
16.

CHEESEMAN, Dick.
The Sennocke Cricket Club, 1942 - 1963:a
short history. Typescript.
16.

CLUCAS, Philip.
The history of Sevenoaks and district.
Design Practitioners Ltd., St. Julian's,
Sevenoaks. 1975.
16

CORKE, C. Essenhigh.
Views of Sevenoaks and neighbourhood.
F.H. Hills. Sevenoaks. n.d.
16.

DEVEREUX, Charles.
Railways to Sevenoaks (Locomotion paper No.102).
Oakwood Press. 1977.
1,2,3,11,15,16,18,23.

DUNLOP, Sir John.*
The pleasant town of Sevenoaks. 3rd impression.
Caxton and Holmesdale Press.Sevenoaks.
1964 reprinted 1975.
16.

ENVIRONMENT, Department of.
List of buildings of special architectural or
historic interest: Urban district of Sevenoaks.
Department of the Environment.H.M.S.O. 1973.
7,11.

FORD, Alan S.
Sevenoaks town trail.
Sevenoaks Society. 1977.
16.

HARRISON, Jeffery Graham.
Sevenoaks gravel pit reserve:a joint WAGBI
Wildfowl Trust Experimental Reserve.
Published by WAGBI with Redland Ltd., and the
Harrison Zoological Museum Trust. 1974.
1,8,11,16,17.

HOLLAND, Josiah Gilbert.*
The Story of Sevenoaks.
Warne. 1876.
11.

KENT COUNTY COUNCIL:COUNTY SECRETARY'S DEPARTMENT,
RESEARCH AND INTELLIGENCE UNIT.
Reorganisation of Secondary Education in Sevenoaks
and Westerham:results of a public opinion
survey carried out in Summer 1975.
K.C.C. 1975.
5,11.

KENT COUNTY LIBRARY: SEVENOAKS DIVISION.
(Societies): a list of organisations in
Sevenoaks, Swanley, Hartley, Edenbridge and
the surrounding district, March,1978.
K.C.L. Sevenoaks Divisional Library. 1978.
11,16.

LOVELAND, Isaac.
Some names of tradesmen who resided in Sevenoaks
about 1848 and later on.
MSS and another copy-typescript.
1927.
16.

MILBOURNE, Raymond A.*
The Gault at Greatness Lane, Sevenoaks, Kent.
(Proceedings of the Geologists.' Association.
Vol.66, part 3, 1956, pp. 235 - 242).
Photocopy.
16.

Notes on the Gault near Sevenoaks, Kent.
(Proceedings of the Geologists' Association.
Vol. 72, Part 4, 1961. pp. 437 - 443). Photocopy.
16.

PIKE, Elsie.
The Story of Walthamstow Hall, a century of
girls' education. Material collected by E. Pike
and arranged by C.E. Curryer. First published,
Carey Press, 1938. Revised edition.
Longmore Press. Ltd. 1973.
16,19.

PONSONBY, Sir Charles.
Ponsonby remembers.
(The author was in The West Kent (Queen's Own)
Yeomanry in World War I and later MP for
Sevenoaks).
Alden Press. Oxford. 1965.
16.

QUINTON, Alfred Robert, C. (1853 - 1934).
The England of A.R. Quinton: rural scenes as
recorded by a country artist. Biographical
details researched by Alan Roger Quinton.
(A.R.C. Quinton completed the bulk of his work
in association with J. Salmon, publishers,
of Sevenoaks, from 1911 - 1934 - 2,300 paintings
for postcards. He visited Salmon in Sevenoaks
frequently. The book includes paintings of
Penshurst, Loose and Groombridge).
J. Salmon Ltd. Sevenoaks. 1978.
16,23.

REGENCY PUBLICITY SERVICE LTD. Publisher.
The Sevenoaks and District Directory of Commerce
and Trade, 2nd edition 1966 - 67.
Regency Publicity Services Ltd. Folkestone. 1966.
16.
The Sevenoaks Book: the Sevenoaks, Kent, and
District Directory of Commerce and Trade.
3rd edition. 1968/69.
Regency Publicity Services Ltd. Folkestone. 1968.
3.16.

RELF, J. Publisher.
Album of Sevenoaks views.
J. Relf. Sevenoaks. n.d.
16.

RUDGE, Charles.*
William Jeffery, the Puritan Apostle of Kent.
(The author was once Baptist Minister of
Sevenoaks).
James Clarke, Kingsgate Press. London. 1904.
11,16.

SALMON, Joseph. Publisher.
Guide to Sevenoaks.
J. Salmon. Sevenoaks.
1881, 1891, 1898, 1901, 1905.   16.
1913.   11.

SENNOCKE, Sir William.
The Will of Sir William Sennocke Knt.,
also copies of, and extracts from, letters,
patents, wills, grants etc. together with
proceedings in Chancery, decrees, statutes,
ordinances relating to the Free School of
Queen Elizabeth and the Almshouses in
Sevenoaks, Kent.
Trustees of the Fund. Printed by T. Clout,
Sevenoaks. 1802.
11.

THE SENNOCKE ALMANACK, DIARY AND DIRECTORY.
1903, 1904, 1905, 1906, 1908.
W. Wicking (later,1908) The Sevenoaks Press,
Sevenoaks.
16.

SEVENOAKS ALMANAC, 1843.
Payne. Sevenoaks.
16.

SEVENOAKS AND DISTRICT CONSUMERS' GROUP.
Sevenoaks consumer:the newsheet of the
Sevenoaks and District Consumers' Group.
July 1971. pp. 1 - 21 assess the Sevenoaks
Library Service.
Sevenoaks and District Consumers' Group.
Sevenoaks. 1971.
11.

SEVENOAKS CHRONICLE.
Old Sevenoaks Calendar. 1977.
Sevenoaks Chronicle. 1977.
16.

SEVENOAKS DISTRICT COUNCIL.
Sevenoaks Official guide.
British Publishing Company. Gloucester.
(1976)   4.11.
1978.   3,12.

SEVENOAKS TELEGRAPH AND KENT MESSENGER.
Popular Calendar 1901, 1909, 1911, 1914.
Sevenoaks Telegraph and Kent Messenger.
16.

SEVENOAKS URBAN DISTRICT COUNCIL.
Guide and Handbook to Sevenoaks and District,*
edited by George Bennett.
Caxton and Holmesdale Press. Sevenoaks. 1948.
1,2,5,11,16,23.

Official Guide to Sevenoaks.
Caxton and Holmesdale Press. Sevenoaks.
1921 8th edition 11.
1947.   11.

SOROPTIMIST INTERNATIONAL CLUB OF SEVENOAKS.
Sevenoaks:a guide for the disabled.
Soroptimist International Club of Sevenoaks. 1975.
16.

SWAN, Peter.
A short history of library services in
Sevenoaks 1905 - 1980.
Kent County Library. 1980.
16,23.

SWIFT, John.
Ducks, ponds and people:a guide to the management
of small lakes and ponds for wildfowl.
(Includes information on Sevenoaks Gravel
Pit Reserve).
WAGBI. 1976.
16.

WARD,Dr. Gordon Reginald.*
Sevenoaks essays.
Metcalfe and Cooper. 1931.
2.

Sevenoaks essays.
(Foreword with biographical details by John N.Ward
added).
Ashgrove Press. 1931 reprinted 1980.
16.

WHITE, Bob.*
Experiments in education at Sevenoaks School,by
B. White and others. Introduced by L.C.
Taylor, contents by boys past and present.
Constable. 1965.
8,11,12,16.

WOODFORDE, John.
Bricks to build a house.
(History of brickmaking with references to
the London Brick Company, District Sales Office
in Sevenoaks and the Redland Group of Companies
whose brick works are in the Sevenoaks area).
Routledge and Kegan Paul for the London Brick
Company. 1976.
11,16.

SHADOXHURST

CHOWNS, L.M.
Shadoxhurst:a village history.
L.M. Chowns. Shadoxhurst. 1977.
1,3,6,7,11,19,22,23.

SHEERNESS

ATKINSON, David A.*
The explosive cargo of the U.S.S. "Richard
Montgomery: a study...a marine wreck in the
Thames (near to Sheerness).
Southend-on-Sea and District Chamber
of Trade and Industry. 1972.
4,11.

BROWN, W. Henry.
A century of co-operation at Sheerness,
being a chronicle of the oldest Co-operative
Society in the United Kingdom.
Co-operative Wholesale Society's Printing
Works.   Redditch 1919?
11.

GREAT BRITAIN, Laws etc. (Geo. III)
An Act for the purchase of certain lands,
tenements, and hereditaments at Sheerness and
Chatham for the use of the Navy. (24th
June, 1816).
Printed by Eyre and Strahan. 1816.
11.

GROSSETT, Harry.
Down to the sea in ships. (Harry Grossett
was trained for deep sea diving and salvage
work at Sheerness Dockyard).
Hutchinson. 1953.
11.

H.M.S.LOCH LOMOND:
Order of service used in seeking the blessing
of Almighty God upon Her Majesty's Ship
Loch Lomond; the last ship commissioned at
Sheerness Dockyard.
1959.
4.

ISLE OF SHEPPEY CHAMBER OF COMMERCE.
Isle of Sheppey and Sheerness-on-Sea official
Guide.
1952. Home Publishing Company. Croydon. 8.
1959. New Century Publications.   8.

KENT COUNTY COUNCIL:PLANNING DEPARTMENT.
Sheerness draft town centre map:explanatory
notes, duplicated sheets.
K.C.C. (196-?).
11.

KENT COUNTY LIBRARY
A list of books and other items in the local
collection at Sheerness Public Library.
Kent County Library. 1978.
11.

MEDWAY PORTS AUTHORITY.
Sheerness Docks.
(Duplicated typewritten sheets).
Medway Ports Authority. (1973).
11.

SHEERNESS. Cont'd

MOYNIHAN, M.
A Place called Armageddon:letters from the
Great War.
David and Charles. 1975.
27.

SHEERNESS:extracted from "Navyworks",
journal of the Civil Engineer-in-Chief's
Department, Admiralty.
(Duplicated sheets). (195-?).
11.

SHEPPEY, URBAN DISTRICT COUNCIL.
Sheerness-on-Sea and the Isle of Sheppey,
compiled by George Beynon.
Sheppey Urban District Council. 1927.
6.

THE WATERING-PLACES OF ENGLAND, PART II.
Gravesend, Sheerness, Southend and
Herne Bay.
(The Travellers' Magazine 180-?).
9.

SHELDWICH

BOREMAN, R.*
A mirrour of mercy and judgement:or an exact
true narrative of the life and death of Freeman
Sonds Esquier, sonne to Sir George Sonds of
Lees Court in Shelwich in Kent. Who being about
the age of 19, for murthering his elder brother
on Tuesday the 7th of August was arraigned
and condemned at Maidstone, executed there
on Tuesday the 21st of the same month 1655.
Published Thomas Dring. Fleetstreet. 1655.
6,11,26.

SHIPBOURNE

GENERAL REGISTER OFFICE.
Census Returns 1841, 1851, 1861, 1871.
Shipbourne.
Photocopy.
23.

PARISH REGISTERS OF SHIPBOURNE, COUNTY KENT.
12th June,1560 - 19th July, 1658.
(Printed).
23.

SHIPS AND SHIPPING

ATKINSON, David A.
The explosive cargo the the U.S.S. "Richard
Montgomery": a study...a marine wreck in the
Thames (near Sheerness).
Southend-on-Sea and District Chamber of
Trade and Industry. 1972.
4,11.

BENHAM, Hervey.*
Down Tops'l: the story of the East Coast
Sailing barges....
Harrap. 1951.
3,4,11,15.
2nd edition 1971. 11.

BENNETT, A.S.
Us bargemen.
Meresborough Books. Rainham. 1980.
11,12.

BLUE CIRCLE GROUP:ASSOCIATED PORTLAND CEMENT
MANUFACTURERS LIMITED.
Barges: 100 years of river trading.
(Published to mark the Blue Circle Group's
Jubilee Celebrations, 1977).
Blue Circle Group. 1977.
4,9,11,23.

BOUQUET, Michael Rome.*
South Eastern Sail:from the Medway to the Solent,
1840 - 1940.
David and Charles. 1972.
3,6,7,12,25,28.

BRETT, Sir Henry.
White Wings.
Vol.I. Fifty years of Sail in the New Zealand
trade 1850 - 1900.
Vol.II Founding of the provinces and old-time
shipping passenger lists 1840 - 1885.
(Includes list of passenger ships to 1886).
Capper Press. New Zealand. 1976.
11.

BUCKNALL, Rixon.*
Boat trains and Channel Packets: the English
short sea routes.
Vincent Stuart. 1957.
11.

BURTT, Frank.*
Cross-Channel and Coastal paddle-steamers.
R. Tilling. London. 1934.
4,11.

Steamers of the Thames and Medway.
R. Tilling. London. 1949.
2,9.

CARR, Frank George Griffith.
Gipsy Moth IV: round the world with Sir
Francis Chichester.
Pitkin Pictorials Ltd. 1969.
11.

Sailing barges.*
Hodder and Stoughton. 1931.   11.
1951. 2nd revised edition. P. Davies. 1951.11.
1971;(1973 reprint) Conway Maritime Press. 25.

Story of the Cutty Sark.
Pitkin Pictorials Ltd. 1970.   5.
                              1976. 11.

CARTER, George Goldsmith (Dover author).
Looming Lights:a true story of the light ships.
Constable (1946).
13.

Spotlight on Sailing ships.
Hamlyn. 1973.
6.

CLARKE, Derrick Harry.
East coast passage: the voyage of a Thames
sailing barge.
Longman. 1971.
11.

CLEGG, William Paul.
British Railways shipping and allied fleets:
the postwar period,by W.P. Clegg and J.S. Styring.
David and Charles. 1971.
6.

European Ferry Fleets.
Marinart. 1976.
28.

Steamers of British Railways and Associated
Companies,* by W.P. Clegg and J.S. Styring.
T. Stephenson. Prescot, Lancashire. 1962.
11.

CROFT, R.J.
Railway shipping services from Dover and
Folkestone to France, 1843 - 1899.
R.J. Croft. Typescript. 1972.
7.

DANCE, Charles.
New Medway Steam Packets, 140 years.
In Sea Breezes, the magazine of ships and the
sea. Vol. 52, No. 393. September,1978,
pp. 569- 579.
11.

DAVIS, Dennis J.*
The Thames sailing barge:her gear and rigging.
David and Charles and International Marine
Publishing Company. 1970.
9,11,23.

DUCKWORTH, C.L.D.
Railway and other steamers, by C.L.D. Duckworth
and G.E. Langmuir. (Includes ferries operating
from Kent ports).
Shipping Histories Ltd. 1948.
13.

SHIPS AND SHIPPING. Cont'd

DUMPLETON, Bernard.
Story of the Paddlesteamer. (includes Medway
and Thames paddle steamers).
Colin Venton. Melksham. 1978.
1,27.
Excerpts from "The Story of the Paddlesteamer".
4.

FINCH, Roger.
Sailing craft of the British Isles.
(Includes Thames barges).
Collins. 1976.
5.

FREESTON, Ewart Cecil.
Modelling Thames sailing barges, by E.C.
Freeston and B. Kent, with an historical
introduction by Richard Hugh Perks.
Conway Maritime Press. 1976.
9,11.

Prisoner-of-War ship models, 1775 - 1825.
Nautical Publication Company. 1973.
4.

GRASEMANN, C.
English packet boats, by C. Grasemann and
G.W.P. Maclachlan.
(Chronological table of ships 1790 - 1939).
Syren and Shipping Ltd. London. 1939.
11.

GREAT BRITAIN:MONOPOLIES COMMISSION.
Cross-Channel car ferry services.
H.M.S.O. 1974.
6.

GREENHILL, Basil.
Archaeology of the boat:a new introductory
study.
A.&.C. Black. 1976.
11.

GRIMSHAW, Geoffrey.*
British pleasure steamers. 1920 - 1939.
Richard Tilling, London. 1945.
15.

GROSSETT, Harry.
Down to the Sea in Ships. (Harry Grossett
was trained for deep-sea diving and salvage
work at Sheerness Dockyard and involved with
shipping on the River Thames and Kent Coast).
Hutchinson. 1953.
11.
HACKNEY, Noel. C.L.
Cutty Sark: classic ships No.3:
their history and how to model them.
Patrick Stephens and Airfix Products. 1974.
11.

HALLAM, W.B.
Blow five:a history of the Alexandra
Towing Company Limited.
Journal of Commerce. 1976.
9.

HAMBLETON, F.C.
Famous paddle steamers.
Percival Marshall and Company. 1948.
4.

Model and Allied Publications. 1977.
11.

HAZELL, Martin.
The sailing barges and the brick and other
industries of Milton Creek, Kent, c.1850 -
c.1970; a social and economic history.
Thesis for Department of Teaching Studies,
North London Polytechnic.
Photocopy of Manuscript. Rough draft completed
May. 1972.
20.

HAZELL, Martin.
Sailing barges.
Shire Publications. 1976.
11,20,23,26,27.

HINES, J.
Barge remains in Kingsnorth Marshes.
In Topsail; the journal of the Society
  for Spritsail Barge Research, Issue
  No.15. Autumn,1976 pp. 48 - 50.
11.

HORLOCK, Albert H. (Chubb).
Mistleyman's log:chronicles of a barging life
as told by A.H. (Chubb) Horlock and written by
R.J. Horlock. (Includes Medway and Thames
Sailing Barge Matches).
Fisher Nautical Press. 1977.
11.

ISLE OF THANET ARCHAEOLOGICAL UNIT.
Wreck of a British man-of-war discovered
on the Goodwin Sands. (Interim Report). 1979.
Isle of Thanet Archaeological Unit. 1980.
13,24.

JONES, Rosemary.
Steam packet trips from London and their
effect on Gravesend between 1810 and 1860.
MS. Thesis. University of Southampton. 1978.
9.

KNIGHT, Charles.*
Shipbuilding at Gillingham. Reprinted from
"Chatham, Rochester and Gillingham News. 1938.
4,8.

KNIGHT, M. T.
A History of J.P. Knight Ltd. (Typescript).
1977.
15.

LEATHER, John.
Spritsails and lugsails, with drawings by
the author.
Adlard Coles. Granada Publishing. 1979.
4.

LIST OF MERCANTILE VESSELS BUILT ALONG THE
MEDWAY 1823 - 1930 and in East Anglia, Kent
and Sussex from 1803.
From a photocopy in Rochester Museum.
4.

LONGRIDGE, George Nepean.
"The Cutty Sark":the ship and the model.
(The ship is now preserved at Greenwich).
Originally published by P. Marshall in
2 volumes. 1933.
Model and Allied Publications. 1975.
11.

MARCH, Edgar James.*
Sailing Trawlers.
David and Charles. 1970.
11.

Spritsail barges of Thames and Medway.
New edition.
David and Charles. 1970.
1,20,25.

THE MARITIME TRUST.
The story of the Cambria.
(Medway barge anchored by Rochester Esplanade)
Ships Monthly with the Maritime Trust. 1973.
4,11,25.

MARSDEN, P.
Wreck of the Amsterdam.
(At Bulverhithe, Nr. Hastings in 1749).
Hutchinson. 1975.
11.22.

SHIPS AND SHIPPING Cont

MARSHALL, M.A.N.
The Armed ships of Dover.
from "Mariners' Mirror", Vol. 42.
No. 1. February,1956.
6.

The Armed Ships of Folkestone.
From "Mariners' Mirror",
Vol. 41. No.1. February,1955.
6.

MILLAR, J.B.
Story of the Medway Queen:a paddle steamer
that went to war,
edited by J.B. Millar.
Paddle Steamer Preservation Society. 1975.
3,4,8,11,20,25,26,27.

PAIN, E.C.*
The last of the luggers and the men
who sailed them.
T.F. Pain and Sons. Deal. 1929.
2.

PERKS, Richard-Hugh.
Sprits'l: a portrait of sailing barges and
sailormen. Written in collaboration with
Patricia O'Driscoll and Alan Cordell.
(The author lives near Faversham. North Kent barge
building centres are given).
Conway Maritime Press. 1975.
3,4,9,11,12,15,20,22,25.

ROBERTS, Bob.
Last of the sailormen (Sailing the East coast
routes with Spritsail barges, including the
"Cambria", now anchored below Rochester Bridge).
Routledge and Kegan Paul. 1960.
11.

ROCHE, T.W.E.*
Ships of Dover, Folkestone, Deal and Thanet...
Adlard Coles. Southampton. 1969.
24,30.

SAGE, Stephen.
Sailing barges of the Medway.
Typescript MS. 1973.
11.

SATTIN, Donald L.
Just off the Swale: the story of the
barge building village of Conyer.
Meresborough Books. Rainham. 1978.
3,12,22,23.

SMITH, Peter C.
Heritage of the Sea.
(Includes seven ships with Medway connections).
Balfour Publications. 1974.
4,11.

SOUTH-EASTERN AND CONTINENTAL STEAM PACKET
COMPANY.
Deed of settlement of the South-Eastern
and Continental Steam Packet Company.
Printed by C. Roworth. London. (1845).
11.

STREATER, Ronald A.
British short sea fleets,by R.A. Streater
and R.W. Jordan.
Marinart Canterbury. 1975.
5,11.

Cross-Channel Ferries from Kent.
2nd edition,edited by R.A. Streater.
Marinart. Canterbury. 1978.
3,5,6,11,13.

Ships and Folkestone.
Marinart. Canterbury. 1973.
6,7.

THORNTON, Edward Charles Bexley.*
South coast pleasure steamers.
1962. 12. Prescot.
1969. 19. Stephenson and Sons.

THORNTON, Edward Charles Bexley.*
Thames coast pleasure steamers.
T. Stephenson and Sons. Ltd. Prescot. 1972.
4,7,8,9,11,20,26,27.

UGLOW, Captain Jim.
Sailorman:a bargemasters' story. (The Author
was born in Gillingham and served on sea-going
barges from Rochester and Greenhithe).
Conway Maritime Press. 1975.
4,9,11,12,15,20,26,27.

VILLIERS, Alan John.
The Cutty Sark, last of a glorious era.
Hodder and Stoughton. 1953.
11.

WILLMOTT, Frank G.
Cement, mud and muddies: a history of APCM
Barges. Photography by Alan Cordell.
(River Industries of the River Medway).
Meresborough Books. Rainham. 1977.
1,3,4,5,7,8,9,11,15,20,23,25,26,27,30.

WOOD, David.
Powder barge W ↑ D.
Wareham and West Country Barge Group of SSBR.
Twickenham. 1977.
(Barges belonged to the Waltham Abbey Royal
Gunpowder Factory, transporting explosives
to and from Faversham, Gravesend, Woolwich etc.)
11.

SHOOTER'S HILL

ELLISTON ERWOOD, Frank Charles.*
Road works at Shooters Hill, Kent, 1816.
Reprinted from Woolwich and District Antiquarian
Society Reports. 1947.
1,2,8,11,12,18.

SHOREHAM

DANKS, William.
The Diary of William Danks of East Down, Shoreham 1806 - 1810. MSS and another copy-typescript.
(Agricultural diary).
16.

REID, Richard.
Shoreham, Kent: a study of a village.
The Shoreham Society. 1975.
1,2,3,11,16,23.

SHOREHAM SOCIETY.
A walk through Shoreham, Kent:a Kentish village
in European Architectural Heritage Year.
Shoreham Society. 1975.
11.

SHOREHAM WOMEN'S INSTITUTE.
Shoreham, Kent:a village booklet.
Shoreham Women's Institute. 1975.
2,16.

SHORNCLIFFE See SANDGATE.

SHORNE

ALLEN, Arthur F.
Shorne Village:a brief historical development.
Shorne Local History Group. 1976.
9.

GRAVESHAM BOROUGH COUNCIL:PLANNING OFFICE.
Chestnut Green, Shorne, conservation area.
Gravesham Borough Council.1976.
11.

SMITH, Victor T.C.
Shorn(e)Mead Fort.
K.D.R.G. 1977.
9,32.

SHORTLANDS

DENCE, Thomas.*
Reminiscences of a Septuagenarian.
(The author was a Bromley businessman
who gave the money for the East Cliff
Pavilion at Herne Bay. He lived at"Kingsbury",
Shortlands).
Sir Joseph Causton and Sons. London. 1911.
11,12.

SIDCUP

AMBROSE, Hilary.
Development of Sidcup since 1840. Thesis.
1971.
1.

BENNETT, Walter.
Sidcup Cricket Club, 1877 - 1977: a history
and reference book, Compiled by W. Bennett
on behalf of the Club. (250 copies printed).
Sidcup Cricket Club. 1977.
1,11.

BEXLEY, LONDON BOROUGH COUNCIL.
The Sidcup Study.
London Borough of Bexley, Borough Engineer's
Department. 1974.
1.

CHISLEHURST URBAN DISTRICT COUNCIL.*
Chislehurst and Sidcup, Kent:the official guide.
E.J. Burrows and Co. Cheltenham. 1954 etc.
5,11,   1954 etc.
1,2,   1951 - 59.
4.   1951

ENVIRONMENT, Department of the.
A20 Sidcup by-pass proposals: Swanley by-
pass to Kemnal Corner.
Department of the Environment. 1974.
2.

LEWIN, Thomas Herbert.
The Lewin Letters:a selection from the
correspondence and diaries of an English
Family, 1756 - 1884. Vols. I and II.
Constable. 1909.
1.

NUNNS, B.N.
Frognal, Sidcup, Kent.
Typescript. 1974.
2.

Notes on early Sidcup.
Duplicated typescript. 1972.
1,2.

SIDNEY, SIR PHILIP
(1554 - 1586) OF PENSHURST

ADDLESHAW, Percy.*
Sir Philip Sidney.
Methuen. 1909.
11,12.

BILL, A.H.*
Astrophel.
Cassell 1938.
12.

BOAS, Frederick S.*
Sir Philip Sidney.
Staples. 1955.
4,12.

BOURNE, H.R. Fox.*
Sir Philip Sidney.
Putnam, 1914.
12.

BUXTON, John.*
Sir Philip Sidney and the English
Renaissance.
Macmillan. London . 1954.
4,12.

DENKINGER, E.M.*
Philip Sidney.
Allen and Unwin. 1932.
12.

LLOYD, Julius.
The life of Sir Philip Sidney.
Longman, Green. 1862.
23.

MUIR, Kenneth.*
Sir Philip Sidney.
British Council and National Book League. 1960.
12.

STODDART, Anna M.*
Sir Philip Sidney:servant of God.
Blackwood. 1894.
11,12,19.

SYMONDS, J.A.*
Sir Philip Sidney.
n.d.
12.

THOMSON, J. Radford.
Sir Philip Sidney. (New Biographical Series No.25)
The Religious Tract Society. n.d.
16.

WILLARD, Barbara.*
He fought for his Queen (Sir Philip Sidney).
Heinemann 1954.
12.

WILSON, Mona.*
Sir Philip Sidney.
Duckworth. 1931.
11,12.

ZOUCH, Thomas.*
Memoirs of the life and writings of Sir Philip
Sidney.
Wilson. 1808.
12.

SISSINGHURST

ASSOCIATION OF FRIENDS OF SISSINGHURST SCHOOL.
Presenting Sissinghurst:a village guide and
quiz-book. Jubilee Year 1977.
Association of Friends of Sissinghurst School.1977.
19.

NICOLSON, Nigel.
Portrait of a marriage.
(That between V. Sackville-West and Sir Harold
Nicolson).
Weidenfeld and Nicolson. 1973.
11,16.

Sissinghurst Castle:* an illustrated history.
Printed by Headley Brothers, Ashford, for
Sissinghurst Castle. 1964.
26.

SACKVILLE-WEST, Victoria, (afterwards
Lady Nicolson)
Sissinghurst:a poem.
Hogarth Press 1931, reprinted by National Trust
1972.
23.

SCOTT-JAMES, Anne.
Sissinghurst:the making of a garden. (The
garden at Long Barn, Nr. Knole is also
described).
M. Joseph. 1974.
3,6,8,11,12,15,16,22.

SISSINGHURST CASTLE.
The National Trust. 1973.
8.

SISSINGHURST CASTLE:guide book.
Printed by R.&.R. Clark Ltd. Edinburgh. n.d.
11.

SISSINGHURST CASTLE ESTATE;
Sale Catalogue. 1903.
11.

SMARDEN

ASKWITH, H.G.
The church of St. Michael the Archangel,
Smarden, Kent.
Printed by Geerings, Ashford. 1965.
11.

THE CHURCH OF ST.MICHAEL THE ARCHANGEL,
Smarden.
Pamphlet copied from typewritten text. n.d
11.

HASLEWOOD, Rev. Francis F.*
Memorials of Smarden.
P.P. 1886.
22.

A "SMARDONIAN" pseud.*
The family names of the Weald of Kent,
particularly Smarden.
Ashford Express. 1901.
1,4,7,11,12.

SMUGGLING

CLARK, Kenneth M.
Many a bloody affray:the story of smuggling
in the Port of Rye and district.
Rye Museum. 1968.
11.

Smuggling in Rye and district.
Rye Museum. 1977.
7.

DOUCH, John.
Smuggling - the wicked trade.
Crabwell Publications. 1980.
6,28.

FINN, Ralph.*
The Kent Coast blockade:"the story of the
days when Kentish Smugglers battled with the
men of the Royal Navy".
W.E. White. Ramsgate. 1971.
2,6,7,12,24,28,30.

LAIGLE, Dominique-Odile.
Smuggling in Kent.
A photocopy of a thesis submitted to the
University of Caen, Normandy.
October. 1972.
11.

LAKER, Rosalind.
The Smuggler's bride.
A novel with mention of the Hawkhurst Gang.
R. Hale. 1976.
11.

LAPTHORNE, William H.*
Smuggler's Broadstairs:an historical guide
to the smuggling annals of the ancient town
of Bradstow, illustrated with old views.
Thanet Antiquarian Book Club.
1970   24.
1971   2nd edition revised 11.24.
1977.   24.

NICHOLLS, Frederick F.
Honest thieves:the violent heydey of English
smuggling.
Heinemann. 1973.
7,8,12,30.

PHILLIPSON, David.
Smuggling:a history 1700 - 1970.
David and Charles. 1973.
7.

"THE SEACOCKS": a brief history of the
smugglers known as the Hawkhurst Gang.
Rother Valley Press. 1976.
8,19.

SHORE, Henry Noel. 5th Baron Teignmouth
(1847 - 1926). *
The Smugglers:picturesque chapters in the
history of contraband,by Lord Teignmouth
and Charles G. Harper. Illustrated by
Paul Hardy, by the authors and from old
prints and pictures.   Volume. 2.
Cecil Palmer. 1923.
3,11.

SHORE, Henry Noel. 5th Baron Teignmouth.*
Smuggling days and smuggling ways.
(Reprint of first edition. Cassell, London 1892).
E.P. Publishing. 1972.
6,11,19.

SNARGATE

SHARMAN, Robert Scott.*
Guide to the parish and church of Snargate, Kent.
P.P. (196-?).
11,30.

SNAVE

CAWLEY, David Lewis.
The parish church of St. Augustine, Snave.
Adams, Rye. 1974.
11.

SNODLAND

CARLEY, James.
The Tunbridge Wells, Snodland and Edenbridge
suspension railway. An abortive scheme of
1825 - 6 with notes on two more.
Meopham Publications Committee. 1979.
2,4,6,13,15,23.

FUNNELL, K.J.
Snodland Paper Mills: C. Townsend Hook and
Company from 1854.
C. Townsend Hook and Co. Snodland. 1979.
4,12,23.

GENERAL REGISTER OFFICE.
Census Returns,1841, 1851, 1861, 1871.
Snodland and Paddlesworth.
Microfilm.
23.

KENT COUNTY COUNCIL:PLANNING DEPARTMENT.
Snodland: informal district plan.
K.C.C. 1976.
11,23.

TRADE, DEPARTMENT OF: ACCIDENTS INVESTIGATION
BRANCH.
Piper PA32R (Cherokee Lance) PH-PLY.
Report on the accident at Holly Hill, near
Snodland, Kent on 29th April, 1978.
H.M.S.O. 1979.
11,23.

WELLS, K.A.E.
Holborough Court, Snodland, Kent. (pamphlet).
K.A.E. Wells. Aylesford.1979.
12.

SOCIETIES See ORGANISATIONS.

SOLE STREET

GRAVESHAM BOROUGH COUNCIL:PLANNING DEPARTMENT.
Sole Street informal district Plan.
Gravesham Borough Council. 1975.
9. 1975 and 2nd edition 1976.
11. 1975.

SOUTHBOROUGH

BROWN, M.D.
David Salomons House: catalogue of mementos
M.D. Brown. 1968.
12.

CATALOGUE OF THE COLLECTION OF PICTURES AT
BROOMHILL, KENT.
A.K. Baldwin. 1881
19.

SOUTHBOROUGH Cont'd

GARDNER, Henry.*
Gardner's Penny Guide:Tunbridge Wells,
Tonbridge and Southborough.
Arthur Dee. Southborough n.d.
19.

GENERAL REGISTER OFFICE.
Census Returns. 1841; 1851; 1861; 1871.
Southborough. Photocopy.
23.

KENT COUNTY COUNCIL:PLANNING DEPARTMENT.
Royal Tunbridge Wells and Southborough
Town Map. Part No. XII.
K.C.C. 1958.
11.

SOUTHBOROUGH ROTARY CLUB.
Silver Jubilee Year 1977:Southborough souvenir.
(A history of Southborough and its Societies).
Southborough Rotary Club. 1977.
11,19.

SOUTHBOROUGH SOCIETY.
Townscape survey of Southborough, Kent.
Southborough Society. 1978.
19.

SOUTHBOROUGH TOWN COUNCIL.
Southborough Official guide. Published with
the Authority of Southborough Town Council.
E.J.Burrow and Co. Ltd. Cheltenham.
11,   1975.
3.   1977.

SOUTHBOROUGH URBAN DISTRICT COUNCIL.
Southborough, Kent:the official guide.
E.J. Burrow and Co. Cheltenham.
1939. 8th edition 11.
1973.   7,11.19.

TUCKER, John.
A sermon preached at the consecration of
Southborough chapel by...George, Lord Bishop
of Rochester, on....August 25th, 1830.
J. Hatchard. 1830.
11.

TUNBRIDGE WELLS DISTRICT COUNCIL.
Southborough official guide.
E.J. Burrow and Co. Ltd. (Cheltenham). (1977).
12.

SOUTH DOWNS WAY

JENNETT, Sean.
South Downs Way.
H.M.S.O. 1977.
6.

SOUTHFLEET

SOUTHFLEET PARISH HALLS WORKING GROUP.
Southfleet Parish Community Halls.
Southfleet Parish Halls Working Group. 1976.
5.

SOUTHWARK

SOUTHWARK CATHOLIC DIRECTORY.
Forty-seventh annual publication, 1975.
Forty-eighth annual publication, 1976.
Pyramid Press for Southwark Catholic
Children's Society. 1975 and 1976.
11.

SOUVENIRS

GARRAD, L.S.
A present from......:holiday souvenirs
of the British Isles.
David and Charles. 1976.
13.

OWEL Jessie.*
Tunbridge Ware.
In "The Lathe and its uses" by Elias Taylor.
Lowe   1871.
19.

PINTO, H.*
Tunbridge and Scottish Souvenir Woodware,
by H. and E.R. Pinto.
Bell. 1970.
2,19.

TUNBRIDGE WARE* - an extract from
Chamber's Edinburgh Journal, 1st December, 1894.
17.

SPAS AND MINERAL WATERS
See also TUNBRIDGE WELLS

ALLEN, Benjamin.
The natural history of the chalybeat and purging
waters of England.
S. Smith. 1699.
19.

BOYLE, Robert.
Short memoirs for the natural experimental
history of mineral waters.
Sam Smith. 1684 - 85.
19.

CAREY, George Saville.*
The Balnea:or, an impartial description of all
the popular watering places in England.
W. West etc. 1799.
13,19.

CARR, Richard.
Dr. Carr's medicinal epistles upon several occasions.
Willian Newton. 1714.
19.

GRANVILLE, Augustus Bozzi.*
The Spas of England and principal Seabathing
places. Southern Spas.
Henry Colburn. London. 1841.
11.

A GUIDE TO ALL THE WATERING AND SEA BATHING
PLACES,by the Editor of "The Picture of London".
Longman. 1815.
13.

JORDEN, Edward.
A discourse on natural bathes and mineral waters;
3rd edition.
S. Parker. 1669.
19.

PHILLIPS, Richard. Publisher
Guide to all the watering and sea-bathing places.
Richard Phillips. 1808.
19.

RUTTY, John.
A methodical synopsis of mineral waters...
Wm. Johnston. 1757.
19.

SAUNDERS, William.
A treatise on the chemical history and medicinal
powers of some of the most celebrated mineral
waters.
Wm. Phillips. 1800.
19.

SEARLE, Muriel V.
Spas and watering places.
Midas Books. 1977.
11.

SLARE, Frederick.
An account of the nature and excellent
properties and virtues of the Pyrmont waters,
which are imported in flasks by Mr. Burges
at the Blue Anchor in Fleet Street, Druggist.
1717.
19.

SMITH, Hugh.
A treatise on the use and abuse of mineral waters.
n.d.
19.

SPAS AND MINERAL WATERS Cont'd

YOUNG, Kenneth.
Music's great days in the spas and watering
places.
Mamillan. 1968.
13.

SPELDHURST

MACKINNON, Donald D.
History of Speldhurst.
1902.* H.G. Groves, Speldhurst. 1.8.11.23.
1930. 2nd edition revised by D. James.
                Printed by
        Warren and Son, Winchester. 2,11.

SPORT

BAILY'S HUNTING DIRECTORY 1900 - 1901
with diary and hunt maps.
Vinton and Co. London. 1900.
11.

BAILY'S HUNTING DIRECTORY 1927 - 1928.
with diary and hunt maps, winners,
meetings and placed horses at point-to-point
meetings.
Vinton and Co. London. 1927.
11.

BROWNING, Robert. H.K.
The Herne Bay Golf Club.
Golf Clubs Association. n.d.
30.

CAMPBELL, Sir Guy.
Golf at Prince's and Deal.
(6 - fold plate describes and illustrates
Prince's course at Sandwich)
Newman Neame Ltd. 195-?
11.

CANTERBURY AND DISTRICT FOOTBALL LEAGUE.
Handbook and Directory of Clubs: Season
1974 - 1975.
Canterbury and District Football League. 1974.
3.

CHETWYND, Richard Walter.
The Environs of London: a guide for team and cycle,
by R.W. Chetwynd and others.
Kegan Paul, Trench, Trubner and Company. 1897.
1.

CRICKET See Separate Section

DARTFORD FOOTBALL CLUB.
Official Handbook, 1972 - 1973.
Dartford Football Club. 1972.
5.

DARWIN, Bernard.*
The Sundridge Park Golf Club (Includes a
history of the Club).
Golf Clubs Association. 1927.
2.

DAY, J. Wentworth.*
Inns of Sport.
Naldrett Press for Whitbread and Co. Ltd.
1949. 3.4.15.
1949. 2nd edition. 15,23.

DEBENHAM, Betty.*
Chestfield (Whitstable) Golf Club.
Golf Clubs Association (G.W. May Ltd). (197-?).
11,30,31.

EAMES, Geoffrey.L.
Bromley Hockey Club...notes on the years
1963 - 1978.
Geoffrey L. Eames. 1979.
2.

EDWARDS, J.P.
History of the Petts Wood Sports Association.
P.P. Printed by Ches. F. Thorn and Son Ltd.
Erith. 1976?.
2,11.

EELES, Henry Swanston.*
The Eridge Hunt.
Courier Printing and Publishing Co. Tunbridge Wells.
1936.
11.

FOXLEY, Gladys L.
A history of Bexleyheath Golf Club. 1907 - 1977.
Bexleyheath Golf Club. 1977.
1.

GOLFING IN KENT: a supplementary issue of
"Kent Life", 1979.
South Eastern Magazines Ltd. Larkfield. 1979.
12,13.

GRAVESEND AND NORTHFLEET FOOTBALL CLUB. LTD.
Official handbook. 1973 - 74.
Football Supporters Publications. 1973.
9.

GREATER LONDON AND SOUTH EAST COUNCIL FOR
SPORT AND RECREATION.
Regional recreation strategy: issues report.
Greater London and South East Council for
Sport and Recreation. 1979.
2,11.

GREATER LONDON AND SOUTH EAST SPORTS COUNCIL.*
Water recreation strategy.
Greater London and South East Sports Council. 1971.
24.

HEATH, Edward.
Sailing; a course of my life.
Sidgwick and Jackson. 1975.
24.

HODGSON, R.D.*
An eye to the ball at Littlestone: the rambling
discourse of a phytopsychologist.
Privately printed for the benefit of the
Littlestone Golf Club. Limited edition-350 copies.
1939.
7,11.

HUNT, F.J.
Deal, Walmer and Kingsdown Amateur Rowing Club.
1927 - 1977.
Kent County Printers. 1979.
28.

JARVIS, Margaret Ada.
Captain Webb and 100 years of Channel Swimming.
David and Charles. 1975.
3,6,7,11.

KENT COUNTY AMATEUR SWIMMING ASSOCIATION.
Handbook. 1979.
Kent Amateur Swimming Association. 1979.
4.

KENT COUNTY COUNCIL: EDUCATION DEPARTMENT.
Kent mountain centre, Glyn Padarn,
Llanberis, Caernarvonshire.
K.C.C. 1973.
4.

KENT COUNTY COUNCIL: PLANNING DEPARTMENT.
Kent County Structure Plan.
a) Formal recreation. b) Informal recreation.
d) Water recreation. d) Tourism
(Serial no 10B).
K.C.C. 1975.
3,4,9,11,13,16.

KENT COUNTY FOOTBALL ASSOCIATION.
Official handbook, 1974 - 75.
Kent County Football Association. Canterbury.
9.

KENT COUNTY LAWN TENNIS ASSOCIATION.
Annual handbook, 1973.
Kent County Lawn Tennis Association. 1973.
9,11.

KENT COUNTY PLAYING FIELDS ASSOCIATION.
Handbook...1972 including the 46th Annual
Report and accounts.
Kent County Playing Fields Association.
4.

KENT SCHOOLS FOOTBALL FEDERATION.
Report. 1947 - 48.
Printed by H.S. Evans, Sheerness. (1947).
11.

LEIGH-BENNETT, E.P.
Some Friendly Fairways.
(pp. 9 - 23, Kent Golf Courses).
Southern Railway. c.1925.
11.

MARGATE ELEMENTARY SCHOOLS' FOOTBALL
AND ATHLETIC ASSOCIATION.
Meetings, 1935 - 1939.
MSS
13.

MARGATE ELEMENTARY SCHOOLS' FOOTBALL
LEAGUE.
Accounts and Players. 1913 - 1923. Ms.
13.
Minutes. 1913 - 1932; 1932 - 1934; Ms.
13.

A MASTER OF HOUNDS:being the life story of
Harry Buckland of Ashford by One Who Knows
Him.*
Faber. 1931.
1,7,11,22.

MEDWAY AREA SUNDAY FOOTBALL LEAGUE.
Official handbook, season 1973 - 74.
4.

MEDWAY ATHLETIC CLUB.
Rules and Constitution, 1974.
12.

MEDWAY PORTS AUTHORITY.
Boating on the River:Medway and Swale.
Medway Ports Authority.
1969. 8 1970. 8. 1975. 8.

Notice to Mariners:Water-Ski-ing and
aqua-planing (Notice No.19 of 1973).
Medway Ports Authority. 1973.
4,8.

MEDWAY TOWNS SPORTS ADVISORY COUNCIL.
Handbook.
Prowles Publications Ltd. Ipswich.
1969. 4.
1972-73. 8.

MEDWAY TOWNS TABLE TENNIS LEAGUE.
Official Handbook, 1974 - 75.
Medway Towns Table Tennis League. 1974.
4.

MEDWAY YACHTING ASSOCIATION.
Water-based recreation in the tidal Medway and
the Swale. A study of the likely requirements...
over the 1970's.
Medway Yachting Association. 1970.
4.

MITCHELL, John.
Kentish Waters.
(Fishing Famous Rivers Series).
E.M. Art and Publishing, Peterborough, for
Angling Times. 1965.
1,2,3,4,5,6,7,8,11,19,20,30.

MOORE, Frank L.
History of the West Kent Golf Club, 1916 - 1976,
by F.L. Moore and Alan Newing. (8p pamphlet).
West Kent Golf Club. (1976).
2.

PARSONS, John.
A fisherman's year:fishy adventures in England
and New Zealand. (Includes the Rivers Darent,
Medway and Thames, and Romney Marsh).
Collins. 1974.
5.

(POUT, Roger).
History of the Herne United Roller Hockey Club
(by Roger Pout).
Herne United Roller Hockey Club. 1976.
3,30.

RANDALL, J.
Captain Webb: the intrepid Champion Channel
Swimmer.
(Originally published by J. Randall 1875).
Salop County Library. 1975.
6.

RIDING IN KENT:* a complete directory of all
riding facilities in the County.
Addison Press. 1954.
4.

ROCHESTER AND GILLINGHAM HOCKEY CLUB.
Brief history and guide.
Rochester and Gillingham Hockey Club. c.1948.
25.

SAUNDERS, D.K.
The centenary history of the Blackheath
Harriers, by D.K. Saunders and A.J. Weeks-
Pearson. (1869 - 1969).
Blackheath Harriers. (1971).
2,11.

SCARTH-DIXON, William.*
The Tickham Hunt.
The Hunts Association. London. 1931.
11.

SHARPE, J.
The archer's register...1877-78, edited by J.
Sharpe. (Tunbridge Wells pp 9 - 18 + Kentish
clubs).
Adnitt and Naunton. 1878.
19.

SOUTHERN WATER AUTHORITY
Fishing available in the Kent area on payment for
permit.
Southern Water Authority.1st May 1975.
4.

Fishing in the South.
Southern Water Authority. 1979.
4.

STOKER, Hugh.*
Sea Fishing in Kent.
E.M.Art Publishing. Peterborough. 1965.
1,2,4,5,6,7,8,11,12,15.
1967 Benn Ltd. 30.
1973 Benn Ltd. 22.

TEICHMAN, Oskar.*
Black Horse Nemo, and other memories.
(Including childhood and youth at "Sitka",
Chislehurst - and West Kent point-to-point).
P. Davies. 1957.
1,2,7.

TEMPLE. C.
Jogging for fitness and pleasure.
(The author lived in Folkestone).
Sunday Times. 1977.
7.

THAMES BARGE SAILING CLUB.
Journal 1971 - 72 Winter.
4.

1977 Jubilee. Thames Sailing Barge and
Smack Match, 4th June,1977.
Souvenir Programme. 1977.
11.

THAMES CONSERVANCY BOARD.
Welcome to the Thames (Regulations and hints on
boating on the River Thames)
1961.
4.

THANET SAILING WEEK, 1974.
Programme.
13.
THE TICKHAM FOXHOUNDS,1950:official handbook.
M. Page. (1950).
11.

SPORT Cont'd

TRIGGS, Roger.
Gillingham Football Club.
(Local history Series No.7).
Gillingham Public Library. 1973.
4,6,11,25.

UNIVERSITY OF KENT:FACULTY OF SOCIAL SCIENCES.
Leisure pursuits in Kent 1850 - 1914.
Group research project, 1973. Completed as
part of the course on aspects of the economic
and social history of Kent in the Faculty
of Social Sciences. Includes horse racing
and Cricket. Duplicated typescript.
University of Kent.at Canterbury. 1973.
11.

VENABLES, Bernard*
Guide to angling waters (South East England).
(pp.36 - 39, Kentish Waters).
Daily Mirror. 1954.
11.

WACHER, John.
Pleasures without change.
(Canterbury author's sporting memories).
Sylvan Press. London. (1946).
3.

WHITSTABLE YACHT CLUB:
Official Handbook, 1972.
G.W. May (1972).
11.

SPRINGHEAD

HARKER, Sydney R.
Vagniacae:the Roman town at Springhead.
Gravesend Historical Society. (1970?).
11.

THE SPRINGHEAD JOURNAL.
Published by the Gravesend Historical Society.
No.1. Spring 1968 - in progress. 4.
Nos. 1 - 3. Spring,Summer and Winter. 1968. 11.

STANFORD-NEAR-ASHFORD.

SPICER, Robert H.
I've seen, said the Stour
(on Stanford-near-Ashford).
Tim Allard. Stanford. 1977.
3,7.

STANFORD SILVER JUBILEE COMMITTEE.
Elizabeth II Silver Jubilee Year Diary, 1977.
(Stanford Silver Jubilee Committee). 1977.
3.

STANSTED

GENERAL REGISTER OFFICE.
Census Returns 1841, 1851, 1861, 1871.
Stansted.
Microfilm.
23.

STANSTED AND FAIRSEAT SOCIETY.
Stansted and Fairseat:a guide to the
footpaths in the Parish of Stansted.
Stansted and Fairseat Society. (197-?).
11.

STAPLEHURST

KEECH, Gertrude C.*
Staplehurst and the Weald of Kent.
Research Publishing Company. 1965.
12.22.

KENT COUNTY COUNCIL:PLANNING DEPARTMENT.
Staplehurst Village:interim district plan (Draft)
K.C.C. 1974.
12.

WALKER, A.J.
Staplehurst church:some notes on All Saint's
Church, Staplehurst.
Eagle Printing Works. 1938.
12.

STOCKBURY

MAJOR, Alan P.
St. Mary Magdalene, Stockbury, Nr. Sittingbourne,
Kent: a brief history and guide.
Duplicated typescript. (1975?).
20.

PUGH, Christine.*
Stockbury:a regional study in north-east
Kent, by Christine Pugh and Geoffrey E. Hutchings.
The Hill Farm. Stockbury. 1928.
2,3,4,5,7,8,11,12,15,20,21.

STODMARSH

NATURE CONSERVANCY COUNCIL:SOUTH EAST REGION.
Stodmarsh National Nature Reserve.
Nature Conservancy Council (1976?).
3.

STONAR

THE HISTORY OF RICHBOROUGH CASTLE, near
Sandwich with historical notices of the ancient
town of Stonar.
Printed and published by Henry Jones. 1843.
24.

STONE-IN-OXNEY

WEALD OF KENT PRESERVATION SOCIETY.*
Stone-in-Oxney, Kent:a village study.
Printed for the Society by Elvy and Gibbs,
partnership.   1970.
2,4,6,8,11,30.

YEANDLE, W.H.*
Historical notes on the Church of Stone-in-
Oxney, Kent.
Church Army Press. Oxford. 1935.
2.

STONE-NEAR-DARTFORD

GRUBB, Geoffrey Watkins.
The Grubbs of Tipperary.
(Alexander Grubb resided at Stone Castle,
between Dartford and Greenhithe. Description
of Stone Castle).
Mercier Press, Cork.
1972.
5.

STOUR, RIVER

BRADLEY, Arthur Granville.
The rivers and streams of England,
Painted by Sutton Palmer. (Includes River Stour).
A.&.C. Black. 1909.
4.

CANTERBURY NAVIGATION AND SANDWICH HARBOUR COMPANY.
Report made by the Directors of the Canterbury
Navigation and Sandwich Harbour Company to
the Proprietors, at their Second General
Assembly held at the Guildhall, Canterbury on
Tuesday the 6th of December, 1825.
Wood, Printer, Canterbury. 1825.
3.

CANTERBURY TECHNICAL HIGH SCHOOL FOR GIRLS.*
The Pastoral Stour.
Barton Court Technical High School for Girls. 1967.
3,11.

DONALDSON, Christopher William.
Save the Stour and other poems.
Scops Press. 1974.
3,11,23.

GOODSALL, Robert Harold.*
The Kentish Stour.
Cassell. 1953.
2,24,25,30.

KENT RIVER AUTHORITY.
River Stour Study. 6 volumes. (By) Sir
M. Macdonald and Partners, consulting
engineers.
Kent River Authority 1973.   11.
Vol.I only:Summary Report.   3.

River Stour flood control: a summary of the
premiminary flood studies of 1974, contained
in the River Stour Flood Relief Study Report,
(by) Sir M. Macdonald & Partners, consulting
engineers.
Kent River Authority. 1974.
11.

River Stour flood relief studies,(by)Sir
M. Macdonald and Partners, consulting
engineers.
Kent River Authority. 1974.
11.

STOUR NAVIGATION AND SANDWICH HARBOUR.*
Prospectus, sketch of the plan; the
report of the engineer, with the estimates,
and a statement of the revenue calculated
on the trade carried on in 1823.
Wood, printer, Canterbury. 1824.
1,3.

STOURMOUTH

SPURLING, Cuthbert Terence."
Stourmouth church.
C.T. Spurling. 1966.
3.

STOWTING

SMITH, Charles Roach.
On some Anglo-Saxon remains, discovered
at Stowting, in the county of Kent:
in a letter from Charles Roach Smith
to Sir Henry Ellis, Secretary. Read to the
Society of Antiquaries of London on
29th February, 1844.
The Society of Antiquaries of London. 1844.
11.

STROOD
See also MEDWAY TOWNS

BLOOMFIELD, Avril.
Strood: a pictorial history.
Meresborough Books. Rainham. 1977.
1,3,4,5,6,7,8,9,11,12,15,16,19,22,25.

BUCKFIELD, Reginald Sidney, Defendant.
The trial of Reginald Sidney Buckfield;
edited, with a foreword and a note on
crime and insanity, by C.E. Bechofer
Roberts. (a murder which took place at
Strood).
Jarrolds. 1944.
11.

ENVIRONMENT, Department of the.
List of buildings of architectural or
historic interest in Rochester and Strood.
H.M.S.O. July,1969.
25.

LONDON AND MIDDLESEX ARCHAEOLOGICAL SOCIETY.*
Visit of the London and Middlesex Archaeological
Society to Rochester and Strood on Thursday,
26th June,1884.   For the London and Middlesex
Archaeological Society, Nichols and Sons. 1884.
11.

PLOMER, Henry Robert.*
The Churchwardens' accounts of St. Nicholas,
Strood. Parts 1 and 2. 1555 - 1600; and 1603 - 1662;
Churchwarden's accounts at Betrysden, 1515 - 1573,
transcribed by H.R. Plomer (Kent Records Vol.5)
Kent Archaeological Society.Records Branch.
1915 - 28.
1,2,4,5,8,10,11,12,15,17,18, 25(part I)

RIGOLD, S.E.*
Temple Manor, Strood, Kent.
(Ministry of Works Guide Books).
H.M.S.O. 1962.
12,20,25.

SMETHAM, Henry.
C.R.S. and his friends, being personal
recollections of Charles Roach Smith, F.S.A.,
and his friends.*
C.W. Daniel. London. 1929.
3,4,9,12,25.

History of Strood.*
Parrett and Neves, Chatham. 1899.
25.
1978 Limited edition, reprinted from the
Parrett and Neves' edition of 1899.
John Hallewell. Rochester.
3,11,22,23,25.

STROOD WATERWORKS COMPANY.
The Strood Waterworks Souvenir.
The Journal Company. Printers. 1903.
25.

STUDFALL

MOULTON, W.R.
Guide to Lympne Church and Castle, Studfall,
Shepway, West Hythe and Court-at-Street.
F.J. Parsons. (c.1926)
7,11.

STURRY

GUIDE TO THE PARISH CHURCH OF ST.NICHOLAS,STURRY,*
with a short history of the village.
1969.
30.

McINTOSH, Kinn Hamilton.*
Sturry:the changing scene,edited by K.H.
McIntosh and others.
K.H. McIntosh Sturry. 1972.
1,2,3,4,5,6,7,11,12,15,24,30.

(SPARKS, Margaret)
A guide to the parish church of St. Nicholas,
Sturry, with a short history of the village.
(duplicated).
(St.Nicholas Church:Sturry)(1978)
3.

STURRY PARISH MAGAZINE. Vol.18. No.6. June,1910.
Sturry Parochial Church Council. 1910.
3.

THE TOPOGRAPHER FOR THE YEAR 1791, containing
a variety of original articles....Vol.IV,
Nos. XXII - XXVII, January - June,1791.
(pp. 119 - 120. Sturry Court).
Printed for J. Robson. 1791.
11.

SUNDIALS

DANIEL, C. St. J.H.
Sundials:the common vertical in North West Kent.
Institute of Craft Education. 1973.
5.

SUNDRIDGE (Bromley).

DARWIN, Bernard.*
The Sundridge Park Golf Club. (Includes a
history of the Club).
Golf Clubs Association. 1927.
2.

SUNDRIDGE. (Sevenoaks)

BAKER, F.A.*
The story of Sundridge Old Hall (Sevenoaks)
Tinsley. n.d.
16.

SUNDRIDGE (Sevenoaks) Cont'd

BREALEY, R.
Sundridge: a collection of historical information
from various sources (Typescript).
1952.
16.

KNOCKER, Herbert W.*
Evolution of the Holmesdale. No.3 Manor of
Sundridge. (Reprinted from Archaeologia
Cantiana, Vol.44. 1933).
Headley Brothers. Ashford. n.d.
11,16.

SUTTON-AT-HONE

FORDRED, Diana.
St. John the Baptist, Sutton-at-Hone:
a short history, by Diana and Derek Fordred.
P.P. D.&.D. Fordred. 1975.
1,12.

ST. JOHN'S JERUSALEM, Sutton-at-Hone, Kent.
National Trust. (1976).
11.

TALLENTS, Sir Stephen.
St. John's Jerusalem, Sutton at Hone.
(Photocopy).
Sir Stephen Tallents , 1944.
5.

SUTTON VALENCE

BLATCHLEY-HENNAH, Frank Tregory Wolfe.*
A short history of Sutton Valence School.
Kent Messenger. 1952.
1,11,12,30.

SWALE

KENT COUNTY COUNCIL:PLANNING DEPARTMENT.
The Swale: coastal and countryside plan.
A report upon the natural resources of the
Swale and the activities within the area,
which could form the basis from an
Informal Local Plan. Approved by the
K.C.C. as Local Planning Authority on the
14th February,1974 for the purpose of
public consultations.
K.C.C. 1974.
11.

MEDWAY PORTS AUTHORITY.
Boating on the River: Medway and Swale.
Medway Ports Authority.
1969.   8.   1970.   8.   1975.   8.

Notice to Mariners: water ski-ing
and aqua-planing. (Notice No. 19 of 1973)
Medway Ports Authority. 1973.
4,8.

MEDWAY YACHTING ASSOCIATION.
Water-based recreation in the tidal Medway
and the Swale. A study of the likely
requirements for yachting facilities
over the 1970s...and of what can be done
to provide them.
Medway Yachting Association. 1970.
4.

STANFORD, Edward Ltd. Publishers.
Coloured charts for coastal navigation.
(Edited by Captain O.M. Watts). No.8. The
River Medway and The Swale. New edition.
Corrected to November. 1974.
Stanford Maritime Ltd. 1974.
4.

Stanford's Harbour Guide: River Medway and
the Swale, Edited by Captain F.S. Campbell.
Stanford Maritime Ltd.
1975.
1,8,9,11,12,15,20,25,26,27.

SWALECLIFFE

GOODSALL, Robert Harold.*
Whitstable, Seasalter and Swalecliffe.
Cross and Jackman. Canterbury. 1938.
17,19,30,31.

SWANLEY

ARNETT, Kathleen.*
St. Paul's School, Swanley. 1862 - 1962.
St. Paul's School. Swanley. 1863.
1,5,11.

BALLS, Horace J.
Historical notes on Swanley Village.
Typescript. Photocopy.
June, 1974.
16.

DRURY, M.*
A socio-economic study of Swanley Junction,
1865 - 1965. Typescript. Photocopy.
(Project for Teachers' Certificate).
1966.
16.

ROBSON, I.S.
The story of the Little Boys.
Homes for Little Boys:Farningham and
Swanley,Kent. 5th edition. (1910).
5.

SWANLEY OFFICIAL GUIDE.
Forward Publicity Ltd., Carshalton, Surrey. 1974.
16.

UNITED REFORMED CHURCH, CHRIST CHURCH SWANLEY.
1878 - 1978.
Tartan Printing Company Ltd. Dartford.1978.
5.

SWANSCOMBE

ROYAL ANTHROPOLOGICAL INSTITUTE: SWANSCOMBE
COMMITTEE.*
The Swanscombe skull: a survey of research
on a Pleistocene site, edited by C.D.
Ovey, with new studies...and some earlier
studies (1937 - 61) reprinted.
Royal Anthropological Institute. 1964.
9.

SMITH, Reginald Ashley.
Stratification at Swanscombe: report on the
excavations made on behalf of the British
Museum and H.M. Geological Survey, by Reginald
A. Smith and Henry Dewey. Read to the Society
of Antiquaries of London on 17th April, 1913.
Extracted from Archaeologia Vol. LXIV, 1913 .
11.

SYDENHAM

PULLEN, Doris E.
Inscriptions copied from the tombstones
of St. Bartholomew's Church, Sydenham.
Unpublished typescript. 1976.
18.

SYDENHAM: from hamlet - part of Lewisham, Kent -
to surburban town - Part of London.
Printed for D.E.Pullen by F.H.Brown,Burnley.1976.
2,11,18.

READ, Joan.
Read about Sydenham Wells.
J. Read. 1977.
2,18.

TANKERTON

KIRBY, O.I.
Tankerton Estate: twenty-one years of development, 1890 - 1911: the origins, aims and
achievements of a property company.
A photocopy of a thesis. n.d.
11,30.

TANKERTON Cont'd

WHITSTABLE AND TANKERTON PUBLICITY COMMITTEE.*
Whitstable, Tankerton and District: on the
Kent Coast in the Garden of England, Compiled
by Arthur Collar.
E.J. Burrow & Co. Cheltenham. 1939. 8th edition.
7,31.

Whitstable, Tankerton and District. The Official
guide. Published by authority of the Committee.
E.J. Burrow and Co. Cheltenham.
1952. 10th edition. 1.4.11.15.31.
1953. 11th edition. 31.

WHITSTABLE URBAN DISTRICT COUNCIL.
The "Borough" Guide to Whitstable and Tankerton-
on-Sea, including a motoring and cycling map
of the district.
E.J. Burrow and Co. Cheltenham.
1910 and 1912. 12.

TELEVISION

INDEPENDENT BROADCASTING AUTHORITY.
Applications for the television franchise for
the South and South East England area.
Independent Broadcasting Authority. Southampton.
1980.
12.

TENTERDEN

THE ASHFORD ADVERTISER AND RIDER.
Ashford 1974: guide to the Borough of Ashford
and Tenterden.
The Ashford Advertiser and Rider. Ashford. 1974.
11.

DIXON, Alan G.
Stockbook: the locomotives and stock
of the Kent and East Sussex railway.
Tenterden Railway Company. (1977?)
11,15.

DUNCAN, Leland Lewis.*
Kentish Monumental Inscriptions at Tenterden,
edited by L.L. Duncan.
Kent Archaeological Society. 1919.
1,3,8,11,12,14,15,17,22.

ELLIS-MACE, J.
Notes on old Tenterden and the Four Churches.*
W. Thomson. 1902.
2,7.

Old Tenterden Road, by J. Ellis-Mace, Esq.,
at the Ashford Road Mutual Improvement Society.
(Reproduced from Thomson's Almanac and
Local Directory for 1891).
W. Thomson. 1891.
11.

ENVIRONMENT, Department of the
List of buildings of special architectural
or historic interest: Tenterden. Kent.
H.M.S.O. 1972.
7,11.

FURLEY, Robert.*
The early history of Tenterden, bound with
Hales, R. Cox. "Brief notes on the Hales
family".
Kent Archaeological Society. (1884).
11.

GREEN, Simon B.
The Kent and Sussex Railway guide.
Tenterden Railway Company. 1974.
11.

KENT AND EAST SUSSEX RAILWAY.
Union Publications. London. 1963.
15,19.

KENT COUNTY COUNCIL:PLANNING DEPARTMENT.*
Tenterden explored.
K.C.C. 1967.
30.

KENTISH EXPRESS
Guide and Directory to Ashford, Romney Marsh,
Tenterden and Elham Districts.
Kentish Express. Ashford. (1923?).
3.

ST.MILDRED'S PARISH CHURCH, TENTERDEN.*
1929.
19.

SMITH, John L.*
Rails to Tenterden.
Lens of Sutton, Surrey. 1967.
1,2,3,4,6,7,8,9,11,12,15,19.

TENTERDEN BOROUGH COUNCIL.
Borough of Tenterden, 1449 - 1974. Souvenir
Programme of the Commemoration Week, 24th -
31st March, 1974.
Adams of Rye, 1974.
11.

Tenterden Town Guide, 1972 - 73.*
Tenterden Borough Council. 1973.
22.

THE TENTERDEN TRUST.
Newsletter No.2. December 1971.
11.

TESTON

BALSTON, John N.
Teston bridge:an appreciation.
(Typewritten material).
John N. Balston. 1978.
11,12.

BARHAM COURT, TESTON,MAIDSTONE, KENT:
Sale of the valuable contents of the residence...
by auction on April 16th, 17th and 18th,1975, by
Finn Kelsey, Collier and Ashenden. 1975.
11.

SEVERN, Joan.
The Teston story: Kent village life through
the ages.
Rufus Fay Publications. Teston. 1975.
3,4,5,6,8,11,12,13,15,16,22,24,25,28.

TESTON PARISH MAGAZINE.
March 1953 - February 1964. Bound volume.
May 1962 - November 1967. Bound volume.
(together with "The Sign" and Rochester
Diocesan News.
11.

THE TESTON SYSTEM OF FARMING...*
together with the Courland method of making
clover....
(Sir Charles Middleton, afterwards Lord Barham,
answers questions concerning his farm).
W. Wildash. Rochester. 1816.
11,12.

TESTON VILLAGE APPRAISAL GROUP.
Teston:an appraisal.
Teston Village Appraisal Group. 1976.
11.

TEYNHAM

ELLISTON-ERWOOD, Frank Charles.*
Teynham Church: architectural notes.
Reprinted from Archaeologia Cantiana,
Vol. XXXV. 1921.
Mitchell,Hughes and Clarke. 1921.
20.

PURSER, Rev. W.C.B.
A short account of the Church of St. Mary,
Teynham.
1935.
12.

TEYNHAM. Cont'd

SELBY, Elizabeth.*
Teynham manor and Hundred, 798 - 1935.
Headley Brothers. Ashford. 1935.
26.

THAMES, RIVER

ALLENDALE, John.
Sailorman between the wars: being the journal
of a Thames, Medway and coastal bargeman.
John Hallewell.Publications,Rochester.1978.
3,4,5,11,12,15,22,23,25.

ANDERSON, Jo.
Anchor and hope.
(Reminiscences of the Thames Riverside).
Hodder and Stoughton. 1980.
4,5.

BENHAM, Hervey.
The Stowboaters:
the sprat fishing industry in the Thames
Estuary.
Essex County Newspapers Ltd. Colchester. 1977.
12.

BENNETT, A.S.
Us bargemen.
Meresborough Books. Rainham. 1980.
11,12.

BRANCH-JOHNSON, William.*
English Prison Hulks.
C. Johnson.
1957. 8,11,15,25.
1970. Revised Edition. Phillimore. 11,12.

BRIGGS, Martin Shaw.
Down the Thames.
Herbert Jenkins. 1949.
11.

BROODBANK, Sir Joseph.
History of the Port of London.
David O'Connor. London. 1921.
9.

CORDELL, Alan.
Old postcard views from the Walter
Dowsett Collection, compiled by Alan Cordell,
Peter Ferguson and Alan Pearsall.
No.1. River Thames.
Nautical Pictorial. 1976.
9,11,23.

CRACKNELL, Basil Edward.*
Portrait of London River:the tidal Thames
from Teddington to the Sea.
R. Hale. 1968.
11.

DAVIS, Dennis, J.*
The Thames sailing barge: her gear and
rigging.
David and Charles; and International
Marine Publishing Company. 1970.
9,11,23.

DICKENS, Charles.
Dickens dictionary of the Thames, from its
source to the Nore, 1893: an unconventional
handbook with maps. (Compiler was eldest
son of the novelist Charles Dickens). Covers
places, activities and organisations for the
whole length of river.
Facsimile reprint of 1893 edition.
C. Dickens and Evans, London. 1893.
11.

DOXAT, J.
The living Thames: the restoration of a great
tidal river.
Hutchinson Benham. 1977.
5,9,20,26,27.

DUMPLETON, Bernard.
Story of the Paddlesteamer (includes
Medway and Thames paddlesteamers).
Colin Venton. Melksham. 1978.
11,27.
Excerpts from "The Story of the Paddlesteamer"
4.

FEARNSIDE, William Gray.*
The Thames and Medway: a series of 80 splendid
engravings from drawings by Tombleson, with
interesting historical descriptions by
W.G. Fearnside.
Thomas Holmes. (183-?).
4,7,11.

FINCH, Roger.
Coals from Newcastle:the story of the
North East Coal Trade in the days of sail.
Terence Dalton. Lavenham. 1973.
11.

FINDLAY, Alexander George.*
A handbook for the navigation of the different
channels of Thames and Medway and the coast
between Folkestone and Orfordness.
R.H. Laurie. 1887.
1,8,11,12.

FREESTON, EWART CECIL.
Modelling Thames sailing barges, by Ewart C.
Freeston and Bernard Kent; with an historical
introduction by Richard Hugh Perks.
Conway Maritime Press. 1976.
9,11.

GOODSALL, Robert Harold.
The Widening Thames.
1965*Constable. 9.26.
1976 Reprint of the 1965 edition by John
       Hallewell, Rochester. 8.25.

GREAT BRITAIN, Laws etc. (Geo.III).
An Act for the better regulation and government
of pilots licensed by the Corporation of
Trinity of Deptford Strand in the County of Kent,
and to prevent mischiefs and annoyances upon
the river of Thames below London Bridge. 1786.
12.

GREAT BRITAIN, Laws etc. (Eliz.II)
Thames Barrier and flood prevention Act 1972.
Chapter XLV.
H.M.S.O. 1972 (1974 reprint).
9,11.

Thames Conservancy Act. 1972. Chapter XLVI.
H.M.S.O. 1972.
4.

GREATER LONDON COUNCIL.*
Taming the Thames:protecting London from
flooding. Amended edition of the Report
of December 1969.
Greater London Council. January,1970.
4.9.

Thames-side conference: Tower Bridge to
Tilbury: an examination of the strategic
possibilities. A report...for Public
consultation.
Greater London Council. 1974.
5,9,11,

GREATER LONDON COUNCIL:DEPARTMENT OF PUBLIC
HEALTH ENGINEERING.
Thames flood protection. Thames Barrier,by
R.W. Horner.
Reproduced from the "Journal of the Institution
of General Technician Engineers, Volume 85. No.2.
February,1974.
4.

Thames Flood Defences.
Greater London Council. (1977).
4.

HALL, Samuel Carter.
The book of the Thames from its rise to its fall,
by Mr and Mrs. S.C. Hall. New edition.
J.S. Virtue and Co. (1877?).
9,11.

HALLAM, W.B.
Blowfire:a history of the Alexandra Towing
Company Limited.
Journal of Commerce. 1976.
9.

HARRISON, Jeffery Graham.
The Thames transformed:London's river
and its waterfowl,by J.G. Harrison and P. Grant.
Andre Deutsch. 1976.
1,2,4,9,15,20,26,27.

THAMES, RIVER Cont'd

HAY, David.*
The Downs from the sea:Langstone harbour
to the Pool of London, by David and Joan Hay.
Edward Stanford. 1972.
4,7,11,12,19,28.

HOUSING AND LOCAL GOVERNMENT:Ministry of.
Pollution of the Tidal Thames: report of the
Departmental Committee on the effects of
heated and other effluent and discharges
on the condition of the tidal reaches of the
River Thames.
H.M.S.O. 1961.
4.

IRVING, John*
Rivers and creeks of the Thames estuary.
Sunday Review,9 King Street,Covent Garden.1927
11.

IRWIN,John.
Sweet Themmes:a chronicle in prose and verse,
edited by John Irwin and Jocelyn Herbert,
with a foreword by W.J. Brown.
Max Parrish. 1951.
11.

JONES, Rosemary.
Steam packet trips from London and their
effect on Gravesend between 1810 and 1860.
MS. Thesis. University of Southampton. 1978.
9.

LINNEY, A.G.
The lure and lore of London's River.
Sampson, Low and Marston. (1932).
11.

The peepshow of the Port of London.
Sampson, Low and Marston (1930).
9,11.

MARCH, Edgar James.
Spritsail barges of the Thames and Medway.
David and Charles. 1973.
1,20,25.

MAXWELL, Donald.
A pilgrimage of the Thames (with line
drawings by the Author).
(Author lived in Rochester and East Farleigh).
Centenary Press. 1932.
4,9,11,25.

NICHOLSON, R. Publisher.
Nicholson's Guide to the Thames from source
to sea. 2nd edition.
Nicholson Publications. 1974.
15,27.

OSMOND, Laurie.
The Thames flows down.
Oxford University Press. 1957.
11.

PENNEY, Stephen.*
Concise navigating directions for the
River Thames, including all the pools, reaches,
and channels from London Bridge to the
South Foreland and Orfordness and the English
Channel to Beachey Head.
J.D. Potter. 1896.
1,9.

PERKS, Richard Hugh.
Sprits'l:a portrait of sailing barges and
sailormen, written in collaboration with
Patricia O'Driscoll and Alan Cordell.
(The author lives near Faversham. North
Kent barge building centres are given).
Conway Maritime Press. 1975.
3,4,9,11,12,15,20,22,25.

PORT OF LONDON AUTHORITY.
Annual report and accounts, year ended
31st,December. 1972.
Port of London Authority. 1973.
9.

PUDNEY, John.
London's docks.
Thames and Hudson. 1975.
9.

REYNOLDS, James and Sons. Publishers.
Reynolds new chart of the Thames Estuary,
engraved by Ralph Welland and compiled from the
new Ordnance and Admiralty Surveys. Scale 1" =
2 nautical miles; Size 24" x 24". Also includes
map of the River Thames from Gravesend to
London. Scale 1" = 1 nautical mile;
Size 4" x 20".
James Reynolds and Sons. London. 1887.
11.

ROBERTS, A.W.*
Coasting bargemaster.
E. Arnold. 1949.
4,11,15.

ROLT, T.*
The Thames from mouth to source.
Batsford. 1951.
9.

THE ROYAL RIVER:the Thames from source to
sea, descriptive, historical, pictorial.
Cassell. 1895.
11.

THE ROYAL SOCIETY.
A discussion on problems associated with
the subsidence of South Eastern England,
26th - 27th May, 1971. Organised by K.C.
Bunham and D.A. Gray.
Contents include The Thames Barrier.
The Royal Society. London. 1972.
4.

SAMPSON, Mrs. P.M.
Social provision in the nineteenth century for
the members of the Company of Watermen and
Lightermen with special reference to the Almshouses
at Penge.
Thesis;photocopy of typescript.
(1974).
2.

SHEPHERD-THORN, E.R.
South East England and the Thames:a field
guide, by E.R. Shepherd-Thorn and J.J. Eymer.
Geo.Abstracts Limited.Norwich. 1977.
5.

SHRAPNEL, Norman.
A view of the Thames.
Collins. 1977.
9,11.

SMITH, Cicely Fox.
Sailor Town days.
(Ports on the River Thames, includes Deptford
and Gravesend etc., Kent. pp. 76 - 102)
2nd edition. Methuen. 1924.
11.

SMITH, Reginald Anthony.
The High Terrace of the Thames:a report on
excavations made on behalf of the British
Museum and H.M. Geological Survey in 1913,
by R.A. Smith and Henry Dewey. Read to the
Society of Antiquaries of London on April
2nd, 1914.
Extracted from Archaeologia Vol. LXV.
The Society of Antiquaries of London. 1914.
11.

SOUTHERN WATER AUTHORITY.
Thames tidal flood defences:do you know?
Southern Water Authority, Worthing. (1975?).
3.

SPURRELL, F.C.J.
Early sites and embankments on the Margins
of the Thames Estuary.
Reprinted from Archaeological Journal Vol.XLII.
1866.
9.
Anglebooks. 1973. 1.

STANFORD, Edward Limited. Publisher.
Stanford's Chart of the Lower Thames -
Richmond to the Nore. New edition. Scale -
1 sea mile = 2½"; Size 37" x 27".
Edward Stanford Limited. 1973.
11.

THAMES, RIVER Cont'd

STANFORD, Edward Limited. Publisher.
Stanford's Chart of the Thames Estuary,
initially prepared under the supervision
of Captain O.M. Watts. Scale 2 sea miles
= 1"; Size 27" x 28".
Stanford Maritime Limited. 1975.
11.

STEWART, Bertram.
The Library and the picture collection
of the Port of London Authority.
Richards Press. 1955.
9.

TEMPEST, Paul.
Down stream to Greenwich:the heritage and
future of London river. A guide to the
river from Westminster to Greenwich and
a guide to Greenwich itself by Paul Tempest.
Conway Maritime Press. 1975.
11.

THAMES BARGE SAILING CLUB.
Journal. 1971 - 72. Winter.
4.

1977 Jubilee. Thames Sailing Barge and
Smack Match, 4th June,1977.
Souvenir Programme. 1977.
11.

THAMES CONSERVANCY BOARD.
Welcome to the Thames (Regulations and hints
on boating in the River Thames).
Thames Conservancy Board. 1961.
4.

THAMES INFORMATION CENTRE.
Handbook of Thames Information:register of
boats, boatyards, hirers, clubs, organisations,
inns, hotels, locks, tide tables.....
Thames Information Centre. 1977.
11.

Index of Information.
Thames Information Centre (1977).
9.

Thames Information Index. 1978.
Thames Information Centre. 1978.
9,11.

THAMESIDE DEVELOPMENT BOARD.
Thameside:Britain's largest workshop.
Thameside Development Board. 1976.
1.

THAMES SURVEY COMMITTEE.*
Effect of polluting discharges on the Thames
estuary:the reports of the Thames Survey
Committee and the Water Pollution Research
Laboratory. (Water Pollution Paper No.12).
H.M.S.O. 1964.
4,5,9.

THOMPSON, A.G.
The Thames and all that:a history of the
river.
General Steam Navigation Company. (1935).
11.

The Thames from Tower to Tilbury.*
Bradley and Son, London. 1939.
11.

THORNTON, Edward Charles Bexley.*
Thames coast pleasure steamers.
Stephenson and Son, Prescot. 1972.
4,7,8,9,11,20,26,27,

TOMBLESON, W.
Panoramic Map of the Thames and Medway.
J. Reynolds. (183-?).
11.

TOMLINSON. H.M.
London River.
Cassell. Popular edition 1925.
9.

TRADE AND INDUSTRY, Department of:
ACCIDENTS INVESTIGATION BRANCH.
Owl Racer 65 - 2G - AYNS:report on the
accident at Greenwich Reach, River Thames
...on 31st May, 1971.
H.M.S.O. 1974.
11.

UGLOW, Captain Jim.
Sailorman:a bargemasters' Story.
(Author was born in Gillingham and served on
seagoing barges from Rochester and Greenhithe).
Conway Maritime Press. 1975.
4,9,11,12,15,20,26,27.

WHEELER, Alwyne.
The Tidal Thames:the history of a river and its
fishes.
Routledge. 1979.
4,9.

WILSON, Charles. Publisher.*
Sailing directions for the rivers
Thames and Medway...
Charles Wilson. 1881.
2,15.

WILSON, W. Eric.
The pilot's guide to the Thames Estuary
and the Norfolk Broads, Compiled by W.E.
Wilson and D. Branson.
Imray, Laurie, Norie and Wilson. 1949.
25.

WOOD, David.
Powderbarge W ⇧ D Wareham and West Country
Barge Group of SSBR Twickenham. 1977.
(The Barges belonged to the Waltham Abbey
Royal Gunpowder Factory, transporting explosives
to and from Faversham, Gravesend, Woolwich, etc.)
11.

WYLLIE, W.L.
London to the Nore, by W.L. and M.A. Wyllie.
Macmillan. n.d.
25.

THAMESMEAD

JONES, Margery R.
Thamesmead: a thesis.
P.P. 1976.
1.

ST CLAIR, Steve.
Thamesmead Social Survey by Steve St. Clair
and Angela Dines.
(Thamesmead is sited on part of the Plumstead-
Erith Marshes).
Greater London Council. 1975.
11.

THEATRE

CANTERBURY CRICKET WEEK:* an authentic
narrative of the origin and career of the
institution, including the programmes of the
"Old Stagers" performances...Vol.I.
Matches recorded. 1839 - 1851.
William Davy, Canterbury. 1865.
1,3,4,11.

DAVEY, Peter.*
Chronicles of the old country theatres of
Southern England.
(Photostat copy of the Folkestone section).
n.d.
7.

DAWSON, Giles E.*
Records of plays and players in Kent,
1450 - 1642, collected and edited by
Giles E. Dawson. Malone Society
Collections, Volume VII.
Malone Society. 1965.
5,23.

ERITH THEATRE GUILD LIMITED.
Erith Playhouse 1973.
1.

GAGE, W.L.
Churchill Theatre,Bromley. Case study,
commissioned by the Arts Council to
assist in teaching arts administration,
by W.L. Gage and others.
(Duplicated typescript).
Polytechnic of Central London. (1978).
2.

KENT COUNTY DRAMA COMMITTEE.
Kent Drama.
Kent County Drama Committee. January 1980.
4.

THEATRE Cont'd

MORLEY, Malcolm.*
Margate and its theatres. 1730 - 1965.
Museum Press. 1966.
1,3,4,6,7,11,13,15,19,23.

RAND, Duncan.
Theatre in Rochester and the Medway area.
Typescript, photocopied.
1971.
4.

THURNHAM

BEARSTED AND THURNHAM HISTORY BOOK COMMITTEE.
A history of Bearsted and Thurnham.
Bearsted and Thurnham History Book Committee.
1978?.
3,11,12,15,23.

TILMANSTONE

WILLIAMS, Eve.
Tilmanstone parish chest.
Eve Williams. 1974.
3,6.

TITHES

BEARBLOCK, James.
A treatise on tithes: containing an
estimate of every titheable article in
common cultivation...5th edition.
J. Hatchard. Piccadilly. 1818.
11.

BOHUN, W.
A tithing table, showing (by way of analysis)
of what things tithes are not due,
cither by common law, custom, or prescription.
Printed by E.&.R. Nutt and R. Gosling for
J. Brotherton...1732.
11.

CANTERBURY CATHEDRAL ARCHIVES AND LIBRARY.
Canterbury Diocesan Tithe Maps, 1837 - 1852.
(photocopy).
Canterbury Cathedral Archives and Library.
(197?).
J.

CULMER, Rev. Richard.
The Ministers hue and cry, or, a true discovery
of the unsufferable injuries, robberies,
cozenages and oppressions now acted against
Ministers and Impropriators: especially
against Ministers placed by Authority of
Parliament, set forth in a dialogue between
four men. (Minister at Harbledown).
Reverend Richard Culmer, printed by Abraham Miller.
London. 1651.
11.

EVANS, Eric J.
Tithes and the Tithe Commutation Act 1836.
Bedford Square Press for the Standing
Conference for Local History. 1978.
11.

KAIN, Roger J.P.
Tithe surveys and landownership 1975.
Extract from Journal of Historical Geography
1975. Use of computers to analyse tithe
surveys in Kent.
11.

PLUMER, Henry R.
Inhabitants of West Kent, 1487 - 8.
(That is, those paying tithes to Sir John Leigh).
Extracted from the British Archivist Vol.I.
No.5. July, 1913.
11.

TONBRIDGE

ANDREWS, S.M.*
Jane Austen...her Tonbridge connections.
Tonbridge Free Press. 1949.
11,12,19.

BLATCHER, Margaret.
The first four hundred, 1570 - 1970:
a history of the firm of Thomson, Snell and
Passmore, Solicitors, of Tonbridge, Kent.
P.P. 1970.
23.

BOORMAN, Henry Roy Pratt.
Tonbridge Free Press Centenary, by H.R.P.Boorman
and E. Maskell.
Tonbridge Free Press. 1969.
2.

BURROW, E.J. and Company Limited. Publishers
The Borough" guide to Tonbridge and
Tonbridge School. No. 416 of the "Borough"
Pocket Guides.
Ed. J. Burrow and Company Ltd. Cheltenham.
n.d. but 1911 census figures included.
23.

CAHIERS DE LA HAUTE-LOIRE: Revue d'etudes
locales année 1977.
(Tonbridge is twinned with Le Puy).
Archives Departementales, Le Puy. 1977.
23.

CHALKLIN, Christopher William.
Early Victorian Tonbridge; edited by C.W. Chalklin.
Kent County Library. 1975.
1,3,4,6,9,11,12,13,16,19.

CHAPMAN, Frank.
The book of Tonbridge: the story of the town's past.
Barracuda Books Limited. Chesham. 1976.
1,2,3,6,7,11,15,16,19.23.

CROFT-COOKE, Rupert.*
The altar in the loft.
Sequel to "The Gardens of Camelot" and includes
the author's schooldays at Tonbridge School.
Putnam. 1960.
8,11,12,23.

(CROMPTON, N.J.).
Yardley Court, 1898 - 1973.
(Preparatory School of Tonbridge School at
Cage Green, Tonbridge).
(1973).
11.

ENVIRONMENT, Department of the.
List of buildings of special architectural
or historic interest: urban district
of Tonbridge, Kent.
H.M.S.O. 1972.
11.

FLEMING, I. Plant.*
Tonbridge Castle to the year 1322, a paper read
before the Kent Archaeological Society on
July 28th, 1865.
Longmans, Green. 1865.
1,2,11,12.

FULLMER, J.Z.
Humphry Davy and the gunpowder manufactory.
In Annals of Science: a quarterly review...
Vol. 20. No.3. September, 1964. pp. 165 - 194.
23.

GARDNER, Henry.*
Gardner's Penny Guide: Tunbridge Wells, Tonbridge and
Southborough.
Arthur Dee, Southborough. n.d.
19.

GASKIN, Valerie.
A comparison of the library services in
Sittingbourne and Milton Urban District provided by
the local council and the library services in
Tonbridge Urban District provided by the County
Council.
Thesis. Typescript. n.d.
20.

.GENERAL REGISTER OFFICE.
Census Returns 1841, 1851, 1861, 1871.
Tonbridge. Photocopy.
23.

GUNTHER, A.E.
John George Children, F.R.S. (1777 - 1852)
of the British Museum. Mineralogist and
reluctant Keeper of Zoology.
(J.G. Children lived in Tonbridge and
collaborated with Sir Humphry Davy in
fonding the Ramhurst Gunpowder Mills).
British Museum (Natural History). 1978.
23.

HILTON, John Anthony.
Tonbridge Castle:a short history,
compiled by J.A. Anthony.
Tonbridge Design and Print Service for
J. Hilton.Hadlow. (1976).
2,6,8,16,19,23.

Tonbridge tales:a series of occasional
papers on the history of Tonbridge and
the surrounding district. Aspects of
Local History.
J. Hilton,Hadlow. 1977.
2,11,12,19.

HODGE, Gwenyth.
Library services in Tonbridge, 1826 - 1975.
(Duplicated typescript).
Kent County Library, Tonbridge and Malling
Division. 1975.
3,23.

HODGE, Sydney.*
The Methodist Church, East Street,
Tonbridge, 1872 - 1972.
Printed by the Wood Press. 1972.
8,19.

HOOLE, G.P.
Sir Humphry Davy:Tonbridge associations.
P.P. by Bridge Chemicals Ltd. Tonbridge. 1978.
2,11,19,23.

KELLY'S DIRECTORIES LIMITED.
Kelly's directory of Tunbridge Wells,
Southborough, Tonbridge and villages in
the neighbourhood. (Photo-copy of Tonbridge
entries only).
Kelly's Directories Ltd. 1889.
23.

Kelly's directory of Tunbridge Wells,
Southborough, Tonbridge and villages in the
neighbourhood. (Photo-copy of Tonbridge
entries only).
Kelly's Directories Ltd. 1898-9.
23.

Kelly's directory of Tunbridge Wells,
Southborough, Tonbridge and villages in the
neighbourhood. (Photo-copy of Tonbridge
entries only).
Kelly's Directories Ltd. 1909.
23.

Kelly's directory of Tunbridge Wells,
Southborough, Tonbridge and villages in the
neighbourhood. (Photo-copy of Tonbridge
entries only).
Kelly's Directories Ltd. 1919.

Kelly's directory of Tunbridge Wells,
Southborough, Tonbridge and villages in the
neighbourhood. (Photo-copy of Tonbridge
entries only).
Kelly's Directories Ltd. 1929.
23.

Kelly's Directory of Tunbridge Wells,
Tonbridge and neighbourhood.
Kelly's Directories Ltd. 1936.
11.

KENT COUNTY COUNCIL:HIGHWAYS AND TRANSPORTATION
DEPARTMENT.
Tonbridge and Hildenborough District Plan:
transport issues and alternatives.
K.C.C. January,1979.
23.

Tonbridge and Tunbridge Wells transportation
study:report on surveys. October. 1976.
K.C.C. 1976.
19.

KENT COUNTY LIBRARY:TONBRIDGE AND MALLING DIVISION.
Building an extension to Tonbridge Central
Library:some questions and answers.
K.C.L. Tonbridge and Malling Division,March, 1980.
4.

KIDNER, Roger Wakeley.
The Reading to Tonbridge Line.
Oakwood Press. 1974.
2,7,11,15,19.

MORGAN, John Scott.
The Colonel Stephens railways:a pictorial history.
(Colonel Stephens operated from Tonbridge,
Chapter 6).
David and Charles. 1978.
3,7,11,23.

THE NEW TONBRIDGE VIEW BOOK, containing the
beautiful views of the town and places of
interest in the vicinity.
J.G. North, 35 High Street, Tonbridge. (190?).
11,23.

PEPPER, Terence.
Monday's children:portrait photography in the
1920's and 1930's. T. Pepper, Librarian of
the National Portrait Gallery wrote this to accompany
an exhibition of the same title. Kent County
Library brought the exhibition to Tonbridge
because Paul Tanqueray (chief of the five
photographers included) and Hugh Cecil were
both pupils at Tonbridge School.
Impressions Gallery of Photography. 1977.
23.

PERCIVAL, Alicia Constance.
Very superior men:some early Public School
headmasters and their achievements. (Includes
Canterbury and Tonbridge).
C. Knight. 1973.
3.

RIVET, Auguste.
La vie politique dans le Département de la
Hante-Loire de 1815 a 1974.
(Note: Tonbridge is twinned with Le Puy).
Publisher: Archives départementales de la
Hante-Loire. Le Puy.

STEVENS, George.
Directory of Tunbridge Wells, Tonbridge and
neighbourhood. (Photocopy of Tonbridge
entries only).
George Stevens. 1886.
23.

THOMPSON, G.C.W.
Tonbridge.(A dissertation presented for the
Degree of B.A., with Honours in Architectural
Studies, at the University of Newcastle-upon-
Tyne).
1974.
23.

TONBRIDGE AND MALLING DISTRICT COUNCIL.
Tonbridge Castle nature trail.
Tonbridge and Malling District Council. 1977.
4.

TONBRIDGE AND MALLING DISTRICT COUNCIL:
PLANNING DEPARTMENT.
Tonbridge and Hildenborough draft district
plan:project report.
Tonbridge and Malling District Council. 1977.
23.

Tonbridge Conservation Area:a conservation study.
Tonbridge and Malling District Council. 1980.
23.

TONBRIDGE CORONATION COMMITTEE.
Official handbook containing the programme of
festivities for the inhabitants of Tonbridge
arranged by the Tonbridge Coronation Committee
for celebrating the coronation of their
Majesties King George V and Queen Mary, June
22nd, 1911.
Tonbridge Coronation Committee. 1911.
11.

TONBRIDGE OAST THEATRE AND ARTS CLUB.
Centenary exhibition of water-colours and
etchings by Martin Hardie (1875 - 1952)
at Tonbridge Castle. (Catalogue).
(The Artist lived at Tonbridge in Retirement)
Tonbridge Oast and Theatre Arts Club. 1975.
11.

TONBRIDGE SCHOOL.*
Tonbridge School and the Great War...Record of
Services...edited by H.R. Stokoe.
Whitefrians Press, Printers, Tonbridge. 1923.
2.

TONBRIDGE URBAN DISTRICT COUNCIL.*
The Official guide to Tonbridge and district.
Pyramid Press.   1963.
30.

TOWERS, Rev. Johnson.
A sermon preached in St. Antholin's Church, before
the Worshipful Company of Skinners, on...
13th June,1754.   (Tonbridge School was
founded by Sir Andrew Judde in 1553 and
vested in the Skinner's Company of London).
Hitch and Harwes. 1754.
11.

WADMORE, Beauchamp.*
Some details in the history of the Parish
of Tonbridge...
M. Stonestreet, Printer, Tonbridge. (1906).
2.

WADMORE, James Foster.
Tonbridge Castle:notes on its history and
architecture.
Blair and Twort.   n.d.
11.

Tonbridge Priory. Reproduced from Archaeologia
Cantiana, Vol. XIV. 1882.
John Hilton. Hadlow. (1976).
23.

WHEELER, Barnaby.
Dry Hill Park, Tonbridge.
(Part II of a thesis on the Mid-Victorian
Suburban House).
1976.
23.

WILLIAMS, W. (Master of the
Boarding School, Yalding).
A sermon written on the death of Miss
Mary Jeffery of Tonbridge.
Waters and Son. Cranbrook.   1818.
19.

TOVIL

KENT COUNTY COUNCIL:PLANNING DEPARTMENT.
Tovil Informal Local Plan.
K.C.C. 1973.
12.

MAIDSTONE BOROUGH COUNCIL:PLANNING DEPARTMENT.
Tovil draft district plan.
Maidstone Borough Council. Maidstone. 1979.
12.

SIX GENERATIONS OF HAND PAPER MAKERS:
the Green family celebrate 150 years continuous
direction of Hayle Mill.   (J. Barcham Green,
Hayle Mill, Tovil, started by John Green,
born in 1669).
From World's Paper Trade Review. 1960.
4.

TRADE   See   INDUSTRY AND TRADE.

TRANSPORT

BAINES, Derek.
TIP Handbook 1977/78. Transport and Industrial
Preservation:a guide to what, where and when.
Edited, produced and published by Derek Baines.
2nd edition.
Derek Baines. Crawley. 1977.
11.

CANTERBURY CITY COUNCIL:CITY ENGINEER.
Canterbury Transportation Study.
Report on Surveys.
Canterbury City Council and K.C.C. (1976).
3.

CIVIL AVIATION AUTHORITY.
A study of general aviation in the South East of
England: a report to the Civil Aviation Authority
and the Standing Conference on London and
South East regional planning.   Kent airfields
mentioned.
Civil Aviation Authority. 1974.
11.

GARRETT, Richard.*
Cross Channel- transport across the channel:
sea, air and discusses the Channel Tunnel.
Hutchinson. 1972.
7,11.

GREAT BRITAIN, Laws etc. (Eliz.II)
London Transport Act.
H.M.S.O. 1977.
5.

KENT COUNTY COUNCIL:EMPLOYMENT OPPORTUNITIES
OFFICER.
Directory of Overseas Transportation Services
by Sea, Air and Road, operating to and from
places in the County of Kent.
K.C.C.
1973.   2,4,6,11,12,25.
1975.   2nd edition. 11.13.20.

KENT COUNTY COUNCIL:HIGHWAYS AND TRANSPORTATION
DEPARTMENT.
Future of Transport in the Medway Towns.
K.C.C. 1974.
4,25.

Maidstone transportation Study:reports on
surveys.
K.C.C. 1974.
11,12.

Medway Towns Transportation Study. Technical Report.
K.C.C. 1974.
4,11,15.
North West Kent Transportation Study*Report on Surveys.
K.C.C. 1977.
5,9.

Tonbridge and Hildenborough District Plan:
transport issues and alternatives.
K.C.C. January,1979.
23.

Tonbridge and Tunbridge Wells transportation study:
report on surveys, October, 1976.
K.C.C. 1976.
19.

Transport policies and programme Submission for
1975-76(Draft report).   K.C.C. 1974.
4.

Transport policies and programme.
Submission for 1975-76. As submitted to the
Secretary of State for the environment in support
of the allocation of Transport Supplement Grant
for 1975-76, July,1974. Presented by A.D.W. Smith,
County Surveyor, 1974.
K.C.C. 1974.
11.
Transport policies and programme:submission
for 1977-78 accepted by Kent County Council
for submission to the Secretary of State for
the Environment.
K.C.C. 1976.
11.

KENT COUNTY COUNCIL:HIGHWAYS AND TRANSPORTATION
DEPARTMENT - PUBLIC TRANSPORT GROUP.
Public Transport Plan.
K.C.C. 1979 & 1980.
1979/80.   4.11.23.
1980/81.   4.6.12.23.

KENT COUNTY COUNCIL:INDUSTRIAL AND COMMERCIAL
LIAISON OFFICER.
Kent - carries it - international, road, rail,
sea, air.
K.C.C. (1977).
3,5,9,11,12.
4.   1979.

TRANSPORT Cont'd

KENT COUNTY COUNCIL:PLANNING DEPARTMENT.
Kent County Structure Plan report on
transport issues. Supplement relating to Cross-
Channel traffic. (Adopted by the Local Planning
Authority in November,1975 for the purpose
of consultations). Serial no. 4B.
(Supplement).
K.C.C. 1975.
3,4,9,11,13,16.

Kent County Structure Plan.Report on transport
issues. Supplement relating to cross-channel
traffic. (Policies adopted by the Local
Planning Authority in May,1978...)Serial 4B
Supplement.
K.C.C. (1977?)
3,15.

Kent County Structure Plan. Report on transport issues. Adopted...July,1975.(Serial No 4B)
K.C.C. 1976.
3,9,11.

Maidstone Town Centre - Transportation.
Maidstone Borough Council. Maidstone. 1980.
12.

MONOPOLIES COMMISSION.
Cross-Channel car-ferry services: a report on
the supply of certain cross-channel car ferry
services.
H.M.S.O. 1974.
11.

(THE) SOUTH-EASTERN AND CONTINENTAL STEAM
PACKET COMPANY.
Deed of Settlement of the South Eastern
and Continental Steam Packet Company.
Printed by C. Roworth. London. (1845).
11.

STREATER, Ronald A.
Cross Channel ferries from Kent. 2nd edition,
edited by Roland A. Streater.
Marinart. 1978.
3,5,6,11,13.

VEALE, Ernest William Partington.*
Gateway to the Continent: a history of
cross-channel travel.
Ian Allan. 1955.
1,6,7,8,11,12.

TRIALS

APOTHECARIES' COMPANY VS. T. RYAN.
A correct report of the trial of the Apothecaries'
Company versus Ryan on March 17th,1831 at
Kent Assizes. (Mr T. Ryan was the defendant
and also wrote up the article. The main characters
are connected with Eynsford and Farningham).
Royal Exchange, Effingham Wilson. 1831.
17.

BELL, John Any Bird. Defendant.*
Narrative of the facts relative to the
murder of Richard Faulkner Taylor in the woods
between Rochester and Maidstone...March 1831...
together with the trial of John Any Bird Bell
for the murder....
Printed by S. Caddell. Rochester. (1831).
11.

BOREMAN, Robert.*
A mirrour of mercy and judgement or an exact true
narrative of the life of Freeman Sonds Esquier,
Sonne to Sir George Sonds of Lees Court in
Shelwich in Kent, who, for murthering his
elder brother was arraigned and condemned
at Maidstone, executed there 1655.
Thomas Dring, Fleet Street, London. 1655.
11,26.

BUCKFIELD, Reginald Sidney, Defendant.
The trial of Reginald Sidney Buckfield;
edited, with a fore ord and a note on crime
and insanity, by C.E. Bechofer Roberts.
(A murder which took place at Strood).
Jarrolds, 1944.
11.

REX VERSUS JAMES MONTAGUE,*
W.L.Newman, John Nelson and four others.
Report of the Trial.
(The defendants cut through the embankment
at Grain Bridge, Yautlet Creek, Isle of Grain)
Corporation of the City of London. 1824.
11.

RIDSDALE, Charles Joseph vs. CLIFTON and others.
Folkestone ritual case: the substance of the
argument, delivered before the Judicial
Committee of the Privy Council by Benjamin
Shaw.
Printed by W.J. Terry. (187?).
11,17.

SAVILL, Mr.*
The trial of Mr. Savill, linen draper,
of Margate, who was falsely and maliciously
charged with assaulting Mary Bayly....
and found guilty...after proving his innocence
at the Quarter Sessions, Dover, on the
7th of June,1800.
Published by Savill. 1800.
6,11.

THE TRIAL AND SENTENCE OF THE KNIGHT OF MALTA,
for perjury, being the second part of the
Canterbury Tale of the year 1833.
(Tracts No.4). (Sir William Courtenay).
Elizabeth Wood. Canterbury. (1833).
3.

THE TRIAL (AT LARGE) OF JOSEPH STACPOOLE,
WILLIAM GAPPER AND JAMES LAGIER for wilfully
and maliciously shooting at John Parker;
tried...1777...Taken in Shorthand by
Joseph Gurney. (An attempted shooting at
the Bull, Dartford on August 17th,1775).
Printed for G. Kearsly. 1777.
11.

TRIAL AT MAIDSTONE SPRING ASSIZES, 1837,
for the possession of a picture, the
supposed portrait of Charles I by Vandyke.
Newspaper cuttings referring to the trial.
1837.
11.

THE TRIAL OF THE RIGHT HONOURABLE LORD
GEORGE SACKVILLE, at a Court-Martial held
at the Horse Guards, February 29, 1760...
Printed for W. Owen. (1760).
11,16.

WHITSTABLE OYSTER COMPANY VS. GANN, THOMAS.*
Trial at Nisi Prius (Kent Lent Assizes,
March 11th,1861)., and subsequent proceedings
relative to the title of the Whitstable
Oyster Company to levy anchorage within the
manor and royalty of Whitstable...and to
distrain for the same.
Publisher - Hibbit. Printed Wm. Davey,
Canterbury, 1861.
31.

TROTTISCLIFFE
(TROSLEY)

ANDERSON, Peggy.
A proposed plan and management scheme for the
North Downs Country Park near Trottiscliffe.
(Discussion papers in Conservation No.10).
University College, London. 1975.
2.

CORKILL, W.H.*
Avebury, Coldrum and Margate.
(A passing reference to the Coldrum Stones).
Harper Company. c.1953.
3,13,24.

FRAMPTON, T.S.
Fifty-eight rectors of Trottiscliffe.
Reprinted from Archaeologia Cantiana,
Vol. XX. 1893.
Mitchell and Hughes. (1893).
11.

GENERAL REGISTER OFFICE.
Census Returns. 1841, 1851, 1861, 1871.
Trottiscliffe. Microfilm.
23.

TUDELEY

GUISEPPI, M.S.
Some fourteenth-century accounts of ironworks
at Tudeley, Kent. Read (to the Society of
Antiquaries) 5th December, 1912. Extracted
from Archaeologia Vol. LXIV and bound.
(Transcripts of accounts 1330 - 1354).
Society of Antiquaries. 1912.
11.

TUNBRIDGE WELLS

ADAM'S WELL: being a circumstantial history
of its origin.
W. Richardson. 1780.
19.

ADVICE TO MR. L-G-N, the dwarf fan painter
at Tunbridge Wells and AN ANSWER TO THE
ADVICE TO Mr. L-G-N. (Thomas Loggon).
(Thomas Loggon, court dwarf to Frederick,
Prince of Wales. Fan painter at Bath and
Tunbridge Wells with a shop in the Pantiles;
painter of the 1748 print of the famous characters
at Tunbridge Wells, including himself. Original
in S. Richardson's letters).
H. Carpenter. 1748.
19.

AMSINCK, Paul.*
Tunbridge Wells and its neighbourhood,
illustrated by a series of etchings, and historical
descriptions.
William Miller and Lloyd. 1810.
2.

ASH, St. George. Lord Bishop of Clogher.
Two sermons preached at Tunbridge Wells.
Dan Midwinter. 1714.
19.

BAKER, Dick pseud.
Guide to Tunbridge Wells, wid summat bout de
Town Hall writ and prented in de old Kentish
Dialect.
J. Richards. 1932.
19.

BAKER, Thomas.*
Tunbridge Walks:or, the Yeoman of Kent, a
comedy by the author of the "Humour o' the
Ape."
Bernard and/or Henry Lintott.
1703, 1714, 1727, 1736 and 1764.
1,11,17,19.

BARNARD, S.
The fruits and effects of God's love...a
sermon preached at the Countess of Huntingdon's
Chapel, Tunbridge Wells, October 21, 1787.
A. Lee, Lewes. 1787.
19.

BATH AND TUNBRIDGE WELLS A CENTURY AGO.
from The Cornhill Magazine, June,1883.
19.

BENSON, Martin.
Tunbridge Wells sermons 1796 - 1828.
19.

BOTANICAL POCKET-BOOK with observations on
some of the rarer plants growing in the
neighbourhood of Tunbridge Wells.
J. Clifford. 1840.
19.

BUMOGRAPHY:or a touch at the lady's tails,
being a lampoon (privately) dispersed at Tunbridge
Wells in the year 1707.
19.

BURR, Thomas Benge.*
This history of Tunbridge Wells.
M. Hingerton (and others). 1766.
1,2,4,6,7,8,11,12,17,19.

CARLEY, J.
The Tunbridge Wells, Snodland and Edenbridge
suspension railway. An abortive scheme of 1825-
6 with notes on two more.
Meopham Publications Committee. 1979.
2,4,6,13,15,23.

CLIFFORD, John Publisher.
A descriptive guide of Tunbridge Wells and
its environs.
Printed and published by J. Clifford.
Tunbridge Wells.
1820, 1826, 1837, 19.
1882.   11.

Tunbridge Wells Guide. 4th edition.
Printed and published by J. Clifford.
Tunbridge Wells. 1825.
19.

Visitors' guide for Tunbridge Wells.
Printed and Published by J. Clifford.
Tunbridge Wells. 1853.
19.

COLBRAN, John Publisher.*
Colbran's new guide for Tunbridge Wells,
being a full and accurate description of
the Wells and its neighbourhood within
a circuit of nearly twenty miles, edited
by J. Phippen.
J. Colbran. Tunbridge Wells.
1839. 19.
1844. 2nd edition 11.

The Handbook and Visitors' Guide for
Tunbridge Wells and its neighbourhood.
J. Colbran, Tunbridge Wells.
1855. 5th edition.   19.
1855.* 5th edition.   11. bound with
        Osbourne's Strangers' guide to
        Hastings and St. Leonards.
        J. Colbran. 1855.
        1857* 6th edition. 2.
        1863 8th edition. 19.

The Tunbridge Wells Visitor, 1833 - 1835.
4 volumes.
J. Colbran,Tunbridge Wells. 1833-35.
19.

COLEBROOK, F.
Royal Tunbridge Wells:the official guide.
Photocrome Company Ltd. Tunbridge Wells (1912?)
11,23.

COPUS, Geoffrey.
The early history of St. Barnabas' Parish,
Tunbridge Wells: notes written for the
parish history exhibition October 16th - 21st,
1967.
19.

COQUETILLA pseud.
A view of the beau monde.
A. Dodd. 1731.
19.

CURLL, Edmund.
A catalogue of books sold by Edmund Curll.
(Tunbridge Wells bookseller).
n.d.
19.

DAILY NEWS Publications Department.
Tunbridge Wells.
Cover Title: Popular Wallet guide to
Tunbridge Wells containing twelve of the best
local   picture postcards. (in back pocket).
Daily News. (1910 - 1918?).
11.

DAVIS, Terence.
Tunbridge Wells: the gentle aspect.
Phillimore and Co. 1976.
2,3,6,15,16,19,22,23.

DEAKIN, Richard.*
The flowering plants of Tunbridge Wells and
neighbourhood.
Stidolph and Bellamy. Tunbridge Wells. 1871.
2.

DERRICK, Samuel.
Letters written from Leverpoole, Chester,
Corke... Tunbridge Wells, Bath. 2 volumes.
G. Faulkner. Dublin. 1762.
19.

DODD, Charles Tattershall.
Charles Tattershall Dodd: artist of
Tunbridge Wells. Centenary exhibition,
Municipal Art Gallery 24th November -
15 December. 1978. (Catalogue).
19.

ELWIG, Henry.*
A biographical dictionary of notable people
at Tunbridge Wells, 17th to the 20th Century,
also a list of local place names.
Stanford Printing Company. Tunbridge Wells.
(1941).
11,19.

ENVIRONMENT, Department of the.
List of buildings of special architectural
or historic interest in the District of
Tunbridge Wells.
H.M.S.O. 1974.
11,19.

FREELING, Arthur.*
Picturesque excursions:containing upwards
of 400 views at and near places of
popular resort, edited by A. Freeling.
(Includes Margate, Tunbridge Wells and
Dover).
William S. Orr. 1840.
24.

GARDNER, Henry.*
Gardner's Penny Guide:Tunbridge Wells,
Tonbridge and Southborough etc.
Arthur Dee, Southborough. n.d.
19.

GEIGER, Erika.
Royal Tunbridge Wells:an example of the
English spa. Origins and rise of the
town to its present status.
(Unpublished thesis. Stuttgart University).
1976.
19.

GISBOURNE,S.
Plan of the Tunbridge Wells Local Act District.1849.
19.

GIVEN, J.C.M.
Royal Tunbridge Wells:past and present.
For the occasion of the Jubilee Congress of
the South-Eastern Union of Scientific Societies,
July, 1946, edited by J.C.M. Given.
Courier Printing and Publishing Company.(1946)
23.

GOULDEN AND CURRY Publishers.
The"Walks Guide" to Tunbridge Wells and the
surrounding country, being based upon the
well-known "Walks and Drives Guide" but
newly revised and amplified.
Goulden and Curry. Tunbridge Wells. 1937.
11.

GREEN, Andrew.
Ghosts of Tunbridge Wells.
John Hilton. Hadlow. 1978.
11,12,19,23.

HALL, Rev. Samuel Romilly.
A Wesleyan minister's address to the members
of society in Tunbridge Wells:being a reply
to "A clergyman's address to the Wesleyan
Methodists in his parish".
John Mason. 1842.
19.

HAMPSON, John. (1760 - 1817?).*
A blow at the root of pretended Calvinism,
or real Antinomianism, in several letters
to a friend. (Minister at the
Dissenting Chapel, Tunbridge Wells).
Jasper Sprange. Tunbridge Wells. 1788.
19.

HARPER, Charles George.*
The Hastings Road and the "Happy Springs
of Tunbridge".
Chapman and Hall. 1906.
2,3,4.

HATCH, P. Henry.
Poetic genius:an essay on poetical character...
a lecture delivered at the Assembly Room, Royal
Victoria and Sussex Hotel, Tunbridge Wells,
February 27th,1839.
J. Colbran. 1839.
19.

HAYNE, Leonora.
The story of Mount Ephraim House, Tunbridge
Wells. 1662 - 1975. Pamphlet.
Leonora Hayne. 1975.
17,19.

HISSEY, James John.
On Southern English roads. pp. 86 - 89
Tunbridge Wells.
Richard Bentley and Son. London. 1896.
11.

IBBETT, MOSELY,CARD AND COMPANY. Chartered
Auctioneers etc.
Royal Tunbridge Wells, Kent.
Property Publications. Croydon. n.d.
11.

JONES, Edgar Yoxall.*
A prospect of Tunbridge Wells and the
adjacent countryside.
Lambarde Press 1964.
1,2,4,5,8,10,11,12,15,19.

KELLY'S DIRECTORIES LIMITED.
Kelly's Directory of Tunbridge Wells,
Tonbridge and neighbourhood.
Kelly's Directories Ltd.
1936. 11.
1973. 7.

KENT COUNTY COUNCIL:HIGHWAYS AND TRANSPORTATION
DEPARTMENT.
Tonbridge and Tunbridge Wells transportation
study: report on surveys. October, 1976. K.C.C.1976
19.

KENT COUNTY COUNCIL:PLANNING DEPARTMENT.
Royal Tunbridge Wells and Southborough
Town Map. Part No. XII.
K.C.C. (1958?).
11.

KENWORTHY, Wesley.
Vale Royal Methodist Church,Tunbridge Wells,
1873 - 1973. (pamphlet).
Vale Royal Methodist Church. Tunbridge Wells.
(1973?).
11,19.

KIDMAN, Brenda.
A handful of tears.
(An account of many travels, with the
beginning of her life spent in Tunbridge Wells).
B.B.C. 1975.
11.

KING, John Thornton.
Buses and bathchairs...but not a tram in sight:
a review of public transport in Tunbridge Wells
from the late Victorian era to the end
of 1914. 9 pages.
Omnibus Society. 1976.
1,8,11,19,23.

LENG, John.
The duty of moderation to all men...a sermon
preach'd at Tunbridge Wells in Kent on
August 21st,1715.
R. Knaplock. 1715.
19.

Knowledge of the nature and providence of God...
a sermon preach'd at Tunbridge Wells in Kent,
September 4th 1715.
R. Knaplock. 1715.
19

LETTER FROM A CITIZEN OF BATH to his
Excellency Dr. R....at Tunbridge.
1705.
19.

LOWE, Jessie.*
Tunbridge Ware.
In "The Lathe and its uses", by Elias Taylor.
Trubner. 1871.
19.

LUTTRELL, Narcissus.
Travels 1677 - 1680. Anno 1680. Travell 13th
to Tunbridge Wells (typescript).
19.

MADAN, Pat(rick).
A phylosophical and medicinal essay of the
waters of Tunbridge. Written to a person
of honour by Pat Madan, M.D. London.
Printed for the author 1687.
11.19.

MAULDON, Jean.
Tunbridge Wells as it was.
Hendon Publishing Co.Ltd. Nelson, Lancs. 1977.
3,6,11,12,15,19,22,23.

MELVILLE, Lewis.*
Society at Royal Tunbridge Wells in the
18th Century - and after.
Eveleigh Nash. 1912.
2.

NORTON,TRIST,WATNEY AND COMPANY.
Plan shewing estates of George Field, Esq.,
Rev. J.J. Saint and John Heugh Esq., and
the land required for the Sewage Works.
November, 1869.
6 chaine = 1 inch
19.

PAGE, Andre.
Kent and East Sussex by Wanderbus:Tunbridge Wells.
Midas Books. Speldhurst. 1973.
1,2,3,6,7,9,11,12,26,30.

PEACOCK, David.
David Peacock's Tunbridge Wells sketchbook,
described by Frank Chapman.
Perspective Press. Tonbridge. 1978.
3,4,5,6,11,13,15,16,19,23,28.

PEARSON, Rev.C.Ridley.
Two sermons preached at the commencement of his
ministry in St. James' Church, 18th May, 1862.
H.S. Colbran. Tunbridge Wells. 1862.
19.

PELTON, Richard Publisher.*
Pelton's illustrated guide to Tunbridge Wells
and the neighbouring seats, towns and villages.
R. Pelton. Tunbridge Wells.
1876.   7th edition.   19.
1883.   (10th?) edition. edited by J.R. Thomson.   3.
1970.   Reprinted 9th edition of 1881, edited by
        J.R. Thomson and with an introduction
        by Jean Mauldon.
        S.R. Publishers. Ltd.   12.

Pelton's shilling directory to Tunbridge Wells.
R. Pelton.   Tunbridge Wells. 1913.
19.

Twenty-four views of Tunbridge Wells.
R. Pelton. Tunbridge Wells. c. 1870.
11.

PINTO, H.*
Tunbridge and Scottish Souvenir woodware,
by H.and E.R. Pinto.
Bell. 1970.
2,19.

POOLE, Keith B.
The two Beaux. (Nash and Brummell).
E.P. Publishing Company. 1976.
19.

RECOLLECTIONS OF TUNBRIDGE WELLS.
A. Newman and Co. London.   (187-?)
11.

RICHARDS.James.
High Brooms: a bit of the history of the place and
its people.
James Richards. 1937.
19.

RICHARDSON, Samuel.
The correspondence of Samuel Richardson.
Volume 3. (Connections with and visits to
Tunbridge Wells).
Richard Phillips. 1804.
19.

ROBERTS, Fred.
Guide to the High Rocks, one mile from
Royal Tunbridge Wells.
Proprietor of High Rocks. n.d.
11.

A ROD FOR TUNBRIDGE BEAUX, bundl'd up
at the request of the Tunbridge ladies.
1701
19.

ROSE, Rev. A.W.H.
Satisfaction in God's likeness. A sermon
preached at Christ Church, Tunbridge Wells,
September 3rd,1843.
W.E. Painter. 1843.
19.

ROWZEE, Lodwick.
The Queene's Welles, that is, a treatise
of the nature and vertues of Tunbridge Water.
1632.   John Dawson.   19.
1656.   Gertrude Dawson.   19.
1670.   Robert Butler.19.

ROYAL ALBUM OF TUNBRIDGE WELLS VIEWS.
Printed in Germany. (c.1900).
11.

ROYAL INSTITUTE OF BRITISH ARCHITECTS:
TUNBRIDGE WELLS AND DISTRICT BRANCH. Tunbridge
Wells Churches:a short architectural appreciation.
Royal Institute of British Architects. 1977.
19.

ROYAL TUNBRIDGE WELLS BOROUGH COUNCIL.
Annual report of the Medical Officer of
Health and the School Medical Officer.
1916 - 1920 and 1931 - 1935.
19.

ROYAL TUNBRIDGE WELLS BOROUGH COUNCIL.*
Royal Tunbridge Wells - Diamond Jubilee, 1969.
Royal Tunbridge Wells Borough Council. 1969.
11.

Royal Tunbridge Wells:the official guide.*
1923.   Ed. J. Burrow, Cheltenham.   11.
(1925). 10th edition. Ed. J. Burrow Cheltenham.11.
(1927). 11th edition.   "   "   "   11.
1929.   13th edition.   "   "   "   8, 11.
1931.   14th edition.   "   "   "   11.
1948.   Clarke & Sherwell.   8.

Tunbridge wells and District:official guide.
G.M. Publications, Bournemouth.
1976.   11,16,20.
1977.   4,13,25.
1978.   11.

ROYAL TUNBRIDGE WELLS CIVIC SOCIETY.
Royal Tunbridge Wells: an architectural
and historical guide map.
Civic Society. 1977.
19.

A royal walk in Tunbridge Wells.
Civic Society. 1977.
19.

ROYAL TUNBRIDGE WELLS CIVIC SOCIETY:
CONSERVATION SUB-COMMITTEE.
A discussion paper:townscape and conservation
in Tunbridge Wells. August, 1977.
Royal Tunbridge Wells Civic Society.
19.

SAINT AUGUSTINE'S NEW CHURCH APPEAL,
September 1974. (Contains history of
the old church).
Saint Augustine's Church, Tunbridge Wells. 1974.
19.

SPREADING THE GOOD NEWS THROUGH THE YEARS:
a short history of the Parish of St. Peter,
Royal Tunbridge Wells. (Centenary booklet).
St. Peters Church, Tunbridge Wells.
Agra-Europe. 1975.
19.

SAVIDGE, Alan.
Royal Tunbridge Wells.
Midas Books. 1975.
1,2,3,4,6,8,11,12,13,15,16,19.

SAVIDGE, Alan.
The story of the Church of King Charles the
Martyr, Royal Tunbridge Wells. 2nd edition.
British Publishing Company. 1978.
19.

SCUDAMORE, Charles.*
An analysis of the mineral water of
Tunbridge Wells, with some account of
its medicinal properties.
Longman, Hurst. 1816.
19.

A chemical and medicinal report of the
properties of the mineral waters of
Tunbridge Wells.
Longman. 1820.
19.

SKINNERS SCHOOL, TUNBRIDGE WELLS.
The Leopard: the Skinners School magazine.
Jubilee edition 1887 - 1937.
1937.
19.

SLIGHT, Rev. B.
The prevalence of Popery considered:
a sermon preached in Mount Sion Chapel,
October 4th, 1835.
W.E. Painter. 1835.
19.

SOUTH EASTERN UNION OF SCIENTIFIC SOCIETIES.
The South Eastern Naturalist and Antiquary,
being the.....Transactions of the South
Eastern Union of Scientific Societies for
1946, including the Proceedings of the Congress
held at Tunbridge Wells.
Seuss. 1946.
19.

SPRANGE, J. Publisher.
On the High Rocks near Tunbridge Wells:
a descriptive poem.
J. Sprange. Tunbridge Wells. 1777.
19.

The Tunbridge Wells Directory.
J. Sprange. Tunbridge Wells. 1792.
19.

The Tunbridge Wells Guide.*
J. Sprange. Tunbridge Wells.
1796.   19.
1801.   2.
1814.   19.

The Tunbridge Wells: or an account of the
ancient and present state of that place...
towns and villages...within the circumference
of sixteen miles.
Printed by J. Sprange. Tunbridge Wells. 1836.
11.

STIDOLPH,T. and Son. Publisher.
Map of Tunbridge Wells showing the principal
houses, places of worship etc.
T. Stidolph and Son. 1839.
19.

STRANGE, Charles Hilbert.
The future development of Tunbridge Wells:
a general survey, edited by C.H. Strange.
Courier Printing Works. 1936.
19.

SYDALL, Elias.
The true Protestant and Church of England clergy...
a sermon preach'd at Tunbridge Wells in Kent on
August 14th,1715...
Printed for John Wyat. 1715.
11,19.

THOMSON, Thomas.
Some observations on the water with which Tunbridge
Wells is chiefly supplied for domestic purposes.
bound with Scudamore, Charles, An analysis of
the mineral water...
Longman, Hurst. 1816.
19.

THORNTON, Rev. F.V.
Church missions:a sermon...preached in the church
of the Holy Trinity, Tunbridge Wells,
August 26th, 1847.
Rivington. 1847.
19.

TOWN AND COUNTY DIRECTORIES.
Kent Trades Directory, 1972.
Margate, Ramsgate and including Maidstone
and Tunbridge Wells.
Town and County Directories. 1972.
11.

TRIMMELL, Charles. Bishop of Norwich.
A sermon preach'd in the Chappel at
Tunbridge Wells upon 19th August, 1711.
D. Midwinter. 1711.
19.

TUNBRIDGE MISCELLANY: consisting of
poems,etc. 2 parts.
E. Curll. 1713.
19.

TUNBRIDGE WARE: an extract from Chamber's
Edinburgh Journal, 1st December, 1894.
17.

TUNBRIDGE WELLS: album (of) views.
c.1900.
11.

TUNBRIDGE WELLS AND DISTRICT COUNCIL OF
SOCIAL SERVICE.
Directory of statutory and voluntary social
services in Royal Tunbridge Wells and
District.
Tunbridge Wells and District Council of
Social Service. October, 1975.
19.

TUNBRIDGE WELLS LOCAL BOARD.
Medical Officer of Health's Reports.1885-1904.
19.

TUNBRIDGE WELLS PUBLIC LIBRARY.
Local History Catalogue, 1966.
Tunbridge Wells Public Library. 1966.
30.

TUNBRIGALIA,*or Tunbridge Miscellanies
for the year....
1719.   19.
1719.   Part I. 2nd edition. 19.
1722.   19.
1733.   19.

WALLINGER, Rev. W.
A sermon preached in Holy Trinity Church,
Tunbridge Wells, June 28th,1840, on the occasion
of the appointed   thanksgiving for the
preservation of the Queen.
J. Colbran. Tunbridge Wells. 1840.
19.

WALTER AND GRIST. Publishers.*
Pictorial history of Tunbridge Wells
and District.
Walter and Grist. 1892.
4,19.

WHITBOURN, Philip.
A look around Holy Trinity: at the arts of
architecture, sculpture, and painting glass.
Published for Trinity Theatre & Arts Association.
1978.
19.
YEATS, G.D.
Some hints on a mode of procuring soft
water at Tunbridge Wells. Excerpt from the
Quarterly Journal of Science, Literature
and the Arts, Vol. XIV, 1823. p.345.
19.

TUNSTALL

BIBLIOTHECA TOPOGRAPHICA,*
Vol 1. No.1. containing.
Queries for the better illustrating the Antiquities
and natural history of Great Britain and
Ireland. and
The history and antiquities of Tunstall in Kent,
by the late Mr. Edward Rowe Mores.
J. Nichols. 1780.
1,2,4,5,6,8,11,12,15,17,20.

MIDWINTER, Arthur Adair.*
Church and Village of Tunstall, Kent.
("Our Village").
W.J. Parrett printer. Sittingbourne. 1937.
1,2.

ULCOMBE

HILTON, John Anthony.
Joseph Hatch:the Ulcombe bellfounder.
J. Hannon and Company. Oxford. 1978.
1,11,12.

STONE, Richard C.
Ulcombe, Ireland and the St. Legers.
Reprinted from Archaeologia Cantiana,
Vol. XCI., 1975.
Printed by Headley Brothers. Ashford. (1976?).
11.

UPCHURCH

JAMES, H.A.*
The church of St. Mary the Virgin, Upchurch.
Church Publishers. Ramsgate. (1973?).
20.

WOODRUFF, Rev.   John (Vicar of Upchurch).
John Woodruff's Journal, 1851-56.
Keith Chare Upchurch Vicarage (1976).
3,20.

UPNOR

EVANS, S.*
Upnor: some notes on the Castle and other
things.
P.P. c. 1951.
25.

SAUNDERS, A.D.*
Upnor Castle, Kent. (Ministry of Public
Building and Works Guides).
H.M.S.O. 1967.
12,20,25,26,27,30.

SHAFTSBURY HOMES:THE ARETHUSA TRAINING SHIP.
The Arethusa.
Shaftsbury Homes and Arethusa Training Ship. n.d.
25.

VINTERS PARK   See   WEAVERING STREET

WALDERSLADE

KENT COUNTY COUNCIL:EDUCATION DEPARTMENT.
Official opening of Walderslade County
Secondary Schools, and Wayfield and Oaklands
(Walderslade) County Primary Schools,by
E.W. Woodhead on Wednesday 22nd June,1960
at 2.30 p.m.   Souvenir booklet.
K.C.C. 1960.
4.

KENT COUNTY COUNCIL:PLANNING DEPARTMENT.*
Walderslade:informal action area plan.
K.C.C. 1972.
4,25.

WALMER

BULLOCK, Charles.
Home Words for heart and hearth.
Bound with Walmer Parish Magazine for 1905.
Home Words Publishing. 1905.
11.

CURZON, George Nathaniel. 1st Marquess Curzon
of Kedleston.*
The personal history of Walmer Castle and
its Lord Warden,edited by S. Gwynn.
Macmillan. 1927.
2,24.

DEAL AND WALMER COMMUNITY ASSOCIATION.
Proposed centre for the Deal and Walmer
Community Association:Report to the
Dover District Council.
Deal and Walmer Community Association. 1979.
28.

DEAL BOROUGH COUNCIL.
Deal and Walmer:the historic holiday resort.
Official Guide.
Deal Borough Council. (1939)
11.

THE EIGHTEENTH OF NOVEMBER, 1852.
Printed for private circulation, 1853.
(Poem about the funeral of the Duke of
Wellington, Lord Warden of the Cinque Ports
and who died at Walmer).
11.

ELVIN, Charles. R.S.
The history of Walmer and Walmer Castle.
(abridged edition).
Cross and Jackman. Canterbury.   1897.
11.

Records of Walmer.... *
Henry Gray. 1890.
2.

FRANKLIN, W.H. Photographer.*
The new view album of Deal and Walmer,
photographed...by W.H. Franklin.
W.H. Franklin. Deal. C.1900.
11.

HUNT, F.J.
Deal, Walmer and Kingsdown Amateur Rowing
Club, 1927 - 1977.
Kent County Printers. 1979.
28.

MINERVA RAILWAY GUIDE AND VISITORS' HANDBOOK
for Deal, Walmer, Sandwich and District.
Minerva.   1907.
12.

PHIPPEN, James. Publisher.
The new handbook to Deal, Walmer, Sandwich
and their environs.
J. Phippen.   1852 etc.
8,11,15.17.

ROGET, John Lewis.*
Sketches of Deal, Walmer, and Sandwich.
Longman Green and Co.   1911.
2.

SAUNDERS, A.D.*
Deal and Walmer Castles. (Ministry of Building
and Public Works Guides).
H.M.S.O.   1963.
3,12,25,30.

WATERINGBURY

BERGESS, Winifred F.
Records of the Crow(e) family of Wateringbury,
Kent, compiled by W.F. Bergess and Carolyn
Duffy.   Manuscript notes.   1973.
11.

GENERAL REGISTER OFFICE.
Census Returns. 1841, 1851, 1861,1871.
Wateringbury.   Microfilm.
23.

LAMBERT, J.R.
Wateringbury - its population and mortality.
Copy of typewritten material. 1975.
11.

WEALD

ABBEY PUBLICITY SERVICE LTD. Publishers.*
Residential and holiday areas of South-West
Kent including the Kentish Weald. 4th edition.
Abbey Publicity Service Ltd. (1939?)
11.

ALLEN, P.*
Geology of the Central Weald: the Hastings beds.
(Geologists' Association Guides No.24).
Benham and Co. Ltd.   1958.
4,12,15,17,30.

ARMSTRONG, J.R.
The Weald and Downland Open Air Museum,
edited by J.R. Armstrong and J. Lowe.
Phillimore   Chichester.
1973. 8.   1974. 11.   1975. 3.

ARMSTRONG, Lyn.
Woodcolliers and charcoal burning.
Coach Publishing House Ltd., and
The Weald and Downland Open Air Museum.1978.
23.

BOLTON, Thomas.
Geography through fieldwork. Book 3.
Studies in Wales, Scotland and England.
pp. 54 - 87. The Wealden District of
South East England.
Blandford Press. 1970.
11.

BRITISH MUSEUM: NATURAL HISTORY- DEPARTMENT
OF GEOLOGY.*
Catalogue of the Mesozoic plants in the
Department of Geology, The British Museum
(Natural History): the Wealden flora
by A.C. Seward. 2 vols.
British Museum. 1894-5.
4,11.

CASTLE, Roger A.B.
Wealden exploration.
Castle Press. Tunbridge Wells. 1971.
19.

CHURCH, Richard.*
The crab-apple tree.
A novel set in the Weald.
Heinemann. 1959.
23.

CLEERE, H.
The Roman iron industry of the Weald and its
connexions with the Classis Britannica.
Reprinted from The Archaeological Journal,
Vol. 131 for 1974. pp. 196-199
Royal Archaeological Institute. (1974?).
3.

DARTON, Frederick Joseph Harvey.*
A parcel of Kent.
Nisbet. 1924.
1,2,3,4,5,6,7,8,9,10,11,12,13,14,15,17,18,
19,20,25.

DAVISON, Ian.*
When night comes. (Essays on the Weald,
written at Branden, Sissinghurst, where
the Author lived).
H. Jenkins. 1936.
4,19.

DEARN, Thomas Downes Wilmot.
An historical, topographical and
descriptive account of the Weald of Kent...
S. Waters. Cranbrook. 1814.
2.

DELANY, Mary Cecilia.*
The historical geography of the Wealden iron
industry.
Benn. 1921.
1,2,3,5,11,15,19,26.

EDMUNDS, F.H.*
Geology of the Wealden District.
(British Regional Geology Series).
H.M.S.O.
1st edition 1935. 1,2,4,7,8,11,17.
2nd edition 1948. 1,3,4,5,6,7,9,11,13,15,19,20,25.
3rd edition 1954.17.

FURLEY, Robert.*
A history of the Weald of Kent, with an outline
of the early history of the County.
3 parts in 2 volumes.
Igglesden. Ashford. 1871 - 1874.
26.

GALLOIS, R.W.*
The Wealden district.4th edition. (British regional
geology), by R.W. Gallois based on the previous
editions by the late F.H. Edmunds.
H.M.S.O. 1965.
1,2.3.4.5.6.7.8.9,10,11,12,15,16,19,20,24,25,30.

KAYE-SMITH, Sheila.*
Weald of Kent and Sussex.
Hale. 1953.
30.

KEECH, Gertrude C.*
Staplehurst and the Weald of Kent.
Research Publishing Co. 1965.
12,22.

KENYON, G.H.*
The Glass Industry of the Weald.
Leicester University Press. 1967.
25.

KING, Geoffrey.
A Country walk:a section of the proposed
'Wealdway' long distance footpath.
Fully illustrated route cards describe the
route from Tonbridge to Uckfield.
Independent Design Executive, Tonbridge,for
Tunbridge Wells CHA And HF Rambling Club. 1976?
8,11.

KIRKALDY, John Francis.*
Geology of the Weald.
(Geologists' Association Guides No.29).
Benham and Co. Colchester.
1958. 1.3.4.5.7.8.9.11.12.15.17.
1960. 25.
1967. 2.6.30.
1976. 3rd edition revised by F.A. Middlemiss.
       3,6,12.

MARGARY, Ivan Donald.
Roman communications between Kent and the
East Sussex Ironworks. Reprinted from the
Sussex Archaeological Collections.
n.d.
11.

Roman Ways in the Weald.*
Phoenix House.
1948. 2.25.
1965 (1968 reprint) revised edition. 2.25.

MARKHAM, Gervase.*
The inrichment of the Weald of Kent: or,
a direction to the husband-man for the true
ordering, manuring and inriching of all the
grounds within the Wealds of Kent and Sussex...
revised, inlarged and corrected...
Printed by Elizabeth Purflow for John Harison,
London. 1649.
11.

The enrichment of the Weald of Kent...
Printed for George Sawbridge. 1675.
2.

The enrichment of the Weald of Kent...
(Facsimile reprint of the 1625 edition).
De Capo Press. Theatrum Orbis Terrarum Ltd. 1973.
11,19.

MASON, Reginald Thomas.*
Framed buildings of the Weald.
1964. p.p. the Author.   24.25.
1969. 2nd edition Coach Printing House
                    Horsham. 2,12,16.
1973. 3rd edition?Coach Printing House
                    Horsham. 16.

MEOPHAM AND DISTRICT FOOTPATHS GROUP.
The Wealdway: a walkers' route from the
Thames to the English Channel:Section I.
Gravesend to Tonbridge.
Meopham Publications Committee. 1973.
9,11.

MILLWARD, Roy.
South-East England. (Landscapes of Britain).
The Low Weald and Downs, by Roy Millward and
Adrian Robinson.
Macmillan. 1973.
11.

Thameside and the Weald, by Roy Millward and
Adrian Robinson.
Macmillan. 1971.
2,3,4,5,9,11,12,16,19,21.

WESTBERE

McINTOSH, Kinn Hamilton.
Chislet and Westbere, villages of the Stour Lathe.
K.H. McIntosh, Sturry. 1979.
2,23,28.

PARISH MAGAZINE FOR WESTBERE AND HERSDEN,
for 1931, 1932, 1933 (except March), 1934-
1939. (Bound in one volume)
3.

WARREN, Charles.
Westbere, Kent: history of the Bread and Cheese
Field Trust from 1833 to 1914. (Photocopy).
Charles Warren? Westbere. (1915).
3.

WESTBROOK See MARGATE

WESTERHAM

BLACK, G.T.*
Westerham Valley (Railway) (Branch line Hand-
book No.8) 2nd edition.
Branch Line Handbooks. Teddington, Middlesex.
April, 1962.
1.2.4.6.8.11.12.15.16.17.

BROWNE, A.M.
Chartwell. An article by A.M. Browne
reprinted from the Illustrated London News
of 25th June,1966.
Illustrated London News for National Trust.1972.
2.

CHARTWELL, Westerham.*
R. Nicholson. 1966.
30.

DENNE, John.
The nature, design and benefits of confirmation:
a sermon preached in the parish church of
Westerham in Kent....1726, at a Confirmation held
there by...Samuel, Lord Bishop of Rochester.
R. Knaplock. London. 1726.
11.

GOULD, David.
Westerham Valley Railway.
(Locomotion paper no.72).
Oakwood Press. 1974.
1,2,3,4,6,11,15,16.

HOOKER BROTHERS Publishers.
Hookers' Directory 1935. (Westerham and
District).
Hooker Brothers, Westerham. 1935.
16.

KENT COUNTY COUNCIL:COUNTY SECRETARY'S
DEPARTMENT:RESEARCH AND INTELLIGENCE UNIT.
Reorganisation of secondary education in
Sevenoaks and Westerham:results of a public
opinion survey carried out in Summer 1975.
K.C.C. 1975.
5,11.

MORAN, James.*
Henry George, printer, bookseller, stationer
and book-binder, Westerham...
Westerham Press. 1972.
2,11,16,19.

NOTES ON THE ANCIENT PARISH CHURCH OF WESTERHAM.
Printed by Hooker Brothers,Westerham. n.d.
11.

QUEBEC HOUSE, Kent.
(the home of General James Wolfe).
National Trust.
1971. 7.8.
1976. 3.12.

SQUERRYES COURT, WESTERHAM:the Kent home of
the Warde family since 1731.*Official Guide.
English Life Publications Limited.
1961/New edition 1971.
4,8,30.

THOMPSON, Gibson.*
Westerham with its surroundings: a hand-book
to Wolfe-land. The Official guide. Previous
editions entitled "Wolfe-land:a handbook to
Westerham and its surroundings")
Warne. n.d. 5.12.15.
Homeland Association. 4th edition 1910. 11.

THOMPSON, Gibson.*
Wolfe-land:handbook to Westerham and its
surroundings.
1898. Beechings. London. 11.
1900 etc. Homeland Association. 1.2.4.7.8.11.12.
                                         15.16.17.
1904. 3rd edition. J.A. Hughes. 2.

TILDEN, Philip.
True remembrances.
Allington Castle, Lympne Castle, Saltwood
Castle, Chartwell.
Country Life. 1954.
7.12.

VICKERSON, Edmund.
Westerham and its associations. The birth
place of Wolfe.
Hooker Bros. Westerham. n.d.
11,16.

WESTERHAM PARISH COUNCIL.
Westerham and Crockham Hill Kent: official
guide published by Authority of The Westerham
Parish Council.
Forward Publicity Ltd. 1975.
4,11.

WESTERHAM SOCIETY.
Westerham.
Westerham Press.
1974. 2.11.16
1974. with errata and updating to November
           1975. 16.

WEST FARLEIGH

SMITH'S HALL, WEST FARLEIGH.
Sale Catalogue. 1921
12.

TUTSHAM FARM, WEST FARLEIGH.
Open day 15 June,1980.
K.C.C. Maidstone. 1980.
12.

WESTGATE-ON-SEA See MARGATE.

WEST MALLING

CRONK, Anthony.*
A short history of West Malling.
A. Cronk. West Malling. 1951.
13.

FIELDING Cecil Henry.*
Memories of Malling and its valley.
Oliver, West Malling. 1893.
25.

GENERAL REGISTER OFFICE.
Census Returns. 1841.1851,1861,1871.
West Malling. Microfilm.
23.

KENT COUNTY COUNCIL:PLANNING DEPARTMENT.
Malling, West:proposed use of West Malling
Airfield.
K.C.C. Maidstone. 1980.
12.

LAWSON, A.W.
The charities of the Parish of West Malling,
Kent.
Printed by Stedman. West Malling. 1918?
11.

A history of the Parish Church of St. Mary
the Virgin, West Malling, by A.W. Lawson and
G.W. Stockley.
Oliver. West Malling. 1904.
25.

MAYCOCK, Alan.*
Saint Mary's Abbey, West Malling.
St. Mary's Abbey. West Malling. 1953.
2.

ST. MARY'S ABBEY, WEST MALLING.
Consecration of the Abbey Church,
June 20th,1966.
St. Mary's Abbey. 1966.
11.

WEST MALLING   Cont'd

TONBRIDGE AND MALLING DISTRICT COUNCIL:
PLANNING DEPARTMENT.
West Malling Conservation Study.
Tonbridge and Malling District Council.
(1979).
23.

WEST PECKHAM

GENERAL REGISTER OFFICE.
Census Returns. 1841,1851,1861,1871,
West Peckham. Microfilm.
23.

WEST WICKHAM

JEFFRIES, E.S.
Short History of West Wickham Allotments
Society...and West Wickham Allotments Association...
Duplicated Typescript.
1975.
2.

KNOWLDEN, P.E.
West Wickham, Kent: land holdings and population
change 1310 - 1484. Typescript dissertation
for extra mural Diploma in History (Local
History Option), University of London. 1980.
2.

LEALE, M.
Glebe House, West Wickham, Kent. (Formerly the
Rectory and from 1977 a short stay home for the
elderly).
Glebe Housing Association Ltd. 1979.
2.

MILLS, Anthony Reginald.*
The Halls of Ravenswood:more pages from the
journals of Emily and Ellen Hall.
(Residents of West Wickham from 1842).
Muller. 1967.
2,8,11.

Two Victorian ladies:more pages from the journals
of Emily and Ellen Hall.
Muller. 1969.
2,8,11.

SHEEN, Alfred L.
To God be the Glory: a history of the Church.
(West Wickham and Shirley Baptist Church 1930 -
1980).
West Wickham and Shirley Baptist Church. 1980.
2.

SHERRARD, Owen Aubrey.*
Two Victorian girls, with extracts from the
Hall diaries, edited by A.R. Mills.
(The Halls of Ravenswood House, West Wickham,
Kent).
Muller. 1966.
2,8,11.

TOPLEY, Peter.
Poems from West Wickham.
(Photocopy of typescript. "Edition" limited
to 50 copies).
Peter Topley. 1978.
2.

WALDEN, Harry.
Early Wickham
(Typescript with Ms. notes (photocopied).)
1971 & 72.
2.

WHITFIELD

WHITFIELD PARISH COUNCIL.
Whitfield Village appraisal.
Whitfield Parish Council. (1979).
6.

WHITSTABLE

BELL, BOOK AND BOYS: one hundred years of the
Whitstable Boys' School.
1977.
31.

BOOTH, Kenneth.
Comparative studies of landscape schemes 1 and 2.
Whitstable Central Area Coast Protection. 1973.
31.

Landscape Scheme!
(Kenneth Booth, FILA, Tunbridge Wells).
Whitstable Central Area Coast Protection. 1973.
31.

C., H.R.*
The Canterbury and Whitstable Railway.
 Article in Southern Railway Magazine Vol.VIII,
No 90. June,1930 .
3,30.

CANTERBURY CITY COUNCIL:AMENITIES AND RECREATION
COMMITTEE.
Canterbury, Herne Bay and Whitstable welcome you:
official Guide.
Canterbury City Council:.
1975. 3,11,12,31.
1977. 3,31.

City of Canterbury, Herne Bay and Whitstable.
(Holiday Guide).
Canterbury City Council: (1978).
3.

CANTERBURY CITY COUNCIL:CITY ARCHITECT AND
PLANNING OFFICER.
Whitstable town centre informal district plan.
Canterbury City Council. April,1978.
3,31.

CHARLES, Frank.*
Coastguards' view. A novel set in "Dymstable",
that is, the Whitstable area. (Local Author).
R. Hale. 1965.
3,31.

COLLARD, Allan Ovenden.*
The oyster and dredgers of Whitstable.
Joseph Collard. 1902.
1.2.3.4.6.7.8.11,12,15,31.

COX, W.J. Publisher.
Coloured souvenir of Whitstable.
W.J. Cox. Whitstable. n.d.
31.

W.J. Cox's guide to Whitstable and its surroundings.*
W.J. Cox. Whitstable. 1876.
8,11,31.

W.J. Cox's illustrated popular guide to
Whitstable-on-Sea and the surrounding neighbourhood.
W.J. Cox. Whitstable. (1884?).
31.

ENVIRONMENT, Department of the.
Town and Country Planning Act. 1971.
Section 54. Twenty-seventh list of buildings of
special architectural or historic interest as
at 20 May, 1977. City of Canterbury...Whitstable.
Department of the Environment. (1977).
3.

FELLOWS, Reginald B.*
History of the Canterbury and Whitstable
Railway.
J.A. Jennings. Canterbury. 1930.
1.2.3.4.6.7.8.11.12.15.17.19.31.

GARNETT, MEPHAM AND FISHER LIMITED. Publishers.
The Canterbury and District, Herne Bay and
Whitstable Local Directory. 41st edition.
Garnett, Mepham and Fisher Ltd. Brighton. 1934.
11.

Canterbury, Herne Bay and Whitstable Local
Directory.*40th issue. 1932 - 33.
Garnett, Mepham and Fisher Limited. Brighton .1932.
11.

GOODSALL, Robert Harold.*
Festival of Britain 1951,Whitstable
a brochure...devised and prepared on behalf
of the Whitstable Historical Society,by
Robert H. Goodsall, Wallace Harvey, and Alexander
W. Jardine.
Whitstable Urban District Council.   1951.
31.

Whitstable, Seasalter and Swalecliffe.*
Cross and Jackman. Canterbury. 1938.
17,19,30,31.

GREAT BRITAIN:Laws etc. (Geo.II).
An Act for repairing and widening the
road leading from Saint Dunstan's Cross...
to the waterside at Whitstable.
1736.
3.

GREAT BRITAIN: Laws etc.(Geo IV)
An Act to authorise the company of Proprietors
of the Canterbury and Whitstable Railway to
raise a further sum of money for completing the
undertaking... (9 Geo 4. CXXIX).
William Gunnell, Agent. Curteis and Kingsford.
11.   Solicitors.1828.

GREAT BRITAIN* Laws etc. (Geo.VI).
Whitstable Urban District Council Act 1948.
An Act to make further and better provision for the
improvement health and local government of the
urban district of Whitstable and for other
purposes. (30 July,1948).
H.M.S.O. 1948.
31.

GREAT BRITAIN, Laws, etc. (Eliz.II).
An Act to provide for the vesting in the urban
district council of Whitstable of the harbour at
Whitstable and the lands of the British Transport
Commission held therewith to confer powers on
the Council with reference thereto...
H.M.S.O. 1957.
31.

GREAT BRITAIN,Laws,etc(Elix.II)STATUTORY INSTRUMENTS
Port Health Authorities, England and Wales.
The Whitstable Port Health Authority order
1978. Made 9th May, 1978. S.I.685.
H.M.S.O. 1978.
3,31.

GREEN, I.W.*
The story of All Saints: a history of the parish
church of All Saints, Whitstable.
Elvy Brothers.   Whitstable.   (1955?).
7,31.

THE HAPPY FISHING GROUNDS:from "All the year
round", Vol.II from October 29,1859 to April 7,
1860 pp.113-116. (about Whitstable). 1860.
31.

HARVEY, Wallace.*
Whitstable and the French Prisoners of War.
Pirie and Cavender. Whitstable. 1971.
2,3,6,7,8,26,30,31.

HASTINGS, Macdonald.
Wheeler's fish cookery book,by Macdonald
Hastings and Carole Walsh. (Whitstable Oyster).
M. Joseph. 1974.
3.

HERNE BAY PRESS.*
The Great East Coast Storm, 1953: damage at Herne
Bay and Whitstable, Kent.
Herne Bay Press. 1953.
30,31.

HERNE BAY URBAN DISTRICT COUNCIL.
Herne Bay and Whitstable.
Herne Bay Urban District Council. (190?).
11.

IGGLESDEN, Sir Charles.
A Saunter through Kent with pen and pencil.
Vol.XI. (Whitstable and environs).
Kentish Express. Ashford. (1914).
31.

KENT COUNTY COUNCIL:PLANNING DEPARTMENT.
Informal district plan:Whitstable town centre.
Proposals map.   Scale 1:2500.   Size 19" x 18".
K.C.C. 1976.
11.

Whitstable town centre:informal district plan.
Draft.
K.C.C. 1976.
3,11,30,31.

McKEE, Alexander.
History under the Sea.
(Includes John Deane of Whitstable, pioneer diver).
Hutchinson. 1968.
3.

MAXTED, Ivan.*
Canterbury and Whitstable Railway.
Oakwood Press . 1970.
3,11,12,15.

NEWELL, G.E.
The marine fauna of Whitstable.
 The Annals and Magazine of Natural History No.77
May,1954 .
(photocopy).
31.

PERKINS, E.J.*
Sea-shore and inshore sea water temperatures at
Whitstable, Kent.
(U.K. Atomic Energy Authority - Production Group).
H.M.S.O. 1964.
4,8,11,15,31.

RATING AND VALUATION ASSOCIATION.*
Rating of site values. Report on a pilot
survey at Whitstable.
Rating and Valuation Association. 1964.
2,11,31.

"REMINISCOR". pseud.*
Fanny Wood, the Whitstable impostor, or the
Clapham Hill Mystery:a story founded on fact.
W.J. Cox. Whitstable. 1884.
11.31.

ROCK AND COMPANY. Publishers.
The 'Princess' album of Whitstable.
 Rock and Company . (c.1875?).
31.

ROYAL BRITISH LEGION:WHITSTABLE BRANCH.
Loyalty and Service:yearbooks and Souvenir
1969-70.
British Legion Press.   (1969).
31.

STEVENS, J.E.
Whitstable natives:a short study of Whitstable
and Oysters.
K.C. Hall, 15 Chinbrook Crescent, London.S.E.12.
1977.
1,3,6,11,23,28,30,31.

VALENTINE AND SONS LIMITED. Publisher.
Photographic View Album of Whitstable
containing views of the flood, November 29th,1897.
Photographed and printed by Valentine and
Sons, Ltd., Dundee. (1897).
11,31.

VAUGHAN, Chester.
The new collotype album of Whitstable Views.
C. Joiner. Whitstable. (c.1900).
11.

WHITSTABLE AND HERNE BAY ALMANACK.
Eastes. Canterbury. 1887.
11.

WHITSTABLE AND TANKERTON PUBLICITY COMMITTEE.*
Whitstable, Tankerton and District: on
the Kent Coast in the Garden of England,
compiled by Arthur Collar.
E.J. Burrow and Co. Cheltenham.
1939. 8th edition. 7,31.

Whitstable, Tankerton and District.
The Official Guide. Published by authority of
the Committee.
E.J. Burrow and Co. Cheltenham.
1952. 10th edition. 1,4,11,15,31.
1953. 11th edition. 31.

WHITSTABLE CIVIC SOCIETY.*
Coastal Preservation and development.
Whitstable Civic Society. 1964.
31.

WHITSTABLE OYSTER COMPANY V. GANN, THOMAS.*
Trial at Nisi Prius (Kent Lent Assizes,
March 11,1861) and subsequent proceedings
relative to the title of the Whitstable
Oyster Company to levy anchorage within
the manor and royalty of Whitstable...and
to distrain for the same. Also a memorial
to the Commissioners of woods and forests
relative to the beach at Whitstable and
otherwise for the answer of the Commissioners
to the complaints and charges embodied in
such memorial.
Wm. Davey. Printer. Canterbury. 1861.
31.

THE WHITSTABLE SOCIETY.
Duncan Down, Whitstable. A case for conservation.
Whitstable Society. December, 1976.
31.

Town Centre Plan.
Whitstable Society. 1975.
31.

Town Walk No.1.
The Whitstable Society. (1978).
3,31.

WHITSTABLE URBAN DISTRICT COUNCIL.
The "Borough" Guide to Whitstable and
Tankerton-on-Sea, including a motoring
and cycling map of the district.
E.J. Burrow and Co. Cheltenham.
1910 and 1912.
12.

Byelaws (selection).
31.

Coast Protection Act. 1949...
Whitstable Works Scheme No.2.
Whitstable Urban District Council. 1954.
11.

Official Guide to Whitstable: Kent's
Garden by the Sea.*
(o.1953) Whitstable U.D.C. 31.
1962, 1963.   31.
1965.   11.31.
1966.   31.
1973. N. Martell. Ramsgate. 4.

THE WHITSTABLE VISITORS' LIST AND GENERAL
ADVISOR. *
Friday September 7, 1877.
Walter Kemp. Whitstable. 1877.
31.

WHITSTABLE YACHT CLUB:official handbook, 1972.
G.W. May. (1972).
11.

WILKINSON, Gladys.J.*
One hundred years on. A history of St. John's
Methodist Church, Whitstable.
(1968?).
31.

WILKS, Hector M.
Some reflections on the second valuation of
Whitstable.
International Union for Land-Value,
Taxation and Free Trade. London. 1973.
8,11,30.

WOODMAN, George.*
Taken at the Flood. A novel based on the
Great Flood at Whitstable, 1953. (Whitstable
author).
Macmillan. 1957.
3,31.

We remember Whitstable,compiled by George
and Greta Woodman.*
Shipyard Press. 1958.
30.31.

WICKHAMBREAUX

ICKHAM, WINGHAM AND DISTRICT RESIDENTS ASSOCIATION.
Wickhambreaux.
Ightham, Wingham and District Residents
Association. Printed by J.A. Jennings Ltd. n.d.
11.

WILLESBOROUGH

"DAY BY DAY" DIRECTORY OF ASHFORD, Kennington
and Willesborough.
Redmans, Ashford.
1965. 5th edition. 12.19.
1970. 6th edition. 11.

WHISSON, J.H.H.
The first hundred years:Christ Church,
Willesborough, 1874 - 1974.
P.P. 1975.
22.

WILLS AND ADMINISTRATIONS See GENEALOGICAL RECORDS.

WINDMILLS AND WATERMILLS

ADAMS, James Whirter Renwick.*
Windmills in Kent.
K.C.C. 1955.
24,26.

CARLEY, John M.*
The Story of Meopham Mill.
Meopham Publications Committee. 1972.
2,4,9,11.

CONNELL, Charles.
Crabble Mill. (Dover).
Printed by Elvy and Gibbs. Canterbury. 1973.
11.

DRAPERS' MILL TRUST.
Drapers Mill (Margate).
Drapers' Mill Trust. 1976.
11,13.

FARRIES, Kenneth G.
The Windmills of Surrey and Inner London,by
K.G. Farries and M.T. Mason.
Skilton. 1966.
1.

FINCH, William Coles.
Vanishing wind and water mills.
(Copied from a scrapbook at Rochester Library).
4.

Watermills and windmills:a historical survey
of their rise, decline and fall as portrayed
by Kent.*
C.W. Daniel and Company.
1933. 3.6.16.20.25.26.30.
1976. (1933 edition reprinted by A.J. Cassell,
     Sheerness). 3.6.16.20.22.25.26.

FULLER, M.J.
The watermills of the East Malling Stream.
P.P. M.J. Fuller. 1973.
11,12,26,30.

HERNE MILL, KENT. (Photocopy).
"An effort to raise funds to enable an
18th Century Smock Mill once more to work
by wind"
1935.
30.

HOPKINS, Robert Thurston.
Old English mills and inns.
Cecil Palmer. 1927.
4,5,11.

KENT COUNTY COUNCIL:ARCHITECTS DEPARTMENT.
Kentish windmills. Brief list-photocopy of
typescript.
May,1972.
4.

KENTISH WINDMILLS.
(The Heritage Series).
Facto Books. 1980.
6,13.28.

WINDMILLS AND WATERMILLS Cont'd

LINDSEY, C.F.
Windmills:bibliographical guide.
C.F. Lindsey. 15 Bournemouth Road. London.1974.
11.

SHORTER, Alfred H.
Water paper mills in England.
Society for the Protection of Ancient Buildings.
1966.
23.

TURPIN, B.J.
Windmills in Kent, by B.J. and J.M. Turpin.
Windmill Publications. Thaxted. 1979.
2,5,6,9,12,23.

WAILES, Rex.
The English windmill.
Routledge and Kegan Paul.
First Published, 1954. 2nd impression 1967,
reprinted 1977.
11. 1954.
23. 1977.

Horizontal windmills.
From the Transactions of the Newcomen
Society, Vol. XL. 1967 - 68.
23.

Water-driven mills for grinding.
From The Transactions of the Newcomen
Society, Vol. XXXIX, 1966 - 67.
23.

Windmills in England:a study of their origin,
development and future.
First published 1948 by the Architectural
Press. Reprinted in 1975 by Charles Skilton.
23.

Windmills in Kent, by R. Wailes and J. Russell,
from The Transactions of the Newcomen
Society, Vol. XXIX.1953 - 54 and 1954 - 55.
24,30.

WEST, Jenny.
The Windmills of Kent.
Charles Skilton. 1973.
1,3,4,5,6,7,8,9,11,14,16,19,20,25,28,29,30,31.
2nd revised and enlarged edition.
Charles Skilton and Shaw. 1979.
2,5,9,13,22.

WHITE MILL FOLK MUSEUM STEERING COMMITTEE.
The White Mill, Sandwich, its history and
workings.
White Mill Folk Museum Steering Committee. 1979.
28.

YOUNG, Percy.
Tide Mill Secret (The Mill was moved from
Buckinghamshire to Luton by barge via
canals and rivers in 1848 i.e. Luton,Chatham).
Stockwell. n.d.
8.

WINGHAM

HUSSEY, Arthur.*
Chronicles of Wingham...
J.A. Jennings. Canterbury. 1896.
2.

KENT COUNTY COUNCIL:PLANNING DEPARTMENT.*
Wingham:village study.
K.C.C. 1967.
16.19.30.

PARKIN, E.W.
Wingham, a medieval town:
Offprint from "Archaeologia Cantiana",
Vol.XCIII,1977,pp. 61 - 79, also issued
as a pamphlet with its own pagination -
copy at Canterbury.
(1978).
3.

WITCHCRAFT

DYER, B.R.
Kent witchcraft.
James Pike, St. Ives, Cornwall. 1977.
3,6,11,19,23,28.

SCOT, Reginald.
The discoverie of witchcraft: being a reprint
of the first edition published in 1584.
Edited with explanatory notes,glossary and
introduction by Brinsley Nicholson.
E.P. Publishing. 1973.
4.

WOLFE, GENERAL JAMES. (1727 - 1759) BORN AT WESTERHAM

AYLWARD, A.E. Wolfe.*
Pictorial life of Wolfe.
Mayflower Press. Plymouth. 1924.
11,12.

BRADLEY, Arthur Granville.*
Wolfe.
Macmillan.
1894. 11.
1904. 12.

GARRETT, Richard.
General Wolfe.
Barker. 1975.
11,12.

POLLEN, J.
The life of Wolfe.
C. Hooker.Westerham. 1890.
16.

QUEBEC HOUSE PERMANENT ADVISORY COMMITTEE.*
Wolfe:portraiture and genealogy.
Quebec House Permanent Advisory Committee. 1959.
11,12.

REILLY, Robin.
Wolfe of Quebec.
White Lion Publications. 1973.
12.

WOODCHURCH

ALL SAINTS' PARISH CHURCH, WOODCHURCH.
Parish Magazine, November. 1977.
11.

MANSELL, M.H.*
The parish church of All Saints, Woodchurch,
Kent.
Printed by Adams of Rye Ltd. 1972.
3,7.

WOOLWICH

CHAMPION, George J.
In the matter of Mrs. Mary Wiseman's Charity,
being partially educational, in the parish
of Woolwich, in the County of Kent, extracted
from official records and compiled...by
George J. Champion.
W.J. Squires. Bookseller, Woolwich. 1886.
11.

CLAYTON, F.S.*
John Wilson of Woolwich:a Baptist pastorate
of fifty years.
Kingsgate Press. 1927.
1.11.

COMMITTEE OF ENQUIRY INTO THE ROYAL ORDNANCE
FACTORIES.*
Reports to the Minister of Munitions, March,1919.
Presented to Parliament by command of His
Majesty.
H.M.S.O. 1919.
11.17.

CONNOLLY, Jane.*
Old Days and Ways.
(Contains reminiscences of Woolwich and Woolwich
Dockyard).
Garsdale. 1912.
1,11.

ELLISTON-ERWOOD, Frank Charles.
Fifty years of commerce in Woolwich.
On Cover Woolwich Chamber of Commerce
diamond jubilee review 1889 - 1949. Signed
by the Author.
Woolwich Chamber of Commerce. 1949.
11.

ELLISTON-ERWOOD, Frank Charles.
John Barker's Plan of Woolwich, 1949:
a description and a commentary.
Kent Archaeological Society   n.d.
1.

The Turn pike roads between Greenwich and
Woolwich:an account of the development
of road cummunications between the Capital
and the town of Woolwich.*
 Reprinted from the proceedings of
the Woolwich and District Antiquarian
Society Vol. XXX. 1954.
Independent Printing Works. 1954.
1,8,11,15,18.

JEFFERSON, E.F.E.*
The Woolwich story 1890 - 1965.
For Woolwich and District Antiquarian Society.
R.A. Printing Press Ltd.   1970.
12.

LANSDELL, Henry.*
Princess Aelfrida's Charity. 3 volumes.
(Lands in Greenwich, Lewisham and
Woolwich which became the endowment of
Morden College).
Burnside Ltd.   Blackheath. 1911 - 16.
2,11,17,18.

LOCKE, M.
Traditions and controls in the making of a
polytechnic:Woolwich Polytechnic 1890-1970.
Thames Polytechnic. 1978.
5.

PRYCE, H. and Son Publisher .*
Views of Woolwich and neighbourhood.
H. Pryce and Son. Woolwich. (c.1900).
1,11.

RIGDEN, Reg.
The floating prisons of Woolwich and Deptford.
London Borough of Greenwich. 1976.
2,4,11,12,25.

ROYAL MILITARY ACADEMY,WOOLWICH.
Records of the Royal Military Acadamy.1741-1892.
F.J. Cattermole,Woolwich.1892.
11.

"SOUTH EASTERN"pseud (i.e. F.M. Atkins,
G.E.Baddeley,R.I.Durrant,R.Elliott & A.A.Jackson)
The tramways of Woolwich and South East London.
Light Railway Transport League. 1963.
2,4,5,8,12.

WILLIAMS Marguerite.*
John Wilson of Woolwich,an apostle to the people.
(Sixty years Pastor of Woolwich Tabernacle).
Marshall,Morgan and Scott. 1937.
1,11.
WOOLWICH BOROUGH COUNCIL
Opening of the gardens at Well Hall by
the Worshipful,the Mayor of Woolwich on
Thursday,25th May, 1933.
11.

WORLD WAR I
BACON, Sir Reginald Hugh Spencer.*
The Concise story of the Dover Patrol.
Hutchinson. 1932.
4.6.11.12.

The Dover Patrol, 1915 - 1917. 2 volumes.
Hutchinson. (1919) 11.
Doran. 1919.   4,6,7,12.

BELL, Ernest W.
Soldiers killed on the first day of the
Somme (Casualties listed by Regiment).
E.W. Bell. Bolton. 1977.
11.

BENNETT, J.J. ("Jackstaff" pseud).*
The Dover Patrol:The Straights: Zeebrugge:
Ostend, including a narrative of the
operations in the Spring of 1918,by
"Jackstaff" (J.J. Bennett).
Grant Richards Ltd. 1919.
11,12.

BORTON, Lieutenant Colonel. A.C.
My warrior Sons the Borton family diary,
1914 - 1918, edited and with an introduction
by Guy Slater.
(The diary of Lieutenant Colonel A.C. Borton
who lived at Cheveney House, Hunton).
Davies. 1973.
11.

BROMLEY CONGREGATIONAL CHURCH.
A short history of our War Work..1914-1918
(photocopy).Bromley Congregational Church. 1919.
2.

CAMPBELL, H.
Belgian soldiers at home in the United Kingdom.
Saunders and Cullingham. 1917.
7.

COXON, Stanley W.*
Dover during the dark days, by a "Dug-out"...
with contributions by other Officers of the
Dover Patrol.
John Lane. 1919.
7,8,11,12,28.

CRESWICK, Paul.
Kent's care of the wounded, by Paul Creswick,
G. Stanley Pond and T.H. Ashton.
Hodder and Stoughton. 1915.
11.19.

CRUNDALL, Edward Duncan.
Fighter-pilot on the Western Front.
(The author is a member of a well known
Dover family and was born at Whitfield,Dover.
His experiences in World War I).
Kimber. 1975.
6.

FIRTH, John B.*
Dover and the Great War.
Alfred Leney. Dover. 1919.
1,2,3,4,6,7,8,11,12,14,15,24.

IGGLESDEN, Sir Charles.
Crimson Glow. A novel set in the Ashford
area during World War I.
Kentish Express.
11. 1925.
4 and 6. 2nd edition. 1940.

THE MARGATE "FRONT" IN THE GREAT WAR, 1914-1918.
Illustrated Peace Souvenir. n.d.
13.

OLIVER, Bernard.
Looking back sixty years:three years service
in Ypres Salient with balloons of the Royal
Flying Corps.
Bernard Oliver. Maidstone. 1979.
12.

PENFOLD, Michael J.
The Unfinished journey.
(Typescript. Loss of H.M.S. Hythe, 1915).
19.

THANET ADVERTISER.*
Thanet's raid history - raids, bombs, shells.
A record of the home line of trenches.
Compiled from Official and private documents.
3rd edition.maps.
Thanet Advertiser. 1919.
11,24.

UNIVERSITY OF KENT-FACULTY OF SOCIAL SCIENCE.
Life in Kent during the first World War:
S214; Aspects of the economic and social
history of Kent. Group research project, 1975.
Duplicated typescript.
University of Kent. 1975.
4,11.

WARNER, Philip.
The Zeebrugger raid.   (The Dover Patrol).
Kimber. 1978.
6.

WEST KENT (QUEEN'S OWN) YEOMANRY.
Roll of honour.
Barnard and Crannis, Printers. c.1919.
2.

WORLD WAR II

BERRY, C.F.
Five years in a pillbox. C6 Area;
memoirs of a part time warden 1939 - 1945.
(Typescript:C6 Area was Southborough
district of Bromley, Kent.
(1975)
2.

BLAIR, Donald.
Clipped wings - the true story of an R.A.F.
pilot's war experiences. (The Author lives at Strood)
Stanhope Press. Rochester. 1947.
25.

BLAKE, Lewis pseud. (G.L. Donnington).
Bromley in the front-line: the story of the
London Borough of Bromley under enemy
air attack in the Second World War...
G.L. Donnington. 1980.
2,5.

BOORMAN, Henry Roy Pratt.*
Hell's Corner, 1940: Kent becomes the
Battlefield of Britain.
Kent Messenger. 1942.
20,25.

Recalling the Battle of Britain:a photographic
essay based upon the records of the Kent
Messenger and other contemporary sources
of World War II,by H.R.P. Boorman and
H.R. Long.
Kent Messenger. 1965.
4,12.

BOWYER, Chaz.
Sunderland at War.
(Sunderland Flying Boats were built by
Short Brothers at Rochester).
Ian Allan. 1976.
11.

BRYANT, Sir Arthur.
The summer of Dunkirk:epic of the little boats
that saved the world, (bound with) Written in
recollection of the great miracle, May-
June, 1940,by Edward Shanks.
The contents were reprinted from the Daily
Sketch of 3rd and 4th June, 1943. Nos 199
and 264 of edition.
Baynard Press. (1949?),
11.

COLLYER, David G.
Battle of Britain Diary:East Kent.
July - September 1940.
Kent Research Defence Group: Kent Aviation
Research Society. 1980.
13.28.

COOK, Raymond A.*
Shell-fire Corner carries on:a graphic
description of the war's events at England's
gateway.
Raymond A. Cook. Printed by Headley Brothers,
Ashford. 1942.
3,6,7,11.

CROSS CHANNEL GUNS.
In "After the Battle" no 29, 1980.
Articles on the heavy guns stationed on
the Cliffs near Dover during World War II).
Battle of Britain Prints International Ltd.1980.
6,28.

DANE, Herbert.*
The War years 1939 - 1945 in Faversham and
District, compiled by H. Dane.
F. Austin. (1971?).
4,6,11,26.

DREW, Bernard.*
Farningham against Hitler, the story of
six years of War in a Kentish Village amid
Barrage, Balloons and Bombs.
Photocopy.
The Kentish District Times Co Ltd. Bromley.1946.
5,11,16.

GRAVES, Charles.
The Home Guard of Britain.
Hutchinson. 1943.
5,

GULVIN, Keith R.
Kent Home Guard:a history.
North Kent Books in Association with
Meresborough Books. 1980.
2,6,12,13,16,22,23,28.

GUY, L.H.
Memoirs of a light rescue leader - ordeal
of Lewisham, 1939 - 1945.
Unpublished Manuscript. 1976.
18.

HERITAGE OF KENT:a special issue of
"Photography" prepared on behalf of the
forces under the care of the Kent County
Welfare Organisation.
Worlds' Press. News Publishing. Company, London,
1943.
4.

ILLINGWORTH, Frank.*
Britain under Shellfire.
(The Author lives in Dover).
Hutchinson. (1941?).
6.11.

IMPERIAL WAR GRAVES COMMISSION.
Civilian War Dead 1939 - 1945, Kent.
Imperial War Graves Commission. 1954.
15.

JONES, G.W.
Chatham in the '40s., by G.W. Jones and
M. Shortland.
Fort Research Group. Chatham. 1978.
4.

JULLIAN, Marcel.
The Battle of Britain, July - September, 1940.
Chivers. 1974.
11.

KENT COUNTY LIBRARY: DOVER DIVISION.
Dover 1939 - 45.
Kent County Library, Dover Division. 1980.
6,13.

MASON, Francis K.
Battle over Britain...(Various Kent references)
McWhirter Twins Ltd. 1969.
2.

MILLAR, J.B.
The story of 'Medway Queen':a paddle steamer
that went to war,
edited by J.B. Millar.
East Horsley Paddle Steamer Preservation Society.
1975.
3,4,8,11,20,25,26,27.

POOLMAN, Kenneth.*
Flying boat:the story of the "Sunderland".
(Short Brothers of Rochester).
Kimber. 1962.
15.

RAMSEY, Winston G.
The Battle of Britain:then and now,edited
by W.G. Ramsey.   Battle of Britain Prints
International Limited. In
'After the Battle' Magazine. 1980.
23.28.

ROOTES, Andrew.
Front line county.
Hale 1980.
2,6,9,12,22,28.

SACKVILLE-WEST, Victoria (afterwards Lady Nicolson)*
The Women's Land Army.
M. Joseph. 1944.
11,12,23.

SCOTT, Sir Peter.*
The battle of the narrow seas:a history of the
light coastal forces in the Channel and
North Sea, 1939- 1945.
Country Life. 1946.
6,11.
Published by White Lion. 1974.   11.

WORLD WAR II Cont'd

STANHOPE-PALMER, R.
Tank Trap 1940 - or No Battle in Britain.
(The German advance to the shores of the
English Channel in 1940).
Arthur Stockwell. 1976.
8.

TOWNSEND, Peter.
Dual of eagles. (The Battle of Britain).
Weidenfeld and Nicolson. 1971.
12.

WEBB, Anthony.
Battle over Kent: a day to remember, 5th
September, 1940.
Kent Battle of Britain Museum, Chilham. 1977.
2,5,6,7,8,12,19.

WILSON, Jack F.
The Royal Observer Corps: a brief history...
and memories of the Bromley Group No.19
Operations room, who guarded the South
Eastern approaches to London.
Typescript. (1975).
2.

WILTON, Eric.*
Centre Crew: a memory of the Royal Observer
Corps. Published privately for the members
of "B" Crew of the Royal Observer Corps
Centre at Bromley, Kent.
Printed by King and Jarrett. 1946.
2,11.

WOOD, Derek.
Target England: the illustrated history of
the Battle of Britain.
Jane's. 1980.
6,28.

WRIGHT, Nicholas.
The Bump: Battle of Britain 40th Anniversary
Reunion: Royal Air Force. 21st September, 1980.
Royal Air Force. Biggin Hill. 1980.
2,12.

YOUNG, Richard Anthony.
The flying bomb.
Ian Allan Ltd. Shepperton. 1978.
12.

WOULDHAM

GENERAL REGISTER OFFICE.
Census Returns. 1841,1851,1861,1871,
Wouldham. Microfilm.
23.

WROTHAM

Annual Handbook for Wrotham and Borough
Green, Kent. 1923.
5.

CARLEY, James.
The Gravesend to Wrotham Turnpike Road.
Meopham Publications Committee. 1973.
2,9,11,23,25.

GENERAL REGISTER OFFICE.
Census Returns. 1841, 1851, 1861, 1871,
Wrotham. Microfilm.
23.

PASCOE, A.P.*
Old ways and days at Wrotham.
Kent Messenger. 1926.
5,11.

THORNDIKE, Russell.
The master of the Macabre. A novel set
in Wrotham.
Rich and Cowan. 1946.
11.

TONBRIDGE AND MALLING DISTRICT COUNCIL:
PLANNING DEPARTMENT.
Wrotham: conservation study.
(E.P. Miller, Planning Director).
Tonbridge and Malling District Council. 1977.
2,11,23.

WROTHAM PARISH COUNCIL.*
Official Guide to Wrotham, Borough Green and
district.
Home Publishing Company. Croydon.
1952 etc.   1.5.
1961.   4.
1965.   19.
1974. Forward Publicity Ltd. 4.11.
1977.   7,11.

WROTHAM: ST. GEORGE'S CHURCH.
Wrotham Festival of Music, 22nd - 29th
September, 1974, in aid of St. George's Church
Organ Restoration Fund.
4.

WYE

BRADE-BIRKS, Stanley Graham.
Wye Church: its history and principal features,
by S.G. Brade-Birks and G.E. Hubbard. Revised
and brought up-to-date in 1976 by the Vicar and
Churchwardens.
Church Publishers. Ramsgate. (1976).
3.

HUBBARD, Gilbert Ernest.*
Old book of Wye: being a record of a Kentish
country parish from the time of Henry the Eighth
to that of Charles the Second.
Pilgrim Press. Derby. 1951.
4,26.

M.,E.W. (MOORE, E.W.). *
A short history of Wye.
Wye Historical Society. (1953,). 1957 reprint.
2.

MORRIS, W.J.*
The history and topography of Wye.
Printed by H. Chivers, Canterbury. 1842.
11,25.

NATURE CONSERVANCY COUNCIL: SOUTH EAST REGION.
Wye and Crundale Downs National Nature Reserve.
Nature Conservancy Council. 1975.
3.

Wye and Crundale Down...Nature Trail.
Nature Conservancy Council. 1977.
7,30.

TOWN AND COUNTRY MAGAZINE
Includes information on Wye.
Virtue. London. 1837 - 38.
4.

WYE COLLEGE: Prospectus 1972 - 74.
Wye College. 1972.
11.

WYE HISTORICAL SOCIETY.
A walk through Wye.
Wye Historical Society. 1977.
3,11.

Wye Local History, Autumn, 1978. Volume 1. No.1.
Wye Historical Society. 1978.
3.

WYE ORNITHOLOGISTS' CLUB.
The Wye and District Bird Report.
No.1. October 1975-September 1976.
No.2. October 1976- September 1977;
edited by Gwyn Williams.
Wye Ornithologists' Club. Wye College.
1977 and 1978.
3.

YALDING

BLUNDEN, Edmund.
English villages. (pp.11 - 21 Yalding).
Edmund Blunden spent his childhood in Yalding.
Collins. 1941.
11.

GENERAL REGISTER OFFICE.
Census Returns - 1851.
Yalding. Photocopy.
23.

HALE, Robert.
Plan of an estate called the Park Farm and
Cat's Place Farm situate in the parishes of
Brenchley and Yalding in the County of Kent.
Scale 21" = 1 mile. Size. 65cm x 90cm.
1837.
11.

KENT COUNTY COUNCIL:PLANNING DEPARTMENT.*
Yalding:village study.
K.C.C. 1967.
30.

KREMER, Tony.
Education in Yalding, edited from local
records by Tony Kremer.
1974.
11.

Origins of Yalding Parish:an account of
manorial history:the derivation of names
and parochial administration, edited
from local records by Tony Kremer.
1975.
11.

TOOTELL, J.
A plan of an estate in the parish of
Yalding and in the hamlet of Old Hay
in the parish of Mereworth in the
County of Kent. The property of Lord
Strafford. Revised from the Tithe Maps...
1860. Scale 1 mile = 26". Size 92 cm x 110cm.
(.744in).
11.

YALDING - a history.
P.J. Mitchell Ltd. (South Croydon).(1977).
12.

YALDING CHURCH FUND RAISING COMMITTEE.
Yalding:articles written by local people
in aid of the Bell and Tower Appeal of St.
Peter and St. Paul.
Yalding Church Fund Raising Committee. (1977).
3,11,19.

ZOOS, ZOO PARKS

ASPINALL,John.
The best of friends.
(Zoo Parks at Bekesbourne and Lympne).
MacMillan 1976.
3,7.

THE ILLUSTRATED HANDBOOK TO THE ROSHERVILLE
BOTANICAL AND ZOOLOGICAL GARDENS, County Kent.
(Rosherville Gardens Company). n.d.
11.

TYRWHITT-DRAKE, Sir Hugh Garrard.
Sir Hugh Garrard Tyrwhitt-Drake's Zoo
Park: official illustrated guide (1938).
(At Cobtree Manor, Maidstone).
12.

BOUNDARY COMMISSION FOR ENGLAND AND WALES: Elections;
Local Government; Rochester.

BOUNDS OF CHATHAM PARISH: Chatham.

BOUQUET, Michael Rome: Coastal Waters; Ships & Shipping.

BOURNE, H.R. Fox: Sidney, Sir Philip

BOWATER PAPER CORPORATION: Industry & Trade-Firms.
See Also SITTINGBOURNE & KEMSLEY LIGHT RAILWAY COMPANY:
Industry & Trade - Firms; Kemsley; Railways; Sittingbourne

BOWATER RAILWAY: See SITTINGBOURNE & KEMSLEY LIGHT
RAILWAY COMPANY: Industry & Trade - Firms; Kemsley;
Railways; Sittingbourne

BOWDEN, Victor E: Kemsing;
See also KEMSING PARISH COUNCIL: Kemsing

BOWEN, Harold Townshend: Rolvenden

BOWRA, Edward V: Ightham.

BOWTELL, John: Bridge; Patrixbourne; Sermons.

BOWYER, Chaz: Aviation; Rochester; World War II.

BOXER, C.R: History - 1501 AD onwards.

BOYD, Derek: Military & Naval History.

BOYD, Hugh: Natural History

BOYLE, A.J: See ADMIRALTY: Sea & River Charts.

BOYLE, John: Kent; Canterbury.
See also Canterbury City Council. Canterbury.

BOYLE, Robert: Spas & Mineral Waters.

BOYS, John: Agriculture & Horticulture

BRADBURN, H: Faversham

BRADBURY, Janet: Biography.

BRADDOCK, Joseph: Footpaths & Commons; Kent, West.

BRADE-BIRKS, Stanley Graham: Agriculture; Geology; Wye.

BRADEN, J.T. Publisher: Isle of Thanet; Margate.

BRADFORD, Ernle: Coastal Waters.

BRADLEY, Arthur Granville: Cinque Ports; Darent, River;
Medway, River; Stour, River; Wolfe, Gen. James

BRADLEY, Donald Laurence: Railways
BRADLEY, Ian: Morris, William.
BRADY, John H: Knole.
BRAMSTON, William: Minster-in-Sheppey.
BRANCH-JOHNSON, William: Medway, River; Prisons;
Thames, River.

BRANSON, Douglas: See WILSON, W. Eric. Sea &
river charts; Thames, River.

BRASIER, W.C. Publisher: Canterbury; Dover;
Isle of Thanet; Margate.

BRASS TO STEPHEN BOROUGH...Chatham.

BRASSELL, K.W: Beckenham

BRAUN, Hugh: Architecture; Castles & Houses.

BRAYLEY, Edward Wedlake: Cinque Ports; History -
General; Isle of Thanet.

BREALEY, R: Sundridge(Sevenoaks).

BRENCHLEY PARISH COUNCIL: Brenchley; Matfield

BRENT, John: Canterbury.

BRENTNALL, Margaret: Cinque Ports; Kent; Romney
Marsh.

BRETHERTON, Ralph Harold: Canterbury; Ghosts.

BRETT, Sir Henry: Genealogical Records; Ships & Shipping

BRETT, Rev. Thomas: See BOUGHEN, Rev. Edward:
Canterbury - Churches; Sermons.

BREWER, Derek Stanley: Chaucer, Geoffrey.

BRIAN LUCKHURST BENEFIT, 1973: See DIMONT, Charles:
Cricket.

BRIDGE-BLEAN RURAL DISTRICT COUNCIL: Kent, East.

BRIDGE, Colin W: Brompton; Footpaths-Country Walks;
Gillingham.

BRIDGE, John W: Maidstone

A BRIEF ACCOUNT OF THE CLOTH TRADE... Industry & Trade;
Maidstone.

BRIERCLIFFE, Harold: Kent.

BRIDGEWATER, Howard: Margate.

BRIGDEN, C.A.T. illustrator: Dickens, Charles;
Kent Artists; Kent Authors & Lit. - Poetry.
See also JOHN, Malcolm: Kent
BRIGG, William: Genealogical Records.

BRIGGS, Asa See MORRIS, William: Morris, William.

BRIGGS, Enid Semple: Broadstairs.

BRIGGS, Martin Shaw: Thames River.

BRIGHTMAN, F.H: Down(e); Natural History.
BRINTON, Thomas, Bishop of Rochester 1373-1389:
Rochester Cathedral-Bishops; Sermons.

BRISTOW, Clement Roger: Geology; Kent West

BRITANNIA: a Journal of Romano-British & Kindred Studies
Canterbury; Richborough

BRITISH ARCHAEOLOGICAL ASSOCIATION: History-Archaeology.

BRITISH ASSOCIATION OF SOCIAL WORKERS: KENT BRANCH.
Health & Welfare; Housing.

BRITISH CHANNEL TUNNEL CO. LTD: Channel Tunnel

BRITISH LEGION See ROYAL BRITISH LEGION: Ditton;
Organisations.
See ROYAL BRITISH LEGION WHITSTABLE BRANCH: Organisations;
Whitstable.

BRITISH LIBRARY: Reference Division
Caxton, William; Printing & Publishing.
See also BRITISH MUSEUM

BRITISH MUSEUM: Bibliography; Dickens Charles.

BRITISH MUSEUM: NATURAL HISTORY. Darwin, Charles.

BRITISH MUSEUM: NATURAL HISTORY - Dept. of Geology.
Bibliography; Geology; Herne Bay; Weald.

BRITISH PETROLEUM COMPANY: Adams, William;
Industry & Trade - Firms; Isle of Grain.

BRITISH PETROLEUM OIL KENT REFINERY LTD:
Industry & Trade - Firms; Isle of Grain

BRITISH PUBLISHING CO LTD: Faversham

BRITISH RAILWAYS BOARD: Channel Tunnel; Railways

BRITISH RAILWAYS BOARD: SOUTHERN REGION. Railways

BRITISH RECORD SOCIETY: See DUNKIN, Edwin Hadlow Wise:
Bibliography; Canterbury Cathedral - Archbishops.

BRITISH RED CROSS SOCIETY: KENT BRANCH. Organisations.

BRITISH REGIONAL GEOLOGY: See SHERLOCK, R.L: Geology;
Kent, N. West.
See also EDMUNDS, F.H: Geology; Weald.

BRITISH ROAD FEDERATION: Roads.

BRITISH SCIENTIFIC INSTRUMENT RESEARCH ASSOCIATION:
Chislehurst; Organisations.

BRITISH SERVICES TATTOO (1951): Folkestone.

BRITISH TOURIST AUTHORITY: Footpaths-Country Walks;
Nature Walks.

BRITON, D.A. Kent-Mid:

BRITTEN, James. Dialects:

BRITTON, John: Canterbury Cathedral.
See also CLARKE, Charles: Barfreston.

BROAD, Lewis: Churchill, Sir W.L.S.

BROADSTAIRS & ST PETER'S ARCHAEOLOGICAL SOCIETY:
Broadstairs.

BROADSTAIRS & ST.PETER'S CHAMBER OF COMMERCE: Broadstairs.

BROADSTAIRS & ST.PETER'S DISTRICT: Local Board
Broadstairs; Health & Welfare.

BROADSTAIRS & ST.PETER'S MAIL: See
EAST KENT TIMES AND BROADSTAIRS & ST.PETER'S MAIL:
Broadstairs; Industry & Trade; Newspapers.

BROADSTAIRS & ST.PETER'S URBAN DISTRICT COUNCIL:
Broadstairs.

BROADSTAIRS PIER: Broadstairs.

BROADSTAIRS PIER & HARBOUR: Broadstairs.

BROME, Rev. James: Dover; Sermons.

BROMEHEAD, C.E.N: See DEWEY, Henry: Geology; Kent, N. West.

BROMILEY, G.W: Canterbury Cathedral-Archbishops.

BROMLEY, Francis. E: Becket, Saint Thomas, Archbishop of Canterbury.

BROMLEY ASSOCIATION FOR THE HANDICAPPED AND BROMLEY COUNCIL OF SOCIAL SERVICE: Bromley

BROMLEY CONGREGATIONAL CHURCH: Bromley; World War I.

BROMLEY, LONDON BOROUGH COUNCIL: Bromley

BROMLEY, LONDON BOROUGH COUNCIL: EDUCATION COMMITTEE Bromley.

BROMLEY PUBLIC LIBRARY: Bromley; Orpington; St. Mary Cray.

BROMLEY SOCIETY FOR MENTALLY HANDICAPPED CHILDREN: Bromley

BROODBANK, Sir JOSEPH: Thames, River.

BROOK, Cyril A: Caves & Tunnels; Dartford.

(The) BROOK PENTAGON: Chatham

BROOKE, John: See GREAT BRITAIN:PARLIAMENT - HOUSE OF COMMONS: Bibliography; History - AD 1501-onwards.

BROOKS, Charles S: Canterbury.

BROWN, Alex: See CANTERBURY COLLEGE OF ART: School of Architecture. Canterbury - Education.

BROWN, Anthony: Aylesford; Organisations.

BROWN, Christopher R: Bibliography; Kent Authors & Literature - General.

BROWN, E.E.S: Geology; Herne Bay; Reculver.

BROWN, H.S: See WENYON, H.J. Military & Naval History.

BROWN, L: Family History.

BROWN, Malcolm Dennis: Bibliography; Southborough.

BROWN, Paul: See ARC Publications. Kent Authors & Lit. - Poetry.

BROWN, Reginald Allen: Dover; Rochester.

BROWN, Samuel: Bridges; Isle of Sheppey.

BROWN, Theodore: Chelsfield.

BROWN, W: See HISTORY OF THE CORPS OF ROYAL ENGINEERS: Military & Naval History.

BROWN, W. Henry: Industry & Trade - Firms; Sheerness.

BROWN, W.J: See IRWIN, John. Thames, River.

BROWNE, A.M: Westerham.

BROWNING, Lieut. G.A. See ADMIRALTY: Folkestone; Sea & River Charts.

BROWNING. Robert H.K: Herne Bay; Sport.

BROWNING, Stella: Kent Authors & Lit. - Poetry.

BROWNING, W.H: Eltham.

BROWNLOW, Margaret Eileen: Seal

BRUCE, Gordon: Aviation.

BRUCE, John: History - 1501AD onwards.

BRUNTON, William illustrator See KNATCHBULL-HUGESSEN, Edward: Hugessen Baron Brabourne: Kent Authors & Lit. -Fiction.

BRUXNER, Mervyn: Education; Music.

BRYANT, Sir Arthur: World War II.

BRYDGES, Sir Samuel Egerton: Kent Authors & Lit - General; Kent Authors & Lit.-Poetry; Letters.

BUCHANAN, Colin, and Partners: Blackheath; Greenwich.

BUCHANAN, James Robert: Herne.

BUCHANAN, Robert Angus: Industrial Archaeology

BUCKFIELD, Reginald Sidney: Defendant. Strood;Trials.

BUCKINGHAM, Christopher: Canterbury-Diocese & Province; Church History; Dover; Family History; Hackington; Lydden. See also MASTERS, John White. Dialects; Kent Authors & Lit. - Poetry.

BUCKLAND, Harry: See A MASTER OF HOUNDS...Ashford;Sport.

BUCKLAND, W.E: See KENT ARCHAEOLOGICAL SOCIETY - RECORDS BRANCH: Rochester Diocese.

BUCKNALL, Rixon: Coastal Waters; Railways; Ships & Shipping.

BUDD, G.L. Culver: Greenwich.

BULL, Christopher: Agriculture & Horticulture; Land Utilisation; Recreation.

BULLEID, Henry Anthony Vaughan: Railways.

BULLEN, A.H: See ARDEN OF FEVERSHAM: Faversham.

BULLOCK, Captain: See ADMIRALTY: Sea & River Charts.

BULLOCK, Charles: Walmer.

BUMOGRAPHY: or, a touch at the ladys tails... Tunbridge Wells.

BUMPUS, T. Francis: Canterbury Cathedral;Rochester Cathedral.

BUNCE, Cyprian Rondeau: Canterbury See also URRY, William. Canterbury.

BUNHAM, K.C: See THE ROYAL SOCIETY. Floods;Thames,River.

BUNYAN, John: Printing & Publishing.

BUNYARD, George: Agriculture & Horticulture; Maidstone.

BURA, Paul: Printing & Publishing.

BURCH, William: See TICEHURST, Norman F: Canterbury Cathedral; Natural History.

BURCHALL, Michael J: Family History; Genealogical Records.

BURCHMORE, L.J: Gravesend; Military & Naval History.

BURGESS, William Engraver: See RAMBLING RECOLLECTIONS OF THE NEIGHBOURHOOD OF DOVER... Dover; Kent, South-East.

BURKE, John: Kent.

BURN, John Southerden: Genealogical Records.

BURNAND, F.C: Coastline.

BURNBY, John: Canterbury Cathedral

BURNHAM, C. Paul: Kent. See also MACRAE, Stuart Gordon: Agriculture; Geography.

BURNHAM, T.G: Bromley; Railways.

BURNETT, Charles Buxton: Isle of Grain.

BURR, Thomas Benge: Tunbridge Wells.

BURRIDGE, William F: Churchill, Sir W.L.S.

BURROUGHS-WELLCOME LTD: See The WELLCOME FOUNDATION: Beckenham; Dartford; Industry & Trade - Firms.

BURROW, Edward J & Co. Publishers: Chatham; Hotels, Restaurants & Clubs; Kent; Rochester; Tonbridge. See Also CHATHAM BOROUGH COUNCIL: Chatham. See Also WHITSTABLE & TANKERTON PUBLICITY COMMITTEE: Tankerton; Whitstable.

BURROWS AND COMPANY, Auctioneers: See BY ORDER OF THE CANTERBURY DIOCESAN BOARD OF FINANCE.. Davington (Sale Catalogue); Faversham(Sale Catalogue)

BURROWS, Montagu: Cinque Ports.

BURT, BOLTON & HAYWOOD LTD: Erith; Industry & Trade - Firms.

CHAMPION, George H.J: Footpaths-Country Walks; Kent,East.

CHAMPION, George J: Charities; Woolwich.

CHAMPION, Mrs. I.K: Kent, North; Natural History;Rochester.

CHANDLER, Marjorie Elizabeth Jane: Natural History.

CHANDLER, Raymond, H: Caves and Tunnels; Crayford.

CHANNEL TUNNEL ADVISORY GROUP: Channel Tunnel.

CHANNEL TUNNEL OPPOSITION ASSOCIATION: Channel Tunnel
See Also AFCO ASSOCIATES: Channel Tunnel.

CHANNEL TUNNEL STUDY GROUP: Channel Tunnel.

CHAPLIN, Howard Douglas: Military & Naval History.

CHAPLIN, Winifred Maud: Sandgate.

CHAPMAN, Frank: Tonbridge.
See also PEACOCK, David: Kent Artists; Tunbridge Wells.

CHAPMAN, T: Aviation; Industry & Trade; Margate.

CHAPMAN, Rev. W. (Curate of Margate):Margate; Sermons.

CHARITY COMMISSION: Canterbury-Almshouses & Hospitals;
Charities; Fordwich.

CHARLES, Frank: Whitstable.

CHARLES, H.R.H. PRINCE OF WALES: See
CANTERBURY CITY COUNCIL: Canterbury.

CHARLTON, John: Greenwich.

CHARLTON PARK, BISHOPSBOURNE: Bishopsbourne.

CHARLTON SOCIETY: Charlton; Genealogical Records.

CHARTRES, J.A: Industry & Trade.

CHATER, G.P: Agriculture & Horticulture.

CHATHAM & DISTRICT LETTER CARD: Medway Towns.

CHATHAM & DISTRICT TRACTION CO: Road Transport.

CHATHAM BOROUGH COUNCIL: Bibliography; Chatham;
Chatham Dockyard.

CHATHAM BOROUGH COUNCIL: BOROUGH ENGINEER & SURVEYOR:
Chatham.

CHATHAM BOROUGH COUNCIL: PUBLIC HEALTH DEPT: Chatham.

CHATHAM BOROUGH COUNCIL:PUBLIC LIBRARIES:
See also KENT COUNTY LIBRARY:Medway Division
Medway Towns; Organisations.

CHATHAM DOCKYARD EXTENSION. 1866: Chatham Dockyard;
Military & Naval History.

CHATHAM FESTIVAL CARNIVAL COMMITTEE 1951: Chatham.

CHATHAM HOUSE SCHOOL:See RUYM: Chatham House School
Magazine; Ramsgate.

CHATHAM NEWS: Medway Towns.

CHATHAM PUBLIC LIBRARIES:See
CHATHAM BOROUGH COUNCIL:Public Libraries See
KENT COUNTY LIBRARY:Medway Division

CHATHAM, ROCHESTER, STROOD & BROMPTON MECHANICS
INSTITUTION: Medway Towns.

"CHATHAM STANDARD": Crime; Medway Towns.

CHATTERTON, E. Keble: Canterbury; Kent Artists.

CHATWIN, C.P: See DEWEY, Henry: Geology;
Kent, N. West.

CHAUCER, Geoffrey: Chaucer, Geoffrey. See also
MANLY, John Matthew: Chaucer, Geoffrey.

CHAUVOIS, Louis: Harvey, Dr. William.

CHEESEMAN, Clive: Footpaths-Countryside; Kent,Mid.

CHEESEMAN, Dick: Cricket; Sevenoaks.

CHELSEA SPELAEOLOGICAL SOCIETY: See
PEARMAN, Harry: Caves & Tunnels; Kent North East;
Kent North West.
See REEVE, Terry: Caves & Tunnels.

CHESTER, J.L: Genealogical Records.

CHESTERTON, Keith: Footpaths-Country Walks; Kent,West.

CHETTLE, George H: Greenwich.

CHETWYND, Richard Walter: Kent, North West; Sport.

CHIDELL, C: See HYTHE BOROUGH COUNCIL:
Bibliography; Hythe.

CHILD and SON (Department Store): Faversham;
Industry & Trade - Firms.

CHILD, Kenneth: Family History

CHILDS, Edmund: Caxton, William.

CHILHAM PARISH COUNCIL: Chilham.

CHISLEHURST URBAN DISTRICT COUNCIL: Chislehurst;
Sidcup.

CHOWNS, L.M: Shadoxhurst.

CHRISTCHURCH PRIORY: Canterbury-Monastic Houses.

CHRISTIE, Rosemary: See HAGUE, Douglas B:
Architecture; Coastal Waters - Safety at Sea.

CHRISTISON, Mc C: See DULWICH COLLEGE: Dulwich.

CHUBB, D.P: See BOLTON, D: Footpaths-Country Walks;
Kent - North-West; Nature Walks.

CHUDLEY, John A: Ashford; Industry & Trade-Firms.

CHURCH, Alfred: J. History to 900 AD.

CHURCH, Derek: Cuxton. See also GOWERS, Edward.
Halling.

CHURCH, Richard: Biography; Canterbury; Kent; Kent Authors
and Lit.-General;Weald.See also LAMBARDE,William:History-
General.

CHURCH, Thomas B: See LIST OF INSCRIPTIONS ON
MEMORIALS...Bilsington; Bonnington; Goudhurst;
Monumental Inscriptions.

CHURCH MISSIONARY SOCIETY: Bromley.

CHURCHILL, Irene Josephine: Bibliography;
Canterbury - Diocese & Province; History - 901AD -
1500 AD; Lambeth Palace.

CHURCHILL, Randolph Spencer: Churchill, Sir Winston.
L. Spencer.

CHURCHILL, Sir Winston Leonard Spencer:
Churchill, Sir. W.L.S.

"A CHURCHMAN OF THE DIOCESE OF CANTERBURY": pseud:
Canterbury Cathedral; Archbishops.

CHURTON, Edward: Railways.

CHUTE, M: Chaucer, Geoffrey.

CINQUE PORTS POETRY SOCIETY: Kent Authors &
Lit. - Poetry.

CITY OF CANTERBURY 1970 FESTIVAL COMMITTEE: Canterbury.

CITY OF CANTERBURY SILVER JUBILEE COMMITTEE: Canterbury.

CITY OF ROCHESTER SOCIETY: Dickens, Charles;
Industry & Trade; Medway Towns; Organisations; Rochester.

CIVIC TRUST: Conservation.

CIVIL AVIATION AUTHORITY: Aviation; Transport.

CLAGUE, John C: Herne Bay.

CLAIR, Colin: History-General.

CLAPHAM, Sir: Alfred William. Canterbury-Monastic
Houses.

CLARE PARK ESTATE: East Malling.

CLARK, F.C: Kent.

CLARK, Gordon W: See
ISLE OF THANET CONSERVATION ASSOCIATION: Margate.

CLARK, Sir Kenneth: Biography.

CLARK, Kenneth M: Cinque Ports; Smuggling.

CLARK, M. Dudley: Birchington.

CLARK, Peter: History - 1501 AD onwards.

CLARK, R.G.A. Dover; Public Utilities.

CLARK, Ronald Harry: Railways.

CLARK, Tim: Crime; Gravesend.

CLARK, W.A: Dickens, Charles.

CLARKE - See MISCELLANEA GENEALOGICA ET HERALDICA:
Bromley; Genealogical Records; Monumental Inscriptions.

CLARKE, Charles: Barfreston.

CLARKE, Dennis: Otford.

C Cont'd.

CONNOR, James Edward: Kent, Northwest; Railways.

CONRAD, Borys: Castles & Houses; Conrad, Joseph.

CONSERVATION SOCIETY (LTD:) Kent Branch: Channel-Tunnel; Conservation.

CONSTAPLE, C.&.D. Ltd. publishers : Kent.

A CONTESTED ELECTION...Kent Authors & Lit. - Poetry.

CONWAY, Agnes E: Allington.

CONWAY, William Martin, 1st Baron Conway of Allington: Allington; Biography.

COODE, FITZMAURICE, WILSON & MITCHELL (Consulting Engineers): Dartford Tunnel; Gravesend.

COODE, WILSON, MITCHELL AND VAUGHAN-LEE. (Consulting Engineers): See COODE, FITZMAURICE, WILSON & MITCHELL (Consulting Engineers): Dartford Tunnel; Gravesend.

COOK, A.M: Dover.

COOK, A.R: East Peckham.

COOK, David: Industry & Trade; Kent, East.

COOK, Graham:See HISTORY OF KENT, Nos 1 - 6: History-General.

COOK, J: Family History.

COOK, Raymond: Biography; Dover.

COOK, Raymond A: Kent, South East; World War II.

COOKE, Arthur O: Coastal Waters - Safety at Sea.

COOKE, Canon Daniel: Kent Authors & Lit. - Fiction.

COOKE, George Alexander: History-General.

COOKE, Robert: See VISITATIONS OF KENT, 1530-31; 1574; 1592. Genealogical Records.

COOKE, Rev. Shadrach: Sermons; Sittingbourne.

COOLE, Albert: Becket, Saint Thomas.

COOLING, Christine M: Geology; Kent East; Kent N.East.

COOMBE, Derek: Medway, River.

COOMBES, Arthur illustrator: See BONE, David: Kent Authors & Lit. - Poetry.

COOMBS, Leonard C: Ickham.

COOPER, Messrs. AUCTIONEERS: See OLD PARK FARM, SAINT MARTIN, CANTERBURY: Canterbury (Sale Catalogue).

COOPER, GORDON: Kent.

COOPER, J.E: Chislet; Natural History

COOPER, John: Chatham; Geology; Herne Bay; Inland Defences.

COOPER, Terence: Road Transport.

COOPER, Thomas Sidney: Canterbury; Kent Artists; Kent, East.

COOPER, W.H. Hewlett: Hayes & Keston.

COOPER-KEY, A: Faversham; Industry & Trade.

COOPER-MARSDIN, Rev. A: Kent Authors & Lit.-General.

CO-OPERATIVE SOCIETY:See BROWN, W. Henry: Industry & Trade - Firms; Sheerness.

COOPERS AND LYBRAND ASSOCIATES LTD: Channel Tunnel; Road Transport. See also BRITISH CHANNEL TUNNEL CO.LTD: Channel Tunnel.

COOTE, C.R: Churchill,Sir W.L.S.

COOTE, Jack Howard: Rivers.

COPE, Michael: Kent Authors & Lit. - Poetry.

COPELAND, H. Rob: Beckenham.

COPLEY, Gordon J. History-Archaeology: See also CAMDEN, William: History-General.

COPLEY, I.A: Music.

COPPEN, John Maurice: Family History.

COPSEY, Alan Charles: Aylesford.

COPUS, G.D: Footpaths & Commons; Green Street Green (Orpington); Pratts Bottom (Chelsfield),

COPUS, Geoffrey: Tunbridge Wells.

COQUETILLA. pseud: Tunbridge Wells.

CORBELL, P.M: Biggin Hill; Military & Naval History.

CORDELL, Alan: photographer. Coastline; Rivers; Thames, River.
See Also PERKS, Richard Hugh: Medway River; Ships & Shipping; Thames, River.
See also WILLMOTT, Frank G: Industry & Trade; Medway River.

CORINA, Maurice: Industry & Trade. - Firms.

CORKE, C. Essenhigh: Hever; Kent Artists; Sevenoaks.

CORKILL, W.H: Margate; Trottiscliffe.

CORNFORTH, John: Kent artists; Maidstone.

CORONATION VISITS OF THE ARCHBISHOP OF CANTERBURY... Isle of Thanet.

CORRAN, H.S: Industry & Trade.

CORRIGAN, Felicitas: See SASSOON, Siegfried. Biography.

CORY, Harper: Margate.

CORYN, M: Edward, The Black Prince.

COTTON, Charles: Canterbury - Almshouses & Hospitals; Canterbury - Cathedral; Canterbury - Churches; Canterbury - Monastic Houses; Kent Authors & Lit.-General; St. Laurence-in-Thanet.
See also GERVASE of Canterbury: Canterbury Cathedral.

COTTRELL, Leonard: Coastal Defences.

COUCHMAN, Conrad: Place-names and Surnames.

COULTER, J.E. Publisher Sittingbourne: See also MOORE, Francis: History-1501AD onwards; Sittingbourne.

COUNCIL FOR BRITISH ARCHAEOLOGY: History-Archaeology.
See also ADDYMAN, Peter: Churches.

COUNCIL FOR KENT ARCHAEOLOGY: History - Archaeology.

COUNTRY MISCELLANY & LITERARY SELECTION See COULTER, J.E. Publisher: Sittingbourne.

COUNTRYSIDE COMMISSION: Footpaths - Country Walks; Maps; North Downs Way.

THE COUNTY OF KENT AND MANY OF ITS FAMILY RECORDS: Genealogical Records.

COURSE, Edwin: Bexleyheath; Railways.

COURT, Alexander Norman: Kent.

COURT OF RECORD MINUTE BOOK: Folkestone.

COURTENAY, Sir William P.H. pseud:
COURTENAY, Sir William P.H. See also TRIAL AND SENTENCE OF THE KNIGHT OF MALTA: Canterbury; Trials.

COUSENS, Ruth, Margaret: Kent Artists; Ramsgate.

COUSINS, David Stanley: Canterbury-Churches.

COUSINS, Herbert Stanley: Hersden.

COWARD, Alice: Hayes and Keston.

COWDREY, Colin: Cricket.

COWELL, M.H: Faversham; Kent, East; Natural History.

COWIE, Leonard W: History - 901AD - 1500 AD.

COWLES, D.M. illustrator:See COWLES, Frederick I: Pilgrims' Way.

COWLES, Frederick I: Pilgrims' Way.

COWLES, Virginia: Churchill, Sir W.L.S.

COWPER, Joseph Meadows: Genealogical Records.

COX, Alan: Industry & Trade.

COX, Charlotte. illustrator: See LIPSCOMBE, Margaret: Printing & Publishing.

COX, H. Publisher: See WHO'S WHO IN KENT, SURREY & SUSSEX: Biography.

COX, John Charles: Footpaths-Country Walks; Genealogical Records; Kent.

COX, Penelope: See B., K. Benenden.

COX, Rosemary: See KENT COUNTY COUNCIL: SOCIAL SERVICES DEPT: Health & Welfare.

318

C Cont'd

COX, Thomas: History - General.

COX, W.J. Publisher: Kent, East; Whitstable.

COXON, Stanley W: Dover; World War I.

COZENS, W.S. Builder & Decorator: Canterbury.

(COZENS, Zechariah): Isle of Thanet; Kent, East.

CRACE, Admiral Sir John Gregory: Chatham Dockyard.

CRACKNELL, Basil Edward: Thames, River.

CRAIG, Ian: See ROOTES, Andrew: Higham.

CRAMP, Rev. Dr. John Mockett: Biography;Broadstairs;
Church History; Kent Authors & Lit. - General;
Letters; Sermons.
See also "A MINISTER OF THE GOSPEL" pseud: Broadstairs;
Sermons.

CRAN, Marion: Benenden; Biography; Gardens; Kent Authors
& Lit. - General.

CRANAGE, David Herbert Somerset: Church History.

CRANBROOK RURAL DISTRICT COUNCIL: Cranbrook.

CRAWSHAR, J.O: Chatham.

CREASEY, Robert: See MARSHALL, Elizabeth:Chatham;
Family History.

CREATON, David: Kent Authors & Lit. - General.

CREER, Stanley: Railways.

CRELLIN, T.D: Dover.

CRESWICK, Paul: Health & Welfare; World War I.

CRESY, Edward: Horton Kirby.

CRISP, Frederick Arthur: See DOVER - THE FRENCH CHURCH:
Dover; Genealogical Records.
See THORPE, John Senior: Biography; Monumental
Inscriptions.
See VISITATION OF ENGLAND AND WALES:Genealogical Records.

CRITCHETT & WOODS: Coastal Waters; Road Transport.

CROCKER, R.J. and PARTNERS: Gravesend.

CROFT, R.J: Ships and Shipping.

CROFT-COOKE, Rupert: Biography; Kent, West; Rochester;Tonbridge.

CROGGAN, Lucy E:Penshurst.

CROMPTON, N.J: Tonbridge.

CROMWELL, Thomas Kitson: History - General.

CRONK, Anthony: Biography; Horsmonden;West Malling.

CROOK, Diane K: Education; Kent, North West.

CROOK, Herbert Evelyn: Margate.

CROSS, Derek: Railways.

CROSS, Francis W: Canterbury.

CROSS CHANNEL GUNS: Kent, South East; World War II.

CROSSICK, Geoffrey: History - 1501 AD onwards;
Kent, North West.

CROSSLEY, David W: Bewl Valley; Industry & Trade.

CROUCH, Marcus: Canterbury; Footpaths - Country Walks;
History - General; History - 1501 AD onwards; Kent;
Kent Authors & Lit. - General; Kent, West; Printing &
Publishing.

CRUDEN, Robert Peirce: Gravesend.

CRUNDALL, Edward Duncan: World War I.

CUBITT, Sir William: Ramsgate.

CULL, Frederick: Chatham, Chatham Dockyard.

CULPEPPER, Sir Thomas (the Elder of Hollingbourne):
Land Tenure.

CULMER, Richard: Church History; Tithes.

CUMBERLAND, Richard: Kent Authors & Lit. - Plays;
Kent Authors & Lit. - Poetry.

CUNLIFFE, B.W. See REPORTS ON THE EXCAVATION OF THE
ROMAN FORT: Richborough.

CUNNINGHAM, Dr. John S: Kent Authors & Lit. - General.

CUNNINGTON, Susan: Caxton, William.

CURLING, P.W.: Hernhill.

CURLL, Edmund: Bibliography; Tunbridge Wells.

CURRYER, Constance. E: See PIKE, Elsie: Education;
Sevenoaks.

CURTIS, Anthony: Biography.

CURTIS, Henry: Cranbrook; Family History.

CURZON, George Nathaniel. 1st Marquess Curzon of
Kedleston: Walmer.

CUST, Lady Elizabeth. See BLIGH, Edward,
5th Earl of Darnley: Letters.

CUSTUMALE ROFFENSE: Rochester Diocese.

CUTTS, Edward L: Canterbury - Cathedral Archbishops

D

D., W.V. (DUMBRECK, William V): Hadlow.

DAILY NEWS Publications Department: Tunbridge Wells.

DALE, Rev. Herbert Dixon: Hythe. See also
HYTHE BOROUGH COUNCIL. Bibliography; Hythe.

DALE, R: Biography.

DALE, Rev. Thomas: Broadstairs; Sermons.

DALESKI, H.M: Conrad; Joseph.

DALY, Augustus A: Isle of Sheppey.

DANCE, Charles: Medway, River; Ships & Shipping.

DANCE, G.W: Bromley.

DANE, Herbert: Faversham; World War II.

DANIEL, C. St. J.H: Kent, North West; Sundials.

DANIEL, Philip A: Footpaths-Country Walks; Kent, North
West.

DANIELS, H.A.W. See ASSOCIATION OF KENT CRICKET CLUBS:
Cricket.

DANIELS, Jack: Maidstone.

DANKS, W: Canterbury. See also WOODRUFF, C. Everleigh:
Canterbury Cathedral.

DANKS, William: Agriculture; Shoreham.

DARELL, William: Dover.

DARK, Sidney: Becket, Saint Thomas; Canterbury
Cathedral - Archbishops.

DARTFORD & DISTRICT CONSUMERS' GROUP: Recipes.

DARTFORD BOROUGH COUNCIL: Darent River & Valley; Dartford.

DARTFORD CONGREGATIONAL CHURCH: Dartford.

DARTFORD CONSTITUENCY CONSERVATIVE ASSOCIATION:
Dartford; Kent, North West.

DARTFORD CRICKET FESTIVAL COMMITTEE: Cricket; Dartford.

DARTFORD DISTRICT ANTIQUARIAN SOCIETY: Dartford.

DARTFORD FIRE BRIGADE: Dartford.

DARTFORD FOOTBALL CLUB: Dartford; Sport.

DARTFORD OVERSEERS OF THE POOR: Dartford; Poor Law.

DARTFORD TUNNEL JOINT COMMITTEE: Dartford Tunnel.

DARTFORD TUNNEL JOINT CONSULTATIVE COMMITTEE:
Dartford Tunnel.

DARTFORD URBAN DISTRICT COUNCIL: Dartford.

DARTON, Frederick Joseph Harvey: History - General; Weald.

DARWIN, Bernard: Railways; Sport; Sundridge (Bromley).

DARWIN, Charles: Darwin, Charles.

DARWIN, Charles Robert: Darwin, Charles; Letters.

DAUBENEY, Rev. Giles: Biography; Family History.

DAUNTON-FEAR, Richard: Gravesend; Pocahontas, Princess.

DAVENPORT, John: Churchill, Sir W.L.S.

DAVEY, Norman: Industry & Trade.

DAVEY, Peter: Folkestone; Theatre.

DAVID - DANEL, Marie Louise: Blean.

DAVIDSON, Diane: Faversham.

DAVIDSON, John: Kent Songs.

DAVIDSON, Randall Thomas Bishop of Rochester: Canterbury Cathedral - Archbishops.

DAVIES & COMPANY. Engravers: See ADMIRALTY: Dover; Folkestone; Medway River; Sea and River Charts.

DAVIES, Rev. Charles Greenall: Broadstairs; Sermons.

DAVIES, Geoffrey Alun: Bibliography; Channel Tunnel.

DAVIES, Griffith James: Chislet; Coal.

DAVIES, Hamlyn L. Rees: Chatham; Military & Naval History.

DAVIES, Michael W: Meopham.

DAVIES, William James Keith: Railways; Romney March.

DAVIS, A.H: See THORNE, William: Canterbury - Monastic Houses.

DAVIS, Arthur G: Geology; Isle of Sheppey.

DAVIS, Cyril: Footpaths- Country Walks; Kent, Mid; Kent, North East; North Downs Way.

DAVIS, Dennis J: Ships & Shipping; Thames, River.

DAVIS, Godfrey Rupert Charles: Bibliography; Land Tenure.

DAVIS, Ralph: History - 1501 onwards.

DAVIS, Terence: Tunbridge Wells.

DAVIS, William J: Dartford.

DAVISON, Ian: Cranbrook; Weald.

DAWN OF THE DAY: Isle of Sheppey.

DAWSON, C.M: Greenwich.

DAWSON, Giles E: Theatre.

DAY, J. Wentworth: Biography; Inns; Sport.

DAY, T.J: Margate.

"DAY BY DAY" DIRECTORIES: Ashford; Kennington; Willesborough.

DEACON, J.L: Cinque Ports.

DEACON, M: Kent Authors & Lit. - Poetry.

DEACON, Richard: Caxton, William.

DEADLINE FOR CHANGE...See KENT MESSENGER: Local Government.

DEAKIN, Richard: Kent, West; Natural History; Tunbridge Wells.

DEAL & WALMER COMMUNITY ASSOCIATION: Deal; Walmer.

DEAL BOROUGH COUNCIL: Deal.

DEAL, WALMER & DISTRICT HISTORY SOCIETY: Deal.

DEANE, John Diver: See McKEE, Alexander: Whitstable.

DEANE, Spencer: Romney Marsh.

DEARN, Thomas Downes Wilmot: Weald.

DE BEER, Sir Gavin. See DARWIN, Charles: Darwin, Erasmus.

DEBENHAM Betty: Chestfield; Sport.

DEBENHAMS, LTD: See CORINA, Maurice: Industry & Trade-Firms.

DE BRISAY, K.W: See ESSEX University of Colchester Salt Conference: Industry & Trade.

DE CARLO, Giancarlo: Morris, William.

DEEBLE, E.B: Architecture; Dover.

DEEBLE, William illustrator: See BRAYLEY, Edward Wedlake: Cinque Ports; Isle of Thanet.

DEFENCE. Ministry of: Land Tenure; Military and Naval History.

DEFEND KENT: Conservation

DEFOE, Daniel: Canterbury; Ghosts. See also AITKEN, George A: Canterbury; Ghosts. See also BAINE, Rodney M: Canterbury; Ghosts. See also SCOUTEN, Arthur H: Canterbury; Ghosts.

DELANY, Mary Cecilia: Geography; Industry & Trade; Weald.

DELAWARE STATE BOARD OF EDUCATION: History - 1501 AD onwards.

D'ELBOUX, R.H: Monumental Inscriptions; Rochester Cathedral.

DELIUS, Nicolaus: Faversham.

DE MONTMORENCY, James Edward Geoffrey; Greenwich.

DENCE, Thomas: Biography; Shortlands.

DENKINGER, E.M: Sidney, Sir Philip.

DENNE, Rev. John: Sermons; Westerham.

DENNE, Rev. Samuel (With W.SHRUBSOLE): History - General; Rochester.
See also DARELL, William: Dover.

DENNESS, Mike: Cricket.

DENNEY, Martyn: Crayford; Dartford; Canals & Waterways.

DEPTFORD BOROUGH COUNCIL, Deptford.

DERBY, Thomas: See POLLEN, John Hungerford: Becket, (Saint) Thomas.

DERHAM, Walter: Fordwich.

DERING, Rev. Cholmeley Edward: Biography.

DERING, Sir Edward: Biography; Church History; History - 1501 AD onwards; Pluckley.

DERRICK, Samuel: Letters; Tunbridge Wells.

A DESCRIPTION OF ENGLAND AND WALES:..History - General.

DE SELINCOURT, Aubrey: Coastline.

DESTOMBES, J.P: Channel Tunnel; Geology.

DE VERE, Aubrey Thomas: Becket, Saint Thomas.

DEVEREUX, Charles: Railways; Sevenoaks.

DEVLIN, Sister Mary Aquinas. See BRINTON, Thomas, Bishop of Rochester 1373 - 1389: Rochester Cathedral - Bishops; Sermons.

DE VRIES, Duane: Dickens, Charles.

DEWDNEY, W.S. Chelsfield: Eltham.

DEWEY, Henry: Geology; Kent, North West.
See also SMITH, Reginald A: Swanscombe; Thames, River.

DEWS, Nathan: Deptford.

DEXTER, Walter: Dickens, Charles; Kent; Kent, Mid; Kent, North West.

DIBDEN, Thomas Frognal: Caxton, William; Printing & Publishing.

DIBDIN, Thomas Frognall; See Also. DARELL, William: Dover.

DIBLEY, George Edward: Geology; Gravesend; Kent, West; Medway, River.

DICK AND SAL:.......See MASTERS, John White: Kent Authors & Lit. - Poetry.

DICKENS, Charles: Broadstairs; Charities; Dickens, Charles; Rochester.

DICKENS, Charles Junior: Thames, River.

THE DICKENSIAN: See CLARK, W.A: Dickens, Charles.

DICKIE, A.J: Agriculture.

DIGGES, Thomas: Military & Naval History.

DILLON, Bert: Chaucer, Geoffrey.

DILNOT, Frank: Ash-next-Sandwich; Kent, East.

DILNOT, George: Newspapers.

DIMONT, Charles: Cricket.

DINES, Angela: See ST. CLAIR, Steve: Thamesmead.

DINES, H.G: Geology; Kent, North East; Kent, West.
See also DEWEY, Henry: Geology; Kent, North West.

DINGWALL, R.G: Coastal Waters; Geology.

DISRAELI, Benjamin Earl of Beaconsfield: Letters.

DITCHFIELD, Peter Hampson: Architecture; Churches; History - General.

DIXON, Alan G: Railways; Tenterden.

DIXON, Staff Commander. J.W: See ADMIRALTY: Medway, River; Sea & River Charts.

D Cont'd

DIXON, Philip: Greenwich.

DIXON-SCOTT, J. Photographer: Coastline; Kent.

DOBELL, Leonora Olive: Kent Authors & Lit. - Collections;
Kent Authors & Lit. - Fiction; Kent Authors & Lit. - Poetry.

DOBSON, F.R: Geography.

DOBSON, Howard E: Deptford.

DOBSON, Jessie: See ROYAL COLLEGE OF SURGEONS OF
ENGLAND: Darwin, Charles; Down(e).

DOBY, T: Harvey, Dr. William.

DODD, Charles Tattersall: Kent Artists; Tunbridge Wells.

DODDS, Norman Noel: Gypsies.

DODSWORTH, Mrs: Kent Authors & Lit. - Poetry.

DOGGETT, Tom: Footpaths - Country Walks; North Downs Way.

DOLBY, George: Dickens, Charles.

DOLDING, C: Kent Authors & Lit. - General.

THE DOMESDAY BOOK FOR THE COUNTY OF KENT....: Census;
Land Tenure.

DONAGHEY, Betty: Kent Authors & Lit. - Poetry.

DONALDSON, Christopher William: Biography; Canterbury -
Churches; Kent Authors & Lit. - General; Kent
Authors & Lit. - Poetry; Stour, River.

DONALDSON, Norman: Gravesend.

DONNE, C.E. Faversham: See also GIRAUD, Francis F:
Faversham.

DONNINGTON, G.L. See BLAKE, Lewis pseud: Bromley;
World War II.

"DORIS": See CHATHAM & DISTRICT LETTER CARD:
Medway Towns.

DORLING, Henry Taprell: Kent Authors & Lit. - Fiction.

DORLING, M.J: Agriculture; Kent,East.

DORRINGTON, J.B: Family History.

DOTTRIDGE, H. Roland: Saltwood.

DOUCH, John: Family History; Ruckinge; Smuggling.

DOUGALL, Donald: Footpaths - Country Walks.

DOUGLAS, Sir George: See WEDMORE, Sir Frederick:
Kent Authors & Lit. - General.

DOUGLAS, Robert. (Vicar of Bredgar): Kent Authors
& Lit. - General

DOUGLAS - JONES, Ian E: Penge.

DOUGLASS, Rev. Douglas Alexander: Gravesend;
Milton-next-Gravesend.

DOVER & DEAL PARLIAMENTARY CONSTITUENCY:
Deal; Dover; Elections.

DOVER BOROUGH COUNCIL: Dover.

DOVER BOROUGH COUNCIL Museum: Dover; Museums.

DOVER COLLEGE: See THE DOVORIAN: Dover.

DOVER COLLEGE, Junior School: Dover; Education.

DOVER CORPORATION TRAMWAYS: Dover; Road Transport.

DOVER DISTRICT COUNCIL: Coastline; Deal; Dover;
Kent, South East; Sandwich. See also
KENT COUNTY COUNCIL & DOVER DISTRICT COUNCIL: Dover.

DOVER DISTRICT COUNCIL: ENVIRONMENTAL HEALTH DEPARTMENT:
Kent, South East.

DOVER DISTRICT COUNCIl:LEISURE AND RECREATIONAL DEPARTMENT.
Kent, South East.

DOVER HARBOUR BOARD: Dover.

DOVER HOSPITAL AND DISPENSARY: Managing Comittee:
Dover; Hospitals.

DOVER RURAL DISTRICT COUNCIL: Kent, South East.

DOVER STANDARD: Dover.

DOVER - THE FRENCH CHURCH: Dover; Genealogical Records.

THE DOVORIAN (Magazine of Dover College): Dover.

DOWKER, George: Reculver.

DOWSETT, Walter (i.e. Walter Dowsett Collection).
See CORDELL, Alan: Coastline; Rivers; Thames, River.

DOXAT, John: Thames, River.

DOYLE, Eric: Canterbury - Monastic Houses; Religious
Denominations.

THE DRAGON: Military and Naval History.

DRAKE, Charles H: Ospringe.

DRAPER'S MILL TRUST: Margate; Windmills and Watermills.

DREW, Bernard: Farningham; World War II.

DREW, Frederic: Geology; Kent, South East; Romney Marsh.

DRUMMOND, Janet See BRADBURY, Janet: Folkestone.

DRURY, M: Swanley.

DU BOULAY, Francis Robin Houssemayne: Church History;
History - 901 AD - 1500 AD.

DUCKETT, E.W: See ASSOCIATION OF KENT CRICKET CLUBS:
Cricket.

DUCKETT, Eleanor Shipley: Canterbury Cathedral;
Archbishops.

DUCKWORTH, C.L.D: Coastal Waters; Ships and Shipping.

DUDENEY, Henry Ernest: Chaucer, Geoffrey; Recreation.

DUDLEY, M.R: Penge.

DUFF, Mrs. A.G: Biography.

DUFF, David: Biography; Chislehurst.

DUFF, Gail: Recipes.

DUFFY, Carolyn: See BERGESS, Winifred F: Family History;
Wateringbury.

DUFFY, Maureen: Biography.

DUGAN, James: Military and Naval History.

DUGDALE, Thomas: Chatham; History - General.

DUGGAN, Alfred: Becket, Saint Thomas.

"DUG-OUT" pseud: See COXON, Stanley W: Dover;
World War I.

DULWICH COLLEGE: Dulwich.

DUMBRECK, William:See D., W.V. (Dumbreck, William V):
Hadlow.

DUMPLETON, Bernard: Medway, River; Ships and Shipping;
Thames, River.

DUNCAN, Archie: See CANTERBURY COLLEGE OF ART: School
of Architecture: Canterbury - Education.

DUNCAN,Leland Lewis: All Hallows; Biddenden; Cowden;
Genealogical Records; History - 1501 AD onwards; Lee;
Monumental Inscriptions; Tenterden.
See also KIRBY, Herbert Charles: Lewisham;
Monumental Inscriptions.

DUNCAN, William Edmonstone: Military & Naval History.

DUNCOMBE, John: Canterbury Cathedral.

DUNDEE ART GALLERY: Kent Artists.

DUNKIN, Alfred John: Eynsford; History - to 900 AD.

DUNKIN, Edwin Hadlow Wise: Bibliography;
Canterbury Cathedral - Archbishops; Canterbury-Diocese
and Province; Kidbrooke.

DUNKIN, John: Bromley.

DUNLOP, Sir John. Sevenoaks.

DUNLOP RUBBER COMPANY LTD: Roads.

DUNNAGE, H. Architect. Eltham.

DUNNING, G.C: History - Archaeology; Kent, East.
See also RIGOLD, S.E: Ospringe.
See also O'NEIL, Bryan Hugh St. John: Deal.

DU-PLAT-TAYLOR, M: Coastline - Sea Defences.

DURRANT, R.J: See SOUTH EASTERN, pseud. Road Transport;
Woolwich.

F Cont'd.

FRIED, Erich: Faversham; Music.

FRIEDMANN, Paul: Biography.

"A FRIEND OF CANTERBURY CATHEDRAL" pseud.
See BABINGTON, Margaret Agnes: Canterbury Cathedral.

FRIENDS OF ALLINGTON CASTLE: Allington.

FRIENDS OF CANTERBURY CATHEDRAL: Canterbury Cathedral.

FRIENDS OF ROCHESTER CATHEDRAL: Rochester Cathedral.
See Also BEST-SHAW, J.K: Rochester Cathedral.

FRISWELL, Laura Hain (Mrs. Ambrose Myall): Bexleyheath;
Biography.

FRITH HALL: East Farleigh (Sale Catalogue).

FROST, Thomas: Kent.

FRY, C. See BATES, Harry: Architecture.

FRY, C.A: See DUNKIN, Edwin Hadlow Wise: Bibliography; Canterbury Cathedral - Archbishops;
Canterbury Cathedral - Diocese and Province.

FRY, Colin Richard: Kent Authors and Lit. - General.

FRY, James: Obituaries: Pembury.

FRY, Plantagenet Somerset: Architecture; Castles
and Houses.

FUEL AND POWER, Ministry of: Coal.

FULLER, M.J: East Malling; Windmills and Watermills.

FULLER, Ronald: Biography.

FULLER, Thomas: Biography.

FULLJAMES, J.A: Maidstone.

FULLMER, J.Z: Industry and Trade: Tonbridge.

FULTON, Hamish: Hythe.

FUNNELL, K.J: Industry and Trade - Firms; Snodland.

FURLEY, Robert: Tenterden; Weald.

FURLONG, Monica: Groombridge.

FUSSELL, L: Coastline.

F(YNMORE), R.J: Sandgate.

G

GAGE, W.L: Bromley; Theatre.

GALBRAITH, Vivian Hunter: History - 901 AD -
1500 AD.

GALLAGHER, Michael Paul: Becket, Saint Thomas.

GALLIPOLI, MACEDONIA, EGYPT AND PALESTINE....See
HISTORY OF THE CORPS OF ROYAL ENGINEERS:
Military and Naval History.

GALLOIS, R.W: Geology; Weald.
See also EDMUNDS, F.H: Geology; Weald.

GALLYON, Margaret: Church History.

GALTON, Captain Douglas: Margate; Public Utilities.

GAMMELL, Christopher John: Railways.

GANN, L.H: Biography.

GANN, P.D: Bibliography; Natural History.

GANN, Thomas: See
WHITSTABLE OYSTER COMPANY VS. GANN, Thomas: Trials;
Whitstable.

GARDINER, Dorothy: Canterbury; Harbledown;
History - General; Kent; Sandwich.
See also OXINDEN, Henry: Letters.

GARDINER, May, illustrator: See
SMITH, Alan: Footpaths - Country Walks;
Kent, Mid; North Downs Way.

GARDINER, Rena: Rochester Cathedral.

GARDNER, Henry: Southborough; Tonbridge; Tunbridge Wells.

GARDNER, John: Chaucer, Geoffrey.

GARDNER, Peter G.A: Broadstairs.

GARDNER, William Biscombe: Kent; Kent Artists.

GARNETT, David: Pocahontas, Princess.

GARNETT, MEPHAM & FISHER LTD. Publishers: Canterbury;
Herne Bay; Whitstable.

GARNIER OF PONT-SAINTE-MAXENCE: Becket, Saint Thomas.

GARRAD, G.H: Agriculture.

GARRAD, L.S: Souvenirs.

GARRETT, Richard: Coastal Waters; Gordon, Gen. C.G;
Transport; Wolfe, Gen. James.

GARRETT, S.R: Railways.

GARRETT, Capt. Thomas: See MOCKETT, John:
Isle of Thanet; Letters; Military and Naval History.

GASKIN, Valerie: Libraries; Milton Regis; Sittingbourne;
Tonbridge.

GASQUET, Cardinal Francis Aidan: History - 901 AD -
1500 AD.

GASTINEAU, H. Illustrator: See SHEPHERD George:
History - General.

GATE, John: Libraries; Maidstone.

GATTIE, George Byng: Goodwin Sands.

GATTY, Richard: Biography; Rolvenden.

GAUSDEN, John: Rochester.

GAYE, P.F: See TURNOR, Reginald: Kent.

GEE, Laurence E: Chislehurst.

GEIGER, Erika: Tunbridge Wells.

GELFAND, M: See GANN, L.H: Biography.

GELL, Francis: Minster-in-Thanet.

GEM, R.D.H: Canterbury Cathedral.

GENERAL BOARD OF HEALTH: See RAMMELL, T.W: Public
Utilities; Sandgate.

GENERAL MOORE AT SHORNECLIFFE: Military and Naval
History; Sandgate.

GENERAL REGISTER OFFICE

Addington;	Paddlesworth
Aylesford;	Paddock Wood;
Birling ;	Platt;
Borough Green;	Plaxtol;
Brenchley;	Ryarsh
Census;	Shipbourne;
Chiddingstone;	Snodland;
Ditton;	Southborough;
East Malling;	Stansted;
East Peckham;	Tonbridge;
Genealogical Records;	Trottiscliffe:
Hadlow ;	Wateringbury:
Hildenborough;	West Malling;
Ightham;	West Peckham;
Leybourne;	Wouldham;
Mereworth;	Wrotham;
Offham;	Yalding.

GENTLEMAN'S MAGAZINE: See GOMME, George Laurence:
History - 1501 AD onwards.

GEOFFREY-LLOYD, Lord Geoffrey W: Leeds

GEOGRAPHIA GUIDE TO SOUTH-EAST ENGLAND: Kent.

GEOGRAPHIA RAMBLERS' MAP: Footpaths - Country Walks;
Maps.

GEOLOGICAL ASSOCIATION See WEALD RESEARCH COMMITTEE:
Geology; Weald.
See - WHITAKER, William: Geology; Reculver.

GEOLOGICAL SOCIETY OF LONDON: See MURCHISON, Sir
Frederick: Geology.

F Cont'd.

FINN, Arthur: Lydd.

FINN, Ralph: Ramsgate; Smuggling.

FINN, Rex Waldon: History - 901 AD - 1500 AD.

FINN, Timothy: Inns; Recreation.

FINN -KELCEY, COLLIER AND ASHENDEN, Auctioneers: See
Bapchild (Sale Catalogue); Faversham; Housing;
Teston (Sale Catalogue).

FINUCANE, Ronald C: Church History.

FIRTH, John B: Dover; World War I.

FISHER, Geoffrey Francis. Archbishop of Canterbury:
Canterbury Cathedral - Archbishops.

FITTER, Richard Sidney Richmond: Kent.

FITZGERALD, Percy: Dickens, Charles.

FITZRANDOLPH, Helen E: Industry and Trade.

FITZSTEPHEN, William: Becket, Saint Thomas.

FLEETWOOD, Serjeant See
BRUCE, John: History and Archaeology - 1501 AD onwards.

FLEMING, I. Plant: Tonbridge.

FLETCHER, Benton: Castles and Houses; Kent, North West.

FLETCHER, Dr. C.M: See MEDWAY AND MAIDSTONE COLLEGE
OF TECHNOLOGY: Industry and Trade.

FLETCHER, F.D: Darwin, Charles.

FLETCHER, Geoffrey: See FOX, Reg: Bromley.

FLETCHER, J. Kent Authors and Lit. - General.

FLETCHER, Joseph Smith: Folkestone.

FLOODGATE, E.E. See CHAMPION, Mrs. I.K: Kent, North;
Natural History; Rochester.

FLOWER, Margaret: Forest Hill.

FOAT, William: Recipes.

FOLKESTONE ART SOCIETY: Folkestone; Kent Artists.

FOLKESTONE BOROUGH COUNCIL: Folkestone; Military and
Naval History.

FOLKESTONE BOROUGH COUNCIL - ENTERTAINMENTS AND
PUBLICITY COMMITTEE: Folkestone.

FOLKESTONE BOROUGH COUNCIL AND PORT HEALTH AUTHORITY:
Folkestone; Health and Welfare.

FOLKESTONE CHAMBER OF COMMERCE: Folkestone.

FOLKESTONE FLOWER SHOW: See BRITISH SERVICES TATOO (1951):
Folkestone.

FOLKESTONE FLOWER SHOW AND FLORAL ACADEMY: Folkestone.

FOLKESTONE HERALD: Folkestone; Hythe; Sandgate.

FOLKESTONE, HYTHE AND DISTRICT HOTEL AND CATERING ASSOCIATION:
Folkestone; Hythe.

FOLKESTONE NATURAL HISTORY AND GENERAL SCIENCES SOCIETY.
See WALTON, John W: Folkestone; Kent, South East; Natural
History.

FOLKESTONE PUBLIC LIBRARY: Bibliography.

FOLKESTONE ROTARY CLUB: Folkestone; Music.

FOLKESTONE SILVER JUBILEE COMMITTEE: Folkestone.

FOLLAND, H.F: See ADAMSON, J.H: Biography; Plaxtol.

FOLLEY, Roger Roland Westwell: Agriculture. See also
DORLING, M.J: Agriculture; Kent, East.

FORBES, Eric G: Greenwich.

FORD, Alan S: Sevenoaks.

FORD, Douglas Morey: Dover.

FORD, Ford Madox: Cinque Ports.

FORDHAM, S.J: Agriculture; Kent, North East; Kent, South
East. See also GREEN, R.D: Agriculture;
Kent, South East.

FORDRED, Derek: See FORDRED, Diana; Sutton-at-Hone.

FORDRED, Diana: Sutton-at-Hone.

FOREIGN & COMMONWEALTH OFFICE: Channel Tunnel.

FORESTRY COMMISSION: See MITCHELL, A.F;
Bedgebury; Forestry.

FOREVILLE, Raymonde: Becket, Saint Thomas.

FORMAN, Joan: Ghosts.

FORREST, Ebenezer: See HOGARTH'S FROLIC:
Isle of Sheppey.

FORSETT, John: New Romney.

FORSTER, John: Dickens, Charles.

FORSTER, John, Lord Harraby: Beckenham; Obituaries.

FORSTER BROWN, Edward Otto: Coal.

FOR THE WIDOW'S SUNDAY SCHOOL...:Music

FORT PITT GIRLS' SCHOOL: Chatham.

FORWARD PUBLICITY LTD: Faversham.

FORWOOD, Michael J: Elham; Kent, South East;
Railways.

FOSTER, M.C: Bexley; Natural History.

FOUGASSE, illustrator: See LEIGH-BENNETT, E.P.
Railways.

FOURNIER, Freda: Kent Authors and Lit. - Poetry.

FOURTEEN WALKS IN AND AROUND TONBRIDGE: Footpaths -
Country Walks; Kent, West.

FOWLE, Dennis: Cricket.

FOWLER, Montagu: Becket, Saint Thomas; Canterbury
Cathedral - Archbishops.

FOX, John: Education; Gillingham.

FOX, Reg: Bromley.

FOXLEY, Gladys L: Bexleyheath; Sport.

FRAMPTON, T.S: Trottiscliffe.

FRANCE, Walter Frederick: Canterbury - Monastic Houses.

FRANCIS, A.J: Industry and Trade.

FRANCIS FRITH COLLECTION: See GREENHILL, Basil:
Greenwich.

FRANCIS ILES GALLERIES: Chatham.

FRANKLIN, Kenneth J: Harvey, Dr. William.

FRANLKIN, W.H. Photographer: Deal; Walmer.

FRANKLYN, Charles Aubrey Hamilton: Chart Sutton;
Family History; Hever.

FRANKS, E: Coal; Kent, South East.

FRANKS, Thomas Leslie Elvy: See FOLKESTONE BOROUGH
COUNCIL: Folkestone.

FRASER, Derek: Poor Law.

FRASER, Fl. Lieut. William: Manston; Military
and Naval History

FREATHY, Hilda C: Gillingham.

FREE THOUGHTS ON THE EXTENT OF THE DEATH OF CHRIST:
Kent Authors and Lit. - General.

FREED, Reginald Henry: See MAIDSTONE GRAMMAR SCHOOLS:
Maidstone.

FREELING, Arthur: Dover; Margate; Tunbridge Wells.

FREEMAN, Charles: Bromley.

FREEMAN, R.B: Darwin, Charles.

FREEMAN, Sarah: Biography.

FREEMASONS See PROVINCE OF WEST KENT:FREEMASONS:
Kent, West; Organisations.

FREESTON, Ewart Cecil: Military and Naval History;
Ships and Shipping; Thames, River.

FREETH, S. See KENT COUNTY COUNCIL:ARCHIVES OFFICE:
Bibliography.

FRENCH, Lt. Col. The Hon. E. Gerald: Gordon,
Gen. C.G., R.E.

FRENCH, Katharine: Canterbury - Monastic Houses.

FRENCH PROTESTANT HOSPITAL: Rochester.

FRERE, Sheppard: Canterbury - Antiquity and
Archaeology. See also WILLIAMS, Audrey:
Canterbury - Antiquity and Archaeology.

E Cont'd.

ERITH THEATRE GUILD LTD: Erith; Theatres.

ERRAND, J: Architecture.

ERWOOD, Guy R: Canterbury.

ESAM, Frank: Architecture; Castles and Houses.

ESCREET, Henrietta Caroline:See MALIM, Mary Charlotte:
Blackheath.

ESDAILE- Katherine Ada: Churches.

ESSEX, University of: COLCHESTER SALT CONFERENCE:
Industry and Trade.

ESTATE PUBLICATIONS: Kent-Mid; Maidstone.

EUROPEAN FERRIES LTD: Channel Tunnel.

EVANS, A.A: Kent.

EVANS, Angela C: Graveney Boat.

EVANS, Bill: See ISLE OF THANET PROMOTION BOARD:
Isle of Thanet.

EVANS, Eric, J: Ti.the.

EVANS, Capt. F.J. See ADMIRALTY: Dover; Folkestone;
Sea and River Charts.

EVANS, Sir Francis H. VS Lord Castlereagh: Elections;
Maidstone.

EVANS, Godfrey: Cricket.

EVANS, Harold: Crayford; Dartford; Industry and
Trade - Firms.

EVANS, John: Cricket.

EVANS, K.A: See ESSEX, University of: COLCHESTER
SALT CONFERENCE: Industry and Trade.

EVANS, Marian: Heath, Edward.

EVANS, Dr.(R.C.T.) of Herne Bay: Kent Authors and
Lit. - General.

EVANS, S: Upnor.

EVERITT, Alan Milner: History - General; History -
1501 AD onwards. See also HASTED, Edward: History-
General.

EVERSON, Don: Brenzett; Military and Naval History.

EVISON, Very Ivy: Lullingstone.

EWALD, Alexander Charles: Biography.

EXTRACTS FROM KENTISH NEWSPAPERS: History - 1501 AD
onwards.

EXTRACTS FROM WILLS, etc: Faversham.

EYMER, J.J: See SHEPHERD-THORN, E.R: Geology;
Thames, River.

EYTHORNE & DISTRICT BAPTIST NEWS LETTER See
ABBOTT, William George: Eythorne; Obituaries.

F

F., R.J: See F(YNMORE) R.J: Sandgate.

FAGG, Brian R: Minster-in-Thanet.

FAIRBAIRNS, W.H: Canterbury Cathedral.

FAIRCLOUGH, Tony: Railways.

FAIRFAX, General Lord Thomas:See RUSHWORTH, John:
History - 1501 AD onwards; Letters; Maidstone;
Printing and Publishing.

FAIRWEATHER, F.H: Rochester Cathedral.

FALK, B: Kent Artists.

FAMOUS OLD INNS...:Inns; Kent, East.

FARLEY, James George Wilson: Agriculture.

FARNBOROUGH, Lady: See LONG, Amelia, Lady Farnborough.

FARNOL, Jeffery: History - 1501 AD onwards;
Kent Authors and Lit. - Fiction.

FARRIES, Kenneth, G: Kent, North West; Windmills and
Watermills.

FAULKNER, P.A: Knole.

FAULKNER, Peter: Morris,William.

FAULKNER, Roger: Kent Authors and Lit. - Poetry.

FAUSSETT, Rev. Bryan: History - Archaeology; Kent,East.

FAUSSETT, Thomas Godfrey: See LARKIN, Lambert Blackwell:
Leybourne; Letters.

FAVERSHAM DISTRICT NATIONAL SCHOOLS: Faversham.

FAVERSHAM & DISTRICT CHAMBER OF COMMERCE: Faversham.

FAVERSHAM BOROUGH COUNCIL: Faversham.

FAVERSHAM BOROUGH COUNCIL:HEALTH DEPARTMENT: Faversham;
Health and Welfare.

FAVERSHAM CENTRAL NATIONAL SCHOOLS: Faversham.

FAVERSHAM INSTITUTE MONTHLY JOURNAL: Faversham.

FAVERSHAM - NATIONAL AND COMMERCIAL SCHOOLS: Faversham.

FAVERSHAM SOCIETY: Faversham; Museums.

FAVERSHAM TOWN COUNCIL: Faversham.

FAVIELL, John: Rolvenden.

FAVRESFELD, Charles: Queenborough.

FAZAN, E.A.C: Military and Naval History.

FEARNSIDE, William Gray: Medway, River; Thames,River.

FEARON, Henry Bridges ("Field Fare" pseud):
Footpaths - Country Walks; Pilgrims Way.

FEGAN, J.W.C: See TIFFIN, Alfred: Biography;
Goudhurst; Prisons.

FELLOWS, Reginald B: Canterbury; Railways;
Whitstable.

FENN-MARSHALL, Vera: Kent Authors and Lit. - Poetry.

FENWICK, Valerie H: Graveney Boat. See also
EVANS, Angela C: Graveney Boat.

FERGUSON, John: Romney Marsh.

FERGUSON, Peter: See CORDELL, Alan: Coastline;
Rivers; Thames, River.

FERGUSON, Rosemary: Industry and Trade.

FIELD, Bartlett: Customs; Kent, East.

FIELD, C: Gillingham; Military and Naval History.

FIELD, Colin Walter; Canterbury - Diocese and
Province; Church History; Religious Denominations.

FIELDER, C: See DORRINGTON, J.B: Family History.

"FIELDFARE" pseud See FEARON, Henry Bridges
("Fieldfare" pseud): Footpaths - Country Walks;
Pilgrims Way.

FIELDING, Cecil Henry: Rochester; West Malling.

FIENNES, Celia: History - General.

FIFTEEN WALKS AROUND FOLKESTONE: Footpaths - Country Walks;
Kent, South East.

FIFTY GREAT DISASTERS THAT SHOCKED THE WORLD: Gillingham.

FIFTY YEARS AGO: Bekesbourne; Bridge; Patrixbourne.

FILMER, Arthur N: Faversham.

FILMER, John L: Family History.

FILMER, Reginald Mead: Family History; History -
901 AD - 1500 AD; History - 1501 AD onwards.

FINANCIAL TIMES: Local Government; Medway Towns.

FINCH, Roger: Coastal Waters; Industry and Trade;
Ships and Shipping; Thames,River .

FINCH, William Coles: History - General; Kent Authors
and Lit. - General; Medway, River; Natural History;
Pilgrim's Way; Windmills and Watermills.

FINDEN, E: Coastline.

FINDLATER, Jane: See A LITTLE BOOK OF RECIPES: Recipes.

FINDLATER, Richard: See TICH, Mary (i.e. POWELL, Mary
Relph): Biography.

FINDLAY, Alexander George: Coastal Waters;
Medway, River; Sea and River Charts; Thames, River.

GOOCH, R: Coastal Waters..

GOOD BEER GUIDE 1977: Inns.

GOODHEW, R.C: Medway Towns.

GOODMAN, Neville: Sandwich.

GOODMAN, P. See CARDOZO, D.A: Ramsgate.

GOODSALL, Robert Harold: Barfreston;
Harrietsham; History - General;
Kent Authors and Lit. - General; Lenham;
Medway, River; Pilgrim's Way; Rother, River;
Seasalter; Stour, River; Swalecliffe;
Thames, River; Whitstable.

GORDON, General Charles George, R.E:
Gordon, General C.G., R.E.

GORDON, Richard pseud: Bickley.

GORE, T.R: Margate.

GORMAN, J.T: Chatham.

GOSNEY, R: Libraries; Medway Towns.

GOSTLING, Frances M: Canterbury Cathedral;
Rochester Cathedral.

GOSTLING, William: Canterbury.

GOTCH, W.J.R. See CAXTON, William: Caxton
William.

GOUDHURST CORONATION BOOK
GOUDHURST JUBILEE BOOK. See
TIFFIN, A.W: Goudhurst.

GOUGH, Benjamin: Kent Songs.

GOUGH, Harold Eric: Herne; Monumental
Inscriptions. See also
PHILP, Brian: Herne.
HASLUCK, Eugene Lewis: Herne Bay.

GOUGH, Richard. See CAMDEN, William:
History - General.

GOULD, David: Kent, West; Railways; Westerham.

GOULDEN AND CURRY Publishers: Footpaths -
Country Walks; Kent, West; Tunbridge Wells.

GOULDEN, H.J. Publisher: Canterbury;
Canterbury - Monastic Houses.

GOULSTONE, John; Cricket; Dartford;
Family History.

GOWERS, Edward S: Halling.

GRADIDGE, Roderick: Chislehurst.

GRAHAM, Norman. See THE NORMAN GRAHAM BENEFIT:
Cricket.

GRAHAM, Norman H: Genealogical Records.

GRAHAM, Rose: Reculver.

THE GRAND HOTEL....: Folkestone(Sale Catalogue).

GRANT, Charles: Kent Authors and Lit. - General.

GRANT, L: Cinque Ports.

GRANT, Peter. See HARRISON, Jeffery Graham:
Natural History; Thames, River.

GRANVILLE, Augustus Bozzi: Coastline;
Spas and Mineral Waters.

GRASEMANN, C: Coastal Waters; Ships and Shipping.

GRAVES, Charles: World War II.

GRAVES, Geoffrey. See HARRISON, Jeffery Graham:
Medway, River; Natural History.

GRAVESEND AND DISTRICT COMMUNITY RELATIONS
COMMITTEE: Gravesend.

GRAVESEND AND DISTRICT COMMUNITY RELATIONS
COUNCIL: EDUCATION SUB-COMMITTEE: Gravesend.

GRAVESEND AND NORTHFLEET FOOTBALL CLUB LIMITED.
Gravesend; Sport.

GRAVESEND BOROUGH COUNCIL: Gravesend.

GRAVESEND BOROUGH COUNCIL: TREASURER'S DEPARTMENT:
Gravesend.

THE GRAVESEND CHRONOLOGY: Gravesend.

GRAVESEND HISTORICAL SOCIETY: Gravesend.

GRAVESEND PUBLIC LIBRARY. See
CONNOLLY, P.A: Airports; Gravesend.
GUNKEL, E.C: Gravesend; Gravesham;
Pocahontas, Princess.
McLELLAN, Doreen: Allhallows; Canals and Waterways;
Dickens, Charles; Gardens; Gordon, Gen.G.C.
Gravesend; Gravesham; Hotels, Restaurants
and Clubs; Railways.
WILLIS, Peter J: Gravesend; Gravesham;
Kent, North West.

GRAVESHAM ADVENTURE PLAYGROUND: Gravesham.

GRAVESHAM BOROUGH COUNCIL: Gravesham.

GRAVESHAM BOROUGH COUNCIL: PLANNING DEPARTMENT:
Chalk; Gravesend; Gravesham; Hook Green;
Industry and Trade; Meopham; Shorne;
Sole Street;
See also WATSON, K: Canals and Waterways.

GRAVESHAM BOROUGH COUNCIL: TREASURER'S DEPARTMENT:
Gravesham.

GRAVESHAM TEACHERS' CENTRE:
Gravesham.

GRAVESHAM VOLUNTARY AIDE SCHEME: Gravesham.

GRAVETT, Kenneth: Architecture.

GRAY, Adrian A: Chatham; Gravesend; Isle of
Grain; Railways; Rochester.

GRAY, Andrew. See
DAVIS, Cyril: Footpaths - Country Walks;
Kent, Mid; North Downs Way.
See
BAILEY, Margaret: Footpaths-Country Walks;
Kent, East.

GRAY, D.A. See THE ROYAL SOCIETY: Floods;
Thames, River.

GRAY, Geoffrey, T: Gillingham.

GRAY, J.A: Road Transport.

GRAY, Patrick: Cliffe.

GRAYLING, Francis: Churches; Milton Regis;
Sittingbourne.

GREAT BRITAIN, Laws etc. (Geo I): Deal;
Dover; Isle of Thanet; Margate.

GREAT BRITAIN, Laws etc. (Geo.II):
Canterbury; Chatham; Chatham Dockyard;
Cinque Ports; Dover; Greenwich; Military
and Naval History; Roads; Whitstable.

GREAT BRITAIN, Laws etc. (Geo. III):
Aldington; Bexley; Blackheath; Broadstairs;
Bromley; Chatham; Chatham Dockyard; Cinque
Ports; Coastal Defences; Coastal Waters;
Deptford; Dover; Faversham; Industry and
Trade; Kent, East; Kent, South East;
Lamberhurst; Maidstone; Medway, River;
Military and Naval History; Poor Law; Roads;
Sheerness; Thames, River.

GREAT BRITAIN, Laws etc. (Geo. IV):
Canterbury; Maidstone; Poor Law; Railways;
Whitstable.

GREAT BRITAIN, Laws etc. (Wm.IV):
Canterbury; Faversham; Roads.

GREAT BRITAIN: Laws etc. (Wm.IV and Vic.)
Canals and Waterways; Roads.

GREAT BRITAIN, Laws etc. (Vic.):
Ashford; Bromley; Charities; Chatham;
Coastal Defences; Dover; Folkestone;
Gravesend; Greenwich; Hoo Peninsula;
Inland Defences; Kent, West; Maidstone;
Margate; Public Utilities; Railways; St. Mary Cray.

GREAT BRITAIN, Laws etc. (Edw.VII):
Broadstairs;   Chatham;   Gravesend;
Kent, West;   Northfleet;   Public Utilities.

GREAT BRITAIN, Laws etc. (Geo.V.)
Broadstairs;   Chatham;   Gillingham;
Public Utilities.

GREAT BRITAIN, Laws etc. (Geo.VI.)
Whitstable.

GREAT BRITAIN, Laws etc. (Eliz.II).
Airports;   Bridges;   Bromley;   Channel Tunnel;
Charities;   Floods;   Medway, River;   Medway Towns;
Rochester;   Thames, River;   Transport;   Whitstable.

GREAT BRITAIN, Laws etc. (Eliz.II):
STATUTORY INSTRUMENTS: Dartford;   Dover;
Folkestone;   Gillingham;   Elections;   Rainham;
Roads;   Whitstable.

GREAT BRITAIN: MONOPOLIES COMMISSION:
Newspapers;   Ships and Shipping.

GREAT BRITAIN:PARLIAMENT: History - 1501 AD
onwards.

GREAT BRITAIN: PARLIAMENT-BILLS: Medway,River.

GREAT BRITAIN: PARLIAMENT-HOUSE OF COMMONS:
Bibliography;   Channel Tunnel;   Folkestone;
History - 1501 AD onwards;   Public Utilities.

GREAT BRITAIN: PARLIAMENT:HOUSE OF COMMONS PAPERS:
Newspapers.

GREAT BRITAIN: PARLIAMENT: HOUSE OF COMMONS:
SELECT COMMITTEE ON THE CHANNEL TUNNEL BILL:
Channel Tunnel.

GREAT BRITAIN: PARLIAMENT: HOUSE OF COMMONS:
SELECT COMMITTEE ON THE CHATHAM ELECTION PETITION,
1853:   Chatham;   Elections.

GREAT BRITAIN:TREATIES Etc: Channel Tunnel.

THE GREAT BRUNSWICK MEETING. See
THE CATHOLIC QUESTION: History - 1501 AD onwards;
Maidstone;   Religious Denominations.

GREATER LONDON AND SOUTH EAST COUNCIL FOR
SPORTS AND RECREATION: Recreation;   Sport.

GREATER LONDON AND SOUTH EAST SPORTS COUNCIL: Sport.

GREATER LONDON COUNCIL: Floods;   Thames, River.

GREATER LONDON COUNCIL: DEPARTMENT OF PUBLIC
HEALTH ENGINEERING: Floods;   Thames, River.

GREATER LONDON COUNCIL:HISTORIC BUILDINGS
COMMISSION: St. Mary Cray.

GREAVES, John: Dickens, Charles.

GREEN AND COMPANY. Publishers: Kent, Mid.

GREEN, Andrew: Ghosts;   Tunbridge Wells.

GREEN, B.H. See NATURE CONSERVANCY COUNCIL:
SOUTH EAST REGION: Natural History;   North
Kent Marshes.

GREEN, E.C. See WALTON, John W: Folkestone;
Kent, South East;   Natural History.

GREEN, E.R: Gravesend;   Place names.

GREEN, Frank: Kent, North West.

GREEN, Henry J: Kent Authors and Lit. - Poetry.

GREEN, I.W: Whitstable.

GREEN, Ivan: Dover.

GREEN, J. Barcham (Hayle Mill).See
SIX GENERATIONS OF HAND PAPER-MAKERS:
Industry and Trade - Firms;   Tovil.

GREEN, J.R: Kent, General.

GREEN, R.D: Agriculture;   Kent, South East;
Romney Marsh.   See also FORDHAM, S.J:
Agriculture;   Kent, South East;   Kent, North East.

GREEN, Simon B: Railways;   Tenterden.

GREENAWAY, George. See FITZSTEPHEN, William:
Becket, Saint Thomas.

GREENHILL, Basil: Graveney Boat;   Greenwich;
Museums;   Ships and Shipping.

GREENSTREET, James: Faversham.

GREENWICH AND LEWISHAM ANTIQUARIAN SOCIETY:
Greenwich;   Lewisham.

GREENWICH FESTIVAL COMMITTEE:Greenwich.

GREENWICH HOSPITAL AND TRAVERS FOUNDATION:
Greenwich.

GREENWICH, LONDON BOROUGH COUNCIL:Greenwich.
See also RIGDEN, Reg: Deptford;   Greenwich;
Prisons;   Woolwich.

GREENWICH:LONDON BOROUGH COUNCIL:LIBRARIES,
LOCAL HISTORY DEPARTMENT: Greenwich.

GREENWICH NATURAL HISTORY CLUB: ZOOLOGICAL
COMMITTEE: Blackheath;   Natural History.

GREENWOOD, C: History - General.

GREENWOOD, E.J: Rochester.

GREY, C.G. See McCUDDEN, James Thomas Byford:
McCudden, James Thomas Byford.

GREY, Edmund, Earl of Kent: Land Tenure.

GREY, H: Coastline.

GREYSMITH, David: Biography;   Kent Artists.

GRIERSON, Elizabeth: Canterbury Cathedral.

GRIFFIN, Ralph: Monumental Inscriptions.

GRIFFITHS, Arthur: Chatham;   Prisons.

GRIFFITHS, Maurice: Coastal Waters.

GRIGSON, Geoffrey. See FITTER, Richard
Sidney Richmond: Kent.

GRIMSDELL, Mrs N.L: Bibliography;   Isle of Sheppey.

GRIMSHAW, Geoffrey: Ships and shipping.

GRIMSON, John: Coastline.

GRITTEN, A.J: Bibliography;   Isle of Thanet;
Margate.

GROOM, J.B: Maidstone;   Natural History.

GROOM, K.N. See   SMITH, P.J: Bromley.

GROSE, Francis: History - to 900 AD.

GROSER, William: Bessels Green.

GROSSETT, Harry: Sheerness;   Ships and Shipping.

GROSVENOR, James: Coastal Waters;   Sea and
River Charts.

GROVE, L.R. Allen: Leeds;   Maidstone.   See also
MAIDSTONE BOROUGH COUNCIL: Maidstone.   See also
KENT FIELD CLUB: Natural History.

GROVES, Roy. See LINDSAY, Philip: History-
901 Ad - 1500 AD.

GRUBB, Geoffrey Watkins: Family History;
Stone-next-Dartford.

GUENTHER, John: Biography.

A GUIDE TO ALL THE WATERING AND SEA BATHING
PLACES: Coastline: Spas and Mineral Waters.

A GUIDE TO THE ISLE OF THANET...: Hotels,etc;
Isle of Thanet;   Margate.

GULVIN, Keith R: Chatham;   Inland Defences;
Medway Towns;   Military and Naval History;
Rochester;   World War II.

GUNKEL, Emuel Charles: Gravesend;   Gravesham;
Pocahontas, Princess.   See also
THE GRAVESEND CHRONOLOGY: Gravesend.

GUNN, Alexander. See TIMBS, John: History -
general.

GUNTHER, A.E: Biography: Tonbridge.

GUNYON, William P: Cricket;   Meopham.

GURNEY, Joseph. See TRIAL (AT LARGE) OF
JOSEPH STACPOOLE: Dartford;   Trials.

GURR, Philip R: Geology;   Herne Bay.

GUY, J: Castles and Houses;   Gardens.

GUY, L.H: Lewisham;   World War II.

GWYNN, S. See CURZON, Nathaniel 1st.Marquess
Curzon of Kedleston: Walmer.

H., W.T: Gravesend; Letters; Milton-next-Gravesend.

H.M.S.KENT: Military and Naval History.

H.M.S. LOCH LOMOND: Sheerness; Ships and Shipping.

HACKETT, Benedict: Biography: Canterbury.

HACKNEY, Noel C.L: Greenwich;

HACKWOOD, John F: Farnborough; Hospitals.

HADFIELD, Charles: Canals and Waterways.

HADLOW PARISH COUNCIL: Hadlow.

HADOW, Grace E: Chaucer, Geoffrey.

HADRICK, Frederick C: Cinque Ports.

HAES, I: Natural History.

HAGGAR, R.J: Agriculture.

HAGUE, Douglas B: Architecture; Coastal Waters - Safety at Sea.

HAILES, W.L.: Family History.

HAINES, Charles: Dickens, Charles.

HAINES, Charles Reginald: Dover.

HAINING, Peter: Channel Tunnel.

HALE, Robert: Brenchley; Yalding.

HALES, Irene: Kent,Mid. See also BALDOCK, Kay: Maidstone.

HALES, R. Cox: Family History.

HALES PLACE: Canterbury (Sale Catalogue).

HALFORD, B.L. See CONNOR, James Edward: Kent, North West; Railways.

HALFPENNY, Harriette: Biography.

HALL, A. See COX, Thomas: History-General.

HALL, Sir Alfred Daniel: Agriculture.

HALL, D.J: Becket, Saint Thomas.

HALL, Eric Foster: Military and Naval History.

HALL, Hammond: Kent, North West.

HALL, John R. See CROSS, Francis W: Canterbury.

HALL, Rev. Joseph: Kent Authors and Lit.- General. Letters. See also "A KENT INCUMBENT" pseud: Church History.

HALL, Peter: Land Utilisation.

HALL, Mr and Mrs. Samuel Carter: Thames, River.

HALL, Rev. Samuel Romilly: Sermons; Tunbridge Wells.

HALL-THERMOTANK LTD: Dartford; Industry and Trade - Firms.

HALLAM, W.B: Industry and Trade - Firms; Ships and Shipping; Thames, River.

HALLEWELL, John Publisher: Rochester.

HAMBLETON, F.C: Ships and shipping.

HAMBRIDGE, H.W. (Bill): Margate.

HAMILTON, Charles. See RICHARDS, Frank pseud: Biography.

HAMILTON, Nigel: Greenwich.

HAMILTON, Ronald: Pilgrims' Way.

HAMMOND, Elizabeth,illustrator. See BACON, Francis: Printing and Publishing.

HAMMOND, F.J: Allhallows.

HAMMOND. Reginald J.W. See WARD LOCK AND CO LTD. Publishers: Coastline; Kent, South East.

HAMO, of Hythe, Bishop of Rochester (1319 -53): Rochester - Diocese.

HAMPSON, John: Letters; Tunbridge Wells.

HAMPTON AND SONS LTD. See COLLEGE OF ALL SAINTS: Maidstone (Sale Catalogue).

HANDBOOK TO THE CATHEDRALS OF ENGLAND: Canterbury Cathedral; Rochester Cathedral.

HANDLEY-TAYLOR,Geoffrey: Biography; Kent Authors and Lit. - General.

HANGER, George: Military and Naval History.

HANNAVY, J.L: Dover; Folkestone; Libraries.

HANNEN, Henry: History - 1501 AD onwards; Maps.

HANSON, Elizabeth. See HANSON, Lawrence: GORDON, Gen. C.G., R.E.

HANSON, Jack: Orpington.

HANSON, Lawrence: Gordon. Gen. C.G., R.E.

THE HAPPY FISHING GROUNDS: Whitstable.

HARDAKER, Rev. Ian Alexander. See THE PARISH CHURCH OF ST. STEPHEN..:Chatham.

HARDIE, Martin: Biography. See also TONBRIDGE OAST THEATRE AND ARTS CLUB: Kent Artists; Tonbridge.

HARDMAN, Frederick William: Place Names.

HARDMAN, G.W: Footpaths - Country Walks; Kent, East.

HARDWICK, Mrs. Hope. See SAUNDERS, Hope: Farnborough.

HARDWICK, Michael: Dickens, Charles.

HARDWICK, Mollie. See HARDWICK, Michael: Dickens, Charles.

HARDY, M.M. See FINN, Arthur: Lydd.

HARDY, Paul,illustrator. See SHORE, Henry Noel 5th Baron Teignmouth: Smuggling.

HARDY, Stella. See KENT COUNTY LIBRARY: Bridges; Medway,River.

HARESNAPE, Brian: Railways.

HARGREAVES, Reginald: Coastal Waters.

HARKER, Sydney R: Gravesham; Springhead.

HARKNESS, Ariel Law: Gillingham.

HARTLEY, J.B. Maps.

HARPER, Charles George: Coastline; Kent; Kent, North West; Roads; Tunbridge Wells. See also SHORE, Henry Noel, 5th Baron Teignmouth: Smuggling.

HARPER, Michael. See ANGLICAN INTERNATIONAL CONFERENCE ON SPIRITUAL RENEWAL: Canterbury.

HARRINGTON, Duncan W: Canterbury; Family Records; Monumental Inscriptions.

HARRINGTON FAMILY MISCELLANY. See HARRINGTON, Duncan W: Family History.

HARRIS, Christopher W.J: Organisations.

HARRIS, Edwin: Charities; Chatham; Customs; Dickens, Charles; Gillingham; Ightham; Inns; Medway, River; Monumental Inscriptions; Rochester, Rochester Cathedral; Rochester Cathedral - Bishops.

HARRIS, G.G: Deptford.

HARRIS, George Robert Canning, 4th Baron: Cricket.

HARRIS, John: Adams, William; Castles and Houses.

HARRIS, Richard: Architecture.

HARRISON, Rev. Benjamin: Canterbury Cathedral; Sermons.

HARRISON, Sir Edward R: Ightham.

HARRISON, James Maurice: Natural History.

HARRISON, Jeffery Graham: Chetney; Medway,River; Natural History; North Kent Marshes; Sevenoaks; Thames, River. See also BOYD, Hugh: Natural History.

HILLS,William; Isle of Thanet.

HILTON, John. (Anthony):
Industry and Trade - Firms; Kent, West; Kent
Authors and Lit. - General; Maidstone;
Medway, River; Nettlestead; Railways;
Tonbridge; Ulcombe.

HILTON, Zella: Marlowe, Christopher.

HIMMELFARB, Gertrude: Darwin, Charles.

HINES, J: Kingsnorth Marshes; Ships and Shipping.

HININGS, Edward: Cinque Ports.

HINKLEY, E.J.F: Charities; Rochester.

HISCOCK, Robert Heath. See BENSON, James:
Gravesend; Northfleet.

HISSEY, James John: Inns; Roads; Tunbridge Wells.

HISTORICAL MANUSCRIPTS COMMISSION: Canterbury Cathedral;
Rochester Cathedral.See also RAYER, Felicity:Bibliography.

HISTORICAL RECORDS OF THE BUFFS, Vol.5: Military
and Naval History.

HISTORY OF KENT, Nos. 1 - 6: History - General.

HISTORY OF PARLIAMENT:POLL BOOKS: Elections.

HISTORY OF RICHBOROUGH CASTLE...: Richborough; Stonar.

HISTORY OF THE CORPS OF ROYAL ENGINEERS: Military and
Naval History.

HOARE, E.N: Kent Authors and Lit. - Fiction.

HOBSBAUM, Philip: Dickens, Charles.

HOBSBAWM, Eric John: History - 1501 AD onwards.

HOBSON, John Morrison: Canterbury - Almshouses and
Hospitals.

HOBSON, Victor G: Kent Authors and Lit. - General.

HODDER AND STOUGHTON, Publishers. See ATTENBOROUGH, John:
Industry and Trade - Firms.

HODGE, Gwenyth; Libraries; Tonbridge.

HODGE, James: Biography; Dartford.

HODGE, Sydney: Tonbridge.

HODGSON, R.D: Littlestone; Sport.

HODSOLL FAMILY: Family History; Loose.

HOELLERING, George. See ELIOT, Thomas Stearns:
Becket Saint Thomas.

HOGARTH, A.C: History - Archaeology.

HOGARTH, William Illustrator. See HOGARTH'S FROLIC:
Isle of Sheppey.

HOGARTH'S FROLIC: Isle of Sheppey.

HOGG, Garry: Inns.

HOGG, Ian Vernon: Coastal Defences.

HOLDERNESS, B.A: History - 1501 AD onwards.

HOLE, Samuel Reynolds, Dean of Rochester:
Kent Authors and Lit. - General; Letters;
Rochester Cathedral - Bishops.

HOLLAND, Josiah Gilbert: Sevenoaks.

HOLLAND, Philemon. See CAMDEN, William:
History - General.

HOLLIDAY, A.C: Dickens, Charles.

HOLLINGBOURNE RURAL DISTRICT COUNCIL: Hollingbourne;
Kent, North East.

HOLLIS, J: Population.

HOLLOWAY, Mark: Harvey Dr. William.

HOLLOWAY, Roger: Military and Naval History.

HOLMES,Martin: Biography; Knole.

HOLMES, R.C: See GILLHAM, Eric Howard:
Natural History; North Kent Marshes.

HOLMES, W. See HAGGAR, R.J: Agriculture.

HOLT, Anita: Faversham.

HOLWORTHY, R. See MISCELLANEA GENEALOGICA ET HERALDICA.
Bromley; Genealogical Records; Monumental Inscriptions.

HOLYCROSS CHURCH:A SHORT ACCOUNT: Bearsted.

HOME, Gordon Illustrator:Canterbury.See also HUTTON,Edward:Kent.

HOME COUNTIES MAGAZINE: History - General.

THE HOME FRONT, FRANCE, FLANDERS....See HISTORY OF THE
CORPS OF ROYAL ENGINEERS: Military and Naval History.

HOME PUBLISHING COMPANY. Publisher: Kent.

HONNORS LTD: Industry and Trade - Firms; Maidstone.

HONOR OAK ESTATE NEIGHBOURHOOD ASSOCIATION: Lewisham.

HOO ST. WERBURGH WOMENS INSTITUTE: Hoo St. Werburgh.

HOOK, Judith Ann: Pratts Bottom.

HOOK, Walter Farquhar: Becket, Saint Thomas;
Canterbury Cathedral - Archbishops.

HOOKER BROS. Publishers: Kent, West; Westerham.

HOOKER, Charles and Co. See HOOKER, Charles E:
Egerton; Industry and Trade - Firms.

HOOKER, Charles E: Egerton; Industry and Trade - Firms.

HOOLE, G.P: Industry and Trade; Tonbridge.

THE HOP GARDEN...:Agriculture.

HOPE, (Anne): Becket, Saint Thomas.

HOPE, Lady Elizabeth Reid. Castles and Houses;
Kent.

HOPE, Sir William Henry St. John: Rochester Cathedral.
See also JEWITT, Llewellyn: Heraldry.

HOPKINS, Jasper: Canterbuty Cathedral - Archbishops.

HOPKINS, Robert Thurston: Architecture; Castles and
Houses; Inns; Windmills and Watermills.

HOPPER, H.C: Churches.

HOPPER, L.T. Illustrator. See HOPPER, H.C: Churches.

HORLOCK, Albert H (Chubb): Ships and Shipping.

HORLOCK, R.J. See HORLOCK, Albert H. (Chubb):
Ships and shipping.

HORN, Alfred Aloysius pseud: Kent Authors and Lit. - Fiction;
Kent Authors and Lit.- General.

HORNER, R.W. See GREATER LONDON COUNCIL, DEPARTMENT OF
PUBLIC HEALTH ENGINEERING. Thames, River.

HORSBURGH, Edward Lee Stuart: Bromley.

HORSLEY, John William: Place-Names.

HORSMAN, Elizabeth: Mottingham.

HOSKINS, William George: Footpaths and Commons;
History-General.

HOTSON, John Leslie: Marlowe Christopher.

HOUGH, Brenda: Hastingleigh.

HOUGHTON, George E. Publisher: Isle of Thanet;
Margate.

HOUSING AND LOCAL GOVERNMENT, MINISTRY OF:
Kent, Mid; Maidstone; Planning; Pollution;
Public Utilities; ·Thames, River.

HOUSTON, Jane: Bibliography; Canterbury Diocese and
Province; Lambeth Palace.

HOVENDEN,Robert: Borden; Chislet; Family History;
Genealogical Records.

HOWARD, Donald R: Chaucer, Geoffrey.

HOWARD, Edwin J: Chaucer, Geoffrey.

HOWARD, Joseph Jackson. See VISITATION OF ENGLAND
AND WALES: Genealogical Records.

HOWE, G.R: Military and Naval History.

HOWE, P.P: Kent Authors and Lit. - General.

HOWELL, S: Coastline.

HOWGILL, Francis. See HAYES, Will: Meopham;
Religious Denominations.

HOWSE, Derek: Greenwich.

HUBBARD, Gilbert Ernest: Wye. See also
BRADE - BIRKS, Stanley Graham; Wye.

JORDAN, K.C. See BARTHOLOMEW, J. Publisher:
Inns; Maps.

JORDAN, R.W. See STREATER, Ronald A: Ships and
Shipping.

JORDAN, Wilbur Kitchener: History - 1501 AD onwards.

JORDEN, Edward: Spas and Mineral Waters.

JOSEPH, Jack: Kent Authors and Lit. - General;
Music.

JOTTINGS OF KENT: History - General.

JOTTINGS OF ST. PETERS...See "A PARISHIONER"pseud:
Broadstairs.

JOURNAL OF KENT HISTORY. See KENT VOLUNTARY SERVICE
COUNCIL: History - General.

JOURNAL OF THE UNITED SERVICES: Military and Naval History.

JOYCE, Alfred.See MAIDSTONE BOROUGH COUNCIL: Maidstone.

JOYCE FAMILY OF CRANBROOK...See CURTIS, Henry: Family History.

JUDGES, K.C. See JANES, Hurford: Hernhill.
See CURLING, P.W: Hernhill.

JULLIAN, Marcel: World War II.

JUSSERAND, Jean Adrien Antoine Jules: History -
901 AD - 1500 AD.

JUSTICES HANDBOOK, 1974: Law.

K

KAIN, Daniel:Maidstone; Road Transport.

KAIN, Roger J.P: Tithes.

KALLA-BISHOP, P.M: Railways.

KAMM, J: Biography; Ramsgate.

KAY, A.M: Margate.

KAYE-SMITH, Sheila: Isle of Oxney; Kent Authors and Lit. -
Fiction; Kent, West; Weald.

KEAN, J.S: Gravesend; Kent Artists.

"KEARSNEY CHRONICLE" JUBILEE ISSUE: Gillingham.

KEATE, George: History - General; Margate.

KEATES, Jonathan: Canterbury Cathedral.

KEBLE, T.H. Publisher: Isle of Thanet.

KEECH, Gertrude C: Family History; Staplehurst;
Weald.

KEELE, Kenneth D: Harvey, Dr. William.

KELLY, A. Lindsay. See KELLY'S DIRECTORIES: Kent.

KELLY, M.B: Bromley; Footpaths and Country Walks.

KELLY'S DIRECTORIES LIMITED: Beckenham;
Folkestone; Isle of Thanet; Kent; Kent, Mid;
Kent, North West; Kent, South East; Kent, West;
Maidstone; Margate; Medway Towns; Penge; Ramsgate;
Sandgate; Tonbridge; Tunbridge Wells.

KEMP, Betty: Biography.

KEMP, John: Biddenden.

KEMSING PARISH COUNCIL: Footpaths - Country Walks;
Kemsing; Natural History.

KENDALL, S.C. See KENT COUNTY YEARBOOK: Kent.

KENDON, Frank: Kent Authors and Lit. - Poetry.

KENDON, Margery: Bilsington.

KENDON, Samuel: Obituaries. See also
THE OLD BETHANIAN: Goudhurst.

KENNEDY, Paul M: Military and Naval History.

KENNETT, John: Eltham; Road Transport.

KENT, Bernard See FREESTON, Ewart C: Ships and
Shipping; Thames, River.

KENT, Joan. pseud: Kent, East: Kent, North East.

KENT, Rockwell Illustrator.See CHAUCER, Geoffrey:
Chaucer, Geoffrey.

KENT AND DOWNS NEWSPAPER ASSOCIATION. See BOORMAN,
Henry Roy Pratt: Newspapers.

KENT AND EAST SUSSEX RAILWAY: Railways.

KENT AND EAST SUSSEX SAND AND GRAVEL WORKING PARTY:
Industry and Trade. See also
STANDING CONFERENCE ON LONDON AND SOUTH EAST REGIONAL
PLANNING: KENT AND EAST SUSSEX SAND AND GRAVEL
WORKING PARTY: Industry and Trade.

KENT AND ESSEX MERCURY: Newspapers.

KENT AND ESSEX SEA FISHERIES COMMITTEE: Coastal Waters;
Industry and Trade; Organisations.

KENT AND SUSSEX BAPTIST ASSOCIATION: Religious
Denominations.

KENT AND SUSSEX BAPTIST ASSOCIATION: MAIDSTONE AND
DISTRICT MISSIONARY AUXILIARY: Maidstone.

KENT AND SUSSEX COURIER AND SOUTHERN COUNTIES HERALD:
Newspapers.

KENT AND SUSSEX POETRY SOCIETY: Kent Authors and
Lit. - Poetry.

KENT AND SUSSEX RAILWAY: Railways; Tenterden.

KENT ARCHAEOLOGICAL RESEARCH GROUPS' COUNCIL: History-
Archaeology.

KENT ARCHAEOLOGICAL SOCIETY: Organisations. See also
ARCHAEOLOGIA CANTIANA: History - General.

KENT ARCHAEOLOGICAL SOCIETY:RECORDS BRANCH: Bibliography;
Rochester Diocese. See also CHURCHILL, Irene J:
Bibliography; History AD901 - 1500.
See also DUBOULAY, Francis R.H: History-AD 901 -
1500.

KENT AREA HEALTH AUTHORITY: Health and Welfare.

KENT AREA TRADES DIRECTORY: Industry and Trade.

KENT ASSOCIATION FOR THE BLIND: Organisations.

KENT ASSOCIATION FOR THE DISABLED: Organisations.

KENT ASSOCIATION OF YOUTH CLUBS: Organisations.

KENT AVIATION HISTORICAL AND RESEARCH SOCIETY:
Aviation.

KENT BATTLE OF BRITAIN MUSEUM. See WEBB, Anthony:
World War II.

KENT BEE-KEEPERS' ASSOCIATION: Agriculture.

KENT BOROUGH AND URBAN DISTRICTS ASSOCIATION:
Local Government.

KENT COLLEGE: Canterbury - Education.

KENT COUNCIL OF SOCIAL SERVICE: Organisations.
See also HARTCUP, Adeline: Organisations.

KENT COUNCIL OF SOCIAL SERVICE:COMMITTEE FOR THE
PRESERVATION OF RURAL KENT: Conservation.

KENT COUNTY AGRICULTURAL SOCIETY: Agriculture.

KENT COUNTY AMATEUR SWIMMING ASSOCIATION: Organisations;
Sport.

KENT COUNTY ASSOCIATION OF CHANGE RINGERS: Organisations.

KENT COUNTY CONSTABULARY: Crime; Police; Roads.

KENT COUNTY CONSTABULARY:TRAFFIC DIVISION: Roads.

KENT COUNTY COUNCIL: Architecture; Channel Tunnel;
Elections; Kent; Kent,East; Libraries; Local Government;
Maidstone; Medway Towns; Music; Roads.

KENT COUNTY COUNCIL: AMENITIES AND COUNTRYSIDE
COMMISSION: Local Government.

KENT COUNTY COUNCIL - ARCHITECTS DEPARTMENT: Windmills
and Watermills. See also ADAMS, James Whirter Renwick:
Windmills and Watermills.

KENT COUNTY COUNCIL:ARCHIVES OFFICE: Bibliography;
Castles and Houses; Cinque Ports; Dover; Faversham;
Genealogical Records; Heraldry; History - General;
Local Government; Maps; Margate.

KENT COUNTY COUNCIL:CHILDREN'S COMMITTEE: Local Government.

KENT COUNTY COUNCIL: CONSUMER PROTECTION DEPARTMENT:
Local Government.

KENT COUNTY COUNCIL: COUNCIL AND COMMITTEE MEETINGS:
Education; Local Government.

KENT COUNTY COUNCIL:COUNTY SECRETARY AND SOLICITORS'
DEPARTMENT: Elections; Local Government.

KENT COUNTY COUNCIL:COUNTY SECRETARYS' DEPARTMENT:
RESEARCH AND INTELLIGENCE UNIT: Agriculture;
Ashford; Dover; Education; Health and Welfare;
Marden; Sevenoaks; Westerham.

KENT COUNTY COUNCIL:DISEASES OF ANIMALS BRANCH: Agriculture.

KENT COUNTY COUNCIL-EDUCATION DEPARTMENT: Dartford;
Education; Health and Welfare; Horton Kirby;
Isle of Thanet; Nent, North West; Medway Towns;
Religious Denominations; Sittingbourne; Sport;
Walderslade. See also DELAWARE STATE BOARD OF
EDUCATION: History and Archaeology - 1501 AD onwards.

KENT COUNTY COUNCIL:EDUCATION DEPARTMENT - ADVISORY
COMMITTEE OF TEACHERS: Education.

KENT COUNTY COUNCIL:EDUCATION DEPARTMENT - CAREERS
SERVICE: Education.

KENT COUNTY COUNCIL:EDUCATION DEPARTMENT - CAREERS
SERVICE:CANTERBURY DIVISION: Education; Industry and Trade.

KENT COUNTY COUNCIL:EDUCATION DEPARTMENT - NORTH EAST
KENT DIVISION: Education; Kent, North East.

KENT COUNTY COUNCIL:EDUCATION DEPARTMENT -
THAMESIDE DIVISIONAL EXECUTIVE: Education, Kent, North West.

KENT COUNTY COUNCIL:EDUCATION DEPARTMENT -
YOUTH AND COMMUNITY SERVICE: Education.

KENT COUNTY COUNCIL:EDUCATION DEPARTMENT -
YOUTH EMPLOYMENT SERVICE: Education.

KENT COUNTY COUNCIL:EDUCATION DEPARTMENT - YOUTH SERVICE:
Education.

KENT COUNTY COUNCIL:EMPLOYMENT OPPORTUNITIES OFFICER:
Industry and Trade; Transport.

KENT COUNTY COUNCIL: ESTABLISHMENT DIVISION:
Local Government.

KENT COUNTY COUNCIL: HEALTH DEPARTMENT: Health and
Welfare; Local Government.

KENT COUNTY COUNCIL:HIGHWAYS AND TRANSPORTATION DEPARTMENT:
Hildenborough; Local Government; Kent, North West;
Maidstone; Medway Towns; Tonbridge; Transport;
Tunbridge Wells.

KENT COUNTY COUNCIL: HIGHWAYS AND TRANSPORTATION
DEPARTMENT - PUBLIC TRANSPORT GROUP: Transport.

KENT COUNTY COUNCIL:INDUSTRIAL AND COMMERCIAL LIAISON
OFFICER: Industry and Trade; Transport.

KENT COUNTY COUNCIL:LIBRARIES, MUSEUMS AND ARCHIVES
SUB-COMMITTEE: Local Government.

KENT COUNTY COUNCIL:MEMBER INFORMATION CENTRE. See
KENT COUNTY COUNCIL: COUNTY SECRETARY AND SOLICITORS'
DEPARTMENT: Elections;Local Government.

KENT COUNTY COUNCIL: PERSONNEL DEPARTMENT: Local
Government.

KENT COUNTY COUNCIL-PLANNING DEPARTMENT:
Agriculture; Airports; Architecture; Ashford;
Aylesford; Biddenden; Brenchley; Canterbury;
Channel Tunnel; Chatham; Chestfield; Cliffe;
Cobham; Conservation; Cranbrook; Deal; Dungeness;
Dymchurch;Edenbridge; Farningham; Faversham;
Forestry; Goudhurst;Gravesend; Gypsies; Halling;
Industry and Trade; Isle of Sheppey; Kemsley;
Kent; Kent,East; Kent, Mid; Kent, North-East;
Kent, North-West; Kent, South-East; Kent,South-West;
Land Utilisation; Larkfield; Lenham; Leybourne;
Local Government;Loose; Lydd; Maidstone; Marden;
Medway,River; Medway Towns; Milton Regis; New Romney;
Penshurst; Planning; Population; Public Utilities;
Recreation; Roads; Sandwich; Sheerness; Sittingbourne;
Snodland;Southborough; Staplehurst; Swale; Tenterden;
Tovil; Transport; Tunbridge Wells; Walderslade;
Weavering Street; West Malling; Whitstable; Wingham;
Yalding.

KENT COUNTY COUNCIL:PLANNING DEPARTMENT AND DOVER
DISTRICT COUNCIL. PLANNING SERVICES: Dover.

KENT COUNTY COUNCIL: PLANNING DEPARTMENT AND FAVERSHAM
BOROUGH COUNCIL: Faversham.

KENT COUNTY COUNCIL:PLANNING DEPARTMENT AND THANET
DISTRICT COUNCIL: PLANNING DEPARTMENT: Hoverports;
Pegwell Bay.

KENT COUNTY COUNCIL: POLICIES AND RESOURCES COMMITTEE:
Local Government.

KENT COUNTY COUNCIL: ROADS DEPARTMENT: Floods; Roads.
See also: KENT COUNTY COUNCIL:HIGHWAYS AND TRANSPORTATION
DEPARTMENT.

KENT COUNTY COUNCIL:SOCIAL SERVICES DEPARTMENT:
Health and Welfare; Local Government.

KENT COUNTY COUNCIL:SUPPLIES DEPARTMENT: Local Government.

KENT COUNTY COUNCIL:SURVEYORS DEPARTMENT: Local Government;
Roads; Transport. See also KENT COUNTY COUNCIL-
HIGHWAYS AND TRANSPORTATION DEPARTMENT.

KENT COUNTY COUNCIL:TECHNICAL EDUCATION COMMITTEE:
Education.

KENT COUNTY COUNCIL:TREASURERS DEPARTMENT: Local
Government.

KENT COUNTY COUNCIL:WEIGHTS AND MEASURES DEPARTMENT:
Local Government.

KENT COUNTY CRICKET CLUB: Cricket.

KENT COUNTY DRAMA COMMITTEE: Theatre.

KENT COUNTY EXAMINER: Ashford.

KENT COUNTY FEDERATION OF YOUNG FARMERS' CLUBS:
Agriculture.

KENT COUNTY FOOTBALL ASSOCIATION: Sport.

KENT COUNTY JOINT COMMITTEE: Local Government.

KENT COUNTY JOURNAL: Kent.

KENT COUNTY LAWN TENNIS ASSOCIATION: Sport.

KENT COUNTY LIBRARY: Austen, Jane; Becket, Thomas;
Bibliography; Biography; Bridges; Canterbury;
Herne; Herne Bay; History - General; Isle of Sheppey;
Kent; Kent Authors and Lit. - Fiction; Libraries;
Maidstone; Reculver; Sheerness.

KENT COUNTY LIBRARY:DARTFORD DIVISION: Dartford.

KENT COUNTY LIBRARY:DOVER DIVISION: Dover; World War II.

KENT COUNTY LIBRARY:GRAVESHAM DIVISION:
See: McLELLAN, Doreen: Allhallows; Dickens,Charles;
Gravesend; Gravesham; Hotels, Restaurants and Clubs;
Libraries; Railways. See
CONNOLLY, P.A: Airports; Gravesham;
See GUNKEL, E.C: Gravesend; Gravesham; Pocahontas,
Princess.
See WILLIS, Peter J: Gravesend; Gravesham: Kent, North
West.

KENT COUNTY LIBRARY:MEDWAY DIVISION: Medway, River;
Medway,Towns; Organisations.

KENT COUNTY LIBRARY:SCHOOL MUSEUM SERVICE:
Kent.

KENT COUNTY LIBRARY:SEVENOAKS DIVISION: Kent, West;
Organisations; Sevenoaks.

KENT COUNTY LIBRARY:SWALE DIVISION: Bibliography;
Faversham. See also
GRIMSDELL, Mrs. N.L: Bibliography; Isle of Sheppey.

KENT COUNTY LIBRARY:TECHNICAL SERVICE.
See GILLHAM, Philip: Kent Authors and Lit. - General

KENT COUNTY LIBRARY:THANET DIVISION: Bibliography.

KENT COUNTY LIBRARY:TONBRIDGE AND MALLING DIVISION:
Libraries; Tonbridge.

THE KENT COUNTY MEETING See THE CATHOLIC QUESTION:
History - 1501 AD onwards; Maidstone; Religious
Denominations.

KENT COUNTY PLAYING FIELDS ASSOCIATION: Sport.

KENT COUNTY SCOUTS ASSOCIATION: Organisations.

KENT COUNTY SHOW See KENT COUNTY AGRICULTURAL SOCIETY:
Agriculture.

KENT COUNTY WAR MEMORIAL: Canterbury; Military and
Naval History.

KENT COUNTY YEAR BOOK: Kent.

KENT FAMILY HISTORY SOCIETY: Family History.

KENT FAMILY PRACTITIONER COMMITTEE See NATIONAL HEALTH
SERVICE:KENT FAMILY PRACTITIONER COMMITTEE: Health and
Welfare.

K Cont'd

KENT FEDERATION OF AMENITY SOCIETIES: Kent.

KENT FEDERATION OF HEAD TEACHERS' ASSOCIATIONS:
Education.

KENT FIELD CLUB: Natural History; Channel Tunnel.
See also MORGAN, G.H: Hothfield; Natural History;
See also GANN, P.D: Bibliography; Natural History.
See also SCOTT, Dr. Ernest: Kent, South East;
Natural History.
See also TITTLEY, Ian: Coastline; Maps; Natural History.

KENT FINANCIAL OFFICERS' ASSOCIATION: Local Government.

KENT FIRE BRIGADE: Local Government.

KENT FIRE INSURANCE COMPANY: Industry and Trade-Firms.

KENT GIRL GUIDE ASSOCIATION: Kent Songs.

KENT, HISTORICAL, BIOGRAPHICAL AND PICTORIAL: Biography.

KENT ILLUSTRATED...History - 1501 AD onwards.

"A KENT INCUMBENT" pseud: Church History.
See also HALL, Rev. Joseph: Letters.

KENT LEISURE GUIDE: Kent.

KENT MATTERS. See KENT FEDERATION OF AMENITY SOCIETIES:
Kent.

THE KENT MEETING. See THE CATHOLIC QUESTION:
History - 1501 AD onwards; Maidstone; Religious
Denominations.

KENT MESSENGER: Canterbury; Castles and Houses;
Kent, Mid; Local Government; Maidstone.

KENT MUSIC SCHOOL: Music.

KENT MUSIC COMPETITIVE FESTIVAL: Chatham; Maidstone; Music.

KENT NATURALISTS' TRUST. See KENT TRUST FOR NATURE
CONSERVATION: Natural History; Ruxley.

KENT NEWSPAPER PROPRIETORS' ASSOCIATION. See BOORMAN,
Henry Roy Pratt: Newspapers.

KENT ORNITHOLOGICAL SOCIETY: Natural History.

KENT PAEDIATRIC SOCIETY: Bexley; Health and Welfare.

KENT POSTAL HISTORY GROUP: Postal History.

KENT RAILWAYS - TWENTY ONE ARTICLES: Railways.

KENT RIGHTS OF WAY COUNCIL: Coastline; Footpaths -
Country Walks; Footpaths - Horse Riding; Maps.

KENT RIVER AUTHORITY: Floods; Rivers; Stour,River.

KENT RIVER BOARD: Floods; Rivers.

KENT SCHOOLS FOOTBALL FEDERATION: Sport.

KENT STANDING CONFERENCE OF NATIONAL VOLUNTARY
YOUTH ORGANISATIONS: Organisations.

KENT TRUST FOR NATURE CONSERVATION. Natural History;
Ruxley. See also JERMY, A.C: Agriculture;
Conservation; Kent Naturalists' Trust;
Natural History.

KENT UNIVERSITY See UNIVERSITY OF KENT.

KENT VOLUNTARY SERVICE COUNCIL:History-General;Organisations.

THE KENTISH COMPANION FOR 1818: History - 1501 AD onwards.

KENTISH EXPRESS: Ashford; Elham; Romney Marsh; Tenterden.

KENTISH GAZETTE; Canterbury; Roads.

KENTISH GAZETTE & CANTERBURY PRESS: Canterbury; Ghosts.

THE KENTISH HOODEN HORSE TODAY: Customs.

THE KENTISH TOURIST..:History - General.

THE KENTISH TRAVELLERS' COMPANION: History - General.

KENWARD, James: Architecture.

KENWORTHY, Wesley: Tunbridge Wells.

KENYON, G.H: Industry and Trade; Weald.

KENYON, J.R: Coastal Defences.

KEPLER, J.S: Church History.

KERIN, Dorothy See FURLONG, Monica: Groombridge.

KERSHAW, J.C See HARPER, Charles George: Kent.

KERSHAW, S. Wayland: Architecture; Castles and Houses;
History - General; Kent, East; Lambeth Palace.
See also MAYHEW, Athol: Birchington; Isle of Thanet.

KERSHAW AND SONS, Engravers and Publishers. See
BARLEY, H. Publisher: Ramsgate.
See SANDERS, J. & CO., Engravers and Publishers:
Margate.

KERSTING, Anthony Photographer. See MASON, John.
Kent.

KESTON FOREIGN BIRD FARM: Bibliography;
Hayes and Keston; Natural History.

KEYNES, Geoffrey: Bibliography; Harvey, Dr. William.

KIDD, Evelyne Rose: Eynsford.

KIDD, William, Publisher: Isle of Thanet.

KIDMAN, Brenda: Biography; Tunbridge Wells.

KIDNER, Roger Wakeley: Kent, North; Kent,West;
Railways; Romney Marsh; Tonbridge.
See also STOYEL, B. Derek: Industry and Trade;
Railways.

KIDWELL & COMPANY. Auctioneers See
ROCHESTER (Sale Catalogue).

KIELY, M.B: Allington.

KIDBURNE, Richard: History - General.

KIMBALL, Katherine: Kent Artists; Rochester.
See also JOHN, Malcolm: Rochester.

KING, Edward See LYON, John: Folkestone.

KING, Geoffrey: Footpaths - Country Walks; Weald.

KING, John Thornton: Road Transport; Tunbridge Wells.

KING, Staff Commander John W. See ADMIRALTY:
HYDROGRAPHIC DEPARTMENT: Sea and River Charts.

KING, Nicholas: Road Transport.
See also MAIDSTONE AND DISTRICT AND EAST KENT
BUS CLUB: Maidstone; Road Transport.

KING, Richard S: Herne Bay.

KING, William Louis: Family History; Kent Authors
and Lit. - Poetry.

KINGSNORTH, Thomas. See PARTICULARS AND CONDITIONS
OF SALE OF..:Bilsington (Sale Catalogue);
Newchurch (Sale Catalogue).

KING'S SCHOOL: Canterbury - Education; Rochester.

THE KINGS' WORK: Broadstairs.

KINNAIRD, Emily: Biography; Bromley.

KIRBY, Rev. F: Letters.

KIRBY, Herbert Charles: Lewisham; Monumental Inscriptions.

KIRBY, John William: Greenwich; Lewisham.

KIRBY, O.I: Tankerton.

KIRK, Barry. See WEBB, Brian: Canterbury Cathedral;
Dover.

KIRKALDY, John Francis: Geology; Weald.

KIRKBRIDE, Lt. Col. William: Biography; Military
and Naval History.

KIRKHAM, Nellie: Pilgrims' Way.

KITCHENER, Geoffrey D: Halstead.

KITCHEN, F.L: See LAMPLUGH, G.W: Geology.

KITTON, Frederick G: Dickens, Charles; Kent.

KLINGER OF MARGATE, LTD:Industry and Trade - Firms;
Margate.

KLOEDEN, Judith L: Beult,River and Valley; Conservation;
Ecology.

KNATCHBULL, Sir Edward: History - 1501 AD onwards.
See also BARTLETT, Rev. Thomas: Letters.

KNATCHBULL-HUGESSEN, Edward Hugessen Baron Brabourne:
Kent Authors and Lit. - Fiction.

KNATCHBULL-HUGESSON, Sir Hughe: Family History;
Mersham Hatch.

KNIGHT, Charles: Gillingham; Industry and Trade;
Inland Defences; Ships and Shipping.

K Cont'd

KNIGHT, Charles Henry Bruere. See
HISTORICAL RECORDS OF THE BUFFS, Vol.5: Military
and Naval History.

KNIGHT, Captain H.R: Military and Naval History.

KNIGHT, M.T: Industry and Trade - Firms; Rochester;
Ships and Shipping.

KNIGHT, Robert: Natural History; Pegwell Bay; Sandwich.

KNIGHT-SWEENEY, Brian: Kent, North West; Meopham.

KNIGHT, FRANK AND RUTLEY, Auctioneers.
Addington (Sale Catalogue); Kent, Mid (Sale Catalogue).
See also CATALOGUE OF THE SYDNEY COLLECTION..:
Bibliography; Chislehurst (Sale Catalogue).

KNOCKER, Edward: Cinque Ports; Dover.

KNOCKER, Frederic See DOVER BOROUGH COUNCIL:MUSEUM.
Dover; Museums.

KNOCKER, Herbert Wheatley: Great Chart; History - General;
Sundridge (Sevenoaks).

KNOCKER, Sir Wollaston: Cinque Ports.

KNOCKHOLT SOCIETY: Footpaths - Country Walks; Knockholt.

(KNOLLYS, E.E.): Folkestone.

KNOTT, Alan: Cricket.

KNOWLDEN, P.E: West Wickham.

KNOWLES, Dom David: Becket Saint Thomas.

KOHLER, David F: Industry and Trade; Lewisham.

KOPS, B: Margate.

KREMER, Tony: Education; Yalding.

KRYNSKI, Audrey See SPAYNE, Janet: Footpaths -
Country Walks.

"KYD" pseud Illustrator (Joseph Clayton Clarke).
See BRIGDEN, C.A.T. Illustrator: Dickens, Charles.

KYD, Tony: Channel Tunnel.

L

LABOUR,MINISTRY OF:JOINT STANDING COMMITTEE FOR
PAPER MILLS: Industry and Trade.

LACEY, Joseph Melville: Coastline.

LAFFERTY, Joan A. See McMILLAN, A. Stewart: Erith.

LAGDEN, G.J: Chislehurst.

LAGIER, James. See TRIAL (AT LARGE) OF Joseph
Stacpoole: Dartford; Trials.

LAIGLE, Dominique-Odile: Smuggling.

LAIRD, A. Bonnet: Agriculture and Horticulture.

LAKE, Phyllis: Kent Authors and Lit. - Poetry.

LAKE, W.E. Photographer. See KIRKHAM, Nellie:
Pilgrim's Way.

LAKER, John: Deal.

LAKER, Rosalind: Smuggling.

LAMB, Cadbury: Inns.

LAMB, John William: Canterbury Cathedral -
Archbishops; Canterbury - Diocese and Province

LAMBARDE, Fane F: Ash-by-Wrotham; Faversham.

LAMBARDE, William: History - General;
History 1501 AD onwards; Law.

LAMBERT, J.R: Wateringbury.

LAMBERT, William M.P. See LAMBARDE, William:
History - 1501 AD onwards.

LAMBETH CONFERENCE. See REPORT OF THE LAMBETH CONFERENCE
1978: Canterbury - Diocese and Province.

LAMPLUGH, G.W.: Geology.

L(AMPREY), S.C: Maidstone.

LANAWAY, Hugh: Coastal Defences.

LANE, GENTRY AND CO. Publishers: Dymchurch;
Isle of Thanet; Margate; New Romney; Romney Marsh.

LANG, Andrew: Dickens, Charles.

LANG-SIMS, Lois: Canterbury Cathedral.

LANGDON, John A: Gillingham.

LANGMUIR, G.E. See DUCKWORTH, C.L.D: Coastal Waters;
Ships and Shipping.

LANGTON, Robert: Dickens, Charles; Rochester.

THE LANGTONIAN: Canterbury - Education.

LANSDELL, Harry: Charities; Greenwich; Lewisham;
Woolwich.

LAPTHORNE, William H: Broadstairs; Smuggling.

LAPWORTH, Herbert: Geology; Kent, East.

LARKEN, H.W: Caxton, William.

LARKING, Lambert Blackwell: History - 901 AD - 1500 AD.
Leybourne.

LARN, Richard: Goodwin Sands.

LATHAM, Albert See GALTON, Captain Douglas:
Margate; Public Utilities.

LATHAM, Charles Photographer: Horton Kirby.

LAVER, C. Architect. See DUNNAGE, H. Architect: Eltham.

LAW, Maurice: Orpington.

LAW SOCIETY: Law.

LAWLER, Ray: Becket Saint Thomas.

LAWRENCE, Margaret: East Peckham; Education.

LAWRENZ, Manfred: Canterbury.

LAWSON, A.W: Charities; West Malling.

LEACH, Peter E: Family History.

LEALE, M: West Wickham.

LEATHER, John: Ships and Shipping.

LEBON, Cicely: Benenden.

LEE, Barbara: Groombridge.

LEE, Laurie: Becket, Saint Thomas.

LEE, Lawrence: Canterbury Cathedral.

LEE-WARNER, Edward. Bishop of Rochester 1637-1666:
Family History; Rochester Cathedral - Bishops.

LEEDS, C.S: Gillingham.

LEES COURT: Faversham; Housing.

LEFRANQ, Paul: Chatham Dockyard.

THE LEGAT SCHOOL DEVELOPMENT FUND: Goudhurst.

LE GEAR, R.F: Caves and Tunnels.

THE LEGEND OF THE HART-DYKES: Lullingstone

LEGOUIX, Susan (Later Mrs Sloman): Bibliography;
Maidstone; Museums.

LEIGH-BENNETT, E.P: Railways; Sport.

LEIGH HOE pseud. See TRIPP, Sir Herbert Alker
("Leigh Hoe"): Coastal Waters.

LE-MAY, Reginald: Family History.

LE NEVE, John: Canterbury - Diocese and Province;
Rochester - Diocese and Province; Religious
Denominations.

LENG, Rev. John: Sermons; Tunbridge Wells.

LENTHAL, Hon. William. See RUSHWORTH, John:
History - 1501 AD onwards; Letters; Maidstone;
Printing and Publishing.

THE LEOPARD See SKINNERS' SCHOOL: Tunbridge Wells.

LERNER, Laurence See SOUTH EAST ARTS ASSOCIATION:
Kent Authors and Lit. - Poetry.

LEROI, David: Channel Tunnel.

LES TAPISSERIES DE LA VIE DU CHRIST...:Canterbury Cathedral.

L'ESTRANGE, Algred Guy K: Greenwich.

LETRASET See CHUDLEY, John A: Ashford; Industry and Trade-
Firms.

L Cont'd

LUCAS, Audrey: Smallhythe.

LUCAS, Meriel: Beckenham; Biography.

LUCKHURST, Brian. See DIMONT, Charles:
Cricket.

LUCY, Sir Henry William: Biography.

LUDLOW, R. Nelson: Margate.

LUGARD, Cecil E: Seasalter.

LUKEHURST, Clare T. See COLEMAN, Alice Mary:
Geography; Kent, East; Maps.

LUMAN, Mrs. Arthur. See LUMAN, Rev. Arthur:
Murston.

LUMAN, Rev. Arthur: Murston.

LUND, Robert: Adams, William.

LUSHINGTON, Lt. Col. Franklin: Military and
Naval History.

LUTTRELL, Narcissus: Tunbridge Wells.

LYALL, Very Rev. William Rowe: Biography;
Canterbury Cathedral.

LYDD CHURCH RESTORATION FUND: Lydd.

LYKIARD, Alexis. See ARC PUBLICATIONS:
Kent Authors and Literature - Poetry.

LYMPNE CASTLE ESTATE: Lympne (Sale Catalogue).

LYNCH, E. Killian: Aylesford; Religious Denominations.

LYNE, R.M: Gravesend; Railways.

LYON, John: Cinque Ports; Dover; Folkestone.

LYSONS, Daniel: History - General.

M

M., E.W. See MOORE, E.W: Wye.

M., J.P: Family History.

MACARTNEY, Sylvia: Hither Green; Industry and Trade;
Lewisham.

MACBRIDE, John. Rear Admiral of the Blue. See
ADMIRALTY: Sea and River Charts.

McCALL, A: Road Transport.

McCALL, Dorothy: Biography.

McCALMAN, Rev. Hugh. See JOHNSON, Miss: Northfleet.

McCLINTOCK, F.H. See BOTTOMS, A.E: Crime; Dover; Prisons.

McCOLL, P.J: Kent.

McCONICA, James: More, Sir Thomas.

McCREA, William Hunter: Greenwich.

McCUDDEN, James Thomas Byford: Gillingham;
McCudden, James Thomas Byford.

McCULLOCH, Joseph: Medway, River.

M'DIVITT, John: Canterbury; Hospitals.

MACDONALD, Gilbert; Beckenham; Dartford; Industry
and Trade - Firms.

MACDONALD, Sir M. and Partners. See KENT RIVER AUTHORITY:
Floods; Stour, River.

MACDOUGALL, Philip: Coastal Defences; Hoo Peninsula;
Isle of Grain.

MACDOUGALL, Mrs. Sylvia (nee Börgstrom). See
WAINEMAN, Paul pseud: Biography.

MACFARLANE, William Angus: Plaistow.

McFEE, William: Dartford.

MACFIE, A.L: St. Margaret-at-Cliffe.

McGREAL, Father Wilfred: Allington.

McINTOSH, Kinn Hamilton: Chislet; Fordwich;
Sturry; Westbere.

MACKAIL, J.W: Morris, William.

MACKAY, W.&.J. Ltd. Printers, of Chatham:
Printing and Publishing. See also
WHYMAN, John: Chatham; Industry and Trade - Firms.

MACKEAN, William Herbert Canon of Rochester Cathedral:
Libraries: Rochester Cathedral.

McKEE, Alexander: Coastal Waters; Whitstable.

MACKENZIE, Jeanne. See MACKENZIE, Norman: Wells,
Herbert George.

MACKENZIE, Norman: Wells, Herbert George.

MACKESON, Charles: Religious Denominations.

MACKIE, S.J: Folkestone; Knole.

McKILLIAM, A.E: Becket, Saint Thomas; Canterbury
Cathedral - Archbishops.

MACKINNON, Donald D: Speldhurst.

MACKLEY, George E: Kent Authors and Lit. - General.

MACKLIN, Herbert Walter: Monumental Inscriptions.

MACLACHLAN, G.W.P. See GRASEMANN, C:
Coastal Waters; Ships and Shipping.

MACLAREN, R: History - General.

MACLEAR, George Frederick: Canterbury - Monastic Houses.

MACLEISH, Kenneth: Canterbury Cathedral.

McLELLAN, Mrs. Doreen E: Allhallows; Canals and
Waterways; Dickens, Charles; Gardens; Gordon, Gen. C.G;
Gravesend; Gravesham; Hostels, Restaurants and Clubs;
Railways.

MACMICHAEL Rev. A.W. See LIVETT, Greville Mavis:
New Romney.

McMILLAN. A. Stewart: Erith.

McNAY, Michael: East Malling.

MACRAE, R. Stuart: Churchill, Sir W.L.S.

MACRAE, Stuart Gordon: Agriculture; Geography.
See also BURNHAM, Paul: Kent.

McVIE, J.D.R. See UPBURY MANOR SCHOOL: Gillingham.

MADAN, Patrick: Tunbridge Wells.

MADDEN, Len: Architecture.

MACE, J. Ellis. See ELLIS-MACE, J: Tenterden;
Roads.

MAGGS, Colin: Railways.

MAGGS, K.R.A: Bromley.

MAGNUS, Philip: Kitchener, Field Marshal H.H., R.E.

MAHIR, Tom: Hayes and Keston; Police.

MAIDSTONE AND DISTRICT AND EAST KENT BUS CLUB:
Hythe; Road Transport; Maidstone.

MAIDSTONE AND DISTRICT CHAMBER OF COMMERCE: Maidstone.
See also THE LINK: Industry and trade.

MAIDSTONE AND DISTRICT MOTOR SERVICES LTD:
Kent, North East; Kent, South West; Road Transport.

MAIDSTONE AREA ARTS COUNCIL: See MAIDSTONE FESTIVAL:
Maidstone.

THE MAIDSTONE BOOK. See REGENCY PUBLICITY SERVICES LTD.
Publisher: Maidstone.

MAIDSTONE BOROUGH COUNCIL: Health and Welfare;
Maidstone; Monumental Inscriptions; Recreation.

MAIDSTONE BOROUGH COUNCIL: BOROUGH ENGINEERS DEPARTMENT:
Maidstone.

MAIDSTONE BOROUGH COUNCIL: INFORMATION OFFICE: Maidstone.

MAIDSTONE BOROUGH COUNCIL: PLANNING DEPARTMENT:
Housing; Industry and Trade; Recreation; Tovil; Transport.

MAIDSTONE CENSUS 1821: Genealogical Records;
Maidstone.

MAIDSTONE COLLEGE OF ART. See RUSHWORTH, John:
Letters; Maidstone; Printing and Publishing.

MAIDSTONE DISTRICT SCOUT COUNCIL: Maidstone; Organisations.

MAIDSTONE FESTIVAL: Maidstone.

MAIDSTONE GRAMMAR SCHOOLS: Maidstone.

MAIDSTONE MUSEUM AND ART GALLERY: Bibliography;
Maidstone; Museums; Road Transport.
See also COLLINS, Kenneth J: Maidstone;
Military and Naval History; Museums.
See also LEGOUIX, Susan: Bibliography; Maidstone;
Museums.

MAIDSTONE PUBLIC LIBRARY: Bibliography; Maidstone.

MAIDSTONE RURAL DISTRICT COUNCIL: Kent, Mid.

MAIDSTONE SCHOOL OF ARTS AND CRAFTS: See
BACON, Francis: Printing and publishing.

MAIDSTONE UNION: Maidstone; Poor Law.

MAIDSTONE WATERWORKS COUNCIL: Maidstone;
Public Utilities.

MAIS, Stuart Petrie Brodie: Cinque Ports.
Footpaths - Country Walks. See also
HOME PUBLISHING COMPANY. Publisher Kent.

MAIZELS, Judith K: Geology.

MAJOR, Alan P: Stockbury.

MAJOR, John B: Erith.

MALCOLM, James Peller: History - General.

MALIM, Mary Charlotte: Blackheath.

MALLING RURAL DISTRICT COUNCIL: Kent, Mid.

MALLING, RURAL DISTRICT COUNCIL: PUBLIC HEALTH
DEPARTMENT: Health and Welfare; Kent, Mid.

MALSTER, Robert: Coastal Waters - Safety at Sea.

MAN OF KENT See SCHEDULE OF KENTISH NEWSPAPERS..:
Bibliography; Newspapers.

MAN WHO SLEW KIT MARLOWE...:Marlowe, Christopher.

MANLY, John Matthew: Chaucer, Geoffrey.

MANN, Sir James: Canterbury Cathedral; Edward,
the Black Prince. See also MILLS, Dorothy:
Edward, the Black Prince.

MANNIN, Ethel: Adams, William.

MANNING, Anne: More, Sir Thomas.

MANNING, Patricia See TONKIN, Nancy: Beckenham.

MANNING, Stanley Arthur: Natural History.

MANSELL, M.H: Woodchurch.

MAPLE AND CO. Auctioneers. See ROCHESTER
(Sale Catalogue).

MARCH, Edgar James: Medway,River; Ships and
Shipping; Thames, River.

MARCHANT, Bessie: Canterbury.

MARCHINGTON, Trevor: Geography, Kent, North East.

MARGARY, Ivan Donald: Industry and Trade; Kent, West;
Roads; Weald.

MARGATE AMBULANCE CORPS: Margate; Organisations.

MARGATE AND THANET PERMANENT BENEFIT BUILDING SOCIETY:
Industry and Trade - Firms; Isle of Thanet.

MARGATE BOROUGH COUNCIL: Birchington; Hotels etc;
Margate; Public Utilities.

MARGATE BOROUGH COUNCIL:EDUCATION DEPARTMENT:
Margate.

MARGATE BOROUGH COUNCIL-ENGINEERS' DEPARTMENT.
Margate.

MARGATE BOROUGH COUNCIL:HEALTH DEPARTMENT:
Health and Welfare; Margate.

MARGATE BOROUGH COUNCIL:PUBLICITY DEPARTMENT:
Housing; Margate.

MARGATE BOROUGH COUNCIL:TREASURERS' DEPARTMENT:
Margate.

MARGATE BOROUGH COUNCIL:WEIGHTS AND MEASURES DEPARTMENT:
Margate.

MARGATE CHAMBER OF COMMERCE: Margate.

MARGATE CIVIC SOCIETY: Margate. See also
STAFFORD, F: Margate.

MARGATE COLLEGE: Margate.

MARGATE CORPORATION: Margate. See also
MARGATE BOROUGH COUNCIL: Margate.

MARGATE DRAINAGE CONTROVERSY: Margate; Public
Utilities.

MARGATE ELEMENTARY SCHOOLS FOOTBALL AND ATHLETIC ASSOCIATION:
Margate; Sport.

MARGATE ELEMENTARY SCHOOLS' FOOTBALL LEAGUE:
Margate; Sport.

THE MARGATE FRONT...Margate; World War I.

THE MARGATE GRAMMAR SCHOOL: Margate.

THE MARGATE HOY, a poem. See BONSFIELD Publisher:
Isle of Thanet; Kent Authors and Lit. - Poetry.
Margate.

MARGATE OPERATIC SOCIETY: Margate.

MARGATE PUBLIC LIBRARY: Libraries; Margate.
See also GRITTEN, A.J: Bibliography; Isle of Thanet;
Margate.

MARGATE SCHOOL BOARD: Margate.

MARILLIER, H.C: Morris, William.

MARITIME TRUST: Medway,River; Ships and Shipping.

MARKHAM, Gervase: Agriculture; Weald.

MARLEY TILE COMPANY LTD: Industry and Trade - Firms;
Kent Authors and Lit. - General.

MARLOW, Louis: Biography.

MARLOWE, Christopher: Marlowe, Christopher.

MARLOWE, John: Biography; Gordon, Gen. C.G.

MARPLES, Morris: Biography.

MARRINER, Edmund Hayes: Chatham; Family History.

MARRINER, Harry Andrew See MARRINER, Edmund Hayes:
Chatham; Family History.

MARRIOTT, Charles Stowel: Cricket; Obituaries.

MARSDEN, P: Ships and Shipping.

MARSH, Ronald J: Kent Authors and Lit. - Fiction;
Libraries; Medway, River; Rochester.

MARSH, William. See MINUTES OF THE COURT LEET: Chatham.

MARSHALL, C.F. Dendy: Railways.

MARSHALL, Elizabeth: Chatham; Family History.

MARSHALL, Emma: Canterbury; Penshurst.

MARSHALL, M.A.N: Dover; Folkestone; Ships and Shipping.

MARSHALL, William:Agriculture.

MARSHALL, William M: Biography; Canterbury Cathedral.

MARSHAM-TOWNSHEND, Robert: Family History.

MARSTON, Louise: Agriculture.

MARTIN, A.R: Blackheath.

MARTIN, Alan R: Canterbury - Monastic Houses.

MARTIN, Bina Elizabeth: Family History.

MARTIN, Charles Wykeham: Leeds.

MARTIN, Elizabeth: Sandwich.

MARTIN, J.E: Geography; Industry and Trade;
Kent, North West.

MARTIN, Kennett Beecham: Ramsgate.

MARTIN, N. Baldwin: Canterbury.

MARTIN, Nancy: Coastal Waters; Rivers.

MARTIN, W. Stanley. See ROW, B. Prescott:
Kent, Mid; Maidstone.

MARTIN, W.W: High Halden; Inns.

MARTON, Mrs. M.E: New Romney.

MARZIALS, Frank T: Dickens, Charles.

MASKELL, E: See BOORMAN, Henry Roy Pratt: Tonbridge.

MASON, Anne. See MASON, John: Kent.

MASON, Francis K: World War II.

MASON, Hilda Claire: Maidstone.

MASON, John: Kent.

MASON, John Neve: Biography; Cinque Ports.

MASON, L: Kent, North East.

MASON, Martin T. See FARRIES, Kenneth G:
Windmills and Watermills; Kent, North West.

MASON, Oliver: Kent.

MASON, Reginald Thomas: Architecture;
Weald.

MASSINGHAM, Betty: Biography; Rochester
Cathedral - Bishops.

MASTER OF HOUNDS...: Ashford; Sport.

MASTERS, John White: Dialect; Kent Authors
and Lit. - poetry.

MATHIAS, Peter: Industry and Trade.

MATKIN, Robert B: Ramsgate.
See also MARTIN, Kenneth Beecham: Ramsgate.

MATTHEWS, Brian: Kent, North West.

MATTHEWS, G.F. See MATTHEWS, John:
Genealogical Records.

MATTHEWS, John: Genealogical Records.

MATTHEWS, W.G: Sittingbourne.

MATZ, B.W: Dickens, Charles; Inns; Kent, North West.

MAUGHAM, H. Hamilton: Folkestone.

MAULDON, Jean: Tunbridge Wells.
See also PELTON, Richard: Kent, West; Tunbridge
Wells.

MAUNDER, E. Walter: Greenwich.

MAURICE, Hon. Mrs. Adelaide See LUBBOCK, Adelaide:
Downe; Family History.

MAURICE, C. Edmund: Biography; Letters.

MAURICE-JONES, K.W: Military and Naval History.

MAXTED, Ivan: Canterbury; Railways; Whitstable.

MAXTON-GRAHAM AND CO., AUCTIONEERS AND ESTATE
AGENTS. See 27 PALACE STREET...:
Canterbury (Sale Catalogue).

MAXWELL, Donald: Churches; Industry and Trade;
Kent; Kent Artists; Kent Authors and Lit. - General;
Medway, River; Obituaries; Pilgrims Way; Roads;
Thames, River. See also
MAXWELL, Gordon S: Kent, North West.
See also MORTLOCK, C.B: Kent Artists.

MAXWELL, Gordon S: Kent, North West.

MAY, Allen: Bromley; Organisations.

MAY, Leonard Morgan: Charlton; Monumental Inscriptions.

MAYCOCK, Alan: West Malling.

MAYCOCK, F.H. See GILBERT R.G: Canterbury.

MAYHEW, Athol: Birchington; Isle of Thanet;
Margate.

MAYLAM, Percy: Family History.

MAYNARD, D.C: Inns.

MAYO, Owen: Chart Sutton.

MEACHAM, John. See GRAYLING, Francis:
Sittingbourne.

MEAD, J. Publisher: Footpaths-Country Walks.

MEADOWS, A.J: Greenwich.

MEASOM, George: Crystal Palace; Greenwich;
Kent, North; Railways.

MEATES, Geoffrey Wells: Lullingstone.

MEDIAEVAL RECORDS OF THE ARCHBISHOPS OF CANTERBURY.
See CHURCHILL, Irene Josephine: Canterbury-
Diocese and Province; Lambeth Palace.

MEDWAY AND GILLINGHAM CHAMBER OF COMMERCE:
Industry and Trade; Medway Towns.

MEDWAY AND GILLINGHAM COMMUNITY RELATIONS COUNCIL:
Medway Towns; Organisations.

MEDWAY AND MAIDSTONE COLLEGE OF TECHNOLOGY:
Industry and Trade.

MEDWAY AND NORTH KENT MARRIAGE GUIDANCE COUNCIL:
Organisations.

MEDWAY AREA SUNDAY FOOTBALL LEAGUE: Medway Towns;
Sport.

MEDWAY ARTS COUNCIL: Medway Towns.

MEDWAY ARTS COUNCIL: FESTIVAL COMMITTEE: Medway Towns.

MEDWAY ATHLETIC CLUB: Sport; Medway Towns.

MEDWAY BOROUGH COUNCIL: Elections; Medway Towns.

MEDWAY BOROUGH COUNCIL: DIRECTORATE OF LEISURE SERVICES:
See MOAD, Michael: Inns; Medway Towns; Museums;
Recreation; Rochester.

MEDWAY CIVIL DEFENCE COMMITTEE: Medway Towns.

MEDWAY COMMUNITY HEALTH COUNCIL. See COMMUNITY HEALTH
COUNCIL: MEDWAY HEALTH DISTRICT: Health and Welfare;
Medway Towns.

MEDWAY CONSERVANCY BOARD: Chatham.

MEDWAY CREMATORIUM COMMITTEE: Medway Towns.

MEDWAY GUIDE AND INDUSTRIAL REVIEW. See
RAND, Duncan: Industry and Trade; Medway Towns.

MEDWAY INDUSTRIES EXHIBITION: Industry and Trade; Medway Towns.

MEDWAY INFORMATION HANDBOOK See MEDWAY BOROUGH COUNCIL:
Medway Towns.

MEDWAY MILITARY RESEARCH GROUP: Military and Naval History.

MEDWAY PAPER SACKS LTD: Industry and Trade - Firms.
See also STOWELL, Gordon: Industry and Trade - Firms.

MEDWAY PORTS AUTHORITY: Industry and Trade; Sheerness;
Sport; Swale.

MEDWAY PRESERVATION SOCIETY: Conservation; Industry and
Trade; Medway River; North Kent Marshes.

MEDWAY REVIEW: Medway Towns.

MEDWAY RIVER USERS ASSOCIATION: Medway, River.

MEDWAY '75 AND MEDWAY '76: Medway, River and Valley.

MEDWAY SOCIETY FOR MENTALLY HANDICAPPED CHILDREN:
Medway Towns; Organisations.

MEDWAY TOWNS BAND: Medway Towns; Music.

MEDWAY TOWNS CONSUMER GROUP: Medway Towns.

MEDWAY TOWNS - M2, M20 and M25: Medway Towns; Roads.

MEDWAY TOWNS ROAD SAFETY COMMITTEE: Medway Towns.

MEDWAY TOWNS SPORTS ADVISORY COUNCIL: Medway Towns;
Sport.

MEDWAY TOWNS TABLE TENNIS LEAGUE: Medway Towns; Sport.

MEDWAY WRITERS CIRCLE: Kent Authors and Lit. - General.

MEDWAY YACHTING ASSOCIATION: Medway, River; Sport; Swale.

MEDWAY YOUTH COMMITTEE: Organisations; Medway Towns.

MEE, Arthur: Kent.

MEIER, Paul: Morris, William.

MELLING, Elizabeth: Agriculture; Architecture; Bridges;
Castles and Houses; Crime; History - 1501 AD onwards;
Industry and Trade; Local Government; Poor Law; Roads.

MELVILLE, Henry: Gardens.

MELVILLE, Lewis: Tunbridge Wells.

MEMOIR OF THE LATE DEAN OF CANTERBURY, WILLIAM ROWE LYALL.
See LYALL, Very Rev. William Rowe: Canterbury Cathedral.

MEMOIR ON HOKEDAY See DARELL, William: Dover.

MEMOIRS OF THE GEOLOGICAL SURVEY OF ENGLAND AND WALES.
See WHITAKER, William: Geology; Public Utilities.

THE MEN WHO TOOK THE MONEY..: Rochester Cathedral.

MEOPHAM AND DISTRICT FOOTPATHS GROUP: Footpaths -
Country Walks; Kent, North West; Kent, West;
Weald. See also BOLTON, D: Footpaths-Country Walks;
Kent, North West; Nature Walks.

MEOPHAM PARISH COUNCIL: Meopham.

MEOPHAM PUBLICATIONS COMMITTEE: Meopham. See also
PRYOR, C.A: Nurstead.

MERCER, Eric: Architecture.

MERCER, Richard C.H: East Malling.

MERCHANT NAVY COLLEGE: Education; Greenhithe.

M Cont'd

MESSENGER AND ADAMS, Architects, Surveyors and Land Agents: Herne Bay.

METCALFE, Leon: Ghosts.

METHODIST CHURCH: Medway Towns.

METROPOLITAN PUBLISHING: Ashford.

MICHEL, Dan: Dialects.

MIDDLEMISS, F.A. See KIRKALDY, John Francis: Geology; Weald.

MIDDLETON, Sir Charles (afterwards Lord Barham) See TESTON SYSTEM OF FARMING..:Agriculture; Teston.

MIDDLETON, John See WIKELEY, Nigel: Architecture; Railways.

MID-KENT WATER COMPANY: Broad Oak; Public Utilities. See also SOUTHERN WATER AUTHORITY AND MID KENT WATER COMPANY: Broadoak; Public Utilities.

MIDWINTER, Arthur Adair: Tunstall.

MILBOURNE, Raymond A: Geology; Sevenoaks.

MILES, Herbert W: Printing and Publishing.

MILES, WALKER pseud (Taylor, Edmunds): Footpaths - Country Walks: Kent, West.

MILLAR, J.B: Medway River; Ships and Shipping; World War II.

MILLARD, Louise: Canterbury - Antiquity and Archaeology. See also CANTERBURY CITY MUSEUMS AND CANTERBURY PUBLIC LIBRARY: Canterbury; Museums.

MILLER, Alastair: Dover; Prisons.

MILLER, Alfred C: Eythorne.

MILLER, Alice Duer: Dover.

MILLER, Derek See RICHARDSON, T.L: Architecture; History - 1501 AD onwards.

MILLER, E.P See TONBRIDGE AND MALLING DISTRICT COUNCIL: PLANNING DEPARTMENT: Wrotham.

MILLER, William: History-General.

MILLGATE'S HANDBOOK....:Reculver.

MILLS, Anthony Reginald: Biography; West Wickham. See also SHERRARD, Owen Aubrey: Biography; West Wickham.

MILLS, Dorothy: Becket, Saint Thomas; Edward, the Black Prince.

MILLWARD, Roy: Coastline; Geography; Hoo Peninsula; Kent, East; Kent, North West; Kent, South; Kent, South East; Weald.

MILMAN, Henry Salisbury: Becket, Saint Thomas; Canterbury Cathedral.

MILNE, F.A. See GOMME, George Laurence; History - 1501 AD onwards.

MILNER, Violet Georgina, Viscountess Milner: Biography.

MILVILLE, H (pseud For Hugh Milville Raven): Broadstairs.

MINAKAWA, Saburo: Adams, William.

MINERVA RAILWAY GUIDE...:Deal; Railways; Sandwich; Walmer.

"A MINISTER OF THE GOSPEL" pseud: Broadstairs; Sermons.

MINSTER PARISH COUNCIL: Minster-in-Thanet.

MINSTER PARISH COUNCIL-VILLAGE STUDY COMMITTEE: Minster-in-Thanet.

A MINUTE JOURNAL OF A SHORT TOUR:..Kent Authors and Lit. - General.

MINUTES OF THE COURT LEET: Chatham.

MISCELLANEA GENEALOGICA ET HERALDICA: Bromley; Genealogical Records; Monumental Inscriptions.

MITCHELHILL, Eileen. See UNIVERSITY OF KENT: CENTRE FOR RESEARCH IN THE SOCIAL SCIENCES: Kent-East.

MITCHELL, A.F See FORESTRY COMMISSION: Bedgebury; Forestry.

MITCHELL, Brian See DEFEND KENT: Conservation.

MITCHELL, Frank: Hayes and Keston.

MITCHELL, John: Rivers; Sport.

MITTON, Geraldine Edith: Railways.

MOAD, Michael: Inns; Medway Towns; Museums; Recreation; Rochester.

MOCKETT, John: Broadstairs; History - General; Isle of Thanet; Letters; Military and Naval History.

MODERN CANTERBURY PILGRIMS: Religious Denominations.

MOLESWORTH, Rev. J.E.N. See CRAMP, Rev. Dr. John Mockett. Church History; Letters.

MOLL, H. Cartographer. See SIMPSON, Samuel, History - General.

MOLLO, Boris: Military and Naval History.

MOLONY, C.V: Military and Naval History.

MONCRIEFF, A.R. See BLACK, Adam and Charles, Publishers: Kent,West.

MONEY, James H: Industry and Trade; Weald.

MONOPOLIES COMMISSION: Coastal Waters; Newspapers; Transport.

MONTAGU(E), Mrs. Elizabeth: Letters. See also CARTER, Mrs Elizabeth: Letters.

MONTAGUE, James defendant. See REX VS.JAMES MONTAGUE; Isle of Grain; Trials.

MONTIER, David J: Kent, North West; Maps; Natural History.

MOODY, George Thomas: Railways.

MOON, John H: Industry and Trade; Inns; Lamberhurst.

MOOR, Nigel: Planning.

MOORE, Doris Langley: Biography.

MOORE, E.W: Wye.

MOORE, Francis: History - 1501 AD onwards; Sittingbourne.

MOORE, Frank L: Kent, West; Sport.

MOORE, John Scott: Weald.

MOOREHEAD, Alan: Darwin, Charles.

MOORHOUSE, M.B: Kent Authors and Lit. - Poetry.

MORAN, James: Industry and Trade - Firms; Westerham.

MORE, Margaret (1505 - 1544): More, Sir Thomas.

MORE, Sir Thomas: Letters; More, Sir Thomas.

MORECROFT, John H: Kent Authors and Lit. - General.

MORECROFT, Victor Wesley: Footpaths - Country Walks.

MORELL, Miss: Erith.

MORES, Edward Rowe See BIBLIOTHECA TOPOGRAPHICA BRITANNICA: History - General; Tunstall.

MOREY, George: Coastal Waters.

MORGAN, E. Victor: History - General.

MORGAN, G.H: Hothfield; Natural History.

MORGAN, John Scott: Railways; Tonbridge.

MORGAN, Verne: Biography; Bromley.

MORGAN, W.L: Hempstead.

MORISON, Stanley: More, Sir Thomas.

MORLAND, William: Lamberhurst.

MORLEY, B.M: Coastal Defences.

MORLEY, Malcolm: Margate; Theatre.

MORLEY, Sheridan: Biography.

MORLEY, Thomas William: Bromley; Kent Artists.

MORRICE, Alexander: Industry and Trade.

MORRILL, J.S. See AYLMER, G.E: History - 1501 AD onwards.

MORRIS, C: Road Transport.See also FIENNES, Celia: History - General.

MORRIS, J.E. See BLACK, Adam and Charles. Publishers: Kent, West.

MORRIS, John: Becket, Saint Thomas; Canterbury; Canterbury Cathedral; Canterbury Cathedral - Archbishops.

MORRIS, Owen James; Railways; Romney Marsh.

MORRIS, P.E: Bexley.

MORRIS, Richard. See ADDYMAN, Peter: Churches.
See MICHEL, Dan: Dialects.

MOSELEY, Mary: Hoo. St. Werburgh.

MOSSIKER, Frances: Pocahontas, Princess.

MOTHERSOLE, Jessie: History - to 900 AD.

MOTSON, Anne: Channel Tunnel.

MOUL, Duncan: Footpaths - Country Walks;
Kent, West. See also THOMPSON, Gibson: Kent.

MOULE, Thomas: Canals and Waterways.

MOULTON, W.R: Court-at-Street; Hythe; Kent, South East;
Lympne; Studfall.

MOUNSDON, David D: Education; Folkestone.

MOUNT, Frank: Hampton.

MOWLL, John H: History - 1501 AD onwards.

MOYLAN, Prudence Ann: Local Government.

MOYNIHAN, M: Sheerness.

MOYSE-BARTLETT, Colonel H: Dover.

(MORRIS, W.J): Wye.

MORRIS, William: Morris William; Letters.

MORRISON, John Harold: Genealogical Records.

MORTLOCK, C.B: Kent Artists.

MORTON, A.L. See MORRIS, William: Morris, William.

MUGGERIDGE, Sidney John: Kent, Mid; Maidstone; Postal
History.

MUIR, Kenneth: Sidney, Sir Philip.

MULLINS, E.L.C: Bibliography.

MUNDAY, C.R: See CONNOLLY, P.A: Airports;
Gravesend.

MUNDEN, Alan Frederick: Education; Faversham.
See also WEEKS, W.R: Faversham.

MUNICIPAL CORPORATIONS COMMISSION FOR ENGLAND AND
WALES, 1834: Gravesend.

MUNRO, A.G: Chatham; Rochester.

MURCHISON, Sir Frederick: Geology.

MURPHY, C.J.V. See DAVENPORT, John: Churchill, Sir W.L.S.

MURR, David: Footpaths- Country Walks; Gillingham.

MURRAY, John Publisher: History - General.

MURRAY, John Oliver: Rochester.

MURRAY, K.M. Elizabeth: Cinque Ports; New Romney.

MURRAY, Walter John Campbell: Romney Marsh.

MURSTON PARISH COUNCIL: Murston.

MUSEUM OF THE CORPS OF ROYAL ENGINEERS: Military and
Naval History; Museums.

MUSGRAVE, George. (Vicar of Borden): Kent Authors and
Lit. - Poetry.

MYALL, Mrs Ambrose See FRISWELL, Laura Hain: Bexleyheath;
Biography.

MYDANS, Sheila: Becket, Saint Thomas

MYNARD, D.C. See COOK, A.M: Dover.

N

NAIL, Martin: Coal; Kent, North West.

NARRATIVE OF THE INGRATITUDE AND ILL-TREATMENT..:
Kent Authors and Lit. - General.

NASH, E.K: Higham.

NASH, Sidney Charles: Railways.

NASH MAUSOLEUM: Farningham; Monumental Inscriptions.

NATIONAL ASSOCIATION OF HEAD TEACHERS: Folkestone.

NATIONAL BOOK LEAGUE: Aylesford; Printing and
Publishing.

NATIONAL COOPERATIVE EDUCATIONAL ASSOCIATION: Margate.

NATIONAL ENVIRONMENT RESEARCH COUNCIL: INSTITUTE
OF GEOLOGICAL SCIENCES. See
BRAZLEY, R.A   Geology;   Kent, West.
BRISTOW, R.A.   Geology;   Kent, West.
DINES, H.G.   Geology; Kent, North East, Kent,West.
HARVEY, B.I.   Geology: Kent, North West.

NATIONAL GARDENS SCHEME: Gardens.

NATIONAL HEALTH SERVICE: KENT AND CANTERBURY EXECUTIVE
COUNCIL: Health and Welfare.

NATIONAL MARITIME MUSEUM: Bibliography; Greenwich;
History - 1501 AD Onwards; Museums.

NATIONAL MASTER FARRIERS', BLACKSMITHS' AND AGRICULTURAL
ENGINEERS' ASSOCIATION: Industry and Trade.

NATIONAL PARKS AND ACCESS TO THE COUNTRYSIDE ACT, 1949:
Broadstairs; Footpaths and Commons.

NATIONAL PARKS COMMISSION:COASTAL PRESERVATION AND
DEVELOPMENT: Coastline.

NATIONAL TRUST- PUBLISHER:
Bibliography (Catalogue of the Working Library...)
KNOLE (Sackville-West, Victoria).
SISSINGHURST (Castle).
SMALLHYTHE (Catalogue of the Working Library...)
SMALLHYTHE (Lucas, Audrey).
SUTTON-AT-HONE (St. John Jerusalem).
WESTERHAM (Quebec House).

NATIONAL UNION OF TEACHERS: Folkestone.

NATIONAL UNION OF TOWNSWOMENS' GUILDS: Organisations.

NATURE CONSERVANCY COUNCIL: SOUTH EAST REGION.
Ham Street; Natural History; Nature Walks;
North Kent Marshes; Stodmarsh; Wye.

"A NAVAL OFFICER" pseud (E. Rogier)
Coastline; Dover; Ramsgate.

NAVY DEPARTMENT: Chatham Dockyard.

NAYLOR, R. See PARNELL, J.W: Bromley; Health and Welfare.

NEAME, Alan: Aldington;   Biography.

NEAME, Harry A. See ONCE A MONTH: Kent Authors and
Lit. - General.

NEIL, E: Harvey, Dr William.

NEILSON, C.P. See SANDWICH BOROUGH COUNCIL: Sandwich.

NEILSON, N. Customs; Law.

NELSON, John. See REX VS. JAMES MONTAGUE: Isle of Grain;
Trials.

"NEMO" pseud. See ADAMS, Henry Gardiner:
Kent Authors and Lit. - Collections.
Kent Authors and Lit. - Poetry.

NETHERSOLE, Susan Colyer: Kent Authors and Lit. - Fiction.

NEVE, Christopher: Canterbury; Kent Artists.

NEVILL, Ralph. See ARNOLD, George Matthews: Gravesend.

NEW ARTICLES OF THE GAME OF CRICKET..:Cricket.

NEW DOVER GROUP. See CRELLIN, T.D: Dover.

THE NEW KENT...See KENT MESSENGER: Local Government.

NEW MARGATE.....GUIDE: Broadstairs; Margate; Ramsgate.

NEW RAMSGATE GUIDE..:Broadstairs; Coastal Waters -
Safety at Sea; Margate; Ramsgate.

THE NEW ST. MARY OF THE CRAYS..:St. Mary Cray.

THE NEW TONBRIDGE VIEW BOOK: Kent, West; Tonbridge.

NEWBY, Donald: Orpington.

NEWCOMBE, Martin J: Blean; Natural History.

NEWELL, G.E: Kent, North; Natural History; Whitstable.

NEWING, Alan. See MOORE, Frank L: Kent, West; Sport.

NEWMAN, Aubrey: Chevening; Family History.

NEWMAN, John: Architecture; Kent, East; Kent, North East;
Kent, West; Weald.

NEWMAN, Leonard Hugh: Bexley.

NEWMAN, W.L: See REX VS JAMES MONTAGUE: Isle of Grain;
Trials.

NEWMAN AND COMPANY Publishers: Canterbury; Kent, East; Ramsgate.

NEWTON, A.P: Gillingham.

NEWTON, David,Illustrator. See NEWTON, Jill: Chiddingstone.

NEWTON, Jill: Chiddingstone.

NEWTON, S.C: Railways; Weald.

NICHOLLS, Frederick F: Smuggling.

NICHOLS, W.N: Cliffe; Cooling; North Kent Marshes.

NICHOLSON, Brinsley. See SCOT, Reginald (Reynalde). Witchcraft.

NICHOLSON, R. Publisher: Sea and River Charts; Thames,River.

NICKLIN, J.A: Dickens, Charles; Kent.

NICOLE, Christopher: Adams, William.

NICOLL, Sir William Robertson: Dickens, Charles.

NICOLSON, J.U: See CHAUCER, Geoffrey: Chaucer, Geoffrey.

NICOLSON, Nigel: Biography; Sissinghurst.

NICOLSON, Phillipa See SACKVILLE-WEST, Victoria (Vita) (afterwards Lady Nicolson):Gardens.

NOAKES, Aubrey: Kent Artists; Rochester.

NOCK, Oswald Stevens: Railways.

NOKES, George Augustus: Railways.

NORBURY, Paul: Adams, William.

NORCOTT, P: Broadstairs.

NORMAN, A.W. See KNATCHBULL, Sir Edward: History - 1501 AD onwards.

NORMAN, George Warde: Biography: Bromley. See also LOYD, Samuel J: Baron Overstone: Biography; Letters.

NORMAN, Geraldine: Biography.

NORMAN, S.N: Kent.

NORMAN GRAHAM BENEFIT: Cricket.

NORRINGTON, John: Family History.

NORRIS, A.G.S: Churchill, Sir Winston L.S.

NORTH, Dudley. 3rd Lord North: Kent Authors and Lit. - General.

NORTH, Jon: Genealogical Records.

NORTH EAST KENT ECONOMIC DEVELOPMENT COMMITTEE: Industry and Trade; Kent, North East.

NORTH-EAST KENT JOINT TOWN PLANNING COMMITTEE: Kent, North East; Planning.

NORTH KENT YACHTING ASSOCIATION: Organisations.

NORTH WEST KENT SPASTICS GROUP: Organisations.

NORTHFLEET URBAN DISTRICT COUNCIL: Northfleet.

NORTON, Ann: Bromley; Poor Law.

NORTON, Jane E: Bibliography.

NORTON, TRIST, WATNEY AND COMPANY: Public Utilities; Tunbridge Wells.

NORWOOD, John C: Kent.

A NOTE OF SUCH AS HAVE BEEN EXPENDITED..:Agriculture; Dartford.

NOTTINGHAM UNIVERSITY: DEPARTMENT OF ADULT EDUCATION: Population.

NOYES, Robert: Cranbrook; Sermons.

NUMISMATIC SOCIETY. See ROLFE, H.W: Coins and Tokens.

NUNNS, B.N: Sidcup.

NUTTING, Anthony: Gordon, Gen. Charles G.

OAKDEN, E.C. See CHAUCER, Geoffrey: Chaucer, Geoffrey.

OAKELEY, R.H: Footpaths - Country Walks; Kent, West.

OAKLEY, E.R. See WILLOUGHBY, David William: Kent, North West; Road Transport.

OAKLEY, Frank A. illustrator. See AYLESFORD PARISH COUNCIL. Aylesford.

OAKLEY, Kenneth P: Heraldry.

OAKSEY, John: Agriculture; Industry and Trade - Firms.

O'BRIEN, Cynthia See RICE, John: Folkestone.

"OBSERVANT PEDESTRIAN" pseud: History - General; Margate.

ODDY, Derek. See RICHARDSON, T.L: Agriculture; History - 1501 AD onwards.

ODLE, Mrs. Rose: Biggin Hill; Biography.

O'DRISCOLL, Patricia See PERKS, Richard Hugh: Medway,River; Ships and Shipping; Thames, River.

OFFHAM PAROCHIAL CHURCH COUNCIL: Offham.

OFFICE OF POPULATION CENSUSES AND SURVEYS: Census; Kent, North; Medway Towns.

O'GORMAN, Richard A: Hythe; Rochester Cathedral - Bishops.

THE OLD BETHANIAN: Goudhurst.

OLD KENT SNAPS: Harrietsham; Kent.

OLD LANGTONIAN NEWSLETTER: Canterbury - Education.

OLD LAWRENTIAN SOCIETY: Ramsgate.

OLD PARK FARM, ST. MARTIN, CANTERBURY: Canterbury (Sale Catalogue).

"OLD STAGERS'" PROGRAMMES.See CANTERBURY CRICKET WEEK. Canterbury; Cricket.

OLIVER, Bernard: World War I.

OLIVER, Lieut. Col. G.E.F. See BRITISH SERVICES TATTOO (1951): Folkestone.

OLIVER, John: Dickens, Charles; Rochester.

ONCE A MONTH: Kent Authors and Lit. - General.

ONE HUNDRED AND ONE VIEWS: Dover; Folkestone; Hythe; Isle of Thanet; Sandgate.

O'NEIL, Bryan Hugh St. John: Deal.

OPPORTUNITIES FOR INDUSTRY...:Industry and Trade; Sittingbourne.

ORDNANCE SURVEY: Church History; History - 901 AD; Maps.

ORDNANCE SURVEY:ARCHAEOLOGICAL SECTION: Chatham; History - Archaeology; Rochester.

ORIGINAL PARISH REGISTERS...:Genealogical Records; Population.

OSBORNE, Brian M: Herne Hill.

OSBORNES' STRANGERS' GUIDE TO HASTINGS...See COLBRAN, John,Publisher: Cinque Ports.

OSBOURN, H.J.L: Kent Authors and Lit. - Poetry.

OSMOND, Laurie: Thames, River.

OSTEOPATHIC EDUCATION AND RESEARCH LTD: Maidstone.

OSTLERE, Gordon See GORDON, Richard pseud: Bickley.

OSWALD, Arthur: Architecture; Castles and Houses.

OSWALD, C.A: Chilham.

OULTON, W.C: Isle of Thanet; Margate.

OUTCROWD See SLUGS: Kent Authors and Lit. - Poetry

OVEREND, Ernest H. See BURROW, Edward J. Publisher: Kent.

OVEREND, G.H: Dover.

OVEY, Cameron D. See ROYAL ANTHROPOLOGICAL INSTITUTE: SWANSCOMBE COMMITTEE: Swanscombe.

OWEN, D.M: Bibliography; Lambeth Palace.

O Cont'd

OWEN, Mrs. J.A. See "A SON OF THE MARSHES" pseud.
Kent Authors and Lit. - General; Kent, North West;
Milton Regis; Natural History.

OXENDEN, Rev. Ashton. (Rector of Pluckley):
Kent Authors and Lit. - General.

OXFORD UNIVERSITY: EXTERNAL STUDIES COMMITTEE:
Education.

OXINDEN, Henry: Letters.

OXLEY, Geoffrey W: Poor Law.

OYLER, Thomas H: Canterbury - Diocese and Province;
Churches; East Sutton; Lydd; Monumental Inscriptions.

P

P-Y-N, Mrs K-TH-N. See NARRATIVE OF THE INGRATITUDE AND
ILL TREATMENT...: Kent Authors and Lit. - General.

PACKE, Christopher: Canterbury.

PACKHOUSE, the story of E.K.P: Industry and Trade - Firms.

PADDOCK WOOD AND DISTRICT YEAR BOOK..: Industry and Trade;
Paddock Wood.

PAGDEN, S: Kent Authors and Lit. - Poetry.

PAGE, André: Kent; Road Transport; Tunbridge Wells.

PAGE, Hugh E: Footpaths - Country Walks.

PAGE, William: History - General.

PAIN, E.C: Ships and Shipping.

PAIN, Nesta: Becket, Saint Thomas.

PAINE, Lauren: Pocahontas, Princess.

PAKENHAM- Walsh, R.P: See HISTORY OF THE CORPS OF
ROYAL ENGINEERS: Military and Naval History.

PALLANT, N: Hither Green; Railways.

PALMER, Cecile: Recipes; Rochester.

PALMER, George Hendy: Rochester Cathedral.

PALMER, Sutton, painter. See BRADLEY, Arthur Granville:
Darent, River.

PAPERS RELATIVE TO AN ASYLUM FOR SHIPS..: Goodwin Sands.

PARISH, William Douglas: Dialects.

PARISH CHURCH OF ST. STEPHEN..: Chatham.

PARISH MAGAZINE..: Hersden; Westbere.

PARISH REGISTERS OF SHIPBOURNE: Genealogy; Shipbourne.

"A PARISHIONER"pseud. (R.R. Schartan): Broadstairs.

PARKER, Hubert H: Agriculture.

PARKER, J.R: Ebbsfleet.

PARKER, John R.A: Isle of Thanet.

PARKER, Louis N: Dover.

PARKER, M.J.R: Orpington.

PARKER, Michael St. John: Canterbury; Dickens, Charles.

PARKER, Richard: St. Nicholas-at-Wade.

THE PARKER CHRONICLE: History - to 900 AD.

PARKIN, E.W: Elham; Wingham.

PARKINSON, W.H: Mottingham.

PARNELL, Emma. See BLIGH, Edward, 5th Earl of Darnley:
Letters.

PARNELL, J.W: Bromley; Health and Welfare.

PARR, Henry: Pilgrims Way.

PARSONS, Capt. Edward: Military and Naval History.

PARSONS, F.G. See DALE, Rev. Herbert Dixon: Hythe.

PARSONS, Staff Captain J. See ADMIRALTY: Folkestone;
Sea and River Charts.

PARSONS, J.A: Footscray.

PARSONS, John: Sport.

PARTICULARS AND CONDITIONS OF SALE OF...:
Bilsington (Sale Catalogue): Newchurch (Sale Catalogue).

PASCOE, A.P: Wrotham.

PASKE-SMITH, M: Adams, William.

PATCH, Rev. John D.H: Becket, Saint Thomas.

PATER, Walter H. See WRIGHT, Samuel: Bibliography.

PATRICK, G: Burham.

PATTEN, Robert L: Dickens, Charles.

PATTERSON, Rev. Robert: Biography.

PAUL, Leslie: More, Sir. Thomas.

PAVING AND LIGHTING RATE 1839 and 1840: Margate.

PAWLEY, Bernard: Religious Denominations.

PAYNE, George: Footpaths - Country Walks; History -
Archaeology; History - General; Kent, North East;
North Kent Marshes; Oldbury Hill; Sittingbourne.
See also ROBERTSON, Rev. William Archibald Scott:
Canterbury Cathedral; Obituaries.

PAYNE, J. Lewin: Hoath; Reculver.

PAYNE, Orlebar D. Bruce: Sandwich.

PEACOCK, Carlos: Palmer, Samuel.

PEACOCK, David: Kent Artists; Tunbridge Wells.

PEAKE, J: Ramsgate.

PEARMAN, Rev. Augustus John: Ashford; Church History;
Rainham; Rochester Diocese.

PEARMAN, Harry: Caves and Tunnels; Kent, North East;
Kent, North West.

PEARS, Chas. (Charles): Coastal Waters.

PEARSALL, Alan. See CORDELL, Alan: Coastline;
Rivers; Thames, River.

PEARSON, Rev. C. Ridley: Sermons; Tunbridge Wells.

PEARSON, Edward: Biography; Kent Authors and Lit. - Poetry.

PECHAM. Johannis, Archbishop of Canterbury: Canterbury -
Diocese and Province. See also PECKHAM, John, Archbishop
of Canterbury: Canterbury - Diocese and Province.

PECK, Alan: Biography.

PECK, W. Emerson: Dover Castle.

PECKHAM, John, Archbishop of Canterbury: Canterbury -
Diocese and Province. See also PECHAM, Johannis,
Archbishop of Canterbury: Canterbury - Diocese and
Province.

PEDDY, D.P.R: Lewisham; Poor Law.

PEEBLES, Ian: Cricket.

PEEL, John Hugh Bignal: Roads.

PEET, J.Michael: Lewisham; Place-Names.

PEGGE, Samuel: Dialects.

PEGWELL BAY COMMITTEE: Footpaths - Country Walks;
Pegwell Bay.

PELHAM, Evelyn Georgina. See BLIGH, Edward. 5th Earl
of Darnley: Letters.

PELTON, Richard. Publisher: Kent, West; Tunbridge Wells.

PEMBERTON, Max: Biography.

PEMBURY PARISH COUNCIL: Pembury.

PENFOLD, Michael J: Military and Naval History; World War I.

PENNANT, Thomas: History - General.

PENNELL, Joseph: Pilgrims Way.

PENNELL, Elizabeth Robins See PENNELL, Joseph:
Pilgrims' Way.

PENNEY, Stephen: Coastal Waters; Sea and River Charts;
Thames, River.

THE PENTAGON (Chatham). See (the) BROOK PENTAGON.

PENTREATH, Guy See UNDERHILL, Francis: Rochester Cathedral.

PENYEATE, John. See CLARK, Tim: Crime; Gravesend.

PEPIN, David: Kent.

PEPPER, Terence: Tonbridge.

P Cont'd

PRICE, Brian P. See MARCHINGTON, Trevor:
Geography; Kent, North East.

PRICE, Daniel: Agriculture; Romney Marsh.

PRICE, F.H: Barham; Natural History.

PRICE, H.I: Kent Authors and Lit. - Poetry.

PRICE, J.H. See TITTLEY, Ian: Coastline;
Maps; Natural History.

PRICE, Leonard Charles: Lyminge.

PRICE, M. See LEBON, Cicely: Benenden.

PRICHARD, John A: Belvedere; Bostall; Erith.

PRIDEAUX, J.D.C.A: Railways.

PRIEST, S. See BROOK, Cyril A: Caves and Tunnels;
Dartford.

PRINGLE, J. See LAMPLUGH, G.W: Geology.

PRITIRWELL, Johannis. See CHRISTCHURCH PRIORY:
Canterbury - Monastic Houses.

PROFESSIONAL PAPERS OF THE CORPS OF ROYAL ENGINEERS;
Military & Naval History. See also CLARKE.G.S: Lydd.
See also AKERS, C.S: Coastal Defences; Dover.

A PROPOSAL TO DEVELOP FORT AMHERST..:Chatham;
Military and Naval History; Museums.

PROPOSED COUNTY BOROUGH: AMALGAMATION..:
Medway Towns.

PROSSER, Arthur: History - General.

PROTHEROE AND MORRIS Auctioneers: Capel-le-
Ferne (Sale).

PROUDFOOT, W. Frank: Fawkham.

PROVINCE OF WEST KENT:FREEMASONS: Kent, West;
Organisations.

PRYCE, H. and son Publishers. Kent, North West;
Woolwich.

PRYER, G.A: Railways.

PRYOR, C.A: Nurstead.

PUBLIC BUILDINGS AND WORKS, MINISTRY OF: Kent.
See also
BROWN, R.A:	Dover and Rochester.
COTTRELL, L:	Coastal Defences.
NEATES, G.W:	Lullingstone.
O'NEIL, B.H. St.J:	Deal.
RADFORD, C.A.R;	Dover.
RIGOLD, S.E:	Eynsford;Ospringe and Strood.
SAUNDERS, A.D:	Deal, Walmer and Upnor.

PUBLIC RECORD OFFICE: Church History.
See also PECHAN,Johannis: Canterbury Cathedral-
Archbishops.

PUCKLE, John: Dover.

PUGH, Christine: Kent, North East; Stockbury.

PUDNEY, John: Thames, River.

PUGH, Edwin: Dickens, Charles.

PULLEN, Doris E: Monumental Inscriptions;
Sydenham.

PUMPHREY, George Henry: Coastal Waters;
History - General.

PURLE, Brenda. See KENT COUNTY LIBRARY:
Bridges, Medway,Rivers.

PURSER, Rev. W.C.B: Teynham.

PUTNAM, Eben: Genealogical Records.

PYATT, Edward C: Footpaths - Country Walks.

PYM, Horace N: Brasted.

Q

QUEBEC HOUSE PERMANENT ADVISORY COMMITTEE:
Family History; Wolfe, Gen. James.

QUEENBOROUGH-IN-SHEPPEY BOROUGH COUNCIL: Isle of
Sheppey.

THE QUEEN'S DIAMOND JUBILEE, 1897: History -
1501 AD onwards.

QUEEN'S DIVISION OF INFANTRY: Military and Naval History.

QUEEN'S OWN BUFFS, ROYAL KENT REGIMENT. See
FOLKESTONE BOROUGH COUNCIL: Folkestone; Military
and Naval History.

QUENNELL, Peter See HICKEY, William: Biography.

QUEX MUSEUM See POWELL-COTTON MUSEUM:Birchington;
Museums.

QUIN, Rev. James. See BARTLETT, Rev Thomas: Letters.

QUINTON, Alan Roger. See QUINTON, Alfred Robert C:
Kent; Sevenoaks.

QUINTON, Alfred Robert C: Kent; Sevenoaks.

R

R.A.C. See ROYAL AUTOMOBILE CLUB: Kent; Maps.

RACKHAM, Bernard: Canterbury Cathedral.

RADFORD, C.A. Ralegh: Dover.

RAGGETT, G.F: Kent Authors and Lit. - General.

RAHTZ, Philip A: Dover.

RAILWAY MAGAZINE. See KENT RAILWAYS - TWENTY-ONE
ARTICLES: Railways.

RAINBIRD, G.M: Inns.

RAIT, Robert Sangster: Canterbury - Diocese and
Province: Rochester-Diocese.

RALPH, Henry Victor (Vic): Newspapers; Printing
and Publishing.

"RAMBLER" pseud (Barry Smith): Dover; Hotels;Inns.

RAMBLERS ASSOCIATION: S.E. LONDON AND KENT GROUP:
Footpaths - Country Walks; Weald.
See also CHEESEMAN, Clive: Footpaths - Country Walks;
Kent, Mid.
See also DOGGETT,Tom: Footpaths - Country Walks;
North Downs Way.

RAMBLING RECOLLECTIONS OF THE NEIGHBOURHOOD OF DOVER..:
Dover; Kent, South East.

RAMMELL, T.W: Public Utilities; Sandgate.

RAMSAY, Arthur Michael, Archbishop of Canterbury:
Canterbury Cathedral.

RAMSEY, Geoffrey. Archbishop of Canterbury:Education.

RAMSEY, Winston G: World War II.

RAMSGATE BOROUGH COUNCIL: ENTERTAINMENT AND PUBLICITY
COMMITTEE: Ramsgate.

RAMSGATE DISPENSARY: Ramsgate.

RAMSGATE HISTORICAL PAGEANT COMMITTEE: Ramsgate.

RAMSGATE IMPROVEMENT COMMISSIONERS: Ramsgate.

RAND, Duncan: Industry and Trade; Medway Towns;
Rochester; Theatre.

RANDALL, J: Dover; Sport.

RANSOME-WALLIS, Patrick: Railways.

RANWELL, D.S. See BOORMAN, L.A. Coastline;
Ecology; Kent, North.

RAPHAEL, Frederic : Biography.

RAPLEY, Hazel E: Medway Towns; Police.

RATING AND VALUATION ASSOCIATION: Whitstable.

RAVEN, David. See RAVEN, Mary: Broadstairs; Family History.

RAVEN, Hugh Milville. See MILVILLE H. pseud.
Broadstairs.

RAVEN, Margaret: Biography.

RAVEN, Mary: Broadstairs; Family History.

RAVEN, Dr. Martin Owen: Biography.

RAVEN FAMILY OF BROADSTAIRS. See
RAVEN, Mary and David: Broadstairs; Family History.
RAVEN, Hugh Milville,(MILVILLE, H. pseud): Broadstairs.
RAVEN, Margaret: Biography.
RAVEN, Dr. Martin Owen: Biography.

RAWLINSON, Richard: Rochester Cathedral.

RAYER, Felicity: Bibliography.

RAYNER, Bryan: Railways.

READ, Conyers:Biography.

READ, Joan:Lewisham; Sydenham.

READ ABOUT BLACKSMITH SHOPS: Industry and Trade.

RECOLLECTIONS OF...: Folkestone; Margate;
Tunbridge Wells.

RECULVER PAROCHIAL CHURCH COUNCIL: Reculver.

REDLAND GROUP OF COMPANIES (Sevenoaks Area).
See WOODFORDE, John: Industry and Trade.

REDMAN, Douglas S.R: Kingsdown.

REDSHAW, Charles J: Dartford; Kent, North West.
See THE INVICTA MAGAZINE : Kent.

REED PAPER GROUP: Aylesford; Industry and Trade-Firms.
See also STOWELL, Gordon: Industry and Trade-Firms.
See also MEDWAY PAPER SACKS LTD: Industry and
Trade - Firms.

REED, W.F: Education.

REES, Jean A: Biography.

REES, Judith Anne: Public Utilities.

REES-DAVIES, W.R: Crime.

REEVE, Terry: Caves and Tunnels.

REEVE AND CO. (Margate) Ltd: Industry and Trade – Firms ;
Margate.

REEVES, Graham: Penge.

REEVES, M: Bromley; Genealogical Records.

REGENCY PUBLICITY SERVICES LTD. Publisher:
Industry and Trade; Maidstone; Sevenoaks.

REGISTER OF THE ARCHBISHOPS OF CANTERBURY:
Canterbury Cathedral - Archbishops; Canterbury -
Diocese and Province.

REGISTRAR GENERALS' OFFICE: Census. See also
GENERAL REGISTER OFFICE and OFFICE OF POPULATION CENSUSES
AND SURVEYS; Census.

REGISTRUM ROFFENSE. Rochester Diocese.

REGNART, Sir H.G. See Rochester (Sale Catalogue).

REID, Ian G: Agriculture; Weald.

REID, Richard: Shoreham.

REILLY, Robin: Wolfe, Gen. James.

RELF, J. Publisher: Sevenoaks.

"REMINISCOR", pseud: Whitstable.

RENNIE, Sir John: Ramsgate.

REPORT OF THE LAMBETH CONFERENCE. 1978:
Canterbury - Diocese and Province.

REPORTS AND DOCUMENTS RELATING TO ROCHESTER BRIDGE:
Bridges; Rochester.

REPORTS ON THE EXCAVATION OF THE ROMAN FORT: Richborough.

REVELL, Alison: Recipes.

REX VS. JAMES MONTAGUE: Isle of Grain; Trials.

REYNOLDS, Charles and Co. Publishers: Canterbury;
Chatham; Margate; Ramsgate; Rochester.

REYNOLDS, Christopher: Coastline; Natural History.

REYNOLDS, Ernest Edwin: Becket, Saint Thomas;
More, Sir. Thomas.

REYNOLDS, James and Sons Publishers: Sea and River
Charts; Thames, River.

RHIND, Neil: Blackheath.

RHOADES, James. See TAYLOR, H.J: Dover; Music.

RICE, John: Folkestone; Kent Authors and Lit. - Fiction.
See also SOUTH EAST ARTS ASSOCIATION: Kent Authors
and Lit. - Poetry.

RICEMANS (Canterbury) Ltd: Canterbury; Industry and
Trade - Firms.

RICHARD OF MAIDSTONE: Kent Authors and Lit. - Poetry.

RICHARD WATTS' CHARITY: Charities; Rochester.

RICHARDS, Frank pseud. (Charles Hamilton):Biography.

RICHARDS, Captain G.H. See ADMIRALTY: Sea and River
Charts.

RICHARDS, James: Tunbridge Wells.

RICHARDS, Peter: History - 901 AD - 1500 AD.
See also KENT COUNTY LIBRARY: Bridges; Medway River.

RICHARDSON,Christopher Thomas:Ramsgate.

RICHARDSON, Herbert See HOPKINS, Jasper: Canterbury
Cathedral - Archbishops.

RICHARDSON, Samuel: Letters; Tunbridge Wells.

RICHARDSON, T.L: Agriculture; History - 1501 AD
onwards.

RICHTER, Michael: Canterbury - Diocese and Province;
Church History.

RICKERT, E. See MANLY, John Matthew: Chaucer, Geoffrey.

RIDDELL, Barbara R.M. See BERGESS, Winifred F:Bibliography.

RIDGE, C. Harold. See INDEX OF WILLS AND
ADMINISTRATIONS: Genealogical Records.

RIDING IN KENT: Sport.

RIDLER, Anne: Downe; Education.

RIDSDALE, Charles Joseph Vs. CLIFTON and others:
Folkestone; Trials.

RIGDEN, George: Canterbury.

RIGDEN, Reg: Deptford; Greenwich; Prisons; Woolwich.

RIGOLD, S.E: Dover; Eynsford; Ospringe; Strood.
See also COOK, A.M: Dover.

RILEY, Peter. See ARC PUBLICATIONS: Kent Authors
and Lit. - Poetry.

RIMMER, Alfred: Dickens, Charles.

RIOS, Dom Romanus: Biography.

RIPPLE VILLAGE APPRAISAL COMMITTEE: Ripple.

RITCHIE, A.E: Coal.

RITCHIE, Carson: Greenwich.

RIVET, Auguste: Tonbridge.

ROAKE, Margaret: History - General.

ROBB, Brian: Kent Authors and Lit. - Poetry.

ROBBINS, Rev. Peter Tyndall: Lower Halstow.

ROBERTS, A.W: Coastal Waters; Thames, River.

ROBERTS, Bob: Coastal Waters; Ships and Shipping.

ROBERTS, C.E. Bechofer See BUCKFIELD, Reginald
Sidney. Defendant: Strood; Trials.

ROBERTS, Fred: Tunbridge Wells.

ROBERTS, Jenifer. See BYEGONE MEDWAY: Medway Towns.

ROBERTSON, James C: Becket, Saint Thomas.

ROBERTSON, Scott See: ROBERTSON, William Archibald
Scott.

ROBERTSON, Rev. William Archibald Scott:
Canterbury Cathedral; Canterbury Cathedral - Archbishops;
Cheriton; Chislehurst;Churches; Church History; Cliffe-
at-Hoo; Obituaries; Orpington; Romney Marsh.
See also WALCOTT, Mackenzie E.C: Churches.

ROBINS, F.W: Bridges; Rochester.

ROBINSON, Adrian See MILLWARD, Roy:
Coastline; Geography; Hoo Peninsula;
Kent,East; Kent, North West; Kent, South;
Kent, South East; Weald.

ROBINSON, Duncan H: Cranbrook.

ROBINSON, J. Armitage: Canterbury Cathedral -
Archbishops.

ROBINSON, Sydney: Public Utilities.

R Cont'd

ROYAL VICTORIA HOSPITAL: Dover; Hospitals.

RUDE, G. See HOBSBAWM, Eric John: History - 1501 AD onwards.

RUDGE, Charles: Biography; Sevenoaks.

RUPP, Gordon: More, Sir Thomas.

RURAL DIRECTORY OF SOUTH EAST KENT: Kent, South East.

RUSHWORTH, John: History - 1501 AD onwards; Letters; Maidstone; Printing and Publishing.

RUSKIN, John: Coastline; Kent Artists.

RUSSELL, Sir. E.J. See HALL, Sir Alfred Daniel: Agriculture.

RUSSELL, John: See WAILES, Rex: Windmills and Watermills.

RUSSELL, J.M: Maidstone.

RUSSELL, P: See ENGLAND DISPLAYED..:History - General.

RUSSELL, R.O: Military and Naval History.

RUSSELL, W. Clark: Coastline; History - General.

RUTTON, W.L: Sandgate.

RUTTY, John: Spas and Mineral Waters.

RUYM: THE MAGAZINE OF CHATHAM HOUSE GRAMMAR SCHOOL: Ramsgate.

RYAN, T. See APOTHECARIES COMPANY V. T. RYAN: Maidstone; Trials.

RYE, Walter: Becket Saint Thomas.

S

S., G: Canterbury Cathedral.

(S.P.Q.R.): Canterbury - Antiquity and Archaeology.

SABINE, William Henry Waldo: History - 1501 AD onwards; Maidstone.

SACKVILLE, Charles, 6th Earl of Dorset. See WILMOT, John. 2nd Earl of Rochester: Kent Authors and Lit.- Collections: Kent Authors and Lit. - Poetry.

SACKVILLE, Thomas. Lord Buckhurst. See BRUCE, John: History - 1501 AD onwards.

SACKVILLE WEST, Victoria (Vita) (afterwards Lady Nicolson): Agriculture; Architecture; Biography; Castles and Houses; Family History; Gardens; Kent Authors and Lit. - Fiction; Kent Authors and Lit. - General; Kent Authors and Lit. - Poetry; Knole; Sissinghurst; World War II.

SACKVILLE-WEST, Vita See SACKVILLE-WEST, Victoria (Vita) (afterwards Lady Nicolson).

SACRED MELODIES: Chatham; Music.

SADLER, A.G: Monumental Inscriptions.

SAGE, Stephen: Medway, River; Ships and Shipping.

ST. AUGUSTINE'S GAOL: Canterbury; Prisons.

SAINT BARTHOLOMEW'S HOSPITAL: Hospitals; Rochester.

ST. BOTOLPH'S CHURCH. See GENEALOGICAL RECORDS: Northfleet.

ST. CLAIR, Steve: Thamesmead.

ST. GEORGE'S GIRLS' SCHOOL: Ramsgate.

ST. GEORGE'S PLACE BAPTIST CHURCH:Canterbury - Churches.

ST. JAMES'S BUDGET NO 911: Margate.

ST. JOHN AMBULANCE ASSOCIATION AND BRIGADE-KENT BRANCH: Organisations.

ST. JOHN THE BAPTIST COLLEGE, OXFORD: Canterbury Cathedral- Archbishops.

ST. JOHN'S COMPREHENSIVE SCHOOL: Gravesend.

ST. JOHN'S SCHOOL: Chatham.

ST. LAWRENCE COLLEGE: Ramsgate.

ST. LUKE THE EVANGELIST'S CHURCH: Charlton; Genealogical Records.

ST. MARGARET'S (SCHOOL) MAGAZINE: Folkestone.

ST. MILDRED, 660 - 725: Minster-in-Thanet.

ST. MILDRED'S HOTEL: Hotels; Restaurants etc; Margate.

ST. PAULS C. of E. JUNIOR SCHOOL: Rusthall.

ST. PETER THE APOSTLE IN THANET: Broadstairs.

SALE CATALOGUES: Addington; Bapchild; Barham; Bibliography; Bilsington; Canterbury; Capel-le-Fern; Chilham; Chislehurst; Davington; East Farleigh; East Malling; Faversham: Folkestone; Kent, Mid; Lympne; Maidstone; Newchurch; Rochester; Sissinghurst; Teston; West Farleigh.

SALMESTONE SCHOOL TREASURY: Margate.

SALMESTONE: THE STORY OF A MONASTIC GRANGE: Minster-in-Thanet.

SALMON, Joseph Publisher : Sevenoaks.

SALMOND, John M. See McCUDDEN, James Thomas Byford: McCudden, J.T.B.

SALTER, Rev. H.E. See TURNER, G.J: Canterbury - Monastic Houses.

SALVATION ARMY: Chatham.

SAMBROOK, Julia. See BEVAN, Anthony: Printing and Publishing.

SAMMES, Edward: History - Archaeology.

SAMPSON, Aylwin: Brabourne.

SAMPSON, Mrs. P.M: Penge; Thames, River.

SAMUELSON, M.K: Recipes.

SANDERS, Frederick: Chatham.

SANDERS, J and Co. Engravers and Publishers: Margate. See also BARLEY, H. Publishers: Ramsgate.

SANDS, Ben Illustrator: See WOODMAN, George: Printing and Publishing; Whitstable.

SANDWICH BAY BIRD OBSERVATORY: Natural History; Sandwich.

SANDWICH BOROUGH COUNCIL:Sandwich.

SANDWICH LOCAL HISTORY SOCIETY: Eastry. See also MARTIN, Elizabeth: Sandwich.

SANDWICH TOWN COUNCIL:Sandwich.

SANDYS, Charles: Gavelkind.

SANDYS, Charles: Canterbury; Gavelkind.

SANGER, "Lord" George. (1825 - 1911): Biography; Margate.

SANGSTER, Alfred: Broadstairs.

THE SAPPER: Military and Naval History.

"SARA" pseud: Kent Authors and Lit. - General.

"SARETAH" pseud: Printing and Publishing.

SARGENT, Miles: Agriculture.

SARTIN, Stephen: Canterbury; Kent Artists.

SASSOON, Siegfried: Biography; Letters.

SATTIN, Donald L: Conyer; Industry and Trade; Ships and Shipping.

SATURDAY MAGAZINE, 1834: Canals; Chatham Dockyard; Cinque Ports; Dover; Reculver.

SAUNDERS, A.D: Deal; Upnor; Walmer.

SAUNDERS, D.K: Blackheath; Sport.

SAUNDERS, Herbert Washington: History - General. See also KENT COUNTY COUNCIL:EDUCATION DEPARTMENT: Education.

SAUNDERS, Hope (later Mrs. Hardwick): Farnborough.

SAUNDERS, William: Spas and Mineral Waters.

SAUTER, R.H: See A LITTLE BOOK OF RECIPES: Recipes.

SAVE OUR SEAFRONT ACTION COMMITTEE: Dover; Hoverports.

SAVIDGE, Alan: Tunbridge Wells.

SAVILL, Mr: Dover; Margate; Trials.

SHORE, W. Teignmouth: Kent. See also
GARDNER, William Biscombe: Kent.

SHOREHAM SOCIETY: Shoreham.

SHOREHAM WOMEN'S INSTITUTE: Shoreham.

SHORROCKS, D.M.M. See KENT COUNTY COUNCIL:
ARCHIVES OFFICE: Bibliography.

A SHORT ACCOUNT OF THE PARISH...:Hernhill.

SHORT BROTHERS (ROCHESTER AND BEDFORD LTD):
Aviation; Industry and Trade - Firms;
Rochester. See also PRESTON, James M:
Aviation; Industry and Trade - Firms; Rochester.

SHORT BROTHERS (ROCHESTER AND BEDFORD LTD):
JOINT SHOP STEWARDS AND STAFF COMMITTEE:
Industry and Trade - Firms; Rochester.

A SHORT HISTORY...See PRESTON, James M:
Aviation; Industry and Trade - Firms;
Rochester.

SHORTER, Alfred Henry: Industry and Trade;
Windmills and Watermills.

SHORTLAND, M. See JONES, G.W: Chatham;
Inland Defences; Rochester; World War II.

SHOWLER, Karl: Religious denominations.

SHRAPNEL, Norman: Thames, River.

SHRUBSOLE, W: See DENNE, Rev. Samuel (with
W. Shrubsole): History - General; Rochester.

SHURY, J.J. engraver. See OULTON, W.G:
Isle of Thanet; Margate.

SIBREE, James: Canterbury Cathedral; Rochester
Cathedral.

SIDE, Alice G: Ecology; Maps; Natural History.
See also KENT FIELD CLUB: Natural History.

SIDNEY, Philip: Family History; Penshurst.

SIFLEET, John See BYEGONE MEDWAY: Medway Towns.

SIMMON, Jack: Biography.

SIMMONS, J.F.C. See THORN, Roland Berkeley:
Coastline - Sea Defences.

SIMMONS, W.T. Publisher: Cranbrook.

SIMON LANGTON HIGH SCHOOL FOR GIRLS: Canterbury -
Education.

SIMPSON, James Beasley: Canterbury Cathedral -
Archbishops.

SIMPSON, Samuel: History - General.

SIMPSON, W. Douglas: Architecture; Castles and
Houses.

SIMS, Richard: Genealogical Records.

SIMSON James: Isle of Thanet.

SINCLAIR, Robert. See BOWATER PAPER CORPORATION:
Industry and Trade - Firms.

SINGLETON, H.G.H: Brasted.

SIR JOSEPH WILLIAMSON'S MATHEMATICAL SCHOOL: Rochester.

SITTINGBOURNE AND KEMSLEY LIGHT RAILWAY:
Industry and Trade - Firms; Kemsley; Railways;
Sittingbourne.

SITTINGBOURNE AND MILTON URBAN DISTRICT COUNCIL:
Milton Regis; Sittingbourne.

SITTINGBOURNE AND SWALE ARCHAEOLOGICAL RESEARCH GROUP:
Kent, North East.

SITTINGBOURNE LITERARY AND SCIENTIFIC ASSOCIATION:
Organisations; Sittingbourne.

SITWELL, Osbert: Dickens, Charles.

SIX, James: Kent Authors and Lit. - General.
Obituaries.

SIX GENERATIONS OF HAND PAPERMAKERS: Industry and Trade -
Firms; Tovil.

SKEAT, Walter William: Dialects; Isle of Thanet.

SKELTON, Geoffrey. Translator. See FRIED, Erich:
Faversham; Music

SKETCH OF THE HISTORY OF THE DIOCESE..:Rochester
Diocese.

SKINNER-FARMER, J.W: East Sutton.

SKINNERS SCHOOL: Tunbridge Wells.

SLACK, Paul: See CLARK, Peter: History - 1501 AD
onwards.

SLADDEN, Dilnot: Kent Authors and Lit - Poetry.

SLARE, Frederic: Spas and Mineral Waters.

SLATER, Guy. See BORTON, Lieut. Col. A.C:
Biography; Hunton; World War I.

SLATER, Humphrey:Channel Tunnel.

SLATER, Michael: Bibliography; Dickens, Charles.

SLIGHT, Rev. B: Biography; Pembury; Sermons;
Tunbridge Wells.

SLOMAN, Mrs Susan.See LEGOUIX, Susan: Bibliography;
Maidstone; Museums.

SLUGS: Kent Authors and Lit. - Poetry.

SMALL, E. Milton: Canterbury.

SMALL, Julia: Agriculture; Customs; Kent, East.

"A SMARDONIAN" pseud: Family History; Place names
and surnames; Smarden; Weald.

SMART, J.G.O: Geology; Kent, East; Kent, South East.

SMEATON, J: Ramsgate.

SMETHAM, Henry: Biography; Churches; Kent Authors
and Lit. - Collections; Kent Authors and Lit. - Poetry;
Strood.

SMITH, A: Agriculture; Canterbury - Monastic Houses;
Geography.

SMITH, A.D.W. County Surveyor. See KENT COUNTY COUNCIL:
HIGHWAYS AND TRANSPORTATION DEPARTMENT: Transport.

SMITH, A.H. See THE PARKER CHRONICLE: History -
to 900 AD.

SMITH, Alan: Footpaths - County Walks; Kent, Mid;
North Downs Way.

SMITH, Alfred Aloysius. See HORN, Alfred Aloysius,
pseud: Kent Authors and Lit. - Fiction; Kent Authors
and Lit - General.

SMITH, Arthur William: Bromley; Industry and Trade - Firms.

SMITH, Baker Peter: Coastline.

SMITH, Barry. See "RAMBLER", pseud: Dover; Hotels;
Inns.

SMITH, C. Leslie W: Faversham.

SMith, C.T. See GILLINGHAM BOROUGH COUNCIL:Gillingham.

SMITH, Charles Roach: Bibliography; Cobham; Coins and
Tokens; Faversham; History - Archaeology; Letters;
Lympne; Reculver; Richborough; Stowting.
See also CATALOGUE OF THE FIRST PORTION OF AN
IMPORTANT LIBRARY..:Bibliography; Davington.

SMITH, Cicely Fox: Thames, River.

SMITH, Clare Sydney: Kent Authors and Lit. - General.

SMITH, Frederick Francis: Rochester.

SMITH, George Barnett: Gordon, General C.G.

SMITH, Gerard Edwards: Bibliography; Natural History;
Kent, South.

SMITH, Hugh: Spas and Mineral Waters.

SMITH, J: Kent,Mid; Maidstone.

SMITH, J.J: Cliffe-at-Hoo.

SMITH, Joanna: Recipes; Weald.

SMITH, John Gilbert: Charlton.

SMITH, John L: Railways; Tenterden.

SMITH, John Russell: Bibliography.

SMITH, L.H. See AYLESFORD PARISH COUNCIL: Aylesford.

SMITH, Logan P: Biography; Boughton Malherbe;Letters.

SMITH, Lucy Toulmin,Translator. See JUSSERAND, Jean Adrien Antoine Jules: History - 901 AD - 1500 AD.

SMITH, P.J: Bromley.

SMITH, Paul R: Milton-next-Gravesend.

SMITH, Peter C: Medway, River; Military and Naval History; Ships and Shipping.

SMITH, Reginald Anthony: Industry and Trade; Northfleet; Swanscombe; Thames, River.

SMITH,Rhonda Madge: Inns.

SMITH, Richard Allington: Rainham.

SMITH, Victor T.C: Chatham;Gravesend;Inland Defences; Shorne.

SMITH, W.E.J: Chatham.

SMITH, W.H. AND SON. Publisher: Coastline; Dover.

SMITH-WOOLLEY AND PERRY Chartered Surveyors. See THE GRAND HOTEL: Folkestone (Sale Catalogue).

SMITHERS, Sir David Waldron: Castles and Houses.

SMITH'S HALL: West Farleigh (Sale Catalogue).

SO, C.L: Geology; Isle of Thanet; Kent, East.

SOCIETY OF ANTIQUARIES OF LONDON: Coastal Waters; History - 900 AD.

SOCIETY OF GENEALOGISTS: Genealogical Records. See also BLOMFIELD, Kathleen: Genealogical Records.

A "SOCIETY OF GENTLEMEN": Isle of Thanet.

SOCIETY OF ST. PETER AND ST. PAUL LTD. Publishers. Broadstairs.

SOIL SURVEY OF GREAT BRITAIN See FORDHAM, S.J: Agriculture; Kent, North East; Kent, South East. See GREEN, R.D: Agriculture; Kent, South East; Romney Marsh.

SOMNER, William: Canterbury - Antiquity and Archaeology; Coastal Defences; Gavelkind; History - to 900 AD: Inland Defences.

SONDS, Freeman. See BOREMAN, Robert: Maidstone; Sheldwich; Trials.

SONDS, Sir George See BOREMAN, Robert: Maidstone; Sheldwich; Trials.

"SON OF THE MARSHES" pseud. (D.Jordan and Mrs.J.A.Owen): Kent Authors and Lit. - General; Kent, North West; Milton Regis; Natural History.

SOROPTOMIST CLUB OF ASHFORD: Ashford.

SOROPTOMIST INTERNATIONAL CLUB OF SEVENOAKS:Sevenoaks.

SOTHEBY AND CO. Auctioneers: Bibliography. See also CATALOGUE OF PRINTED BOOKS..:Bibliography. CATALOGUE OF THE INTERESTING AND EXTENSIVE LIBRARY..:Bibliography; Appledore.

SOUTHEBY, WILKINSON AND HODGE. Auctioneers. See CATALOGUE OF THE FIRST PORTION OF..:Bibliography; Davington.

SOUTHAM, B.C: Austen, Jane.

SOUTHBOROUGH ROTARY CLUB: Southborough.

SOUTHBOROUGH SOCIETY: Southborough.

SOUTHBOROUGH TOWN COUNCIL: Southborough.

SOUTHBOROUGH URBAN DISTRICT COUNCIL: Southborough.

SOUTH-EAST ARTS ASSOCIATION: Biography; Kent Authors and Lit. - General; Kent Authors and Lit. - Poetry; Recreation. See also ABERCROMBIE, Nigel: Recreation.

SOUTH-EAST ECONOMIC PLANNING COUNCIL: Kent, South East, Planning.

SOUTH-EAST ENGLAND DEVELOPMENT BOARD: Industry and Trade.

SOUTH-EAST ENGLAND TOURIST BOARD: Industry and Trade - Firms; Kent; Medway Towns.

SOUTH-EAST JOINT PLANNING TEAM: Planning.

SOUTH-EAST METROPOLITAN REGIONAL HOSPITAL BOARD: Hospitals.

SOUTH-EAST THAMES REGIONAL HEALTH AUTHORITY: Chartham; Health and Welfare; Hospitals.

"SOUTH EASTERN" pseud: Road Transport; Woolwich.

SOUTH-EASTERN AND CHATHAM RAILWAY COMPANY:Railways.

SOUTH-EASTERN AND CONTINENTAL STEAM PACKET COMPANY: Ships and Shipping; Transport.

SOUTH-EASTERN ELECTRICITY BOARD: Public Utilities.

SOUTH-EASTERN ELECTRICITY BOARD:CANTERBURY DISTRICT: Kent, East; Public Utilities.

SOUTH-EASTERN ELECTRICITY BOARD:KENT EAST DICTRICT: Kent, East; Public Utilities.

SOUTH EASTERN ELECTRICITY BOARD:MAIDSTONE DISTRICT: Kent, mid; Public Utilities.

SOUTH-EASTERN, FOLKESTONE AND DISTRICT PROPERTY REGISTER: Folkestone; Housing; Kent, South East.

SOUTH-EASTERN GAS CONSULTATIVE COUNCIL: Public Utilities.

SOUTH-EASTERN GAS CONSUMERS' COUNCIL: Public Utilities.

SOUTH EASTERN NATURALIST AND ANTIQUARY. See SOUTH EASTERN UNION OF SCIENTIFIC SOCIETIES: Folkestone; Natural History; Tunbridge Wells.

SOUTH EASTERN RAILWAY COMPANY: Footpaths and Country Walks.

SOUTH-EASTERN SOCIETY OF ARCHITECTS: Architecture.

SOUTH EASTERN UNION OF SCIENTIFIC SOCIETIES: Folkestone; Natural History; Tunbridge Wells.

SOUTHERN ENGLAND WITH COLOURMASTER: Kent.

SOUTHERN HISTORY:History - General.

SOUTHERN RAILWAY COMPANY: Kent; Railways.

SOUTHERN RAILWAY:SOUTH-EASTERN AND CHATHAM SECTION: Railways.

SOUTHERN WATER AUTHORITY:Floods; Public Utilities; Thames, River.

SOUTHERN WATER AUTHORITY AND MID-KENT WATER COMPANY: Broadoak; Public Utilities; Sport.

SOUTHFLEET PARISH HALLS WORKING GROUP:Southfleet.

SOUTHOUSE, Thomas: Faversham.

SOUTHWARK CATHOLIC DIRECTORY: Kent, North West; Religious Denominations; Southwark.

SOUTHWARK, LONDON BOROUGH OF: LIBRARIES DEPARTMENT: Dulwich.

SOUVENIR ALBUM OF VIEWS: Folkestone; Hythe;Sandgate.

A SOUVENIR FROM STONE STREET..:Petham.

SOUVENIR GUIDE TO THE HOUSE ON THE CLIFF..:Broadstairs.

SPAIN, A. See MORGAN, G.H: Hothfield; Natural History.

SPAIN, R. See GROVE, L.R. Allen: Maidstone.

SPARKS, Margaret: Sturry.

SPARLING, H. Halliday: Morris, William.

SPARROW, Gerald: Gordon. Gen. C.G., R.E.

SPAYNE, Janet: Footpaths - Country Walks.

SPEAIGHT, Robert: Becket, Saint Thomas.

SPENCE,Jeoffry: Railways.

SPENCE,Keith: Kent.

SPENCER, Herbert, R: Biography.

SPENCER, Nathaniel: History - General.

SPICER, R.H:Hythe; Industry and Trade - Firms. See also SPICER, S: Hythe; Industry and Trade - Firms.

SPICER, Robert H: Stanford-nr-Ashford.

SPICER, S: Hythe; Industry and Trade - Firms. See also. SPICER, R.H: Hythe; Industry and Trade-Firms.

354

SUMNER, John Bird. Archbishop of Canterbury, (1848 - 1862). See HALL, Rev. Joseph:Letters.

SURVEYOR'S INSTITUTION: Dover.

SUSSEX, John: Prisons.

SUTCLIFFE, Sheila: Coastal defences.

SUTTON, Aubrey: Nonington.

SWAIN, F.A: Natural History.

SWAINE, Anthony.See KENT COUNTY COUNCIL: PLANNING DEPARTMENT AND FAVERSHAM BOROUGH COUNCIL: Faversham. See also THANET DISTRICT COUNCIL:Margate.

SWAINSON, Charles: Legends and Folklore.

SWALE DISTRICT COUNCIL: Kent, North East; Local Government; Lower Halstow.

SWALE FOOTPATHS GROUP: Footpaths - Country Walks; Isle of Sheppey; Kent, East; Kent, Mid; Kent, North East. See also BAILEY, Margaret.
    CHAMPION, George H.J.
    DAVIS, Cyril.
    SMITH, Alan.

SWALE RURAL DISTRICT COUNCIL: Health and Welfare; Kent, North East.

SWAN, Kenneth Raydon. See SWAN, Mary Edwards:Biography.

SWAN, Mary Edwards: Biography.

SWAN, Peter: Libraries; Sevenoaks.

SWANN, Edward: Canterbury.

SWANZY, Henry: Adams, William.

SWEET, Henry: History - to 900 AD.

SWEETMAN, Rev. D.H. See HARVEY, C: Eynsford.

SWEETMAN, H.S: Addington; Family History.

SWIFT, John: Natural History; Sevenoaks.

SWING, Francis: History - 1501 AD onwards.

SWINGLEHURST, E. See ANDERSON, J: Coastline.

SYCKLEMOORE, J.P: History - 1501 AD onwards.

SYDALL, Rev. Elias: Sermons; Tunbridge Wells.

SYKES, Joseph Donald: Agriculture.

SYMES, Rodney: Agriculture; Railways.

SYMS, W. See GRAVESEND BOROUGH COUNCIL:Gravesend.

SYMONDS, J.A: Sidney, Sir Philip.

T

T., B: Margate.

"T.F.": Canterbury Cathedral.

TAIT HOMES, ST PETER'S, ISLE OF THANET: Broadstairs.

TALBOT,Miss Catherine SeeCARTER, Mrs Elizabeth: Letters.

TALLENTS, Sir Stephen: Sutton-at-Hone.

TALLIS, John. Publisher: Gravesend.

TAMES, Richard: Adams, William; Gordon, Gen. C.G: Morris, William.

TANNER, Terence Edmund: Dover.

TANQUERAY, Paul Photographer. See PEPPER, Terence: Tonbridge.

TARBUTT, William:Cranbrook.

TATE, Rosemary: Lee.

TATTON-BROWN, Tim: Canterbury - Antiquity and Archaeology.

TAYLOR, Alfred D: Cricket.

TAYLOR, Arthur: Military and Naval History.

TAYLOR, Cottington,Illustrator.See MAXWELL, Donald: Kent Authors and Lit. - General.

TAYLOR, Edmund S.See MILES, WALKER pseud: Footpaths - Country Walks; Kent, West.

TAYLOR, Elias. See LOWE, Jessie: Souvenirs; Tunbridge Wells.

TAYLOR, F.N. See BARNARD, H.C: Ramsgate.

TAYLOR, H.J: Dover; Music.

TAYLOR, H.M: Canterbury Cathedral; Reculver.

TAYLOR, J.C: Rochester.

TAYLOR, John: Hotels and Restaurants; Inns;Road Transport.

TAYLOR, L.C. See WHITE, Bob: Education;Sevenoaks.

TAYLOR, Leonard: Kent.

TAYLOR, Margaret: Biography; Eltham.

TAYLOR, Michael Minter: Davington; Railways.

TAYLOR, Richard Faulkner.See BELL, John Any Bird, Defendant: Chatham; Maidstone; Trials.

TAYLOR, Silas:Gavelkind.

TEICHMAN, Oskar: Biography; Sport.

TEICHMAN-DERVILLE, Max: New Romney.

TEIGNMOUTH, 5th Baron. See SHORE, Henry Noel, 5th Baron Teignmouth: Smuggling.

TELESCOPE, Thomas pseud: Elections.

TELFER, R.L. See WITTON, A.M: Kent, North West; Road Transport.

TELFER, William:Faversham.

TELFORD, Christopher: Genealogical Records.

TEMPEST, Paul: Greenwich; Thames, River.

TEMPLE, C: Sport.

TEMPLE, Frederick; Archbishop of Canterbury (1896-1902). See BARBER, Melanie: Bibliography; Canterbury Cathedral - Archbishops; Lambeth Palace; Letters.

TEMPLE, Henry John. Viscount Palmestone See HALL, Rev. Joseph: Letters.

TEMPLE, William. Archbishop of Canterbury(1942-1944): See IREMONGER, F.A: Canterbury Cathedral - Archbishops; Letters.

THE TEMPLE HILL LINK:Dartford.

TENISON, E.M: Biography.

TENNYSON, Alfred. 1st Baron Tennyson:Becket,Saint Thomas.

TENTERDEN BOROUGH COUNCIL:Tenterden.

THE TENTERDEN TRUST:Tenterden.

TESTER, P.J: Bexley; Cobham.

TESTON SYSTEM OF FARMING..:Agriculture; Teston.

TESTON VILLAGE APPRAISAL GROUP: Teston.

TETLOW, E: Cinque Ports.

TEXTUS ROFFENSIS: Rochester Diocese.

THAMES BARGE SAILING CLUB: Sport; Thames, River.

THAMES CONSERVANCY BOARD: Sport; Thames, River.

THAMES INFORMATION CENTRE: Thames, River.

THAMES SURVEY COMMITTEE: Pollution; Thames, River.

THAMESIDE ARCHAEOLOGICAL GROUP: Gravesend; Inland Defences.

THAMESIDE CONFERENCE.See GREATER LONDON COUNCIL: Thames, River.

THAMESIDE DEVELOPMENT BOARD: Industry and Trade; Thames, River.

THANET ADVERTISER: Isle of Thanet; World War I.

THANET CATHOLIC ANNUAL: Isle of Thanet; Religious Denominations.

THANET DISTRICT COUNCIL: Isle of Thanet; Margate.

THANET DISTRICT COUNCIL:AMENITIES DEPARTMENT: Broadstairs; Isle of Thanet; Margate; Ramsgate.

THANET DISTRICT COUNCIL:AMENITIES DEPARTMENT: PUBLICITY DIVISION: Isle of Thanet.

THANET DISTRICT COUNCIL:PLANNING DEPARTMENT:Margate. See also KENT COUNTY COUNCIL:PLANNING DEPARTMENT AND THANET DISTRICT COUNCIL:PLANNING DEPARTMENT: Hoverports; Pegwell Bay.

THANET EAST AND WEST CONSTITUENCIES:Elections;
Isle of Thanet.

THANET FIGARO: Isle of Thanet.

THANET FREE PRESS AND GENERAL ADVERTISER:
Isle of Thanet.

THANET GLOWWORM:Isle of Thanet.

THANET ITINERARY: Isle of Thanet.

THANET SAILING WEEK: Coastal Waters;Isle of
Thanet; Sport.

THANET TIMES; Isle of Thanet.

THANET VOLUNTEER YEOMANRY. See
LETTERS CONCERNING THE...YEOMANRY; Isle of Thanet;
Letters; Military and Naval History. See
MOCKETT, John: Isle of Thanet; Letters;
Military and Naval History.

THANET WATER BOARD: Isle of Thanet; Public Utilities.

THEOBALD, C.R See CHAMPION, George H.J:
Footpaths - Country Walks;Kent, East.

THIRTY EIGHT (38) EIGHTEENTH CENTURY VIEWS OF
KENTISH CASTLES: History - 1501 AD onwards.

THOM, John Nichols (also spelt Tom). See
COURTENAY, Sir William P.H pseud: Courtenay, Sir
William P.H.

THOMAS, Bernard G: Maidstone.

THOMAS, Charles A: Pocahontas, Princess.

THOMAS, D.M. See ARC PUBLICATIONS: Kent Authors
and Lit. - Poetry.

THOMAS, Denis: New Ash Green.

THOMAS, Helen: Agriculture; Weald.

THOMAS, Louise: Hollingbourne; Kent Authors and Lit. -
Poetry.

THOMAS, R.L. See KENT COUNTY CONSTABULARY:Police.

THOMAS, Richard: Kent.

THOMAS, Ronald H.G: Greenwich; Railways.

THOMAS, William. See POLLEN, John Hungerford:
Becket,(Saint) Thomas.

THOMAS MORE THROUGH MANY EYES: More, Sir Thomas;
Sermons.

THOME DE GAMOND, N.A: Channel Tunnel.

THOMPSON, A.G: Thames, River.

THOMPSON, Donald: See THAMESIDE ARCHAEOLOGICAL GROUP:
Gravesend; Inland Defences.

THOMPSON, E: Recipes.

THOMPSON, Edward Pett: Natural History.

THOMPSON, Fred: Chatham.

THOMPSON, G.C.W: Tonbridge.

THOMPSON, Gibson: Kent; Westerham.

THOMPSON, Henry Percy: Hayes and Keston.

THOMPSON, P.A; Cricket; Hayes and Keston.

THOMPSON, Paul: Morris, William.

THOMPSON, Philip: Chatham Dockyard; Military and
Naval History.

THOMPSON, R.H: Coins and Tokens.

THOMPSON, Robert Anchor: Becket,Saint Thomas.

THOMPSON, W.H: Churchill, Sir Winston L.S.

THOMSON, A.A: Biography.

THOMSON, Hugh Illustrator. See JERROLD, Walter: Roads.

THOMSON, Ian Hugh White.See CANTERBURY CITY COUNCIL:
Canterbury.

THOMSON, J. Radford: Sidney, Sir Philip. See also
PELTON, Richard Publisher: Kent, West; Tunbridge Wells.

THOMSON, Thomas: Tunbridge Wells.

THORN, Roland Berkeley: Coastline - Sea Defences.

THORNBURGH, Roger: Loose.

THORNDIKE, Russell: Rochester; Romney Marsh; Wrotham.

THORNDYCRAFT, Colin: Frindsbury.

THORNE, John: Kent.

THORNE, William: Canterbury - Monastic Houses.

THORNEWELL, David. See CHEESEMAN, Clive: Footpaths -
Country Walks; Kent, Mid.

THORNHILL, J.F.P: Geography.

THORNTON, Edward Charles Bexley: Coastline; Ships and
Shipping; Thames, River.

THORNTON, Rev. F.V: Sermons; Tunbridge Wells.

THORNTON, W. Pugin: Becket, Saint Thomas; Canterbury.

THORPE, Bernard and Partners Auctioneers: See
FRITH HALL; East Farleigh (Sale Catalogue)

THORPE, J.F: Hernhill.

THORPE, John Junior. See CUSTUMALE ROFFENSE:
Rochester Diocese.

THORPE, John Senior: Bibliography; Monumental
Inscriptions. See also REGISTRUM ROFFENSE:Rochester
Diocese.

THORPE, Teresa: Coastline; Kent, East.

THRELFALL, W: Bexley.

THURLEY, Elizabeth Fusae: Bromley; Education.

TICEHURST, Norman F: Canterbury Cathedral; Dungeness;
Natural History.

TICH, Mary (i.e. POWELL, Mary Relph): Biography.

THE TICKHAM FOXHOUNDS: Sport.

TIFFIN, A.W: Goudhurst.

TIFFIN, Alfred: Biography; Goudhurst; Prisons.

TIFFEN, William Publisher: Folkestone; Hythe; Sandgate.

TILDEN, Philip: Allington; Lympne; Saltwood; Westerham.

TILLEY, Ernest W: Coins and Tokens; Gravesend; Milton-
next-Gravesend.

TILLOTSON, John. Archbishop of Canterbury 1630 - 1694.
Canterbury Cathedral - Archbishops.

TIMBS, John: History - General.

THE TIMES. Dickens, Charles; Kent.

TIMES OF EDWARD, THE BLACK PRINCE..:Canterbury
Cathedral; Edward, the Black Prince.

TIMMIS, L.B: Orpington.

TIMPSON, Thomas: Religious Denominations.

TIP HANDBOOK. See BAINES, Derek: Industrial Archaeology;
Transport.

TITTLEY, Ian: Coastline; Maps; Natural History.

TIZARD, Staff Captain, T.H. (later Staff Commander).
See ADMIRALTY: Dover; Medway, River; Sea and River
Charts.

TODD, A: Sandgate.

TOKE, Nicholas (of Goddington, or, Godinton):
Letters; Poor Law. See also KNOCKER, Herbert W:
Great Chart.

TOM, John Nichols (Also spelt Thom). See
COURTENAY, Sir William P.H pseud: Courtenay, Sir
William P.H.

TOMASZEWSKI, N.E: Deal.

TOMBLESON, W. Illustrator: Maps; Medway, River;
Thames, River. See also FEARNSIDE, William Gray:
Medway, River; Thames, River.

TOMLINSON. A.W: Hotels, Restaurants and Clubs.

TOMLINSON, Fred: Biography.

TOMLINSON, H.M: Thames, River.

TOMLINSON, Norman: Biography; Gillingham; Military
and Naval History.

TOMPSETT, B.P: Matfield.

TONBRIDGE AND MALLING CONSTITUENCY:Elections.

TONBRIDGE AND MALLING DISTRICT COUNCIL: Kent, Mid;
Kent, West; Nature Walks; Tonbridge.

T Cont'd

TONBRIDGE AND MALLING DISTRICT COUNCIL:PLANNING
DEPARTMENT: East Malling; Eccles; Hildenborough;
Ightham; Ivy Hatch; Tonbridge; West Malling; Wrotham.

TONBRIDGE AND TUNBRIDGE WELLS SOCIETY FOR
MENTALLY HANDICAPPED CHILDREN: Organisations.

TONBRIDGE CORONATION COMMITTEE: Tonbridge.

TONBRIDGE OAST THEATRE AND ARTS CLUB: Kent Artists;
Tonbridge.

TONBRIDGE SCHOOL: Tonbridge.

TONBRIDGE URBAN DISTRICT COUNCIL: Kent, West; Tonbridge.

TONKIN, Nancy: Beckenham.

TOOKEY, G.W : Beckenham.

TOOKEY, Geoffrey. See FORSTER, John,Lord Harraby:
Beckenham; Obituaries.

TOOTELL, J: Mereworth;Yalding.

TOPLEY, Peter: Kent Authors and Lit. - Poetry;
West Wickham.

TOPLEY, William: Agriculture; Coastal Waters; Geology;
Hythe; Weald.

THE TOPOGRAPHER,Canterbury; Goodnestone; Greenwich;
Nonington.

THE TOPOGRAPHER FOR THE YEAR 1791..: Canterbury-
Churches; Chilham; Sturry.

TOPOGRAPHICAL ACCOUNT OF THE HUNDRED OF DEWSBOROUGH..:
History - General; Kent, South East.

TOPOGRAPHICAL MISCELLANIES: Canterbury - Monastic
Houses; Nonington.

TOPOGRAPHICAL QUARTERLY: Land Tenure. See also
TELFORD, Christopher: Genealogical Records.

TORR, V.J. See BOORMAN, Henry Roy Pratt:Churches.

TOUR THROUGH THE ISLE OF THANET...See COZENS,
Zechariah: Isle of Thanet; Kent, East.

TOURISTE: Kent.

TOUT, Thomas Frederick: Becket, Saint Thomas.

TOVEY, Sir John Cronyn, Admiral of the Fleet.See
GILLINGHAM BOROUGH COUNCIL: Gillingham.

TOVEY, W: Greenhithe.

TOWERS, Rev. Johnson: Sermons; Tonbridge.

TOWN AND COUNTRY MAGAZINE: Allington; Eltham;
Hackington; Hadlow; History - General; Isle of
Sheppey; Legends; Minster-in-Thanet; Wye.

TOWN AND COUNTY DIRECTORIES: Industry and Trade;
Kent, North; Maidstone; Margate; Ramsgate;
Tunbridge Wells.

THE TOWN CRIER: Gravesend.

TOWNROE, S.C: Railways.

TOWNSEND, Rev. George: Kent Authors and Lit. -
General.

TOWNSEND, Peter: World War II.

TOWNSEND, William, Artist. See NEVE, Christopher:
Canterbury; Kent Artists.

TRADE AND INDUSTRY: Department Of: Coastal Waters.

TRADE AND INDUSTRY, Department of: ACCIDENTS
INVESTIGATION BRANCH: Airports; Aviation;
Leigh; Snodland; Thames, River.

TRADE AND INDUSTRY, Department of: WARREN SPRINGS
LABORATORY: Health and Welfare; Industry and
Trade; Pollution.

TRADESMEN'S TOKENS ISSUED IN THE ISLE OF THANET...
AND THE CINQUE PORTS: Cinque Ports; Coins and Tokens;
Isle of Thanet.

TRANSPORT, Ministry of: Channel Tunnel; Medway, River.

TRANSPORT 2000;KENT GROUP: Hoo Peninsula; Railways.

TRANSPORTATION PLANNING ASSOCIATES:Bromley; Road Transport.

TRAPP, J.B: More, Sir Thomas.

TRAVERS, Samuel (Foundation). See GREENWICH HOSPITAL AND
TRAVERS FOUNDATION:Greenwich.

TREANOR,. Rev. Thomas Stanley:Goodwin Sands.

TREASURES OF THOUGHT: Kent Authors and Lit. - General.

TREBILCOCK, Clive: Crayford; Dartford; Industry and
Trade - Firms.

TRENCH, Charles Chenevix: Gordon, Gen. C.G.

TRENCHARD, Hugh M. See McCUDDEN, James Thomas Byford:
McCudden, J.T.B.

TRENDELL, John: Deal; Military and Naval History;
Music.

TRESIDDER AND CO. Auctioneers. See LYMPNE CASTLE
ESTATE: Lympne (Sale Catalogue).

TREVELYAN, John. See DOGGETT, Tom: Footpaths -
Country Walks; North Downs Way.

TREVITHICK SOCIETY: Dartford.

TREVOR-ROPER, Hugh Redwald: Canterbury Cathedral -
Archbishops.

TRIAL AND SENTENCE OF THE KNIGHT OF MALTA:
Courtenay, Sir William P.H; Trials.

TRIAL AT LARGE OF JOSEPH STACPOOLE etc:
Dartford; Trials.

TRIAL AT MAIDSTONE SPRING ASSIZES, 1837: Maidstone; Trials.
TRIAL OF THE RT. HON.LORD GEORGE SACKVILLE...:Trials.

TRIGGS, Roger: Gillingham; Sport.

TRIMMELL, Charles.Bishop of Norwich:Sermons;Tunbridge Wells.

TRIPP, Sir Herbert Alker ("Leigh Hoe"): Coastal Waters.

TRISTRAM, E.W: Canterbury Cathedral.

A TRUE AND PERFECT TERRIER: Bekesbourne.

TRUMANS,Gwyn and Co. Brewers. See EAST KENT TIMES
AND BROADSTAIRS AND ST PETERS MAIL: Broadstairs;
Industry and Trade - Firms.

TSCHUDI, Clara: Chislehurst.

TUCKER, John: Sermons; Southborough.

TUNBRIDGE EPISTLES: Kent Authors and Lit. - Poetry.

TUNBRIDGE MISCELLANY: Kent Authors and Lit. - Collections;
Tunbridge Wells.

TUNBRIDGE WARE: Souvenirs; Tunbridge Wells.

TUNBRIDGE WELLS AND DISTRICT COUNCIL OF SOCIAL SERVICE:
Health and Welfare; Kent, West; Organisations;
Tunbridge Wells.

TUNBRIDGE WELLS HEALTH DISTRICT: COMMUNITY HEALTH CENTRE:
Health and Welfare; Kent, West.

TUNBRIDGE WELLS LOCAL BOARD: Health and Welfare;
Tunbridge Wells.

TUNBRIDGE WELLS PUBLIC LIBRARY: Bibliography; Tunbridge
Wells.

TUNBRIGALIA: Tunbridge Wells.

TURNBULL, Patrick: Gordon, Gen. C.G.

TURNER, G.J: Canterbury - Monastic Houses.

TURNER, J.M.W. See RUSKIN John; Coastline;
Kent Artists.

TURNER, J.T. Howard: Railways.

TURNER, Keith: Coastline; Herne Bay; Hythe; Railways.

TURNER, R: Dover.

TURNOR, Reginald: Kent.

TURPIN, B.J: Windmills and Watermills.

TURPIN, J.M. See TURPIN, B.J. Windmills and Watermills.

TWENTY-SEVEN (27) PALACE STREET.:Canterbury(Sale
Catalogue).

TWISDEN, Sir John Ramskill: Family History.

TWIST, Syd: Faversham.

TWO BRASSES...See CAIGER, John E.L: Darenth;
Monumental Inscriptions. See GOUGH, Harold Eric:
Herne; Monumental Inscriptions.

TWO SCHEMES RELATING TO FAVERSHAM..:Charities;
Faversham.

TWYMAN, Frank: Family History; Kent, East.

T

TWYSDEN, Sir Roger: History - 1501 AD
onwards.

TYE, D.F: Boughton Monchelsea.

TYRWHITT-DRAKE, Sir Hugh Garrard: Biography;
Customs; Kent Authors and Lit. - General;
Maidstone; Zoo and Zoo Parks. See also
MAIDSTONE MUSEUM AND ART GALLERY: Maidstone;
Museums; Road Transport.

TYSON, R.G and Co. Publisher: Maidstone.

U

UGARTE, F. Perez: Cobham.

UGLOW, Capt. Jim, Biography; Medway,River;
Ships and Shipping; Thames,River.

ULANOFF, Stanley M. See McCUDDEN, James Thomas
Byford: McCudden, J.T.B.

ULLYETT, Henry: Folkestone; Natural History.

UNDERHILL, Francis: Rochester Cathedral; Rochester
Cathedral - Bishops.

UNDERWOOD, Derek: Cricket.

UNITED KENT LIFE AND ANNUITY INSTITUTIONS.
See KENT FIRE INSURANCE COMPANY: Industry and
Trade - Firms.

UNIVERSITY OF KENT: Bibliography; Bridge;
Canterbury; Canterbury - Education; History - General.

UNIVERSITY OF KENT: CENTRE FOR RESEARCH IN THE
SOCIAL SCIENCES: Kent, East.

UNIVERSITY OF KENT:FACULTY OF SOCIAL SCIENCES:
History - 1501 AD onwards; Recreation; Sport;
World War I.

UNIVERSITY OF KENT - STUDENTS' UNION: Canterbury -
Education.

UNWIN, T. Fisher. Publisher: Blackheath; Footpaths - Country
Walks; Greenwich; Kent, North West.

UPBURY MANOR SCHOOL:Gillingham.

URRY, William: Becket,Saint Thomas; Canterbury;
Canterbury Cathedral. See also SOMNER, William:
Canterbury.

V

VALENTINE, Alan: Biography.

VALENTINE & SONS,LTD. Publisher:Floods;Whitstable.

VALLANCE, Aymer: Churches;Cranbrook;Morris,William.
See also LAMBARDE Fane F: Faversham.

VANSITTART, Nicholas, 1st Baron Bexley(1766 - 1851).
See ANIMADVERSIONS ON LORD BEXLEY'S LETTER:
Church History; Letters; Religious Denominations.

VARLE, Captain G. Illustrator.See OULTON, W.G:
Isle of Thanet; Margate.

VAUGHAN, Chester: Whitstable.

VAUGHAN, John: History - General.

VEALE, Ernest William Partington: Coastal Waters;
Transport.

VENABLES, Bernard: Sport.

VERKAIK, John: Folkestone.

VERNIER, Jean Piere: Wells, H.G.

VESEY, Mrs. See CARTER, Mrs. Elizabeth: Letters.

VETCH, Captain James: Ramsgate, See also
RENNIE, Sir John: Ramsgate

VICKERS BROS., ARMAMENTS. See TREBILCOCK, Clive :
Crayford; Dartford; Industry and Trade - Firms.

VICKERSON, Edmund:Westerham.

VICTORIA AND ALBERT MUSEUM: Dickens, Charles;
Kent Artists.

VICTORIA HISTORY OF THE COUNTY OF KENT. See
PAGE, William: History - General.

VIDGEON-WILSON ALMSHOUSES See CHARITY COMMISSION:
Canterbury - Almshouses and Hospitals.

VIDLER, John: Maidstone; Prisons.

VIDLER, Leopold Amon: Cinque Ports.

VIEW ALBUMS...See town or village.

VIGAR, J.E: Aylesford.

VILLIERS, Alan John: Greenwich; Ships and Shipping.

VILLIERS, Oniver G: Saltwood.

VINE, Francis Thomas: History-to 900 AD.

VINE, Paul Ashley Laurence: Canals; Inland Defences;
Military and Naval History; Roads.

VISITATION OF ENGLAND AND WALES: Genealogical Records.

VISITATIONS OF KENT: Genealogical Records.

VISITORS' GUIDE TO THE WATERING PLACES..:Coastline.

VITA ET PROCESSUS S. THOMAE: Becket, Saint Thomas.

VULLIAMY, Lawrence: Kent.

W

W., D: Fordwich.

W., F.A. See WATERHOUSE, F. Aelred: Margate.

W., J.A (Willmore, J.A): Fordwich.

WACHER, John: Sport.

WADDAMS, Herbert Montagu: Becket, Saint Thomas;
Canterbury Cathedral.

WADE, Virginia: Biography.

WADHAMS, Leonard J. See COOMBE, Derek:Medway, River.

WADMORE, Beauchamp: Tonbridge.

WADMORE, James Foster: Tonbridge.

WAILES, Rex: Cranbrook; Windmills and Watermills.

WAINEMAN, Paul pseud. (Mrs. Sylvia Macdougall nèe
Börgstrom): Biography.

WAINWRIGHT, Clive: Davington.

WAINWRIGHT, J.G: Anerley; Education.

WAINWRIGHT, Richard: History - Archaeology.

WAITE, H.E: Anerley.

WAKELEY, R.H: Biography; Rainham.

WAKELEY, Thomas S. See WAKELEY, R.H:Biography;
Rainham.

WAKEMAN, Norman: Railways.

WALCOTT, Mackenzie E.C: Church History; Churches.

WALDEN, Harry: West Wickham.

WALFORD, Edward: Dover; Leeds; Rochester.

WALKER, A.J: Staplehurst.

WALKER, Alfred T: Birchington.

WALKER, Jack: Paddock Wood.

WALKER, James: Ramsgate.

WALKING IN KENT: Footpaths - Country Walks.

WALL, Nicholas.See GROVE, L.R.A: Maidstone.

WALLENBERG, J.K: Place Names and Surnames.

WALLER, J.G: Cobham.

WALLINGER, Rev. W: Sermons; Tunbridge Wells.

WALSH, Carole.See HASTINGS, MacDonald:Recipes;Whitstable.

WALTER AND GRIST. Publishers; Kent, West; Tunbridge Wells.

WALTER AND RANDALL, Auctioneers. See CATALOGUE OF THE
COLLECTION OF ANTIQUE FURNITURE....:Rochester
(Sale Catalogue).

WALTER, J.C. Engraver.See ADMIRALTY:Sea and River
Charts.

WALTER DOWSETT COLLECTION. See CORDELL, Alan:
Coastline; Rivers; Thames, River.

WALTERS, John: Margate.

WALTON, George Chapman: Folkestone; Natural History.
See also WALTON, John W: Folkestone; Kent, South East;
Natural History.

WALTON, Hugh Mersey: Margate.

WALTON, Izak. See WOTTON, Sir, Henry: Kent Authors
and Lit. - Collections.

WALTON, John W: Folkestone; Kent, South East;
Natural History.

WARD, Adolphus William: Chaucer, Geoffrey.

WARD, B.R: Brompton; Military and Naval History.

WARD, Bernard: Canterbury Cathedral - Archbishops.

WARD, C.H. Dudley. See TWISDEN, Sir John Ramskill:
Family History.

WARD, D.J: Geology; Herne Bay.

WARD, Gordon Reginald: Canterbury - Monastic Houses;
History - to 900 AD; Lewisham; Sevenoaks.

WARD, H. Snowden: Canterbury Cathedral.

WARD, Henry, Publisher: Canterbury; Canterbury -
Monastic Houses.

WARD, Paul L. See LAMBARDE, William: History and
Archaeology - 1501 AD onwards.

WARD LOCK AND CO LTD. Publishers, Coastline; Kent, East;
Kent, North East; Kent, South East.

WARLOW, G.H: Knockholt.

WARNER, Harold William: Canterbury; Cricket.

WARNER, Kenneth: Canterbury - Churches.

WARNER, Oliver: Cricket.

WARNER, Philip: Dover; World War I.

WARNER, S.A: Canterbury Cathedral.

WARNICKE, Retha M: Biography.

WARREN, Charles: Charities; Westbere.

WARREN, Clarence Henry: Kent Authors and Lit. - General;
Mereworth.

WARREN, Judy. See BURCHALL, Michael J: Family History.

THE WASP. See MAIDSTONE GRAMMAR SCHOOLS: Maidstone.

WATERHOUSE, F. Aelred: Margate.

WATERING PLACES OF ENGLAND, PART II: Gravesend; Herne Bay;
Sheerness.

WATERING PLACES OF GREAT BRITAIN: Coastline.

WATERS, H. Bookseller: Cranbrook.

WATERS, S.C: Farnborough; Local Government; Orpington.

WATKINS, Albert Henry: Bibliography; Bromley; Wells, H.G.
See also BROMLEY PUBLIC LIBRARY: Bromley.

WATKINSON, J: Herne Bay.

WATSON, Basil: Greenwich.

WATSON, Sir Charles M. See HISTORY OF THE CORPS
OF ROYAL ENGINEERS: Military and Naval History.

WATSON, Julian. See GREENWICH: LONDON BOROUGH COUNCIL:
LIBRARIES - LOCAL HISTORY DEPARTMENT: Greenwich.

WATSON, K: Canals and Waterways. See also
GRAVESHAM BOROUGH COUNCIL - PLANNING DEPARTMENT: Gravesham.

WATSON, William W: Canterbury; Herne Bay; History - General.

WATT, F: Canterbury.

WATT, John: Bibliography; Dickens, Charles.

WATTS, Alan Wilson: Biography; Chislehurst.

WATTS, Capt. O.M. See STANFORD, Edward Ltd. Publishers:
Coastal Waters; Medway, River; Sea and River Charts;
Swale; Thames, River.

WAUGH, Marlene: Kent Authors and Lit. - Poetry.

WAUGH, Mary: Agriculture.

WAYLEN, Barbara: Biography; Prisons. See also
BANKS, Frances: Education; Prisons.

WAYMARK, Peter: Petts Wood.

WEALD OF KENT PRESERVATION SOCIETY: Channel Tunnel;
Conservation; Footpaths - Country Walks; Organisations;
Stone-in-Oxney; Weald.

WEALD RESEARCH COMMITTEE: Geology; Weald.

WEALDEN IRON RESEARCH GROUP: Industry and Trade; Weald.

WEAVER, G: Ghosts; Inns.

WEBB, A.E: Harrietsham; Lenham; Natural History.

WEBB, Anthony: World War II.

WEBB, Brian: Canterbury Cathedral; Dover.

WEBB, M: Kent.

WEBB, W: Coastal Waters; Safety at Sea.

WEBB, William: Architecture; Castles and Houses.

WEBBER, C.J: Chislehurst.

WEBBER, Ronald: History - 901 AD - 1500 AD.

WEDD, Mary R: Education.

WEDMORE, Sir Frederick: Kent Authors and Lit. - General;
Kent Authors and Lit. - Poetry.

WEDMORE, Millicent: Kent Authors and Lit. - Poetry.

WEEKS, W.R: Faversham.

WEEKS - PEARSON, A.J. See SAUNDERS, D.K: Blackheath;
Sport.

WEINER, J. Ltd. Publisher: Canterbury; Kent, East; Medway
Towns.

WEIR, A.H: Geology; Pegwell Bay.

WELBY, Douglas: Dover; River.

WELCH, Denton: Biography.

WELCH, Kate: Farnborough; Natural History.

WELLAND, Ralph, engraver. See REYNOLDS, James and
Sons. Publishers: Sea and River Charts; Thames, River.

WELLCOME FOUNDATION LTD: Beckenham; Dartford; Industry
and Trade. See also MACDONALD, Gilbert: Beckenham;
Dartford; Industry and Trade - Firms.

WELLS, Arthur G: Industry and Trade; Railways; Sittingbourne.

WELLS, George: Dickens, Charles.

WELLS, Mrs. Hester: Hayes and Keston.

WELLS, K.A.E: Snodland.

WELSBY, Canon. Paul A: Rochester Cathedral.

WENBAN, A.A: Family History; Sandhurst.

WENYON, H.J: Military and Naval History.

WERF, Philip van der Bromley; Industry and Trade.

WEST, Jenny: Windmills and Watermills.

WEST, John: Blackheath; Deptford; Newcross. See also
MACARTNEY, Sylvia: Industry and Trade; Lewisham.

WEST, R. George: Canals; Penge.

WEST KENT BORDER ARCHAEOLOGICAL GROUP: Hayes and Keston.

WEST KENT FEDERATION OF WOMEN'S INSTITUTES: Recipes;
Kent, West; Organisations. See also LEWIS, Mary:
Agriculture.

WEST KENT POLL BOOK: Elections; Kent, West.

WEST KENT (QUEEN'S OWN) YEOMANRY: Military and Naval
History; World War I.

WESTALL, A.W. See MITCHELL, A.F: Bedgebury; Forestry.

WESTERHAM PARISH COUNCIL: Crockham Hill; Westerham.

WESTERHAM SOCIETY: Westerham.

WESTERN MOTOR WORKS (Chislehurst Ltd): Chislehurst;
Industry and Trade - Firms.

WEYBURN, S. Fletcher: Family History.

W.G. MASON COLLECTION See CATALOGUE OF THE COLLECTION
OF ANTIQUE FURNITURE..: Rochester (Sale Catalogue).

WHARTON, Florence Ann: Dartford.

WHARTON, Captain W.J.L: See ADMIRALTY:
Medway,River; Sea and River Charts.

WHATMAN, Susanna. See BALSTON, Thomas: Maidstone.

WHATMORE, Rev. Leonard E: Canterbury - Diocese and
Province; Church History; Religious Denominations.
See Also MORRIS, John:Canterbury.

WHAT'S ON..:Folkestone; Hythe; Sandgate.

WHATS ON AND WHERE..:Kent.

WHEATLEY, Rev. Sydney William: Bridges;Heraldry;
Rochester; Rochester Cathedral.

WHEELER, Alwyne:Natural History; Thames,River.

WHEELER, Barnaby:Housing; Tonbridge.

WHEELER, Clifford: Becket, Saint Thomas.

WHEELER, J.M: Biography; Family History;
Kent Artists.

WHEELER, Sir Mortimer. See WOOD, Eric Stuart:
History - Archaeology.

WHEELER, Terence: Kent Authors and Lit. - Fiction.

WHIBLEY, Joan. See KENT, Joan pseud: Kent, East;
Kent, North East.

THE WHIGS DEFENDED...:Gravesend.

WHISSON, J.H.H: Willesborough.

WHITAKER, William: Geology; Public Utilities;
Reculver.

WHITBOURN, Philip: Tunbridge Wells.

WHITBREAD AND CO LTD:Beltring; Hotels,
Restaurants and Clubs; Industry and Trade - Firms;
Inns; Kent. See also RAINBIRD, G.M: Inns.
HILL, Brian: Inns. DAY, J. Wentworth: Inns;Sport.

WHITE AND CULMER-WHITE FAMILY.See BARBER, T:Broadstairs.
See also WHITES OF COWES:Broadstairs;Industry and
Trade - Firms.

WHITE, Bob: Education; Sevenoaks.

WHITE, Charles: Footpaths - Country Walks;
Pilgrims Way.

WHITE, Dorothy: Groombridge.

WHITE, Gabriel: Kent Artists.

WHITE, H.J Osborne:Geology; Kent, East; Kent, South East;
Kent, South West.

WHITE, Henry Patrick: Railways.

WHITE, J.T:Isle of Thanet.

WHITE, John Baker:Biography.

WHITE, John Talbot: Gardens; Kent; Weald.

WHITE, Joseph William Gleeson: Canterbury Cathedral.

WHITE, Judy. Illustrator. See CAUDWELL,Hugo:Printing and
Publishing.

WHITE, Th(omas) Henry: Kent Authors and Lit. - General.

WHITE - THOMSON, Very Rev. Ian Hugh. See CANTERBURY
CITY COUNCIL: Canterbury.

WHITEHEAD, Rev. ALFRED. See ST. PETER THE APOSTLE IN
THANET: Broadstairs.

WHITEHEAD, C.J: Herne Bay.

WHITEHEAD, Sir Charles: Agriculture.

WHITEHEAD, J.G.O: Military and Naval History.

WHITEHEAD, R.A: Agriculture.

WHITEHOUSE, Archibald: McCudden, James Thomas Byford.

WHITEMILL FOLK MUSEUM STEERING COMMITTEE: Sandwich;
Windmills and Watermills.

WHITES OF COWES:Broadstairs;Industry and Trade - Firms.

WHITESIDE, Thomas: Channel Tunnel.

WHITFIELD PARISH COUNCIL: Whitfield.

WHITING, Crispin: Dartford; Poor Law.

WHITING, William: Ford; Minster-in-Thanet; Ospringe.

WHITLOCK, Ralph: Customs.

WHITNEY, C.E: Cinque Ports.

WHITNEY, John: Darent, River; Medway, River.

WHITSTABLE AND TANKERTON PUBLICITY COMMITTEE:Tankerton;
Whitstable.

WHITSTABLE CIVIC SOCIETY: Coastline; Conservation; Whitstable.

WHITSTABLE OYSTER COMPANY VS. GANN,Thomas: Trials; Whitstable.

THE WHITSTABLE SOCIETY: Whitstable.

WHITSTABLE URBAN DISTRICT COUNCIL:Tankerton;Whitstable.

WHITSTABLE VISITORS'LIST AND GENERAL ADVISOR:Whitstable.

WHITSTABLE YACHT CLUB:Whitstable; Sport.

WHITTA, Terry:Medway Towns; Recreation.

WHITTAKER, Joseph: Kent Authors and Lit. - Poetry.

WHO'S WHO IN KENT:Biography.

WHO'S WHO IN KENT, SURREY AND SUSSEX:Biography.

WHO'S WHO IN MAIDSTONE:Biography; Maidstone.

WHO WAS CAXTON:Caxton, William.

WHYLER, Fred:Farnborough;Hospitals.

WHYMAN, Colin.See CITY OF ROCHESTER SOCIETY: Industry
and Trade; Rochester.

WHYMAN,John:Chatham;History-1501AD onwards;Industry and
Trade-Firms;Rochester Cathedral. See also ROAKE,Margaret:
History-General.See also JACOB,Edward:Faversham.

WIBBERLEY, Gerald P. See BULL, Christopher:
Agriculture; Land Utilisation; Recreation.
See SYKES, Joseph Donald; Agriculture.

WICKHAM, W: Reculver.

WICKWIRE, Franklin: History - 1501 AD onwards.

WICKWIRE, Mary. See WICKWIRE, Franklin: History -
1501 AD onwards.

WIGAN RICHARDSON INTERNATIONAL LTD:Agriculture.

WIGGINS TEAPE:Dartford; Industry and Trade - Firms.

WIGHTMAN, Ralph: Kent.

WIGNALL, George Wilding: Gillingham.

WIKELEY, Nigel: Architecture; Railways.

WILDIFE CONSERVATION....:Natural History.

WILDASH, W. See DENNE, Rev. Samuel (With W. SHRUBSOLE):
History - General; Rochester.

WILDE, Laurie A:Margate.

WILDISH, W.T: Rochester.

WILES, H.V: Morris, William.

WILKES, R.E: Gillingham; Military and Naval History.

WILKINSON, Gladys J: Whitstable.

WILKS, Brian: Austen, Jane.

WILKS, George: Hythe.

WILKS, Hector M: Whitstable.

WILL ADAMS MEMORIAL: Adams, William.

WILLARD, Barbara: Sidney, Sir Philip.

WILLEMENT, Thomas: Davington. See also
CATALOGUE OF THE FIRST PORTION OF..:Bibliography; Davington.

WILLETT, William: Kent Authors and Lit. - General.

WILLIAM, OF BYHOLTE: Legal Customs.

WILLIAM DOWSETT COLLECTION.See CORDELL, Alan:
Coastline; Rivers.

WILLIAM MORRIS SOCIETY: Morris, William.

WILLIAMS, Alan:Railways.

WILLIAMS, Audrey: Canterbury - Antiquity and Archaeology.

WILLIAMS, Emlyn: Dickens, Charles.

WILLIAMS, Eve: Tilmanstone.

WILLIAMS, Geoffrey: Cinque Ports; Heraldry.

WILLIAMS, Guy R: Kent, North West; Land Utilisation.

WILLIAMS, Gwyn.See WYE ORNITHOLOGISTS CLUB:Natural
History; Wye.

WILLIAMS, Harry: Kent, North West.

WILLIAMS, Marguerite; Biography; Woolwich.

WILLIAMS, R.H. Isaac; Elham.

WILLIAMS, Rev. W: Sermons; Tonbridge.

WILLIAMSON, Catherine; Kent Authors and Lit. - General.

WILLIAMSON, Catherine Ellis; Canterbury.

WILLIAMSON, George C. See WEDMORE, Sir Frederick:
Kent Authors and Lit. - General.

WILLIAMSON, Hugh Ross: Becket, Saint Thomas.

WILLIAMSON, James Alexander: Coastal Waters.

WILLIAMSON, W.S: Medway, River; Sea and River Charts.

WILLIS, Arthur J: Canterbury, Diocese and Province;
Church History; Genealogical Records.

WILLIS, Peter J: Gravesend; Gravesham; Kent, North West.

WILLIS, Robert: Canterbury Cathedral.

WILLMORE, J.A. See W., J.A: Fordwich.

WILLMOTT, Frank G: Industry and Trade - Firms;
Lower Halstow; Medway, River; Rainham; Ships and
Shipping.

WILLOUGHBY, David William: Kent, North West;
Road Transport.

WILLS, Alan. See FAIRCLOUGH, Tony: Railways.

WILMOT, John: 2nd Earl of Rochester: Kent Authors
and Lit. - Collections; Kent Authors and Lit. - Poetry.

WILSON, Angus; Dickens, Charles.

WILSON, Charles. Publisher: Medway, River; Thames, River.

WILSON, Geoffrey: Communications.

WILSON, Jack F: Bromley; Military and Naval History;
World War II.

WILSON, Mona: Sidney, Sir Philip.

WILSON, Peter. See GEOFFREY-LLOYD, Lord Geoffrey William:
Leeds.

WILSON, S. Gordon: Canterbury; Canterbury - Almshouses and
Hospitals; Dickens, Charles; Pilgrims Way.

WILSON, Sydney: Faversham.

WILSON, W. Eric: Sea and River Charts; Thames, River.

WILTON, Eric: Bromley; Military and Naval History;
World War II.

WINBOLT, Samuel Edward: Folkestone; Kent.

WINCHELSEY, Archbishop. See GRAHAM, Rose: Reculver.

WINDUS, William Edward: Kent Authors and Lit. - Fiction;
Kent Authors and Lit. - General; Kent Authors and Lit.-
Plays. See also ARMIGER, Will: Kent Authors and
Lit. - Fiction.

WINGFIELD - STRATFORD, Esme: Biography.

WINIFRID, Charles. See BLAXLAND, George Cuthbert: Family
History.

WINNIFRITH, Rev. Alfred: Biography.

WINNIFRITH, Sir John: Appledore.

WINSPUR, Catherine: Medway Towns.

WINSTANLEY, Michael J: History - 1501 AD onwards.

WINSTON, Richard: Becket, Saint Thomas

WISDEN, John. See ASHLEY-COOPER, F.S: Cricket.

WISEMAN, Mrs. Mary. See CHAMPION, George J: Charities;
Woolwich.

WITCOMBE, Oliver: Chatham Dockyard.

WITHERS, Hartley: Canterbury Cathedral; Minster-in-Sheppey;
Rochester Cathedral.

WHITNEY, K.P: History - to 900 AD; History - 901AD -
1500 AD; Weald.

WITTON, A.M: Kent, North West; Road Transport.

WOLFE, C.S: Railways; Romney Marsh.

WOLFF, Michael. See VIDLER, John: Maidstone; Prisons.

WOLFFRAM, H: Blackheath; Lee; Military and Naval History.

WOLLASTON, Rev. Mr. See Six, James: Kent Authors and Lit.-
General.

WOLVERHAMPTON CENTRAL ART GALLERY: Cranbrook; Kent Artists.

WOMEN'S ROYAL VOLUNTARY SERVICE: Organisations.

WOOD, David: Industry and Trade; Ships and Shipping;
Thames, River.

WOOD, Derek: World War II.

WOOD, Dorothy: Kent Authors and Lit. - General.

WOOD, Eric Stuart: History - Archaeology.

WOOD, J.C: Downe.

WOOD, John D.AND COMPANY.Auctioneers. See
AMOS AND DAWTON, Auctioneers: Chilham (Sale Catalogue).

WOOD, Margaret: Plaxtol.

WOOD, T.P.S: History - 1501 AD onwards.

WOODCOCK, D.G. Illustrator. See BLAXLAND, Gregory:
Military and Naval History.

WOODFORDE, John: Industry and Trade; Sevenoaks.

WOODGATE, Mildred Violet: Becket, Saint Thomas.

WOODLANDS ART GALLERY: Greenwich.

WOODMAN, George: Floods; Kent Authors and Lit. - Fiction;
Printing and Publishing; Whitstable.

WOODMAN, Greta. See WOODMAN, George: Whitstable.

WOODRUFF, Charles Everleigh: Canterbury Cathedral;
Canterbury - Monastic Houses; Fordwich.

WOODRUFF, Cumberland Henry: Dover.

WOODRUFF, Rev. John: Upchurch.

WOODS, Frederick: Bibliography; Churchill, Sir Winston S.

WOODS, Nancy: Kent Authors and Lit. - Poetry.

WOODS, Walter T.W: Gravesham; Local Government.

WOODS, William: History - 901 AD - 1500 AD.

WOODTHORPE, T.J: Isle of Sheppey; Medway, River;
Military and Naval History; Queenborough.

WOODWARD, Grace Steele: Pocahontas, Princess.

WOODWARD, Matthew: Folkestone.

WOOLF, Mrs. Virginia (Stephen): Biography; Kent Authors
and Lit. - Fiction.

WOOLLEY, Frank: Cricket.

WOOLLEY, Martha Wilson. See WOOLLEY, Frank: Cricket.

WOOLNOTH, William: Canterbury Cathedral; Canterbury -
Monastic Houses.

WOOLWICH AND DISTRICT ANTIQUARIAN SOCIETY: Erith.

WOOLWICH BOROUGH COUNCIL: Gardens; Woolwich.

WORKERS' EDUCATION ASSOCIATION - S.E. DISTRICT:
Gravesend.

WORKS, Ministry of: ANCIENT MONUMENTS AND HISTORIC
BUILDINGS: Reculver.
See also: BUSHE-FOX, J.P: Richborough.
            CLAPHAM, Sir Alfred William: Canterbury -
                                  Monastic Houses.
            MEATES, G.W: Lullingstone.
            RIGOLD, S.E: Ospringe; Strood.
            SAUNDERS, A.D: Deal; Walmer.

WORMALD, H: Agriculture.

WORSFOLD, Frederick Henry: Barfreston.

WORSSAM, Bernard Charles: Geology; Kent, Mid; Rivers;
Weald.

WORTHAM, H.E: Gordon, Gen. C.G.

WOTTON, Sir Henry: Kent Authors and Lit. -Collections.
See also SMITH, Logan P: Biography; Boughton Malherbe;
Letters.

WRAY, (OPTICAL WORKS) LTD. See SMITH, Arthur William:
Bromley; Industry and Trade - Firms.

WRIGHT, Christopher John: Footpaths - Country Walks;
North Downs Way; Pilgrims Way.

W Cont'd

WRIGHT, I.G. Publisher:Medway Towns.

WRIGHT, Nicholas: Biggin Hill; Military and Naval
History; World War II.

WRIGHT, Samuel: Bibliography.

WRIGHT, Thomas. See RICHARD OF MAIDSTONE:
Kent Authors and Lit. - Poetry.

WRIGHT, Tom: Agriculture; Gardens.

WROTHAM:ST.GEORGE'S CHURCH: Music; Wrotham.

WROTHAM PARISH CHURCH: Borough Green; Wrotham.

WYATT, George: Boxley.

WYATT, Sir Stanley Charles: Allington; Chilham;
Family History.

WYATT, Sir Thomas: Kent Authors and Lit. - Poetry.

WYE COLLEGE: Agriculture; Bibliography; Wye.
See Also. BEST, Robin Hewitson:Agriculture.
          BODDINGTON, M.A.B: Agriculture.
          BULL, Christopher: Agriculture.
          CHATER, G.P: Agriculture.
          DORLING, M.J: Agriculture.
          FOLLEY, Roger Roland Westwell:Agriculture.
          HAGGAR, R.J:Agriculture.
          IRVING: R.W: Agriculture.
          McRAE, Stuart Gordon: Agriculture.
          REID, Ian G: Agriculture.
          SYKES, Joseph Donald:Agriculture.
          YOUNGMAN, James: Agriculture.

WYE COLLEGE:CENTRE FOR EUROPEAN AGRICULTURAL STUDIES:
Agriculture and Horticulture.

WYE COLLEGE:SCHOOL OF RURAL ECONOMICS AND RELATED
STUDIES:Agriculture.

WYE HISTORICAL SOCIETY:Wye.

WYE ORNITHOLOGISTS CLUB:Natural History;Wye.

WYLLIE, M.A:Biography; Kent Artists. See also
WYLLIE, William Leonard: Thames, River.

WYLLIE, William Leonard: Thames, River.

WYMER, Norman: History - General.

WYNDHAM, Richard: Kent.

Y

YALDING AND NETTLESTEAD PRESERVATION SOCIETY:
Footpaths - Country Walks; Kent, Mid.

YALDING CHURCH FUND RAISING COMMITTEE:Yalding.

YANDELL, Elizabeth: Biography; Weald.

YATES, E: Churches.

YE OLDE LEATHER BOTTLE:Cobham;Inns.

YEANDLE, W.H: Stone-in-Oxney.

YEATS, G.D: Tunbridge Wells.

YELLOLY, Margaret: Health and Welfare.

YOKOSUKA,CITY COUNCIL:Adams, William.

YOUDEN, George H. See EMBRY, Bernard:
Kent, South East; Natural History.

YOUNG, Arthur: Agriculture; Kent, North.

YOUNG, Kenneth: Coastline; Music; Spas and Mineral Waters.

YOUNG, Percy: Chatham; Windmills and Watermills.

YOUNG, Richard Anthony; World War II.

YOUNGMAN, E. and Son. Publishers Canterbury; Canterbury
Cathedral.

YOUNGMAN, James: Agriculture.

Z

ZOUCH, Thomas: Sidney, Sir Philip.

RECREATION AND ENTERTAINMENT.

RELIGIOUS DENOMINATIONS.

RESTAURANTS See HOTELS, RESTAURANTS AND CLUBS.

RIDING See FOOTPATHS - HORSE RIDING.
      See SPORT.

RIVER CHARTS See SEA AND RIVER CHARTS.

RIVERS See also INDIVIDUAL RIVERS. e.g.MEDWAY,River.

ROAD TRANSPORT.

ROADS.

ROLFE, Mrs. John See POCAHONTAS, Princess
(1595 - 1617).

ROYAL AIRFORCE HISTORY See MILITARY AND
NAVAL HISTORY.

ROYAL OBSERVER CORPS See MILITARY AND NAVAL HISTORY.

SCHOOLS See TOWNS, VILLAGES.

SEA AND RIVER CHARTS.

SEASIDE RESORTS See COASTLINE, TOWNS AND VILLAGES.

SERMONS.

SEWERAGE See PUBLIC UTILITIES.

SHIPS AND SHIPPING.

SHIPPING See SHIPS AND SHIPPING.

SIDNEY, Sir Philip (1554 - 1586). See also PENSHURST.

SMUGGLING.

SOCIAL SERVICES. See HEALTH AND WELFARE.

SOCIETIES See ORGANISATIONS.

SOIL SURVEY See AGRICULTURE.

SONGS See KENT SONGS.

SOUVENIRS.

SPAS AND MINERAL WATERS.

SPORT.

STATIONS See RAILWAYS.

STREET NAMES See PLACE NAMES AND SURNAMES.

SUNDIALS.

SURNAMES See PLACE NAMES AND SURNAMES.

SWIMMING See SPORT.

TABLE TENNIS See SPORT.

TALLIES See COINS AND TOKENS.

TAVERNS See INNS.

TELEGRAPH See COMMUNICATIONS.

TELEVISION.

TENNIS See SPORT.

THEATRE.

T(H)OM, John Nichols See COURTENAY, Sir William P.H.
pseud.

TIDE MILLS See WINDMILLS AND WATERMILLS.

TITHES.

TOKENS See COINS AND TOKENS.

TOPOGRAPHY: PRE 1900 See HISTORY - GENERAL.

TOPOGRAPHY: POST 1900 See KENT.

TRADE See INDUSTRY AND TRADE.
         INDUSTRY AND TRADE:FIRMS.

TRAMWAYS See ROAD TRANSPORT.

TRANSPORT.

TRAVELLING PEOPLE See GYPSIES.

TRIALS.

TROLLEY BUSES See ROAD TRANSPORT.

TUNBRIDGE WARE See SOUVENIRS.

TUNNELS See CAVES AND TUNNELS.
       See CHANNEL TUNNEL.
       See DARTFORD TUNNEL.

VISITATIONS (ECCLESIASTICAL) See CANTERBURY - DIOCESE
AND PROVINCE.

VISITATIONS (HERALDS) See GENEALOGICAL RECORDS.

WAR DEAD See WORLD WAR I.
         See WORLD WAR II.

WASTE DISPOSAL See PUBLIC UTILITIES.

WATERMILLS See WINDMILLS AND WATERMILLS.

WATER SPORTS See SPORT.

WATER SUPPLY See PUBLIC UTILITIES.

WELFARE See HEALTH AND WELFARE.

WELLS, Herbert George (1866 - 1946).

WILLS See GENEALOGICAL RECORDS.

WINDMILLS AND WATERMILLS.

WITCHCRAFT.

WOLFE, General James (1727 - 1759). See also WESTERHAM.

WORLD WAR I.

WORLD WAR II.

ZOOS AND ZOO PARKS.

DOUGLAS, James (1753 - 1819).   JESSUP, Ronald Frederick.

DYER, Albert.

EDWARD THE BLACK PRINCE (1330 - 1376)   See SECTION: EDWARD, THE BLACK PRINCE.

EDWARD AUGUSTUS, H.R.H. DUKE Of KENT. (1767 - 1820).   DUFF, David.

EHRMANN, Rev. Louis Emil Augustus.

ELWYN, Richard.   PATTERSON, Rev. Robert.

ERASMUS.   LONG, G.S.

EVANS, Godfrey.

FEGAN, J.W.C.   TIFFIN Alfred.

FISHER, John. (Bishop of Rochester)   UNDERHILL, Francis.

FORSTER, Lord John of Harraby   - OBITUARY.

FRISWELL, James Hain.   FRISWELL, Laura Hain.

FRY, James Hockett.   - OBITUARY.

GARNET, Henry.   CARAMAN, Philip.

GERMAIN, Lord George. See SACKVILLE, Lord George.

GORDON, Alastair.   TENISON, E.M.

GORDON, General Charles George, R.E. (1833 - 1885).   See SECTION: GORDON, General Charles George.

GRACE, W.G.   HAWKE, Martin Bladen. Baron Hawke.

GRAHAM, Norman.

HALFPENNY, H.   HALFPENNY, Harriette.

HALL, Ellen   MILLS, Anthony Reginald.
HALL, Emily.   SHERRARD, Owen Aubney.

HAMILTON, Charles.   See RICHARDS, Frank.

HAMO OF HYTHE (Bishop of Rochester).   O'GORMAN, Richard A.

HARRIS, George Robert Canning. 4th Baron Harris 1851 - 1932

HARVEY, Dr. William (1578 - 1657)   See SECTION: HARVEY, Dr. William.

HAYES, Richard   ARNOLD, Ralph.

HEATH, Edward Richard George (1916 -)   See SECTION: HEATH, Edward Richard George.

HESELTINE, Philip Arnold See WARLOCK, Peter.

HICKEY, William.

HILDER, Rowland.   LEWIS John.

HILL, Octavia: HILL, William Thomson. MAURICE, C. Edmund.

HOLE, Very Rev. Samuel Reynolds.   MASSINGHAM, Betty.

HOBBS, Rev. John.   SPOONER, T.G.M.

HOOPER, Very Rev. George.   MARSHALL, William M.

HUGGINS, Godfrey 1st Viscount Malvern and Bexley.   GANN, L.H.

IGGLESDEN, Sir Charles.

IVY, Bill.   PECK, Alan.

JEFFERY, William   RUDGE, Rev. Charles.

JELF, George Edward.   JELF, Katherine Frances.

JOBSON, A.

JONES, Henry YANDELL, Elizabeth.   YANDELL, Elizabeth.

KEATING, Tom   NORMAN, Geraldine.

KENDON, Samuel (1864 - 1945).   - OBITUARY.

KENT, Duchess of See MARINA, H.R.H. DUCHESS OF KENT.

KENT, Duke of See EDWARD AUGUSTUS H.R.H. DUKE OF KENT. (1767 - 1820).

KEYES, Sidney   GUENTHER, John.

KIDMAN, Brenda.

KINNAIRD, Emily.

KIRKBRIDE, Lieut.Col.William.

KITCHENER, Field Marshall Horatio Herbert, R.E. 1st EARL KITCHENER OF KHARTOUM. (1850 - 1916)   See SECTION: KITCHENER, Field Marshal Horatio Herbert.

KNATCHBULL, John   RODERICK, Colin.

KNOTT, Alan.

LAMBARDE, William   WARNICKE, Retha M.

LEE, Jimmy.   PEARSON, Edward.

LEYBOURN, Sir Roger de.   LARKING, Lambert Blackwell.

"LITTLE TICH" (Harry Relph)   TICH, Mary (Powell, Mary Relf)

LOYD, Samuel J. Baron Overstone

LUCY, Sir Henry William.

LUCKHURST, Brian   DIMONT, Charles.

LYALL, Very Rev.William Rowe.

McCALL, Dorothy.

McCUDDEN, James Thomas Byford, V.C.   See SECTION: McCUDDEN, James Thomas Byford, V.C.

MACDOUGALL, Mrs Sylvia (née Börgstrom). See WAINEMAN, Paul.

MARINA, H.R.H DUCHESS OF KENT.   CATHCART, Helen. DAY, J. Wentworth.

MARLOWE, Christopher. (1564 - 1593)   See SECTION: MARLOWE, Christopher.

MARRIOTT, Charles Stowell (1895 - 1966).   - OBITUARY.

MARTIN, J.E.   HIGGS, Lionel F.

MASON, John Neve.

MAUGHAN, W. Somerset   CURTIS, Anthony. RAPHAEL, Frederic.

MAXWELL, Donald.   - OBITUARY.

MILNER, Sir Alfred.   MARLOW, John.

MILNER, Violet Georgina. Viscountess Milner.

MONTEFIORE, Sir Moses.   KAMM, J.

MORE, Sir Thomas. (1478 - 1535)   See SECTION: MORE, Sir Thomas.

MORGAN, Verne.

MORLEY, Thomas William. (1883 - 1931).

MORRIS, William (1834 - 1896).   See SECTION: MORRIS, William.

MORRISON (1789 - 1857).   GATTY, Richard.

MOTHER MARY OF THE HEART OF JESUS.   RIOS, Dom Romanus.

MURRAY, Lady Augusta.   GILLEN, Mollie. MARPLES, Morris.

NASH   POOLE, Keith B.

NESBIT, E.   BELL, Anthea. MOORE, Doris Langley. TAYLOR, Margaret.

NICOLSON, Sir Harold.   NICOLSON, Nigel.

NORMAN, George Warde.
NORMAN, George Warde.   LOYD, Samuel J.
   Baron Overstone.

NORTHCLIFFE, Lord.   PEMBERTON, Max.

ODLE, Mrs. Rose.

PALMER, Samuel   See SECTION:
(1805 - 1881).   PALMER, Samuel.

PAYNE, George.   BARRY, T.B.

PEPITA (OTILA).   SACKVILLE-WEST, Victoria.

PERFECT, William   SPENCER, Herbert R.
(1737 - 1809).

PETT, Phineas.

PETTIE, John   HARDIE, Martin.

PITT, William   See SECTION:
The Elder (1708-1778)   PITT, William
The Younger (1759-1806)   (The Elder and The Younger).

PLACE, Francis   HOWSE, Derek.

POCAHONTAS, Princess   See SECTION:
(Mrs John Rolfe)   POCAHONTAS, Princess.
(1595 - 1617).

POINTER, Thomas James.

POLLEY, Margery.   JENNINGS, Letitia.

PONSONBY, Sir Charles.

POPE, Douglas.

RAVEN, Margaret Maxwell.

RAVEN, Dr. Martin Owen.

RAVEN FAMILY.   RAVEN, Mary.

REES, Tom.   Rees, Jean A.

RICHARDS, Frank.

ROBERTSON, Rev. William.- OBITUARY.
Archibald Scott.

ROHAN, John J.

ROLFE, Mrs. John   See SECTION:
   POCAHONTAS, Princess.

ROLLS, C.S.   BRUCE, Gordon.

ROSE, Rev. George

ROWE, Rev. John Tetley   ROWE, Mrs. Mercy Elizabeth.

SACKVILLE FAMILY   WOOLF, Mrs Virginia.

SACKVILLE, Lord George.   MARLOW, Louis.
   VALENTINE, Alan.

SACKVILLE, Viscount George.
See
SACKVILLE, Lord George.

SACKVILLE-WEST   ALSOP, Susan Mary.
Lady Victoria
(1862 - 1936).

SACKVILLE-WEST, Victoria. NICOLSON, Nigel.
(Vita). afterwards Lady STEVENS, Michael.
Nicolson. (1892 - 1962).

SANGER, "LORD" George.
(1825 - 1911).

SASSOON, Siegfried.

SHEARS, Sarah.

SIDNEY, Sir Philip   See SECTION:
(1554 - 1586).   SIDNEY, Sir Philip.

SIX, James   — OBITUARY.
(1730/1 - 1793).

SMITH, Charles Roach   SMETHAM, Henry.

SMITH-MARRIOTT,   CRONK, Anthony.
William Marriott.

SPENCELAYH, Charles.   NOAKES, Aubrey.

STONE, John (Saint).   HACKETT, Benedict.

STRANGER, John.   GROSER, William.

SUSSEX, Duke of   See AUGUSTUS FREDERICK,
   H.R.H. DUKE OF SUSSEX.

SWAN, Sir Joseph Wilson. SWAN, Mary Edwards.

SYDNEY. Hon. Algernon.   EWALD, Alexander Charles.
(1622 - 1683).

TEICHMAN, Oskar.

TEMPLE, John Henry   ASHLEY, Evelyn.
Viscount Palmerston.

T(H)OM, John Nichols.   See SECTION:
   COURTENAY, Sir William P.H.

THOMAS, James Henry.   BLAXLAND, Gregory.

THORNDIKE, Sybil.   CASSON, John.
   MORLEY, Sheridan.

TREVITHICK, Richard.   HODGE, James.

TRITTON, Clara   DONALDSON, Christopher
Elizabeth.   William.

TURNER, J.M.W.   FALK, B.
   RUSKIN, John.

TYRWHITT-DRAKE, Sir
Hugh Garrard.

UGLOW, Capt. Jim.

UNDERWOOD, Derek.

VANE, Sir Henry (Harry).   ADAMSON, J.H.
The Younger, 1613 - 1662.

WADE, Virginia.

WAIN, Louis.   DALE, R.

WAINEMAN, Paul

WAKELEY, Rev. Thomas S.   WAKELEY, R.H.

WALSINGHAM, Sir Francis.   READ, Conyers.

WARLOCK, Peter.   TOMLINSON, Fred.

WARNER, John   LEE-WARNER, Edward.
(Bishop of Rochester).

WATTS, Alan Wilson.

WELLS, Herbert George   See SECTION:
(1866 - 1946).   WELLS, Herbert George.

WELLS, James William   LUCAS, Meriel.

WELLS, William Frederick   WHEELER, J.M.
(1764 - 1836).

WHITE, John Baker.

WILSON, John.   CLAYTON, F.S.
   WILLIAMS, Marguerite.

WOOLFE, General James   See SECTION:
(1727 - 1759).   WOLFE, General James
   See also WESTERHAM.

WOOLLEY, Frank.   PEEBLES, Ian.
   WARNER, Oliver.
   WOOLLEY, Martha W.

WOTTON, Sir Henry.   SMITH, Logan P.

WYLLIE, W.L.   WYLLIE, M.A.

YEVELEY, Henry.   WHITEHEAD, J.G.O.

COLLECTED BIOGRAPHY

CHURCH, Richard.

ELWIG, Henry (Tunbridge Wells).

FULLER, Thomas.

HANDLEY-TAYLOR, Geoffrey.

KENT COUNTY LIBRARY (Library Staff).

KENT, HISTORICAL, BIOGRAPHICAL AND PICTORIAL.

POLE-STUART, Dr. E. (Folkestone)

SIMMON, Jack. (County Historians)

SOUTH EAST ARTS ASSOCIATION (Directory of Writers).

THOMSON, Arthur Alexander.

WHO'S WHO IN KENT.

WHO'S WHO IN KENT, SURREY AND SUSSEX.

WHO'S WHO IN MAIDSTONE.

WINNIFRITH, Rev. Alfred.